Gospel of John

Expository and Homiletical Commentary

by

William H. Van Doren

Two Volumes in One

KREGEL PUBLICATIONS
Grand Rapids, MI 49501

Gospel of John by William H. Van Doren,
Copyright © 1981 by Kregel Publications, a division of Kregel, Inc. All rights reserved.

Library of Congress Cataloging in Publication Data

Van Doren, W. H. (William Howard), 1810-1882.
  Gospel of John.

  Reprint. Originally published: A suggestive
commentary on St. John. London: R. D. Dickinson,
1872.
    1. Bible. N.T. John—Commentaries.
  I. Title.
BS2615.V26   1981   226'.507   80-8080
ISBN 0-8254-3953-1   AACR2

CONTENTS

FOREWORD

Over one hundred years ago there began a remarkable series of helps for the pastor designated *The Homilist*. They were edited by two gifted men, Dr. David Thomas of London and Urijah Rees Thomas of Bristol.

The design of some thirty volumes is stated in the preface: "The mission of *The Homilist* is not to supply sermons for indolent or imcompetent preachers but stimulus and tonic for the truehearted, hard working teacher. It does not deal with the ready-made but with the raw material ... *The Homilist*, in one word, proceeds upon the principle that the author serves his reader best, not who gives, but who suggests the most thought, and thus brings out, from the reader's own soul, thoughts and thought-producing powers of which before he was utterly unconscious."

When one spends time with Van Doren's work on the *Gospel of John* he must experience what the editors of *The Homilist* hoped for all those who read their unique publication. Van Doren is different. As you travel over terrain that is familiar, you suddenly realize that you are being confronted with truths that somehow you have missed. Spurgeon said when he pursued this volume on John, "If men who read this volume do not preach better for so doing, it is not Mr. Van Doren's fault; they must be Van Dolts by nature, though they may ignore the family name."

When you open the door to this remarkable exposition of John's Gospel you are thrust immediately into a sample of the riches that can be mined in this fruitful study volume. Here are ten pages that are jewelled with a presentation of the life of the Apostle John and the uniqueness of his writings. This sample stirs one to pursue with expectation all that will follow. As you do so you will discover that W. H. Van Doren's commentary on the Gospel of John is *exhaustive* without being *exhausting*. He provides sound, reliable exposition of the text, accented with refreshing insights for application to daily living.

Van Doren's exposition of the text is supported by a thorough understanding of the original languages, history, culture, and theology. Woven throughout his exposition are an abundance of cross references by which he ties the Gospel of John into the fabric of the whole of Scripture.

Although having occasional technical discussions for the scholar, he is not so technical as to exclude the layman. It is deep enough for the Biblical professor and the pastor to swim in and never touch bottom, yet navigable enough for the beginning student to plunge into without fear of drowning.

Van Doren's commentary is sprinkled with quotations from great church leaders. The pastor and Bible teacher will also find sermonic seed thoughts throughout. His work is not a compilation of dry doctrinal dust, but it pulsates with living truths. The student who spends time in the Word of God with the aid of Van Doren will find his mind enriched, his heart warmed and his soul stirred to a new devotion to His Lord.

DR. HOWARD F. SUGDEN

INTRODUCTION

John, the Apostle, son of Zebedee, a fisherman, and of Salome. Matt. iv. 21 ; xxvii. 56 ; Mark xv. 40 ; xvi. 1.

Probably younger than his brother James, whose name commonly precedes his.

Certainly younger than his friend Peter, and younger, as it is supposed, than the Lord.

Traditions of fourth century make Salome daughter of Joseph by a first wife, and consequently half-sister to Jesus. *Epiphanius.*

Some modern critics identify her with the sister of Mary, mother of the Lord, mentioned John xix. 25. *Ewald, Wieseler.*

It is probable John was born at Bethsaida on the Lake of Galilee.

Although in humble life, his parents appear to have been in easy circumstances.

Zebedee, his father, employed hired servants in his occupation. Mark i. 20.

Salome, his mother, was of the number of those women who contributed to the maintenance of Jesus. Luke viii. 3; Matt. xxvii. 56.

John's acquaintance with the high-priest also indicates the same thing. John xviii. 15.

Moreover, we find that he received Mary, the Lord's mother, into " his own house " (probably in Jerusalem) after the Lord's death. John xix. 27.

Although not taught in the Rabbinical schools, he was doubtless taught the Scriptures.

His writings show an intimate acquaintance with the Alexandrine version and with the Hebrew text.

Bound by the law, there would be at the age of thirteen the periodical visits to Jerusalem.

He would become familiar with the grand ritual of the temple, with the sacrifice, the incense, the altar, and the priestly robes.

Ideas suggested by this stately worship are often reproduced in the imagery of the Apocalypse.

His occupation also as a fisherman was adapted to promote religious meditation.

He must have passed whole nights in stillness upon the waters of the lake.

Above him the heavens, sparkling with countless stars, of surpassing beauty and glory.

Around him scenery as charming as the environs of the Lake of Lucerne.

Doubtless at such times he would reflect on the glowing visions of the Prophets.

He would also feel the inspiration of the hope that their fulfilment was close at hand.

His very name seems a sign of that yearning and expectation which then animated not only the devout, but the whole people. *Plumptre.*

Hence, when the voice of the Baptist was heard in the wilderness, John was one of the first to attach himself to the Forerunner.

On the banks of the Jordan this Messianic HERALD directed him to Jesus as " THE LAMB OF GOD."

With a prepared heart, he at once became the Lord's disciple, and followed Him to Galilee.

Arrived there, he at first resumed his trade, but afterward was permanently called to the apostleship.

In all lists of the TWELVE the names of the sons of Jona and Zebedee stand foremost.

They form the innermost circle of the Lord's friends, and are with Him when none else are.

In the chamber of death, in the glory of the transfiguration, in the agony of the garden.   Mark v. 37 ; Matt. xvii. 1 ; xxvi. 37.

Peter is the leader of the band, but to John belongs the memorable distinction of being " the disciple whom Jesus loved."

This love John received and returned with all the earnestness of his deep nature.

Peter showed his love more by outward, busy action ; John, by inward, quiet devotion.

Peter loved the Lord in His official dignity as the Messiah and King.

John loved Him in His personal character as the source of spiritual light and life.

Peter was more a friend of THE CHRIST, John a *bosom* friend of JESUS.

Peter sees the glory of Christ chiefly in the unfolding of the glory of His kingdom.

John sees all the glory of His kingdom in the single glory of His personal exaltation, and His future appearing.

One aspect of this feeling appears in his consuming zeal for the Lord's honour.

He flames into indignation against all that seemed to outrage or even touch it.

Like a fiery gleam it runs through the whole of his protracted life.

To him there can be no neutrality between Christ and Antichrist.

He is intolerant of all compromises and concessions : he will have no half-heartedness.

It harmonizes with his character, that, as *Polycarp* records, meeting with Cerinthus, the arch-denier of our Lord's Divinity, in the public baths of Ephesus, he fled from him, crying that "*he feared the walls of the bath would fall.*"

Church traditions declare also that divine love so absorbed his soul, there was no room left for the lower, and hence they attribute to him a life of celibacy.

He treasures up as priceless every word and accent of our Lord's conversations and dialogues.

He is the Apostle of love because he has grown more and more in the image of Him he loved so truly.

His inmost spirit is filled with the thought of that Son of Man who is also the Son of God.

Hence he is a living mirror, receiving the full glory of the Lord and reflecting it back on others.

This made him pre-eminently the "THEOLOGUS" or "DIVINE" of the Apostolic circle.

As his love is so deep and tender, and his believing knowledge intuitive vision, the popular notion, fostered by Christian art, represents his nature as *feminine.*

But he was *feminine* only in *that character* of mind proper to all religious emotions and exercises of faith—perfect receptivity and self-surrender of spirit.

He was great not merely in receiving and feeling, but in reproduction and statement.

It is impossible to conceive of more sublime compositions than the fourth Gospel and the Apocalypse.

The name BOANERGES given to him and James (Mark iii. 17) implies natural vehemence, fiery zeal, and passionate intensity.

This spirit breaks out when they join their mother in asking the highest places in the kingdom of Christ.

When they declared they were ready to drink of His cup and be baptized with His baptism.

When they rebuked one for casting out devils in their Master's name because he was not of their company.

When they sought to call down fire from heaven on a village of Samaritans.

John's subsequent humility, gentleness, and love were the fruit of Christ abiding in him and he in Christ.

The impressions the Lord made on him the first time they met remained vivid till death.

The words of that evening (John i. 37—40), though not recorded, were mighty in effect.

Then began that glowing devotion which burned brighter and brighter to the end.

He is happy to be known as "that disciple" or as "the disciple Jesus loved."

As the favoured one, he reclines at table on the Lord's breast, and rests on that Eternal heart which now beats "in the midst of the throne." Rev. v. 6.

From that INFINITE FOUNTAIN of truth, purity, and love he drew all his excellence.

At the table it is to him Peter makes signs that he shall ask what probably no one of the rest would dare.   John xiii. 24.

As they go out to the Mount of Olives the chosen three are nearest the Lord.

They alone are within sight and hearing of the awful conflict in Gethsemane.

After the betrayal Peter and John follow Jesus, the former, " afar off "— all the rest have fled.

Of the apostolic band John alone goes through the terrors of that night with any measure of firmness.

Peter remains in the porch of the high-priest's house, but John presses into the council chamber.

He stands upright and faithful, while Peter, suddenly tempted, falls.

He follows his Master even into the prætorium of the Roman governor.

He appears at the cross, and becomes a son to the desolate and broken-hearted mother.

The dying Lord bequeaths to him the most precious of all legacies—the reward of a " love stronger than death."   John xix. 26.

Doubtless he spent that sad Sabbath in loving sympathy with her whose heart the sword had pierced.   Luke ii. 35.

Notwithstanding Peter's denial, he receives him on the old terms of friendship.

The more ardent, he is the first to reach the tomb the morning of the resurrection.   John xx. 4—6.

Peter, the least restrained by awe, the first to enter and look in.

At the Sea of Galilee John is the first to recognize in the dim form the risen Lord.

" O wonderful power of love, organ of all spiritual knowledge, eye of the soul by which we gaze on God ! " *Novalis.*

Peter the first to plunge into the water and swim to the shore to meet Him.

The two friends are together at the Lord's ascension, and on the day of Pentecost.

They are fellow-workers in the first great expansive action of the Church.

Those who wanted to call down fire on Samaritans now receive Samaritans in brotherly love.

Paul (Gal. ii. 9) describes Peter, James, and John as " pillars of the Church."

In the persecution under Herod Agrippa the brothers are separated— James is put to death.   Acts xii. 2.

The *first* of the apostolic band who received the crown of martyrdom.

His brother, " the beloved disciple," the *last* " to enter into the joy of his Lord."

John seems to have resided at Jerusalem till the death of the Lord's mother, but when this took place we can only conjecture.

Fifteen years after Paul's first visit he was still there, and helped to
settle the controversy between the Jewish and Gentile Christians.
Acts xv. 6.

But there are no signs of his presence in Jerusalem at the time of Paul's
last visit. Acts xxi.

We know that afterward he became bishop (pastor) of the Church at
Ephesus.

It would seem that some persecution, local or general, drove him to Patmos.

Tradition affirms that he was condemned to work in the mines in that
island.

Patristic writers generally attribute this to the Emperor Domitian.

In Patmos, according to Rev. i. 9, he saw and recorded the visions of the
Apocalypse.

There the Lord appeared to him in His personal majesty and glory.

There the Spirit instructed him to warn and counsel the Seven Churches,
and through them the whole Church to the end of time.

There the successive periods of earth's history arose and passed in pano-
ramic vision before him.

There he beheld the glorious transformation scene to which the ages
hasten: " The kingdoms of this world are become THE KINGDOMS of
CHRIST." Rev. xi. 15.

Patmos, so rugged and bare, seems a suitable theatre for so awful and
sublime a drama.

Only one palm-tree remains, and it stands in a valley called " the saint's
garden."

On a hill is the celebrated monastery which bears the name of " JOHN
THE DIVINE."

Half-way up the hill is the cave or grotto where it is said he received the
Revelation.

" The sea was still as the grave. Patmos reposed in it like a dead saint.
John is the thought of the island. It belongs to him; it is his
sanctuary. Its stones preach of him, and in every heart he lives."
Tischendorf.

The Gospel requires the Apocalypse, the Apocalypse presupposes the
Gospel.

On the accession of Nerva (so tradition reports) John was liberated from
his island prison, and permitted to return to Ephesus.

Here, according to the unanimous testimony of antiquity, he wrote his
Gospel. Probably here also he wrote his Epistles.

The spiritual character of this Gospel and its references point decidedly
to Ephesus.

It is also the unanimous tradition of the ancients that it was the *last*
written.

As it is the latest, so it is the ripest and the most original of all the
Gospels.

Thoroughly independent of the other Evangelists, it presupposes and
confirms them.

Although each Gospel is invaluable and indispensable, this is the Gospel of Gospels.

It is the conclusion, the completion, and the crown of the Gospels.

It is the most remarkable as well as the most important book ever written.

"It can be comprehended only by those who lean on the bosom of Jesus, and there imbibe the spirit of John." *Origen.*

"It is a voice of thunder, and yet more love-bewitching and elevating in its influence than all the harmonies of music." *Chrysostom.*

"It but pours forth the water of life John himself had drunk from the bosom of Jesus in secret." *Augustine.*

"It is the unique, tender, genuine, leading Gospel." *Luther.*

"It reveals the soul of Christ; the others seek rather to describe His body." *Calvin.*

"The most important portion of the New Testament." *Lessing.*

"The heart of Christ." *Ernesti.* "Written by the hand of an angel." *Herder.*

"Eternal, childlike, Christmas joys pervade John's soul." *Schleiermacher.*

"It possesses a peculiar originality and charm to which there is no parallel." *Tholuck.*

"The diamond amongst the Gospels, which reflects the glory of the God-head, even in the crown of thorns." *Lange.*

It introduces us to the Holy of Holies, so that we behold the glory of "THE ONLY BEGOTTEN" face to face.

It is the communication of the deepest and highest self-revelation of the Lord.

"Clear as crystal" in the view of His Incarnate Divinity and perfect man-hood.

Doctrine of the LOGOS or WORD one of the most important and glorious doctrines ever revealed.

It is the ground, the harmony, and the crown of all known truth.

Christ is the Eternal WORD, source of all life and organ of all revelations.

He is the LIGHT of the world, illuminating the darkness of sin and error.

He is the FOUNTAIN of living water, quenching the thirst of the soul.

He is the BREAD of life—bread imparting life—life which becomes bread.

He is the RESURRECTION and the LIFE, destroying all death's terrors.

This Gospel breathes the air of peace, and yet sounds at times like thunder from the unseen world.

It is the plainest and yet the profoundest portion of the Bible.

"A river deep enough for an elephant to swim, with shallows where a lamb may wade." *Owen.*

"It is a Gospel from the height and likewise from the depth." *Da Costa.*

"It is the noiseless completion of the inner and holier places of the temple of faith." *Alford.*

"It is the Gospel of the world, resolving reason into intuition and faith into sight." *Westcott.*

"Compared with the Synoptists—'Thou hast kept the good wine until now.'" *Wordsworth.*

Yet this very Gospel is now made the main point of attack by unbelievers.
We are not surprised at this: "It is the most conspicuous written attest-
ation of our Lord's Godhead." *Liddon.*
As in the days of His flesh, His claims must always call forth adoring
love or relentless enmity.
Human nature is the same now it was eighteen hundred years ago.
Men cannot remain neutral on the great question, "WHAT THINK YE OF
CHRIST ? "
They will either declare for Him or against Him, accept Him or reject Him.
Hence modern Scribes, Pharisees, and Sadducees " crucify Him afresh."
No book of ancient Greece or Rome or of recent times is so well attested.
Not a shadow of doubt has ever been entertained in the Church either
as to its authorship or canonical authority.
No book of the New Test. more strongly impresses the mind with the
thought of union and integrity.
The internal evidence is overwhelming : THE HEART OF CHRIST VIBRATES
IN IT.
Yet this Divine sublimity is now the *alleged* ground of suspicion !
Is it not undeniable that the writer moves as a familiar acquaintance
amongst the Lord's friends, and in every case appears to know more
than his predecessors relate ?
Note the minor details implying personal intimacy between the writer
and Jesus.
Note the demeanour of Martha and Mary at the tomb of Lazarus.
Note the characteristic declaration of Peter when Christ would wash his
feet.
Note the answer to John at the last supper which seems to direct his at-
tention to Judas, and yet is not heard by the others.
Note Christ's dying recommendation of His mother to the care of His
disciple.
Note the character of Mary Magdalene, depicted with such life-like
touches.
Note the account of her distress in the garden of the sepulchre.
Note the character of Thomas, his unbelief, and the Lord's loving dealing with him.
" Criticism " committed *suicide* when it asked us to believe that a Gospel
originating in the middle of the second century (as it is affirmed this
Gospel did) would dwell so much and so incidentally on the traits of
private and personal character exhibited by the various apostles and
disciples, or would show so little trace of the ecclesiastical development of Church authority during that period.
" The author possessed such knowledge as could only be found in an eye-
witness of that time." *Ewald.*
" The holy city had fallen, yet the writer paints it with its localities and
inhabitants in living colours." *Oosterzee.*
" His accounts are like a freshly plucked cluster of grapes, on which the
morning dew still glistens." *Ibid.*

No cne in the second century—no one since—could have written such a work.

Of all men John alone could have written it, and he *only* by the inspiration of the Holy Spirit. John xiv. 26.

Summary of the evidence of the genuineness and authenticity of this Gospel : —

1. Unanimous testimony of antiquity—heretical and orthodox—reaching to the beginning of the second century, i.e. almost to John's lifetime. 2. Language and style, " a pure Hebrew soul in a pure Greek body." 3. Familiarity with Jewish nature and Palestine localities. 4. Minute circumstantiality of account. 5. Number of graphic touches and incidental details which unmistakably betray an eye-witness. 6. Express and solemn testimony that the writer witnessed the issue of blood and water from the Lord's pierced side. 7. Indirect and delicate self-designation as the most favoured among the twelve. 8. High and lofty tone of the whole narrative. 9. Perfect picture of the purest and holiest being that ever lived. *Schaff's* Introduction to *Lange's* Comm., Amer. Edit.

Sceptical " criticism " has exhausted its armoury, and not one point has proved vulnerable.

"Not a feather has been plucked from the mighty wing of this eagle." *Meyer*.

The " fierce light " which has beaten upon this Gospel has served but to bring out more clearly its Divine character.

Its bitterest and most scholarly assailants (the *Tübingen* School) are now obliged to admit that " *the fundamental ideas of the Fourth Gospel lie far beyond the horizon of the Church of the second century, and indeed of the whole Christian Church, down to the present day.*"*

"Thus to each succeeding attack of scepticism we may apply the words, ' Behold the feet of them that shall carry it out dead are already at the door.' " *Oosterzee.*

John sets out from the manifestation of the personal God in the WORD. He ends with the personal manifestation of the *glorified* CHRIST.

Between these he places the biography of the *historical* CHRIST.

This biography extends through seven chronological sections.

Over all shines God Himself in the threefold radiance of the Holy Trinity,—the FATHER, the SON, the COMFORTER.

It was a true feeling which led the later interpreters to symbolize John by the eagle that soars into the highest heaven and gazes at the midday sun. Thus sings *Adam* of St. Victor who died about 1192 :

" Volat avis sine meta
Quo nec vates nec propheta
Evolavit altius :
Tam implenda, quam impleta,
Nunquam vidit tot secreta
Purus homo purius."

"Bird of God ! with boundless flight
Soaring far beyond the height
Of the bard or prophet old :
Truth fulfilled, and truth to be,—
Never purer mystery
Did a purer tongue unfold." *Washburn.*

" Above all, I like to read the Gospel of John. There is something truly

---

* Quoted in *Schaff's* Introduction to *Lange's* Comm., Amer. Edit.

beautiful in it: twilight and night; and athwart flashes the vivid lightning. A soft evening sky, and behind the sky, in bodily form, the large full moon! something so sad, so sublime, so full of presage, that one can never weary of it." *Claudius* of Wandsbeck.

" John the typical representative of the perfect ideal Church of the future." *Fichte, Schelling.*

That John died in Ephesus is attested as early as the middle of the second century. *Polycrates.* He had lived in Ephesus nine years before his exile in Patmos, spent fifteen years in exile, lived twenty-six years after the exile, and died at the age of a hundred years and seven months, in the seventh year of the reign of Trajan. The *Chronicon Paschale.*

He died in the reign of Trajan. *Irenæus.* He attained the age of one hundred years. *Jerome.* A hundred and twenty. *Suidas.*

The remarkable reply to Peter (John xxi. 22) has given rise to some strange conjectures.

Our Lord's words will be best interpreted in the light of Matt. x. 23; xvi. 28.

In that earlier announcement John is evidently referred to " There be some standing here," &c. Matt. xvi. 28.

The destruction of Jerusalem was the mightiest, most dreadful, and most significant catastrophe.

Most truly, though invisibly, THE COMING OF THE SON OF MAN to execute judgment. Matt. xxiv. 34.

Then the *old* Jewish " earth and heavens " passed away " with a great noise."

At the same time it was the most blessed event the world has ever seen.

The dissolution of the *old* made room for " the *new* earth and heavens " of Christ's Kingdom.

John *only* of the TWELVE survived that event, and *tarried* far into the glorious age which succeeded.

Moreover his whole life and ministry was in harmony with this peaceful end.

He was not ordained to tread the rougher paths : his was another discipline.

Martyr in will, but not in deed, a calm and honoured old age was crowned with a natural and peaceful death. *Trench.*

CHURCH TRADITIONS. At Rome he was cast into a caldron of boiling oil, but taken out unhurt. *Tertullian.* This unsupported tradition not entitled to credit. *Kitto, D. Brown,* &c. Yet *Polycrates* called him a " martyr." *Eusebius.* He was accustomed to play with a partridge, which he made the emblem of the blessing of recreation. *Cassian.* Illustrates the truth—

> "He prayeth best that loveth best
> All things, both great and small." *Coleridge.*

He drank the cup of hemlock which was intended to cause his death, and

suffered no harm. *Pseudo-August.* Memory of this deliverance
preserved in the symbolic cup, with the serpent issuing from it, which
appears in the mediæval representations of the Evangelist. *Smith's*
Dict. Near Ephesus John found a youth whom he loved. On
leaving, he committed him to the pastor in presence of the flock.
After a long absence the Apostle returned and cried to the pastor,
"Restore to me the pledge which I intrusted to thee." The pastor
was alarmed, thinking it must have béen a sum of money. "I
demand the youth !" exclaimed John. Sighing heavily, the pastor
replied, "He is dead : he became godless, and finally a robber."
Calling for a horse, the Apostle hastened to a mountain cave, and at
length found him, the leader of a band of robbers. Recognizing John,
the culprit fled through shame. "Why do you fly from me, an unarmed
old man ? Stop ! believe Christ hath sent me." The robber returned, weeping bitterly, but held back his right hand. Finally,
overcome by love, he gave his hand, and was another prodigal restored, kindling joy and praise among the angels of God. *Clemens
Alex.* When all capacity to work and teach were gone, the aged
Apostle would have himself carried intò the Church, and holding up
his trembling hands, would say, "Little children, love one another."
On being asked why he constantly repeated this one saying, he
replied, "Because it is the command of the Lord, and enough is done
if this is done." *Jerome.* He caused his grave to be prepared while
he yet lived, and laid himself in it, as in a bed, to die ; and, on the
ground of the expression in John xxi. 22, it was believed he did not
actually die, but only slept. *Augustine.* In the middle ages, and
even in modern times, the saying has been widely spread, that he
still lives. Certainly in his writings. *Lücke.* So late as the six-
teenth century an enthusiast or impostor was burnt at Toulouse,
who gave himself out as St. John ; and in England some of the sects
of the Commonwealth were looking for his return to revive and
reform the Church. *Trench.* He is reserved to reappear again in
conflict with the personal Antichrist in the last days. *Suicer.* See
also *Smith's* Dict., *Fairbairn's* Dict., *Kitto's* Cyclopædia, *Lange's*
Comm. Amer. Edit., *Lange's* Life of Christ, *Leathes'* Witness of St.
John, *Oosterzee* on John, *Bengel, Alford, Olsh., Tholuck, Hengst.,
Brown, Schaff's* Hist. of the Apost. Church, *Hutton's* Theological
Essays, *Trench* on the Miracles, *Jameson's* Sacred and Legendary
Art, &c.

John 1

1. IN the beginning was the Word, and the Word was with God, and the Word was God.

A simple and sublime introduction.
No other evangelist commences in this manner.
A strange Eastern fragrance hovers over all John's writings.
He lived to an epoch somewhat different from that of the other apostles.
The springtide of the apostolic mission had passed away.
Christianity had now to combat the errors of philosophy.
It was a time of great intellectual speculation.
An age when reason was asserting its power.
Remarkable providential preparation for divine truth.
This Gospel a complete theological treatise illustrated by history.
Discloses the Eternal Divine Word as historically incarnate.
By the apostle of Love divine inspiration is completed.
John resorts to no argument, he condescends to no proofs.
His utterances are the profoundest spiritual axioms.
A surpassing glory clothes this revelation.
We hear not the voice of an apostle, but of the great Inspirer Himself.
The Spirit sends out this record like the sun, a living fountain of light.

He who denies inspiration might as well deny the light of the sun.

Divine source of the Bible is like sunlight—SELF-EVIDENCING.

" He who believeth not God hath made Him a liar." 1 John v. 10.

In Scripture one plan, one revealing Spirit, is manifest.

Unity in variety, as in the works of God in creation.

Molten gold adjusts itself to various models, and still is gold.

Mental character may affect the *form* of truth, but the *substance* is
eternal.

There are *many* countenances, yet but *one* human face.

The *same* word may be written in a different manner by *many*
hands.

A sunbeam is reflected according to the medium it passes through.

Its presence seen as really in the dew-drop as in the ocean.

In the beginning. This Gospel the complement of the evangelical history.

Matthew, writing for Jewish Christians, traces our Lord's genealogy from Mary to Abraham.

Mark opens with the *beginning* of His public life and ministry.

Luke, writing for the Gentile world, traces Him to Adam and to
God.

But John goes back before all time, and opens his Gospel in eternity.

" This is thunder brought to us by the son of thunder." *Bengel.*

The other evangelists appear to walk on the earth.

John soars, like the eagle, above the clouds of human infirmity.

They are principally concerned to relate the words and works of
Christ in the flesh.

John contemplates eternal truth, and gazes at our Lord's Divinity.

He opens his account of the new creation as Moses that of the old.
Gen. i. 1.

Hence this Gospel has been called the *Genesis* of the New Test.

Our conception cannot comprehend infinity and eternity.

We are obliged to conceive of a commencement or *original* beginning.

Hence " *the beginning* " Moses signifies of the initial moment of
time.

But " *the beginning* " of John rises to that which is independent of
time.

Augustine has well said, *This is a beginning which had no beginning.*

" From everlasting to everlasting, Thou art God." Psa. xc. 2.

" Whose goings forth are of old, from the days of eternity." Mic. v. 2.

John starts from the hidden depths of uncreated glory.

And closes his Apocalypse with the consummation of all things.
Thus the circle is restored, and God again becomes all in all.
1 Cor. xv. 28.

Was. This carefully excludes the idea of creation.
The world was *created* in time, but the Word *was* from eternity.
Chrys.
John at once leads us to the topless mount of God. *Augustine.*
No attempt is made to prove the Divine existence.
Atheism is either moral or intellectual insanity.
"The fool hath said in his heart—no God." Psa. xiv. 1.

The Word. One of the most celebrated titles of our Lord.
Not the name by which He is generally designated.
Used principally and emphatically in the opening of this Gospel.
John assumes his readers to be familiar with the meaning.
How came he to find the term so ready to his hands as to need no
explanation ?
1. In the gradual development of the idea in the Old Test.
The whole form and expression of the revelation, that of THE WORD
OF GOD.
God is seen to create by the Word, " LET THERE BE ! " Gen. i.
The Word spoke to our first parents in the garden. Gen. iii. 8.
The Word called Abraham to go out from his native land. Gen.
xii. 1.
The Word came unto him in a vision. Gen. xv. 1.
The Word or Angel of the Lord called to him on Mount Moriah.
Gen. xxii. 11.
The Word or " Voice " is distinctly recognized by Samuel. 1 Sam.
xv. 22.
" For Thy Word's sake—hast Thou done all." 2 Sam. vii. 21.
In the Book of Psalms the Word appears in a personal form.
" The word of the Lord is tried ; He is a buckler to all who trust
in Him." Psa. xviii. 30. See also Psalms cxix. 89, 105 ;
cvii. 20 ; cxlvii. 15, 18, &c.
It is the Word in all revelations, and in all the Divine dealings.
2. The idea of the WISDOM of God is found in the Old Test.
Used to designate revelations of the Divine essence and attributes.
Personified in Job xxviii., and also in Prov. viii., ix., in striking
terms.
This personification not merely poetical but practical.
Ascribes to WISDOM all revelations of God in creation and providence.

Nothing wanted but Love, the highest attribute, to complete the idea.

In Christ the WORD of God and the WISDOM of God are united.

The LOGOS of John embodies and unfolds these glorious titles.

3. The Apocryphal writers use similar forms of thought in reference to WISDOM.

The "Targum," or Chaldee paraphrases, clearly represent the sense of the Jews of that age.

They speak of "Memra," or the Word, and apply the name to God Himself.

Psa. cx. 1 is rendered, "The Lord said unto His Word."

Isa. xlv. 12, "I by my Word made the earth, and created man upon it."

Gen. i. 27, "The Word of the Lord created man."

In the Sept. "Shaddai," the Omnipotent name, is changed into "the Word." Ezek. i. 24.

In many other passages the Sept. has *Logos* or Word.

These facts account for the familiarity of the term to the Jewish mind.

4. Faint rays of truth had penetrated the Gentile world.

We meet with the term Logos in the Platonic philosophy.

Philo, the celebrated Alexandrian Jew, had given the term wide currency.

He endeavoured to show the harmony between Plato and Moses.

The writings of Plato and Philo known at Ephesus where John resided.

John's teaching wholly independent of the schools of philosophy.

His LOGOS and that of Plato and Philo altogether distinct.

Their Logos a mere group of Divine ideas or causes.

A purely impersonal quality included in God.

Or some sort of imaginary representative of the Divine agency.

A kind of emanation mediating midway between the infinite and finite.

Shadowy, distant, indistinct : a mere abstraction.

The ideas of time, history, and corporeality totally foreign to it.

A yawning gulf fixed between "Word" and "Flesh."

On the contrary, the LOGOS of John is real, present, personal, incarnate God.

No vacillation or hesitancy with John : his doctrine clear, compact, majestic.

It is stamped with the image and superscription of Divinity.

He lifts the LOGOS conception infinitely above all Jewish and Gentile thought.

He fills it with the glory of EMMANUEL. Matt. i. 23.

Henceforth and for ever it enshrines the *great mystery of Godliness.*

Christianity not only a refining fire, it transfigures and consecrates all truth.

All things subserve the kingdom of God in the world.

Philosophy, notwithstanding its follies and errors, helped to pave the road for the rapid advance of Christ's Chariot.

Classical writers use Logos for the inward thought, and the outward form by which the inward thought is expressed.

The Biblical Logos is the creating, revealing, active Word of God.

Identified by John as the eternally existing Son of God. Chap. i. 4.

Christ is the Word of God both in His being and office.

Thought and speech are one : there is an essential identity.

Thought is inward speaking, and speech is audible thinking.

Thinking and speaking, spirit and speech, are necessarily associated.

Human speech is effected psychically and corporeally.

But speech in pure spirit, even in the Godhead, is inseparable from thought.

The word is the comprehension of the thought.

Christ is the inward and expressed thought of the eternal mind.

" He is the brightness of His Father's glory : the express image of His person." Heb. i. 2.

" He that hath seen Me hath seen the Father." John xiv. 9.

" The image of the Invisible God, the Firstborn of every creature." Col. i. 15.

He who is " *the image* " of Paul's writings is the *Logos* of John.

Each exists before creation : each is the one agent in creation.

Each is a Divine person : each is equal with God : each is really God.

James calls Christian doctrine "the Word of Truth." Chap. i. 18.

He describes it as having an effectual regenerating power.

Correspondent to God's creative Word in physical nature.

He calls Christian truth also " the engrafted Word." Chap. i. 21.

Capable of being livingly united with the life of the soul.

Peter speaks of "the Word of God which liveth for ever." 1 Pet. i. 23.

The Apocalyptic name given to Christ is " THE WORD OF GOD." Rev. xix. 13.

The relation of human thought to speech and action is a mystery.

This relation of the Word to the Father is a sublime mystery.

Mystery is the shadow of eternity falling upon time.

Mystery the skirts or train of the cloud of the Divine glory.

To all eternity there must ever be an altar to " the Unknown God."

Word was. "Was" not emphatic either in this or next clause.

"Let there be light, and there was light." "*Light*" emphatic, not
"*was.*"

With God. The Word was *with* God, not merely *in* Him.

God's Companion: The Man who is Jehovah's "Fellow."

Distinction of personality is affirmed. God means the Father.

A real independent " I " filled with the Divine life.

The Word is here declared co-eternal with the Father.

Was without time, but never without God. *Chrysostom.*

The Holy Ghost neither confounds the Person, nor divides the
substance.

The Greek word for *with* signifies more properly *towards* God.

The face of the Word is ever directed towards the face of the
Father.

Implies fellowship in nature, perfections, and works. John xvii.

The Lord Himself had often spoken upon this profound subject.

Christ, absolutely God, is yet relatively and personally the Son of
God.

A man may be a father, a son, and a spirit at the same moment.

Was God. Implies participation in Divine substance or essence.

Not merely a divine being, but in the absolute sense God.

From His eternal existence we ascend first to His distinct personality.

Then to the full truth of His substantial Godhead.

"John comes round again and knits up the ring." *Luther.*

The Word : Where ?—" In the beginning." How ?—" With God."
What ?—" Was God."

There are not two Gods, but one God, although two persons are
here named.

The first eighteen verses, axioms, affirming Christ's true and proper
Divinity.

The remainder of the Gospel, demonstrations, based on those axioms.

Doctrine of Christ's Divinity depends on a truth beyond itself.

It presupposes *real* distinctions in the essence of the Godhead.

Revelation discloses the existence of three such distinctions.

Not merely three varying relations of God in His dealings with man.

Scripture affirms eternal distinctions independent of creation.

The term " person " applied to these distinctions by the Western
Church. (See note to verse 2.)

The most expressive term, yet its use demands caution.

Divinity of Christ interwoven with the whole course of revelation.

Impossible to abstract or deny it and preserve Christianity.

As well destroy the sun in the heavens, and hope for light and vitality

He is called God in the highest sense. Rom. ix. 5; Matt. i. 23.

The *true* God, 1 John v. 20; the *great* God, Tit. ii. 13; the *mighty* God, Isa. ix. 6.

He is called JEHOVAH, Mal. iii. 1. The *only wise* God, Jude, verse 25.

Divine attributes are given Him: Eternity, Mic. v. 2. Immutability, Heb. xiii. 8. Omniscience, John xxi. 17. Omnipotence, Rev. i. 8. Omnipresence, Matt. xxviii. 20. Supremacy, Rom. ix. 5.

Divine works are ascribed to Him: Creation, Col. i. 16, 17. Upholding all things, Heb. i. 3. Redemption, Heb. ix. 12. Miracles, John xi. 47. Forgiving sins, Mark ii. 5. Raising the dead, John v. 28, 29. Judging the world, 2 Cor. v. 10.

Divine worship is paid Him. John v. 23. (See note to verse 2.)

Baptism to be administered in His name equally with the Father and Spirit. Matt. xxviii. 19.

Faith to be put in Him. John xiv. 1. The only Mediator. 1 Tim. ii. 5.

His name associated with the Father and Spirit in apostolic benediction. 2 Cor. xiii. 14.

Doctrine of Christ's Divinity protects the idea of God in human thought.

Deism cannot guard, and Pantheism destroys the idea.

This doctrine involves and insures Christ's infallibility as a teacher.

It communicates infinite virtue to His atoning death.

It imparts supernatural power to the ministry of the Gospel.

It irradiates with glory the kingly office of the Lord.

It alone secures the true dignity of man.

Belief of it has created the loftiest and purest piety.

Faith in a Divine Christ the Church's strength in all dangers.

Impugners of His Divinity generally deny the need of salvation.

If His Godhead is admitted all else is proved and established.

It is eternal life to know the Father and the Son. John xvii. 1—3.

This verse disproves *Atheism*, for it assumes the Being of God.

It disproves *Polytheism*, for it incontrovertibly declares the Unity of God.

It disproves *Fatalism*, for it discloses the free activity of the independent One.

8 / Gospel of John

It disproves *Pantheism*, for it clearly recognizes the existence of God apart from and before all things.

It disproves *Arianism* and *Socinianism* in every form.

The Divine unity a glorious complex social unity.

Doctrine of the Trinity embraces the entire Christian view of Revelation.

Creation and Redemption rest upon this immutable and eternal foundation.

'Εν ἀρχῇ. Expressive of a Being not in time. *Origen.* Before the world was. *Lücke, De Wette.* Beginning of all things. *Alford, Bengel.* From eternity. *Tholuck.* Beginning of the Old Covenant. *Many expositors.* Before any creation. *Meyer, Hengstenberg.* "John led me to a solitary spot frequented for prayer. Amid lightning, thundering, and earthquake John said, 'Take pen and parchment and write—In principio,'" &c. *Procorus*, a disciple of John, in *Barradius.* ἦν. The existence of an enduring and unlimited state of being, implied in ἦν, is contrasted with ἐγένετο in ver. 3. *Alford.* Verbum ab eterno *erat.* Those denying it *errant. Ambrose.* ὁ λόγος. From the time of Ptolemy I. (300 B.C.) there were Jews in Egypt in great numbers. Philo estimates them at a million in his time (A.D. 50). Aristobulus, about 150 B.C., endeavoured to unite the ancient doctrines of Wisdom and the Word of God with a form of Greek philosophy. This effort culminated in Philo, a contemporary with Christ. *Bengel.* The term before John predominant only in Philo. *Tholuck.* St. John found the term universally applied to Christ, and guarded and rightly expounded it. *Prescott, Burton.* Impossible to mistake the historical connection of John's doctrine with the Alexandrian as presented in Philo. *De Wette, Lücke.* The term familiar to John's readers. *Witsius.* He describes the incarnation, and uses it no more in his Gospel. *The Author.* Philo's Logos *not* a distinct person. *Dorner, Jowett.* Historical connection with Philo, but no doctrinal dependence. *Alford.* Philo did not know his own mind; his Logos is sometimes impersonal and sometimes not. *Liddon.* John derived the term from the Old Test. *Hengstenberg.* Denial of connection with Jewish and Alexandrian philosophy destroys the historic meaning. Logos, a term furnishing a common point of thought. *Meyer, Neander, Olshausen, Tholuck.* ὁ λόγος. The eternal revelation of the Divine essence—the fountain of all truth for all men. *Justin Martyr.* A real Being in whom the Divine essence is represented. *Tatian.* Always concealed in God as the reason of the Divine Spirit. *Theophilus.* The νοῦς and the λόγος, the revelation of the νοῦς, are to be thought of as one. *Athenagoras.* The Logos an image of the Divine reason. *Clement.* The medium of the life that flows from the essence of the Father. *Origen.* Inadequately rendered into English by "Word," although better than verbum. It has not the frequent classical meaning of "reason." A word before uttered must be indwelling. The Word the exponent of the will of God whether by speech or works. *Prescott.* Comprehends both *ratio* and *oratio. Lid. and Scott.* No other translation of this great word possible. *Luther.* "Speech." *Calvin.* "Reason." *Plato.* "Act of reasoning." *Plotinus, Philo.* Νοῦς and λόγος, in the way of likeness, stand in necessary essential relation as God the Father and God the Son. *Delitzsch.* As in man is *Logos creatus*, God the Father has *Logon æternum increatum. Nicolai.* God as object of Himself is the Word. The Word is the principle through which God is revealed to Himself. Creation mirrors God's thoughts. Logos mirrors Divinity. *Tholuck.* Philo made Θεός and Κύριος unite in the Logos. *Dorner.* Fundamental idea of first fourteen verses is, that *the original, all-creating*, and *all-enlightening Logos*, or personal Word of God, became man in Jesus Christ. *Lücke, Meyer, De Wette, Alford, Neander, Tholuck, Olsh.* As used by John, it means throughout the Word ; sometimes the individual word, as an expression of Jesus, John ii. 22 ; of God, x. 35 ; of the prophet, xii. 38 ; of the Scripture, xv. 25 ; of the people generally (proverb), iv. 37 ; sometimes of the entire word of Jesus, viii. 31 ; or of God, xvii. 17. Thus also John i. 1, 1 John i. 1, and Rev. xix. 13 will signify respectively the Word, the word of life, the word of God. Elsewhere it is the word of the proclamation, John vi. 68 ; Rev. i. 2, 9. The word of the proclamation, and the word that appeared in Jesus, are distinguished in such a way, that the latter is the personal Word, which preceded the former. In it God has from everlasting given His Counsel of love an objective existence, and not only His Will, but His Nature. *Delitzsch.* The Rabbis never called Messiah Interpreter of God's Will. *Melancthon.* Jews and Gentiles disliked the term υἱὸς θεοῦ. *Arrowsmith.* All the Father speaks comes from the Son. *Erasmus.* Brightness derived from the sun but contemporary with it (Heb. i. 2). *Council* of Ephesus. πρὸς τὸν. He does not say " *God was with God*," for there is but one God. *Musculus.* Consubstantiality with the Father. *Erasmus.* In two subsistences exists the one absolute Godhead. *D. Brown.* πρὸς τὸν, not ἐν τῷ θ. *Basil.* πρὸς, *unto*, for παρά, *with*, denotes a perpetual tendency of the Son to the Father. *Bengel, Besser.* πρὸς refers to an inner relationship of nature. *Brückner.* πρὸς, as indicative of space, designates the idea of distinction. *Tholuck.* In the Father's bosom. *Theoph.* Zech. xiii. 7. The word rendered " My Fellow " does not mean only an associate. It is used eleven times in Leviticus, strictly for a *fellow-man*, one who is as himself. When applied to the relation of an individual to God, that individual can be no mere man, but must be one united with God by an Unity of Being. The "Fellow" of Jehovah is He who said, "I and My Father are One." *Pusey, Hengstenberg.* καὶ Θεός ἦν ὁ λόγος. The form of this sentence is strictly parallel with πνευμα ὁ Θεός, chap. iv. 24. But the sense is as weighty a consideration as the form. Had John intended to say, " *God was the Word*" (Luther's translation), he would only have contradicted his last assertion. *Alford.* Θεός without the article means God as a *nature* or *essence*. *Tholuck.* Means strictly God; not merely *Divine*, or a God in a lower sense; of which no instance in the New Test. *Lücke, Meyer, De Wette.* Theodotus, a tanner of Byzantium in the second century, seems to have been the first who denied our Lord's proper Divinity. Other heresiarchs of the same name have been confounded with him. *Mosheim.* Arians look upon the Logos as an emanation from God. Unitarians apply the term to God Himself, or to certain of His attributes ; as Reason or Intelligence. The absurdity of such interpretations has been well exposed by *Dwight* (System of Theology). The eminent Hebrew scholar, *Junius*, was converted by this chapter. *Henry.* Papists hang the first verse round the neck as a charm against fevers. Each truth affirmed in the first fourteen verses refutes some error of ancient or modern times. Religious errors repeat themselves from age to age. The Word is a "two-edged sword." Heb. iv. 12. *The Author.* The first verses of St John's Gospel "worthy to be written in letters of gold." A *Platonic philosopher* quoted by *Augustine.* This barbarian comprised more stupendous thought in three lines than we in one volume. *Amelius in Eusebius.*

2. The same was in the beginning with God.

The same. Gr. HE. HE *alone.* He, and no other.

This verse a summary and repetition of the three propositions preceding.

First proposition characterizes the special subject.

Second affirms the personal distinction between the Logos and God.

Third declares the essential unity and consubstantiality of the Divine nature.

The three propositions form a solemn gradation :—

The Logos eternal, the Logos the antitypical expression of God, the Logos God. *Lange.*

Was, &c. Not at some time in the beginning included *in* God.

Did not become a self-subsistent person at the time of creation.

Nor yet when He was made flesh and dwelt among us.

As God of God He was " in the beginning with God."

Declares His eternal personality, in unity, with the Father.

Shows that His relation to God was the first and highest.

The Father could not be personal if the Son were not. *Origen.*

Before a creature existed who could be brought to blessedness,

The eternal Logos or Word was life and blessedness in Himself.

Only in virtue of His eternal existence could the Logos be the Creator of all things.

Scriptural repetition intentional.—1. In prayer it denotes affection. 2. In prophecy celerity. 3. In threatenings suddenness. 4. In precepts certainty. 5. In truth eternal importance.

Οὗτος. Christ adored as God by the ante-Nicene Church. "On a stated day they (the Christians) meet before daybreak and sing hymns to Christ as God." *Pliny* to the Emperor Trajan. "The population of Alexandria divided between the worship of Christ and the worship of Serapis." Emperor *Adrian* to Servian. "The Christians are still worshipping that great man who was gibbeted in Palestine." *Lucian.* "Christians worshipped a dead man." *Celsus.* A remarkable caricature of the adoration of our crucified Lord, was discovered not long since under the ruins of the Palatine palace. It is a rough sketch, traced, in all probability, by the hand of some Pagan slave in one of the earliest years of the third century of our era. A human figure with an ass's head is represented as fixed to a cross ; while another figure in a tunic stands on one side. This figure is addressing himself to the crucified monster, and is making a gesture which was the customary Pagan expression of adoration. Underneath there runs a rude inscription : *Alexamenos adores his God. Transactions of Royal Soc. of Lit.*, Lond., vol. ix., second series. The oldest Christian hymn which has come down to us in a complete form is preserved by *Clement of Alexandria* in his Pædagogus. It celebrates our Lord as "the Dispenser of Wisdom," "the Support of the suffering," the " Lord of immortality," the

"Saviour of mortals," "the Mighty Son," "the God of peace." It thrice insists on the "sincerity" of the praise thus offered Him. It concludes :—

> "Sing we sincerely
> The Mighty Son ;
> We, the peaceful choir,
> We, the Christ-begotten ones,
> We, the people of sober life,
> Sing we together the God of peace."

The Tersanctus and the Gloria in Excelsis both belong to the second century, and both pay Divine honours to Christ. As each morning dawned, the Christian of primitive days repeated in private the Gloria in Excelsis. Each evening, too, the Christian offered another hymn addressed to Jesus in His majesty :—

> "Hail ! gladdening Light, of His pure glory poured,
> Who is the Immortal Father, heavenly, blest,
> Holiest of Holies—Jesus Christ our Lord !
> Now we are come to the sun's hour of rest,
> The lights of evening round us shine,
> We hymn the Father, Son, and Holy Spirit Divine !
> Worthiest art Thou at all times to be sung
> With undefiled tongue,
> Son of our God, Giver of Life, Alone !
> Therefore in all the world, Thy glories, Lord, they own."
>
> *Lyra Apostolica.*

The original is given in *Routh's* Reliquiæ Sacr. It is still the vesper hymn of the Greek Church. The Te Deum is at once a song of praise, a creed, and a supplication. In each capacity it is addressed to our Lord. In its present form it is clearly Western, whether it belongs to the age of Augustine, with whose baptism it is connected by popular tradition, or, as is probable, to a later period. But we can scarcely doubt that portions of it are of Eastern origin, and that they carry us up well-nigh to the sub-apostolic period. *Liddon's* Bampton Lectures, 1866. Our Lord's *Manhood* especially assailed in the second century, His *Godhead* in the third and fourth. In the fifth the Personal *Unity* of His two natures. *Wilberforce.* ἐν ἀρχῇ. Prov. viii. 22, 23. Arius corrupted the text from ἔκτησε (possessed) to ἔκτισε (created). *Trapp.* "Ancient of Days," Dan. vii. 9. πρεσβύτατον τῶν ὄντων (the most ancient of anything that hath being). *Thales.* πρὸς τὸν θεόν. That the term "Trinity" is not Scriptural furnishes no argument against the doctrine so long as it is asserted and reasserted in the Scriptures. So the terms "Divinity," "Deity," "Humanity," "Incarnation," even "Christianity," are not less true because not found in the Bible. *Huntington.* Theophilus, Bishop of Antioch, appears to be the first writer who used the term. *Riddle.* Father, Son, and Spirit not qualities, not powers or activities of the Divine nature ; they are *hypostases*, that is, distinctions, expressing not merely single " aspects," single "rays " of the Divine nature, but each expressing by itself the entire Essence ; each for itself at the same time, and in equal degree, reveals the whole of God, the whole of Love, though each in a different way. *Martensen.* Christian doctrine of the Trinity, in its peculiar characteristics, opposed to Judaism, in that, instead of an impassable gulf between God and creation, it realizes the consciousness of Divine communication with creation ; and opposed to Paganism, in that it teaches the elevation of God above creation. *Neander.* The Trinity has its analogies in nature, and above all in man, who is body, soul, and spirit. *Baxter.* Existing ideas, Pagan, Oriental, Platonic and Neo-Platonic, and the amalgamation of the Jewish, Oriental, and Platonic, in Alexandria, furnished a junction, and served as a substratum for the development of this great Christian doctrine. *Hagenbach.* The Osirian myth was the great mystery of the Egyptian religion. Osiris is fabled to have come upon the earth for the benefit of mankind, with the title of "Manifester of good and truth," to have been put to death through the malice of Typhon the Wicked One, to have risen from the dead, and to have become the Judge of all. He is called the ineffable Osiris; the son who, having fought on earth the battle of his father, the lord of the invisible world, had risen and become the only being in the firmament. As judge of the dead, he received the soul of the perfect or the justified, purified and blessed, to himself. *Birch.* "PERSON." This word must not be taken to signify the same thing when spoken of God and of ourselves. *Howe.* Must be understood as an intelligent agent, having the distinct characters I, Thou, He. *Waterland.* The *finite* individuality which supplies our standard of thought is no adequate measure of the *infinite.* *Wilberforce.* Since Revelation is the entrance of Divine realities into this lower world, human conceptions cannot give them adequate expression. *Aquinas.* As applied to men, "person" implies the antecedent conception of a species. But this conception is utterly inapplicable to that one Supreme Essence which we name God. Christ, $\dot{\alpha}\pi\alpha\dot{\nu}\gamma\alpha\sigma\mu\alpha \ \tau\tilde{\eta}s \ \delta\dot{\delta}\xi\eta s$ (Heb. i. 3), that is, He is one with God, as having streamed forth eternally from the Father's essence, like a ray of light from the parent fire with which it is unbrokenly joined, and He is also $\chi\alpha\rho\alpha\kappa\tau\dot{\eta}\rho \ \tau\tilde{\eta}s \ \dot{\upsilon}\pi\sigma\sigma\tau\dot{\alpha}\sigma\epsilon\omega s$, that is, both personally distinct from, and yet literally equal to, Him of whose essence He is the adequate imprint. *Liddon.* The insufficiency of Unitarianism (so called) has received the following striking testimony from a gifted writer, Rev. James Martineau (Unitarian), England. "I am constrained to say that neither my intellectual preference nor my moral admiration goes heartily with their heroes, sects, or productions of any age. Ebionites, Arians, Socinians, all seem to me to contrast unfavourably with their opponents, and to exhibit a type of thought and character far less worthy, on the whole, of the true genius of Christianity," &c. *Huntington's* Christian Believing and Living, page 355.

---

3. All things were made by him; and without him was not any thing made that was made.

All things. Of wide import : denotes the whole universe. Col. i. 16 ; Heb. i. 2.

Gives the idea of something earlier than the completion of the world and the creation of man.

Perhaps a glance of inspiration at the wonders revealed by modern science.

He who made one world in space made all worlds in space.

He who made one world in time made all worlds in time.

He who gave matter its forms gave it also origination, the ground of all its forms.

Were made. "In the beginning God created the heavens and the earth," &c. Gen. i.

The Bible opens with this inspired Psalm of Creation.

It is a brief summary of an inconceivably vast series of events.

A rapid sketch of prominent features in the history of creation.

Intended to impress on the Hebrew people, prone to idolatry, the existence of one supreme Being.

To bring home to a race, rude and uncultivated, God's almighty power and dominion.

Commemorates therefore only the most impressive and striking acts.

Has no rivals, no competitors. It absolutely stands alone.

Ancient mythologies and cosmogonies gross and silly.

Different attempts to explain the origin of the world and of man refuted by intrinsic absurdity.

Gentile nations had no conception of creation in the Scriptural sense.

Wisest of them failed to discover that there is one God, the Maker of all things.

Chaldean philosophers familiar with the courses of the heavens.

But could not rise from the contemplation of creation to the Creator.

The creatures themselves the gods Chaldea worshipped.

Egypt great enough to conceive and execute the idea of the Pyramids.

Yet in its palmiest days Egypt adored beasts and reptiles

Greece peerless, mistress of arts, source of refined taste, storehouse of intellectual power, great nurse of genius.

Yet ignorant of the One God, Giver of all gifts, who had so richly endowed her.

Imperial Rome no exception to the common character of the Gentile world.

Bible alone proclaims what philosophy and science were never able to teach.

From age to age, with marvellous simplicity, it accommodates itself to all true progress.

In perfect accord with each view of God's manifold power which human science brings to light.

Creation a revelation of God—1. In His omnipotence. 2. In His wisdom. 3. In His goodness.

The world according to its various forms. 1. As Creation (Rom. i. 20). 2. As Nature (Rom. ii. 14). 3. As Cosmos (John i. 10). 4. As Æon (Eph. ii. 2).

Outlines of creation :—Heaven and earth : 1. Heaven and earth in union. 2. Earth for heaven. 3. Heaven for earth. *Lange.*

Creation in its progressive stages a picture of redemption—1. In the order of revelation. 2. In the individual soul. 3. In the history of the Church. 4. In the history of the world.

14 / Gospel of John

By Him. John discloses the relation between the Logos and creation.

Through His Word God created the world. Gen. i.

His Word is a personal Divine life. John, and N. T. generally.

According to Genesis everything is created with a view to man in the image of God.

According to the N. T. it is through the idea of Christ, and with a view to Him.

Adam the principle of creation; Christ the principle of humanity.

The growth of the world points back to the eternal existence of the WORD.

The eternal WORD the foundation for the growth of the world.

The Word echoes through time in creation, in redemption, and in glorification.

Relation of the Word to the created universe threefold :—

All things created *in* Christ, *by* Christ, and *for* Christ.

In Him. All archetypal forms and sources of creative life eternally reside in Him.

By Him. He is the one Producer and Sustainer of all created existence.

For Him. He is the end of created things as well as their immediate source.

"Whether they be thrones, or dominions, or principalities, or powers." Col. i. 16.

Creation in the most absolute sense ascribed to Christ. Heb. i. 10—12.

Living for Him, the explanation and the law of every creature.

For " He is before all things, and by Him all things consist." Col. i. 17.

Christ the root, the flower, and the fruit, of all the works of God.

" And I beheld, and lo, in the midst of the throne," &c. Rev. v. 6.

And without Him, &c. Expresses something more than that which precedes.

A distinct denial of the eternity and uncreatedness of matter.

Not even one thing was made without the Divine WORD.

Now, whatever has a being was either made or not made.

Whatsoever is not made is God ; whatsoever is not God is made.

One uncreated independent essence ; all others depending on it.

One eternal and necessary existence ; all others derived from it and by it.

The Word, Jesus Christ, not made, Maker of all things.

Jesus Christ therefore absolutely very and eternal God.   Heb. iii. 4.
Christ our Saviour, Maker of all things, a precious truth.
1. Associates His Name with all existence, past and present.
Furnishes the key to the dark problems of nature and providence.
Gives to science and Christianity a common foundation.
Science reveals the eternal power and God-head of the WORD.
Christianity, the means of mercy to fallen man through the WORD.
Compartments of one great fabric reared to the glory of God.
Science the outer court of the temple : admire and adore.
Christianity, the holy place : kneel, pray, praise.   Heb. iv. 16.
Shadow of the Cross thrown back upon the whole course of nature.
   1 Pet. i. 20.
The WORD, " the Lamb slain from the foundation of the world."
   Rev. xiii. 8.
2. It affords to faith the greatest assurance and encouragement.

> " His every word of grace is strong
>   As that which built the skies ;
> The voice that rolls the stars along
>   Speaks all the promises."—*Watts.*

3. It inspires the humblest with confidence.
He cares for, and provides for, the lowest of His creatures.
" These all wait upon thee : thou givest them their meat," &c.
   Psal. civ. 27.
" How much more shall your Father give good things ? " &c.
   Matt. vii. 11.
4. It irradiates the future with glorious hope.
" And I saw a new heaven, and a new earth," &c.   Rev. xxi. 1.
" Behold, I make all things new."   Rev. xxi. 5.

πάντα :—without the article more suitable than τὰ πάντα. *Lange.* Equal
to τὰ πάντα (1 Cor. viii. 6; Col. i. 16), and to ὁ κόσμος (verse 10). *Alford.*
ἐγένετο. Came into being. *Besser.* Creation in its proper sense was never so
much as dreamt of by the Gentile world. *D. Brown.* Springing of seed comes
nearer to their idea of creation. *The Author.* A child of our day knows and
has learned more from Genesis i. than all the philosophers without it ever
knew. *Jones.* The doctrine of a creation—the absolute free act of Divine omnipotence—the highest elevation of the human mind, to which no philosophy of
heathenism could attain. *Neander.* Ancient Greek writers begin with a dark
and formless chaos, in whose womb all beings slumbered as fermenting germs.
With them all is birth,—there is no creation. *Martensen.* Heathen cosmogonies all very similar. Chaos develops itself into the world-egg. This egg only
a conception called forth by the apparent form of the earth, so that the sky
presents itself as the shell and the earth as the yolk of this great egg. With

this shaping of chaos into a world-egg, arises the first being, or *the first man*. This first man, or being, the father and founder of all life, is a giant-like being. From himself he develops the various parts of the world-organism, heaven and earth, sun and moon, mountains and rivers. Now, by dividing or killing this first being, or by mingling its generating parts with earthly things, especially water, the lower life of nature begins, and things can multiply in sexual division and separation. Behind, beside, or over the chaos, usually stands a mysterious form of the highest divinity. This is the nucleus of all heathen cosmogonies. *Lange.* Chaldean myth of the creation, as given by *Berosus*, is found in *Eusebius ;* Phœnician myth, as given by *Sanchoniathon*, in *Eusebius ;* Egyptian myth in *Diodorus Siculus ;* a Grecian myth in *Hesiod ;* Indian myth in *Von Bohlen*, &c. ἐγένετο. Geological science claims an immense antiquity for the earth. The Bible gives no chronology of *creation*. It simply states that it took place "*in the beginning*," Gen. i. 1; Heb. i. 10. Here is ample scope for all that can be demanded. No language can be more indefinite. The word used by the sacred writer in Gen. i. 1 is *Bara*, which strictly means to create out of nothing ; whereas in describing the operations of the six days the word is *Hasah*, which means to *form* or *fashion* out of pre-existing materials. In Exodus xx. 11 the word is also *Hasah*. The early Christian Fathers commonly held the existence of created matter prior to the work of the six days. *Basil*, *Chrys.*, *Ambrose*, *Bede*, &c., and the most eminent doctors in the schools. The "days" of creation regarded as—1. Ordinary days of 24 hours. 2. Representative days. Days of the *description* ordinary days, but days of the *reality* Divine days. 3. Vast periods of time, according to Scriptural phraseology, Gen. ii. 4; 2 Pet. iii. 8. Remarkable coincidence between the order of creation given by Moses and that set forth in geology. Three days especially distinguished for the creation of vegetable and animal life. On the third day plants and trees (Gen. i. 11). On the fifth, reptiles, fish, and birds (Gen. i. 20). On the sixth, cattle, and beasts, and towards the end, man himself (Gen. i. 24—28). Harmony between the Mosaic history of creation and the science of this age can only be accounted for by Divine inspiration of Scripture. *Wiseman*, *Buckland*, *Chalmers*, *Harris*, *Pye Smith*, *Hugh Miller*, *Molloy*, *Paul*, *Kurtz*, *Lange*, *Delitzsch*, &c. διά αὐτοῦ. Opposed to "*without Him.*" *Bengel*. By, by means of, through. Christ is not said to have *created*, but the *Father by Him. Olshausen.* He did not make the world as an ὑπουργὸς, but as ὁμοούσιος τῷ Θεῷ. *Cyril.* Oriental Church assigned particles διά, σύν, and ἐν, to the Three Persons in the Trinity. Basil opposed it. *Hales.* χωρὶς. Implies the Father does nothing except as through the Son. *Jansen.* Denotes perfect unity of the first and second persons. *Denton.* οὐδὲ ἕν. This repetition excludes the ὕλη of Philo. Gnostics set *matter*, as a separate existence, over against God, and made it the origin of evil. *Neander*, *Lücke*, *Olshausen*, *Alford.* John exalts the Logos above all orders of spirits. *Augustine*, *Tholuck.* ὃ γέγονεν. The preterite implies something more absolute than the aorist. *Bengel.* Some place a stop after οὐδὲ ἕν. Whatever was made in Him was life. *Origen.* Whatsoever was made, its life was in Him. *Cyril.* But this might lead to the error of the Manicheans. *Aug.* Placing the period after οὐδὲ ἕν injures the sense of the passage, and renders it weak and inconsistent with analogy. *Lange*, *Alford.*

---

4. In him was life; and the life was the light of men.

In Him. From simple *creation* to the higher idea, communication of *life*.

" In Him we live, and move, and have our being." Acts xvii. 28.
Was life. Word LIFE occurs some *sixty* times in the brief books
of John.

Christ, *Prince of Life.* Acts iii. 15. Source of all life. Col. i. 16.
Author of spiritual life. 1 John v. 12. Of natural life. Ver. 3.
On Him all created life depends, and by Him it was imparted.
By Him, also, a new moral existence is effected. Eph. ii. 10.
" As I live : " The ordinary oath by Jehovah. Isa. xlix. 18.
No element of death can ever be found in Him. Psa. lxviii. 20.
He is the *pattern* of all life, so far as moral being is concerned.
Grace and glory of all believers are traceable to Him, as all rays
are to the sun.
" Our life is hid *with Christ* in God." Col. iii. 3.
By nature men are " dead in trespasses and sins." Eph. ii. 1.
" For He is thy life." Deut. xxx. 20 ; Psa. xxvii. 1.
The everlasting Fountain of all Life, without loss to Himself.
A boundless ocean of life ever-flowing, yet full as at the first.
However exalted His creatures, Christ alone hath infinite " FUL-
NESS." Col. i. 19.
Christ has life in Himself. John v. 26. More cannot be said of
Jehovah.
" With Thee is the fountain of LIFE ; in Thy light shall we," &c.
Psa. xxxvi. 9.
" She is a tree of LIFE to those that lay hold upon her." Prov.
iii. 18.
" Whoso findeth Me findeth life." Prov. viii. 35. Eternal sal-
vation. Luke ix. 24.
It is a far greater work to renew a soul, than to create a world.
Creation, like a scaffolding, is but temporary, salvation is eternal.
Prophets uttered oracles which they did not understand.
Apostles wrought miracles, but could do nothing of themselves.
They could not at times comprehend their own words. Acts iii. 7.
None but the Creator can *understand the mind,* much less regen-
erate it.
Men are " alienated from the life of God through ignorance." Eph.
iv. 18.
All boasting of life apart from Christ is only *death masked.*
Our Lord connects Himself continually with *Light* and *Life.*
The WORD breathed into man's nostrils, and he became a living
soul. Gen. ii. 7.
Hence our Lord's name is " THE WORD OF LIFE." 1 John i. 1.

Light. Christ is to the soul what light is to the body.

The naturally blind, the *saddest;* spiritually blind, the *darkest* of men.

Heathenism had its unconscious prophecies of an approaching Light.

As time rolled on they multiplied, as lamps when nearing a mighty city.

Like Socrates, some sought after the Lord, if haply they might find Him.   Acts xvii. 27.

Christ in the *conscience* is the only solution of heathenism.   John i. 9.

Among Jews some looked for "glory, honour, and immortality."   Rom. ii. 7.

By the light of the WORD Abel sacrificed and Enoch walked with God.   Heb. xi. 4, 5.

Life points out the *Author* of human salvation, *the* Sacrifice.

Light indicates a *Teacher* and *Preacher* of salvation.

In all languages light is a figure either for happiness or its author

Christ the WORD, Jehovah heard ; the LIGHT, Jehovah seen; the LIFE, Jehovah felt.

"*I am the Light of the world.* My followers shall not walk in darkness."   John viii. 12.

"The Dayspring from on high hath visited us."   Luke i. 78.

"Who dwells in light unapproachable."   1 Tim. vi. 16.

Our life has its *origin* in this "fulness of God," and it *flows* in communion with Him.

In the midst of a pining and perishing world life proceeds from Him, whose Breath of Life renews the face of the earth. Psa. civ. 30.

In Christ is the *light* of *life.*   Out of Christ is the *night* of *death.*

"These words are thunder-claps against moralists trusting in their own works." *Luther.*

Classical Greece and Rome were in misery, though a *brilliant* misery.

Light of Christ unlike the light of the sun :--

1. It illumines the midnight cell, Acts xvi. 26, and dark mountain caverns, Heb. xi. 38.   Knows no limits.   John i. 9.

2. It takes no time to travel from heaven to earth. Matt. xxviii. 20

3. No obstacle, though dark and cold as a "shadow of death," can arrest it.   Luke i. 79.

4. Its source is not created, nor liable to any possible failure.

5. Earthly objects must borrow the sun's rays, in order to disclose their beauty. Grace and truth from the Lamb of God have a *native, inherent* beauty.
6. The most perfect likeness reflected on an earthly mirror is defective.

The image of Christ, traced on the heart, is perfect. 2 Cor. iii. 18.

Clothed in corruptible flesh, we cannot show the world this celestial image wrought on the soul.

7. Light of the sun falling on cold hard objects, *leaves* them cold and hard still.

Light divine *warms, transforms, quickens* into life and light. Eph. ii. 1.

8. Light of the sun sometimes mocks the hope of the traveller.

The author saw in the *Arabian Desert* a singular illusion, the *mirage.*

In the distance appeared a lake of enchanting loveliness and beauty.

Ripples, reflecting the rays of the sun, seemed to lave its mossy banks.

Islands rose in velvet green, and trees loomed out, trailing their branches in the water.

Yet there was neither tree, nor isle, nor water, nor mossy bank.

In an instant the vision vanished, and left a wild barren desert stretching as far as the eye could see.

Thus Barry, the celebrated painter, while on his deathbed, mistook the reflection of the rays in his chamber for the glories of the golden city, flashing over its jasper walls.

But the light of Christ never deceives or betrays those following HIM.

Like light, Christ is His *own witness—self-evidencing.* 1 John v. 10.

Thus the Bible, beaming with divine radiance, will ever be its own witness.

Life in the heart will give *light* in the head. 2 Cor. iv. 6.

Bible understood and valued in proportion to depth and fulness of piety.

ζωή. Life, really life, opposed to death. *Rostlin.* Life in the rational creation by the Logos. *Hengstenberg.* All physical, moral, and eternal life have their source in Christ. *Lücke, Meyer.* Without Him all things would fall back into nothingness. *Calvin.* βίος is life extensive, the period of life, means of sustaining, and manner of spending it. βίος, ethical word in classics. ζωή, higher term and nobler in the Scriptures, Eph. iv. 18. πηγὴ ζωῆς, Fountain of life. Psa. xxxvi. 9. Absolute life implies freedom from sin and all death. *Trench.* Life and light, darkness and death, are constantly associated. *Bengel.* Source of spiritual life. *Luther, Lampe, Lightfoot.* Recovery of blessedness. *Alford.* Providence. *Calvin.* φώς, sunlight, Rev. xxii. 5. φέγγος, moonlight, Mark xiii. 24; Matt. xxiv. 29. Λύχνος, a hand-lamp fed with oil. Λαμπάς, a torch. John was a λύχνος : Christ τὸ φῶς τὸ ἀληθινὸν. *Trench.* φώς, supreme source of blessedness. *Quesnel.* It frequently denotes true religion. *Lampe.* Revelation, with the glittering fragments of light scattered among the heathen. *Alford.* The Logos in general history. *Hengstenberg.* He became the light of the world at the Incarnation. *Heumann.* All is dark in the mind, until Christ illumines it. *Quesnel.* Contrasted with light and life boasted by Jews in their law. *Lightfoot.* Through the creative energy of the WORD, consciousness and insight into highest truth were unfolded in humanity. *De Wette.*

---

5. And the light shineth in darkness; and the darkness comprehended it not.

The Light. Christ Himself. John ix. 5. Salvation. John viii. 12.
Shineth. From the moment of creation this light hath shone.
There is to the earth twilight before the actual rising of the sun.
So by conscience, by prophecy, by vision, by angels, by revelation,
   He caused dawn to precede the morning of the Incarnation.
Without any other light conscience speaks out for God so clearly
   that all men are without excuse. Rom. i. 20.
Yet so intensely depraved are men, that they hear it not. Eccles.
   vii. 20.
" Lord, I have nothing for thee to pardon." *Isidore,* a monk.
Light of Old Test. from the *unrisen* " Sun of Righteousness."
Same Light *risen* shines in the New Test. 1 John ii. 8.
Darkness the state of all out of Christ. Matt. iv. 16.
Shadows of sin deepen into the gloom of death.
Christ's Light conducts through the gloom of the grave to heaven.
The Law is a light, but a dim half-light only. Prov. vi. 23.
The gospel alone brings life and immortality to light. 2 Tim. i. 10.
This Light reflected " from the face of Jesus Christ " on the heart.
   2 Cor. iv. 6.
Paradise itself, according to Rabbinical tradition, was radiant with
   heaven.
God not far from the heathen,—their conscience His representative.
   Rom. ii. 15.
Numberless and costly sacrifices reveal His hand with them.
All earthly sounds fail to drown the sound of God's secret, awful
   march among the nations.
His righteous judgments, like lightning, flashed on heathen consciences, amid all their darkness.

Above the raging sea of passion He made His thunder-voice heard.
Else why did the Greeks erect a temple to the *Eumenides ?*
Why was *Orestes* for his mother's blood haunted from land to land ?
Why was the sacrilege of *Prometheus* visited with the rock, the
 vulture, and the chain ?
Why did *Cleomenes* expiate his guilt by cutting himself piecemeal ?
Why did the plague spot cling to *Megacles* and his seed for ever ?
Why was *Agathocles* said to have been placed on the funeral pile
 while still alive ?
Why was *Dionysius,* who boasted with a jest that the gods smiled
 on sacrilege and prosperity, so punished that the world
 looked on with astonishment ?
Fulvius-Flaccus robbed Juno's temple, and they noted that he died
 a madman.

Darkness. Bible use of the term, thorough alienation from God.
Spirit of God did not find a deeper darkness on the face of chaos
 than the moral gloom which the WORD found enveloping our
 race.
Want of light self-incurred, the *state :* depriving of light, the *result.*
Darkness in Egypt, and darkness at the crucifixion.
The symbol of misery, adversity, death.   Job iii. 5. ; Joel ii. 2.
Of God's mysterious providence. Psa. xviii. 11.   Of the downward
 road of sin. Psa. xxxv. 6.
Of Satan's dark power. Col. i. 13.   Of a wilful choice of error.
 1 John ii. 11.
Of idolatrous rites. Ezek. viii. 12.   Of ignorance. Matt. vi. 23.
Of Divine judgments. Isa. xiii. 10.   Of the soul. Isa. xlix. 9.   Of
 works of the wicked. Rom. xiii. 12.
The atmosphere of rebellion and depravity.   "They sit in dark-
 ness and in the shadow of death."   Luke i. 79.
Here signifies collected humanity unilluminated and unsanctified
 by truth.
Saints freed from it at death.   *" There shall be no night there."*
 Rev. xxi. 25.
The *Word* the light of " the law, a shadow of good things to come."
 Heb. x. 1.
He was the Light of prophecy, " a light that shineth in a dark
 place."   2 Pet. i. 19.
The dim light of Jewish revelation gives place to the gospel blaze.
" If I had not come and spoken unto them, they had not had sin."
 John xv. 22.

The *majesty* of the *Deliverer* proves the depth of our ruin and misery.

The *vastness* of His *sacrifice* proves the depth and burden of our sin.

How false the deceitful promises of the world. Jer. vi. 14.

How absurd to suppose that man, an *alien*, unreconciled to his Maker, can be happy.

Heaven and all its inhabitants ever have light. Psa. civ. 2 ; Isa. xxx. 26 ; Dan. ii. 22.

"And the city had no need of the sun." Rev. xxi. 23.

The glory of God doth lighten it, and the Lamb is the light thereof.

In the first and second verses we have the state of things before creation.

In the third, creation ; in the fourth, man's condition in Eden.

In the fifth, the fall of our race—*the interpretation of Genesis by the Holy Spirit.*

Comprehended. Gr. " *Did not take it in.*"

The presence of the Almighty effected no change in chaos.

The Spirit *must* MOVE. Chaldee, " breathed " life or *quickened* the mass.

The fountain was not found by Hagar until pointed out by the angel. Gen. xxi. 19.

Christ is called the TRUE LIGHT. John i. 9. The TRUE BREAD. John vi. 32.

The TRUE VINE. John xv. 1. All others were but types of the truth. Heb. ix. 24.

Sunlight at noonday, yet the blind perceive it not.

The renewed see first at conversion, but the light was there *before.*

At the darkest hour, when Satan had crushed and chained our race, LIGHT appeared in the Incarnate One.

Men may sink so deep in darkness as to cease to desire light.

They will " *love darkness rather than light.*" John iii. 19. Desperate depravity.

Jew and Gentile refusing to own God *in heaven*, He came down in the flesh.

Not seeing His light proves our *blindness*, not Christ's want of light. Prov. i. 22, 29, 30 ; 1 Cor. ii. 14 ; Eph. iv. 18 ; Rev. iii. 17.

Darkness *repels* the light. John iii. 20. *Imprisons it.* Rom. i. 18.

Spurns it, as did Balaam. Num. xxiv. 2. Some *curse* the sun, as
Ethiopians.
To such Christ " is set for their fall." Luke ii. 34. To them He
is " the shadow of death."
Instead of growing weaker after shining 4000 years, our SUN waxes
stronger.
This light shines for the "little flock : " the millions of earth prefer
darkness.
The strivings of man after moral good had miserably failed.
1 Cor. i. 21.
This prepares the way for announcing the Incarnation of the *Word*.
Each object in creation is a *hand-board* to the inquirer pointing to
the Saviour.
Thus Mary made the gardener a guide to her Lord. John xx. 15.
"1 sought Him, but I found Him not. Saw ye Him whom my soul
loveth ? " Cant. iii. 2, 3. The spouse to the watchmen.

φαίνει. The agency of the historical Christ. *Hengstenberg*. This verse the
key to the Gospel of John. *Lange*. 1. Shining of this light over the world. 2.
The historical manifestation among the Jews. *Alford*.
Σκοτία. By nature all was light. Sin darkened all. *Theophylact*. Darkness is not created, light is. *Bengel*. From simple ignorance to daring, devilish
resistance. *Brückner*. Darkness of Judaism hinted at. *Lampe*. The almost
tragic tone of this verse is prevalent through the Gospel and First Epistle.
Lücke. Our Lord's conflict with the darkness of Jews in Jerusalem John's
special design. *Fromann*.

---

6. There was a man sent from God, whose name was John.

A man. John the Baptist, or Baptizer. See on John i. 15.
So illustrious a person could not visit our world without being an-
nounced.
John was the subject of prophecy 416 years before he was born.
Mal. iii. 1.
He had no knowledge of the Messiah until specially revealed.
John i. 33.
At Bethany (not Bethabara) he pointed out the Lamb of God.
He baptized after Christ began to preach. John iii. 30 ; iv. 1 ;
Acts xix. 3.
He taught his disciples prayer and fasting. Matt. ix. 14 ; Luke
xi. 1.
Sent. As a divine Legate whose errand was one word, " LIGHT."

He found nearly all Judea sunk in the grossest darkness.

The Spirit of God roused the nation to listen to his proclamation.

The last witness belonging to the Old Test. whose finger stretches over to the New.

Sent from God. A definition of a prophet.

Reference to the prediction, " Behold, I send my messenger," &c. Mal. iii. 1.

Jonah declined going after he had been divinely sent.

Some, however, attempt to run before they are sent. Jer. xxiii. 32.

" The time to favour Zion, yea, the set time, had come." Psa. cii. 13.

John, the Baptist, as forerunner of Christ, was honoured above all prophets.

Ministry lasted about three years, half of which was spent in prison.

God at times accomplishes more by a minister in jail than by 1000 in the pulpit. (John Bunyan.)

'Εγένετο, not ἦν; not " was," but "began to be." *Denton.*

Άνθρωπος. These three verses in parenthesis. *Rosenmuller.*

'Ιωάννης, Heb. Jehovah-given. *Gesenius.* As harbinger of grace. *Hawkins.* Was born six months before our Lord. *Wieseler.* The Evangelist does not quote O. T. fully, but alludes to the prophecies. *Hengstenberg.* The Baptist's knowledge of Christ specially revealed. *Jackson.* No knowledge verifying Him as the Messiah. *Mill.*

---

7. The same came for a witness, to bear witness of the Light, that all men through him might believe.

Came. Though sent, came freely to testify.

Like the morning-star, a herald and ornament of the approaching King of Glory.

Witness. Not the " person," but the " testimony given."

Jesus declared that he was more than a prophet. Matt. xi. 9.

Christ needed no forerunner, any more than the great orb of day, for who needs a star to seek the sun?

The Baptist was "a burning and shining light," John v. 35, reflecting Christ's light.

To bear witness. The Evangelist's manner to repeat, to make truths clear and strong.

Verb and noun used 38 times in the Gospel, 17 in the Epistles, and 18 times in the Apocalypse.

Light. Christ. John i. 4. Salvation. John viii. 12.

A strange fact ! *Does the sun seek lanterns? Augustine.*

Yet the Son of God seeks a *poor, frail, sinful mortal* to testify of
His Incarnation.

So brilliant was the *lesser*, that the Jews mistook him for the
greater, Light.

John, like the watchman before day, cried, "The morning cometh."
Isa. xxi. 12.

He resembled the star guiding the wise men of the East to Christ.

Not the Bridegroom, but the friend of the Bridegroom. John iii. 29.

Those are oft of great use who shine in *borrowed* light.

Some are in danger of overvaluing, as well as undervaluing, God's
ministers.

All men. None are excluded who do not exclude themselves.
Luke vii. 30.

Through him, i.e. through John the Baptist, not through Christ,
the Light.

When we see a mountain-top irradiated at dawn, we know by such
witness that the sun will soon rise upon us.

We may be able to look on a mountain of snow illumined by the
sun, yet we cannot gaze steadily upon the blazing orb itself.

Believe. John vii. 38. Faith is, 1. A special divine gift. Eph.
ii. 8.

2. A duty comprehending all other duties—*the duty of duties.*

" *This is the work of God, that ye believe on Him whom He hath sent.*"
John vi. 29.

Much idle controversy has sacrificed one to the other or misrepresented both.

The *link* between *duty* and *grace*, the human and divine, is not yet
reached by the mind of man.

The Holy Spirit defines faith to be the " substance (confidence) of
things hoped for." Heb. xi. 1.

1. The gospel is a record of life through the Son of God. 1 John v.
5—13.

2. Design of this record or witness is to beget belief. John i. 17.

3. Faith in that thus witnessed " our testimony." 2 Thess. i. 10.

Abraham believed according to that which was spoken. Rom.
iv. 18.

" He that hath received His testimony hath set," &c. John iii. 33.

" He that believeth not God hath made Him a liar," &c. 1 John
v. 10.

Personal object of faith is God. *Special personal,* object is Jesus
Christ.

μαρτυρίαν. Not a prophet to announce only, but testify. *Hugo de S. Charo.*
πάντες. Heathen. *Luther.* Jews. *Tholuck.*
πιστεύσωσι, in the Light understood. *Lücke, Alford.* Anabaptists affirmed
the written word useless, and that all are taught by the Spirit in our time.
Besser.
Αὐτοῦ. Refers to John and not to the Light. *Hengstenberg.*

---

8. He was not that Light, but was sent to bear witness of that Light.

Was not. What moral splendour has this morning star !
The evangelist tells us " *He was not* " *the Sun* of Righteousness !
Thus the morning rays on the mountain-top tell us the sun is risen.
Thus an angel coming seemingly *at midnight*, it appeared like the
> dawn of day, for " the earth *was lightened with His glory*."
> Rev. xviii. 1.

Not that light. Not the promised *Light* of the world ; not a light,
> lighting others—but a light, *lighted* by another. *Augustine.*
Hero worship has been the religion of many men in gospel lands.
In the presence of Jesus the highest of mortals is less than vanity.
The shading of John was to heighten the light of Christ. *Herder.*
John rejoiced his glimmering taper would be lost in the effulgence
> of this Light.

1. The Gentiles had a light which, carefully observed, might lead
> them to God. Rom. i. 20 ; ii. 15.
2. The light of revelation through inspired prophets. Heb. i. 1.
3. The Shechinah and pillar of fire illustrated the truth. Psa. xcix. 7.
4. The Saviour bringing the gospel typified by the sun. Mal. iv. 2.

Bear witness. He was sent as a watchman to proclaim the com-
> ing dawn to a city asleep.
In all ages man had uttered this heart-cry amid the moral gloom,
> " Watchman, what of the night ? " Isa. xxi. 11.
He was sent to announce and commend the Saviour, the true office
> of gospel ministers.
They are not mediators, as Romish priests blasphemously claim.
They are witnesses of the truth and stewards of the mysteries of
> God. 1 Cor. iv. 1.

οὐκ ἦν. Superfluous, as earliest traces of John being deemed the Messiah,
were in the second century. *Tholuck.* Is man to judge what Jehovah ought
or ought not to record ? *The Author.* τὸ. Greek article denotes distinction,
as *that* bread, John vi. 32. φῶς. Archetypical light, not partial or derived.
Alford. Many Jews believed John the Messiah on account of the prestige
of his birth, and popularity of his ministry. *Corn. à Lap.* He who gives light
must be divine. *Grotius.* Polemically to prevent too high an estimate of
John. *Olshausen.*

9. That was the true Light, which lighteth every man that cometh into the world.

True Light. John i. 4.   Uncreated, eternal, underived source of
   light.

In comparison John was a mere lamp, a feeble and failing light.

Christ not only imparts light, but vision, ability to see the light.
   Luke xxiv. 45.

As Herostratus took fire from the altar at Ephesus to burn the temple, so *infidels* owe their entire powers used in battling JE-
   HOVAH JESUS to the very Being they would destroy.

John the Baptist, a burning and shining light to the Jews *alone*.

Christ the true Light to Jews and Gentiles in every age to the end
   of time.

1. Christ is a divine Light.   Prov. xxx. 4.   2. He is a transforming light.   2 Cor. iii. 18.   3. His kingdom is one of
   light.   Eph. v. 8.   4. His inheritance is light.   Col. i. 12.

(1.) Light of reason.   (2.) Of the everlasting gospel.   (3.) Operations of His Spirit.

This name given our Lord was claimed by Him also.   John viii.
   12 ; ix. 5 ; xii. 46.

" He that seeth ME seeth Him that sent me."   John xii. 45.

Lighteth.   Gr. *continually is lighting*.   This word used 11 times
   in New Test.

This Light hints at the *source* of the *soul*.   The body as a case
   was made of clay.

But the soul could not be created from matter ; no air, no earth,
   no water was here used.

We are in debt to nothing but the Logos for our soul.   He who
   breathed upon the apostles and imparted the Holy Ghost gave
   to us a living spirit.

Knowledge and righteousness were the image, the essence, the
   light of the soul when first created.

What of our glorious inheritance is left to us prodigals Christ is
   the blessed author.

Our Lord alone is the True Light illuminating all believers.

Christ as the Messiah does not lighten the heathen in their blindness.

But He lightens *all men* by means of conscience.

Our Lord's *vicegerent* can *alone meet the demands of this text. Calvin.*

The eye sees by *light*, but takes no account of this *medium* in the act.

Thus conscience decides the right and wrong at the *first* glance.

Its office is to declare not what *is*, but what *ought* to be.

It speaks *one language at Athens and at Rome,* and hath a sanction in every heart. *Cicero.*

Infidels have *in vain* controverted this great fact.

It *declares virtue never can be vice,* nor *vice virtue.*

It *solemnly and faithfully declares evil to be evil,* and announces its doom.

Had it power as it has authority, it would rule the world. Butler.

Conscience looks to the LAW above it, as the eye does to the sun.

As the mind's foundations are torn up and become deranged, so can the conscience be *distorted.*

Sin is moral insanity, and conscience often outraged becomes "madness." Ecc. ix. 3.

Conscience is the master power of the soul, and never moves without a *retinue.*

Devoted benevolence, patriotism, or piety, these attendants *cheer* and *gladden.*

Violated, they become *avenging furies,* and remorselessly pursue with scorpion lash.

Our Lord, who reaches "every man," thus renders the soul *sensible* of its connection with virtue or vice, as the needle is sensible of the approaching magnet.

Conscience does not render one virtuous, but judges of moral acts.

Conscience is often perverted. *The novel is stained by tears of those who never weep over real misery.*

Thousands weep over trials of chastity in *the theatre* and *go forth to the* SAME SIN.

They multiply the victims of lust, yet shed tears over their ruin *on the stage.*

Sterne wept over a dead ass, yet treated his mother *unkindly.*

Millions think themselves virtuous because they admire the good.

A grand error that *hero-worship* and *heroism* are the same, or that to *admire* a martyr is to *deserve* the martyr's crown.

Every man. Revelation was designedly withheld from some of our race.

" If the mighty works which were done in you HAD BEEN DONE in Tyre." Matt. xi. 21.

But where prophecy did not go, *He sent conscience:* all are "without excuse." Rom. i. 20.

It is a *narrow* exegesis which confines this to the gospel revelation.

Enlightened conscience is as truly God's work, and in degree as
  radiant with divinity, as the Bible.
They are both mere reflections of the great Central Light, or
  echoes of the higher law.
Conscience, the lesser light, leads men like " the sun shining in its
  strength."
The Bible beams as the combined " LIGHT OF SEVEN DAYS." Isa.
  xxx. 26.
All who walk in darkness put out the light given, and *create their*
  own night of woe.
Hence the inference : In that day " every mouth will be stópped."
  Rom. iii. 19.
Cometh into, &c.   Hebrew periphrasis for a man, meaning all
  mankind.

φῶς.   Light of reason. *Ed. Irving.*   Inward light. *Fox, Pelagius.*   Conscience. *Calvin, Augustine, Quesnel, Lampe, De Wette, Lücke, Tholuck.*
Christ gives all men sufficient light for salvation. *Chrysostom, Lightfoot.*   All
the treasures of human knowledge worth the name are the fruit of the *Pure*
Reason, or the categorical imperative (i.e. conscience). *Kant.*   Living according to conscience secured salvation to Socrates, Heraclitus, and other virtuous
heathen. *Rosenmuller.*   Universal intuitions. *Brown, Aristotle.*   Primitive
judgment. *Cousin.*   Fundamental idea. *Whewell.*   A hundred of the best and
profoundest thinkers agree in this. *Sir W. Hamilton.*   Monarch faculty.
McCosh.   Gospel powerless without the *living* LOGOS. *Denton.*
    It is the province of Christ to lighten. *Jacobus.*   By no means exhausts the
sense of the text.   How could "the world" (ver. 10) know *Him* apart from
Revelation ? *The Author.*   ἀληθινόν.   That which answers to its idea.
Tholuck.   Original. *Alford.*
    φωτίζει.   Heb. says it was *done,* when *intended. Pearce.*   Dawning salva-
tion. *Hengstenberg.*   Explains what John says of himself.   Verses 31, 33.
Wordsworth.
    ἐρχόμενον.   Refers to the Coming One, Christ. *Lampe, Lücke, Tholuck,*
Alford, D. Brown.   Others more properly to ἄνθρωπον. *Bengel, Luther,*
Erasmus, Calvin, Beza, Meyer, Van Oosterzee.

---

10. He was in the world, and the world was made by him, and the world
knew him not.

He was.   Added, lest any one should suppose the I·ight *had not*
  been in the world.
The very nature of God's love causes Him not to abandon
  man.
But apostasy ever drives man, a prodigal, *from* his Father.
God abides by man even in *punishing* him here and hereafter.

In the world. He was here by thousands of witnesses,—the *rains*, fruitful seasons, the nightly *dew*, the healthful *breeze*, the genial *sun*, and cheerful *morn*, but with an infatuation utterly wild, *men worshipped these gifts as God.*

"The world by wisdom knew not God" as its Creator and Preserver. 1 Cor. i. 21.

For 4000 years He had been promised to an afflicted, waiting Church. Gen. iii. 15.

From creation He was guiding, sustaining, and unfolding all things.

He was the "Angel of the Covenant," oft revealing Himself to the Patriarchs.

The creature may forget the Creator, but He never forgets the creature.

"A woman may forget her sucking child, yet will I not forget thee." Isa. xlix. 15.

"My Father worketh hitherto, and I work." His arm never wearies. John v. 17.

Even the ungrateful share His continued, but forfeited favours. Matt. v. 45.

Being in the world, the world ought to have *known* Him as DIVINE.

Because the world did not see Him in His Godhead, He came in the flesh.

Word "world" occurs 68 times in the course of John's Gospel.

It seems always associated with the thought of *pain* or suffering.

Darkness of sin has marred the lightsome work of Christ, changing it into "*the world.*"

The *whole* world is a *lost* world ; continuing such will be a *rejected* world.

World denotes the *desperate alienation of the heart from God.*

Every conscience for 4000 years before Christ *clearly* and strongly testified for God, against the sinner, as it does *now.*

But men boldly and defiantly refused to inquire.

Refused to ask for more light, or more convincing truths.

Roman and Greek writers, with an *honesty rare* among "Liberals" and infidels, confess *they did not do what they knew to be right.*

Seneca gives the unanimous verdict of the thoughtful heathen, *Eamus ad communem errorem,* "for company let us sin on."

Was made. Repeated, in order to deepen the impression. Rev. iv. 11. (See on verse 3.)

He claims to have been upholding and governing all things.

Yet the Jews understood Him not, *did not wish to know Him.*

The world. In the Bible this word points out the *impious vanity of the human race.*

Knew Him not. His ETERNAL POWER and GODHEAD were written on the very heavens. Psa. xix.

Yet the heathen sinned on, and *knew they sinned,* because they loved their sins, and gloried in their shame. Phil. iii. 19; Rom. i. 20.

In nature, Christ puts forth the *arm of a Creator* before the heathen.

In *men's consciences,* He puts forth the VOICE of a REVEALER. *Chalmers.*

Hence, in judgment, each soul condemned, will give its everlasting *Amen* to the act of the righteous Judge.

The world's Maker WALKING ON IT, *yet ignored by the world He made!*

"The starry heavens, monuments of Almighty power, by their very commonness, have grown contemptible." *Augustine.*

God had hid His Son under the form of a carpenter's son.

Hid His saints under humble artificers, shepherds, fishermen, &c.

Monarchs in exile; His elect princes in banishment. Psa. xlv. 16.

Melchizedek "*King,*" having received his crown from his Maker, and thus his heraldry guaranteed by Jehovah Himself, does nowhere appear in *tables of royalty* of earthly thrones.

The Church, like the moon, is ever full-orbed to *the Sun,* her REDEEMER.

So the Church ofttimes shows her dark side towards the earth.

If the earth knew not her Lord, much less the Lord's servants. 1 John iii. 1.

Note the climax. *He was in the world* (as the sun risen), therefore the world should have known Him.

The world was made by Him. Much more should they have *known* their Creator.

Yet the world knew Him not. Cared not to know their best Friend.

Knew Him not. He was here governing, sustaining, quickening all things.

But men's foolish hearts were darkened. Rom. i. 21.

His *Wisdom,* infinite, seen in every leaf, bud, and flower.

His *Power* in wheeling the changes of spring, summer, and autumn.

His *Justice* that fell ever and anon like a thunderbolt on the impious.

His revealed *Will* in the oracles of the prophets and in His living Church they saw not.

The love of the *world* blinds, though that world was made to reveal its Maker.

" The ox knoweth its owner," &c. Isa. i. 3. But men did not know God.

Man cannot, if he would, separate from God. *Vinet.*

He cannot put off his moral nature and be a mere *animal.*

He may only cease to be a man, by becoming a *demon.*

The *wicked* are bound to have to do with God, as well as the *good.*

Even in their *blasphemies they cannot leave God alone.*

Many essaying to fling off all religion, become *fiercer enemies of themselves.*

Trust, becomes mistrust ; peace, rancour ; prudence, error ; good-will, hatred.

Not the scorched brain, but the burning heart, is needed.

Those " not of the world," even before the Incarnation, knew Him.

Abraham saw His day, and was glad. John viii. 56. David called Him Lord. Psa. cx. 1.

Seven thousand besides Elijah had not bowed the knee to Baal. Rom. xi. 4.

ἐν τῷ κόσμῳ. The created world here represented by man. *Alford.* The Logos before His Incarnation. *Bengel.* Light was not in the world before the Incarnation. *Hengstenberg.* The light of conscience was. *Calvin, Augustine.* Old dispensation. *Burgon.*

---

11. He came unto his own, and his own received him not.

Came. He had in truth never left the world after making it.

But now He comes in the flesh, that men might better know Him.

His errand was foretold so plainly by the prophet, Isa. liii., that sceptics affirm it was *written after* the events had taken place.

His own. Gr. refers to *things*, as fields, cities, dwellings, &c., in Judea.

The second " **His own** " to *persons*, those enlightened and exalted by Divine Revelations. Psa. lxxviii. 71.

Jacob was the lot of His inheritance. Deut. xxxii. 9.

The Evangelist calls the Jewish people Christ's " inheritance."

The Lord's "people." 1 Pet. ii. 9. "His glory." Isa. xlvi. 13. "Heirs of the kingdom." James ii. 5.

Dear to God, though despised by the world. Jer. xxxi. 20.

A "peculiar treasure." Ex. xix. 5. "A special people unto Himself." Deut. vii. 6.

God's "first-born." Psa. lxxxix. 27. Rom. ix. 4, to them pertained :—

The *glory.* Shechinah, dwelling-place of the Angel of the Covenant, fiery pillar.

The *covenants.* With Abraham and the patriarchs, and at Sinai in the law. Ex. xx.

The giving of the law. Statutes of Moses, legal, ceremonial, and political.

The promises. Made to Abraham and to his seed for ever.

Every leaf of this precious book drops myrrh, and is fragrant with mercy.

Jews confessedly were privileged above all nations. Rom. iii. 2.

"I have nourished and brought up children, and they have rebelled against Me." Isa. i. 2.

"Touching the election, beloved for the fathers' sakes." Rom. xi. 28.

But the more He loved them, the less was He loved. 2 Cor. xii. 15.

Received Him not. They longed for a Deliverer to free them from Herod and the Romans.

But the liberty He offered was from the chains of sin, which they loved.

A yoke on their hearts, they had not felt heavy.

They did *not* grudge the tribute which they paid to Satan.

Our Lord's supposed allusion to civil bondage, they hurled back with scorn.

He promised to make the "poor in spirit," holy and happy.

But they did not know they were *wretched, miserable, poor, blind, naked.* Rev. iii. 17.

The height of guilt—His *own brothers* did not believe in Him. John vii. 5.

He came to a people "stiff-necked and uncircumcised in heart." Acts vii. 51.

His consolation remained : "Though Israel be not gathered, yet shall I be glorious." Isa. xlix. 5.

Many, whose friends were healed of blindness, lameness, sickness, let Him be led to execution, and raised no arm or voice for Him.

Did He not fulfil every prophecy as to *lineage, birth, life,* and *death ?*

Did He not show all the mighty signs and wonders due to a Messiah ?

Did not His doctrines and wisdom come up to those of the Shiloh ?

He came as a *Saviour* offering deliverance, but they denied their danger.

He came to *redeem,* but they denied their bondage.

He came to offer eternal *life* as a gift : they denied their fear of any loss by death.

He came to make them *sons of God,* but they refused Him who alone could give them this power.

He came to be a *fountain,* but they denied their need of cleansing.

He came to be their *physician :* they affirmed they were not sick.

The rightful *Ruler* was treated as an *intruder* by his subjects.

There was anarchy in the soul, where there ought to have been obedience.

A usurper had reduced our Lord's freedmen to spiritual slavery.

In vain had the Incarnation hymn sounded out over Bethlehem.

In vain had the silver trumpet of the second Elijah been heard among the dwellers in Judea, "Prepare ye the way of the Lord."

No joyful applause, no submissive homage welcomed the King.

The world, cold and dark, *knew* Him not. Israel cared not to know Him.

Extreme wickedness had combined with judicial blindness.

Storm of God's wrath was even then gathering over these Christ rejecters.

But in the next verse John's eye falls on a *remnant* of humble believers.

To some He was " a light to lighten the Gentiles." Isa. xlii. 6.

But from the self-hardened, He *hid* himself. John xii. 36.

" I am come, that they who see may be made blind." John ix. 39.

Therefore they " denied the Holy One, and desired a murderer." Acts iii. 14.

The nation said, " This is the *heir ;* come, let us kill Him." Matt. xxi. 38.

For this sin, by common consent of nations, they are cast out.

God's mercies will cause eternal joy, or unending woe.
Hence the " *Justice* of heaven is *Divine love* in *flames.*"

τὰ ἴδια.   Own things. *Henry.*   Messianic rights. *D. Brown.*   Judea.
Alford.   House of Israel. *Wetstein.*   His elect people. *Bede.*   ἴδια expresses
more than ὁ κόσμος. *Tholuck.*   His vineyard. *Ferus.*   The world made by
Him, and especially the Jews. *Cyril, Chrys., Aug.*

ἦλθε.   Utrum Christus venisset, si Adamus non peccasset? a question of
the Schoolmen. *Aquinas.*

God would somehow have allied Himself to man, even if man had not sinned.
Malebranche.

παρέλαβον.   Jesus is the Jehovah of the O.T. identical with the " Angel of
the Lord." *Hengstenberg.*

----

12. But as many as received him, to them gave he power to become the sons
of God, even to them that believe on his name.

As many.   Although as a nation they were " a disobedient and
   gainsaying people," a few rejoiced in His Advent.   Rom.
   ix. 27.
Received Him.   As the " Word " of God, as the "Light" of men.
The nation not waiting to receive either the power of adoption, or
   such a Messiah.
A Gideon or a Samson to deliver them from their foes would have
   been welcomed by a long, loud, universal shout of triumph.
The Roman yoke broken, they cared for no higher, no purer
   liberty.
He gave.   " By nature we were children of wrath, even as others."
   Eph. ii. 3.
An act of the highest *sovereign grace* and power to make sinners
   sons of God.
It pertains to THE LIGHT to make children of the light.
Power.   It does not mean *authority* only, but *ability* also.   John
   vi. 44.
Without strength imparted, the depraved soul has not the *power*
   to repent.   John vi. 44.
Without grace bestowed, the sinner has not the *desire* to be made
   holy.   John v. 4.
Our Lord does not *compel* obedience, He only invites.
He does not *create* them *sons*, He gives them *power* to become sons.
Yet when His Spirit renews, the heart is " made willing."   Psa.

The Spirit the *agent*. Tit. iii. 5.   The Word the *instrument*. 1 Pet.
i. 23.

Heathen deities came with empty pretensions : Christ full-handed.

" Blessed are they that have *right* (Gr. *power*) to the tree of life."
Rev. xxii. 14.

Become sons.   They were *aliens* before, and must be *adopted* to
become sons.

An adopted person in Greece must have been an *Athenian* citizen.

But though " Abraham be ignorant of us," God has promised to be
our Father.   Isa. lxiii. 16.

" I care not for the petty deities, if only Jove is my friend."   *A
Latin Proverb.*

Romans, in adopting, first selected a *slave*, then obtained his emancipation.

In the presence of witnesses, flung his father's mantle around him,
and then registered his name among the citizens.   John
viii. 35.

" If sons, then heirs." Rom. viii. 17.   Kings can only constitute
their first-born *heirs*.

Here *all* are " heirs of God, and joint-heirs with Christ." Rom.
viii. 17.

Least faith can be joint *possessor*, but *no* faith, however great, can
be a joint *purchaser*.

As the weakest hand can receive a sceptre, so the feeblest mind
can receive faith, " the gift of God " (Eph. ii. 8) ; but a
legion of angels cannot obtain it by force.

An act of God's free grace.   " Behold, what manner of love," &c.
1 John iii. 1.

That any believed was the sovereign work of God, and not of
man.

Many receive Him as *man merely*, which avails nothing.

Grace does not run in the blood, as corruption does.

Fallen man " begat a son in his own likeness."   Gen. v. 3.

Of God.   What a stretch to the human mind, *to realize such a relation* to the Infinite, Eternal, Unchangeable Jehovah, as to
call Him Abba !

Father !   The mind sinks under the effort to measure the height
and depth, the length and breadth, of this Love.

For an humble slave to be adopted as son and heir of some million-
naire might well turn his head.

Add to that wealth, the honours of a long ancestry—to that noble blood—to that royal line—prospective sceptre, a crown, throne, palace, kingdom of loving subjects.

But few could preserve their reason to be exalted thus.

A clerk once drew a prize in a lottery of a few thousand pounds, went and purchased a pistol, and committed *suicide* the same day.

A young man, simply for *his name*, received a large inheritance. The sudden greatness and change shattered his mind and sent him for *seven years* to a *lunatic asylum.*

Adoption into God's family implies—

1. We have no right to this honour   Gal. iv. 4, 5, 6.
2. Freedom from fearing the rod, more than loss of His love.
3. Filial confidence, the fruit of the Father's love, free access to Him at all times. Rom. viii. 15.
4. A title to the heavenly inheritance. 1 Pet. i. 2—4.
5. The Spirit witnessing with our spirit. Rom. viii. 16.

" How shall I act? " said Antigonus to Menedemus. " Like a king's son," was the admirable reply.

1. God's children have the *provision* of sons. God promises all they need.

" All things work together for good." Rom. viii. 28. Their " hairs are all numbered." Matt. x. 30.

In adversity they enjoy heavenly peace, in prosperity sunshine of God's favour.

Friendless or persecuted, in health or sickness, in life or death, *all is well.*

2. They have *education* of sons, " led by the Spirit," purified from stains. Rom. viii. 14; 1 Thess. v. 23.

Disciplined gently or severely, " God dealeth with them as sons." Heb. xii. 7.

3. Their *inheritance* is that of sons. "Heirs of God, joint-heirs with Christ." Rom. viii. 17.

" It is your Father's good pleasure to give you the kingdom." Luke xii. 32.

" An inheritance incorruptible, undefiled, and that fadeth not away." 1 Pet. i. 4.

If God's sons, what inconceivable folly to trouble ourselves about earth's honours.

Children not in *name and dignity*, but *nature* also. 2 Pet. i. 4.

Note the transcendent grandeur of the humblest saint related to the King of kings.

Thus the tenderest bud derives life from the mighty trunk.

Believe. Faith, John i. 7 ; vii. 38. In Him as our Wisdom,
Righteousness, Sanctification, complete Redemption. 1 Cor.
i. 30.

On His name. A phrase never used in Scripture of any created
being.

Signifies that *trust* proper to be placed in God only.

Name. As manifested in the Joshua, Jesus, Saviour from sin.

Whole *content* of faith in *name* of Being believed in.

Whole *confession* of faith in that name *uttered. Meyer.*

ὅσοι. Both Jews and Gentiles. *Chrysostom.* Primarily among the Jews,
but also in all the world. *Alford.*

ἔλαβον, took. Differs from καταλαμβάνειν, ver. 5, and παραλαμβάνειν,
ver. 11. Is for the Gentiles, to whom *grace* belongs. *Bengel.*

ἐξουσίαν. Privilege or prerogative. *Chrys.* The adoption itself. *Bengel.*
Potestas et potentia. *D. Brown.* Power to love as sons. *Tittmann.* Power to
complete the filiation at the resurrection. *Theophylact.* Power to co-operate
with God. *Denton.* Capability, inner enabling. *Lücke.* Power through
baptism. *Lamy.* Not through faith, but because of faith. *Luca Brug.* Fiunt
non nascuntur Christiani. *Tertullian.* Believers are daily renewed. *Bourgon.*
Involving all the actions and states needful to their so becoming and removing
all obstacles (e.g. the wrath of God, guilt of sin). *Alford.*

τέκνα Θεοῦ. A more comprehensive expression than υἱοὶ τ. Θ., and involves the *whole generation and powers* of our life in the Spirit, as being from
and of God, and consequently our *likeness* to God. *Alford.* Adoption can be
lost. *Hugo de S. Charo.* Not if Phil. i. 6 is true. *Author.* Heathen and
Jews had an idea of human beings having Divine descent. *Lücke.*

γενέσθαι. "Become," demands time, not all at once. *Euthymius.* There
is no moment when the soul is neither *in* the kingdom, nor *out* of it. *Author.*
Reformation gradually affects it. *Rosenmuller.* God's work, and instantaneous.
Calvin.

πιστεύουσιν. *Credo languidâ fide, sed tamen fide. Cruciger,* on his death-
bed.

---

13. Which were born, not of blood, nor of the will of the flesh, nor of the
will of man, but of God.

Born. This new birth in Scripture not new honour, but *change*
of *nature.*

To these things before he was a total stranger—an alien. Eph.
ii. 12.

Though this birth is a secret in its nature, its signs are manifest—.
  " Love, joy, peace, longsuffering, gentleness, goodness, faith,
  meekness, temperance." Gal. v. 22.

Not of blood. Denoting the infinite superiority of the spiritual over the natural birth.

A commendation of a far nobler lineage than princes can boast. Psa. lxxxix. 27.

In this line of nobility are found PATRIARCHS, PROPHETS, KINGS, the ADORABLE REDEEMER!

The oldest genealogies of any race of kings reach back less than 1000 years.

This genealogy of the saints reaches to the Eternal Father, the Everlasting God.

Will of the flesh. Birth into the family of God is traceable to no human instrumentality, for "*faith is the* GIFT OF GOD." Eph. ii. 8.

This birth is heavenly in its *origin, nature,* and *evidences.*

Will of man. A threefold denial of an earthly source of this new birth.

How emphatic does the following declaration of its real source become!

Will of the flesh and will of man bring *power, rank,* and *nobility*

Of these three the Jews were wont to boast.

But it shows how little man has of himself except sin and shame.

But of God. "The Father, of whom the whole family in heaven and earth is named." Eph. iii. 15.

Of that LOVE whose Son is "the First-born of every creature." Col. i. 15.

How far Christ incarnate assumed sanctified humanity we know not.

Neither do we know the nature of the relation the adopted ones bear to the Son of God.

But we do know that the Holy Ghost compares the union to that of Eve taken from Adam. "*Members* of HIS BODY, and of HIS FLESH, and of HIS BONES." Eph. v. 30.

Spiritual birth, a regeneration, *alone* gives value to our natural birth.

God brought Abraham and family into *covenant,* and his children, and slaves.

True nobility, where God is the top of the kindred, and religion the root.

No birth equal to the new birth, no privilege like that of the Spirit.

οὐκ ἐξ αἱμάτων. "Not of bloods:" a Hebraism. *Lücke.* Superior human descent. *D. Brown.* Blood is the seat of life; hence connection between child and parents called *blood* relationship. In classic usage "to spring from the *blood*," that is, "from the seed of any one." *Tholuck.* Refers to the rite of circumcision. *Lightfoot.* Generally used in a derogatory sense. *Hengsten-berg.*

οὐδὲ, a climax:—"*not* of blood, *nor* yet of the will of the flesh, *nor* yet of the will of man, but of God." *Alford.* ἐκ denotes, the first time, the *material ;* the second and third time, the *mediate* cause; the fourth time, the *immediate* cause, of the generation. *De Wette.* θελήματος. In Hebrew, *father, he willed, he loved,* are kindred words. Col. i. 13, 15, "Son of His love," &c. *Bengel.*

---

14. And the Word was made flesh, and dwelt among us, (and we beheld his glory, the glory as of the only begotten of the Father,) full of grace and truth.

Word. The last time the Evangelist uses this term. Henceforth it is "Jesus" or "Lord." (See on verse 1.)

The thirteen verses introduce us to the great climax, the INCAR-NATION.

He does not say "the Light (ver. 4) became flesh," because Light, the essential element of Jehovah, embraces the Father and Spirit.

He does not say "Son," for then some would refer it to the Son of Mary.

He "slept," "wept," "hungered," "thirsted," "marvelled," "grieved," "wearied."

In His body, He bore our sicknesses ; in His soul, He carried our sorrows.

Was made. Constituted thus by assuming the nature of frail, infirm man.

Jehovah had often visited our earth. Jer. i. 2 ; Hosea i. 2.

But He became *man*, VERY MAN, was clothed in flesh, but *once*.

A mystery hung around His birth—"Who can declare His gener-ation ?" Isa. liii. 8.

He might have come to our vale of tears in the full splendour of His Deity.

The mountains might have rejoiced, and the stars shot forth pe-culiar glory.

The trees might have assumed another bloom, and another vintage might have grown.

The ocean might have rejoiced, and all creatures gathered around Thee.

All the angels of heaven might have accompanied Thee in Thy journey of benevolence.

As a hero, resplendent with spoils, Thou mightest have come to
earth : but *none of these things !*

The Divine splendours were laid aside at the threshold of time.

The homage of kings and all nature Thou didst not desire.

Thou didst assume "the form of a servant." Phil. ii. 7.

Thus boundless dignity blended with infinite humility.

A *necessity* for it. And infinite *wisdom* chose this method of the
Incarnation. 1 Cor. i. 30 ; Heb. ii. 10.

" Without controversy great is the mystery of godliness." 1 Tim.
iii. 16.

He has not come *in vain.* The unrighteous must become like
Him.

If the vast scheme of redemption has been completed by such a
costly sacrifice, the destiny of our race *cannot be, as though
that had not been.*

The prophets have not spoken *in vain.* Angels sang not *in vain*
His birth-song. The Spirit did not descend *in vain* at His
baptism.

Flesh. Why not write man ? Because " flesh " indicates *falli-
bility* and *weakness.* Psa. lxxiii. 26.

Denotes humanity without Jewish or Gentile peculiarity.

The mighty God contrasted with feeble flesh !

An interval between Divinity and fading grass, wider than the
mind can span. Isa. xl. 6.

Infidels ask why our Lord never alludes to this miraculous
birth ?

We answer, He was seen to be a perfect man. Men needed *no
proof* of His spotless *humanity.*

Made flesh, but only " in the likeness of *sinful* flesh." Rom. viii. 3.

His Incarnation did not dim His Divinity, nor His Divinity nullify
His humanity, since it will eternally share His throne.

Sceptics deny His Divinity because He humbled Himself.

They resemble the madman in his cell, who denied a *small gnat*
could ever be created by a *great God.*

He did not cease to be what He was before, but He became what
He was not before. *Augustine.*

These very words were adopted by the Fourth General Council.

John did not exist before the announcement of his birth. Luke
i. 13.

But the WORD was before Mary or Abraham, even before Gabriel
who announced Him. John viii. 58.

He assumed our pitiable nature *as it now is,* excepting the taint of sin.

For three years apostles saw a mysterious Being moving by their side, in human form.

But ever and anon the flashings of Omnipotence proved " the MYSTERY of GODLINESS." 1 Tim. iii. 16.

He was "seen of angels : and all flesh shall see the salvation of our God." 1 Tim. iii. 16 ; Luke iii. 6.

By the power by which He adopts sinners into His family He became incarnate, " made of a woman." Gal. iv. 4 ; Heb. ii. 14.

To reject our Saviour because of His humiliation resembles the patient, who should blush at the sight of the physician who cures him.

Incarnate Lord, yet " holy, undefiled, separate from sinners." Heb. vii. 26.

Our nature in Him is redeemed, quickened, ennobled, transfigured.

A hereditary curse is here opposed by a mightier hereditary blessing.

The Evangelist finds a prophecy of His Incarnation in Isa. vii. 11 ; Matt. i. 22.

Christ, the child of a poor traveller, is born upon a journey.

A humiliating sight—the Lord, hungering, thirsting, sleeping, weeping, despised, chastened, slain, and buried.

Divinity and dust were united, *truly,* to oppose *Arians ; perfectly,* to confute *Apollinarians; undividedly,* against *Nestorians ;* and *unmixedly* against the *Eutychians.*

He became *partaker* of our fallen humanity and *Restorer* too.

Dwelt. Gr. *Tabernacled.* Hints at His humility and transient stay.

He had no settled home on earth, though He remained 33 years.

The angel Gabriel, the instant his brief errand ends, darts back to heaven,—nothing can detain him.

" Let them make me a sanctuary ; that I may dwell (Heb. tabernacle) among them." Ex. xxv. 8.

Dwelling in the Shechinah *typical.* In Christ in flesh it attained its *fulness.*

Glory streamed through His human garb, on Mount Tabor.

Thus the Shechinah glorified the tabernacle, and afterwards the temple.

He found the tabernacle of our humanity overthrown, and He repaired it, making it a meet dwelling for the infinite God.

The high and lofty ONE will *dwell* with the contrite and humble.
Isa. lvii. 15.
Not in a palace. "He had not where to lay His head." Matt.
viii. 20.
Patriarchs "confessed themselves strangers," by dwelling in tents.
Heb. xi. 13, 14.
It was a type of the body, in which His Godhead was enshrined.
1 Cor. iii. 16.
GOD! what term more *glorious!* FLESH! what word more *vile!*
Sceptics ask, "Why did not Jesus by reasoning prove His
Divinity?"
Amid the blaze of His miracles this were to place a label over the
sun.
Among us. He appeals to living witnesses who saw and heard
Him.
Exposed to all temptations, yet remaining perfectly SINLESS.
David mourned because he was compelled to dwell in Mesech.
Psa. cxx. 5.
Ezekiel afraid because he "dwelt among scorpions." Ezek. ii. 6.
Church of Pergamos grieved that it dwelt "where Satan's seat is."
Rev. ii. 13.
Beheld. Gr. *revealed to our gaze;* but not to our sense.
Emphatic: we beheld with admiration and delight.
Blind *unbelief* beheld, and saw only the *carpenter's son*, but *faith*
spiritually discerned Infinite *Majesty!* 1 Cor. ii. 14.
"Beheld" implies the actual fulfilment of prophecy.
"The glory of this latter house shall be greater than that of the
former." Hag. ii. 7, 9.
John here gives the experience of the Church. Some hold only
renewed ones saw His true glory.
Carnal affections had overgrown and smothered all spiritual life.
His glory. The royal robes of uncreated splendour were seen by
Peter, James, and John, Moses and Elias. Mark ix. 3.
His wonders seen by the 70, and His resurrection by 500 brethren.
1. Earth His home for a season. 2. His Divine glory seen. 3.
The Father's glory reflected in the Son. 4. Grace and truth
supreme.
The sun pours forth oceans of living splendour, clouds and darkness
notwithstanding.
Thus neither blindness of men, nor gloom of sin, can dim Christ's
Divine glory.

" All nations gathered shall come and see my glory." Isa. lxvi. 18.
In the Incarnation appeared the LOGOS the Jehovah of the O. T.
Moses' glory at Sinai was veiled to prevent it dazzling Israel.
But what can fully express the GLORY GIVEN by the EVERLASTING
GOD TO HIS ONLY SON ?

We saw His glory. They saw lepers cleansed, sick healed, blind
cured, deaf ears opened, demons cast out, winds and waves
calmed, sun darkened, graves opened, rocks rent, tomb sealed
and guarded, made empty, and the *buried* ONE rising, changed,
ascending up to His throne.

What overpowering splendour will be forced upon His *foes* when
He comes as Judge ?

During His earthly life the *Shepherd*, the *Lamb*, the *Servant*, were
seen.

Myriads have received His Spirit, and lived as " *strangers in the
world*." 1 Pet. ii. 11.

Myriads have felt in their dark minds " a light above the brightness of the sun." Acts xxvi. 13.

Millions of martyrs, like Stephen, have died praying for their
murderers.

These are scattered rays of that GLORY Christ caused first to
shine.

Multitudes live and trade on earth with " *their life hid in Christ*."
Col. iii. 3.

As of. Not as comparison, but as confirmation and clear definition.
Conformable to the character of so sublime a person.

Only begotten. Because the *only Son, therefore* tenderly beloved.
" As one mourneth for an only son,"—a very bitter grief. Zech.
xii. 10.

So a love for an only begotten is the most *intense love* known.

" He will rest in His love." Zeph. iii. 17. Heb. be *silent* in His
love.

Note the infinite *depth* of meaning in this term applied to the
Saviour.

Incorporating *His own name* in the formula of baptism all analogy
of relation between human beings fail.

" Show and explain to me an eternal Father, and I will explain
and show to you an eternal Son." *Augustine.*

None beside Him had this relation. He alone had the *whole glory*
of the Father.

Seraphim, cherubim, angels, saints share, but dimly indeed.

It was not given *by measure* to Him who filleth all in all.   Eph. i. 23.

" He was anointed with the oil of gladness ABOVE His fellows." Psa. xlv. 7.

Angels are the sons of God, but of none of them did the Father ever say, " *This day have I begotten Thee.*" Heb. i. 5.

The fourth in the fiery furnace had "the form of the Son of God." Dan. iii. 25.

Father. Godhead of the Trinity one.   Glory equal.   Majesty co-eternal.

Grace, or mercy and truth, the key-note of the Bible.

The entire riches of God's redeeming love to sinners in Christ.

Before fulfilment it was *promise;* after fulfilment, *the truth.*

GRACE, as the result of His infinite love to mankind, His obedience and death.

Truth, as to the unity, purity, and light of His character.   John xiv. 6.

" Pavement of burning sapphire," an emblem of Infinite truth, seen under Jehovah's feet by the Elders of Israel.   Ex. xxiv. 10.

Λόγος, not θεός, yet Sabellians affirm the Father became incarnate. σάρξ ἐγένετο, but θεὸς ἦν. *Henry.* ἦν becomes ἐγένετο the moment He passes from the pre-existent to the incarnate state. The *Fathers. D. Brown.* Orientalism for the whole man. *Luther.* The Incarnation would have taken place, even if man had not sinned. *Albertus Magus, Duns Scotus, Rupertus, Osiander.* Questioned. *Aquinas, Calvin.* John hints at the Docetæ, who held an apparent Incarnation. He alludes again to those heretics, 1 John iv. 3. *D. Brown.* Our Lord here becomes second Adam. *Olshausen.* Alien to John's habit of thought, but implied. *Lücke.* Referring to gospel times. *Cocceius.* All former Theophanies culminate in a historical manifestation. *Neander.*

ἐγένετο. Nowhere in literature is the shade of meaning between εἰμί and γίνομαι more sharply defined. *Trapp.* ἐσκήνωσεν: technically of God's dwelling among men. Judges viii. 11, &c. *Alford.* As the dweller differs from the tabernacle, so Christ from the flesh He inhabited. *Chrysostom.* δόξα, properly the essence of the Shechinah. *Lücke, Tholuck.* Refers to O. T. tabernacling by Jehovah, and stretches forward to the *rest* of heaven. *Ber. Bibel.*

ὡς, as it were. *Glassius.* As pertaining to the only begotten. *Wordsworth.* Befitting. *Lücke.*

μονογενής. See ver. 18. Christ only by John is thus named. *Luther.* The complement of the other. An inconceivable loving nearness to the Father. *D. Brown.* ἀγαπητος, Sept. Jer. viii. 26. Kings called sons of God. *Hesiod, Callimachus, Homer.* παρὰ, not ἐκ, forth, not from. *D. Brown.* ἀληθείας added gives it a supernatural force; greater in love and faithfulness. *Knobel.* Abundant in truth. Ex. xxxiv. 6. Thoroughly God. *Hengstenberg.* All created things are but the shadows of realities. Substance alone found in the Kingdom. With John it implies both the *good* and the *true. Neander.*

15. John bare witness of him, and cried, saying, This was he of whom I spake, He that cometh after me is preferred before me: for he was before me.

John. Heb. *gracious*, as Theodore, in Gr., *God given.*

The Baptist, a Baptizer, son of Zacharias and Elisabeth, cousin of Mary, tribe of Levi.

Zacharias visited by an angel, while sacrificing in the temple.

Angel *Gabriel* foretold his birth, name, and Nazarite training.

Josiah's birth and reign were foretold 350 years before his birth. 1 Kings xiii. 2.

John six months older than Jesus; his *second cousin*, humanly speaking.

John a great religious reformer and forerunner of the Messiah. Isa. xl. 3.

At his birth, friends wished to call him Zacharias, but his mother called him *John.*

Zacharias, dumb for nine months, spake first at his child's circumcision.

"Thou, child, shalt be called the prophet of the Highest, and go before the face of the Lord and prepare His way." Luke i. 76; Mal. iii. 1.

"John waxed strong in spirit, and was in the desert" for 30 years. Luke i. 80.

Fifteenth year of Tiberias, he began the life of an O. T. prophet, with camel's hair garments, locusts and honey for food.

He summoned the Jews to repentance, especially the rulers and priests.

People were in expectation, and mused whether John were the Christ. Luke iii. 15.

Our Lord, knowing John had announced him, as come. Matt. xi. 14.

John's humility prompts him to *ask* (instead of *performing*) baptism from Christ.

Christ baptized, heaven was opened, and the Father and Spirit witnessed. Matt. iii. 17.

The Baptist the first to learn the particulars of the Messianic office as belonging to the son of Mary.

John's followers acted *apart* from the Christian Church for some years after the death of their master. Acts xix. 3.

Having rebuked Herod publicly for incest, he was imprisoned.

A divine warrant for ministers *warning* rulers and subjects, and publicly enforcing the duties of people and magistrates. 1 Tim. ii. 2.

What must have been the lustre of John's moral character, for he wrought no miracle !

The number of disciples baptized, the purity of his life, the spirituality of his doctrines, all directed men to the *earthly side* of the Messianic signs.

Many, like Herod, attributed our Lord's miracles to John risen from the dead. Matt. xiv. 1.

John was beheaded by Herod through the influence of Herodias.

During a feast at the castle of Machaerus, in Perea, near the Dead Sea.

Herodias, like another Helen, the cause of Herod's war with Aretas.

Bear witness. The morning-star heralds the sun, and disappears as the luminary rises.

Gradually and mysteriously this servant retires into prison to be a martyr.

Cried. Gr. *hath cried*, and is still crying ; his trumpet gave no uncertain sound.

Jubilee introduced by voice of a crier, and by sound of a trumpet.

Implied public testimony, a loud proclamation to all men.

With confidence and joy. Sign of decision. Rev. vii. 2.

False teachers entice *secretly*. Wisdom is heard in the streets. Prov. i. 21.

Spake. Happy are they who, like Paul, can appeal to the witness of conscience. Rom. ix. 1.

COMETH AFTER, and yet GOES BEFORE, a kind of divine paradox.

He, who entered His name among those coming to my baptism.

He, whom a celestial voice declared to the " SON OF GOD."

He followed, yet preceded me—is my SAVIOUR and my GOD.

Preferred. Signifies to esteem, and also advance or promote.

For. Gr. *because*. A clear and definite proof of Christ's *pre-existence*.

Before me. Christ comes after His messenger, and yet is before him, and mightier than he.

He who is baptized as the less is greater than he who baptizes.

Not only was He before John, but before Abraham, Adam, Angels, Cherubim, Seraphim, Principalities and Powers. Coeval with the eternal God.

Jews looked for a great Prince, a kind of angel to deliver them
from tyranny.

Was not David to have an heir on his throne?

John subject of such miracles at his birth, no wonder that men
became confused as to who was actually the Messiah.

John was "the prophet of the Highest." Luke i. 76. Christ "Son
of the Highest." Luke i. 32.

John, "greatest born of woman." Matt. xi. 11. Christ, "Creator
of all," born. John i. 3.

John, *minister* of the New Test. Christ, *Mediator* of the New Test.

Christ's birth announced after John's; born after, circumcised after,
entered office after.

He began to preach after John, and baptized after him.

"*Was before,*" said not of His *Divine* nature, but Messianic office.

Foundation of preference, the infinite excellence of His person.

A prince is preferred to the servant that ushers him in.

Such depths of humility are the fruit of the gospel only.

Thus Farel besought Calvin to remain at Geneva, and the poet
Klopstock's genius was defended by the pure-hearted Bodmer.

'Ιωάννης. Born at Hebron. *Rabbis.* At Jutta. *Reland.* Tradition: Zach.,
questioned by Herod, as to the place of John's concealment, was slain for refusing an answer. *Beard.* Elisabeth dying, angels trained John for his work.
Fabricius. Zebedee an uncle of the Baptist. *Theophylact.*

ὀπίσω. John did not retire on Christ's appearing. *Winer.* His mission
was to satisfy his *disciples. Alexander.* John beheaded by Herod through
jealousy of his growing influence over the people. *Josephus.*

κέκραγεν. This testimony clear proof that many Jews believed John the
Messiah. *Lampe.* Designates the historical sphere of his first witness. *Hengstenberg.* The writer owes his clear perception of the Baptizer to the vividness
of his youthful reminiscences. *Maurice.* To the Holy Ghost; inspirations
never depend on a frail human memory. *Author.* ἔμπροσθέν never refers to
precedence in dignity. *Hengstenberg.* Always of position. *Bengel.* The pre-
existence of Christ. *Lücke, Hengstenberg.* His dignity. *Calvin, Lampe.* He
continued to baptize, and did not join Jesus. *Ebrard.* "My successor has
become my superior, for he was my Predecessor," illustrates the enigmatical
character of the original. *D. Brown.*

ὅτι. Assuredly. *Lampe.* John gives fuller account of the Baptist's testimony than the Synoptists, having ample material. *Alford.* Had he any more
material than the Holy Spirit supplied? *Author.*

---

16. And of his fulness have all we received, and grace for grace.

Fulness. Not the words of the Baptist, but of the Evangelist.
"It pleased the Father that in Him should all fulness dwell." Col
i. 19.

He received not the Spirit of God by measure.   John iii. 34.

He has a boundless supply for all the millions of His subjects. Prov. viii. 21.

As all the planets are said to light their fires at the sun's blaze, so all the saints derive their kindling, cheering, quickening, warming, enlivening grace from Christ.

When in nature a thing is filled, its capacity can receive no more.

What Christ filleth, He *enlargeth* in *capacity* to *receive more* and more.

Take even a drop from the ocean and it is so much the less, but Christ's fulness is inexhaustible.

The fulness of the sun is such that though it light a thousand worlds it suffers no loss.

Yet what to us availeth fulness, if inaccessible ?

The treasures of the Redeemer can be reached by all, and are shared by all through His empire.

From His fulness, the apostles brought their weapons of celestial temper.

From Him they acquired power to " *ring the great bell of the universe.*"   Acts iii. 16.

By His fulness, they were " enriched in all utterance " for the gospel.   1 Cor. i. 5.

He is *wisdom*, the Light of the world.   He is *power*, He controls nature.

Saints may find—1. An open fountain.   2. A copious fountain. 3. An inexhaustible fountain.   4. An ever-increasing fountain. 5. A fountain of blessedness.

This is one of the golden texts of the Apostle John.

Its complete meaning, " eye hath not seen, nor ear heard."

When the King of kings rewards as a King, His saints will know it.

When the one city multiplies into five, and the five into ten cities, faithful ones will begin to realize the height and depth, the length and breadth, of His fulness.

A flowing fountain, at which angels, cherubim and seraphim, drink for ever.

Grace.   Gr. *anything which imparts joy*, body or mind.

One of the many words lifted by inspiration from the region of sense to that of a spiritual character.

As the original word embraced everything that could *charm*, so *grace* in the N. T is the chosen term for all blessings in Christ that cheer and save ; and like all *love* worth the name, must be *unbought* love.

Grace for grace. In successive communications, as the glass receives lineaments, one after another, until " facĕ answers to face."

Special grace is electing, redeeming, justifying, pardoning, adopting, sanctifying. Rom. viii. 30.

Common grace, light of nature, reason, conviction of conscience. Rom. ii. 4.

1. The freeness of this grace, a gift according to grace. Rom. xii. 6.
2 The fulness, " plenteous redemption." Psa. cxxx. 7.
3. Grace for advancing others. 1 Pet. iv. 10.
4. From a low degree of grace to a higher, " from glory to glory." 2 Cor. iii. 18.
5. From grace in sense to grace in Christ ; image of the earthly, to that of the heavenly. 1 Cor. xv. 49.

The " for " or *instead* implies a new grace always succeeds an old.

Christ is not rich in supplies merely *once*, and afterwards lets saints *want.*

He is constantly giving His people cause for " a new song." Rev. v. 9.

New works, new wonders of redeeming love are ever multiplied. Psa. xiv. 7.

Grace of preservation in this wilderness of sin and sorrow. Psa. xxiii. 2.

Grace of the believer now in possession before the throne. 1 John iii. 2.

The living olive-tree in the temple ever supplied oil for the lamps. Zech. iv. 3.

καὶ, retained. *Hengstenberg.* Cancelled, and ὅτι substituted. *Tischendorf, Lach., Tregelles, Alford, Cod. Sin.* This text the words of John the Evangelist. *Chrys., Meyer, De Wette, Alford, Tholuck, Bengel, Ols., Lampe, D. Brown.* He confirms the Baptist by his own experience. *Lücke.* Words of the Baptist. *Origen, Erasmus, Hutcheson, Strauss.*

πληρώματος. In saints *plenitudo vasis*, in Christ *fontis*. They differ as ignis, et ignitæ. *Trapp.* Refers to Gnostics and Corinthians. *Waterland.*

πάντες. All who have been saved. *Melancthon.*

χάριν ἀντὶ χάριτος. New covenant for the old. *Euthymius.* Contrast between the law and the gospel. *Chrys., Beza, Elsley, Wetstein.* Gratiam gloriæ pro gratia militiæ. *Bernard.* Habits of faith, hope, and love. *Saurin.* New grace superseding the former grace. *Alford.* Grace of God as a special favour towards His Son. *Melancthon.* Grace proportioned to that of Christ. *Calvin.* A pleonasm, means " grace gratuitous." *Grotius.* Grace upon grace. *Doddr., Wesley.* Abundance of spiritual blessings. *Scott.* More grace given to those who thankfully receive. *Le Clerc.* Grace to advance grace. *Henry.* Each grace overwhelmed by the accumulation and fulness of that which follows. *Lücke, Meyer, Thol., Ols., De Wette.* Faith first and eternal life afterwards. *Aug.*

---

17. For the law was given by Moses, but grace and truth came by Jesus Christ.

Law, which worketh wrath, hath a shadow of good things. Rom. iv. 15.

Divine provision. Psa. xix. 7. It threatened, but helped not.

It commanded the leper to be cleansed, but did not heal. Deut. xxiv. 8.

It revealed sins reigning, but did not subdue their power. Gen. vi. 5.

It uncovered the soul's pollution, but showed no Siloam's pool. 2 Cor. iii. 6.

It told us of our utter feebleness, but imparted no strength. Eccles. vii. 20.

The law embraced legislation for husband and wife, master and slave, strangers, land, debt, taxation.

Original laws concerning God, man, royal power, reverence.

Criminal laws. Sacrifices ordinary and extraordinary, holiness of persons.

Holiness of places, of things, of times, festivals, priests, tabernacles.

There were no laws relative to suicide ; no sumptuary laws for luxurious living.

Yet house, dress, food, and family affairs are determined.

Jewish law recognizes dignity of women, rights of slaves : deaf and blind are protected.

Even cruelty is noted ; a *kid* is *not* to be seethed in his *mother's milk.* Deut. xxii. 7.

Protracted death or torture not allowed ; corners of fields left un-reaped.

The reading of this law was forbidden by *Antiochus Epiphanes* under penalty of death.

A pure theocracy,—" The land is mine, and ye are sojourners with me." Lev. xxv. 23.

Given. While Moses received it, Sinai trembled in flames.

Blackness, darkness, and tempest enveloped the *pulpit* of the law.

Moses. Heb. *drawn out*, B.C. 1722. Son of Amram, great grandson of Levi, son of Jacob.

Rescued from the Nile by Pharaoh's daughter, who adopted and educated him.

Trained in all the learning of the Egyptians. Acts vii. 22. His mother his nurse.

Taught by her, he knew his lineage, and the fear of the God of his fathers.

Having slain an Egyptian oppressor, he fled to Midian, in Arabia, at 40 years of age.

There he married Jethro's daughter, and remained 40 years.

At 80 God appears in the burning bush and sends him to free Israel.

Met by Aaron at Horeb, they announced to Pharaoh God's word.

Miracles. 1. Water into blood. 2. Frogs. 3. Lice. 4. Flies. 5. Murrain. 6. Boils. 7. Thunder and hail. 8. Locusts. 9. Darkness. 10. Death of the first-born.

Celebrates the Passover. Israel departs. Spoiling of the Egyptians. Pillar of cloud.

Red Sea divided. Egyptians drowned. Water of Marah sweetened.

Encamps one year at Sinai : third day he receives the Ten Commandments from God : fasts 40 days on the mount.

Came down and saw Israel and the calf : He breaks the two tables of stone.

Spends 40 days again in Sinai, and receives another copy of the Decalogue.

Lustre of his face concealed by a veil : Jethro visits the camp.

Miriam murmurs at his Ethiopian wife : at Kadesh he sends 12 spies to Canaan.

People murmur : Caleb and Joshua are faithful.

Conspiracy of Korah and company. Earth opens, and swallows them up.

Israelites remain here 32 years. Murmur for water. Rock yields it.

Miriam dies, aged 130. On Mount Hor Aaron dies, 123 years of age.

Sihon and Og defeated. Balaam, by daughters of Moab, seduces the Israelites.

Plague slays 24,000. Moses dies at Nebo, aged 120 years, and God buries him.

Grace (ver. 14).   That *unmerited goodness of God* shown to the fallen.

Grace cannot be shown by one created being to another, since there is an element of *duty* not found in the act of Jehovah.

It embraces glory, honour, immortality, eternal life.   Rom. ii. 7.

The law worketh wrath. Rom. iv. 15.   A curse on all violating it. Gal. iii. 10.

"The law a *shadow* of good things to come" in the *gospel*.

Law tells us what boundless treasures we by sin have lost.   Gal. iii. 10.

Grace comes to fill the vast empty void found in every sinner's heart.   John i. 12.

At the apostasy the four Divine attributes parted:—Mercy, truth, righteousness, and peace.   They met again at Calvary.   Psa. lxxxv. 10.

These are the watchwords of Moses, Num. xiv. 18, and of David, Psa. c. 5, as they have been for ages of the sacramental host of God.

"By the works of the law shall no flesh be justified."   Gal. ii. 16.

Yet is "the law a schoolmaster, to bring us to Christ."   Gal. iii. 24.

A criminal, denying his guilt, confident of escape, becomes sullen.

But an *unlooked for witness* coming, and clearly proving his guilt, his spirit fails, his conscience shrinks, and death's terrors subdue him.

Thus the Spirit by the law overwhelms the proud *will-worshipper*.

"The law came, sin revived, and I died."   Rom. vii. 9.

But sooner or later "every mouth will be stopped, and all the world become guilty before God."   Rom. iii. 19.

Mankind will meet both law and lawgiver.

The law demands perfect *obedience*, so Christ offers perfect *forgiveness*.

What use does the law serve ?   1. The law is God's *will* respecting us.   Our Saviour kept it perfectly.   It is our rule that we may have a "conscience void of offence."   Acts xxiv. 16.

2. The law the *commands* of God : if we were judged by their holy precepts, who could stand ?

3. Do we desire or strive to honour this known law of God ?

4. Those loving Christ best are the most careful observers of the law.

The *covenant* of grace turns *precept* into *promises,* and the spirit of grace turns both into *prayer,* and grace turns all into *glory*

The famine in our land has made ours a *salvation-craving heart*.

We have hungered and thirsted from age to age after *peace*, not *holiness*.

Truth. When complete righteousness is sought in the law, it fails.

The law is not sent to give light, but to bind and make us feel our chains.

Came. John well weighs his words. Law is *given;* grace *came*.

Jesus Christ. Divinity and names. See on verses 1, 2, 41. Acts, life, and miracles. See on John iv. 25.

Christ not a proper name, but official title. Heb. MESSIAH, both *" anointed."* John i. 41.

Attraction of love, not terrors of law, the *genius* of the *gospel*.

It is *grace teaching*. Tit. ii. 11. *Grace reigning*. Rom. v. 21.

Christ is the *fulfilment* of all the O. T. promises.

Christ is the *substance* of all the O. T. types and shadows.

Jesus, name of none of His mother's relatives.

Not given by *chance*, but by Divine command. Matt. i 21.

Mary and Joseph were not disobedient. Matt. i. 25.

1. Deliverer from folly. He is our WISDOM.
2. From guilt. He is our RIGHTEOUSNESS.
3. From sin's pollution. He is our SANCTIFICATION.
4. From sin's power. He is our REDEMPTION. 1 Cor. i. 30.

MESSIANIC PROPHECIES

The Bible for 4000 years foretold the coming of an *illustrious personage*.

To bruise the serpent's head. Gen. iii. 15. His coming as Judge foretold by Enoch. Jude 14. In whom all nations are to be blessed. Gen. xxii. 18.

A Prophet like unto Moses. Deut. xviii. 15.

A Priest of the order of Melchisedec. Psa. cx. 4 ; Heb. vii. 21.

A rod from Jesse's stem. Isa. xi. 1. "A virgin shall bear a son." Isa. vii. 14.

Branch of Jehovah. Isa. iv. 2. Angel of the Covenant. Mal. iii. 1.

Lord of the temple. Mal. iii. 1. His goings forth from everlasting. Mic. v. 2.

Wonderful Counsellor, Mighty God. Isa. ix. 6. A child born of the tribe of Judah. Gen. xlix. 10.

Of the family of David. Isa. xi. 1. A Light for Jews and Gentiles. Isa. xlix. 6.

Cut off, but not for Himself. Dan. ix. 26. Wounded for our transgressions. Isa. liii. 5.

By His stripes we are healed. Isa. liii. 5. The Lord laid on Him
our iniquity. Isa. liii. 6.

He made His soul an offering for sin. Isa. liii. 10. Shall see of the
travail of His soul, and be satisfied. Isa. liii. 11.

By His knowledge (knowledge of Him) He shall justify many.
Isa. liii. 11.

He is PROPHET, PRIEST, and KING, sole ruler of conscience and
heart.

Divinely accredited and anointed Saviour of the world. Isa. lxi. 1, 4.

Set up from everlasting in the eternal counsels of God. Prov.
viii. 23 ; 1 Pet. i. 20.

By His appearing in humanity " grace and truth " are become the
portion of all men.

νόμος. Talmud makes the laws 613 : females subject to only 100. Doctrine
of future life not taught. *Warburton.* The law produces wrath and has a
shadow. *Bengel.* Opposite of grace and truth. *Tholuck.* Contrasted with
grace, in so far as it merely condemns. *Meyer.*

Μωυσέως. Miriam older than Aaron or Moses, the wife of Hur. *Josephus.*
Tradition : Pharaoh's daughter, a leper, was cured by the sight of the beautiful
child. Labourers left their work to gaze on his beauty. *Josephus.* Educated
at Heliopolis. *Manetho.* Taught Orpheus, called by Greeks Musæus, and by
Egyptians Hermes. *Clem. Alex.* At three years of age he trampled upon the
crown, playfully put upon his head. *Josephus.* A bond of union established
between Moses and the shepherds lately expelled. *Ewald.* His shepherd's
staff wrought wonders ; resembled the cross in Christianity. Cushite wife
(Num. xii. 1) was his second wife. *Ewald.* Supplied water at Meribah by
wild asses leading to a spring. *Tacitus.* Passage of the Red Sea due to his
local knowledge. *Eusebius.* Song at the Red Sea was adapted to the sanctuary
at Gerizim. *Ewald, Bunsen.* 100 psalms written by him. *Origen, Jerome.*
Only Psalm xc. Questioned by *De Wette, Olshausen.*

Moslems pointed out his grave on the *west* side of Jordan to the *Author*, but
he died on the *east* side.

Babylon being captured by Alexander, Aristotle examined the libraries as
to ancient chronology. Babylonian chronology fell short of that of Moses by
2000 years.

χάρις. Fulness of Christ set against narrow limits of law. *Alford.* John's
words are selected with rare skill as to minute distinctions in this chapter.
Bengel. Distinctions questioned by *Lücke.*

ἀλήθεια. Not ψευδος, but imperfection attaches to the law. *Lücke.* With
John both the good and the true. *Neander.*

'Ιησοῦς. Original form in Heb. *Jehoshua.* Num. xiii. 16. Immanuel and
Jesus are equivalent. *"Jehovah will save."* Isa. vii. 14. John drives from
trust in good works, to grace of Christ. *Hengstenberg.*

Supplemental note as to the time of our Lord's birth. In February.
Wieseler. The day undecided. *Ellicott.* Year 750 A.C. *Tischendorf.* 749.

Robinson. 754. *Ideler, Winer.* 749. *Clinton, Wordsworth.* Ignorance of historical dates should make us more meek with regard to supernatural truth. *Wordsworth.*

---

18. No man hath seen God at any time; the only begotten Son, which is in the bosom of the Father, he hath declared him.

No man. The Shechinah filled the tabernacle, overflowing and apparently covering it with a cloud of unapproachable glory.

Nor dare Moses approach, till God called him with a call of *love.* *Rabbis.* Lev. i. 1.

Thus God visibly and gloriously consecrated His dwelling-place.

Solomon's temple so filled with God and glory the priest could not enter. 2 Chron. vii. 1, 2.

Hebrew people thought the flash of Divine glory would destroy. Judg. xiii. 22.

Hath seen. That is, as He is, by immediate gaze. Jacob saw "God face to face." Gen. xxxii. 30.

Isaiah "saw the Lord," the second Person, the Angel of the Covenant. Isa. vi. 1 ; John xii. 41.

The Invisible, "whom no man hath seen, or can see," faith sees. 1 Tim. vi. 16 ; Heb. xi. 27.

O. T. revelation of God obscure, compared with that of the New.

The Angel of the Lord, the God seen by Jacob at Peniel. Gen. xxxii. 30 ; Hos. xii. 4.

Elders saw the God of Israel. Moses calls it "similitude." Num. xii. 8.

Moses' prayer, "Show me Thy glory," only partly answered.

No man can see the absolute Divinity. "Thou canst not see my face, and live." Ex. xxxiii. 20.

"O Lord, let me die, that I may see Thee ; let me see Thee, that I may die." "I would not live, but die, that I may see Christ." *Augustine.*

If we trust to know God by *direct intuition,* as some have essayed, we shall be like those who, gazing at the sun, *turn noon into darkness.*

Thus *Milton* and *Watts* became *dazzled* to *partial blindness* in their old age, by gazing too *daringly* on the SUN of RIGHTEOUSNESS.

Only begotten. After the preceding truth these words are intensely emphatic.

He is the golden *key*, unlocking at will all the boundless riches of the Infinite God, and His life the highest continued act of adoring *Love.*

If no *created* eye *hath ever gazed on* GOD, WHO IS HE WHO HATH SEEN HIM ?

Implies an inconceivable, personal, and loving nearness to the Father.

The Son is " *in the bosom of the Father*," i.e. has access to the very heart of the Father. Luke xvi. 23.

Christ, then, has *absolute,* i. e. *infinite knowledge of Jehovah.*

Which is. The present indicates *essential truth,* not regarding *time.*

In the bosom. Reclining in one's bosom, as anciently at feasts.

In human relations intimacy of heart is indicated by *bodily nearness.*

" Render," &c. Psa. lxxix. 12. Punishment carried *home to the heart* and feelings.

" Carry," &c. Isa. xl. 11. *Borne tenderly* as a lamb by a kind shepherd.

John remembered how he himself lay on Jesus' bosom, and can think of no more tender expression to describe the most intimate, ever-blessed communion of the Son with the Father. *Besser.*

God's saints are in His *hand,* but His Son is in His *bosom.*

The Son is in the Father's bosom because there never was a time in which He was not. *Bengel.*

Apostles sat at Christ's feet as scholars ; Christ is in the Father's *bosom* as His " fellow." Zech. xiii. 7.

The Lord allows us to speak of Him with our poor words that we may lift up our hearts to embrace His greatness. *Chrysostom.*

Christ's *word* a perpetual *hymn of praise.*

Christ's *work* a *high festival* that must have been lived to be recorded.

He, an emphatic pronoun in the Gr. HE, and no *one else.*

Declared Him. As the *expression of His own infinite nature.*

Dwelling in the very Being of God, He descends from heaven and becomes man.

" He that hath seen me hath seen the Father." John xiv. 9.

Through the only-begotten Son we look God straight in the face.

He declared by His life and death—1. God's JUSTICE. He will by no means clear the guilty. Ex. xxxiv. 7.

2. His IMMUTABILITY. " The soul that sinneth, it shall die." Ezek. xviii. 4.

This would ruin our race without an atonement.

3. His MERCY. " Herein is love, not that we loved God, but that He loved us," &c. 1 John iv. 10.

4. His SEVERITY. "Behold, ye despisers, and wonder, and perish." Acts xiii. 41.

Jesus is "worthy to take the book, and open the seals thereof." Rev. v. 9.

His DEEDS are WORDS, and His WORDS DEEDS; such as are *worthy of God*.

A solemn beauty beams in His life, a Sabbath glory rests on Canaan.

A stream of eternal peace seems to well up in His path.

Gethsemane becomes sacred, and the accursed tree radiant with glory.

The touch of His holy head makes it a badge of honour to millions.

His life, the concentrated impression of the history of the world.

His words have founded an empire, lasting 18 centuries.

Embracing many of the *wisest*, *greatest*, and *best* of mankind.

God's words are facts, like the *sun* and *stars*, radiant with His *glory*, and with proofs of His *power*, and far more lasting in their nature.

At creation, His word formed laws for the guidance of nature.

Incarnate, His word established laws binding all His moral kingdom.

Bethlehem, Bethany, Nazareth become consecrated through all time.

He invests with sad interest the names of *Judas, Herod, Pilate*.

His light manifests their dark traits, and the depths of their sin.

Every man He touched became a *living mirror to the world*.

His finger brings forth from everything a sound corresponding to His word.

His Spirit glorifies His cross, revealing His victory in His resurrection.

His sorrow sheds a glory on all holy sorrow.

Henceforth *afflictions* are *dispensations* of *God's hidden kindness*.

Atoning grace illumines earth's terrible depths, by its victory over sin.

The Incarnate Word, the living exposition that GOD IS LOVE.

God has placed His glory wholly and solely in His Son.

Sceptics affirm John invented this Gospel. As well might we believe that a plain mechanic wrote *Paradise Lost*.

ἑώρακεν. Fully discovered as to essence or attributes. *Sumner*. Not only bodily sight, but intuitive and infallible knowledge, enabling Him to declare the will of God. *Alford*. Patriarchs and prophets saw angels who revealed the will of God, but never saw God. *Chrysostom*.

A decided distinction between *hearing* God and *seeing* Him. The first is attributed to men in general, the second to the Son alone. *Hearing* causes perception of the object in *motion ;* vision perceives the object in the condition of *rest*, and consequently is better adapted to express that knowledge which springs from personal unity with God. *Tholuck*.

μονογενὴς, more than well-beloved—only one of its kind. *Tholuck*.

τοῦ ἰδίου υἱου, Rom. viii. 32, depends for its whole force on His being His *essential* Son, or partaker of His very nature. *D. Brown*.

υἱός. *Cod. Alex., Tisch., Alford*, and nearly all critics. Thoroughly Joannean. *D. Brown*. Θεὸς. Adopted by *Tregelles* in deference to *Cod. Sin., Cod. Vat., Cod. Eph.*, and other authorities. Seems to have arisen from a confusion of the contracted forms of writing υἱὸς and θεὸς. Would introduce great harshness into the sentence, and a new and strange term into Scripture. *Alford, Brown*, &c. ὁ ὤν, used to signify *essential truth* without any particular regard to time. *Alford*. Ever existent. The peculiar name of Jehovah in the O.T., as written in the Sept. *Wordsworth*. A continuous present. *Winer*.

τὸν κόλπον. Sedes consilii pectus est. *Calvin*. He gives and receives confidential communications. *Tholuck*. Kindred and oneness of essence. *Chrysostom, Alford*. In the loins—one unborn. In the bosom—one born. Hence Christ born from eternity. *Bengel*. Being placed in the bosom, remains there. *Winer, Lücke*. Does not refer to His exaltation. John iii. 13. *Hengstenberg*. Closeness of relation not disturbed by Incarnation. *Luther*. Knows Him with absolute intimate perception. *Brown*.

ἐξηγήσατο. Classic use specially referred to Divine matters. *Alford*. Here to χάρις and ἀλήθεια. *Lücke*. Requires an object "it," (Auth. Ver. "Him,") not expressed in Greek or Hebrew. *Tholuck*.

---

19. And this is the record of John, when the Jews sent priests and Levites from Jerusalem to ask him, Who art thou ?

And. Here this sublime introduction closes.

The record. For 40 days our Lord had been in the desert.

Louder and louder had John's voice echoed through Judea.

The inquiry of aching hearts had run—" How shall we escape from the wrath to come ? " Matt. iii. 7.

The Sanhedrim, proud oligarchs at Jerusalem, watched and wondered in dismay.

They knew that Daniel's 70 weeks were now expiring.

That *Jews, Greeks, Romans* were in high expectation of some great PERSONAGE.

They knew King Herod's jealous inquiry, and the answer to the Magi. Matt. ii. 4.

They knew that supernatural wonders had lighted up the heavens some 30 years before ; and that signs of the coming Shiloh had multiplied, as lights increase when we are approaching a mighty city.

That they themselves, restless under the Roman yoke, sighed for a DELIVERER.

Hence the message of the priests to John near Jordan, " Who art thou ? "

They might hope that Zacharias' son was indeed their Messiah.

They thus flatter John : " offer him an apple for a kingdom." *Luther.*

Surprise increased, as no prophet had appeared for 400 years.

This is the second testimony of John to Christ's mission.

The first was given to His disciples and to the crowds rushing to his baptism.

He does not feel authorized to announce Christ publicly.

Fear doubtless prevented them from bringing John to Jerusalem.

Jews. Abraham, the founder of the Jewish nation, a pious, wealthy man of Ur, born 2153 B.C.

At God's command he came and dwelt in Canaan, aged 60.

Abraham died, aged 175. Isaac and Jacob dwelt in Canaan.

Jacob, aged 130, goes to Joseph, who is Vizier of all Egypt.

A new Pharaoh oppresses the Hebrews ; Moses under God releases them.

Israelites cross the Red Sea : Pharaoh and his army perish.

Manna falls in the desert of Zin. Rock at Rephidim yields water.

Amalekites defeated. Law given at Sinai. Soldiers numbered 603,550.

Quails sent at Taberah : Korah's conspiracy ; Kadesh-Barnea.

Aaron dies on Mount Hor, 1609 B.C. Moses dies same year.

Joshua leads Israel over Jordan, 1607 B.C. ; dies, aged 110.

Judges : Othniel, Ehud, Deborah and Barak, Gideon, Tola, Jephthah, Samson, Samuel ; Saul chosen king ; David crowned.

Solomon crowned 1030 B.C ; Rehoboam, Jehoshaphat, and other kings of *Judah.*

The kingdom lasts 388 years.

Jeroboam, Ahab, and other kings of *Israel,* for 254 years.

Hezekiah, Josiah, and others reign from 708 B.C., over Judah alone.

Captivity under Nebuchadnezzar : Daniel and others, 586 B.C.

Jeremiah prophesies 586 B.C. Ezekiel prophesies 590 B.C.

Kingdom of Judah continued 468 years; the 70 years' captivity
begun 584 B.C.
By permission of *Cyrus* Jews returned under Nehemiah and Ezra,
536 B.C.
Second temple built under Zerubbabel.
Nation saved through Queen Esther, from the ruin designed by
Haman, 516 B.C.
Darius Ochus carried many Jews captive to Babylon.
Alexander the Great visited Jerusalem. Sends many Jews to
Alexandria, 341 B.C.
Ptolemy Lagus carries 100,000 Jewish prisoners to Egypt, 335
B.C.
Seleucus Nicator builds 30 cities; sends many Jews thither.
Ptolemy Phil. bought the freedom of all Jewish slaves, 246 B.C.
Antiochus Epiphanes murdered 40,000 Jews for rejoicing at the
report of his death, 166 B.C. The *Maccabees* won their
liberty, 160 B.C.
Jews conquered by Rome under *Pompey*, who entered the *Holy of
Holies*, 63 B.C.
Crassus pillages the temple, 54 B.C. Herod crowned king, 37 B.C.
Begins to rebuild the temple, 20 B.C. Jews now hold the following
tenets :—
1. There is but one God. 2. He created all things. 3. He is a
Spirit. 4. He alone is worthy of worship. 5. The O. T.
Scriptures are true. 6. Moses head of all prophets. 7.
Author of the Law. 8. Law unchangeable. 9. God is
omniscient. 10. God will punish or reward all men. 11.
Messiah is yet to come. 12. There will be a resurrection.
13. The souls of the dead are to be prayed for.
Modern Jews are mostly *Pharisees*. A few *Sadducees* dwell at
Gaza, Damascus, Cairo, and Sychar or Nablus.
Many Jews at present *Infidels* as to their own creed.
Failure of their expectations as to Messiah the chief cause.
Jews under pain of death excluded by Emperor Hadrian from
Jerusalem.
They had to bribe the guard for admission until A.D. 700.
20,000 Jews sold as slaves, A.D. 605, for massacring Christians of
Antioch.
Cruelly and bitterly persecuted, A.D. 845, in Spain and France.
Crusaders in Germany, Hungary, and Asia *hung* and *burned* mul-
titudes, A.D. 1188.

Terrible pestilence taking place, Jews were charged with poisoning wells.

1,500,000 were put to death in Europe, A.D. 1270.

At the Coronation of Richard I. mobs murdered large numbers of Jews.

500 destroyed themselves by fire in the palace of York, after killing their wives and children.

Caliph Nassar destroyed all he found in Mesopotamia.

At Toledo all put to death who refused to renounce their religion, A.D. 1349.

160,000 banished from England by King Edward, A.D. 1291.

In Persia any Jew might be put to death not escaping to Turkey.

600,000 banished from Spain, A.D. 1392 ; from Bohemia, Bavaria, Cologne, Nuremberg, Augsburg, Moravia, and Bonn.

150,000 banished from Portugal, A.D. 1492.

John's frequent mention of the " *Jews* " indicates that the *separation* of the *Christian Church* had taken place, which continues to this hour.

Persecution in spirit or deed is antichristian. Rev. ii. 9, 10.

Priests. John vii. 32. Among Greeks and Romans they performed rites, but never preached.

Levites. Distinguished from priests, the sacerdotal tribe. Ezra ii. 40.

Patriarchal custom to set apart the first-born of each family as a priest doubtless the result of Divine revelation. Ex. xxiv. 5.

Aaron's family first chosen by God's express command. Ex. xxviii. 1.

They made a *terrible consecration* of themselves to God's service. Ex. xxxii. 28, 29.

The first-born males of the 12 tribes, 22,273. Census of Levites, 22,000.

The tabernacle the sign of the *presence* of their *unseen King* in the desert.

Levites, as the royal guard, were continually waiting upon Him.

Not numbered in the army, nor in the census of the people. Num. xvi. 62 ; ii. 49.

Could not sacrifice, or see holy things uncovered. Num. iv. 15.

They took down the tabernacle and set it up when halting. Num. i. 51.

They entered service at 30, and finished at 50. Num. iv. 23.

Their clothes first washed, they themselves were sprinkled or baptized. Num. viii. 7.

The Levites laid their hands on the victim, and then entered on
duty. Num. viii. 12.

Levites had no *land*. Num. xviii. 20. Received one-tenth of all
produce. Num. xviii. 21.

Dwelt in *forty-eight* cities. Num. xxxv. 2.

Heliopolis, Thebes, Memphis, Benares, were also anciently sacred
cities.

They transcribed and kept the laws. Deut. xvii. 9, 10. Guardians
of the tabernacle. Num. i. 51 ; xviii. 23.

Read the law every seventh year at the feast of Tabernacles.

Waiters to the priests, provided the shew-bread and fine flour for
offerings.

Levites stood and acted as choristers every morning and evening
to Jehovah.

Aided the priests in all burnt-offerings.

Teachers of the nation. 2 Chron. xvii. 7, 9. They also instructed
adults in the Lord's judgments. Deut. xxxiii. 10.

Levites, by study, were often *advanced* to the *priesthood.*

Jerusalem. See John v. 1 for its history, and John vii. 25 for
its topography.

Then the high watch-tower : the home of religious expectation
and hope.

Ask him. His claim to teach without their permission angered
them.

Jealous of his popularity, they would suppress him if possible.

Who art thou ? The whole nation, at that time, looked for a
Messiah.

They knew John was a Levite, but Christ must be of David's line.

They wished to know his office, and views, or plans : Art thou the
Christ ?

The emphasis is on " *thou.*" Question of unbelief and inquisitorial
spirit.

His priestly lineage secured far higher honours than our *Lord.*

They never sent priests to ask Him His authority and office.

Jerusalem never honoured Him with such a delegation.

Yet under Providence Jerusalem's great ones *unconsciously* became
witnesses for Christ.

μαρτυρία. A frank protest in answering a question. *Rosenmuller*. John's
entire life a testimony to Jesus. *Denton.*

οἱ Ἰουδαῖοι. Sanhedrim. *Lampe, Alford.* Hostile community in contrast with οχλος. *Lücke, Ellicott.* John's frequent use of Ἰουδαῖοι shows that he wrote at a distance from Palestine. *Hengstenberg.* Proves they had ceased to be politically a nation. *Bleek.* John writes concerning the Jews as it were *ab extra :* proves that his Gospel was written after the Synoptists. *Words-worth.* John generally means by the term *the Jews,* the *opponents of Jesus,* as a body. *De Wette.*

ἱερεῖς. In classic usage, *priests, sacrificers,* to whose office the divination from the victim's entrails also belonged. *Lid.* and *Scott.* Priests in Greek temples made known the oracles of the gods. *Plato.* Heb. word *côhên :* root-meaning uncertain ; referred to the idea of prophecy. *Gesenius.* Meaning belongs to the Arabic, not to the Heb. form ; signifies to array, put in order (Isa. lxi. 10) ; reference to the primary office of the priests in arranging the sacrifice on the altar. *Ewald.* To minister. *Saalschütz.* To draw near. *Bähr.* One who may "draw near" to the Divine presence (Ex. xix. 22 ; xxx. 20), while others remain afar off. *Smith.* Jewish priests were upbraided with ignorance of their own God by *Varro. Augustine.*

Λευείτας, became half mendicants. Judges xvii. An Israel within an Israel. *Ewald.* Tradition makes the tribe of Simeon teachers of the people. *Godwyn.* Levites had no peculiar dress. *Lewes, Heb. Rep.*

---

20. And he confessed, and denied not; but confessed, I am not the Christ.

Confessed. John here resisted a strong temptation.

The miracles accompanying his birth might well have kindled his *ambition.*

His powerful eloquence attracting immense crowds, and baptism of his disciples, as *no one* had ever done before, caused multitudes to mistake him for the Messiah.

John's disciples, after his death, unduly honoured their master.

They appear to have persistently refused to recognize the claims of Jesus.

And even some think they baptized in their master's name as though he had been the Messiah. Acts xix. 3. *Piscator.*

It is no great virtue to be humble in deep misery.

But it is most difficult to decline honours when *pressed* on us.

It was only human nature for the Athenian orator to confess his satisfaction on hearing one of the crowd whisper to another " *That* is *Demosthenes.*"

" *Confessed.*" Not written to *prove* John's deep humility, but to show the importance of his testimony officially given.

His unhesitating promptness must have surprised them.

He might have declined answering, or left his dignity to his disciples.

He might have claimed to be Elijah, as he could boldly denounce Herod and Herodias, as Elijah denounced Ahab and Jezebel.

They paid homage to John, and tempted him to declare himself the Christ.

Denied not, implies he shrank with holy indignation from the thought.

The mere idea seemed to *pain* this holy, humble, but honoured servant of God.

The Evangelist uses this double affirmation 19 times. 1. To strengthen our belief. 2. To avoid the use of an oath. 3. For the greater certainty of a thing.

It implies that the nation's hopes were intensely roused just at that time.

He denied *himself*, but did not deny his *Master.* Matt. xxvi. 70.

" Whosoever shall *confess* me," &c. " But whosoever shall *deny* me," &c. Matt. x. 32, 33.

A Christian goes out of his way, to undeceive others with regard to himself.

Silently to receive honours belonging to another is to *act a falsehood.*

I am not. Brief reply, resembles his rugged, ascetic character.

Yet these *side winds* from the world wreck many a hopeful craft.

" All the fat must be sacrificed to God." Lev. vii. 25, 30.

Christ. Gr. *anointed.* See notes on " Messiah." John i. 41. For His life, see on John iv. 25.

ἠρνήσατο; affirmation intensified by a negation common in John. *Maldonat.* Possibly because of the course of John's later disciples. *Olshausen.* To show the vast importance of his testimony. *Alford, Tittmann.*

οὐκ εἰμὶ ἐγώ. Received text, and so *Tischendorf.* ἐγὼ οὐκ εἰμί. *Lücke, Alford, Cod. Sin.*

---

21. And they asked him, What then? Art thou Elias? And he saith, I am not. Art thou that prophet? And he answered, No.

Elias. Heb. the *Strong Lord*, undaunted courage, fiery zeal, brilliant triumph.

" The Tishbite," in reference to his dwelling-place ; the locality unknown.

His hair long and thick, implying endurance. 2 Kings i. 8.

His raiment, a skin mantle, in which he hid his face. 1 Kings xix. 13.

Denounces heavy judgments on the idolatrous court and people.

Oriental freedom permitted the prophet to enter the king's presence.

Drought of three years and six months. He abides at Cherith, fed by ravens.

Goes to Zarephath, near Tyre, as the *first apostle* to the Gentiles.

Met by a widow who entertains him; her son dies; she calls Elijah "Man of God;" her son restored to life. 1 Kings xvii. 18.

400 prophets of Baal, and 400 of Ashtoreth, collected at *Carmel.*

Splendid vestments, mad fury, and disappointed hopes, distinguish the prophets of idolatry.

They appeal to their false gods by loud cries and self-mutilation, but there is no voice nor any to answer.

Jehovah answers the prayer of Elijah by fire, the well-known symbol of His presence.

The king feasts while Elijah puts his prophets to death.

"Subject to like passions," &c. James v. 17. He failed in faith and duty.

In the desert prayed for death ; was fed by an angel, and travelled 40 days "in the strength of that meat."

God appeared to him at Horeb, and taught and restored him.

Finds Elisha ploughing with 12 yoke of oxen, and casts his mantle on him, a sign of adoption.

Ahab murdering Naboth, meets Elijah and is doomed.

Jehu, 20 years after, in the chariot of the king, repeats this fearful curse.

Together Elijah and Elisha travel to Gilgal, Bethel, Jericho, and the Jordan.

Elijah smites the waters and they divide, the two prophets passing over.

Elijah conditionally promises Elisha "*a double portion of his spirit.*"

Horses of fire and chariots of fire suddenly burst upon them and separate them.

Elijah ascends to heaven in a whirlwind : a suitable and glorious departure.

Enoch in the old world, Elijah in the old covenant, Christ in the new.

Life and immortality are *brought to light* in the gospel. 2 Tim. i. 10.

"*Brought to light*" in the sense of clear and complete revelation.

Enoch and Elijah witnesses to the glory of final victory over death and the grave.

Our Lord and John the Baptist both mistaken for Elijah. Matt. xvi. 14.

John came in the *spirit*, though not in the person, of Elijah. Luke i. 17.

Both austere, self-denying, wore similar raiment, ate similar food, stern in manner, and bold in appeal.

Misunderstanding Mal. iv. 5, Jews expected, and *still expect*, Elijah to come personally before the Messiah.

They expect that he who sits at the banquet with Abraham, &c., Matt. viii. 11, will leave the festal scene, and mingle again with men.

I am not. Personally he was not, and in *their sense* his answer was given and received.

Had they asked him if he came "in the spirit and power of Elijah," he must and would have answered "Yes." Matt. xi. 14.

His mission was a far higher one than that of Elijah. Luke i. 17.

It was to testify of the COMING ONE as come, and although unknown to them, as then standing in their midst.

That prophet. "The Lord thy God will raise up unto thee a PROPHET." Deut. xviii. 15.

That prophet was no other than the MESSIAH Himself.

Yet many of the Jews at this time supposed him distinct from Christ and even inferior to Elias.

In Matt. xvi. 14 Jeremiah is mentioned as this expected prophet.

Jews held that all the prophets would *rise* at the coming of Messiah.

They understood not His two advents :—1. In humiliation. 2. In glory.

Answered, No. 1. He was not that prophet predicted by Moses.

2. He was not one of the old prophets restored to life.

3. He was not a prophet at all in the sense of a foreteller of future events.

His simple "No" shows the holy zeal with which he strove after Christ and the confession of His Name.

As if he had said : Let us come at once to HIM who really is worth asking for.

'Hλίας. Born in the town Thisbe. *Hiller, Reland.* The name naturally points to a place called Tishbeh. *Fürst.* Tishbi of Gilead. *Ewald, Bunsen.* Jabesh Gilead. *Lightfoot.* The Hebrew word may be so pointed as to mean

"the stranger." *Michaelis. Tishbite*, from *dishbi*, "converter." *Lightfoot.*
Tradition makes him oft appear to pious Rabbis as an Arabian merchant.
Eisenmenger. Arab tradition places his tomb near Damascus. *Mislin.* Jews
expected a general baptism before or at the coming of the Messiah. *Lightfoot.*
Rabbis say Elias' coming would solve all doubts. *A. Hales.* Jews meant the
Tishbite in proper person : τὸν Θεσβίτην is interpolated by the LXX. in Mal.
iv. 5. *Wordsworth.* Jews believed in the doctrine of a second body. *Origen.*
Elias will preach the second advent as John the first. *Gregory.* Jews and
some of the Fathers affirm that Elias will appear in person before Christ's
second advent to judgment. *Rosen., Alford, Wordsworth.* He must come in
the *flesh ;* he has come in the *spirit. Ryle.*

προφήτης (πρόφφημι). 1. Properly *one who speaks* for another, esp. *one who
speaks for a God*, and interprets His will to men. 2. An *interpreter, declarer.*
In N. T. *an interpreter of Scripture, preacher. Lid. and Scott.* Ordinary
Heb. word for *prophet is Nabi*, "to bubble forth like a fountain." One who
announces or pours forth the declarations of God. *Gesenius, Ewald, Bleek,
Lee, Pusey,* &c. The man *to whom announcements are made* by God, i.e. inspired. *Davidson, Bunsen.* Read "a prophet." *Augustine.* The one foretold.
Deut. xviii. 15. *Chrysostom.* An angel. *Kimchi.* Others made Elias an angel.
Jews divided as to whether he was the Shiloh or not. *D. Brown.* Applies exclusively to Messiah. *Kurtz, Tholuck.* Succession of O. T. prophets. *Hoffman.* Similar prediction to Gen. iii. 15. *Von Gerlach.* Christ is included.
Ewald. The passage repeatedly held to be Messianic. *Hengstenberg.* They
looked for Jeremiah, Matt. xvi. 14, or one of the old prophets. *Alford.* His
wisdom would equal Solomon's. *Maimonides.* John was not a prophet to *predict* events. *Hammond.* Pharisees try to induce him to assume to be something. *Lampe.* Jews had so far lost their hold of truth that they did not apply
this prediction to Christ. *Rupert.* John's denial reaches to either meaning.
Cyril.

---

22. Then said they unto him, Who art thou ? that we may give an answer to
them that sent us. What sayest thou of thyself ?

Who art? Conjecture exhausted, they demand a positive reply.

Thou. Their question persistently refers to his person. But he
is a "*voice.*"

His answer as persistently only refers to his office. He hid behind
his calling.

An answer. An answer had been demanded by the people,
especially the Jewish chiefs.

Every man who enters on a special undertaking ought to be able
to give a reason for it.

These legates were intensely anxious to retain their vain ceremonies.

The right of establishing baptism, they held, was confined to the
Messiah.

Hence, disappointed, they indignantly ask, " Why baptizest
thou ?"

John felt bound to answer them in an official communication.

Some were officers in authority, claiming respect, "sitting in Moses' seat." Matt. xxiii. 2.

He acknowledges their authority while he unmasks their scheme.

Our Lord and His messengers seemed to live in the atmosphere of the Bible, and the Holy Spirit gave them power to pierce the designs and scatter the devices of foes.

Thyself. He knew the danger of speaking well or ill of himself.

If well, the world will charge us with *flattering* ourselves.

If ill, they think we seek compliments from others.

The conquerors in Olympic games waited for *others* to place the garlands on them.

---

23. He said, I am the voice of one crying in the wilderness, Make straight the way of the Lord, as said the prophet Esaias.

He said. He answers in Scripture language. Isa. xl. 3.

The voice. Our Lord was the WORD, John the voice declaring the WORD.

The sound precedes the knowledge of the word, and makes it known.

This *herald* hints at the *majesty* of the Saviour.

The law was proclaimed by angels, but no angel's coming or errand was foretold, as was John and his office, centuries before his birth.

John's teaching would have been useless, without the Incarnate WORD.

A proof of John's humility : the *voice* passes, but the WORD remains.

" He must increase, but I must decrease." John iii. 30.

The voice rouses the attention of the hearer. So John calls to all Judea.

He knew himself to be the *incarnation* of the foretold voice.

The voice an *echo* of the WORD, the name of the Divine Eternal Son.

A shining lamp, John v. 35, preceding the LIGHT of the world.

Yet how empty is the mere voice, without *mind* being *enshrined* in the word !

How feeble a mere lamp, to dispel the darkness before sunrise.

Happy if the minister can thus forget himself in the message.

" He lends his tongue to the Lord." *Gregory Nazianzen.*

Crying. The author has often heard amid the overcrowded narrow streets of oriental cities the voice crying, " Make way for the Howadji."

Public testimony given in an earnest, importunate manner.

Bells of pure gold, hung on Aaron's garments, rung sweetly during service.

But John rebuked Herod *severely ;* Pharisees *roughly ;* his own disciples *gently,* thus charming ever so wisely. Psa. lviii. 5.

Wilderness. Generally an immense broken plain, with flinty mounds of rock, varying from ten to forty feet in height.

Camel or horse leaves no foot-print on the stubborn ground.

The flinty sands among these flint hills, after being traversed for thousands of years, *bear not a vestige that any one ever passed that way.*

The water obtained a few feet beneath the soil is very *briny.*

These dreary, desolate solitudes have *nothing that lives or moves.*

The curse reigns amid those desolations in terrible grandeur.

The cattle, as well as hosts of Israel, were sustained by *miracle.*

" *Wilderness of Judea.*" Matt. iii. 1. The desert valley of the Jordan, thinly peopled and bare in pasture, a little north of Jerusalem.

Wilderness. The spiritual and bodily wretchedness of Israel.

In the wilderness there is no ploughing or hoeing, no reaping or sowing.

No springing, no shooting, no growing, no blossom or fruit.

No one dwells in the wilderness, but the traveller hastens on.

No highway along which one can travel,—all is barrenness and desolation.

Thus John found mankind barren of any grace or virtue.

No meekness, no kindness, no self-denial, no repentance, no faith.

As the wilderness cannot of itself yield flowers and fruit, neither can sinners transform themselves into God's children. John vi. 44.

But we can " PREPARE THE WAY OF THE LORD," " break up the fallow ground." Jer. iv. 3.

Make straight. Remove all obstacles. Couriers thus announced the progress of kings.

Angels cried as harbingers of Messiah, " Lift up your heads, O ye gates ; and the King of glory shall come in." Psa. xxiv. 7.

Each of the four Evangelists quotes and applies the prophecy to the mission of John : a connecting link between the Old Test. and the New.

Our Lord, like the great ones of earth, must have a herald.

John would cry, "·I do not want disciples to follow me, but my Master."

All obstacles are to be removed for the Lord of Glory "travelling in the greatness of His strength." Isa. lxiii. 1.

All unbelief, spiritual pride, avarice, anger, vanity, uncleanness, must be removed.

The way. That wonderful road which angels had travelled so often.

A pathway leading from an unseen Being, to the heart of man.

A way which the prophets had tried to prepare, ages gone by.

A way in which the burdened heart might travel and find repose.

A way which the Eternal Spirit would move on in mercy to our race.

A way in which the ransomed of the Lord would return with everlasting joy.

1. A way divinely planned and opened.
2. A way ever open, and which no man or angel can ever close.
3. A way of truth, peace, and eternal life.
4. A way of light, which no cloud or darkness can finally conceal.
5. A way the wicked never know, nor care to travel.
6. A way exalted, a " highway " rising until it reaches the throne of God. Isa. xxxv. 8.

Esaias. *Salvation of Jahu;* a shortened form of Jehovah.

The prophet refers to the signification of his own name. Isa. viii. 18.

Son of Amoz. Nothing more is known of his tribe or ancestry.

Surnamed, for his full predictions of Christ, " THE EVANGELICAL PROPHET."

A rabbinical tradition says he was sawn asunder in the trunk of a tree by order of Manasseh.

Apparently confirmed by Heb. xi. 37, which can be referred to no other known fact.

Yet it is doubtful whether Isaiah was alive when Manasseh ascended the throne.

If he began his career at 30, the usual period for a priest to enter upon his office, he must have been 90 years of age when Hezekiah died, and 90 when his son Manasseh (surnamed the bloody) began to reign at 12 years of age.

Hostility of those opposed to Jehovah sufficiently excited against the prophet to prompt them to the murder during the reign of Manasseh's predecessor. *Smith.*

His audience were dwellers at Jerusalem and in Judea.

They had become the *sole home* of Hebrew hopes and blessings.

Grandeur of his thoughts and sublimity of his style render him worthy of the name of the " KINGLY PROPHET." *Ewald.*

Φωνὴ. This prophecy fulfilled by the activity of Jesus Christ. *Hengsten-berg.* Christ never spake a word to Herod for killing this herald. *Trapp.* Words quoted of John by Matt. and others here spoken by him. *Alford.*

ἐρήμῳ. Wilderness where John was brought up, Luke i. 80, not strictly a *desert*, but thinly peopled, and abounding in pastures for flocks. *Alford.* Wilderness of the wandering, a perfect waste. *Seetzen.* Flocks could not be sustained. *Stewart.* Psa. cvii. 35—38, a poetic description of the *miraculous* supplies amid utter and complete desolation. *Ritter.* 6000 Bedouins dwell in the wilderness. *Hamilton.* And obtain less sustenance than 6000 mariners from the ocean. *Author.* Here spiritually understood. *Hengstenberg.*

Εὐθύνατε. Heart reform. *Lücke.* Penitence. *Luther.* Renovation of life. *Hengstenberg.*

Κυρίου, Luke iii. 6. May have been understood by John to refer directly to the Messiah. *Tholuck.*

Ἡσαΐας. Rabbis use the Hellenistic form. Amoz, his father, confounded with the prophet Amos by *Clem. Alex.* A brother of King Amaziah ; tradition of Rabbis. Nothing known of his race or tribe. *Kimchi* (1230 A.D.). The traditional spot of the martyrdom is a very old mulberry tree which stands near the pool of Siloam on the slopes of Ophel, below the S.E. wall of Jerusalem. *Smith.*

---

24. And they which were sent were of the Pharisees.

Pharisees. A religious party or school among the Jews at the time of Christ.

So called from *Perishin* (Heb. *Perûshîm*), meaning " separated."

The name does not occur in the Old Test. or in the Apocrypha.

Usually considered that the Pharisees were the same with the Assideans (i.e. *chasidim*, godly men, saints), mentioned in Maccabees.

Our Lord's teaching in many respects thoroughly antagonistic to theirs.

He denounced them in the bitterest language as " hypocrites," " vipers," " murderers," &c.

The most intense *formalists* the world has ever seen : " whited sepulchres." Matt. xxiii. 27.

They treated men like children, formalizing and defining minutest particulars of ritual observance.

" Made the Word of God of no effect by their traditions: "—

1. Purest form of religion in Old Test. incompatible with their endless ceremonies.
2. Some of their traditions decidedly at variance with genuine religion.

They held that God had given Moses an oral law on Sinai to complete and explain the written law.

This statement so incredible they seem to have maintained in the following way :—

The Pentateuch, they say, contains 613 laws, including 248 commandments, and 365 prohibitions.

But contains no allusion to *future* life, or to the *duty* of prayer, except Ex. xxiii. 25.

But as these are most important matters, God was alleged to have given Moses commands concerning them orally.

To these alleged oral laws they added three other classes of traditions.

1. Opinions on disputed points, the result of a majority of votes.
2. Decrees said to have been made by prophets and wise men in different ages.
3. Legal decisions of ecclesiastical authorities on disputed questions.

Some of the most characteristic laws of the Pharisees related to what was clean and unclean.

A saint must not eat nor drink with the multitude.

Hence our Lord violated their most deeply-rooted prejudices.

Animals, unless slaughtered with prayer, were strictly forbidden as food.

Jews forbidden to pay money to Gentiles three days before heathen festival.

Forbidden to show the way or point out a spring of water to the *uncircumcised*.

Or to assist a heathen mother in the labours of childbirth.

Pharisees prayed at 9 o'clock, at 12, and at 3, as Mohammedans do at present.

Forgetting their devotions, they must return from the field for prayer.

The Decalogue must be read once a day, without moving foot, hand, or eye, in a clean place, four feet from a grave.

Some beat their heads against the wall until the blood came.

They put thorns in their garments, to prick themselves.

They lay on planks, or stones, or thorns, to do *penance*.
They would as soon eat swine's flesh as a Samaritan's bread.
They hated the presence, the fire, the fashions, the books, of the
Samaritans.
If a Samaritan simply touched a Jew, he plunged into the water
to cleanse his clothes.
Jews said if *two only went to heaven*, one must be a Pharisee, and
the other a Sadducee.
Their contest with the scribes was very bitter.
" They were far fiercer in their fanaticism than other sects, and
they took more pains to go to hell." *Bishop Hall.*
Their boasted purity required water drawn of their own labour.
Self-righteousness, as *casuistic*, was peculiar to them.
Sadducees were *rationalistic;* Essenes *ascetic*, the Puritans of their
day.
The very heathen saw the malignity of the Pharisees, and dreaded
them.
Grossly sensual, they hated John's searching preaching, and fled
from the burning words of the Redeemer.   John viii. 9.
So it has ever been : those trusting to their own self-righteousness
are incapable of repentance.

οἱ cancelled. *Alford.* Omitted. *Cod. Sin.* Retained. *Tischendorf.*
ἀπεσταλμένοι. The reason added because of their hostility. *Lücke.* The
deputation of that sect. *Luthardt.*
φαρισαίων. Bigotry became malignant after the captivity. *Judaism* stood
out as apart from *Hebraism. Winer.* Sadoc inferred that there would be no
future retribution. *Lange.* The Sadducees undermined all prophecy. They
were the most hopeless sceptics. *Neander.* Peculiar jealousy of the Pharisees
as to *new* religions here hinted at. *D. Brown.* Talmud, i.e. Doctrine, Jerusalem and Babylon. The text is called Mishna. Comments Gemara. Written
about 500 A.D. 6 vols. Amsterdam, 1703. Hillel and Shammai, surnamed
the *reaper* and *binder*, had just died before Christ. Their decisions of the
highest authority. *Smith.* Moses received the Talmud from God at Sinai.
Pirke Abôth. A specimen of "traditions" of the Pharisees: "The oil and
wick of Sabbath-candle. Not with moss, nor cedar, nor undressed flax, nor
rushes, nor leaves of the wilderness, nor moss that has grown on the waters,
nor pitch, nor wax, nor cotton-seed oil, nor fat of the tail or entrails of beasts,
nor suet, nor train oil, nor nut oil, nor radish-seed oil, nor fish oil, nor gourd-
seed oil, nor resin, nor gum." *De Sola & Raphall.* At the present day a strict
orthodox Jew may not eat meat of any animal unless it has been killed by a
Jewish butcher. The butcher searches the animal for any blemish, and on his
approval causes a leaden seal, stamped with the Heb. word *câshâr* (lawful),
to be attached to the meat, attesting its cleanness. *Disraeli.* A seal is recorded
to have been used for a similar purpose by Egyptian priests, to attest that a
bull about to be sacrificed was " *clean.*" No Egyptian would salute a Greek

with a kiss, nor use a Greek knife, or spits, or cauldron, or taste the meat of an ox which had been cut by a Greek knife. They drank out of bronze vessels, *rinsing them perpetually.* And if any one accidentally touched a pig, he would plunge into the Nile without stopping to undress. The Egyptians derived the idea of clean and unclean from the Jews. *Herodotus.* Pharisees mainly filled the *Sanhedrim. Grotius.* Several kinds. 1. *Shechemites,* i.e. circumcised for profit. 2. *Dashing* Pharisee, moved blindly, so his toes dashed against a stone. 3. Those who let *out blood :* press the wall so as to press out blood. 4. *Mortar*, shape of his hat. 5. *Sinless* Pharisee as to the law. 6. Pharisee for *love :* obeyed the law for love. 7. Pharisee for *fear.* A sect of female Pharisees who, under the veil of sanctity, resembled Spanish nuns in morals. *Lewes, Heb. Rep.*

---

25. And they asked him, and said unto him, Why baptizest thou then, if thou be not that Christ, nor Elias, neither that prophet ?

Why ? By what right, or what calling ?

A general purifying of the people was expected in Messiah's time.

They regarded baptism as a token of the approach of Messiah's kingdom.

But the right to baptize could only be given by a Divine commission.

John gives the Pharisees no satisfaction upon this point.

Baptizest ? That is, If thou art no forerunner of the Messiah.

They expected Messiah or His attendants, Elias or Jeremias, to baptize.

For baptism formed a new obligation, such as that which was formed by proselytes.

An ancient religious rite : Priests of Egypt bathed twice a day ; Greek priests bathed before sacrificing. Those entering on the *Eleusinian* mysteries were required to wash. The guilt of the homicide was thus expiated (*Sophocles*).

Pollution of battle stains were thus cleansed (*Ovid*).

Baptism was observed in the wilderness before the giving of the law. Ex. xix. 10.

Mosaic law enacted " washings," numerous and frequent.

All kinds of ceremonial pollutions required purification by water.

Necessary, also, to prepare for taking part in sacred services.

Aaron at his consecration, Ex. xxix. 4, and on entering the sanctuary, Ex. xxx. 20.

Solomon's temple had *ten lavers* for the various cleansings. 2 Chron. iv. 6.

Priests at their ordination were sprinkled with water. Num. viii. 7.

Our Lord solemnly confirmed this rite by adopting it in His Church.

Whether by *sprinkling* or *immersion* it points to "the washing of regeneration."

"Then shall I sprinkle clean water upon you, and you shall be clean." Ezek. xxxvi. 25.

Children admitted to baptism in accordance with the spirit of Christianity.

Passage of Israelites (including children) through the Red Sea called baptism. 1 Cor. x. 2.

We bring our children to the font in faith that God will cleanse their hearts.

The waters of a thousand Jordans cannot take away *one sin*.

"Wash me throughly from mine iniquity, and cleanse me from my sin." Psa. li. 2.

"In that day there shall be a fountain opened for sin and uncleanness." Zech. xiii. 1.

"I will wash my hands in innocency: so will I compass," &c. Psa. xxvi. 6.

Pilate, condemning the innocent One, "washed his hands" before the people. Matt. xxvii. 24.

At the Lake of Lucerne, where he is said to have committed suicide, popular belief represents his ghost as rising from the waters and going through the process of washing its hands. *Smith.*

Pharisees blinded by carnality gave baptism a wholly external character.

Imagined they could enter Messiah's kingdom without sincere repentance and faith.

Converting the miracle of the new birth into a kind of *magical* transmutation.

If thou. John denying himself to be the Messiah, or Elias, or one of the old prophets, Pharisees deny his right to baptize.

Baptism in ordinary use admitted proselytes to *Judaism;* but John was baptizing *actual Jews.*

Jews held that none but Messias Himself could add to the ritual. Ezek. xxxvi. 25.

John's baptism a kind of transition from *Jewish* baptism to *Christian.*

Τί οὖν. John's modesty was turned against himself. *Henry.* These delegates proceed from flattering to threatening. *Luther.*

βαπτίζεις. Tingere. *Tertullian.* Mergere. *Ambrose.* Literally immersion. Mark vii. 4. *Lightfoot ;* but used classically and by Josephus of sprinkling and pouring. *Dale.* Baptism practised before the captivity. *Bengel, Kuinoel.* A symbol of repentance. *Meyer.* Of purifying and sifting. *Tholuck.* John understood Christian baptism. *Ebrard.* Waters of the Deluge type of baptism, 1 Pet. iii. 21. *Augustine.* Right of baptizing only to the herald of the Messiah. *Lücke.* Not derived from sprinkling proselytes, but from ceremonial washings. *J. A. Alexander.* Christian baptism not properly instituted until after His Resurrection, Matt. xxviii. 19. Yet those baptized before were not re-baptized after the Resurrection. *Hengstenberg.* John's baptism neither of Moses, nor of Christ, but the *twilight* between night and morning. *Robert Hall.* "Whenever a Gentile desires to enter into the Covenant of Israel, and place himself under the wings of the Divine Majesty, and take the yoke of the law upon him, he must be circumcised, and baptized, and bring a sacrifice ; or if it be a woman, she must be baptized and bring a sacrifice." *Maimonides.* Men, women, and children (proselytes) were all baptized, and either two or three witnesses required to be present. *Lightfoot.* Doubted or denied that this baptism of proselytes had been in use amongst the Jews from times so early as those of the Gospel. *Lardner, Ernesti, De Wette.* Highly improbable that after the rise of Christianity the Jews should have adopted a rite so peculiarly Christian as baptism had then become. *Smith.* All baptisms by Christ's disciples were into the name of the *Trinity. J. A. Alexander.*

---

26. John answered them, saying, I baptize with water: but there standeth one among you, whom ye know not.

Answered. An indirect but complete answer to the demands of the priests.

John implies he did not act on his own authority.

I bear a commission from ONE who has power and authority.

I come simply baptizing with water, but *He* will baptize the *heart.*

Water. Note the forcible and severe brevity of his reply.

As water *cannot* cleanse the soul, you will need another baptism.

I am the Messenger foretold by Malachi. Mal. iii. 1.

I only gather the sheep and the lambs, the Shepherd alone can fold them.

My baptism fulfils Ezek. xxxvi. 25. Christ's baptism will fulfil Ezek. xxxvi. 26, 27.

As the brazen serpent foreshadowed the cross and its victim, so circumcision, passover, and baptism foreshadowed *sacraments.*

Compared with Him they are husks and shells ; Christ alone is the heart kernel.

It seems that but a few of John's converts ever came to the Redeemer.

A sad premonition of the number of mere professors in the Christian Church.

Refusing this, there is another baptism of fire and of judgment. Luke iii. 16.

God's mercies and ministrations of justice are knit together.   Isa.
iv. 4.

Standeth.   Gr. *Hath stood for awhile, and is still standing.*

" Having done all, to stand," Eph. vi. 13, i.e. as *victors* over foes.

An orientalism used for a *herald* making a proclamation, and for
a witness before a court.

Jews had asked John a sign of his being sent of God.   He points
to the fact of the Messiah standing in their midst.

One among.   As the tree of life stood in the midst of the garden,
so Jesus among men.

A mysterious Being who has authority to command and power to
compel obedience.

One in visible form, too, they inferred from the "latchet of the
sandal."

But one whom they did not know, nor would they if His name
was given.

One whom, if He should flash His lightning amid their darkness,
they would still be ignorant of.

After three years of stupendous wonders in Judea, looking upon
the sun He had darkened and standing on the earth that had
trembled for Him, they knew Him not, nor the day of their
visitation.   Acts iii. 17; 1 Cor. ii. 8.

His disciples alone, of all the human family, had the privilege of
beholding Him in HIS ROBES of MAJESTY ON TABOR.

God is often nearer to us than we are aware; often nearest when
thought most distant.

Our Lord had really left the private walks of life at Nazareth.

Know not.   Because they only looked with a *carnal* eye for a
conqueror.

They neither knew Him *personally* nor wanted to know Him
officially.

Had He told His aim as marching to a cross, they would have
spurned His claims as those of one insane.

God's saints His hidden ones.   Psa. lxxxiii. 3.   The world knows
them not.

It might have been supposed the Pharisees would have inquired
intently—

"Where is that wondrous person of whom you speak in such
terms ? "

Christ is still *standing* among men as Prophet, Priest, and King.
Rev. iii. 20.

Unbelief, worldliness, sensuality prevent men seeing their Lord. 2 Cor. iv. 4.

He will soon *sit* upon His great white throne as Judge Eternal. Rev. xx. 11.

In that day " every eye shall see Him." " Small and great shall *stand* before God." Rev. i. 7 ; xx. 12.

ἀπεκρίθη. The Messiah, standing among them then, was a sign that he, the Baptist, was sent from God. *Olshausen.* This fact was authority for John's baptism. *Alford.*

ὕδατι. Initiation by water, used long before Christ. *Selden, Godwyn.* Probably this said immediately after Christ's baptism. *D. Brown.* The sacrament of baptism itself purifies the soul. *Council of Trent.* John's disciples did not follow Jesus after their master's death. *J. A. Alexander, Denton.* μέσος. As to His human nature. *Luca Brug.* In public office. *Tholuck.* As to His Divinity. *Jansen Ypres.* As the light of men. *Beau Amis.* Not as the Baptist, but in the midst of the cities of men. *Chrys.* The "Voice" indicates the WORD. *Origen.* As Mediator. *Theophylact.* My baptism is only anticipatory. *P. Anton.*

ἔστηκεν. Hath taken His stand. *Bengel.* δέ, omitted. *Tisch., Alford, Tregelles.*

---

27. He it is, who coming after me is preferred before me, whose shoe's latchet I am not worthy to unloose.

Coming after. John's birth preceded the Saviour's six months.

Our Lord's ministry began doubtless while John was still baptizing, although the exact chronology is unknown.

Preferred. Gr. *Existed before* the Baptist.

Before :—1. In station. 2. In dignity. 3. In glory.

He was not authorized *publicly* to announce the Messiah.

In proclaiming his own unworthiness he publishes Christ's Divinity.

Nothing so full of sublimity as humility, because no virtue indicates so clearly the work and presence of Divinity.

Shoe. *Sandal,* the article ordinarily used for protecting the feet.

No description of the sandal in the Bible itself.

Talmudists say materials employed for the sole were either leather, felt, cloth, or wood, and that it was occasionally shod with iron.

Palm leaves and papyrus stalks used in Egypt in addition to the leather. *Herod.*

Egyptian sandals usually turned up at the toe like our skates.

Assyrian sandals formed of wood or leather; heel and side of the foot encased.

Jewish sandals different in form : a heel-strap essential to a proper sandal.

Great attention paid by ladies to their sandals; made of skins of hyenas, badgers, and seals.

The thongs were handsomely embroidered, as were those of Greek ladies.

Sandals worn by all classes in Palestine, even by the very poor.

Hence sandal and thong so cheap and common, they became a proverb for insignificant things.

Not worn at all periods ; dispensed with indoors ; put on for a journey, military expedition, going from home, &c.

On such occasions persons carried an extra pair. Objected to by our Lord as far as the apostles were concerned. Matt. x. 10.

During meals feet uncovered. John xiii. 5, 6. Paschal Feast special exception. Ex. xii. 11.

Approaching a sacred place the shoes were withdrawn. Ex. iii. 5 ; Josh. v. 15.

Rabbis forbade persons to pass through the temple with shoes on.

Cybele at Rome, and Isis at Herculaneum, were worshipped bare foot.

Mohammedans now thus enter mosques, and especially *Kaaba* at Mecca.

Samaritans thus walk the summit of Mount Gerizim.

Mourners went barefoot, as David at the Mount of Olives. 2 Sam. xv. 30 ; Isa. xx. 2.

Romans, Conscript Fathers and people, went barefoot at Augustus' death.

" Over Edom I will cast my shoe," Ps. lx. 8, implies *subjection.*

Modern Yezidis of Mesopotamia enter the tomb of their patron saint barefoot.

Not worthy. Yet Christ *must* submit to be baptized by John, Matt. iii. 15.

Not worthy, a sentiment of adoration, a bending of the knee.

It is a lowly but just perception of thorough truthfulness.

Archangels and Cherubim feel and confess the same thing. Isa. vi. 2, 3.

Can any Christian, however lowly, humble himself thus before a created being and be innocent ?

Unloose. The most servile office one could render to another.

A disciple, it is said by some, might perform any office for his
  teacher, unloosing of shoes excepted.
Only the meanest slave with Greeks carried the sandals of his
  master.
On entering a house the slave unloosed them and washed the
  guest's feet.
Yet we have our Lord's words that he who thus speaks was inferior
  to none of men. Matt. xi. 11.
With one full of the Spirit such words amount to an act of
  adoration.
Hence acts of prostration to the Virgin Mary and the Pope are
  idolatries.

αὐτός ἐστιν, omitted. *Gries., Tisch., Lach., Alford, Cod. Sin.,* &c.
ὀπίσω. The Lord's ministry began after John's imprisonment. *Denton.*
They laboured contemporaneously. *Greswell, Andrews, Alford.*
ὃς ἔμπροσθέν μου γέγονεν. Omitted. *Gries., Lach., Tisch., Alford, Tregelles, Cod. Sin.,* &c.
ἄξιος. For his humility, says one, John was exalted to the seat vacated by
Lucifer. *Trapp.*
ὑποδήματος. Properly applies to the sandal exclusively, as it means what
is bound *under* the foot. Jews went barefoot in Egypt in the time of Christ.
Bochart. Priests are said to have conducted their ministrations in the temple
barefoot. *Theod.* Use of the shoe in transfer of property noticed, Ruth iv. 7,
8, and a similar significance attached to the act in connection with the repudiation of a Levirate marriage, Deut. xxv. 9. Terms applied to removal of the
shoe, Deut. xxv. 10; Isa. xx. 2, &c., imply that the thongs were either so
numerous or so broad as almost to cover the top of the foot. *Smith.* Shoemaking, or strap-making, a recognized trade among the Jews. *Mishna.*
Clothes and shoes grew with the growth of children in the wilderness, Deut.
viii. 4, as shells of snails. *Justin Martyr, Grotius.* A miraculous durability.
Calvin.

---

28. These things were done in Bethabara beyond Jordan, where John was
baptizing.

Bethabara. Without any authority substituted by Origen, A.D.
  329, for *Bethania.*
His reason was, in visiting the Jordan, he could not find the place.
300 eventful years had changed the face of Palestine since these
  things occurred.
We might as well change the names Bethsaida and Capernaum
  because we cannot find these places.
He laboured and preached far from Jerusalem, the *mother,* and also
  the *altar,* of the saints.

" Amos must not prophesy at Beth-el, for it is the king's court."
Amos vii. 13.

Bethania, a precious spot where first the LAMB OF GOD was pointed
out to a fallen world.

There the Church of the Saviour Incarnate began its blessed
career.

There first was preached Him whom kings and prophets desired to
see. Matt. xiii. 17.

Beyond Jordan. This shows it was not *the* Bethany at the foot
of Olivet, but a village on the east side of Jordan.

JORDAN. Heb. *the descender.* Arabs call it *Esh Sheriah*, i.e.
watering-place.

First allusion,—" Lot saw the plain of the Jordan well watered."
Gen. xiii. 10.

Abraham forded it coming from Charran; Jacob with his staff passed
over it. Gen. xxxii. 10.

Joshua led Israel through it on dry ground, over against Jericho.
Josh. iv. 12.

The distance is nine miles, and the space barren swales of sand.

Elijah and Elisha passed over by a miracle. 2 Kings ii. 8.

Naaman, in returning to Damascus, must have passed an upper
ford.

But *one boat* is ever named in regard to Jordan. 2 Sam. xix. 18.

Jordan overflowed its banks during the barley harvest. Josh.
iii. 15.

In March, by the rising of the waters, the lion was driven from his
lair. Jer. xlix. 19.

" This side Jordan " is always the *west ;* " beyond the Jordan " the
east side, or Moab.

A great altar built on its banks. Josh. xxii. 10. Near it our Lord
was baptized.

The Jordan in a straight line is 60 miles ; the course is 200
miles. *Lynch.*

The Dead Sea, receiving the Jordan, is 2600 *feet lower than the
Mediterranean.*

From the roots of Anti-Lebanon to the Dead Sea, it falls 3000 feet
in 27 rapids.

The width varies from 80 to 150 feet; depth from 5 to 12 feet.

No town ever was built on its banks. An extinct crater is near its
source.

It is *useless as to watering the barren valley,* and, from its rapids, useless for *navigation.*

There are hot springs near Magdala, Emmaus, and Gadara.

In "the clay ground," near Succoth, were the brass foundries of Solomon. 1 Kings vii. 46.

On its immediate banks are seen corn-fields, palms, vines, figs, melons, cedars, &c.

Apart from its immediate banks, the sand extends for miles on either side.

This is furrowed into countless channels resembling huge waves of the ocean. In other parts they assume other forms.

These white sand cones resemble gigantic tents : in the hollows are dwarf trees and shrubs.

The "sweet fields beyond the swelling floods" of Jordan have no real ground in nature. But faith beholds them, and the Christian will still sing—

> "Could we but climb where Moses stood,
>   And view the landscape o'er,
> Not Jordan's streams nor death's cold flood
>   Should fright us from the shore." *Watts.*

βηθαβαρά. Heb. place of crossing. House of passage, Jos. iv. 8, 9 ; Judg. vii. 24.

βηθανία. "Shiphouse." *Cod. Sin.*, and all the Codices. Ubi Johannes baptizabat. *Jerome.* Place had two names. *Lücke.* Changed from Bethania to Bethabara. *Lange.* As Joshua here passed the Jordan. *Lücke.* The vast number of the army renders the spot indeterminate. *Lightfoot.*

'Ιορδάνης. Altar built by Joshua, 50 stadia from the river. *Josephus.* In the river. *Clark.* In Gilgal. *Kennicott.* Two altars of 12 stones each. *Pool, Patrick, Geddes.* On the banks. *Rosenmuller.*

---

29. The next day John seeth Jesus coming unto him, and saith, Behold the Lamb of God, which taketh away the sin of the world.

Next day. The day following his explanations to the hierarchical party.

The deputation had departed and the crowd dispersed John is alone with his disciples.

John. For his character and life see on verse 15.

Seeth Jesus. The Lord is returning from the wilderness in holy triumph.

He comes on the scene a Conqueror. "ministered unto by angels."

Probably on His way from the scene of His temptation to His Galilean home.

From this time till John's death they appear to have had no direct intercourse.

While John had been preaching, Jesus had been living in retirement.

Coming. It shows our Lord was absent the day before, at the meeting with the deputation.

The vanquisher of Satan walks in sublime silence on the shores of the Jordan.

Why or *whence* He came no hint whatever is given in Scripture.

Conjectured it was solely to receive this glorious testimony.

One of those instances of *reticence* peculiar to Divine inspiration.

Humanity babbles on, but God alone knows how and when to be silent. Prov. xxv. 2.

Hence there are many problems awaiting solution in eternity.

Behold! Glorious consolation for John *to see* Him whom kings and prophets longed to see. Matt. xiii. 17; Luke x. 24; Heb. xi. 13.

Augustine wished to see Solomon in his glory, Paul in the pulpit, and Christ in the flesh.

All generations to the end of time are here addressed with his disciples.

Every word is emphatic. 1. "*Behold!*" A summons to the world. 2. The object, "*the Lamb.*" 3. The character of this object, "THE LAMB OF GOD." 4. The office, "*to take (bear) away.*" 5. The burden, "*sin.*" 6. The magnitude and weight of this burden, "*the sin of the* WORLD."

BEHOLD! In this word lies the sum and substance of the Gospel ministry.

"We preach not ourselves, but Christ Jesus the Lord." 2 Cor. iv. 5.

Lamb. (See on ver. 36.) Socinians and others say this refers to His meekness as a man.

Doubtless His meekness is included in His sin-expiating and atoning character.

But the Gospel has for its root a truth so deep that angels desire to look into it. 1 Pet. i. 11, 12.

This name given Jesus by the Holy Spirit to point Him out as THE SACRIFICE. Isa. liii. 7.

Morning and evening, from the hour of deliverance from Egypt, a lamb had been offered.

Witnessing Jews hearing this, needed no explanation of the words.

Christ is here the GOD-ORDAINED, GOD-GIVEN, GOD-ACCEPTED SACRIFICE.

Called a " Lion " because of His strength and courage, and yet a Lamb, the chosen emblem of innocence, meekness, patience. 1 Pet. i. 19 ; Rev. v. 5.

In the midst of the throne there stands a LAMB adored by heaven and earth, as the remedy appointed and approved by God. Rev. v. 6.

Priests daily laid their *hands* on the victim offered in token of *transferring the sins of the people.* Lev. i. 4; iii. 2 ; iv. 4.

Each Jew paid a yearly tax of a half-shekel, to provide this daily victim.

Thus Christ is said to bear our sins. 1 Pet. ii. 24. Made a sacrifice. 2 Cor. v. 21.

How many lambs for ages had to be slain, to remind them of their deliverance !

How often had poor sinners read, " He is brought as a lamb to the slaughter " ! Isa. liii. 7.

Yet all the thousands of lambs slain could give the conscience *no repose.*

All the Paschal lambs ever eaten could not satisfy the hungering spirit.

A *suffering* Messiah Jews still *deny* to be revealed in the *Scriptures.*

Yet Isaiah's harp seems to have been strung on the summit of *Calvary itself.*

Simeon gave a prophetic glance at it, by the Spirit of God. Luke ii. 34.

Those denying the atonement deny thereby the Divine origin of the New Testament.

Inspiration of the Bible and Christ's atonement cannot be separated.

A scarlet thread saved the believing heroine of Jericho, and on a scarlet thread which runs through the whole Bible hangs ALL THE PROMISES.

The Baptist calls Judea and the world, to *behold with faith and love* the suffering and atoning Lamb.

1. He is a SAVIOUR. He came not as a Divine Teacher or Exemplar only, nor to grant pardons merely, but to *atone for sin.* " He bare our sins in His own body on the tree." " Was made a curse for us."
2. He is a *complete* SAVIOUR. He finished His work, and " by one offering hath perfected for ever them who are sanctified."
3. He is an *almighty* SAVIOUR. Jew or Gentile " He saves to the uttermost."
4. He is a *perpetual* SAVIOUR. " He *ever* lives to make intercession ; He became the author of *everlasting* salvation ; He has obtained *eternal* redemption for us."

Sufficient for the sins of the *world, efficient for all who believe.*

The LAMB OF GOD chosen by God for the purpose of atonement. Rom. iii. 25.

The lot falling on the goat, was called the " Lord's lot." Lev. xvi. 8, 9.

Blood of the Lamb. 1 Pet. i. 19. Strictly and absolutely *vicarious* sacrifice. " Blood of God." Acts xx. 28.

This sacrifice *alone* gave value to all previous sacrifices, foundation of all others.

My WELL-BELOVED is white (innocence) and ruddy (blood-dyed garments). Sol. Song v. 10.

Of God. *Hebraism* implying intensity as foreordained of God, or well-pleasing to God, or in the *most tender relation* conceivable to God.

Taketh away. That which the sinner's *faith* lays on the Redeemer.

The Baptist's word shows that he had *the key* of the mysterious worship of God.

All Christ's rejecters defiantly *give the lie* to their Maker's solemn word :—

" Without the shedding of blood there is no remission." Heb. ix. 22.

The *atonement idea* has prevailed through the entire history of our race.

The ground tone of all sacrifices among nations of every clime.

The life of this Lamb a sublime *Messiahad* which no poetry can equal.

A drama, where the curse of the Adamic race falls on a holy child.

His history, full of mortal agonies and heavenly victories, breathes the quickening influence of the Spirit of God.

Its wondrous secret power *charms* all who trust in His *blood,* but *disturbs* the peace of *all who resist His claims.*

Conscious guilt has extorted horrible sacrifices from human frenzy.

Moloch received the fairest and fondest from the arms and hearts of parents as a bloody tribute; "the fruit of the body for the sin of the soul." Mic. vi. 7.

This failing to bring peace, they oft sacrificed themselves.

Dark and horrible as these rites were, they pointed to the necessity of an atonement.

A necessity felt so keenly that no price was too costly to gratify it.

Hence altars have smoked with blood in all lands and in all nations.

The sacrifice of life and the hope of Divine forgiveness mysteriously blended in all religions.

"I will meet with the children of Israel." A *sad separation existed.*

"Thou shalt offer daily two lambs on the altar, and THERE WILL I MEET," &c. Ex. xxix, 38—43.

"Taketh away." Not *has* merely, but still bears them away,—a continuous present.

In the centre of the infinite glory He appears as the slain Lamb. Rev. v. 6.

Christ was delivered by the "determinate counsel and foreknowledge of God." Acts ii. 23.

Since He cried "*It is finished,*" these sins as a burden no longer oppress Him.

Since the baptism of blood was completed, He bears them as a *trophy.* Col. ii. 15.

Thus the risen and exalted King abides *for ever* the Lamb of God. Heb. vii. 24.

The power of the atonement is that derived from the shed blood of the *Son of God,* therefore an *eternal power.*

On this vital subject the gospel trumpet gives forth no uncertain sound.

Where this is not preached men are left without God and without hope. Eph. ii. 12.

Reconciliation can only be obtained through the "Blood of His Cross." Col. i. 20.

Paschal Lamb speaks—1. Of deliverance from bondage. 2. Of a deliverance which God alone can secure. 3. Of an offering to Jehovah of those redeemed from slavery. 4. Of a glorious liberty that can never be lost.

John, like all true converts, had felt the burden of sin.

An actual *load, too heavy* to be borne, is here plainly hinted at.

In that matchless allegory, the Pilgrim's Progress, this idea is beautifully brought out.

This burden every one feels ; it belongs to every human being.

Every humble mechanic in our land feels this burden.

The gay, dashing pleasure-seeker only *disguises his load.*

Under that smiling mask God knows he hides an aching heart.

Who can bear that burden when God forsakes the soul?

The closing hours of *Altamont, Spira, Voltaire, Paine*, will give the answer.

Hence this great central truth is an arrow of no doubtful power.

The wicked, chained by Satan, rage and denounce, but *peace* they have none.

Its publication arraigns all minds, either for or against it. Matt. xii. 30.

It is a sign by which the thoughts of many hearts are revealed. Luke ii. 34, 35.

In the wide universe of God there *is not*, there *cannot be* NEUTRALITY.

God could have taken away sin by taking away the sinner, as justice was satisfied by the taking away of men by the deluge.

" Taketh away." A continuous act. Includes justification and sanctification.

The double salvation represented by " the water and the blood." 1 John v. 6.

God multiplies pardons. He healeth our backslidings. He restoreth the soul.

The process of " taking away sin " extends over the whole life.

It is only in heaven we read of " the spirits of just men made perfect." Heb. xii. 23.

Before Pentecost not one of the apostles uttered so advanced a word as this of John.

The sin. The singular number with the article gives great force. *Bengel.*

The *one* plague of all He bore : not a *part* merely, but the *whole.*

The world. All the world, all related to Adam, He died for. 1 Cor. xv. 22.

Some speak of redemption as a failure, affirming that more are lost than saved.

But no one can estimate the extent to which the great Sacrifice has taken effect.

Half the human race die in infancy, and are saved through the imputed righteousness of Christ. Rom. v. 14.

The redeemed will ultimately be a *great multitude* which no man
can number.

The gates of the celestial city face the *four* cardinal points of
heaven. Rev. xxi. 13.

They shall come from the east, and from the west, and from the
north, and from the south. Luke xiii. 29.

Christ has bruised the serpent's head. In all things He is to have
pre-eminence.

His blood is *weighty :* it turns the scale when weighed against the
world. Augustine.

Bible points to a consummation of redeeming grace inconceivably
glorious. Eph. i. 10.

No soul is excluded from this salvation who does not exclude himself!

Not since creation, nor ever shall there be a more glorious announcement.

What sweet consolation to the Redeemer Himself to hear these
words!

τῇ ἐπαύριον. Heb. any future time. *Hammond.* Chosen with an ulterior
design unknown to us. *Meyer.* John denotes the exact day and even the hour,
ver. 39. *Hengstenberg.* A regular diary of the Messiah seems to have been kept
until Christ became well known. *Ber. Bib.*

ὁ 'Ιωάννης, omitted in all the Codices. *Ἴδε, Ecce agnus Dei,* ECCE *qui
tollit, &c. Vulg.* The heretics were *unborn* at whom John pointed. *Augustine.*

ὁ ἀμνὸς. Before the sacrifice John calls Him ἀμνός, a *living lamb.* After
he calls Him τὸ ἀρνίον, Rev. xxi. 22, a slain lamb. *Wordsworth.* The
former is used four times, the latter 30 times in the Apocalypse. See 1 John
iii. 5. No reference to atonement. *Meyer, De Wette, Luthardt.* A clear proof
of the atonement. *Calvin, Tholuck, Olshausen.* He refers to Isa. liii. *Origen,
Lücke.* Agnus in passione. *Leo.* Resurrectione. *Bernard.* The scenery
around John might have suggested another image, viz., the scape-goat.
Maurice.

τοῦ Θεοῦ. By the genitive this Lamb is more particularly characterized :
destined by or *well-pleasing* to God. *Tholuck, Calvin.*

ὁ αἴρων occurs in the N. T. 103 times : take, take up, take away ; 82 times
a continued act, as the sun shining, the spring flowing. His blood never dries.
Rollock. Neither biblical nor classical usage gives the idea of *taking upon
one's self,* Matt. xvi. 24 ; xi. 29. *Doddridge, Hengstenberg.* The Hebrew
synonym used frequently in O. T. in the sense of *peccati pœnas luere.* The
word is also used in the sense of "*taking away of sin and its guilt,*" but taking it away *by expiation.* This conception in the Baptist the result of Divine
teaching. *Alford.* Means something more than *taking away ;* it means also
supporting the *burden,* bearing the weight of. Hence it is used in about 200
places in the Sept. for the Heb. "*nasa,*" to *carry,* to *lift, bear a weight.*

Wordsworth. Atonement flashed through John's soul. *Lange.* The atoning act prophetically seen as present. *Meyer.*

John's knowledge a *higher type* than that of the apostles, until after the resurrection. *Tittmann.*

ἁμαρτίαν, sing. Not confined to any race; all kinds of sin. *Calvin.* Embraces the race from creation to judgment. *Musculus.* Takes away the universal condemnation of the race. *Melancthon.* Opens the door for the return of all penitents. *Author.*

---

30. This is he of whom I said, After me cometh a man which is preferred before me : for he was before me.

This is He. The Spirit gradually reveals the Messiah's character to the Baptist.

A man, called a " BRANCH," shall build the LORD's temple. Zech. vi. 12.

" Against the man that is my fellow," Zech. xiii. 7, that matchless Man.

Mystery of an Incarnate God the root of Christianity.

The Gospel, God descending into the world in our *form,* and conversing with us in our *likeness. Cudworth.*

Value of John's Gospel as a testimony to Christ's Divinity increases every hour the Christian Church stands.

Was before. He does not mean born before, for Christ was born six months after him.

Means His pre-existence, " Before Abraham. was, I am." John viii. 58.

A " *man,*" " before me." *Human and Divine natures* are here in *one sentence.*

Was before him in Israel, was before him in time and eternity.

The Lamb of God is the Eternal Son of God. This gives perfect joy to the soul. (See on verse 1.)

ἀνὴρ, not ἄνθρωπος. Christ is the Husband of the Church and of every soul, as Paul says, "I have espoused you to one *man* (ἑνὶ ἀνδρὶ), Christ," 2 Cor. xi. 2. *Wordsworth.* Here John takes up the declaration of the previous day. *Hengstenberg.* A strange announcement rousing curiosity as to this *gigas geminæ substantiæ. P. Anton.*

πρῶτός μου ἦν. Precedence in rank, because his essential chief. *Fürst.* Confirmed by Paul, Acts xiii. 25. Refers to verse 27.

---

31. And I knew him not: but that he should be made manifest to Israel, therefore am I come baptizing with water.

Knew Him not. John doubtless knew Jesus as a prophet highly honoured of God.

But he did not even suspect Him to be the true Messiah until the descent of the Holy Ghost and announcement at His baptism.

He had no *certain* knowledge of his mighty kinsman who should "baptize with the Holy Ghost and with fire."

Thus the garb of the cross wrapped around the saints conceals them.

The wise men of earth see not under this disguise *future kings.* Luke xxii. 29.

But the power and malice of earth or hell cannot wrest from them their crown. Rom. viii. 38.

John's relationship proves nothing : cavils of sceptics are utterly groundless.

The plain declaration of the Holy Spirit is against the *inferences and surmises* of men.

His previous ignorance of our Lord's true character was *full warrant* for the assertion.

Lest any should suspect collusion, God has chosen to reveal the reason.

Mary and Joseph dwelt with their SON in Galilee at Nazareth.

John's parents sent him into " the desert till the day of his showing unto Israel."

No one can ever learn so much of Christ, that they need not learn more.

Angels, after gazing at the throne of God for thousands of years, still desire to learn more. Eph. iii. 10.

It was *revealed* to John. There are many *heavenly students at the cross.*

Cherubim adoringly gazed on the ark of the tabernacle : " which things angels desire to look into." 1 Pet. i. 12.

Manifest. John's ministry was to introduce Christ to men.

This assurance of results nerved this New Testament Elijah to diligence.

God had so ordered it that his witness should be founded on a revelation coming immediately from heaven.

Our Lord's baptism is here supposed as already past.

οὐκ ᾔδειν. Refers to Him as Messiah. *Tholuck.* Does not exclude personal acquaintance. *Chrysostom, Brückner.* Seeming contradiction to Matt. iii. 14. Knowledge here is relative : compared with the present, he never knew Him before. *Hengst.* By inspiration. All other knowledge but idle conjecture. *Neander.* John's knowledge, due to his deeper acquaintance with Christ at

His baptism. *Ewald.* Youthful acquaintance waits for an infallible sign.
Lange, Riggerbach. "Even *I* knew Him not." *Besser.* Knew Him to be he
Son of God, but not the Redeemer. *Jerome.* Had no acquaintance whatever.
Maurice. May have known Him from his youth up, but not as the *heaven
sealed* Messiah. *Alford.* He knew His innocence, but not His dignity as
Messiah. *Hess, Tittmann.* Made infallibly certain by baptism. *Bengel.*

---

32. And John bare record, saying, I saw the Spirit descending from heaven
like a dove, and it abode upon him.

Record. A solemn attestation with the reverence due to witness-
bearing.

Exalted privilege to *see*, but far higher to *record*, this vision.

The Evangelist *omits* both the baptism and the temptation of our
Lord.

I saw. Gr. *I have seen.* Justifies the announcement that this " man "
is " *the Lamb of God.*"

Many saw the wonders of the day of Pentecost, yet mocked. Acts
ii. 13.

Many heard the voice of God in the temple, yet persisted in unbelief. John xii. 28, 29.

The Baptist heard the voice of the Father, touched the body of
Christ at His baptism, saw the Spirit as a dove, and thus understood, grasped, and embraced the TRINITY. *Chrysologus.*

Spirit. That in the form of a dove representing the Spirit. Luke
iii. 22.

They who saw Christ saw not the Divinity indwelling. John
vii. 39.

Descending. Every good and perfect gift from *above.* All evil
from *beneath.*

Believers known here by their *graces*, above by their *glory*. Mark
xii. 25.

A precious pledge of greater blessings during Pentecostal times.
Acts ii. 3.

Heaven. See on John i. 51. The place of God's glory.

Like a dove. Not in *manner* merely, but IN THE BODILY SHAPE
OF A DOVE. Luke iii. 22.

Symbol of purity and innocence, noted for rapid flight. Psa. lv.
6. A carrier-dove will fly 72 miles in 2½ hours.

Noted also for beautiful plumage. Psa. lxviii. 13. Dwelling in
rocks. Jer. xlviii. 28. Mournful voice. Isa. xxxviii. 14.
Harmlessness. Matt. x. 16. Simplicity. Hos. vii. 11.

Modesty. Cant. ii. 14. Beauty of eyes. Cant. i. 15. Emblem of peace. Gen. viii. 11. Offered as a sacrifice. Lev. v. 7.

Supposed to have been placed on the Assyrian and Babylonian standards in honour of Semiramis.

Will explain Jer. xxv. 38, "From before the fierceness of the dove." (See *Smith's* Dict.)

No representation of it, however, has yet been found amongst the sculptures of Nineveh.

Lamb and dove most honoured of irrational creatures : symbols of the Son of God and the Holy Spirit.

Luther once bestowed the name of " *teacher* " on a bird because it had taught him to confide entirely in God.

A dove proclaimed to Noah the time for returning to the earth ; but Israel forbidden to take omens from the voice of a bird.

Abode. Descent of the Spirit predicted. Isa. xlii. 1 ; lxi. 1.

Abode, not as a flash of lightning, but as the sunlight of a clear day.

Expresses the tranquil movement of the *Spirit's* power in Him compared with the detached impulses given to prophets.

Upon Him. As a crown gently placed on the brow of a king is at once an ornament and badge of sovereignty, so this sacred symbol pointed out the Son and Heir to the throne of the universe.

By-and-by that same sacred brow will be pressed with MANY CROWNS gathered from the countless " Principalities and Powers,"—He will reign KING of KINGS !

Had His been a mere creature's baptism, would all these high wonders have occurred ?

The Father and the Spirit endorse the glorious sacrament of baptism. Matt. xxviii. 29.

Father, Son, and Holy Ghost are still present with those who are baptized in faith.

1. Our Lord owned at baptism, so are believers. 2. As the dove typified the Spirit, so believers are to be pure and harmless also. 3. The Spirit renders the baptism of Christ and His followers of value. 4. As circumcision was the seal of the Old, so baptism is the seal of the New covenant. 5. In baptism believers put on Christ. Gal. iii. 27. 6. Heavens opened to Jesus, so the Church to believers. 7. The Spirit present at Christ's and invoked at believers' baptism.

Union of symbols, *lamb* and *dove* in Christ and the Spirit, should
teach us what manner of spirit to be of. Jam. iii. 17.

ἐμαρτύρησεν. As though he witnesssed it alone. *Bengel. Punctum
saliens* in Baptist's discourse. *Hengst.* Simply to emphasize the testimony.
Meyer, Tholuck. Witnessed by hundreds as they did His ascension. *Tittmann.*
A spiritual vision to John and Jesus alone. *Lücke, Alford.*
τεθέαμαι. If they did see it they could not understand it. *Ryle.* Why
not ? John xii. 28. *The Author.* A vision of the Synoptists, rendered objective
by tradition. *Meyer.* Not real, but in the *likeness* of a dove. *Ambrose.* A
mild white lustre, like the flutter of a dove on the wing in the sunbeams.
Lange. In symbolic figure. *Rosenmuller.* A symbol of the simplicity of the
Spirit. *Clement* of *Alex.* Did not the Creator embrace in His plan at the beginning, this very use of these creatures as signs of mystical truths ? *Bauer.*
John trusts to signs, but does not forget their signification. *Maurice.* Form
was real. *Ellicott.* Bodily shape witnessed to by the Four Evangelists. *Alford.*
The corporeal form of a dove. *D. Brown.* Visible form of a dove. *Besser.* A
real appearance like the tongues of fire. *Dods.*
περιστεράν. Origin of the Heb. word, from an unused root, signifying " *to
grow warm.*" *Gesenius.* Gen. i. 2, " *Hovered* " or " *brooded*," after the
manner of a dove, who spreads her wings over her young to impart warmth and
vitality. *Besser.*

---

33. And I knew him not : but he that sent me to baptize with water, the
same said unto me, Upon whom thou shalt see the Spirit descending, and remaining on him, the same is he which baptizeth with the Holy Ghost.

Knew Him not. I know Him now, as formerly I knew Him not,
tone of sadness.

A previous revelation enabled him to understand this vision.

One Divine act interprets and confirms another.

Thus Samuel heard the Spirit, " Arise, anoint him : for this is he." 1
Sam. xvi. 12.

The knowledge of Christ is gradual, as the steps of the temple,
as the trumpet sounded gently at first, then louder and
louder.

Path of the just is as the shining light, which shineth more and
more. Prov. iv. 18.

A sad word for a minister on his death-bed to use,—" I knew Him
not."

A sad word for him by whom youth are trained for the duties of
life

A sad word for a father dying with his family all around.

Saddest of all, to hear the Judge say in that day, " I KNOW YOU
NOT."

Sent me. His warrant from heaven for what he did.

Some hasten to go, whom God hath never sent. Jer. xxiii. 21.

The true minister hath the promised aid of an Almighty Agent. John xiv. 16.

When he speaks to the *dead*, the Spirit can *quicken dry bones*. Ezek. xxxvii. 9.

Baptize. Why did not Jesus Himself personally baptize?

Answered by some, The subjects would have *boasted;* by others, He must have baptized in His *own name*, being one with the Father.

Christ baptized with the *Spirit;* He left the outer sacraments to others.

Same. Reference to the record of the other three Evangelists, for John had not before alluded to this office of the Messiah.

Remaining. As the anointing *remained* on kings and priests, when the oil disappeared.

This was the *inauguration* of Jesus as KING in Israel.

Thus also the *Transfiguration* was the inauguration to the MESSIANIC work.

" I have set (i. e. constituted by anointing) my king in Zion." Psa. ii. 6.

Holy Ghost, i.e. Spirit, an immortal, immaterial, thinking Being.

Supreme Godhead of the Spirit proved by His Divine *names, attributes*, and *works.*

" God anointed Jesus of Nazareth with the Holy Ghost." Acts x. 38.

But had He not the Spirit from all eternity as the LOGOS or WORD ?

Yes! It was *for us* He received the Holy Ghost, when *for us* He was baptized.

As the HEAD He has received it for the blessing of His members.

Christ had no need of baptism, but baptism needed the strength of Christ. *Chrys.*

Here is evidently the turning-point between the two dispensations.

The teachings of the forerunner melt away into those of our Lord, and the witness of the servant is changed for the witness of the Son.

οὐκ ᾔδειν. Does not exclude personal acquaintance. *Brückner.* Does not refer to our Lord's person, but to Messianic dignity. *Tholuck.* " Even I, intimate with Him, did not know Him as He *is*, and as I now preach Him."

Wordsworth. Not from personal knowledge, but Divine revelation. *Theoph.* Not from human attachment, but the Divine will. *Cyril.*

βαπτίζειν. Neither Apollos nor the apostles were rebaptized. "Upon whom," &c., i. e. whilst thou art baptizing Him. *Meyer.* It remained, as though it would dwell there. *Patrick.* Water implied, but the Holy Ghost included. An Orientalism. *R. Hall.*

---

34. And I saw, and bare record that this is the Son of God.

I. By special revelation John learned whom to call the LAMB OF GOD.

"The word of God *came unto John* the son of Zacharias in the wilderness." Luke iii. 2.

I saw. Gr. *I have seen.* We " were eye-witnesses of His majesty." 2 Pet. i. 16.

A solemn repetition of the testimony after a stupendous miracle was wrought.

"I believed, and therefore have I spoken." 2 Cor. iv. 13. "Knowing, therefore," &c. 2 Cor. v. 11.

I saw, and bare. A tone of triumph and thanksgiving : Blessed privilege coveted by millions but shared by few.

Yet " Blessed are they that have not *seen,* and yet have believed." John xx. 29.

This privilege will all believers finally share, for He bears *our nature* on the THRONE.

" When He doth appear, we shall be like Him ; for we shall see Him as He is." 1 John iii. 2.

Bare record. Gr. *Afterward signified,* and John exemplified it by dying a martyr.

Son of God. Adam was thus named as having no earthly father. Luke iii. 38.

But the Word who became flesh was no created being. (See notes on John i. 1—3.)

Not only not created, but absolutely and solely CREATOR.

SON OF GOD—1. By His miraculous conception. Luke i. 35. 2. By His designation to the Mediatorial office. John x. 34—36. 3. By His resurrection. Rom. i. 4. 4. By His exaltation to glory and being made Heir of all things. Heb. i. 3—5. 5. By impartation of Divine essence from the Father whereby He is " very God of very God." Prov. viii. 22 ; Psa. ii. 7 ; Micah v. 2 ; John i. 14.

Second Psalm makes trust in Him, whose wrath is destruction, a *duty.*

In infancy, childhood, youth, maturity of manhood still the " Son of God."

The Holy Ghost was given Him without measure.   John iii. 34.

Prophets, with their limited, created capacities, received *with measure.*

" In Him dwelleth all the fulness of the Godhead bodily." Col. ii. 9.

This great central truth of Christianity *revealed* from heaven. Matt. xvi. 16, 17.

No human mind could conceive, or build up, the system of Christianity.

μεμαρτύρηκα.   Testimony closed, and its validity firmly established. *Tholuck.*   Divine Mediator was fully revealed at the beginning of His ministry. *Lampe.*   Jesus baptized at the close of the summer, U.C. 780. *Wieseler, Lange, Tisch.*   Near Dec. 779. *Lichtenstein.*   Jan. 6th, U.C. 780. *Friedlieb.*   Last of Jan. *Greswell.*   Oct. *Lightfoot.*   Nov. *Usher.*   Spring. *Clinton.*   7 Oct. *Sepp.*   Autumn. *Robinson.*   Interval between baptism and passover two or three months. *Andrews.*   6 months. *Hales.*   2¼ years. *Usher.* An *inference* that priests entered on duty at 30, because Levites did. *Andrews.*   Full vigour of body and mind. *Greswell.*

ὁ υἱὸς τοῦ Θεοῦ. A profounder sense than ordinary Jewish theology. *Hengst.* Known only by a special revelation from heaven. *Bengel.*   Until now all His relations believed Him a mere *man. Tittmann.*   Except His mother, John ii. 3. *The Author.*

---

35. Again the next day after John stood, and two of his disciples.

Next day.   Precision as to dates a marked characteristic of this apostle.

After this introduction, the record is of what he had seen and heard.

John.   His life and character, see on verses 6, 15.

Stood.   Ministers of Christ on Zion's watch-tower are to wait for the Lord.

As Paul at Athens, in the *market-place,* ready to preach to every one he met.   Acts xvii. 17.

The ancient cynics could afford to *lose time* in winning disciples.

Stood, or was standing, probably at his accustomed place, where he baptized.

He stood, a herald, announcing his message to the Jewish nation.

He stood as *victor* over his tempters.   " Having done all, to stand." Eph. vi. 13.

Two. Andrew and John the Evangelist were probably the persons.

Disciples. He thought all led to Christ found the best master.

Andrew and John willing " to follow the Lamb whithersoever He goeth." Rev. xiv. 4.

τῇ ἐπαύριον. Great days! First the day of testimony to Jesus as Messiah (ver. 15, &c.) ; second, of testimony to Him and to His passion (ver. 29, &c.) ; third, that of the three disciples joining Him; fourth, that of the gaining Philip and Nathanael (ver. 43, &c.). *Bengel.*

εἰστήκει. Mystically, Law ceasing, Christ brings grace. *Alcuin.* The constancy of the ministry. *Ludolphus.* In expectation of Jesus. *P. Anton, Hengst.*

μαθητῶν. Most of our Lord's disciples were first followers of John. *Hammond, Lightfoot.* These two were absent the previous day (ver. 29). *De Wette.*

δύο. The second the Evangelist. *Lücke, Meyer.* Andrew the other. *Trench.*

---

36. And looking upon Jesus as he walked, he saith, Behold the Lamb of God!

Looking. He saw One pure, meek, holy, benevolent.

Divine, self-sacrificing love ever commands admiration of the good and envy of the evil.

Jesus. Heb. *Joshua,* Gr. *Jesus.* Saviour occurs 750 times in N. T.

This name given Him before His Incarnation. Luke i. 31. For other names, see on John i. 41.

Walked. As if engaged in holy meditation.

Yet evidently designing to bring about the interview with two of John's disciples.

As the humble Nazarene, but in truth the *Judge of the world.*

He was gathering His disciples, but not working miracles.

He was not *coming* to John this time. Once was condescension enough. Ver. 29.

Waiting for His hour, and the Father's command ; the plans of Jesus *take in the sweep of everlasting ages.*

Equipped with tested armour for His great spiritual conflicts.

Though *unknown* on earth, sure of a victory that would rejoice angels.

A Christian's very steps should be radiant with holiness.

Looking. Gr. *with steadfast gaze.* Great singers' first notes tremble.

Cicero turned pale when he was ascending the Rostrum.

John felt that in the presence of the Lamb of God he was less than *nothing.*

His *first adoring look.*   Kings and prophets longed for this sight in vain.   Luke x. 24.

Some believe a *halo* of Divine Majesty ever surrounded our Lord.

John certainly knew he saw *One* before whom *all the hosts of heaven bow.*   Rev. iv. 10.

Human curiosity was never more intensely taxed than here.

No other human being had received a direct revelation from heaven as to our Lord's Messiahship and Divinity.

Behold.   A brief repetition of that wonderful proclamation, ver. 29.

The two disciples addressed represent Christ's whole circle of followers.

This seems a gentle hint that they should follow Jesus.

Lamb of God.   John i. 29.   For our Lord's various names, see on John i. 41.

Lamb, in His passion, but the Lion of the tribe of Judah in His resurrection.

John speaks as though he saw the sin-bearing Victim on His way to Golgotha.

The Atonement alone satisfies the law of God and the deepest necessities of man.

Paschal lamb a striking type of Christ and His salvation :—

Chosen out of the flock ; a male of the first year ; without blemish or spot—

Christ " a Son given ; " taken from His brethren ; holy, harmless ; put to death in the prime of life.

The paschal lamb killed before the Israelites were delivered or the Mosaic sacrifices appointed—

Christ, the Lamb, fore-ordained and slain from the foundation of the world.

A bone of it not to be broken—The soldiers brake *not* the legs of Jesus.

Killing the paschal lamb not enough : its blood to be sprinkled and flesh eaten—

Blood of Christ must be sprinkled on the conscience.   Jesus the Bread of Life.

Paschal lamb to be eaten with unleavened bread and bitter herbs—

Christ must be received in sincerity of heart and with repentance toward God.

Israelites to eat the passover prepared to go forth from Egypt—
Christians strangers and pilgrims here, looking for a city in heaven.

"An ordinance for ever" commemorating cruel bondage and Divine deliverance—

Redemption by Christ to be had in everlasting remembrance; *theme* of glorified saints. Rev. i. 5.

Lamb of God. End of the law and fulfilment of prophecy.

In Him all preceding dispensations are solved and glorified.

To cry "Behold the Lamb!" the divinely appointed office of the Christian ministry.

ἐμβλέψας. Fixing his eyes as with significant gaze. *D. Brown.*

περιπατοῦντι. A royal divine Hero in John's eye. *Jerome.* As the youthful Cyrus was crowned by the infant shepherds on the mountains. *Ber. Bib.* Virgil notes a regal step: "Incessu patuit Venus." A minister's words, deeds, vestments a lesson to the people. *Jerome.* Passing avoids the appearance of collusion. *Hengstenberg.*

Ἰησοῦς, from ἴασις, healing. *Eusebius.* He was not acquainted with the Heb. original, Jehoshua, contracted into Joshua. Gr. Jesus. *The Author.*

ἀμνὸς. Divine justice is satisfied and God's government sustained. *Outram, Le Clerc.*

---

37. And the two disciples heard him speak, and they followed Jesus.

Disciples. Andrew and John are believed to be the two. John i. 40.

Speak. We have none of the Baptist's sermons, only the heads of one or two discourses.

He had no stated hour for teaching. Instant in season, out of season. 2 Tim. iv. 2.

Pentecostal blessings come not as seed time and harvest, but as angels' visits.

Thus the proclamation of this *last* prophet of the Old Test.

Followed. Even on this, the first day of following Jesus, they enjoy the sweetness of fellowship.

The Lord sent His disciples on their mission "*two and two.*" Luke x. 1.

Followed, in silence, without any introduction whatever.

It was the Father drawing to the Son. The effectual call of grace.

Conversion, in a calm, quiet attraction of the heart to God, suited to *contemplative* minds.

Thus Lydia, " whose heart the Lord opened." Acts xvi. 14.

Thus *à Kempis, Melancthon, Calvin, Bengel, Zinzendorf, Martyn.*

Paul illustrates the strong impetuous type, such as *Tertullian, Augustine, Luther, Farel, Bunyan.*

Luther was drawn by the memorable words of Staupicius, " Predestination begins at the wounds of Christ."

The martyr Bilney's confession converted Latimer, and Peter Martyr's appeal brought Caracciolus to plead for mercy.

These two disciples were doubtless the first-fruits of our Lord's harvest.

Love needs not chains to draw where the heart is free. Rev. xiv. 4.

In following Jesus, they must necessarily forsake John.

Some go to *Paul* for a text, and to *Addison* for a sermon.

Some leave the " rose of Sharon " to gather only the wild flowers of the field.

Others draw the " sword of the Spirit," and wreath it with garlands of human device.

Sinners grow weary hearing of human valour and its heroes, of the achievements of science and philosophy, but *never* of *salvation:* an incidental proof of the divinity of the gospel.

Myriads attend the sanctuary, make sacrifices to sustain Christianity, yet live and die without an interest in its offered blessings.

" Most men have a certain madness about religion." *Gibbon.* Yes, and philosophers also have often strange misgivings on their death-bed.

The Church is upheld and increased by the same WORD which gathered its first members.

Faithfulness to truth never without fruit. Even a cup of water in HIS NAME, &c. Mark ix. 41.

Paul hints that good was wrought by the *mere report* of his *bonds* in Cæsar's palace. Phil. i. 13, 14.

Followed Jesus. Central object in the visions of Patmos,—the Lamb as though newly slain.

First-fruits of God and the Lamb follow Him whithersoever He goeth. Rev. xiv. 4.

" If any man will come after Me, let him deny himself," &c. Luke ix. 23.

ἠκολούθησαν. They accounted John the Lamb, but he repelled the idea, and cried, " Why look to me ? I am not the Lamb." *Augustine.* Not in the narrower sense when they *left all and followed Him :* here only a *mechanical going after Him. Alford.* Baptist, as the friend of the Bridegroom, gives away the Bride to Christ. *Chrys.* They wished to know something of Him. *Euthym.*

---

38. Then Jesus turned, and saw them following, and saith unto them, What seek ye ? They said unto him, Rabbi, (which is to say, being interpreted, Master,) where dwellest thou ?

Turned. Omniscient, He felt each pulsation of their trembling hearts. Isa. lxvi. 2 ; Luke xv. 20.

Unconsciously they yielded to the attraction of the Son of God, as the needle yields to the influence of its beloved star.

He notes the first breathings of faith. He suffers not the wind to break the bruised reed or quench the smoking flax. Matt. xii. 20.

Beautiful subject for the pencil of some *Raphael*––the Lord looking, as though saying, " Will not some one come to me ? "

That question implied in His silent *turning.* Is He not thus looking at us all ? Luke xxii. 61.

What He says at this crisis, the beginning of His ministry, will be full of import.

Saw them. Gr. *Looked upon them as they followed.* He looks upon the two first disciples given Him by the Father.

What seek ye ? He knew well enough that they sought *Him.*

But they must *confess what* it was they sought in Him.

On this " why we seek Christ " hinges a blessed finding or not.

What for centuries had patriarchs, prophets, judges, kings, saints, sought ?

John, standing on the mountain-top between the Old and New Test., points Him out.

What seek ye ? A gentle, winning question : His second public utterance. Luke ii. 49.

God's unchanging promise is,—none shall ever seek Him in vain. Isa. xlv. 19.

To every passer-by He saith, " BEHOLD ME!" Isa. lxv. 1 ; Psa. xxxiv. 15.

Under ordinary circumstances this had repelled them.

As though He meant, " Leave me to my own pleasure ; " but His look and tone convert it into " *Come !* "

He came to seek us. His entire life from the manger to Calvary was one long, pressing invitation to lost ones, "COME!"

The question regards not *Himself*, but *their* spiritual character.

Note the incomparable sweetness of the Spirit of Jesus.

If we follow, He graciously turns about and asks us what *we* seek?

"When the Lord saw he turned aside, God called." Exod. iii. 4.

Every inquirer receives a warm welcome from the true Shepherd.

Pastors not yearning for souls may well doubt their call to the ministry.

Conscious or unconscious, it was the Lord seeking *them.*

"Adam, where art thou?" sought to bring back the fallen son.

"Fleeing from *Me*, ye seek *death*. Return unto Me,—I have redeemed thee."

Rabbi. "Thou meetest him that rejoiceth, and worketh righteousness." Isa. lxiv. 65.

They felt the face of the Teacher turned full upon them. Ver. 49.

As one coming out of a cold cavern first feels the warm sun shining on him.

Like Moses with unsandaled feet, they reverently draw near.

The only Rabbi "in whom were hid all the treasures of wisdom." Col. ii. 3.

This Lamb is "worthy to take the book and open the seals." Rev. v. 9.

"*Lord*," more expressive of Messianic dignity, was soon applied.

Rabbi interpreted implies the readers of John ignorant of Jewish customs.

Hence we infer he wrote while dwelling out of Judea at Ephesus.

Dwellest? Indifferent words, but of value to Him looking on their hearts.

They wanted to say "We seek the Messiah," but dare not.

They act modestly. Loving Christianity never rudely intrudes itself.

Their answer implied that, merely as a human teacher, they were willing to be numbered among His disciples. It seems somewhat abrupt, but full of *trust.*

We are Israelites waiting for the coming of the Shiloh. Luke ii. 25.

They do not feel satisfied with a transient interview, but desire a longer and more thorough communion with Him. It is a word of the heart, craving rest and peace.

" Sooner shall the heavens fall, than I forsake my Christ." *A martyr's words.*

The tender vine winds round its support, following the course of the sun.

Change its course, and it will rather *break* than *yield.*

Ruth clave to Naomi, " Thy people shall be my people, thy God my God."

Dwellest? As though they would say, " Lord, that question requires leisure."

If thou hast a calm hour in private, we would gladly tell our case.

Matters of such moment cannot be discussed on the highways of earth.

In secret, sacred confidence, they would unburden all their hearts.

Though all the palaces of earth were His, He had no home.

The Lord of Glory indebted to His subjects for a cradle, a resting-place, and a grave !

Strange extremes centre in Him : Himself the strangest of all.

Στραφείς. With designs of grace. *Hengst.* He understood the sounds of their footsteps. *Lange.* ζητεῖτε. Our Lord would search their motives by His *word,* but cheers them to come by His *tones. The Author.*

" She bade me so sweet a ' farewell,'
I thought she bade me return." *Shenstone.*

This expression won their hearts. *Bengel.* ποῦ. Capernaum. *Lightfoot.* μένεις. Where dost thou pass the night ? *Euthymius, Alford.* Words having pretium affectionis. *Hengst.* We, too, could abide there. *Lange.* Be disciples of the inner circle. *Lampe.*

---

39. He saith unto them, Come and see. They came and saw where he dwelt, and abode with him that day : for it was about the tenth hour.

Come. This His third public utterance more winning still.

This invitation of the Son of God the burden of all His sermons and all His sufferings.

Spoken in lowliness as profound as their majesty is sublime.

They have a *simple human aspect,* but a *Divine background.*

" I heard one of the four living ones saying, COME AND SEE." Rev. vi. 1.

" Come and see the works of God, terrible in His doings." Psa. lxvi. 5.

Church's privilege to see heathen idols shattered. Psa. xlvi. 9.

He teaches that all delays in duty are attended with loss.   Psa. lxiii. 1, 2.

It matters not where the mercy-seat is, if we do not *go to see.*

Christianity challenges all to put her claims to the severest trial.

Duties enjoined in God's Word are our reasonable service.   Rom. xii. 1.

All other religions rest on custom, civil law, or secular power.

The Bereans inquiringly searched the Scriptures, and God calls them noble.   Acts xvii. 11.

To the sons of earth mad upon their idols these words would have been nought.

To no one but Elijah did that hand-breadth cloud portend a glorious shower.

Happy day for those who come where Jesus dwells, not for a day or a week, but for ever.

See.   He would, in His humble state, quench all ambitious hopes.

Never can there be a better time than " JUST NOW."   2 Cor. vi. 2.

See all, experience all, and find all that ye seek.

This phrase, of ordinary, every-day intercourse, here endorsed by the Son of God, becomes one of friendly acceptance and of eternal solemnity.

They found the Lord's glory a *self-evidencing testimony.*

A man leaving a dark cave at mid-day needs no one to tell him to look for the sun.

They came.   The nearer we approach, the more we see of the King's beauty.

And saw.   What they saw is buried in silence.   It was enough. Ver. 41.

Where.   Our Lord had much more in view than simply the *where.*

The perverse blindness of unbelief does not want to find Christ dwelling humbly in Capernaum.   Matt. iv. 13.

How blessed a thing to dwell with Him, and commune with Him where He dwelt !

What they heard who will ever tell us ?

Was there no listening angel to record the words of the heavenly King ?

Did not their hearts also " burn within them as He opened the Scriptures " ?   Luke xxiv. 32.

By-and-by we, by faith, may dwell with Him and *hear His voice in heaven.*

I asked Him with aching heart, "Where dwellest Thou ? "   He said, "COME AND SEE." I went and saw, and now *all my life have I sung*,—"BLESSED IS THE MAN WHO DWELLETH IN THY COURTS, EVEN IN THY HOLY TEMPLE." Psa. lxv. 4.

The meeting of these two men with Jesus of Nazareth is the *first step* in that which has changed the LIFE, GOVERNMENT, LAWS, AND RELATIONS OF MANKIND FOR 1800 YEARS!

The infidel still madly denies Him to be more than mere man.

We KNOW Him to have been THE LIGHT of the world in darkness.

Abode. A blessed evening, and a precious interview to those disciples.

Let us prepare a dwelling in our hearts, where Christ may enter and hold converse with us. *Augustine.*

Day. Thrice happy day! Blest spirits have such a day for ever!

Tenth hour. 10 o'clock A.M. if *Roman*, 4 P.M. if *Jewish* time.

Morning, noon, and evening were the original Heb. modes. Gen. xix. 1 ; Psa. lv. 17.

Dividing the day into hours was an invention of the Chaldeans.

Day was divided into 12 equal parts by Babylonians, Egyptians, Jews, Greeks, and Romans.

These hours were shorter or longer, changing with the season.

Their first hour 6 A.M., their third 9, their sixth 12, their ninth 3 P.M. Acts ii. 15 ; Matt. xxvii. 45 ; Acts iii. 1.

Darkness at the crucifixion lasted from 12 to 3.

Night divided into three watches : anciently by the Romans into four.

It was the tenth hour when they came, not when they left.

This was, indeed, one of the never-to-be-forgotten "days of the Son of Man." Luke xvii. 22.

Henceforth is kept, by this Evangelist, a regular diary of the Messiah.

It was a decisive hour to John, remembered in eternity.

On the dial-plate of human hope it was the natal hour of the Christian Church.

John could no more forget that hour than the mother the hour her child was born.

Luther could not forget the hour he nailed the 95 theses to the church door.

Our Lord's presence left an impression on all present, such as will be felt in judgment.

This alone can explain that invisible influence so often seen in the background of the inspired record.

Twice this Divine presence became insupportable : on Tabor,
Matt. xvii. 6, and in Gethsemane, John xviii. 6.
A different, but mighty influence swept over the crowd, Luke
xxiii. 48.

Tenth hour. Moslems appoint each part of the day to particular
prayers.
Dial of Ahaz was doubtless brought from Babylon. Isa. xxxviii. 8.
Shadow on the dial noted for the Romans the hour for their
favourite luxury, the bath.
Their water-clock appeared like a globe of brass with a neck, and
was used to measure *speeches in courts of justice.*
A public water-clock was built in Rome B.C. 159.
In parts of India water-clocks are still used. Servants notify the
intervals.
The Jews after their subjugation by the Romans adopted the four
Roman watches. Luke xii. 28 ; Matt. xiv. 25.
Fourfold division of the day continued in the temple after they
had adopted the 12 hours.

ἔρχεσθε. A formula in Rabbinical writers demanding special attention.
Lightfoot.
ἴδετε. So also *Cod. Sin.* ὄψεσθε. *Tischendorf, Alford.* The Bible has
more marks of authenticity than profane history. *Isaac Newton.* It contains
more sublimity, purer morality, more important history, and higher eloquence
than all other books together. *Sir Wm. Jones.*
εἶδον. *Cod. Sin.* has ἴδον. A dwelling peaceful, neat, frugal, without a
beggarly array of vases and books (2 Kings iv. 10), worthy of Him and of Him
alone. *Bengel.*
ἡμέραν. November. *Lightfoot.* December. *Robinson.* John followed the
Jewish division of time. *Alford.* Jewish day lasted until complete darkness.
Hengstenberg.
ὥρα. Romans divided the day into 12 hours, though not the legal method.
Lücke. Next day spent with Christ, the Sabbath. *Lightfoot.* Here the day
extends to the time of going to rest. *Hengst.* δὲ, omitted. *Lach., Tisch.,
Alford.* δεκάτη, Roman time, 10 A.M. *Olshausen, Tholuck, Ebrard, Ewald,
Wordsworth.* An hour-glass at Rome noted a speech in court five hours long,
another six, another nine hours. *Pliny, Martial.*

---

40. One of the two which heard John speak, and followed him, was Andrew,
Simon Peter's brother.

One of the two. The other is believed to have been the Evangelist John. John xx. 2, 3.
Andrew, Peter, Nathanael, Philip, are all named.

John's fraternal relation to Peter is historically attested. Ver. 41.
Only two poor men *the* BEGINNING OF THE CHURCH OF CHRIST !
Yet at that time the promise was, " *I will give the heathen for thine
  inheritance, and the uttermost parts,*" &c.   Psa. ii. 8.
Despise not therefore " the day of small things."   Zech. iv. 10.
The hand-breadth cloud may soon spread over the whole
  heavens.   1 Kings xviii. 44.
" The stone cut out without hands shall become a great mountain,"
  &c.   Dan. ii. 35, 45.
The dry root of Jesse shall, like Nebuchadnezzar's tree, fill the
  earth.   Dan. iv. 11.
" A handful of corn upon the mountain-top, its fruit shall shake
  like Lebanon."   Psa. lxxii. 16.
Sleeplessness of Ahasuerus brings the Jews before the world and
  saves them from the wicked designs of Haman.   Esther vi. 1.
Two poor monks, *Huss* and *Luther*, instrumental in the glorious
  Reformation.
Followed.   They left their master, the Baptist, to enter the school
  of Christ.
This reverential timidity of walking in silence behind the Saviour
  characteristic of John, who never names himself in his Gospel.
  John xx. 4.
Andrew.   Elder brother of Simon Peter, dwelt in Bethsaida.
He had been a disciple of John the Baptist.   Ver. 35.
He pointed out the lad having five loaves and two fishes.   John
  vi. 8, 9.
Accompanied by Philip he reported to Jesus the desire of certain
  Greeks.   John xii. 22.
One of those who asked the Lord on Olivet when the judgment
  would descend on Jerusalem.   Mark xiii. 3.
Name of the second not given, but recorded in the *Book of Life.*
Simon Peter.   See on ver. 42.   He belonged to the inner circle
  named in Luke ii. 38

'Ανδρέας, intimates a Hellenistic connection. *Alford.* Preached in Scythia.
Eusebius. In Achaia. *Jerome.* In Thrace. *Nicephorus.* Crucified on St
Andrew's Cross [×] in Achaia. Doubted by *Lipsius.* Andrew older than Peter.
Bengel. Peter older than our Lord. *Olshausen.* δύο. One was John. *Alford.*
Thomas. *Lightfoot.* Some obscure disciple. *Euthymius.* Companion, not
disciple. *Kuinoel.*

41. He first findeth his own brother Simon, and saith unto him, We have found the Messias, which is, being interpreted, the Christ.

First. He was the first to *find* for Christ. The words have a festival freshness.

Andrew found his brother, Simon Peter, before John could find his brother James.

The Spirit lets neither rest until Simon becomes sharer of their joys.

" I could not endure now to be saved *alone* " is the feeling here shown. *Löhe.*

An unlettered fisherman, probably literally *uneducated*, boldly tells his brother that he has found the Christ.

A scribe would proudly exclaim, " What fanatical ignorance and conceit ! "

What had convinced Andrew ? He had seen *no* miracles.

He could not have heard Jesus say, " I am THE CHRIST." John iv. 26.

The Light of the world *made him feel* that *He was His* LIGHT.

The Church has been *founded by Him* and exists *by Him.*

Peter the foreman of the band of apostles, but Andrew first came to Christ.

James first received the martyr's crown ; John first in our Lord's love.

Findeth. He speaks exultingly, as of a treasure found.

Having found it, he announces it to others, as the lepers did. 2 Kings vii. 9.

Believers have none the less spiritual life for sharing it with others.

Unlike earth's treasures, where the more numerous the heirs the smaller the inheritance.

Implies that he had been seeking for his brother, and could not rest until he found him.

Yet Peter afterward outstripped Andrew in faith.

Luther's zeal surpassed his teacher in theology, Staupicius.

A loadstone magnetizes one ring, and that another, until many are magnetized.

Christ's questions at the last day, " What hast thou done for me ? What hast thou suffered for me ? Whom hast thou won for me ? "

Andrew bringing others is thrice noted. John i. 41 ; vi. 8, 9 ; xii. 22.

If we would discover those most instrumental in blessing the world, we must *unlearn* our admiration of heroes.

Sacrifices of love are least in danger of the leaven of pride.

His own. There is a nearer relation than blood. " My brother Jonathan," the words indicating David's depths of love for the son of Saul. 2 Sam. i. 26.

John was the brother of Peter *in Christ.* 1 Cor. xvi. 20; Phil. iv. 21.

Simon. For Peter's life and character, see on ver. 42.

Saith. Notice how universally the Jews knew the promises of the O. T.

When Andrew named the Messiah he knew they all understood him.

Even the poor polluted Samaritan was well instructed in this. John iv. 25.

Relations increase both our *opportunities* and *obligations.* 1 Cor. vii. 16.

We. " John and I (Andrew) have found Him whom we have sought by prayer."

Found. The Church had been looking for Him for 4000 years.

A bold confession. None else had made it : by the Word he had surpassed his teachers. ·Psa. cxix 99.

Messias. Heb. root, *anointed* with oil : receiving God's great seal. A chosen name with the people.

Kings, as channels of grace to the nations, were called *anointed*, 2 Sam. xxiii. 1.

An essential characteristic of the King of kings. Isa. lxi. 1.

The oil had its antitype in the Holy Ghost. Acts x. 38.

" God hath anointed thee with the oil of gladness," &c. Psa. xlv. 7; Heb. i. 9.

" Seventy weeks are determined upon to anoint the Most Holy," &c. Dan. ix. 24.

" Thy *Holy Child Jesus*, whom Thou hast *anointed.*" Acts iv. 27.

" How God *anointed Jesus of Nazareth* with the Holy Ghost." Acts x. 38.

Andrew can say but little as yet of His person, office, or value.

He brings this brother to Jesus, as a bell calls us to God's house.

We, too, can bring men to Him, as they brought the *palsied* man on his bed.

He was to be a *suffering* Messiah. Psa. xxii., lxix.; Isa. liii. ; Dan. ix. 24—27.

Moses representing the law, and Elijah prophecy spake, of His death. Luke ix. 31.

Many names are given our Lord :—Last Adam. 1 Cor. xv. 45. Advocate. 1 John ii. 1 ; John xiv. 12. Amen, faithful and

true Witness. Rev. iii. 14. Apostle, High Priest. Heb. iii. 1.
Author and Finisher of faith. Heb. xii. 2. Bishop of souls.
1 Pet. ii. 25. Bread of God. John vi. 33. Brightness of
the Father's glory. Heb. i. 3. Shiloh. Gen. xlix. 10. Lord
our Righteousness. Jer. xxiii. 6. Desire of all nations. Hag.
ii. 7. Jehovah's Fellow. Zech. xiii. 7. Messenger of the
Covenant. Mal. iii. 1. Sun of Righteousness. Mal. iv. 3.
Captain of salvation. Heb. ii. 10. Door of the sheep. John x.
7. Emmanuel. Matt. i. 23. Firstborn from the dead. Col. i. 18.
Forerunner. Heb. vi. 20. Foundation. 1 Cor. iii. 11. Head
of every man. 1 Cor. xi. 3. Heir of all things. Heb. i. 2.
Holy Child. Acts iv. 27. Holy One of God. Mark i. 24. Our
Hope. 1 Tim. i. 1. Image of the invisible God. Col. i. 15.
Judge of quick and dead. Acts x. 42. King. Luke xix. 38.
Lamb of God. John i. 29. The Branch. Zech. vi. 12. Mes-
siah. Dan. ix. 25. Light of the world. John viii. 12. Lord
of all. Acts x. 36. A Man approved of God. Acts ii. 22.
Your Master. Matt. xxiii. 8. Mediator. 1 Tim. ii. 5.
Morning star. Rev. xxii. 16. A Nazarene. Matt. ii. 23. Our
Passover. 1 Cor. v. 7. Resurrection and Life. John xi. 25.
Son of David. Mark x. 48. Good Shepherd. John x. 11.
Saviour of the world. 1 John iv. 14. God's beloved Son,
Matt. xvii. 5. Teacher from God. John iii. 2. The Way,
the Truth, and the Life. John xiv. 6. True Vine. John xv.
1. Son of Man. John i. 51. Wonderful, Counsellor, Mighty
God, Everlasting Father, Prince of Peace. Isa. ix. 6. Lion
of the tribe of Judah, Root of David. Rev. v. 5. Jesus. Matt.
i. 26. Our Peace. Eph. ii. 14. &c.

A Saviour determined in the counsel of God, and promised at
creation.

Now sent and sealed with absolute commission and fulness of
power.

Interpreted. John, writing in Ephesus, explains the Heb. and
Chal. names.

This is the interpretation: THE ANOINTED. It should not be "the
Christ."

The Christ. 1. As Priest. Priests should purge or expiate.

Priests among Greeks had a threefold office,—to purify, instruct,
perfect.

2. As Prophet. Prophets should illuminate and teach.

3. As King. Kings should set right and keep right.

Aaron, the priest ; Elisha, the prophet ; David, the king, were
anointed.

The Christ. 1. Priest after the order of Melchizedek. Psa. cx. 4.

2. Prophet, to be heard when Moses was silent. Deut. xviii. 18.

3. King, whose name should be Jehovah, and who should save
His people. Jer. xxiii. 6.

The Holy Spirit made conviction a quick work in their simple
hearts.

Εὑρίσκει. *Active* faith shows it genuine. *Calvin.*

πρῶτος qualifies οὗτος. *Lücke, Alford.* Other disciple was Peter's friend
also ; he had gone in another direction to find him. *Henry.*

τὸν ἴδιον indicates the other disciple, a brother in a wider sense. *Hengst.*
Jews were angry because of Jesus calling God πατέρα ἴδιον. *Lampe.* John
did not seek Peter, but Andrew his brother. *Meyer.*

Εὑρήκαμεν, a great and joyful finding, for which the world had been waiting 4000 years. *Bengel.*

Μεσσίαν. Symbolized in O.T. the impartation of the gifts of the Holy
Spirit. *Hengst.* In N.T. χριστός (from χρίω) used as equivalent to Messiah.
Smith. Our Lord not anointed before the Ascension. *Jackson.* Called χριστός
by anticipation. Heathen expectations seen in Virgil. *Horsley.* In
works of Suetonius. *Trench.* In Tacitus and the Sibylline oracles. *Faber.*
Jewish Rabbis speak of two Messiahs,—a suffering Messiah, Ben Joseph, and
a conquering Messiah, Ben David. *Buxtorf, Kimchi, Ben Ezra.* Targums all
ignore a suffering Messiah. *Onkelos, Payne Smith.* They look for the Messiah
yet to come. *Maimonides.* After each meal they say, "Make us worthy of the
days of the Messiah." *Holmes, Alexander, Herzog.* Jewish despair changed
for Christian hope. *Isaac da Costa.* A learned Jewish infidel rebuked the Jews
for hoping for a coming Messiah. *Salvador.* He quotes as proof the great
authority of *Hillel* the *Reaper. Pye Smith, Herzog.* David's priest, Moses's
prophet, Jeremiah's king. *Andreas.*

---

42. And he brought him to Jesus. And when Jesus beheld him, he said,
Thou art Simon the son of Jona : thou shalt be called Cephas, which is by interpretation, A stone.

He brought. May have let himself be brought in haste.

Possibly he even outran Andrew, and came first to Jesus.

Having received a pound, they gave it back with usury. *Cyril.*

In the dawning hour of the Church mission life is in youthful
vigour, and there is an angel's joy over the heavenly secret
of Christian fellowship.

Happy brothers! now bound by a tie stronger than blood.

If Peter surpassed his elder brother, that brother called him to
Jesus.

Beheld. Gr. *looked on him with fixed gaze,* in the power of the
Spirit.

That same look afterwards brought him to repentance and tears.

Now, doubtless, it transforms from being *carnal* to *spiritual.*

We too often forget that *Jesus lived, moved,* and *acted* as *Jehovah !*

Art Simon. Heb. *obedient.* He will make out of Simon a man that
will deserve to be called Cephas (Peter), a rock.

A proof of our Lord's omniscience. " He knoweth them that are
His." 2 Tim. ii. 19.

A proof of God's favour. " I know thee (Moses) by name." Ex.
xxxiii. 17.

Son of Jona. Heb. *dove.* It occurs only in the O. T. in Jonah.

" A new name " indicates a new character, Rev. ii. 17 ; and
adoption also, Isa. lxii. 2.

To change a name is the prerogative of one in authority. Dan. i. 7.

Abram was called Abraham. Gen. xvii. 5. Jacob called Israel.
Gen. xxxii. 28.

Orientals mark a great event by a peculiar *surname.*

Called. Creatures were brought to the first Adam, that he might
name them.

The second Adam alone could say " This is thy name, and learn
hence thy work."

Cephas. Aramaic, *stone.* Firmness of his renewed character.

He was known at Corinth and among the apostles by this name.
1 Cor. ix. 5.

In earnestness, depth, and nobility of soul, John towers above him.

Our Lord's word a promise that he shall become what He calls
him.

Peter a " *stone* of *stumbling* " when yielding to temptation. Gal.
ii. 9, 14.

Alas, also, that millions calling themselves Christians should put
him in the place of Christ !

All that Rome has built on Peter's *primacy* is a fabric of delusion.

Birth-place and residence, Capernaum ; his mother-in-law dwelt
there. Matt. viii. 14.

His father and brother Andrew associated as fishermen with him.

Andrew, and probably *Peter,* were disciples of John the Baptist.

He walks on the sea. Matt. xiv. 29. Avows Jesus to be the
Messiah. Matt. xvi. 16.

The Lord makes his confession a foundation of the future Church.

Rashly, but affectionately, he rebukes the Lord. Matt. xvi. 22.

Earnestly and with horror, he at first refuses to allow the Lord to wash his feet. John xiii. 8.

He and John provided the paschal lamb. Luke xxii. 8. Judas had the bag. John xii. 6.

Boasts of his ardent love to Christ, and disgracefully denies Him. Mark xiv. 29.

His deep repentance. Matt. xxvi. 75. The Lord's forgiveness. John xxi. 15.

After his fall, his piety matures ; his love becomes ardent.

Interpretation. John writing in Ephesus explains Heb. and Chal. names.

A stone. Should have been rendered " PETER " in the English translation.

Signifies he will hereafter be renowned by this name. Matt. v. 9 ; Luke i. 76.

" As an adamant have I made thy forehead : fear them not." Ezek. iii. 9.

Peter is believed to have died a martyr before John wrote these lines.

Peter's temptation presupposes his rock-like character.

καὶ and δὲ omitted. *Tisch., Alford, Cod. Sin.*
Σίμων. An evidence of our Lord's omniscience. *Stier, P. Anton.* To prove Himself the same who changed Abram's name. *Chrysost.* For Ἰωνᾶ Ἰωάννου. *Tisch., Alford, Cod. Sinai.* Here, as in Matt. xvi. 17, the full name gives solemnity to the language. *Tholuck.*
κληθήσῃ. In O. T. in the change the old name stands before the new one. *Hengst.* Persians and Jews give a name at circumcision. *Chardin.* He is called *Petrus,* "a stone," from *Petra,* "the ROCK." 1 Cor. x. 4. *Augustine, Bede.*
κεφᾶς, Matt. xvi. 18, refers to Christ. *Jerome, Chemnitz, Witsius, Beza, Schultz.* A heaven-taught confessor. *Origen, Chrys., Luther, Beza, Erasmus, D. Brown.* A type of the Church. *Augustine.* To Peter as representative of the apostles. *Pearson, Hammond, Bengel.* *Passaglia,* the latest Romanist writer, opposes this view. To Peter's primacy. *Baronius, Bellarmine, Bossuet,* and Church of Rome generally. Name changed to what He would make him. *Calvin.* A prophetic reference to the Papal apostasy. *Lightfoot.* Inflexible, unbroken corner-stone. *Sumner.* Hellenists never use the Attic dialect in their appellatives, Acts ix. 36. *Grotius.* Three popes in their ignorance mistook κηφᾶς for κεφηλὴ. *Nifarius.* Even Bellarmine trips here. *Calovius.* Peter was primus inter pares : never claimed any authority. *Smith.* He aided Mark in his Gospel. *Papias, Clem. Alex., Tertullian.* Our Lord took these young disciples into fellowship immediately. *Neander.* Tradition calls his wife Concordia, or Perpetua. She is said to have suffered martyrdom, her husband encouraging her to be faithful unto death, "Remember, dear, our Lord." *Clem. Alex.* Peter crucified at Rome. *Tertullian, Lactantius.* Probably at Rome.

Neander, Winer, Wieseler. At his own request crucified with his head downward, declaring himself unworthy to suffer as his Lord; buried in the Vatican,
near the triumphal way. *Jerome.*

---

43. The day following Jesus would go forth into Galilee, and findeth Philip,
and saith unto him, Follow me.

Day following. Fourth day after ver. 19. Girded for this. John
  xvii. 19.
Our Lord toils on unceasingly. He never could say, with Tiberius,
  "*I have lost a day.*" A Moravian pastor was asked once,
  "Why thus alone ? " He answered, " Because I would have
  it so." Not thus our Lord. Where the perishing are there
  He is to seek and save.
Go forth. Since leaving Nazareth He had dwelt in Judea.
Is now on His way back to Galilee ; calling of Levi a subsequent
  act. Matt. iv. 18.
Thus begins the *personal history of the Redeemer of the world.*
Modestly and quietly the Son of God moves, *unknown among men.*
Nothing could more delicately show this Divine meekness than the
  happy expression, " He thought it *not robbery* to be EQUAL
  WITH GOD." Phil. ii. 6.
The CREATOR of the sun and stars, in human form, walks along the
  shore of the lake to seek some humble fisherman to begin the
  work of a Church that should outshine and outlast the sun.
Clad in that armour lately tested in the great conflict. Luke iv. 2.
He seems resolved to find all given Him. " None to be lost."
  John xviii. 9.
Divine grace makes the word "the rod of His strength." Psa. cx. 2.
Philip. (Ver. 44.) The name is Greek. Jews and Gentiles had
  begun to mingle.
One of the 12 apostles of our Lord ; though born a Jew, he bears a
  Greek name.
Proves how much Judea had become Hellenized by Greek customs.
Andrew and John found the Messiah, but Jesus found Philip.
Before these two found Christ, *His Spirit* had found them through
  the Baptist.
Galilee. In the O. T. a small circuit among the mountains of
  Naphtali.
In the N. T. a province embracing one third of Palestine, 50 miles
  long, 25 wide.

Asher dipped his foot in oil. Deut. xxxiii. 24. Olive trees still abound here.

Once lower Galilee was famous for grain-fields, and Judea for vine-yards.

Galilean, a term of *reproach* among the Southern Jews. Matt. xxvi. 73.

Into this miserable, dark Galilee, the great Light was to shine. Isa. ix. 2.

It was then the most densely peopled portion of Judea. *Josephus.*

Our Lord's home for 30 years was in Galilee.

After His baptism and temptation He returned to Galilee.

He had parables of the tares and sower for peasants, of pearls and treasures for merchants.

His mission successful. First three Gospels confined mainly to His labours in Galilee.

Herod Antipas, a weak, crafty voluptuary, was king.

Findeth. Our Lord finds Philip ; the three, however, may be said to have found Jesus.

Yet in all cases " We love Him, because He *first* loved us." 1 John iv. 19.

" When Saul saw any strong or valiant man, he took him unto him." 1 Sam. xiv. 52.

Thus David may have filled the ranks of his worthies.

Thus David's *greater Son* drew by a *Divine attraction* toilers, con-fessors, and martyrs—future heroes of His young empire.

Follow. Our Lord here for the first time calleth a disciple.

It may imply a *new* creation begun : Philip now renounces the world as his portion.

His affections being crucified to it, henceforth he will live to Christ.

How much of this Philip understood we know not, for the Power went with the Word.

Heathen were either amazed or angered at such words as these.

Emperor Julian and Porphyry fiercely *railed* at the apostles for following Him : " The Evangelists were either deceivers or foolish to think ONE WORD COULD HAVE SUCH POWER !"

Hierocles first attacked Christianity by crying down miracles.

Celsus ridiculed Christ's followers as mechanics and fishermen.

The same voice that said, " Let there be light," and caused the orbs sweetly to follow their central sun, now, as a familiar friend,

calls and draws a loving heart to His sacred circle, to share
His cross and crown.
How sublimely noiseless are the footsteps of a ministry, that in-
volves the interests of myriads through eternity !
Each one is called in God's own way.   1 Cor. xii. 6.
John and Andrew, after being trained by the Baptist, are won by
the words :—" Behold the Lamb of God ! "
So it is still.   The central power is ONE : the grace is ONE.
Thus sunshine and dew fall on all, yet no two flowers bloom alike.
The glorious key-note struck by the Baptist is the great proclama-
tion in every age.
Never was any ministry divinely blessed, of which this was not the
Alpha and *Omega*.
Follow me.   This one word expresses the disciple's life.
It begins the Saviour's work and song, and is the closing note.
John xxi. 19—22.
His method of effectual calling various,—He is *tied* to none.
" Ye shall walk after the Lord your God, and obey His voice."
Deut. xiii. 4.

ἐπαύριον.   The fourth from that mentioned in ver. 19. *Meyer.*   Our
Lord's labours begin and end with seven well-defined days. *Luthardt.*
ὁ Ἰησοῦς. Omitted. *Tisch., Lach., Alf., Tregelles.*
Ἀκολούθει, refers to an external calling. *Hengst.*   Internal also.
Author. Follow His doctrines. *Chrys., Lampe.*

---

44. Now Philip was of Bethsaida, the city of Andrew and Peter.

Philip.   The fourth disciple who attached himself to Christ.
His first act was to bring Nathanael to the Lord.   Probably the
same as *Bartholomew.*   Ver. 45—51.
Our Lord asked him, " Whence shall we obtain bread ? " John vi. 5.
Weakness of his faith seen in the request, " Lord, show us the
Father, and it sufficeth us."   John xiv. 8.
Greeks (proselytes of the gate), desiring to see Jesus, went to him.
John xii. 21.
He was present with the assembly after the resurrection.   Acts
i. 13.
Ancient commentators identify him with the disciple who said,
" Suffer me first," &c.   Luke ix. 59.

Philip, like Andrew, made manifest the savour of the Gospel, 2 Cor. ii. 14.

He does not seem, however, to have followed our Lord *literally.*

This is inferred from the next verses, and explains an incident in John vi. 5.

Neglecting the Lord's teachings exposes us to His scrutinizing questions.

Bethsaida. Aramaic, " *house of fishing,*" in Galilee. The exact location is unknown.

In the plain of Gennesaret. Mark vi. 45, 53. *Supposed* site nearly one mile N. of the *supposed* ruins of Capernaum.

Sandy beach answers to Matt. iv. 18—22. A sheltered bay is still found, and near by are ruins of fountains, aqueducts, and mills.

A woe pronounced upon it. Matt. _i. 21. Yet a remnant was there.

Another Bethsaida, at the lake near the head of the Jordan, was called *Julias,* after the abandoned daughter of Augustus. *Josephus.*

Founding new and altering old cities the pastime of oriental monarchs.

Philip would not fail to proclaim salvation at home, in Bethsaida.

But in vain. Hence, " Woe unto thee, Bethsaida!" Matt. xi. 21.

Our Lord would not suffer even the blind man cured to go thither. Mark viii. 26.

The city. Not only of the same town, but of the same *school* of *repentance.*

Happy moment! when these three friends found themselves with Jesus.

Probably the city of their birth, for they resided at Capernaum. Mark i. 29.

Andrew. Gr. *a strong man,* native of Bethsaida, disciple of John the Baptist.

Led to Christ by John's announcement, " Behold the Lamb of God!" Ver. 36.

Φίλιππος. Ancient Greek. *Winer.* Heb. *Olshausen.* Believed to have been a disciple of John. *Bengel.*

Βηθσαϊδά. Two towns of that name. *Reland, Porter.* One on the eastern, the other on the western side of Galilee, on the Lake. *Jerome, Eusebius.* Khan Minyeh ruins called Batzaida. *Ritter, De Velde.* But one place, i. e. Tell

Hum. *De Saulcy.* Divided by Jordan into two parts. *Thompson.* Ruins half a mile north of the ruins of Capernaum. *Robinson.* Philip died there and was buried there in a costly tomb. *Winer.*

---

45. Philip findeth Nathanael, and saith unto him, We have found him, of whom Moses in the law, and the prophets, did write, Jesus of Nazareth, the son of Joseph.

Findeth. These were blessed days of finding, after thousands of
    years of seeking.
The Spirit leads John to *dwell* on the gathering of the firstlings of
    the flock.
Five times in the context he uses the same beautiful phrase.
Nathanael and Philip called while travelling from Jordan to
    Galilee.
Each convert in succession becomes a preacher of the glad news.
Seed hath a natural life and warmth, producing more seed.
Thus God's word in the heart, like fire, kindles a warmth in others.
Philip called, finds Nathanael : The woman found, calls *all the town.*
    John iv. 28.
Mary, and even the angels, hasten to tell the news to their friends.
Nathanael. Identical with Greek name *Theodorus,* i. e. God's
    gift.
Believed to be the same person as Bartholomew, one of the
    twelve. John xxi. 2.
John mentions Nathanael twice, but never names Bartholomew.
Bartholomew named by the other Evangelists immediately after
    Philip the apostle.
Having so promptly confessed Christ, would he have been left out ?
He seems to have been of the band waiting for the Messiah.
In heart-stirring words, he soon will hear of his joy fulfilled.
He distrusted Nazareth because not named in the O. T., as the city
    of Messiah.
His humility, simplicity, sincerity, are endorsed by One, who could
    read the heart.
Our Lord uses terms of praise concerning him, such as He uses of
    no other person.
The fig-tree scene proved to Nathanael that he stood near the
    Searcher of hearts.
We. Andrew, Simon Peter, and John. John vi. 5, 8 ; xii. 21,
    22.

Found. Gr. implies *coming suddenly*, and that he *had been seeking.*

"I have found," rewarded the life-long labour of *Archimedes* of Syracuse.

Thus Columbus, seeking, toiling, enduring, at last found *a world.*

Thus the diligent Franklin, after many trials, found the secret of *electricity.*

Thus the merchant seeking goodly pearls, found THE PEARL *of great price.*

A believer's first transport : he does not say *where* they had found Him

It was He, of whom they had so often talked, hoped, and waited for.

We cannot think of these humble men, with such faith, without wonder.

They had left their homes and trades to follow the Baptist.

They were not called to become *apostles,* because they answered the call to be *believers.*

If humble Bethsaida contained three men qualified to be apostles, surely among our toilers on sea and land there may be such also.

Of whom. Christ is the KEY to all the Scriptures of the Old and New Testaments. Deut. xviii. 15—19.

As a beam brings the sun (though 95,000,000 miles distant) near the eye, so prophecy brought Christ near to the O. T. saints.

Moses. His life and character. See on ver. 17.

The law. History and antiquities. See on John vii. 19.

Prophets. Office and history. See on John i. 21 ; iv. 19.

These messengers from God dwelt among men, but the Messiah, still on His throne, shed more lustre than they.

Thus lamps in our neighbours' chambers are visible and near, but the moon, 200,000 miles away, gives more light.

Did write. "In thy seed shall all the nations of the earth be blessed." Gen. xxii. 18.

"The sceptre shall not depart from Judah, until Shiloh come." Gen. xlix. 10.

"A prophet will I raise up unto them, like unto thee." Deut. xviii. 18, 19.

"Thou art my Son ; this day have I begotten thee." Psa. ii. 7 ; Heb. i. 5.

"Thy throne, O God, is for ever and ever ; a sceptre of righteousness," &c. Psa. xlv. 6 ; Heb. i. 8.

" Worship Him, all ye angels." Psa. xcvii. 7 ; Heb. i. 6 ; Dan. vii. 9, 10, 13, 14.

" Thou art a priest for ever after the order of Melchizedek." Psa. cx. 4.

" The Lord our Righteousness," or " Jehovah our Righteousness." Jer. xxiii. 6.

Old and New Testaments, like the Seraphim in the temple, ever are crying to one another. Isa. vi. 3.

Testimony of Jehovah, of angels, and prophets forms one grand chorus to this sublime anthem—

" JESUS CAME INTO THE WORLD TO SAVE SINNERS." 1 Tim. i. 15.

Jesus. See on ver. 17. This name, given in prophecy, Matt. i. 21, has clung evermore to the same Lord.

Pronounced by demons, Luke iv. 34 ; nailed to His cross ; uttered by angels, Mark xvi. 6.

Claimed by the Lord of Glory ; miracles wrought in it. Acts iii. 6.

Rationalists fancy that Philip was *unversed* in O. T. prophecies.

But the apostle Peter, after His ascension, boldly spake the same word. Acts x. 43.

From what place the Saviour came was nothing to this disciple.

He had PROVED HIMSELF KING OVER HIS HEART !

Hereafter this humble origin may be harmonized with His royal name.

Nazareth. See on ver. 46.

Son. He talks as one ignorant of the miracle of Nazareth.

His mistake as to the Redeemer causes Nathanael's doubts.

But far better to be like Peter on Tabor, who spake " not knowing what he said," than preserve the sullen *silence* of Ahab, 1 Kings xxi. 4.

" Have I been so *long time with you,* and yet hast thou not known Me, Philip ? " John xiv. 9.

Joseph. See on John vi. 42.

Jesus as the *son of Joseph* may have been *personally* known to these men.

A carpenter's son might be Messiah : a shepherd boy became a *king.*

A *suffering Messiah,* which Jews despised, would have explained all these apparent contradictions.

Our Lord throws a veil over their weakness, and to these Galilean fishermen, unknown to the proud Sanhedrim, unknown to the philosophers, statesmen, and heroes of the world, He will *show His glory*, and that glory will soon FILL THE EARTH.

εὑρίσκει. On the same day. *Lampe.* Disciples in the interval disperse and the miraculous draught occurs. *Neander.* Not first in Cana. John xxi. 2. *Hengst.* Implies it was in a strange place. In Cana of Galilee. John xxi. 2. *Alford.* Nathanael seems to have sat down to rest under a fig-tree. Philip begs Jesus and the three brothers to wait a little, and hastens back and announces to Nathanael. *Besser.*

Ναθαναὴλ. Bartholomew, a second name derived from his father, Tholomy, or Tolomæus, as Simon from Jona, Bar-Jona. *Bengel, D. Brown, Besser, Trench, Smith, Meyer.* Christ chose illiterate persons (1 Cor. i. 26), while Nathanael is believed to have been learned in the law. *Augustine, Gregory.* Tradition makes him the bridegroom at Cana. One of the two disciples on their way to Emmaus. *Epiphanius.* He preached the gospel in India. *Jerome.* More probably Arabia Felix, sometimes called India by the Ancients. *Mosheim.* Some allot Armenia to him as his mission-field, and report him to have been there flayed alive and then crucified. *Assemann.*

λέγει, with a loud joyful voice. Ver. 48. *Bengel.*

τὸν υἱόν. Jews used the Messianic psalms in praying for the Messiah. *Chandler.* Up to this time the youthful Jesus only known to these parties as the carpenter's son. *Besser.*

'Ιωσήφ. John knew nothing of the histories of Matthew, Mark, and Luke. He simply gives the current word. *Olshausen.* Christ's Divine conception is taught, John i. 14; iii. 6. *Neander.* The two disciples did not permanently join our Lord's band. *Greswell.* John ii. 2 indicates they did. *Maldonatus, Ellicott.*

Ναζαρέτ. Philip believed Nazareth His birth-place. *Trench.* Did Peter believe He was born there? Acts x. 38. *Author.* Evangelist did not know that He was born at Bethlehem. *De Wette.* Philip only knew Christ as the son of Joseph. *Beza.* He knew Bethlehem must be the birth-place of the Messiah, and, as a disciple of the Baptist, had heard of Jesus' superhuman nature. *Hengst.*

---

46. And Nathanael said unto him, Can there any good thing come out of Nazareth? Philip said unto him, Come and see.

Can? Is it possible á prophet should appear in our neighbourhood?

Galileans well knew they were despised by others, and must have learned to despise themselves.

Jerusalem he thought might produce the Messiah, but not Galilee.

Cana, his home, was but two hours distant from Nazareth, yet he had never heard of Jesus dwelling there. But this was not sin.

Nazareth not hallowed by anything in the past, nor even named in the O. T.; not founded until after the exile.

Difficulties at every step will be met by the thoughtful mind.
Thus alone can the discipline of faith be accomplished.
In the sunlight of heaven all shadows will for ever flee away.
Any good thing. There may be prejudice without malice.
Nathanael erred as to this, and Philip erred as to the son of
Joseph.
Nathanael thought greatness must have a natural foundation.
" Who is like the LORD our God, who raiseth the poor out of the
dust ? " Psa. cxiii. 5—7.
He denieth it not, but only wonders at the strange ways of God.
Our Lord in sovereign wisdom passed by the learned of Jerusalem,
the eloquent of Athens, and the mighty of Rome, and chose
His disciples from wretched villages.
He collects fishermen, uncultured ones, to be the human founders
of His kingdom.
He asks not after kings or heroes, that His empire may be founded
in *grace alone.*
Hence "no flesh ever can glory in His presence." 1 Cor. i. 29.
A largeness of soul ever puts the best construction on things *un-
known.*
Had he forgotten Isaiah's words concerning ONE " despised and re-
jected of men ? "
ONE " lightly esteemed," ONE " without form or comeliness," ONE
" a root out of dry ground ? "
Nazareth. A despised town, of a despised province, of a despised
people.
"God hath chosen the weak things of the world to confound the
mighty."
He does not say out of Bethlehem, Messiah's birthplace.
Of all places, the *bad reputation* of this made it the most unlikely.
Nazareth, the home of Mary and Joseph ; scene of the annunciation.
Here our Lord spent His childhood and the first 28 years of His
life.
Nazareth is linked with Bethlehem and Jerusalem in holy alliance.
Intense devotion has led to the erection of great structures to mark
the spot.
Thousands of pilgrimages for 1800 years have been made to
Nazareth.
Angel Gabriel was sent here to a virgin named Mary. Luke i. 26.
Joseph and Mary left Nazareth to be taxed (enrolled) in Bethle-
hem. Luke ii. 4.

They return to Nazareth on arriving from Egypt. Matt. ii. 23.

Having visited the temple at 12 years of age, Jesus returned hither with his parents. Luke ii. 51.

Left Nazareth to be baptized by John in Jordan. Mark i. 9.

After His preaching at Nazareth, His neighbours try to destroy Him. Luke iv. 16, 29.

Of the identification of the ancient site there can be no doubt.

Name of the present village *en-Názirah*, same as of old.

Surrounded by hills. Some of the hills rise to 400 or 500 feet. Luke iv. 29.

From its situation Nazareth enjoys a mild atmosphere and climate.

Hence all the fruits of the country ripen early and attain a rare perfection.

" Fountain of the Virgin " at the north-eastern end of the town, where, according to tradition, the mother of Jesus received the angel's salutation.

The well-worn path has been trodden by the feet of countless generations.

A cliff near the Maronite Church, perpendicular, and 40 feet high, probably the one over which Nazarenes attempted to hurl Jesus. Luke iv. 29.

Epiphanius states that no Christian dwelt in Nazareth till the time of Constantine.

Helena, mother of that emperor, is said to have built the first Church of the Annunciation here.

No Jews reside in Nazareth at present. Population about 4000.

Houses all stone, and cleanly. Streets about six feet wide, and filthy.

This Nazarene prejudice—1. Powerful. 2. Foolish. 3. Common. 4. Pernicious.

Philip. (See on ver. 43.)

Come and see. Disputing is useless. Some know enough to *satisfy* themselves, but not enough to silence cavils.

Philip, unable to solve the question, knows where it can be done.

Nathanael wisely follows his advice. John vi. 68.

" Come and see " is thought to be evidence that a *mild lustre, a supernatural glory, beamed* around Him.

Philip had only to say " Come and see." He seemed assured that Nathanael would see, under the young Galilean's humble form, the GLORY of the MESSIAH.

Nathanael did *see* and *hear* enough : hence his confession, " Rabbi, thou art the Son of God."

Christian circles cannot show Jesus, but the *witness* is there.

Whoever comes in faith, will ever find Immanuel, *God with us.*

Philip's answer seems to have been learned from Christ. Ver. 39. Or from David, "O taste and see that the Lord is good." Psa. xxxiv. 8.

Heat of the sun, though so distant, tested by coming into its rays. Sweetness of honey proved by its taste. Psa. xix. 10.

" Come and see " the best remedy against pre-conceived opinions.

Nevertheless there are a few familiar truths we cannot submit to such a test, such as the doctrine of the Trinity, immortality of the soul, attributes of God, &c.

Thus faith is evermore solving difficulties by bringing them into the sunlight of the THRONE of GRACE.

He was a Pharisee, but, shielded by the fig-tree, he prayed in secret.

Our Lord's incarnation and death reveal the infinite peril of sin : Then let the *careless* sinner COME AND SEE.

He alone has that peace, which can calm the fears of the broken-hearted : Let the *anxious* sinner COME AND SEE.

He alone can satisfy the justice of God : Let the *guilty* sinner COME AND SEE.

1. *Religious* inquiry is rendered necessary by prejudice. Ver. 46.
2. *Religious* inquiry ought to be encouraged by Christians. Ver. 46.
3. *Religious* inquiry is an excellency : Christ commended it. Ver. 47.
4. *Religious* inquiry should issue in profession of Christ. Ver. 49.
5. *Religious* inquiry is rewarded by glorious discoveries. Ver. 51.

Ναζαρέθ. Matt. ii. 23. Heb. Sprout. *Robinson, De Wette, Meyer, D. Brown.* Crowned. *Bengel.* Consecrated. *Tertullian.* Contemptuous epithet. *Ebrard, Lange.* In the 7th century it had two churches and the fountain and house of Mary. *Reland.* Romish tradition affirms Mary's house was carried through the air by angels to Dalmatia, and thence to Loretto, Italy, 1200 A.D.

τι ἀγαθὸν, ἀγαθὸν τι. *Cod. Sin.* This sentence reads affirmatively *Augustine, Cyril, Origen.* A common saying, " a Galilean is a block." *Besser.* As Nathanael was a native of Galilee, he may have referred to the village merely in the sense of its smallness. *Hengst.*

---

47. Jesus saw Nathanael coming to him, and saith of him, Behold an Israelite indeed, in whom is no guile !

Saw Nathanael. Three things point out our Lord's omniscience.
1. I saw thee before Philip called thee. Luke xix. 4, 5.

2. I saw thee under the fig-tree, hid from all the world.

3. I saw thee in thine inmost heart to be without guile.   Jer. xxiii. 24.

Our Lord's omniscient glance detected Zacchæus' hiding-place.

Coming.   A friend invites, and he resolves to test the reality of the word.

He soon loses his prejudice in a happy experience of sight.

But he had doubtless wrestled, like Jacob, for this very proof.

Zacchæus, by urgent prayer, may also have won, "This, also, is a son of Abraham."

Saith.   He could have solved the difficulty about the nativity.

John, here as elsewhere, shows Christ's power of *looking into the soul.*

Of him.   Not *to* him.   Our Lord never praised a mortal to his face.

Behold.   No evidence of any allusion whatever to the previous question.

The hint that Jesus *overheard* the question, ignores or forgets His Omniscience.

Not long since John had cried "*Behold !* "   Now Christ Himself is the crier.

" *Behold !* " Of such rare virtue the Searcher of hearts alone could be the *herald.*

Nathanael is thought to have been learned in the sacred law.

But our Lord first chose the " foolish things of the world."   1 Cor. i. 27.

Afterward He chose *orators,* but they knew He had first chosen " unlearned and ignorant men."   Acts iv. 13.

Afterward He chose *rich* men, but they knew He had first chosen the *poor.*

Afterward He chose *Emperors,* but laying aside their diadems, they *wept at the tomb of fishermen.   Augustine.*

Is not Christ's Church still a " little flock"?   Has it ceased to be true in our day, that "few there be that find it "?   Matt. vii. 14 ; Luke xii. 32.

As to the upright, " Behold " for imitation : the hypocrite, for detestation.   Psa. xxxvii. 37 ; lii. 7.

Israelite.   It was a theocratic title won.   Acts ii. 22.

Won from God Himself, by Jacob's fervent pleading and agonizing prayer.   Gen. xxxii. 28.

Nathanael was an Israelite *after the flesh,* as Paul boasts.

A far higher honour to be an *Israelite* than an *Abrahamite*. Isa.
lxiii. 16 ; Gal. vi. 16.

There were Israelites with and without pure hearts, in the time
of Asaph. Psa. lxxiii. 1.

Some calling Jacob father *here* do not call God Father *there*. Psa.
xxiv. 6.

Those alone were sons of Abraham who walked in his steps. Rom.
iv. 12.

How did the Lord *know* Nathanael to be so free from guile ?

The question can only be asked by one who has *yet to learn* WHO *is
the Lord?*

JESUS as EMMANUEL needs no circumlocution to find *who* or *what*.

Jacob seems to have been a discoverer of angels. Gen. xxviii. 12 ;
xxxii. 1, 2, 24—30.

A wonderful commendation from ONE to whom he thought his face
and heart were entire strangers.

Had they not met before ?   Had he not wrestled for Light ?

Had he not agonized for the scattering of his enemies, pride, covetousness, falsehood ?

Truly His ministry is blessed.   In two days five souls are gathered
by Him.

No guile.   The only one of our race who lived and died *sinless*
was the man Jesus Christ.   1 Pet. ii. 22.

He does not say *no guilt*.   The mark is not sinlessness, but sincerity.

Such a character Jehovah pronounced blessed ages before.   Psa.
xxxii. 2.

It excludes all denial, extenuation, or apology for want of inward
truth.

Falsehood was then the fundamental disease of the people of the
Jews.

How *thoroughly devoid* of truth as a principle are heathen and
Papal nations in our age !

Ten Hindoos solemnly pledged their truth to come and work on
the morrow.   Only *one* came.   Where were the nine ?   *Dr
Newton* of Lodiana, India.

Pharisees concealed their true character from themselves and others.

Nathanael, a sinner, confessed himself to be a sinner.

The physician, therefore, judged him *curable*, not *whole*.

The Pharisees judged themselves *whole*, therefore were filled with
guile.

Christ's *omniscience* a joy to the upright, a terror to hypocrites.

Samuel, like Nathanael, was ready to follow truth wherever it led him. "Speak, Lord ; for thy servant heareth," implies thorough obedience 1 Sam. iii. 10.

" Without deceit" one of the great characteristics of Christ as foretold.   Isa. liii. 9.

Confessors daring to stand amid obloquy and persecution are guileless.   Rev. xiv. 5.

ἀληθῶς.   Nathanael heard the words and was embarrassed. *Stier*.

Ἰσραηλίτης.   No evidence of its being an honorary title. *Tholuck*, *De Wette*.   A name given by his friends before. *Lightfoot*.

δόλος.   He might have spots, but not painted. *Hengst*.   Light of Jesus pierces all folds of character. *Quesnel*.   Distinct reference to Psa. xxxii. 1. *Trench*.

---

48. Nathanael saith unto him, Whence knowest thou me ? Jesus answered and said unto him, Before that Philip called thee, when thou wast under the fig-tree, I saw thee.

Whence ?   He seems to think at first that Philip had informed the Lord as to his thoughts.

The reply convinced him that it came from no human source.

Nathanael's question reveals the very simplicity and integrity just named.

One can decline praise without affectation : it is here *admiration*.

Knowest.   Modestly inquires, "Who am *I*, O Lord God?" 2 Sam. vii. 18.

The dawning recognition of a superhuman nature in Jesus.

Conscious that his very heart had been penetrated and read.

Willing Omniscience should search his inmost heart.   " O Lord, search me," &c.   Psa. cxxxix. 23.   And his *simple, sincere, ardent* desire was to know and hold the truth.

Answered.   This answer no mere random shot.

Before.   Christ thinks of us when we little think of Him.   Rev. iii. 20.

Called.   Our Lord relates a circumstance of which we *know nothing*.

Messiah was foretold to be of " quick understanding in the fear of the Lord."   Isa. xi. 2, 3.

Nathanael, in a highly-favoured moment, may have had a *vision* of Messiah.

Thus Isaac walking in the field communed with God. Gen. xxiv. 63.

Doubtless *consecrated* himself by a *solemn, inviolable covenant.*

Jacob was conscious of *Divine presence* when he wrestled. Gen. xxxii. 24.

Our Lord does not directly answer his question.

He names a fact, thereby proving His knowledge more than psychological acuteness.

Nathanael knew none but an OMNISCIENT GOD could *reveal* this fact.

Without OMNISCIENCE how did Jesus know he was there at all ?

The Evangelist had said nothing about the fact.

Christ tells him not only that he *was there*, but what *he was doing !*

I saw thee. We can do nothing without millions of unseen witnesses.

Our CONSCIENCE is a THOUSAND WITNESSES, and GOD is a THOUSAND CONSCIENCES !

It is an awful moment when one meets God's all-searching eye in secret.

Hence hypocrites will ever dread the place of secret prayer. Job xxvii. 10.

What a moment when first, at death, the soul meets the burning *eye* of an all-knowing God !

To the *faith* of the two blind men our Lord adds *sight*. Matt. ix. 27.

To the humble *prayer* of Nathanael He adds open *vision* of the Son of God.

Nathanael heard with adoring wonder and profound awe.

He questions no more about Galilee, Judea, Bethlehem, or Nazareth.

A flood of light has entered his soul, not through the crevices of prophecy, but from the clear open heaven, where God dwelleth.

Nothing impresses the mind so much as to know that the depths of one's tender and secret emotions are laid open.

"I saw thee," i.e. "this is not the first time we have met ! "

In sacred, holy communion, Nathanael had felt the presence of God.

But he did not then know MESSIAH was the hearer of his prayer.

These words an answer to both Nathanael's questions (verses 46, 48), and above all to his *memorable prayer under the fig-tree.*

He was as thoroughly convinced of the Saviour's SUPREME GODHEAD as Thomas when he made his glorious confession. John xx. 28.

" I have loved thee with an everlasting love: therefore with loving-kindness have I drawn thee." Jer. xxxi. 3.

Religion is now also a self-evidencing experience in the soul.

The sun needs no witness, its radiance being self-evident ; so the believer hath the witness in himself. " Christ in you, the hope of glory." Col. i. 27 ; 1 John v. 10.

There had been a solemn transaction known alone to him and his God.

Would that Nathanael's fig-tree stood by *every* house !

Not a single sigh breathed forth from a contrite heart in solitude, but brings the EYE of the Son of GOD right on the soul in love.

The angel that showed Hagar the fountain in the wilderness, will direct such to a fountain of pure and holy joy. Gen. xxi. 19.

Nathanael may reveal his sweet secret to us, when all secrets shall become known.

Most believers have their moments of high and holy communion, *fig-trees and Tabors.*

" The secret of the Lord is with them that fear Him." Psa. xxv. 14.

Confession of Peter, Matt. xvi. 16 ; of Martha, John xi. 27 ; of Thomas, John xx. 28, breathes the same adoring faith and love.

Under. Sitting under a fig-tree oriental symbol of peace and plenty. 1 Kings iv. 25.

Israelites often there, as under a leafy roof, read the law. Mic. iv. 4 ; Zech. iii. 10.

Fig-tree. The fruit precedes the leaves. Bloom invisible except by a microscope.

The fruit is found in all stages, from the first kernel to the ripe fig.

It is bluish or yellowish in colour, and of a luscious taste.

Some hang on the branch all winter ; chosen king of trees. Judg. ix. 10.

Baskets, dishes, umbrellas, aprons, are still made of the leaves Gen. iii. 7.

A sign of fertility. Deut. viii. 8. Smitten, a token of Divine wrath. Psa. cv. 33.

It makes an almost perfectly concealed shelter for one praying.

It yields fruit for ten months in Palestine, from March to December. Height of the tree about 8 or 10 feet ; leaf is lobed.

γινώσκεις. Nathanael at that time a young man. *Tholuck.* Judged as Adam unfallen would by physiognomy. *Lavater.* As a wise prince studies

men to select for office. *Braunne.* He overheard our Lord's remark. *Alford.*
Nathanael's question *inspired,* to bring out the answer revealing Christ's
OMNISCIENCE. *Author.*

συκῆν. An Indian monarch wrote to Antiochus, " Send me sweet wine,
dried figs, and a sophist." *Athenæus.* This may point to the *home* of Philip.
Lange. In angello, cum libello. *A Kempis.* " In a nook, with a book."
Jones. Students frequented such shady spots to sit and study. *Lightfoot.*
Philip and he had *talked* of Christ there alone. *Chrys., Tittmann.*

εἶδόν, actual vision. *Lücke, Hengst.* A supernatural sight. *Alford.* An
internal perception. *Bengel.* Nathanael perhaps engaged in wrestling with
temptation. *Trench.* It means far more than merely seeing him under a fig-
tree. *Wordsworth.* The fig-tree a type of the fruits of faith and love which
Israel should bring to Messiah. *Besser.*

---

49. Nathanael answered and saith unto him, Rabbi, thou art the Son of God ;
thou art the King of Israel.

Rabbi. Our Lord's first words astonished and quite overpowered
him.
This title is recorded to have been given to our Lord 16 times
during three and a half years.
Rab, master ; Rabbi, my master ; Rabboni, our master.
The last only given to seven illustrious doctors, all of Hillel's
school.
To Nathanael Christ was more than the Messias. He was the Son
of God.
But *few* Israelites deemed the Messiah to be such.
It was doubtless by inspiration Nathanael uttered this great word
touching the Messiah.
He owns himself a true Israelite by loyally confessing his King.
Thou art He whom I have waited for and sought with cries and
tears.
Thou alone knowest how often Thou hast been with me before.
Thou art. He felt the eye of Him who searcheth the heart and
reins. Rev. ii. 23.
The Samaritan woman also believed on the ground of His omnis-
cience. John iv. 19.
Son of God. See on verses 18, 34. The first ascription refers
to the dignity of Christ's person, the second to the greatness
of His office.
This title aroused intense hostility in the Pharisees. John v. 18 ;
x. 30, 39.
The Jews never attempted to stone Him until He assumed it.
The full meaning of this *august term* was not understood, until it

was unfolded by the Spirit unto the Churches.   Psa. ii. 7, 12 ;
Isa. ix. 6.

Our Lord from the beginning did not conceal His glory.

Why if not Son of God did He not reject this flattery as blasphemy ?
What prophet was ever thus addressed ?

He knew well that the Jews attached to it the idea of supreme
Godhead.   John v. 18.

Yet our Lord never refused this august title during His life.

No one could honestly receive it, and none but a blasphemer could
intentionally offer it to one less than Jehovah.

The King.   Gr. article implies " *that* expected King."

The great future King of Israel here bears the name "Son of God."
Isa. ix. 6.

The Messiah foretold as THE BRANCH shall judge Israel, and His
name is "THE LORD OUR RIGHTEOUSNESS."   Zech. vi. 12 ; Jer.
xxiii. 5, 6.

" Rejoice, O daughter of Zion : thy King cometh unto thee." Zech. ix. 9.

Gabriel foretold He would have " the throne of His father David."

The sages from the east asked, " Where is the King of the Jews ? "

Pilate's title was an unconscious prophecy, " King of the Jews."

Nathanael acknowledges Jesus as RABBI, the promised prophet,
Deut. xviii. 18.   He confesses Him SON OF GOD and MESSIAH,
Psa. ii. 7 ; lxxxix. 27 ; and he bows before Him as KING OF
ISRAEL, Zech. xiv. 9 ; Jer. xxxiii. 15.

Swiftness to believe brings a splendid portion ; slowness is censured.
Luke xxiv. 25.

How much loftier this than anything said or implied by Philip !

> " As the great Sun, when he his influence
>   Sheds on the frost-bound waters—The glad stream
>   Flows to the ray and warbles as it flows." *Coleridge.*

Souls like Nathanael and Thomas, when divinely touched, gush
forth into the freest and highest faith.

Henceforth Nathanael must have clung to Philip by ties stronger
than blood.

It was a bond for *life.*   " *Philip* and Bartholomew " went forth
two and two.   Mark vi. 7.

It was a bond for *eternity.*   " Having *loved* His own, *He loved them
to the end.*"   John xiii. 1.

This is the *first simple creed* of the Christian Church, and the lofty
key-note of all revealed truth from heaven to our race.

καὶ λέγει αὐτῷ, omitted. *Tisch., Alford, Tregelles.* καὶ ειπεν. *Cod. Sin.*

---

50. Jesus answered and said unto him, Because I said unto thee, I saw thee under the fig-tree, believest thou? thou shalt see greater things than these.

I saw thee. Christ declares His omniscience by a new proof.

Believest? Faith, John i. 7; vii. 38. Highest idea of faith among Greeks was being *sure,* but our Lord lifted this word from its low estate, and made it the passport to the golden city.

Here it is faith in Christ's Divinity and Messiahship.

The Lord's words imply admiration at the ready faith of Nathanael.

True disciples need no greater miracle than the *word of the Searcher of hearts.*

This hath power over the soul above all signs and wonders. Matt. iv. 19; Luke ix. 39.

Shalt see. His faith, now in advance of his countrymen, and even of the apostles, was to grow, and receive richer promises and higher revelations.

"Who hast done great things: O God, who is like unto Thee!" Psa. lxxi. 19.

This promise holds good to the end of time with all believers in its widest sense.

Greater things. Possible reference to the miracle at Cana, which immediately follows.

To him that hath shall be given, and he shall have more abundantly.

A law which operates everywhere, but especially in the kingdom of Christ.

Greater things to be seen till all is consummated in the vision of God.

Whatever revelation of glory here, others yet "to be revealed." Rom. viii. 18.

Matchless mysteries for ever unfolding the "manifold wisdom of God." Eph. iii. 10.

Our Lord doubtless refers to the PLAN OF REDEMPTION, in which the attributes of the Triune God would be revealed, as they had not been since creation. 1 Cor. i. 24.

The word is as true to us as Nathanael. "Ye shall seek Me, and find Me, when ye shall search for Me with all your heart." Jer. xxix. 13.

ὅτι before εἶδον. *Tischendorf, Cod. Sin.*
πιστεύεις. Nathanael slightly blamed for hasty belief. *Von Gerlach.*
Such childlike faith is praised. *Stier.*
πιστεύεις. Interrogatively. As in the Auth. Vers. *Bengel.* Historically.
Hengst. As reproof. *Chrysostom.* Commendation. *Alford.*
μείζω. His faith would increase. *Tittmann.* Glories unfolding, not completed even at this day. *Alford.* More remarkable proofs of my mission. *Benson.*

---

51. And he saith unto him, Verily, verily, I say unto you, Hereafter ye shall see heaven open, and the angels of God ascending and descending upon the Son of man.

Verily, verily. This double "*Amen*" occurs 25 times in John's Gospel.

Never used by any one but Christ, and always at the opening of a sentence.

Prophets began with, "Thus saith the Lord." Christ takes the highest position,—"I SAY." Ex. iv. 22, 23.

"He sware by Himself because He could swear by no greater." Heb. vi. 13.

He utters this as the Son of God in mysterious but eternal union with the Father.

Our Lord, distinguished from all prophets, speaks in His own name.

He clearly shows Himself to be that Jehovah who spake by the prophets.

Our Lord is called THE AMEN. Rev. iii. 14. God of truth. Isa. lxv. 16.

All God's promises are YEA and AMEN in Christ. 2 Cor. i. 19.

Unto you. Not to Nathanael merely, but spoken to *all present*, and meant for all believers to the end of the world.

Hereafter, or from henceforth. These glories are still being unfolded.

At His Incarnation the heavens were opened, and since His Baptism in the Jordan they have not been shut.

Opened *over* all, *to* all, and *for* all believers. *Ambrose.*

As citizens of the New Jerusalem in communion with angels. Heb. i. 14 ; xii. 22.

Ye shall see. When this prophecy was specially fulfilled is unknown.

As on mountain tops at noon-day, stars invisible to dwellers in valleys are seen to sparkle in the heavens; so Nathanael, on some Tabor in this dark world, saw revealed what our Lord promised.

In like manner many prophecies have been fulfilled. We know all have been or will be.

When lifted to the heights of holiness *faith becomes vision.* Matt. v. 8.

A gracious intercourse between heaven and earth through the mediation of our Lord. John xvii. 20.

Where Immanuel was angels were, His unseen LIFE-GUARD clustering around Him, waiting and watching His will. Matt. xxvi. 53 ; Luke ii. 13.

Heaven, called *Paradise.* Luke xxiii. 43. *Abraham's* bosom. Luke xvi. 22. *New Jerusalem.* Rev. xxi. 10 ; Heb. xii. 22. *Being with Christ.* Phil. i. 23. *"My Father's House."* John xiv. 2. *Building.* 2 Cor. v. 1. *A better country.* Heb. xi. 16. *An Inheritance.* Acts xx. 32. *A crown.* 2 Tim. iv. 8. *Glory.* Psa. lxxxiv. 11. *Peace, Rest.* Isa. lvii. 2.

Heaven a *state.* 1 John ii. 25. Heaven a *place.* Christ, Enoch, Elijah, are bodily present.

Degrees of glory in heaven taught. Dan. xii. 3 ; Matt. x. 41, 42 ; xix. 28, 29 ; Luke xix. 16—19 ; Rom. ii. 6 ; 1 Cor. iii. 8 ; xv. 41, 42.

Christian recognition taught. Matt. xvii. 4 ; Luke xvi. 9—23 ; 1 Thess. ii. 19.

Firmament called *heaven.* Popularly thought of as hammered out like a metallic arch.

" Windows of heaven " opened at Deluge. We read of " Bottles of heaven." Job xxxviii. 37.

Place of the stellar universe called *heaven.* Stars, lamps, leading up to the Temple of God.

Above all this the *third heaven.* Place of God's dwelling and glory.

To this region Paul was caught up, and also caught into Paradise. 2 Cor. xii. 1—4.

Heaven concealed by curtains. Psa. civ. 2 ; Isa. xl. 22. Heaven of heavens expression of infinity. Neh. ix. 6.

Open. Fulfilled at His *Baptism, Temptation, Transfiguration, Ascension.*

Embraces especially the mediatorial work as revealed to men.

In O. T. times of type and shadow the heavens may be said to have been shut.

" In the thirtieth year the **heavens** were opened, and I saw visions of God." Ezek. i. 1.

" The dear angels take our prayers to heaven and bring back the answers." Rev. v. 8. *Luther.*

An open communication established. Angels ascended and descended on the ladder Jacob saw. Gen. xxviii. 12—17.

So in Christ angels are our ministers, and there is " the house of God and the gate of heaven."

Angels. When our Lord became incarnate the gates of heaven opened ; as when the doors of a palace, highly illuminated, are opened at midnight, and the monarch steps forth, the blaze within beams on the outer gloom.

Thus when our Lord was born, light from heaven came forth through the portals.

When He was baptized the gates of pearl were again opened.

When tempted in the desert and in peril by wild beasts, angels guarded Him. Mark i. 13.

When agonizing in Gethsemane an angel appeared to strengthen and cheer Him.

The morning of His resurrection His tomb was surrounded by angels.

Sometimes one and sometimes two of the shining ones appeared.

When ascending, two addressed the men of Galilee on Olivet, and a radiant host met Him returning with the song, " Open, ye gates, ye everlasting doors," as He moved on to the golden city. Psa. xxiv. 7.

The very armour of the angelic host is lustrous with glory, and cherubim use flaming swords. Gen. iii. 24.

They are known by various *names*, although all are called *"angels,"* i.e. God's messengers.

Sons of God. Job i. 6. Gods (Heb. *Elohim*). Psa. viii. 5. Thrones, Dominions, Principalities, Powers, Living Ones, Morning Stars, Seraphim, i.e. *burning ones;* Cherubim, i.e. *knowing ones.*

Prophets are called angels. Isa. xlii. 19. Priests also. Mal. ii. 7.

Heb. name implies an incorporeal and invisible essence, SPIRITS. Heb. i. 14.

Their appearance glorious. Dan. x. 6. Like Christ's. Rev. i. 14—16. Oft in human form. Gen. xviii. 2 ; Luke xxiv. 4. " Chariots and horses of fire." 2 Kings ii. 11.

They ever behold Jehovah's face. Matt. xviii. 10. An orientalism for *nearness to the throne.*

Being finite and compared with God, called imperfect. Job iv. 18.
Capable of being tempted. 2 Pet. ii. 4.

Some have fallen. Matt. xxv. 41 ; Rev. xii. 7—9. Others are confirmed in their obedience and blessedness. 1 Tim. v. 21.

Saints and angels both called "Holy Ones." Dan. iv. 17 ; Matt.
xxv. 31.

Agents of God's Providence. Slew the first-born. Ex. xii. 23.
Guarded Paradise. Gen. iii. 24. Gave the law at Mount Sinai.
Ex. xx.; Heb. ii. 2. Slew the murmurers in the wilderness.
1 Cor. x. 10. Punished David's pride. 2 Sam. xxiv. 16.
Destroyed 185,000 of the Assyrian army. 2 Kings xix. 35.
Slew Herod. Acts xii. 23. Endued with power : " Bless the
Lord, ye angels who *excel* in *strength.*" Psa. ciii. 20. Every
angel equals an army of 185,000 soldiers, and how much
mightier we can only infer. 2 Kings xix. 35 ; Isa. xxxvii. 36.
Adoring Jehovah. Isa. vi. 3. Great activity : He maketh His
ministers a flaming fire. Heb. i. 7. Gabriel came from heaven
to earth during *one sacrifice.* Dan. ix. 21. "The speed of angels
time counts not." Loveliness and high personal dignity ; immortal youth ; the two at the sepulchre at least 4000 years old.
Mark xvi. 5. Perfect in holiness. Matt. vi. 10. Celebrated
earth's creation. Job xxxviii. 7. Welcomed the Messiah's return. Psa. lxviii. 17. Students of God's works. 1 Pet. i. 12.
" Minister to them who shall be heirs of salvation." Heb.
i. 14. Watch over children. Matt. xviii. 10. Rejoice over
penitent sinners. Luke xv. 10. Present at Christian worship.
1 Cor. xi. 10. Present at our prayers. Rev. viii. 3. Bear
the souls of the redeemed to Paradise. Luke xvi. 22. Their
number great. Dan. vii. 10 ; Matt. xxvi. 53 ; Luke ii. 13 ;
Heb. xii. 22, 23. " Host of God." Gen. xxxii. 2.

Fellowship with the unseen world, closed by sin, again opened by
Christ.

> " Angels now are hovering round us,
>   Unperceived they mix the throng :
> Wondering at the love that crowned us,
>   Glad to join the holy song—
>   Hallelujah ! glory doth to God belong."

Painters borrow the *radiance* around them from the *heathen*
poets.

Ascending. Nathanael probably saw them at our Lord's resurrection and ascension. John xxi. 2.

Israel in a dream saw them. Gen. xxviii. 12. This true Israelite had his faith confirmed.

Heavenly ladder broken in Adam, restored by Christ, and now God and angels are at work.

A hint at their boundless energy and transcendent interest in believers.

Mediation, reconciliation, and re-union cause increasing movements of angels.

Our Lord may sleep in the storm, but awakes for others.

Our rest is not due till all toils, temptations, conflicts, are ended.

> " And when the shore is won at last,
>   Who will count the billows past ? "

The dying Bishop Wilson exclaimed, " Don't you see the angels ascending and descending on those trees ? "

Faith bridges the chasm between heaven and earth. What Israel saw, the true *Israelite* shall see.

Then God was a God afar off, and the Lord stood above the ladder.

Now, Incarnate, He stands at the foot and thus speaks to men.

Then shall earth be changed to heaven : all the interests one ; one kingdom, one joy, one redemption, the golden clasp binding heaven and earth into one, and the tabernacle of God shall be with men. Rev. xxi. 3.

Descending. They are left in their *descending* office, as if they only *went up, to come down on other errands* of love.

Every groan from burdened Christian hearts goes up this ladder.

Every ray of light cheering the stormy billows of earth descends it.

As Jacob saw the ladder just by the place he lay, so will each aching, breaking heart, find the *mercy-seat* and the *foot* of the *ladder* ONE !

When the curtain drops what a crowded ladder will be seen !

Contrast these living links of love, with the *dead, useless,* golden chain said to hang from the classic heaven of Jove.

Believers are *citizens of heaven in exile* here, but *served* by angels. Heb. i. 14.

Son of man. John v. 27. The disciples are introduced to our Lord in a quiet domestic way.

It fulfils " He shall not strive nor cry, neither shall his voice," &c. Matt. xii. 19.

Human nature and incident bring Immanuel near to our hearts.

Kindred and friendship, with noiseless hands, under God, lay the everlasting foundations of the kingdom of heaven.

The Baptist looked on Jesus and thus hinted to some the presence of the Lamb of God.

They introduce themselves to His notice, and go in silence to His abode, and are received by Him as a man receives his friends.

The *door closes on them, and they are with Christ. But what passes remains to be revealed* IN HEAVEN.

The grain of mustard-seed is committed to the mercy of the winds till it takes root.

He who calleth the stars by name is calling and adorning His Church below.

Twenty-one DIFFERENT NAMES *are in this chapter given to Christ.*

1. Word. 2. God. 3. Life. 4. Light. 5. True Light. 6. Only Begotten. 7. Full of Grace and Truth. 8. Jesus Christ. 9. The only Son. 10. Lord. 11. Lamb of God. 12. Jesus. 13. A man. 14. Son of God. 15. Rabbi. 16. Teacher. 17. Messiah. 18. Christ. 19. Son of Joseph. 20. King of Israel. 21. Son of man. *Aretius.*

'Αμὴν ἀμὴν. Spoken in His co-equality with the Father. *Stier.*

ἀπ᾿ ἄρτι omitted. *Cod. Sin.* Cancelled. *Lach., Alford, Tregelles.* Retained. *Tisch.* From henceforth. *Lightfoot.* The key to these words is Jacob's vision. *Trench.* Refers to Daniel's vision, vii. 13, 14. *Witsius.* The saying not yet completed at this day. *Alford.* Change to the plural ὑμῖν remarkable; although in answer to Nathanael, the words were intended for all. *Prescott.*

οὐρανὸν, οὐρανοί, a plural of excellence. *Schleusner.* "*Firmament,*" supposed to be a solid barrier between celestial and terrestrial waters, Gen. i. 6. *Smith.* Jews divided heaven into three parts, viz.: 1. Nubiferum, the air or atmosphere, where clouds gather; 2. Astriferum, the firmament in which sun, moon, and stars are fixed; 3. Empyreano, or Angeliferum, the upper heaven, abode of God and His angels. *Grotius.* Rabbis spoke of two heavens, "the heaven and the heaven of heavens," Deut. x. 14. Also of seven heavens. *Clem. Alex.* 1. Velum; 2. Expansum; 3. Nubes; 4. Habitaculum; 5. Habitatio, 6. Sedes fixa; 7. Araboth, or sometimes "the treasury." *Resch Lakisch.* Some locate heaven in the sun, others in the new earth, Rev. xxii. 1. *Winthrop, Ryle.* All languages will be understood by saints. *Ridgely.*

ἀνεῳγότα, opened at His baptism. *Lücke.* His ascension. *Hammond.* At judgment, Matt. xxvi. 64. *Elsley.* Symbolical expression. *Alford.* No allusion to the Transfiguration or Passion. *Olshausen.* The Son of man Himself the gate of heaven. *De Wette.*

ἀγγέλους, πνεύματα, Heb. i. 14. Same name for soul when separated from the body, Luke xxiv. 37; 1 Pet. iii. 19. Belief in angels satisfies the cravings of the mind. *Winer.* Prayers addressed to them, Gen. xlviii. 16. *Rabbis.* Each saint has a guardian angel now. Ancient Jews had also, Psa. xci. 11; Acts xii. 15. *Barry.* A superstition not in the text. *J. A. Alexander.* Pure spirit. *Peter Lombard.* Not necessarily such. *Meyer.* Have appetites, Gen. xix. 1—3. *Milton.* It demands a sunny eye to see the sun. Stars are ethereal and angels dwell in those bright abodes. *Lange.* Minerva visible to Ulysses, invisible to Telemachus. *Homer.* But one sex named. *Kitto.* Messengers of the New Covenant. *Augustine.* 1. A created ángel. 2. A sign by which Jehovah made known His will. 3. A form of Jehovah's manifestation. 4. The Logos of John. *Hengst.* Angel of the presence same as Gabriel. *Havernick.*

ἀναβαίνοντας. No reference to miraculous events : the opening up of a gracious intercourse between heaven and earth through our Lord's mediation. *Origen, Calvin, Lücke, Ols., Stier, Alford, Tholuck.* Does not signify that the angels *now* begin to descend : the scene displayed to view that of existing intercourse between earth and heaven. *Lücke, Winer.* Special providences towards the Church. *Hengstenberg.* Spirits bear the prayers and sacrifices of mortals to the gods. *Plato.* An unfulfilled prophecy. *Ryle, Gomarus.* Unbroken revelations of Divinity. *Luther.* A prophecy constantly fulfilled. *Trench.* The bridge between heaven and earth narrow as the edge of a razor. *Koran.* υἱὸν ἀνθρώπου. See notes on John v. 27.

Nathanael not immediately numbered among the apostles, lest his learning should be made a ground of reproach. *Augustine, Gregory.* No proof of his learning. *Ryle.*

John 2

1. AND the third day there was a marriage in Cana of Galilee; and the mother of Jesus was there.

Third day. After He had returned from the wilderness.

About two days' travel (oriental style) from the Jordan to Cana.

This parting from the Baptist was final till they met in Paradise. Luke xxiii. 43.

Three first chapters of Genesis and John describe the creation of all things, and each occupies a week of history.

In both the *sixth* day was signalized by a marriage.

In the beginning, the Lord Jesus *instituted*, now He *honours* it with His presence.

Marriage, at creation.   1. *Unity*—one flesh. Gen. ii. 24.   2. *Indissolubleness*. Matt. xix. 9.   3. *One wife* original law. Matt. xix. 5.   4. *Social equality*. 1 Pet. iii. 7.   5. *Subordination* of wife. 1 Cor. xi. 8, 9.   6. *Respective duties*. Eph. v. 22, 23.

Apostasy begun by the wife, therefore she was put in a state of subjection.   Gen. iii. 16 ; 1 Pet. iii. 6.

Polygamy leads to jealousies, as in the case of Jacob, Abraham, Elkanah, &c. 1 Sam. i. 6 ; Gen. xvi. 6.

Celibacy first practised by Essenes, Therapeutæ, and Gnostics.

Romanism affords sad proof of Infinite Wisdom requiring pastors to be married.   1 Tim. iii. 2.

Celibacy has led to *unbounded corruption and ruin in society*.

" Forbidding to marry " a sign of *antichrist*. Infidels and libertines often joined with Papists in *war against social purity*. 1 Tim. iv. 3.

Here is a solemn, loud, enduring protest of the Son of God against Romish abominations.

Blood relationship or near of kin forbidden to marry. Lev. xviii. 6—18.   Athenians married half sisters, Egyptians full sisters, as Ptolemy Philadelphus, Cambyses the Persian, &c.

Abraham married his half sister. Gen. xx. 12.   Amram, his aunt. Ex. vi. 20.

Jacob married two sisters at the same time. Herod, his half sister.

Archelaus, his brother's widow. Antipas, his brother's wife. Matt. xiv. 3.

Bride was chosen by the parent, or by a friend, as Eleazar. Gen. xxiv. 3.

In oriental lands bridegroom seldom sees features of bride before the wedding.

Espousal was confirmed by an oath and the giving of presents to the bride. Ezek. xvi. 8.

A parent often received a *dowry* for his daughter.

Boaz says, " Ruth have I purchased to be my wife." Ruth iv. 10.

Removal of the bride from her father's house was the ceremony of marriage.

A bath was a formal proceeding in ancient marriages. Ruth iii. 3; Ezek. xxiii. 40.

A veil the characteristic attire of the bride, covering her whole person. Gen. xxiv. 65 ; xxxviii. 14, 15.

A girdle, also, which no bride could forget. Jer. ii. 32. A gilded chaplet on her head. Psa. xlv. 13. A virgin's hair was flowing.

Robes white. Rev. xix. 8. Covered with jewels. Isa. xlix. 18; lxi. 10. Highly perfumed. Psa. xlv. 8.

Musicians led persons bearing torches. Jer. vii. 34; xvi. 9 ; Matt. xxv. 7; Rev. xviii. 23.

At the bridegroom's house a feast was prepared. Gen. xxix. 22. Robes for guests. Matt. xxii. 11.

Greeks offered a sacrifice at marriages, the bridegroom officiating as the priest.

Feast lasted from one to fourteen days. Judg. xiv. 12.

The revelry was the voice of the bridegroom and bride. Jer. vii. 34.

Newly-married man was exempt from military service for one year. Deut. xxiv. 5.

Married females went unveiled ; talked with strangers. 1 Sam. i. 13 ; ix. 11.

Appeared in courts of justice. Num. xxvii. 2. Held office ; Miriam, Deborah, Huldah, &c. Entertained guests. Judg. iv. 18.

Our Lord, the son of a virgin, honoured widowhood in Anna at the temple, and at a marriage feast " showed forth His glory."

Oh that Jesus were invited to all our marriage feasts !

In the expressed judgment of Infinite Wisdom "It is not good for man to be alone."

Our Lord places the *golden crown* on the marriage state, by working, in its honour, His first miracle.

God thus shelters holy wedlock from the scorn of wicked men.

Infidelity, denying Christ's Divinity, has dared to *assault* this institution.

Any one should suspect his virtue when tempted to undervalue this ordinance.

When lust broke down the marriage altar the flood swept men away from the earth. Gen. vi. 2, 3.

Cana. Heb. *place of rest.* Once mentioned in the O.T. Josh. xvi. 8; xix. 28.

Its supposed site lies about eight miles north of Nazareth, and about 17 miles from Capernaum.

Many ancient cisterns, but no architectural ruins are seen. Home of Nathanael. John xxi. 2.

Bethlehem our Lord's chosen birth-place, Nazareth His home, obscure Cana the scene of His first miracle; illustrating His *humility*.

Christ's Light and Galilee's darkness foretold. Isa. ix. 2.

Mary, wife of Cleopas, resided at Cana, and the wedding is thought to have been at her house.

Galilee. See notes on John i. 43.

Mother. Mary dwelt at Nazareth : was the daughter of Heli.

Joseph, son-in-law to Heli, took his wife's name, and, according to Jewish custom, was called son of Heli. Luke iii. 23.

She was of the lineage of David. Psa. cxxxii. 11. A relative of Elisabeth.

Betrothed to Joseph, a carpenter, she dwelt at Nazareth.

Angel Gabriel announced to her that she should have a child to be called the SON OF GOD !

As a sign Gabriel also announced the conception of Elisabeth. Luke i. 36.

Angel leaving her, Mary went to the city of Elisabeth, probably *Hebron.*

Her feelings at the meeting prompted her to utter the inspired song. Luke i. 46—55.

" Henceforth all generations shall call me blessed." Gen. xxx. 13.

Mary returned to Nazareth, and with Joseph, went to Bethlehem for enrolment.

In a stable the Redeemer of the world was born, four years before the Common era.

She was visited by the shepherds and by the Magi also, who were led by THE *miraculous* STAR.

She took her son to the temple to present Him to the Lord.

Her poverty was seen in the offering of the poor,—a pair of birds. Luke ii. 24.

Simeon's song and Anna's thanksgiving deeply aroused her interest.

Warned by the angel of the Lord, the holy child is taken to Egypt.

Returning, Mary dwells in Nazareth 23 years.

At His twelfth year she took Jesus to Jerusalem to the Passover.

She retires to Nazareth until the marriage at Cana.

At Capernaum, Mary and her sons James, Joses, Simon, and Jude, and her daughters, desired Him to come and speak with them.

On the cross the Lord committed Mary to the care of John, in preference to her own sons, since John had a *home* at Jerusalem. John xix. 27.

Mary the mother of Jesus appears at the place of prayer. Acts i. 14.

During 40 days *ten* appearances of Christ are recorded, *not one to His mother*.

Her characteristics : *Earnestness*. Luke i. 39. *Submission*. Luke i. 38. *Gratitude*. Luke i. 48. *Thoughtfulness*. Luke ii. 19. *Fidelity*. Luke ii. 51. *Humility*. John ii. 5.

Our Lord's intercourse with His mother was refined, and was reflected in her graces.

The conflict of the *Jew* with the *Israelite* in her breast was intense.

She could not pierce the holy night of His childhood.

She saw the dew of Paradise resting on all His youthful ways.

She led her Son to the temple, but she could not go with Him, as He entered within the veil to commune with HIS FATHER.

He gave the most touching and lovely testimony to her character when, on the cross, He bequeathed the DEAREST LEGACY EVER LEFT BY LOVE to the devoted John.

His love was infinitely instructive, fruitful even in the agonies of death.

She could see His whole life was *one prayer of infinite depth*, a deep sigh for the world's salvation, a loud Hallelujah for saving love.

John does not name Jesus' mother, nor his brother James, nor himself.

Mary has not appeared before in this Gospel, and will not again until we meet her at the cross.

It seems that our Lord and His disciples were invited to the wedding, but not His mother.

A fair inference that she was present, either as a *relative*, or *manager*, especially as she gave commands which were obeyed. Ver. 5.

Mother. Her most honourable title. Joseph probably was dead.

τρίτη. The Passover, 15th Nisan, year of Rome 781; 30th of March. *Wieseler.* Of April. *Greswell.* The road for Jesus to Capernaum went through Cana. *Tholuck.* Journey required two days for 50 miles from Bethabara. *Robinson.* The third day after arriving in Galilee. *Meyer, Lichtenstein, Andrews.* After the call of Nathanael. *Alford.* Same as last day named. *Lange.* From the end of the day in which Nathanael came to Jesus. *Hengst.*

γάμος. "Help meet for him," Gen. ii. 20, over against or before him. *Heb.* ὅμοιος αὐτῷ. *Sept.* Simile sibi (exact counterpart of himself). *Vulgate.* 18 wives allowed a king. *Selden.* High priest sanctioned bigamy, 2 Chron. xxiv. 3. Rabbis allowed four wives. *Selden.* Mahomet also. *Niebuhr.* Honorius forbade it. *Selden.* No one joined a marriage procession without a hand lamp. *Trench.* Veil used by Greeks and Romans. Word "nuptial" derived from *nubo*, "to veil." Modern Egyptians envelope the bride in an ample shawl. *Smith's Dict.* Old *Pomeranian Church Guide* calls Satan a foe to wedlock, desiring to reduce men to a herd of beasts. *Besser.*

Κανᾶ. Heb. *place of reeds.* Joseph's family had settled in Cana. *Ewald.* Jesus and His disciples sought Mary there. *Hengst.* Eight miles north of Nazareth. *Robinson.* Doubtful. *Stanley.* This town had, through the monks, lost the honour of this miracle. It was restored by Dr Robinson. *Trench.* Marriage at the house of Cleopas. *Lightfoot, Greswell.*

μήτηρ. Luke's genealogy Mary's. Her father was Heli. *Greswell, D. Brown.* Tradition makes her parents Joachim and Anna. It alleges she walked up to the temple at three years of age and remained there until 14, ministered to by angels, &c. Also that the house at Nazareth in which the angel came to Mary was carried by angels to Dalmatia, in Illyricum, and from thence to Loretto, Italy. Tradition makes her live 22 years after the Ascension, says that Gabriel and Michael fanned her when dying, and then bore her spirit to heaven. *Melito.* Jewish blasphemy invented the story of Pandera in the Toldoth Jesu, which was repeated by Voltaire. The immaculate conception of Mary was a Mahometan doctrine six centuries before any Christian theologians or schoolmen maintained it. *Smith's Dict.* Mary not named by John out of reverence. *D. Brown.* Being well known. *Alford.* She was dead when John wrote. *Author.*

---

2. And both Jesus was called, and his disciples, to the marriage.

Jesus. We infer the *piety* of the host in his calling one so holy.

Also his *hospitality* in the number of his guests, contrasted with his limited means.

As a rule, wealth intensifies selfishness, and the poor are more hospitable than the rich.

Our Lord's *public character* could not at that time have been the ground of this invitation.

John had just announced, " Behold the Lamb of God ! " John i. 29.

Yet crowds had begun to curiously watch so singular a Personage.

Anything that reminded of the Messiah set the nation's heart on fire with dreams of regal splendour, triumphant armies, and unending glory.

A few fishermen, fast bound to Him, were present with Him.

They were lately John's disciples in the desert ; now they go to a wedding feast.

The Lamb of God, however Royal and Divine, touches earthly interests.

Invited by Nathanael, perhaps, who was of Cana, of Galilee. John xxi. 2.

Chastened feasting and joyful communion. Scorners hint that our Lord sanctioned midnight revelry by His presence and miracles, because, forsooth, *Essenes* were monastic in their habits.

He came not to abolish, but *sanctify*, times of joy and times of sorrow to believers, and thus struck the *key-note* of His future ministry.

He is not to retire like the Baptist : His is the harder and higher task to mingle with and purify the fountains of common life of men.

Cave, spectat Cato. " Beware, Cato is looking on," was the old Roman proverb.

How much more solemn the EYE OF THE INFINITE GOD.

He foresaw the licentiousness sanctioned by Rome and family ties dishonoured.

He begins His ministry at a wedding feast while attracting His disciples to future glory on His *way to the cross*.

Called. His mother was there without being called, doubtless as a near relative.

Was the Saviour at *thy* wedding, reader ? One answers *Yes.*

Was He an *invited* guest ? At many He is an unbidden guest.

Sooner or later He will reveal Himself either in a *blessing* or a *curse ;* either the Saviour or Avenger of the state. 1 Cor. vii. 39 ; Job xviii. 15.

Rome, with her usual impiety, changes the ceremony into a *sacrament*, and vilifies the marriage state by refusing it to her ministers.

While professing to receive, she nullifies *every gospel truth,* proving
herself the organized enemy of all righteousness. 2 Thess.
ii. 9, 10.

Those who sacrifice for Christ shall never lose by Him.

Believers a community, the dawn of a new world of love, called
into life only by Christ.

Called. Three kinds of guests were found at ancient feasts.

1. Acquaintances and relatives invited. 2. Those who were able
and willing to bring presents. 3. Others, who, under cover
of a feast, came as *flatterers* and *buffoons* for the sake of sharing
the dainties remaining.

Among Greeks and Romans the revelry became highly licentious.
Cyprian.

Disciples. They had the same invitation as that given to the
angels by Abraham. Gen. xviii. 2—5.

Those who invite the Saviour will ever welcome His *disciples.*

There were but *five.* They were all His family—the foundation of
a Church destined to fill earth and heaven. Eph. iii. 10.

They soon learn that though He had no *wealth,* they need fear no
want.

John the Baptist's austere teachings *contrast* with marriage festival
shared by Christ and His disciples.

Idolatrous ideas of celibacy condemned in the germ by the Holy
Spirit. 1 Tim. iv. 3.

Disciples their first name ; then called *servants ;* then *friends.*
John xv. 14, 15.

12 in number. 12 altar pillars. Ex. xxiv. 4. 12 stones at Gilgal.
Josh. iv. 3. 12 jewels in breastplate. Ex. xxviii. 21. 12 tribes.

He gave them power to cast out devils, Mark iii. 15 ; and the keys,
Matt. xvi. 19.

He promised the Spirit to rule the Church. John xiv. 16. He renewed it. Matt. xviii. 18.

" As my Father hath sent me, even so send I you." John xx. 21.

Disciples called apostles. Matt. x. 2.

Essentials of an apostle—1. To have seen Christ in the flesh.
John xv. 27. 2. They must have been called immediately
by the Lord. Gal. i. 1. 3. Inspiration was essential to the
exercise of this office. John xvi. 13. 4. Power of working
miracles. Mark xvi. 20. 5. Universality of mission. Acts i. 8.

These characteristics, being supernatural, prove that they had *no
successors* in the Apostolic office.

Marriage. He came not to annul human obligations.

As the foundation of all society, He hallows what He first founded. Psa. lxviii. 6.

A holy family circle intelligently and actively engaged in doing good is the nearest approach on earth to the exalted society of heaven.

Our heavenly Bridegroom bears a conjugal relation to the Church. Rev. xix. 7.

Only a sacred state can be a type of the holiest of all relations.

Believers learn from this the innocence of such festive gatherings.

But we are never to go where *He* would not have gone.

There are companies where believers cannot bring the *salt of grace*.

We should *avoid a feast where we cannot show our colours*.

If we go where our Master went we must go in our Master's Spirit.

Can we go *with His Spirit* to the dance, card-table, theatre, &c. ?

ἐκλήθη. As a relative. *Kuinoel*. Not as a religious Teacher. *Ryle*. Philip and Nathanael present. *Trench*. Jesus and five disciples typified by the six water-pots. *Luthardt*. Our Lord's first disciples originally converts of the Baptist. *Olshausen*. Our Lord took pleasure in attending wedding feasts *Renan*.

μαθηταί. Couriers, conveying letters, called apostles. *Oecumenius*. Andronicus and Junia mentioned, Rom. xvi. 7, as "of note among the apostles." Some think this means "noted apostles." *Calvin, Luth., Bengel*. Others more properly regard the phrase as "persons esteemed by the apostles." *Beza, Grotius, DeWette, Stuart, Hodge, D. Brown*. μαθηταί. Disciples from various localities, not friends. *De Wette*.

γάμου. At the house of Mary, wife of Cleopas. *Lightfoot*. Alphæus, and the sister of Mary, the mother of our Lord, were the parties. *Greswell*. Another tradition, the Apostle John the bridegroom. *Jerome, D. Herbelot*. Another, Simon the Canaanite. *Nicephorus*. "Marriage a condition especially exposed to temptation." *Nicole*. A slander on the author and Divine founder of marriage by an amiable Jansenist. *The Author*. A symbol of Christ's relation to His Church shadowed in the Canticles. *Augustine, Hengstenberg*.

Modern religionism keeps the leaven from the lump, lest the leaven become unleavened. *Alford*. Fashionable marriage feasts afford believers a very *doubtful* occasion for doing the work of the Master. *The Author*. The time 6th of Jan. *Epiphanius*.

---

3. And when they wanted wine, the mother of Jesus saith unto him, They have no wine.

Wanted. Gr. *wine having failed.* More guests perhaps than expected.

Domestic cares begin very early in wedded life. 1 Cor. vii. 33.

Modern Jews send gifts of wine to their friends at wedding feasts.
Providence surely arranges for the first of the Lord's miracles.
Wine may be absent, and Christ Himself present.
Bread may be wanting, even though Christ is at the board.
But the hidden manna is ever present, and in our Father's house
　　there will be enough.
What though we beg our bread here, Heaven will make up for all.
Humanity needs many mercies, and luxuries are the inheritance of
　　but very few.
But our Lord sanctions festal hours with festal goods.
Consciousness of the wants and woes of millions should moderate
　　even innocent pleasures.
The cravings of the body, though ever so severe, do not equal those
　　of the soul.
There is a hunger which God did not create.　Luke xv. 14.
Wants of the soul oft make a famine amid festal plenty.
This craving of the spirit is beyond the reach of earthly friends and
　　treasure.
Belshazzar's feast was a mockery, while *the hand moved on the wall.*
The flame causing Dives to thirst had been kindled by cravings
　　on earth.
Wine. The well-known juice, oft called the " blood of the grape."
Grapes were eaten, but it is supposed no wine was made, before
　　the flood.
Wine first noted in the time of Noah. Gen. ix. 20. Lot's inebriety.
　　Gen. xix. 32.
Vines grow luxuriantly around Ararat, where the ark rested.
Jacob blessed by Isaac with "corn and wine." Gen. xxvii. 28.
　　Pharaoh's butler.　Gen. xl. 11.
Vintage and drinking scenes are carved on Egyptian temples at
　　Thebes.
The Lord required wine among His most sacred offerings.　Num.
　　xv. 5, 7, 10.
This the key to the words, " Wine cheereth the heart of God and
　　man." Judg. ix. 13.
Wine forbidden priests during service, Lev. x. 9, hints at Nadab's
　　fatal sin.
Forbidden to Nazarites during the obligation of their vows. Jer.
　　xxxv. 14 ; Rom. xiv. 21.
Israelites free to use wine at their national festivals.　Deut. xiv.
　　22—26.

Medicated or mixed wine anciently given to criminals. Prov. xxxi. 6 ; Mark xv. 23.

Mixed wine with Jews was strong, with Romans was diluted. Isa. v. 22 ; Psa. lxxv. 8.

"Royal wine" fit for Persian kings, " wine of Lebanon." Esther i. 7.

Nehemiah kept only enough for a ten days' supply. Neh. v. 18.

Romans kept wine stored in large Amphoræ, seen at present in the house of Diomedes, Pompeii, ranged round the cellar walls, with the lees which they contained 18 centuries ago.

Scripture at times discriminates between strong and weak wine.

Corn, oil, milk, and wine constantly named among blessings. Isa. lv. 1, 2.

Our Lord was no ascetic. He came " eating bread and drinking wine." Luke vii. 33, 34.

Timothy enjoined by Paul to use it. 1 Tim. v. 23. Created at Cana. Ver. 8.

Believers in certain cases bound to *abstain* out of *love*. Rom. xiv. 21 ; Matt. xviii. 6.

An enlightened conscience is the rule. Paul circumcised Timothy, and refused it to Titus.

Solemn warnings—" *Wine is a mocker, strong drink is raging.*" Prov. xx. 1.

"Who hath woe ? who hath sorrow ? who hath contentions ? *They that tarry long at the wine ; they who seek mixed wine.*" Prov. xxiii. 29, 30. " Woe to them who rise early to follow strong drink ! " Isa. v. 11.

" *Come ye,* say they, *we will fill ourselves with strong drink.*" Isa. lvi. 12.

If any man called a *brother be a drunkard, leave him.* 1 Cor. v. 10, 11 ; Eph. v. 18.

Drunkards shall not inherit the kingdom of God. 1 Cor. vi. 10 ; Hab. ii. 15.

Self-denial in *things indifferent* is often imperative. 1 Cor. viii. 13.

His mother. It was her first and last attempt to control His Divine power.

It is not for us to set the sun by our dial.

It is not fit to send for the *king by a letter through the post.*

Jehovah never did, and never can, allow any *familiarity from a creature.*

Witness His solemn charge against Israel's curiosity at the mount. Ex. xix. 21. Nadab and Abihu's doom for trifling, Lev. x. 1, and Uzzah's for touching the ark. 2 Sam. vi. 6 ; Col. ii. 18.

Said. Many scholars think that she did not intend a miracle in her request.

But our Saviour's answer implies that she did.

Some say she wished to gratify maternal vanity, and secure a display of His power.

Others, she knew Him to be the subject of several great miracles.

Others, she had learned from the Scriptures who and what He was, as Messiah.

Others, a mere neighbourly request, simply to oblige the host.

Others, a hint for Him and His disciples to withdraw on account of the scarcity.

She *felt* He had a *supernatural power* as she *knew* He had a *supernatural nature*, and longed that He would give proof of it.

Had she not seen some *domestic wonder* she would hardly have expected one now. *Bp. Hall.* But we are told that this was " the beginning " of His miracles. Ver. 11.

She might have drawn on her credit to purchase the supplies.

But she will not go to the shallow stream when she can get to the Fountain Head.

She had seen in that wonderful child the daybreak of Israel's help.

How modestly she now calls His attention simply to the want of wine.

A proof that her visions were fresh and her hopes not given up.

A mother's request ordinarily binds a *son* as a *command.*

They have. Was her request really a prayer ? If so, how seldom, in approaching the mercy-seat, do we remember our infirmities, or realize the rebukes of our Lord !

She was herself the subject of a miraculous maternity.

An angel had announced the birth of a son whom she knew to be *more* than *mortal.*

She heard Elisabeth, while inspired, call her unborn babe " MY LORD." Luke i. 43.

She knew that the Eternal Spirit was the only Father of her child.

She knew that angels had sung the birth-song of her SON !

She knew that the midnight had become mid-day at His nativity.

She knew that strangers from distant lands had offered *royal gifts* and *worship.*

She knew that at 12 years of age He had called Jehovah " MY FATHER " in the Temple.

She knew that God the Father at Jordan had acknowledged Him as His Son.

She knew that John had publicly proclaimed Him the MESSIAH.

She knew that Nathanael, sure of His omniscience, had hailed Him "the Son of God, the King of Israel."

Shall she not, therefore, look for a crisis soon ? Is it not a fit hour to prove THY might in a miracle ?

Thirty years had passed, but to the mother the wonders of His birth were *ever present*.

They have no wine. These words convey a hint, a question, and a supplication.

She has herself a feeling of the impropriety of the request.

She does *not dare* to express *directly*, but only suggests a *desire*.

So great, even now, was her regard, and so profound her reverence for her son.

Her own and Joseph's sons shared their mother's vain or ambitious impatience. John vii. 3.

She had good reason to expect from prophecy that He would be greater than Moses or Elias.

During those 30 years how many solemn investigations of the prophecies had they together !

No wine. Enough for a meal, but not enough for a feast. The bridegroom was richer in hospitality than in purse.

Wedding banquet usually lasted *seven* days among Jews of the upper classes.

With the poor but *one*. Wine was provided accordingly.

The feasters here had doubtless prolonged their stay beyond the time intended.

If there was not wine enough, there was water enough.

In a world hungry and thirsty, boundless grace has provided all that is *necessary* for life, if not luxuries.

Want at a *wedding* proves that this earth's pleasures are *hollow*.

" Even in laughter the heart is sorrowful." Prov. xiv. 13 ; Ecc. ii. 1; vii. 3.

A flashy mirth, that moistens the lips, but leaves the heart thirsty still; that smoothes the brow, but leaves a hollow in the soul.

Even the festal wreaths of the ungodly become chains to bind and burn.

ὑστ. οἴνου. Sudden invitations had been issued by the bridegroom. *Lange.*

This feast lasted several days. *De Wette, Lücke.* Wine was boiled down and
mixed with water for use by Greeks and Romans. *Ammon.* Departure before
the proper time an insult. *Stier.* οἶνος. 6 Gr. and 12 Heb. words used for
wine :—Yayin, Gen. ix. 21, is intoxicating. Among the high blessings. Permitted Israelites at their feasts, Deut. xiv. 23—26. Tirosh, Hos. iv. 11.
Shecar, Lev. x. 9. Asis, Isa. xlix. 26; Joel i. 5. Sobe, Isa. i. 22.
Mesec, Psa. lxxv. 8. All intoxicate when used too freely.

Egyptians honoured Osiris as inventor of the vintage ; Greeks, Bacchus ;
Romans, Saturn. Wine kept close in skins soon matures its strength. *Silliman.*

λέγει. The Fathers here dwell on the virtues of *silence.* Many fall through
speech, few or none by silence. *Ambrose.* Humility, Queen of virtues, brings
forth her first-begotten son, *Silence. Bernard.* She had witnessed His miraculous power. *Maldonatus.* John calls this the first miracle. *D. Brown.* She
certainly saw Him the *subject* of several splendid miracles. *Author.* To gratify
her vanity. *Chrysostom.* Slightest possible touch of pure, womanly, motherly
complacency to see her son honoured. *Stier.* Eagerness to see His power.
D. Brown. Satisfied of His Messiahship. *Lücke.* No reference to His working a miracle. *Luthardt.*

μήτηρ. Social interviews led many to expect a miracle. *P. Anton.* " So
good and gracious is my son, I need only name to Him our need." *Luther.*
With all her faith and humility, still He was displeased. *Lampe.* She desired
a miracle. *Maldonatus, Tholuck.* Went for counsel. *Cocceius, Lücke.* Desired
Him to perform a miracle, but not from experience. *Alford.* Hint for Him
and disciples to depart. *Bengel.* He should now give His wedding present.
Stier. She knew from His leaving His trade and going abroad, the time was
near. *Taylor.* Desires Jesus to excuse the want. *Henry.* Improves the time
by instruction. *Calvin.*

οὐκ ἔχουσιν. A hint that He should purchase additional wine. *Meyer.*
Miracle occurred the same day our Lord arrived. *Lücke, Wordsworth.* A
single feast alluded to. *Ellicott.* She desired Him to borrow. *Kuinoel.* According to human wisdom, Jerusalem should have witnessed His first miracle.
Tholuck.

---

4. Jesus saith unto her, Woman, what have I to do with thee ? mine hour
is not yet come.

Woman. She as mother claimed a miracle. He answers,
" Woman."

So far from harshness, the address has something solemn in it.

It does not imply she bears the relation of *woman* to *God*, but that
of a *mother* to a *son*.

His period of subjection was ended for ever.   Luke ii. 51.

This was not a question between Mary and her son, but between
God and His Son.

At the age of twelve He protested against " *thy father* " with a
" My Father ! "

His reproof a refusal to perform a miracle on *the ground* of the request.

It implied that He might work a miracle, but it could never be at her bidding, founded on *her relation* to Him.

No longer before the world is He to be known as *Mary's son ;* His relations henceforth are with the ETERNAL GOD.

" He lifted up His eyes, and said, FATHER, I THANK THEE." John xi. 41.

A Bible reader would as soon think of an angel calling a *man* Father as our Lord calling any *created* being FATHER !

Once He pointed to His apostles, saying, " Behold my mother," &c.

On the cross He said to John, " Behold *thy* mother." But He never, so far as recorded, said, " My Mother."

Divine wisdom evidently would not permit a phrase which blind Superstition has so terribly abused among millions of Papists.

No shade of disrespect belonged to the term " Woman " at that day.

He used it on the cross to Mary while providing for her a home. John xix. 26.

Used kindly to Mary Magdalene. John xx. 15. Used for *mother*. Isa. xlv. 10.

She clearly had not yet learned her exact relation to her *exalted* SON.

He takes this first occasion to teach her it, once for all.

He thus disengages Himself from every mere human relation. Luke xi. 27, 28.

His human nature was " a holy thing." Luke i. 35. Eminently so from its union with Deity.

The Saviour assumed human *nature*, not a human *person*.

The *woman*, having borne Him as a *virgin*, became Joseph's *wife* and *widow*.

He who was not Joseph's son, but the Son of God, shows that He deems Himself no longer *the son of Mary*. Matt. xii. 48—50.

That Mary can interfere with Him in heaven is an idolatrous assumption of the superstitious devotees of Rome.

On the cross, while burdened with " the sin of the world," He proves His loving interest in her by providing her with a *son* and a *home*.

To do with thee. In officiously interfering with Him, she is gently but decidedly repelled.

That nature which could work miracles was not born of her.

The least rebuke implies that He had been unreasonably spoken to.

" Only as the SUPREME GOD can I do such a thing as thou askest."

" For thirty years have I been subject to thee, but I AM THY GOD."
" Thy state of heart rather *impedes* the manifestation of My glory "
" Thou shouldst, in quiet resignation, have waited for it."
Yet we doubt not His manner must have been inimitably tender.
She never used her parental authority again, so far as we read.
Not even on earth can she mingle with His mighty doings.
How much less on the mediatorial throne, as Papists profanely
    teach !
As God He had no mother ; none must claim that relation.
He partook of her flesh and its infirmity to bear the curse of sin.
But the miracle was by the power of *Divinity*, not by the weakness
    of *humanity*.
" In My official duties it is for thee to forget that thou art My
    mother."
He is not to be at her beck whenever she is pleased to call.
In the very nature of the formula a censure is implied.
He who never turned a suppliant away, seems to frown on her who
    bare Him.
Mine hour. While it proves His mother expected a real miracle,
    it is by no means certain what was His meaning.
His HOUR. The time selected by Himself to begin to act as
    Messiah.
It proves that all He said and did was *predetermined.*
His words have the perfect clearness of an *Alpine lake,* with an
    unfathomable depth of meaning.
A world-breadth comprehensiveness, and always hint a something
    more profound.
They ever ring in our inner being, like a voice from a higher
    world. *Ullmann.*
Having received the Spirit without measure, His acts were to be
    regulated by HIS FATHER'S BUSINESS.
This stern word to one who, of all the world, knew Him best, was a
    censure, rather than a *rebuke.*
She claimed nothing above the strong faith of one praying.
Thus if our prayers are not answered we should remember God is
    not bound to regard us.
His own time when He will grant any favour is fixed. Ecc. iii. 1.
His gentle reproof for assuming authority or showing unreason-
    able haste does not lessen her faith as to His performing a
    miracle.
At the appointed time want on earth will cease in universal plenty.

He hints that her request, nevertheless, shall not be neglected.

Mary's words to the servants show she thus understood Him.

He consecrates with His foot-prints the path described, Deut. xxxiii. 9.

Mine hour, &c.—1. To hear petitions of human selfishness. 2. To listen to the murmurings of dissatisfied, unhumbled spirits. 3. To hear forced prayer. 4. To regard prayers screamed at Him.

He will resist all, even the appearance of human dictation.

Rome strikes her out of the catalogue of *sinners* by the miserable dogma of the " *immaculate conception.*"

Though to a child parental power is the greatest on earth, it ceases when God's word and work begin.

Mine hour, notes the entrance of a crisis. John xvi. 21 ; vii. 30 ; xiii. 1.

Not come. He declined her jurisdiction, but grants her request.

He repeats this same word to His brethren when going up to the feast. John vii. 6.

"They sought to take Him. but His hour was not yet come." John vii. 30 ; viii. 20.

The error common to His disciples His mother also participated in.

They mixed up an element of earthly kingship with the heavenly kingdom.

An hour to bear the burden of the curse and an hour for glory. Isa. xvii. 1 ; John xii. 27.

The time when the better wine of a more glorious banquet shall be drunk *new.*

As surely as the hour of suffering, so surely did the hour of glory come.

Delays of mercy are not to be interpreted as *denials* of prayer.

Providence is to be met unconditionally, obediently, resignedly, joyfully.

The most simple sayings of Christ reach through time and eternity.

Come. It *would* never have come at all unless her heart had changed.

But the moment all is right, help bursts in like an overflowing stream.

He delayed going to Bethany until Lazarus was dead four days, and now He delays until the exhaustion is complete.

She felt assured that it would come in time, if it did not then come *publicly.*

The miracle was wrought *privately*, none but servants being present,
and even they did not *see* the change wrought.
Not until they drew out the wine did they discover the miracle.
So privately that the three Evangelists, Matthew, Mark, and Luke,
have taken no notice of it in their records.
Neither ruler, host, nor guest knew of it until it was *finished*.
It *confirmed* the disciples of the inner circle in their faith. Ver. 11.
It showed forth His glory in their increased devotion.

λέγει. Eight volumes have been written on this answer. *Prescott.*
Τί ἐμοί. That is my concern, not thine, or, leave that to me, thou troubled, tender-hearted one. *Mann, Ebrard.* What is that to me and thee? *Douay Version.* Being strangers here. *Rhemish* notes. A wilful mistranslation. *Fulke.* What have I in common with thee? *Stier, Prescott.* The moment God's will is concerned. *Luther.* A perpetual warning against superstitious regard of Mary. Her glory must never obscure His. *Calvin.* Romanist authors vindicate her from all wrong. *Bossuet.* What does it concern us that there *is* no wine? *Trench.* Higher interests of His kingdom decided His course. *Bernard.* Indignation at interruption. *Schleusner.* Modified by the tone of voice. *Kuinoel.* Thy thought and mine different. *Bengel.* Obtrude not thyself in my concerns. *Tholuck.* What have I, as God, to do with thee, a woman? *Wordsworth.* The language of gentle rebuke. *Law, Pearce, Newcombe, Doddridge.*
γύναι. In ancient languages used to females of the first rank. *Bloomfield.* Greeks accustomed thus to address their queens: may be rendered, "my Beloved." *Tittmann.* Augustus thus addressed Cleopatra. *Dion Cassius.* Gentlewoman. *Lange.* An opinion unsupported. *Stier.* "Mother." *Sumner.* γύναι, no synonym in Latin or German language. *Bengel.* Nor in the English. *Author.* Papal Rome prays, "Holy Mother of God, Refuge of Sinners, Queen of Heaven, of Angels, of Patriarchs, of Prophets, of Apostles, of Martyrs, of Confessors, of Virgins, of all Saints, PRAY FOR US." Endorsed by *Bishop Walsh, Wolverhampton,* "Garden of the Soul," p. 317, London, 1839. In three pages there are 103 prayers to Mary, and but two to the Saviour.
ὥρα. His own time as determined by the Father. *Lange.* The seasonable time for performing the miracle, i.e. when the wine was entirely gone. *Rosenmüller.* Is not my hour come of deliverance from your authority? *Gregory Nyssen.* Whole doctrine of Divine delays herein contained. *Ber. Bib.* Delay was neither of indolence nor carelessness: in due time He would attend to it. *Calvin.* He would work wonders when *unsought. Augustine.* The manifestation of His glory. *Trench.* The great marriage feast in the kingdom of God. *Stier.* John vii. 6. Hour of human infirmity on the cross. *Wordsworth.* ὥρα fixed for showing His glory, ver. 11. *Lücke.*

---

5. His mother saith unto the servants, Whatsoever he saith unto you, do it.

Mother. She made no reply to Him. Evidence of faith and humility.

It is best to *need* no reproofs of Christ : next best to be *meek* under them.

Like Abraham, " against hope " she " believed in hope." Rom. iv. 18 ; Psa. lxii. 5.

Saith. Something of the incident is omitted, since she is thus encouraged. *Alford.*

This is not a right estimate of her knowledge of all the miracles of His birth, and does injustice to her *inspired faith* in the RE-DEEMER.

Humbled, her faith forms the *precious link* between the denial and the granting of her prayer.

The most energetic faith draws encouragement out of rebuke. Matt. xv. 27.

Her faith catches at a little word ($ο\mathring{v}πω$, " *not yet* ") and infers it *will* come.

Her *impatience* stayed the wonder-working power of the Almighty.

Yet in Mary we see the sublime submission which knows not, but only *trusts.*

When " *No* " meets the ear, He often whispers " *Yes* " to the heart.

The Lord *resigns Himself to be vanquished* by the *violence* of faith.

" Let me go, for the morning breaketh ; " and yet the Angel was at that *very moment* kindling Jacob's faith and girding him to perseverance for the *victory.*

Servants. Gr. *deacons.* The word represents a servant in active toil. Eph. iii. 7.

Not another word to her son, though publicly reproved by Him.

"Once have I spoken ; but I will not answer." Job xl. 5 ; Psa. xxxix. 9.

Jonah, rebuked by Jehovah, closes his prophecy in *silence.*

Let God come into the heart, and the storm of passion is hushed.

There is a silence of *revenge.* When Saul noted the insult to his crown.

Of *force.* Philip II. when God scattered and destroyed his invincible armada at sea.

A *sullen* silence. Ahab when failing to purchase Naboth's vineyard.

A *despairing* silence : a dying Pope, shown the crucifix, "I have too often *sold the cross.*"

A *stoical* silence. Codrus warmed his hands at the flames of his burning home.

Whatsoever.   Neither does the hour come (*how much like God!*) until Mary testifies her faith and subjection.

She neither appoints time, nor manner, nor place, nor measure, nor person, nor name, leaving Him to do as He pleases.

" Speak, Lord, thy servant heareth. " Samuel a type of all Christians.

Jesuits, those fierce tyrants, demand just what God demands.

Christian discipleship obeys *implicitly*, not *blindly*, but in *love*.

This word is one of unconditional faith in her son's Divine power.

Pharaoh said to the Egyptians, " Go to Joseph ; what he saith to you, do." Gen. xli. 55.

No one great virtue comes single : those "that be her fellows will bear her company."

If she had not expected a *miracle* what mean these words ?

It would be a heartless judgment to suppose that she desires Him to *prove* His mission.

Do it.   Through their obedience our Lord will show His power.

He appeared with a drawn *sword* to Joshua, as Captain of the Lord's host.   Josh v. 13.

He appeared in a *flame* of *fire* to Manoah.   Judg. xiii. 20—22.

He appeared in a *tempest* to the disciples.   Matt. xiv. 24—27 ; Mark vi. 48.

He appeared at the door of the *tomb* to the angels and to Mary Magdalene.   John xx. 11—18.

He appears in the *wine*, at a wedding feast, during a time of innocent delight.

"Lo, I am with you alway, even unto the end of the world."   Matt. xxviii. 20.

" For He hath said, I will never leave thee, nor forsake thee."   Heb. xiii. 5.

Here reason lies in a small room, obedience in less.

Do it.   Most holy and excellent counsel.   Angels alone *do it.*

1. Without merit we rest on His sovereign grace :—" What have I to do with thee ? "

2. Realizing our deep necessity :—"They have no wine."

3. Patience, submission, and obedience.   Mary was submissive :— " Do it."

A model prayer :—

1. She left to the Lord His own *pleasure* to do it or not.

2. She left to His sovereign pleasure His *own way* of doing it.

3. She left to Him to do it in His own *time.*

4. She left to His own choice *what* to do.

As Messiah He reproved her, as a son He complied with her request.

διάκονος, the servant in activity. δοῦλος, the same in his servile relations.
θεράπων, one in voluntary servitude, Matt. xxii. 2—14. ὑπηρέτης, a rower
on a war galley, distinguished from a soldier. *Trench.* Hereafter we may
learn where our Lord had given her a previous hint: her fault was a rash
hastening of His fixed purpose. *Alford.* Not sustained by the record. *Author.*
λέγη. His motive a remedy for the shame of the humble host, when the Son
of God was guest. *Hengst.* This was the *result.* But the *cause* was ground
for the *faith* and *glory* of His *Church.* Our Lord's miracles have ever some
great principle underlying them. *Author.*

---

6. And there were set there six water-pots of stone, after the manner of the
purifying of the Jews, containing two or three firkins apiece.

Six water-pots, or amphoræ, of stone, earthenware, copper, silver,
or gold.

Those found in Pompeii, 1800 years old, have two handles, stand
about 3 feet high, and contain some 12 gallons each.

Springs or wells being very rare in the East, water had to be *carried,* as it is now, throughout Palestine and Egypt.

Infidels cavil at the amount, but that precludes all *collusion.*

The bountiful Giver here, as in autumn, pours forth an abundance, but who dare charge the Holy One with placing temptation before men by the vine or the corn yielding in pro-
fusion ?

Who dare charge the Lord with encouraging *surfeiting* by the
divine abundance of bread for the 5000 ? John vi. 13.

The wedding may have been at the house of Cleopas, with our
Lord, and Mary, the mother of Jesus, Zacharias, Simeon, and
such like believers as guests.

Scoffers, therefore, have no right to enter so sacred a circle. Mark
v. 40.

Some refuse His bounty to save the trouble of seeking the grace.
Alford.

The manner. See on John i. 25, 26. This intimates that John
wrote at a distance from Judea.

Purifying. See on John iii. 25. Mahometans are required to
wash five times each day before their stated prayers.

When water cannot be had conveniently, *sand* is used.

Aaron and his sons were purified by washing before putting on
   priests' robes.   Lev. viii. 6.
Israelites commanded to wash raiment and person before receiving
   the law.   Ex. xix. 10—15.
All priests washed before offering sacrifice on pain of death.   Ex.
   xxx. 17—21.
Ministers in the primitive age all washed their hands before com-
   munion.
Levitical law notes eleven kinds of pollution needing purification;
   touching a leper, a dead body, a slain animal, &c.   Lev.
   xii.—xiv.
"I will wash my hands in innocency: so will I compass thine
   altar."   Psa. xxvi. 6.
Pilate is thus seen washing his hands according to Greek and
   Roman custom.   Matt. xxvii. 24.   (See on John i. 25.)
Jews, in our Lord's time, washed before entering their own house
   and before eating.   Mark vii. 1—5.
Cups not easily cleansed were broken.   A house infected with
   leprosy to be taken down and all removed.
Two or three.   The evangelist nicely indicates between two and
   three firkins.
Firkins.   If the Jewish "bath," a measure containing about seven
   and a half gallons.
If in Attic measure, it held nine and a half gallons.
Each of these huge water-jars, then, must have held some 20 gal-
   lons.
Six, one for our Saviour and each guest that came with Him.
A lasting memorial of strangers entertained proving angels.   Heb.
   xiii. 2.
Our Lord was about to pour into the six apostles the wine of the
   gospel, and they would present in turn, to each guest at the
   marriage supper of the Lamb, the good wine of the kingdom.
   Matt. ix. 17 ; Rev. xix. 9.
An humble family was furnished with many large vessels for purifying, as if sin could be washed away by cleansing the skin !
" Purge me with hyssop, and I shall be clean: wash me, and I shall
   be whiter than snow."   Psa. li. 7.
Superstition, full of the spirit of the world, is pompous and ambitious.
These huge vessels at hand and not brought, shows there was no
   premeditated plan.

Great want of water in the East renders large supplies necessary for crowds of guests at feasts.

The number of *uninvited* ones was in proportion to the greatness of the giver.

Jews. Their history and character, see on John i. 19. About 2,000,000 in Europe, 700,000 in Asia, 500,000 in Africa, 2,000,000 in America.

ὑδρίαι. "I saw stone jars, large and massive, lying about, not regarded as antiquities by the people, with whose original use they were unacquainted." *Ed. Clarke.* Broader than deep. κείμεναι, "lying." *Bengel.*

ἔξ, enough to supply 175 men and as many women, requiring 100 sheep for proportionate meals. *Bengel.*

καθαρισμὸν. Those admitted to the Eleusinian mysteries were purified by bathing. *Smith's Dict.* Persons were fumigated with sulphur. *Dollinger.* Greeks had ideas of moral uncleanness. *Thucydides.* A custom of human origin among the Jews. *Ford.* He forgets scores of passages in the Pentateuch. *Author.* Egyptian priests bathed every third day. *Herodotus.* Three times each day. *Porphyry.* Ebion tried to bring this into the Church. But its origin is traced to *Juvenal*, 6th sat. *Baronius.* μετρητὰς. When used for a Jewish bath, about 7½ gallons; if Attic, 9½ gal. *D. Brown.* 8¾ gal. *Robinson.* 126 gal. *Alford.* From 90 to 135 gal. *Hengstenberg.* About 135 gal. *Wordsworth.* All the water not made wine. *Lücke.* A seeming argument against frugality. Answer—Our sins alone abuse His rich blessings. *Calvin.* The surplus would maintain His disciples some days. *Lampe.* A fine marriage-gift to the humble pair. *Meyer.*

---

7. Jesus saith unto them, Fill the waterpots with water. And they filled them up to the brim.

Fill. How unpromising every step towards getting the wine ! Let us ever distrust our judgment when God is speaking. "Hath He said, and shall He not do it?" Num. xxiii. 19.

> " Blind unbelief is sure to err,
> And scan His work in vain :
> God is His own interpreter,
> And He will make it plain." *Cowper.*

Obedience ever inherits a blessing under our Divine Master. 1 Sam. xv. 22.

No small gifts from great hands. James i. 5.

They might have had good cheer with water only, but boundless grace supplies not only our wants, but our superfluities.

He had not only the guests, but the bridal party to think of, who
were exposed to shame, because of the failure of the wine.

Our Lord notes the grace and beauty of life, as well as its sterner
realities.

If He thus feasts His friends here, what a banquet will He spread
above !

Could not He have made bread out of stones, as well as wine out
of water ?

Yet in the desert He suffered hunger, while making our cup overflow.

He does all for love, but nothing, *absolutely nothing*, at the instance
of Satan.

Even in His miracles of CREATION our Lord used something as a
basis.

Bread must have bread. John vi. 11.   Wine must have water.

This basis of water and loaves makes the miracle more easily
comprehended by finite minds.

We, in our weakness, cannot grasp the mode of creating a thing
from nothing.

Hence He takes a diseased body for a groundwork of perfect
health.

He takes a corpse, and summons back the spirit to quicken it.

Some see in these two glorious miracles the elements of bread and
wine consecrated through all coming time to the *two* sacraments.

He gives in superfluity : " The river of God is full of water."   Psa.
lxv. 9.

Infidels object that an impulse was thus given to *luxury.*

Providence, sending a good vintage, might as well be blamed.

A trial of our sobriety is moderation amid abundance.

" I have learned to be full and to be hungry."   Phil. iv. 12.

He came upon earth and found the law empty, and hearts void.

He poured the true wine of His kingdom into the vessels of earth.

He came to teach no new doctrine, but to quicken the old.

He is the true PLEROMA, or " fulness," of the promises of the old
covenant.   Col. i. 19.

He intends the greatness of the miracle shall supply a *dowry.*

Thus Elijah's gift ceased not until vessels were *wanting* to contain
the oil.

The smitten rock flowed on, until its streams met the Jordan.

The answer to Abraham's prayer ceased not till he ceased asking.

Happy is that wedding where Christ is the guest, for they who "marry in the Lord" cannot marry *without* Him. 1 Cor. vii. 39.

Filled. The vessels were so large, that they could not carry them to the fountain.

They were used by the ancients instead of *barrels* as among us.

They might have said, "We want wine ; why bring water ? "

Not flagons of wine to the tables, but pails of water to the vessels.

One firkin would have sufficed for all the wants of the *guests*.

Divine goodness regards not so much our need as His *boundless fulness*.

Same bounty that provides so much, secures its *excellence* also.

He can do nothing without indicating exquisite *perfection*.

Even His *rods* of discipline bear the *workmanship* of a *divine hand*.

While the water flows in the firkins His eye beholds them filling with the blood of the grape.

Note : Our Lord touches nothing. The same *silent, omnipotent will*, working daily in our gardens and vineyards, was here working in the same way. The miracle was not more mysterious than that which occurs yearly in the processes of nature.

Because we witness it and name it, we THINK we *understand it*.

As He *lived in the promises* which He had Himself inspired while redeeming the world, so His stupendous miracles are in the line of His *daily Providence*.

Brim. So that any one might see first the water, then the wine.

This augments the miracle : the possibility of deception excluded.

These minute circumstances are most wisely written :—

1. They establish a wide interval between true and false miracles.
2. They impress the mind with the reality of the Divine work.
3. They prove the stupendous nature of this act of the Son of God.

The servants, not the disciples, are directed to fill the vessels.

Γεμίσατε. A Divine Being could have drawn wine from empty waterpots. *Paulus.* Neither piping nor dancing will satisfy. Even Horace, a heathen, rebukes this German sceptic. *Author.*

---

8. And he saith unto them, Draw out now, and bear unto the governor of the feast. And they bare it.

Saith unto them. The servants, who are gazing on the Lord, wondering what will come next.

Draw out. The inconsistency of infidels·hath a melancholy madness in it.

They try to discredit this great miracle, although they find a *blade* of grass at their feet, as *utterly beyond their comprehension* as the *eternity of Jehovah.*

Romish priests pretend that in the *mass* a miraculous change occurs.

A wonder of Divine forbearance that this *lie* is *so often enacted under such solemn circumstances !*

He need not now bear witness of Himself, for His *work* testifies.

Love is reflected from every angle of His life, and no motion of hand or foot is seen save of His own *will.* 2 Kings v. 11.

Sometimes He uses a sigh, sometimes a tear for others' sake. John xi. 33 ; Luke xix. 41.

This is not a solitary example of our Lord conforming kindly to human customs.

He had the attributes of the supreme Godhead and perfect humanity.

Yet He never once, for 33 years, *violated the proprieties of either.*

With all human goodness He ever lived and moved as God !

" He bare our infirmities." He slept, rested, laboured, ate, drank, and died as *man.*

Here He exercises His Divine power to promote innocent social enjoyment.

" Religion does not banish mirth, but moderates and sets rules to it." *Herbert.*

" Proper recreations recruit mind and body for renewed application to the serious business of life." *Jebb.*

These guests, like our Lord's disciples, must have shared the spirit of the friends of the Lord of Heaven, else *He had never been there.*

Filling the heart all day with *earth,* one cannot draw out *heaven* at night.

The old and the new wine came from the same vineyard.

The Messiah *promised* in the Old Test., and *incarnate* in the New, is the same Redeemer.

Now. Indicates the moment of the wondrous change being complete.

" The *conscious* water saw its Lord and blushed." *Milton.*

Note the Divine *reticence.* Not a word describing the miraculous change which is silently presupposed.

It took place outside, not inside, the hall, for it was not known by the bridegroom, nor by the governor.

Their surprise and ignorance prove the change was as *silent as the rising of the sun.*

The miracle appears covered by a transparent veil, so that we can only conjecture whether *all* the water had changed to wine.

Not a syllable is recorded as to the impression made on the guests, nor even on Mary herself.

The writer seems *as impassive as an angel.* Do men write history after this fashion ?

On the lake, the elements in a storm hear and obey His Almighty voice.

Here in these vessels, the tasteless element obeys, and becomes wine.

The same simple but mysterious grandeur is seen in *nature.*

Every year a similar miracle is *secretly* and *sublimely* wrought in silence.

He pours showers from the clouds, and He fills clusters from those showers *changed into wine.*

Bear. The servants knew the reality of the miracle ; the governor attested the excellence of the wine.

Mark there was *no* command, nor was there a *prayer* that it might be changed : *He simply* WILLED ITS *change.*

Governor. Among the Greeks and Jews he first blessed the wine.

How many baptized ones neglect any act of recognition !

Too many ignore all idea of a *Giver*, and seem to *stumble on* their daily mercies.

He first tested the wine, then sent it round to all the guests.

How the Lord gracefully gives " honour to whom honour," &c., thus shaming pedants. Rom. xiii. 7.

Although not the master of the feast, He surely was its best benefactor.

He complies with custom, and lets the ruler discharge his office of tasting the food.

Feast. For articles of food used by the ancients, see on John iv. 31.

Each guest was followed by a footman, who received the presents for his master.

Parasites followed the rich man to clear the way, and to adjust his raiment.

Usually females were not invited, or, if so, were feasted in another room.

Hands and beards of males, and tresses of female guests, were perfumed by female slaves.

Incense was offered on an altar in the festal hall to the gods.

Even heathen could say, Where I have a *table* the gods shall have *an altar.*

Greeks esteemed such a *feast* in the light of a *sacrifice.*   *Theocritus.*

Romans always began their great annual *feast* by *sacrificing* to the gods.

Seldom did an ancient general presume to begin a battle without a *sacrifice.*

Alexander feasted 400 officers in seats of wrought silver.

Purple carpets were provided for all, and white garments.

Having poured out a libation to the gods, the feast ended.

A supper of Lucullus in Apollo's Hall cost 5000 drachmæ, equal to $20,000 in our day.

30,000 festal garments for guests hung in the wardrobe of his palace.

Greeks would not profane the *sanctity* of their table by idle converse.

Emperor Severus used to *read* during his *family meal.*

Instead of being invited to card-playing, guests were invited to read.

Scythians had their bow-strings made to sound during their feasts, lest they should become enfeebled by pleasure.

22,000 tables were spread by Cæsar for the Romans after a victory.

Coronation dinner of Edward III. cost £200,000 in gold.

Ἀυτλήσατε. "Numen convivæ, presens agnoscite numen Lympha pudica *Deum* vidit, et *erubuit.*" *Crashaw,* 1634. This thought has been attributed to *Milton,* a contemporary of *Crashaw.* The moment of the miracle is understood, not expressed. *Lücke, De Wette.*

ἀρχιτρικλίνῳ. *Triclinium,* a room with three κλίναις, or sets of cushions. The person who presided over this, and arranged the feast called by the Romans *triclinarches. Tholuck.* One who superintends the tables, and preserves order. *Athenæus.* Convivii Magister, Modimperator. *Varro.* Arbiter bibendi. *Horace.* Dictator. *Plautus.* Greeks called them Sumposiarchs. Romans, Dictators. *Trapp.* His duty was to regulate the wine taken, and prevent all inebriation. *Theophylact.* A head servant. *Lampe.* No authority for this opinion, and the etymology of the word against it. Besides, his words to the bridegroom are not those of a servant, but an equal; he must have been one of the guests. *Wordsworth.* A person chosen from the priests. *Jer. Taylor.*

Chosen from the guests. *Alford.* Chosen by lot. *Horace.* Servants, often young female slaves, mixed the wine. Athenian law limited the number of guests to 30. *Athenæus.* Females excluded. *Cor. Nep.*

---

9. When the ruler of the feast had tasted the water that was made wine, and knew not whence it was : (but the servants which drew the water knew ;) the governor of the feast called the bridegroom.

Ruler. Gr. *chief of three couches.* In our Lord's day guests reclined.

Romans, Greeks, and Jews followed the custom of the Persians.

Tables formed three sides of a square. In the open space in the centre servants waited on guests.

Usual number of guests nine, the number of the Muses.

Sometimes, however, as many as 13, as at the Lord's last meal.

To recline on the bosom of the host the privilege of the favourite guest. Luke xvi. 22 ; John xiii. 23.

Couches of Romans after Punic war were mattresses stuffed with rushes.

In Tiberius' time costly *woods* and *tortoise-shell* were used to veneer couches.

Roman tables made of *citron* wood from Mauritania, inlaid with *gold and ivory.*

Feast. The time for the banquet was between 5 and 6 P.M.

Company invited some time previous to the banquet by cards.

A second and verbal invitation announced the feast ready. Matt. xxii. 3.

Masters of families slew their own meat, and kings and princes in early ages cooked their own simple meals. Gen. xxvii. 31.

Each hero used a table for himself, and a *sword* for his carving-knife. *Homer.*

Warm climates required animal food to be eaten promptly. Hence search was made in the highways for guests, to use up the meat. Matt. xxii. 9.

Pledging to *accept* the invitation, then *declining*, was an *insult* to the host.

Servants stood at one door and received the guests with their invitations.

In the East great crowds hover around with familiar impatience.

Guests were offered water for washing, and perfumes for anointing.

Perfumed waters were sprinkled over them during the banquet.

A gay-coloured and richly-embroidered robe was offered each guest. Rev. iii. 4, 5.

Jews, Greeks, and Romans all ate with their *fingers*, folding the wafer-like bread, and dipping it in the sop before eating.

Meat was cut into small pieces and put into broth, as Gideon gave the angel. Judg. vi. 19.

To *give the sop* to a guest was an oriental act of *delicate friendship*. John xiii. 26.

Two-thirds of the table covered ; the other left bare for dishes and food.

The wine-cup, by courtesy, was filled to running over. Psa. xxiii. 5.

Hands soiled by food cleaned by soft part of *bread* and dropped for dogs. Matt. xv. 27.

Monks of St Swithin complained to Henry II. that three out of 13 daily dishes had been taken away.

Canterbury monks had 17 dishes daily, besides their dessert.

The fine wines of oriental monasteries have for ages been noted.

Guests were crowned with garlands given to them by the host.

Wine spiced was drunk, always, however, preceded by a libation to the gods. Prov. ix. 2.

Jews poured out some blood before God on slaying each animal.

Marriage, the birth of a son, weaning, birth-days, sheep-shearing, return of friends, were the occasions of feasts.

Banquet lasted from one to fourteen days. Portions sent to friends. Neh. viii. 10 ; Esther ix. 17—22.

Pilgrims should use pleasures as rations, not their chief good.

Christianity, though enjoining sobriety, is no melancholy thing.

Believers should not regard the supercilious despisers of God's blessings. 1 Tim. iv. 3, 5.

Religion does not draw water from every desert-rock in this world, nor does it sweeten the bitter streams of every Marah.

It does not find manna in every wilderness, nor create a cloudy pillar in every desert.

Neither can we hope to find all the waters of earth changed to the wine of heaven.

We should ever infuse a bunch of myrrh into our festive goblet.

" Remembering the days of darkness, for they are many." Eccl. xi. 8.

Tasted. Romish priests, knowing that persons could taste wine as wine, cunningly withhold wine at the mass.

Nevertheless the unchanged wafer is a constant educator of every
such participant *in falsehood* at the *communion table.*

The melancholy fruits of such frauds are seen in all countries where
Antichrist " hath his seat."

Water made wine.   A foreshadowing of the Lord's Supper.

Modern infidelity, putting on airs of a pietist, censures the miracle
as encouraging *luxury.*

None but Judas the *traitor* censured the act of Mary at Bethany.

Saints, having a covenant right to the blessings of God, do not
complain.

Neither should they meanly scant themselves, where God has been
liberal.

γεγευημένον. Their minds in a state of ethical ecstasy. *Lange.* Change
magnetic between our Lord and the guests. *J. Fisker, Lange.* Servants had
great faith in Christ. *Lange.* They gave evidence of obedience, but not of
faith. *Author.* Why did not the bridegroom call the servants? *Chrysostom.*
Ans. He never conceived of any miracle. *Author.*

φωνεῖ, not summoned, but hailed him reclining on his couch. *Maldonatus.*

------

10. And saith unto him, Every man at the beginning doth set forth good
wine ; and when men have well drunk, then that which is worse : but thou hast
kept the good wine until now.

Every man.   Custom, or fashion, an invisible tyrant.

The world denounces it with its breath, yet bows to receive the
gilded chains.

Beginning.   Moses's first sign was turning water into *blood.*

Christ's first sign which reveals His glory turns water into *wine.*

Glory of the Law inflicts *wounds ;* glory of the Gospel *heals.*

It was predicted that Shiloh should wash his garments in wine.
Gen. xlix. 11.

Beginning low ends high.   " They that sow in tears shall reap in
joy." Psa. cxxvi. 5.

Evil things here ; good things in eternity.   Luke xvi. 25.

" Heaviness may endure for a night, but joy cometh in the morning." Psa. xxx. 5.

Christ's works commend themselves, though the Author be unknown.

Good wine.   Had a stronger body, richer and higher flavour, than
ordinary.

When our Lord does any work, however minute, it is ever perfect. Gen. i. 31.

The governor's ignorance of the miracle was a warrant for the *excellence* of the wine.

The servants' knowledge warrants the *reality* of the miracle.

In His kingdom *want* vanishes in the *riches* of His boundless love.

A signal of His world-transforming heart-power.

He gives His children to drink of the mysterious fountain of His highest LIFE-POWER.

Christ's miracles add both beauty and value to Nature's fruits.

Their richness ever abides, but Satan's pleasures are bitter, and sting at last.

Satan's delights, sweet at first, become as deadly poison by-and-by.

Blessed Saviour, what wine wilt Thou give to drink in Thy Father's kingdom ! Matt. xxvi. 29.

Well drunk. Gr. *drank freely*. Cant. v. 1.

Ruler of the feast is speaking of the general practice.

His remark has no application to the company then present.

Note how the pleasures of earth pall on the appetite ; the longer they are enjoyed the less pleasure they yield, though we, like the luxurious Greeks, dip golden ladles into our wine.

A warning is needed, " Let not your hearts be overcharged," &c. Luke xxi. 34.

Our mercies, the fruit of Divine bounty, cannot be *abused* without *impiety*.

Believers eat bread before God. Ex. xviii. 12. Sinners feed themselves without fear. Jude 12.

Wine of this world's joys gives its colour first, but bites at last. Prov. xxiii. 32.

Religion has a present joy and a " glory to be revealed." Rom. viii. 18.

The fact of our Lord's miracle is a proof of the sobriety of the guests.

Their perception of the " good wine " an additional proof.

How would infidels exult if they could fix even a solitary stain upon the Redeemer's life.

The abundance of a Christian's goods excites gratitude, not indulgence.

We are to be victorious *in* temptation, as it is impossible we should be exempt from it. 1 Cor. v. 10.

OUR LORD A KING, GAVE AS A KING. James i. 5.

The ruler of the feast notes what was then, and is now seen at some weddings.

But they who imagine our Lord would provide wine for men *intoxicated* will find *difficulties everywhere*, and *inspiration nowhere*.

In the case of such cavillers it is better to attend to the advice, "Answer him not." 2 Kings xviii. 36.

Which is worse. The palate becomes after a while dull, and can not distinguish.

Earth's pleasures resemble the image in Nebuchadnezzar's dream.

Its head was gold, but its material became baser and baser, till it ended in iron and clay. Dan. ii. 31, 33.

Each sin carries a smile on its face, and honey on its tongue, but a lie on its lips.

"In the end it biteth like a serpent, and stingeth like an adder." Prov. xxiii. 32.

Christ reverses all this. It is true He causes tears of repentance, but by-and-by He inspires "strong consolation." Heb. vi. 18.

Thou hast. Returns thanks to the host in his ignorance.

"She did not know I gave her corn and wine." Hos. ii. 8.

Alas! too many are like the horse and ox, who drink of the stream, but care not for the spring.

Until now. God moves by a higher law than man understands. "My thoughts are not," &c.

Man thinks *how* God should act, and often presumes to dictate to his Maker.

Development of Providence and economy of salvation confound all *human* ideas.

God ever astonishes His people by displays of surpassing love.

Sometimes we think God cannot exceed *this* or *that;* but behold He rises higher still.

In the path of life He scatters on our way one gem brighter than another.

We should never imagine we have received the *best* God can give.

Man is sometimes praised for that which comes from the hand of God.

The guests praised the bridegroom ; no higher hand was recognized.

So it is in politics, legislation, science, morals, art, religion.

We stop short in *second* causes, or mistake them for primary ones.

In every advancement in life we should recognize the Divine hand.

As we approach nearer and nearer the eternal throne we shall realize God has always something better in reserve for His children.

In the marriage of the Lamb the features of this feast will be restored.

Around that banqueting table the guests of the KING of KINGS will say: Verily *our Atoning Benefactor has kept the good wine till now.*

The severe brevity of the record is full of footprints of Divinity.

No word of regret from host or guest at the failing of the wine cheer.

Not a syllable of pleasure attending so unexpected a supply.

No surprise of servants, no expression of satisfaction from the company.

No thanks from the bridal pair for the splendid gift.

No hint as to *how* the fact was revealed to them.   All is *utterly unlike human ways and thought.*

The record stands, like an Alpine mountain, in its naked dignity and divine grandeur.

Yet is Christ ever turning water into wine in Christian life.

Ever consecrating and transfiguring by His presence the commonest blessings.

To those who have Christ in heart and home every meal is a Eucharist.

" All this and Jesus too ! "   The words of a pauper over black bread and water.   *Chalmers.*

καλόν. Feelings of the company raised as on Tabor. *De Wette.* Their frame of mind made water *taste as wine. Tholuck.* Required a certain state of mind to enjoy the miracle. *Lange, Dods.* Many may have enjoyed both the *miraculous* bread and wine without either faith or grateful gladness. *Author.* Not nectar, but a divine beverage. *Lange.*

μεθυσθῶσιν. Inebriated. So used in *Odyssey.* Thoroughly soaked. *Homer.* Drunk freely. *Dᴉ Brown.* Infidels, determined to cavil, affirm the quantity *tempted* to drink too much. *Strauss, Bauer.* Temperance is not in the paucity of the supply, but in the restraint of our desires. *Augustine.* No reason here to *press* its ordinary meaning, neither is there any to shrink from it. *Alford.* " When men be dronke." *Cranmer, Tyndale.* " Cum inebriati fuerint." *Vulgate.* " Drunk to the full." *Wickliffe.* The governor did not refer to the inebriating effect, but to the *large* quantity consumed. *Lees, Tholuck.* Drunk sufficiently. *Lampe.* Not excess, but satisfaction. *Hutcheson.* Cheered with drink.

Gesenius. Till the taste is blunted. *Trench.* Superfluities belong to believers if to any; the Church is not quite an almshouse. *Lange.* Excess sometimes disgraced marriage feasts anciently as now. *Cyprian.* Some hosts bring in different wine from that which they drink. *Pliny.* Language of the governor half sportive. *Lücke.* An idle, merry observation. *Maurice.* His remark refers to one day's feast. *Ellicott.*

---

11. This beginning of miracles did Jesus in Cana of Galilee, and manifested forth his glory ; and his disciples believed on him.

Beginning. Parable of the sower the beginning of parables.

This beginning of miracles implies that more would follow.

Miracles the predicted character of Messiah and seals of His doctrine.

Our Lord did nothing to create *surprise or display* His power.

He began His wonders in an obscure village, remote from Jerusalem.

" He sought not honour from men." John v. 41.

How could the sun seek honour from a glow-worm ?

The plain honest Galileans did not oppose Him, as the priests and Rabbis.

He will provide an everlasting banquet for the Church, His bride.

Nothing like this is said of any of the prophets, though mighty in word and deed.

It could not be said of a mere creature without *blasphemy*.

For 30 years God had hid Himself from the world He came to redeem.

His *not* doing a miracle was the greatest of His miracles.

The founder of marriage in Paradise bestows His first miracle on a bridal party.

No other miracle *so prophetic* as inaugurating His future work.

Miracles. See on John ii. 23; iii. 2. Works of God that appear to suspend the ordinary course of nature.

A grain of corn presents a *visible likeness* of a miracle.

Its dying, germinating, springing are all *supernatural*, but repeated so often it is called *natural*.

His miracles, not *isolated* facts, but *integral* parts of His life.

Proved His doctrines to be from God by their character and tendency.

Jesus' miracles were WONDERS OF LOVE for soul and body.

Although miracles surrounded His infancy and baptism, and He

ever had the ability, yet there " was a *hiding* of *His power.*"
Hab. iii. 4.

Miracles the ringing of the great bell of the universe, to call attention to His doctrine. *Foster.*

Miracles reflected in nature. Water is changed into wine, wine
into blood, and blood into milk.

His life a stupendous miracle, a vision of God ; and the Church He
founded a miracle of world-wide lustre.

The *supernatural,* with a Divine Being, becomes of necessity
natural.

Each Divine thought might prove a thunder-bolt of life or death.

With equal power He could extinguish the sun, as easily as wither
a fig-tree.

He restored life to Lazarus ; at creation He kindled a world into
being.

Laws of being are not broken, but resolved into higher laws :
miracle is not creation, but freeing earth from the bonds of
sin.

Apostles anointed with oil ; Christ simply spake, or touched.

He ever concealed and softened the sublimity of His wondrous
acts.

Faith in His power to *forgive sin* a prominent trait in those cured.

His miracles had a double aspect,—works of power and works of
redemption.

The wonder of disciples and guests, as they saw this first miracle,
we can little comprehend.

He who made the vines grow on a thousand hills stood before
them.

He who was older than the earth or sun was at their marriage
feast.

The Creator of men, of angels and of stars, was their *Teacher* and
Friend.

As He changed the *dust* of the ground into a living man (Gen.
ii. 7), so here He changed the Mosaic Law, cold as water,
into gospel grace, which, like wine, is generous, full-flavoured,
and cheering. *Corn. à Lap.*

Jews had a right to ask, " What sign showest Thou ? "

God saw fit to change the order of nature, to prove Moses' call.

He suspended the laws of the universe to give *Joshua* credentials.

And now, to prove the *Divinity* of the *Son of Man,* water becomes
wine.

The order of nature is one long and grand series of miracles.

Grapes in six months are as surprising as wine in six moments.

A hundred-fold harvest is as great a wonder as an increase of bread in a few seconds.

The sensitiveness of the child's ear as mysterious as the instant hearing of one deaf.

The first fish created, or the first grain of wheat created, was as miraculous as the feeding of the 5000, and the one is as profound a mystery as the other.

All the science of earth cannot comprehend the secrets of a single bud ; then why cavil at any of God's works ?

Did. Wrought not by His *hands*, but by His mightier *words*.

They made a stronger appeal than had He, on a given night, created another planet in our system in the presence of a million of spectators.

His glory. Of none but a Divine Being could this be said without blasphemy.

Peter and John simply showed forth the glory of their Master. Acts iii. 6.

His *power.* By His mere word He changed one substance into another.

His *mercy.* He wrought this wonder to supply the want of the poor.

His *truth.* He fulfilled the predictions made 1000 years before.

His *justice.* Seen in punishing the covetousness of the Gadarenes.

Did any heavenly splendour cover the Divine act ?

Did the guests witness any flashings forth of the Deity ? Answer :—

" *We beheld* HIS GLORY, the glory as of the only-begotten of the Father, full of GRACE and TRUTH." John i. 14.

As marriage lies at the foundation of order and progress in His Church, His first miracle sanctions that institution, and guards it by proving His authority over it as OUR LORD.

Romish priests and infidels unite in efforts to stain the glory of God as seen in this institution.

But this miracle has stood, and to the end of the world will stand, as a rebuke of Divine Power and Love to all its foes.

During 30 years our Saviour was hidden from the world, and this miracle was the *breaking through* the fleshly covering.

His glory—1. As the Fountain of Life. 2. As Treasure of the Father's Love. 3. As the Beam of the Father's Light.

Christ's constant work on earth is ennobling all He touches.

Saints are made out of sinners, and angels out of saints.

He makes a paradise out of the cold barren wilderness of this world.

In the humble marriage banquet are the elements of the festal table of heaven. Rev. xix. 9.

A prophecy that His people shall drink new wine with Him in His kingdom. Matt. xxvi. 29.

He will not suffer His host to say, " If there be no wine let them drink water."

He will save him the shame of the exposure that his hospitality was larger than his purse.

No one shall ever regret inviting the Son of God under his roof.

This happy bridegroom knew not that the CREATOR OF ALL THINGS *was his guest.*

How utterly unconscious was he when inviting Jesus, that he was providing instruction and consolation for all family circles to the end of time !

Disciples. Where is the crowd of guests ? Did *they* not witness the sign ?

But *not one* seems to have been led by it, to Christ, as the Messiah.

A terrible comment on the hardness and blindness of the human heart.

Believed. Faith, John i. 7 ; vii. 38. Gr. *thoroughly believed.*

Faith has a definite moment of beginning, but is *not finished,* like Jonah's gourd.

His mother had already believed. John i. 45. His brothers not yet. John vii. 5.

Carnal men looked and longed for *signs,* and *look for them still.*

Without repentance, the only signs for 1800 years have been, " *They are joined to their idols : let them alone."* Hos. iv. 17.

The sign proved HIM to be the SHILOH, and the Shiloh to be the ETERNAL GOD.

Such a miracle begets faith in those in need of Divine aid.

It seemed cold comfort to call for water when wine was needed.

Yet was the wine nearest when the pots were filled with water to the brim.

So Divine help is often nearest when afflictions are at the highest.

When Christ pours water let none be discouraged, for what the water so will the wine be ; what the crosses, such the comforts. Psa. xc. 15.

178 / Gospel of John

Though succour be delayed it will be *timely*, abundant, and glorifying to God.

τὴν cancelled. *Tisch.*, *Alford.* Retained. *Cod. Sin.*
ἀρχὴν. Miracles ascribed to Him in youth, and in Egypt, are prophetically
excluded. The first in which He showed His glory. *Maldonatus.* Star of the
Magi the first; Spirit at the Baptism the second, and this the third Epiphany.
Ferus. The beginning of *public* miracles. *Chrysostom.* John's design seems
to have been to sweep away all unreal ideas about our Lord, seen in Docetic
books. *Trench.* Excludes as unworthy of credit all the Apocryphal miracles.
Alford.
σημείων. Historic reality. *Lange.* Has allegorical significations. *Dods.*
This word and the following are all used to characterize the supernatural works
wrought by our Lord in the days of His flesh, viz. τέρας, Acts ii. 22; John iv. 48;
δύναμις, Mark vi. 2; Acts ii. 22; ἔνδοξον, Luke xiii. 17; παράδοξον, Luke
v. 26; θαυμάσιον, Matt. xxi. 15; while the first three, by far the most usual,
are employed to denote the supernatural works wrought in the power of Christ
by His Apostles (2 Cor. xii. 12). Among all the names the miracles bear
their ethical end and purpose comes out in σημεῖον with the most distinctness.
It ought always to be translated " sign," for it is a kind of finger-post of God ;
valuable not so much for what it is as that which it indicates. *Trench.*
Miracles exceed the laws of nature known to us. *Spinoza.* But with God they
are nature. *Author.* The conflict of Moses was not with Magi, or the king,
but with the power of Satan underlying their deeds. *Calvin, Hengst., Arnold.*
Jews charged our Lord with collusion with Satan, Matt. xii. 24. Christ as
God incarnate made miracle natural. *Augustine, Young* (Christ of History).
Miracles performed by Christ through the Father. *J. Müller.* Simple
omnipotence of Christ. *Neander, Ullmann.* Spirit the agent. *Dods.* Canaanite
mother an *electrical* conductor of health to the daughter. *Lange* (Life of Jesus).
Sometimes the Lord inquired into the symptoms of the disease. *Ewald.* 40
definitions of a miracle are given by *Alexander* (Christ and Christianity).
Had He emptied the amphoræ He would have rejected salvation by the O. T.
Augustine.
ἐφανέρωσε, equivalent to—in order that He, &c. *Calvin.* Only a prelude to
the greater going forth of His Divine power. *Lampe.* A hastening of natural
process. *Olshausen, Hase.* The miracle made water taste as wine to the guests
in ecstasy of mind. *Neander, Lange* (Life of Jesus). This miracle and that
of the loaves prophecies of the Lord's Supper. *Irenæus.* Of the marriage
supper above. *Hoffmann.* Wine of the higher Messianic glory. *Erasmus,
Luthardt.*
δόξαν. Had Christ a plan? Yes. *Rheinardt, Neander.* He had not.
Ullmann. Discussed with an unbecoming freedom. *Ellicott.* He certainly
had a very definite plan, and one that embraces all things. *Author.* We infer
all living processes have their first power in Him. This belief carries us to
great heights and depths. But it gives *solemnity* to the *investigations of science,*
and forbids trifling. *Maurice.*

---

12. After this he went down to Capernaum, he, and his mother, and his
brethren, and his disciples : and they continued there not many days.

Went down. Cana stood on the hilly part of Judea.

Capernaum. *Village of Nahum* on the western shore of the Sea of Galilee.

The exact site of Chorazin, Bethsaida, and Capernaum now *unknown*.

The ruins at Tell Hum contain remains of a marble church. Also a splendid ruin 105 feet long and 85 feet broad. Pillars single and double with elaborate Corinthian capitals, architraves, and pedestals. Door-posts 9 feet long, and $4\frac{1}{2}$ wide. These ruins extend half a mile along the shore, and as far back.

" Exalted to heaven," had reference to privileges, not situation. Matt. xi. 23.

Called a city, Mark i. 33. Had its own synagogue, built by a Roman centurion, in which Jesus taught. Luke vii. 5 ; John vi. 59.

Capernaum had also a garrison and custom-house.

Here He chose Matthew, Matt. ix. 9 ; healed the centurion's servant, Luke vii. 1, and Simon's wife's mother, Mark i. 30.

Peter and Andrew resided here. Here He healed the paralytic. Mark ii. 1. Also a man with an unclean devil. Luke iv. 33. And the nobleman's son. John iv. 46.

The incident, Mark ix. 36, occurred here. Our Lord's discourse, John vi. 26, spoken here. Its doom pronounced. Matt. xi. 23.

His mother and her children had doubtless gone to settle here. Jesus was *Pastor* here. *Luther.*

Lake of Gennesaret, on the west, had great bustle and activity at that time.

Three great roads passed southward in vicinity of the lake :—1. Damascus road ; 2. Egyptian ; 3. The Perea route.

Brethren. His mother and brethren seem to have left Nazareth and followed Him.

Being of blood kindred, they are named before His disciples.

The Greek term for brethren used about 80 times by the Evangelists in *this sense.*

Superstition has led many good men to deny the natural sense of the text, and to affirm that they were children of Mary's *sister having the same name.*

Sufficient reason to believe they were the sons of Mary and Joseph, born after the Lord.

Jehovah thus places His seal on His own divine ordinance of marriage.

He thus utters in the Scriptures an eternal protest against all
Mariolatry.

The Evangelist has just finished the record of a splendid miracle.

We are now to be presented with another. Miracles were our
Lord's ordinary life-work.

Between the two occurs the mention of *mother* and *brethren.*

Thus the sacred writers blend the Divine and human, His Godhead and His humanity.

For their Master's nature united the elements of earth and heaven.

Continued. Note His transition from private to public life.

Demand for tribute money proves our Lord a legal resident and a
subject of Cæsar. Matt. xvii. 24.

His mother and brethren were drawn by *nature,* His disciples were
attached by *grace.*

Not many days. He loses no time, for his work is great, and
His time is short.

"And how am I straitened till it be accomplished!" Luke xii. 50.

κατέβη. After the temptation He remained at Capernaum. On returning
He stayed at Cana, John iv. 46, where Mary had retired. *Ewald, Ellicott.*
Moved and settled there with His mother's family. *Wieseler.*

Καφ ρναούμ. Village of Nahum, or village of consolation. *Besser, Winer.*
Khan Minyeh, the present site of the city, about the middle of the western shore
of Gennesaret. *Greswell, Robinson, Stanley, Porter.* Tell *Hum,* or hill of
Hum, site of the ancient city, lies an hour and twenty minutes north of *Khan
Minyeh. Pococke, Bochart, Wilson, Ritter, Thompson, Winer, Reland,
Tristram.* Joseph had property there. *Lightfoot, Ewald.* Central and easy
of access. *Andrews.*

Peter took a house for our Lord and His apostles. *Norton, Alexander.* The
whole family, except sisters, married in Nazareth. *Alford.*

ἀδελφοί. See also on John vii. 5. 1. Joseph's sons by his first wife. *Epiphanius, Gregory Nyss.,* &c. 2. They were cousins of our Lord. *Augustine, Jerome,
Besser, Bengel, Wordsworth, Lange, Lardner, Pearson, Ellicott, Tischendorf,
&c.* 3. They were the children of Joseph and Mary. *Eusebius, Tertullian,
Luther, Fritzsche, De Wette, Meyer, Tholuck, Hase, Wieseler, Neander, Winer,
Alford, Stier, &c.* 3. The arguments for their being our Lord's uterine brothers
are numerous, and *taken collectively,* to an unprejudiced mind almost irresistible, although singly they are open to objection, Luke ii. 7; Matt. i. 25;
xii. 46; Mark iii. 31. The opposite view easily accounted for by the
general error on the inferiority of the wedded to the virgin state. *Smith's Dict.*
Suits the text best in all the places where the parties are referred to. *D. Brown.*

ἔμειναν. This preceded John's imprisonment. *Abode* followed it. *Bengel.*

---

13. And the Jews' passover was at hand, and Jesus went up to Jerusalem.

Jews'. History and character, see on John i. 19.

Passover. See on John i. 29, 36. John wrote for Gentiles.
Called " unleavened bread." Luke xxii. 7 ; Acts xx. 6 ; 1
Cor. v. 8.

John notices four passover feasts during our Lord's life. John
v. 1 ; vi. 4 ; xii. 1 ; xiii. 1.

The passover instituted in Egypt at the death of the first-born.
Ex. xii. 21.

On the 10th of Abib, afterwards called Nisan, answers to our
April.

Each family selected a lamb or kid, without blemish, a male of the
first year.

Slain while the sun was setting ; the BLOOD SPRINKLED ON THE
DOOR-POSTS. Deut. xvi.

Ancient Egyptians for ages marked their sheep with red to protect
them. *Epiphanius.*

Ancient Peruvians sprinkled their door-posts with blood in the
spring. *Von Bohlen.*

Roasted whole ; no bone broken ; ate with unleavened bread and
bitter herbs.

Ate in standing posture : loins girded, shoes on feet, staff in hand.
Ex. xii. 11.

After entering Canaan they ate it reclining. John xiii. 23 ; Luke
xvi. 23.

No uncircumcised person dare eat ; all leaven was put away.

Every male to attend this feast unless ceremonially impure, or
bodily infirm. Devout women also. 1 Sam. i. 7 ; Luke
ii. 41.

All work was suspended on the 15th day after the holy convoca-
tion.

First sheaf of the harvest was waved by the priest before the Lord.

Origin and object : leaving Egypt Israel, late a nation of slaves,
became free.

It was called " redemption : " horses and chariots were overthrown.
Ex. xiii. 14, 15.

First-born was consecrated to the Lord. Ex. xiii. 14, 15. A
kingdom of priests. Ex. xix. 6.

Sanctioned patriarchal priesthood ; was more ancient than the law.
Ex. xix. 6.

" Through faith Moses kept the passover, and sprinkling of blood."
Heb. xi. 28.

Bone not broken a symbol of unity. God with Israel.

Rather a *prophetic type* selected for *identifying* the *Christian Paschal Lamb*. John xix. 36.

Leaven excluded, to render it more intensely sacrificial.

Fermentation a sacred symbol of decomposition and ruin. 1 Cor. v. 6, 8.

Offering of the Omer of wheat a type of deliverance from *winter*.

" Christ was the first-fruits of them that slept," in the winter of death. 1 Cor. xv. 20.

Deliverance from Egyptian bondage a type of deliverance from sin's slavery.

Blood on the door-posts foreshadowed Christ's atoning blood. Heb. xi. 28.

A lamb exhibits the most perfect of peace-offerings. Isa. liii. 7.

" *My sacrifice.*" Ex. xxxiv. 25. Peace with God. Eph. ii. 13—17.

Points to Calvary, the foundation and top-stone of all *propitiatory* sacrifices.

The unleavened bread a type of a sanctified heart. 1 Cor. v. 8.

Girded loins, staves and shoes, point to the Christian pilgrimage.

Provision made for receiving Gentiles into the Church at the national birth.

" A mixed multitude " through circumcision might share the passover. Ex. xii. 44.

Went. With His disciples: five already called : John, the writer, was one.

Matthew, Mark, and Luke make no allusion to this visit.

Our Lord's memorable discourses recorded by John were given at the Passover, Tabernacle, and Dedication feasts.

Jerusalem. For its history, see John v. 1. For its topography, see John vii. 25.

If Lord of the Sabbath LORD of the feasts, and free from temple tribute, because LORD of the *temple*. Matt. xvii. 26.

Prophecy foretold that He would come to the daughter of Zion. Matt. xxi. 5.

The entire nation of Jews was represented at Jerusalem at the passover.

To the temple for a thousand years prophets had come in the old dispensation.

Being under the law, He observed the passover. " It becometh us to fulfil all righteousness." Matt. iii. 15.

The true Paschal Lamb came to confirm and fulfil the covenant. Dan. ix. 27.

" The dwellings of Jacob " must pale before " the gates of Zion."

ἐγγὺς. From our Lord's baptism a half-year is ended. *Lightfoot.* Jesus' first passover and cleansing of the temple about the same time. *Robinson.* Identical with Matt. xxi. 12. A repetition. *Robinson, Andrews.* Passover on the 9th of April. *Greswell.* The 11th. *Friedlieb.*

πάσχα. Aramean form in Greek letters. *Howson.* Death of first-born of beasts, aimed at the *gods* of Egypt, sacred ox, &c. *Michaelis, Kürtz.* Ex. xii. 6. πρὸς ἑσπέραν, Sept. At twilight. *Geddes.* Sunsetting. *Rosenmüller.* Interval between sunsetting and dark. *Gesenius, Winer.* Lamb roasted on a transverse spit to resemble a cross. *Justin Martyr.* Pure superstition. *Author.* Object and origin astronomical. *Baür.* Change of seasons. *Hupfield.* A sacrament. *Calov.* A sacrifice. *Bochart, Cudworth, Vitringa,* and divines generally.

No bone broken, symbol of natural and spiritual union. *Howson in Alexander.* Passover points to a greater deliverance than from Egyptian bondage. *Lange.* The rejoicing combined with a sacrifice celebrated by Christ. *Lightfoot.* Questioned by *Lücke.* Gentiles called resurrection feast, Pascha. *Irenæus.* Thirteen points of coincidence with Christ our Passover. *Godwin.* Seventeen. *Lightfoot.* Nineteen. *Keach.* Army of Sennacherib smitten on passover night. *Rabbis.* New moon type of the brightness of Messiah's reign; lengthening days, the increasing love of the Redeemer's kingdom; hour of the supper, fulness of time; roasting, God's wrath against sin; thorough cooking, well-digested doctrine; unfermented bread, humility. *Vitringa.* Call to the Gentiles made at the beginning, Ex. xii. 44. *Kürtz.* Festive throng favourable for our Lord's Messianic mission. *Hengstenberg.*

---

14. And found in the temple those that sold oxen and sheep and doves, and the changers of money sitting.

Found. In the outer court,—the court of the Gentiles.

At 12 years of age He visited the temple and called it " My Father's."

Now He visits it as Prophet and Judge in His own name and by His own authority.

Temple. The most celebrated building the world has ever seen.

First erected by Solomon, King Hiram, of Tyre, builder, in $7\frac{1}{2}$ years.

Stood on Mount Moriah on the spot selected by God Himself.

An enlarged pattern of the Tabernacle : exactly double its dimensions.

Description of this famous structure given in 1 Kings vi.; 2 Chron. iii.

Plundered by Shishak, King of Egypt, 30 years after its erection. 1 Kings xiv. 25.

Destroyed by Nebuchadnezzar 588 B.C., having stood 424 years.

Lay in ruins 52 years.   Rebuilt by Zerubbabel, under Cyrus.

The people wept, remembering the glory of the first temple.

Second temple lacked five things :--1. The Ark and Mercy-seat.
2. The Shechinah.   3. The Holy Fire.   4. The Urim and
Thummim.   5. The Spirit of Prophecy.

Yet it was foretold that the glory of the latter house should exceed
that of the former.

Fulfilled in the presence of the Only-begotten of the Father, the
Lord Himself.

Zerubbabel's temple rebuilt, enlarged, elevated, and beautified by
Herod.

Cloisters and other buildings not finished till after his death.

Holy Place and Most Holy of their original length and breadth.

COURT OF THE GENTILES. Immediately within the circuit of cloisters.

Ran round the enclosure with a width of 25 cubits, i.e. 37 feet 6
inches.

Limit of this court on the inside a low balustrade 3 cubits high.

Bore inscriptions in Greek and Latin, warning Gentiles not to pass
within it.   Acts xxi. 28.

INNER COURT.   This contained the COURT OF ISRAEL and the
PRIESTS' COURT with the Temple and Altar.

Was surrounded by a lofty wall with a cloister on the inside.

Entered by 7 gates: 3 on the north, 3 on the south, 1 on the
east.

Eastern gate very richly adorned, supposed by *some* to have been
" the Beautiful Gate."

No woman or Gentile of either sex could enter the COURT OF IS-
RAEL.

COURT OF THE WOMEN.   On the east of the Court of Israel on a
lower level.

Into this court men undefiled and their wives could enter.
Josephus.

It had four gates, one on each side.   Contained the Treasury.
Mark xii. 41.

The great eastern gate a wonderful piece of work : the pride of the
temple area.

Covered with carving, richly gilt, having apartments over it.
Generally believed to have been " the Beautiful Gate."   Acts
iii. 2.

Here Pharisee and publican prayed.   Here our Lord delivered His
discourse.   John viii. 1—20.

Here the lame man healed followed Peter. Acts iii. 2. Here Paul
   was seized. Acts xxi. 26.
Solomon's Porch was on the east. John x. 23. It was here Peter
   preached so successfully.
Colonnade on the south side, built by Herod, called the ROYAL
   CLOISTERS.
Had three aisles, comprising 162 Corinthian pillars of surpassing
   height and richness.
Beauty of the temple in our Lord's time called forth universal
   admiration.
But through national apostasy it had ceased to be *God's* house
   and had become *theirs.* Matt. xxiii. 38.
Sold. A sacred traffic allowed; Jews dwelling afar might sell
   their own lambs. Deut. xiv. 21.
At the passover people balanced accounts with the temple claims.
Spirit of traffic the bosom sin of the Jews. *Hengstenberg.*
Even a heathen said, "Put off thy shoes when sacrificing."
   Pythagoras.
"Make religion, not your pastime, but business." *Numa Pompilius.*
"Not purple garments, Priests of Athens, are needed, but pure
   hearts at the sacrifice." *Æschylus.*
"Keep thy foot when thou goest to the house of God." Eccl. v. 1.
Spiritual meaning of the passover lost in desire for trade and gain.
The presence of the Holy God rendered such deeds a kind of
   sacrilege mingled with treason.
But priest and people, mastered by covetousness and licentiousness,
   had banished Jehovah from their hearts and from His temple
   too.
At the root of this Godless worship the axe was to be laid first by
   the Baptist, then by the Son of God.
Oxen and Sheep. See on ver. 15. Animals to be offered in sacrifice.
Doves. See on John i. 32. The purification offering of the poor.
   Lev. xii. 8 ; xv. 14, 29.
Changers. See on ver. 15. They supplied strangers with the
   half-shekel, in which the temple tax must be paid, converting
   Roman into Jewish money.
Money. This market began after the captivity. This tax was
   generally paid at Jerusalem. Sometimes elsewhere.

τῷ Ἱερῷ, not τῷ ναῷ. Ἱερόν is the whole compass of the sacred enclosure, but ναός, from ναίω, "*habito,*" as the proper habitation of God; the οἶκος τοῦ Θεοῦ, is the temple itself. Into the ναός the Lord never entered during His earthly course. *Trench.* Immensæ opulentiæ templum. *Tacitus.* No one could enter the temple—1. With his staff 2. Nor with shoes on. 3. Nor with scrip. 4. Nor with dust on his feet. 5. Nor money in his purse, but in hand. 6. No one dare spit in the temple. 7. Nor make an irreverent gesture. 8. Nor use it for thoroughfare. 9. Every one must move slowly. 10. Feet to be drawn close, eyes down, hands on the heart. 11. No one could sit, however weary, *except kings.* 12. Every one to pray with head uncovered. 13. To retire with face to the altar. *Lightfoot.* Temple of Zerubbabel described by Hecatæus just after Alexander's death. *Josephus.*

The temple resembled the Escurial. *Jesuits.* Resembled Egyptian temples. *Trench.* Those of Persepolis. *Botta, Layard.* The Egyptian corresponds in many particulars. *Author.* Whatever the exact appearance of its details, the triple temple of Jerusalem—the lower court, standing on its magnificent terraces— the inner court, raised on its platform in the centre of this, and the temple itself, rising out of this group and crowning the whole—must have formed, when combined with the beauty of its situation, one of the most splendid architectural combinations of the ancient world. *Ferguson.* πωλοῦντας. A pious Jew looked on this traffic as a pious Briton would on the sale of a "*living*" advertised. *Maurice.* None entered Diana's temple without first taking off the shoes, probably derived from Ex. iii. 5.

κερματιστὰς. Bankers sat in court of the Gentiles to supply Jewish change to those who came to pay their half-shekel and other offerings. *Lightfoot.* Before the great fire St Paul's Cathedral, London, was similarly desecrated, by what was called *Poule's Walk.*

---

15. And when he had made a scourge of small cords, he drove them all out of the temple, and the sheep, and the oxen; and poured out the changers' money, and overthrew the tables.

Scourge. The cord may have been used in binding or driving cattle.

Not the *instrument* so much as the *emblem* of His Divine displeasure.

Such a weapon must have been powerless in other hands.

Here Almighty power wields it, and directs the crowd to His word of mercy and warning.

He bore the symbol, but did not use it; the rod is ever in His hands, and love ever in His heart.

Sinners prepare the scourge with which they are driven by *conscience.*

The time to scourge the wicked had not yet arrived.

Contrast His loving-kindness to Mary at the humble Galilean festival, with His *judicial severity* to the faithless rulers of the temple. Rom. xi. 22.

The glory that was full of *grace*, was also full of *truth.*

Heavenly wisdom is " first *pure*, then peaceable." James iii. 17.

Aaron was washed before being anointed.   Lev. viii. 6.

He who brought peace and joy to the world, has a fan for the threshing-floor.   Matt. iii. 12.

He does not begin with a miracle, but with an act of *authority*.

The Angel of the covenant now comes to His temple, but they cannot abide it.   Mal. iii. 1, 2.

He does not merely speak ; no simple word alone would suffice.

He uses a scourge to discipline the wayward of our race.

He will one day wield a two-edged sword against incorrigible foes.

The *scourge* is typical of the *absolute purity* demanded of the heart.

At times our sins become our scourges, to lead us to penitence.

" It is good to be zealously affected in a good thing." Gal. iv. 18.

" I will not give sleep to mine eyes, until I find out a place for the Lord."   Psa. cxxxii. 4, 5.

Drove out.   The Greek word does not mean by *force*, but by *authority*.

He faces the rude crowd of traders,—on fire with love of lucre— and compels them, *against their interest*, to fly—by a mere wave of His scourge.

This has ever been esteemed one of our Lord's mightiest miracles.

It far surpasses Elijah's gaining Israel's permission to slay the prophets of Baal, for He who answered by fire, could wield *the will* of myriads.

His acts, like His words, had always a tone of *kingly* decision.

The trafficking crowd fled, panic-stricken, before the awful PRESENCE of Him in whom they could not see their future Judge.

We speak of Him as meek and lowly, and such He truly was, but here His uplifted hand scattered the profane like summer chaff.

It was distinctly foretold that the Lord should suddenly come to His temple and purify it.   Mal. iii. 1 ; Matt. iii. 12.

Zeal in behalf of godliness is attended by vengeance towards *sin*. 2 Cor. vii. 11.

He never *drives* any into the temple ; He draws with cords of love. Hos. xi. 4.

He refines as silver in the fire, individually, socially, nationally. Mal. iii. 2.

He might have taken them as trespassers on His Father's ground.

At the beginning and at the close of His ministry this act was repeated.   Matt. xxi. 12.

The other Evangelists are silent as to the *first* cleansing.

Temple. See on ver. 14. See also on John v. 14.

Sheep. For characteristics as noted in Scripture, see on John x. 2. An important item in oriental wealth in every age.

Used in sacrifices. Ex. xx. 24. Lambs of the first year. Lev. ix. 3. None killed under 8 days old. Lev. xxii. 27.

Article of food. 1 Sam. xxv. 18. Wool used as clothing. Job xxxi. 20; Prov. xxxi. 13. Horns used for trumpets. Josh. vi. 4.

Skins dyed and used in Tabernacle. Ex. xxv. 5. Lambs as tribute. 2 Kings iii. 4.

Sheep of Bozrah. Isa. xxxiv. 6. Of Bashan and Gilead. Mic. vii. 14. Flocks of Kedar. Isa. lx. 7.

A large flock of sheep and goats feeding together, following one shepherd on the mountains near *Bethlehem*, was seen by the *author*. John x. 4 ; Psa. viii. 7.

Orientals give names to sheep, as dairy cattle and horses are named in England. John x. 3.

Fat tails of Syrian sheep alluded to, Lev. iii. 4. Fat is used instead of butter.

Oxen. No animal held in higher esteem by ancient Orientals generally than the ox.

Kine or cattle used in ploughing. Horses not used in the East. Deut. xxii. 10.

Oxen tread out grain. Hos. x. 11. Used for draught generally. Num. vii. 3. Beasts of burden. 1 Chron. xiii. 9.

Flesh eaten. Prov. xv. 17. Used in sacrifice. Ex. xx. 24. Not to be muzzled. Deut. xxv. 4 ; 1 Cor. ix. 9.

Not allowed to work on the Sabbath, that they might have *rest*. Deut. v. 14.

Oxen were stall-fed and pastured by Hebrews. Ancient monuments show that the Egyptians stall-fed oxen.

The worshippers had a right to buy sheep and oxen for sacrifice, but in the temple it became *sacrilege*. Deut. xiv. 24.

Poured. By this He showed His estimate of silver and gold.

Changers'. See on ver. 14. Noted among Orientals for impiety avarice, and fraudulent dealing.

None but the sacred-coined *half*-shekel was received, $15\frac{1}{2}d.$ (31 cents) in value.

Paid by every Israelite who had reached or passed the age of 20. Ex. xxx. 13 15.

Strangers gave Cæsar's coins for the sanctuary half-shekel.

Money. In Egypt, Assyria, and Babylonia no coined money was found.

Egyptian money was made into *rings* of gold and silver. Babylonian into wedges (or tongues, Heb.).

Spits or skewers of silver or gold—six of which made a handful. " Bundles." Gen. xlii. 35. *Sept.* " chains " or links of rings fastened together. Josh. vii. 21.

The Daric was the first coined money brought into Palestine. Ezra ii. 69.

Previously the uncoined metal was *weighed :* by Abraham. Gen. xxiii. 16. By Joseph's officers in Egypt. Gen. xliii. 21.

By Moses' law cattle, houses, lands, &c., determined by money. Lev. xxvii. 17, &c.

Jews' ear-rings and bracelets made of specific *weight.* Gen. xxiv. 22.

Friends of Job brought pieces of money and ear-rings of gold. Job xlii. 11.

Threshing-floor of Ornan was bought by David for 600 shekels of gold. 1 Chron. xxi. 25.

Jews' coinage ceased under *Hadrian.*

Capture of Jerusalem commemorated by coins marked "JUDEA CAPTA," struck by Vespasian.

Money in Greek answers exactly to our *coined* money.

Overthrew. Shows authority mingled with righteous indignation.

It was a thorough reformation : He drove the traders *out* of the temple.

He did not complain to the priests, knowing that for selfish purposes they *sanctioned* the traffic.

φραγἑλλιον, made of the ropes holding the oxen. *Lampe.* Used naturally, not symbolically. *Ebrard, Meyer.* A symbol of His power. *Neander.* A prelude to the reformation under Christ. *Calvin.* Divine majesty scattered them. *Grotius.* The first of *two* similar events. Second found Matt. xxi. *Wieseler, Greswell, Wordsworth, Alford, Robinson, Ebrard, Meyer.* No rod ever inflicted less injury. *Bengel.*

πάντας, including owners as well as stock. *Origen.* His face flashed with Divine majesty. *Jerome.* A greater miracle than turning water into wine. *Origen.*

ἐξέβαλεν. A type of exorcising the human soul of evil spirits. *Olshausen, Trench.* Not forcible, but authoritative driving. *Lampe.*

πρόβατα. Carmel, Bashan, Gilead, are covered now with countless flocks. *Thompson.* Dogs in Greece watched flocks. *Theocritus.* See Job xxx. 1.
βόας. Cattle herds near Jerusalem now of an inferior kind. *Schubart.*
κέρμα. Coined money in Phœnicia B.C. *Robinson.* Not found in Homer's time. Unwrought masses of metal. ὀβελίσκος, pyramidal in form. *Leake.* Probably large nails. *Rawlinson.* A coin bearing figure of a lamb, as pecunia a pecus. *Bell in Alexander.* Phidon, King of Argos, B.C. 748, introduced copper and silver coinage. *Smith, Grote, Clinton.* Lydians. *Herodotus, Rawlinson.* Jewish silver coins were struck. A "shekel of Israel" with a chalice. Another, "Jerusalem the Holy," with a triple lily, Hos. xiv. 5. A copper "Redemption of Zion," a palm-tree between two baskets. *De Saulcy.* Herod left Salome 500,000, Cæsar 10,000,000, and others 5,000,000 of coined silver. *Josephus.* Egyptian money was composed of gold and silver rings, and the standard weights were *metal heads* of lions, bulls, geese, and antelopes. *Wilkinson's* Egypt, vol. ii., p. 148.

---

16. And said unto them that sold doves, Take these things hence ; make not my Father's house an house of merchandise.

And said. The world could not contain all His sayings. John xxi. 25.

The selection and arrangement were not left to human minds.

Doves. See on John i. 32 ; ii. 14.

Doves and swallows in God's providence are welcome to the temple. Psa. lxxxiv. 3.

But not even innocent doves can be tolerated when used to promote filthy lucre.

Decorum ever characterized our Lord ; the doves were not *let loose.*

Besides, they were offered in sacrifice by the poor, when unable to purchase a lamb.

These animals left no room for the poor and wretched who came to Christ to be blessed and healed, or for the children who sang Hosannas in His praise.

Our Lord was a true reformer : He cast out abuses, but enjoined duties.

He scourges the mercenary intruders, but retains His ministers.

He overturns the tables of the changers, but disturbs not the treasury.

Take. Note the delicate touch of Divine compassion that leaves the cages of *living birds* undisturbed.

His eye saw through a few years, the heavy judgments of God coming on the nation.

He proved, by His miraculous power over these fierce sons of mammon, that He was " Lord of the temple."

We need wonder no more that He seldom attended *such* feasts. John vii. 8.

That He *lingered* as if dreading to be present, amid so depraved and reckless a crowd.

These things. Language of emotion, kindled by a holy, divine jealousy.

These things belong not here. He wields " the sword of the Spirit, the word of God." Eph. vi. 17.

Court of Gentiles open to all nations for the worship of Jehovah.

But to compel " sons of strangers " to herd with cattle was an insult to humanity.

A trait, however, in the character of Pharisees of all ages and generations.

Cattle considered of more value and importance than the poor and the outcast.

Many professing Christians of to-day as guilty in this respect as the ancient Jewish rulers.

Mammon and religion, though apparently united, cannot blend. Amos viii. 5 ; Ezek. xxxiii. 31 ; Acts viii. 18.

" Who shall stand when He appears? " Mal. iii. 2, 3.

An evident miracle, the temple guards even did not attempt to interfere.

Conscience of the sinner often the reformer's best and surest friend.

The sin was not in the *trade*, but in the profanation of the place and in the spirit in which the traffic was conducted.

My Father's. He had frequent favourable opportunities for declaring himself the Messiah.

As on His first visit, the words " MY FATHER'S HOUSE " sound out in the Temple of God.

In each case He expresses the same consciousness of *real relation to the temple.* Heb. iii. 6.

In childhood a son *in* His own house, now a son *over* His own house.

He publicly calls God HIS FATHER, which, to those wicked Jews, was a compound blasphemy, in that He claimed to be *both* the MESSIAH and the SON OF GOD !

Connected with the bold confession of Nathanael, the miracle at Cana, and these words of loftier meaning, no one not hardened could doubt His claim.

To all listening it was a word of new and mighty significance.

It was a direct answer to the question put by Nathanael and the Scribes, "WHO ART THOU ? "

Jews, in their blindness, thought the temple *theirs*, and our Lord, amid tears and judgments, calls it "*your house*," God's House no more for ever.   Luke xiii. 35.

But one now in their midst calls it " MY FATHER'S HOUSE."   The Judge is very near.

If the lowly Nazarene could *thus* call it, the humblest publican might claim a right, and the exiled Gentile feel there was a *home for him, too, in his Father's house!*

House.   See on John vii. 53.   He, "as a Son, was faithful over His own house."   Heb. iii. 5, 6.

Merchandise.   He softens " den of robbers " to " house of merchandise."   Jer. vii. 11.

At the first purging they had made it " a house of merchandise."

At the second He charged them with making it a " den of thieves."

The first purification did not last long ; they returned to their old practices.   Matt. xxi. 13.

To commit new sins, pretending to bewail old ones, a mockery of God.

Though sacrifices have ceased, the sanctity of God's house remains.

This race of Jews, driving their unhallowed trade under the wings of the Cherubim, still live.

If there be those found in the sacred name of religion who *sell indulgences* and place a *market price on all ordinances of God's house*, then do we see in our age a Church of God changed into a " *den of thieves*."

ἐμπορίου.   Covetousness a thievish passion. *Theophylact.*   A place to gather their money as robbers their booty. *Fritzsche.*   Dove-sellers are those who, like Simon Magus, trade in spiritual things. *Augustine, Origen, Hall.*

---

17. And his disciples remembered that it was written, The zeal of thine house hath eaten me up.

Disciples.   He had but five as yet.   John i. 40, 41, 43, 45.   For character and history, see Sugg. Comm. on Luke vi. 13—16.

Remembered.   An original faculty by which the mind retains the knowledge of past events or past ideas.

There is an important distinction between *memory* and *recollection*.

Memory retains past ideas without any, or with little, effort.

Recollection implies an effort to recall ideas that are past.

A retaining of past ideas in the mind is remembrance.

The process or order of this mental power is wrapped in mystery.

Because we give certain names to facts and faculties, we foolishly suppose we understand them.

This is the case with much that proudly boasts its scientific character.

Reminiscences are less distinct than the impressions originally made.

On earth there seems to be a constant decay of all our ideas, as figures and forms *photographed* become more and more dim, until they finally disappear.

Two or more senses render the task of the memory easier than one.

Memory is capable of being greatly strengthened or weakened.

It appears, however, that after death memory possesses its full power in the soul. Luke xvi. 25.

As a rule, the clearer the mind comprehends a thing, the better it is remembered.

By His Spirit " He would bring all things to their remembrance," John xiv. 26.

The dulness of those who cannot see a stupendous miracle is rebuked by the Spirit, who foretold this act of our Lord.

Happily we have an inspired interpretation both of the prophecy and its fulfilment.

Prophecies are of use after they are fulfilled by God, their INTERPRETER.

Seed covered out of sight is of great use after the harvest.

Fulfilment of prophecies in the past inspires faith concerning the *unfulfilled*.

Written. For antiquities, materials employed, &c., see on John v. 47.

This passage, Psa. lxix. 9, could not have been quoted at the second purification.

It peculiarly and pre-eminently belongs to THE ANGEL OF THE COVENANT.

" The LORD shall suddenly come to His temple, even the messenger of the covenant." Mal. iii. 1—3.

Shall come to annul carnal ordinances : in driving out the legal victims, He showed them a *better Victim.*

Zeal. Holy love and holy wrath constitute justice, and *Divine justice is* DIVINE LOVE IN FLAMES !

Disciples called it *zeal.* Jews would call it madness or demoniacal possession.

Zeal of apostates often becomes the *malice* of persecuting fanaticism.

Let not zeal eat up our wisdom, nor pride eat up our zeal.

The holy zeal of a Josiah or an Ezekiel was *renewed in Him.*

His look, His voice, showed a fire burning, that will at length consume the chaff of the threshing-floor.

Our Lord flew, like the seraphim, in a constant flame of zeal.

Elijah cried, " I have been very jealous for the Lord of hosts." 1 Kings xix. 10.

In this act repeated, He exercises His supreme *kingly* authority.

An offence chastened by the King's *own hand* is no small sin.

Moses' zeal broke the tables of stone. Ex. xxxii. 19.   David wept for Israel. Psa. cxix. 136.

Levity over discipline in the dust is a false and dangerous *charity.*

" The reproaches of them that reproached thee fell on me." Psa. lxix. 9.

Three years after, the repetition of this act proved the Jews had not reformed.

Pastors finding the labour of years destroyed by the course of one malicious person, feel this truth. *Luther.*

The stream is stopped in vain, if the poisonous fountain flows on.

House. A well-ordered mind, sanctified, cannot be detained from the Sanctuary.

Retired worship avoids temptation in the rush of the crowd.

If such storms assault us in the harbour, what will we do when launching out in the sea of domestic and public life ? *Chrys.*

" I had rather be a doorkeeper in the house," &c. Psa. lxxxiv. 10.

Eaten. Not outward consequences, but inward intensity of emotion.

It *was* the zeal of love for His temple ; it might have been anger to His foes.

This zeal did in the end literally *consume* Him.

All may share the Saviour's *zeal*, but may not, like Him, take up the *scourge.*

ζῆλος, a symbolical act. *Hengst.* We should pray for young zeal with old discretion. *Trapp.*

This purification of the temple differs from the account given by the Synoptists. 1. One occurred at the outset, the other at the close of His ministry. 2. One with, the other without, a scourge. 3. First has not the rebuke expressed in Matt. xxi. 13. 4. A sign sought at the first, not at the second. 5. In the last the priests sought His life, proving a crisis at hand. *D. Brown.*

κατέφαγέ. Codices Sin., Vat., and Alex. have καταφάγεταί. So also *Tisch.* and *Alford.* δὲ omitted. *Tisch., Alford.* Deep grief mingled with anger. *Lampe.* Wrathful love. *Luther.*

---

18. Then answered the Jews and said unto him, What sign showest thou unto us, seeing that thou doest these things?

Jews. See on John i. 19. The rulers controlling the temple-police.

As spiritual teachers they were solemnly bound to stand by Him in His holy zeal.

What sign? See on John iv. 48. As well might the survivors of a hurricane, amid the ruins of their homes, demand of Providence what it meant.

A sign? Were not the selfish crew driven out by an humble Nazarene?

A sign? Were not the Jews paralyzed before the power of the terrible ONE?

A sign? Had not their fleeing, like a flock of *timorous* sheep, proved a sign?

A sign? Could they not hear His word thundering in their consciences?

Alas! they stifled their convictions, although quailing under His power.

They demand, like the reckless scoffer, *miracle to be proved* by *miracle.*

Why not inquire about their *sins,* just rebuked?

The Sanhedrim alone claimed the right to rectify these proceedings if wrong.

Our Lord, just returning from the wilderness, was still a *stranger* in Jerusalem.

"Without office, do you, as a prophet, arrogate a right to purify the temple?"

When kings and priests were condemned by prophets, signs vindicated their divine commission.

John had warned them, but left their temple-trading undisturbed.

Our Lord never showed the Jews a miracle on their demand.

Although He gave signs many and glorious, *He had none for cavillers.*

Armed with Divine power, these bold intruders were hurled out of the temple.

An effect somewhat similar was produced the night of His apprehension in the garden.

" As soon as He said, I AM HE, they went backward, and fell to the ground." John xviii. 6.

If His presence caused such consternation to His enemies in His *humiliation,* what will it cause in HIS GLORY !

Jewish presumption trusted Heaven would lavish miracles at their will : there had been no miracle for 400 years.   No prophet since Malachi : hence the Jews suspected His claims.

He will give them a prophecy, and three years will fulfil it.

What sign?   This question a captious interference of men disturbed in their sin.

Those dissatisfied with our Lord's miracles could not be satisfied with any others.

They were reckless as to His credentials : the nation was *infatuated.*

Satan was never a friend to God's temple and work.   Ezra iv.

Our Lord's works were veils, screening the mystery of His holy work.

Sign enough to those able to see Almighty power in this miracle of ejectment.

But not enough to subdue the incorrigible hardness of such men.

Like owls, they hoot and ask to see the sun at noon.

These things.   In general this incident, but especially the words, " MY FATHER'S HOUSE."

An unknown man, wielding both power and authority *supernaturally,* raised lofty expectations in the people.

He had condemned the nation in its idolatrous and profane rush after gold.

In rebuking their priestly traffic, He had dared to rebuke the *Sanhedrim itself.*

Nothing but a pressure from the rulers prevented the people from acknowledging Him as a Divine Messenger.

Nothing but His Almighty power prevented them in their malice and rage from putting Him to death.

ἀπεκρίθησαν. Jews would never suddenly change any supposed wrong in the temple service. *Calvin.* No one now, without God's authority, can change things in Christ's Church. *Quesnel.*

σημεῖον. What *proof* by miracle? *Bloomfield.* What evidence for exercising such authority? *Hammond.* Our Lord rebuked not their desire for proper credentials, but their rejecting such as He gave, Matt. xii. 39 *Stillingfleet.* They used the same expression at the end of His ministry, Matt. xxi. 23. *Alford.*

δεικνύεις, signifies really to give or bestow. *Thucydides.*

ὅτι, quoniam. *Lampe.*

---

19. Jesus answered and said unto them, Destroy this temple, and in three days I will raise it up.

Destroy. Prophetic of what will certainly be done, as " Fill ye up," &c. Matt. xxiii. 32.

They criminally charged Christ with saying He would destroy the temple. Matt. xxvi. 61 ; Acts vi. 14.

No one disappoints God. His word will and must for ever stand. Psa. xxxiii. 11.

What the sinner *will* do, he *is* to do. Acts ii. 23; 1 Pet. ii. 8.

The counsel of God fully and freely allows men to carry out their own plans. Isa. xlvi. 10.

Our Lord spoke *permissively* and *prophetically :* " Let it be destroyed."

A hint that those who should have been the natural *defenders* of the temple would prove its *destroyers.*

" You that defile one temple will destroy another and a nobler temple."

If they would not believe what they saw, let them *wait.*

He clearly predicts His own *violent death* by these very Jews.

From the beginning, He had a clear foresight of His passion.

He now *purges* what they had *defiled ;* He will *raise* what they had *destroyed.*

The ruins of their temple were " the riches of the world." Amos ix. 11 ; Acts xv. 16 ; Rom. xi. 12.

He will completely vindicate His *authority* over their glorious House.

His enemies found abundant food for speculation and cavil.

He knew they *would not* (because they *desired not*) comprehend this prophecy until fulfilled.

In the end His enemies seem to have had a glimpse of the real meaning of this enigma. Matt. xxvii. 63.

Especially recollecting that He had called the temple " My Father's
House."

The nation had long gloried far more in the *temple* than in the
God of the temple.

Their inward thought was, " *When the temple perishes God must
perish.*"

Hence one day the money-changers convert it into a *market*, and
on the next, Stephen is *murdered* for hinting that God had
left it. Acts vi. 14.

A mystical connection between the *house* of the temple and the
house of clay enshrining Christ's Divinity at that time.

This. That He then pointed to His body is a mere conjecture.

Yet even had He done so they would *not* have comprehended His
meaning.

Their question referred to what had just taken place in the temple,
and His answer pointed to the same.

Jews thus doubtless understood Him. Matt. xxvi. 61 ; Mark xiv.
58 ; Matt. xxvii. 40.

Temple. See on John ii. 14 ; v. 14.

Allusion to the material temple *did not exhaust the meaning of His
words.*

Our Lord's sayings have all a *heavenly echo.*

When one class of truths is perceived, another rises and passes
before the mind.

In the soul where we now see ruin we may read, " *Here God once
dwelt.*"

But, alas! the lamps are gone out, the altar is overthrown, the
temple is desolate.

The golden candlestick of light and love, that shone with celestial
radiance, is displaced.

Instead there is the throne of the prince of darkness.

The intruder *Sin*, with sacrilegious hammer and axe, has broken
down the carved work of this sanctuary.

Yet its exquisite ruins prove the original structure was wrought
by the FINGER of GOD.

No longer sacred incense sends up its sweet perfume, for " the
house of prayer " has become " a den of thieves."

Behold what desolations! Yet the remains of pillar and arch,
foundation and dome, prove that the Divine Being dwelt
there.

Vain builders have tried to rebuild these fragments into beauty and symmetry ; but what one age erects, the next dashes to pieces.

There was a still nobler temple—the INCARNATE ONE. This, also, traitors to truth and God will attempt to destroy.

His body a temple enshrining His Godhead. Col. ii. 9.

Jews believed a portion of the Divine Spirit dwelt in the temple then standing.

As Lord of the Temple, He goes to prepare among the "many mansions" a home for His followers.

His every word at once foretells the malice of His crucifiers and His own Divinity.

Every claim He put forth while living received God's seal when He rose from the dead.

The temple a symbol and pledge of God's union with and sympathy for believers.

"In the tabernacle of the congregation, there will I meet with you." Num. xvii. 4.

The children of Israel dwelt spiritually with the Lord in the Tabernacle. Lev. xvi. 16.

Sparrows and swallows, emblems of helpless believers, found rest there. Psa. lxxxiv. 3.

Jews inferred that the Messiah would be called THE TEMPLE. Dan. ix. 24.

He utters this mainly for the disciples' sake standing around Him.

He knew it would lead them to believe the Scriptures after a season.

The great sign implied, "*He shall be cut off for His people;*" yet as Messiah never see corruption. Isa. liii. 3 ; Dan. ix. 26.

Hence the multiform proofs from friends and foes of His resurrection.

Temple means the sacred *shrine*, not the splendid courts surrounding it.

Three days. Not proverbial for a short time, but actual prophecy. 1 Cor. xv. 4 ; Matt. xii. 40.

Afterwards He repeats His hint, as to the prophet *Jonah.* Matt. xii. 39.

I will raise. The resurrection of His humanity attributed to the Father, but *was the act of His own Divinity.*

This word would have been *blasphemy* had He been merely a *man.*

It proves His Godhead, since all *creatures* have to be raised by *another.*

How deep His consciousness of the main *object and end* of His
short stay!

What consummate insight into all His Father's plans!

He thus begins the decreed warfare against the masters of the
temple.

Calmly and sublimely He dedicates Himself through blood to a warfare certain to lead to victory.

Yet even when He had risen from the dead they still refused to
believe, and had recourse to palpable falsehoods to account for
His empty tomb.

Like their fathers of old, who for forty years, though under the
blaze of the pillar of fire, resisted the Holy Ghost and despised
God's promises.

The mockery at the cross, and their accusations against Stephen,
prove how widely this saying of our Lord must have circu-
lated.

John alone gives us its key, as none of the other Evangelists allude
to this incident.

A prophecy uttered at the threshold of His ministry, yet not understood at His death nor even at His resurrection.

Λύσατε. Sometimes a future force. *Lampe, Tittmann.* An instance of the
prophetic imperative so frequent in the Psalms, not imprecating, but foretelling.
Pearce. The permissive imperative : " *Make* the tree good." *Alford, Tholuck.*
Distorted after three years at His trial. *Lücke.*

ναὸν, not ἱερὸν, sacred court. *D. Brown.* Refers to His body and the temple.
Stier. To His body, the temple and the N. T. Church. *Hengst.* Hebrews
called the body a mansion. *Rheinhardt.* Jews did not know His meaning.
Chrysostom. Others think they did. *Stier.* Messiah was the "*Holy* of
Holies," Dan. ix. 24. *Aben Ezra, Abarbinal.*

τοῦτον. He did not point to His body. *Stier.* A groundless hypothesis.
Hengstenberg. Alluded to His body. *Alford, Bengel.* His enemies never heard
Christ utter the words in Matt. xxvii. 63, but they understood these words
better than the apostles. *Lange.* Questioned by *Hase.*

ἐγερῶ. Destroy my body, and in three days I will raise up my body, and,
with it, the *essence* of the outward temple. *Hengstenberg.*

If their falsehood and treason to God caused the ruin of the temple by the
Romans, " a house not made with hands" would remain. They would try to
destroy *this* temple, but it would spring from the tomb. *Maurice.* He would
raise the antitype, His own body, destroyed by them. *Bede.* "Carry on your
desecration to the destruction of the temple itself, and in a little space of time
I will establish a new spiritual temple in its place." *Hencke, Herder, Lücke,
Bleek, Tholuck.*

---

20. Then said the Jews, Forty and six years was this temple in building, and
wilt thou rear it up in three days?

Then said. Why did they not humbly ask for instruction ?
Men resolved at all hazards to cavil, will cavil on till they perish.
Jews. For history and character, see on John i. 19, 24. The
  Evangelist here speaks of the Sanhedrists.
Forty-six years. From the time Herod commenced rebuilding
  the temple.
Solomon's temple was 7½ years in building. (See on ver. 14.)
Zerubbabel's temple begun in 2nd year of Cyrus ; completed in
  32nd of Artaxerxes : made precisely 46 years. *Lightfoot.*
Herod's temple begun in the 18th year of his reign ; to that present
  time was 46 years.
Temple of Diana was 220 years. St Peter's Church of Rome, 350
  years. 43 popes reigned and died while it was building.
Temple. For history and antiquities, see on John ii. 14 ; v. 14.
Herod's temple was not a *third,* but a glorification of the *second.*
Building. It had been in progress 20 years before Christ's birth,
  and was not finished until 30 years after His death, being
  84 years in building.
Christ's body to Herod's temple was as the substance to the
  shadow.
There is no temple in heaven, " for the Lord God Almighty and the
  Lamb are the temple of it." Rev. xxi. 22.
No Holy Place where all is Most Holy. Heb. ix. 8, 24.
Emblematic of God's residence, the temple is perfectly formed in
  the New Jerusalem.
Wilt thou ? They might have known that it was He who built
  the universe in " six days."
They were blinded by unbelief; stupidity often aids malice.
They falsely interpreted these words before Caiaphas. Matt.
  xxvi. 61.
He said to them, " Destroy *ye* this temple." They alleged He said,
  " *I will destroy.*"
How little do sinners realize the far-reaching influence of crime!
Every stroke of the hammer nailing Jesus to the cross was a
  thunder-stroke upon their own *idolized* temple.
Their wrath, shown to the temple of His body, was returned
  in deeper vengeance on their sacred house.
A nation on this earth without a sanctuary is a magazine of
  powder exposed to the lightning, without a rod to protect it.
Our boasted Constitution without the Bible and God's sanctuary may
  be said to rest on a volcano for a foundation.

Illustrated in the first French Revolution. Civilization is not Regeneration.

ὠκοδομήθη. Herod's reign dated from Rome's authority. We have 20 years to Christ's birth and 30 years since that event. Take four years from that date, our era being four years too late, and we have 46 years. *Alford, Wordsworth.* They seem to have taken His words more literally, because He was called a *workman. Bengel.* They simply show curiosity. *Semler, Lücke.*

ναός. Christ's body was the true temple. Herod's had ceased to be Christ's living temple. *Luther.* The words refer to the temple of Zerubbabel. *Beza.* To the temple of Herod. *Lightfoot,* and commentators generally.

---

21. But he spake of the temple of his body.

He spake. He makes no reply, but would force them to reflection.
Body. In which was enshrined the glory of the eternal Word. John i. 14.
His Godhead dwelt, *tabernacled, among us.* John i. 14.
The veil was rent at His death. Paul makes it figurative of His flesh. Heb. x. 20.
His flesh, the chosen veil, concealing the indwelling Divinity.
The temple and His body—1. Both were built by Divine directions. 1 Chron. xxviii. 19 ; Heb. x. 5. 2. Both were holy. Psa. v. 7. "That holy thing." Luke i. 35. 3. Deity dwelt in both. 2 Kings xix. 15 ; 1 Tim. iii. 16. 4. Both the medium of communion with God. 1 Kings viii. ; Eph. ii. 18.
Jewish temple was perishable, but the union between the Godhead and manhood seems to be *indissoluble.* Col. ii. 9.
Godhead dwells in Him bodily ; He dwelt in the temple sacramentally, and dwells in the soul spiritually.
This Tabernacle, like Daniel's stone, was " made without hands."
The patriarchs knew they dwelt in " houses of clay whose foundations were in the dust." Job iv. 19.
Our earthly tabernacle (Gr. *tent house*) is taken down. 2 Cor. v. 1. A picture of the sad process of death.
As one with Christ, "our building shall again be fitly framed," Eph. iv. 16 ; for by His power the believer becomes a temple of the Holy Ghost. 1 Cor. iii. 16, 17.

σώματος. Quod semel assumpsit nunquam deposuit. *Brownrigg.* God abode with Christ's spirit in Paradise, and with the body in the grave. *Clark. One*

Person holds the sword and scabbard. *Trapp.* Neither Jews nor disciples comprehended Him *at the time. Meyer.*

---

22. When therefore he was risen from the dead, his disciples remembered that he had said this unto them ; and they believed the scripture, and the word which Jesus had said.

Risen. See on resurrection, John v. 29. Immortality of the soul taught in Scripture.

Soul after death lives on, independent of the body. See on life, John v. 24.

Soul's future existence taught in Enoch's translation and Elijah's ascension.

" God of Abraham, &c. Not the God of the dead, but of the living." Luke xx. 37, 38.

Our Lord's parable of the rich man and Lazarus. Luke xvi. 19.

Appearance of Moses and Elias on the Mount of transfiguration. Luke ix. 30.

Our Saviour's reply to the penitent thief on the cross. Luke xxiii. 43.

Paul being " caught up to the third heaven." 2 Cor. xii. 2.

Paul " willing to be absent from the body and present with the Lord." 2 Cor. v. 8.

Remembered. See on ver. 17. Our Lord often uttered sayings not intelligible at *first* to those who heard them.

But becoming *clear* afterwards, He thus displayed His Divine *prescience. Chrys.*

In due time they learned that to patient waiting the Word becomes plain.

It appeared no answer at the time, but, like seed cast on the waters, it yielded and will continue to yield a glorious harvest.

Many Divine promises are like riddles, until solved by experience.

Some things seem to die entirely out, and to be utterly forgotten.

Thoughts received during pain, pleasure, wonder, surprise, curiosity, or any other strong emotion, remain longest.

A youth in England heard Mr Flavel pronounce a *benediction* with this singular addition,—" Whoso loveth not the Lord Jesus Christ, let him be Anathema," &c. At fourscore years of age, removed to America, he confessed that that *malediction* had

been sounding in his *ears* for *threescore years*. It then led
him to believe in the Redeemer.

Believed. Faith. John i. 7; vii. 38. Infidels claim the right
of rejecting revelation after a fair investigation, but no one
honestly continues to doubt after a *prayerful searching*.

Some at first *slow* of heart to believe, afterward believed *surely*
and preached.

Apostles founded their faith in our Lord's resurrection on Old Test.
prophecies. 1 Pet. i. 11.

Prophets boldly *guaranteed* the resurrection of the Lord. Psa.
xvi. 10; Isa. ix. 7; Micah v. 2.

Scriptures. See on John v. 39; see, also, Sugg. Comm. on Rom. i. 2.
Here the O. T.—1. The Law. 2. The Prophets. 3. The Psalms.

At first sight it appears difficult to fix on a passage wherein it is
directly announced.

But the Holy Spirit gave and still gives the deeper understanding
of Scripture.

Such prophecies as those in Psa. xvi. and Hos. vi. 2 are fulfilled
in Christ alone.

Word, &c. Our Lord's sayings of equal authority with those of
the Old Test. John xiv. 1.

Under the cross God's promises often sound to us like dark enigmas.

But when trial has accomplished its end the sense of the promises
dawns upon us.

Disciples afterwards perceived mysterious connection between the
temple at Jerusalem and the temple of His body.

It is by *degrees* the Spirit leads us on to perception of truth.

Divine revelation is essentially progressive. 2 Cor. iii. 18.

ἠγέρθη. Transmigration of souls held by *Pythagoras*. Soul's pre-existence
held by *Plato*. Souls emanations of anima mundi. *Virgil*. Souls had the
fiery element of the stars. *Aristotle*. Home of spirits was under the earth.
Homer. In the air. *Orpheus, Origen, Ossian*. Heathen uncertain whether the
living or the dead were better off. *Socrates* in *Plato*. This Greek expected a
divinely-commissioned person to inform mankind whether sacrifices were acceptable to the gods. *Plato* in *Alcibiades*. Achilles prefers to be a slave to
some poor hind that toils for bread, than live a sceptred monarch of the dead.
Homer. A belief in a future life puerile and pernicious madness. *Pliny*. The
soul perished with the body. *Epictetus*.

ἐμνήσθησαν. Apostles based their belief of the resurrection of our Lord
on the witness of the O. T. *Hengstenberg, Alford, Tholuck*. αὐτοῖς, omitted.
Lach., Tisch., Alf., Tregelles.

23. Now when he was in Jerusalem at the passover, in the feast day, many believed in his name, when they saw the miracles which he did.

When, &c., proves their faith not deep : it was too dependent on outward circumstances.

Jerusalem. History, John v. i.   Topography, John vii. 25.

Passover. See on John i. 29, 36 ; ii. 13.

Feast. Feasts made a great part of the religion of Greeks and Romans.

Celebrated at Olympian, Pythian, and Nemæan games : days divided between sacrificing, banqueting, and sports.

Jews had three great feasts.   Called in the Talmud "*pilgrimage feasts.*"

1. The Passover.   2. Pentecost, called also Feast of Weeks, and of First-fruits.   3. Feast of Tabernacles, or of Ingathering.

On each of these occasions every male Israelite was commanded to "appear before the Lord."

Attendance of women voluntary, but the zealous often went up to the passover.

Thus Hannah attended it, 1 Sam. i. 7 ; ii. 19 ; and thus Mary, Luke ii. 41.

Besides their religious purpose, these feasts largely maintained national unity.

Times of their celebration ordained in wisdom so as to interfere as little as possible with the industry of the people.

Passover was held just before the work of harvest commenced.

Pentecost at conclusion of the corn-harvest and before the vintage.

Tabernacles after all the fruits of the ground were gathered in.

In winter, when travelling was difficult, there was no festival.

There was a stricter obligation of the passover than of the other feasts.   In fact, *all* Israel assembled at Jerusalem.

Many.   There were not many Nathanael-like souls amongst them.

The seed may soon joyfully spring up and yet have taken no root. Matt. xiii. 20, 21.

Believed.   Faith.   See on John i. 7 ; vii. 38.

In His.   As a prophet, or as the long-promised Messiah.

They had historic faith, but not a loving trust in the Redeemer.

Their intellect was *convinced,* but their will was not *subdued* to obedience.

Name.   See on John i. 12.   The name indicates Messiah's calling and renown.   Isa. lxiii. 14.

Just then His name was gloriously displaying itself in His miracles.

Many, like Nicodemus, were hesitating between belief and scepticism.

They saw.   We note these remarks as quite peculiar to John.

The three other Evangelists record facts and sayings as *Amanuenses.*

John, writing nearly 50 years after the Ascension, takes *a review* of things.

Miracles.   See on John ii. 11 ; iii. 2 ; iv. 48 ; vi. 30.

Not one of the Evangelists has recorded these miracles.

The Synoptists do not mention any *public* visit of our Lord to Jerusalem but the *last.*

A *whole world of wonders* may be wrapped up in this one short verse.

Miracles are not *hints*, but *prophecies*, of the hidden glory of the Incarnate Word.

Omnipotence is the real FACTOR in all miraculous signs.

Miracles on nature, on man, and on the spirit world proclaim His absolute Divinity.

His Resurrection the fundamental and crowning miracle of the Gospel.

In it all other forms of miraculous working are included.

Nicodemus confesses " We know that thou art a teacher come from God," &c.   John iii. 2.

Yet " though He did so many miracles, they believed not on Him." John xii. 37.

But these attestations from Jehovah Himself left unbelievers without excuse.

Our Lord appealed to His miracles as proof of His Divine mission.

" If I had not done among you the works which no other man did," &c.   John xv. 24.

He did not rest the *truth* of His doctrine on His miracles, but intended them to assure men that He was indeed THE SENT OF GOD.

Miracles are not for believers, but unbelievers. *Chrysostom.*

True faith is founded on GOD'S WORD, not on *wonders.*   *Theophylact.*

Sanhedrim generally remained in guilty unbelief, while Nicodemus and Joseph of Arimathæa yielded to the evidence.

How natural the record that splendid wonders won the *many.*

ὡς δὲ.   The particular time designated proves the cleansing of the temple anterior to the passover. *Lampe.* Purifying the temple coincided with the putting away of the leaven. *Hengstenberg.*

πάσχα. See on John ii. 13. Embraces the whole seven days of the feast. *Hengstenberg, D. Brown.*

ἑορτῇ. Romans had Saturnalia, Lupercalia, Liberalia, Vulcanalia, &c. ἐπίστευσαν. As those in chaps. viii. 30; xii. 42. *Bengel.* Must be understood of theory and disposition, rather than of assured conviction. *Grotius.*

---

24. But Jesus did not commit himself unto them, because he knew all men.

Not commit. Gr. *Did not* TRUST *Himself.* Belief in Christ is
    TRUST.
1. They were *weak.* 2. *Timorous.* 3. *Turbulent.* 4. *Treacherous.*
The faith of many cannot stand the storm of public opposition.
"When tribulation or persecution arise, they are offended." Matt.
    xiii. 21.
Many in foreground turned to Christ, with alienation in background.
Nicodemus at first recoiled from regeneration, the simplest of truths.
Our Lord did not trust them, since faith must be reciprocal.
In His intercourse He still maintained a wise reserve.
The words imply that a dangerous opposition even thus early *began* to show itself.
They "believed" in Him, but He did not confide in them.
We find them continually obtruding themselves on Him.
None so lacking in modesty and humility as those thus deceiving themselves.
Not a single instance of a hypocrite's conversion in the Bible.
Their ideas of the Messiah were crude and gross.
They rejected every sign or wonder that pointed not to a temporal sovereign.
They could not be faithful to Him, a spiritual King.
His conduct an example of the wisdom He commended to His disciples. Matt. x. 16.
He knew. To know all the thoughts even of *one man demands omniscience.*
Who, then, is He who *knows all the thoughts* of all mankind?
God knows the very *roots.* We only know the tree by the *fruit* it bears. *Calvin.* They alone learn to know *themselves,* who follow Christ.

He knew. He had *omniscience*, an attribute of *God* alone.
We know not our nearest friends, indeed, scarcely know ourselves.
Christ's knowledge is infallible. " He trieth the hearts and reins."
    Heb. iv. 12, 13 ; Psa. vii. 9. This is His prerogative. Acts
    i. 24 ; xv. 8 ; Psa. cxxxix. 2.
Prophets knew many secrets by revelation from heaven. 2 Kings
    vi. 8—12.
But Jesus alone knows all *things*, in Himself. Rev. ii. 23.
The Creator of man knows of man, what the man created knows not.
If we may be so fearfully ignorant of ourselves, our Lord's judg-
    ment may reverse our own at the last day.
A warning not to trust our own heart as the fool does. Prov.
    xxviii. 26.
Friendly with all but intimate with few, seems a selfish maxim.
Yet our ignorance of mankind renders such a rule of life prudent.
He left Judea for Galilee, where there were but few Pharisees. John
    iv. 3.
They speedily felt an irreconcilable opposition between Him and
    them.

ἐπίστευεν. They had only a milk faith which cannot remain steadfast. *Luther.* He did not acknowledge Himself their Messiah. *Macknight.* He did not intrust His life to them. *Lampe.* He refrained from further dis-closures. *Tholuck.*
    γινώσκειν. Their hearts unchanged He would not trust them. *Clarke.* He knew whether they were trustworthy or not. *Euthymius.* Nothing less than Divine knowledge is here set forth. *Alford.* Our Lord had often four classes or grades of hearers. 1. Those for whom miracles had no other than a selfish and sensuous object, John vi. 26. 2. Those a step higher, who demanded miracle, indeed, from personal interest, but who were led by it to a loftier aim, John iv. 53. 3. A yet higher grade were those who felt the need of faith, but who required the mediation of such proofs of Divinity as addressed the senses, John iii. 2. 4. Highest of all, those who, by the word and appearing of Christ, were enabled to believe, John x. 38; xiv. 1. *Tholuck.*

---

25. And needed not that any should testify of man: for he knew what was in man.

Needed not. The Divine nature cannot stand in need of any-
    thing. Col. ii. 9.
To no *created* being does God give the key of His hidden treasures.
To His Son exclusively He has given power to create and up-
    hold the universe. John i. 3 ; Col. i. 16, 17 ; Heb. i. 10.

To God alone is due the *adoring* love of all His creatures.   Luke
   x. 27 ; Lev. xix. 18.
With Him alone is the right to execute vengeance : " It is mine,
   saith the Lord."   Rom. xii. 19.
To Him alone belongs the time, circumstances, and mode of the
   final Judgment.   Matt. xxiv. 36.
To Him alone is it to know and record the thoughts of the heart.
   Jer. xvii. 10.
To Him alone is it reserved to pardon sin.   Mark ii. 7.
Knew.   John loves to give prominence to our Lord's profound
   knowledge of men.   Chaps. v. 42 ; vi. 61, 64.
By this repetition he affirms again the omniscience of Christ.
The 30th verse of the preceding chapter teaches His *omnipresence.*
Artificers of a watch know the working of spring and wheels.
Christ knows perfectly all the springs and wheels of the human soul.
God knows our thoughts before they are formed in our minds.
A gardener knows what *flowers* will grow, because he well knows
   the roots and the seed.
These words contain the strongest possible affirmation of Christ's
   absolute knowledge of MAN.
What a truth to the self-deceiver, who clings to his sins !   But a
   precious comfort to the soul struggling with a corrupt nature.
Our Redeemer on the throne *knows* all our sins and *hears* all our
   prayers.
He is able to grant an answer, and *pardon* all our iniquities.
The Maker knew far better what was in His work than the work
   knew what was in itself.   Luke xxii. 33, 34.
No prophet ever dared to put forth this God-like claim.
And yet so natural does it seem, that we should feel disappointed
   if He claimed anything less.
This proves—1. That His sufferings and death were wholly voluntary.
2. That neither our duties nor our trials shall be suffered to exceed
   our capacities.
3. That no religion is of any value in His sight but that of the
   heart.
4. That the gospel must be in harmony with man's spiritual nature.
5. That the last Judgment will be conducted on a thorough
   knowledge of all the facts.
Man.   In man exists what is *human ;* in the new man what is
   divine. Bengel.

John's Gospel not only an inspired *History*, but an inspired *Comment* on that History. *Wordsworth.*

τῷ ἀνθρώπῳ. Man is a great deep, yet his hairs are numbered, whilst they are outnumbered by his thoughts. *Augustine.*

From this proof of omniscience His Divinity was defended against infidelity by *Chrysostom, Cyril, Augustine, Lampe.* He possessed this knowledge intrinsically, not from revelation. *Jerome* in *Wetstein.* Not the result of observation, but omniscience. *Liddon.*

τῷ before ἀνθρώπῳ denotes each particular man. *Winer.*

John 3

1. THERE was a man of the Pharisees, named Nicodemus, a ruler of the Jews.

There was. We have here an advance on the preceding chapter.
There it was shown how the Son of God out of human failure could
    bring in better things.
A fit introduction to the miracles of grace to be accomplished by
    the Son.
Special miracle of the new birth prepares the way for the indwell-
    ing of the Spirit. Chap. iv.
With Nicodemus it is " the birth of water and the Spirit."
With the woman at Jacob's well it is " the well of water within,
    springing up unto everlasting life."
John records *eleven* conversations of our Lord, of which this is the
    first.
Man. Represents a large class of worldly-minded persons.
Pharisees. See on John i. 24. They considered themselves
    righteous, and despised others. Luke xviii. 9.
As a Pharisee, Nicodemus believed himself safe in God's favour,
    and as to the law, blameless. Phil. iii. 6.
His surprise must have been very great, to hear our Lord's reply.
John the Baptist had called them a " generation of vipers.' Matt.
    iii. 7. Corrupt trees, which bore the fruit of eternal death.
Christ solemnly pronounces the " seven woes " upon them. Matt.
    xxiii.
He warned His disciples against the " leaven of the Pharisees."
    Luke xii. 1.
Nicodemus. A purely Greek name in frequent use among the
    later Jews.
His character is drawn by one touch of the pencil of inspiration :—
    " Came to Jesus by night." John vii. 50.
He dared to speak in behalf of our Lord in the Sanhedrim. John
    vii. 51.
A secret but *timid* follower of the Lord, in due time he became a
    bold confessor. John xix. 39.
After the crucifixion he joined with Joseph in bringing a mixture

of myrrh and aloes, about 100lbs. weight, and they buried
Him.   John xix. 39—42.

Shared with Joseph in honouring the remains of Christ, but did
not join in begging the body for sepulture.   Matt. xxvii. 57.

*Every man in the four Gospels appears in the light reflected on him
from the Lord !*

So this character of *fearfulness* is reproduced in every age.

We are Nicodemus, the man at Bethesda, the Samaritan woman,
&c.   Bible mirrors all ages and all characters.

Divine grace seizes his spirit, vibrating between pride and sincerity.

Ruler. Ver. 10,· " Ruler" is exchanged for "Doctor " or "Teacher."

Titles are not given by the Spirit, to flatter his memory, but to hint
at the great hindrances he had to overcome.

His office, his social position, all rendered his salvation *a hard
problem.*   Matt. xix. 24 ; Luke ix. 47.

It cannot be denied humble position, and the absence of glittering
temptations, are *far more favourable* to securing eternal life.

Can we doubt that Dives found salvation a harder problem than
Lazarus ?

Although knowing this, how many rush after pleasure and honour,
and multiply impediments.

From the Augustinian monks Luther, a witness of Christ, arose.
Paul and Nicodemus sprang from the self-righteous Pharisees.

Ruler.   Gr. *One invested with power and dignity.*   In Luke
xviii. 18, it probably signifies a *magistrate.*

Here signifies a member of the Sanhedrim.   Acts xiii. 27 ; John
vii. 26.

Rulers generally are harassed by a feverish fear lest they should
lose the praise of men.   John xii. 43.

The president of an humble synagogue may be in as much spiritual
danger as a monarch.   Luke viii. 41.

Neither the learned Nathanael, nor Nicodemus, a Master in Israel,
is excluded from Christ.

Had He received none but the *ignorant*, it might have been said
they were deceived by their own simplicity.

Yet not many " wise after the flesh " are called.   1 Cor. i. 26.

He rebukes the pride of boasting philosophers by calling the
humble to be the " *pillars* of the Church." Gal. ii. 9.

Jews.   History and character, see on John i. 19.

'Ην. The connecting particle δὲ should not have been omitted. "But (or

'Now') there was a man," &c. *D. Brown.* ἄνθρωπος, not *ἀνήρ*. A representative of man. *Stier.* Questioned by *Luthardt.* He came with a mind deeply prejudiced. *Dräscke.* His sincerity is undoubted. *Lücke.* Νικόδημος. Heb. sceleris purus. *Wetstein.* He was baptized by Peter, and expelled from office and from Jerusalem, and found refuge with Gamaliel. Nicodemus, one of the three rich men in Jerusalem. *Otho.* Some vindicate him from charge of timidity. *Niemeyer.* Our Lord encounters a rationalist in Nicodemus. *Lossel.* Old man's humble greeting, desires only instruction, but his earnest longing after life is manifest. *Lange.* Awakening before conversion. *Fresenius.* Nicodemus' face towards Jesus, but his heart goes another way. *Dräscke.* He came, having evidence of His Divinity. *Augustine.* John derived this account from Nicodemus. *Maurice.* From our Lord Himself. *Alford.* Some writers seem to forget that the Scriptures are inspired. *Author.* Some think him proud and artful, and that under the mask of an inquirer he sought cause of accusation. *Schwartz, Koppe.* Our Lord's reply endorses his motive as honest. *Tittmann.*

---

2. The same came to Jesus by night, and said unto him, Rabbi, we know that thou art a teacher come from God : for no man can do these miracles that thou doest, except God be with him.

Came to. It would have been unreasonable to invite Him to his house.

He came, not officially, but voluntarily ; not to criminate, but to learn Christ's doctrine.

His curiosity, perhaps his fears, had been aroused by the splendour of our Lord's miracles. John iv. 45.

We have no record of a solitary person coming to Christ with a burdened spirit, seeking peace.

The young ruler came to *display* his treasures of morality, not to .seek *life eternal.* Mark x. 17.

Night. Darkness : symbol of ignorance. See on John vi. 17.

Like the gates of the celestial city, the door of Christ was open always. Rev. xxi. 25.

Night noted by the Holy Ghost as a symbol of the darkened mind. John iii. 19.

How dark Nicodemus found out only by coming to the LIGHT of the world.

Had he come to improve the time, while others were sleeping, as David did in watching, then were it praiseworthy. Psa. lxiii. 6.

The Spirit alone knew his motive as no human historian could inform us.

The Lord was watching for him, knowing that he was wearied of his good works.

How unconscious was he of that very Prophet's Spirit *drawing* him
to His side.   Cant. i. 4.

His soul vibrates between humble sincerity and the fear of man.

He had not the faintest conception of our Lord's Divinity.

Gideon, the patriot, began his work of deliverance by night.
Judg. vi. 27.

Timidity of Nicodemus not remote from the spirit of Peter,—"I
know not the man."   Matt. xxvi. 72.

He came to seek light in the midst of natural darkness.   Eph. v. 8.

Many a rationalist since has " sought the living among the dead."
Luke xxiv. 5.

A mind spiritually proud cannot see although amid a blaze of
light.

Poor humble-minded Galileans could come to the Lord even at
noon-day.

High position obliges some to *seek for mercy,* "like a thief in the
night."

Bowing to Christ utterly spoils ambitious ones in the world's eye.

Two mountain-barriers stop them,—the love of praise, and their own
morality.

Too many, like Nicodemus, would carry religion in a *dark lantern.*

Many dread to drop the sounding line, to learn how shallow are
their hopes.

But how gently our Saviour encourages and leads him onward !

He will not " break the bruised reed nor quench the smoking flax."
Matt. xii. 20.

He is the only one on the earth to whom his failings are fully
known.

One can calculate the motions of the stars, but not those of his own
heart.

Can predict eclipses, but cannot see the spots in his own soul.

Can analyze metals, but cannot discover the motives which sway
him.

Many fear to cast out the sounding line, and drift along until it is
too late.

The merchant dreads to have his accounts examined when on the
verge of bankruptcy.

The God of truth solemnly affirms " *men love darkness,*" protest as
they may.   John iii. 19.

Nay, sadder still, men " LOVE DEATH," Prov. viii. 36, and deny
it also.

Rabbi. John i. 38. A complimentary title, very similar to "Reverend" with us.

Myriads now approach Him in a similar patronizing spirit.

He shows his fearful ignorance of our Lord by this human flattery.

He saw His works were beyond human power, and *God was with Him.*

His words were true in a far higher sense than he intended.

Every pastor ought to be like our Lord—1. A Rabbi, to learn truth, where Jesus learned it. 2. His commission from God, countersigned by the same Spirit. 3. His holy life should compel the same word, "God is with him."

We know. Had he said "I know" it would have compromised him. It would have been too personal, too close.

He is yet too proud to let the haughty Sanhedrist down to the level of an humble inquirer.

He thus hides himself behind his fellow-rulers in Israel.

There "will be no concealment" before the same Christ "at that day." 2 Tim. ii. 3.

We. The appointed guardians of the temple and law.

He candidly, in secret, expresses the *conscience* of his *order.*

The people thought *no ruler* had believed in our Lord. John vii. 48.

He modestly intimates his rank and dignity, in a patronizing manner.

A proud, learned member of a faculty cannot easily shake off his habits.

He comes not in the spirit of Nathanael, although with a question.

He uses "Rabbi" not as a learner, but as a Master in Israel.

But some "*will not know.*" Hence the unpardonable sin. Matt. xi. 23.

Satan, full of objective knowledge, commits this sin every day.

How Nicodemus reasons! Doubtless he had seen the unrecorded cluster of miracles. John iv. 45.

"The works that I do bear witness of Me, that the FATHER hath *sent* me." John v. 36.

"*We know,*" a self-sufficient speech, but he is soon forced to confess he knows nothing.

Teacher. Probably a cautious retraction after a sudden avowal.

We learn from the young ruler's question the *kind* of *instruction* our Lord gave.

Not what Nicodemus *sought,* but verily such as he *needed.*

He enlightened the heart not merely as a " Teacher sent from God," but as *God Himself.*

Nicodemus doubtless expected an answer similar to the question, " What good thing shall I do ? "   Matt. xix. 16.

He would increase his present treasure of holiness.

He seems uncertain whether to call Him teacher or prophet ; perhaps He might be the Christ.

He would nevertheless show his learning and piety to Jesus.

Come.   In public official character, for He had openly before the people called the temple "My Father's House."   John ii. 16.

Nicodemus knew that for four hundred years Israel had had no prophets except false ones.   John x. 8.

The Sanhedrim questioned John, if *he* were " THE COMING ONE."   Matt. xi. 3.

From God.   This implies more than a simple fact.   It admits that our Lord was a scholar not of the schools, nor trained by human teachers.

A Prophet from heaven, with authority over priests and kings ; also Comforter and Ruler, Law-giver and Judge of the quick and dead.   John xiv. 18.

It was a good beginning, when a Pharisee made such a confession.

For the first time in his life he feels in his heart the searching glance of Omniscience.

This phrase stands here alone in all the Bible : it is *un-Israelitish,* for the Jews then expected far more than a *teaching* Messiah.

No man.   So far this shows candour and honesty. " He that doeth truth, cometh to the light."   John iii. 21.

A Pharisee, yet in *secret* an humble, fervent, prayerful man, seeking light !   This is the true key to'this visit, of so unlooked-for a guest.

How deficient when compared with Nathanael,—" Rabbi, thou art the Son of God."   John i. 49.

He does not at once fully yield himself up to the truth.   The sacrifice is still too great.

By way of *apology*, he gives his reason for yielding even thus far.

Miracles.   Gr. *signs*—i. e. of Divine working.   John ii. 11, 23 ; iv. 48 ; vi. 30.

1. Wrought to confirm Divine truth. 2. In harmony with revelation. 3. Produce definite results. 4. Overthrow Satan. 5. Wrought without any concealment. 6. Supernatural. *Stillingfleet.*

Our Lord thus "*rings the great bell of the universe,*" summoning

angels, men, and demons to witness the laying of the foundations of His Church.

Satan can work " signs and lying wonders " (Greek " miracles "),
2 Thess. ii. 9, as " Prince of the power of the air." Eph. ii. 2 ;
Matt. iv. 5.

But Satan never wrought wonders in the way of *benevolence.*

Biblical miracles are the revelation of the almighty freedom of AL-
MIGHTY LOVE.

God in miracles restores the moral order disturbed by man's sinful
abuse of freedom.

Neither Divine wisdom nor Divine unchangeableness injured in the
slightest degree.

Miracles an advantage to the eternal order of the world destroyed
by sin.

The whole question of miracles : Is it conceivable that God should
interfere for the redemption and restoration of a race corrupted
and made miserable by sin ?

Our Lord rebuked sinful demands for miracles. John iv. 48;
Matt. xvi. 4.

He even pronounced those blessed who believed without them.
John xx. 29.

MIRACLES OF OUR LORD. I. MIRACLES ON NATURE : *Water
made wine.* John ii. 1—12. *Bread multiplied* (1.) Matt. xiv.
15—21 ; Mark vi. 35—44 ; Luke ix. 12—17 ; John vi. 5—
14. (2.) Matt. xv. 32—39 ; Mark viii. 1—10. *Walking on
the water.* Matt. xiv. 22—26 ; Mark vi. 48, 49 ; John vi. 16—
21. *First miraculous Draught of Fishes.* Luke v. 1—11.
Storm stilled. Matt. viii. 23—27 ; Mark iv. 35—41 ; Luke viii.
22—25. *Stater in the Fish's mouth.* Matt. xvii. 24—27.
Second miraculous Draught of Fishes. John xxi. 1—23. *Fig-
tree cursed.* Matt. xxi. 19 ; Mark xi. 20. II. MIRACLES ON
MAN. *Two blind men in the house.* Matt. ix. 29—31. *Bartimæus.* Matt. xx. 29—34 ; Mark x. 46—52 ; Luke xviii. 35—
43. *One Leper.* Matt. viii. 1—4 ; Mark i. 40—45 ; Luke v.
12—16. *Ten Lepers.* Luke xvii. 11—19. *Woman with the
Issue.* Matt. ix. 20—22 ; Mark v. 25—34 ; Luke viii. 43—
48. *Blind.* Mark viii. 22—26. *Deaf and dumb.* Mark vii.
31—37. *Nobleman's son.* John iv. 46 — 54. *Centurion's
servant.* Matt. viii. 5—13 ; Luke vii. 1—10. *Man borne of
four.* Matt. ix. 1 — 8 ; Mark ii. 1 — 12 ; Luke v. 17 — 26.
Blind man. John ix. *Fever.* Matt. viii. 14, 15 ; Mark i.

29 — 34 ; Luke iv. 38 — 41. *Dropsy.* Luke xiv. 1 — 6.
Withered hand. Matt. xii. 9—13 ; Mark iii. 1—5 ; Luke vi.
6—11. *Impotent man.* John v. 1—17. *Woman with Spirit
of Infirmity.* Luke xiii. 10—17. *Girl raised.* Matt. ix. 18 ;
Mark v. 22 ; Luke viii. 41. *Young man raised.* Luke vii.
11—18. *Lazarus raised.* John xi. III. MIRACLES ON THE
SPIRIT WORLD : *Dumb man possessed.* Matt. ix. 32—34. *Man
blind and dumb.* Matt. xxii. 22 ; Luke xi. 14. *Syrophœnician's
daughter.* Matt. xv. 21—28 ; Mark vii. 24—30. *Lunatic boy.*
Matt. xvii. 14 ; Mark ix. 14 ; Luke ix. 37. *Man in the Synagogue.* Mark i. 21—28 ; Luke iv. 31—37. *Man with legion.*
Matt. viii. 28—34 ; Mark v. 1—17 ; Luke viii. 26, 27.

Thirty-four distinct miracles, including those in Acts, *forty-four,*
and of *benevolent tendency.*

The greatest miracles of all appeared in the Redemption plan. 1.
His Incarnation. 2. His Resurrection. 3. His Ascension.

His *works illustrate His words* as the ocean reflects the splendour
of the sun.

" Goodness is a foreland ; godly deeds are hills ;
And faith's efforts in God's strength the lower mountain height ;
But in Christ's miracles the Alpine world begins,
O'er which His resurrection-peak sheds dazzling light."—*Lange.*

God be with him. This appeal from an aged leader of the
Sanhedrim came in the form of a compliment amounting to
flattery.

The venerable Nicodemus confronts a young man from Galilee
with honied words.

Perhaps he would draw the Son of Mary to join the Theocracy and
become a Pharisee.

This plausible scheme would make Jesus stand high with the
guardians of religion in Jerusalem.

Nicodemus' spirit was of the earth, and he speaks both as an Elder
and a man of the world.

In a word, he meant " *Be one of us,* and you shall have all the
honour you desire."

For Ἰησοῦν, αὐτόν. *Lach., Tisch., Alf., Cod. Sin.* It does not imply the
three apostles were not present. *Hengst.*
νυκτός. Fear, a result of a lower faith. *Hengst.* Our Saviour's evenings His
only leisure. *Bede, Maldonatus.* Not to give umbrage to his colleagues. *Grotius.*
Desired a private interview. *Lightfoot.* Censured for not desiring open baptism

and confession. *Wetstein.* By chance found himself in Jesus' home, on his way over the Mount of Olives. *Tisch.* Not timid. *Herder.* He acts sincerely and consistently. *G. Müller.* The colour of a time-server. *Eichorn.* Prudence dictated a private interview. *Kezel.* Our Lord did not condemn his night visit. *Bahrdt.*

'Ραββὶ. He had a full conviction of our Lord's divine commission. *Lampe.* Remarkable, as our Lord's social position was very humble. *Doddridge.* He was not certain, but that He might lead to rebellion. *Maurice.*

οἴδαμεν. Of singular import, embracing the people. *Lightfoot, Crusius.* Plural "we" may be merely an allusion to others who had come to the same conclusion, e. g. Joseph of Arimathæa. *Alford, Bengel, Stier.* If he spake for all the Sanhedrim, he must have been too sanguine. *Luthardt.* He expressed the opinions of his peers. *Prescott.* He represents believers in Christ's miracles then wrought. *Hengst.* Implies the Sanhedrim would conceal the knowledge of His miracles. *Ferus.*

Θεοῦ ἐλήλυθας. Our Lord not "*sent*" as the Baptist. John i. 6. The expression "come from God" nowhere used for a merely human messenger. *Luthardt, Brown.* A recognition of His Messianic mission. Not a mere authentication of His mission. *Stier.* Promised by all the prophets. *Schleiermacher.*

διδάσκαλος. Two great teachers here met, one from Jerusalem, the other from heaven. *Herberger.* A concealed request to lead him to the Messiah. *Hengst.*

σημεῖα, τέρατα, δυνάμεῖς, are frequently common events chosen as signs, not necessarily miraculous. (See critical notes to John ii. 11.) *Trench.* Miracle, a *violation* of the laws of nature. *Hume.* Something *different* from those laws. *Butler.* *Contrary* to nature. *Douglas.* *Above* nature. *Trench.* Done to attest truth. *Sam. Johnson.* To restore moral order destroyed by sin. *Oosterzee.* Can evil spirits work miracles? Some answer, No. *Formes, Bekher.* Some answer, Yes. *Jerome, Lactantius, Tertullian, Augustine* with reserve.

---

3. Jesus answered and said unto him, Verily, verily, I say unto thee, Except a man be born again, he cannot see the kingdom of God.

Answered. Our Lord anticipated rather than interrupted Nicodemus, to introduce His own theme.

No purely *political* or *philosophical* theme was ever introduced by Christ.

Reveals the solemn spiritual atmosphere created by His life and teaching.

In John He oft seems to answer *thoughts,* not words, yet He never drew a bow at a venture.

Nicodemus does not introduce at first his object in coming, but our Lord, with an omniscient glance, *reveals the secret* to him.

He would not allow the motive *curiosity* to come out more plainly, and thus mar the supreme object of the Gospel scene.

A craving unsatisfied desire might also have been another motive.

The answer to his heart, instead of his words, probably convicts him.

Not mainly doctrine, but *life itself* is concerned here.

Not merely admiring the Christian system, or sustaining Christian rules.

Balaam's mind glowed with wonder at the beauty and loveliness of the Church.

Rousseau became grand as he described the scene of Calvary.

Not of being *different*, but of being *new born*, Christ speaks. *Luther*.

How may I enter life ? was in his heart, but not on his lips.

As a Jew and a Pharisee he believed that when the kingdom appeared, he would unquestionably be one of its members.

He wishes to hear of heavenly things, but our Lord brings him down to *repentance* in *dust* and *ashes*.

His aching heart was a surer guide than his head ; but the fear of man ensnared him, and held him in fetters.

Our Lord avoids all circumlocution ; immediately and plainly He makes the solemn announcement.

The hour was brief, and eternity for Nicodemus depended on the issues.

He must speak no more complimentary words to the TEACHER ; he must look within himself.

Verily, verily. See on John i. 51. An expression not found in any of the other Gospels.

John emphatically, " the disciple who testifieth." Chap. xxi. 24.

The one who caught most of the manner of Him who is " the faithful and true WITNESS."

This solemn asseveration implies Nicodemus' ignorance of this great truth.

It indicates his *resistance* to its hearty acknowledgment.

Indeed, some hold he came secretly to make friends with One he supposed might be the long-expected Messiah.

It is used at the end of prayer, blessings, curses, or vows. Num. v. 22.

Words uttered on Divine authority, and therefore truth itself.

Nicodemus possessed of a common, but radical error, that the kingdom of God would *be visible to the eye.* Luke xvii. 20.

Yet our Lord kindly receives this timid inquirer,—a parable of the future Church.

I say unto. An emphatic formula. Contains two emphatic pronouns, I, the Son of God, say unto YOU.

I, the Teacher sent from God, will answer thine inmost soul.

Thou wouldst begin at the *Omega*, I will begin at the *Alpha*.

Thee. The Pharisee, the " separated," esteeming thyself better than others.

" Thee," a member of the chief Council, reputed as pre-eminently *virtuous* and *zealous !*

With a diamond-pointed truth, the Spirit alone knows how to reach the mind. Witness Nathan's parable, Elisha to Hazael, &c. 2 Sam. xii. 1 ; 2 Kings viii. 13.

All his hopes seemed reduced, in an instant, to a heap of ashes.

Except a man. The Lord's insight into the heart explains the abruptness of the answer.

This draws him out from behind his " *We*," and places him a sinner among sinners.

Before Omniscience, all human classes and castes disappear.

Thus the Saviour's reply answers Nicodemus, as though he would learn how to be saved, and to the Omniscient Lord, this *might* have been his unconscious motive, and the Holy Spirit's purpose.

The great Searcher of the heart sees this venerable man rooted by education in formalism.

He would win him by the shattering stroke of one mighty truth.

He does not *limit it to Nicodemus*, but makes it general as the human race.

He deliberately shakes down the whole edifice of *his* religion.

Most persons, like Paul, have what they call " *Our Religion*." Acts xxvi. 5.

Nicodemus may have looked for compliments for his candour.

He is told that he cannot solve his own question, until all his powers are *reconstructed*.

Born again. Gr. implies *a second birth*, and that of a heavenly origin.

Equivalent to " Thou art not yet born again."

Our Lord uses a strong metaphor to hint at his terrible ignorance.

Why did He abruptly introduce regeneration ?

Because He thought of new *fruits*, and hence begins with new *roots*.

It is not of doing new works He speaks, but of a new *heart* to do them.

Not of *living* in a new way, but of being *born* into a new life.

Not a life of mere *lea n'ng*, but of holy *obedience*.

Not even of another *life* only, but of another *birth*, a new nature.

As the *kingdom* is God's and God is Spirit, so must the birth be
spiritual.

When a young Brahmin has the " *sacred string*," he is said to be
born, and the putting on the sacred string is IRI PURAPPATI,
i. e. " *twice born.*"

The ancient Egyptians called one of their deities " sun-begotten."
This child of light must ever be radiant as its sire.

Thus " Spirit-born " will be spiritual, as the Holy Ghost by whom
he is begotten.

Had He said, " Except a Gentile," &c., Nicodemus would have
understood it.

Origin of spiritual life like origin of natural life,—a mystery.

The fact we know, but the mode is lost in God's almighty fiat.

Spiritual life grows ; its germ is implanted in regeneration.

Nicodemus thought *that* a *command*, which was promised as a
gift.

No question of moral *reformation*, but of VITAL RENOVATION.

Not a medicine to cure a sick soul, but a creating of a new man.
2 Cor. v. 17.

Many ages before David cried, " CREATE *in me a clean heart.*" Psa.
li. 10.

Nicodemus in practice utterly ignored the fact of his depravity,
and this was the foundation of his error.

Unrenewed men believe not that " the wrath of God abideth on
them." John iii. 36.

Claiming to be *innocent*, they boldly deny that " they must be born
again." John iii. 3.

The three " R's " of Baxter : Ruin, Redemption, Regeneration, blaze
on the very door-posts of the Bible.

Men hate these humbling truths, as they ring the death-knell of
self-righteousness.

Sage and hero must begin life anew, just as at the first, a CHILD.

The eye with which one sees was not *made* by the seer, but was
born ; the power to *breathe* was not *acquired*, but results
from our *birth.* Psa. civ. 30.

Thus to see the beauty of the Redeemer, or hear His call as the
Shepherd Divine, both eye and ear must be born in the soul.
Cant. v. 10 ; John x. 16.

Hence there are men who having ears, are deaf, and having eyes,
are blind. Isa. xliii. 8 ; xlii. 18.

A blind man fondly trusted that if the letters were enlarged he could read : not the words, but his eyes needed to be changed.

A question might have arisen with any unrenewed heart,—"Is it not better to renounce the kingdom of God, at such a price ? "

Our Lord's words the severest conceivable indictment against human nature.

On the natural soil NO FRUIT of righteousness CAN GROW.

Some dream of baptismal regeneration, but our Lord *knew it not.*

The penitent malefactor was assured of heaven, and yet was never baptized.

To legally inherit from a parent, one must be born of that parent.

Thus, to *inherit heaven*, our Father's patrimony, we must be *born of God.*

Cannot.   No man, however innocent, not even a Master in Israel, is excepted.

Regeneration, as the act of God, is *not* commanded, but AN-NOUNCED.

Pardon is not commanded to rebels, but PROCLAIMED by the herald.

By nature we have reason, but it is blinded; a will, but it is paralyzed.

We *love*, but it centres in self ; we seek *pleasure*, but not in God.

We can *hate* anything, save sin ; we fear, but it is *servile.*

No new faculty is added, but all are *renewed* or *re-created.*   2 Cor. iv. 16.

" We are His *workmanship*, CREATED in Christ Jesus."   Eph. ii. 10.

As a man is born *but once*, so we are *renewed but once.*   Eph. iv. 23 ; Tit. iii. 5.

See.   To know the way to heaven and travel therein no one need even try to see this kingdom at *a distance.*

Jacob attained this *seeing* while wrestling with the ANGEL of the Covenant.

Kingdom.   By experience, not discussion ; by the heart rather than the head, we find this kingdom.

No polluted steps ever soiled or can soil the golden pavement.

Our Lord in speaking of a kingdom lays hold of a *foundation* hope of every Jew.

Prophets had predicted its reality and coming for ages.

All the nation's *expectations at that hour* were aglow.

The departing Simeon uttered the universal hope.   Luke ii. 30.

Our Saviour's words hint this kingdom was near.

It was even then begun, in the night visit of Nicodemus.

In it God rules; the Spirit, the supreme *law* of life; union with
   Christ, *the vital element.*
The Jewish idea was transformed by His Love.
Christ's Incarnation was this " kingdom at hand."
Justice honoured, Mercy celebrates its festal glory in heaven.
The kingdom will be complete, the reprobate shut out for ever!
Parable of the *sower,* shows the *culture* of heaven, imaged in that of
   earth.
That of the *tares,* shows the positive *hindrances,* to be overcome by
   His kingdom.
That of the *leaven,* its inherent power to overcome and *assimilate*
   to itself. Matt. xiii. 33.
That of the *net,* the final *separation* of all unfriendly elements.
Mercy, Invincible Love, Redeeming Grace, elements in this kind-
   dom. Luke x. 30 ; xiv. 16 ; xv. 11.

ἀπεκρίθη. Our Lord never interrupted the meanest person speaking.
Stier. Probably some remark made by Nicodemus, unrecorded. *Lightfoot.*
An unjustifiable conclusion. *Author.* Nicodemus secretly intended such an
inquiry. *Doddr.* The Evangelist omits other questions. *Kuinoel.* He had
spoken of the Messiah's kingdom. *Glassius.* Our Lord anticipated his desires.
Beza, Chemnitz. No evidence he intended to inquire about his salvation.
Lampe. Such matter for thought and investigation, as his Pharisee's life never
gave him. *Dräscke.*
   Ἀμὴν. Hebrew adjective "*sure,*" an ejaculatory particle of assent. *J. A.
Alexander.*
   λέγω. Our Lord denies He is *merely* a prophet, but claims essential Godhead. *Cajetan.*
   γεννηθῇ. Differs from μετάνοια, a word not used by John. *Bengel.* A
new being, more rigorously demanded. *Hengst.* Not repentance, but renovation.
Calvin. Proselytes at baptism received a new soul. *Rabbis, Selden.* 1. A
change in the Jewish law intimated. 2. Instead of servants, sons henceforth.
3. Jews and Gentiles could enter Jerusalem. 4. All through Christ. *Toletus.* A
thorough giving up of views, connections, plans, &c. *Michaelis.*
   ἄνωθεν. No ambiguous term in the Aramaic. *Grotius.* On high, from
heaven, from God. *Erasmus.* The Syro-Chaldee used by our Lord has no
obscurity. *Lightfoot.* Baptismal regeneration. *Rheimish Notes.* From the
beginning. *Blenker.* A moral reformation, πάλιν ἄνωθεν. Gal. iv. 9. A
change of religion called a regeneration by Jews. *Wetstein.* Born again among
Romans was adoption. *Justinian.* Our Lord's remarks aimed rather at the
teachers of that age. *Cyril.* First be unmade, 1 Pet. ii. 24. *Trapp.* Spiritual
generation. *Hilgenfeld.* Not synonymous with πάλιν, δεύτερον, but altogether
new. *Stier.* Again, anew. *Luther, Lampe, Calvin, Neander, Tholuck, Luthardt.*
Afresh. *Alford.* From above and again. *Maurice.* From above. *Origen,
Erasmus, Lightfoot, Bengel, Meyer, De Wette, Lücke, Lange.* Begin life
anew in relation to God. *D. Brown.* Renatus denuo. *Vulgate.* Nicodemus
had no idea of it at all. *Meyer.* The characteristic of Pharisaism is to ignore
regeneration. *Hengst.* The doctrine of regeneration is found in *Justin Martyr*
firty years after John wrote. *Tholuck.*

ἰδεῖν. Clearly perceive. *Stier.* To enjoy. *Bengel.*
βασιλείαν. Heaven resembled a state, God its Sovereign, angels its citizens; the dead must rise to share it. Hence he must receive a new principle of life to enter it. 1. Christ's offices executed past and present. 2. Ordinances for redemption. 3. His work in redemption, on earth, and heaven. *Tittmann.* He saw in it those miracles. *Luthardt.* Kingdom lies in the background. *Tischendorf.* Something more than being children of Abraham. *Lightfoot.* The essential relations of humanity culminate in Christ their Head. *Lange.* Our Lord did not entirely reject the Jewish idea of a kingdom. Luke i. 32, 33. *Author.*

---

4. Nicodemus saith unto him, How can a man be born when he is old? can he enter the second time into his mother's womb, and be born?

How? The "how" and "why" of ignorance and pride often make faith to stumble.

Thus Sarah in the folly of her heart laughed at God's promise.

But after centuries of thought and study we know no more of the mode of regeneration than we do of the springing of corn, 1 Cor. xv. 36, or the creation of Adam's soul.

Nicodemus but imperfectly understood our Lord. "He saw men as trees walking." Mark viii. 24.

He knew the Lord meant *him*, and that *his* seeing the kingdom was involved in a new birth.

This utter annihilation of all to which he had clung so long was more than the old man could bear.

He seems to excuse himself from the possibility of compliance.

Yet Pharisaism gave him no *rest* of heart before God. Jer. vi. 14 ; Isa. xlviii. 22.

He longs for the blessings of the kingdom, but the needle's eye is too narrow for his ecclesiastical pride.

He writhes in mental anguish, dreading the inevitable inference.

" Even *thou, the aged Nicodemus, must be born again, must become a child!* "

How hard the words of Jesus to the young wealthy ruler! Luke xviii. 24.

But how much harder to this venerable Pharisee, high in office, and long flattered by the fawning crowd!

Yet he denies not the *fact*, but questions the *mode*.

He could not conceive how the soul could be changed except by re-framing the body.

Alas, the body might be created anew a thousand times and the soul remain the same guilty dark thing.

He evidently came confident of obtaining new light.

But his reply seems to say, since a new birth in my case is impossible, am I to be shut out ?

He hears he has no eyes *to see* the kingdom, until *born again.*

A momentary doubt only strengthens the depth of conviction.

Conscience responds like a flash of lightning in the night of his soul.

He had come, perhaps, to flatter his pride of learning, or to gratify his curiosity.

But our Lord's words had dashed his hopes to pieces, and he stands convicted of *utter ignorance.*

This blow was heavy in proportion to the splendour of the "*miracles,*" which he referred to in ver. 2.

As a " natural man, he could not receive the things of the Spirit of God." 1 Cor. ii. 14.

As well ask how God at first created man, or how the *same soil* produces the night-shade and the grape.

He was not called to comprehend *how,* but to *believe* the *fact,* and *obey* the *law.*

He is old. " Although one of our Lord's first converts was an old man, yet by far the greater number are gathered in youth." *Jon. Edwards.*

He goes not beyond the unlearned Samaritan woman. John iv. 11.

She mistakes "the living waters " for earthly streams.

The ignorant crowd cried, " Evermore give us this bread." John vi. 34.

Nicodemus begins to dispute instead of humbly asking for light.

Doubtless his confusion was increased by the abrupt manner of the Lord.

The Great Teacher has suddenly broken through all barriers of reserve.

He clearly saw the " *thee* " was an arrow aimed at *himself.*

His command of words as a scribe reveals itself; he conceals his personal convictions under " one being old."

He first questions the possibility of a new birth, and then asks if an impossibility can be realized ?

Enter. He now goes on to a still stronger protest.

He hangs perpetually upon the *letter,* with a faint tinge of irony.

He is of the earth, earthy; his views are earthly.

A musician being asked what was the soul, answered " *Harmony.*"

Plato's disciple, trained in mathematics, when asked the same question, answered " *Number.*"

Simon Magus, long accustomed to buying and selling, offered
silver for the Holy Ghost.

Our Lord's sacred paradox was intended to humble the pride of
Nicodemus.

His reply evinces fear, and the obliquity of a mind in spiritual
darkness.

Many Nicodemuses now ask, "Cannot I repent whenever I choose?"

Others turn away in scorn and go to Judgment, to learn their folly,
when it is too late. Prov. i. 28.

Second. Our Lord had said he must be "*born from above.*"

Nicodemus entirely changes the sense, by bringing in a new term.

Like all Jews, he believed that Gentile proselytes must be changed,
but that "the seed of Abraham" was already and always
fit for the kingdom.

His surprise, therefore, is intense, for, like Paul, he could boast that
he was "a Hebrew of the Hebrews." Phil. iii. 5.

Πῶς δύναται. The Jewish nation could not renounce their Messianic view.
Kuinoel. Would you have a Jewish doctor go through a change as great as a
heathen renouncing his impure faith and practice? *Wetstein.* He feels himself
addressed as a Hebrew of culture, and not an ignorant Gentile, and thinks birth
means birth. *Maurice.* If only reformation is meant, what was plain before is
now obscured. *Wesley.* Very doubtful if the new birth was an obvious truth
in Nicodemus' age. *Stier.* Imitated sensibility. *Lange.* Some see a prompt
self-application of the truth. *Ford.* The proud ruler feels injured, expecting a
different reply to his acknowledgment of the Nazarene. *Ebel.* He seems offended
by repeating δύναται, which the Lord had given him back. *Stier.*
γέρων ὤν. He would not understand that he should begin anew. *Stier.* He
ridicules any such change. *Alford.* You don't mean literally. What then?
Lücke, Olshausen. How can this kingdom come, if men must renounce their
whole past life? *B. Crusius.* Our Lord's ἄνωθεν differed widely from his
δεύτερον. *Stier.* To become a little child in one's view is as impossible as,
&c. *Ebrard.* He knows no more of this truth than a cow-herd of astronomy.
Trapp.

---

5. Jesus answered, Verily, verily, I say unto thee, Except a man be born of
water and of the Spirit, he cannot enter into the kingdom of God.

Answered. Our Lord's replies were always the fruit of Infinite
wisdom.

His second answer is more distinct, and more severe, than the first.

He regarded the questioner much more than the question.

Nicodemus seemed to hint, that waiting for an entrance by new
birth into the kingdom, was a hopeless thing.

Under apparent repulsion, he is drawn closer to the Lord.

In like manner the Syrophœnician woman and the Samaritan were attracted also.

Joseph spake roughly to his brethren while love was overflowing in his heart.   Gen. xlii. 7.

Our Lord's answer proves profound condescension and grace.

Verily. Nicodemus doubted the possibility, our Lord re-asserts the *absolute necessity of this new birth.*

He knew how hardly the Pharisee resisted this truth.

With the same spirit for 1800 years, unbelievers have fought against this and other evangelical doctrines.

Regeneration involves faith in all the essential truths of Christianity.

Adoringly, we admire our Lord's spirit of love, not provoked or offended by a question of unbelief.

Unfavourable as it looked, there was an ear, in the deep recesses of his conscience, listening.

The same power that *created* the soul was *then re-creating it.*   Psa. li. 10.

I say.   The Son of God working miracles is God's endorsement of His words.

Our Lord intended no one should ever misunderstand His object.

His mission is written as plainly in the Bible, as the sun in the heavens.

Each answer is pointed by this deeply significant word ;

For the conditions of entering the kingdom are *unchangeable.*

Nicodemus represented the best instructed Judaism of that day.

Modern unbelievers act as though the Lord must retract all such words.

They will insist on entering heaven on their own terms.

But "the word of the Lord endureth for ever," whether mortals understand it or not.   Rom. iii. 3, 4.

Born.   There is not a birth by water, and another by the Spirit.

But ONE birth of water AND *the Spirit.*

But ONE REGENERATION.   "What therefore God has joined together, let no man put asunder."

Water.   See on John i. 25 ; ii. 6.   Regeneration of the soul is beautifully illustrated by the cleansing influence of water.

The Spirit is compared to water in the Old Test.   Isa. xliv. 3 ; Joel ii. 28.   And the same figure is used in the New.   Tit. iii. 5 ; 1 Cor. vi. 11.

Recoiling from the superstitious dogma that the sacraments are

saving in their nature, some deny baptism is here alluded to.
Clem. Alex., A.D. 200, was the first to broach the dogma of bap-
tismal regeneration.
Council of Trent anathematizes all who deny it.
They who "preach another gospel," Gal. i. 8, are here condemned.
He who refused to celebrate the Passover was to be " cut off," that
is, perish under a visitation of God.   Exod. xii. 19.
But Philistines or Moabites may have shared the Passover a score
of times.
Yet, instead of a blessing, the curse would have followed.
A stung Israelite might have " looked " at the serpent in scorn and
must have died !
Hypocrites sharing the sacraments, enter the Church, but before His eye,
wear no mask.
They share the ordinances, like Judas, only to deepen their con-
demnation.
Baptism is here as solemnly enjoined as the Lord's Supper.   John
vi. 53.
Yet baptism can no more *secure a new heart* or be a *substitute for*
it, than sprinkling holy water could exorcise a demon.
This new rite stripped the Jew of all *confidence* in circumcision or
faith in Abraham's blood.
It was the *link* between the Old and New Test. economies.
A Jew no longer, the chosen child of God must be baptized, and
thus renounce Judaism before he can share the blessing.
The crescent is the badge of Islamism.
Baptism is the *badge* of the *Christian.*
It binds to the Redeemer by a (" sacramentum ") solemn oath.
Those who falsely assume this symbol are guilty of *treason* to
God.   Acts v. 2.
A great reformer had arisen, and Jerusalem and all Judea went out
to be baptized.
But the proud members of the Sanhedrim refused to acknowledge
him.
Infatuated with their Israelitish blood, and blind through fanati-
cism, they despised all reformation, and disregarded John the
reformer !
The coming of this herald, foretold 400 years before his birth.   Mal.
iii. 1.
Our Lord greatly honoured him, and indirectly enjoins the proud
Pharisee to own him also.

While Nicodemus had neglected John's baptism, even the spotless Jesus had submitted to it.

He thus vindicated the *binding solemnity* of Christian sacraments, while honouring that of His forerunner.

Had Nicodemus obeyed, he *now* would have understood the Lord.

Circumstances may render baptism impossible, as in the case of the penitent thief. Luke xxiii. 43.

Yet Romanists affirm " the blood from Christ's side *sprinkled* him."

Even under the O. T. the necessity of spiritual purification was taught. Ezek. xxxvi. 25.

But this Divine teaching had been lost during the long reign of formalism.

Prominence given to water is a fatal blow to Nicodemus' pride.

How exceedingly *defiled*, if he needed it to cleanse him.

The Lord, in His sovereign wisdom, *makes an external act a condition of acceptance.* Matt. ix. 21.

The bitten Israelite must look to the brazen serpent, or perish. Num. xxi. 6, 9.

The rich young man's discipleship depended on making *an external sacrifice.* Matt. xix. 21.

Yet beggaring one's self, as an act of *will-worship*, would only deepen guilt and ruin.

This fatal delusion filled scores of monasteries and convents with lazy, licentious monks and nuns. *Bernard.*

The impotent man's cure at Bethesda depended on an *external order*, and the ten lepers' in obeying an *external duty.*

Water is a symbol of Divine influence cleansing from guilt and pollution. 1 John v. 6 ; Isa. xliv. 3 ; Eph. v. 26.

The washing of Aaron and his sons a most solemn and significant symbol. Lev. viii. 6.

" Wash me throughly from mine iniquity, and cleanse me from my sin." Psa. li. 2.

Wisdom and mercy seen in selecting *bread* for the communion and *water* for baptism, both being generally accessible at all times.

He would sanctify these COMMON *blessings,* and exalt our daily festal board into a holy table.

Spirit. See on John i. 32, 33 ; vii. 39. He is the manifestation of the LOVE of the Godhead.

This stroke of the Redeemer levels the entire fabric of Pharisaical hopes to the dust.

They placed their religion in external forms, things which the world could *see* or *hear*.

They were the *Romanists* and *Ritualists* of that day.

Our Lord repeats the same truth as in ver. 3, but adds the *nature* of this change.

The soul must be *re*-created to be freed from its dregs of sensuality and sin. Psa. li. 10.

Cavillers say the means employed bear no proportion to the end.

True, but faith in the ALMIGHTY supplies the *difference*. 1 John v. 4.

Enter in. Our Lord makes no further reference to water.

This proves that it was used merely as a *point of departure*.

The *entire burden* of the interview refers to a *spiritual birth*.

But refusing to submit to a divinely-appointed external duty indicates the lack of an earnest *desire* for salvation.

Baptism is the door God has appointed for *entering the Christian Church.*

Regeneration is the only door appointed for *entering* HEAVEN.

Note a marked change of language : " *see* " is dropped for " *enter.*"

Seeing implies *comprehending*, entering implies becoming a *subject*.

By nature we are subjects of God's kingdom, and bound by its laws.

Hence they avenge themselves on us, when we violate them.

But consciousness and life proclaim that we are rebels against God.

No theory for 6000 years has enabled men to get rid of these facts.

Until we return to our allegiance to God we must have war in our souls.

How we can regain peace, our Lord professes to tell.

Israel leaving bondage was baptized in the Red Sea.

Elijah about to ascend in the chariot of fire, must first pass through Jordan. 2 Kings ii. 8, 11.

So the believer entering the kingdom must enter on God's own terms.

ὕδατος. Heavenly light. *Zwingle, Vitringa*. Cleansing involved. *Tholuck*. All Christ enjoins. *Kuinoel*. Baptism, most ancient authors. *Wall, Hooker*. Water a sign, the Spirit is signified. *Alford*. Water, an emblem. *Olshausen*. Indicates the cleansing of the soul. *Neander, Lücke*. Baptism of the Spirit. *Luther, Calvin, Turretin*. Signaculum. *Isidore*. Emblem of regeneration. *Sumner*. Word sacramental. *Stier*. Baptismal regeneration ex opere operato. *Rheimish Notes, Council of Trent*. Baptismal sanctification shows edifying examples in Zinzendorf, Spener, Scheibel, Tschierley. *Besser*, a Lutheran. Quakers strangely out of the circle if it be baptism. *Ryle*. Is the Lord's Supper not binding because ignored by Quakers? *Author*. Water used in baptizing proselytes before John the Baptist. *Goodwyn.* Denied. *J. A. Alexander.* Lord's Supper and baptism both found in John. *Hilgenfeld.* Persons desiring baptism and dying without are accepted. *Burgon.* Martyrs, unbaptized by the Church, are accepted through the baptism of blood. *Bingham.* Water, the seal of access to the Spirit. *Hengst.* Testifying great moral pollution. *Anton.* Baptism is an indenture, only executed by one party. *Waterland.* Death the penalty of violating the sacrament of Paradise, and this guilt no less. *King.* Baptism succeeds circumcision. *Gerhardt.* A mere figure for the truth. *Lampe, Cocceius.* Baptism embodies the simple truth here announced. *D. Brown.* Is baptism necessary to salvation? Yes. *Rheimish Notes.* No! It is applied invisibly. *Augustine, Calvin,* and all evangelical commentators. Objection: Baptism had not yet been established. Answer: John had for months been baptizing all the hosts who came. Nicodemus understood as much as any of them what it implied. *Author.*

Πνεύματος. Spirit brooding over chaos, the air. *Erasmus.* Mystical element. *Schubert.* A renewed man becomes πνευματικος. *Wetstein.* Three births in the New Test.—1. National birth. 2. At conversion. 3. At the reunion of soul and body. Matt. xix. 28. *Toletus.*

εἰσελθεῖν. To *see* (ver. 3) signifies to believe in, to *enter* is to become subject to. *Maurice.*

---

6. That which is born of the flesh is flesh; and that which is born of the Spirit is spirit.

That. The neuter makes its application universal and absolute.

So that even if it could be so, it would avail nothing.

Born. The origin of natural life is mysterious, so is the origin of spiritual life.

The infant's first cry shows another *evil thing* has come into being.

We enter the world seemingly under the *frown* of our Maker. Gen. iii. 16.

As if our Lord had said, Dost thou not know, proud ruler, that thou art but a *common sinner?*

A principle universal: That which is begotten partakes of the nature of its sire.

Adam begat a son in his likeness. Gen. v. 3. David mourned it also. Psa. li. 5.

Job asks, "Who can bring a clean thing out of an unclean?" Job xiv. 4.

Even the sinless flesh of Christ recoiled from agony. Matt. xxvi. 39.

The mind is carnal (Gr. fleshly) sold under sin. Rom. vii. 14.

Allusion to Romans selling captives as SLAVES, *under the spear.*

Flesh. Not the mere material body, but all that which comes into the world by birth.

"Born" refers to the natural relation of child to parent.

"Flesh" refers to humanity in its depraved corrupted condition.

Human nature through the fall in entire subjection to "the law of
sin and death." Rom. viii. 2.

As *carnal* "flesh and blood cannot inherit the kingdom." 1 Cor.
xv. 50.

Nor could transmigration into another body renew a fallen soul.

Nor can cutting winds and penal fires eradicate its ingrained corruption.

Millions of ages of suffering could not consume enmity and produce love.

The descent of a soul from a soul is a secret too deep for our
minds.

If an angel falls, he falls alone, or if the last of a race fall, none
suffer with him :

But if the first of a race fall—the guilt and the penalty cling to all
the race.

Yet the depth of our misery in the end displays the depth of God's
mercy.

A flesh-birth at once reveals the *source* of our depravity.

It also shows the *necessity* of our change by a spirit-birth.

Not that the soul unrenewed, "*dead in sin*" (Eph. ii. 1), has no
power.

Its energies grow fiercer, stronger, and stouter against God continually.

The transmission of evil a profound mystery, although a palpable fact.

We inherit more than a nature : we inherit sinful dispositions and
tendencies.

Spirit. See on John iii. 8 ; vii. 39. The love of the unrenewed heart is *selfishness*, all its power is *impotence*, all its
science *blindness*, all its wisdom *folly*.

Its true life, life in a spiritual kingdom, has not begun.

Men generally admit their *guilt*, and yet often deny their *depravity*.

The "*would nots*" and "*cannots*" of Paul are deeply emphatic. Rom.
viii. 3, 8.

As the fevered patient dreams of strength, so do the unrenewed.

The *Spirit* produces, by this new birth, a nature similar to His own.

He who is *born of God* is *uncorrupt, spiritual*, and *divine*.

σάρξ. Natural depravity. *Tittmann.* National birthright of sin. *Barhdt.*
Carnal nature. *Hodge.* Like produces like. *Erasmus.* First used by Adam,
Gen. ii. 23 ; ever since an idea of accessory weakness. *Stier.* Mixture of the
sons of God with the daughters of men. Gen. vi. 2. *Nitzsch.*

το γεγεννημένον. Neuter denotes rudiments of new life. *Bengel.* Mystery of original sin revealed as plainly as one's face. *Luther.*

πνεύματος. A spirit is created, liable to corruption, without involving the Creator. *Stier.* Denied by *Hegel.* A most weighty truth. *Olshausen.* Partakers of the Divine nature of the Spirit. *Erasmus.*

---

7. Marvel not that I said unto thee, Ye must be born again.

Marvel not. Doubtless He noticed signs of deep astonishment in Nicodemus.

No dreamer ever *wondered* more than the youth at the words, "Go, sell all," &c. Mark x. 21.

Nicodemus did not marvel at the necessity of baptism so much as at the doctrine of the new birth.

The Samaritan woman *wondered* at the "living water."

The Jews, offering the Lord a crown, *wondered* at His refusal.

So the Pharisee, proud of *his* birth, *wonders* at this new demand.

Wonders that he had lived so long, and *heard so much, yet never knew of this great mystery before!*

His earlier spirit of disputation is humbled.

He doubtless felt the *omniscient glance searching his heart.*

He finds *deeper* signs of ONE present "come from God."

He now first feels the AWFUL DISTANCE man by nature is from God.

He knows no man can be "just with God" unchanged. Job ix. 2.

Our Lord implies,—Receive this testimony with confidence as of eternal moment.

Ye must. Necessity of regeneration denied by rationalists and sceptics.

These words the weightiest that ever fell on that listening ear.

Especially as our Lord expressly includes Nicodemus as under the "*flesh.*"

Can we doubt the Holy Spirit carried it home to his heart?

1. It is *unreasonable* that the *holy* God would admit the *unholy* into heaven.

The sinner hates what God loves ; and labours to defeat His designs.

To confer favours on the wicked would be to *approve* their wickedness.

It would be equal to a Divine declaration that sin and holiness are the same.

That the law was enacted, and redemption accomplished, to no end.

2. Regeneration necessary to render us capable of *enjoying* heaven.

Our entire happiness hereafter is dependent on our personal holiness.

Sinners cannot relish the pursuits, affections, and company of saints.
God's worship is burdensome, nay, loathsome to sinners *here.*
How much more so in its perfect state in the heavenly temple !
3. For *usefulness* in heaven. " To give is more blessed than to
   receive."
But sinners' designs, affections, interests, are *supremely selfish.*
Hate, fraud, lust, oppression, injustice, violence, cannot enter there.
4. Regeneration must take place *here.* Death *parts,* but *changes not.*
Here sinners are " *prisoners of hope."* Zech. ix. 12. There, *prisoners*
   of " *despair."*
" No work, nor device, nor knowledge in the grave." Eccl. ix. 10.
Nicodemus desired to be the representative of his associates' senti-
   ments.
He imagined that Jesus would, with glad surprise, accept their
   homage.
Jesus intimates that He can HAVE NO INTERCOURSE WITH THEM UN-
   CHANGED.
God must either become like the sinner or the sinner like God.
It is a vestige of a fallen, but once noble nature, the wish to be
   numbered with the good.
Hence " Liberals " *vehemently* claim to be called Christians, and to
   be numbered with God's people.
Ye. The Incarnate One spotless (John viii. 46) could not say "we."
He never includes Himself among *sinful* men in all His intercourse.
Ye Jews, ye Gentiles of human birth, not I, who came down from
   heaven.
Born again. Three times is this solemnly said, as though the
   Father, the Son, and the Holy Ghost had each endorsed a
   truth of deep moment to all the millions of earth.
Circumcision of the heart, the same doctrine taught at Sinai. Deut.
   x. 16 ; xxx. 6.
We meet it, as it were, bodily in Abraham, Isaac, and Jacob.
" I will put a new spirit within you." Ezek. xi. 19.
Zion is said to be the place of the second birth of the children of
   God. Psa. lxxxvii. 5.
Born again. A most remarkable sentence when taken in connec-
   tion with principles so absolute.
Next to the *atonement,* no truth has encountered more intense
   hatred.
The great have sneered at it, and the learned have scoffed.
But conversions and revivals are not fanaticism nor enthusiasm.

They are as plainly *the great work* of the SPIRIT, as CREATION is *the work* of the WORD. John i. 3.

This Divine truth follows, enrobes, and fills all the Scriptures, as light fills, enrobes, and follows the sun.

Wherever men live, move, and have their being, we know, sunlight is around their steps :

So HOLINESS, another word for the new birth, pervades every book, chapter, verse line nay, syllable of Inspiration.

θαυμάσης. His countenance indicated surprise. *Kuinoel.*

δεῖ. From δέω, to bind. The Greeks held their gods were *bound* by Fate which was supreme. *Æsch.* in *Prom.* Gods themselves submit to irresistible destiny. *Agrippa* in *Dionys* Fortune rules and scatters her gifts blindly. *Seneca.* Necessity with God is the chain of His decrees, every link of which is Love, 1 John iv. 8. *Author.* A moral and intellectual necessity. *Ferus.*

ὑμᾶς. Not "we," although a man He was sinless. *Bengel.* Never alienated from His Father. *Alford.*

γεννηθῆναι. Times, modes, measures of the Spirit are variable, mysterious, and indefinable. *Ford.* Natural birth once in a century would be esteemed quite miraculous. *Trapp.* Verses 7 and 8 imply that Nicodemus thought the thing quite impossible. *Tholuck.*

---

8. The wind bloweth where it listeth, and thou hearest the sound thereof, but canst not tell whence it cometh, and whither it goeth: so is every one that is born of the Spirit.

The wind. "Wind" of the Lord and "Spirit" of the Lord are convertible terms. 1 Kings xviii. 12 : Acts viii. 39.

Air, ether, spirit, breath, life, names given the atmosphere.

It covers the globe about 50 miles high ; is composed of oxygen, nitrogen, and moisture.

Clouds, mist, rain, snow, various forms of water, which constitute that overhanging sky-scenery, which curtains the heavens at morn and even.

A human adult requires a gallon of fresh air every minute.

Confined in the same air, or deprived of it, he must die.

In 1756, in Calcutta, 146 English merchants and soldiers were placed in a room 18 feet square, and in one night all except 23 perished for want of pure air.

The leaves of trees, like the lungs, are vivified by contact with air.

Galileo discovered the pressure of air on all things, but the higher we ascend the more pressure decreases.

The night wind may then have been *audible* to the Lord and His guest.

Jehovah, in the *beginning*, may have designed the wind to be a perpetual symbol of the Spirit's work.

Thorns are a type of the cares and temptations of life.

Light is a type of truth, and *darkness* a type of error and ignorance.

Water is a type of moral purity, and a *rock* a type of abiding rest and repose.

So a mighty wind typified the Spirit's power and accompanied His presence.   Acts ii. 2.

Up to this time He had spoken in parables, to humble the Pharisee.

The blind feel the warmth of light without comprehending its radiance.

Things revealed are *above*, but not *contrary* to reason.

Men, sowing the fields in spring, act with wisdom and faith.

Yet no man knoweth *how* the seed, dying, springs again.   1 Cor. xv. 36.

We must die to mere *reason*, as we must die to the *law*.   Gal. ii. 19.

Philosophers, *boasting* their reason, oft act most *unreasonably*.

" Vain man would be wise, though born like a wild ass's colt."   Job xi. 12.

The path by the cross is the only way to understand scriptural truth.   Job xlii. 6.

Bloweth.   Gr. *A gentle breeze* rustling among the leaves without any special direction.

Listeth.   Gr. *willeth.*   The Bible often *personifies* things in nature.

" The stone shall cry out of the wall, the beam shall answer it."   Hab. ii. 11.

Abel's blood spilt cried to God from the ground.   Gen. iv. 10.

1. *Where* He listeth, a lesson of charity. 2. *How* He listeth, a lesson of discretion.   3. As *much* as He listeth, a lesson of humility.   4. On *whom* He listeth, a lesson of hope to all.   5. *When* He listeth, a lesson against despair.

We can only pray, " Awake, O north wind ; and come, thou south, blow," &c.   Ezek. xxxvii. 9 ; Cant. iv. 16.

His ways various : Lydia, Cornelius, Philippian jailor, Paul, &c.

With Sarah He reasons when she laughs at what Abraham embraced with faith.

God "gathers the winds in His fists," and He alone gives the
Spirit.

"A broken heart" the magnet that attracts the Eternal Spirit.

He can be "*resisted*," "*grieved*," "*quenched*." Acts vii. 51 ; Eph.
iv. 30 ; 1 Thess. v. 19.

As our will cannot *control* the wind, neither can we the Spirit.

The wind is mysterious in its risings, fallings, and frequent changes.

We can use its power on sea and land, but it is divinely *free*.

So we can yield to the Holy Spirit, but His influence will ever be
free. Psa. li. 12.

This distinctly implies the sovereignty of God.

The priest *waved* the offering pointing to God's *universal* empire.
Ex. xxix. 24.

Thus the priests in Greece turned *East*, *West*, *North*, and *South*,
while offering the sacrifice.

God's sovereignty is the deep background revealing every flash of
conscience. Rom. ii. 15.

"He doeth according to His will in the armies of heaven and
amongst," &c. Dan. iv. 35.

All laws binding on us must have a *Lawgiver*, and thus are linked
with God.

"I am God, and there is none like Me. I WILL DO ALL MY PLEA-
SURE." Isa. xlvi. 9, 10.

The thunders of vengeance and the treasures of boundless love are
His.

The power of the artist over canvas and colour is to paint what he
will.

The power of the potter over the clay, to mould what vessel he
pleaseth. Rom. ix. 21.

So in perfect sovereignty God "*hath mercy on whom He will have
mercy*," &c. Rom. ix. 18.

To all cavillers Paul puts the question, "Who art thou, O man, that
repliest against God?" Rom. ix. 20.

Hearest. A practical and experimental knowledge of things.

The evidences of spiritual life are seen in ourselves and others.

But we cannot trace the beginning or course of the Spirit's work.

"Faith comes by *hearing*," soul-hearing, Rom. x. 17, and "faith is
the gift of God." Eph. ii. 8.

Sound. A reference to the voice of the preacher and prophets.

As the gentlest murmur may increase until it become the loud roar
of the tempest.

So with the Spirit's influences. It is the LIFE OF GOD *in motion.*
Its Divine fulness, like that of the atmosphere, is immeasurable.
The *spring wind* was even then blowing through the soul of the
    aged ruler.
All that the gospel prescribes to us is plain ; all that is mysterious
    is God's part.
Watch the gales of grace,—they cannot be purchased with money.
Not tell. Partial discoveries have indeed been made, but the
    causes and laws of daily winds are as profound a secret as in
    the days of Nicodemus.
The precise moment the wind begins or the place it starts from is
    unknown to the wisest meteorologists.
They can only guess at changes. After thirty years' careful observ-
    ation of its signs and motions, a distinguished *scientific man*
    gave up the few rules he had at the beginning.
God alone can measure the winds, Job xxviii. 25, and He alone
    knows from whence He bringeth them. Psa. cxxxv. 7.
Over-anxiety as to the changes of the wind is condemned in Eccl.
    xi. 4.
The Cave of *Æolus* proclaims the confessed ignorance of the ancients.
" Thou knowest not the way of the wind," Ecc. xi. 5 ; not " spirit,"
    as in Eng. version.
Water illustrates the Spirit's divine *cleansing* power.
Wind illustrates the Spirit's divine *quickening* power.
A *stone* illustrates God's method of accomplishing His purposes,
    Dan. ii. 34, and before it the mightiest monarchies crumble and
    disappear.
Wind—1. An emblem of the Spirit, *uncontrolled* by none save
    Jehovah. "God's gift."
His control of the mind's motions shows the same sovereignty as
    its creation.
2. It pervades *all* nature, as the Spirit reaches all kinds of hearts.
3. Wind invisible, but effects visible. So the Spirit is unseen, and
    yet all the world see its fruits.
4. Wind brings both life and disease. So the gospel is a savour of
    life or of death. 1 Cor. ii. 16.
5. Wind at times silent, at others in motion. So is the Spirit in the
    heart and in the Church.
6. Wind comes and goes we know not how. Thus with the Spirit.
7. Wind or air is absolutely *essential to life.* No spiritual life apart
    from the Holy Ghost.

8. Wind *is* irresistible. The Spirit of God is Almighty. *"Create in me a clean heart."* Psa. li. 10 ; Rom. ix. 18.

This supplies an answer to the demand often made for time, place, and circumstances of conversion.

Some can comply with all, as Paul, Acts ix. 3, but as a rule the testimony of eminent saints confirms the text.

The all-important matter,—"One thing I know, whereas I was blind, now I see." John ix. 25.

So is. He in whom the Spirit breathes, breathes of the Spirit. Jas. i. 8.

Marvellously manifold are the modes of the Spirit in changing hearts.

They defy observation, and reduce all opposition to silence.

Practical treatises are but faint echoes of the wonders of HIS POWER.

A prophecy of the mighty revolutions in character, society, government wrought since that hour.

The humble Galilean has left His impress as wide and deep on the last 18 centuries, as *though the race had been created to illustrate it!*

Just as the millions of trees, vines, plants, animals, illustrate the Divine power and wisdom.

To Nicodemus He appeared an humble worker of miracles.

A deep mystery rested on His designs as well as on His origin.

But lowly as He was, before His influence *idolatry* was doomed to *fall,* and even the cherished and beloved *temple* at Jerusalem to be *destroyed.*

His gospel, combating wealth, rank, eloquence, philosophy, and the most ancient religious systems, would *mate* and *master* all opposing powers.

In every age since the scene on Calvary the learned and great have resisted and wondered, but *each word of our Lord is moving on to a sure and glorious fulfilment.*

πνεῦμα, *aura,* a gentle breeze; ἄνεμος, strong wind or gale. *Trench, Alford.* The height of our atmosphere first inferred by *Pascal.* Air in union with metals forms our ores discovered by *Priestly.* Spirit of nature. *Beck.* Latent power divinely imparted. *Meyer.* Our Lord chose a thing *midway* between spirit and body. *Euthymius.* Hebrews by comparing anything with wind indicated *obscurity. Wolfius.*

τὸ πνεῦμα. Heb. *ruach,* used, as πνεῦμα, for wind, and also for the Holy Spirit, Gen. i. 2; vi. 3, 17; vii. 15; viii. 1. *Wordsworth.* τὸ πνεῦμα, the Holy Spirit exclusively. *Origen, Augustine, Bengel.* But the *form* of the sentence, as well as its import, is against it. τὸ πνεῦμα, the wind. *Thol.*, *De Wette*, *Meyer*, *Stier*, *Ols.*, *Robinson*, *Schleusner*, *Lücke*, *Alford*, and commentators generally. Three points usually noted : 1. Free action by the Spirit. 2. Man's experience of His influence. 3. Its incomprehensibleness. The last the only one made by the Lord. *Hengst.*

ὅπου θέλει. Imputes *will* to the wind. Translate "The breathings of God's Spirit are free, you hear His voice," &c. *Maurice.*

φωνὴν, voice of the various divine heralds. *Estius.* The articulate voice of a living being, here a natural sound. *Maurice.*

οὕτως, as conscious of regeneration as the breathing of the wind on us. *Rheinhardt.* " I honestly confess I never received any such testimony of the Holy Spirit." *Michaelis.* His *sceptical* views will explain his sad experience. *Author.*

οὕτως implies moral evidence. *Stier.* Spirit's influence discernibly Divine to a believer's friends. *Pfemminger.* Homo, in quo Spiritus spirat, Spiritu respirat. *Bengel.* Mysteries of the winds and natural birth are joined here. *Lampe*, *G. Müller.* In spiritual birth physiognomies are as *varied* as in natural. *Dräscke.* The Spirit's renewal *evident* as the air moving, but the *how* is concealed. *Calvin.* True faith asks no *quids*, no *quares*, no *quomodos.* *Clerke.* It is not intelligendi vivacitas, sed credendi simplicitas. *Augustine.* There are regular causes for the course of the wind. *Sumner.* But we know of none for the Spirit, but God's sovereignty. *Author.*

ἐστί πᾶς, of Himself. *Stier.* Only inclusively with the saints. *Alford.*

---

9. Nicodemus answered and said unto him, How can these things be ?

Nicodemus. This is the third and last time he spoke during this visit.

How? Our Lord's words are so plain to us, we wonder how he could *misunderstand* them.

Yet He would have to create new powers to enable us to *comprehend* the *nature* of this work.

Questioning may denote unbelief, or wonder, or scorn, but not frivolity.

The longer he listened, the less he seemed to understand the Lord.

It is just so with the Nicodemuses of our day.

A dead " orthodoxy " or a shallow " theology " is always annoyed at the mysteries of a spiritual experience.

Although he comprehends not Christ's words, Christ's words " apprehend " him. Phil. iii. 12.

He has been long accustomed to exclude the truth from his conscience.

Therefore he imagines he must know *how* before he can believe the fact that he must be born again.

The actual longing of his heart is *masked* by his *words.*

His question, however, has no longer any *ecclesiastical* opposition in it.

242 / Gospel of John

He surrenders the proud "*we*" (ver. 2), and asks for further help.

Thou knowest full well, "Speak, Lord, Thy servant heareth."

These things. As we know the sun quickens the herb and the tree *by* the leaves, flowers, and fruit, so is the presence of the Spirit known. Matt. vii. 16 ; Gal. v. 22.

It is evident the Saviour's yearning heart leaps to receive and adopt him.

Christ seems almost ready to draw the veil and reveal the mystery of redemption.

Nicodemus appears to sigh out, " How late I came to know THEE, THOU INCARNATE GLORY ! "

From this moment Nicodemus is silent ; he becomes a disciple.

Like Job, he seems to say, " Behold, I am vile ; what shall I answer Thee ? " Job xl. 4.

This night-scene for graphic vividness and interest as a historical picture has never been approached by uninspired genius.

Two figures appear on the canvas,—the youthful Redeemer and the aged Rabbi.

The minute details and life-like touches rivet youth and old age alike.

The heights and depths of these lessons never seem to lose their interest.

Their grandeur, unaffected by time, arrests, astonishes, and delights.

This Gospel was doubtless written some sixty years after the interview, and yet it is fresh, new, and warm, as though John wrote it that very night.

Nicodemus heard on that occasion announcements from the Son of God *more wonderful than had been heard since creation* by any of our race.

Had he been the only accession to His band, it would have been enough.

Like Mary, he came to qualify himself against the Lord's death, for uniting with Joseph in *fulfilling a prophecy*, and laying Him in a virgin tomb. Isa. liii. 9. Note—

1. Our Lord separates Himself from the entire human family.
2. How lofty is the style He uses, " God so loved the world," &c.
3. He discriminates between His humility as " *Son of man* " and dignity as " *Son of God.*"
4. His patience and meekness in dealing with one, in whom candour and caution struggled for the mastery.

Here, also, is a directory for all preachers as to the *what* and *how.*

1. NO SALVATION WITHOUT REGENERATION! This *qualifies* for the kingdom of God.
2. NO SALVATION WITHOUT ATONING BLOOD! This constitutes the meritorious *right.*
3. The Spirit comes under laws divinely ordained, but to us inscrutable.

Let us beware of tying down or limiting the grace of the Spirit. Psa. lxxviii. 41.

Let us *pray for, expect,* and *hail* those sacred breathings of love. Ezek. xxxvii. 9.

Definite, sharp, authoritative, spiritual teachings will be blest.

Are the pointed truths, the weighty brevity, and the loving manner here inimitable?

"My speech and my preaching were *not* with enticing words," &c. *Paul.* 1 Cor. ii. 4.

Our only hope of reaching the *dead* is through the *power* of God. Eph. ii. 1.

But a preacher must be "alive unto God" himself before he can awaken others. Rom. vi. 11.

A ministry "full of faith and of the Holy Ghost" the great want of the times. Acts xi. 24.

Πῶς. An exclamation. *Luther.* Our Lord makes no attempt to explain the *whence* and *whither* of the Spirit's influence. *Stier.* The old nature, like old Sarah, asks, "Shall I of a surety" be born again? Gen. xviii. 13. Admitting the necessity, he would now know *how,* &c. *Luthardt.* At Maria ipsa quæsivit, "*Quomodo?*" *Beza.*

---

10. Jesus answered and said unto him, Art thou a master of Israel, and knowest not these things?

A master. Gr. *the teacher.* Our Lord recognizes his *position* and *dignity.*

High-sounding titles were given to Jewish doctors at that period.

"Guide of the blind." "Light of the ignorant." "Instructor of babes." Rom. ii. 17, 19, 20.

These learned sinners were styled "princes of this world." 1 Cor. ii. 8.

Great scholars, in their pride, they would not bow to the truth found in Rom. iv. 4—6. Note—

A ruler among God's people *might* and *ought* to have known these things.

All intelligent heathen admitted the necessity of some kind of *attiring at death*, for the presence of the dwellers on Olympus.

If Joseph changed his dress to appear before Pharaoh, how much more we for entering the presence of the King of kings!

Those denying this necessity, prove either their ignorance or dishonesty.

The infallible Spirit affirms "their thoughts accuse," &c. Rom. ii. 15.

No wonder Israel was "dying for lack of wisdom" with such teachers. Hos. iv. 6.

In Israel. They were the sole inheritors of the oracles of God among all nations.

The gloom of midnight oppressed all the world except Judea.

Those dwelling under the wings of the cherubim are "exalted to heaven." Matt. xi. 23.

Surely God and men have a right to expect more fruit from such planting. Matt. v. 47.

Knowest not? Confessing his ignorance atones for the proud "*we know.*" Ver. 2.

He alike admits his ignorance of the movements of the wind, and of the Spirit.

Hence the Lord's words contain a slight commendation joined to a gentle *reproof*.

He, professing to be a spiritual guide, knows not the way himself.

The "bondage," spoken of at Sinai, prefigured *spiritual redemption*.

Moses spoke of "the circumcision" of "the heart" to the fathers of Israel. Deut. xxx. 6.

God commanded the circumcision of the heart. Deut. x. 16; xxx. 6.

David speaks of God "creating a clean heart." Psa. li. 10.

Jeremiah speaks of God writing "the law on their hearts." Jer. xxxi. 33.

Ezekiel of a "stony heart taken away and a fleshy heart given them." Ezek. xi. 19.

Hence our Lord strikes mightily on that key, "Is it not written?" "Have ye not read?" Matt. xii. 3; Mark xii. 10, 26.

A Papal bishop of great name said he could not find in the Bible "a promise of pardon for sin confessed *to God!*"

Carlstadt had taught theology for 78 years before he found *it* out.

These things. The knowledge of our guilt is as clear as that of our being.

The new birth was demanded essentially under the Old Testament.
A holy obedience divided saints and sinners then, as now.
Carnal-minded parents became estranged from believing children.
Who knows not *necessary* things is *ignorant*, however much besides
he may know. *Pascal.*
Our Lord did neither depose not anathematize this teacher.
His light obeyed would have led him, and will lead all faithful
souls.
If modern Nicodemuses ceased attempting to teach until they them-
selves were taught, how many desks would be *vacant !*

Σὺ εἶ. His ignorance of the Old Testament no more surprising than that of
Arius, Pelagius, Kant, Hegel, Michaelis the Elder, &c., concerning the New.
ὁ, the article rhetorical. *Lücke.* Gentle tinge of irony. The only
master in Israel ? *Stier.* Sharply definite. *Lange.* Indefinite. *Kuinoel.*
ὁ διδάσκαλος. Ille Magister. *Erasmus.* That teacher. *Winer, Trench.*
The President of the Sanhedrim. *B. Crusius.* So termed by way of contrast.
Winer. Nicodemus elected to receive this instruction. *Beza.* He represents
the *entire class. Hengst.*
οὐ γινώσκεις. Such pointed words must have decided Nicodemus for or
against the truth. *Hengst.* These words to a proud member of the Sanhedrim,
were thorns in his heart. *Anton.* Regeneration not taught before Christ's time,
and many—*Belsham, Channing, Parker,* and others—don't think the Scriptures
even now teach it. *Author.* ταῦτα, emphatic. *Calvin, Luther.*

---

11. Verily, verily, I say unto thee, We speak that we do know, and testify
that we have seen ; and ye receive not our witness.

Verily, verily. This assurance of the Divine WORD is three
times repeated.
The *first* anticipated his objection, and was aimed at humbling him.
The *second* confuted his objection by a familiar illustration from
nature.
The *third* introduces him to the Messiah as Son of God, and
Saviour of men.
In the first answer our Lord severely closed the door of hope to the
proud.
But to the humble, He flung wide Mercy's " golden gates."
I say. Note the majestic " *I*," not the form of the Old Test.
prophets, " Thus saith the Lord."
We speak. The regal style : that adopted by kings. Mark iv.
30.
We. The act of Deity, classifying Himself as one of the Trinity.

We do know. "*We*" and "*our*" in emphatic contrast with "Rabbi, we know." It implies absolute knowledge and immediate, perfect vision of God.

"The only begotten Son" exclusively claims this as *His own.* John i. 18.

The high priest alone entered and knew what transpired in the Holy of Holies.

Our High Priest came from the depths of Infinite knowledge and Love,—the Father's bosom. John i. 18.

Have seen. Sight the most certain of our senses giving evidence.

Having seen a thing we almost *compel* those hearing to believe us.

And ye. The class to which Nicodemus belonged and from whom he was now beginning to separate himself.

Chaff and wheat begin on earth to part. Luke iii. 17.

Receive not. Rather as a question to the lingering, hesitating ruler.

Not Nicodemus *personally*, but *prophetic*, of the rejection of the Messiah by the infatuated Jews.

His countenance and tone of voice indicated the compassionate lamentation of Incarnate Truth.

The *sorrow* of the Spirit, that they having eyes, will not see; and ears, will not hear. Jer. v. 21.

The *supplication* of the only Begotten, that they will turn from eternal ruin.

Our witness. Gr. *testimony*, connecting it with the same truth, verse 32. (Authorized Version here is inexact. *Trench.*) Our Lord joins Himself with the noble band of prophets.

How many wonder at the simple ignorance of this ruler.

Is it not a more difficult task and more daring guilt *now* to *keep out the light* of the *Messiah ?*

The light of the Old Testament moon has become as the sun, and the light of the sun as the light of seven days. Isa. xxx. 26.

λαλοῦμεν. I and John the Baptist. *Luther, Tholuck.* I and all believers. *Maldonatus, Sepp, Lange.* I, the Father, and Spirit. *Chrys., Lampe, Stier, Alford.* Himself and Spirit. *Bengel.* Himself and prophets. *Beza, Tholuck, Calvin.* Style of royalty. *Lücke, Theoph., Doddr.* Men know I teach. *B. Crusius.* Teachers like Himself. *Meyer.* It may as well be taken "verecundiæ gratia" as dignitatis gratiâ. *Bloomfield.*

λαλοῦμεν and μαρτυροῦμεν taken together express the complete knowledge of Omniscience. *Doddr.* Vain labour to simplify the mysteries of God; let us rather bring our reason to the adorable Throne. *Lord Bacon.*

λαμβάνετε, a reflection of the Evangelist himself. *Sepp.* "Ye," sudden turning of the discourse to Nicodemus' companions. *Ols.* Used interrogatively. *Stier.* His exceeding slowness. *Lücke.* This verse contrasts the sure truths with Rabbinical dreams. *Melancthon.* No teacher *in doubt* ought to teach. *Bucer.*

---

12. If I have told you earthly things, and ye believe not, how shall ye believe, if I tell you of heavenly things?

Earthly things. However far we may prosecute our inquiries into the causes and nature of earthly things, we must at length reach the *insoluble* and the *unknown.*

Necessity of faith, repentance, regeneration, are things taught and believed on *earth.*

In eternity these exercises of the soul will be *too late*, but their fruits endure for ever.

Regeneration, though an earthly fact, occurs on the *verge* of heaven.

As with the crucifixion, its sweep embraces eternal *results.*

Each gospel sound seems to have an echo in heaven, as, "If any man be in *Christ*, he is a new creature." 2 Cor. v. 17.

He has not received his crown, but an heirship, *issuing in a* "KING-DOM." Luke xxii. 29.

The things of the Spirit of God are *spiritually* discerned. 1 Cor. ii. 14.

We are God's workmanship, created anew in *Christ Jesus.* Eph. ii. 10.

The Christian has ever been a *mystery* to the world, for his conversation (*citizenship*) is in heaven. Phil. iii. 20 ; 1 John iii. 1.

Believers live under the same law as angels, and the world wonders why *its* glory and honour attract them not.

The citizens of Zurich anciently took an oath twice a year, never to *receive* a *gift* from a *foreign* prince or power.

Our Lord's words imply, If the A B C of the gospel confound you, how can you receive the knowledge of "the deep things of God?" 1 Cor. ii. 10.

Believe not. Faith its nature and fruit. See on John i. 7 ; vii. 38.

This *great word* takes the place of "know."

It is not only our duty to listen, but refusing to exercise our faith is the wilful *bankruptcy* of the understanding.

The unrenewed mind ever *stumbles* at the doctrines of *depravity*, *inability*, and salvation by grace. Jer. xvii. 9 ; John vi. 44 ; Matt. xvi. 16, 17.

He does not say " comprehend,"—that were quite impossible.

We believe a thousand facts *as mysterious* as regeneration or the Trinity.

" O taste and see," Psa. xxxiv. 8.   Our experience is the fruit of faith, and he was righteously rebuked for his unbelief.

His acknowledgment of Christ as a Divine Teacher is *implied*, and our Lord thus gave the death-blow to the dying unbelief of Nicodemus.

He was, we may hope now, made the subject of redeeming grace.

How shall ?   The complete moral ruin of our race a great truth of the Bible.

Since the first preaching of the gospel men disbelieving *depravity* have always renounced the *Divinity* and atoning work of the Son of God.

Ignorance of one's *own heart* is a fatal barrier to receiving Bible truth.

Laboured and learned evidences and apologies never converted a soul.   The sun need not shine brighter.

If we cannot, without our eyes being blinded, look at the *sun*, His creature, how can we hope to pierce the mysteries of its CREATOR, the INFINITE and ETERNAL GOD ?

In both earthly and heavenly things the appeal is not to reason, but to faith.

Heavenly things.   His Divine origin, person, and work, &c.

He distinctly forewarns him that more will stumble at these than at the doctrine of regeneration.

The proud sneering world has fiercely resisted, age after age, the humiliating truth,—SALVATION BY THE BLOOD OF CHRIST.

One of the Presidents of the U.S., a man of transcendent ability, is said to have exclaimed, " What have I to do with an obscure citizen of an obscure province in Asia ? "

Men who will speak kindly of *God*, of *Brahma, Vishnu*, &c., kindle into a fierce passion at the *thought* of the Redeemer.

Voltaire proclaimed himself to the world as the *defender* of the rights of *God* against the claims of Jesus Christ. *Letters from Geneva to D'Alembert*, Feb. 25th, 1758.

A human echo of the demoniac shriek, " Art thou come to torment us ? "   Matt. viii. 29.

The enemies of this truth are the *organized antichrist,* whether called Papists, Liberals, Rationalists, Pantheists, or by any other of the Protean forms of infidelity.

Their writings from Celsus and Julian down to Renan and Strauss illustrate this, and the most poisoned shafts have been pointed at *this gospel.*

Until John the Evangelist is proved a writer of fables, Christ's DIVINITY and ATONEMENT stand like the Pillar of Fire and Cloud in our desert world.

ἐπίγεια. About earthly things. *Luther, Cyril.* Holy Spirit. *Ambrose, Augustine.* Doctrines well known to the Jews. *Hegel.* Truths naturalized on earth. *Lange.* Things easily known. *Chrysostom, Tittmann.* Some truths are criteria of our faith in God. *Coleridge.* Earthly things, regeneration; heavenly, atonement for sin. *D. Brown.*

πιστεύετε. Equivalent to receiving My testimony. *Jacobi.* Evangelical faith. *Stier.* One can never believe until he has learned to doubt. *Kant.* Then angels could never have believed. *Author.* He that will not believe it, let him experience it. *Dräscke.*

πῶς. How would ye believe? &c. *Luther's* version. "Wilt thou then believe?" &c. *Stier.*

ἐπουράνια. Satan's fall, &c. *Voss.*

μυστήρια of Paul, 1 Cor. iv. 1, or Peter's δυσνόητα, 2 Pet. iii. 16. *Tittmann.* Things contained in 13th and following verses. *Lampe.* Mysteries of the Trinity and their relations to the soul. *Estius.* Eternal generation of the Son. *Theophy.* Mysteries of redemption. *Ferus.* Heavenly things without a veil. *Beza, Maldon.* Hypostatic union of Father and Son, Christ's glory after resurrection. *Euthy.* Designs of God as to man's salvation. *Lange.* Internal nature of Christ's kingdom. *Kuinoel, Doddr.,* 1 Cor. ii. 10. How can ye believe spiritual truth without a heavenly image? *Alb. Magnus.* "Earthly." That side of things of the new birth, which is upon earth. "Heavenly," from the heavenly side. *Alford.* He brought heavenly things with Him, but did not reveal them. *Ols.* Things easily and hardly to be interpreted. *Lücke.* "Liberals" and others affirm they believe nothing in religion, without first comprehending it. *Christian Teacher,* passim. London, 1839—1842.

---

13. And no man hath ascended up to heaven, but he that came down from heaven, even the Son of man which is in heaven.

Ascended. Man by nature longs after immortality. Gen. iii. 22. Ancient fables made Prometheus ascend to heaven, and steal fire from the gods.

Men have in every land sighed after the lost bliss of a *golden age.*

"Who hath ascended up into heaven?" &c. Prov. xxx. 4.

Here the *water,* the *wind,* and "*The Son*" seem to be alluded to by Solomon.

Beside our Lord, the angels alone have visited earth and heaven. John i. 51.

Aristotle said a little knowledge of heaven equalled much of other knowledge.

Ascending was *natural* to Christ,—it was merely returning home. John xiv. 2.

This shows how *highly figurative was much of our Lord's discourse.*

Since the Fall, there have been many *heaven-ascenders,* climbing spirits. Gen. xi. 1—4.

" Thou hast said in thine heart (Lucifer), I will ascend into heaven." Isa. xiv. 13.

With the Hebrews a question was a strong denial:—" Who hath measured the waters? " &c. Isa. xl. 12.

He attributes to Himself a residence in heaven previous to His Incarnation.

His former glory with His Father. John xvii. 5. Coming from above. John iii. 31.

Man had shut himself out from heaven, yet desires to return.

Happiness without holiness is the great *solecism* of our race.

Men seem resolved to *force* an entrance through the guarded gate and past the armed cherub to the tree of life. Gen. iii. 24.

But alone by *faith* can we regain the lost inheritance, or see the chariots God will send to bring us home. Gen. xlv. 27.

Our Lord intends to link, unchangeably and eternally, the WELL-BEING of mankind WITH HIS INCARNATION !

Paul was " caught up," 2 Cor. xii. 2 ; saints rising shall be " caught up " also. 1 Thess. iv. 17.

But none but our Lord ascended to *open the way* for others.

If we ever ascend, it can only be by virtue of *His* ascension.

God's way of raising us is by humbling us in the dust and causing us to cry, " God be merciful to me a sinner."

Heaven. See on John i. 51. God, the Father and Son, carry heaven with Them wherever They are.

He was man, as though he had ceased to be God, and God, as though He had never become man.

No man. Save Him whose proper habitation, in His essential and eternal nature, is heaven.

Enoch's and Elijah's were receptions, rather than ascensions.

Jesus came down from heaven on the double errand of teaching the world and sustaining the law, by suffering the penalty due to sin.

Son of man. John v. 27. There was nothing deficient either in
His humanity or Divinity.
Son of God reflects the infinite exaltation of His humanity.
Son of man reflects the infinite humiliation of His Divinity.
Thus we attribute *creation* to the " Son of man," as to His God-
head.
And salvation to the death of the " Son of God," as to His incarnate
humanity.
To the one we attribute *mortality*, to the other absolute ETERNITY.
His humanity *veiled* His heavenly majesty from men.
" Though as a man I stand before you, as Divine I alone ascend."
" One like the Son of man came with the clouds of heaven." Dan.
vii. 13.
He " descended " as to His Divinity, His humanity was of the
earth. Eph. iv. 10.
Yet He did not *leave* heaven at His Incarnation, but as the WORD
eternally *dwells in heaven.*
All men, as sinners, are shut out of heaven. John viii. 21.
But Christ and His believing people *are one.* John xvii. 21.
The Church is called by Paul the " *fulness* of Christ." Eph. i. 23.
A challenge to the world, to place unlimited faith in the promises
He makes.
Which is, &c. Gr. *being in heaven* (essentially), *who appertains to
heaven.*
At the time of His Incarnation, and at the moment He addressed
these words to Nicodemus, He was in heaven.

οὐδείς. Attained knowledge of Divine things. *Kuinoel.*
ἀναβέβηκεν, aoristically. *Stier.* Present. *Luther.* Perfect. *Hengst.*
Change it to future middle. *Bengel.* Properly of the Gods. *Elsner.* Im-
properly of eminent persons. *Lactantius.* Brings knowledge from heaven.
Doederlein. Perfect tense forbids reference to the ascension. *Lücke.* The
knowledge derived from His union with the Father. *Ols.* The mind only
capable of ascending. *Ebrard.* " None but I can reveal heavenly things."
Meyer. Christ's Divine nature evidently taught here, else His being born
of a Virgin were a *platitude. Lampe.* He was caught up to heaven and instructed. *Socinus, Norton.* Jewish tradition said *Moses* had ascended to
heaven to receive the Law. This Christ contradicts. *Whitby.* The necessity of
being taught by the Spirit. *Calvin, Quesnel, Lightfoot.* No man can possibly
justify himself. *Zwingle, Melancthon,* and others. Although descending, the
Son holds the inmost union with God. *Lücke.* " I am not merely the teacher,
but the Messiah foretold." *Rollock, Ryle.* He speaks of His Passion as past :
Nestorians here condemned, A.D. 431. *Dollinger.* Cerinthus denied His pre-
existence, in the first century. Manes, His humanity, A.D. 277. *Shedd.*

ὤν. Continuous present. *Hengst.* An exposition of the predicate ὁ υἱὸς τοῦ ἀνθρ. *Lücke, Winer.* The relative proprieties of dignity preserved accurately in word. *D. Brown.*

καταβάς. Not literally, but the sphere of absolute knowledge, result of unity with God. *Tholuck.* 1st clause proves Christ's knowledge ; 2nd, loving, suffering, and doing ; 3rd, heavenly being and inner life. *Lange.*

---

14. And as Moses lifted up the serpent in the wilderness, even so must the Son of man be lifted up.

As. No capricious resemblance, but actual interpretation of Scripture by its Inspirer.

Moses. See on John i. 17. Our Lord for the first time mentions the great Jewish lawgiver.

He will now *correct* Nicodemus' Jewish ideas of the Messiah.

He will *not* prove an avenger of Jewish wrongs, an earthly monarch.

He will be the author, not of a *temporal*, but a *spiritual* salvation.

He clearly hints that the revealed truth will not attract the nation's faith.

He knew the idea of a suffering Messiah was *opposed* to all their long-cherished hopes.

Had our Lord revealed *all* at the first, *not one would have followed Him.*

His disciples, after three years' *schooling* by sermon and miracle, were scarcely won from this *earth-born* trust. Acts i. 6.

Therefore to Nicodemus, *He veils* the great truth under a type.

Our Lord often, after alluding to His *glorification,* speaks of His *passion.*

An exaltation, indeed, preceded by a most profound abasement.

He now leads Nicodemus to the cross, the source of all these gifts.

He implies that the gospel is not opposed, but in harmony with, Moses.

He teaches a doctor of the law, by an illustration from the law.

Doubtless the fiery serpents were sent both as a *punishment* and a *type.*

When the bitten Israelites were directed to "look and live," God's purpose embraced at that moment both the serpent of brass and the victim on the cross.

Lifted up the serpent. Wearied with the way, the Hebrews murmured in the wilderness, and the Lord sent fiery serpents, and many of the people died.   Num. xxi. 6.

Providence selects His own messengers, now " serpents," afterwards "hornets."   Josh. xxiv. 12.

Thus the *stars* from their golden tresses shed ruin on Sisera's host.

Thus He caused great *stones* from heaven to crush His foes.

Thus He armed the *sun* and *moon* to engage in the work of avenging His people.

Thus in Egypt the *thunder* and *lightning* took up the cause of their injured Sovereign.

Thus *water* executed His terrible decree in the days of Noah.

Thus *fire* made clean work in the time of Lot.

All nature, in the twinkling of an eye, might arm against mankind and entomb its millions before the sun has set.

Serpents and scorpions abounded in the Wilderness of the Wandering.   Deut. viii. 15.

TYPICAL CHARACTERISTICS OF THE BRAZEN SERPENT, &c.

1. Its sting was death.   " At last it bites like a serpent."   Prov. xxiii. 32.

Sin has a sting, " the sting of death," and its " strength is the law." 1 Cor. xv. 56.

2. The serpent was cursed in Paradise.   " Christ was made a curse for us."   Gal. iii. 13.

3. In the wilderness no medical aid was accessible.   Earth has *no cure* for the serpent bite of sin.

4. Many Israelites were perishing.   *All* mankind are from sin.

5. The brazen *serpent* and the *cross* both of *Divine* appointment for healing.

6. As did the brazen serpent, so the cross, cures in a way *unknown* to reason.

7. The brazen serpent was made like the fiery serpent, yet *without a sting.*

So Christ was made like unto sinning man, yet without sin.

8. The metal passed through a *furnace,* to be moulded into the serpent form.

So the " Captain of our salvation was made perfect through suffering."   Heb. ii. 10.

9. Both lifted up, the serpent on a pole and Christ on the cross, as objects of *faith* to the dying.   John xii. 32.

254 / Gospel of John

THE REMEDY, &c.

1. Only those who were stung would look to the remedy.

So sinners must be *convinced* of their misery and guilt.

2. One could not *look* for another ; each must look for himself.

So sinners must not rest on the experience of others. " Search ME, O God." Psa. cxxxix. 23.

3. No qualification was required of the wretched victim to look.

All the fitness the sinner requires is to feel his need of the Saviour.

4. The Jew feeling himself dying gladly accepted the remedy.

So the convicted sinner gratefully receives the gospel as the " good news " of salvation.

5. Looking by faith, the fiery poison kindled in his blood was extinguished.

However numerous the wounds, however far advanced the issue, the look restored him.

So Christ by one offering perfects for ever all who believe in Him.

He is able to save to the uttermost ; even the chief of sinners.

6. Doubtless some had weaker, others stronger eyes, yet all were healed who *looked.*

So Christ saves all who believe on Him, though in some faith is weaker, and in others stronger.

7. The Jew cured once, would henceforth hate a serpent in any form.

So the rescued sinner dreads the touch or sight of sin or the tempter. Col. ii. 21.

8. The healed Hebrew attributed his restoration to the gift of God.

So the saved sinner ascribes his salvation to the free sovereign grace of God.

9. Doubtless many made light of a method of cure apparently so *unreasonable.*

So to many the cross of Christ is a *stumbling-block,* and to others *foolishness.*

10. Though the brazen serpent was lifted up, only those who *looked* were *healed.*

So though Christ is lifted up, none are saved save those who look, i.e. believe.

POINTS OF DIFFERENCE : 1. The brazen serpent had no power in itself to heal.

But Christ has inherent power in Himself to heal all that believe.

2. The brazen serpent healed only one particular disease,—the serpent's sting.

But Christ heals all the diseases of His people. He is the good Physician, in whose hands no one is incurable.

3. The brazen serpent healed only one people,—the Jews.

Christ is for the healing of all nations. "Look unto me, all ye ends," &c.

4. Though the brazen serpent healed all who looked at it, it could not give eyes or light.

But Christ gives the eyes and the light, by which the dying sinner looks and is saved.

5. The brazen serpent after a time lost its healing efficacy and was destroyed.

But Christ's healing power is eternal. The same yesterday, to-day, and for ever.

6. Though the Israelites looking were healed, they nevertheless afterward died.

But "whosoever believeth in Christ shall never die." "I give unto them eternal life," &c.

Serpents are said to have a power of charming the bird they select as their victim.

But it is no delusion as to the power of the old Serpent to assume the "*form* of an angel of light," and in angelic *accents* charming his victims to their ruin. 2 Cor. xi. 14.

The event our Lord refers to occurred in the 40th year of Israel's wandering, at Zalmonah, near Canaan, in the month of August.

Hitherto Israel had been most wonderfully protected from the perils of the wilderness. Deut. viii. 15.

The Lord had just given them victory over the Canaanite king.

Yet were they unbelieving, ungrateful, and rebellious.

Sore discipline was necessary to refine their graces and quicken their faith.

The Lord has a treasure of afflictions as well as of blessings.

Two upliftings of Christ: 1. On the cross. 2. From the Mount of Olives. Acts i. 9.

A profound mystery to unbelieving sages, how the CRUCIFIED ONE can overcome an old living Serpent with all his black kingdom of demons. Rev. xii. 9—17.

In the desert the command was, "Look and live." Num. xxi. 8.

Thus *they knew* that their *disease* and *remedy* both came from *God*.

Serpent. Characteristics mentioned in Scripture : Subtilty. Gen.
iii. 1. Wisdom. Matt. x. 16. Poisonous. Psa. lviii. 4. Tongue
instrument of harm. Job xx. 16. Habit of concealing itself.
Eccl. x. 8. Dwells in sand. Deut. viii. 15. Oviparous. Isa.
lix. 5. Tamed anciently by "charming." Jer. viii. 17 ; Eccl.
x. 11. Mischievous, malignant craftiness. Matt. iii. 7. Eats
dust. Isa. lxv. 25 ; Micah vii. 17.

An emblem of evil with the Greeks. Adored by the Phœnicians.

Symbol of great wisdom and power with the Chinese.

Egyptians represented the eternal spirit Kneph, the author of all
good, under the serpent's mythic form.

But Tithrambo, god of revenge, and Typhon, had also a serpent's form.

Tripod of wreathed serpents, now at Constantinople, taken among
the spoil of the Persians at Platæa, is 3000 years old.

A clear *traditional link* between the actors and scenes of Eden, and
the Scriptures of to-day, revealing the record of the serpent in
the wilderness with Israel.

The *Eumenides* or Furies had their locks wreathed with serpents.

Hindoos and ancient Romans made *house-pets* of them.

Brazen serpent *impaled* by Moses as a *trophy* of Divine medical skill
over diseases.

Constant emblem of a *physician* among Greeks and Romans.

Æsculapius, *god of medicine,* is always seen with a rod wreathed
with serpents.

Nehushtan (the brazen serpent) was destroyed in the days of
Hezekiah as a relic of idolatry. 2 Kings xviii. 4.

Must. Not *shall,* historic, but *must,* prophetic and *decretory.*

God's decrees not rigid icy chains of *fate,* but golden links of *love.*

Each grain of wheat must die before it will germinate and bear
fruit ; and as each believer must die unto sin, so Christ must
die to bring eternal life to believers.

The Father has voluntarily *bound His hands* by eternal JUSTICE !

Christ, His Eternal Son, voluntarily binds Himself to the cross to
open those hands by LOVE !

This was not understood by Nicodemus at the time, but his mind
was prepared, and at the cross light flashed into his soul.

Son of man. See on John v. 27. Our Lord first introduces Himself as Divine.

Nicodemus *understands Him* as referring to *the Messiah.*

What this ruler had said was honourable, but far short of the real
dignity and majesty of the Redeemer.

Lifted up. Not as Solomon was to the throne, but as a malefactor
on the tree, and exhibited to all God's empire. Rev. v. 6.

Distinct reference to His death as an atonement. John i. 29.

As the *guilt* could neither be transferred nor assumed, He bore the
penalty of sin. 1 Pet. ii. 24.

Thus "*a door was opened in heaven*" to all believers. Rev. iv. 1.

How *different* was all this from what Nicodemus had expected.

The *Messiah* of the Jews was to be *immortal :* this Jesus was to
die as a slave and a felon.

Lifted. A common expression for death by crucifixion. John
viii. 28 ; xii. 32.

Crucifixion a punishment familiar among Roman subjects.

Here, as often, our Lord's words have an earthly and a heavenly
meaning.

"Lifted up," to be crucified as a slave ; "lifted up," to be *crowned,*
KING of KINGS and LORD of LORDS ! Rev. xvii. 14.

Was the brazen serpent intended to be to the Jews in our Lord's
day a type of Himself?

The Jews did not believe the *Messiah was to die,* as here taught.

But John expressly explains the "lifting up" to refer to the Redeemer's death. John viii. 28 ; xii. 32, 33.

The Lord Himself said, " I will give my life for the world." John
vi. 51.

A sublime scheme, for on this " ransom for all," 1 Tim. ii. 6, the
entire Bible turns as on a hinge.

That which healed was the same in form as that which had slain,
and *death was to be put to death by dying.*

The crucified One, who saves, was *only in appearance* a sinner or
malefactor. Rom. viii. 3.

These *doctrinal details* were not for *Nicodemus* only, but for the
more complete instruction of the *future Church.*

Jehovah might have *destroyed the serpents* rather than have *cured
their bite.*

He might have annihilated evil spirits, instead of delivering us from
temptation.

" But his ways are not as our ways, nor his thoughts as our
thoughts." Isa. lv. 8, 9.

ὕψωσε. Our Lord used Syriac. *Knapp.* Exaltation after death. *Lampe.*
To confirm His gospel. *Socinus.* Comparison alone in the "lifting up."
Lücke, De Wette. Complete analogy. *Alford, Calvin,* and most authors.

258 / Gospel of John

Body-healing and *soul*-healing followed looking at the brazen serpent. *R. Erskine.*

τὸν ὄφιν. Tradition makes it *erect* before the fall, and that its poison was then first inserted by the Creator. *Josephus.*

> "Not
> Prone on the ground as since, but on his rear
> Circular base of rising folds, that towered
> Fold above fold, a surging maze."—*Milton.*

Boa constrictor has rudimentary *feet*, but nothing of the kind found in fossil ophidia. *Drake* in *Smith.* Ahriman the type of evil with Persians. *Zoroaster, Winer.* In Num. xxi. 6, 8, and Deut. viii. 15, where the transaction our Lord refers to is recorded, not a word is said about the serpents having been flying creatures. There is, therefore, no occasion to refer the venomous snakes in question to the kind of which *Niebuhr* speaks, and which the Arabs at Basra call "flying serpents," from their habit of springing from branch to branch. The Heb. term (saraph) rendered "fiery" by the Auth. Ver. is in the Sept. represented by θανατοῦντες, "deadly." *Onkelos*, and the *Vulg.* translate the word "burning," in allusion to the sensation produced by the bite. *Smith's Dict.* Brass material indicates the colour of the serpent. *Kitto.* Its indestructible continuance. *Fikenscher.* Must have been of colossal size, seen by 2,000,000. *Drake.* Israel reminded of the serpent in paradise, whose enmity is immortal. *Besser.* The brazen serpent a type of Christ. *Justin Martyr, Theophylact.* Difficulties may be started concerning any other type which we cannot solve, the plain word of Christ is our warrant. *Deyling, Lampe, Witsius.* A type of His crucifixion. *Lücke.* Of salvation. *Lampe.* A type of Satan tempting and of Christ saving. *Jackson.* Brass, symbol of Christ's humanity, and gold of His Divinity. *Meyer.* Israel themselves took it as a type of Messiah. *Menken.* Fiery serpent hardened into dead brass. *Hengst.* God binds Himself to no sign, as working miracles, ex opere operato. *Cocceius.* An undertone reference to the serpent in paradise. *Vitringa.* Brazen serpent cannot refer both to the Saviour and to Satan. *Lücke, Hoffmann, Stier, Gerlach.* A sign of their guilt and remedy. *Jacobi, Meyer, Lange.* Suspended, implies the poison overcome. *Tholuck.* John's allusion to death connects it with glory. *B. Crusius.* Crux scala cœli. *Aquinas.* The *primum cognitum* is our depravity; the Lord then taught Nicodemus τὰ ἐπουράνια. *Anton.* There *vide et vive*, here *crede et vive. Trapp.*

οὕτως. Dialectics of Jesus with Nicodemus the dialectics of the whole gospel. *Kahnis.* Gravitating points of the gospel: 1. His person. 2. His work. *B. Crusius.* Our Lord hints at a systematic typology. *Stier.*

ὑψωθῆναι. Shown as a saving sign. *Ebrard.* Men can thus see our Lord's sufferings. *Hoffmann.* Nicodemus first thought it a type of the Messiah's dignity. *Ammonius.* Only a type of Christ as openly exhibited. *Luthardt.*

δεῖ. Based on cited Scripture. *Stier.* Denied by *Lücke.* God could not save without THE CROSS. *Athanasius.* O.T. prophecies. *Hengstenberg.*

τὸν υἱὸν, analogy to the ὄφιν as well as ὕψωσε. *Jacobi, Stier.* Type of Christ's person. *Heller.*

----

15. That whosoever believeth in him should not perish, but have eternal life.

Whosoever. Gr. *every one.* Sufficient for all the world, efficient only for believers.

A plain *type* of the *manner*, but especially the benefit of His death.

Israel perishing in the wilderness is a type of *humanity.*

Their encampment, with its serpents and dying victims, a symbol of the *world.*

With every new wound, there came to the believing Israelite a new cure.

Thus the cross is ever repairing the evils of Satan's conflict with saints.

The promise embraces all mankind and welcomes their return.

Believeth. John i. 7 ; vii. 38. Faith appropriates the *crucified One* as its *own Saviour.*

Anguish of the serpent's bite a shadow of the anguish of a guilty conscience.

The way in which the bite was healed paradoxical to the Hebrews.

So a life of faith in the crucified One seems *a fable* to unbelievers.

Men are not saved *because* of faith, but *through* faith.

The brazen serpent did not change the nature of the serpent's sting.

But obedience to the Divine command not only prevented the effects of the poison, but imparted life.

Peter and Judas looked on the Saviour—one in the garden and the other in the Prætorium.

Peter's look was one of faith, Judas' of unbelieving despair. Luke xxii. 61 ; Matt. xxvi. 49.

A cure by a look in the wilderness was no greater miracle than salvation by faith now.

Salvation by the *cross* pre-eminently magnifies the POWER of God. Rom. i. 16.

The crown of *glory* shines forth most brightly amid the crown of *thorns.*

In Pilate's superscription is heard an echo of the voice of God.

The brazen serpent was wholly *unconscious* of the benefits conferred.

But our Lord rejoices to *intercede* as a *living, loving, triumphant* Redeemer.

In Him. Mark the dignity and majesty of this Son in contrast with all human deities.

Ancient Greeks imagined it required nine gods to hurl a thunder-bolt of Jupiter to *destroy life.*

Here the Son of God with boundless grace and ease does an act in-finitely greater.

He draws all men to His cross by LOVE to *give life* immortal. John xii. 32.

Eye of the bitten Israelite saw *many things beside.*

But it was the sight of the *brazen serpent* alone that could heal and cure.

These words have ever been on the lips of preachers of the gospel.

They have inspired precious hopes in the broken hearts of millions.

They have been signally honoured in bringing multitudes to God.

They have kindled undying love in martyrs even in the flames.

Reference is here made to the " *look* " of the bitten Israelite at the brazen serpent.

It was a small thing, a trifle which the profane doubtless sneered at.

An act having no medicinal virtue, but on the performance of which hung life.

Not perish. By the poison of sin. Immortality without Christ is eternal death.

Have. Promise postponed, Dan. xii. 2, is spiritually realized under grace.

If looking in faith to that which never had life could save, how much more looking in faith to Him who is LIFE itself? John xi. 25.

Faith the *hand* of the soul, which *lays* hold of the cross. *Luther.*

Faith the *mouth* of the soul, by which the believer *feeds* on Christ. *Augustine.*

Faith the *feet* of the soul, whereby when Christ says, " *Follow* Me," we come. *Trapp.*

Faith the *tongue,* wherewith we make confession unto salvation. *Paul.* Rom. x. 10.

Eternal life. The first time these great words are named.

He takes it for granted the Old Testament taught it.

The eleventh of Hebrews proves that patriarchs and prophets through successive ages firmly believed in and hoped for eternal life.

He obscurely alludes to His *passion*, but plainly and triumphantly declares its *fruits.*

Nicodemus received sharp answers at first from the Lord.

But once subdued, humbled, and believing, he henceforth was silent.

Eternal life in its *power* belongs to the *future*, but its *possession* to the present. John vi. 54.

πᾶς. Universality of redemption intimated. *Tholuck.* Just as universal **as** *faith ;* where it stops there are the limits of the Spirit's work. *Augustine,* *Beza, Turretin, Calvin.*

πιστεύων. To become one with Him, as He is one with the Father. *Stier.*
A figure of life temporal, but also a type of life eternal. *Augustine.* Not
merely looking, but being grafted in Him, as the branch into the olive-tree.
Rom. xi. 24. *Chrysostom.*

ἔχη. Promise of Old Testament now realized. *J. Müller.* Nicodemus is
silent because subdued and humbled. *Anton, Ber. Bib.* Divine counsel shown
negatively and affirmatively. *Kuinoel.* Miraculum fuit in miraculo. *Wetstein.*
This word eventuated in Nicodemus' conversion. John xix. 39. *Tholuck.*
These words were to him as *speaking in an unknown tongue. Jacobi.* But
soon *interpreted* by the Spirit to his *soul. Author.*

μὴ ἀπόληται, ἀλλ'. Omitted. *Tisch., Tregelles, Alford, Cod. Sin.*

---

16. For God so loved the world, that he gave his only begotten Son, that
whosoever believeth in him should not perish, but have everlasting life.

For. "These words are *the Bible in miniature.*" *Luther.* When
this immortal hero of the Reformation was dying, he repeated from the *Vulgate* the words, "Sic enim Deus dilexit
mundum, ut Filium Suum," &c. He had learned them in the
childhood of his faith, and they were his comfort and hope in
passing into eternity.

The Dialogue form has ceased, for Nicodemus no longer questions
our Lord.

God so, &c. John i. 2. With adoring gratitude we receive these
words from the lips of Christ.

So loved. Indefinite past time, denotes THE UNIVERSAL ETERNAL
EXISTENCE OF THIS LOVE!

LOVE is the *one ground* of the Divine purpose, and salvation the
one aim.

So loved. Words inexpressible, inexhaustible, and beyond all
others.

Love is the joy, the purpose, the nature, the essence of God, for
"GOD IS LOVE." 1 John iv. 8.

In Love He *created* the world; and though it has fallen, in Love
He *upholds it.*

The greatest miracle that has ever been seen on earth is God's
kindness to sinners. Rom. v. 8—10.

The believer, once learning it, can never through all eternity forget
it.

The greatness of God's love is seen—

1. In its object—a fallen, miserable world.
2. In its plan, embracing and harmonizing such opposing interests.
3. In its agent. No higher could be found than the second Person
in the glorious Trinity.

4. In its manifestation. "He spared not His own Son," &c.
5. In its results. "Now are we the sons of God, and it doth not yet appear," &c.
6. In its conditions. "Whosoever believeth shall be saved."
7. In its disinterestedness. No adequate *return* is possible.
"*Behold, what manner of love.*" 1 John iii. 1 ; Eph. iii. 18. The highest intelligences in the universe stand amazed at the vastness of this love. Eph. iii. 10.
The missionary Nott announced this text to Tahitians. They asked "*Is this really true?*" He repeatedly affirmed it. "Oh !" they exclaimed ; "and canst thou speak of such love without *tears ?*"
These poor heathen *wept* and *wondered at such matchless love !*
These Divine words can make mourners joyful, and the dead live.
God's absolute Love is not inconsistent with His immutable Justice.
"The wrath of the Lamb" is love in flames.
God can have no motive to malevolence, nothing to fear, nothing to envy.
He has provided remedies for the evils under which we suffer, and freely offers them to all.
"The Lord is good to all, and His tender mercies are over all His works." Psal. cxlv. 9.
Christ, like sunlight, is given "without money and without price" for a *world's* good.
He claims our regard in behalf of a Being of infinite *Love.*
Beyond this life all irregularities will be adjusted, and "every mouth stopped." Rom. iii. 19.
World. All men share either *temporal* or *spiritual* blessings through the cross.
God so loved, &c. 1. Love in its grandest *source*—"GOD." 2. Love in its purest *form*—"SO LOVED." 3. Love in its widest *sphere*—"THE WORLD." 4. Love in its highest *purpose*—"SALVATION." *Morris.*
Vain Jews believed that God loved them only, and hated the Gentiles.
The sole conditions of salvation are *repentance* and *faith*, and as its benefits are not limited by their Author, they must not be by us.
The *General Assembly* of the Church of *Scotland* having censured *Erskine* for offering Christ too freely, *were silenced* by *his appeals to these words.*

He gave. Christ did not die, as infidels falsely say, *that* God *might
love* men.

But He died *because* God loved men, for the ATONEMENT is not the
cause, but the *effect*, of God's love.

Gave. Not to the *world* only, but absolutely *gave* Him up,—
" spared not." Rom. viii. 32.

An undoubted allusion to Gen. xxii. 16, " Because thou hast not
withheld thy son," &c.

He gave. Christ the highest, greatest, best gift of God. Even
Jehovah could give no greater. John iv. 10.

With His Son also " This cup which my Father hath *given* Me," &c.
John xviii. 11.

Then our CREATOR was constituted our SAVIOUR, our JUDGE became
our ADVOCATE.

Man gives to man when urged by a cry for help, or when desirous
of procuring favours.

But God gave His Son to *enemies :* the world had neither asked nor
cared. Rom. v. 10.

Not because Justice demanded it, nor of any necessity in government.

But pure sovereign grace, with the Son's full consent. Eph. ii. 4.

The Spirit hints that this *love* is incomprehensible to man, and *a
study*, exercising the mightiest powers of heavenly intelligences.
Eph. iii. 18 ; 1 Pet. i. 12.

This *revelation* of mercy embraces *all* mankind as sinners.

It removes every barrier, and invites all the children of Adam, as
prodigals, to return to their Father's house.

No sinner has ever yet perished through God's *unwillingness* to save.

" As I live, saith the Lord God, I have no pleasure in the death of
the wicked." Ezek. xxxiii. 11.

" Ye will not come to me, that ye might have life." John v. 40.

" O Jerusalem, how oft would I have gathered you, but ye would
not ! " Matt. xxiii. 37.

We have no proof that any one ever refused to trust in God's mercy
because of the doctrine of *election*.

Only begotten. John i. 14. SON OF GOD. John i. 41. Prophetic type. Gen. xxii. 2.

The eternal Sonship of Christ is clearly taught in Scripture.

" God of God, Light of Light, very God of very God, begotten, not
made, of one substance with the Father." *Nicene Creed.* Matt.
xvi. 16 ; Heb. i. 5 ; John vii. 29.

A pledge in this that when He *requires* the dearest, He will also *give* the dearest.

Nicodemus would see—1st, the love required; 2nd, the substitution made; 3rd, the prophecy uttered to Abraham, Gen. xxii. 2, foreshadowing the Messiah.

Son. As Son of man He could sympathize in all our trials; as Son of God, save to the uttermost.

Not an apostle nor a prophet, nor an angel nor a cherub, but the Son.

The mightiness and inexhaustibleness of the Father's love seen in giving not a creature, for that were a *finite* love, but the CO-ETERNAL, CONSUBSTANTIAL SON !

South African converts call the *Bible* "THE BOOK OF BEAUTIFUL WORDS," referring to this epitome of the gospel.

Man's salvation: 1. The *originating cause*—God's love. 2. The *efficient cause*—gift of God's Son. 3. The *material cause*—His death. 4. The *instrumental cause*—man's faith. 5. The *final cause*—eternal life.

Whosoever. The Greek is "*every one*," limited only by the circle of humanity.

This invitation is broad and mighty, but availeth *nothing* to those baptized, or in Church communion, *without faith !*

"I thank God for the word, 'whosoever.' Had it read, there was mercy for Richard Baxter, I am so vile, I would have thought it meant *some other* Richard Baxter, but 'whosoever' includes the worst of all Richard Baxters."

Nicodemus must have been astounded to hear the Gentiles included.

Bigoted Jews malignantly hated the *breadth* of this offer.

"Liberals" and infidels equally scorn its *conditions,*—faith in the blood of atonement.

For ages Jews called Gentiles "dogs," and treated them as excluded from God.

Messiah's coming was to bring *morning* to Israel, and *light* to all the world.

"The *propitiation* for our sins: and not for ours only, but for the sins of the *whole world.*" 1 John ii. 2.

It has been said that the ruin and annihilation of our race would never have been known to the universe save by express revelation. But we know that dwellers in other worlds deeply sympathize with the redeemed on earth. Heb. i. 14.

Believeth, &c. Faith. John i. 7 ; vii. 38. The golden key to the riches of redemption.

" Faith is the substance (*confidence*) of things hoped for, the evidence (*conviction*) of things not seen." Heb. xi. 1.

The condition of regeneration, noted in verse 3, is a proof of Christ's Divine nature.

To assert believing on a *creature* would *secure heaven* were *blasphemy*. A creature, though ever so holy, can only answer for himself, and has no power to save others.

Our Lord condenses the entire gospel into this *single verse*.

1. THE WORLD, objectively in its widest sense, and as ready to perish.
2. THE LOVE OF GOD as measured and measurable only by the gift of love.
3. THE GIFT. His only begotten Son, the brightness of His glory, the express image of His person.
4. THE FRUIT of this stupendous gift, negatively and positively.
5. THE MODE, by which this gift becomes available to the sinner, viz. *faith*.

How would Nicodemus's narrow Judaism pale before this " SUN OF RIGHTEOUSNESS rising with healing in his wings ! " Mal. iv. 2.

οὕτω refers to the mode of the gift, " on this wise," as here described. *Mattoon.* " A ship laden with God's love, sailing through thousands of years, drops anchor in Bethlehem. The treasures of her cargo are unladen at Golgotha." *Tauler.* Sic, i.e. tam vere, tam fideliter. *Garranus.*

οὕτω. A continuation of our Lord's discourse. *Knapp, Meyer.* The words of the Evangelist. *Tholuck.*

γάρ always connects the following with the preceding. *Hengst.* Strange to give the Lord's words to another. *B. Crusius.* A child must feel the *Lord* is speaking. *Richter.* Otherwise Nicodemus is left where we found him. *Alford, Luthardt.* Words of our Lord, otherwise the strength and beauty of the admonition is destroyed. *Doddr.,* and all other critics of note. Appended as warning to John's disciples. *Ols.* Denoting intensity, with such an excess of affection. *Lampe.* Directed against Pharisaical exclusiveness. *Stier.* Till now He had spoken as it were in strange tongues. *Jacobi.* A sic without a sicut, without a parallel. *Trapp.*

ἠγάπησεν. Names both the fact and the mode of love. *J. J. Müller.* " Reconciliation of God," an improper word. *Gerlach.* That God so abhorred sin as to surrender His Son is a " *typus doctrinæ* " inadmissible. *Munch, Meyer.* The imputation that Christ's death *induced pity* in God is a slander on evangelical theology. *Author.* The fire which Christ sent. *Salmeron.* God is not the author of sin, nor was He obliged to prevent its existence, nor can it be proved that, in the end, it will be detrimental to the universe, as the well-being of the universe and God's glory are *identical.* He will, by-and-by, show us how to comprehend this great mystery. Natural evil checks iniquity. Good men need afflictions. The world, as created, had neither natural nor moral evil in it. *Dwight,* vol. i. p. 180.

κόσμου, fallen race. *Stier.* Properly the universe, but here limited to the world. *Hengst.* Mundus electorum. *Synod of Dort, Swiss Formula, Hutcheson, Lampe, Gill.* Some men draw ti e lines closer than the Spirit of inspiration. *Davenant.* No discrimination between renewed and unrenewed. *Heumann.* Salvation offered to all. *Wolfius, Koecher.* Confined to the Jews. *Rosenm.* The Lord resists this very narrow opinion. *Grotius, Lightfoot.* Nicodemus' prejudices confined this blessing to Priests and Levites especially ; outsiders would be cast into a kind of Tartarus. *Kuinoel.*

πιστεύων, added to show descent or blood brings not salvation. *Wetstein.* 1. *Prius nos dilexit.* 2. *Tantillos dilexit.* 3. *Tales.* 4. *Tantos.* 5. *Tantum dilexit.* 6. *Sui gratiâ.* *J. Hacket.*

ὁ Θεὸς. As a *man*, He loved us in our misery. But the Love sending Him was *infinite*. *Denton.*

ἔδωκεν, i.e. to death. *Ols.* Hath given. *Markland.* The infinite freedom of the gift hinted. *Corn. à Lap.* In the sacrament of the altar. *Pusey.* A papal dogma revived. *Author.* Not the incarnation chiefly, but the atonement. *Hengst.*

μονογενῆ, John's peculiar phraseology. *Lücke.* John's phraseology derived from the Master. *Luthardt.* Reference to offering of Isaac. *Stier.* Direct inspiration of the Spirit. *Hengst.*

πᾶς. Paul calls himself πρῶτός, a first-rate sinner. *D. Brown.* Isaiah embraces those *crimsoned* by crime. Isa. i. 18.

---

17. For God sent not his Son into the world to condemn the world ; but that the world through him might be saved.

Sent. To all mankind, not to Jews alone, as Nicodemus held.

Never used of the second Advent. He will *come*, but not be *sent*.

To die for sinners, the Son is *sent* as a *servant*, but in majesty He will *come*.

His first, a coming in mercy ; the second, in judgment.

His incarnation made His being sent evident to mankind.

He had always been in the world, but " the world knew Him not."

Condemn. To abandon one judicially to merited ruin. There was reason to fear the worst.

The blood of all nations had been *tainted* with the guilt of a fearful leprosy.

A guilt like that of the Amalekites, with whom " God made war from generation to generation."

All Old Testament prophecies of the Messiah ruling and punishing, especially those describing Him as *final Judge*, were applied by the Jews to His first coming.

With ineffable presumption on Divine favour, the Pharisees *challenged* God's avenging justice.

They expected to stand and see the heathen destroyed, fearing no separation at judgment.

" I came not to judge," John xii. 47, will characterize His relationship to the world to the close of this dispensation.
Judgment springs not from *Love's* primal design, but because of
unbelief.

Condemn. Gr. *judge*, John ix. 39. It is the *unfolding of character*,
anticipating the last day.
" Fear not," said the angel ; " I bring you good tidings of great
joy." Luke ii. 10.
He was not sent *now* to be the Judge, but the SAVIOUR of *the*
world. 1 John iv. 14.
Sentence had already been passed, Gen. ii. 17, 18, but the measure
of iniquity was not full.
His first coming was to *make* satisfaction for sin. His next will
obtain it.
Many will not be *constrained* by love to live happily, and reign
eternally. Judg. ix. 13.
Though, alas! condemnation is the *issue* of Christ's mission to them,
yet the *object* of His mission is solely a *saving* one.
He is appointed for " the *fall* and *rise* of many in Israel." Luke
ii. 34.

But that. God " desireth not the death of the sinner, but rather,"
&c. Ezek. xxxiii. 11.
If men will perish, they " must force their passage to the flames ! "
Cowper.
The gay worldlings cannot be persuaded that what they call " their
good things" cost dearer, and demand greater sacrifices, than
" the way of life." Jer. xxi. 8.
" There is NO PEACE, saith my God, to the wicked ! " Isa. lvii. 21.

Through Him. " For there is no other name under heaven
given amongst men." Acts iv. 12.
During 6000 years men have tried a thousand schemes, but all
have failed.
It is enough to make one weep to read the longings and yearnings
of earnest hearts in heathendom for peace.
A heathen praying, said, " I despise the little gods ; I want aid
from *Jove alone.*"

Saved. Immeasurable thought, THE WORLD MIGHT BE SAVED!
Divine counsel provided for it in *Redemption as* POSSIBLE.
Foundation of this great truth is found in the promise in Paradise
(Gen. iii. 15), where the *avenue to mercy* is as wide as the
road to ruin.

" I am come that they might have life, and have it more abundantly."   John x. 10.

But *rejecting* the Saviour, those already dead under the law die eternally.   Heb. x. 29.

Unbelief converts our Lord's advent in *mercy* into an advent in *judgment.*

" A savour of life or a savour of death " is He to *all* who hear the gospel.   2 Cor. ii. 16.

He does not offer life in vain for God *cannot be mocked.*   Gal. vi. 7.

Those rejecting the offered crown, must wear the burning chains.

Little children can learn Christ died for them that they may be saved.

Yet an intellect, sweeping the universe on angel-wings, cannot go beyond it.

The scheme of redemption, stretching from eternity to eternity, is a *thesis* involving the deepest problems of God's moral government, and will test the highest powers of created intelligence. 1 Pet. i. 12.

ἀπέστειλε.   Cannot refer to His second coming.   *Stier.*   Second is not for remission of sins, but for judgment.   *Chrys.*

κόσμον.   Reprobate heathen.   ἵνα, the one design, normal use of the particle.   Luke ix. 56; Matt. xviii. 11, 14; John ix. 39.   *Stier.*

κρίνῃ.   The verb signifies to judge, sentence, inflict punishment.   *Robinson.*

κρίνειν equivalent to κατακρίνειν.   *Tittmann.*   Our Lord's use of the word not to sentence but punish.   *J. Brown.*   Not to begin His Messianic kingdom with judgment.   *Nonnus.*   The sentence had been passed, the sword lifted, only the word was not given.   *Luther.*   He speaks of His first advent, not His second, to glory.   *Beausobre.*

σωθῇ.   To save from eternal death.   *Gesenius.*   Such a doctrine, *maintaining* itself, despite all the evil passions and perverse wills of a wicked world, proves it from God.   *Hammond.*   Luke xiii. 23.   Free-will of man set forth. *Alford.*   But free-will, left to itself, invariably leads to perdition.   John v. 40. *Author.*   Christ so died for the lost, that they need not have been lost.   *Stier.*

---

18. He that believeth on him is not condemned : but he that believeth not is condemned already, because he hath not believed in the name of the only begotten Son of God.

Believeth.   John i. 7 ; vii. 38.   Faith a saving grace.   " Believing, ye might have life," &c.   John xx. 31.

The Saviour is received by faith.   " As many as received Him," &c. John i. 12.

Salvation comes through faith. "Saved through grace." Acts
xv. 11.

"Justified by the faith of Christ we have peace with God." Gal.
ii. 16; Rom. v. 1.

No true gospel faith without resting on the SACRIFICE *for sins.*
1 John v. 10, 11.

God's *general* Benevolence will not save: it would be at the expense
of Justice.

He cannot scatter pardons from His throne to men, whether they
repent or not.

A higher law binds consistently with His own word, to let the incorrigible perish.

Faith, *resting* on *works* of the law, avails nothing to save the soul.
Gal. iii. 10—12.

Faith, *mixing* our works with Christ's merit, will avail nothing.
Rom. ix. 31—33.

Salvation from the *guilt, penalty,* and *dominion* of sin, the end of
faith.

Men, living without God, imagine it their interest to deny His
Being.

Those, disliking the restraints of religion, would fain get rid of its
truths.

Hence unbelievers in every age assault the Bible, supposing that if
they can subvert its claims, they need fear nothing.

Their cry is, "Let us break His bands in sunder, and cast away,"
&c. Psa. ii. 1—3.

Man's unbelief is not because he *is* a sinner, but because he refuses
the light of truth.

The great *God-dishonouring sin* is UNBELIEF, under the gospel dispensation. Mark xvi. 16.

1. It aims to nullify all the glorious purposes of Infinite LOVE.
2. It aims to impute folly to all the designs of Infinite WISDOM.
3. It aims defiantly to oppose all the operations of Infinite POWER.
4. It aims to falsify all the promises of Infinite TRUTH
5. It proclaims to the universe that DARKNESS IS BETTER THAN
   LIGHT. See verse 19.

Unbelief is traceable—1. To PROFLIGACY. Sinners of this class
are defiant, and refuse to give up their sensual indulgences
for any cause. 2. To RECKLESSNESS. Sinners of this class
take time and pains to think about worldly profits, pleasures, honours, but will not about religion. 3. To PRIDE.

Sinners of this class have made up their minds, and to change they think would imply fickleness, self-ignorance, or guilt. 4. To INFATUATION. Sinners of this class seem bereft of reason as to their *eternal* well-being. Madness is in their hearts while they live. Eccl. ix. 3.

Condemned. Gr. *judged.* Unbelief locks and bars the gate of Infinite mercy.

It strikes at the heart, not of man, nor of angel, but of the Son of God.

As redemption does not reject *believing* heathen, Rom. ii. 14, 15, so judgment will not spare *unbelieving* Jews. Rom. xi. 22.

The terrible sting of the sentence is its *desert.* The soul is *self-condemned.*

Man is NOT *lost* BECAUSE *he has* SINNED, *but because he* PERSISTS *in* KEEPING HIS SINS.

Men do not perish because RUINED by the FALL, but for REFUSING the offered REMEDY.

An awakened conscience approves the law of God, and acknowledges the righteousness of the sentence. Ezek. xviii. 4.

Every gospel-despiser perishing must confess the justice of his doom.

All unbelievers are fighting their own convictions, as well as resisting the Spirit of God. (See on *Conscience*, John i. 9.)

What perdition is we know not, but eternal loss of heaven must break the heart.

Future misery is not so much *objective* as *subjective*, a *malignant conscience.*

Twenty-eight murderers in one year were put in *solitary cells* in one prison.

They had no companions but God and a guilty *conscience !*

In twenty-one months SEVENTEEN became RAVING MANIACS *for life !*

"There is now no condemnation to them which are in Christ Jesus." Rom. viii. 1.

But a solitary *thread*, as feeble as the *pulse*, suspends the sinner over ruin.

Subjects in rebellion are offered pardon, if they lay down their arms.

Their *refusal of the offer* proves they *are* "*condemned already.*" John iii. 18.

Not accepting terms of reconciliation causes this decree to *abide.* John iii. 36.

Some might say, "*We do not know the messenger's credentials.*"

The answer will not avail. They refused to *examine* the evidences offered.

The very *willingness* to examine Christ's claims *is submission begun.*

The main reason why unbelievers refuse to examine the Bible is because they know IT WILL CONVICT AND CONDEMN THEM ! Luke xi. 45 ; John ix. 41.

Mark how a *father* and a *son* received a message from Jehovah. 2 Kings xxii. 11.

Josiah found the book of the law, and called the nation to the house of God to hear.

He stood by a pillar and covenanted to walk before the Lord with the people. But his son *Jehoiakim* took the roll, " *cut it into pieces,* and *cast it in the fire.*" Jer. xxvi. 21 ; xxxvi. 28.

" He that doeth evil *hateth the light,* neither cometh he to the light." John iii. 20.

Already. Gr. *by this time.* Though judgment is RECORDED, it is not yet EXECUTED.

The traitor by his own act is condemned even before his treason has come to light.

So Adam was condemned the moment he sinned, even before judgment was pronounced. Gen. ii. 17.

The first sentence, " Thou shalt surely die," Gen. iii. 4, remains in full force against *all unbelievers.*

Because. Nicodemus having seen the *excellence* of faith is now taught the fearful results of unbelief.

Not believed. The Greek perfect sets forth *deliberate choice* of the man. 2 Thess. ii. 11, 12.

It has been said that Judas in refusing to *believe* in Christ, was guilty of a greater sin than in *betraying Him.*

Unbelief shuts the door of mercy against the soul beyond the arm of man or angel to open. Gal. iii. 11 ; Isa. lxi. 1.

The name. See John i. 12 ; ii. 23. JESUS, " He shall save His people," &c. Matt. i. 21.

Only begotten. See John i. 14. " Only Son." Rom. viii. 32. " Well-beloved." Mark xii. 6.

As there is but one Son, and one Saviour, so there is but " *one ark.*" Acts iv. 12.

Rejecting the only life-boat in an ocean of danger, what hope for the wrecked mariner?

πιστεύων. Justification by faith the test of a standing or falling Church. *Luther.*

οὐ κρίνεται. Is not judged, does not come into punishment. *D. Brown.* He, by unbelief, punishes himself. *J. Brown.* " Ille nocens se damnat, quo peccat, die." *Wordsworth.*

μὴ πιστεύων. In the wilderness, serpent and peril drove nearly all to believe. *Stier.* Sin of heathen is violating the law of conscience, Rom. ii. 14, 15 ; sin of impenitent Christendom is unbelief. *Anton.* Unbelief condemned anticipating the Judgment. *Estius.*

πεπίστευκεν. Perfect tense. Decided finally and deliberately. *Lange.*

---

19. And this is the condemnation, that light is come into the world, and men loved darkness rather than light, because their deeds were evil.

This is. To His omniscient eye, all men are ever moving to the one or other side of the dividing line ; in truth, "*judgment is begun* on earth." 1 Pet. iv. 17.

" Let both grow together until the harvest." Matt. xiii. 30. Character is ever unfolding here.

He could have revealed the awful mystery, the origin of evil, but His silence is Divine.

He, however, tells us plainly why men are condemned.

The. By way of high and solemn emphasis, THE condemnation !

The Christ-rejecters and gospel-despisers have no *common* doom. Luke xii. 47.

Condemnation. Decision and separation implying guilt.

Condemnation is perdition, and it seals up under it those remaining incorrigible.

He condemns to darkness those who love darkness. This disappoints not God, but rather *fulfils* His eternal laws.

Light is sent to guide, but if rejected, it takes part with God against man.

Water, the *home* of finny tribes, becomes the *winding-sheet* of a wicked world.

The *stars* made for radiance, enter into alliance with God, and *fight against* Sisera.

The *sun* and *moon* take up their Creator's cause, and battle against the hosts of the Amorites. Josh. x. 12.

The *sea* rolling in peace makes a grave under its dark depths for Pharaoh.

The *flames* of His justice vindicate His holiness in Sodom's ruins.

The *hail* pours destruction on the enemies of Jehovah's people. Josh. x. 11.

Man's *conscience*, God's friend in the bosom, will prove a tormentor in eternity.

Christ's *blood*, the highest proof of mercy, will, rejected, become the most painful element of woe.

Unbelief turns His *Incarnation* into judicial ruin. Luke ii. 34.

He veiled His truth before Jews generally as strangers, or profane. Matt. xiii. 11 ; Mark iv. 11.

Light. John i. 4. The conversation with Nicodemus took place in the night season.

Christ the essential, everlasting SOURCE OF LIGHT leaves a creature with whom He deigns to converse, to *infer* what He meant.

The universe is full of countless glowing orbs, but *this Light* is the LIGHT OF LIFE. John viii. 12 ; ix. 5.

The unrenewed, like Nicodemus, desire the *light* without the *life.*

Light of love purifies, cheers, illuminates, and elevates the soul.

Light. 1. Kindled by God in creating man a living soul. Gen. ii. 7 ; Psal. iv. 6. 2. In inspiring holy men to write the Holy Scriptures. Psal. cxix. 105. 3. In raising up living witnesses for the truth in every age. 4. In Christ incarnate, in whom all light is concentrated and perfected.

Is come. Every child of Adam has light sufficient to leave him without excuse. John i. 9 ; Rom. i. 20 ; iii. 19.

World. Points to the natural corruption of fallen humanity.

The unrenewed constitute a large majority of adult mankind.

Loved. Instead of coming to the light that comes to them, they flee from it.

An awful revelation, confirmed by *eighteen centuries* of history.

A depraved *heart* paralyzes the *will;* this is mankind's deepest ruin.

Persistent unbelief of the Jews a continuation of their fathers' treason.

It implies *an effort to shut out* the light of truth through fear of disturbing conscience.

As the sluggard closes the shutters, to keep out the morning rays.

Convictions stifled, lead to " holding truth *in unrighteousness.*" Rom. i. 18.

To *have sin* is not the danger, but boldly insisting that we have *no sin* ruins so many. *Luther.*

Among all the birds of beauty and song, the night-loving owl is the *solecism* in natural history.

Not ignorance, but the *love* of *darkness,* brings doom on the world.

Men hate the light because it robs them of all good opinion of their *morality.*

As a man fights for the title-deeds of his inheritance, so men fight for this " morality."

The sick man thanks the physician for unfolding a disease concealed.

The traveller thanks the stranger for revealing his danger from lurking robbers.

But the sinner strangely hates those friends who would rescue him from the evil which will ruin him for ever.

This will be a CAUSE of WONDER to the LOST THROUGH ETERNITY !

Hating the light and loving the darkness, proof of HEART MADNESS ! Eccl. ix. 3.

Thus the insane often strangely hate their *best friends.*

The sinner, conscious or unconscious, never had such a Friend as Jesus, and if hated, never will have such a Friend again.

Men sin, some say, from necessity of organization or constitutional infirmity. *Combe.*

This is the cloven foot of infidelity, under the guise of spiritualism or phrenology.

Men not only love darkness rather than light, but REJOICE in loving evil because it is evil.

"THEY HATE GOD WITH ALL THEIR HEART, SOUL, AND MIGHT." *Burke.*

A mere child finding it can utter a *bad word,* will repeat it as it never does a *good one.*

"Evil, be thou my good," were a speech worthy the prince of fiends. *Milton.*

Men deliberately turn from Christ as one insane does from a physician.

Hypocrisy and deceit follow sin, as the shadow follows a body.

Not that men love darkness for its *own sake,* but for that which it *conceals.*

"They that hate ME love death," but not death for its own sake. Prov. viii. 36.

They love the bowl *sparkling with wine,* "but in the end," &c. Prov. xxiii. 32.

They love "sweet stolen waters," but they lead to death. Prov. ix. 17, 18.

They love their ease, and will not *give up the world.* Luke xviii. 23.

Two wonders—one from above, the other from the depths of Satan :

The first, God so loved the world ; the other, men reject God's only begotten Son.

Some perish *ashamed* to stand before their companions *serious minded.*

Others perish too *proud* to acknowledge they have sinned at all.

Others perish too *busy* in their rush after the glittering prizes of earth. Rev. xviii. 14.

Others perish too *insolent* to acknowledge God their superior and their Judge.

There is a *fearful, fiery energy* in man's pursuit of sinful objects.

Darkness. John i. 5 ; vi. 17. Light filled them with wonder, but they were bound down by the *love* of darkness.

The discerning of truth is a thing of the honest *heart,* not of the deceitful *brain.*

Divine light is first obscured, then repelled, then hated.

Thus infidels travesty the truth, and then reject the inspired Book of God.

Thus martyrs were first *slandered,* then *slaughtered.*

Witness Stephen, Jerome of Prague, Cranmer, &c., and even the Lord Himself.

Revealing the terrible truth, that man's hatred to holiness increases in proportion as the holiness itself increases.

To love *light* with a *false love* is to love darkness really.

This is God's saddest judgment, *permitting* men to "*put darkness for light.*"

Heathen sages have all noted the *poison* in the cup of humanity.

Man being so miserable, the marvel is he dislikes to hear of *help.*

The wicked hail new inventions for sin as the Ethiopians now welcome our cards, oaths, and intoxicating drinks, but reject our Bible, our Sabbaths, and salvation.

The thirsty Bedouin is glad to find the willow pointing out the spring.

But sinners are not glad to see the river of Life flowing from the throne of BOUNDLESS LOVE.

Rather. "They loved the praise of men more than the praise of God." John xii. 43.

That is, they cared not to have the praise of God *at all.*

Thus the Pharisee was not justified *at all* in the parable. Luke xviii. 14.

Deliberate rejection of the Light reveals a fearful preference for darkness.

None but *Antichrist* teaches that "ignorance is the mother of devotion."

Deeds. Outward acts the mere index of man's inner being.

Deeds, here transpiring, are the ground of final judgment. Rom. ii. 16.

Are evil. Gr. implies those which are of *Satan's* nature, and all are evil.

Human depravity had reached a terrible height in the time of Christ.

Rome's emperors became so frantic in crime, they ceased to remember virtue.

The ruins of Herculaneum, destroyed A.D. 79, reveal even now the terrible intensity of its sin.

There and in Pompeii we find the *key-note* of the terrible doom of Sodom.

Moral blindness—1. The effect of *passion:* " Fleshly lusts war against the soul." 1 Pet. ii. 11. 2. Effect of evil *habits:* " Can the Ethiopian change his skin ? " Jer. xiii. 23. 3. Effect of *fanaticism:* " I persecuted the Church of God." Gal. i. 13. 4. Effect of *impenitence :* " The last state of that man is worse than the first." Luke xi. 26.

A possibility of eternal blessedness, involves that of eternal misery.

The Moslem cultivates *sensuality*, and thus veils God from His soul.

The Deist exalts the laws of *nature* into the place of God.

The Papist cleaves to his *rites* and *dogmas*, and thus *nullifies* the gospel.

The unbeliever holds up *self*, and therefore cares not for and cannot see the cross.

κρίσις, κρίμα. John ix. 39. It embraces verse 21. Men not receiving light are condemned to darkness. *Lücke.* Separation of the lost from life. *Stier.* Not punishment, but occasion and cause of punishment. *Beza.* Cause of eternal condemnation, or the *manner* of incurring it. *Schoettgen.*

φῶς. See on John i. 4. φῶς, not φέγγος, true antithesis to σκότος. *Doederlein.* Evidently the Redeemer Himself. *Schleiermacher.*

ἐλήλυθεν. Christ, the light, the *occasion*, not the cause of condemnation. *Kuinoel. Religion* the *occasion* of the death of millions of martyrs. *Author.* Not controlled as to His *will* by the Father. *Cajetan.* Not because fallen man could *claim* Him, but of sovereign grace. *Calvin.* Not because we sought Him. *Jans. Gand.*

ἄνθρωποι. Jews principally. *Hengst.*

ἠγάπησεν, successive acts, definitely establishing a habit. *D. Brown.*

μᾶλλον. Comparison very appropriate. *Bengel.* It has a sharp tone of mournful complaining irony. *Stier.* Curiosity prevents a love of ignorance. *Stier.* To love it absolutely would be devilish. *Lücke.* In the background, a complete want of love to the light. *Hengst.* Man's moral nature torn up, all is perverted. *Oetinger.* Not one among the finally lost but felt drawings towards the light. *Besser.*

πονηρὰ, πονος, causing labour or pain, positive malignity. φαῦλος, vile worthless. Satan is ὁ πονηρός, author of all evil, Matt. vi. 13; Eph. vi. 16. φαῦλα contrasted with ἀγαθὰ, John v. 29. The sinner's life *worthless* as to virtue, and *barren* as to result. *Trench.*

---

20. For every one that doeth evil hateth the light, neither cometh to the light, lest his deeds should be reproved.

Doeth. Persistently practising it, evil is ever restless, busier than truth.

It is a *habit* of doing evil, not a *single* act of guilt, that enslaves the soul.

One crime is not decisive of wickedness, nor one good act of piety.

Evil. Gr. indicates both *worthlessness* and *contemptibleness.*

Opposed to the proffered treasures; God's love and eternal life.

Although not malicious, yet for ever barren of good results.

The wicked vehemently deny they hate light, and yet nothing so excites their rage as a revelation of their depravity.

Their cry is, " Peace, peace ! " Ezek. xiii. 10. They demand, " Prophesy not unto us right things," &c. Isa. xxx. 10.

Hateth the light. It is as though they would say, " God's light is no light for men."

" His words I regard not, His thunders I fear not." 1 John v. 10.

The sinner IDENTIFIES himself with HIS SIN.

The covetous man sees, hears, thinks of nothing but his treasures.

These are not merely parts of his being,—he loves them as HIM-SELF ! his LIFE ! his ALL ! his GOD !

His treasures lost, his staff is broken, hope faints, and his god dies, leaving him in despair.

He hates—1. God, who is LIGHT itself. 2. The light's *living energy.* 3. The *children* of light. 4. The *fruit* of light.

He loves—1. *Works* of darkness. Eph. v. 11. 2. *Ways* of darkness. Prov. ii. 13. 3. *Treasures* of darkness. Isa. xlv. 3.

Sinner hates light—1. Because it reveals to him the *misery* of his own heart.

2. Because revealing his *corruption*, it makes him despise himself.

3. Because revealing his *guilt*, it awakens fear of punishment.

4. Because it condemns his sensual pleasures, aims, honours, &c.

Men prefer to remain the prey to consuming passions, those " fierce vultures of the mind."

Some fancy amiable tempers, correct manners, external morality will save them.

LIGHT HATED, LIKE ITS AUTHOR.

Covetous deride it, as it writes *idolater* under their own name.

Envious reject it, as it writes *misery* in those condemned by conscience.

Hateful despise it, as it writes *murderer* over causeless passion.

Lustful scorn it, as it writes *none such can enter the kingdom of heaven.*

Self-righteous refuse it, because it proclaims *salvation by grace.*

Infidels of all kinds abhor it, because it reveals *a God and future retribution.*

" Wilfully ignorant," the condemnation of many gospel despisers. 2 Pet. iii. 5.

" He that is not with Me is against Me " shows neutrality impossible. Matt. xii. 30.

Montesquieu says, " I must either love a man or hate him."

Neither cometh. By natural corruption the mind is darkened.

A course of perseverance in evil ripens into actual *hatred* of light.

Allusion to wicked men *working* during the *night* in all lands.

Men habitually sinning laboriously strive to exclude all convictions.

They dread truth, and avoid going where it might disturb their peace.

The light. A distant hint to Nicodemus coming by night to see Jesus.

Light. A chosen type of the Deity. 1 John i. 5. Flaming sword. Gen. iii. 24. Burning lamp. Gen. xv. 17. Burning bush. Exod. iii. 2. Divine Majesty. Exod. xix. 18. Divine wrath. Num. xi. 1. Angel Jehovah. Judg. xiii. 20. Consuming the sacrifice. 1 Kings xviii. 38. Divine vengeance. 2 Kings i. 10. Chariots of God. 2 Kings ii. 11 ; Psa. lxviii. 17. Spirit's energies. Acts ii. 3. Purifier. Mal. iii. 2. Divine truth. Jer. xxiii. 29. David's offering at Araunah. 1 Chron. xxi. 26. Victim on the altar consumed by fire from heaven. Lev. ix. 24. Elijah's offering at Carmel. 1 Kings xviii. 38.

Julian, the apostate, acknowledges God kindled these sacrifices.

In humble imitation, *priests of Apollo* laid their sacrifices on the Vulcanian hills of Syracuse to be consumed by hidden fire. *Solinus.*

" God, accepting them," became a standing formula in devotion. Psa. xx. 3.

Nadab and *Abihu* took strange fire, and perished by the stroke of God. Lev. x. 1, 2.

" Fire of *the Lord*," or lightning discharged on Sodom in vengeance. Gen. xix. 24.

Spoils of the heathenish Midianites were purified by *fire*. Num. xxxi. 23.

The Holy Ghost appeared in *fiery tongues* on Pentecost. Acts ii. 3.

Faith, Hope, and Charity are the " *tongues of fire* " kindled in our day.

πράσσων, ποιῶν. Former indicates restless activity in sin, latter toils quietly. *Bengel.*

ποιεῖν, doing good, producing permanent results. *Alford.* Nicodemus intended. *Wetstein.*

φαῦλα. See John iii. 19. Empty of good. *Reiger.* Subtle allusion to φῶς. Originally a good, passed entirely to an evil sense. *Wahl.* Its origin signifies *little*, as the old Latin word "paulus." *Donnegan.* Our Lord alludes not to really flagrant sins, but to heathen virtues. Its wisdom, folly; its pleasures, sensualities; its justice, revenge. *Brenz.* Simple abstinence from lust is purity. *Chrys.*

μισεῖ. Light attacks the man, and the man attacks the light, and puts it out. *Anton.* Men dread to uncover their secret sin. *Calvin.* Ethiopians curse the heat of the sun. *Herodotus.*

ἔρχεται. Nicodemus came honestly. *Reiger.* His coming by night reproved. *Herder.* Tacit praise to Nicodemus coming at all. *Lampe.*

φῶς. A decision that will stand the light hinted at. *Ebrard.* Words spoken at the door, as Nicodemus was parting. *Lange.* Heathen borrowed from Jews, and claimed that their god answered by fire. *Dionysius Hal.* Nadab and brother may have taken too much *wine*. *Maimonides, Outrance.* Magistrates forbidden wine while on duty in ancient Greece. *Plato, Eusebius.*

ἔργα, of which he knows he will not be ashamed. *Bengel.* A very divine consciousness. *Stier.*

---

21. But he that doeth truth cometh to the light, that his deeds may be made manifest, that they are wrought in God.

Doeth. Gr. applied to that which *results in good.*

His aim and energy are such, that " his works do follow him." Rev. xiv. 13.

Truth. In *nature* conforming to God's *works ;* in *morals,* in harmony with His *will.*

A good man—1. *Listens* to truth. 2. *Acts* truth. 3. *Seeks* truth. 4. *Abides* in truth. 5. *Loves* truth. 6. *Reflects* truth. 7. Is *approved* by the God of Truth.

His supreme aim in life is *to be* and *to do* what bears the light of eternity.

" Heathen habitually and knowingly utter falsehood." *Dr John Newton.*

" More systematic, determined liars cannot be found than the dwellers in the East." *Dr Jos. Roberts.*

A man's words may be living truths, his deeds may be enacted lies.

How many make their devotions mere *stage performances !*

Mexicans, cruelly tortured by Spaniards, asked, " What God do these men serve ? " and yet those men called themselves *Christians !*

A coat of mail taken from a *bishop* in battle was sent by the King of Hungary to the Pope, with these words : " Know now whether this be thy son's coat or no." Gen. xxxvii. 32.

Hypocrites are the scorn of the very heathen as well as of a holy universe.

Diogenes seeing a wild youth clad in a philosopher's cloak, plucked it off, saying, " Why do you pollute that garment ? "

Christianity is a DIVINE LIFE, as well as a system of DIVINE TRUTH.

He who, beginning with the *least* duties, is sincerely desirous to do *all,* grows from being a " babe in Christ," to be a heroic martyr. 1 Cor. iii. 1.

Cometh. As if He had said, Only come thou to the light, thou visitor in the night season !

Light. Our cold hearts, like winter days, have more light than heat.

An invitation to Nicodemus to come in future in clear daylight.

His first deed of light was done at *night.*

With what a gentle hand the Lord reproves his weakness !

He presses him not to a *decision,* but kindly points out the way, and encouragingly says, " *Go on in the light,*" &c.

In Infinite wisdom He leaves him to resolve and work in *silence.*

LIGHT—1. Of truth. 2. Of love. 3. Of power. 4. Of glory.

Deeds. These have the character of truth or falsehood, so that one must *live* the truth, as well as *believe* the truth.

Faith, hope, charity, patience, humility, self-denial, are a part of God's light, and cannot be hid.

Manifest. Nicodemus, exposed to the contempt and scorn of the Sanhedrim, and to the fierce fanaticism and daring unbelief of a profane age, needed some sustaining assurance of Divine friendship.

Thus the Spirit greets every true penitent with *grace, mercy, and peace.*

By the death of our Lord his faith was made manifest to all Jerusalem. John xix. 39.

One of the first with *martyr spirit,* he was not ashamed of *the
cross.*

In other cases the Lord commands *immediate confession* of faith in
Him. Matt. xii. 13; Mark v. 30; John iv. 16.

In any case His followers must be willing to bear His mark in
their foreheads. Rev. vii. 3.

Hypocrites receive the mark in their hands—that they may conceal
it at pleasure. Rev. xiii. 16.

"Give me thy heart," said Gregory XIII. to his followers, " and
your allegiance to whom you will."

"One may as well worship at the altar of Jupiter as presume to
conceal his faith, and be innocent." *Zwingle.*

Victorinus, a Roman lawyer, desired to be a *secret Christian,* but
Simplicianus, an aged saint, repeated to him Matt. x. 32, and
he confessed on the morrow, and was baptized before the
people.

In God. The believer lives, moves, and has his being in God.

Saints are soldiers in the service of a glorious leader, whose name
is Conqueror. Rev. vi. 2. And His followers are surnamed
" *conquerors.*" Rom. viii. 37.

Mahomet told his followers that " wounds in his cause would hereafter be as resplendent as vermilion." *Koran.*

Sins of believers are cancelled and the record destroyed.

The " handwriting against us blotted out; nailed to the cross."
Col. ii. 14.

" No one shall ever dig up our sins out of Christ's grave." *Besser.*

God is LOVE, and God is LIGHT, and God is TRUTH. 1 John iv. 8,
John viii. 12 ; xiv. 6.

Day of eternity alone will reveal the blessed results of this night
interview to millions who have since studied it.

Nothing to gratify mere curiosity, a strong proof of Divine inspiration.

We are led to infer that Nicodemus remained for some time a
secret believer. John xii. 42.

With this touching farewell, Jesus dismisses him to meet him in
the light.

This ruler learned more in one night than Judas, a disciple, in three
years.

Strauss has denied the truth of this narrative, and says it is a *myth,*

designed to take away the *reproach* that the early Christians
all belonged to the *lower class.*

Neander has replied, THIS FACT was and is to this hour one of the
chief GROUNDS of CHRISTIAN GLORY. 1 Cor. i. 26, 27.

Celsus and *Julian* had made the same *charge* more than a thousand
years before.

The Lord, in this chapter, teaches a *proud* Pharisee, and in the
fourth an *ignorant,* abandoned, Samaritan woman.

Learn that no one is beyond the power of sovereign grace or the
might of redeeming love.

ποιῶν. This great point was left with Nicodemus' conscience. *Dräscke.*
Truth is told, not done. *Schoettgen.* A true word is a *thing immortal. Luther.*
He leaves the seed in the heart, and gives it time to take root and spring.
Reiger.

ποιῶν points to the moral tone of the spirit, πράττειν to the work. *Lücke.*

ἀλήθειαν. See on John i. 14. φῶς. Nicodemus needed a clear perception
of the difference between truth and error. *D. Brown.*

ἔργα. Well-pleasing to God. *Nonnus.* Preparatory to repentance and
faith. *Meyer.* Consequences of conversion interwoven with the change itself.
Stier. Last words uttered under the evening sky, as Nicodemus was leaving.
Lange. This record not minutely detailed. *Weisse.* A poetical free reproduction. *De Wette.* There is *beauty* as well as *truth* in the golden setting of
the sun. *Author.* The account derived from Nicodemus. *Tholuck.* How
many critics seem to forget that the Bible was *inspired ! Author.*

---

22. After these things came Jesus and his disciples into the land of Judæa;
and there he tarried with them, and baptized.

After, &c. The Evangelist had once been a disciple of John the
Baptist.

His finger first pointed out to him the loving "Lamb of God."

The Baptist's death as a martyr was now near, and hence the
testimony which follows is like " the note of the dying swan."
Verses 27—36.

Our Lord was returning from Jerusalem, homeward towards Galilee.

The Evangelist passes over our Lord's *first year* of ministry briefly.

He is totally silent as to His designs in Judea, found in Mark and
Luke.

The land. The sacred band retired from the Passover at Jerusalem, and came to the banks of the Jordan.

He appears to have gone to the northern part of the Jordan valley.

Jews esteemed all dwelling outside their limits unholy and impure.

Hence, returning from abroad, they " shook the dust from off their feet." Acts xiii. 51.

Our Lord confined His labours to Judea, but they *embraced* A WORLD. John xii. 23.

Judæa. Its position preserved it from contact with *Babylonian* idolatry, its monotheism from *Egypt's* learning, and its festal life from *Phœnician* splendour.

Judea lay midway between the nations of Europe, Asia, and Africa, and was traversed by the great caravan routes.

Easily fortified, Jerusalem itself a Gibraltar, Gerizim and Tabor natural fortifications.

Its caves of Carmel and Adullam shielded Elijah and David.

Its seas are Galilee and Sodom. Eastern borders seem *volcanic.*

Of Mount Hermon, in the range of Lebanon, Arabs say, Winter rests on its head, spring sits on its shoulders, autumn lies in its lap, and summer slumbers at its feet.

Valley of Jordan has a tropical clime,—palms formerly flourished there. Also willows, poplars, and tamarisks : nightingales, wood-pigeons, and turtle-doves in the branches.

Gardens of Jericho bloomed like oases bounded by the desolations of Quarantania.

Hills, once terraced and covered with harvests and pastures are now desolate, too poor even to bear the " curse of thorns."

Its valleys of Sharon, Esdraelon, and Jordan, with the deserts around, show both the primeval blessing and the shadow of the curse.

Jordan, though diminutive, ranks in renown with the noblest of earth's streams.

At present the desolation, almost universal, appears as the result rather of a *miraculous judgment* than of natural causes. Isa. vi. 11, 12 ; Jer. xlv. 4 ; Isa. v. 6 ; Deut. xxviii. 33.

About *one third* of the valley of Sharon, *one tenth* of the valley of Jordan, *one sixth* of Jezreel or Esdraelon, are now cultivated.

Canaan's highest consecration derived from the *journeyings* of JESUS.

He followed the call of need, the paths of the poor, and the sheep that were lost.

Transformed the rugged path of temple service into a happy pilgrimage.

His chosen sanctuary for worship was on Galilee's shores and heights.

He revealed the believer's rich inheritance when He Himself *had not where to lay His head.*

He could rest on the Father's bosom, though earth only offered Him
a cross and a tomb.

By His birth the pasture fields of BETHLEHEM became fields of
light.

NAZARETH, symbol of earth's obscure corners, its solitary valleys
of white rock and its luxuriant meadows, He often trod.

CAPERNAUM, full of wealth, publicans, soldiers, and travellers, His
second home.

Here He paid tax, and met the caravans of Phœnicia going to Syria.

Here He taught and displayed His miraculous power.

At CANAAN his first miracle became an antepast of the Lord's Supper.

He offered light and peace to the darkened *Gergesenes* beyond the
sea.

Between Mount Tabor and Sea of Galilee stood KURUN HATTIN,
where the Sermon on the Mount was preached.

Tradition alleges TABOR is the honoured spot of His *transfiguration.*

Mount of OLIVES was consecrated by the Redeemer's tears.

GETHSEMANE witnessed His deepest woes, His agony and sweat of
blood.

The voice of the sorrowing Saviour issuing from GETHSEMANE hallows the earth, as a place of suffering for believers in all
coming time.

CALVARY has communicated its sacredness to the whole of Palestine.

Ascending, His sacred feet pressed OLIVET last of earth, making it
a bright hill of victory !

To this hour the children of the crucifiers long for a grave in the
same sacred soil.

Baptized.   For its history and meaning, see on John i. 25, &c.

John's work finished, he no longer invites men to be baptized.

Thus lanterns are put aside when the morning is seen to dawn.

" Christ will have His people know that baptism by His servants
is His baptism."   *The Fathers.*

This sacrament, repeated from age to age in the Church, must ever
be traced directly to *Jesus Christ.*

Believers, like their Master, should be ever doing, walking while
the day lasts.   John ix. 4.

If Moses cannot execute judgment in Egypt, he will do it in Midian.
Ex. ii. 17.

If *John Howe* is in his cell, he will pen the " *Blessedness of the
Righteous* " for the Church.

If *Bunyan* is in gaol, he will write the "*Pilgrim's Progress*" for all coming time.

" I had rather be sick than have nothing to do." *Seneca*.

In the last twenty verses we find a complete " system of theology."

1. The work of the Father, Son, and Holy Spirit ; 2. Depravity of man ; 3. Nature and necessity of regeneration ; 4. Efficacy of faith ; 5. Way to escape eternal ruin ; 6. True marks of an anxious inquirer.

μετὰ ταῦτα. Our Lord began His ministry in Bethabara, went to Galilee, thence to Jerusalem, then to Judea, apart from the capital. *Hengst*.

'Ιουδαίαν. Some parts of the shores of the Dead Sea covered with vegetation. *Schubert*. Hadrian, who decreed no Jew should approach within sight of the land under penalty of *death*, was unconsciously the angel to keep this race out of the land. *Lewis' Heb. Ant.*

ἐβάπτιζεν. Why did not John join the Saviour? Ans. He did virtually become His disciple. Matt. xi. 11 refers to those *relatively less*. *Author*. John's baptism an introduction to Christ's. *Cyril*. Why was baptism practised, since the Church was not established? *Bretschneider*. The full form, Matt. xxviii. 19, used by the apostles from the beginning, showing the Church *begun*. *J. A. Alexander*. They used only John the Baptist's form. *Tertullian*. Christ's Messiahship confessed, made it diverse. *Tholuck*.

----

23. And John also was baptizing in Ænon near to Salim, because there was much water there: and they came, and were baptized.

John. Life and character, see chap. i. 6. He is never called Baptist or Baptizer by the Evangelist, since his baptism had passed away.

Ænon. These localities entirely *lost*. Hebrew for *fountains*.

Salim. Eight Roman miles south of Scythopolis. *Eusebius, Jerome*.

Much water. The universal wants in the East are fuel and water. John iv. 6.

The depth to which wells must be sunk in Judea renders it costly work, and it is always uncertain whether the waters will be *fresh* or *salt*.

There are few or no brooks in Palestine, as understood in England and America.

The crowds (Matt. iii. 5) who gathered around him required a daily supply such as wells could not furnish.

To this day, American rural gatherings are held where water is *abundant*.

Came. Gr. *kept coming* and getting baptized.

Baptized. He had left Bethania, where he usually baptized, John i. 28, and retired to a secluded spot, near his own country.

Our Lord veiled His baptism of fire (Luke iii. 16) under the water image.

But the Baptist's work was nearly closed as a messenger of Christ.

Δὲ. Now or but. *D. Brown.*

'Ιωάννης. Those holding John's differed from Christian baptism think he should have ceased when Christ began. But they bore the same relation as the morning's dawn and sunrise. *Author.*

Αἰνὼν. Abounding in springs. *Lücke.* Adjective. *Ewald.* Beyond Jordan in Judea. *Alford.* By Arabian desert. *Hengst., Ritter.* 8 Roman miles south of Scythopolis. *Raumer.*

Σαλείμ, nearly east of Nablous. *Robinson.* In Galilee. *Lightfoot.* Wady Farah 6 miles N.E. of Jerusalem. *Barclay.* At the base of Tell Redghah. *De Velde.* Near Hebron. *Lichtenstein.* Not in the vicinity of Jordan. *Andrews.* In the wilderness of Judea. *Wieseler.* Near Scythopolis, a palace of Melchizedek being there. *Jerome.* Followed by *Greswell.* There are ὕδατα πολλὰ there. *Porter.* Many rivers. *Beza.* Baptism was generally, but not universally, by immersion. *Lightfoot.* The mode not named by Scripture. *J. A. Alexander.*

---

24. For John was not yet cast into prison.

For. He had ceased inviting, but doubtless he baptized until arrested. John iii. 22.

In full armour and out in the field, he falls, a faithful soldier.

Not yet. Allusion to the more complete histories of Matthew, Mark, and Luke.

Prison. Durance, " *in ward*," occurs Lev. xxiv. 12 ; Num. xv. 34. " In the king's house." Jer. xxxii. 2. Jehoiachin in Babylon. 2 Kings xxv. 27. Some imprisoned in private houses. Jer. xxxvii. 15. Prisoners sometimes retained years. 2 Chron. xvi. 10 ; 1 Kings xxii. 27. Some tormented until debts were paid. Matt. xviii. 34.

Stocks used, wooden trammels, locking the feet by a key. Jer. xx. 2 ; Acts xvi. 24.

Under the Herods *prisons* and *palaces* were built together. Mark vi. 27 ; Acts xii. 4, 10.

At Jerusalem, Antonia was used as a prison ; at Cæsarea, the Prætorium.

Formerly fortresses and palaces of Europe generally had prisons under them, where the *chained ones oft heard the revelry of music and dancing above.*

Priests also had prisons. Acts v. 18. Friends had usually access to prisoners. Jer. xxxvi. 5.

At times, a dry well was used as a prison. Gen. xxxvii. 24.

Levitical law required certain sins to be punished by being " CUT OFF." Num. xv. 30. Uncircumcision. Gen. xvii. 14. Neglect of passover. Num. ix. 13. Sabbath-breaking. Ex. xxxi. 14. Neglect of atonement. Lev. xxiii. 29. Children offered to Moloch. **Lev. xx. 3.** Trifling with holy things. Num. iv. 15.

Modes of punishment mentioned in the Bible: Hanging. Num. xxv. 4. Stoning. Ex. xvii. 4. Burning. Lev. xxi. 9. Sword and spear. Ex. xix. 13. Crucifixion. John xix. 18. Drowning. Matt. xviii. 6. Torn asunder. 2 Sam. xii. 31. Precipitation from a rock. 2 Chron. xxv. 12 ; 10,000 Idumeans thus perished. Pounding in a mortar. Prov. xxvii. 22.

Like John, we must preach the truth, whether they pay, slay, or imprison us.

Elijah was weaker in endurance than in action. 1 Kings xix. 4.

Luther, being confined for ten months in Wittenberg Castle, murmured.

We learn the Church is *immortal* without human instruments.

Primitive pastors far oftener found in prisons than palaces.

" I'd rather be with Cato in prison, than with thee in the Senate." *Petronius* to Cæsar.

" I'd rather be with Paul in prison, than rapt to the third heaven." *Chrys.*

With this brief allusion, John dismisses the imprisonment and martyrdom of the Baptist. Matt. xiv. 3—12 ; Luke iii. 19, 20.

He lay two whole years in the dungeon of Machaerus, where the ruins of Herod's palace are still found, while Herod was feasting and sporting in a right royal style. Mark vi. 21.

"In thy life-time thou receivedst thy *good* things, but Lazarus *evil* things." Luke xvi. 25.

φυλακήν. Prison houses kept by private speculators in Persia, where prisoners paid their own board. *Chardin.* O.T. punishment "cut off " literally put to death. *Gesenius, Furst, Ewald, Kiel.* By God's hand. *Schultz.* Banishment. *Le Clerc, Michaelis.* Stoning to death. *Jahn.* Deprived of covenant rights. *Baumgarten.* Pounded to death in a mortar practised in Ceylon. *Sir E. Tennant.* Sawing asunder in Barbary. *Shaw.* Jewish rulers 40 years before the city's destruction forbidden to take life. *De Wette.* Machaerus found by Seetzen N. E. shore of Dead Sea. *Ewald.* Questioned by *Robinson.* John's prison in Livias. *Wieseler.* In Queen Mary's time the martyrs merrily called their prison "Bocardo," a "college of *Quondams.*" *Trapp.* Six weeks after our Lord preached, John is still baptizing. *D. Brown.* Period too short. *Tischendorf, Ellicott.* John seems to refer to the records, the sources of the Synoptics. *Alford.* The only record he needed was the mind of the Spirit. *Author.* Exact date of John's imprisonment uncertain. *Winer.* At the Feast of Purim, March 19, A.U.C. 782, and beheaded April 17, 4 weeks later. *Wieseler, Ebrard, Ellicott.* Slain Sept. 22, 781. Feast of Tabernacles. *Greswell, Lichtenstein.*

---

25. Then there arose a question between some of John's disciples and the Jews about purifying.

A question. Peaceful discussion, a quarrel not implied in the original.

For eighteen centuries the relation of outward religious acts to the inner man have agitated good and evil men in the Church.

A master move of the tempter, to divert men's minds from "the things which belong to their eternal peace."

Millions, it is feared, have perished for ever while disputing about the truth under the very shadow of the sanctuary.

Ritualism, with all its hollow pretensions, still deludes myriads.

Surprise, perplexity, and perhaps indignation, rendered John's disciples jealous of their beloved teacher. Matt. xiv. 12.

Unrenewed men may, and do often, love the devotedly pious.

John's disciples seemed to boast their *master's* baptism possessed greater dignity than that of the disciples of Christ.

Jews. See on John i. 19. This incident appears to have occurred at Bethabara.

Jews craftily combined to set these envious disciples against Christ

Thus Jesuits maliciously joined with *Lutherans* to estrange them from *Calvinists.*

Wicked ones ferment evils among Christians, as "Satan loves to fish in troubled waters."

Purifying. For Jewish modes, uses, &c., see on John ii. 6.

Purifying always connected with sacrifices among *Greeks.*

Water was sprinkled by a priest on all who entered a Roman temple, and the custom borrowed hence by Papists.

A marble vase with holy water stood at the door of each heathen sanctuary.

Greek priests took a torch from the altar, dipped it in the sacred
water, and sprinkled the *people.*

The head of the *victim* about to be sacrificed was also sprinkled.

The farmer sprinkled water on his *fields,* asking fertility of the
gods.

The shepherd sprinkled water of security over his *flock* towards
evening.

Roman generals before battle sprinkled their *legions.*

Commanders before sailing sprinkled their *fleets* when about founding a new colony.

Every five years Romans assembled in Campus Martius, were all
purified by the flamens with prayer, sacrificing, and sprinkling.

Jesus and John were the only teachers who baptized Jews.

Some, like Nicodemus, seemed to *refuse* submitting to *either.* Ver. 5.

'Ιουδαίων. *Cod. Sin.*
'Ιουδαίου. *Hengst., Lach., Tisch., Alford.* They call a Jew to account for
preferring Christ's baptism to John's. *Hammond.*
οὖν indicates the contest arose from the nearness of the two baptisms. *Hengst.*
καθαρισμοῦ. The question of John's baptism in relation to Jewish purifications. *W. & W.* A purifying preservative. *Trapp.* Whether purification
was to be sought by Christ's baptism or John's. *Hengst.* First baptism into
the *future* Messiah, second into *the* Messiah, third into the *Trinity. Tholuck.*
John's agreed in essentials, but differed in circumstances. *Calvin, Turretin,
Witsius.* Affirming them the same is anathematized by *Council of Trent.* Our
Lord's doctrine, illustrated by miracles, attracted the populace more than John's.
Wetstein. John's friends held *all* must be baptized by their master, but the
Messiah authorized it in His own name. *Alford.* John's disciples start the
question, Acts xix. 4. *Semler.* Settled in the second century. *Tittmann.*
Even for Levitical baptism this Evangelist uses *purifying. Bengel.*

---

26. And they came unto John, and said unto him, Rabbi, he that was with
thee beyond Jordan, to whom thou barest witness, behold, the same baptizeth,
and all men come to him.

Came. The Baptist's disciples did not cling to him, as Christ's
did to their Master.

Rabbi. For account of this and similar titles, see on John i. 49.

Envying is one of the fruits of the flesh, and always follows glory.

They envied for John's sake, as Joshua did for Moses's.

John's disciples began to be jealous of the brilliant miracles of
Jesus.

Their master performed no miracles. Still his birth was prophecy
fulfilled, and his life as the HERALD OF THE LORD surpassed a
miracle, and shone with the *reflection of the Godhead.*

To John's carnal disciples our Redeemer appeared an ambitious
  rival.
They had heard John's testimony, but in their state of mind it had
  become quite obscured.
Taking their seats with the scorners, Jesus appears Jesus no more.
There are certainties of the past, which shine through Time, *like
  stars.*
The Incarnation makes not only Bethlehem, but the entire earth,
  radiant.
But to " Liberals" *Bethlehem* has not the tithe of the interest of
  Mount Vernon, and they feel far more kindly towards *Wash-
  ington* than *Jesus.*
He that was.   They speak disrespectfully, unconscious of His
  Infinite Majesty.
They implicitly assert what the Pharisees also had learnt.   John
  iv. 1.
Avoiding mentioning His name is a suspicious sign, for *envy*
  makes men *malignant.*
There were no spots in our Lord's character, no defects in His life.
He moved holy and harmless as an angel of God, yet men *envied*
  His spotless loveliness.
The chosen spirits in the school of John had been *dismissed* to Jesus.
The *greatness* of John, and the *littleness* of his disciples, stand in
  contrast.
Their conduct, even after the crucifixion, seems to prove they had
  no true piety.
With thee.   As though the Lord Himself had once actually
  followed in *the train* of their teacher.   The WORD, Creator of
  heaven and earth, was *with* a poor humble creature, who lived
  by His favour !
As well speak of a SUN that *followed* the morning and evening STAR.
Jordan.   For description, see on John i. 28.
Witness.   Gr. *hast been all the time bearing witness.*
As though our Lord had taken advantage of John's testimony.
How *soon* was our Saviour wilfully and maliciously misrepresented!
And from that hour countless enemies have striven to *tear* from
  His thorn-scarred brow its " *many crowns.*"   Rev. xix. 12.
Detraction is a poison instilled in a golden cup, with sweet wine.
A certain bee can neither eat nor pluck fair fruit, but stings it.
The reply of John was one of the noblest and most affecting
  utterances ever made.

All men. That Christ was attracting the people was good news to John.

But jealous of the Saviour's fame, they wish Him to be forbidden. Num. xi. 28.

As much as to say, " He is requiting thy generosity by drawing away all thy followers, and at this rate thou wilt soon have no disciples at all."

The Redeemer's matchless WISDOM and boundless LOVE so veiled themselves in the depths of humility, that these men actually pretended to believe Him less than their master.

Two causes of offence—1. Asking baptism of John, they supposed He had become John's disciple. 2. One unknown, but commended by John, had outshone their master.

μεμαρτύρηκας. We call the battle of *Waterloo* the deciding point, but the Prussians speak in the same strain of *La Belle Alliance.* Vespers of Palermo to a Papist commemorate a *victory*, to a Christian a massacre. ὃς ἦν μετά. They do not say, thou with him. *D. Brown.* John's disciples seem to have had no true idea of religion. *J. A. Alexander.* Confused ideas of their master's baptism, as well as Christ's. *Besser.*

οὗτος. "This fellow" among Greeks showed supreme contempt. *Wetstein.* Some hold they took their master for the Messiah, baptized, were austere, and were called *Sabeans*, or Christians of St John, and many dwelt at Ephesus. *Overbeck, Storr.* Questioned. *Eichorn.* Those Sabeans were Mahommedans. *Adler, Niebuhr.*

πάντες for πολλοί. *Kuinoel.* An hyperbole common to all languages. *Author.* Not John's converts, but multitudes besides. *Alford.* This complaint merely a respectful inquiry for explanation. *Hanmann.*

---

27. John answered and said, A man can receive nothing, except it be given him from heaven.

Answered. John had been the conscious, divinely-chosen herald of Christ.

How he rises in loyalty to his King, and stands firm for Jesus.

He sees the temptation in the half-jealous, half-doubting complaint.

" He resists unto blood, striving against sin," and hints no envious word.

He would far rather die a martyr than take one ray of glory belonging to the Redeemer.

His brief work will soon be over for ever. He is hastening to his crown.

His own divinely appointed humiliation was as certain as the greater Majesty of Him WHO WAS TO COME after him.

The same Spirit, imparting princely gifts to John, could render his
    humility radiant as an angel's in exile.   Rev. xviii. 1.

Solemnly, and with an inspired presentiment of his death (Num.
    xx. 26) and of the coming glory of the Messiah, he again
    testifies.

Receive.   Or assume anything lawfully with hope of success.

Nothing.   Either an humble admission of his own inferiority and
    dependence, or a vindication of our Lord's exalted claims.

Be given.   What countless heart-burnings *die out* when this
    sentence is written on the soul!

" For what hast thou which thou didst not from God receive ? "
    1 Cor. iv. 7.

Counting over gifts and mercies *not* acknowledged from God,
    what have we left ?   Answer—sin, shame, death.   Rom.
    vi. 21.

What myriads dishonestly claim that which is not their own,
    and how many more *desire*, but *dare not*, steal from God.

Heaven.   Jesus takes nothing from heaven : brings all down with
    Him.

As each ray of light can be traced back to the great source, so all
    our graces come from the Sun of Righteousness.

Every divinely-commissioned person has his own work assigned
    him.

Even Christ Himself came under this *Law of Jehovah's empire.*
    Acts ii. 23.

εἶπεν, ipsissima verba in the main are given. *Stier.* Translated into John's
style. *Ebrard.* Faint traces of the Evangelist's subjectivity. *Luthardt.* The
phraseology is the Evangelist's, the matter all the Spirit's. The gold cast in the
mould is *heavenly*, the *mould* itself is earthly. Hence the difference of style.
Author.

δύναται, not mere moral possibility, but λαμβ, denotes a real receiving.
Hengst.

ἄνθρωπος sets forth the miserable poverty, moral and spiritual, of man
by nature. *Beza.* Greeks, to intensify one's misery, called him τρίσανθρωπον.
Trapp. I cannot claim more than God has given. *Wetstein.* One ought to
be content with the honour Providence allots. *Kuinoel.* If His glory and
followers eclipse mine, His Divinity is the cause. *Chrys.* This idea in the
background. *Alford.*

οὐρανοῦ, a general instead of a special term, implies meekness. *Bengel.*

---

28. Ye yourselves bear me witness, that I said, I am not the Christ, but that
I am sent before him.

Yourselves. Consciousness of a life beyond reach of suspicion, an inheritance above rubies.

Moses had not taken a hoof. Num. xvi. 15. *Samuel* not an ox. 1 Sam. xii. 3.

Paul appealed to his past life. Acts xx. 18. *Melancthon* made the same appeal.

The renowned *Gustavus Adolphus*, of Sweden, at his death called the world to witness that "he had not enriched himself, to the price of a *pair of boots*."

Witness. The praise of the virtuous more precious than the honours of an ungodly world.

"Demetrius hath a good report of the truth itself." 3 John, verse 12.

John hides himself in the Saviour, as a star is lost in the sun.

Before Him. "I will send my messenger, and he will prepare the way before me."

The Baptist never called Jesus plainly *Christ*, or the *Messiah*, but by implication it is inferred.

Him, specially emphatic, John being the messenger foretold. Mal. iii. 1, 2.

εἶπον. I can only stand where God has placed me. *Lücke, Neander.* Jesus rises just where God exalts Him. *Chrys., De Wette.*

ἐκείνου and οὗτος are antithetical as here really in one sentence. *Buttmann.*

οὗτος concealed under ἐγώ. *Hengst.* Refers not to *the Christ*, but to a personal Jesus. *Alford.*

---

29. He that hath the bride is the bridegroom : but the friend of the bridegroom, which standeth and heareth him, rejoiceth greatly because of the bridegroom's voice : this my joy therefore is fulfilled.

Bridegroom. The prophets had used this Oriental figure for another bond.

The domestic tie ever pointed the Jews to a higher relation.

All breaches of the marriage vow indicate infidelity to an unseen HUSBAND.

He leaves all previous prophetic teachings behind, as he declares his Lord's relation, BRIDEGROOM OF HUMANITY !

Name given by the Spirit to the Lord. Rev. xix. 7; Matt. ix. 15.

Names of Christ constantly and magnificently advance in dignity.

MAN. John iii. 27. CHRIST. Ver. 28. BRIDEGROOM. Ver. 29. SON of THE FATHER. Ver. 35.

To Jesus belongs the Church of God, in its noblest first-fruits.

Every pastor's office, as "friend of the bridegroom," is to woo for Christ.

"Thy Maker is thine husband; the Lord of hosts is His name." Isa. liv. 5.

"As the bridegroom rejoiceth over the bride, so shall thy God rejoice," &c. Isa. lxii. 5.

New Jerusalem comes down from God "as a bride adorned for her husband." Rev. xxi. 2.

Disciples heard the Saviour a year hence claim this very title. Mark ii. 19.

Friend.   In Oriental lands the friend *negotiates* between the parties, and settles the preliminaries of marriage, and has the conduct of the *feast*.

The perfect seclusion of females still renders the intervention of a paranymph necessary, and almost universal.

The minister's office makes him instrumental in bringing souls to Christ, and equally interested in both.

A severe but triumphant test of John's loyalty, since he rejoices in the gathering of converts, though Christ's *increase* be his *decrease*.

Standeth.   Implies John's part was now finished.   Henceforth he must follow in the Saviour's blessed train.

Brief was the interview between John and Jesus. Only *one* expression of our Lord reported, "*Suffer it to be so now: for thus it becometh us to fulfil all righteousness.*"   Matt. iii. 15.

Still it was the Bridegroom's pleasure His friends should be present.

Rejoiceth.   Paul rejoiced that Christ was preached, even if through envy.   Phil. i. 15.

Moses was grateful if Eldad and Medad did also prophesy.   Num. xi. 27.

"Let not those three dogs follow you into the pulpit,—pride, covetousness, envy."   *Luther* to Pastors.

Having accomplished his own work, his joy was complete.

Thus Simeon, having seen God's salvation, longed to depart.   Luke ii. 29.

When Paul's hard battle for Christ's "crown and covenant" was fought, he desired "to depart, and be with Christ."   Phil. i. 23.

The Baptist seemed willing as a single drop to be lost in a sea of glory that Christ might become "ALL in ALL."   Col. iii. 11.

The seeming envy of those casting out devils was rebuked by our
Lord.   Luke ix. 49.

The celestial dove honoured Jesus in the presence of John's disciples.   Matt. iii. 16.

The Incarnation one of the great festal days of the Church.

A contract between heaven and earth was solemnized.

Divinity is espoused to humanity, which, it is believed, will *continue
on* THE THRONE ! John xvii. 24.

The " Bridegroom in royal apparel is come forth out of His chamber." Rev. xix. 7.

The pledge of the soul's espousal to Christ is the remission of sin,
and a sacred and solemn endorsement of the *divine institution
of marriage.*

John, though self-denying and an ascetic, yet rejoices in others' joy.

His abstinence and life were so severe and mysterious, the world
called him the Messiah.

Our Lord eating and drinking, they called a *prophet.*

" Do you say my followers leave me, to go to Him ?   Ye bring me
good tidings of great joy."

The happy and jubilant tone of the Bridegroom's voice moves to
greater gladness.

Voice.   The mechanism of the human voice is one full of wonder
and mystery.

The art of 6000 years has failed to make an instrument able to
articulate a single letter in combination.

The *will* behind this mechanism controls it.

Physiologists are compelled to confess their ignorance of the *mode*
by which the tones of the voice are regulated, or even what
kind of *instrument* the human voice is.

Some make it like *a flute,* others *a horn,* others *a wind instrument,*
others find it to be like a *clarionet.*

The *muscles employed by the voice* are susceptible of 16,000 *changes.
Dr. Barclay.*

Voice is of three kinds,—monotonous, discordant, musical.

Voice of the *bridegroom* which gently attracts the *bride.*

Joy fulfilled.   Gr. *complete.*   A joy without sorrow or envy.

Few lines of Scripture have a deeper, diviner music than these.

Christ is ever bestowing the infinite treasures of His love on His
saints.

He is ever forming souls into His own image of immortal beauty
and perfection.

By faith we should hear His voice in the accents of humiliation, in the notes of thanksgiving, in the confessions of penitence, in the joyous prattle of childhood, in the silence of the forest and field, and in the glorious tidings of Zion's victories in every land !

Our Bridegroom's voice through the Church shall yet be "as the sound of many waters."

" THE KINGDOMS OF THE WORLD ARE BECOME THE KINGDOMS OF OUR LORD AND OF HIS CHRIST ! " Rev. xi. 15.

νύμφην. Coincidence of thought with the late marriage at Cana. *Luthardt.* Psa. xlv. and Canticles allude to this relation. Canticles inspired. *Josephus.* Referred to Matt. ix. 15; xxv. 1; Rev. xxi. 2, 9; xxii. 17. *Stier.* Some, speaking one word for Christ, and two for themselves, are not friends, &c. *Trapp.*

φίλος. 1. Ex castitate. Prov. xxii, 11. 2. Ex similitudine morum. 3. Ex similitudine voluntatis. 4. Ex officio. *Hengst.* To prepare the Church for her living spouse. *Austin.* The vision of a king is before him, contrasting with the tyrants of earth. In the place of a *Deioces* hidden in the recesses of a Median palace, in the place of a *Tiberius* governing the world by spies, he sees " One fairer than the sons of men," &c. *Maurice.* Our Lord's humanity as intercessor continues on the throne. *Aquinas.*

ἑστηκὼς disproves that John avoided close relation to Christ. *Hengst.*

φωνήν. The mechanism, causing vibrations, resembles a flute. *Aristotle.* *Galen.* Tone due to the length and mouth of the instrument. *Savart.* A horn. *Dodart.* A stringed instrument. *Ferreira, Young.* Vocal chords shortened or strengthened, a clarionet, a reed. Tones due to the varying the length of the aperture. *Cuvier, Biot, Magendie.* We neither know how the voice is produced or modified. *Huxley's* address at Cambridge on Descartes. The tone of the voice heard through the stethoscope. Some ignorance exists as to ventriloquism. Those who practise it do not understand the *rationale. Von Mengen.* Result of inspiration. *Haller, Nollet.* Of expiration. *Rich.* Skill in using the voice. *Mason Goode.* Jubilee of wedding festivities. *De Wette, Lücke.*

πεπλήρωται. The Church was presented to Christ and the ministry intrusted to me. *Euthymius.*

---

30. He must increase, but I must decrease.

Must. Founded on divine counsel, revealed in prophecy. Isa. lii. 13.

" Behold, my servant *shall be* exalted and extolled very high."

Increase. Evident allusion to the humble origin of the Babe of Bethlehem.

Our Saviour's Incarnation was not as the morning sun bursting on the world.

For thirty years the faith of His mother and the shepherds slowly
strengthens.

From the hour of the Magi's visit to the Lord's ascension to glory
gradual increase witnessed by John the Baptist.

Jesus, first thought to be a mere prophet, was at length acknowledged as Messiah.

John, at first supposed to be the Messiah, dwindles to a mere
prophet.

Ezekiel commended Daniel, his contemporary, placing him side by
side with Noah and Job, for his power and faith in prayer.
Ezek. xiv. 14.

Peter highly praises Paul, who had publicly rebuked him. Gal.
ii. 11 ; 2 Pet. iii. 15, 16.

Decrease. Only comparatively. The Baptist's fame did not
diminish, but increased, until he ascended in a martyr's
fiery chariot to glory, where he shines more and more for
ever.

Not thus with Christ at death : His glory, flashing forth, shone on
over the grave, up to heaven.

Higher and greater Jesus ascends and becomes, until John disappears with no hint as to his rising again.

This decrease depressed his disciples, fearing they should be
humbled also.

It rejoiced the heart of John ; one's shadow shortens the nearer
one approaches the sun.

So our self-conceit diminishes the nearer we approach Christ.

Love drives out fear from the soul ; so Christ, entering, drives out
pride.

Divine majesty realized makes us small in our own eyes.

His glorious perfections show our virtues to be mere gilded sins.

His power shows our *weakness*, His wisdom our deep *ignorance*.

His holiness our *vileness*, His justice our *depravity*.

His goodness our supreme *selfishness*, His truth our *deceitfulness*.

John like the morning-star melts away in the light of heaven.

The Baptist beheaded is forgotten, the Saviour, on the cross, *draws*,
until *nation after nation glories in the name* and joy of a *Christian.*

His almighty power is a pledge this " stone shall fill the whole
earth." Dan. ii. 35.

From that hour, Christ's glory has advanced through friends and
through foes.

Pagan emperors, by *persecution,* published the gospel to the ends of
the earth.

EACH MARTYR WAS EQUAL TO TEN THOUSAND SERMONS FOR CHRIST.

" Liberals" and other infidels, in their fierce assaults, only *proclaim the Saviour's honour.*

As the retiring storm-cloud, having *obscured* the sun for a season,
now bears on ITS BOSOM A NEW proof of his glory.

αὐξάνειν. John born in Midsummer, when the days are shortening, Christ
in January, when the days are lengthening. *Augustine.* Born in the night, to
be a light to the Gentiles. *Tertullian.* So Plato commends Aristotle as ἀναγ-
νώστην et νοῦν. Aristotle is said to have erected an altar to Plato's memory
inscribing, " NULLA FERENT TALEM SECLA FUTURA VIRUM." But *Luther* envied *Carlstardt's* services at Wittenberg. *Trapp.* Pompey was to Sylla as the
rising sun to the waning moon. *Plutarch.* The one overshadows and thus
obscures the other. *Ammonius.*

---

31. He that cometh from above is above all : he that is of the earth is earthly,
and speaketh of the earth : he that cometh from heaven is above all.

Cometh. Some critics make the Evangelist here speak.

These sentiments, they think, are far too advanced for the Baptist.

But they are homogeneous, uniform, consistent, and continuous with
the whole testimony of the Baptist.

Cannot the Holy Ghost inspire one servant quite as easily as
another ?

This is the last testimony the noble martyr was permitted to bear
to His Lord.

From above. Not a heavenly mission merely, but the Divine nature, for hitherto Christ had been compared with John.

But now He is exalted above all men, " chief amongst," &c. Cant.
v. 10.

The standard-bearer is selected for his great prowess, and woe to
the " host whose standard-bearer fainteth."

Above all. He stands in need of none, is absolutely sufficient in
Himself, incomparably and unapproachably ABOVE ALL, i.e.
JEHOVAH !

John well knew Him as the LAMB and the BRIDEGROOM.

Christ's words are not only those of the " WORD made flesh," but of
Him who " was anointed with the oil of gladness above his
fellows." Psa. xlv. 7.

This was foretold by Isaiah (chap. lxi. 1), and acknowledged by
  our Lord, Luke iv. 18.
He spake and wrought miracles by the Spirit of God, as by a power
  not foreign, but of Himself.
Prophets and apostles spake truths as they received from above.
But in Christ's words " we hear a voice as from the excellent glory."
  2 Pet. i. 17.
Of the earth. As such he will remain, notwithstanding their
  wishes.
" Head of Syria is Damascus," Isa. vii. 8; as such it will remain, and
  not rise.
Although flashes of heavenly light shone on his path, the
  Baptist remained, on the whole, bound to the earth, in his
  words.
From heaven. The FAITHFUL AND TRUE WITNESS cometh from
  His proper element.
Although mingling with men of earth, He is not of it, either in
  person or words.

ὃ ἄνωθεν, κ. τ. λ. Words of John the Evangelist. *Bengel, Lücke, Tholuck.*
Strauss' denial of these words to the Baptist "more impertinent than true."
Hug. Not noticing the change to his own, result of mysticism. *Tholuck.* Hard
to explain well that which never was. *Author.* Other words mingle with those
of the Baptist. *De Wette.* Altogether the Baptist's. *Hengst., D. Brown,
Meyer.* 1. In harmony with the Baptist's time and position. 2. Sentiment and
diction John's. 3. Internal evidence. *Alford.*
  Involves His pre-existence. *Kuinoel.* Since John is proving our Lord's superiority to all the prophets. *Wetstein.* Merely a divinely-commissioned legate.
Rationalists.
  ἐκ τῆς γῆς. Homo, from humus, bids him be humble. *Clarke.* Homo
terræ filius, nihili nepos. *Augustine.* Every son of earth bears the image of
the earthly. *Besser.* Designates the unchanging state of the earthly. *Hengst.*
This earthiness of John explains the after perplexity about Christ. *Hengst.*
Matt. ix. 14. Terræ est. *Augustine.* Fish in the gospel either dumb or nothing
but gold in its mouth. *Trapp.* No tautology, an evident antithesis between
Christ and all mortals. *Lightfoot.*
  πάντων, in dignity, power, and speech. *Bengel.*

---

32. And what he hath seen and heard, that he testifieth; and no man receiveth his testimony.

Seen and heard. Orientalism for *exact accuracy* of detail.
The EASE and FREEDOM of our Lord as of one perfectly at home

when He speaks of the wonders of eternity strikes all thoughtful readers.

A prince alludes to the splendours of court in a way which astonishes the humble peasant, and that peasant could with difficulty describe the same things to his companions at home. *Pascal.*

No man. They said "all men come to Him." John answers, "Would it were so ; but, alas ! they are so few, we may say, scarcely one."

Nay, so perverse are men, they would prefer John to the Lord Jesus. Once even a murderer was preferred. Matt. xxvii. 21.

So vast is the multitude who reject God's offer, that but " a little flock " really receive it.   Luke xii. 32.

Receiveth.   How many *approach*, but how few *receive !*

To receive it demands a higher baptism than water. "No man can come to Me, except the Father draw him."   John vi. 44.

That great and good man *Chrysostom* standing in a church of Antioch, a city of some 500,000 inhabitants, sorrowfully exclaimed, "*I don't think one in a hundred will be saved.*"   "In Antioch fashion was the only law, and pleasure the only pursuit."—*Gibbon.*

καὶ omitted. *Tisch., Tregelles.*
οὐδεὶς. Vix quisquam. *Erasmus.*   Few or none. *Markland.*   Refers to disciples. Ye receive it, but, alas, how feebly ! *Ber. Bib.* Comparatively none. *Alford.*

---

33. He that hath received his testimony hath set to his seal that God is true.

Testimony.   A singular evidence of the divinity of Scripture, that *God's authority* is the only proof hinted at from Genesis to Revelation.

" THUS SAITH THE LORD " should satisfy the conscience of every *rational* being.

In judgment each gospel-rejecter *will acknowledge this fact.*

Set his seal.   As metal cold and hard refuses to receive the seal, and must be melted, so the human heart needs the Spirit's fire to enable it to receive the image of the Lord.

Things are sealed either for *security* or *confirmation.*

It is in the latter sense the Son is " sealed by the Father " to the work of redemption.   John vi. 27.

Divine call of the apostles sealed by the Spirit's converting grace.
1 Cor. ix. 2.

Seal. Phrase borrowed from *royal edicts:* they were confirmed
by a seal, commonly a signet-ring.

But *few* understood how to sign their name, as now only one in a
thousand in Egypt, one in thirty in Italy, one in twenty
in Spain, a few years ago. In Naples, the desks of letter-
writers stand in the public square.

A seal had the same authority and legal validity as a name. Gen.
xxxviii. 18. Used by Pharaoh and given to Joseph. Gen. xli.
42. Arabs carry it on a *string* from the neck.

Ancient Egyptians used a scarabæus or beetle as a sacred symbol;
it was engraved on a cylinder made of precious stone, gold,
silver, or terra-cotta.

One in Alnwick Museum bears date of Osirtasen 1, or between 2000
and 3000 B.C.

Seal of Ilgi, a Chaldean king, now in the British Museum, about
2050 B.C.

State seal of the great Sennacherib is also in the British Museum,
and a small tablet, on which we read how he had recovered a
signet-seal which had been captured by the King of Babylon
600 years previously.

One of Sabaco, King of Egypt, dated 711 B.C., has been found at
Nineveh by *Layard.*

The impress of the seals of *So,* King of Egypt, and the *Assyrian
monarch,* were found on a tablet of clay in the ruins of
Sennacherib's palace,—a clear allusion to the *treaty of peace
after the war,* B.C. 721. 2 Kings xvii. 4.

The seal of *mail-clad warrior* transferred to the SHIELD, *identified*
him.

Engraved seals used by Hebrews, 1451 B.C. Ex. xxviii. 11. Doors
of tombs and other places sealed with clay.

The image of the Spirit stamped on the heart identifies the believer.
Eph. i. 14.

Seals of God's covenant, the sacraments and His Spirit, and a
living faith.

Packages of value have the *tied cords* sealed now as formerly. Isa.
viii. 16.

God is true. With special reference to His promises in Christ.

Believer has experimental evidence,—"the witness within."

Spirit in the heart and Spirit in the word agree.

λαβὼν implies his disciples were prejudiced against our Lord. *Hengst.*

εσφράγισε. George IV., unable to set his royal seal, had a *stamp engraved* and affixed in his presence. *Layard.* Used now by Arabs. *Chardin.* Emblem of authority still among Persians. *Knobel, Niebuhr.* Coedwalla, a Saxon king unable to write, put his cross × to a charter. *Ency. Brit.* Charter of Westminster Abbey signed by *Edward* the Confessor with a cross ×. *Signum quasi signillum.* Heb. word *seal*, to fasten. *Bloomfield.*

ἀληθής. True to His promise in the prophets. *Wetstein.* A revealer of truth. *Euthymius.*

---

34. For he whom God hath sent speaketh the words of God : for God giveth not the Spirit by measure unto him.

He whom. Equivalent to this person, i. e. Jesus Christ.

Words of God. All truth, but especially revelation.

What a vain conceit to suppose we have comprehended all these words !

Who can grasp the idea of a God of goodness, without bounds ?

The difficulty of difficulties to believe in a *God*, a LIVING GOD, who loves His creatures, and yet has permitted moral evil.

A difficulty that no human arguments remove, and one that the progress of ages does not diminish in the least, and that nothing less than Infinite Wisdom can overcome.

Yet no difficulty emerges in theology that has not first arisen in philosophy. *Sir W. Hamilton.*

There are many sounds on earth, but all the witnesses of science, &c., are but solemn mockeries of the wants of the soul, " dead in trespasses and sins."

"I will raise up a prophet, and put My words in his mouth." Deut. xviii. 18.

" The words I speak unto you they are spirit, they are life."

John concludes that Christ is the SON OF GOD because " He speaks the words of God."

Giveth. Denotes the ever-renewed communication of the Spirit by the Father.

Spirit. The third person of the adorable Trinity. See on John vii. 39.

Measure. That is, by limited measure,—such measure as the creature can receive.

An exceedingly definite line is drawn between Jesus and all created teachers.

He can receive no increase of being. " In Him dwelleth ALL THE FULNESS of the GODHEAD." Col. ii. 9.

But unto man " He divideth to every one severally as He will."
1 Cor. xii. 11.

Contrast *the unlimited* gifts of the Spirit to Him from *above,* with
the *limited* sharing of that same Spirit by those from *below.*
Rom. xii. 3—8.

Plotinus says, " A good man differs from God only in *age.*"

What angel can bridge the mighty chasm between *creature* and
Creator?

Our Lord's words agree with all the words of the prophets.

As the flower agrees with the bud and the fruit with the blossom.

John the Baptist and John the Evangelist received the Spirit's
fulness according to measure.

But Jesus had it as the fulness of the sunlight, or of the waters of
the ocean.

An unsearchable sufficiency for all created beings!

Nor did He receive this by any particular revelation.

For " all the treasures of wisdom and knowledge " are hidden in
Him.   Col. ii. 3.

As Messiah, He beareth these boundless gifts *"for the Church."*
Eph. i. 22.

Thus the clouds bear rain not for themselves, but for the fields and
meadows.

ἀπέστειλε is emphatic. *Hengst.* A regnum naturale. He is co-essential
with the Father. A regnum economicum, as Mediator. *Reynolds.* Prophetic
dignity. *Grotius.* Internal call to the Messiahship. *Tholuck.*

ἐν τῷ κόσμῳ implies more. *De Wette.* In the visible world. *B. Crusius.*
Processi a Deo, eternal generation ; veni, Incarnation. *Augustine.* Both refer
to Incarnation. *Maldonatus.* Generally to redemption. *Bucer.*

δίδωσιν αὐτῳ. Pronoun omitted by Greeks, where we look for it. *Erasmus.*
ἐκ μέτρου. What one man lacks, another has. *Augustine.* The entire
fulness of the Divine life and power. *Ols.* Means sparingly. *Raphelius.*
Abraham's inheritance was *in mensurâ ;* Jacob's *sine mensurâ,* and to the
prophets by measure. *Rabbis.*

πνεῦμα. Knowledge of facts and the skill of imparting them to the Church.
Rosenm. Paul could not speak spiritually to the men of Corinth, 1 Cor. iii.
1, 2. because of weakness. *Euthymius.*

ὁ Θεὸς in the last clause omitted. *Tisch., Alford.*

---

35. The Father loveth the Son, and hath given all things into his hands.

The Father.   Reveals mysteries to babes, but Christ alone reveals
the FATHER.   Matt. xi. 25—27.

Loveth the Son. A Father *loves* a son, but only *esteems* a servant. This love of the Father implies that we should " kiss the Son," &c. Psa. ii. 12.

All things. Is to be interpreted in the strictest and widest sense. John xiii. 3 ; 1 Cor. xv. 27.

Even final decision concerning our eternal salvation or damnation. How terrible to oppose Him, who hath all things in His hands.

He is an enemy to his own well-being who neglects to make Him his *Friend*.

" As the FATHER hath life in Himself; so hath He given to the SON to have life in Himself." John v. 26.

He, in His own *sovereign right*, offers the water of life to the Samaritan woman. John iv. 10.

Christ is the redeeming arm of God's power, and the bestowing hand of God's love.

He Himself is both the *Giver* and the Divine *Gift* to believers.

This " *all things* " proves that the Son is as great as the Father. John xvi. 15.

The Son Himself says, "All things are delivered to me of my Father." Matt. xi. 27.

Eternity, Micah v. 2 ; *Immutability*, Heb. xiii. 8; *Omniscience*, John xxi. 17 ; *Omnipotence*, Rev. i. 8 ; *Omnipresence*, Matt. xxviii. 20, are ascribed to Christ.

Among " all things " given by the Father to the Son is "ETERNAL LIFE."

Hence the next verse declares the connection established by God Himself, between faith in the soul and immortal blessedness.

ἀγαπᾷ. See on John xxi. 15—17. As I sufficiently learned from the voices of Jordan. *Ber. Bib.* Differs from φιλεῖ: the latter love is of the person, the former of character ; former *diligit*, latter *amat. Doederlein.*

χειρὶ. Hebraism for power. *Bloomfield.*

---

36. He that believeth on the Son hath everlasting life : and he that believeth not the Son shall not see life; but the wrath of God abideth on him.

Believeth. Faith in its full and saving exercise. See on John i. 7 ; vii. 39.

Hath. Already hath it. " *I am* the God of Abraham," i. e. living and dying. " *Hath it* " as the seed contains the ripe fruit.

He has "the earnest of the inheritance." " Christ in you, the hope of glory." Eph. i. 14; Col. i. 27.

He has it in union with Christ by the indwelling of the Spirit.

He has it in "righteousness, peace, and joy in the Holy Ghost." Rom. xiv. 17.

Be not deceived. There is but *one* blessedness, but *one* life.

It never begins *after* death,—it always *embraces* life and death.

If thou wilt ever have peace, it must become thine *here* or *nowhere.*

Life that begins not this side the grave is no life,—it is the *second death.* Rev. xx. 14.

" He that hath the Son *hath* life : and he that hath not the Son," &c. 1 John v. 12.

Faith is the Substance of heaven's joys and glories. Heb. xi. 1.
    And heaven is begun, as to its *peace, assurance, serenity, joy, love.*

"Substance of things hoped for " involves all the realities of the Paradise of God, as well as all the *truths* which lead to and all the *promises* which irradiate " those blest seats."

The light of Paradise flashes over the crystal walls, and falls on the believer's soul.

The music of heaven flows down from golden harps to the believer's ear.

" Angels are ministering spirits to heirs of salvation " in this vale of tears. Heb. i. 14.

Hath life. It is now a possession of the believer, and will be completed at the coming of Christ. Rom. viii. 23.

This heaven begun, marks the fruit of a soul all *inflamed* with love.

As birds are said never to pollute a sacrifice *burning* on the altar, so earth-born passions pollute not the soul *on fire* in God's service.

A believer seeking up and down in *his experience* for proof of conversion is like as if an eagle with its pinions spread and flying up the mountain, against adverse winds, should ask, Do I make progress ?

There may be stormy blasts, delaying and wearying the soul, but the summit will be reached at last.

Everlasting. It implies more than endless. See on verses 16, 17.

Believeth not. The believer already has a life that will endure for ever.

But the unbeliever not only has it not, but as an unbeliever never shall have it.

On the Son. Most remarkable word. Had it been " on Christ," it might refer to His testimony.

BUT FAITH IN THE SON OF GOD can be nothing less than faith in Him, as sent by the Father, to be the *Saviour of men.*

The Son of God is the great administrator of the kingdom of grace.

Our destiny, a blissful or baleful eternity, depends on our relation to Him.

Not see life. See on John i. 4. Man by nature has not the life of God. Eph. ii. 1.

The soul is spiritually dead. 1. Death terminates all desires. Thus all longings after higher life die out of the soul as conscience becomes finally *seared.* 1 Tim. iv. 2. 2. Death destroys all *vision.* The beauty of nature and art are a blank to the dead. So to those dead in sin Christ seems a dry *withered* root. He has no " comeliness." Isa. liii. 2. 3. Death destroys hearing,—all the music of earth and sky falls in vain on the ear. So to all tender invitations of mercy and thunders of law the sinner is dead.

Wrath. Passions agitating human breasts cannot enter God.

Difference between wrath in God and wrath in man. 1. In man it is an exciting passion. 2. A malignant passion. 3. A painful passion. 4. A selfish passion.

Agreement, for there must be some things common to both. 1. Repugnance. Sin is repugnant to the Divine nature and procedure. 2. Retribution. The wrath of God is retributive.

As the law " thou shalt love " when broken leads to death, so wrath in God is the wrath of the LAMB.

Words are but dim shadows of what is passing in the Infinite Mind.

God's face toward unbelief is *wrath,* its *judicial expression* is *vengeance.*

A fearful penalty to be for ever excluded from God's presence, but infinitely worse to be under the ABIDING WEIGHT of wrath Divine !

And yet some venture to teach that God does not hate sin, and needs no atonement. John i. 29 ; x. 15.

They admit *men* must be morally changed, even should the Bible be no revelation.

But if it is God's word, then He must be gained to us, as well as we to Him.

Neither Christ's death nor our faith makes God *willing* to save, as " we be slanderously reported to affirm." Rom. iii. 8.

God's will *lay beneath the scene* at Calvary. " Him being delivered
by the determinate counsel," &c. Acts ii. 23.

Both parties must meet at the cross, and till this reconciliation
takes place God's yearning over the sinner WILL NOT, CANNOT
REACH HIM.

It is a fatal error, that under the gospel *wrath of God* has no
place. Heb. x. 29.

If His Son reveals this wrath, He reveals the *fact* of a hell.

A fearful truth, to which some professing to be guides shut their
eyes.

The blind rider *not seeing* the bridge was gone, perished nevertheless !

Of God. He does not say of the " Son," but God the Father will
for ever vindicate the *Son of His love* from *neglect* and *scorn !*

The final word of promise is God's solemn *oath.* Heb. vi. 17.

Opposite of faith is unbelief,—here it is treasonable *disobedience.*

As the lightning-rod attracts the fire-charged clouds to itself, so
the sinner draws upon himself the righteous vengeance of God.

Abideth. It was on him before, and not being removed by the
only way, believing on the Son, it, *of necessity*, REMAINETH ON
HIM.

" And now also the axe is laid (is lying) at the root "—and
will *remain there.* Matt. iii. 10.

The ark was built, but those refusing to enter perished.

The cross attracts, but only those who will *look* to its VICTIM.
Isa. xlv. 22.

The gate of the Refuge city was open day and night, yet the man-
slayer perished if only just outside its walls.

A rebel unpardoned is under the ban of a law broken.

Unpardoned guilt and unchangeable truth illustrate " There is no
peace, saith my God, to the wicked." Isa. lvii. 21.

God's wrath abides, for the *suffering* it inflicts *is no atonement.*

As eternal life follows holiness, so eternal death follows sin. Isa.
xxxiv. 10.

He who persistently sins against the Spirit renders this *abiding*
perpetual. Matt. xii. 22.

God's government reveals itself against the incorrigible in fire.

Wrath of God abides for evermore. To the lost " hope never comes
that *now* comes to all." *Milton.*

Sodomites, blind by passion, saw not the cloud charged with storm
and flame, but it was there.

Black and damning as their sin was, unbelief is far worse.
They rejected the warnings of conscience and of righteous Lot.
But the gospel-despiser rejects even the pleadings of DYING LOVE !
The curse of sin is written over everything here below—1. In the
vanity of the creature. 2. In the accusations of conscience.
3. In the fear of death and judgment. 4. In the grave. 5.
In the corruption of the believer. 6. In the many afflictions
of life. 7. In the threatenings of Scripture.
So faithfully did the Baptist give his evidence as to the Messiah.
Here closes the testimony he was permitted to bear his beloved
Lord.
This denunciation the last utterance of the Old Testament economy.
This peal of thunder from the Sinai of the New Testament.
With these awfully solemn words, the Baptist dismissed his dis-
ciples.
We may hope the result was the same as with Nicodemus.
Like him, they are *silent*, laying their hands upon their mouth.
" Once have I spoken ; but I will not answer." Job xl. 5.

πιστεύων. An effectual principle of sincere obedience. *Doddr.* Rendered
"obeying," Rom. x. 16 ; 1 Pet. ii. 7, 8, and may be here. *Alford.*

ζωὴν. 1. In promisso. 2. In pretio. 3. In primitiis. *Trapp.*

ὀργὴ corresponds to ὀργὴ εἰς τέλος, 1 Thess. ii. 16. This confusion of soul
internal and immediate as punishment. μένει, conditional on refusing repentance after death. *Ols.* After death no sinful being can repent, Rev. xxii.
11. *Hengst.*

ἀπειθῶν, a descending series magnificently awful. The believer hath already
eternal life. The unbeliever hath not life. Persisting in not obeying the Son,
he cannot *possess*, nor even see life. So the wrath of God is the eternal possession of the disobedient. *Jebb.*

John 4

1. WHEN therefore the Lord knew how the Pharisees had heard that Jesus made and baptized more disciples than John.

When. Chap. iii. 22 is here resumed. Jesus attended the feast at Jerusalem in March.

The Lord. See on chap. i. 41. Here for the first time the Evangelist gives this title to Jesus.

It recalls all that is written of His glory in the three first chapters.

He knew that the Pharisees hated Him more than they hated John.

Yet he openly speaks, as though the world acknowledged His divinity.

Knew. Although no one had told Him. See on chap. ii. 24, 25.

Pharisees. See on John i. 24. They confidently expected Messiah would show entire cordiality toward themselves as the guardians of the Theocracy, and reserve for them His highest honours.

They had been called by Him " a generation of vipers " before the Jewish nation.

They firmly denied the right either of Jesus or John, or their disciples, to baptize, and they pretended to hate the Baptist on principle.

Baptized. See on John i. 25. What is done by one's followers is said to be done by their Leader.

The offence was that He had instituted baptism in His own name.

He returned to Galilee about seed-time, Nov. or Dec., and passed right through Samaria, despite the scruples of the Jews.

He had ended one of the longest of His recorded discourses.

The Baptist had sounded the trumpet of repentance, and was now in prison.

The ministry of our Lord had begun by miracle, not preaching, six months before.

The first of the four Passovers under His ministry was now ended.

More. Pharisees did not desire to become John's disciples.

Neither were they jealous of his honour, satisfied he was not the Messiah.

All expected Messiah's advent, yet their envy was aroused when

they heard that Jesus was gathering disciples to His standard.
John. See on chap. i. 6. The Baptist was now in prison.

ὡς. Journey to Galilee Nov. or Dec. *Lange.* Jan. *Wieseler.* Dec. *Meyer, Lichtenstein.*

ἔγνω rises above ἤκουσαν. Intuitive knowledge. *Stier.*

οὖν connects with the last. John had doubtless already been sacrificed to their jealousy. *Hengst.*

βαπτίζει. John, of a priestly family, less obnoxious than the Galilean, Jesus. *Grotius.* What John's disciples in envy conjectured, Pharisees would take for granted. *Maurice.* Through envy they had told an untruth. *Chrys.* John baptized to repentance. Christ's baptism was always according to the form, Matt. xxviii. 19. *J. A. Alexander.*

---

2. Though Jesus himself baptized not, but his disciples.

Jesus. The Logos, John i. 1. His titles, John i. 41. His parables, John x. 6. His sinlessness, John viii. 46.

Baptized not. He who baptizes with the Holy Ghost ordains the outward symbol.

Believers rejoice in this rite by His servant's hands as though by His own.

He connects His ministry with the Baptist, and interferes not with John's peculiar mission, which He had publicly acknowledged.

His ordained servants bearing His seal are to be acknowledged. Matt. xxviii. 19.

Our Lord Himself baptized not, lest undue importance should be attached to those who received the rite at His hands.

John foretold that He should baptize with the Holy Ghost and with fire. John vii. 39.

Disciples. For names and character, see on John i. 40—45. See also Sugg. Comm. on Luke vi. 13—16.

"The least in the kingdom of heaven was greater than the Baptist." Matt. xi. 11.

Preparation for the Messiah, and His actual coming, run parallel.

Our Lord turns away from the fanatical Sanhedrim, and bends His course to His favourite field, among the honest Galileans.

οὐκ ἐβάπτιζεν. John's baptizing at the same time a key to the history of the Church. *Stier.* It would have interfered with our Lord's preaching. *Schleiermacher.* His office, like Paul's, was to teach. *Alford.* John's disciples were rebaptized, Acts xix. 3. *Doddr.* This implies Christian baptism embraced the formula, Matt. xxviii. 19. *J. A. Alexander.* Even baptism by Judas might be said to have been by Christ. *Wordsworth.*

---

3. He left Judæa, and departed again into Galilee.

Left. A glimpse of the unwearied activities of our Lord's life.

A hint at the future universal diffusion of the gospel.

We should use all lawful means to preserve our lives.

But Christ's cause, at times, demands resistance even unto blood. Acts iv. 19, 20.

At others He commands us to fly from threatened danger. Matt. x. 23.

An *humble retreat* is, sometimes, more difficult than a *proud resistance.*

Some retire from fear, some from fidelity to their Master.

Opposition so early organized, might have marred His work.

Departed. At this time the Baptist had been cast into prison.

Here John takes up the narrative of Matthew, Mark, and Luke.

Period of His stay in Judea appears to have been eight months. Ver. 35.

Galilee. See on John i. 43. Pharisees had less influence there than in Judea.

Rome, content with taxes paid, indulged the Pharisees in Judea.

But Herod despised the Pharisees, and rejoiced at the victory which John's ministerial success had won over them.

He never disturbed John until he had boldly rebuked him.

During the three following weeks our Lord proved His Divine power—1. Over the elements. 2. Over death. 3. Over evil spirits. One Church was formally founded, and a number of lost sheep folded.

ἀπῆλθε. John being imprisoned no motive for Christ leaving. Pharisees and scribes mainly instrumental in John's execution. Matt. xvii. 12, *Hengst.* His stay in Judea about 8 months. *Hengst.* Departs late in Jan. *D. Brown.* πάλιν only found in *Cod. Alex.* Omitted. *Tisch.*

---

4. And he must needs go through Samaria.

Needs. Mercy, guided by eternal wisdom, leads Him to this neglected field.

No intention to abandon Israel, and betake Himself to the Gentiles
in Galilee, where many Jews dwelt.

He does not nullify His counsel to the disciples, " Into any city of
the Samaritans enter ye *not*." Matt. x. 5.

Geographically the direct route. But there is a higher reason.

By avoiding the Samaritans He would appear to sanction Pharisaic
bigotry.

He is in no special haste, for He remained in Samaria two days.

This conversation, and the miracle recorded in Matt. xv. 21, occurred during this journey.

He could, by His own rule, leave Israel and visit the heathen. Matt.
x. 5.

His parable, Luke x. 30, was spoken to condemn national prejudice
and intolerance.

Go. " He went about doing good." Acts x. 38. He sought out
the needy.

He visited not only those who needed Him, but those who needed
Him most. *Wesley.*

The tabernacle a travelling " mercy-seat," a type of Christ.

He never refused any asking help. He received every beggar
coming.

Had each one healed sent a thousand more, all would have been
welcome.

His boundless treasures flowed free as the sunlight of heaven.

His only caution was, lest bigotry might lessen the number of His
guests.

Pressure of affairs, distance of object, or greatness of favours already
shown, never deterred Him.

And when He went not, He sent His almighty grace to save, though
He was " not sent but to the lost sheep of the house of Israel."
Matt. xv. 24.

If mercy reaches Samaritans, it is a crumb falling from the children's table.

Samaritans went out to Him, and being urged, He spent two days
with them.

He only aided aliens as they pressed their claim. Matt. xv. 25 ;
Mark vii. 24.

Samaria. See on verse 5. On Samaritans, see on verse 9.

The deep malignant obstinacy of the Jews makes them reject
Christ.

But their *sin* brings Jesus and *salvation* to the Samaritans. Acts xiii. 46.

"I will give Thee for a light to the *Gentiles*" indicates this fact. Isa. xlix. 6.

Our Lord classes Samaritans with the heathen. Matt. x. 5, 6.

Yet thrice favoured were they who lay in the Saviour's way.

He arrives the first day of His journey at the spot where Abraham found his first resting-place in the promised land. "He passed through the land unto the place of Sichem." Gen. xii. 6.

The patriarch saw Jehovah in vision who said, "Unto thy seed will I give this land," and on this spot our Saviour entered upon His promised inheritance.

The people of Sichem were the *first* to enter the heavenly Canaan.

Heathen in Canaan were the first-fruits of the world of Gentiles.

δὲ, "now." *D. Brown.*

ἔδει, not because the nearest and most direct road. *Wetstein.* This implies otherwise He would have avoided it. *Stier.* Any design to show His power is excluded. *Luthardt.*

διέρχεσθαι. He was now in north of Judea. *Meyer.* From April to Oct. had elapsed. *Lichtenstein.* Baptized during this period by sprinkling, John by immersion. *Sepp.* Time about a month. *Greswell.* Two or more weeks. *Norton.*

---

5. Then cometh he to a city of Samaria, which is called Sychar, near to the parcel of ground that Jacob gave to his son Joseph.

Samaria. Heb. "Watch mountain," name of a district and city.

Palestine was divided into three parts, each about the size of an American county. Samaria the central one.

Tribes carried into captivity by Hazael. 2 Kings x. 32, 33. Heathen put in their stead. 2 Kings xvii. 27.

"I will stretch over Jerusalem the line of Samaria," i. e. utter ruin. 2 Kings xxi. 13.

Samaritans claimed Esar-haddon as their founder. Ezra iv. 2, 10.

"Lions sent among them," they applied for religious teachers. 2 Kings xvii. 25.

Our Lord calls them "strangers," not of Jewish blood. Luke xvii. 18.

They were treacherous to the Jews, "adversaries of Judah." Ezra iv. 1.

They frustrated the building of the temple, until silenced by Darius Hystaspis, B.C. 519.

Manasseh, deposed as a priest, built a temple on Gerizim under Darius Nothus, B.C. 409.

Cæsarea was made capital of Samaria by Theodosius, A.D. 409.

Samaria city, capital of the kingdom of Israel : first capital after the secession was Shechem.

Omri built Samaria, 920 B.C. Ahab built a palace of ivory. 1 Kings xxii. 39.

Also a temple of Baal which Jehu destroyed. 2 Kings x. 27.

Samaria captured by Shalmaneser, 2 Kings xvii. 2—6, B.C. 720. City rebuilt by Cuthites.

Captured also by Esar-haddon; planted by Syro-Macedonians under Alexander the Great. Ezra iv. 2.

Taken by Hyrcanus, B.C. 109 ; restored to Samaritans by Pompey, B.C. 54.

Rebuilt by Herod the Gréat, to whom Augustus gave it, and who called it *Sebaste,* after his patron.

Colonized by 6000 Roman veterans, A.D. 210.

An episcopal see probably as early as the third century. Taken by Mahommedans, A.D. 637.

A splendid colonnade of the temple erected by Herod, still standing, a noble ruin.

" I will make Samaria as a heap of the field." Mic. i. 6 ; Hos. xiii. 16.

Now about 200 Samaritans remain : only 60 pay capitation tax ; population 8000.

Sychar. Called Shechem, after Hamor's son. Gen. xxxiv. 2. Now *Nablous.*

About 34 miles north of Jerusalem, between Ebal and Gerizim.

A valley 500 yards wide parts them. Mountains within calling distance.

10,000 of the Shechemites destroyed by the Romans at one time.

It was called the " Paradise of the Holy Land " by Mahommed.

Here God first appeared to Abram in the promised land, and here the patriarch first tented under an oak. Gen. xii. 6.

Under the oak at Shechem, Jacob buried his household idols. Gen. xxxv. 1—4.

Near this Joseph was sold, a slave, to the Ishmaelites. Gen. xxxvii. 12.

Here also his remains rest, until the morning of the resurrection.

Here the *eleven brethren were buried* at the time Joseph's ashes were
brought up from Egypt.   Acts vii. 16.

Under the plain of the pillar (oak of the monument) Abimelech was
made king.   Judg. ix. 6.

Assigned to the Levites and became a city of refuge.   Josh. xxi. 20.

Joshua here gave his counsels before death to gathered Israel.
Josh. xxiv. 1—24.

The city is twice named, for its dignity and strength, by David.
Psa. lx. 6.

Israel here met and crowned Rehoboam, Solomon's son, king.

Here the ten tribes renounced him and made Jeroboam king.
1 Kings xii. 16.

From its vicinity to their place of worship it kept its rank as
principal city till the destruction of their temple.

Population about 5000.   150 are Samaritans.   Houses are of stone.

Samaritans have a small synagogue 400 years old.

Parcel.   A fact not expressly stated in the O. T. concerning his
grave.

The Jews inferred it from Gen. xlviii. 22 ; xxxiii. 19 ; Josh. xxiv.
32.

Joseph had a better resting-place than his brethren were willing
to give him.

Jacob, second son of Isaac and Rebekah.

His mother heard the prophecy that her offspring should be founders
of two nations, and that the elder should serve the younger.

Jacob was domestic and affectionate.   Rebekah openly preferred
him to her elder son, Esau.

Jacob's cunning prompted him to demand Esau's birthright for a
mess of pottage.

Jacob, led by his mother, deceived blind Isaac, and secured his
blessing.

This blessing had the force and solemnity of a *modern will* at death.

Jacob went to Mesopotamia, 600 miles, to his Uncle Laban.

Served 14 years for his two wives, Rachel and Leah.

He set out for Canaan.   Passing Mount Seir, he met Esau.

Jacob wrestled with the Angel (the Lord Himself) at Peniel.
Name changed to ISRAEL.

Escaping the rage of the Shechemites, he travels to Bethel and
rears an altar.

At Beth-lehem Ephratah his beloved Rachel dies after Benjamin's
birth.

Visits his father Isaac at Mamre.   Gen. xxxv. 27.

Afterward, taught by a divine vision, he goes to Egypt : Joseph met him at Goshen.

Jacob enters Pharaoh's presence, and with great dignity blessed the king.   Gen. xlvii. 8—10.

After dwelling in Egypt 17 years, he dies, aged 147, B.C. 1836.

His the patriarch character. With a staff only he goes over Jordan.

The earth is his bed, a stone his pillow, but angels are his companions.

He deceived his father, and was deceived himself by Laban in turn.

" He is consumed by the frost by night, and by heat in the day."

If the righteous prosper not, they are despised ; if successful, envied.

Laban followed him with one troop, Esau met him with another.

God, sooner or later, makes fools of all the enemies of His saints.

Laban leaves Jacob with a kiss, and Esau meets him with an embrace.

He lost a joint by the angel, but he gained an immortal blessing.

His children wounded his soul.   Reuben is guilty of incest, Dinah is disgraced, Simeon and Levi are murderers, Er and Onan are struck dead, Joseph is lost, Simeon is imprisoned, Benjamin proved the death of Rachel.

Jacob himself was driven by famine, in his old age, among the heathen Egyptians.

But, out of all his sorrows, delivered by the Angel of God, he dies in peace.

His grave at Machpelah, Hebron, Gen. l. 13, was visited by the author, A.D. 1855.

Gave.   A mere tradition : Jacob bought it, paying for it 100 lambs. Gen. xxxiii. 19.

Joseph was buried here, and it became the inheritance of the children of Joseph.   Josh. xxiv. 32.

This was the only land Jacob really owned in Canaan.

He gave what he first earned by his sword and bow.   Gen. xlviii. 22.

Like Jonathan's bow, it never returned empty.   2 Sam. i. 22.

Joseph, son of Jacob and his beloved Rachel.   Born 1906 B.C., in Mesopotamia.

Raised by Providence from a prison cell to be governor of all Egypt.

His father, in unwise partiality, gave him a coat of many colours.

His brethren envied him, and visiting them in Dothan, they cast him into a pit.

Taking him out, they sold him to Ishmaelites going to Egypt.

His coat, torn and bloody, was brought to his distressed father.

Jacob comforted himself with the prospect of meeting him in eternity.

Joseph sold to Potiphar, captain of Pharaoh's executioners. *Kalisch.*

The Lord blessed the house of the Egyptian for Joseph's sake. Ezek. xiv. 14.

Egyptian temples still show great care and exact records of stewards' labours.

He was placed "in chains" at the beginning of his imprisonment. Psa. cv. 17, 18.

The dreams of the cup-bearer and baker revealed the hand of Providence.

Pharaoh's dream brought the imprisoned prophet to court.

Six years in slavery and imprisonment had disciplined Joseph's faith.

Pharaoh invested Joseph with a royal robe, and gave him the royal signet ;

A collar of gold and a chariot next the royal cortège in public processions.

Joseph purchased all the land of Egypt during the seven years of famine.

Joseph had two sons, Manasseh and Ephraim, during these seven years.

The monarch, from that day to this, receives one fifth of the produce.

Thirteen years after he is sold a slave his brethren arrive.

Joseph receives their *obeisance,* and so his *prophetic dreams are fulfilled.*

At the sight of his own brother Joseph is overcome, and retires *to weep.*

Inviting them to dine, he placed them according to their age.

He makes himself known, to their confusion and joy.

He sends chariots and guards to bring down his venerable father.

The meeting was one to be *conceived,* not *described.*

Pharaoh welcomed Jacob and his family, and settled them in Goshen.

Joseph dies aged 110, and his brethren sware to take his bones to Canaan. Heb. xi. 22.

High resolution, strong faith, patient endurance, great modesty, in-

flexible honesty, unwavering purity, deep affection, and benevolence were his characteristics.

JOSEPH A TYPE OF CHRIST.   Typical characteristics :—

1. Joseph's character so far as recorded was blameless.   Christ
   without spot.
2. He was greatly loved by his father.   So was the Lord Jesus.
3. His knowledge and piety were of the highest kind.   The Lord's
   infinite.
4. He was deeply humbled by being in great danger.   So was
   Christ.   Heb. v. 7.
5. He was sold as a slave.   Christ was sold, and for the same price.
6. He was cast into prison.   Christ was bound and led away captive.
7. Envy was the ground of hate in Joseph's brethren.   So of the
   Pharisees.
8. Covetousness was also an element in the betrayal of *both*.
9. God designed the affliction of each should save many people.
10. Both were delivered by several wonderful miracles.
" The Lord taketh the wise in their own craftiness."   1 Cor. iii. 19.
11. His exaltation.   " Only in the throne," said Pharaoh, " will I
    be greater."
Our Lord from the cross, advanced to the *central* THRONE.   Rev. v. 6.
12. Joseph saved the lives only of grateful Egyptians.
Our Saviour redeems the souls of countless adoring millions.
13. His treatment of his brethren with forgiving clemency and
    love.
Thus our elder Brother collects and blesses the wandering, envious
    race.

Συχάρ, wages. *Bengel*. Falsehood, a husk without a kernel. *Trench.* A
mere provincialism. *Lücke*. Heb. drunkenness, Isa. xxviii. 1, *Lange*. Their
boast of being descended from Jacob a falsehood. *Hengst*. Fountain of Sychar,
Wieseler. Delicious fountains are at Sychem (Nablous). *Thompson*. Sychar
identified with Shechem by all writers but *Ewald* and *Eusebius*. Hymns of
Samaritans discovered by *Gesenius*. Their great boast is that their law is in the
Heb. character. The Jews employed the Chaldee. They curse Ezra as an im-
poster, not restorer of the law. *Kitto*.

Σαμαρείας, burial-place of Elisha and Obadiah. *Reland*. Had Samaritans
Jewish blood ? The fathers always answered, " Yes." Modern writers answer,
" No ; " Jews called them " Proselytes of the lions." *Trench*.

πλησίον. " By my sword's bow." Gen. xlviii. 22, i. e. by fair purchase,
not by violence. The scenery is like the environs of Heidelberg. *Richter*.
Transcendently beautiful. *Ed. Clarke, Robinson, Van de Velde*.

χωρίον. John hints at the sanctity of the spot. *Momus, Stier*. Reference
to Joseph's goodly portion, Deut. xxxiii. 13. *Lightfoot*. A great famine took

place in Egypt during the reign of Sesostris I. *Bunsen.* Infidelity hints grapes never grew in Egypt. Temples at Thebes abound with proof to the contrary, as seen by the *Author*.

---

6. Now Jacob's well was there. Jesus therefore, being wearied with his journey, sat thus on the well : and it was about the sixth hour.

Jacob. For his history and character, see on verse 5.

Jacob's well. Not thus named, Gen. xlix. 22. Among ancient shepherds a *well was a land title.*

Jacob's well the *only spot known where our Saviour actually stood.*

It is a mile and a half from Nablous, the ancient Sychar, and was lately bought by Russia for a site for a Greek church.

A spot held sacred by Jews for Jacob's sake, by Arabs, Greeks, Latins, Samaritans, and Christians for this interview.

Water is precious, and at times worth more than its weight in gold.

In the deserts of Arabia and Sahara water is obtained everywhere a few feet from the surface by digging, but it is *brine.*

Egyptians obtain their water not from wells or springs, but from the Nile.

Hence they cannot conceive of heaven without a *celestial Nile.*

A well, the scene of several transactions in the history of the Covenant.

Isaac, Jacob, Moses, each found his future wife beside a well.

The Son of God takes to Himself His alien spouse, the Samaritan Church, at this well.

Water being scarce in Oriental lands, wells involve grave questions of property.

To give name to or destroy a well a mark of conquest. Gen. xxi. 30, 31.

Abandoned wells, sign of a nation's desolation.

To acquire wells dug by others a promise of favour to the Hebrews. Deut. vi. 11.

To be the owner of one a mark of independence. Prov. v. 15.

In Arabia one well supplies a whole tribe with water. *Burckhardt.*

The well near Beersheba, cut through the solid rock, cannot be destroyed, but filled up, and is an undoubted witness to sacred history.

Wells in Palestine have steps descending, as a spiral staircase. Gen. xxiv. 16.

An ancient sarcophagus is frequently found used as *a trough* for water.

Buckets are either of skin or of grass, never of wood or tin.

Water carried by females. " A man bearing a pitcher " a strange sight. Luke xxii. 10.

Neighbourhood of wells selected as battle grounds among the Orientals.

Wearied. At night He welcomed Nicodemus, and now He welcomes a Samaritan during His noonday rest.

He with whom Jacob wrestled and prayed, to whom he erected an altar, and in whom he trusted for salvation, was *exhausted* by the cares and burdens of a world's salvation.

His death is our life, His humiliation our exaltation, His thirst our refreshment, and His weariness our eternal rest.

Hunger is once, thirst twice, recorded of the Son of God.

In His own experience He was conscious of our wants, which the perfection of His nature is thought to have greatly intensified.

But the disciples, judging by man's fallible tests, believed He hungered and thirsted for the meat and drink of Sychar.

He, Himself a sufferer, knew how to sympathize with others.

He who has been shipwrecked, knows well how to pity those at sea.

Journey. Believers wearied, find comfort in thinking of their Divine Head.

Drinking from the " pure river flowing from the throne of God " gives rest. Rev. xxii. 1.

Sat. The Maker of heaven and earth glad to rest on a stone !

Thus. The fatigue of a wearied but never idle man is expressed in these words.

Amid dust and heat He will appeal to her human sympathies.

Our Lord thus intimated He was the true LIVING WATER.

His rest is as mysterious, and as abundant in mercy, as His weariness.

He watches to meet and give rest to those wearied in the ways of sin.

He seeks not exquisite meat or delicate wine ; purple and fine linen were not among His wants. Luke xvi. 19.

It is a divine art to turn our repose, as well as toil, to the glory of God.

He sat on the rocky curb-stone to share the bread of need. Phil. ii. 6.

Oppressed with hunger, and yet He freely fed thousands in the desert.

Weakened by thirst, and yet He cried, " *Whosoever is athirst, let him come to Me and drink.*" John vii. 37.

Orientals usually halt at wells for refreshment, rest, and company. There being no hotels on the highways, the wells are rallying points.

On the. Gr. *by the.* An instance of the graphic style of John.

The most human of all the scenes of our Lord's earthly history.

Much appears as if the record of an *angel's life on earth.*

With the human, Divine majesty, grace, patience, pity are blended.

In that tropical clime even the flocks rest at noon. Cant. i. 7.

" I must work the works of Him that sent me, while it is day." John ix. 4.

His words have been more than music to myriads of wearied, crushed hearts on the dusty highway of life.

" Come unto ME, all ye that *labour* and are *heavy laden,* and I will give you rest." Matt. xi. 28.

Sixth hour. 12 o'clock. Darkness at the crucifixion from the sixth to the ninth hour, i.e. 12 to 3. Matt. xxvii. 45.

Truth delights in minute particulars. Falsehood in generalities.

πηγὴ and φρέαρ, former, fons, a springing well; latter, puteus, water is stationary. *Trench.* In 1843 bottom scarcely covered with water. *Eb. Smith.* Identified as really Jacob's well by *Robinson.* Empress Helena, A.D. 325, built a church over it. The well was built among many fountains, to have an independent supply. *Robinson.* The fountains may not have been there 1800 years ago. *Author.*

οὕτως, as you may fancy. *Webster.* Without ceremony. *Euthymius.* Incuriose. *Grotius.* Indicates His humility. *Ber. Bib.* Sat thus as one wearied. *Lightfoot.* So then. *Thol.* Immediately. *Doddr.*

ὥρα ἕκτη. In the morning, after a night's travelling. *Rettig.* The evening. *Ebrard.* Jewish, not Roman time. *Lange.* Six in the evening. *Townson.* The woman being alone, evidences it was not the usual hour. *Alford.* Indicates the cause of our Lord's weariness. *Bengel.* Deep significance of the following fact. *Hengst.* John has in view its prophetic character. Travelling midday proves it autumn. *Neander.*

ἐκαθέζετο, avoided entering the town, for yet He would not offend the Jews. *Stier, Brown.*

---

7. There cometh a woman of Samaria to draw water: Jesus saith unto her, Give me to drink.

Cometh. The Spirit had just shown how the Lord dealt with a self-righteous formalist.

Now He shows how He dealt with an ignorant, depraved female.

Alone, at an unusual hour and in an unusual manner, He speaks words, to a solitary woman, which have shed a stream of light through our dark world for 1800 years.

This reveals the cause of that strange word, "He must *needs* go through Samaria."

A woman. See on John iv. 27 ; viii. 3. How utterly thoughtless was she of that day's eternal issues.

Of Samaria. Of the country, as the city was 6 miles north of Sychar. Acts viii. 5.

The blessing here lay, as it were, in ambush for her.

She came to the well, and found a spring that she never expected.

Henceforth, amid the outward and inward toil of life, she is to have, *within herself*, a fountain that will flow for ever.

Yet myriads in every age, through guilty pride, *wrongly seek*, and therefore find not.

To draw. No apparatus provided for drawing proves that it was not commonly used.

Pumps are unknown in that land ; a rope and bucket of skin generally employed.

A *Sakiyeh* is a wheel with a set of buckets turned by oxen.

Our Lord's garb would betray the fact that He was a Jew.

It would seem she neither observes nor greets Him, doubtless dreading the scorn sure to follow from a common Jew.

Said. A divinely perfect example of wisdom in a missionary.

Our Lord knew, what no minister ever could, the *exact state* of her heart.

Sovereignty illustrated. He turns from proud Pharisees, to talk with a lowly outcast of an alien race.

Give me. That our Lord had a human body, was denied by the *Docetæ.*

But His actual human wants and supplies are often mentioned in the Gospels.

He sought to quench His real thirst, but still more to kindle faith in a poor woman, and, through her, instruct unborn millions of our race.

His hunger and thirst are seen disappearing *in joy.* Verses 31, 32.

His act a protest against the narrow-hearted bigotry of the Jews, and especially the Rabbis, who would scorn intercourse with a woman. Ver. 27.

Against the Pharisee forbidding contact with a sinner, Luke vii. 39, and against the vulgar prejudice, that refuses to ask a favour of an inferior.

In *proportion* as the creed is evangelical, will the *spirit* be catholic.

History shows those holding the most Puritanic theology, like their Master, *exercising the largest charity.*

The fifty millions of martyrs, with a few exceptions, were of the class holding *evangelical* doctrines.

Whatever doctrines various errorists have held, they have never shown a willingness to seal their *faith* with their *blood.*

With the tact of heavenly wisdom He obviated her prejudice, and awakens her attention.

His request appeals to a *good will* already existing.

But, like His other words, it has a spiritual echo, for afterwards the wants of the body are entirely disregarded. Ver. 32.

This request to a depraved woman shows the *freedom* and *grandeur* of *His love !*

Drink. As a human being, He experienced thirst and hunger. Matt. xxi. 18 ; John xxi. 5.

But out of water, the gift of God, He will bring both *text and sermon.*

Thirsty and exhausted, He cannot forbear His chosen work.

As though He would say, "Refresh my soul also with thy penitence ; I am seeking thee, thou poor sinner." *Augustine.*

Holding the *thread* in His hand, in Divine sovereignty He drew her there, to be present at *that time,* Hos. ii. 23, and intends to make her *thirst* for the living waters ere He leaves her.

Rejected by His own, John i. 11, He seeks His lost sheep among strange people. Isa. lxv. 1.

Our Lord, in this Oriental way, plainly *requests fellowship* with her.

He here begins the " breaking down of the middle wall of partition." Eph. ii. 14.

To what blessings of eternal import to all coming generations does *His* EYE see this simple request open the door !

How our concern in the affairs of empires dwindles, when compared with the world-wide and immortal interests here unfolded.

He Himself is thirsty, while holding the fountains of earth and skies in His hand.

From Him the wants of all the saints have been and ever will be supplied.

" Enough for all, enough for each, enough for evermore." *Wesley.*

Compared with Him, the springs of all created worlds dwindle into rills.

" In the last day, that great day of the feast, Jesus stood and cried,

saying, If any man thirst, let him come unto ME, and drink."
John vii. 37.

Such an offer resembles His promise of crowns and kingdoms, only
a few hours before *being bound,* and led on the way to the
cross. See Sugg. Comm. on Luke xxii. 29.

ἔρχεται. Two testimonies to Christ by Himself after John's prologue:
Nicodemus and woman of Samaria. *Stier.* Others make threefold arrange-
ments. *Luthardt.* She was from Shechem, a representative of her people.
Hengst.
  γυνὴ without an article, a poor woman. *Neander.* A poor tankard-bearer.
Festus.
  ἀντλῆσαι, surrounded by many springs. Why come so far? A mark of piety.
Robinson. Waters medicinal, as Jacob's spring is now. *Bargis.* To meet her
neighbours and hear the news, *custom* in the East. *Author.* Roman Calendar
names her "Photina." Tradition says she preached in Carthage, and died a
martyr. *Corn. à Lapide* tells us he saw her head at Rome!
  Δός μοι double sense. *Augustine, Quesnel.* A close connection between the
request and a fruitless ministry. *Hengst.* He spoke designedly seven words
here, as well as seven on the *cross. Bengel.* A witness against the *Docetæ,* who
denied His humanity. *Trench.*

---

8. For his disciples were gone away unto the city to buy meat.

Disciples were gone. See on John i. 35—51. There were but
five disciples chosen at this time.

He parted from them probably to be *alone,* to hold communion
with His Father.

His heart sick at the sight of the guilt and misery of our fallen
race.

Religion runs deeper in *solitude* than in "the *market-place.*"

As Abraham sent away his servants, Gen. xxii. 5, and Jacob his
herdsmen, Gen. xxix. 7, so the disciples were absent, that
this lost daughter of Samaria might be gathered into the fold
of the good Shepherd.

The dew and the sunshine are not *clearer facts,* nor more full of
Divine *wisdom* and *goodness,* than our Lord's acts and words.

The Samaritan woman would have been embarrassed by the presence
of a number.

He made this solitude and appointed this meeting to win a poor
soul.

To *study* these *designs* of grace will fill the redeemed with adoring
wonder.

Unto. Not " *into* " the city. Our Lord went *unto* a mountain to pray, not " *into*."
Neither did the apostles *enter* Samaritan towns when going to preach. Matt. x. 5.

Buy. Judas carried the bag, as treasurer of the little band. John xiii. 29.
Our Saviour never lived upon alms, though so poor. 2 Cor. viii. 9.
His friends, stimulated by His own burning love, supplied His wants. Luke viii. 3.

Meat. See on verse 31. For kinds of food sold in ancient market, see on John vi. 5.
Food of Hebrews, beans, honey, syrup from grapes, spices, nuts, almonds, cucumbers, melons, leeks, onions (longed for in the wilderness).
Flocks and herds were used. Beasts parting the hoof and chewing the cud were clean. Lev. xi.
All fish that have scales and fins. All fowls except carnivorous.
Locusts, beetles, grasshoppers, the only insects used for food. But flesh offered to idols, Exod. xxxiv., and animals that had died of disease or had been slain by wild beasts, and all blood, were strictly forbidden.
Eating such things punished by being " *cut off.*" Lev. vii. 20. Thought by some to have been death, by others excommunication. *Lewis' Heb. Antiq.*
Manna from heaven for forty years supplied the twelve tribes with bread. John vi. 31 ; Deut. xxix. 6.
Birds (quails) also miraculously given them. Exod. xiv. 11.

μαθηταί. Since Mark omits this incident, Peter must have been absent. *Townsend.* One or two must have remained. *Schleiermacher.* Not one. *Stier.* John's account hints he remained. *Hengst.*

γὰρ, the key to the " no dealings " in the next verse.

ἀγοράσωσι. They left wherewith to draw water in their sacks. *Hengst.* Carried it with them. *Alford.* How unlikely such should be their travelling gear. *Trench.* A concealed Providence dispatched them to be absent. *Corn. à Lapide.* " Quærens me, sedisti lassus." *Dies Iræ.*

τροφὰς. Hebrew regulations simply sanatory. *Michaelis.* A wall between them and heathen. *Lewis.* Reasons wise, but unknown. *Cunæus.* Those articles forbidden sacred to Minerva, Apollo, Zeus, Hecate, &c. *Lewis.* Eaters of the thigh punished. Gen. xxxii. 31. *Selden.* Swine forbidden, for its filth. *Maimonides.* It produces leprosy. *Cunæus.*

9. Then saith the woman of Samaria unto him, How is it that thou, being a Jew, askest drink of me, which am a woman of Samaria? for the Jews have no dealings with the Samaritans.

Woman. Oriental females, see on ver. 27. Their morals, see on John viii. 3.

Jew. For history and character, see on John i. 19.

His dress, probably the gift of some disciple, may have been of the form worn by Rabbis. John xix. 23.

His *dialect* was softer than hers, and the unchanging features of Jewish *physiognomy* declared His nation. Rom. ix. 5.

How is it? Not curiosity alone, but gratification at being noticed.

Such a request would not often be refused by one in Palestine.

" Can a Jew humble himself so much as to ask drink of a Samaritan woman?"

She wondered at the request, but He had more wonderful things in store.

She thought He was dependent on her for a cup of water.

The relations between a creature and Creator here become visible.

We need not wonder at our darkness of mind while communing with our God.

The more *lowly*, the more *sensitive* persons are to slight or insult.

Jewish pride stronger, and therefore Jewish fanaticism fiercer than that of Samaritans.

The singular ill-will felt by all nations for so many ages against the Jews, arises from the *fulfilled prophecy* of their being resolutely and defiantly *insulated* from mankind. Deut. xxx. 7 ; xxviii. 37.

Rome received all nations as citizens save the Jews, and death was the penalty for attempting to obtain it.

As the Jews scorned the Gentiles, the Gentiles in turn scorned the Jews, using terms degrading to the last degree. See testimony from Tacitus and Ammianus Marcellinus, in *critical* notes on John vii. 35.

No dealings. A remark of John to explain her apparently unkind retort.

Not intercourse, but intimacy, was refused.

True followers of Christ, of every name, have always lived in love, while infidels have ever proved *contentious*. Luke xvii. 1.

The *image of Christ*, wherever found, the *true* Christian gladly recognizes.

He *proves* himself antichrist who refuses to commune with one
  Christ has received.
Persecution, though often hypocritically inflicted in the name of
  Christ, is of the devil. *Augustine.*
Hence the charge "that CHRISTIANS *persecute one another*" is one
  of the slanders our Lord foretold.   Matt. v. 11.
The national antipathy noted here gives point to our Lord's parable.
  Luke x. 30—37.
The record of this interview, like a *miracle of grace*, was intended to
  heal a thousand heart-burnings.
The same grace led back the healed alien leper to preach to the
  world a sermon on gratitude.   Luke xvii. 16.
We may be sure she offered her water-pot to His parched lips,
  since He had so far humbled Himself as to ask a favour at
  her hands.
Mungo Park bears noble testimony to the characteristic kindness
  of females, for even among the degraded tribes of Africa its
  generous impulses had not been extinguished by barbarism.
Samaritans.   They were of heathen blood. Christ calls them
  "*aliens*," Luke xvii. 18.   Yet they claimed to be descended
  from Joseph.
Their temple, in rivalry to that at Jerusalem, was built on Gerizim,
  409 B.C.
Schismatics, they claimed the Pentateuch, as their sole sacred
  writings.
They refused hospitality to pilgrims, going to worship at Jeru-
  salem.
They scattered dead men's bones to pollute the temple at Jeru-
  salem. *Josephus.*
They gave the Jews false signals, by beacon lights, as to the time
  of the Passover.
They requested *Alexander* to waive taxes every Sabbatical (seventh)
  year.
Enraged by their duplicity, the Macedonian conqueror destroyed
  Samaria.
Everything touched by a Samaritan was polluted, as swine's flesh.
They were annually anathematized in all the Jewish synagogues.
Their testimony would not be taken in a Jewish court.
Heathen, *but no Samaritans*, were allowed to be Jewish proselytes.
At one time some of our Lord's apostles, treated inhospitably,

wanted to call down fire from heaven to consume them.
Luke ix. 54.

Samaritans repaid hate and insult with scorn and outrage.

Jews prayed that Samaritans might have no share in the resurrection of the just.

Entertaining a Samaritan was laying up judgment for one's children.

During many centuries their nationality has been preserved.

They annually celebrate the Passover on Mount Gerizim.

If a Samaritan but touched a Jew, he washed off the pollution with all speed.

Every sacrifice offered by Samaritans, Jews esteemed a *sacrilege*.

In Nehemiah's day Jews enjoined to put away Samaritan wives, refused, and went and dwelt among them.   Neh. xiii. 23—30.

Ἰουδαῖος.   He probably dressed after the manner of the Rabbis. *Stier*.

λέγει.   National prejudices flattered. *Lange*.   Capricious desire of bantering. *Lücke*.   Her curiosity defers drink, until He explains His request. *Luthardt*.   Gratifies her humoursome spirit. *Klee*.   Surprise mingled with contempt. *Thol*.   Jesus in the background, seems above an ordinary Jew, and she refuses out of curiosity. *Hengst*.   All the replies to our Saviour providentially, perhaps supernaturally, directed to unfold the Saviour's mission. *Author*.

συγχρῶνται.   Bigotry *alone* entertained by the enemies of Christ and religion. *Author*.

Σαμαρείτιδος.   Samaritans of pure heathen extraction. *Origen, Eusebius, Chrys., Cyril, Hammond, Maldonatus, Hengst., Robinson, Trench*.   Mixture of Jewish blood. *Winer, Davidson, Stanley*.   Distinction recognized by the *Theodosian Code*.   It was lost after an outrage on Christians, in the fifth century, in reign of Zeno.   Samaritans corresponded with *Scaliger*, 1592 A.D.   Also with *Job Ludolph*, 1681 A.D.   The letters are in *Eichorn's* Repert.   They claim to spring from Joseph. *Robinson*.

οὐ γὰρ, κ. τ. λ. Omitted. *Cod. Sin.* Jews use their labour, lodge in their towns, and say "*Amen*" to their salutations. *Lightfoot*.

---

10. Jesus answered and said unto her, If thou knewest the gift of God, and who it is that saith to thee, Give me to drink ; thou wouldest have asked of him, and he would have given thee living water.

Answered.   His urgent desire is, to finish in love His work. Luke xii. 50.

Instead of stirring the embers of the wretched national quarrel, He gently leaves contest and the water untouched, until He had won her soul.

Then the pitcher is left behind, for she has more important matters in hand.

Many Christians would refuse fellowship with such a character, but the heavenly Physician dreads not contact with the leprous soul.

If thou knewest. He graciously softens down the reproach of ignorance.

In Infinite love He desires to make Himself known to her.

He who makes the *request* for water can bestow a far greater thing than He asks.

An *Otaheitan* refused a handful of *guineas* for a *hatchet,* saying he could not think of selling it for a few gilded buttons.

Gift of God. Had she come so oft to the well, and yet never knew that *water* is a *gift* of God ?

Had no soul-thirst taught her *that* common blessings are types of higher good ? Amos viii. 11.

Perhaps the Saviour's glance had reached and awakened her conscience.

He HIMSELF was the GIFT, which God had sent in mercy.

The gift of the SAVIOUR always includes the gift of the SPIRIT. John vii. 37—39.

That fountain of living immortal joy in the soul, the golden, gracious time of communing with the Messiah, and finding in Him our Redeemer, the Fountain of Life. *Hooker.*

" Unto us a SON is GIVEN." Isa. ix. 6. There can be but ONE such GIFT !

" None but CHRIST, none but CHRIST," cried the martyr in the flames.

Our Lord had already said " God *gave* His only begotten Son." John iii. 16.

Who it is. He speaks of Himself with modesty and in the third person, and puts Himself in the place of the unacknowledged GIVER of the GIFT OF GIFTS.

The second step in the conversation intimates that He is far from being the person she supposes Him.

Who can impart the GIFT OF GOD but One who is HIMSELF ALMIGHTY ?

This arouses her mind, and deepens her interest in the stranger.

Thou wouldest. His unchanging testimony for all those in want.

The condition of prayer is of necessity the heart's condition for this gift.

Asked. Asking of God is *prayer*. How gently He teaches this woman to pray !

" Instead of wondering, of thine own accord thou wouldest have asked."

Our Creator *ever links* ASKING by US *with* GIVING by HIM.

" What God has joined together let no man put asunder."

A *creature* too proud to beg of his Creator will, remaining such, be for ever unworthy to receive.

For even the ETERNAL SON "*asks* for the heathen as an inheritance." Psa. ii. 8.

None too high, none too low to be excluded. " Ask, and it shall be given." Matt. vii. 7.

An archangel's holy *desire*, in heaven, is a prayer heard on the THRONE !

Her error was, that He was the petitioner, and she the granter.

Given thee. This offer of the secret resources of the mysterious stranger surprised her.

There was something which no ordinary rules could reach, for in claiming this power to Himself, He boldly claims the attributes of Jehovah.

Jehovah alone is the " Fountain of *living waters*." Jer. xvii. 13.

An evidence of sovereign grace ; an adulteress is chosen to life eternal. Heb. xi. 31.

Living water. With design He uses a word of *double* meaning ; it is more than " running water."

" Living water " meant a fountain, in contrast with a cistern, so common in Oriental lands, supplied from rain.

Water and *bread* and *light* are—1. Necessary ; 2. Common ; 3. Healthful.

He links the heavenly to the earthly, and uses earth as a ladder, to rise to heaven.

Spiritual life is a flowing fountain, a blessed Divine existence, and its source is " hid with Christ in God." Col. iii. 3.

" And he (the angel) showed me a pure river of water of life." Rev. xxii. 1.

"I will give him that is athirst of the fountain of the water of life freely." Rev. xxi. 6.

" In that day the living waters shall go out of Jerusalem." Zech. xiv. 8.

She had hesitated conferring the smallest gift, but He speaks of a priceless gift.

He saw one lost in sensuality, yet He seeks to inspire her with a deep, ardent longing after holiness.

To those at Capernaum seeking *bread*, He offers the " Bread of heaven."

To *shepherds*, as Moses and David, He offers " His flock " to be guided.

To *fishermen* He promises success while *fishing* for souls with God's net.

The Magi, star-gazers, He leads to the manger by a miraculous *star*.

To over-taxed hearts, crushed by the legal burdens of the exacting Sanhedrim, He cries, " *My* yoke is easy, and *My* burden is light."

To a *thirsty* lonely female He speaks of the living unfailing *water*.

He gently reproves her for hesitating a moment to grant His request.

He claims to be the Sovereign Giver, and Dispenser of peace.

A well-spring of joy in the soul, that shall never cease to flow. Isa. xii. 3.

" Everything shall live whither the river cometh." Ezek. xlvii. 9.

" The Lamb shall lead them unto living fountains of waters." Rev. vii. 17.

The consolations of earth, at best hollow and vain, come from reservoirs, needing constant filling.

But the Redeemer shows by this "living water" the spirituality, vitality, joy, and perpetuity of heart-religion.

In all the Bible no such word ever escaped from *creaturely* lips.

In *Jesus* we feel it *appropriate, majestic,* and *rightfully* His.

Reading this dialogue, we feel in the presence of *grace enshrined,* INCARNATE GOODNESS !

δωρεὰν Θεοῦ. The gift of God to all who thirst. *Pfemminger*. Any blessing God can, and man cannot give. *Cyril*. The Holy Ghost. *Augustine, Alford*. This very interview. *Meyer*. An hour of grace. *Bucer*. Christ Himself. *Rollock, Lightfoot, Hengst*. Eternal life and gift of the gospel proclaimed. *Lampe, Calvin*. The hunger and thirst of the soul an element of heaven and hell. *Rieger*. Living water. *Stier, Trench*.

ᾔτησας. Anticipated by asking. *Winer*.

αἰτεῖν, a word from an inferior to a superior, differing from ἐρωτᾶν. He uses λέγων of Himself, an implied claim to *dignity* of person, that marks all His intercourse with mortals. *Ullmann*.

ζῶν. Not necessarily same as water of life. Rev. xxi. 6. An energy inde-

pendent of the substantial ὕδωρ. *Luthardt.* As He calls the Spirit " fire "
denoting the burning glow of grace, so here " water " denoting its refreshment.
Chrys. Baptism. *Theodoret.* Any blessing that cheers the soul. *Tittmann.*

---

11. The woman saith unto him, Sir, thou hast nothing to draw with, and
the well is deep : from whence then hast thou that living water ?

Sir. At first she calls Him a " Jew," but now it is " Sir " or
" Lord."

It denotes a suspicion that a person of high dignity is standing before her.

Nevertheless she believes Him in real need.

Nothing. Do not all streams of life flow from the word of this
same Jesus ?

Nothing ? Who filled the oceans from the hollow of His hand ?

Nothing ? Who causes the clouds and makes them treasuries of His
rain ?

Nothing ? Who for thousands of years has opened fountains of
joy in myriads of hearts ?

What this woman said in ignorance has been practically endorsed
by all unrenewed hearts, and thus human infatuation from
age to age would limit the Holy One of Israel.

To draw with. Gr. *a bucket.* Not a common village well, or
it would have had these conveniences.

A bucket of skin and sticks, with a rope of goat's hair, are now
found at the wells in Palestine.

Earthly minds cling with pertinacity to things of sense.

So some birds never lift a wing towards heaven while they can
find a twig to rest on.

Whence ? She begins to *contrast* the two kinds of water.

This supposed superiority was simply in the background.

Her answer referred to the wonderful " water " He announced.

How little avail at last is Jacob's well without Jacob's piety.

There are few sadder sights on earth than one *exact as to religious
rites,* and yet " *without holiness.*"

Κύριε. In that day the usual form of courtesy. *Tholuck.* His mysterious
words change her Ἰουδαῖος into Κύριε, and flow out of His τίς ἐστίν. *Stier.*
She thinks Him some great man. *Euthymius.* He had attained a certain
supremacy over her mind. *Ber. Bib.* Thou hast nothing to draw with, as I
have. *Stier.*

ἄντλημα. The woman did not necessarily come from the village. *Robinson.*
Gerizim has 375 springs. *Samaritan Tradition.*
τὸ ὕδωρ τὸ ζῶν. Double article, *that* living water. *Stier.* Equivalent to
ζῶν ὕδωρ. *Middleton.*

---

12. Art thou greater than our father Jacob, which gave us the well, and drank thereof himself, and his children, and his cattle?

Art thou? Poor proud humanity resents this grace, as though it lacked nothing.
Greater. She sees nothing in His words but unseemly depreciation of a well hallowed by ages.
She little suspected the Infinite Majesty of the Stranger in Jewish garb.
This seems zealously and warmly spoken, since she understood Him not.
Dost thou slight us Samaritans, or our Jacob's well?
Our father. Alas! this idolatry of *heroes* has been man's infirmity for ages.
Nearly all the scores of gods and goddesses of the ancients were mere heroes deified.
The inventors of useful arts, or successful leaders in war.
Of what avail the relics of all the sainted martyrs treasured by superstition?
Samaria, the dwelling of Jacob and tomb of Joseph, was a land of *darkness* still.
She would learn to what mysterious *greatness* He aspired.
" *Our father.*" Contradicting pride assumes what the Jews denied.
In this false claim she shows herself a dweller in Sychar, i.e. falsehood.
Not unwilling to grant the favour, she thinks that *He* comes in *Jewish pride.*
She stands before Him as a daughter of Jacob to defend his honour.
Jacob. See on ver. 5. A wise, industrious, and prudent shepherd.
He knew well the value of good water in a thirsty land.
For more than 1600 years it had given sufficient for all who came.
Gave us. No historic authority for this statement—a mere tradition.
Drank. The patriarchs drank water rather than *wine.*
She means that Jacob being satisfied with this, wished not better.
" They looked for a city whose builder and maker is God." Heb. xi. 10.

334 / Gospel of John

Will men of the world *ever comprehend* the deep spiritual necessities,
which, amid their all, leave them *hungry and thirsty* still ?
Children. The twelve patriarchs and an only daughter, Dinah.
When it went well with the Jews, Samaritans claimed kindred,
but when unfortunate, they disowned them.
Cattle. Sheep, oxen. See on John ii. 15.
Marvellous simplicity ! Could such water suffice for *all* the wants
of MAN ?

μείζων. The woman faintly apprehends the spiritual meaning of the Lord.
Schleiermacher.

φρέαρ. It lay in Joseph's tract, and Samaritans boasted of descending from
Joseph. *Trench.*

πατρὸς ἡμῶν. She claims Jacob so strictly for the Samaritans, as almost
to deny him to the Jews. *Lange.* Samaritans all cherished this falsehood.
Bengel. Their round features prove they are not Jews. *Wilson* in *Ritter.*
Critically the same decision reached. *Robinson.* They were of Jewish descent.
Kiel. Samaritans did not pretend to be, till after the captivity. *Hengst.*

θρέμματα, pecora. *Vulgate, Lampe.* Anything nursed. *Gesenius.* Includes servants. *Trench.*

---

13. Jesus answered and said unto her, Whosoever drinketh of this water
shall thirst again.

Answered. He never for a moment forgets His majesty, nor the
relation He bears to creatures.
He perceived in the woman a weak, candid, docile mind.
Still He does not answer her reply, but her deep spiritual long-
ings.
He will not confound her by saying, " *I am* greater than Jacob."
For this she will in due time be prepared. "He ever sits as a
REFINER," &c. Mal. iii. 3.
He holds her mind firmly to the greater truth.
Yet He does reply, He who gives water for the soul must be greater
than Jacob.
Drinketh. Burning thirst of sensuality, fierce grasping of the
cup of earthly pleasure.
The parched earth receives the shower and remains thirsty still.
This water. Earthly things reach only the *superficial* wants of
our nature.
The deeper necessities of our being are not reached at all.

Thirst again. He clearly hints that Jacob had other water than this well.

He must have drawn from *higher* springs than those his *cattle* shared.   Heb. xi. 21.

They are poor indeed to whom their father Jacob left no *better inheritance* than this well.

There is a famine, but not of bread,—a thirst that God never made. Amos viii. 11.

To " thirst again " in *this* world is to thirst for ever in the *next*.

The supply of to-day will be no supply for to-morrow.

But what could an uncultured mind understand of a spring *within ?*

Her answer shows that thus far the spiritual idea had not entered her mind.

Yet *Luther* called John's Gospel the " CHILD'S GOSPEL."

A little more training, and the gospel sunlight breaks on her soul.

Whenever God in mercy imparts light, He creates *a capacity to receive it.*

This water in reality cannot hinder either thirst or death.

An inspired " *Inscription* " for every creaturely fountain of good.

No school of human wisdom has ever discovered the LIVING WATER.

All this world can offer only deepens the thirst it professes to allay.

In all the joys of earth there is in the background a note of dissatisfaction.

" O God, *Thou* art my God ; my soul thirsteth for THEE." Psa. lxiii. 1.

With believers no fear of future want should ever agitate the heart.

This is our Lord's wonted manner   He rouses a soul from its sleep.

He denounces not her guilt, but points to her own conviction, of the *empty* hopes of evil courses.

How often earth's devotees conceal an *aching* heart beneath a smiling face.

The variety of human misery is as astounding as it is deplorable.

There is a *fountain of* " *gold*," to which myriads continually resort.

A sparkling *fountain of* " *glory*," whither many battle their bloody way.

A fountain of " *pleasure*," which attracts millions, only to poison their peace.

These all only dull or deaden man's cravings ; by-and-by they
    burst forth more fiercely than ever.

In these the worldling finds enough to sink, not satisfy, him.

Here we sow, but reap not ; hope, but receive not ; we gather, but
    possess not ; oft possess, but enjoy not.

In the cup of Christ afflictions and persecutions become drops of
    joy.

As the drop of water falling in a cask of wine loses its nature.

At the foot of the throne, the spirit is quiet under its holy shadow.

Living waters flow from the Rock, Christ, smitten by the rod
    of God ; on these waters the *Angel* of the *Covenant* ever
    broods.

It *never can be* denied that very many persons have all that heart
    can wish, yet are *weary of life.*

If manna (angels' food, Psa. lxxviii. 25) could not stay hunger,
    much less earthly springs.

> " My days are in the yellow leaf,
>   The flowers and fruits of life are gone,
>   The worm, the canker, and the grief
>   Are mine alone.
> The fire that in my bosom preys
> Is lone as some volcanic isle ;
> No torch is kindled at its blaze,
>   A funeral pile."—*Lord Byron*, on his last birthday.

Mere *ennui* led persons of culture and wealth in *Paris*, previous to
    the first revolution, to commit suicide, *to get rid of themselves !*

Every Ahab has a Naboth's vineyard hard by his palace.

Every Haman sees a Mordecai at the gate.

If we begin to drink of this living water, we shall be satisfied
    with nothing else.

Hence to seek *first* the kingdom is to care for nothing *second.*

Christ slakes the spirit's thirst, and slakes it for ever.

πᾶς ὁ πίνων. " Whosoever drinketh," &c., an inscription over a public fountain in Pall Mall, London. *Author.* The woman understood none of these things. *Cyril.* The impenitent often comprehend far more than they are willing to acknowledge. *Author.* Spoken for the Church through all time. *Stier.* And for all out of the Church. *Author.*

14. But whosoever drinketh of the water that I shall give him shall never thirst; but the water that I shall give him shall be in him a well of water springing up into everlasting life.

Drinketh. Gr. *shall have drunk*, i. e. a continued, earnest, full, thorough drinking to the end. Not those who merely taste.

It sets forth that, having once " tasted," he will continue to drink " living waters."

" To drink water from one's well " is to be one's disciple among Orientals.

The water. " The words which I speak unto you, they are spirit, and they are life." John vi. 63.

No father Abraham or Jacob, no father *Luther* or *Calvin*, can give this.

The Church of God is *" a spring shut up, a fountain sealed,"* Sol. Song iv. 12, to which no one can have access except through *faith.* John x. 9.

I shall give. While offering this cup, He is *creating*, by His sovereign grace, *a thirst* for the same.

He gives this water by the act of giving HIMSELF to death.

This life-stream began in the promise in Eden, and it will increase, and become deeper and broader for ever. Ezek. xlvii.

The saints perfected shall drink it in the Paradise of God. Rev. xxii. 1, 17.

True, the believer daily thirsts for fuller, deeper draughts, Psa. xlii. 2, but that source of thirst is a source of joy, and is *ever being satisfied!* John vii. 38.

While the thirst of the wicked ever torments, and is a prelude to eternal thirst! 1 John iv. 18.

If thirst return in the believing soul, the *fault* cannot be in the FOUNT. John vi. 35.

Unbelief alone can hinder the blessedness of this living spring.

The river of life, proceeding out of the throne of God, Rev. xxii. 1, in the Jerusalem above, is one with that below.

With the saints it is a *river* of life, with angels a *river* of glory, with Christ an *ocean* shoreless and infinite of life eternal.

Our Lord gathers the whole of O. T. promises to Himself. Deut. xxxiii. 28.

" Ho, every one that thirsteth, come ye to the waters, and he that," &c. Isa. lv. 1.

He adopts as His own the name " FOUNTAIN OF LIVING WATERS." Jer. ii. 13.

" With Thee is the fountain of life," Psa. xxxvi. 9, is fulfilled in Christ.

Never thirst. Gr. *shall thirst no more* for ever,—shall have the spring at home. Isa. xlix. 10.

I, in my grace and power, I who alone can, will preserve him.

The prodigal, amid the dainties of his father's table, never again longed for husks.

There will be no *satiety*—the relish will endure with the soul's nature.

" My soul is athirst for God, even for the living God." Psa. xlii. 2.

Believers yearn for the same thirst, and mourn their craving is so languid.

" Blessed are they who hunger and thirst after righteousness." Matt. v. 6.

There is a foolish longing, as *David* longed for the waters of Bethlehem, and *Balaam* for a believer's death,—*Pilate* for a knowledge of truth, and *Herod* to see Christ.

But the heart " panting for the water brooks," must find, or perish. Psa. xlii. 1.

" My soul breaketh for the longing," &c., Psa. cxix. 20, like the famished servant of the Amalekite. 1 Sam. xxx. 12.

" Not riches of earth, but a TREASURE of *this sweet longing after Christ.*" The martyr *Saunders.*

In His kingdom " they neither hunger nor thirst any more." Rev. vii. 16.

But God gives no " letters of credit " for *happiness* in *this world* of *sin*, Mark x. 30, but a pledge of *perfection hereafter.* " Not that I have already attained," &c. Phil. iii. 12.

Well of water. It becomes a *perennial* fountain in the believer's heart.

A soul " filled with God's fulness " on earth, becomes God-like. Eph. iii. 19.

Thus our Lord's *raiment* on Tabor *shared* its Master's effulgence. Mark ix. 3.

Springing up. Not periodic, a figure taken from the bounding elasticity of a being full of life, divine life.

Its author being LIFE INFINITE and ETERNAL, its nature is to rise.

" Springing," gushing forth, from the indwelling of the Holy Ghost

The *eternal freshness* and *vitality* of the *ocean* of *Divine Love!*

In a secondary sense a believer's life becomes a fountain *to others,*

but it must be fed, and fed for ever, from the " upper springs."
A spark falling, kindles a flame, and rises higher than before.
Piety, " like a torch, the more 'tis shook it shines."
Like the *taper fabled* to float on the *ocean*, passing under billow
after billow, its flame became clearer, and its light blazed
higher and higher, the longer and louder raged the storm.
The seed, taking root, spreads," until its fruit shakes like Lebanon."
Psa. lxxii. 16.

Into. It *issues in* life eternal, as well as *springs from* life eternal.
All of life, worth the name, is from God, and ends in His love.

Everlasting. She well knew that Jacob's well could not do this.
We cannot, if we would, ignore the continual gnawing of a sense
of want.
" The heart knoweth its own bitterness," and seldom tells it ALL to
the world. Prov. xiv. 10.
" A *perpetuity* of bliss is *bliss*," all our goods have bounds, life its
end.
We must daily confront the dreadful fact, that DEATH stops all
plans of pleasures, a word never failing to reach man's inmost
conscience.

Life. This promised well—1. Mysterious as to its source. 2. Unfailing as to its supply. 3. Unfathomable as to its depth.
Earth's streams rise and then *flow back*, but this hath an eternal
impulse.
The DIVINE FOUNTAIN. 1. It never fails; all else are broken cisterns. 2. It always satisfies. No craving void, no restless
desire left. 3. It imparts eternal satisfaction. Nothing
claims *to be or do* what it does. 4. It increases as it flows, a
confluence of many streams. 5. It cannot be arrested. It
flows on to the ocean, which is GOD !
Christ, its AUTHOR, gives " grace for grace " until it reaches a sea
that knows no storms.

ὃς δ' ἄν. An echo of the son of Sirach, Eccles. xxiv. 19. *Meyer.* No
evidence our Lord ever *borrowed* from such a source. *Author.*
    πίῃ. Drink often and deeply, as wine. *Homer, Hesiod, Pindar.*
    ἀλλομένου. Springing or bounding. The imperial philosopher notes the
expansive nature, but not the SOURCE of virtue. *Plutarch.* Salientes. *Vulgate.*
A spring flowing towards eternal life. *Luthardt.* Eternal life in the soul flowing on. *Stier.*
    εἰς ζωὴν αἰώνιον, as the Spirit is its heavenly source, hence it rises. *Bur-.*
gensis.
    διψήσῃ. The thirst of grace must increase. *Whitby.* But it will not per-

mit him to perish. *Lightfoot.* Rather the *aching void* will harass no more. *Author.* With her dark mind, in heavenly self-denial the Lord still communes. *Tholuck.*

---

15. The woman saith unto him, Sir, give me this water, that I thirst not, neither come hither to draw.

Sir. Water becoming a living fountain suits the soul's wants.

Critics make our Lord and apostles speak above the understanding of their hearers.

Sunlight comes from on high ; and while the wisest are ignorant of its nature, the humblest and meanest *move by its light.*

Nicodemus doubtless ever found a sermon in the *wind,* and this Samaritan in the *water.*

The words flow silently through the soul, and will to eternity instruct and illumine.

Give me. Her reply seems to involve the assumption that the promise could not be made good.

Willing to enjoy any comfort, but careless as to results.

Nicodemus' earnestness had advanced further,—his *conscience* was more active.

The woman's words—1. A half prayer. 2. An imperfect prayer. 3. A sinner's prayer. 4. No prayer, judged by the rules given among men.

Still a prayer. 1. It was heard. 2. Quickly heard. 3. Effectually heard. 4. Gloriously answered. Ver. 32.

EARTH'S JOY a FAILURE ! 1. How short its pleasures. 2. How trifling its recreations. 3. How false its friendships. 4. How fleeting its glories.

Contrast with these God's service ! 1. How sustaining His promises. 2. How charming the communion of saints. 3. How glorious their hopes. 4. How gracious His dealings. 5. How gentle His corrections.

This water. Dreaming of some magical means of quenching her bodily thirst.

Half perhaps in frivolity and half in earnest, she will test His power.

Thirst not. The very means the human heart uses to allay thirst only render its demands stronger and fiercer.

Desiring spiritual life from this motive none will obtain it, since many pray for deliverance from *all kinds* of *evil,* but *sin !*

Those trusting they *deserve* life, or that they can give a *price* for it,
 never obtain it.
The soul originally was filled with longings after immortality.
" Lest he put forth his hand, and take of the tree of life." Gen. iii.
 22.
All nations sigh for the golden age, which ever appears to belong
 to the past.
Man can neither give up *his God,* nor *his idols,* nor *his lusts !*
Neither cruel laws nor fierce persecutions can burn out this longing
 of the soul.
Man's immortal spirit cannot act as its nature demands, in a life of
 sense.
Even the eagle, with her broad and powerful pinions, cannot swim
 through the sea.
Rapidly-moving wheels heat themselves by their own velocity.
Thus man's unsatisfied longings become more and more fierce.
But becoming angel-like, Luke xx. 36, they hunger not, nor thirst.
 Rev. vii. 16.
Each one would beg an immortality here on earth.
A Greek youth (so the fable reads) found in his wanderings a foun-
 tain, whose water conferred immortality. He returned and
 told the tidings, and all Greece flocked around him, beseech-
 ing him to tell them *where* it was.
There *was* a youth who once found that long-sought fount when
 the voice of the Baptist cried, " BEHOLD the LAMB OF GOD ! "
 John i. 36.
" Thirst not " might denote a soul longing after life eternal, but the
 next word shows she had only *carnal ideas.*
Ignorant of her true wants, she fails to ask for the true supply.
" Man, with energy, draws water from the depths of hell, yet
 thirsts on." *Augustine.*
Come hither. A wondering desire after this unknown gift, from
 the mysterious stranger.
She wants a fountain *at home.* What a fearful error when men go
 from the fountain unseen at their side.
The angel ready to show them the spring, as he did Hagar, is
 disregarded.
It must indeed be a fountain close at hand, to which the *helpless,*
 the *feeble,* the *blind,* the *lame,* &c., can have access.
His Spirit probably *prompted* the reply, " Yet the dogs eat of the
 crumbs that fall from their master's table." Matt. xv. 27.

So, also, the prayer of the sinking Peter, " Lord, save mə." Matt. xiv. 30.

So that what seems but dull apprehension in this woman may have been an inspired word to draw forth counsel for millions unborn.

The carnally-minded question about manna (John vi. 34) was a *text* for *a sermon* of world-wide interest to all coming time.

Many baptized persons offer prayers quite as *mixed* as those of this woman.

The daily blessings sought are often *vague* and *carnal*.

How many would be free from all the *harassing vexations* of life.

1. *Hilly* ways are *wearisome*, and tire the ambitious man.

2. *Carnal* ways are *polluted*, and tire the licentious man.

3. *Covetous* ways are *thorny*, and tire the grasping man.

4. *Emulation's* ways are *dark*, and tire the envious man.

" There is no (or there shall be no) peace to the wicked, saith my God." Isa. lvii. 21.

We retire at night, weary with our toil, and on the morrow we begin the same sinful labour, toiling up the barren mount, that lies pining under the curse of God.

λέγει. A mere method of putting an end to the conversation. *J. G. Müller.*
δός μοι. A wavering between the spiritual and earthly meaning. *Stier.* A certain jesting, naïveté. *Lightfoot.* She believes the waters of Jacob's well far more efficacious than common water. *Hengst.* Meritorious sanctity in them. *Lange.*
διψῶ. The gods in their celestial abodes, having vacated their chariots, human souls mounted them, and attempted to drive round the circuit of the heavens; but dashing against one another, became disabled, and fell to the earth,—where ever since they *long after their lost immortality!* *Plato.*
μηδὲ ἔρχωμαι. A glimmering of doubt, something akin to irony. *Schweizer.* Sarcasticum quid subesse videtur. *Lampe.* A bantering word. *Luthardt.* Shows ignorance. *Davidson.* Candid and sincere. *Erasmus.*

---

16. Jesus saith unto her, Go, call thy husband, and come hither.

Go, call. A curious and startling break in the dialogue, but verse 15 explains it.

Our Lord simply begins to *answer her request* made in that verse.

That water she unconsciously asked was *repentance* and *faith*.

What connection had it with Jacob's well or living water?

It was *His divine method* of arousing her conscience, and granting her request.

She now first felt the flash of the Spirit's glance, kindling conviction.   Luke xxiv. 32.

God, in His usual mysterious way, in a moment had dashed her hopes.

The new-born powers of the regenerate soul began to move.

" Give me this water " was a petition *that reached into eternity*, although she knew it not.

Our Lord's command showed He saw *through* and *through* her guilty soul.

He illustrates this omniscience in every conversation held with men.

His words are *words of earth*, but they are *echoes of the eternal world*.

He intends to *bring out* the very answer He knew she would give.

He would penetrate her secret sinful life, as He had already broken through the foolish rules of the Talmud, which forbade conversation in public with a woman.

Our Lord's freedom, dignity, purity, and fidelity, could not be affected by such rules.

His prophetic glance runs parallel with spiritual convictions.

He utters the word with *look* and *tone*, that reach her soul at once.

He waits for the answer, " I have no husband," and by means of this *invisible shaft* He will pierce her *slumbering conscience*.

His plain design is by *her own lips* to awaken self-knowledge and *repentance*.

Our Lord, with deep humility, permitted a sinful woman to wash His feet with her tears.

Now, with greater humility, He invites a harlot to come into the kingdom of heaven.

" The grace of our Lord is exceedingly abundant."   1 Tim. i. 14.

Husband.   What a Master, touching *the key* among a thousand.

The answers of our Lord are unequalled for their *adaptation* to the mind.

He alludes to such minute details, proving to her *He knew* ALL !

Thus He prepares her for receiving the wonderful stranger as her SAVIOUR.

How easy would examinations in our human courts be, if one *knew all secrets*, as did this Divine questioner.

Bring with thee the partner in thy sin, that we may proceed to speak further.

An echo in the background of yearning for his salvation too.
Boundless wisdom and grace preach mercy, not condemnation.
He lays His finger on the wounds, but only in LOVE, to HEAL.
Her answer hints at the deep corruptions then found in the
world.
First chapter of Romans applies to the *civilized Greeks and Romans*,
and also to the Jews, if Josephus is to be trusted.

ὸ 'Ιησοῦς, omitted. *Tisch., Alford.*
φώνησον. A concealed question put to the woman. *B. Crusius.* Her incapacity for understanding His dialogue. *Cyril.* He would thus arouse her
conscience. *Alford.* Even rough natures appreciate truth. *Calvin, Melancthon.*
A request bearing hard on the sinful Samaritan. *Bretschneider.* The Lord's
dignity not the least compromised. *Stier.* The woman's answer awakens our
Lord's prophetic gift. *Lücke.* Our Lord, intuitively omniscient, never asked
through ignorance. *J. A. Alexander.* He aims at the emotion called by
Mystics "momentum compunctionis." *P. Anton.* About to be a disciple, the
husband should be present. *Lange.* He would make him a sharer with the
wife's consolation. *M. Henry.* He would draw out her answer. *Trench.*

---

17. The woman answered and said, I have no husband. Jesus said unto
her, Thou hast well said, I have no husband.

Answered. Note our Lord's wisdom and modesty in not abruptly
telling her all.
Supposing Him a *man*, she vainly attempts to cloak her guilt.
How many even of high culture daily treat God as though Om-
niscience could be deceived as easily as a neighbour.
Achan acted as if he believed God could not see under ground
covered by his tent. Josh. vii.
Jeroboam's wife under her mask thought God could not discover
her. 1 Kings xiv. 5.
God need never ask, with Jehu to Jehonadab, "Is thine heart
right?" 2 Kings x. 15.
Cain really thought Jehovah would have to *find out* his brother.
Words spoken in the Syrian king's bed-chamber were revealed to
Elisha. 2 Kings vi. 12.
Man looketh on the outward appearance, but God on the heart.
1 Sam. xvi. 7.
"Sin is acted on earth, but it is recorded in heaven on Jupiter's
parchments,"—the saying of a heathen *sage.*

Cyrus was named several hundred years before that heathen
monarch was born. Isa. xliv. 28.
Three hundred years before Josiah's birth he was named as the
destroyer of an idolatrous altar. 1 Kings xiii. 2.
No husband. She modestly denies it, but with a smitten consci-
ence.
As though she would say, " I have indeed some one, but not a
husband."
She told the truth, but only half of it, *intending so far to deceive.*
In the Gr. *Husband have I none.* " Husband " is emphatic.
Her life is spread out before His eye, and she vainly tries to
conceal it.
Thus our first parents *prevaricated* when they heard God's voice.
It is hard even for the *renewed* heart to frankly confess its sin.
Well said. This time thou hast spoken the truth, but not fully.
A gracious look and tone encouraged her to be candid.
He intends for her the *same evidence* of His *Godhead* that He gave
the guileless Nathanael. John i. 48.
Certain unrevealed impressions may have flashed on both minds
the great truth.
Or His Spirit may have disclosed to them, what the *soul will feel
at judgment.*
She will soon be thoroughly conscious she had the ALL-SEEING EYE
on her heart.
Omniscience found Nathanael a *guileless*, this woman a *sinful*, being.

οὐκ ἔχω ἄνδρα. The emphatic word ought to have been noted in the translation. *Alford.* The ancient Hebrew copyists emphasized a word by enlarging
the letters. *Author.* Under the ambiguity of this word, she hides her shame.
Hengst. She had deserted the five, and could not legally marry the sixth.
Grotius.
καλῶς. Ironical. *Tholuck.*

---

18. For thou hast had five husbands ; and he whom thou now hast is not thy
husband : in that saidst thou truly.

Five husbands. How gently He unrolls the blotted and blurred
scroll of her life.
The eye of the *Searcher* of *hearts* pierces all the *specialities* of her
guilt.
" Thou knowest my downsitting and mine uprising, thou under-
standest my thoughts afar off." Psa. cxxxix. 2.

" I am He who searcheth the reins and the heart," Rev. ii. 23, said of Jesus Christ.

Five despotic husbands might easily, by Samaritan law, have divorced a wife.

Or death might have released some, and lawless passion the rest.

But the word " *thou hast* " implies the depravity was greater in the woman.

Memory brings all the dark chapters of life up in a moment, a midnight flash of lightning reveals the ocean in a storm.

What a moment, when ETERNITY *fixes* and *reveals* a *lifetime* of *sin !*

He who will then fill the Judgment Throne *stood* before her.

Divorces *then* and *now* were frequent and easy in Judea. Deut. xxiv.

No dweller in Jerusalem would be surprised at this record or custom.

Missionaries had collected some thirty divorced females to instruct them, none of whom were over twenty-five years of age, who were visited by the author at Jerusalem in 1855.

Not thy husband. Clinging to one man discriminates her from one utterly abandoned.

She seems to have felt no interest in him, as we do not read that she made any announcement to him of the Saviour. Ver. 28.

Saidst truly. To Nathanael the Lord disclosed his *secret place* of prayer.

To Nicodemus He unfolds the *great laws* of his spiritual being.

To the woman His omniscience reveals her *secret* course of *crime.*

Scripture speaks to every condition of sinner with the words, " Thou art the man." 2 Sam. xii. 7.

The sword of the cherub turning *every way* was a type of the law of God. Gen. iii. 24.

Though the heart makes many windings and turnings, it cannot shun the strokes.

He accuses not to condemn, but to save. The eagle, though loving her young, beateth them out of her nest. So faithful ministers will beat men out of their pleasure nests. *Trapp.*

πέντε. We cannot but impute evil, even if all had died a natural death. *Stier.* No husband, but all paramours. *Chrys., Maldonatus.* All legal, but divorced. *Tittmann.* All lawful husbands but the sixth. *Hengst.* Through

divorce, death, or impropriety. *Meyer.* Certainly lawful husbands. *Alford.*
Roman wives counted years by husbands divorced. *Seneca.* A woman in Rome
had ten husbands. *Martial,* Ep. vi. 7. Another had eight in five years,
Juvenal, Sat. vi. 230. A Roman wife had thirteen husbands. *Jerome,* Epist.
lxii. A woman in Haarlem had to be checked *by law* from marrying again,
after her tenth. *Evelyn's Diary.* We find Macænas, Cato, Augustus, Cicero,
divorcing for mere trifles. *Lecky's* History. Allegorical reference to five-fold
idolatry of Samaritans. *Lücke, Lange.* A representation of their half-wor-
ship. *Sepp.* Five senses. five books of Moses. *Origen.*

ὃν ἔχεις. He read their number on her spirit like rings on a forest tree.
Lange. These wood marks questioned. *Pelt.* His omniscient glance knew all.
Author.

ἀληθές. The objective truth without regarding the circumstances. *Hengst.*
We need not suppose that our Lord knew all the details of each one's history
He met. *Trench.* A marvellous word, indeed, concerning an omniscient Lord.
Author.

---

19. The woman saith unto him, Sir, I perceive that thou art a prophet.

Saith. She was but *half* in earnest when she said, " Sir, give me
this water."

But she is *wholly* in earnest now. Yet our Lord presses not a confession.

It lies beneath the surface, and her seeming indifference only betrays the depth of the wound, made by the Divine archer.

Her word is a confession of the entire truth, for she does not attempt to escape from the Lord's rebuke.

His Spirit's grasp holds her, until the work of God is complete.

Some suppose a pause, since our Lord would reveal no more of her
life.

We know that with His *words* there went forth *a power* secretly
compelling. Matt. iv. 19, 20.

Perceive. She illustrates the truth that *sin* is the parent of all
our misery.

She had silenced conscience in part, now its voice rings out clearly.

" There is *no peace*, saith the LORD, unto the wicked." Isa. xlviii.
22.

Prophet. See on John i. 21. Since the fall, men have vainly
sought to pierce the future. 2 Kings xxi. 6.

Hence we find oracles sought by monarchs, sages, and hinds, to
obtain some disclosure of futurity.

Future events were professedly foretold by divination among
Greeks and others by consulting the entrails of beasts, flight
of birds, &c.

Ancient *Druids* would slay a man, and watch the way he fell.

Some *enchanters* pretended to reveal secrets by magic or charms, Lev. xix. 26 ; others by the planets, eclipses, clouds, &c., Deut. xviii. 10.

Sorcerers, by occult science and by arts, of which the multitude were ignorant. Ex. vii. 11

Magicians used familiar spirits, pretending to commune with devils.

Necromancers pretended to call up the dead, and obtain their secrets.

Narrative of witch of Endor shows how Saul had thus offended God.

Some of the prophets had *direct* communication with God, 2 Kings xvii. 13 ; Jer. xxv. 4, and others by visions and dreams. Job iv. 13.

From Samuel, 1100 B.C., to Malachi, 410 B.C., there was a regular succession.

Not prophets, but Levites, had charge of the religious instruction of the people.

False prophets fostered idolatry,—idolatry flattered the oracles in turn.

Hence necromancy, passing through fire, &c., were forbidden. Deut. xviii. 10, 11.

Prophecy oft connected with music. 1 Sam. x. 5. Miriam. Exod. xv. 20.

About a *hundred* years after the Babylonian exile prophecy ceased.

Sacred books having been collected, prophets were no longer needed.

Ark of the Covenant had been taken away for the same reason.

Schools of the prophets at Bethel and Gilgal were taught by Elijah, Elisha, and Samuel. Amos had not this training, vii. 14, 15.

They were national poets, historians, preachers of patriotism, extraordinary exponents of the moral law.

Their duty was to reprove kings and denounce judgments on nations.

THE PROPHET of ALL AGES, JESUS CHRIST, THE ETERNAL SON of GOD !

Our Lord spoke to the hidden man of the heart. 1 Pet. iii. 4.

Jews looked chiefly for a *kingly* Messiah, Samaritans for a *prophet.*

All was not right. He knew it, and He made her know it also.

She had sinned against heaven, perhaps He might tell her how to obtain forgiveness.

Light and darkness fought for the mastery, but the undertone of her words is, " Yea, Lord, I am a sinful woman."

λέγει. With woman's dexterity, she turns to a foreign theme. *J. G. Müller.* Profoundly ashamed, she would divert His attention. *Hase, Ebrard.* Neither diversion nor evasion. *Stier.* The question with her is confession. *Luthardt.*
προφήτης. ENCHANTMENTS by serpents. *Gesenius.* OBSERVERS of TIMES, from the moving of clouds. *Lee.* By birds. *Fuller.* SORCERY, speaking magic words. *Gesenius.* Sleight of hand. *Patrick.* MAGICIANS, mutterers. *Bochart.* Divined by fire. *Lee.* CHARMERS, gathering a crowd, &c., e.g. serpents or beasts. *Ludolphus.* Out of fascination. *Gesenius.* FAMILIAR SPIRIT. Calls forth the dead. *Gesenius.* Spirit of damnation. *Lee.* PROPHETS. Sprang up after the age of Samuel. *Stanley.* Questioned by *Hengst.* A man to whom announcements were made. *Bunsen, Davidson.* " Nàbi," officially of the prophetic order. *Havernick.* Prophecy connected with poetry. *Steinberk.* All prophecies conditional. *Koster.* Questioned by *Hengst.* Symbolic deeds a part of their vision, not really done. *Calvin, Hengst.* Samuel not a priest nor a Levite. *Stanley.* Both Levite and priest. *Meyrick* in *Smith.* These things had been unknown to her countrymen. *W. H. Mill.* She had given up her life of sin. *Williams.* There is no evidence of this. *Author.*

---

20. Our fathers worshipped in this mountain ; and ye say, that in Jerusalem is the place where men ought to worship.

Our fathers. Some refer to the founders of the Samaritan worship and nation, rather than the patriarchs.

The profane heart ever prefers *tradition* to revelation.

But the fathers are often charged with rites which they would have abhorred.

Jacob was actually *slandered*, instead of *honoured*, by this Samaritan.

A man hating a *spiritual* service will, like Saul, go to the Bible for authority.   Acts xxii. 3 ; Gal. i. 14.

Reviving rites of ancient Judaism is like lighting up candles at noonday.

Even a profligate is glad at times to claim acquaintance with some known Christian.

Having acknowledged Him a prophet, we look for her to *confess her sin.*

But it is hard to humble the carnal mind when it is disturbed.

" My wicked heart would slight the word of God."   *Henry Martyn.*

Religious discussion united with *profligacy* is one of the curious conditions of our fallen nature.

Stranger still, the very *pirates* and *robbers* of *Italy, Greece,* and *Spain* offer up daily prayers.

They use these things as a *shield* for conscience.

This verifies the sad truth, " The heart is deceitful above all things, and desperately wicked." Jer. xvii. 9.

Worshipped. Gr. *salute* with profound reverence, to adore.

Greeks always used this word in their approaches to their gods.

Anciently, and at present, many worship by *prostrating* the body. Rev. xix. 10.

" He fell on his face to the ground." 1 Sam. xx. 41. Elijah cast himself upon the earth. 1 Kings xviii. 42.

Our Lord Himself went forward and fell on the ground. Mark xiv. 35.

The writer saw an *Armenian* in *Jerusalem* prostrate himself on the floor 24 times before the image of Mary.

At times they clasped *the knees.* Matt. xxviii. 9. Greeks consecrated the ears to memory, and the eyes to faith, but the knees to mercy.

Others kissed the ground. Psa. lxxii. 9. In the Mosques all must either *stand* or *kneel.*

Standing during prayer formerly and still practised by Jews in their synagogues.

Our Saviour's words imply that the custom was general, " When ye stand praying." Mark xi. 25.

Among the Romans *prostration* was exclusively an act of *adoration.* Acts x. 25.

It is still so understood by those approaching the Pope.

Hebrew word " *bow* " means also to *bless,* persons thus received blessing.

However lost to virtue, she and the Pharisees, *yet they must worship God.*

Conscience holds strange supremacy over the *good and vile.*

Greek pirates who had murdered a crew, testified in court at Malta that they had rigidly avoided tasting meat during the whole of Lent. *Dr. Goodall.*

This mountain. Mountains selected for their silence, shade, solemn grandeur, and nearness to the gods.

Samaritans circumcised their children in the name of Gerizim.

Abraham met Melchizedek here, who was buried on this mount.

The Jews in their turn appealed to " the fathers " also. John **vi.** 31.

No sin in its *power* and *subtilty* equals hypocrisy.

It is expressly condemned as " a form of godliness, but denying the power." 2 Tim. iii. 5.

" *This mountain.*" Gideon and Manoah built altars by divine command on high places, as well as Elijah.

Her words imply, " Before I can receive the gift of God I must know where I shall pray for it."

Although their temple was ruined, the sanctity of the place remained.

Mount Gerizim is unsurpassed in beauty of scenery, except by Mount of Olives.

Tradition is divided between Gerizim and Olives as to Abraham's offering.

Gerizim was to the Samaritans as Jerusalem to Jews, or Mecca to Moslems.

She might say, We have *sinned with our fathers* in this place, and we are resolved to remain in our ignorance.

Mark how her mind turned to the *place, His* to the mode of worshipping.

She seems stunned by the unexpected revelation of her past life.

She saw herself all disclosed, but rallied to parry the home-thrust.

She is not prepared to confess her guilt, hence she seeks to change the topic.

But she is tempted to ask the wonderful stranger to settle the question, that had for ages parted Jew and Samaritan.

How the heart contests every inch, in its thorough humiliation.

Our Lord tersely and pertinently led her on. Common teachers would have said, " That is not the point now," but He sheds light where it was dark, until she saw standing before her the *object* of *worship* in HEAVEN AND ON EARTH.

Ye say. Religion no *hearsay suppositions*, nor penance, nor aught of will-worship, but a HOLY LIFE.

Her words almost involve, If this be so, we have no right in the well of Jacob, nor in the life of God.

Jerusalem. The site of the temple, home of God's worship, was chosen by a miracle. 2 Chron. iii. 1.

Mount Moriah was the divinely-appointed place for Isaac's sacrifice. Gen. xxii. 2.

" I have chosen Jerusalem, that my name may be there." 1 Kings ix. 3.

In the calendar of prophecy our Lord beholds millennial times, when every place on earth shall become a real Jerusalem.

" From the rising to the setting of the sun, in *every place*, incense,"
&c. Mal. i. 11.

Worship. Prayer at morning and evening sacrifice, 6th and 9th
hours, that is, at 12 and 3 P. M.

Some devout Jews prayed three times a day. Dan. vi. 10.

Moslems, like Peter, are often seen praying on the house-top. Acts
x. 9.

They may remain invisible if they choose (Deut. xxii. 8), but they
are the Pharisees of the heathen world.

οἱ πατέρες. Samaritan ancestors. *Meyer, Alford*. Ephraimites. *Mede*.
Adam, Seth, Noah having no kin to Hebrews. *Trench*.

τούτῳ τῷ ὄρει : τούτῳ, omitted. *Cod. Sinai*. Samaritan Pentateuch has
(Deut. xxvii. 4) Gerizim instead of Ebal. An interpolation of the Samaritans.
Gesenius, Kiel, &c. Daring change. *Usher, Prideaux*. Ebal correct. *Rosenm.,
Gesenius, Kuinoel, Stier*. Gerizim. *Whiston, Kennicott, Michaelis*. Mount
Gerizim is the Riblah. Tradition of Samaritans. *Ritter*. They call it the
house of God, nor did the deluge cover it. *Josephus*. Altars never ceased to be
built on high places. *Ewald*. Jews limited to *one* altar, to counteract this
superstition. Deut. xii.

τῷ ὄρει. On no spot on earth has worship been sustained so many thousand
years as on Gerizim. *Stanley*. Moses commanded an altar there. *Dathe*.
Samaritan tradition is, Paradise was on this mount. Adam was made of its
dust, and reared his first altar here. Here Isaac was offered. *Petermann* in
Herzog.

προσεκύν. Greek, to kiss toward God with the hand. Job xxxi. 27.
Adored by sacrifice. *Rheimish Notes*. No warrant for the statement. *Author*.

προσκ. Never is used in N. T. with sacrifices. Jews prayed with a veil,
but Paul rebukes. 1 Cor. xi. 4. Greek priests prayed bareheaded, Romans
veiled. *Hodge*. Hebrew wives veiled out of reverence to husbands. *Lewis' Ant*.
Mahommed enjoins " *standing* " as the posture. *Michaelis*. Eight things ; 1.
Stand. 2. Face the temple. 3. Compose the body. 4. Adjust the dress. 5.
Fit his place. 6. Order his voice. 7. To bow. 8. To worship. *Maimonides*.
Prostration considered improper save for a holy man, like Joshua. *Lewis' Ant*.
She hesitated to commune further with a Jew, until that point is cleared up.
Hengst. Her question honestly put for information. *Stier, Alford*.

---

21. Jesus saith unto her, Woman, believe me, the hour cometh, when ye shall
neither in this mountain, nor yet at Jerusalem, worship the Father.

Saith. His answer is from a far higher standpoint than she expected.

No one, uninspired, could have looked for such a sublime prediction.

His prophetic glance beheld the Spirit strike off these fetters.

He saw Circumcision enlarged to Baptism, and the Passover to the

Lord's Supper, proving that the " Free Spirit," Psa. li. 12, confers liberty. 2 Cor. iii. 17.

His prophecy embraced all the Samaritan converts. Acts viii. 1, 25.

Believe me. Faith. See on John i. 7 ; vii. 38. A phrase nowhere else used by our Lord as far as recorded.

A fact new, and quite incredible to this ignorant Samaritan.

He does not add, in the spirit of the Jews, " We worshipped in the right place."

His words refer to her admission, " Thou art a prophet," and imply that she should confess faith in Him.

" The hour cometh " when heathen, Samaritan, and Jew will " see my glory." Isa. lxvi. 18.

Hour. John iv. 52. A customary formula of prophetic announcement.

Not that the period will be brief, but the commencement is near.

Ye shall. He did not say " *we*," but " *ye*," Jews and Samaritans.

He ever maintained His dignified DISTINCTION FROM ALL HUMANITY !

He is ever consistent, an incidental proof of His *Divinity*.

Neither. She asks as to the place, our Lord replies as to the manner and the object.

He would turn her mind entirely from mere forms.

He introduces a new name, apart from the God of Abraham, and speaks of " Father."

He *abrogates* with the sovereign right of Jehovah Himself, Deut. xii. 5, 6, and 2 Chron. vii. 12, " I have chosen this place."

The ark, Shechinah, and altar were there, and there must they bring their offerings.

As if He had said, This point of dispute, of so much importance to you *now*, will lose all its significance.

This levels for ever the " middle wall of partition " between Jew and Gentile. Eph. ii. 14.

He lifts the dispute into a higher sphere, where its conditions are unknown.

An instructive contrast with that exacting zeal, ever shown by ritualists.

The Christian Church takes the place of the demolished synagogue and temple. Heb. vii. 27.

He would not dash her hopes by saying she and her people were all in the wrong, until He had told her how *soon* all this would come to an end.

The Church hitherto had moved among worldly elements, Gal. iv.
  3, and had not disdained owning a worldly sanctuary, Heb.
  ix. 1, but soon it will be divorced for ever. Mal. i. 11.

God is only known by those to whom He reveals Himself.

He is only worshipped by those whom He has taught how to worship Him.

Samaritanism, like Paganism, was an *invented* religion, and all such
  empty forms are like a temple without Deity.

The altar they reared was built " TO THE UNKNOWN GOD ! "   Acts
  xvii. 23.

Mountain.   See on John iv. 20 ; vi. 3. " The high and lofty *One*
  inhabiteth eternity," Isa. lvii. 15, " yet He hath respect unto
  the lowly." Psa. cxxxviii. 6.

Men have ever thought mountains nearer to God, and prayers there
  more quickly heard.

But here He corrects this delusion,—the " lowly," the " humble,"
  those in the valleys, are first heard.

Hence He withdraws from the Pharisee pressing close to the
  " HOLY of HOLIES," and goes to the publican " afar off."

The Father.   First person in the adorable Trinity. Rom. xvi.
  27 ; 2 Cor. xiii. 14 ; Matt. xxviii. 19.

An implied antithesis between " our fathers " and " THE FATHER."

This was a chord in her heart, touched by a Master's hand.

She who had had five husbands, had a FATHER in *heaven !*

It was the dawn of a new day to her, to feel that the God of the
  distant hills and sky bore that tender relation to her.

She had said " worship," our Lord adds " THE FATHER."

Jerusalem destroyed, no religious *centre* was left to superstition.

Christianity is designed for the world, and would make every city
  a *Jerusalem.*

The *heart*, not the surroundings, renders our worship acceptable.

No word of the Lord afterward sounded so strangely in apostolic ears.

Like a thunder-bolt it dashed the towering pride of the Jews, for
  everything known to the nation rendered such a thing *improbable.*

SPIRIT worship is spiritual, reverential, free from idolatry. 1 Pet.
  ii. 5.

His INFINITY assures that worship may be offered in any place
  and under any circumstances.

His ETERNITY, that the righteous will rejoice, and incorrigibly
  wicked will mourn.

His UNCHANGEABLENESS, that His purposes of love and justice are
immutable.

His WISDOM, that all will result in good to the holy, and in retribution to the unbelieving.

His POWER, that His friends are safe, but woe to those who resist
His will.

His HOLINESS, that repentance, faith, and obedience are absolutely
necessary.

His JUSTICE, that sin cannot pass with impunity,—and a day of
judgment a certainty.

His MERCY, that we should be grateful for His kindness, and resigned under the evils of life.

His TRUTH, that the careless have reason to fear. He cannot be deceived.

Samaritans were not *forced* to go to Jerusalem to worship.   Acts
viii. 14.

The crusaders needed not the sepulchre to aid them to heaven.

All local superstitions are thus swept away for ever. 1 Tim. ii. 8.

" YE SHALL WORSHIP THE FATHER."   He graciously admits her to
the household of faith.

πίστευσόν.   " *Dico nobis* " to His disciples. " *Crede mihi* " to the Samaritan.   He addresses them according to their privileges. *Bengel.*
τῷ ὄρει.   The temple was burnt despite all Titus' efforts, at the *same hour*
that at Delphi was consumed by thunderbolts, and torn by earthquakes.
Goodwyn's Moses and Aaron.
προσκυνήσετε.   Our Lord predicts the conversion of Samaritans. *Brucker.*
All mankind. *B. Crusius, Stier.*   Our Lord's *expansive views above* all na-
tionalities, admitted even by Spinoza. *Dorner*, vol. iii, p. 262.   Spiritual worship by all converted heathen. Mal. i. 11. *Hengst.*   Every place except Egypt
and Assyria. *Michaelis.*   Local sacredness abolished even *preferences* for other
places than Jerusalem, hinted at. *Bengel.*
τῷ πατρί, expression well-nigh equivalent to " My Father." *Stier.* Tacita
oppositio noted by *Calvin.*

---

22. Ye worship ye know not what : we know what we worship : for salvation is of the Jews.

Ye worship.   They *sincerely* believed they were right.

" Liberals " affirm they were therefore safe, but our Lord definitely
pronounces that *sincerity of heart* will *not* avail as a plea in
judgment.

A worship of their own invention was honour not paid to *Jehovah.*

Rejecting all promise of a Messiah, they cut themselves off from hope.

Nadab and Abihu lighting the altar with common fire, God refused altar, fire, priest, and sacrifice.

The same fire which before consumed the sacrifice now consumes the sacrificers.

The sons of a ruler of Israel for the first sin are struck dead.

Their father set up a false god, and they bring false fire to the true God.

Turks hold themselves the only true Mussulmen, i.e. believers.

The Stoics thought themselves the only wise men on earth. *Lucian.*

The Chinese assume theirs to be the celestial empire, and their books the perfection of wisdom.

Worshippers of the Virgin Mary deem themselves the only true Church, and infidels boast themselves as liberal and free above all others.

Ye know not what. There was one flaw in their devotion, but that was *fatal.*

One single defective link in the anchor chain, and woe to the vessel in a storm.

It is the *nature of love to call evil, evil.* Hence He will not disguise their wilful folly.

Their worship rested on *no* Divine ground, hence they knew neither *how, where,* nor *whom,* and were without hope in GOD.

They imposed upon themselves a *mere mask,* and hence were void of consolation at death.

Without a living trust in Christ, each sinner bears an empty aching heart.

Every form of *will-worship,* whether of circumcision or baptism, of mass or communion, is here condemned, and its fruit is *ever-increasing darkness and misery.*

Heathenism, Liberalism, Rationalism, and Formalism differ only in name.

Hence Jews, rejecting Jesus, to this hour worship they know not what.

He who dwelt between the Cherubim had appointed " THE WAY OF LIFE." Jer. xxi. 8.

But the Samaritan religion was a device, and could render no help to finding God.

Three hundred years they had been offering vain oblations. Isa i. 13.

Hence the uncompromising *severity* of the Saviour's verdict.

Samaritans offered aid for the erection of the temple, but the Jews refused. The time for their adoption and union was yet afar off. God, not man, must determine when that hour should arrive.

Samaritans resented the refusal of the Jews, and the mutual antipathy has lasted *two thousand years.*

Their land was ever the home of superstition, of Baal worshippers, of enchanters, of fanatics.

The Jew was cold and formal, measuring all things by profit.

He grew a worshipper of Mammon, yet he clung to the shadow of a glorious substance.

Many who verily *believe* they worship *God*, will find their error too late.

Because they have never humbly asked God for light.

Man is responsible for his religious opinions and practices, although virtually *denied* by *Lord Brougham.*

In this, as in all other things, " Whatsoever a man soweth, that shall he also reap." Gal. vi. 7.

Salvation is the key-note of all true worship. Rev. vii. 10.

God revealed and intrusted to Abraham His plan of mercy.

The dying Jacob trusted it : " I have waited for thy salvation." Gen. xlix. 18.

Aged Simeon knew it : " Mine eyes have seen thy salvation." Luke ii. 30.

Our Saviour here places *His Divine seal* on the O. T. economy.

It was the *aloe-tree*, unsightly, but blossoming in *one consummate flower*, and having fulfilled its mission, it was doomed to wither and die.

We know. He well knew the depths of Jewish apostasy, but they had the true revelation.

Our Lord speaks more favourably of the Jews to aliens, than to themselves.

He asserts this claim at the very moment He seemed breaking down all distinction of nations before the FATHER.

He makes Himself the representative of the elect of God among them.

We. Our Lord takes common part with the chosen people.

The only place in the Gospels in which He *identifies Himself* with the Jewish race.

He refers to a *class* among the worshippers of God. With them He was one.

Worship. Our Saviour as *man* must have some nationality.

Although Divine, no prophet or martyr *actually* or more *fervently* ever served his God.

" *He went into a mountain to pray, and continued all night.*" Luke vi. 12.

Yet as God, *He* is also worshipped even by angels : " Let all the angels," &c.   Heb. i. 6.

Salvation.   His answer embraces the character of God as revealed in His atonement.

Greeks had often used this term, but *how wide* were they from the true meaning.

Of the Jews.   John' i. 19. This knowledge is alone found in Moses and the *prophets*.   Isa. ii. 3.

Proud philosophy and unbelief in every age are offended.

Celsus and *Julian* seem to feel insulted to be in debt to poor Galileans.

Yet Judea, an humble province in Asia, was the source of salvation to the world.

Divine counsel has been attesting this truth for 1800 years.

The world's salvation will ever be linked with the Jewish people. Zech. viii. 23 ; Rom. xi. 12.

All nations were to be blessed through this line.   Gen. xlix. 10.

" I will give thee for a light to the Gentiles, that *thou* mayest be MY salvation to the ends of the earth."   Isa. xlix. 6.

Samaritanism and all "isms" without an atoning Saviour have no *salvation* for their disciples.

Since Jews can only be saved by *faith* in *revelation*, none can be safe without it.

If salvation be linked with Christ, all Christ-rejecters will be found related to His " many mansions " only as the despisers of Noah were to his ark in the flood.

Millennial glory will be connected with the restoration of the ancient people.

" The Lord will build up Zion when He shall appear in His glory."

The faith of Abraham, of Daniel, of Isaiah, is not now found with Jews.

Their creed and religious life show *not* the signature of the living God.

Perhaps the rich man (Luke xvi. 29) may have had an orthodox creed, although after death " he opened his eyes in hell."

Mark our Lord's infinite prudence : He did not assault the open impiety of Sadducees in presence of Pharisees.

Nor the pomp and hypocrisy of Pharisees to soothe the conscience
  of Sadducees.
Among Sadducees He established the doctrine of the resurrection.
Among Pharisees He inculcated charity and a holy life.
Among Samaritans He vindicated the truth sacredly held by Jews.
Sectarian bigotry makes each article of faith a ground of quarrel,
  every quarrel a faction, every faction zealots, and all zealots
  pretend to be for God.
Zealots and Ritualists outnumber believers, since these false lights
  flatter the human heart.
Our Lord honours the Jewish *faith*, while He calls *them* a " gen-
  eration of vipers."   Matt. xxiii. 13, 33.

ὅ, neuter, hints their ignorance of God's personality. *Alford.* Samaritans
doubtless were heathens, as *Latins, Copts, Greeks,* at present in Palestine.
Author.
οὐκ οἴδατε, what man may hope from Him, i.e. He is a Saviour. *Luthardt.*
A significant want of an object. *Stier.*   Why were they left in ignorance of the
true God?   Only another form of the question, Why are any left to heathenism
now ? Rom. ix. 18, 19, 20. *'Hengst.*
ἡμεῖς.   The only instance of our Lord thus speaking.   Infidels early began
to torture this into a confession of His mere humanity, used as the word "weary,"
verse 6. *Tittmann.*   We Jews. *Chrys.*   Because He speaks as a Jew. *Alford.*
He actually worshipped in Jerusalem. *Author.*   Only the Lord and His disciples. *Semler, Henke.*   All Jews. *Stier.*   We know, since Providence has
revealed it to me. *Barhdt.*   Touching the family He belonged to. *D. Brown.*
ὅτι.   Not simply a consequence, but cause.   σωτηρία equivalent to σωτήριόν,
Luke ii. 30. *Tittmann, Olshausen.*   The Saviour of Jewish extraction. *Kuinoel.*
His advent. *Chrys.*   The salvation, a prophecy distinctly denied by Samaritans.
Alford.   Messianic *method* of salvation, not merely the Messianic *idea. Hengst.*

---

23. But the hour cometh, and now is, when the true worshippers shall worship the Father in spirit and in truth : for the Father seeketh such to worship
him.

Hour.   Here not brief duration, but near approach.
Our Lord had spoken of the *place,* now He speaks of the *manner.*
This future, already commenced, was long foretold.   Jer. iii. 16 ;
  Hag. ii. 7—10.
Cometh.   In all its strength, lustre, and perfection, the dawn will
  yield to noon-day.
It was even then opening through the speaker, but the world
  knew Him not.

The veil of shadows and types which had obscured it for many ages, was about to be rent.

A worship wide and deep as the heart of humanity was about to be set up.

The rending of the temple veil from the top to the bottom the signal note.

True worshippers. Once they sacredly and rightfully used *forms, vestments, rites,* &c., but now a new order of things under the New Covenant is at hand.

The great question will not be *where?* but *how* can God be served?

Worshippers at Jerusalem will not be *accepted* for praying there.

Nor the Samaritans of Gerizim *rejected* for worshipping there.

He *can't miss the place* who *knows, honours, trusts,* and *loves* God.

Rejecting all but Moses, they knew not the prophecies of the Messiah.

Now the time is come when ceremonial observances will yield to spiritual ordinances, for legal services were *figures* of the true. Heb. ix. 24.

The Church of God of all ages is a family, same in *spirit,* same in *faith,* same in *love.*

" Ye are come unto Mount *Zion,*" Heb. xii. 22, instead of *Sinai,* pointing to those under the *cloud* of types and shadows.

In spirit. An antithesis to all externals of place, time, or circumstances.

Implies dependence on the Eternal Spirit for *strength, sincerity, truth,* and *zeal.* Psa. li. 6.

Man needs *forms* of thought and faith as *vehicles* for devotion.

But poor human nature is ever prone to rely on the *form,* thus practically denying the *power* of godliness. 2 Tim. iii. 5.

True devotion is not confined to holy *places.* Noah in the ark, Abraham in Egypt, Jacob in the desert, Moses in the wilderness, David watching sheep, Joseph in prison, Joshua amid wars, Josiah on the throne, Daniel in the den, Hebrew youths in the furnace, thief on the cross, Stephen stoned, all *worshipped in spirit.* God blessed the dwelling of Abinadab and Obed-edom. 1 Sam. vii. ; 1 Chron. xv. 18 ; 1 Kings viii. 27.

A tree with leaves and fruit, but *girdled,* is a dead tree, doomed to the flames.

A purely ritual worship will only suit a *ritual* god.

Sacrifices instead of thanksgiving. Psa. l. 8, 14. Rivers of oil instead of justice, &c. Mic. vi. 7, 8.

Paganism of Greeks and Romans *needed* pompous ceremonies. Being nothing themselves, they must *seem* to be something.

Long-continued rites, even those of Christian Churches, have darkened into a very midnight among Copts, Greeks, Armenians, and Latins in the East, until they differ in nothing from the heathen.

A poor Spartan, travelling from his mountain hut, and seeing the posts of houses *squared* and *carved*,—asked if the trees thus grew ?

" *Thou desirest* NOT *sacrifice.*" " *Thou delightest* NOT *in burnt-offerings.*" Psa. li. 16.

In truth. This regards the outward form : " **In spirit,**" the inward power.

The first strikes at *idolatry*, the second warns against *hypocrisy*.

Contrast this with the *heartless irreverence* found among " Liberals " and other enemies of the gospel.

The Lord is far from those failing to call upon Him in truth. Psa. cxlv. 18.

Yet *sacramental* forms are binding, although so sadly abused.

But *no rite can claim authority* without " Thus saith the Lord."

" To obey is better than sacrifice." 1 Sam. xv. 22. " Offer unto God thanksgiving." Psa. l. 14. " I will have mercy, not sacrifice." Hos. vi. 6.

The Epistle to the Hebrews is an extended commentary on this text.

Father. In the beatitudes it is " *your* Father ; " in the Lord's prayer " *Our* Father ; " at Lazarus' tomb " Father ; " in Gethsemane " MY FATHER."

By nature He is our *Creator*, but rebels cannot call their king father. Rom. viii. 15.

By grace He is our Father. Children alone can presume to use this name.

All unrenewed ones are children of wrath. John iii. 36. Children of Satan. John viii. 44.

Every man's instinct makes him feel himself *God's fallen child*.

Seeketh. How should this *kindle* devotion ! God is *seeking* for such ; alas, they are few, for the gate is strait. When God comes to inquire for His people, the question will not be, who worshipped at Jerusalem, or Gerizim,—another touchstone will be used.

Our Lord notes His own mission. At that very moment " He came to seek," &c. Luke xix. 10.

God's boundless compassion in this redemption is the wonder of
angels ! 1 Pet. i. 12.

Spirit of God ever " seeking " implies His grace is ever making true
worshippers. 1 Pet. i. 11.

The woman felt this stranger was seizing her heart for God.

Such. " Let me see thy face and hear thy voice." Cant. ii. 14.
He solicits suitors.

Him. Divine personality, worship must receive its perfect expression.

ἐν πνεύματι. The Holy Spirit. *Basil, Athanasius, Chrys.* Integrity in
the human soul, *usus loquendi,* and sense. *Tittmann.*

ἐν πνεύματι refers to the Jews, ἀληθεία to the Samaritans, in earnestness.
Luther. Inwardly and sincerely. *Stier.* *Deus est animus, hic tibi præcipue
sit purâ mente colendus. Cato* in *Lampe.*

ζητεῖ signifies loving as well as seeking. *Euripides.* Requireth. *Tyndale,
Cranmer,* and *Geneva.*

καὶ construed with ζητεῖ. *Meyer.* Who then seeks as well as the Father.
Stier. The woman felt the mysterious stranger's equality with God. *Roos.*

ὁ πατήρ. He never spoke thus to unbelieving Jews. *D. Brown.*

ἐστιν added to show the spot was not in Judea. *Bengel.*

---

24. God is a Spirit; and they that worship him must worship him in spirit
and in truth.

A Spirit. Gr. *Spirit,* article omitted. Hebrew and Greek express
the infinite perfection and glory of the Divine nature.

It suggests the *vital, overflowing, abounding energy* of Jehovah.

Our Lord implies that Jerusalem as well as Gerizim will have a
purer worship.

Samaritans held more strongly than the Jews *the unity of God.*

Spirit. The profoundest word in human language.

Invisibility, immateriality, omnipresence, eternity, are abstrac-
tions to us.

But **Spirit** implies truth, wisdom, holiness, power, mercy, unchangeableness.

To the idea of a *living God living worship* must be added. Heb. ix.
14 ; Rom. xii. 1.

God is the ONLY PURE SPIRIT. He is *energy, life, mind, will,
activity,* infinitely and eternally.

In vain do we attempt to grasp the fulness of this word.

Had He revealed the *essence* of *Divinity, we* could not comprehend it.

Light enters and fills the eye, but no man understands it.

The sun is as deep a mystery now as 6000 years since.

" In a temple wouldst thou pray ? pray within thyself." *Augustine.*

Only be thou first a temple of God, since He will hear thee in His temple. 1 Cor. iii. 17.

To become this temple is *the* " gift of God." John iv. 10.

God's spirituality the ground-tone of all O. T. revelation.

Man was spiritual at first, Gen. ii. 7 ; became *carnal* by the fall ; and by THE SPIRIT he returns to *spiritual* life. Eph. i. 19 ; 2 Cor. iv. 13.

Honouring God with the mouth enjoined, but as the expression of the *spirit.* Isa. xxix. 13.

The same word signifies *spirit* and *wind,* in Greek. See on John iii. 5—8.

The wind "bloweth where it listeth," on hill, vale, or ocean. So God is everywhere, on Gerizim and Mount Zion.

Who can without impiety " limit the Holy One of Israel"? Psa. lxxviii. 41.

Essentially *free,* but a *living power* to all that dwell on the earth.

Worship. Only as His *children* can we worship our *Father* in spirit.

Our love *for* Him can only proceed *from* Him.

The conversation with Nicodemus is thus here reproduced.

Philosophy false and boastful, is put to shame before the truth.

For four thousand years all the sages of earth could not evolve this one simple but sublime truth.

All their learning and thought must pale before the humble teacher of a female outcast, at the solitary well in Samaria.

What a comment on the vain-gloryings of philosophy and science. 1 Cor. i. 20.

Humanity, to turn to God, must know it has a Son of God in heaven.

Gerizim, Mecca, and Jerusalem can never satisfy the soul's longings.

Nicodemus, equally with the woman of Samaria, will ever remain *without* until ONE comes and *opens the door.*

In spirit. Mere *forms* and *rites* can no more satisfy a spiritual God, than *incense* can appease a hungry man.

As the Angel of the Covenant consigned Manoah's feast to the
flames, so does God, a Spirit, consume all ritualistic schemes
that have no " Thus saith the Lord."

Yet spiritual worship does not reject material expression and form.

He alone who bows the knees of his *heart* bows the *bodily* knees
aright.

Our Lord humbles this sinner, by drawing aside the veil of the
false worship she *trusted* in.

How many within the church doors worship a God *afar off*.

Here the worshipper must become one with God : " I IN THEM, and
THOU IN ME." John xvii. 23.

As God's omnipresence, so His Spirit, and praying in the Spirit
is the highest act of life.

Syrians confessed they could not contend with the gods of the
hills.

The believer in the vale, or on the mount, or in the cave, or on
the ocean, saith, " Thou, God, seest me."

" Surely God is in this place," exclaimed Jacob, " and I knew it
not." Gen. xxviii. 16.

Worship stripped of its vestments and sacrifices, preserved its
essence, spirituality.

A solemn standing *protest* of the Lord against mere ritualism.

Spiritless forms, like tall, fair, dead trees, are hollow and sapless.

Formalists act religion as a *pageant of piety*. " God desireth truth."
Psa. li. 6.

The ostrich hath wings, but never leaves the earth, to fly towards
heaven.

The Lord shows that specially sacred places passed away with types.

Yet the house of the Lord will ever be precious to pious hearts.

Those who refuse attendance on the ordinances of God's house
soon neglect all devotion.

Private worship will not be long maintained when *public* worship
is disregarded.

Truth. The inseparable accompaniment of all *real* worship.

All other is a mockery, a " form without power." 2 Tim. iii. 5.

Penance in a thousand modes, by Protestant, as well as Papist, is
trusted.

In manifold ways men still " give the fruit of the body for the sin
of the soul." Micah vi. 7.

Blood of lambs, temple services, new moons, sabbaths, and spread
hands were all *commanded*. Isa. i. 10—15.

But without the *heart* God calls them an abomination.   Isa. i. 13.
Cain's gift, Gen. iv. 5, and Saul's sacrifice, were irreligious and
    profane. 1 Sam. xv. 30.
" Wherewith shall I come before the Lord ? " Micah vi. 6.   Poor
    depraved human nature ever dreams of merit.
This wondrous dialogue begins with a cup of water, and ends with
    the most sublime revelation of the NATURE of GOD and HIS
    WORSHIP.
A sign of plenary inspiration :   To the mind of this woman and
    the approaching disciples, our Lord had but one solitary
    hearer—while *He knew* His words were reaching untold
    millions of listening angels, and would reach millions of men
    and women to salvation.
He spent more time and patience in preaching this sermon than in
    building up the Alps or Andes.
The third chapter interprets these words.—GOD BECAME ONE FLESH
    WITH US, THAT WE MAY BECOME ONE SPIRIT WITH HIM !

Πνεῦμα, only incorporeal. *Chrys.* Necessary source of all life. *Tittmann.*
Embracing truth, knowledge, wisdom, and power. *Bengel.* Spirit, ἀλήθεια.
Christ absolute truth. *Athanasius.* Spirit, essence, not personality. *Alford.*
Frame of mind. *Luther, Calvin, Melancthon.* He opposes the outer to the
inner sanctuary. *Augustine.* A cultus without any form. *Tholuck.* God's
absolute sufficiency. *Rothe.* Spirituality the great anti-heathen principle.
Hoffmann. Connection established between the worship and His nature. *J.
Müller.*
   πνεῦμα does not fully express the Divine nature. *Fichte.* Man is not God's
temple, but made so by the Spirit. *Neander.* Spiritual element of worship noted
here as *new. Luthardt.* The old covenant spirit unable to overcome carnality.
Hengst. One being asked, What is God? answered, Si scirem Deus essem. *Plutarch.* "I think I know God, but attempting to explain, I find I know
nothing." *Augustine.* Persons, places, and times were chosen by Divine
wisdom, to this hour. *D. Brown.*
   προσκυνεῖν. As to forms, "the wine of devotion, without vessels to hold it,
will unavoidably be lost." *Trench.* But no vessel contains the *wind*, neither
can it the *Spirit.* Without His presence there can be no wine of devotion, Isa. i.
passim. *Author.* Boasted reason can produce no spirituality in *man*, but remains
flesh. Gössner.
   δεῖ. This cheerless δεῖ remains an insupportable barrier to all going to Gerizim or Jerusalem to seek after peace. *Stier.* Spirit and truth only distinguished by internal notes. *Oetinger.*
   ἐν σαρκί καί σκιᾷ is the antithesis. *Lücke.* All sensible worship is but
typical. *Gerlach.* The New Test. does not transform the Church into a meeting of Quakers, but imperatively demands the body should be used. *Roos.* A
living, holy, acceptable sacrifice unto God, Rom. xii. 1. *Author.* In this
sublime truth, uttered to an ignorant woman, the aristocracy of culture is overthrown. *Neander.*

25. The woman saith unto him, I know that Messias cometh, which is called Christ: when he is come, he will tell us all things.

I know. These traditions from prophecy floated among the common people.

Like legends of saints among the baptized heathen of Romish lands.

Messias. See on John i. 17, 41. A gently expressed question, " Art thou the Messias ? "

She hints she is not so ignorant as He intimated.

How quickly under His teaching was the heart of this sinful woman made capable of grasping exalted truths.

Cometh. Jacob's *Shiloh* was thus still found at Jacob's well. Gen. xlix. 10.

Proof from prophecy of the Messiahship of Jesus is complete.

For 1600 years God had sent a succession of prophets to testify, and the dispersed Jews scattered these prophecies through the heathen world.

Christ. This allusion would indicate she had *concealed* her suspicions He was the Christ.

Thus worldlings are *too proud honestly to confess* their convictions, even while their hearts are aching under the burden of sin.

Not unfrequently in the dying hour, a *seeming bravery* is assumed by infidels, since *consistency* requires they should be *heroes to the last.*

Her faith in the *near advent* of the Messiah as a spiritual teacher differed from the Jewish hope of a conquering hero.

Samaritans acknowledged the Pentateuch only ; Jews, all Scripture.

Will tell us, &c. She candidly confesses that darkness hangs over her mind.

She hopes Messiah's advent will reveal the whole depth of truth and duty.

In response to this longing, our Lord reveals Himself to her adoring wonder.

She knew He would be a Divinely enlightened teacher. Deut. xviii. 15.

Her views of Christ were far more Scriptural than those of the Jews generally.

The Jewish mind was immersed deeply in sensuality.

They looked for a Messiah—a worldly *king ;* Samaritans for a Messiah —a Divine *Teacher.*

Μεσσίας. First used by Hannah, 1 Sam. ii. 10. Not found in Pentateuch. *Augustine.* Here a proper name. *Hengst.*

Χριστός. His word had quickened the miserable germ of Samaritan Messiah hope into life. *Lange.* Her ἔρχεται an echo of the Lord's ἔρχεται, verse 23. *Stier.* Speaks of a Samaritan restorer. *Sepp.* She uses a specific name not found in the Samaritan Canon. *Hengst.* Learned it from the prophets. *Ernesti.* Samaria's boundary only 14 miles from Jerusalem. *Author.* Samaritans dreamed of a returning Moses. *Von Raumier.* She founded her word on Deut. xviii. 15. *D. Brown.* Words of the woman, not the Evangelist. *Alford.*

ἀναγγελεῖ, a fact announced by authority. *Campbell, Alford.*

ἔρχεται. Christ called ἐρχόμενος, "The sent." It occurs but twice in N.T. *Trench.* She becomes dizzy under the Lord's sublime words. *Chrys.*

---

26. Jesus saith unto her, I that speak unto thee am he.

I. As if He had said, "Look for no other. Ask for no outward sign. I have uncovered thy secret life, and revealed to thee the truth. This is the *proof* of my Messiahship."

His manifested omniscience was intended to be to her instead of a miracle. Luke xvii. 17.

That speak. Our Lord observed studied reserve among the Jews as to His Messiahship, lest they should have rebelled against Rome.

Hence He enjoins secrecy on those to whom He did reveal it. Matt. xvi. 20.

I am. It took a long time for the disciples to learn this glorious fact. John xvi. 31.

I am : " He " not in the Greek. Name of Jehovah given to Moses. Ex. iii. 14.

This is the most explicit recorded declaration our Lord ever made of His Messiahship.

Why did He not respond to the question, " If thou be the Christ, tell us plainly " ? John x. 24. Because the Pharisees asked in malice, but this woman sought the truth in simplicity.

How promptly is her half-prayer answered, and how gloriously !

A wonderful proof of Divine sovereignty ; the Lord passes by the learned scribes and Pharisees, and reveals this truth, foretold for four thousand years, to an outcast from Samaria.

The next time it was to the *blind* beggar, He had met on the way and cured. John ix. 37.

Our Lord concealed His Messiahship from all but His disciples.

1. Only by His resurrection was the whole evidence completed.

2. Place and time strictly observed in the kingdom of God.

He *sealed* absolutely the lips of the witnesses of His transfiguration. Matt. xvii. 9.

In His entire ministry He was careful to avoid all parade or excitement. John vi. 15.

How perfectly God-like and how different from man. In the same
grandly silent manner He clothes the earth with verdure, and
causes the celestial machinery to move noiselessly. No one
observes the action of the sunbeam which enrobes the forests.
" His voice shall not be heard in the street." Isa. xlii. 2.

It is a *sad error* when teachers of the gospel refuse to impart its
mysteries to those the world calls ignorant.

An ancient, but wicked *jealousy*, " This man receiveth sinners."
Luke xv. 2.

Reception and belief of the truth depend on the presence and influence of the Spirit of God.

Luther's work, confined to the Church of God, remained, while that
of *Savonarola* came to nothing.

Had our Lord yielded to their pressure (John vi. 15) and become
a King, His plans would have been frustrated.

I am He! Equivalent to " *Ask, and receive the living water.*"

A solemn tender earnest of the time coming, " Behold me," &c.
Isa. lxv. 1.

To the outlying world of Samaria He first discloses His Messiahship.

The woman longed after the Revealer of heavenly truth. *He stands
before her.*

No sooner do we desire Christ, than He is at our side.

If our prayers be swifter than words, Christ is in the advance.

In tropical lands the sun rises without a dawn, but the Sun of
Righteousness had ages of prophetic dawn to precede Him,
and ages of miracles to follow Him.

Our Lord held His peace before *Herod*, but freely spoke to a despised *Samaritan.*

To the Jews He *proves*, but does not PUBLISH, this great fact.

To the *simple* and *docile* He reveals His grace and glory.

In Samaria no seditious tumults need be feared, for they cherished
no dreams of a conquering Messiah.

λέγει. He hastens to announce Himself before His disciples return. *Bengel.*
Questioned by *Stier.* The seventh and last word to the woman. *Anton.*
'Εγώ εἰμι indicates eternity. Equal to Ex. iii. 14. *Grotius, B. Crusius.*

Elohim refers to the outward character. Jehovah to His personal, moral
nature. *Hengst.*
    'Εγώ εἰμι. Not classical Greek. *Lücke.* Heathen thoughts never took
such a range. *Author.*

---

    27. And upon this came his disciples, and marvelled that he talked with the
woman: yet no man said, What seekest thou? or, Why talkest thou with her?

Disciples marvelled.   Instead of wondering why He talked with
    this poor woman, they might rather have asked why did He
    converse with themselves?
In Judea His conduct would have awakened no surprise, in
    Samaria jealousy is kindled.
To murmur in ignorance at God's sovereign acts is a sign of an
    envious heart.
Reverential silence prevented any one asking Him what He
    sought of her.
Sinister surmisings were hushed by the sight of INFINITE PURITY
    and INFINITE LOVE attracting the humble.
The neglected waterpot suggests no idea of a spiritual transaction,
    but how much more would they have wondered could they
    have read the heart-joy of the Divine Shepherd at finding
    this lost sheep.
Well may *we* marvel, also: Who but the SON of GOD could have
    invested *so simple an incident* with an *interest enduring as
    eternity!*
Talked.   The Oriental contempt for women here comes out
    strongly.
The disciples themselves had not unlearned this great wicked-
    ness.
Our Saviour has a claim on the adoring gratitude of every *female.*
The woman.   See on John viii. 3.   Article wanting in the Gr.,
    wondered He talked with *any woman at all.*
Dependence of the female fosters the tenderest mutual affection.
The high Bible standard of female relations shows its *Divine origin.*
Orientals make her a toy or a slave, flattering her in her gilded
    bondage.
Islamism, true to its savage spirit, holds her in perpetual child-
    hood.
Her *passions* receive excitement, her soul is ignored.
Anciently women tended flocks, Gen. xxix. 9; Exod. ii. 16, and
    ground corn, Job xxxi. 10.

They drew water for family use as well as for the flocks.   Gen.
xxiv. 20.

Thousands of females may now be seen thus employed, but not a
single *man*.   Luke xxii. 10.

Females are esteemed just in proportion as the Bible is believed
to be the Word of God.

Thus in Prussia and England the Bible lifts females to their
proper sphere, while in France and Spain, where the Bible is
neglected, women are degraded.

No man.   Some few at times were insolent (John viii. 48), but
levity generally seemed awed by the *indescribable majesty*
of the SON OF GOD.

It is a remarkable fact that while *no person* of eminence escapes
ridicule, our Saviour alone of all the race of Adam NEVER WAS
THE SUBJECT OF A SINGLE JEST.

Notices of *profound reverence*, John xii. 20—22; xiii. 22—24;
xvi. 17—19 ; xxi. 12 ; Mark ix. 32.

Said.   Dared to say.   He made men *feel* the presence of
Divinity.

Seekest ?   That is, no one asked her what object she had in addressing their Master.

Lowly as she was, she would hardly have dared first to accost
Him.

The *Syrophœnician* experienced His divine compassion, and the
Samaritan found Him ready to reveal His glory, as he had
never done to Jews.

Why ?   That He should have imparted spiritual gifts to a woman
never flashed through their minds.

ἐπὶ τούτῳ. The critical moment. *Peschito.* While He was speaking.
Stier.

ἐθαύμασαν. This was mingled with so much reverence, they dared not
judge Him. *Ber. Bib.* Esteemed Him a wonderful person. *Chrys.* "Cave,"
cried the Roman monks. Abraham may see Sodom burning, Lot may not.
Trapp.

γυναικὸς. Article understood. *Beza.* So poor a woman, therefore, omitted.
Tittmann. Females among Moslems and most barbarous tribes are esteemed
mere animals. A woman ought not to be wise above her distaff. *Rabbi Eleazar.*

λαλεῖς. Did the disciples hear His 'Εγώ εἰμι ? No. *Stier.* Had He asked
for food or drink ? *Grotius.* The dispute was about the national question.
B. Crusius. After many years, the scene is as vivid as though the Evangelist
was at Sychar rather than amid the tumult of Ephesus. *Maurice.* To the
Spirit that inspired him *past* and *future* are *present* and vivid too. *Author.*

28. The woman then left her waterpot, and went her way into the city, and saith to the men,

Woman. From the first her mind is impressed and her interest deepened, but His last word sealed her solemn resolve.

In the depths of her soul is heard, "I HAVE FOUND," "I HAVE FOUND," with emotions such as the *Sicilian* philosopher never conceived.

Her new-born rapture was responded to by the angels of God. Luke xv. 7.

Left. Our Lord well knew her object, and she retired in silence, as the disciples came.

Her feelings were too deep and overpowering to be continued, and one touch of the pen, " she left her waterpot," tells volumes.

The living water was already welling up from the depths of her soul.

Yes, she found, what millions of believers have rejoiced to learn, that " *man doth not live by bread alone.*"

> " There is a stream whose gentle flow
> Supplies the city of our God."—*Watts.*

Her waterpot would now only prove an encumbrance, as she hastens to tell her friends.

Went. Confidential solitude is disturbed,—Jewish countenances are on her.

Her gentle self-possession is gone. Her departure is a flight.

She neglects her waterpot, and the Lord His bread. Ver. 32.

The pitcher of earthly pleasure is for ever abandoned, as unsatisfactory.

Saul, under the Spirit, forgets his father's errand, just as grace made Peter and James forget net, ship, and gain, and this woman even Jacob's well.

Thus the healed in all places at once publish abroad the grace received. Mark vii. 36.

She had greater things on hand. Man can live awhile without bread.

Alexander, departing for India, scattered kingdoms among his generals, and when asked what he retained for himself, answered, HOPE.

The *urgency* of the Divine sender will make His messengers *urgent.*

All shame as to her immoral career is lost in a *mightier* emotion.
One forgets an ailing limb in efforts to save his burning home.

And saith. She becomes almost an apostle, and with far more
active zeal than Nicodemus.

She calls not only her friends, but nearly a whole village, to the
Redeemer.

She and Zacchæus met the Lord, *strangers* to their own hearts and
to God.

Note the expansive and creative power of grace : Matthew leaves
the receipt of custom. Matt. ix. 9. Peter, James, and John
forsook their nets. Mark i. 19. Saul gave up all. Acts ix. 20.

The woman who was "a sinner," Luke vii., the adulteress,
John viii., and the penitent malefactor, Luke xxiii., show
that the Holy One *cannot* be *limited* in His sovereignty.
Psal. lxxviii. 41.

ἀφῆκεν. Our Lord's method and its results : 1. He hints obscurely the
wants of the soul. 2. ʹDiscovers personal sin. 3. The woman shows a half
submission to omniscience. 4. Repentance. *Stier.* A sign she was coming
again. *Richter.* She left her waterpot, that the Lord might drink, and thus
ministered unto Him. *Bede.* In her joy she forgets it, as the disciples did their
nets, Matt. iv. 20. *Trench, J. Müller.* Messiah's thoughts absorbed her soul.
Chrys.

---

29. Come, see a man, which told me all things that ever I did : is not this
the Christ ?

Come. A new-born soul in its first spring of joy would bring *the
world* to Jesus.

Melancthon fondly believed the love of Jesus need only be told to
win the world to faith.

She joyfully knows and *triumphantly* proclaims that the Messiah has
come.

Words of Naaman's "little maid " were more powerful than those
of *Elijah* the prophet. 2 Kings v. 13.

A wonderful *paradox,* the Messiah announcing Himself in Gerizim.

Haughty Jews at Jerusalem would have laughed to scorn a Galilean announcing himself thus.

See. Gr. means *judge,* as well as *see,* i.e. search into and hear,
as I have done.

All things. In the disclosure of one thing her guilty conscience
heard all.

To a conscience aroused even *one sin fills the entire field of vision.*
She rests not so much on His declaration as on her own consciousness.

Some think our Lord told her many things not recorded.

But at midnight, *one* flash of lightning reveals a whole landscape.

The Divine glance made the page of her whole past life visible.

There stood one who knew all that was wrong, or right, in her.

Thus conscience began its solemn work in Eden : " Who told
thee ? " &c. Gen. iii. 11.

Conscience is immortal, as the memory of God, its *Author.*

Note the growth of her faith. 1. " I perceive thou art a prophet."
2. The question of high import, " *Is not this the Christ ?* "

Solomon answered the hard *questions* of the Queen of Sheba.

But our Lord, *without* a question, told her " all things " in her past
life.

Is not ? Her question presupposes " It is impossible He can be
any other."

Under this modest inquiry she conceals her *conviction* of His being
the Messiah.

A question gently arouses attention. Had she said, " This is the
Christ," all their *bigotry* would have been aroused.

" Must He not be the Christ for you, as He is for me ? " " Must
He not know all you ever did also ? "

He might not have the *marks of the king* looked for by the Sanhedrim. But for the poor despised dwellers in Samaria *He
is* THE CHRIST.

Christ. John i. 17. This is the theme of all N.T. preaching.
" We preach Christ." 1 Cor. i. 23.

She seems not to hint at the wonderful things revealed by Him,
but only to what referred to herself.

Her life being well known in a small village, their prejudices are
disarmed and her testimony received.

Δεῦτε. Requiring their judgment to confirm her supposition, since she is
about to join the female followers of Christ. *Braune.* Not implied. *Stier.*

πάντα. Prudence seen in withholding Christ's confession concerning Himself, leaving them to judge of evidence. *Isidore.*

μήτι. Perhaps. *Buttmann.* Expression not of doubt, but of modesty.
Hengst. Can this be the Christ ? *D. Brown.* Authorized version inexact.
Is this the Christ ? expecting an affirmative answer. *Trench.*

30. Then they went out of the city, and came unto him.

They went. Gr. *were coming.* They had not arrived when that which follows occurred.

What a deep reproach to the Jews hesitating to believe the Baptist, the chosen messenger of God.

Those ignorant Samaritans believe the word of a lately infamous female.

Fruit not *ripened* is *shrivelled* and *destroyed* by the sun.

How many objections might have been made against their going.

How utterly improbable that the Messiah would appear to *such* a person at such a *place*, without witnesses or previous notice.

How earnestly must they have plied her with questions and pressed her with difficulties.

But the quickening breath of heaven had begun to move upon the slain. Ezek. xxxvii. 9.

The city. Samaria. A woman may found a Church of God, a woman was the first person baptized in Europe by Paul. Acts xvi. 15.

A poor ignorant woman of Samaria goes forth, and by grace leaves a record that has cheered thousands of humble labourers in all lands for 18 centuries.

Females are not called to preach in public (1 Cor. xiv. 35), but by a thousand means they can make their influence felt.

Came unto him. Their willingness to receive light was quickly and richly rewarded.

Why did they *believe* the word of one who had been infamous in morals?

There is an earnestness of manner, which cannot be resisted.

Constituted for sympathy, we cannot be indifferent to deep feeling.

A messenger in breathless haste once entered a village assembly with the cry, " A child is drowned."

There were many mothers present, but there was *one* who threw up her hands and uttered a wail, that told its own sad tale.

Doubtless the Spirit of God mightily moved the hearts of these " strangers." Luke xvii. 18.

οὖν, omitted. *Tisch., Alford.*

---

31. In the mean while his disciples prayed him, saying, Master, eat.

Mean while. Disciples had returned with supplies from the market.

But our Lord had carefully and effectually concluded the interview.

Prayed. Gr. *reasoned.* Not impatience, but tender care of Him.

Human *folly* oft incidentally led to the most precious sayings of our Lord.

He neglected Himself to serve us; thirsted, that we may have drink.

He gave the hungry bread out of His mouth to nourish them.

He sighed and groaned in spirit, to see men so reluctant to be saved.

Eat. Eternal interests burdened His heart, while the disciples could not rise above bread.

How man's judgment of pleasure differs from that of angels and the Redeemer! Luke xv. 10.

Absorbed in His great work of mercy, His natural appetite was forgotten.

They besought Him to eat, if only they might eat also.

Fatigue and *thirst* were not unknown to the Lord of Glory, while incarnate.

Food of Orientals is always simple and light. John vi. 5.

Orientals sparingly use animal food, and only on festive days.

Heat of climate makes it unwholesome and expensive.

It was doubtless eaten before the flood. Flocks of Abel. Gen. iv. 2.

Blood being the life, was prohibited under penalty of death. Lev. iii. 17.

Prohibition extended to strangers, and even Gentile converts were laid under the law. Acts xv. 29.

Sinew of the hip not eaten, on account of what happened to Jacob. Gen. xxxii. 32.

μαθηταί. All had left but John. *Hengst.*

φάγε. Tradition excludes animal food before the flood. *Diod. Sic.* Flesh used before, contrary to the will of God. *Keil, Delitzsch.* Legalized after the flood. Gen. ix. 3. *Lange.* First grant enlarged. *Basil.* Man had become contumacious. *Gregory Nys.* Because not food enough without animals. *Abarbanel.* Orientals offer refreshments out of courtesy, and feel insulted if you offer pay. *Russell, Maundrell.*

ἠρώτων, "ask," constantly used for "*pray*." *Chrys.*

ἐρωτάω, αἰτέω. Former used only by our Lord to the Father, as having authority to ask, as one king asks of another. Luke xiv. 32. *Lampe.* Latter is the submissive request of an inferior. *Trench.* They had reluctantly bought food of Samaritans, and wonder, after being sent, why He refuses meat. *Stier.*

---

32. But he said unto them, I have meat to eat that ye know not of.

He said unto them. Not spoken in blame, but in the depth of an earnest heart, as one called from the exalted privileges of a communion table, to attend to the dull duties of earth.

Meat. His spiritual satisfaction at times rose to a Divine rapture.

Even *our* human joy and grief will sometimes overpower hunger and thirst.

" I " and " ye" sharply marks the contrast between *His* thoughts and *their* thoughts.

" As for me, I have been sharing a banquet such as ye think not of."

" My meat is to do the will of Him that sent me." Verse 34.

Saints of all ages have found this " hidden manna " to be " sweeter than honey." Psa. xix. 10.

Their preparations completed, and the Samaritans perhaps already in sight, they desired to know *why* He refused.

He was anxious to inform them, for He would have them (as angels) to rejoice with Him over the lost one found.

To eat. His bodily wants not to be compared with the longings of His soul.

But all this His disciples had yet to learn.

They knew not that the humble water-carrier would bring a whole town to the feet of their Master.

Ye know not. They were amazed at this word, for it implies if they knew *His* food, they would also forget *their* meat.

No wonder the woman understood not the *water*, when they understood not the *meat*.

The world becomes bitter to us when tasting the sweetness of Christ.

" How rich a prize even for the sacrifice of a man's whole life, the rescuing of ONE SOUL ! " *Hammond.*

Eliezar, servant of Abraham, refused to eat till his errand was completed. Gen. xxiv. 33.

Samuel refused to eat until he had anointed the young king. 1 Sam. xvi. 11.

Seek *first* the kingdom, and you will want nothing *second.*

εἶπεν. The following conversation in the plan of the Evangelist. *Stier.*
It had no independent signification. *Luthardt.*
βρῶσιν used for mental food. Pastus animorum. *Grotius.*
οἴδατε. My temporal wants must yield to others' spiritual necessities. *Ber. Bib.*

---

33. Therefore said the disciples one to another, Hath any man brought him ought to eat?

Disciples. The twelve chosen as companions and heralds, of whom but five are thought to have been present.
One to another. The record abounds with tokens of profound respect.
His *presence* never allowed the *least* familiarity on their part.
Cherubim "covered their faces with their wings," Isa. vi. 2, not presuming to address the Infinite Majesty, and "cried one to another." Isa. vi. 3.
Brought him. He waited their return, but no ravens had brought Him food. 1 Kings xvii. 6.
No angel had remembered His wants, as in the case of Elijah under the juniper tree. 1 Kings xix. 6.
No stones of the wilderness had, by command, become bread. Matt. iv. 3.
Are not these yet "carnal and talk as men"? 1 Cor. iii. 3. As if one Almighty to CREATE *bread* and *wine* could want!
Can we wonder at the midnight ignorance of Greek and Roman sages?

μήτις. A citizen had. *Nonnus.* Possibly an angel. *Stier.* Disciples were thinking of Elijah and ravens. *Origen.*

---

34. Jesus saith unto them, My meat is to do the will of him that sent me, and to finish his work.

Jesus saith. In answer to a question they *thought*, but dared not *put*.
Meat. This places in the background His need of *food*, as ver. 10 his need of *water*.
Sons of earth know but little of this emotion, as it is peculiar to dwellers in heaven.

Job, in holy devotion, preferred this *meat* to festal joys.　Job xxiii. 12.

Gladness of heart cheers ploughers and sowers, and the shout of " harvest-home " crowns the reapers in the end.

Thus, not finding fruit on the barren fig-tree, He entered the temple, certainly not a place for *bread*.　Matt. xxi. 23.

But full well He knew the *Divine gladness* of doing *Divine works.*

The will.　Plan of redemption embraces the whole range of the Divine purposes, from the promise in Eden to the judgment.

Complete submission to the DIVINE WILL implies angelic perfection.

" I and my house will serve the Lord " is a picture of a *good father.*　Josh. xxiv. 15.

" I put on righteousness, and it clothed me "—a *good ruler.*　Job xxix. 14.

" I watered my couch with my tears "—a picture of a *true penitent.*　Psa. vi. 6.

" No obedience more painful than unrestrained liberty."　*Hammond.*

Were there no laws of God, each sinner would have a *tyrant* for his *master.*

He would multiply more sorrows than thorns and briars did.

Adam was a slave in the open world, a free man in the enclosure of Eden.

Barbarians in Appian begged the Romans to take them as *slaves.*

We best " taste the goodness of God " by doing His will.　Psa. xxxiv. 8.

Sent me.　Possible allusion to John iii. 17.　Joy now beamed from His features, that the eternal work of mercy was already begun.

Doubtless a heavenly radiance illuminated His face as He spake these words.　Mark ix. 15.

Even a martyr at the stake would hardly venture to make these words his own.

But of Jesus they are absolutely true : doing His Father's will was His daily bread, and absorbed His ordinary wants.

The master passion of His soul was love to God, and pity to fallen man.

Finish.　A prospective glance at the cross, and its *pentecostal results.*

No believer knows perfectly *what* is his work, *how* to do it, or *when* it is finished.

He thus answered the disciples' *thoughts*, and His *omniscience* enabled Him to foresee *all possible duties*.

What His Father willed He did, and did *perfectly*.

His life and death bear the stamp of eternal completeness.

His work. *One* work. A great work for Samaritans, Jews, and all nations.

A servant of His God, in form and fidelity, finishing His task, He bestows pity, patience, wisdom, love on one poor soul, an humble female, and in some respects one repulsive too.

Salvation is peculiarly and essentially the WORK OF GOD. "The pleasure of the Lord." Isa. liii. 10.

βρῶμά. Elegant term among Greeks. *Tittmann.*

ἵνα, His meat and drink the endeavour. ὅτι, His will actually done. *Lücke.*

ἵνα pointing onwards to each step to the end. *Stier.* Questioned by *Meyer.*

θέλημα. Though independent, yet always coincident with the Father's. *Stier.* Disciples yet ignorant of their own instrumentality. *Brandt.* To the tempter, "*Non licet*" a good answer, *non vacat* is stronger and surer. Neh. vi. 3. *Sanderson.*

τελειώσω. Changing the tense to that of a completed work. *D. Brown.* I will finish my work on the Sabbath, whether you will or not. *Brandt.* Not only finish what was begun, but in all its parts and qualities. *Lampe.*

---

35. Say not ye, There are yet four months, and then cometh harvest? behold, I say unto you, Lift up your eyes, and look on the fields; for they are white already to harvest.

Say not ye? A glorious noon-day scene is about to unfold itself to His disciples.

Mark the difference between the eye of faith and common experience.

Four months. Jews divided the year into twelve *lunar* months. Every *third year* they *intercalated* a month. *Smith's Dict.*

"Four months" a proverbial phrase for the ordinary time between sowing and reaping.

Harvest. By way of eminence, *wheat* harvest; barley was two weeks earlier. Palestine: 1. SEED TIME, October to December. 2. WINTER, December to February. 3. COLD, February to April. 4. HARVEST, April to June. 5. HEAT, June to August. 6. SUMMER, August to October.

Rain falls in November; grass springs, oranges, lemons, citrons, bloom in January.

Towards the end of January almonds bloom. In February and March, pears and plums. In May, apricots and melons in the valley of Jordan and around Galilee. In June, figs and cherries. In August, grapes, peaches, figs, and pomegranates. In September, grass is parched, trees look grey, soil becomes dust, and the whole land appears like a *desert*. The valley of Sharon, and a few spots watered by man, are excepted.

"Former rain" begins in October, "latter rain" ends in April.

It rains nearly every day, more or less, during this period.

"Ye are God's husbandry," 1 Cor. iii. 9. God has a field,—"the world." Matt. xiii. 38.

He has vineyards, corn-fields, shepherds, flocks, herds, winepress, threshing-floor, ploughers, sowers, reapers, garners, and place for burning chaff!

Pastoral life prevented local attachment. "The land is mine." Lev. xxv. 23.

Inheritances were inalienable, except till Jubilee, for forty-nine years.

This fostered patriotism, and every seventh year of rest fostered piety.

It was a kind of *sacred rent*, reserved for the DIVINE OWNER.

Reaping. Valley of Jordan lies 3000 feet lower than the springs of the river. Hence harvest-time varies more than two months. Along Jordan, March; in the hill country, April; about Lebanon, June.

Soil needs constant watering. Grass, by heat, turns to hay, hence it needs to be artificially irrigated. Psa. lxv. 10; Prov. xxi. 1; Isa. xxx. 25.

Grain, when short, was plucked up by the root.

Sheaves were collected into shocks, and drawn by carts to the threshing-floor.

No rain ever fell during harvest, except as a *miracle*. 1 Kings xviii. 1.

Gleaning, a provision ordained by Providence, for the poor. Deut. xxiv. 19.

Threshing-floor, a *beaten spot* of *ground*. Oxen used unmuzzled. Deut. xxv. 4.

Wooden rollers with iron teeth, break the straw used for fodder.

Winnowing done in the evening. Ruth iii. 2. By forks or fans. Matt. iii. 12.

Grain is *still watched*, as seen by the author in Egypt. Ruth iii. 4, 7.

Various seeds connected with magical rites led to idolatry, and hence were forbidden. Deut. xxii. 9.

I say. This formula shows that His language is figurative. In contrast with " *Say ye*," who look on outward things.

Lift up, &c. " Behold, all these gather and come to Thee." Isa. xlix. 18.

Harvest of *nature* is more distant than the harvest of the *gospel*.

White. A harvest of another husbandry is already ripe for the sickle.

The transparent simplicity of thought only equalled by the glow of holy emotion.

The Redeemer's soul seemed kindled with uncommon joy at the sight.

He begins with holy satisfaction to " see the travail of His soul." Isa. liii. 11.

" A handful of corn on the mountains, the fruit shall shake like Lebanon." Psa. lxxii. 16.

Then apostate Samaria shall be brought back to the faith.

" The ploughman shall overtake the reaper," seed-time and harvest blended. Amos ix. 13.

The coming crowds of Samaritans typified all Gentiles coming. Matt. ix. 37.

The lesson of our Lord is—" Life is the time for *toil*, not for *reward*."

There is a rest *remaining*, but not until life's toils are closed. Heb. iv. 9.

Heavenly chemistry extracts lessons of wisdom from growing grain.

Nature and its laws are types and shadows of the spiritual world.

λέγετε. Not comparison, but a contrast. *Stier.* Our Lord spoke this in December. *Hengst.*

θερισμός. From 1846 to 1859 only *two* slight showers fell in Jerusalem between May and October. Average fall of water 56 inches. *Barclay.* 65 inches. *Whitby.* This harvest, a result of a spiritual sowing. *Hezel.* Questioned by *Stier*. Harvest began 16 Nisan. *Lightfoot, Wieseler*. No good grounds for chronological inference. *Alford*.

τετράμηνόν. It was now about Dec. 15. *Hengst*. Jan. or Feb. *Stanley*. In Palestine period from sowing to reaping is 6 months. *Jahn*. Varies from 5 to 7 months. *Porter, Ritter*. Agriculture the basis of the Mosaic economy. *Michaelis*. "Do you not usually say there are four months to the harvest?" *Wieseler*. First reaping of barley sown in Nov. is in June. *Lücke*.

λευκαί. Pointed to crowds of Samaritans coming clothed in white. *Chrys*. Questioned. *De Wette, Stier*. Not impossible. *Ebrard*. No allusion to the harvest *season*, but the *fact* that the Saviour's labours would produce immediate fruit. Possible allusion to Joshua xxiv. 13. *Alford*. Time eight months after the first Passover, December some four months before the actual harvest. *Robinson*.

ἤδη and ἔτι unqualified, the seed time January. *Stier*. In Nisan or April. *Bengel*. Connected with the next verse. *Tisch., Tregelles*. Belongs to ver. 35. *Alford*. "If you could see with right eyes, you would," &c. *Ber. Bib*.

ἐπάρατε. May have pointed with His finger. *Hengst*. Some must have been present. *Lücke*. It seems that the following harvest would be gathered after the ascension. *Author*.

---

36. And he that reapeth receiveth wages, and gathereth fruit unto life eternal : that both he that soweth and he that reapeth may rejoice together.

Reapeth. Harvest ever a season of joy among all nations. Isa. ix. 3.

" They that sow in tears shall reap in joy." Psa. cxxvi. 5.

Serving the Church of God in tears issues in eternal joy. Acts xx. 19.

Ancient tradition says that the tears of the vine branch cure the leprosy.

The olive is most fruitful when tears distil from its leaves.

Sadness is turned to gladness, sighing to singing, and musing to music.

Our Lord had the fruit of Pentecostal glories in His eye,—the Churches.

Receiveth. Souls won to Christ by prayers and tears " the joy and crown " of apostles and of all true and faithful labourers in the Lord's field. 1 Thess. ii. 19.

Wages. Harvest-men receive higher wages than other toilers.

They labour under a burning sun, and are more exposed to fatigue in their toil.

Their work completes that of plougher and sower, and all who have gone before them.

" They that turn many to righteousness shall shine as the stars for ever and ever." Dan. xii. 3.

The ordinary reaper wrought for his master, and was paid, and the harvest he gathered perished afterward ; but ye shall reap a harvest garnered to eternity, and therefore a source of *immortal* joy. Deut. xvi. 11 ; 1 Thess. ii. 19.

What lofty promises, and in what contrast to His *humble* band.

What *an echo* has come down the valleys and hills of time, from the toilers for God who have borne the burden and heat of the day.

In nature he who sows is often the reaper, but in God's field it is seldom so.

A believer's greatest joy, he is not working for *himself*, but for his MASTER.

"The Lord is not unjust to forget your work of faith and labour of love." Heb. vi. 10 ; 1 Thess. i. 3.

The Son of God is the great *Administrator* of the kingdom of grace. Rev. xxii. 12.

Gathereth. Our Lord never repeated His visit to Samaria, and expressly forbade the disciples going. Matt. x. 5.

This shows His design a prelude of scenes after the Ascension.

Life eternal. The converts shall be eternally saved, and the *reward* of the faithful labourers shall be everlasting.

Soweth. Prophets had sowed in tears and blood, and apostles reaped their harvest.

In the kingdom of God the reaper also sows, but the sower does not always reap of that which he has sown.

Sowing in Judea produces a harvest in all the world for 1800 years.

Sower, with unselfish hope, anticipates the joy of the reaper following.

The reaper, possessed of the same spirit, responds to the sower's joy.

John the Baptist aroused thoughts among Samaritans of the coming Messiah.

Reapeth. *Shows* more than sowing, but the JUDGE cannot err in bestowing due reward.

Rejoice. The joy of the harvest will be the harvest of joy. Isa. ix. 3 ; Matt. xiii. 39.

Precious issue of the husbandry is the interest alike of sower and reaper.

He sees beyond the bloody seed-time of Calvary, a glorious harvest.

Now the husbandman dreads the perils of the season : *then*

blight, mildew, frost, and storms will cause anxiety no more
for ever.

Patriarchs and prophets of the ancient dispensation will rejoice
with apostles; and angels will rejoice with all over redeemed
souls.   Luke xv. 7—10.

This evangelist gives us the song of the *redeemed*, when robed and
crowned :—

" UNTO HIM THAT WASHED US FROM OUR SINS IN HIS BLOOD."   Rev.
i. 5.

" He that goeth forth and weepeth, bearing precious seed, shall
come again," &c.   Psa. cxxvi. 6.

Together.   A common joy will extinguish all rival jealousy.

The bridegroom went forth, leading home his bride with songs.
Jer. xxv. 10.

The Levites chanted before Jehoshaphat, going to war with
Ammon.   2 Chron. xx. 19, 20.

With music they celebrated their victories and triumphs.   Ex. xv.
21 ; Judg. v. 1 ; 1 Sam. xviii. 6.

With hymns, they worshipped Jehovah and celebrated His praise.
Psa. lxviii. 25.

Four thousand musicians were appointed by David to praise the
Lord.   1 Chr. xxiii. 5.

The grand chorus of redemption will be heard throughout the universe as " the voice of many waters."

From star to star the Hallelujah echo shall roll for ever and ever.

Angels and archangels with the redeemed will SHOUT THE ETER-
NAL HARVEST HOME !

Order of verses 36, 37, 38 should be inverted. *B. Crusius.* Profound prophetic
power reverses natural order. *Stier.*

μισθὸν often used for the reward of free grace.   Matt. v. 12, &c. *Trench.*
Faithful servant's own salvation but a small part of the Εὖ, δοῦλε, Matt. xxv.
21. *Stier.*   God's glory, not joy, the ultimate end of a Christian. *J. Scott.*

καὶ συνάγει even in this, he receiveth wages.

σπείρων.   Sower did not sow his own lands, nor reaper reap his own fields.
Gossner.   Our Lord Himself both sowed and reaped. *Schleiermacher.*   He
intends virtue to be its own reward here, as well as hereafter. *Quesnel.*
Saints may look to another reward, Heb. vi. 10.   Prophets are denoted. *Lange.*

ὁμοῦ, emphatic. *Trench.*

χαίρη.   The μισθός of the θερίζων is in the χαρά here implied, just as the
βρῶσις of the σπείρων was His joy already begun. *Alford.*   Their labours
were at different times, the reward will be given at once. *Origen.*

37. And herein is that saying true, One soweth, and another reapeth.

Herein is. Maxims of men as a rule are *selfish* and injurious.
As if He had said, To gather is not mine, but your blessed work.

One soweth. For ages patriarchs, priests, prophets, and kings had laboured, but apostles reaped the reward, of seeing Messiah and His kingdom. Matt. xiii. 17.

Rich encouragement to toilers in God's field, for to human appearance some have had no success.

How little of the harvest in the field of Samaria was seen, save by the Lord Himself.

So may the desert, in an unexpected moment, burst out in bloom.

Ofttimes the sower toils and *dies*, before the harvest hour arrives.

In Tahiti missionaries laboured 20 years without *one* known convert.

The field was about to be abandoned, but *shortly* after that idolatry was quite overthrown.

Pilgrim fathers, amid want, cold, and other terrible trials, cast in the seed, whereof we, their children, under God, reap a glorious harvest.

Another. Seek not to know why the Messiah did not come sooner or why He has different dispensations. " The Judge of all the earth " sooner or later will for ever *satisfy* every trusting soul. Gen. xviii. 25 ; Rom. v. 6.

In the annals of eternity " one day is with the Lord as a thousand years," &c. 2 Pet. iii. 8.

For even Israel, the prince with God, and the poor Samaritan woman are parts of one harvest.

Reapeth. Among the severest, but noblest sorrows, are those of Christ's husbandmen.

But a rich eternity will equalize this disproportion.

Moses had sown during 40 years, and then Joshua reaped the harvest.

David and Isaiah sowed the seed, and Ezekiel, Daniel, and Malachi reaped in their stead.

And the aged Simeon and Anna *saw* what all had longed for in vain.

ἐστίν the only predicate. *Bengel, Winer.*

ἀληθινός. True in a much higher relation. *Olshausen.* In Matt. xiii. 39 harvest and reapers have another meaning. *Stier.* Multos sæpe alieni laboris fructum percipere. *Calvin.*

σπείρων. I was the sower in conversing with the woman, and you shall reap. *Trench.* Alludes to the labours of Greek philosophers in preparing the way for Christianity. *Clem. Alex.*

---

38. I sent you to reap that whereon ye bestowed no labour : other men laboured, and ye are entered into their labours.

I sent. The majestic " **I** " appropriates all that Jehovah could demand.

Our Lord's omniscience embracing the *future*, He oft alludes to it as *past*.

The Greek word refers to their past calling, and to their future duty.

Here begins their *name*, " *apostles*," i.e. *sent*, though they were not yet thus called.

No labour. Compared with our Lord's agony, the disciples endured nothing.

They had not shared at all in the toil that produced the present ingathering.

The same law still prevails : pastors reap what former pastors had sown.

At Peter Weiker's ordination, scarcely had the preacher announced this text when the flock *burst into tears*, for their beloved but sainted pastor *Hollatz* was present to every mind. His fervent zeal, his exalted piety, his untiring diligence, his self-sacrificing devotion, had made " the field white for the harvest." The sobbings were so loud, they drowned the voice of the preacher. *The Spirit was there!*

Thus John the Divine sowed seed for *Polycarp* to reap, he for *Athanasius*, he for *Augustine*, he for *Anselm ; Bernard* for *Tauler, Luther* for *Calvin*, and he for *Chemnitz ; Wickliff* for *Tyndale*, and he for *Coverdale* and a glorious army of reapers.

The O.T. labourers and the Baptist are kept in the background, as our Lord never *identifies* Himself with *man* as such.

Other men. Prophets who wept between the porch and the altar, and died without seeing any fruit.

Moses and Elias, Daniel and Ezekiel, as certainly sowed as Peter and Paul.

The former actually rejoiced with Peter and other reapers on Tabor.

Laboured. A luminous glimpse at the work of redemption.

When He said, " Let there be light," there was light.

The starry heavens are " the work of His fingers," Psa. viii. 3, a figure taken from *embroidering* or tapestry.

But in redemption "He TRAVAILETH in the GREATNESS of His STRENGTH ! " Isa. lxiii. 1.

Divine as He was, He bowed down in Gethsemane under the awful task of sustaining justice and opening the door of mercy to a lost world.

Although angels had often ministered unto Him, none ventured near the cross : " He trod the wine-press alone." Isa. lxiii. 3.

" His own right hand and His holy arm hath gotten Him the victory," and hence " He bears the glory." Psa. xcviii. i ; Zech. vi. 13.

ἀπέστειλα. Not indefinite aorist. *Hengst.* He often speaks of a thing being ended when not begun. *Alford.* Because there can be neither past nor future to omnipresence. *Author.* Hebrew past equivalent to future. *Greswell.* Appointed to confirm the faith of believing Samaritans. *Schleiermacher.* To baptize them. *Hezel.* Samaria not yet on a level with Israel. *Stier.* Mission began with their calling, but completed afterwards. *Lampe.*

ἄλλοι, John the Baptist with Christ, Law and Prophets. *Calvin, Lampe, Luthardt.* Old Test. the seed, New Test. the harvest. *Olshausen.* Our Lord the only sower. *Herder, Tholuck, Stier.*

κόπου. Men are the grain, and eternal life the granary. *Tholuck.*

ἐγὼ concealed in the ἄλλοι, Christ also the seed. *Schleiermacher.*

---

39. And many of the Samaritans of that city believed on him for the saying of the woman, which testified, He told me all that ever I did.

Samaritans. For their history and character, see on John iv. 9.

Believed. John i. 7 ; vii. 38. Marvellous promptitude, she must have testified with power, " the Holy Ghost also bearing witness."

What a contrast ! His own nation repelled Him. Luke iv. 29. Heathens of Samaria invited Him. Luke xvii. 18.

Note the Divine seal on labours among the abandoned. Those believers were the foundation of the Church of Samaria.

Those in Jerusalem believed through miracles ; but with a freer faith, Samaritans trusted the word of this woman, although Jews would not receive the testimony of the Baptist.

The Lord had opened to her the register of her criminal life ; and

John unfolded to the Jews their sins, but they would not trust him.

Saying. Human testimony an important instrument in gospel work.

The Lord had used no elaborate argument, no burning eloquence, but simple truth.

As the skilful hand of David made the sling do its work.

Prayerful, believing obedience made Gideon's lamps and pitchers victorious. Judges vii. 20.

God can honour any humble believer, *with* or *without* authority from the Church.

He told. Had she said, " He unfolded to me the *prophecies,*" who would have cared ? or had she said, " He wrought a miracle before me," they might have replied, " Enchanters have often deceived wiser persons than thou."

What pains by the SON of GOD, for the conversion of one poor soul !

Thus Philip was taken from a revival, and sent on the desert road to Gaza, to instruct and baptize a *stranger* of Ethiopia. Acts viii. 26.

Converting a sinner " saves a soul from death, and hides a multitude of sins." Jas. v. 19, 20.

How casually, as we would say, was this woman won,—she and our Lord were on their own affairs.

He desired to assuage His thirst, and rest His wearied limbs. But He cannot remain silent,—the opportunity is too precious to be lost.

We need the same *burning* LOVE : " My meat is to do the will of Him that sent me." Ver. 34.

Who can calculate the result of one faithful word or act ? Remember " the little maid." 2 Kings v. 1—14.

It is said that Junius, the illustrious scholar, was converted by a conversation with a farmer near Florence, on John chap. i., and from an infidel became a mighty defender of the faith.

These things enlarged the charity of the apostles, and prepared them for their world-wide ministry.

As one wave of the sea causes another, so " no man liveth unto Himself." Rom. xiv. 7.

With what warm quivering emotion does His humanity reveal itself.

" In all points made like unto His brethren," sin alone excepted.

Undying faith in His SINLESSNESS, upheld martyrs in their agony.

Even " little ones " admire and feel the beauty of the scene, and
yet this is the loftiest and deepest of all the Gospels.

Thus a child can admire and enjoy the sun's glorious light equally
with the philosopher.

This narrative may be compared to a net-work of gold, covering
rarest jewels.

In Him we behold DIGNITY, AUTHORITY, PATIENCE, PENETRATION,
GRACE.

In His petitioner curiosity, perseverance, conviction, penitence,
faith, love, zeal.

ἐπίστευσαν. In authorized instruction. *Augustine.* Small means often result in great things. Even Chaucer's poems were givers of light to some.
Fox's Martyrs. Note the simple record of faith. 1. Credere Deum. 2. Credere
Deo. Credere in Deum. *P. Lombard.* 1. Faith in doctrine. 2. Faith in
promises. *J. Damascenus.* 1. Cognitio. 2. Affectus. *Hugo St Victor.*
Opinions of Fathers, Mediæval Doctors, Reforming Doctors weighed and adjusted, are of little value to the reader of this verse. *Maurice.*

---

40. So when the Samaritans were come unto him, they besought him that he
would tarry with them ; and he abode there two days.

Samaritans. For their history and character, see on John iv. 9.

Besought. Jews exalted in privileges, besought Him to depart,
Matt. viii. 34, but *never* to remain.

They drove Him out with *violence*, Luke iv. 29, or plotted against
Him by *fraud*, Luke xiii. 31, 32.

How many hopes hung on that earnest prayer, how many homes
were blest with wells of " water of life," and how many hearts
were won for God, eternity alone will reveal.

What would the travellers to Emmaus have lost had they not
prayed, " Abide with us " ?

Yet how different was the conduct of Samaritans nine months
after, Luke ix. 54, when His face was turned *toward* Jerusalem.

Tarry. All His life. They would never willingly part with Him.

Abode. Our Lord at one time forbade His disciples to visit any
Samaritan city. Matt. x. 5, 6.

But after they had received the Holy Ghost they were to be " witnesses for Him in Samaria," &c. Acts i. 8.

It is remarkable that the home of these grateful Samaritans can
still be identified, while Capernaum and Bethesda have
wholly disappeared.

Two days. If the record of this visit existed, how intensely would
we peruse its details.

But the *silence* of the Bible is as *Divine* as its *revelations.* It is so
like God in His works and ways.

What occurred during *thirty years* of our Lord's life, with one
exception, is unknown.

Neither can we tell how Paul, the burning convert, spent his *three
years* in *Arabia.* Gal. i. 17.

δύο. Remained two days at Sychar, where He healed the youth, John iv.
51. And two days at Bethabara before going to awaken Lazarus, John xi. 6.
Typical of His own resurrection, Hosea vi. 2. *Bourgon.*

---

41. And many more believed because of his own word.

Many more. A quiet blessing rested on that harvest-field of
Samaria.

But the harvest was also a time of sowing, which had its ripening
after Pentecost.

From Sychar came forth *Justin Martyr,* one of the noblest heroes of
the Church.

Although we read of only a few believing in other places, yet,
after His resurrection, He appeared to 500 brethren in Galilee.
1 Cor. xv. 6.

Believed. Faith, nature and evidences. See on John i. 7 ; vii.
38.

The simple, unreasoning, loving faith of a *little child* is Christ's
chosen model.

Men of Cana believed because of His miracles, but these Samaritans
because of the truth He revealed.

The *Holy Spirit* doubtless drew them, and wrought in their hearts
their simple faith.

Such faith saints have had in all ages. "Blessed are they who
have not seen, and yet have believed." John xx. 29.

When the people were uninfluenced by their leaders, our Lord had
constant success.

Samaritans believed while priests and Pharisees, possessing the
highest religious privileges, rejected the testimony of God.

So is it still,—nominal Christians continue in unbelief while poor
   heathens gladly enter the kingdom of God.

His own word. The Spirit showed each one his own heart, as he
   had never seen it before.

He caused the Light to enter their souls, and gave them a *new
   sense* of fellowship.

His Light scattered their ignorance, falsehoods, superstitions.

Divinity of Christ as self-evident to believing hearts as the power
   of the sun when he bathes the earth in the beauty and glory
   of a summer's day.

πλείους. Our Lord spends only two days with Samaritans, while months
are spent among Galileans. *Lange.*

ἐπίστευσαν. Prejudice taken on trust, conviction upon evidence. *Berkeley.*
Samaritans received Him on His teaching alone. *Chrys.* He might have
unfolded heart *secrets*, with an omniscient glance, as with Nathanael. *Author.*

---

42. And said unto the woman, Now we believe, not because of thy saying:
for we have heard him ourselves, and know that this is indeed the Christ, the
Saviour of the world.

Woman. She had doubtless been summoned to that spot by the
   Spirit.

Her questions and answers also were overruled by Infinite wisdom,
   for the benefit of the world.

Representing a large class of saved ones, she now disappears from
   the gospel history.

Believe. Faith. See on John i. 7; vii. 38. They put faith in
   the word of this sinful woman.

A most cheering encouragement to the humble labourer for Christ.

Many have an historical faith, yet perish *without* a *Saviour.*

EXTERNAL EVIDENCES OF CHRISTIANITY: 1. Revelation *possible.*
   The Creator of a thinking soul can disclose objects of thought.
   2. Revelation *probable.* Ancient lawgivers, *Zoroaster, Minos,
   Pythagoras, Solon, Lycurgus, Numa,* pretended they had laws
   from the gods. Men were *conscious* of the need of such intercourse. 3. Revelation *desirable.* Socrates and Plato longed
   for a teacher from heaven. 4. Revelation *necessary.* Unaided
   human reason has not and cannot attain to truth. Even the
   most polished heathen nations were spiritually ignorant,

superstitious, and depraved ; licentious and cruel, often offering *human sacrifices.*

They knew nothing of *creation,* or of the *origin of evil,* or of a way of *reconciliation* with God, or of *immortality,* or of the rewards and punishments of another life.

Revenge was considered praiseworthy, and *suicide* proof of a noble mind.

MIRACLES : performed before *friends* and *foes,* and attested by multitudes of eye-witnesses who sealed the truth with their blood.

YET NO MAN WILL WILLINGLY DIE A MARTYR BY MISTAKE.

Hence error has had no real martyrs. Those pretending to be so were executed as *any other great criminals.*

PROPHECIES were delivered foretelling unexpected changes in empires, and so *minute,* that scoffers pretend they were written *after fulfilment.*

INTERNAL EVIDENCES. Language and style prove the books of the Bible to be genuine and authentic.

Unity of purpose amid authorship so diverse and extending over 1600 years an evidence of inspiration.

Complete harmony between all the parts, facts, doctrines, laws, and predictions.

Sublimity and excellence of its teaching, tendency to promote man's highest interests.

LIFE and CHARACTER of JESUS the most marvellous of all miracles.

That a Judean peasant should have risen so far above his own times and above the greatest efforts of the greatest sages is wholly inexplicable on any known law of life or history.

To this day the mightiest and most highly-trained intellects have endeavoured in vain to exhaust the teaching of the Nazarene.

Wonderful *preservation* of the records also, despite many attempts to *destroy* them.

Emperor *Diocletian* struck a medal to *celebrate the ruin* of Christianity with the inscription, "NOMINE CHRISTIANORUM DELETO," but he might as well have boasted that he had extinguished the sun.

" Attacks of infidelity on the Bible as ineffably ridiculous as if a mouse should attempt to nibble off the wing of an archangel." *Robert Hall.*

Thy saying. Nothing rude is here found,—they indeed confirm her word.

But their word seals the *power* and *grace* Divine of the Redeemer's truth.

" The children and servants of the true God are not strangers to the *vernacular* of their home." *Melancthon.*

Ourselves. Their ground of faith not miracles overpowering with proofs of His Divinity.

What miracles had the ancient Jews,—wonders in Egypt and the Red Sea ; grandeurs of Sinai : pillar of cloud and fire day and night ; the rock, and stream flowing therefrom ; manna six days out of seven ; their clothing never wearing out ; quails flocking where no living thing was ever found before : still they *murmured,* and *rebelled,* and *perished.*

Not miracles, but privileges improved through grace, turn the heart to God.

Evidence that He was a true prophet satisfied the honest, but the special work of the Spirit must explain the faith of so many.

If the woman's testimony wrought such an interest, what should have been the effect of the presence of the Son of God ?

Indeed. Perhaps a hint at false Messiahs, who may have mocked them.

Christ. Gr. order, " *That is indeed the Saviour of the world, the Christ.*" John i. 17.

Saviour of the world. The phrase is alone found here and in 1 John iv. 14.

It had a depth of meaning to those outside the Jewish Church of which we have but a faint idea.

Jews had no thought of it, nor had the idea risen above the horizon, even in apostolic minds.

Whence, then, did these despised dwellers in Sychar obtain it ?

Although all are not saved, yet " by the grace of God Jesus tasted death for every man." Heb. ii. 9.

The promise, also, is to *all who believe,* without any difference as to nation, rank, or character. Rev. xxii. 17.

The world *might be* saved. Room in the love of God, in the work of Jesus, in the grace of the Spirit, in the promises of the gospel, in the Church, in heaven, for ALL. Luke xiv. 22.

World of believers shall be saved, not one wanting (1 Cor. xv. 22), for as *all* related to Adam died, so *all* related to Christ live.

A more ample confession of the Lord's mission is not found in the New Testament.

This made by a half-heathen race, and not by Jews, a proof of sovereign grace. Rom. ix. 15.

The Lord had unequivocally reckoned them with the heathen, and ignored their right to the covenant. John iv. 22.

Mark their rapid growth in charity under the Divine Teacher. Thus true piety strikes off the trammels of bigotry. "The world" included even Jews.

Some spend their lives not in *cultivating* their lot, but in building *fences*, and their *party* walls are so high, they cast a shadow on their own garden.

γυναικὶ. Her conversion clearly inferable. *Stier*.

πιστεύομεν. Their creed derived from Moses. *Grotius*. From Jesus' words. *Stier*. Pentateuch has a few Messianic references. *Hengst*. Most believe on the *self-evidencing testimony* of the Scriptures. *Boyle*. The gospel plan in two days was more spread out than even at Jerusalem. *Calvin*.

λαλιάν. Not keeping silent, λογός the sentence uttered. *Bengel*. Our Saviour's use (John viii. 43) of λαλιάν disproves its being *garrulity*. λαλεῖν, loqui, the simple fact of utterance, λαλιά not so well weighed. *Trench's Syn*. Allusion to her diffuse and eager report to them. *Alford*.

Χριστός. Omitted. *Lach., Tisch., Alford, Cod. Sinai*. Samaritans did not utter it, but included it in their testimony. *Stier*.

σωτὴρ κόσμου. Jews held the Messiah the Saviour of Jews only. *Lightfoot*. Samaritans expected Him as a *Teacher*. *Tholuck*. Were prepared for admission into the kingdom by Philip. Acts viii. 5. *W. H. Mill*. Samaritans *now* refer Gen. xlix. 10 to Solomon, but of old to Messiah. *Hengst*.

κόσμου. They had no idea of the salvation of the *Gentiles*, of which the disciples were also ignorant. *Le Clerc*. They were Gentiles, like Ishmaelites, circumcised. *Grotius*. Our Lord repeated the interview to His disciples. *Tholuck*. Inspiration enough to account for the record. *Author*.

---

43. Now after two days he departed thence, and went into Galilee.

After two days. He goes to gather the harvest, though limited, of the seed sown.

No *mention* of miracles, no evidence, however, that *none* were wrought.

Departed. Our Lord continues the journey mentioned in verse 3.

How few ministers have ever so denied self as to leave a flock where they were caressed, and go and dwell among those who despised them.

Hints at high significance, attached by John to the Lord's *Presence*.

Those who earnestly entreated the mysterious stranger to stay, surely did not fail to urge Him when *known* as the SAVIOUR.

Pressing entreaties of friends must not detain those called to serve the Master elsewhere.

To fly from duty is sinful cowardice ; to court suffering, pride and folly.

Galilee. John i. 43. Doubtless to Nazareth, as that was His home. John i. 46 xix. 19.

The disciples having heard the saying recorded in the next verse, must have supposed He would never return.

Rulers said to Nicodemus derisively, " Art thou also of Galilee ? " John vii. 52.

ἐξῆλθεν. John's omissions the result of abbreviation. *Hengst.* Used by this Evangelist more than all other N.T. writers. Section of history closes with 4th chapter. *Luthardt.* With the 6th. *Stier.*

Γαλιλαίαν. The τῇ ἰδίᾳ πατρίδι of verse 44. Luke iv. 24. *Hengst.*

---

44. For Jesus himself testified, that a prophet hath no honour in his own country.

Testified. Our Lord *had* testified at Nazareth, and goes there no more.

A minister unable to accomplish any good in a particular place has a hint from Providence he might be useful elsewhere.

No honour. A most remarkable reason : the Lord leaves where they *honoured* Him, and goes where they *contemned* Him.

How utterly beyond the circle of *human* experience was this act of humility.

We often see a principle *flashing out* of the Redeemer's history, as unlike the ordinary order of life as the advent of an *angel*, in a *family circle.*

" Prophesy not in the name of Jehovah, lest thou die." Jer. xi. 21.

Thus was Jeremiah threatened by the murderers of Anathoth.

The Lord's friends could not comprehend One, with His *claims* and His *origin.* Matt. xiii. 54, 56.

Own country. Nazareth, Matt. xiii. 54, where He dwelt 28 years.

This sentiment was expressed by Jesus Himself in Nazareth. Luke iv. 23.

Men sadly fulfil the adage, " Familiarity breeds contempt."

Jews had, as a rule, persecuted God's prophets. Matt. xiii. 57 ; Acts vii. 52.

Nazarenes had upbraided Him for neglecting them, His own people, while other cities were filled with the renown of His miracles.

It is evident that He *never* returned thither, thus acting on His own principle, " Cast not that which is holy to the dogs." Matt. vii. 6 ; Luke iv. 16.

Jerusalem would seem the place for showing His glory, but God's thoughts and ways are above ours.

He spent nearly the whole of the first year of His ministry in despised Galilee, and there delivered the Sermon on the Mount, and wrought many miracles.

ἐμαρτύρησεν. John refers to a hint antecedent in Luke iv. 23. *Lampe.* Our Lord refers to His rejection by Nazarenes. *Beza.* Proverb arose from their impious habit of persecuting God's messengers. *Calvin.*

πατρίδι. Cana. *Grotius, Ols.* Capernaum. *Chrys., Stier.* Galilee. *Ellicott.* Signifies both a city and region, one's native land. *Tittmann.* To Judea, as this explains His leaving *Galilee. Origen, Lücke, Ebrard.* Bethlehem. *Wieseler.* Nazareth. *Calvin, Lampe.* Adopted city. *Hengst.*

---

45. Then when he was come into Galilee, the Galilæans received him, having seen all the things that he did at Jerusalem at the feast : for they also went unto the feast.

Come. Because of the fierce enmity of the Jews.

No minister is bound to battle with bigotry, when other fields invite him to peaceful labour.

He had remained in Cana for some time, and those in Capernaum hearing of it, sent for Him.

Received. Luke ix. 11, Gr. an *honourable welcome*, although they rejected Him at His *first* visit.

But having seen His wonderful works at Jerusalem, they now gladly welcome Him.

Our Lord did not despise them on this account. He will not quench the smallest spark of grace. Luke xix. 3.

All the things. Miracles done and parables spoken, although not recorded. John xxi. 25.

The 34 distinct miracles recorded are doubtless a typical *selection* from many others, for we read that He healed *whole crowds at a time.*

Nazarenes were so besotted by covetousness or prejudice, they would not hear.

This is the third time John alludes to miracles unrecorded, wrought at Jerusalem.

These wonders caused Nicodemus to leave the Sanhedrim, to seek the night conference with the Lord.

How much more honest were these Galileans, than those of Capernaum.

"Except ye see signs and wonders, *ye will not believe.*" John iv. 48.

Jerusalem. For its history, see on John v. 1. For its topography, see on John vii. 25.

Went, &c. An explanatory clause. Those outside Judea knew not that the Galileans also attended the feasts in Jerusalem.

ἐδέξαντο. The proverb quoted verse 44 was illustrated during His first visit. His miracles at Jerusalem, however, won them over. *Neander.*

πάντα. His fame at Jerusalem had its usual influence on the provincial people. *Alford.*

---

46. So Jesus came again into Cana of Galilee, where he made the water wine. And there was a certain nobleman, whose son was sick at Capernaum.

Cana. See on John ii. 1. Its site at present unknown. The distance is believed to have been some twenty-five miles, a day's journey on a camel. John iv. 52.

The Lord probably visited at Cana the newly-married pair. *Stier.*

The prestige of His miracles opened the hearts of people to receive Him.

The Lord had *in His eye* the concealed faith of the Roman officer.

He was on the direct road to meet the suffering father, but he knew it not.

Thus it is often with the tried and half despairing children of God.

God in sovereign grace selects the time and means of mercy.

Seneca, losing a friend, sadly exclaimed, "The gods have neither the power nor the will to help us."

Water wine. This miracle is recorded in John's Gospel only. See on chap. ii. 1—11.

Nobleman. Ruler, *Tyndale.* Probably a courtier in the king's household, like Chuza. Luke viii. 3.

Perhaps he had come to the mountains of Judea for the benefit of his family

In the order of *Providence* his life was so arranged that he was *here* at this time.

We see the same Divine hand that placed a Jewish *slave* in the house of Naaman. 2 Kings v. 2.

None of the princes of this world, as far as we know, *came* to Christ while on earth.

Those " princes" who did meet Him did *not know* Him. 1 Cor. ii. 8.

Yet kings will one day be "nursing fathers," and queens " nursing mothers," of the Church. Isa. xlix. 23.

This nobleman did not come to the Lord till compelled by his son's sickness.

He who chose fishermen and publicans as the founders of His kingdom required not the proud rulers or sages of earth.

Countess of Huntingdon often thanked God that in 1 Cor. i. 26 it is not " any," but " many."

The first called were " fishermen," then a proud Pharisee, then a fallen daughter of alien Samaria, now a " nobleman." This illustrates His sovereignty. Rom. ix. 15.

Bereans reading and investigating the Scriptures God's true NO-BILITY. Acts xvii. 11.

Whose son. Blessings *descend*. There is no record of a *son* or *daughter* coming to Christ for their *parents*.

How hard for youth to realize the possibility of death, yet the records of cemeteries prove that few live to see fifty.

The *first grave ever dug* was that of a *young man*, and the first who died on earth was the *son*, not the *father*.

At one stroke, Aaron saw *two sons perish* before the Lord, and David followed one after another to the tomb.

The patriarch Job was bereft of all his children in a day.

Death of the first-born subdued Egypt, after successive wonders and plagues had failed.

Sick. Not even a nobleman's cup can be protected from the bitterness instilled by sin.

Many, alas ! confound fortune with felicity. Psal. lxxiii.

Yet all the joys of earth vanish at the approach of a fever.

Prosperity and rank do not remove the *cause* of afflictions, and they have but little power tc *soothe* the aching heart or fevered head.

What avails all the pomp of life ? When the gaudy, flaunting curtain is lifted, anxious cares are seen flitting through the gilded rooms.

Those deemed the most fortunate are often the most miserable of our race. A sad comment on external splendours.

David was far happier tending his father's flock than enthroned in Jerusalem.

The loftier the tree the more exposed to lightning, and the wider its branches the more danger from the fury of the blast.

One of these blasts had brought this nobleman to his knees, as a suppliant for aid.

Every hour the disease, advancing, was baffling all medical skill, and the father becoming more and more *despairing* when he hears that the wonder-worker of Galilee is on His journey of mercy.

Little did that father know that his son's life was threatened to force *him* to his knees, or that every step of the Redeemer to Cana was to meet *him* and bring salvation to his house.

Each act of the Saviour is chapter, book, and lesson to all coming ages.

Capernaum. See on John vi. 24. In vain did he expect our Lord's return thither.

Κανᾶ. Came to confirm the faith implanted by the miracle. *Chrys.*
βασιλικὸς. A relative of Herod Antipas. *Chrys.* Palatinus. *Jerome.* Regulus. *Vulg.* Mistake for βασιλίσκος. *Hammond.* A royal official. *Josephus, Lange.* Probably Herod's steward and a Herodian. Luke viii. 3. *Lightfoot, Chemnitz.* A royal servant. *Hengst.* A Jew. *Bengel.* One of Cæsar's household. *Origen.* This miracle and that recorded by Matthew different—1. As to place: Matthew's Capernaum, this Cana. 2. As to time: Matthew's at the beginning of His ministry, here after many miracles. 3. As to person: Matthew's a servant, here a son. 4. As to religion: Matthew's a Roman, here a Jew, verse 48. 5. As to faith: Matthew's rare energy of faith, here little faith. *Hengst., Lücke.* The few noblemen who believed are like black swans. *Trapp.*
υἱός. Probably his only heir. *Bengel.*

----

47. When he heard that Jesus was come out of Judæa into Galilee, he went unto him, and besought him that he would come down, and heal his son: for he was at the point of death.

Jesus. See on John i. 17, 41 ; iv. 25. Personal name.
Went unto. Doubtless risking his honour as a courtier.
But what is honour when his beloved child's life is in peril ?

A nobler motive to have come for his own *salvation*.

But there is not a *recorded* instance of one coming to our Lord for this exclusive object.

He applied to Him as a miracle-worker, but not as a *Saviour* from *sin*.

He sends no messenger, though he must have had many servants. Ver. 51.

Besought. *Darius* gave command to the saints of the Most High that prayer should be made for the king's life. Ezra vi. 10.

We learn from a heathen historian, *Ctesias*, that the king had *lost several children*.

Emperor *Maximinus*, on his deathbed, begged Christians whose friends he had murdered to pray for him.

The Lord's two days' delay at Sychar, and His halt at Cana, severely tested his faith. Jas. i. 3.

So the long journey from Mamre to Moriah tested Abraham's faith and obedience.

Come down. In person. He believed such a work could not be done at a distance.

" Am I a God at hand, and not a God afar off ? " Jer. xxiii. 23.

Wicked seem to think God's rod is so far off, it cannot reach them.

Penitents often tempted to suppose His arm is so distant He cannot *save* them.

Naaman thought Elisha must *come out* and *smite* upon the place.

The ruler thought that his daughter must *have the Lord's hand* laid on her. Matt. ix. 18.

Death. " It is appointed unto men *once* to die," Heb. ix. 27. The " *second* death " is not " appointed." Matt. xxv. 41.

In death by old age the weary wheels of life stand still at last.

We might all have left the world as *Enoch* and *Elijah*.

But convulsions, fears, and agonies of death show *God's mind* towards *sin*.

With life ends the pleasures of the worldling : " In thy life," &c., Luke xvi. 25, and also the sufferings of the righteous, " He is comforted." Luke xvi. 25.

Death—1. As the desert of sin. 2. As the effect of Divine decree. 3. As the sentence of the law.

Death is, by *conscience*, made the most sensible mark of God's *wrath*.

Bondage through fear of death embitters all the enjoyments of life. Heb. ii. 15.

Some in death seem to begin their perdition on this side the grave.

Herod's protracted disease increased his frantic tyranny to the last.

Saul, a brave man, trembles before a female sorceress, at the idea
of death. 1 Sam. xxviii. 20.

With a hundred lords, and a horde of concubines, Belshazzar fears
death. Dan. v. 6.

Death appears as a *conqueror*, ruling with vast power over men.
Rom. v. 14.

The earthly mind clings to the fleshly prison, and still loves to
look through the *gratings*.

A believer dying is like an infant, who fears not to go to sleep in
its loving parent's arms.

Why do children suffer, seeing that in God's kingdom none ever
suffer except for sin ? Doubtless on account of the connection
between fallen parents and their offspring.

Parents are thus *often chastened through their children*, and He, who
best knows *what keys* in the heart to touch, *reaches His ends in
the wisest way*.

Faith of Abraham, consecration of Aaron, fervour of David, resignation of Job, victorious prayer of the Syro-phœnician woman,
all developed through family affliction.

A shepherd is often seen to carry the lamb into the fold to induce
the mother to follow.

So the death of a child is often made the means of turning hearts
of parents to God and eternity.

καταβῇ. Curiosity to see the cure at home. *Bengel.* The strong faith of
the centurion, Matt. viii. 6, contrasted with this nobleman's unbelief. *Augustine.*

ἀποθνήσκειν. Life, a mystery. *Hippocrates.* Generative principle. *Aris-
totle.* Archæus. *Von Helmont.* Anima. *Stahl.* Vital principle. *Hunter.*
Organic germs. *Buffon.* Formative appetences. *Darwin.* Formative forces.
Needham. Formative nisus. *Blumenbach.* Pre-existing monads. *Leibnitz.*
Semina rerum. *Lucretius.* Plastic nature. *Cudworth.* Sensibility, irritability.
Haller. Correlative forces. *Owen.* Protoplasm. *Huxley.* Protogenes.
Hæckel, Herbert Spencer. Vital force a *mystery of the Creator*, like magnet-
ism, gravitation, light, &c. *Author.* Four vital principles,—sensibility, mobil-
ity, assimilation, and vital resistance. *Dumas.* Blood is vital. *Magendie.* Body
called a σκῆνος by *Paul*, 2 Cor. v. 1, and by the *Pythagoreans.* Death, ἐκδύ-
σασθαι, 2 Cor. v. 3, 4, ἀναλῦσις, Phil. i. 23. *Wetstein.* Death ends all things.
Cicero. Sleep and death twin brothers. *Homer.*

---

48. Then said Jesus unto him, Except ye see signs and wonders, ye will not
believe.

Jesus said. Unlike human founders of sects, our Lord often
seemed to repel applicants.

He did so with Nicodemus, John iii. 3, and the hasty scribe, Matt.
viii. 19, and the devoted Syrophœnician mother, and blind
Bartimæus. Matt. xv. 26 ; Mark x. 46.

Thus He sifted the chaff from the wheat, and tested purity of
motives.

All hearts are in His hands, and He could as easily convert a *nation*, Isa. lxvi. 8, as *a tax-gatherer*, Luke xix. 9.

Him. This rebuke would not have been given had he not been
a Jew.

"Ye Jews, so unlike the alien Samaritans I have just left."

Except. As much as to say, Had it not been for dire necessity,
thou wouldst not have applied.

With one exception (healing of the ear of Malchus), our Lord
never wrought a miracle on a person until He had brought
him or her into *spiritual relation* with *Himself* or truth.

This nobleman expected the Lord at his request to leave His *fixed
circle* of operation.

The tide of the ocean does not rise with a bound, nor the seasons
ripen the harvest in an hour.

Our Lord moved with similar *Divine, silent power*, avoiding all
excitement, hurry, and confusion.

We might as well think of hastening sunset, or delaying sunrise,
as dream of dictating *our* time or *our* ways to the Son of God.

This man must learn that the Redeemer of the world can never be
a nobleman's *retainer*.

If any claim be greater, it is that of the helpless, friendless outcast. Isa. v. 7.

And this nobleman shall *know* and *feel* these things ere his prayer
is answered.

Signs. See on John ii. 11, 23 ; iii. 2, contrasting with the
prompt faith of the Samaritan woman.

The word which disclosed the secrets of her life was to her a sign.
John iv. 29.

Our Lord first chides this nobleman for delaying his profession.

He saw his *unbelief needed a rebuke*, even when his child was dying.

He must learn that some things are more important than health
or life.

Even raising the child from death would have been a miracle
wasted, had not the father's mind been prepared.

His *education* as a believer began and was completed during this
interview.

" Lying wonders " are no mere illusions ; they are pillars built by
the Evil One to support the kingdom of darkness. 2 Thess. ii. 9.

Egyptian priests contended not with Moses, but demons contested
hand to hand with the Son of God.   Matt. iv. 1—10.

Our Lord attached but little importance to a faith produced by
miracles only.

" An evil and an adulterous generation seeketh a sign "—a mere
refuge for *unbelief.*   Matt. xii. 39.

He mourned over such hardness of heart, for we read, " *He sighed
deeply in His spirit.*"   Mark viii. 12.

He has miracles, *many as the stars,* but NONE for the UNBELIEVER !

Petitions of all kinds were welcomed by Him, but *this* for more
miracles was *rebuked.*

Though the present applicant was high in station, and entreating
not for a *servant,* but for a *son.*

Doubtless the Lord saw some *haughtiness lingering,* needing humbling.   Isa. ii. 17.

Perhaps a profane desire that " the gift of God might be purchased
with money."   Acts viii. 20.

The loftier his social position, the deeper the impression must this
rebuke have made on his mind, and on the disciples.

He was the highest in station of all those *recorded* to have applied to the Lord for aid.

Not only the highest harmonies, but the deepest discords, are
reached by His hand.

When the doctrine is heavenly, the miracle seals it *Divine.*

Revelation presupposes the power in man of *recognizing truth* when
shown.

" He that is of God heareth God's word," and knows it from God.
John viii. 47.

A miracle-worker professes to be *a messenger in immediate connection with* GOD, who is TRUTH, and miracles *are his credentials.*

Jesus claims *unreserved acceptance* of *truths,* which *transcend* (not
contradict) the reason of man.

Pharaoh had a *right* to say to Moses, " Show a miracle," Ex. vii.
9, and it was a mark of Ahaz's *unbelief* refusing to ask a
miracle.   Isa. vii. 10, 13.

Had he loved the PROMISE, he would have esteemed the SEAL, confirming the promise.

No miracle could prove that which is condemned by *conscience.* Deut. xiii. 12, 13 ; Gal. i. 8.

Ignorant of the unseen world, we must judge of miracles by their *moral* character.

God's miracles are REDEMPTIVE ACTS, works not merely of POWER, but of GRACE !

All our Saviour's miracles were prophecies of man's spiritual deliverance from the dark tyranny of sin.

Nature symbolizes man's rebellion. Hence Christ treads on the stormy sea, and makes warring elements His willing servants.

The curse of barrenness was removed by the miraculous supply of fishes.

These were part of the evidences of our Lord's Divinity—proofs of His *power.*

His works of grace and words of purity show Him to be the Son of God. See on John i. 1—3.

We can no more think of Jesus without them than of the *sun* without *effulgence.*

He points the inquiring Baptist to His miracles of mercy, as Messianic *proof.* Matt. xi. 4, 5.

" If I do not the works of my Father, believe me not." John x. 37.

" If I had not done among them the works which no other man did," &c. John xv. 24.

But the Searcher of hearts here gave a *severe* answer, with *merciful* intention.

Nothing so offensive to Jehovah as that one who is surrounded day and night by myriads of His wonders should yet *hesitate* to trust HIM.

Those who exalt Jesus *highest* find their prayers answered *soonest.*

Believe. See on John i. 7 ; vii. 38. Would they really have believed had He wrought them more signs ? John xiv. 11.

How few *did* believe His teaching, even though endorsed by so many glorious miracles.

Mary and Martha thought His absence prevented their brother's recovery. John xi. 32.

The centurion, a Roman officer, believed He could heal if He were actually absent. Matt. viii. 8.

But the nobleman's faith was so weak, that he seemed to have no such belief.

Little did this parent think *he* stood more in need of a physician than his dying *child.*

Our Lord opposes his precipitate *haste* with His own Divine tranquillity, as though He would say, "Who made me your
physician ? "
In the case of the centurion He first calmed his *mind*, and then
gently instructed him.
Although rebuking the nobleman, in the background, the request
is granted.
What a contrast to the late scene at the well ! He gave no rebuke
there. Yet He was an utter stranger, and His listener
a woman of a despised race.

σημεῖα. See on John ii. 11, 23 ; iii. 2. Denotes supernatural works. May
be a wonder, but is also a prediction. *Klee, Origen.* A miracle may be under-
valued as well as over-valued. *Munch.* Christ does not say that signs and wonders
draw men to the truth. *Schleier.* Unless I perform signs in your presence.
Pfenninger. Can demons work miracles? Some answer, Yes. Dæmones possunt
facere miracula. *Aquinas.* The Church denies not, but contemns miracles of
Satan. *Gregory.* Heathen rejected Christ's miracles, because they witnessed
Satan's " lying wonders" ! *Cyprian.* Wonders performed by Satan, confirmed
by *Lactantius, Tertullian.* Partially admitted by *Augustine*, and nearly all
the Fathers.
πιστεύσητε. After miracles our Lord required purer faith. *Gerlach.* Not
condemned for asking a miracle, but for not believing until *compelled* to ask for
one. *Ebrard.* Implication, "If Thou restore my son, I will believe." *Stier.*
Faith of Galileans contrasted with Samaritans. *Glassius.*
ἴδητε, the nobleman and Jews. *Stier.* Men of the world. *Rieger.* Courtiers
and politicians. *Oetinger.* The petition hardly dealt with. *Bruno Bauer, C. F.
Barhdt.* Goethe charged the latter with writing to the effect, If I had been
Jesus, I would have spoken thus and thus. *Oosterzee.*

---

49. The nobleman saith unto him, Sir, come down ere my child die.

Nobleman. He was not repelled by a seemingly severe reply.
In his deep affliction he but presses his suit more earnestly.
He will soon learn that afflictions, deepening after prayer, proves
prayer *heard.*
Was not his perseverance caused by the influence of the Holy
Ghost ? Eph. ii. 8.
Such *new crosses* are tokens of a Saviour's love to His chosen.
"After these things (repeated trials) God did tempt Abraham."
Gen. xxii. 1.
"Whom the Lord loveth He chasteneth." Heb. xii. 6—11.
Come down. He speaks as if the dread emergency left no time
for considering the Lord's words.

His whole faith lay in this, that for one *in death* he was seeking
    One who had *life*.

With the Syrophœnician, he would say, " Yea, Lord—but—"

Faith of Mary and Martha was only a few degrees higher in kind.

His fear was that it would be for ever too late, if the child died.

How his faith hesitates and drags along the ground. *Augustine.*

He little knew that Christ's miracles were to build up *faith* in men !

His persistent importunity points to Jesus as His *only trust*.

He suffers the word of exhortation (Heb. xiii. 22), for he knows, if
    the Lord refuse, there is no other hope.

Die.   This stroke of the pen paints his very heart.

Fierce diseases appear as death knocking at the door.

" Alas ! while we talk my child is dying.   If Thou come not *now*,
    all will be over for ever."

He believed the Lord was a great physician, and a greater prophet,
    but it never flashed through his mind that he was talking
    and pleading with the CREATOR of ALL WORLDS !

In the presence of actual death he could not think of ONE who is
    THE RESURRECTION AND THE LIFE.

κατάβηθι.   Not accustomed to be controlled, the great generally are irritable. Tange montes, et fumigabunt. *Trapp.*

------

50. Jesus saith unto him, Go thy way ; thy son liveth. And the man believed the word that Jesus had spoken unto him, and he went his way.

Go thy way.   The Lord saw instruction and reproof were not lost
    on the father.

" My personal presence is not needed." He thus corrects his prayer,
    then answers it graciously.

Our Lord sends him away without personal knowledge of the result ; and takes away every ground for any thought of remuneration.

Sovereign grace is as clearly an element in all our Saviour's acts of
    mercy as light is in a sunbeam.

Hence a proof of His Divinity, that of the hundreds miraculously
    ealed, not one ever presumed, like **Naaman**, to offer a remuneration.

Elijah and Elisha were not thought above the reach of gold and goodly raiment.

But men would as soon *think of paying the sun for shining* as Christ for His act of love.

They knew and felt that adoring gratitude alone was to be offered to the Son of God.

Before He spoke this word, the Lord made a solemn *pause*, sinking the nobleman where none but God could help.

Our Lord thus refusing to go, would avoid seeming to pay honour to the *great*.

Christianity never bows before human rank, but loves to honour those on whom the world frowns.

Here, as everywhere, it *offers everything*, but *yields nothing*. " My kingdom is not of this world." John xviii. 36.

The Lord went with the centurion to his house, because he confessed his *unworthiness*. Luke vii. 6.

There a strong faith is crowned, *here* a weak faith is strengthened.

Our Lord answers his prayer, but *humbles* his pride, with one word, " Go."

A new trial, and perhaps the hardest yet to his faith.

But the command was a message of authority to the *ear*.

With it went Almighty grace, a secret consolation to his aching heart !

When our Lord commands, to the *believing*, He offers *strength*. Matt. xii. 13.

The nobleman would have credited Christ's *presence*, with that which was alone due to His DIVINE POWER.

By granting and yet denying He fanned the spark of faith into a flame.

In the case of the woman at the well " He breaks not the bruised reed," and now " He quenches not the smoking flax."

Here domestic ties are blest, as at Cana marriage joys were sanctioned by the Lord of heaven.

Here for the *bridal* we have the *funereal* aspect, and in each miracle family life is hallowed and beautified by the Creator of both.

He " manifested His *glory* " at Cana, and unveiled His *power* at Capernaum.

Liveth. Not merely a command, " Let him live."

Our Lord meekly *conceals* the might of His own arm Isa. xlv. 15.

Sceptics vainly object that our Lord knew his son was recovering and *informs* him of the change.

The time will come when the cavils of sceptics will for ever cease. "Every eye shall see Him." Rev. i. 7.

Thus our Lord meets those *in the end* whom He crosses *in the way.*

A double miracle : 1. On the distant *body* of the son. 2. On the *heart* of the father.

And the man. The trembling grateful emotion of the parent seems felt by the Evangelist, as he writes with a rejoicing heart.

Believed. See on John i. 7 ; vii. 38. To sweetly incline a soul resisting is the mightiest outgoing of power. Psa. cx. 3.

His disciples will henceforth know that a distance wide as heaven from earth cannot hinder His instantaneous help.

The word of Christ went swifter than a flash of lightning from Cana to Capernaum.

The cure was complete, the child was restored to perfect health, before the word was finished.

His faith resembled Abraham's,—he went, because God's PROMISE LED. Rom. iv. 20.

1. We must have the same sense of utter helplessness. Psa. x. 17 ; Rom. viii. 26. 2. The same hatred of that destroying our peace. Heb. i. 9. 3. The same trust in Christ's Almighty strength. John xiv. 13. 4. The same earnest wrestling in prayer. Psa. cxix. 147.

"The effectual (Gr. *working*) prayer availeth much." Jas. v. 16.

Went his, &c. In token of his faith, the joyful father departed homewards.

The faithful servants, sharing the pleasure, hasten to tell the welcome news.

His faith was begun when he *came* to ask a miracle.

It was *enlightened* and *purified* when the Lord reproved his slowness to believe.

It increased when the word was *spoken,* "Go ; thy son liveth."

It was perfected when the *servants said,* "Thy son liveth."

A singular error some make, in thinking he went *leisurely.* See on ver. 52.

Πορεύου. He declines to go down, as contrary to his present plan. *Schleier.* A considerable pause between πορ. and υἱός σου made by the Lord. *Lange.* Contrary to evidence. *Stier.*

ζῆ. Neither imperative, for that would make a display of His power, nor
future, for that would defer an assured boon. " Has now good health."
Trapp.

ἐπορεύετο. Two cures were wrought by this one word. *Brenz.* Occurred
at one o'clock. He went leisurely, since he could ride 25 miles that day. *Maldonat, Alford.* A remark that shows the writers were not familiar with Oriental travel. *Author.*

---

51. And as he was now going down, his servants met him, and told him,
saying, Thy son liveth.

Going. He was hastening with all speed to learn the result of
his errand.

Servants. Gr. *slaves.* Slavery was recognized, but not established, by the Mosaic law. Gen. xvii. 13.

Hired service, unknown among Jews, Greeks, and Romans, was
thought incompatible with personal freedom.

A slave occupied a modern *labourer's place*, except as to political
rights.

SOURCES of SLAVERY :

1. *Poverty.* Creditors could seize the debtor, and sell him as a
slave. Lev. xxv. 39 ; Neh. v. 5.

A person could sell himself into voluntary servitude. Lev. xxv. 47.

Cases mentioned in 2 Kings iv. 1 ; Neh. v. 5 ; Isa. l. 1, are instances of illegal violence.

2. A *thief* was sold into slavery if unable to make restitution. Ex.
xxii. 1, 3.

According to *Josephus*, he must be sold to a Jew, not to a stranger.
But this is very doubtful.

Under Roman law, the thief became the *actual slave* of his creditor.

3. A *parent* could sell a daughter to be a secondary wife. Ex.
xxi. 7.

4. *War.* Captives as a rule were to be put to death, but if they
could find purchasers they were (*servi*, preserved, hence
servants) sold to the highest bidder at auction—the sign of
which was two spears crossing (sub hastâ) among Romans
in the time of Christ.

Hebrew slave became free- –1. By obtaining remission of all
claims. 2. By the Jubilee. 3. By the Sabbatical year, six
years after he had been a slave. The Rabbis add, If a master
died leaving no son as heir.

A slave unwilling to be free, had his ear bored with an awl.   Ex. xxi. 6.

Mesopotamians and Lydians bored the ear for a similar purpose.

To a freedman the master was bound to give out of his flock, his floor, his winepress.   Deut. xv. 13.

Being free, his wife and children remained slaves.   Ex. xxi. 4, 5.

A Roman father could sell his child, and if freed, he again became his father's, and could be sold a second time as a slave.

At any time he could take his son's property or *life*.

Cato advised masters to sell their *aged* slaves.   " So many slaves, so many enemies," became a Roman proverb.

A Roman master being murdered, all his slaves were put to death.

Flamininus killed a slave, to gratify a curious guest.

Vedius Pollio fed his fish with the flesh of the children of his slaves.

Augustus had a slave crucified, for killing a *favourite quail*.

Their testimony was never received in court, except under *torture*.

Superannuated slaves were left on an island in the Tiber to starve.

Their souls were thought essentially corrupt, and hence were despised.   *Plato*.

A master might feel friendship for a slave, but there could be no equity between them.   *Aristotle*.

Rings in Pompeii still seen, where *porters* were *chained to the gate*.

Fields were cultivated by slaves in chains.   Many slept nightly in *prison*.

By Mosaic law a man wilfully murdering a slave, was to be put to death.   Lev. xxiv. 17, 22.

If he punished him till he died, the crime was to be avenged.   Ex. xxi. 20.

If he lost an eye he gained his freedom.   Some were kindly treated.   Prov. xxix. 19.

Slaves were circumcised, Gen. xvii. 12, and as such shared the Passover.   Ex. xii. 44.

Female slaves ground at hand-mills, gleaned, and did other menial work.

Slaves often became stewards, tutors, physicians, artists.   2 Sam. ix. 2, 10.

Slaves dared not offer incense, or sacrifice, or use the lustral bowl in the temple.

Cruel masters would shut them out, even from the pity of God.

Many captives were freed in six years,—their gains were theirs.

Sometimes masters and slaves sat at the same table, since a differ-
ence of colour was unknown, and slaves often were the *fairest.*
Pliny consoled himself on the death of a favourite, that he died
free.
Epictetus, a slave freed, became a warm *friend* of the *Emperor*
Hadrian.
Some slaves nobly sacrificed life itself to save a beloved master's.
Petronian law forbade masters selling their slaves as *gladiators.*
Christianity ameliorated their condition and raised it so much, that
*dying masters asked the comfort and prayers of Christian slaves
in their last hours.*
But Cicero *apologizes* for noticing the death of a slave.
" *Bond and free* are one in Christ," 1 Cor. xii. 13, and will be one
in heaven.

Met.   Voices from Providence come oft as an *echo* of our prayer
and faith. Col. Von M——, a prisoner in Silesia, at midnight
took his Bible, which he had always neglected. He read,
" *Call upon me,*" &c., Psa. l. 15. That very night his *king*
could *not sleep ;* all efforts were vain. He rose, wrestled an
hour in prayer, and found peace ! " Who," cried the king to
his wife, " is the man that lives, and has done me the *greatest
harm ?* This very day I will forgive him." In the morning,
after inquiry, the king wrote out the *pardon* of Col. Von
M——, a state prisoner. That day that convert praised the
Lord for a *double pardon.* The God of grace still lives who
remembered *Mordecai* and the *king.* Esther vi. 1.

High station of the nobleman may be inferred from this fact.
His household was complete, and yet several servants were sent
with tidings to their lord.
The astounding suddenness of the recovery, doubtless, urged them
to utmost haste, to rejoice their master's mind.
This very errand hints a kind treatment. Hence their gratitude.

Thy son liveth.   Could they have known their master's errand
to the Lord ? had they *faith* as well as knowledge to *anticipate
his success ?*
How many masters have learned from their " slaves " the *way to
heaven !*
Children to the third and fourth generation are blessed for their
fathers' sake. Ex. xx. 6.
They greet him, as it were, with an echo of the Saviour's word
in verse 50.

δοῦλοι. " *Slaves.*" Some deny the right of Hebrew creditors to sell the debtor. *Michaelis, Maimonides.* He had no right until he needed food and clothing. *Selden.* If one sold to a strange tribe, his kindred bound to redeem him. *Diodorus.* Lev. xxv. 39 should be read, "sell himself." *Gesenius.* Not as Auth. Vers., "to be sold." *Bevan,* in *Smith's* Dict. Slaves were to go to the tabernacle for their inheritance. Ex. xxi. 6. *Ewald.* The word "for ever" meant till the Jubilee. *Josephus, Rabbis.* This custom obtained among Arabs. *Bochart.* Master killing slave, Ex. xxi. 20, punished by death. *Rabbis, Selden.* Slaves dare not sacrifice. *Pliny.*

ἀπήγγειλαν. Omitted. *Cod. Sinai.*

---

52. Then inquired he of them the hour when he began to amend. And they said unto him, Yesterday at the seventh hour the fever left him.

Inquired. It might have been *accidental,* but he must know all, especially if the time *corresponded* with that of the word of Christ.

Cana was a whole day's journey from Capernaum, or 25 miles distant.

The works of God in nature and grace challenge investigation.

The more men or even angels search, the more they will for ever wonder. 1 Pet. i. 12.

Amend. His trembling faith does not rise to so much as a complete *cure.*

Yesterday. Jewish day ended at sunset, began at sunrise. John i. 39.

He arrived home the next day. Oriental travelling is slow for *private* persons.

His intense desire to realize the Saviour's pledge, and see his son restored, prevented *the least delay.*

Seventh. Or 1 o'clock, P.M. Day divided into twelve equal parts.

Exhausted by painful anxiety, he must have urged his way with all possible speed.

"One wonders he stops during *night* on the road home." *De Wette.*

Such a remark is simply the result of ignorance of Oriental travel.

If *Roman* time, 7 P.M., and he must have journeyed *all night.*

It is curious how some authors will tax themselves to explain a tardiness which *never existed.*

Camels, travelling 20 miles a day, make a *laborious journey* for the *rider.*

Fever. One hundred and seven fevers are indexed by *Dr Dunglinson.*

All the diseases treated by the same author (Pathology and Thera-
peutics) are 3500.

Left. That is, he was suddenly and entirely restored.

This thorough work shows God gives more than we ask. Eph. iii. 20.

The lesson of this miracle is seen in a father despairing who throws
himself on the *possible power* of the Lord.

κομψότερον. Implies he was not prepared for so sudden a cure. *W. & W.*
ἐχθὲς, after sundown. *Brückner.* About 2 o'clock P.M. *Stier.* 1 P.M.
W. & W. His faith calmed his mind, and he went leisurely. *Leigh.*
πυρετός, from πῦρ, fire, a burning fever.
ἐβδόμην. Kernel of this miracle is the elevation of a *wonder-seeking faith* into, &c. *Alford.*
ὥραν. If Roman time, 7 P.M. ; if Jewish, 1 P.M. He had time to reach home
that day. *Alford.* The learned critic could not be familiar with Oriental travel.
Author. He took a long route home. *Bengel.*

---

53. So the father knew that it was at the same hour, in the which Jesus said
unto him, Thy son liveth : and himself believed, and his whole house.

Father knew. The one word brought healing at once to two souls.

The hand of *Love* brought this child to the brink of the grave.

" Your fathers cried unto the Lord, and the Lord sent Moses," &c.
1 Sam. xii. 8.

" God saw the affliction of our fathers in Egypt, and sent them," &c.
Neh. ix. 9.

" He smote the first-born of Egypt, but made His own people," &c.
Psa. lxxviii. 51, 52.

" Ask what I shall give thee," the Lord to Solomon in Gibeon. 1
Kings iii. 5.

" Call upon me in the day of trouble, and I will deliver thee."
Psa. l. 15 ; Isa. lv. 6.

Believed. A much higher faith than that noted in verse 50.

Here it is *absolute faith in Jesus as the Messiah*, the SON OF GOD.

Who can doubt that *servants* and *children* were included ?

Who can disprove that the " *household* of Stephanas," 1 Cor. i. 16,
and " *the household* of Lydia," Acts xvi. 15, had children of
various ages embraced in the covenant ?

" The promise is to you, and to your children " (Acts ii. 39,) of all
ages.

Every reason to hope that all children INDENTURED to the Lord, like Samuel, will be saved. 1 Sam. i. 28.

The nobleman must have called his family, and then rendered thanks to God. Job i. 5.

God's testimony concerning Abraham: " I know him, that he will command his household after him." Gen. xviii. 19.

Thus Jacob had family devotions. Gen. xxxv. 3. Samuel at the house of Jesse. 1 Sam. xvi. 5. David. 2 Sam. vi. 20. Noah. Gen. viii. 20. Abraham. Gen. xii. 7. Isaac. Gen. xxvi. 25. Joshua. Chap. xxiv. 15. Jesse. 1 Sam. xx. 6. Families prayed " apart." Zech. xii. 12—14. Cornelius. Acts x. 2.

Aquila and Priscilla had *a Church in their house.* Rom. xvi. 3, 5.

Primitive Christians began and closed the day with prayer. *Tertullian* in *Neander.*

A gracious law in Israel, " Fathers should make known to their children," &c. Psa. lxxviii. 5.

Whole house. The light kindled on the hills shines down on the valleys.

Covenant blessings reach the children also: " *This day is salvation come to this house.*" Luke xix. 9.

Family religion the ground and source of all the blessings and glories of the Church of God.

The golden thread of the covenant runs through the entire Church history.

" Keep thy soul diligently, and teach thy sons and thy sons' sons." Deut. iv. 9.

" Thou shalt talk of them when thou sittest in thine house." Deut. vi. 7 ; Prov. xxii. 6.

" Set your hearts unto all these words which ye shall command your children." Deut. xxxii. 46.

Even Esau received only a lesser blessing, as *father* of *many princes.*

When all Israel but two died in the wilderness, the nation, like a river checked for a while, flowed on afterwards.

The priesthood was changed from line to line, and the crown from family to family, through their national sins and rebellions, yet GOD FORGOT NOT HIS COVENANT with their *father* Abraham. Matt. xxiv. 35 ; Jer. xxxiii. 20.

On account of idolatry, ten tribes were carried into Assyria, and never returned.

Two tribes still inherited the blessing, until, owing to their sin, they also were led away.

Yet God brought them back, and the covenant stood, until they
killed *a* GREATER *than Abraham !*

" Touching the election, they are beloved for the fathers' sakes."
Rom. xi. 28.

For FIFTEEN HUNDRED YEARS Abraham's posterity enjoyed the
fruits of this covenant.

Another covenant was an inheritance of the curse, first noted in the
second commandment.

Eli's seed inherited it, and the males died in *the flower* of their
youth. 1 Sam. ii. 33.

Beggary was to be their portion, and the loss of the priesthood
their punishment.

It began with Hophni and Phinehas, and went down in a series of
calamities.

Dying, the wicked *leave arrears for their descendants to pay.*

Some men so live, that at last they only leave an *inventory* of *wrath
to their heirs.*

Athenians rejoiced on seeing *Simon,* a *martyr* for patriotism, honoured
in his *children.*

When the children of *Lachares* were banished, they placed *their
hands on their mouth,* and, in silence, acknowledged the justice
of the gods.

The pious loving Jonathan lost his throne and life for his father
Saul's sin.

A *traitor* loses his estate and life, and leaves his innocent children
beggars.

ἐπίστευσεν. He believed before. This is the acknowledging of Jesus as
the Messiah. *Trench.* An augmenting of his faith ; there are grades in the
strength of faith. *Beza.* Faith was completed when his servants announced the
cure. *Bede.*

οἰκία, after such a stupendous act of kindness our Lord was doubtless persuaded to remain some days with this nobleman. *Hengst.*

---

54. This is again the second miracle that Jesus did, when he was come out of
Judæa into Galilee.

Second. Gr. *this second miracle* again Jesus performed.
God registers all our mercies, and all neglects of the same.
This second miracle aggravates the infidelity of the Jews.

The Lord takes account how souls are won by a *tract*, or a *sermon*, or a word fitly spoken.

Miracle. See on John ii. 11, 23 ; iii. 2. Doubtless many were wrought in this neighbourhood. John iv. 45.

That of Cana was confined to an humble village company.

But this on the nobleman's son was a blazing torch, lighting Galilee's capital.

That of the *loaves* sent forth five thousand *heralds* of His majesty and power.

Galilee. For geography and history, see on John i. 43.

πάλιν, a favourite term with John, and not necessary here. *Hengst.* It occurs about fifty times in this Gospel. In Luke it occurs but twice. This again a second miracle, i.e. the second *Galilean* miracle. John iii. 2 ; iv. 45. *Alford.*

Γαλιλαίαν. What became of our Lord, or where He stayed for a season, we cannot tell from the narrative. *Schweizer.* This Gospel is a paralipomena to the preceding Evangels. *Hengst.*

John 5

1. AFTER this there was a feast of the Jews; and Jesus went up to Jerusalem.

Feast. Probably the second passover of four in our Lord's ministry. John ii. 13; vi. 4.
Indifference of inspiration to chronology proves it of no especial use in teaching men the " way of life."
" Let my people go, that they may hold a feast unto me." Exod. v. 1.
Blessings flowing from Christ should crown our lives with many feasts.
A good man keeps every day as a *holyday. Diogenes.*
" Eat thy bread with joy, &c., for God now accepteth thy works." Eccl. ix. 7.
Jews. History and character, see on John i. 19.
Went up. Our Lord's life is filled with mysterious transitions.
From glory to humiliation, and from humiliation to glory.
His complex personality, Divine and human natures, not sufficient to account for all.
Underneath His whole history lies the great fact that by His obedience He was to make many righteous. Rom. v. 19.
Jerusalem. See on John vii. 25. Heb. *Vision of peace.*
Called Salem. Gen. xiv. 18. Jebus. Judg. xix. 10. Ariel, or Lion of God. Isa. xxix. 1. Holy City. Matt. iv. 5
Arabic authors call it " *El Makdis,*" which means *sanctuary,* and " *Esh Sherif,*" the *venerable.*
At present they call it by the name " *El Khuds,*" the *Holy.*
Jerusalem 37 miles east of Joppa, 18 from the Jordan, 20 from Hebron, and 36 from Samaria.
Its elevation is 2400 feet above the sea on the mountains of Judea.
Stands on a promontory 500 feet above the valleys of Hinnom and Jehoshaphat.
Occupies Mount Moriah, 2429 feet, Mount Zion, 2537, and Mount Acra, 2610 feet high.
Walls $2\frac{1}{2}$ miles in length, 60 feet high, 8 feet thick, built 1534 A.D.

With four gates, 2000 houses, 5000 Jews, and 25,000 Turks, Greeks, and Latins.

Taken by David, 2 Sam. v. 7, and made the capital of Judea, 1048 B.C.

Taken by Nebuchadnezzar, and Jews led captive to Babylon, 588 B.C.

Rebuilt by Zerubbabel, 526 B.C.   Taken by Alexander, 352 B.C.

Taken by Ptolemy, 324 B.C.   By Antiochus, 170 B.C.   Retaken by Maccabees, 163 B.C.

Taken by Pompey, 63 B.C.   Destroyed by Titus according to prophecy, 70 A.D.

In the rebellion of Bar-Cocheba 580,000 Jews perished, 132 A.D.

Jews banished by Hadrian. City called Ælia Capitolina, 136 A.D.

For a time the very name of Jerusalem seems to have been forgotten.

Helena, mother of Constantine, built a church over the pretended sepulchre, 325 A.D.

Emperor Julian vainly attempted to rebuild it to *dishonour* Christ, 363 A.D.   (See on verse 14.)

An earthquake suddenly scattered both workmen and their work.

Taken by Chosroes, 614 A.D., by Heraclius, 628 A.D., by Omar, 637 A.D.

By Ahmed Turk, 868 A.D., by Saracens, 969 A.D., by Crusaders, 1099 A.D.

By Saladin, 1187 A.D., by Raymond's treachery restored to Latins, 1242 A.D.

Sultans of Egypt, 1291 A.D., Selim, 1517 A.D.   Present walls built by Suliman.

The Turks have held it from 1517 A.D. to this time, 1871 A.D.

A Protestant mission is now sustained in it by Prussia and England.

Destruction of Jerusalem clearly foretold by our Lord.   See Sugg. Comm. on Luke xxi. 5—20.

The writer saw the Jews bewailing the desolation of their temple as they sat by the foundations of the first temple, swaying to and fro, and mournfully reading the prophecies.   Isa. lxii. 1, 4, &c.

" Jerusalem above," Gal. iv. 26, " Heavenly Jerusalem," Heb. xii. 22, " New Jerusalem," Rev. xxii. 2, names given to the home of the glorified.

μετὰ ταῦτα.   Remote succession. *Lücke.*

ἑορτὴ. If this feast is the Passover, then John names four. This gives our Lord 3½ years. Dan. ix. 27. *Hengst.* Opinions : 1. PENTECOST. *Chrys., Theoph., Erasmus, Calvin, Beza, Bengel.* 2. Second PASSOVER of our Lord's ministry. *Irenæus, Luther, Scaliger, Hengst., Greswell, Robinson, Trench, D. Brown, Lightfoot.* 3. PURIM, going right before the second Passover. *Jacobi, Kepler, Hug, Olshausen, Wieseler, Winer, Stier, Meyer.* Purim feast too crude in its idea and celebration. *B. Crusius.* 4. Feast of TABERNACLES. *Cocceius, Ebrard.* 5. DEDICATION. *Petavius.* Cannot with any probability gather what feast it was. *Lücke, De Wette, Tholuck, Alford.*

'Ιεροσόλυμα. Same as Salem. Gen. xiv. 18. Jews quote as proof, Psa. lxxvi. 2. *Rabbis.* Salem 8 miles from Scythopolis. *Jerome.* Beyond Jordan near Sodom. *Ewald.* Testimonies balanced. *Smith.*

---

2. Now there is at Jerusalem by the sheep market a pool, which is called in the Hebrew tongue Bethesda, having five porches.

Now. John wrote A.D. 96, first year of the Emperor Nerva.

There is. This Gospel was written after the ruin of the city, and that pool is there to this day.

Pools were sunk so deep and built so strong, conquerors had not time to destroy them.

Romans would have spared Bethesda for the convenience of their garrison.

Sheep. " Market " added by the translators, others would more properly insert " gate." Neh. iii. 1.

Pool. Immense reservoirs elaborately built of hewn stone. See on John ix. 7.

Hebrew. Eber, or Heber, great grandson of Shem. Gen. x. 24.

The language spoken by the Jews from Abraham, 1996 B.C.

The oldest form of speech known to us. Abraham found it in Canaan.

Aramaic a modification of the Chaldee used in our Lord's time. But few fragments remain.

Aramaic learned by the Jews during their captivity.

Hebrew Scriptures, however, were still read in their synagogues.

Remains of Hebrew now mainly found in the comments of Rabbis on the old Testament.

Mishna, tradition of the law written or collected, 230 A.D.

Gemara, commentary on the Mishna, written 290 A.D.

Targums, Chaldee paraphrases of the Hebrew Scriptures.

Masora, critical remarks on these Targums, 850 A.D.

Bethesda. Heb. " House of Mercy," a splendid ruin, still seen on Moriah.

Few, *very few,* of the New Testament localities can be *identified.*

Yet this pool, near the temple, seems to be one of the few.

Its length 360, breadth 130, and depth 75 feet, covering something more than one acre.

Built of large blocks of stone of remarkable beauty and finish.

A course of concrete covers these stones, and a coat of fine plaster covers the concrete.

Supplied once with water from Solomon's pools, 8 miles distant.

Those pools, beyond Bethlehem, three in number, are perfect.

138 feet in depth, and made of very large stones, they cover about six acres, and would now cost millions.

A spacious pool in perfect order still exists in Hebron.   2 Sam. iv. 12.

These works are nearly 3000 years old, proving their massive structure.

Proximity of this pool to the temple crowd was very favourable to those begging *alms*.

Here the impotent man found bread ; possibly he may find a cure for his disease.

To leave would be to give up alms, and all hope of being healed.

To wait he is resolved ; and when Christ comes, lo ! he is abiding his time.   Isa. xxx. 18.

The "Angel of the covenant" came when hope seemed past.

What an attitude for a sinner, ever to wait at mercy's gate !

Just before Jesus came he might have said, " I'll return and die at home."

But he waited a little longer, and his perseverance was crowned with a glorious blessing.

Five porches.   Formerly splendid tokens of *luxury* and *wealth* in Oriental cities.

The colonnades at Samaria and Baalbec are superb ruins.

Millions spent on tombs, temples, circuses, theatres, baths, but no hospitals or asylums.

Ridley preached on *charity*, and Edward VI., that youthful wonder of piety and patriotism, consecrated two *palaces* for hospitals.

ἐστι ; ἦν in Syriac, Arabic, Persic, and Armenian versions. *Author*.   The scene after two score years was fresh in John's mind. *Maurice*.   More so in the mind of the Spirit. *Author*.   Gospel written before destruction of Jerusalem. *Lücke, Bengel*.   No evidence. *Hengst., Alford*.   Indicates that Jerusalem ruined had been restored. *Lange*.   That Jerusalem may have perished, but the pool remained. *Author*.

προβατικῇ, supply πύλῃ. *Wetstein, Lampe, Rosenmüller, Alf*.   Jerusa-

lem had a sheep gate, Neh. iii. 1; xii. 39, but not a sheep market. *Campbell.*
No wall built there till Agrippa. *Alford.* Prison gate belonged to the temple
same as the present " golden gate." *Von Raumer.*

Βεθεσδά. House or place of Mercy or of the flowing of water. Eusebius describes it as existing in his time as two pools. *Grove.*

κολυμβήθρα, a name given baptistries during middle ages. *Burgon.* Medi-
cal baths still near the mosque, and fed by subterranean fountains. *Walcott,
Tobler, Ritter.* The same as the fountain of the Virgin. *Robinson, Trench.*
Both pool and fosse. *De Saulcy.* Undoubtedly the pool near the temple site,
one of the traditions found true. *Ellicott, Williams.* Built for the sick.
Bengel. The water red in the time of Eusebius. Mirum in modum rubens.
Jerome.

Ἑβραϊστί, Aramaic, spoken by the Jews after returning from exile, substantially the same as Chaldeé. Books of Tobit, Judith, Maccabees, written
in Aramaic. *Jerome.* Phœnician and Punic closely related to the Hebrew.
Nicholson in *Kitto.* Hebrew the primitive language. *Löscher, Havernick,
Ewald, Hengst.* Aramaic. *Gesenius.* Hebrew ceased as a living tongue during the captivity. *Kimchi, Buxtorf, Walton.* Slowly expired during the age
following. *Pfeiffer, Robinson, Löscher.* Ancient Hebrew character still used,
B.C. 143. *Jerome, Origen, Talmud.* Change ascribed to Ezra. *Gesenius.*
Masoretic points invented A.D. 700, by Jewish Rabbis. *Nicholson.* Being un-
known to Jerome and Origen. *Hupfeld.* Septuagint translated from the
Samaritan copy. *Eichorn.*

πέντε. Half of ten, symbol of incompleteness. *Hengst.* Five books of the
law. *Augustine.* Five senses, five wounds of Christ. *Morus.*

στοάς, cloisters called οἶκοι as well as porticos. *Tittmann.* A wall on one
side like the porch (ποικίλη) at Athens. *Tholuck.* Cloisters or colonnades
round artificial tanks common in the East. *Smith.*

---

3. In these lay a great multitude of impotent folk, of blind, halt, withered,
waiting for the moving of the water.

Multitude. A picture of the nineteenth century in the West as
well as East.

Thus we have witnessed crowds of *invalids* around some celebrated
spring.

Suffering is the background in the great picture of human life

Impotent. Medical term is *atrophy*, or emaciation, arising
from deficiency in nervous action, want of blood, and other
sources.

Blind. In Egypt to this day blind are tenfold what they are in
Britain and America.

The greatest bodily calamity. No sense wherein we enjoy so
much as sight.

Sight gives form, colour, body even to our ideas.

The most pitiable beggars to be met in Palestine and Egypt are
blind.

In Cairo, one in five is either blind or diseased in the eyes. *Lane.*

So far ·as the writer could observe, Egyptian teachers are mostly blind.

Causes assigned are fine sand, saline particles from the Desert, southern winds, bad diet, or sleeping on the roof in open air.

Mahommedans neglect all remedies, being strict fatalists.

European soldiers suffered terribly from this disease while in Egypt.

Out of a population of 5000 in Jaffa 500 are estimated to be blind.

Jews forbidden to curse the *deaf*, Lev. xix. 14, or make the blind to wander. Deut. xxvii. 18.

Persons imprisoned anciently often had their *eyes put out*. Judg. xvi. 21 ; 2 Kings xxv. 7.

Ceylonese attribute their blindness to sins of a former state.

A blind man said he thought scarlet colour must be like the sound of a trumpet. *Locke.*

Blind are generally *timid,* afraid of unseen dangers, and *nervous,* because *sedentary.*

Negligence and wantonness of others often exasperate their temper.

Blind often exhibit the highest order of abstract thought and calculation.

Nicholas Saunderson, an eminent English mathematician, although blind, was appointed professor in Cambridge University in 1711.

John Metcalf, 1788, an engineer in Derbyshire, although blind, laid out the highways with admirable skill.

The immortal poets *Homer, Ossian,* and *Milton* were blind.

Blind asylums still send forth many of the best musicians.

Diodotus was blind, and yet he taught Cicero the art of eloquence.

Halt. Crippled in the feet, limping, lame.

Withered. Loss of vital power in the limbs by paralysis or stiffness.

To this class of paralytic the " impotent man " Jesus cured belonged.

Waiting. A picture of our race. Diseases are thousands in number.

How patiently, yet often how hopelessly and weariedly, do the afflicted look for some angel to relieve them.

Moving. Creation pervaded by the energy of the living God.

Water. Note the laver of regeneration here typified. Tit. iii. 5.

" A fountain opened to the house of David and to the inhabitants of Jerusalem." Zech. xiii. 1.

τυφλῶν. A blind Arab acted as a guide through the desert of Arabia. Dr Moyes found touching red disagreeable; he knew a voice after two years' absence. *Encyc. Britt.* It is remarkable that Prof. Saunderson, with so terrible an affliction, was profane and an atheist. *Chalmers,* Bio. Dic.

κίνησιν, daily. *Doddr.* Often in the year. *Euthymius.* The time was always well known. *Lampe.* Period marked out by God as the sound among the mulberry trees. 2 Sam. ii. 24. *Author.*

πολὺ and ἐκδεχομένων τὴν τοῦ ὕδατος κίνησιν omitted. *Cod. Sin., Tisch., Alford, Meyer, Tregelles.*

---

4. For an angel went down at a certain season into the pool, and troubled the water: whosoever then first after the troubling of the water stepped in was made whole of whatsoever disease he had.

For an. Although there is weighty *external* evidence against the genuineness of this verse, the *internal* in its favour is overwhelming.

Without it the seventh verse, admitted to be genuine, is meaningless.

Impossible to see how such a verse could have crept into the text.

Why should not the healing powers of nature appear to the profound spiritual vision of John to be directed by an angel?

Had we John's eyes we should doubtless be aware of many such blessed agencies. *Besser.*

Angel. For nature and office of these celestial beings, see on John i. 51.

Physical science has as yet shed no light on intellectual or moral *force.*

Though in every step we are compelled to admit such forces. Job xxxviii. 33.

The *source* of all power seems hidden among the secrets of God. Prov. xxv. 2.

ORDINANCES of HEAVEN are written out, but not yet translated for man. Jer. xxxi. 35.

An angel brought the food to Elijah, and here gave to the water its healing efficacy. 1 Kings xix. 5.

An angel strengthened our Lord's body, not adding strength to His spirit. Luke xxii. 43.

Angelic presence reassured Him of His Father's love in that awful hour.

Angels carried Lazarus to heaven ; their aid ever seems *outward.*

They do *not* appear to have *any power* BETWEEN THE SOUL AND GOD.

Their ministry to saints never reaches to *salvation heights.* Heb. i. 14.

Papal *Rome*, in this as in many other points, nullifies God's truth.

Troubled. Ministration of angels clearly taught in Scripture. See on John i. 51.

The Jews having age after age rebelled against their God, and become exceedingly corrupt, the angel came no more, after they had rejected the Lord. *Tertullian.*

Roman world scorned their religion as a senseless superstition; and Jews as the worst of slaves.

Yet their prophets, through faith, saw the boundless healing power of a fountain Divine. Zech. xiii. 1.

The angel appears to have descended at the seasons of the three great feasts, but there was a Divine *limitation* to the virtue.

For more than 400 years no prophet's voice had been heard in Israel.

First. Those coming first and those coming last to Christ are healed.

Made whole. Fountains of earth's pleasures are soon exhausted.

Earth's health-springs only heal the body, water of life heals the soul.

The world believes not in the efficacy of this gospel pool.

Abana and Pharpar could only cleanse the *external* man.

Fountain of Christ heals wounds inflicted by *the fire of sin* in the inmost soul.

A leper like Naaman, though clothed in purple, is a leper still.

" Though your sins were as scarlet, I will make them as wool, and though red," &c. Isa. i. 18.

ἄγγελος. This verse is cancelled by *Ebrard, Tischendorf, Alford, Meyer, Tholuck, Olshausen, Lücke, Lange, Tregelles.* Omitted in *Cod. Sin., Vat.* Retained in *Cod. Alex.,* in *Syriac, Ethiopic,* and *Arabic* versions. Retained. Tertullian, Ambrose, Chrysostom, Cyril, Nonnus, Augustine, Lachmann, Brückner, Ellicott, Wordsworth. Energy of nature personified. *Martensen.* Oriental figure for Providence. *Rosenm.* Evangelist would not leave us to guess how the sick were healed. *Hoffmann.* Parallel with Rev. xvi. 5. *Hengst.* In the Gospels angels only appear in ethical spheres. *Lücke.* Baptismal angel. *Tertullian.* Prophecy of the Spirit's descent. *Ambrose.* A marginal note little by little increasing. *Trench.* Strange legendary air of the miracle may account for its omission, but not its insertion. Verse 7 has no point without it. *D. Brown.*

κατὰ καιρὸν, appointed time. Rom. v. 6. *Hengst.* At their great feasts. *Stier.* Sometimes evil angels trouble the clear stream of justice. *Trapp.*

κατέβαινεν, showed himself active then. *Winer.* Was wont to descend. *D. Brown, Wordsworth.*

ἐτάρασσε. Spring probably gaseous, and bubbled at intervals, like that in Kissingen. *Tholuck.* John would have found an angel in the sparkling waters of Carlsbad. *Hengst.* Natural efficiency increased by the angel's presence. *Olshausen.* Divine efficacy frequently bestowed on baths. *Bengel.* Sick trusting in the troubling of the waters were superstitious. *De Wette.* A tradition states that one in a year was cured. *Chrys.* Sacrificial carcases washed here imparted medical virtues. *Hammond, Richter.* A notion opposed to all principles of materia medica. *Author.* Miraculous. 1. Only the first entering were healed. 2. Every kind of disease healed. 3. Healing instantaneous. *Lampe.* A report not vouched for by the Evangelist. *Kuinoel.* Demanded skill in application, as vaccine to resist small-pox. *Maurice.*

ὑγιὴς ἐγίνετο. This atheistic age fixes its eye on that monstrum ingens cui lumen ademptum, a Cosmos without a God. *Hengst.* Had we the inspired eye of John, we too could see angels in our health-giving springs. *Besser.* Scholars are sceptical, mankind are trustful as to the existence of angels. *Maurice.* Students worship idols of the cave, the people idols of the market-place. *Lord Bacon.* Angels still work miracles at martyrs' festivals and other places. *Rheimish Notes.*

---

5. And a certain man was there, which had an infirmity thirty and eight years.

Infirmity. Literally without strength, probably a stroke of paralysis, a type of Israel under the curse in the wilderness for thirty-eight years. Deut. ii. 14.

Thirty-eight. A generation had passed away, and the population of the globe had changed, while he suffered.

Deprived of the use of his limbs, chained to his wretched couch, he was God's prisoner for nearly forty years.

Mankind subject to 3000 diseases, so many visible and invisible *fetters* by which God can bind us.

Christ suffered the curse to ravage the world for 4000 years.

He waited three full days after the sisters of Lazarus mourned his death.

The work of the Saviour became more *marked* by delay.

In mysterious wisdom God waited for " the fulness of time." Gal. iv. 4, 5.

A long period to be the victim of suffering, but what is that to ETERNITY ?

Some will never think of leaving sin until *disabled.*

Many, like Byron, " see their household gods dashed around them," and yet, like him, harden under the blow instead of repenting.

" I thank thee, O God, for a discipline of *fifty-eight years*," said *Baxter.*

King Alfred prayed for the rod if necessary to *drive* him to God.

This poor man's perseverance showed his faith fastened on that which was *above.*

None less than an *angel of God* could bring him a remedy.

It is likely he was the most miserable of all the patients assembled
there.

Jesus knew He should meet this poor creature, and selected him as
the sermon for the morning.

δέ. Now. *Brown.*
τριακονταοκτώ refers to Israel's journeying in the wilderness. *Apollinaris*
in his catena. *Hengst.* The duration of the disease. *Trench, De Wette.*

---

6. When Jesus saw him lie, and knew that he had been now a long time in
that case, he saith unto him, Wilt thou be made whole?

Saw him. Mark the sovereignty of His mercy. Rom. ix. 15.

How many other sufferers did He see, but passed by?

How like God! He visited the lowly, those whom the world neglected and despised.

His eye moved His heart. Lam. iii. 51. He shows mercy in
proportion to one's misery. Heb. v. 2.

On the cross, as on the throne, His heart thrills with pity and compassion.

On one occasion He thanked the Father for hiding these things
from the wise, &c. Matt. xi. 25.

" I will be gracious to whom I will be gracious, and will show
mercy," &c. Exod. xxxiii. 19.

Knew. Gr. *knowing by intuition*, direct and perfect as of omniscience. See on John ii. 25.

Although He *knew*, He yet puts the strange question.

Did He see true faith in the sufferer's heart? He will *create* it
there, if it is not. Psal. li. 10.

Long time. Verse 14 proves his disease the fruit of his personal
sin.

Had he *sinned* at twenty, he would now be nearly threescore.

A picture of the race. Man's inveterate obstinacy had widened
the distance between him and God.

Man had fully tested every scheme for *rising*, and proved all vain.

But as in the case of the deaf mutes healed by our Lord, He saw
their *silent plea.*

So our groaning world could only make silent signals that all was
lost.

The Spirit ever begins in a man's heart before man begins with
Him.

" I am found of them who sought me not." Isa. lxv. 1.

Unto him.   All the multitude of patients were intently longing
for aid.

He singled out one who seemed to be without friend on earth.

Wilt thou ?   Without our desire being aroused by His love,
heaven comes not.

Could there be a possible doubt of his desire for a cure ?

But the Lord would thus call the poor man's attention to Himself.

As he turned his gaze on the stranger, he saw not the long-
wished-for *angel*, but the LORD OF ANGELS !

Detailing his disease reminds him of his utterly *desperate* case,
" for hope deferred maketh the heart sick."

Why had no such question before been heard by him ?

Because the Saviour as GOD does things not as *man*.

The question could not have been asked in mockery, and the poor
man felt a deep meaning was concealed under these simple
words.

" Art thou here with an *earnest desire* to be made whole ? "

Our Lord would bring out clearly and definitely the conscious
sense of need.

And He would awaken *faith* by giving a presentiment of a cure.

He would also attract all eyes and hearts to Himself, the INCARNATE
GOD.

Not the HEALER only, but the CREATOR of body and soul, stood before him, and he knew it not.

Our Lord did not rebuke his hopeless lying and waiting.

The question implies, " Hast thou done *all that thou couldst* or
sought relief by fervent prayer ? "

" Hast thou *courage, confidence, and hope* enough to believe that thou
canst ever be cured ? "

He must confess his case hopeless as to any aid from the pool.

The *desire* to be saved is as much of *grace* as the plan of *salvation*.

THE SIN to be removed is the WILFULLY CHOSEN STATE of all
unrenewed minds.

Instead of parting with it, all their energies are put forth to
RETAIN it.

The sinner covered with leprosy, insanely refuses to be cured.

" All they," says Christ, " that hate ME love death."   Prov. viii.
36.

The sensual insanely cling to their destroyer, and wist not that
" the dead are there, and that her guests are in the depths of
hell."   Prov. ix. 18.

Whole. Awakens a full sense of that great change needed, though he thinks only of a bodily cure.

Our Lord's miracles seldom if ever stopped with *temporal* aid.

Lepers, paralytics, blind, lame, dumb, demoniacs, were doubtless healed of the *greater disease*,—SIN IN THE SOUL.

He seems to gently hint, perhaps, ANOTHER may assume the angel's office.

It was now no mere *experiment* of successful entrance into the " troubled " pool.

There is no *peradventure* in obeying the voice of God. Deut. xxx. 19.

"He that believeth shall be saved." It is the word of the omnipotent God.

All the attributes of Jehovah are *pledged to secure* that result.

His heart may have been withered, through the long burnings of rebellion.

It was something to convince him One stronger than an angel did pity him.

But Divine LOVE persuaded him, for Divine MIGHT had created trust in his heart.

ἰδών. Crowds of wretches throng the temples of idolatry in Asia, and are passed by the steel-hearted visitors as though they were so many blocks of wood. In *one night a score of them have been known to die. Medhurst.*

ἰδών. Hopelessness probably seen in his face. *Alford.*

γνούς, i.e. ἐν ἑαυτῷ. Superhuman knowledge, of which we have so striking an example in the Samaritan woman. John iv. 17, 18. *Alford.*

θέλεις. His aspect was that of feeble will and self-abandonment. *Lange.* Reproved for not using his remaining strength. *Schleiermacher.* A sluggish and dull-minded man. *Richter.* Chief object of the question to correct the soul. *Stier.* To awaken a yearning after the remedy. *Trench.* To establish a *point of connection* between his mind and the object of mercy. *Alford.*

γενέσθαι, refers to healing of the spiritual maladies. *Meyer.* Some supply " although it be the Sabbath day." *Semler, Lightfoot, Rosenm.* But this is very improbable. *Alford.*

---

7. The impotent man answered him, Sir, I have no man, when the water is troubled, to put me into the pool: but while I am coming, another steppeth down before me.

Answered. Without churlishness, he simply states his desperate case.

His answer shows he understood all in an *external* sense.

Doubtless he had made his case the ground for pleading for *alms*, and now hoped this kind stranger would help him into the

pool when the angel came, or else would give him generously
out of his purse.

Little did he think the CREATOR of angels and LORD of life stood
before him.

I have no man.   Unlike the palsied one, had no kind friends to
bring him to Christ.

He repeats for the hundredth time his piteous, plaintive tale.

All his efforts have been for 38 years *useless,* and now his case is
hopeless.

When our hopes are low our prayers are languid : " we are saved
by hope." Rom. viii. 24.

Yet he will not give up coming, for here by the temple he might
get *alms.*

The universal cry of humanity is one of *misery, helplessness,* and
hopelessness.

Put me.   Gr. *cast me in ;* it must be done with energetic promptness.

The kingdom of heaven demands higher energy and more prompt
action.

Coming.   Slowly must the wretched friendless one have dragged
himself along.

But no such weary steps are needed to the throne of grace.

Nor does infinite compassion appoint such terms of mercy.

In seeking salvation each of earth's millions may be first at the
throne of grace.

We too often think God must work by our rule or not at all.

But He will not *tie* Himself to any sacramental means of grace.

He often bestows His highest favours here without sacramental
signs.   Num. xi. 17.

Another.   Either the rushing crowd or narrow porch prevented
him.

A picture of the world in its rush after things of sense.

How many Jacobs defraud their brothers and sisters by over-
reaching !

To supplant others and gratify selfishness the rule now rather than
the exception.

But a time is coming when all the millions of wronged ones will
have justice.

" I know," cried Job, " that my Redeemer (Vindicator or Avenger)
liveth." Job xix. 25.

The gospel bids us " prefer one another," " love our neighbour as
ourself." Rom. xii. 10 ; Matt. xix. 19.

A hard selfish mind battles on, but sensitive spirits are pushed to the wall.

To such Christianity brings gentle, blessed relief.

The wretched seldom find a human ear patient to hear their woes.

But there is ONE to whom they can " make their request known." Phil. iv. 6.

This poor man's words breathe a sad feeling of abandonment.

Yet he complains not of man, nor murmurs against God.

He seems to have accepted the link binding his *sin* to his *suffering*.

He who heard the agonized father's plea, John iv. 50, will not refuse the silent entreaty of a poor victim, resigned to his misery.

Such a trust some call *superstition,* but true faith in the INVISIBLE has ever been called fanaticism. Acts xxv. 19.

Having buried their master, John's disciples " *went and told Jesus.*" Matt. xiv. 12.

Before me. In earth's narrow pools but one at a time. With Christ " a nation may be born at once." Isa. lxvi. 8.

ἀπεκρίθη. Not a categorical desire to be cured is here intimated. *Lange.* His charges against others' neglect, not confirmed by our Lord. *Steinmeyer.*

οὐκ ἔχω. Loathed by men for the notorious punishment of his sin. *Tischendorf.* Questioned by *Stier.*

ὅταν ταραχθῇ. Indicates the attempt was merely experimental. *Hengst.* No more than obedience to all Divine commands. *Author.*

πρὸ ἐμοῦ, instead of me, pushing me aside. *Lange, Hirsch.* " *Yea, Lord,*" implied. *Syriac* and *Arabic* versions. His indirect reply was more pointed than if he had said, " *Yes, indeed,*" &c. *Grotius.* Why could not the person bringing him put him in? *Bauer.* He could so slowly move himself. *Alford.* His trust was superstition. *De Wette, Tholuck.* Go to your priests with your troubles. *Gregory.* Vain refuge for a broken heart. *Author.*

---

8. Jesus saith unto him, Rise, take up thy bed, and walk.

Jesus saith. One year since He proved to His foes His lordship over the *temple.*

Now to the same He is to prove His lordship over the *Sabbath.*

And yet the Sabbath had been instituted by Jehovah Himself in the morning of creation, and re-enacted amid the solemnities of Sinai.

Helpless and hopeless the poor man lies at the pool, but the Lord's power ignores the troubled water and the descending angel.

Rise. This *thunder-clap* of omnipotence suddenly bursts from the Saviour.

A glorious type of the great saying, "The dead shall hear," &c.
John v. 25.

The word of this strange visitor works an almighty change.

Our Lord does not first demand faith and repentance.

He heals the man in his sins, but his soul is not forgotten. Ver. 14.

Divine command *binds* with faith, or without faith, and it shall be
seen by the *visible act* whether the *invisible* is also His.

The only criteria the Church has to judge by are *fruits.* Matt. vii. 20.

The Lord of the Sabbath intentionally puts His foot on Pharisaism.

Jews, as Romanists now in Europe, made the *Sabbath a curse to the
well-being of the nation.*

Love to God makes a holy Sabbath daily, while formalism destroys
the Sabbatic law.

Take up. 1. To *proclaim* his cure. A person carrying a bed
through Jerusalem on the Sabbath was so *unusual* a violation
of the law, that the whole community would inquire the
reason.

2. The Lord will enter His protest against the superstitions and
cruelties of the Jewish rulers.

3. He will show Himself Lord of the Sabbath, and therefore
Jehovah.

4. To test the faith of the man who risked being scourged in the
synagogues.

It was our Lord's custom to direct the manner of *proving* the
miracle.

A symbol of victory over the disease that had long enchained
him.

Zacchæus converted, says to his gold, "Once thou hadst *me,* but
now I have *thee.*"

The tresses of the Magdalen that once allured to sin, wipe the
Saviour's feet. Luke vii. 38.

The impotent man must, on condition of being cured, break the
Pharisee's Sabbath.

Not for the sake of doing a servile work, but to prove his *obedience*
to the Lord.

Bed. A mat or rug is used by common people in the East for a
seat by day, a bed by night, and a garment when travelling.

The writer saw hundreds of both sexes asleep at night on the
harvest-fields, on the pallets brought with them. Ruth iii. 4.

Chairs are unknown in the East ; low couches are used by day for
seats. Esth. i. 6 ; 2 Kings iv. 10.

432 / Gospel of John

Orientals neither anciently nor *now* change their dress on retiring
 to rest.
A frame generally used by kings, sometimes of iron, Deut. iii. 11,
 of ivory, Amos vi. 4, or of palm wood.
Our body, fretted by the curse, is *this bed* of unrest and sorrow.
This man shall carry his bed, a present memento of past sin.
Walk. He who was healed, Acts iii. 8, leaped. Here the healed
 one must walk.
Thus all the people will have opportunity of seeing the reality of
 this miraculous cure.
Pool of Bethesda a picture in miniature of the world :
1. The human world is greatly afflicted. (1.) Effects of sin.
 (2.) Often the means of salvation.
2. The human world has alleviating elements. (1.) Medicinal
 properties of the earth. (2.) Soothing influences of nature.
 (3.) Offices of social love. (4.) The gospel of Christ.
3. The human world is sadly selfish. (1.) Selfishness is injustice.
 (2.) Impiety. (3.) Misery.
4. The human world has a glorious Saviour. (1.) He cures the
 greatest of sufferers. (2.) He cures by His own word. (3.)
 He cures by the earnest desire of the patient. *Thomas.*

Ἔγειραι. Our Lord might show him by gesture. *Kuinoel.* Under this
word is couched the command to believers. *Calovius.* Having never heard of
miracles, developed faith was not required. *Grotius.* He would impart entire
health of soul to those who entirely trust Him. *Ber. Bib.*
 κράββατόν, a litter or couch. Emperor M. Antoninus preferred a couch
covered with skins. *Cicero, Gesner.* A little wooden couch for the sick.
Tittmann. Ulysses' bed of olive wood was inlaid with gold and ivory. *Homer.*
Bedsteads were made of solid silver. *Plato.* Of ivory embossed and carved.
Athenæus. Veneered with tortoise shell inlaid with gold. *Lucian.* In Thessaly
beds stuffed with grass. Some with sponges at Athens. *St John's* Gr. Antiq.
 περιπάτει. He intends to prove His lordship over the Sabbath. *Ellicott.*
To condemn the hypocritical burdens imposed in the name of the fourth com-
mandment. *Lightfoot.*

---

9. And immediately the man was made whole, and took up his bed, and
walked : and on the same day was the sabbath.

Immediately. " The Lord spake, and it was done." Psa. xxxiii.
 9. " Let there be " produced the universe.
The omnific word carried the curative power into the man's being.
Medicinal waters have cured myriads, but not one, INSTANTLY.
But the *blind, lame, halt,* have *never* been *cured* by any water.

God never commands, but He implies grace is ready to aid us. In regeneration, the same almighty word is needed. Jas. i. 18.

The man. Our Lord healed one here and many in Galilee. Matt. iv. 23.

In Capernaum He healed all that love and sympathy could bring. Matt. viii. 16.

Near Tabor myriads were healed without a word or touch.

His infinite virtue went forth as light from the sun. Luke vi. 19.

Sabbath. See on verse 10. Our Lord healed on the principle that " the Sabbath was made for man." Mark ii. 27.

He will make His miracle a text and sermon to bigots.

He will show them that He dares to set at naught their miserable Sabbath rules, and yet by performing a work which none but God can do.

There was no crisis in the man's disease nor danger in postponement.

He would certainly find the patient in the same place to-morrow.

But His love brooks no delay : He delights to show mercy.

Moreover, He ever " makes the wrath of man to praise Him." Psa. lxxvi. 10.

This miracle became noised abroad by the rulers taking it up.

Our Lord wrought several miracles on the Sabbath day. Mark iii. 1—5 ; Luke iv. 31, 35, 38, 39 ; xiv. 1—4 ; John ix. 14.

Thus JEHOVAH our ETERNAL REST has come, foreshadowing THE TRUE SABBATH.

---

10. The Jews therefore said unto him that was cured, It is the sabbath day : it is not lawful for thee to carry thy bed.

Jews. See on John i. 19 ; v. 10. Generally means adherents of the Sanhedrim.

Those who evidently had not witnessed the miracle at the pool.

Doubtless the rulers were at once informed what had been done.

If the healed one hastened to bear the joyful tidings to his friends, he soon returned to the temple, to offer his grateful sacrifice. Verse 14.

Sabbath. First mentioned at the close of the record of creation. Gen. ii. 3.

Six days' work clearly indicate a *succession of acts* by the Creator.

The first formal notice of the Sabbath occurs in Ex. xvi. 23—29.

Sabbatic law was re-enacted at Sinai before assembled Israel, with indescribable grandeur and solemnity.

"**Remember:**" Implies their previous knowledge of the day.

Creation and *deliverance* from *bondage*, are the two reasons given.

Jewish tradition says in the 6000th year the world will be destroyed, then the Sabbath of heaven will begin. *Talmud.*

Prophetic warnings against its violation are oft repeated.

Sabbath desecration represented as among the highest acts of guilt. Ezek. xx. 12—24.   [trary rules.

Pharisees and Rabbis burdened the day with many silly and arbi-

Rich Jews generally *feasted* on the Sabbath day on a sacrifice.

Each seventh day, each seventh month, and each seventh year, were sacred.   [year.

Labour forbidden on the seventh day, *land rested* on the seventh

Each 49th year closed up a week of years, viz. the JUBILEE.

This Sabbatic year affected the foundations of the social and civil state.

Announced by a peal of trumpets. No sowing, ploughing, or reaping done.

All servants (slaves), whether born or purchased, were set at liberty.

The fields yielded and the trees bore fruit *spontaneously*, perhaps supernaturally.

Title-deeds, mortgages, and all inheritances were restored at the Jubilee period.

The Lord said, "FOR THE LAND IS MINE." Lev. xxv. 23.

Refusing to keep. His Sabbath, *God made* HIS LAND DESOLATE, by sending Israel 70 years into captivity. Deut. xxix. 23—25.

It was a standing proof that neither their time nor their land was their own.

They were God's stewards. So are all now, but it does not so palpably appear.

On the Sabbath the Israelites were not to gather manna, Ex. xvi. 23, nor light a fire, Ex. xxxv. 3, nor gather sticks, Num. xv. 32, nor travel beyond 6 furlongs, about three quarters of a mile, but each was to abide in his place, Ex. xvi. 29.

There was *no* Sabbath in sacred duties,—sacrifices were *doubled.*

"Priests profane the Sabbath, and are blameless." Matt. xii. 5.

A *third* of man's life is spent in sleep, the symbol of death.

The Sabbath gives one *seventh* of life to repose of nerve and brain.

It lifts the wheels of the soul out of the deep ruts of earth.

Suspension of labour in Sabbath rest, a positive gain to a nation.

Plough standing in the furrow and factories closed increase wealth.

Man, "the machine of machines," is repairing and winding up.

With many, life is either exhausting toil, or unconscious slumber.

Our Lord consecrated the first day of the week by His resurrection and appearances to His apostles.

Their observance of the day after Pentecost a divinely-authorized endorsement of the change.

" I was in the Spirit on the *Lord's day*." Rev. i. 10.

Great principle of Sabbatic law, consecration of one seventh of time to God.

This principle fully recognized and asserted in the Christian Sabbath.

Creation consummated and perfected in Christ.

Redemption the head and crown of all the works of God.

Hence, as Jesus rose the *first* day, that day is the Sabbath of the universe.

Sabbath a type of the rest that remaineth for the people of God.

Desecration of Sabbath and national corruption go hand in hand.

Superior cleanliness of Sabbath keepers over neglecters generally observed. See Sugg. Comm. on Luke vi. 5 ; xiv. 5.

Not lawful. Not sincerely said, they cared not for the Sabbath.

The miracle excited their envious malice, rather than adoring wonder. [peril. *Rabbis.*

Medical attendance forbidden on the Sabbath, unless life were in

The Jews had *apparently Old Test.* sanction for their rebuke. Jer. xvii. 21, 22.

To carry. Triumphant testimony of enemies to an instantaneous cure. Neh. xiii. 15. [cure.

He hereby proved at once his faith in Christ, and reality of his

This charge of Sabbath-breaking was false and malicious.

Doing good, rather than leaving it undone, is true Sabbath-keeping. Luke vi. 9.

God, whose beneficial activity never ceases, ordained the Sabbath.

But the Jews had no true reverence for this or any other law of God.

They envied Christ's miraculous power, and hated His spotless holiness.

They had made many fine-spun and subtle distinctions.

This plain man neither knew nor cared for the casuistries of rulers.

Yet the world of fashion in religion and etiquette binds its votaries.

Christ's followers are declared authoritatively to be free. John viii. 36.

The religion of Jesus issues from a divinely free spirit. Psa. li. 12.

" He alone is *a freeman* whom the *truth* makes free." *Cowper.*

Σάββατον, *rest.* Origin found in Ex. xv. 25. "Ordinance." *Rabbis, Selden.* Day honoured from the beginning, but first noticed, Ex. xvi. 23. *Grotius.* One might feed an animal found in a pit, but not draw him out. *Rabbis, Buxtorf.* Some Samaritans maintained a man should remain in whatever spot or circumstance found on the Sabbath. *Heylin* in *Smith.* All *work* forbidden, servile or business. *Michaelis, Gesenius.* Heathen believed Jews fasted on Sabbath. *Tacitus.* Because meals were postponed till after sacrifice. *Heylin.* A "luxus sabbatarius." *Sidonius Apollinaris.* Given to hilarity in the days of *Augustine.* Sabbath instituted after the apostasy. *Lightfoot.* Sacredness attached by Greeks to the seventh day. *Hesiod.* Same by Egyptians. *Herodotus.* Primitive disciples discouraged Sabbatizing. *Buxtorf.* Rome adopted Egypt's week in Hadrian's reign. *Dion Cassius.* Extra sanctimoniousness made an excuse for breaking other commands. *Fuller.* All slaves went free Sabbatical year. *Mede, Lewis'* Heb. Ant.

---

11. He answered them, He that made me whole, the same said unto me, Take up thy bed, and walk.

Answered. We may give a similar answer, when the world demands why its rules have been violated. Another model answer is found in Neh. vi. 3. [Lord."

He that, &c. Happy for us also if we can say, " Thus saith the This healed cripple had already risen far *above* the rulers of the nation.

He calmly rested on the Lord's word, and trusted His arm to protect him.

Made me whole. He does not say " healed me."

It implies something *lost* was restored, perhaps a limb.

He did not even know the name of the wondrous physician.

How often the worldling receives blessings without caring to know the giver.

Alas! how often they *never inquire* not even with the zeal of Baal's friends. 2 Kings i. 2.

Said. Our Lord gave him not only health, but an obedient heart.

There is something heroic in his answer, for he must have known the danger he exposed himself to. [*authority.*

His curing him proved Him a prophet, and His command a *prophet's* " I have a powerful warrant for carrying my bed."

In a similar strain Abraham, ascending the mount to the dreaded sacrifice, might have spoken.

Thus are broken the chains of tradition and ecclesiastical authority.

Thus the Christian finds a liberty of which no man can deprive him.

The key-note of the miracle is not so much that we may do deeds

of mercy on the Sabbath, but that Jesus Christ is THE ABSOLUTE
LORD of the Sabbath.   [healed him.
Hence the Jews transferred the blame from the man to Him who
Take up.   He did not command him to enter the pool; Christ's
  WORD was HEALTH and SALVATION !
He that can thus cure must have *power* to change or suspend the
  laws of the Sabbath.

᾽Αρον. This shows the power of God was claimed by our Lord, and the
miracle began and ended in Himself. *Dodd*, on Miracles.   That the author of
the miracle must be the supreme law-giver, lies in the background of this
reply.   But the man himself might not have seen it. *Alford.*   Many answers
in the N. T. seem as if *inspired* by God.   Luke xxi. 15. *Author.*

---

12. Then asked they him, What man is that which said unto thee, Take up
thy bed, and walk ?

What man ?   As though a mortal man could do the works of GOD!
They pretend to be very ignorant of Jesus, the wonder-worker.
They might as well have asked, WHENCE DID SUNSHINE COME ?
All intelligent persons in Palestine knew very well that none but
  JESUS of Nazareth had done and could do such miracles as this.
They malignantly omit to ask, *Who made thee whole ?*
Said.   Wicked men pass over the bright and better side, and
  love to fasten on the unfavourable point of any case.
This question was asked to confuse and torment the healed one.
They do not inquire that they may admire and adore, or bring
  their afflicted friends for health.   [noble.
Fire of fanaticism burns out in the soul all that is tender, true, and
Such cold-blooded ones would rather the wretched were *not* healed,
  than that their miserable superstitions should be violated.
They would silence all songs that did not speak their praise.
  Luke xix. 40.
Had persecutors displayed as much zeal in seeking salvation
  as in hunting the lambs of Christ, how many would have
  escaped eternal woe !   [cruelty.
Dissembling their malice, proves their *hypocrisy* as well as their
Their purpose was to undermine this man's trust in Jesus.
Take up.   How transparent their hatred and deceit.
Had their question sprung from earnestness and integrity, they
  would have inquired concerning this stupendous work of God.
The miracle demanded their adoring wonder, gratitude, and love.

" Who is He, having such God-like power, who has deigned to
    visit this people ? "
" Who is He who has wrought on this wretched creature a *cure*
    equal to CREATION ? "   [people."
" For 400 long dark years God has not so wondrously visited His
"Praise His holy name, Abraham's God still lives, to bless and save!"
No such grateful emotions arise in their cold malignant bosoms.
They had no anthem of love for such a heavenly messenger.
No sympathetic word for the relieved object of 38 years' woe.
If their narrow bigotry can be enforced, the miserable man might
    suffer on another cycle.   Verily " the *tender* mercies of the
    wicked are cruel."   [not yet extinct.
Ever seeking for something to find fault with belongs to a race

---

    T*is*. Malice of this question proposes to find ground for an *arrest*, not
praise. *Grotius.* They teach the " healed " to despise his benefactor, by calling Him a " *man*," when they well knew *no created being* could do such a
miracle. *Lampe.*

---

13. And he that was healed wist not who it was: for Jesus had conveyed
himself away, a multitude being in that place.

Wist not. Imagined not or knew not. " Wist " a Saxon verb,
    obsolete.
The crowd themselves may not have known the Lord's person.
The man only knew some one with Divine power, equalled by
    compassion, had done the deed.   [benefactor.
But in his abject desperate misery he knew not the name of his
For our Lord's *fame* was far more familiar to the nation than His
    features.   [not unknown.
His use of the word " Jesus " (verse 15) proves it a name to him
Conveyed. A metaphor from swimming. Multitude, like water,
    closing behind him. A rapid gliding away.
Our Lord at the proper time cries, " I am He." John xviii. 5.
But He now avoids alike the praises of friends and the envy of
    malicious foes.
We have no word in our poor tongue to express the retiring of
    Deity. " It is the glory of God to conceal a thing." Prov.
    xxv. 2.
The secret descent of the nightly dews, and the noiseless move-
    ments of the mighty orbs of heaven, illustrate this feature.

No one hears the sunlight or the operation of those laws that
bind atoms and worlds.
All creation, for aught we know, rose into being as silently as the
spheres now revolve.   [thing.
Multitude.   Crowds soon assemble in a large city at any strange
After such acts, our Lord often loved to retire into secret places.
Men might find the Lord in their secret chamber, but they dread
solitude.
Hence the rush of myriads after any pleasure where they can be
rid of themselves. *Young.*
We may live in *a crowd*, but we must die *alone. Jay.*
Retirement has many temptations, but society more. *Kempis.*
Tendency of society : 1. To stir up and strengthen the impulses
of our animal nature. 2. To produce habits of superficial
thought. 3. To destroy the sense of individual responsi-
bility. 4. To promote forgetfulness of God. *Thomas.*
" Arise, go forth into the plain, and I will there talk with thee."
Ezek. iii. 22.
Ministers, above all men, require seasons of devout solitude. *Monod.*
True solitude is in the heart; he that finds it not there finds it no-
where. *Vinet.*

ἤδει. None of the crowd would tell him. *Tisch.* Why? The Saviour,
especially after miracles, retired. *Lücke.* Impression that Jesus was going
round alone, and that John did not witness the miracle. *Weisse.* Jesus told
him of it. *Lange.* Our Lord avoided applause. *Grotius.* The dialogue might
gather a menacing crowd. Our Lord retired, His hour being not yet come.
Trench. That our Lord withdrew before the man had time to see Him, is required by the context. *Alford.*

---

14. Afterward Jesus findeth him in the temple, and said unto him, Behold,
thou art made whole : sin no more, lest a worse thing come unto thee.

Jesus.   His Divinity, John i. 1—3 ; His names, i. 41 ; His mira-
cles, iii. 2 ; His moral character, vii. 46.
Temple.   See on John ii. 14, 20. It was the object of the nation's
idolatrous pride and glory.
An *insult* to it was wiped out by the blood of the offender. Acts
vi. 13.   [xiii. 2.
Our Lord foretold its utter overthrow, and continued ruin. Mark
Terentius Rufus, of the tenth legion, ploughed up the foundation.
Fulfilling the Divine word, " Zion shall be ploughed as a field."
Jer. xxvi. 18.

Julian the Emperor madly *tried* to *falsify* the *prediction*. A.D. 362.

Jews, hating Christians, aided him with shovels of *solid silver*. *Gibbon*.

But fireballs bursting from the earth, scattered the foundations and workmen. *Marcellinus.* [*Chrys*.

A portico, sheltering some, fell and crushed them and many others.

A clear judgment of heaven against the impious attempt. *Warburton*.

No building on earth ever was subject to such terrible changes.

Nothing remains but the splendid *foundations* of marble, laid by Solomon to enlarge the area of mount Moriah, now called the "*place of wailing.*"

The author saw grey-headed men sitting on the ground reading the prophets and swinging their bodies to and fro, as they mourned over the ruin of their house and nation.

The temple a fit place for restored health and a grateful heart.

To the temple Hezekiah, when healed, hastened for praise. Isa. xxxviii. 22. [Psa. lxvi. 13.

"I will go to thy house and pay my vows which I have," &c.

Yesterday, an object of *healing* mercy, to-day, of *enlightening* grace.

Even Pagan Greeks and Romans, recovering from danger, crowded their temples with votive offerings.

Mark, he found Christ in the temple, not in the crowd. *Augustine.*

Said. He proved to the healed one His omniscience ; He knew all his past.

Sin no more. Our Lord points to his restored health, and lovingly warns him against his besetting sin.

He who would risk another curse after such a miracle must be desperate indeed.

God's strokes to the living should awaken penitence for our sin.

"I have deserved all," soon changes stripes into a Father's blessings.

For thirty-eight years God's hand had lain heavily on him in affliction.

Terrible diseases the fruit of sin. Lev. xxvi. 16 ; Deut. xxviii. 15 ; 1 Cor. xi. 30 ; Luke xiii. 1.

As the Deluge followed sinners of the old world from valley to hill, and from hill to mountain, so does the wrath of God still pursue the wicked. Rev. xxvi. 15.

Apostolic authority settles the point : "*The wages of sin is death.*" Rom. vi. 23.

Church of Rome affirms some sins *venial*, and others *mortal*.

But the Divine word proclaims each sin worthy of *death*.

A worse thing. " If we sin *wilfully* after we have received," &c. Heb. x. 26.

A relapse is far more dangerous than the first disease.

" A worse thing," than thirty-eight years of suffering, gives an awful glimpse of the severity of God's judgments.

No matter how miserable any being has been or is, he can be more so.

Our Lord plainly hints special sin brought special punishment.

This infirmity had found him a youth, and left him a withered old man.

What his sin was we know not, *but he knew that Jesus knew.*

Our Lord incidentally reveals His omniscience, as the sin was committed before He was born. [ignorant.

Conscience interprets many a *warning*, of which all the world is

The eagle is often struck down by a shaft feathered from its own wing. [God.

So do men's sins cause and procure the righteous judgments of

Ahab's blood and his grandson's are shed in Naboth's vineyard. 2 Kings ix. 26.

God pointed all Israel to the *sin* of Korah and his company, by having *their censers beaten into plates, and laid on the altar.*

How oft is the deceiver deceived, as Jacob by Laban, and Laban by Jacob.

" The mills of God grind slowly, but they grind exceeding small."

Virtue and vice are only rewarded here, just so far as *to prove* there is a PROVIDENCE. [against sin.

All human calamities are dark revealings of the wrath of God

Some say all suffering *must* be reformatory, but experience proves the contrary.

Are jails and penal settlements known to reform criminals ?

Neither " cutting winds nor penal fires " can change the evil heart. [spires love.

It is grace, sovereign grace alone, that takes away enmity, and in-

---

ἱερῷ includes all the courts and porticoes of the building. Christ always was in the ἱερόν, never in the ναόν. In the ἱερόν were the money-changers, there was the brazen altar. Matt. xxiii. 35. ναόν, proper shrine and home of the Deity. Samaritan aid was refused in building ναόν, but not ἱερόν. No Gentile, under penalty of death, could enter the ναόν. Acts xxi. 29, 30. Zacharias entered the ναόν, people bowed in the ἱερόν. Luke i. 10. *Trench.* No flies ever infested the temple. *Rabbis.* No one with staff, or shoes, or scrip, or

dust on his feet, or money in his purse, could enter the temple. *Lewis'* Heb.
Ant.

μηκέτι. Thirty-eight years of energetic usefulness lost. *Tisch.* A lamentation that such a punishment had not led to repentance. *Stier.*

ἁμάρτανε. Guilty of some great sin, causing this malady. *Trench.*
Questioned by *Hengst.* Omniscience detected a tendency to relapse to old sin.
Lange.

χεῖρόν. No evidence of a special judgment. *Sumner.* Loss of place in the
kingdom of the Messiah. *Meyer.* Ancient Greeks gave the name ADRASTEIA
to Divine vengeance, signifying that none can escape. *Smith.*

---

15. The man departed, and told the Jews that it was Jesus, which had made
him whole.

Told. Some think he went to betray his benefactor as a Sabbath-
breaker, but the idea of such perfidy is monstrous and incredible.

Much more likely he desired to honour Jesus.

Little did he think his tidings would arouse such malignity.

Perhaps he intended to encourage them to bring *their* sick to Jesus.

Mary Magdalene seem to have thought the gardener *should have
known her* LORD as well as she. John xx. 15.

Made him whole. It is on this the healed one *emphatically* dwells.

He does not repeat the words " Take up thy bed," as this had
offended them.

As our Lord's cures on the body were generally accompanied with
healing to the soul, it is highly probable he began to preach
Jesus to the people. [able.

Holding civil as well as sacred authority made their enmity formid-

---

ἀπῆλθεν. An evidence of an utterly reprobate mind. *Schleier., Paulus.* A
very suspicious circumstance. *Ber. Bib.* A combination of weakness and
goodness. *Stier.* Obedience to authority. *Bengel.* Our Lord would not have
healed a miscreant. *Hengst.* Surely good intent, " probi ex suâ naturâ
cæteros fingunt." *Trapp.* Ingratitude to the physician who had healed him.
Calvin, Chrys. He would stop the mouths of gainsayers. *Trench.* Utterly
ignorant of the treachery of the Sanhedrim. *Lampe.* He thought they inquired
out of curiosity. *Kuinoel.* Words "made me whole," ver. 11, prove no ingratitude here. *Alford.* An excuse for this act. *Meyer, Luthardt.* Not
sufficient proof of his gratitude. *Ellicott.*

---

16. And therefore did the Jews persecute Jesus, and sought to slay him,
because he had done these things on the Sabbath day.

Persecute. See on John ix. 15, &c. Our Lord's activity of love
was met by sleepless foes.

In the *professional* pride of doctors of the law, they condemn Him.
They were utterly alienated in heart from the God of the Sabbath.
And yet to the ignorant they seemed exceedingly zealous for God.
Ritualists in proportion to their exactness in forms are often want-
ing in sincerity.

No class so self-sacrificing in their *outward* devotions, yet none so
supremely wicked as the Jesuits. *Steinmetz's* History.

Xavier boasted of millions of converts, yet the Church of Rome
has never *to this hour* given the bread of Life, the BIBLE,
translated to a heathen tribe. [2 Tim. iii. 5.

Jehovah loves the "*power*" far more than the "form of godliness,"
"*Your* new moons and solemn feasts, my soul hateth." Isa. i. 13, 14.
"*Your*" sacrifices, and not "mine." All was *hypocrisy*, and there-
fore abhorred.

Slay Him. "The wicked watcheth the righteous, and seeketh to
slay him." Psal. xxxvii. 32.

As this miracle was wrought *by God's power*, in aiming their
assaults at Christ they struck at GOD HIMSELF.

Practical atheists, though of the seed of Abraham, what cared they
for Abraham's God, if they could only wreak their vengeance
on Christ ? [vii. 19—21.

Our Lord plainly charged them with murderous designs. John

Note the blindness of Pharisaic bigotry : In pretended zeal for the
Sabbath, they seek to commit murder !

Yet we must not refuse to work, though we know the enemy
will blaspheme.

The Church is the TRUE HEIR TO THE CROSS, therefore the world
hates it. [head.

These things. Stupendous miracles revealing His supreme God-
Things which had not been done by man or angel since creation.
Things which gladdened the hearts of thousands relieved.
Things which pleased Jehovah, the Lord of the Sabbath.
Such divine wonders did *over-awe* all honest minds. [deed.

Sabbath. An ironical allusion to the folly and daring of such a
He might most righteously have silenced them with a thunderbolt.
But His long-suffering is only brought out in more sublime relief.
His proceeding seemed to be in the character of a *deep joy*.
What, to blinded hypocrites, is the most glorious miracle ?
Departing from *their traditions* was unpardonable even for such
an act.
He proposes to them an opportunity of raising the first public

controversy, that His claims as the MESSIAH might reach the people.

Healing of this man in connection with water is thought by some to point out baptism.

Others contrast the healing of one now and then at distant intervals with the vastness of redemption.

Bethesda was a confined spot for the crowd, waiting for the angel, but salvation's stream is boundless as the compassion of God.

The healing element in Bethesda was exhausted by the *one* who entered it, but the fountain opened in Christ can heal all and yet remain inexhaustible for ever.

A crisis has now come in the Lord's history. His preaching will be tolerated no more, and the city of David will no longer be a safe place for the Son of David. [Son.

His " Father's house " is no more to echo the voice of the eternal

---

ἐδίωκον too vague, μᾶλλον, ver. 18, presupposes the fact. *Hengst., Lücke.* Never used in the sense of *legal* prosecution in the N. T. *Alford.* A forensic term, accuse and prosecute. *Æschines.* At that time death was inflicted for a wilful desecration of the Sabbath. *Lightfoot.* Matt. xii. 2. Some suppose an official summons before the Sanhedrim. *Lange.* He was not standing before a tribunal during verses 17—38. *Lücke.* Informally resolved. *Ellicott, Lampe.* He would not have made such a direct attack on their conscience. *Stier.* Persecution, the devil that dogs the gospel. *Trapp.* Ecclesia hæres crucis. *Luther.* .

καὶ ἐζήτουν κ. τ. λ. Omitted in *Cod. Sinai.* Cancelled. *Tisch., Tregelles, Meyer, Alford, Lange.* Inserted from ver. 18, in more modern copies. *Bengel.* Retained. *Lachmann, D. Brown.* Unsettled as to the chronology of this attack. *Stier.* Their only alternative was to acknowledge Him as Messiah or kill Him. *Lampe.*

---

17. But Jesus answered them, My Father worketh hitherto, and I work.

Answered. For grandeur, weight, and terseness, this reply is unapproachable.

He requites their malignity with boundless mercy.

He well knows they will not believe, but still He pleads.

In the day of Judgment the universe will see how true the challenge, " What could have been done more ? " Isa. v. 4.

My. Mark, He does not say " Our : " " MY " implies equality John x. 30, 33, 36. [*nature.*

Father. Father and Son, distinct in person, but *indivisible in* For any mere creature thus to speak were shocking blasphemy.

Worketh. If Jehovah did not work, how could the Sabbath occur ?
Our Lord thus corrects a foolish notion as to inactivity in God.
He does not, as in Luke xiii. 15, speak from a human stand-point.
He rests His acts solely on His glorious relation to His Father.
God's rest, Gen. ii. 3, signifies He *ceased* to work in creation.
He who is never weary can never need rest.
Our Lord, sharing the supreme Godhead, is free from Sabbatic
limits.
His act of healing was only the continuous activity of the Creator.
Did Jehovah rest, as the Jews demanded, all the wheels of nature
would stand still.
Unceasing Divine activity illustrated by the movements of the
heavenly bodies, as well as by the minutest processes.
The microscope reveals spherical atoms moving on atoms, and at-
taching to the living mass.   [tect.
Beyond this there are doubtless other changes our eye cannot de-
Life is of such tenuity, that it can climb up through water, and
probably through the air also. *Beale.*
Of all God's works, the organic mechanism of the *nerve* is the most
wondrous and elaborate.
With these nerves, the WILL works, yet how great is the chasm
between the *nerve* and the WILL.
Instinct seems half way between the *nerve* and MIND.
But the *vital power* has hitherto perfectly eluded human analysis.
The cause of life, the modes of life, and scores of the common
movements of the body, are as deeply mysterious as eternity.
The confessions of ignorance in a standard work on Physiology
were noted by the author, and they numbered *hundreds.*
This gives emphasis to those sublime words, Acts xvii. 28, " In
HIM WE LIVE, AND MOVE, AND HAVE OUR BEING."
God marvellously uses the *wrath* of man to unfold the noblest truth.
He instructs His Church, while apparently refuting His enemies.
He vindicates His own act of healing, and the healed one also in
carrying his bed.
Greeks and Romans, while denying Providence, taught *influences of
hell,* mingled in affairs of the gods.
Ate poured violence and discord over the affairs of men.
Alecto and her infernal sisters united to scourge and torment man-
kind.
Men's *crimes* were prompted by the gods, and were by them avenged.
Men trembled at an evil omen, and then insulted their gods.

Deities cared for *sages* and *heroes*, but common men were disregarded.

At the words, " *The gods, though real beings, care not for men's affairs*," the Roman theatre trembled with the applause of 40,000 persons.

" I see no reason to trust the gods, when my enemies triumph," Cato cried, and then fell on his sword.

The Stoics taught that consolation in affliction was to be found, not in *submission* to the gods, but in *resistance!*

Fortune or *Chance* had a Temple at Ægina, in Greece, and was blind. *Pliny.*

Poor *Codrus*, the stoic, warmed himself at the flames of his burning home.

A particular Providence has ever been a subject of contest and hate among sceptics.   [doctrine.

Even *Lord Macaulay* cannot hide his sneers at believers in this

Hitherto. Indicates the perpetuity of His Almighty Providence.

God of creation never slumbers or sleeps on His throne.

On the seventh day He ceased to create, but never ceased His Divine activity.

I work. In their presence stood ONE who had in their sight created bread, healed the lame, blind, and sick, and even raised the dead.

Here for a *moment* the vail trembles, as though the Almighty hand could be seen by men!   [days. Gen. i.

The Father rested in His crowning work, man, after working six

Now He rests in His Son, but His deepest repose is the silent, perpetual activity of infinite goodness.   [mercy.

Our Lord *hallows*, not breaks the Sabbath, by works of love and

Man's shattered moral powers need rest, to collect his spirit for God.

My Father's energy knows no Sabbath, and that is the law of My working. Neither works without the other.

Jesus Christ claims to be the embodied essence and perfections of Jehovah.

With this word, at a stroke, He lays bare the heart of the question.

Although He had set at naught *their* Sabbath. He never even hints at *abrogating* God's Sabbath.   [Sabbath.

Jewish Doctor *Hillel* held the sick should be comforted on the

Shammai denied it. Infidelity freezes the *heart* and benumbs the head.

To do good is a festal Sabbath for the infinitely loving Redeemer.

Divine working does not disturb Divine rest.

God rests, and yet the heavens move in their courses, the sun rises, shines, and sets, the rain descends, the dew falls, the rivers run, the tides ebb and flow, and all the processes of life are carried on with uninterrupted energy and completeness.

Even the waters of Bethesda's sacred pool bubbled on holy time.

And now the Lord of nature and of angels heals the diseased, and bids him take up his couch.

Not working is far from constituting a real Sabbath in the *soul*.

Saints enjoy in God the ceaseless rest of worshipping festivity.

The four living ones keep an eternal Sabbath, yet "*rest not day or night,* saying, Holy, holy, holy," &c.   Rev. iv. 8.

The SON claims for HIMSELF alone the SUBLIME UNITY of AN UNCEASING FESTAL LABOUR IN GOD, which He transfigures and glorifies.   [Jewish mind.

This word, "MY FATHER AND I ALSO!" was too high for the

THE FATHER IN ME hath wrought this work, therefore I AM THE SON!

He binds to a stupendous miracle His claim to supreme Godhead, as a *preface* to the following sermon.   [*plans.*

My FATHER works in His ever-unfolding and wide-embracing

I work in the scheme of *redemption,* and the SPIRIT works in the application.

Healing that cripple is no more a profaning of the Sabbath than the shining of the sun.   [no rest.

If acts of mercy, you call works, then *I work,* and the Sabbath is

Faith keeps no "holiday" Sabbaths ; man must, indeed, cease from *his* work, but it is to perform GOD's nobler work, in sleepless watchfulness, unremitting energy, and untiring love.

ἀπεκρίνατο. An anticipated attack. *Stier.* Presupposes a question. *Lampe.* Refers to a public prosecution. *Grotius, Kuinoel.* The scene was probably in the temple. *Lampe.*

Ὁ Πατήρ. He corrects the Jewish error, that God had *rested* since creation. *De Wette.* Our Saviour rests His right to work on the relation He sustains to God. *Hengst.* He vindicates Himself, and the healed paralytic. *Calvin.*

ἐργάζεται. Not simply in one act, but in vocation, justification, sanctification. *Augustine.* He grasps the very root of the error. *Neander.* He imparts to nature His invigorating forces. *Herder.* Creation, involving preservation, is an eternal work. *Brückner.* Where, then, is the rest of the Creator? Heb. iv. 10. *Stier.* Can one better sanctify the Sabbath than by doing the work of God? *Tisch.* As to Providence, "The gods themselves are subject to fate:" Agrippa to the Romans. *Dionysius Hal.* Fate is superior to Jove. *Æschylus.*

Proud Fortune kindly scatters her gifts. *Seneca.* Gods abandon everything to chance. *Euripides.* Jupiter, desiring to save Patroclus, inquired of Destiny. *Homer.* Destiny of man is written on adamant. *Ovid.* "I cannot change your destiny, but I will manage to avenge your death."—Diana consoling the dying Hippolytus. *Euripides.* Achilles' destiny was twined with the thread of his life, hence the mightiest gods were his friends. *Homer.* Three destinies spin the fates of gods and men. *Plato.* Romans stoned their gods' statues when their beloved Germanicus died. *Suetonius.* "I think the human race does not share the notice of the gods." *Ennius,* approved by *Cicero.*

---

18. Therefore the Jews sought the more to kill him, because he not only had broken the Sabbath, but said also that God was his Father, making himself equal with God.

Jews. For history and character, see on John i. 19.

Broken. That is in their estimation, by word, ver. 17, and by deed, ver. 8. [Job xiii. 15.

Duty is ours, results are God's. Dan. iii. 18 ; Acts vii. 54—57 ;

Our Lord *knew* His word would rouse the murderous resolve, yet calmly spoke it.

He had violated *their* superstitions, but *not* God's day.

They were breaking Sabbath solemnities by their murderous thoughts. [have said.

Said. Jesus had really said what they had understood Him to

God His Father. They understood the meaning of this luminous word.

Vain philosophers in our day have been speculating on the mystery of the Incarnate Deity, but have not found out who Jesus was.

His Father. Gr. " His own Father," corresponds to " His own Son." Rom. viii. 32.

They charged Him with blasphemy, although they themselves were committing the very sin.

They well knew none but God could heal with a word !

They must first make the *laws* of their being *lies*, before such a miracle can be believed to be *man's* work.

His claiming to work as the Messiah deepened their rage.

This was probably transacted before the Sanhedrim, and instead of correcting them He sets His seal to it.

Deniers of His divinity must in logical consistency deny His moral excellence.

If no more than man, connivance at the claim of divinity was a fearful crime. [consistency.

Hence *Renan* and all such critics stand convicted of gross in-

They hold Jesus to have been only " the best of men," and yet
allow He claimed to be God !   [faculty.
But conscience in infidels is often a very elastic and accommodating
Making Himself. Their resolute persistent protestation is, *He
was only a man.*   [alleged offence.
His *vindication* of Himself is incomparably worse than the *first*
Had they misunderstood Him, He would instantly have corrected
the grave error.   [zeal for God.
The Pharisees chose the Sabbath as the *easiest test* of their false
They had nullified the first commandment by " covetousness,"
the third by " swearing by the gold of the temple," the fifth
by a " corban," &c.
But Jesus, as Lord of the Sabbath, claimed superiority to the
Sabbatic institution.
Here He encountered them to vindicate the law and make it
honourable, for on this command the truth of the Mosaic
covenant turned.
Their *answer* to His question, " Is it right to do good on the
Sabbath ? " was a conspiracy *to murder Him, an innocent being.*
In a similar manner has the Church of Rome ever answered the
men she had denounced as " heretics."
Proving His sovereign right to work on the Sabbath with the
Father, He brings out that word revealing the full-orbed
splendour of His Godhead :
" MY FATHER WORKETH HITHERTO, AND I WORK."
No angel would have dared to claim such a seat beside the throne
of God !
His offence was not that He dispensed with the law, or gave the
law a *new sense*, but that He boldly *enforced* the law, and
showed the *nature* of God's rest, and God's works by HIS OWN.
Our Lord brought the Jewish conscience so near to the burning
mount, Exod. xx. 19, that in their guilt they recoiled from
the light and flame Divine.
Equal with God. Thus our Lord's enemies unconsciously confirm one of the highest and holiest doctrines of Christianity.
Is all of the Father ? All is also of the Son. Did the Father
create the world? So did the Son. Does the Father up-
hold the universe ? So does the Son. Is the Father the
Saviour of the world ? So is the Son.
He claims co-essential and co-eternal Godhead, although some
pretend to find no Divinity here.

Thus *Satan* boldly challenged Jehovah's justice, and still more
blasphemously His truthfulness. Gen. iii. 1—4.

A citizen of London once became angry with the sunlight, and he
vowed "no sun should ever again shine within his home."
Closing the door and shutters, and lighting the lamps, he
lived many years and died as though there had been NO SUN.
The world with one voice justly pronounced him INSANE.

In a similar spirit "Liberals" and infidels deny Christ's supreme
Godhead.

ἔλυε. Hillel the "reaper" denied, Shammai the "binder" affirmed, works
of mercy proper for the Sabbath. *Lightfoot.*

ἀποκτεῖναι. Supply an outcry, "Stone Him, stone Him!" *Tisch.* Christ's
example authorizes us to preach truth, regardless of consequences. *Calvin.*

ἴδιον. His own. *Alford.* Same in nature, dignity, and glory, grammati-
cally implied. *Tittmann.*

πατέρα. Manifestation of God in Christ. *Hoffmann.* He claims here
far more than an equal right over the Sabbath. *Stier.* God called Father of
Israel in a few passages of the O. T. *Tholuck.* Not the calling God Father,
but in *such* a *sense* as to free Him from the Sabbath command. *Hengst.*
Sceptics fail, but the Jews perfectly understood Him. *Calvin.* Calling God
peculiarly "His Father." *Campbell.* Peculiar personal sonship. He made
God *sharer in His breaking* the Sabbath. *Alford.*

---

19. Then answered Jesus and said unto them, Verily, verily, I say unto you,
The Son can do nothing of himself, but what he seeth the Father do: for what
things soever he doeth, these also doeth the Son likewise.

Answered. Here our Lord begins a discourse the height and
depth of which no human being has ever fully comprehended.

We feel our utter nothingness in the presence of such a MIND.

As one gazing on the heavens can only take in a small portion,
and cannot COMPREHEND even THAT.

He has been charged with blasphemously *claiming* equality with
God, and He will now surely *disclaim* any such pretension.

Far from it, He confirms it, and vindicates His right to it.

He repeats the "offence," CLAIMING TO DO SOMETHING AS GOD.

Verily, verily. This solemn, oath-like word, is repeated three
times in this chapter.

No mere peradventure, but knowledge, absolute, Divine!

He persistently and triumphantly calls Himself THE SON!

The Son. See on John i. 1, 2, 14, 18, 49. This great word He
never for a moment retracts, but makes it the foundation of
all He has to say.

The humble Son of man softens His indispensable testimony.

He does not at once say, " I AND MY FATHER ARE ONE." John x. 30.

If there is a SON above angels, and that SON INCARNATE, all their views of God *must* be entirely changed.

Heathen supposed to have been hitherto abandoned by God as orphans, must then actually be *brethren of one blood* with the chosen people.

This laid the axe at the root of their pride of race. Matt. iii. 9.

Can do. The Son's very person implies the Father's will and counsel, and the Son's perfect knowledge of that will.

Nothing. That is, nothing independently, for that would be presumptuous and sinful.

Every creature as a creature may pervert its freedom.

Even angels may lose their fidelity. " Some kept not their first estate." Job iv. 18 ; Jude 6.

But the eternal Son cannot do wrong, but only and eternally right.

God is infinitely *free*, and yet God is infinitely *holy*.

Christ as the SON OF GOD possesses this glorious excellence of the Divine nature.

Of Himself. In this word " Himself " lies the sting of their accusation.

In *their* sense of it, He solemnly repudiates the charge.

" Himself " to their dark minds was merely a presumptuous *man*.

He comes, not in His own name, but in His Father's. John viii. 42. [mysterious.

We have here the key to many passages, which otherwise are

Seeth. By such terms alone can God reveal heavenly mysteries.

Jehovah speaks to mankind, as we speak to little children.

We tell them the truth, and when grown up, they reproach us not for our terms.

They, in turn, use the same terms to the next generation.

The Father. Trinity, see on John i. 1, 2. The Father originating, and the Son acquiescing; the Son not only doing WHATEVER the Father does, but as He does it.

Doeth the Son likewise. He is co-operator with the Father in the government of the universe.

How could more *absolute equality* with the Father be claimed ?

Jews, opposing our Lord, dreamt they were taking part with God.

Men, under this delusion, are found fighting against God. Acts v. 29 ; xxiii. 9.

452 / Gospel of John

Their charges had nothing to do directly with Him, but were
against the Father, who moves in the Son.

ἀπεκρίνατο. A discourse that would scarcely be tolerated in a *Neological*
Consistory in our day. *Ber. Bib.* The reckless Sanhedrists, against their own will,
had to listen. *Pfenminger.* An unparalleled testimony to our Lord's Divinity.
Zeller.

'Αμὴν, ἀμὴν. Indicates the high import of the following word. *Heumann.*
ἀφ' ἑαυτοῦ. In quotation marks, as taken from His opponents. *Hengst.*
As used by the Jews, they had a poison in them. *P. Anton.*

οὐ δύναται. *Arius* inferred from this Christ's inferiority to the Father. It
refers to Christ simply in His humanity. *Calvin.* Moral impossibility. John
xii. 39. *Bengel.* A physical impossibility. *J. Brown.* An indistinct reference
to the human. *De Wette.* A sign of omnipotence, as when we say of God, He
cannot die. *Author.* Trinity involves revealed subordination of second and
third persons with equality of nature. *Waterland.* How can man comprehend Divinity, when he cannot comprehend his own soul? *Augustine.*

οὐδὲν, ἐὰν, nothing contrary to the Father's will. *Chrys.* Only that which
the Father, not all that, &c. *Ferus.*

βλέπη. His eternal generation. *Augustine.* A figure for the inseparable
communion of Father and Son. *Diodati.*

ὁμοίως, with the same power. *Gregory Naz.* In imitation of Him. *S. Clarke*
(Arian). In like manner. *D. Brown.* Not subordinate, if He acts the same as.
Chrys. " An admirable apology, which makes the matter worse." *Luther.*

---

20. For the Father loveth the Son, and showeth him all things that himself
doeth: and he will show him greater works than these, that ye may marvel.

Loveth. *Love* is ingenuous and open-hearted, concealing nothing.
God cannot possibly be an unfruitful unity. " GOD IS LOVE." 1
John iv. 8.

There is a peculiar reciprocal relation of eternal, energetic love.

The infinite perfections of the Father are reflected in the Son.

" He is the brightness of His glory, and the express image of His
person." Heb. i. 3.

The Son. See on John i. 1, 2, 14, 18, 49. He re-affirms His
Deity, though He well knows it offends them.

Showeth. Denotes the eternally inherent power of doing all that
the Father does.

From perfect fellowship love has no concealment.

Their nature and interests ONE. By glorious inheritance the Son
participates in the counsels of the Father.

Doeth. In all worlds, from the creation to the judgment.

With the Father willing is doing. The Son alone acts *in time.*

Greater. Regeneration and sanctification of the soul transcend
miracles.

Perhaps a hint at the glories of the resurrection and judgment.

Works. He calls His miracles " works," because with Him they
were *natural*.   [*cles.*
But to us every act and every word, nay, His very being, are *mira-*
Miracles only the sign or symbol of His proper work.
RIGHTEOUSNESS, LOVE, LIFE, are GOD'S REGALIA, worn by the
FATHER and SON.

Ye. Some refer this to the witnesses of Lazarus's resurrection,
seeing many of them wondered and believed. John xi. 45.

May marvel. He rebukes their stupidity and blindness for not
appreciating the miracle just wrought.
As miracles in Egypt rose higher and higher, so those wrought
around the cross and Olivet left Jerusalem without excuse.
All wonder will culminate in the majesty of His second advent.
Those who recklessly, defiantly, and blasphemously reject God's
Son, neither ministry nor miracle can change them.
" Behold, ye despisers, and wonder and perish." Acts xiii. 41.

φιλεῖ. See on John iii. 35. Qui amat nil celat. *Bengel.* Idea of love is
that of uniting distinction, and distinguishing unity. *Tholuck.*
δείκνυσιν. Conceptional, not dogmatic expression. *Hengst.* To knowledge
it adds *impulse. Bloomfield.* Perfect knowledge of Jehovah's plans. *Doddridge.*
μείζονα. Regeneration of the soul and resurrection of the body. *Augustine.* As Saviour He would do greater things than the miracle just performed.
Calvin. His work in the unfolding of His person, such as resurrection and
judgment. *Ebrard.*

---

21. For as the Father raiseth up the dead, and quickeneth them ; even so
the Son quickeneth whom he will.

Raiseth. " Why should it be thought a thing incredible that
God should raise the dead ? " Acts xxvi. 8.
Implies we have a right to doubt that any but *God* could do it.
Our Lord's works were wrought on *this life* and on the *life beyond
this.*   [*death.*
" Talitha cumi," " Lazarus, come forth," prove Him LORD over
Yet the salvation of Zacchæus, and the Magdalene, and the dying
thief proves *equal power.*   [of His people.
His own resurrection was the pledge and type of the resurrection
His life-imparting words to the dead, show all His words to be
full of life.
" Thy sins be forgiven," Matt. ix. 2, sustained by a miracle,
proved He could forgive sins.

The dead. " Death, the wages of sin," first seized the living
  spirit, then poisoned the whole *body*.   [mankind.
Presence of death an abiding witness to the spiritual death of
Quickeneth. The Son had healed a man, and shortly He will
  raise Lazarus from the dead.   [in time.
Restoring the sick a *sign* of His *health-giving*, *life-giving* influences
And by raising the dead He *lifts the veil* and shows His power in
  eternity.   [dust.
Thus He will one day loose the chains that bind all sleeping in
Quickening also embraces the raising of those dead in sins.
  Eph. ii. 1.
Illustrating His resurrection power in *its innermost* and *deepest sense*.
" With Thee is the fountain of life." Psa. xxxvi. 9. " Fountain
  of salvation." Psa. xvi. 11.
His word doubtless includes not only those in their graves, but those
  " having a name to live, and yet dead."
Quickening of grace begins in this life, and ends in eternal life.
He will. Those securing the Son's favour absolutely certain of
  eternal life.
Though infinitely sovereign in His acts, He is ever controlled
  by the law of love.
As the Father quickens by an omnipotent act of will, Jas. i. 18,
  so the Son does the same by an act of His own sovereign
  will. Matt. viii. 3.
Prophets are mere *instruments*, God's hand alone works miracles.
While His will is sovereign it is infinitely removed from *arbitrari-
  ness*. Eph. i. 11.   [His acts.
Sooner or later we will know God has *infinitely wise reasons* for
As to POWER, it is a light thing for Him to raise the dead.
He *desires* the salvation of all, but only *effectually wills* that of those
  that *believe*.   [so.
He might have raised many from the grave, but did not will to do
Those raised were witnesses that HE IS THE RESURECTION AND THE
  LIFE.

ἐγείρει. Moral and physical resurrection. *Lücke, Neander, Olsh., DeWette,
Calvin.* God's entire activity for man through the mediation of the Son.
Tholuck.
  ζωοποιεῖ. 1. Awake the dead. 2. Impart life. *Gesenius.* All Divine
works included in producing, sustaining, restoring, *quickening. Stier.* Not a
mere rising, but resurrection. *Beza, Bucer, Simpson.* Intentionally capable of
figurative or literal exegesis. *Bourgon.* Noting a three-fold kind of energy :

1. Miraculous. 2. Converting. 3. The resurrection. *Lange.* Life in the
O. T. interchangeable with salvation. *Hengst.* The quickener qualified to
judge. *Grotius.* *Souls* raised by the Father and the Son, *bodies* by the
humanity of the Son. *Augustine.*

νεκρούς. Dead in body, not referred to till verse 28. *Meyer.* Morally
dead. *Chrys., Tittmann.* Christ's agency affirmed in both. *Tholuck.*

οὓς θέλει. Present used as the future. *Buttmann.* Divine sovereignty.
Stier. Opposing Jewish exclusiveness. *Lücke.* Prophets wrought miracles
not by their *own will.* Our Lord did. *D. Brown.* Jews held the Messiah
would resuscitate all the dead. Isa. xxvi. 19. *Wetstein.* A distinction
between the Son working in heaven (i.e. creation) and His working in humiliation. *Alford.*

---

22. For the Father judgeth no man, but hath committed all judgment unto
the Son.

Judgeth. The Father called "the Judge of all the earth." Gen.
xviii. 25 ; Psa. cv. 7.

No man. Jews connected judgment with the resurrection.
He anticipates their objection as to keeping the thoughts apart.
Our Lord here reveals the great truth, that judgment is involved
in the office of REVEALER of TRUTH.
The moment the soul is enlightened its character is unfolding for
eternity. Matt. xiii. 30. [Matt. xxiv. 14.
The formal decree will not be announced until "the end cometh."
Even now the testimony of our hearts is the *echo* of the VOICE of
the JUDGE.
" *He told me all things that ever I did.*" This work of conscience is
begun. John iv. 29.

Hath committed. Infidels object that the Father gives the Son
what He is assumed to have had.
The distinction is between *possessing* and *exercising* the right.
Nor does it involve any withdrawal of the presence of the Father.
The Son is the essential manifestation of Himself, His express
image. Heb. i. 2, 3.
This redemption begins and ends in the action of the Holy Trinity.
Judgment. In its most comprehensive sense, i. e. *administration.*
All human destiny will depend on relationship to the Son.
Even *now* judgment is recorded of the believer and the unbeliever.
But a day is appointed in which this Judgment will be publicly
declared. [the future.
Men deceive themselves by loose and undefined hopes concerning
" He that believeth *hath* life : he that believeth not, the wrath of
God *abideth* on him." John iii. 36.

Heaven and hell are *now* begun, for there are but the two classes.
He will " come to be glorified in His saints, and admired in them
that believe." [gether lovely."
To those who have known Him as JESUS He will appear " the alto-
To those who have rejected Him He will appear " in flaming fire."
All the dark mysteries of Providence will then issue in glorious
light.
From the astonished universe will go up the exultant shout, " He
hath done all things well." [angels'.
An accumulation of glory, His Father's, His own, and His holy
Then He will be glorified in His *righteousness.* None will perish
undeservedly. Rev. xx. 13.
He will be glorified in His *mercy.* Saints will for ever praise His
grace. Rev. i. 5, 6.
He will be glorified in His *omniscience.* He "searcheth the
hearts." Rev. ii. 23.
He will be glorified in His *immutability.* " The same yesterday,"
&c. Heb. xiii. 8.
He will be glorified in His *power.* " He has the keys of death and
hell." Rev. i. 18.
Those not ashamed of Him now, He will confess before the uni-
verse. Luke xii. 8.
To the righteous, " Come, ye blessed." To the wicked " Depart."
Matt. xxv. 34, 41.
So far as revealed, this scene will surpass all other scenes in
solemnity.
Men will then have views very different from what they now have.
The *miser* will see a life spent in gathering gold, with terror.
The *ambitious* will wonder he could barter his soul for office.
The *sensualist* will dread to review his luxury and lewdness.
The *sophist* will argue no more for ever against Divine truth.
The *impenitent* will be amazed at his madness in clinging to his
sins. [things.
The *mocker* will be heard uttering no more jests about sacred
The *profane* will howl over the folly that insulted his God.
In a crowd men may live, but they die and are judged *alone.*
There no voice of mercy will be heard by gospel-despisers. Prov.
i. 30. [x. 16.
The day of grace will never return to the Christ-rejecter. Luke
" The day of wrath is come ; and who shall be able to stand ? "
Rev. vi. 17.

" Thou Monarch of Life and Death, my lot is in Thy hands.
" Punish me in this world, O, Jesus, but not in that to come."
    Quesnel.
Our Lord is commissioned to do His Father's will in that day.
Judgment is the close of the great drama of time and life on this
    earth.
With it the curtain falls to rise on " a new heavens and a new
    earth, wherein shall dwell righteousness."

κρίνει. Begins in this life, as shown by verse 30. *Hengst.*
κρίσιν. The mere withholding of life as to predestination. *Ebrard.* Distinguishing between these or those at judgment. *Schleier.* Sanctification of
believers. *Stier.* Final condemnation of impenitent. The entire ruling of
His Father's kingdom. *Calvin.* A priori, " The Judge of all the earth," the
Father is not excluded. *Hengst.* Pater non judicat solus. *Bengel.* Grace
withdrawn, Spirit grieved—is Christ judging. *Quesnel.* No allusion to the
general judgment. *Oeder, Eckermann.* No reason for rendering κρίσις judgment, ver. 22, and condemnation, ver. 24. " Shall not come " render " doth
not come." *Maurice.* Raising the dead implies the Son is to be Judge hereafter. *Alford.*

---

23. That all men should honour the Son, even as they honour the Father.
He that honoureth not the Son honoureth not the Father which hath sent him.

All men. How can self-called " Liberals " believe this verse, and
    yet deny Christ's Divinity ?   (See on verse 18.)
Jews rightly regarded each word as blasphemous, if Jesus is not
    very and ETERNAL JEHOVAH !
Honour. Given to creatures may be mere *respect,* but to God
    must always be WORSHIP.   [sult.
All professions of honour to Jesus Christ, short of WORSHIP, are in-
He now gives the reason why judgment is transferred to Him.
Adoring the Father implies adoring the Son.   1 John ii. 22, 23.
Rejection of the Son implies rejection of both Father and Son.
Even as. Equality in judging, quickening, creating (John i. 3),
    involves equality in nature, unity of work, and unity of glory,
    Hos. iii. 5.   (See on John i. 1—3.)
The Father. See on John i. 14, 18 ; iii. 35 ; iv. 23.   Maker, Up-
    holder, and Governor of all things.
Honouring the *Father* involves much more : " Father of our Lord
    Jesus Christ."   1 Pet. i. 3.
1. As FATHER, He so loved the world as to purpose its *redemption.*
2. As FATHER, He gave His only begotten Son to die under the
    law.

458 / Gospel of John

3. As FATHER, He will ever listen to His Son's intercession for us.
4. As FATHER, He waits to receive every fallen child of man.
Why do sinners repel so *universally* the Saviour's claims?
Because His Divinity is inseparably connected with His atoning
     sacrifice.
And that implies the inexorable demands of the law of Jehovah.
And that implies man's responsibility, guilt, and condemnation.
The Father never "gives His honour to another, nor His praise to
     graven images." Isa. xlii. 8. Hence the Son is not "*another.*"
He will *require* every "knee to bow" to that Son, "of things in
     heaven, and things on earth." Phil. ii. 10.   [43.
"The enemies of the Son shall be made His footstool." Luke xx.
Jews professing to honour the Father, but refusing to honour the
     Son, perished. Deut. xxviii. 63; Matt. xxvii. 25.
Our Lord will be glorified either in salvation or destruction. Rev.
     xix. 1.
If men will not *sing* His praise, they must *weep* His praise!
A terrible sight, a "scorned" Jesus sitting on a "mocked" Judg-
     ment throne!
When He condemns, to whom will gospel-despisers appeal?
CONDEMNATION by the SAVIOUR will be the bitterest woe in the
     cup of the lost.
Amphilochius entered the palace of *Theodosius,* and bowed to the
     Emperor, but not to *Arcadius,* his son. The Emperor remind-
     ing him of his neglect, the good man still refused, and on his
     showing great displeasure, Amphilochius replied, "Oh, king,
     how much more will Jehovah abhor those rejecting His Son!"
Honoureth not. "Whoso denieth the SON, the same hath not the
     FATHER." 1 John ii. 23.
Those "denying the Lord who bought them" bring upon them-
     selves "swift destruction." 2 Pet. ii. 1.
No one can believe in the UNITY of God while denying the TRINITY.
Plutarch said he would rather persons denied there was a Plutarch
     than deny his character.
Refusing openly to render allegiance is treason on earth.
Toward our Maker and Redeemer, it is treason toward heaven.
And involves all the results,—conflict, death, and ruin.
Here our Lord unequivocally CLAIMS DIVINE WORSHIP.
This claim was sealed by JEHOVAH HIMSELF in EVERY MIRACLE!
Out of Christ there is nothing but idolatry and false imaginings of
     God. *Luther.*

καθώς. Denotes strictly equality of Divine honour. *Stier.* This realized in any ambassador plenipotentiary. *Pfenninger.* His relation to His work. *B. Crusius.* Men begin with opposing Christ, and end with atheism. *Müller.* The Son separated idealistically from Jesus. *Herder.* Apart from each other neither can exist. *Klenker.* Jesus is no saint, whom as Papists we may invoke. *Stier.* That all men should honour the angel "*Gabriel*" as they do God, would sound strange. *Toplady.*

---

24. Verily, verily, I say unto you, He that heareth my word, and believeth on him that sent me, hath everlasting life, and shall not come into condemnation; but is passed from death unto life.

Verily, verily. At this solemn moment these words were an oath. *Augustine.*

They point to a leading thought in the discourse.

A strengthening confirmation of His lofty claims to Divinity.

Repeated here and directly after (verse 25) intimates He is about to say something *difficult of apprehension.*

That believers on earth and in heaven are one.

That *regeneration* completed here is the *resurrection begun.*

Heareth. The ear has been called the mouth of the soul.

The soul receives nourishment from the truth, as the body from food.

As death first came in by the ear, so doth life eternal. Isa. lv. 3.

God the Father on Mount Tabor said, " HEAR YE HIM." Matt. xvii. 5.

Here it implies *faith*, an experimental evidence of Divine grace.

Millions through curiosity would like to see the Son incarnate.

But *hearing* is the great test of obedience from age to age.

" The Lord thy God will raise up a Prophet; *unto Him shall ye hearken.*" Deut. xviii. 15.   [the dead.

My word. The gospel voice (verse 25), word of power raising

His word is the real principle of life.   " The incorruptible seed."

Believeth. Faith, its nature and evidence.   John i. 7 ; iii. 15, 16, 18 ; iv. 39, 42 ; vii. 38.

Salvation begins in hearing and is perfected in believing.

The constant victory of truth in convincing and converting the soul.

Shows at once the majesty and grace of the testimony of God.

Incarnate Love stands and pleads to win His murderers.

Him that sent. Not belief in the Father merely, but that the Son was sent by Him.

That redemption and judgment are committed to Him.

Hath. See on John iii. 36.   Not " *shall have.*"   The elements of heaven and hell are found on earth.

Everlasting life. See on John iii. 15, 16, 36. Life is of many
degrees, the lowest is in the *sponge*.   [worm.
Then in the polypus, then in the oyster, and higher still in the
Through a long and beautifully graduated series we come to man,
partly material and partly spiritual, the link between earth
and heaven.

Life is absolutely perfect in God only, the great SOURCE of LIFE to
all created beings.

" And this is life eternal, to know THEE the only true God, and
Jesus," &c. John xvii. 3.

This life in its fulness implies—1. Freedom from all the guilt and
pollution of sin, and from all known and possible evils. 2.
The possession of all good, perfect love, perfect purity, perfect youth, perfect activity, perfect blessedness.

Glimpses of this glory seen in Moses and Elijah on the Mount.

Though morn's first blush leaves all the earth still in night.

But Christ Himself is the perfect model : " We shall be like Him."

And all this in uninterrupted and everlasting perpetuity.

Instability casts a shadow on all the joys and glories of earth.

Believers having "tasted the powers of the world to come," begin
to live here.   Heb. vi. 5.   [Col. iii. 3.

Life of God hid in the soul has its source and perfection in eternity.

Men speak of laying down at death " the burden of life."

But the Bible speaks of saints laying down " the burden of death."
2 Cor. v. 4.   [Rev. ii. 7.

" To him that overcometh I will give to eat of the tree of life."

The glory given the Son by the Father the Son gives His saints.
John xvii. 22.

All are children of ONE FATHER through the merit of ONE LORD
and by the grace of ONE SPIRIT.

All are " heirs of Christ," and " kings and priests unto God."

" To him that overcometh will I grant to sit with Me in My
throne."   Rev. iii. 21.

Alexander the Great said to one overwhelmed with his generosity,
"I GIVE AS A KING."   Jehovah gives as the INFINITE GOD.

" Eye hath not seen, nor ear heard, neither have entered into the
heart of man, the things that God hath prepared for them
that love Him."

" But God hath revealed them to us by His Spirit."   1 Cor. ii. 9.

" Life, or death, or things present, or things to come ; ALL ARE
YOURS ! "   1 Cor. iii. 22.

Not come. "All, both good and evil, will stand before the Judge."
Into condemnation. Shall enjoy a life of authorized right to
stand in God's presence.
From death. A state of impenitence and unbelief a state of death.
The soul a temple in ruins. Inscription, "HERE GOD ONCE DWELT."
Divine presence withdrawn. Lamps extinct. Altar overthrown.
Affections, once filled with love and light, now cold and dark.
Golden candlestick displaced. Prince of darkness enthroned.
Sacred incense displaced by poisonous vapours.
House of prayer now a den of thieves, as *lust, hate, and covetousness.*
Carved work of the sanctuary broken by axes and hammers.
Scattered fragments prove they were engraven by the finger of God.
BEHOLD THE DESOLATION ! *John Howe's* Living Temple.   [ONE.
1. Dead, having eyes, but *blind* to all the beauty of the ANOINTED
2. Dead, having ears, but *deaf* to all the music of His voice.
3. Dead, having a heart, but no *throbbings* of love more than the
   grave.
4. Dead, having no more *hope* of the inheritance than one buried.
The young man " went away sorrowful." He must *die* to the world
   if he would *live* to Christ.   [vi. 11.
" They only can be alive unto God who are dead unto sin." Rom.
This new life bestowed on each believer is a resurrection.
Without this change the resurrection only reveals and finishes death.
Resurrection : 1. From a death of unbelief, to a life of faith.
2. From a death of falsehood, to a life of truth.
3. From a death of sin, to a life of righteousness.
4. From a death of misery, to a life of blessedness.
The Son of His own inherent, sovereign will, imparts our faith in
   Him. 1 John iii. 14.
" As I heal the sick and raise the dead, so I quicken whom I will."
To life. As all believers died through *sin,* so they live through *faith.*
" The sting of death is sin," but in Christ the sting is taken away.
Bodily death, when the guilt of sin is purged away by Christ's
   blood, is "falling asleep in Jesus."
Our Lord's death secures life, and hence THE WAY OF DEATH IS BUT
   THE WAY OF LIFE.

ἀκούων. Hearing begins faith, ends man's agency. *Fikenscher.* Faith
never matured below. Refers to labours and trials only. *Stier.*
τὸν λόγου. Refers to Deut. xviii. 15. λόγος here differs from φωνῆς, verse
25. *Hengst.* Two propositions to be confirmed with emphasis. *Lücke.*

Christ's life-giving activity here, and bestowal of life hereafter. *Hengst.*
The Jews would have murdered Him then, but He discourses on earnestly and
lovingly to win them. *Anton.*

οὐκ ἔρχεται. Comes but remains not in condemnation. *Chrys.* Comes not
to trial. *Wetstein.* Is not sentenced to death. *Kuinoel.* Hath passed : *perfect*
sense of μεταβέβηκεν, not to be weakened. *Alford.* Others regard it as a confirming of the decision made at death. No other judgment than that of
condemning the believer's sins. *Stier.*

κρίσιν. Used in a restricted sense. *Erasmus.* Unless he fall from grace.
Wesley. As well say Elijah reached heaven in his chariot of fire, if he met
with no accident on the way. IF INDEED CHRIST'S, all else is secured.
John x. 28, 29. *Author.*

θανάτου. Physical death. *Chrys., Tertullian, Tittmann, Tholuck, J. Brown.*
Spiritual death. *Eichorn, Lampe, D. Brown.* Literally and spiritually understood. *Calvin, Lücke, Neander.* Believers have passed from death to life, for
the incorruptible seed (1 Peter i. 23) abides in them, and they are already with
Christ. Col. iii. 3. *Calvin.* The conversion of sinners by Christ's ministry.
Doddr. No allusion to the miserable doctrine of purgatory. *J. Taylor.* A
present thing of faith. *Zwingli, Beza.*

ζωήν. The souls of saints shine through their glorified bodies as wine
through a glass. *Aquinas.*

---

25. Verily, verily, I say unto you, The hour is coming, and now is, when
the dead shall hear the voice of the Son of God: and they that hear shall live.

Hour. Measure of time. John iv. 52. An epoch in the future.

Dead. See on ver. 24. Repentance is called LIFE. Eph. ii. 1.
Impenitence, DEATH. Col. ii. 13. [really live.

The righteous who have "fallen asleep" (1 Cor. xv. 6) alone

That hear. See on ver. 24. An Oriental expression for obedience
to God's will.

His voice penetrated the eternal world when He raised the dead.

"Lazarus, come forth," reverberated through the hosts of disembodied spirits.

To the wicked He will say, "I am the resurrection," but to His
saints, "I am the resurrection and the life." *Harris.*

There is no sinner now, however dead and corrupting, that His voice
cannot reach. [even of the vilest !

What encouragement to prayer and humble effort for the salvation

Live. See on John ii. 22 ; v. 29. Love of life a constitutional
instinct of man's nature. Gen. iii. 22.

Poets of Greece and Rome had their *Elysium* and *Tartarus.*

Socrates inferred a life to come from the *necessity* of future rewards
and punishments. [coming.

Jews, for ages, had looked for a resurrection, at the Messiah's

As there is a *soul* resurrection, so a *bodily* resurrection is taught in
the O. T. Dan. xii. 2.

Not *the* body sown in the grave, but a new body springing
from it.
Animated by the same mind; conscious of its own identity.
Remembering its thoughts and feelings as we do after a night's sleep.
Energy of God will be visible as in the creation of man at the first.
Shall live, a great truth. Even " The sea shall give up her dead."
" Death and hell *(hades)* shall deliver up the dead which are in
them." Rev. xx. 13.
" LIVE " in contrast with " THE SECOND DEATH " from which be-
lievers are saved.
As the height of a mountain is only fully measured by the *depths
around*, so until the redeemed reach the golden city they
will never wholly know the *length, breadth, height,* and *depth*
of salvation.
Divine LOVE and MERCY are deeper than hell, and higher than
the glorious summits of heaven.

νῦν ἐστιν. Spiritually understood. *Stier.* No reference to Lazarus. *Lücke.*
ὥρα. Bodily resurrection as the spiritual is pre-supposed. *Olsh.* Jews had
long expected a resurrection, when Messiah appeared. *Lightfoot.* Resurrection of the soul from spiritual death partial, this universal. *Andrews.* *Time*
continues till His appearing. *Meyer.* Often refers to the calling of the
Gentiles. *Elsley.*
φωνῆς instead of λόγος, proves spiritual raising. *Stier.*
φωνῆς, resurrection call. *Tholuck.* Calling of the Gentiles. *Cocceius.* Same
as λόγος in verse 24. *Lücke, Hengst.* From " hearing,' verse 24, He rises to the
grander expression " as soon as they shall hear," &c. *Stier.*
οἱ limits the number. *B. Crusius.*
ἀκού. Not the voice at Lazarus's tomb. *Hengst.* The call of the trumpet
will not have died away before all the rising dead shall have heard it. *Grotius.*
Heard spiritually in regeneration, and will be corporeally in the last day.
D. Brown.
ζήσονται. Preliminary individual resurrections. Regeneration goes on to
the complete and final resurrection. *Stier.* Immediate blessedness of the
saints not taught, but sure of everlasting life. *Tholuck.* Future existence
somewhat and somehow the universal opinion among men. *Cicero.*

---

26. For as the Father hath life in himself; so hath he given to the Son to
have life in himself.

Father. Trinity. See on John i. 1, 2, 18, 49 ; iii. 16, &c. ; iv. 21, 23.
Life in Himself. Life unoriginated, independent, absolute,
eternal life. With God is the fountain of life. Psa. xxxvi. 9.
1. Spiritual ; 2. Ever flowing ; 3. Overflowing ; 4. All-satisfy-
ing to men and angels.

Given the Son. By eternal impartation of the Godhead as "THE
ONLY BEGOTTEN." Hints also at His office as Saviour, "I
give unto them eternal life."

The Son. See on John i. 18, 49. Son of God and Son of man,
the Divine and human inseparable in one person.

In Himself. Heathen called Jove STATOR, but Christ is the
STATOR of the universe. [all things.

As the LOGOS (see John i. 1—3), He created, and still upholds
"As the living Father hath sent me, and I live by the FATHER."
John vi. 57.

"In Him dwells all the fulness of the Godhead bodily." Col. ii. 9.

Not in types, or cloud, or shechinah, or temple, but in the *glories*
of the *kingdom of grace.* [spirit world.

His miracles proclaim Him Lord of nature, of man, and of the
"He shall change our vile bodies, and fashion them like," &c.
Phil. iii. 21.

Paul founds this hope on that Infinite energy by which He is
"able to subdue all," &c. Phil. iii. 21.

The eternal life of our Lord, as co-equal with the Father, is constantly blending with His mediatorial character as INTER-
CESSOR. John xvii. [man.

He gives life as the Son of God, and is Judge as the Son of
Such is His fulness, that He has inexhaustible and everlasting
treasures for all.

ζωὴν. Life-giving power. *Theoph.* Purpose of God that it should be in
the Son. *Lücke, Luthardt.* A subject beyond human judgment. *Author.*
Refers to the essential life of the Son before all time as the Λόγος. Thus understood by nearly all the *Fathers. Olsh., Stier, Alford, &c.* To His human
nature. *Athan., Calvin, Beza, Lampe.*

ἐν ἑαυτῷ. An immovable boundary definition in *well-measured words* in
relation to the Trinity. *Stier.*

ἔδωκεν, anterior to Creation. *Stier.* From *eternity* the Father *gave*, and
from eternity the Son *receiveth* life. *Burgon.* A perfect likeness, save one is
Father, the other Son. *Chrys.* Christ from eternity was a light and life.
Augustine. "Given to have,"—i.e. appointed to be Messiah. "In Him (the
LOGOS) was life." John i. 4. *J. Brown.*

---

27. And hath given him authority to execute judgment also, because he is
the Son of man.

Authority. Complete investment for the mediatorial office which
consummates in resurrection and judgment.

Embracing all the intervening course of the affairs of time.
The reward of His humiliation and obedience unto death.   Phil.
 ii. 6—11.
Grace despised converts mount Zion into another Sinai.
" In flaming fire He will take vengeance on those that obey not
 the gospel." 2 Thess. i. 8.   [save.
" Ye would not " is the bitter cry of Divine love that still waits to
Execute judgment.   See on verse 22.   *Judgment* is exhibited
 as the higher idea.   [His humanity.
Because Son of man.   Significantly and strikingly emphasizing
As the compassionate elder Brother, He will judge.
He hath exercised mercy toward all the members of His family.
He will finish that kindness by final absolution from all their
 sins.
To those on His left hand He will judicially say, "I know ye not,"
 because "ye would not come unto ME for life."
We shall be judged as men by Jesus *as a man.*
As a man, His life will condemn our life ; His humility our pride,
 His temperance our indulgence ; His forbearance our im-
 patience ; His chastity, our sensuality ; His piety and devo-
 tion our ungodliness and earthly-mindedness.
But with loving *trust* in His offer of life, as one bearing our
 NATURE, what favour may we not expect at His hands.
He once promised thrones and kingdoms to His humble followers.
 Luke xxii. 29, 30.   [His saints.
He who is Creator and Upholder of the universe, will not forget
He who will be our future JUDGE, is now our ADVOCATE and IN-
 TERCESSOR in coming to God.
Now MERCY as great as MAJESTY sits upon that throne.
Those knowing Him as JESUS " shall be caught up to meet Him "
 when He comes as JUDGE.   1 Thess. iv. 17.
Son of man.   Denotes His relative humanity, *the human appearance
 of* Him who is the Son of God, and always implies this.
Jews surmised " *Messiah* " was concealed under this name.   John
 xii. 34.
He must become Son of man, by being born among men.
By virtue of His birth, we can truly say " OUR BROTHER."
This true and proper humanity certifies the fulfilment of all the
 promises.   [sons of God.
For our sake He became Son of man ; we, for His sake, become
By this title He ever reminds us of His deep humiliation.

He appropriated the name in presence of the Sanhedrim just
before He was adjudged to die. Matt. xxvi. 64.

It identifies Him with the Glorious One seen in Daniel's vision.
Dan. vii. 13, 14.   [55 times.

It *stands alone* as His *chosen designation*, and is used by Himself
The Spirit permits not the Evangelists to give Him this title,—
only Jesus of Himself.   [" SON OF GOD."

Used in John 11 times, being overshadowed by the more august
It constantly refers back to and contrasts with His Divinity.

As " Son of God," it declares His humility in *humanity*.

The Son. The second Adam, representative of man's recovery, as
the first was of the fall.

Called by the apostles generally, " SON OF DAVID."

O.T. prophecy points to Him as upholding the birthright of all the
race.   Luke iii. 23—38.

Son of God promised and given to man.   Gen. iii. 15 ; Isa. ix. 6 ;
John iii. 14.   Sprung from man, Heb. ii. 11, known as a *true
man*.   To be a *marked man* on the scale of human misery.
Mark viii. 31 ; Heb. v. 7.

Called " SON OF MAN " in His exaltation, John i. 51 ; as being *in*
heaven while on earth, John iii. 13 ; as "Lord of the Sabbath,"
Matt. xii. 8 ; as blasphemed, Matt. xii. 32 ; as coming in
glory, Matt. xvi. 27 ; as suffering, Matt. xvii. 12 ; as rising,
Mark ix. 9 ; as Saviour, Matt. xviii. 11 ; as sitting on His
throne, Matt. xix. 28 ; in His second advent, Matt. xxiv. 30 ;
as made under the law, Gal. iv. 4 ; as subject to God's
decrees, Matt. xxvi. 25 ; as forgiving sins, Matt. ix. 6 ; as
houseless, Matt. viii. 20 ; as wearing a golden crown, Rev.
xiv. 14; as Lord of angels, Matt. xiii. 41 ; as supreme Judge at
the last day, Rev. i. 7 ; as Head of the Church, ever walking amid the seven golden candlesticks, Rev. i. 13.

A heavy cross for Jewish pride, the rock on which the Jews
stumbled.

His humanity the *very ground* of His being appointed Judge.

If men plead the infirmity of the flesh, He can say, " I also was a
man."

As SON OF MAN a wondrous flower on the decaying tree of
humanity.   John iii. 31.

ἐξουσίαν, founded on His incarnation. *Hengst.*

κρίσιν ποιεῖν. To exercise mild judgment. *Wetstein.* Judgment an essential part of Messiah's office. *Lücke, Kuinoel.* Because He humbled Himself to take flesh. *Grotius, Lampe.*

ὅτι υἱός, reference to Dan. vii. 13, 14. *Stier.* Reference to His mediatorial humanity, since man is to be judged by a man. *Meyer.* The omission of the article very significant. *Brückner, De Wette.* The phrase occurs above seventy times, but here the only time without the article. Only a man. *Beza, Michaelis.* Reference to His Divinity, humanity did not originally belong to Him. *Middleton.* Principle of life in humanity, He perfectly discriminates each soul. *Lange.* A faint estimate of the omniscient Judge. *Author.* By virtue of the Divine union, His mind perfect, Isa. xi. 2, 3. His body also, Psa. xlv. 2. Highest in favour, Luke ii. 52. Use of the article separates Him from all mankind. Indwelling of Divinity in humanity as ground and medium of life-giving and judgment. *D. Brown.* Equivalent to Messiah. *Lightfoot, Lücke.* Humanity to be glorified. *Olshausen, Neander.* Refers back to His Divine nature. *Justin Martyr, Irenæus, Tertullian.* An antithesis to higher nature. *Tholuck.* Our Lord called so out of contempt by the *Rabbins.* *Le Clerc.* By this name He was concealed from Satan. Indicates immortal youth. Dan. vii. 13. *Bengel.* Psa. viii. 4 has *Bar-enosh,* i.e. humanity in its frailest and weakest form. Phil. ii. 5—11. Docetæ, Valentinus, and Marcian denied Christ's proper humanity. *Wordsworth.* The human appearance of the Son of God. *De Wette.* Jews had not grasped *this* thought. A demon-like Jew of extraordinary power, were their hope. *Lange.* Suitable for his incognito among nations. The term a protest against Gnosticism, Sabellianism, monkish contempt of life, and against the perversions of the doctrine of election. *Dorner.* Since He is the Messiah. *Origen.* A title not yet given to the Messiah of the Jews. *Wilson, Ellicott.* An ideal man. *Neander.* Verse 25 assumes, and 26 and 27 unfold, that Messiah and the Father have the same fulness of life and power. *Lücke.* Conscious of a complete participation in humanity. *De Wette.* Pointless, if not used in a sense inapplicable to other men. That He would glorify humanity. *Author.*

---

28. Marvel not at this: for the hour is coming, in the which all that are in the graves shall hear his voice.

Marvel not. It would seem as if their wonder had appeared in their *looks.*

Sublimely and serenely He utters still more wonderful words.

Instead of *wondering,* it is far better to foster the habit of *believing* unto salvation. [wonders.

His name being "WONDERFUL," Isa. ix. 6, He may well utter

Of Him alone it can be said, He was created, and yet uncreated; without beginning, and yet begotten in time; a Jew, and yet God over all. [noted.

The hour. Not brevity of period, but time of beginning thus

Is coming. Close of the present dispensation of mercy is indicated.

All. Now He calls to faith and repentance, and men *can* refuse.

Then the archangel's voice will pierce every grave, and none will disregard.

As in a certain war there is no discharge (Eccl. viii. 8), so there will be none from that call.

Now men can obtain *substitutes* in law, in battle, in office; but *that summons* will bring to the bar every child of Adam.

Graves. See John xi. 38. Includes earth and sea; wherever remains of humanity have found a " last home."

The myriads of that vast realm over which death has held dominion.

Our Lord condemns the error of some who in later times denied the second resurrection, because the first of faith is passed. 2 Tim. ii. 18.

Shall hear. Determinate prophetic certainty ; shall hear and obey the call.

"Many that sleep in the dust shall awake, some to everlasting life," &c. Dan. xii. 2.

Raising the wicked equivalent to summoning them to the *bar*.

They will indeed see Christ " whom they pierced "—a *look* of *despair*.

They will hear His voice in the irrevocable sentence, " DEPART ! "

A happy glorious morn will then dawn on the graves of the just.

To those who loved Him it will be the gladdest sound ever heard by man.

The consummation of all their faith and penitence and hope.

The rich and glorious harvest of a field often sown in tears and cries.

His voice. John iii. 29. Voice of the SON OF MAN; Jesus Christ's own voice.

What higher claim could he make, to show that He is God Himself ?

His voice is even now heard—1. In the whisper of grace. 2. In the thunder of condemnation.

Even the voice of Peter, in Christ's name, awoke from the sleep of death Tabitha at Lydda. Acts ix. 40.

But He whose word hushed storms, cast out devils, healed diseases, raised the dead, will now speak, and earth, heaven, and hell shall hear. [glory ?

If His word in humiliation was so powerful, what will it be in

---

μὴ θαυμάζετε. Merely an unbelieving wonder. *Luthardt.* A state of mind suddenly affected for good. *Stier.* Wonder mingled with anger, perhaps show of gesture. *Bloomfield.* Pharisees forgot their scorn in their wonder at such words. *Tisch.* Connected with the last verse. *Chrys.*

μνημείοις, μνῆμα, a memorial; bodies, not souls, are in these graves. *Augustine.*

φωνῆς. Called κελεύσμα, 1 Thess. iv. 16. The sound made by the ancient rowers as the oars kept time. *Trapp.*

---

29. And shall come forth; they that have done good, unto the resurrection of life ; and they that have done evil, unto the resurrection of damnation.

Shall come. Not as something *done* to them, but as their own
act, the fruit of new life. *Kling.*

Millions *now* hear His call in nature, providence, and grace, but
heed not.

But no laggart will be there *then*,—no hiding-place for the wicked.
Gen. iii. 8. [forth their trust.

The sea will yield up her charge, and earth's cemeteries will send

Done good. A wide-spread and wilful delusion prevails as to duty.

Vain man cares not to do good, unless it be on a *grand scale*.

This very test will decide for ever the doom of myriads.

It is doing good to make one person holier or happier, or even to
give brutes a better home.

Even a cup of cold water given in His náme will have a reward.

The widow's mite more honoured than all, because " she did what
she could."

Yea, so good is God, that what we *would* do is reckoned as if *done.*

" It is well that it was in thine heart to build Me a house."

No meritorious sufferings here alluded to,—moral character alone is
recognized. [xxv.

" Inasmuch as *ye did it*, &c. Inasmuch as *ye did it not*," &c. Matt.

Romish dogma of a purgatory after death a flat contradiction of
Scripture. [hood.

Invented to give *power* and *purse* to an ignorant and corrupt priest-

Our Lord alludes not to the *cause* of salvation, but to the *works* of
grace. [Lord.

In verse 24 it is, They that " *hear* " His voice, that is, *obey* the

Doing good is another phrase for " hearing His voice." " Faith
works by love," &c., producing a *holy life.*

Charity the flower and fruit of faith ; " The beauty of the Lord."

A Christian shows mercy to all, is provoked by no insult.

Suffers not the weak to be oppressed, relieves the wretched.

Comforts the mourner, and mingles tears with the bereaved.

He is ready to help the weary, teach the ignorant, lift the fallen,
warn the guilty.

He spreads his table for the hungry and thirsty, and points them
to the bread and water of life. [God.

Not unwilling to be poor in this world, if he can be rich towards

An humble follower of Him of whom it is recorded " He went
about doing good." Acts x. 38.

Resurrection. See on John ii. 22 ; v. 25. Implies the soul's
immortality and the body's restoration.

Enoch's translation must have left a tradition among the *whole race.*
Ancient Egyptians, Greeks, and Romans hoped for life beyond
    death.   [departed.
Hottentots leave the hut of the dead furnished for the ghost of the
The great question with heathen sages, "If a man die, shall he live
    again ? "   Job xiv. 14.
Revelation answers, " Thy dead shall live." Isa. xxvi. 19. "Many
    that sleep shall awake."   Dan. xii. 2.
" I will ransom them from the power of the grave." Hos. xiii. 14.
Doctrine of the resurrection in all its details fully taught by Paul.
    1 Cor. xv. 35—58.
A Christian's life is tainted with death until the resurrection.
An immortality of bliss begins immediately after the resurrection.
"This day shalt thou be with ME in paradise." Luke xxiii. 43.
A clear prophecy, for the malefactors were put to death by "break-
    ing their legs."   [on the cross.
According to *Roman* custom they would have lived several days
Resurrection an act of sovereign authority toward both righteous
    and wicked.
Of life.   See on John iii. 15, 16, 36.   He claims to be the WORD,
    and to possess LIFE and LIGHT.   [hearts.
Faith in Christ shows us His knowledge of every throb of our
Without this faith all thoughts of the tomb are dark as midnight.
Its abysses are *dreaded* by all the millions of the race of Adam.
But these words will yet shed sweet summer on the graves of His
    saints.
Here the voice of the Son of Man reigns in LOVE, to the holy.
" I AM the RESURRECTION AND THE LIFE."   These are thy trophies,
    O FAITH !
Done evil.   All wish to know what will be their lot hereafter.
The fearful mistake is to examine our wishes rather than our lives.
An expression involving many and various shades of character.
Some think none but the openly profane and criminal will be con-
    demned.
But the "slothful servant" is classed with the " wicked " in doom.
" To him that knoweth to do good and doeth it not, it is sin."
" To do no harm," a merely negative state of life, will not be ac-
    cepted for "*doing good.*"   [pensable.
" Love to God and man," present and active in the soul is indis-
Not to have this is to *do* evil, for " the carnal mind is enmity
    against God."

Damnation. Gr. *Judgment.* Pharisees held none but the just
would rise.
This word condemns—1. Those who hold death is the termination
of being.   [world.
2. Those who deny punishment of the impenitent in the eternal
3. Those teaching that saints only rise, and that the wicked are
annihilated.
4. Those holding that a faith without works will save. Jas. ii. 26.
How awfully grand and of absorbing interest are these unfoldings !
In what light does the trifling of myriads in gospel lands appear ?
In what, the studied contempt of many shown towards the Holy
Judge ?
No language can describe what will be the self-condemnation of
this madness, when too late.
How few take time to think to what joys the holy shall rise !
How few consider what may be suffered through eternity !
He, who here spoke, knew all the woe comprehended in " damn-
ation."
But men divert their thoughts from subjects distressing to them.
Satan again whispers as of old, " Ye shall not surely die."
But if there be *no* reality in hell or heaven, *would Jesus have died ?*
If the worm that dieth not be no dreadful truth, would the Holy
Ghost strive ?
It is no imaginary scene.   The throne of judgment will be set.
No mere painting !   The heavens passing away, and worlds
vanishing, systems dissolving ;
Monarchies breaking up, thrones crumbling, crowns and sceptres
lying as neglected things.   [state.
The supreme Judge in glorious apparel, moving forth in solemn
The splendour of His vast and countless retinue, an obedient throng
of holy beings, doing homage to their Eternal King.
The swift flight of His royal guards, sent forth to gather the
elect, covering the heavens with their expansive wings.
Silence and universal attention to the loud sounding of the trumpet,
as it shakes the pillars of the world, pierces the caverns of
earth, and resounds through the encircling heavens.
Myriads of joyful expectants, arising, changing, putting on glory,
ascending upwards to join the triumphant host.
Judgment set, books opened, terror of the lost, final sentence,
heavens rolled up as a scroll.   Earth and all things in it
burned up. *John Howe.*

Thus the curtain falls to rise upon a "new heavens and a new earth, wherein shall dwell righteousness."

ἀνάστασιν. Spectres of frequent occurrence according to *Homer* and *Virgil*. Among Mahommedans. *Bruce.* Among modern Europeans. *Glanville.* Transmigration of souls to brutes or men. *Pythagoras.* The elements of souls similar to that of stars. *Aristotle.* Soul and the material of the body both *eternal. Plato.* "Principal ideas connected with the earlier part of the 'Ritual of the Dead' are the living after death, and the being born again as the sun, which typified the Egyptian resurrection." *Birch.* Enough of the body resists putrefaction to be seed for the next body. *Mahomet.* Fathers held that the dead were in abditis receptaculis. *Irenæus.* The soul went into the air. *Orpheus, Origen, Ossian, Dodwell.* Achilles dreaded the spirit world.

> "Rather I'd choose to be
> A slave to some poor hind that toils for bread,
> Than live a sceptred monarch of the dead."—*Homer*.

Elysium allotted to the friends or relatives of the gods. But Sisyphus, Tantalus, and Ixion are sent to suffer in Hades. A purgatory hinted at by *Pythagoras*, was plainly taught by *Plato* and *Virgil*, and adopted by *Gregory* the *Great*, 590 A.D., and ratified by the Council of Trent, 1545 A.D. The same person, but not the identical body, will be raised. *Locke.* Cannot literally be same body—1. Science shows that in seven years the human body has so totally changed, that not one atom remains ; so that a man seventy years of age has had ten bodies. 2. Shows that immediately after death the various particles begin to liberate themselves and mix up as parts of other bodies. 3. In oriental lands the dead are burned, not buried, and in process of combustion the greater portions of the body pass off in gases, to mingle with other forms of existence. 4. In the case of cannibals, the parts of the body eaten assimilate with and become integral portions of other human bodies. St Paul says, "Thou sowest not that body that shall be." *K.* What the Bible calls the resurrection body takes place at death. *Bush, Maurice.* In the buried body exists an indestructible germ. *Origen, Watts, Drew.* An "immortal bone." *Ancient Jews and others.* A monad. *Leibnitz, Goethe.* In the spirit lies an ideal form of the body. *Lange.*

ἀνάστασις. Acts xvii. 18, taken by Athenians for a deified mortal. *Chrys., Hammond.*

ποιήσαντες, πράξαντες. Former "*wrought*," latter "*practised*." ἀγαθά. Good works named, since there are some who never knew the gospel. *Stier.* A grave error. *Munchmeyer.* Good works of heathen dependent on a Redeemer unrevealed to them. *Schleier.* Resurrection itself will be their regeneration. *Stier.* Resurrection is restored union of body and soul, no spiritual change. Dan. xii. 2. *Author.* Resurrection to death doubted, since all unbelief will have ceased. *Schleier.* A groundless inference. *Stier.*

κρίσεως. Kind of irony, since the death of the lost, instead of changing to life, is death consummated. *Stier.* Wicked annihilated because there is life in Christ only ; man's natural immortality denied. *White, Leask, Minto, Birks.*

ζωῆς. Which imparts life. *Bengel.* But one verse (Acts xxiv. 15) speaks of the wicked rising. *Tholuck.* What about Dan. xii. 2, 3 ? *Author.*

---

30. I can of mine own self do nothing : as I hear, I judge : and my judgment is just ; because I seek not mine own will, but the will of the Father which hath sent me.

I. The discourse passes into the majestic I, and yet is natural!
Mine own self. He denies doing these things as a human being,
  things which God *alone* could perform.
Things which involved their faith, their life, their eternal peace.
They could not say, as the philosopher to the jealous Dionysius,
  " We of this academy have no *leisure* for minding your affairs."
In these things interests of eternity were involved if true.
Do nothing. My decisions are all anticipated in the Father's
  mind.   [His.
By Me they are only reflected, and eternally just because certainly
He connects His present acts with His deeds as Judge.
Before it was " What I see, I do," now it is " What I hear, I do."
As I hear. Listening to the words of our Lord is one great duty
  of man.
As He listened to the words of His Father, and spoke them to us.
" Trouble about many things " disqualifies us from hearing Christ.
Martha rebuked for her inordinate agitation of mind. Luke x. 41.
Stayed on God; the mind has perfect rest in hearing God., Isa.
  xxx. 15; xxxii. 17.
Always " from the Father," I must always *hear right.*
As a consequence, right hearing leads to infallibly right judgment.
If I judge, my Father *in Me* commands Me thus to judge.
This is in sublime contrast with the humble appeal of an Apostle.
  Acts iv. 19.
I judge. "Give the king Thy judgments, O God." Psa. lxxii.
  1, 2; Isa. xi. 3, 4.
This the first great official work of the Messiah. Isa. xi. 3, 4.
Not mine own will. Pure freedom from self, " He lived, moved,
  and had His being " in God.
He asserts here His perfect sinlessness. " Not My will, but Thine
  be done." Luke xxii. 42.
Note—1. There is a moral difference in the judgment of men concerning Divine truth. 2. Diversity of judgment is dependent
  on moral condition. 3. Moral condition is resolvable into
  one of two great principles of action,—*self-seeking* or *God-seek-
  ing.* 4. Adoption of the Divine will is the essential condition
  of just judgments.
These principles—1. Explain the perversion of the Bible by its
  avowed disciples. 2. Indicate the method in which the
  gospel should be preached. 3. Supply a test of fitness for
  the work of the gospel ministry. 4. Show the necessity of

Divine influence. *Thomas.*

The only way to feel and know Christ is to be Christlike.

Love God and each other, and the God of love will teach you
   Divinity. *Archer Butler.*

ἀπ' ἐμαυτοῦ. Judicial. *Euthym., Grotius.* Apart from: with no
separate interest of my own. *D. Brown.*

ἀκούω. Present tense in John is often understood of the future. *Tittmann.*
As *I hear*, spoken of His humanity. *Beza.*

πατρός. Omitted. *Cod. Sinai., Lach., Tisch., Alford, Stier.*

θέλημα. Judges following their own passions are often hurried away from
justice. *Grotius.* This looks backwards and forwards. Satan's malice would
divorce Christ's will from God's. *Besser.*

δικαία. Sin and error are essentially the same. *Stier.* He can only speak
the pure truth of God. *Winer.* Even in such a glorious Being submission is
good. *Ber. Bib.* Christ does not only speak of His Divinity, but that incarnate,
we should not judge of Him by outward appearance. *Calvin.*

---

31. If I bear witness of myself, my witness is not true.

If I. Our Lord not only answers the thoughts of His foes, but
   also the objections they will *hereafter* bring up, by Him *foreseen.* John viii. 13.

Bear witness. *Law terms* have a definite meaning, e.g. one
   guilty means one who has been *proved* guilty.

A man's testimony may be " *true*," but in law it must be supported
   by *other evidence.*

As one witness is not enough, neither is one text sufficient to settle
   a point in theology. 2 Pet. i. 20.

He adduces three proofs as testimony to His relation with the
   Father : 1. John's mission. 2. His miracles. 3. Old Test.
   prophecy. [is void."

" If my miracles from God fail to prove me a prophet, my testimony
This is conclusive against all impostors, like Mahomet.

Our testimony must be in harmony with God's word and Church.

If it differ from these, Divine *miracles* should be *demanded.*

Prophets of the Old and New Test. must bring to the Church
   something besides their own word before being believed.
   Chrysostom. [witnesses.

Even Christ, speaking out of the law and prophets, offers other

Persons now claiming to speak in the name of Christ and the
   Holy Ghost are to be rejected unless they speak *according
   to the Scriptures.* [John viii. 14.

Still our Lord's record was true, though He testified of Himself.

Not true. The Jews already had asked Him, "Art thou the Christ?"
He did not answer them, because it would have been *no* answer.

It would have led them to think Him *another person* than He was ;
in fact, the Messiah that Jehovah sent was not the Messiah
the Jews *expected.*

The Evangelist has given the key-note : "Light shone, but the
darkness comprehended it not." John i. 5.

Baptist's testimony, though coming *through* man, was *not of* man.

Our Lord ever reflected, *and could not but* reflect, the Father's will.

For He was "the BRIGHTNESS OF THE FATHER'S GLORY, and EXPRESS
IMAGE of HIS PERSON." Heb. i. 3.

μαρτυρῶ. An interruption of those contradicting : "*Thou* bearest witness
of Thyself." *Tisch.* Rabbis held a similar sentiment. *Tholuck.* Roman law
refused such witness. *Pomponius, Lücke.* Two witnesses required by the law,
one being insufficient. *Grotius.* 2 Pet. i. 20. No one passage can be taken by
itself. *Jer. Taylor, Horsley.* Miracles alone vindicate a prophet's claims. *Le
Clerc.* He repudiates all self-glorification. *Tholuck.*

ἀληθής. Validus in foro humano. Concessio rhetorica. *Beza.* Testimony
ruled out of court is forensically *no evidence. Campbell.* This was the custom
for ages, that no one could be acquitted or condemned on his *own evidence.*
American law now admits *the person's* testimony. *Author.* Independent
testimony without regard to the Father would not be true. *Alford.*

---

32. There is another that beareth witness of me ; and I know that the witness which he witnesseth of me is true.

Another. The Father, distinctly declaring different personality.
See John i. 1, 2.

God alone can testify touching the nature of a Divine relation.

1. He has the witness of the Baptist, His predicted forerunner.
2. The witness of His own numerous and stupendous miracles.
3. The witness of the FATHER, given at His baptism, Matt. iii. 17,
transfiguration, Luke ix. 35, and in the temple, John xii. 29.
4. The witness of the Holy Scriptures, as full of Christ as the
heavens are full of stars. [to do them.

Witness. The miracles just performed required ALMIGHTY GOD

The Jews had the alternative of admitting—1. The testimony of
God to all Christ had said, or 2. That Jesus Christ, who performed them, was Jehovah, the Supreme God.

Is true. How affecting this allusion ! What depth of humility He
has reached when He must thus vindicate Himself !

Thus under the gathering cloud of persecution He cheered His
spirit !

476 / Gospel of John

" Ye are my witnesses, saith the Lord."   Isa. xliii. 12.

What a terrible doom will be that of false witnesses.

Such, returning from Canaan, perished miserably in the desert.

Hypocrites disgrace religion, as false witnesses injure a cause.

Worldly professors are *Satan's witnesses* in the court of the Messiah.

Do *we* bear true testimony for our Master, or is it against Him ?

ἄλλος.   Our Lord here is dealing with the Sanhedrim, or a section of them. *Lange.*   Sublimely distinguishes Himself from the Father. *Stier.*

ἄλλος.   John Baptist. *Chrys., Eras., Grot., De Wette, B. Crusius, Tisch.* The Father, as it would be beneath His dignity to rest His claims on human authority. *Aug., Bengel, Hengst., Lampe.*

μαρτυρία.   Mallem obedire quam miracula facere. *Luther.*   Antipater, a Greek profligate, wore a white cloak.   Diogenes said to him, Virtutis stragulam pudefacis. *Trapp.*

---

33. Ye sent unto John, and he bare witness unto the truth.

Ye sent.   Supposing John to be the Messiah, ye sent officially to learn the truth.   John i. 19.

He testified that *he* was not Messiah, and that I am Hᴇ.

Though the Lord was not personally present, His Spirit followed them.   Jer. viii. 6.

He would show the Jews they preferred fixing their hopes *anywhere* but on Christ.

John.   The Baptist.   For his life and character, see John i. 15.

He reminds them of a testimony to His Messiahship, kept back by them.

But they believed not John, although a faithful witness of the truth.

This act significant, since by it the Sanhedrim acknowledged John's *prophetic character.*

Witness.   John's testimony was supported by Jerusalem and all Judea, coming down to Jordan to be baptized by him, confessing their sins.

Through blind obstinacy or malice, this testimony they rejected.

Unbelief renders the heart ungrateful, and ingratitude soon grows to enmity.

Strange infatuation of sin, it *blackens* those whom it *wrongs.*

Wine is the remedy for hemlock, yet mingled it intensifies the poison.   [desperate.

The gospel, mingled with unbelief, renders the case of man more

---

Ὑμεῖς.   " You mean John the Baptist," interpolated by the crowd. *Tisch.*

He now points out—1. Testimony of the Baptist. 2. Of His works. 3. Of the Scriptures. *Stier.* Ye believed not John's testimony, to whom ye sent. Human testimony is not wanting. *Kuinoel.* Ye hear me, and my Father through me, but believe me not. Now search the Scriptures.

    μεμαρτύρηκε. The mission sent to John had suppressed his testimony to Christ. *Lange.* Doubtful. *Stier.*

    ἀληθεία. See John i. 14. Truth guides us back to God, whence it first came. *Herder.*

---

34. But I receive not testimony from man: but these things I say, that ye might be saved.

But I. This was a claim far above any demanded by prophets.
He who can assert this with truth cannot be less than God.
John, inspired, had echoed Moses' testimony. Deut. xviii. 15.
Concerning Moses all Jews believed his inspiration and mission were
    Divine.

Receive not testimony. Yet it was as certainly from God as the
    voice from heaven. Matt. iii. 17.   [tion.
That He permitted the Baptist to bear it seemed to need explana-
The full-orbed sun needs no glimmering star to announce its
    presence.
Not the *human* messenger, but the *Divine* Sender, gave John's tes-
    timony its dignity. Matt. iii. 3.   [MESSIAH!
That testimony believed would lead all to the light of TRUTH,—the
Jehovah might have sent angels to gather the sheep to His fold.
But He reserves to Himself all the glory in the humble instru-
    mentality of *men*.

From man. I receive no honouring testimony from man, even
    if that man be John.
Whoever I am, I am independent of human authority.
Ahaz sinned in rejecting the word of the *prophet* of the Most High.
But sinned yet more grievously in rejecting the sign of *Jehovah*
    Himself.
God, for ages, by man's instrumentality, revealed His will.

These things. Concerning John, who earnestly wished for your
    salvation.   [Me.

I say, &c. I mention John's testimony that ye might believe in
It would also aid the faith of those who had already believed.
Prophecy fulfilled is God setting His seal to His own word, uttered
    by inspired creatures.

λαμβάνω. Not only allow, but urge as evidence. *Stier.*

μαρτυρίαν. John's testimony being inspired, had the weight and seal of the Holy Ghost. *Hengst.*

ἀνθρώπου. Christ received not testimony from John as a man. *Zeller.*
Our Lord's words in accommodation to their misunderstanding. *Stier.*

------

35. He was a burning and a shining light: and ye were willing for a season to rejoice in his light.

He was. Suggests that the Baptist had left the scene ; was either in prison or had suffered death.

A burning. Gr. *the light burning and shining.* John iii. 20 ; ix. 5.
Implies the light he gave was kindled from above.

Light in the temple was kindled from heaven, and never suffered to go out.

Rabbis held it to be an emblem of the *light* of prophecy.

Christ was not *a* light, but THE LIGHT of the Church.

John was not *a* lamp, but *the* lamp borne before the bridegroom.

His fiery zeal proved him to have the spirit of Elijah. Luke i. 17.

A candle or oil in a lamp is *consumed* in giving light.

Thus believers can only give light by *burning until burnt out.*

But their light is not extinguished in the gloom of the grave.

Burning. Like the sword of celestial temper, it burned into the heart. [Lamb of God.

But it *illumined* as well as pierced, and would lead men to the

Indicates John's fervent zeal, glowing piety, and usefulness to the Church. [truth.

No cloistered selfishness, but toiling to bless *the million* with the

And. As contrasted with Christ's *underived, self-existing, Eternal* LIGHT ! [of his light.

Shining. Gr. *lighted,* hints at the derived and transient nature

Fathers of the Church held there was heat without light in *perdition.*

Some shine, but do not burn, others burn, but do not shine.

True grace in the soul both burns and shines.

Basil thundered in his preaching and lightened in his life.

Of the martyrs *Rogers* and *Bradford* it was difficult to decide whether their eloquence or holiness shone the brighter.

Light. Gr. *hand-lamp.* Candles of tallow were used at first.

Lamps with wicks of flax were then universally substituted.

Ancients, in the absence of tables, used candlesticks from 12 in. to 5 ft high.

Made of wood, bronze, marble, silver and gold, with several branches.

That of Antiochus was adorned with jewels set in chains.

They were made in the form of *lilies, seals, vines,* and other figures.
Lamps were used in *marriage* ceremonies ; placed also in *sepulchres.*
Olive oil was used ; on festive occasions it was highly perfumed.
Domestics stood around the table, holding lamps up, in time of
    Charles V. [1848.
The writer shared at a supper where lights were held by slaves, in
Ministers of God called " candles " in the Scriptures. Zech. iv. ;
    Rev. i. ; xi. 4.
Rabbis were often called "Candle of the law," "Lamp of the light."
Light and fire in the O.T. were emblems of God. See John i. 4 ;
    iii. 20. [disappears.
Lamps only used in the sun's absence, so at Christ's coming John
The Church of God is symbolized under the sign of a candlestick.
    Rev. i. 20.
" Let your light shine," &c. Caravans in the desert at night are
    always preceded by a brilliant lantern, which lights all who
    follow : [all.
Should the bearer be careless, " Let your light shine " sounds from
Christ never called, as was His holy servant, a " light-bearer."
The Greek word " LIGHT," applied to Christ, John i. 4, is entirely
    different.
We call an illustrious person " the luminary of his age."
Willing. Their willingness soon ceased. Believers endure.
    Phil. iv. 4.
Whatsoever the unbelieving will or will not, alike opposes God.
Season. They were pleased for a while, but no conversion was
    effected. [rejecting him.
Our Lord reprehends their inconstancy, first receiving him, then
Israel in Ezekiel's day boasted of their prophets, and disobeyed
    their words. [and baptism.
Rejoice. Pleased with the thrilling excitement of his ministry
Experiencing the delight of a new and powerful sensation.
When John began to strike deep they forsook him,—none cared
    for his chains, none mourned when the martyr perished.
As children sport with fire until they are burnt, then cast it aside.
As to the people of Judea, his divinely-authorized mission was *in
    vain.*
They crowded to his baptism without faith or repentance.
A clear evidence of the *deep impression* made by John on the nation.
As he foretold the coming Messiah, they dreamed of a full release
    from Rome's oppression.

Rejoice. Joy a dangerous ground of confidence, and used by the
    tempter to deceive myriads.
Ignorance and self-flattery render it doubly perilous.
Thus multitudes crowd to hear the word proclaimed, but come not
    to Christ.   [the Master.
They fatally imagine that listening to the messenger is loyalty to
The moment he bore testimony for Christ they rejected and
    slandered him.   Luke vii. 30, 33.   [tion.
Light. You were attracted by his brilliancy, not warmth of devo-
Thus the Athenians sought *profane amusement* in Paul's preaching.
    Acts xvii. 19.
Thus popular preachers are followed by thousands who will the
    next day be found at the gaming-table, the race-course, or
    the theatre.   [seek for.
Not *admiration* but *regeneration* the evidence a minister should

---

ὑμεῖς. In verse 34 the Sanhedrim, here the people. *Stier.* Before the former as a tribunal. *Lange.*

ἠθελήσατε. Classically either to desire or take pleasure in a thing. *Butt-mann.* Sharp ironical reproof. *Stier.*

πρὸς ὥραν. People's willingness very brief. *Cyril, Chrys., Bengel, Lange.* Does not imply that he was dead, but that they had deserted him before his course was run. *Lange.* Simply that he was removed from the scene. *Author.*

ἦν. Indicates John's work complete. *Stier.* Past used because he retired, the Jews being weary of him. *Bengel.*

ὁ λύχνος. Article emphatic. *Stier.* The light which ought to guide you, &c. *De Wette.*

φῶς, a self-giving light like the sun. φέγγος, radiance of the self-giving orb. φωστήρ, a heavenly luminary. Phil. ii. 15. *De Wette.*

λαμπάς, a torch. John xviii. 3. λύχνος, a hand-lamp fed with oil. Candle, *candela*, Ital., white wax-light, not used until centuries after in Italy. Ille erat *lucerna* ardens, et lucens. *Vulgate.* Christ the φῶς ἀληθινὸν, John i. 9, and φῶς ἐκ φωτός, the Eternal Light. The Baptist a lamp kindled by another, antithetical to φῶς. *Trench.* Our A.V. loses the distinction between the *light* and the *vessel* containing it, which the Evangelist carefully preserves. *Maurice.* The poverty of our language is the cause. *Author.* On a candlestick, to lead to Christ. *Augustine.* The Church animated by the Spirit. *Hengst.* The light which should go before Me. *Luthardt.* The article extends the meaning. *Bengel.* Ardere prius est, lucere posterius. *Wilkins.* The great light of his day. *D. Brown.*

ἀγαλλιας. To hear that the Messiah (a temporal one) was come. *Stier.* Used ironically of their mirth, ending in *scorn. D. Brown.* Much leaping in the dance. *Gesenius.* Theatres, schools of Satan, are in our day at times deserted for popular preachers. *Besser.*

---

36. But I have greater witness than that of John : for the works which the Father hath given me to finish, the same works that I do, bear witness of me, that the Father hath sent me.

Greater. God's works are great, greater, greatest, even in His
    least.

The microscope reveals the perfections of God in the minute, as
    the telescope does in the vast.

But the wondrous mysteries of life go on beyond all human search.

No human science can possibly *comprehend*, much less *imitate*, the
    least of them.   [minds?

If the structure of an *insect*, how much more does a soul, baffle our

Even John was not needed long; the sun being risen, lamps are
    removed.

We cannot dig deeper when we have come to the *rock*. 1 Cor. x. 4.

John. The Baptist. For life and character, see John i. 6—8, 15.

Works. The miracles of Christ. See on John ii. 11, 23 ; iii. 2 ;
    iv. 48, 54.

Some refer to His great work of atonement, but the reference is to
    miracles exclusively.

This Gospel records fewer miracles than the others, and yet oftenest
    appeals to them.   John x. 25, 32 ; xiv. 11 ; xv. 24.

In miracles His *will* is seen to be sovereign, His authority *absolute*,
    His power almighty, His majesty divine, His grace infinite.

Stupendous as His miracles were, they availed but little in sub-
    duing unbelief and carnality.

He appealed to His miracles as witnesses of His Divinity, and
    ancient saints appealed to their lives as witnesses of the
    excellency of Christian faith.   [heathenism.

Justin Martyr saw their holy life and death, and renounced

The moment Nicodemus saw His omniscience he believed.

Had they shared his *honesty*, the entire Sanhedrim would have
    resigned.

When all Bible readers are *honest*, the Son will be worshipped
    even as the Father.

Finish. His miracles prove Him not only God, but the MESSIAH.
    Isa. xxix. 18 ; xxxii. 3, 4 ; xxxv. 5, 6 ; xlii. 6, 7.

Our Lord's most divine and greatest work was QUICKENING SOULS,
    to which miracles were the mere *preface*.   [POWER.

The REGENERATION of an immortal spirit demands ALMIGHTY

And ISSUES IN RESULTS TRANSCENDING THE CREATION OF A WORLD !

Bear witness. John's lamp was filled and kindled by our Lord.

For a while they had hailed its cheerful beams as full of hope.

It strengthened them in faith that God had not quite forgotten
    them.

Our Lord's last miracle on the Sabbath was, the Father's solemn
   witness to Him as Son.   [munion.
A witness of filial power, of filial obedience, of filial love and com-
A witness also to the heart of suffering humanity, which the high
   strains of the Baptist never reached.

μείζω. Testimony of the Scriptures. *Stier.* All Divine testimonies are
alike, but some are more palpable. *Hengst.*
   μαρτυρίαν. First witness (verse 35), the Baptist; second (verse 36), the
works; third (verse 39), the Scriptures; fourth (verse 45), Moses. *Luther,
Chemnitz, Neander.* Only a two-fold witness, the works and the Scriptures.
Augustine, Maldonat., Grotius. Direct testimony, the witness of the prophets.
Calvin, Cocceius. To the direct testimony of the Father. *Lampe, Bengel.*
Word of God. *Lücke, De Wette.* Direct operation of the Spirit in man.
Olshausen.
   ἔργα. Wonders wrought. *Olshausen.* Instructive symbols of the Spirit.
Church laid too much stress on outward signs. *Stier.* Entire sphere of the
Messiah's activity. *Stark, Lücke.* They teach His words and doctrines to be
Divine. *Lampe.* Each act one of imminent Divinity. Hence ἔργα alone used.
Beck. Not His *miracles* alone, but *the whole of His life and course of action.*
Alford.
   τελειώσω. I will finish all on the Sabbath, despite your complaint
Brandt. Some believers' lives seem angelic in their heavenly-mindedness.
Chrysostom.

---

   37. And the Father himself, which hath sent me, hath borne witness of
me. Ye have neither heard his voice at any time, nor seen his shape.

Father. Trinity. See John i. 1, 2, 18, 32, 49. In my daily words
   and works Divine, the Father is tenderly speaking to you,
   testifying of Himself to you.
Having no visible form, He reveals Himself by His Son, the WORD.
Hath sent me. He tells them this fact six times in this chapter.
Borne witness. Past time, but reaching to the present ; " hath
   ever, and still doth."
1. By prophecy. " Testimony of Jesus is the spirit of prophecy."
   Rev. xix. 10.
2. By a voice from heaven, viz. at His baptism, transfiguration,
   and in the temple.   [baptism.
Some strangely infer none but the Baptist heard the voice at His
3. By miracles, which He wrought through the power of the Father.
The Hand that creates and upholds all things is seen in His
   miracles.
Wine at Cana ; we have wine each year in the *clusters* of *grapes.*
Gathering of fish into the net is constantly taking place in all our
   seas and *rivers.*

Stilling of the tempest is still seen in His *control* of the elements.

Giving sight to the blind, in the natural *sight* of millions.

Paralytic healed, in the *restoring power of nature*, curing countless diseases.

Raising the widow's son, in the constant *creation* of immortal beings.

Feeding of 5000, in all the harvest-fields waving with grain.

Healing the impotent, in the strength imparted to our bodies.

The GOD of NATURE can be none other than the AUTHOR of CHRISTIANITY.

Heard. Spiritual deafness and blindness was their fathers' sin. Isa. xxix. 11, 12.

Yet at Sinai (Ex. xx. 18 ; Deut. v. 26) Israel had heard God's voice, but it was the voice of the ANGEL JEHOVAH, and not the Father.

Voice. " Thou heardest His word out of the fire." Deut. iv. 36.

The Father's word, " This is my beloved Son, in whom I am," &c. Matt. iii. 17

Never heard apart from, or independent of, our Lord Himself.

Seen. Moses prayed to see the Divine glory. God promised a transient view.

" For there shall no man see ME and live." Ex. xxxiii. 20.

God's glory passing, Moses had to be protected from the splendour.

Hence God placed him in a cleft of the rock, and covered Him with His hand. [xxxiii. 22.

The prophet saw the mere fringes of Jehovah's robe of fire. Ex.

The glory of God broke through the cloud at Sinai, and appeared like a devouring flame on the *seventh* day. Ex. xxiv. 17.

Jacob said, " I have seen God face to face, and my life is preserved." Gen. xxxii. 30. [2 Chron. vii. 2.

This glory filled the temple, so that the priests could not enter.

The elders saw the God of Israel. Ex. xxiv. 10. Isaiah saw the glory of Christ. Isa. vi. 1—8 ; John xii. 41.

John the Baptist saw the form of a dove in the descent of the Holy Ghost. Matt. iii. 16.

Shape. In ME, the ETERNAL WORD, you behold the FATHER'S *only* " shape " and hear His *only* " voice."

But ye have neither eyes to see nor ears to hear. Deut. xxix. 4.

Those rejecting the testimony of Christ reject the Father's also.

To this day the Jews, forsaken of Father and Son, are buried in deception, darkness, and spiritual death.

Strangers visiting Socinian chapels have often borne witness that there seemed no influence of the Spirit, no presence of the Father with the worshippers.

καὶ. Therefore. *Grotius.* The Father beareth witness, although ye have never heard His voice. *Kuinoel.*

οὔτε φωνὴν. Interrogatively. *Campbell.* An objection hinted by our Saviour. *Markland.* Father's voice at His baptism. *Chrys.* Words "at any time" forbid this. *Lücke.*

εἶδος. Not the φωνή and εἶδος at His baptism, but *sensible* revelation of God. *Tholuck, Neander.* Law and prophets a mysterious paradox they never heard nor saw *aright.* *An undertone* meaning was " apart from *Himself.*" *Stier.* Designedly mysterious. *D. Brown.* Simply a repetition of truth uttered 15 centuries before. Deut. iv. 12. *Author.* "My goodness," Ex. xxxiii. 19; Heb. "my beauty." *Patrick.*

μεμαρτύρηκε. A fourth witness at Jordan. *Lampe.* 1. God's voice at baptism heard by the people. *Chrys., Bullinger, Chemnitz, Rollock, Trapp, Baxter, Hammond, Lampe, Bengel.* 2. Old Test. prophecies. *Theophylact, Calvin, Tholuck, Brown, Alford, Lücke, Meyer, Luthardt.* 3. Witness of the Spirit. *Bucer, Olshausen.* Ye believe in God whom ye have not seen, yet ye *hear* Me not, speaking in His name. *Rosenm.* By not believing in My miracles, ye prove ye do not believe in the God of your fathers. *Wetstein.* Blindness here results from unbelief of the word. *Besser.*

---

38. And ye have not his word abiding in you : for whom he hath sent, him ye believe not.

Have not His word. Passing from the witness-bearer to the sacred oracle, the Father's testimony.

He affirms them strangers to both, proved by their rejecting Him.

But the chief witnessing intended is that *in* THE HEART *of* A BELIEVER.

This INVISIBLE CHURCH, however, for the creation of which all else is but scaffolding, the Jews at this time had no perception of. Therefore He points them to their own Scriptures, the inspired word.

Abiding. See on verse 42. Finding no real lodgment in the heart, as an "engrafted word." Jas. i. 21. [iv. 2.

" The word was not mixed with faith in them that heard it." Heb.

Not entertained and prized as a precious treasure, as the " incorruptible seed " of life.

They honoured " the letter," and ignored " the Spirit," whereas " the letter killeth," &c. 2 Cor. iii. 6.

Thousands now profess reverence for the Bible, and freely give to promote its circulation in the world, and yet remain, like these Jews, in spiritual ignorance and death.

Whom He hath sent. Our Lord invariably recognized and assert-
ed His Divine mission. [stronger.
His claim to faith and obedience is thus made immeasurably
As the door hangs on the hinge alone, so all blessings and hopes
of Jew and Gentile hang on Christ.
Believe not. Faith, its nature and fruits, see John i. 7 ; vii. 38.
The fallow ground must be broken up and the Lord sought.
Hos. x. 12.
The heart must be circumcised, the nature regenerated. Jer. iv. 4.
The Jews had the entire range of the oracles of God. Rom. iii. 2.
But practical atheism left and leaves them still *without a revelation.*
2 Cor. iii. 14, 15. [qualities.
Judaism is now like the Dead Sea, without life, beauty, or salutary
A similar awful state of things may be seen in parts of Christendom
through unbelief and formalism.

λόγον. Inward revelation in conscience. *Olshausen.* Converting work of
the Spirit. *Lücke.* His Logos. *Locke.* But our Lord nowhere calls Himself
by that name. *Bloomfield.*
ὅτι for διά, as Luke vii. 47. *Stier.*
τούτῳ, as a prophet, in the dative, who testifieth of God as His Father.
Stier.

---

39. Search the scriptures ; for in them ye think ye have eternal life : and
they are they which testify of me.

Search. Gr. implies *inquiry* and *examination.* Truth will bear
the most thorough investigation.
To " search " was an old command given the Church by the
prophet. Isa. viii. 20.
" Ye sent in vain to John, he sent you back to Me."
" I now therefore send you back to *your own Scriptures.*"
Would ye learn *how* to search, *observe the heirs reading a will.*
Many skim over their Bible, but few search as for *hid treasure.*
Many praise its morality, its purity, its benevolence. its eloquence,
its poetry.
Not a few Protestants *idolize* the *Book,* and boast of it as their
whole and sole religion.
Alas ! while many would *fight* for it, how few of its millions of
admirers are willing to *live* by it ! [blinded.
Jews at this time slavishly read the Scriptures, but their eyes were
Deceived Pharisees held the *key* of knowledge, but in the day of
judgment will find it useless to unlock the gates of pearl.

Through Christ alone the Old Testament really becomes SCRIPTURE.
A melancholy but instructive fact, that all denying Christ deny
the Bible to be God's word.
These words, uttered as a *rebuke* to Jews, become a *precept* to us.
Withholding the Bible is the daring rebellion of *Antichrist.*
Rome, with her hundreds of missionaries, never yet translated the
Bible.   [languages.
The Church of Christ has published the Bible in nearly 80 different
Without the Bible there is no evangelical faith, no true worship
of God.
No Divine sacraments, no Holy Spirit in the hearts of believers.
The Living Redeemer eternally opposes the trust of the carnal
heart in *the letter.*   [xxvi. 9.
Saul of Tarsus believed he had read the Scriptures aright.   Acts
Moses and Elijah found a SUFFERING MESSIAH in the Old Test.
Luke ix. 31.
These great prophets on Tabor, having come *from heaven*, surely
read aright.
Yet they found what no living Jew says can be found.
Scripture abused or misused will prove a " savour of death unto
death." John ix. 29—35 ; 2 Pet. iii. 16.
Our Lord shuts us up absolutely to the REVEALED WORD OF GOD.
If we would know the SON we must go to Scripture and study the
FATHER'S TESTIMONY.
Yet Council of Trent pronounces an *anathema* on all who use the
Bible without priestly direction.   [in ignorance.
Search. Infidels sneeringly assume that Christian faith flourishes
Yet the lives and opinions of infidels show that of all men they
are the most *credulous.*
One beam from the eternal world, and their boasted valour is
turned into wretched cowardice.
Facts of Christianity triumphantly exclaim, " This thing was not
done in a corner." Acts xxvi. 26.
" Prove all things ; hold fast that which is good,' the apostolic
motto. 1 Thess. v. 21.
Christian faith courts the fullest and most complete inquiry.
Men are not infidels because they *reason*, but because they are
unreasonable.
Flippancy and shallowness characterize all forms of infidelity.
Reason is consummated and glorified when it passes up into faith
in the testimony of God.

Scriptures. John ii. 22. Inspired writings or books of the Old Test.

O.T. writings the only inspired Scriptures in our Lord's time.

Supplemented, not superseded, by the books of the New Test.

Jews who had the O.T. properly the first to receive the gospel.

O.T. the promise, the dawn, the bud ; N.T. the fulfilment, the perfect day, the flower.

O.T. called "holy," Rom. i. 2 : 1. From their author, God. 2. Their matter, His will. 3. Their design and tendency. 4. To distinguish them from other writings.

O.T. divided by Jews into—1. Law. 2. Prophets. 3. Psalms.

All written in Heb. except parts of Daniel and Ezra, and Jer. x. 11.

These parts written in Chaldaic, language used by Jews in Babylon.

O.T. canon complete in our Lord's time as we have it at present.

Jews, no longer speaking Heb., had a Greek translation (the Septuagint) and Chaldee paraphrases.

Apocrypha no part of Scripture, though declared to be so by the Church of Rome. 1. Never considered inspired by Jews. 2. Never quoted by our Lord or His apostles. 3. Found only in Greek language. 4. Contains doctrine opposed to inspiration. 5. Not included in any list of sacred books in the first four centuries.

Read in the Churches, but not used as of Divine authority. *Jerome.*

Holy Scriptures now include the N.T. as well as the O.T.

N.T. canon completed as we now have it at a very early period.

Earliest MSS. of the N.T. the Vatican, Alexandrian, and Sinaitic.

Last recently discovered by *Tischendorf*, and possesses great value.

Books composing N.T. underwent in first two centuries most rigorous examination.

Only those admitted whose authenticity was beyond all question.

Other similar writings were rejected as doubtful or apocryphal.

Those admitted bear marks of their own genuineness, and are quoted by Christian writers from the time of the apostles downwards. [or life.

No difference in the MSS. essentially affecting any point of faith

First complete translation (English) made by Wickliffe in 1380 A.D.

Before that a copy cost a man's wages for fifteen years, or about £300.

Coverdale's Bible the first in England sanctioned by royal authority.

Tyndale's translation chiefly ; dedicated to Henry VIII. in 1535.

Our present translation, King James's Bible, begun in 1607, finished in 1611.

Division of O.T. into chapters and verses made by Hugo of St Caro in the 12th century ; that of the N.T. by Stephens in his edition of 1551. [Scriptures.

Greatest intellects have borne testimony to the excellency of the " Tell the prince this is the secret of England's greatness." *Queen Victoria,* presenting a Bible to the ambassador of an African prince. See Sugg. Comm. on Luke xxiv. 27, 44 ; Rom. i. 2.

The Jews nullified the Scriptures by spiritual *blindness* and *hypocrisy.*

By fanaticism, unbelief, and unbounded pride of heart.

All the light of a noonday sun is useless to one *closing* his eyes.

All the spiritual instruction of the Bible to unbelievers is a *dead letter.*

Bereans " more noble " than Thessalonians, because they searched the Scriptures. Acts xvii. 11.

Those ignorant of or unskilled in Scripture rebuked. Matt. xxii. 29.

This book alone able to make wise unto salvation. 2 Tim. iii. 15.

If we do not see the *scarlet thread* of Christ's blood running through all the Bible, we read it amiss. *Cecil.*

The Old Testament interests no reader finding no Christ there. *Augustine.*

Think. In this " *thinking* " they were perfectly right as to the *value* of Scripture.

But to *have* a treasure in charge, and *to use* it are things essentially diverse.

Eternal life was there revealed, but, alas ! they esteemed it not.

We may turn the sacred leaves a thousand times, like Jews, and yet perish clasping the Bible. *Luther.*

Moses and Paul can never see God, except as SINNERS SAVED BY FAITH IN THE REDEEMER ! [on His lips.

Even our blessed Lord *lived* in the sacred word, and *died* with it

The Jews read Scripture only that they might spin out curious doctrines, or form opinions.

There is no space for mere *opinion,*—it is FAITH or NO FAITH.

Eternal life. See on John v. 24. Men have everywhere and always desired eternal life.

Not in the special and glorious sense of the gospel, but in the general sense of immortality.

The idea comprehends two things : 1. Existence. 2. Happiness.

This idea, in all ages and amongst all peoples, held in connection
with the notion of a revelation of some kind.
Brahmin has his Shaster, Mahommedan his Koran, and the
followers of Joseph Smith study the " Book of Mormon."
Even those tribes who have no written record fancy they have
communications from the Great Spirit.
Everywhere men have hoped for life beyond the grave, and have
associated it with the idea of a revelation from their Deity.
Some deny that the ancient saints were acquainted with eternal life.
But the eleventh chapter of Hebrews proceeds entirely on this
knowledge.

And.   That is the undiscovered truth, they were too blind to see.
Testify of Me.   See John i. 4.   That which they emphatically
teach proves Me the Messiah.
This truth, missed, left all else *worthless knowledge!*
The Bible, read rightly, i.e. with prayer, always leads to Christ.
The Jews found the *Law*, Christ found the *Gospel*, in the O. Test.
" While our foes burned us for reading the Scriptures, we burned
to read them." *Moulin*, Protestant Pastor, Paris.
As Micah's gods, Bibles neglected will be witnesses against men.
The doctrines He taught were witnesses of His Messiahship.
Types, shadows, history, laws, feasts, sacrifices, prophecies, psalms,
of Old Test. are *full* of *Christ.*
The babe of Bethlehem is bound up in these swathing bands.
He is both the Author and the Hero of these sacred books.
The pages of inspiration reflect the Godhead of the atoning Saviour,
as the great ocean reflects the glory of the noonday sun.
" A prophet like Moses " God had literally raised up in His Son.
Deut. xviii. 15.   [Lord."
A voice in the wilderness had cried, " Prepare the way of the
A " *virgin* " had conceived and borne a Son.   Bethlehem was His
birthplace.
At the exact time He came, but " they saw no beauty in Him that
they should desire Him."

Of Me.   He claimed to be Messiah. See on John i. 41 ; iv. 25,
26.   Sent by the Father. See on chap. vii. 29.
Scriptures testify that He is the AUTHOR and DISPENSER of LIFE to
man.   [*of life.*
1. As making atonement for sin, and thus providing *the ground*
2. As procuring the influences of the Spirit, and thus providing
the means of life.

3. As exhibiting a perfect humanity, and thus providing *the model of life.*

4. As overcoming death, and thus providing *the triumph of life.* Because He lives, His people shall live also.   John xiv. 19.

'Ερευνᾶτε. Indicative. *Athanasius, Eras., Lücke, Meyer, De Wette, Bengel, Lange, Olsh., D. Brown.* Imperative. *Chrys., Augustine, Theophy., Calvin, Beza, Wetstein, B. Crusius, Campbell, Stier, Hengst., Luther, Grotius, Maldon., Alford.* Search with the greatest exactness into subtleties. *Tholuck.* Track game in the chase. *Homer.* Inquiry superficial, not deep. *Krebs.* Learned curiosity drove out spiritual life from the Jews. *Lücke.* Would they now be constrained? *Hoffmann.* Proud Pharisees boasted they studied the law "humbly." *Josephus.* But dared not attempt great questions. *Justin Martyr.* A "thorough mining." *Chrys.* An investigation of the πνεῦμα, not γράμμα. *Stier.* Jews were tearers, not investigators, of the Bible. *Ber. Bib.*

ἐρευνᾶτε. Directed against their ἀκριβείας. Ye grovel in the Scriptures. *Tholuck.* Greek usage opposed to a bad sense. *Stier.* In our day it is a command. *Gossner.* Holding the words of the law, one has future life. *Rabbis. Lightfoot.* O. Test. contained the λόγος. *Hilgenfield.*

μαρτυροῦσαι. Our Lord showing Himself to be intended, confesses Himself the Messiah. *Schleier.* WORD of *Jehovah* is found speaking and appearing from Gen. to Malachi. *Zeller.* Prophets say little of heaven, yet all their types and shadows clearly allude to it. *Horneck.*

δοκεῖτε. Imagine ye (emphatic) in them (emphatic). *Besser.* Bibles lie unread, while play-books—those devil's catechisms—are worn out by perusal. *Trapp.* Ye search the Scriptures and think to earn heaven by this, yet they testify of me. *Lampe.* Heretics are ever talking, turning, and shuffling the Scriptures, but are most ignorant of them. *Rheimish Notes.*

---

40. And ye will not come to me, that ye might have life.

Ye will not come.   There is a deep lament of the heart of God in these words.

His tears were flowing unseen, while mourning their ruin.

It was not His loss that wrung His compassionate heart, but their persistent, hopeless, incorrigible madness.

"*How often would I have gathered thee!*" will echo through eternity.

They had searched diligently for the *shell*, neglecting the *kernel.*

Hence they understood not the Messiah, when He did appear.

Self-blinded and deaf, they heard not the voice of Almighty Love. John x. 27.   [ix. 28.

He had tenderly appealed to the weary and heavy laden.   Matt.

He had uttered loud cries in the ears of the spiritually *dead.* John xi. 25.   [final "No"!

To all combined voices and testimonies, they gave a fearful and Such words as those in the text from the lips of Sovereign Mercy, have solemn emphasis.

A strong proof of the responsibility of man, even although his will is enslaved. [fall.

Man's intellect weakened and his moral powers paralyzed by the Depraved, not only passionately, but frantically, cling to their sins.

All unrenewed men sin in opposition to their *judgment, interest, peace.*

Heathen scholars boldly confessed " *They knew the right, but did not wish to do it.*"

Over this deliberate choice of evil some of them made *merry.*

They boasted the same right to sin as the ox to his master's crib.

Jews' damning sin, rejection of the mighty Son of God and merciful Son of man.

Ye will not. Thus mourns His love, piercing the secret principle of guilt.

While Mercy stands beseeching and winning some to Himself.

The time is coming for the lamentation, " *But ye would not !* "

A terrible discovery, at the last day, to learn one had a *guide,* but never found " the way of life."

His Divine holiness *condemns* their vows and sacrifices.

They professed themselves desirous and anxious to come to the Father.

He cries and forces their conscience to the decision, " *Ye will not.*"

The rulers were zealously busied about the Scriptures, but missed their aim.   Verse 16.

" That word testifies of ME, but to ME ye will not come."

" That word announces ME the DISPENSER of ETERNAL LIFE." Acts xvii. 11, 12.

Rejection of Christ not an act of the *intellect,* but of the *heart.*

To me. Why go to Him, if He holds not the key to unlock Paradise ?

If, as " Liberals" affirm, He is not God, He only mocks our hopes.

In these lofty demands on the faith of the world, we feel HE ONLY CLAIMS HIS OWN.

Crucifying our pride, we must receive HIM as well as His *promises.*

Thankful to be *holy,* as well as *happy ;* to be *subjects* as well as *saints.*

To reject so true, so loving, and so powerful a Friend is guilt, is infatuation at which JEHOVAH *Himself* WONDERS.   Psa. ii. 12.

Those reading the Scriptures and professing to find no atoning Saviour resemble the idiot on the shore, complaining he could find no ocean.

The life of all such cries, " We desire not a knowledge of thy
    ways." Job xxi. 14.
Every word spoken against Christ's Divinity is an echo of the
    dwellers in Gadara, " Depart out of our coasts."
Men, like Adam in the garden, try to hide from the presence of
    God.   [soul.
Unmistakable evidence of the nature and awful power of sin in the
Thus " Cain went out from the presence of the LORD." Gen. iv. 16.
Thus the prodigal could not abide the eye of his holy father.
Proud licentious Romans would not retain God in their thoughts.
    Rom. i. 28.   [Heb. iii. 12.
Hardened, incorrigible Hebrews, departed from the true God.
It matters not what their professions ; in heart and life they deny
    God. Tit. i. 16.   [*way*."
Hating God's presence, so they do His prophets : " *Get ye out of the*
" Cause the HOLY ONE of Israel to cease from before us." Isa.
    xxx. 11.
" *Who* is the Lord, that I should obey *His* voice ? "
" I know not the LORD " (Ex. v. 2), because he *would not*.
But that proud monarch learned, too late, when sinking in the
    depths of the sea !
" MADNESS is in the heart of the sons of men while *they live*."
    Eccl. ix. 3.
Nothing but the realities of eternity will arouse them to reason.
Hating light and loving darkness is to run blindfold to hell.
Such rush through *inner*, onward to " *outer* darkness." Matt.
    xxv. 30.
They refuse the gentle reign of grace, because they hate the
    King. Luke xix. 27.
If the kindness rejected were from some prince or angel, it would
    be a grievous sin.
" Of how much sorer punishment suppose ye, &c., who have
    trampled under foot the SON OF GOD?" &c. Heb. x. 29.
Life. See on John v. 24, 39. He who cannot find in the word
    the ruin wrought by sin will never think of looking for the
    redemption therein revealed.

θέλετε. A power of the mind enabling it to consider or refuse to consider.
Lücke. A capability of energy is power, hence the will. *Reid.* The will pos-
sessed of a self-determining power. *Clarke, King, Law, Butler, Price, Bryant,
Wollaston, Horsley, Erasmus.* The will governed by law. *Collins, Hume,
Leibnitz, Luther, Kames, Hartley, Edwards, Priestley, Locke, Kant, Augus-*

tine. Will is not a mere determination of the mind, but a state of the feelings and judgment. *Hodge.* Rom. vii. 15. Araspes the Persian : " Certainly I must have two souls. I will now to do evil, and now to do good." *Xenophon.* "My mind is better than my desires." *Euripides.* "I knew that it was proper, but wretch, I could not do it." *Plautus.* Video meliora probo que, deteriora sequor. *Ovid.* Hoc quod volo, me nolle. *Seneca.* They would not come to Him, but they ran greedily after impostors. *Tholuck.* Stiff-necked unbelief everywhere in the Gospel confronts our Saviour. *Luthardt.* Occasionally, beginnings of faith, and fitful tendencies to listen, are excited by the Lord's words. *Stier.*

θέλετε. Addressed to rulers. *D. Brown.*

---

41. I receive not honour from men.

I receive not.   No ordinary member of our race could *honestly* say this.

To deny that we love the praise of men proves not superior holiness, but profound self-ignorance.

Our Lord's words imply *they* received and intensely loved to receive such honour.   Verse 44.   [worms.

The fear of God uproots the *desire* of praise from our poor fellow-

Some esteem gold as dust, others make it a god.   Job xxxi. 24.

Others make business their net, and offer sacrifice to their net. Hab. i. 16.

As we transform things, so do they with power *transform* us.

It were mockery to speak of human applause to one of whom Jehovah said, " LET ALL THE ANGELS OF GOD WORSHIP HIM."

Honour.   That honour which sinners can only give to sinners He could not share.

The proud offer incense to those still prouder than themselves.

After they had seen the miracle of the loaves and fishes, they clamoured to make Him a king.   John vi. 15.

But when He announced that His kingdom was not of this world, they crowned Him with thorns and gave Him a cross for a throne.

Satan had in vain offered Him the glory of the world.   Luke iv. 6.

In the day of judgment earthly crowns and sceptres will lie as neglected things.

All pining, panting, and battling for earth's fading honours will then cease for ever.   [*I've been!*"

One, having toiled a life-time for these baubles, cried, " *What a fool* "Is this all ?" said Cæsar.   " *All this avails me nothing !* " exclaims proud Haman.   Esther v. 13.

A Prussian monarch was miserable because a Theban *captive* would not salute him.

> " O Cromwell, Cromwell,
> Had I but served my God with half the zeal
> I served my king, HE would not in my age
> Have left me naked to mine enemies." *Wolsey, in Shak.*

The experience of one who " drank every cup of joy, heard every trump of fame, drank early, deeply drank, drank draughts that common millions might have quenched," is, that " all is vanity and vexation of spirit." Eccles. ii. 11.

From men. That is, I neither desire nor need honour from you.

Though all were to perish, Christ's glory remains eternal.

Human honour offered to Christ is like bringing out a taper to give light to the midday sun.

All-sufficient in Himself, He is for ever the *infinitely blessed God.* Rom. ix. 5.

Yet He is pleased with the grateful praise of the humble loving heart. Isa. lvii. 15. [performed.

Pleasing God and the world at once often attempted, but never

The world besought Jesus to accept a crown, and He fled from it. John vi. 15.

In His Father's service He was offered the thorns, the nails, and the cross, and He accepted them.

Δόξαν instead of μαρτυρία advances one step further. *Stier.*

λαμβάνω. He repudiates the eager desire after it. In the milder sense, I may not, I cannot. *Stier.* This verse a parenthesis. *Kuinoel.*

---

42. But I know you, that ye have not the love of God in you.

I know you. For our Lord's omniscience, see on John i. 48; ii. 24, 25 ; iv. 29 ; vi. 64.

Doubtless He made them feel that at that moment He was searching their thoughts.

Yet being mad against Him, they hardened into incorrigibleness.

" I know the Father, and that you are strangers to Him."

He had borne with them for many generations, as a kind parent, year after year, bears with a petulant child. Acts xiii. 18.

" These things saith the Son of God, whose eyes are as a flame of fire." Rev. ii. 18.

Have not. With what holy indignation did His eyes pierce their pretended zeal for God's law and glory !

Love of God. Love is life, and here takes its place. See verse 40.
" Thou shalt love," &c., the first great command and ground of all
    others. Matt. xxii. 40.
Principle of obedience to God in all worlds, on earth and in heaven.
It is this which distinguishes between *saving* faith and all other
    kinds of faith.
" The devils believe and tremble," James ii. 19. Saints " believ-
    ing, rejoice with joy unspeakable," because, although " having
    not seen, they love." 1 Pet. i. 8.
Breaking this first link of the chain, all others hanging to it fall too.
Not only the *decalogue*, but all the promises and precepts of the
    prophets.
As a farthing placed against the eye hides all the earth and the
    heavens ; so self, a very small idol, hides all that is due to
    Father, Son, and Spirit, to our neighbour, and, alas, even to
    ourselves !   [love.
The love. By which I am recognized as the Son of the Father's
God's love toward man to which man's love responds. Rom. v.
    5 ; viii. 32 ; 2 Thess. iii. 5 ; Tit. iii. 4 ; 1 John ii. 5.
Happy are those who can appeal with the Apostle, " Lord, Thou
    knowest all things, Thou knowest that *I love* Thee." John
    xxi. 17.
In you. See on verse 38. Gr. *in yourselves.* True religion must go
    further than the *head,* the *intellect.*
It is more than dry formalism, cold assent, barren orthodoxy.
It is essentially a " matter of the heart," the " fountain of life."
Its home is "the inner man," the kingdom of heaven is " *within* you."
It is a " power of godliness," a *spirit* created by THE HOLY SPIRIT,
    a *life* from THE SOURCE OF LIFE.

ὑμᾶς, emphatic. *Grotius.*
ἀγάπην. Spoken not of an ungodly mind in general, but of an absence of
that love which God's covenant people should have for Him. " They would
none of Jesus, for they were not true Israelites." *Luthardt, Alford.* Their
high pretensions, with hollow hearts, resembled Egyptian temples, splendid
without, but a cat, or beetle, the god within. *Trapp.*
ἀλλ'. Forcibly draws the distinction. *Alford.*

---

43. I am come in my Father's name, and ye receive me not : if another shall
come in his own name, him ye will receive.

My Father. His hearers understood Him to claim *equality* with
    God.

Loving GOD, we receive and love all bearing HIS image.

Receiving those not having God's image proved they loved not God.

Receive Me not. They did not receive Jesus but persecuted Him to death. [miracle.

Our Lord's disciples were few, though He fed 4000 and 5000 by Yet a boasting impostor led forth to Olivet 30,000 followers. *Josephus.*

Our Lord, in gospel lands is not received without being *sought.*

Jewels of the mine are not found on the surface of the earth.

Highways of earth are not paved with gold.

Receive Me not. A terrible realization of Deut. xviii. 19, "Whosoever will not hearken," &c.

Another. In strong contrast with the "another" in verse 32.

Shall come. Upwards of sixty pretended Messiahs noticed by historians.

Chief of those pretenders was Bar-Cocheba in the second century.

It is said that in the rebellion under him more Jews perished than in the war of Titus.

Jews so often deluded by "false Christs," that Messianic hopes are now nearly lost. [Thess. ii. 10.

"For this cause God shall send them a strong delusion," &c. 2

There is light for those loving light, and darkness for those loving darkness. *Pascal.*

In his own name. An orientalism for one's own authority.

Him ye will receive. Punishment for not receiving Him who came in God's name. [day.

Same law of the Divine government seen through all ages to this

Men refusing "the true light," surrender themselves to "false lights," which lead to ruin. Isa. l. 11.

Men either enlightened by the Spirit from *above* or blinded by the spirit from *beneath.*

He who despises the *dove* (John i. 32) falls a prey to the frogs. (Rev. xvi. 13). *Besser.*

Robert Owen rejected Christianity, and died a believer in table-turning and spirit-rapping.

ἐλήλυθα. The ερχόμενος. John iii. 2. Promised for ages. *Stier.*

ἄλλος. Sharp antithesis of the ἄλλος in verse 32. *Stier.*

οὐ λαμβάνετε. Prophecy in Hag. ii. 7 only fulfilled at His second coming. *Augustine.* Jews rejected Him, and heathen did not receive Him. Nevertheless *all* nations did long for peace, joy, prosperity, and bliss, which He in reality brought. Unconsciously He, the source of all these, was desired, and the prophecy fulfilled. *Anton.* God in mercy excludes none save those who exclude themselves. *Lake.*

ἐν τῷ ὀνόματι. The fathers held that the Jews would receive antichrist when he came. *Whitby, Wordsworth.* Upwards of thirty pretended Messiahs. *Basnage.* Sixty-four false Messiahs. *Schudt.* Spoken primarily of antichrist. *Alford.*

---

44. How can ye believe, which receive honour one of another, and seek not the honour that cometh from God only ?

How can? Oriental mode, expressing strongest denial by a question.

" Cannot " and " will not " (verse 40) represent different aspects of the same state of mind.

Man's moral powers weakened at the fall. Gen. vi. 5 ; the will is paralyzed and in bondage to Satan. Eccl. vii. 20 ; Gen. viii. 21 ; Jas. iii. 8.

Hence pretended world-menders are hailed, although coming in their own name and folly. Verse 43.

While the only RESTORER of the heart to original purity and peace is rejected.

How can men, catching and grasping the earthly, obtain the heavenly ?

Ye believe. Faith, its nature and effects, see on John i. 7 ; iii. 16 ; vii. 38.

Receive. Gr. *seizing upon.* This passage has a secret, revealed to us, concerning ourselves.

The heart longing for honour from men is *not right* with God.

Hence knowing men's hungering after these honours, it may be predicted who will practically ignore God's favour.

Those professing to serve the true God with the design to *please men* commit this sin.

Desiring to please God by religion, they choose a religion *the world approves.*

Sin perverts and blinds the mind, and prevents men from seeing the truth.

AN HONEST MIND IS ESSENTIAL TO JUDGMENT AS TO SCRIPTURE TRUTH.

Honour. Gr. *glory*, a specious word. Those deserving most receive least.   [age.

Men desire, through interest, not to break with the spirit of their

Hence men's passions, prejudices, and depravity are *flattered.*

How few like ABDIEL !

> " Among innumerable, false, unmoved,
> Unshaken, unseduced, unterrified,
> His loyalty he kept, his love, his zeal ;
> Nor number nor example with him wrought
> To swerve from truth, or change his constant mind,
> Though single."—*Milton.*

Selfishness is the worm that gnaws at the root of faith in God.

The cure is not Stoical stupidity, or proud contempt of the world.

Cynics, monks, and nuns, under professions of deepest humility and self-renunciation, often the proudest and vilest.

Pleasures intoxicate the soul, but none so fatally as earth's flatteries.

The path of life lies amid snares and along the verge of precipices.

Pharaoh said of the escaping Hebrews, " Surely they are entangled in the land," &c.   Ex. xiv. 3.   So are those immersed in fashion.   [than the TRUTH.

One of another.   Flattering *lies* please the unrenewed far more

Influence of some men due to their success in making persons satisfied with themselves.

Jewish pride was fostered by God's choice of their father Abraham.

In God's eye friendship with the world is enmity to our BEST FRIEND !

Beggarliness of human honour seen in that one poor sinner gives and receives flattery.   [another.

One hypocrite or liar rejoices to have his falsehood confirmed by

Men, " holding the truth in unrighteousness," bolster up one another against conscience.

How much of the world's biography is a mere whitewashing of sepulchres of corruption !   [*shame.*

This craving for human honour a secret confession of *poverty and*

If we know our own value, of what avail our neighbour's testimony ?

It is *idolatry*, in that it is bringing incense to our own altar.

It violates the first command, by placing SELF before Jehovah.

Many are "*men*-pleasers," and all unrenewed are *self*-pleasers. Col. iii. 22.

How much toil, treasure, blood, and principle are sacrificed on the altar of desire to shine among men !

Cicero candidly confessed he was "*too fond of glory.*"

" Love of honour crowds out of the soul every other rival."
  Rochefoucauld.
" Vanity the last infirmity of noble minds."   *Milton*, after *Tacitus.*
Hume called pride " *self-valuation.*"   God hates pride.   Prov. viii.
  13.   We must " give honour to whom honour is due," but
  not seek it.   Rom. xiii. 7.
And seek not, &c.   In the language of heaven, honour from
  men only is *disgrace.*   Prov. xxix. 23.
Honour, the god of the ambitious, *dies* and *is buried* with them.
True honour is linked to service of the Saviour here, and through
  eternity.   [xii. 26.
" IF ANY MAN SERVE ME, HIM WILL MY FATHER HONOUR."   John
From God only.   Gr. *God alone.*   Declaring the unity of the
  Triune God as revealed in the New Test.
To seek honour elsewhere is an act of treason against heaven.
In earthly courts subjects are not allowed to receive foreign
  honours without the consent of their own sovereign.
The unrenewed heart ever seeks to be worshipped by others and by
  ITSELF.
Ancient Greeks and Romans held it right to boast of one's learn-
  ing, grace, eloquence, heroism, prudence, generosity, furni-
  ture, &c.
To have given " a cup of water in the name of Jesus " will bring
  in the day of judgment more honour than all the world's
  boasted glory.

πιστεῦσαι.   Proof of faith being a moral disposition. *A. Knox.*   Faith the
gift of God, Eph. ii. 8;   Phil. i. 29;   John vi. 45;   Rom. x. 17;   1 John v. 1.
Author.   Qualifies ἀληθινὸν, John xvii. 3. *Schleusner.*
  πῶς.   Contains a strong denial, the inability arises from malignity. *Lampe.*
μόνου.   God alone. *Jelf.*   Jews accused (v. 45) of rejecting O.T., whose
central truth was God's unity. *Alford.*   The brave general asking a favour of
Louis XIV., was abashed by the splendour of his sovereign, and said, " Sire, I
trust your Majesty will believe I do not *thus tremble before the enemy.*" *Author.*

---

45. Do not think that I will accuse you to the Father: there is one that ac-
cuseth you, even Moses, in whom ye trust.

Do not think, &c.   So intensely did He desire their salvation,
  He could speak of nothing else.
A deep condemnation remains to the scorners of God's honour.
Judgment is the expressed voice of justice over the despisers of
  mercy.

The office which Christ *now* sustains is that of *Mediator* and *Intercessor.* 1 John ii. 1.

He had not come to collect evidence against them. The writings of Moses, unregarded, condemned them.

They refused, by that self-same guide, to be led to the LAMB OF GOD.

Moses *predicted their unbelief,* and it was placed in the ark with the law. Deut. xxxi. 21—26.   [them.

The very one who was their constant glory was the witness against

What unlooked-for accusers will rise at the last day against the sinner !

There is one. He sends them to read anew a book they could not have loved.

He warns them that the LAW they boasted of would for ever *condemn them.*

There is a conscience which will accuse all gospel-despisers and unbelievers at that day.

How many now flatter themselves conscience *is with them.*

Those thus building on the *sand* and imagining it is *rock,* are legion.

Many refuse either to study Moses or listen to conscience.

The rich man " in hell " seemed unwilling to remember Moses had written. Luke xvi. 30.

Even to the last hypocrites will hope for admission to heaven by crying, " Lord ! Lord ! "   [the law.

Moses. For his life, &c., see on John i. 17. He is here put for

An intimation that the Jews brought Moses to *accuse the Lord.*

Our Lord's self-justification now becomes a *condemnation* of His judges.

Externally the Jews honoured Moses's law to actual idolatry.

They never touched it but with the *right hand,* and a *kiss* of reverence.   [*fasted.*

They carried it carefully in their bosoms, and dropping it, they

Proof of the " desperate deceitfulness " of the human heart (Jer. xvii. 9), they fondly dreamed that for *their trust* in Moses God would receive them at last.

And yet the loudest witness against them in judgment will be that very Moses, *whose trust,* living and dying, *was in this very Jesus,* whom these Jews scorned, insulted, and crucified !

Trust. A zealous attachment to gospel dogmas will not avail with our Judge for a life of holy love.   [17, 23.

" They made their boast of God, and rested in the law." Rom. ii.

And yet that *boast* and that *rest* will be the ground of their con-
  demnation.
Moses as a *vail* blinded their minds, so that they could not see
  Christ. 2 Cor. iii. 14, 15.
" There is *a way* seeming *right* in a man's eyes, but the end is
  death." Prov. xiv. 12. [Jas. v. 3.
Those trusting in *riches* will find their trust a witness against them.
The *throne* coveted at the sacrifice of life, witnessed against Jehu.
  2 Kings ix. x. [Kings ix. 25.
The *garden* of Naboth was a witness against Ahab's avarice. 2
The retained *gold* witnessed against Ananias and Sapphira. Acts
  v. 10. [Matt. xxvii. 4.
The guilt of Judas found a witness in the thirty *pieces* of silver.
Papists, who trust to *Mary and other saints,* will find them swift
  witnesses against their idolatry.
Protestants who trust to the *letter* but have not the *spirit* of the
  Bible, will find the Bible chief witness to their condemnation.
Nothing will stand the fiery trial of judgment but that which is
  from GOD, *by* GOD, and *in* GOD.

κατηγορήσω. Forensic term, Satan, called an accuser. *Stier.* One brought
before their tribunal, stands their accuser. *Lange.* Imagine Me not as yourselves, a complainer, because you refuse Me honour. *Bauer.* Not their ruin,
but redemption, He came to seek. *Kuinoel.*
Μωσῆς. No obscure hint. The Jews had already endeavoured to condemn
our Saviour by quoting Moses. *Hengst.* Here used for the Scriptures generally.
Gerlach.
ἠλπίκατε. No intercession is here implied. *Hengst.* External idea of
false confidence. *Stier.* He diligently studying the law here, need not fear the
judgment. *Pirke Aboth.*

---

46. For had ye believed Moses, ye would have believed me: for he wrote of me.

Believed Moses. Faith. See on John i. 7 ; vii. 38. No sinner
  can place his hope in Moses.
That would be to rush on one's own sword. *Brenz.*
A vain desire and endeavour to ascend to heaven by Sinai, rather
  than by Calvary.
The law as a schoolmaster must ever lead to Christ. Gal. iii. 24.
A want of sincere *subjection* to the law will lead to *rejection* of the
  gospel also. [race.
The Pharisees believed not Moses's record of the apostasy of our
They believed not his record of Abraham's faith and piety.

Else would they not have walked in Abraham's steps and shared
his reward? [Moses.
They believed not in the *heart-piercing* severity of the law, given by
Else they never would have endorsed a self-righteous scheme.
Rom. x. 3.
They believed not that the *sacrifices* were to lead to repentance.
Simeon, believing Moses, was prepared and waiting for the Messiah.
Moses first wrote of the coming Messiah, and all prophets follow
him. John i. 45; Rom. x. 19.
Our Saviour's teachings are continuations of the prophecies.
The gospel is no *new* religion, but a continuation of the *old*.
Moses's vail removed, shows the platform of the gospel laid in the
law.
Jerusalem and Mounts Zion and Moriah were types of New Test.
blessings. Heb. xii. 22; Rev. iii. 12.
Sinai looks to Calvary, and Calvary looks back on Sinai.
Every drop of sacrificial blood had a voice, and cried concerning
the LAMB OF GOD.
In His temptations our Lord vanquished Satan by words of Moses,
"Thus it is written," &c.
On Tabor, Moses and Elijah, the great representatives of law and
prophecy, appeared "talking with Him of His decease."
Luke ix. 31.
From their radiant seats they hastened to confess and adore Him,
in whom law and prophecy find their consummation and per-
fection. [advent.
For 4000 years a Divinely-appointed class of men had foretold His
For 4000 years, through persecution and slavery, an entire nation
had testified its hope in this advent. *Pascal.*
But modern Jewish despair seldom resolves into Christian hope.
Believed Me. Our Lord is certain of His spirit being *identical*
with *Moses.* [Test. flower.
Hence we know that the New Test. is only the fruit of the Old
Our Lord read Moses with *another* and *deeper* spirit than modern
sceptics. [word *spoken.*
For he wrote of Me. Men respect more a word *written* than a
If ye believe not his writings inspired by God and hallowed by
prophets, how can ye receive my words?
Moses was a guide leading to Me. Refusing the guide, how can
you ever reach the end?
Unbelief shuts up the eyes, and blinded ones stumble and perish.

Moses wrote of the ark of the covenant, and of the Shechinah resting over it.

He wrote of the mercy-seat sprinkled with the blood of the victim covering the law within.

All pointed to Christ and His atoning blood, and to the throne of grace where the Holy God will *only* meet with sinners.

The Epistle to the Hebrews is the inspired exposition of these words, " He wrote of ME."

" The Lamb is the light " of all dispensations and ages, even of the heavenly Jerusalem itself.

He who has Christ in his heart has the key to all mysteries of time and eternity.

Our Lord here endorses the authority of the Pentateuch, and the inspiration of Moses as its author.

ἂν, forsitan. *Vulgate.* Earnestly denied. *Erasmus.*

Μωσῆς. Scriptures in general. *B. Crusius.* Our Lord followed the ruling opinion. *Neander.* Not this or that word alone, but all the Pentateuch. *Luthardt.* Moses's words substantially the contents of the O. T. *Stier.* Moses the ocean of theology, from whom all others watered their gardens. *Theodoret.* The " fierce light " of modern science and criticism has beaten hard on the Pentateuch, but only to bring out more clearly that it is in essential harmony with the facts of nature and history. See on John i. 3, and critical notes.

---

47. But if ye believe not his writings, how shall ye believe my words ?

Believe not. Faith, its nature and effects, see on John i. 7 ; vii. 38.

Our Lord had already proved that, professing to honour John the Baptist, they had despised him.

He now proves, that professing to believe Moses, they had rejected him also.

His words do not imply that Moses was more worthy of credit than Himself, or that his mission stood not on independent evidence, but that those not believing writings acknowledged from God would reject His claims also.

Many, like those Jews, now boast their attachment to *creeds* which will prove swift witnesses against them in judgment.

His writings. An incidental allusion to his words, committed to writing.   [years.

No allusion to writing in the Book of Genesis, a period of 2429

Yet the signet of Judah mentioned Gen. xxxviii. 18 must have had some *device.* See on John iii. 33.

Pharaoh's ring had a name or sign. Gen. xli. 42 ; Ex. xxxix. 30.
Ring of Thothmes III., in the Brit. Mus. (B.C. 1550), has one of his
   names.
Writing is first distinctly mentioned Ex. xvii. 14,—a war record.
We read that the two tables of the law were written by the finger
   of God.   Ex. xxxi. 18 ; xxxii. 15.   [xxiv. 12.
Probably the first material used for writing on was stone. Ex.
Letters were cut in the rock by an iron graver, and melted lead
   poured in.   Job xix. 23, 24 ; Jer. xvii. 1.
Discovery of key to Egyptian hieroglyphics and to ancient cunei-
   form inscriptions proves the antiquity of writing.
Parts of the book the " Ritual of the dead " of the ancient Egyp-
   tians, now in the British Museum, bear date 2250 B.C.
Books and writing must have been familiar to Moses. Acts vii. 22.
Profession of scribe first named Judg. v. 14.   He held a high
   rank even among the *judges.*
Solon's laws were written on triangular *stones* and placed on
   square tables of wood.   [*ivory.*
The twelve tables of Roman laws were made of *oak* overlaid with
" Write them upon the table of thine heart."   Prov. iii. 3.
" Sin of Judah written with pen of iron and with point of diamond
   upon the table of their hearts."   Jer. xvii. 1.
Reason to believe letters, like language, of Divine origin.
Our Lord affirms the office of the O.T., preparing the way for His
   coming.
Links of chain connecting the Old and New Test., held in the hand
   of God, and here recognized as Divine.
How shall ye believe ?   See on John i. 7.   The interrogation
   an oriental mode of denial.
Men refusing to believe Moses's writings would refuse to believe
   Christ's words, were He to come again from heaven.   Luke
   xvi. 31.
All the Divine goodness in the gift of the Scriptures had been
   nullified by their perverseness.   [xvi. 31.
This word seems an echo of part of the parable of Dives.   Luke
To the sincere the Bible, like the sun, carries with it its own
   evidence.
The owl cannot see at noon, because its eyes are closed.
" Liberals " and infidels, blind with pride and " sin's madness,"
   fail to see the plenary inspiration of the Book of Books.
   Eccl. ix. 3.

My words. He deliberately assigns to His *words* authority equal to the words of Jehovah recorded in the Old Test.

Carnal minds are ignorant alike of Christ's majesty and humility.

Causes of Jewish unbelief still in the world, and operating now as of old.

Wise men from the East followed the star, and it led them to Jesus.

To every soul that obeys its light God will assuredly give the LIGHT OF LIFE.

Men rejecting light grow unable to perceive light when it comes.

The last year of our Lord's ministry occupies nearly the entire Gospel of John.

γράμμασιν. "Sôpher" in Judg. v. 14, equivalent to "Shôphêt," *Judge.* Indicating the exalted estimate of the knowledge of writing. *Ewald.* Kirjath-sepher, "Book town," Josh. xv. 15, where the Hittites discovered the art of writing. *Hitzig.* Square Hebrew invented about the 4th century. *Kopp.* About the 1st century. *Whiston.* Modified by copyists of different nations. *Kennicott, Eichhorn.* Samaritans preserved it better than Jews. *Hupfeld.* During the Maccabæan period. *Havernick.* Shemitic, at first 16 letters. *Lepsius, Donaldson.* Ancient round, Phœnician. *Wright.* Square are later. *Buxtorf.* Sacred and profane, as in Egypt. *Hartmann.* Cadmus brought letters into Greece. *Herodotus.* Invented by Assyrians. *Pliny.* Some say by Mercury among Egyptians. By the Syrians. *Diod. Sic.* Phœnicians derived letters from Egypt. *Tacitus.* Originated in Babylon. *De Wette.* Names of letters indicate a pastoral origin. Aleph (ox), Gimel (a camel), Lamed (an ox-goad), Beth (a tent), Daleth (a tent-door), Vau (a tent-peg), Cheth (a hurdle or pen). *Gesenius.* Vowel points introduced by Ezra. *Martini, Nicholas de Lyra, Luther, Calvin.* A few attached to doubtful words. *Prideaux, J. Michaelis, Eichhorn.* Karaites held to their being inspired. *Kalisch.* Not known in the sixth century. *Hupfeld.* The idea of the law having been written on stone ridiculous. *Voltaire.* Monuments of ancient Egypt and Assyria now in the Museums of Europe show the "ridiculous" character of infidel criticism. *Author.* When was writing first practised? Thoth lived before Menes, 2412 B.C. *Josephus, Hales.* Thoth or Hermes said to have invented letters. *Wilkinson.* But inscriptions on the first pyramid are as old as 2450 B.C. *Birch.* Memnonium, erected at Thebes 1571 B.C., has a library inscription, "Balsam for souls." Library had "President of the Library." *Champollion.* Pyramid, erected 2123 B.C., has writings in the chambers. *H. Wyse.* Paper still exists, made before Abraham's time. *Wilkinson.* Psammeticus placed two children with a shepherd to be trained without hearing a human voice. They pronounced βακκος, *Phrygian* word for bread. *Herodotus.* Language is of human origin. *Dio. Siculus, Horace, Lucretius, Condillac, Roth, Agassiz.* Of *Divine* origin. *Warburton, Humboldt, Müller, Bunsen, Hincks.*

ῥήμασι, emphasized. *Hengst.*

γράμμασι and ῥήμασι are set in opposition to one another. *Stier.*

πιστεύσετε. A solemn and alarming note of interrogation. *Zeller.* A question of hopelessness. *Meyer.* Shows degree of dependence Jews placed in Moses's testimony. *Gerlach.* God has and will again authenticate Moses's writings. They reject Christ, pretending it is—1. Love to God. 2. Reverence for Moses. Our Lord refutes both. *Lightfoot.*

John 6

1. AFTER these things Jesus went over the sea of Galilee, which is the sea of Tiberias.

After. Between chapters fifth and sixth nearly a year has
      elapsed.   [saida.
After hearing of John's martyrdom, the Lord visited near Beth-
John had been beheaded, and Herod desired to see Jesus. Luke
      ix. 8, 9.
The record of His life, from one passover to another, is found in
      Matthew, Mark, and Luke.
This is one of the few points where the four Evangelists touch and
      meet. Matt. xiv. 13 ; Mark vi. 30 ; Luke ix. 10, &c.
It occurred just before the *third* of the *four* passovers named.
A similar coincidence, their histories uniting, takes place before
      the last passover. John xii. 12.
John's silence confirms the testimony of the others, and when he
      speaks he harmonizes with them.
This gospel *historically* a " *Supplement* " to the other Evangelists.
Went. Departed from Capernaum, lest He should irritate the
      Jews. Mark vi. 3.   [vii. 30.
To avoid the fury of Herod. " His hour was not yet come." John
In mercy also He would not hasten the filling up of the cup of
      national guilt. Gen. xv. 16.
And as His silence deepened and drew forth the Syro-Phœnician's
      faith, Matt. xv. 23, so would He excite and sharpen the
      desire of the people.
Sea of Tiberias. So called from the celebrated city which bore
      this name. See on John vi. 23 ; xxi. 1.
This name used by John only, probably because it was more
      familiar to those out of Palestine.
John constantly translates Hebrew names and terms into the
      language of Gentiles.
Called in the O.T. " Sea of Chinnereth " or " Chinneroth," Num.
      xxxiv. 11 ; Josh. xii. 3, from a town of that name which
      stood on or near its shore. Josh. xix. 35.
Called " Gennesaret," Matt. xiv. 34, from a beautiful and fertile
      plain at its north-western angle. Luke v. 1.

Called " Sea of Galilee," Matt. iv. 18, from the province of Galilee
    on its western side.   [shore.
All the names given to this " sea " were from places on its western
It is of an oval shape, about 13 geographical miles long, and 6
    broad.
Jordan enters it at its northern end, and passes out at its southern.
Bed of the " sea " is a lower section of the great Jordan valley.
It is remarkable for its deep depression, being 700 feet below the
    level of the ocean.
Of volcanic origin. The scenery has neither grandeur nor beauty.
On the east the banks are nearly 2000 feet high, without verdure
    or foliage.   [at work.
Frequent earthquakes prove the elements of destruction are still
The great depression makes the climate of the shores almost
    tropical.   [" sea."
Most of our Lord's public life was spent in the environs of this
On its shores stood Capernaum,—" His own city." Matt. iv. 13.
On its shore He called His first disciples from their trade as
    fishermen. Luke v. 1—11.
Near its shores He spake many of His parables, and wrought
    many of His miracles.
This region was then the most densely peopled in all Palestine.
Nine cities stood on the shores of the " sea," and numerous
    villages dotted the plains and hill-sides around. *Smith's* Dict.

Μετὰ. Nearly a year has elapsed. *Light., Hengst.* Showing the fragmentary character of this gospel as to mere narration. *Lücke, Alford.*
    ἀπῆλθεν. Starting-point Jerusalem. *Meyer.* Capernaum, or some place
on sea of Tiberias. *Hengst.*
    θαλάσσα. John, a Galilæan, uses the most stately term for this lake.
Hengst. Luke seems intentionally to refuse calling it a "*sea*." Our Lord
crossed from the west to the east side of the sea. *Meyer.*
    Τιβεριάδος. Called Gennesaret by *Josephus.* Founded on ruins of *Kinne-
roth. Jerome.* Messiah will rise from the waters of the sea of Tiberias, go to
Safed, and erect His throne on the mountains of Galilee. *Hackett.*

---

2. And a great multitude followed him, because they saw his miracles which
he did on them that were diseased.

Multitude. An oriental crowd the most excitable and curious
    of mankind.
This multitude crossed the sea to follow Him. Having no supplies,
    it is probable they had left their camp equipage and food
    on their passover journey.

Through a " sea of tribulation " another " great multitude, whom
no man can number," follow Him. Rev. vii. 9.

Followed. Followed Him to a desert near Bethsaida.

The "Sun of Righteousness" could not be hid,—there was " healing
in His wings." Mal. iv. 2. [iii. 2; iv. 48.

Saw His miracles. Gr. *sign wonders.* See on John ii. 11, 23 ;

Miracles not signs to believers, but to those who believe *not.*
1 Cor. xiv. 22. [Matt. vii. 28.

Those astonished at His *doctrine*, had sounder heads and hearts.

Although the faith of this multitude was feeble, their zeal in
following Him into the wilderness rebukes indifference.

He manifested His mercy by *deeds* of *power* and words of grace.

However hard the road He goes, His people find He gives more
than the cold world.

That same LOVE in redemption's plan outruns our conscious needs.

He oft sends famine of various kinds to *force* us to look to Him in
our wants. Luke xv. 14.

αὐτοῦ, omitted. *Tisch., Alford, Cod. Sinai.*

σημεῖα. No extended remarks were made at His two first miracles. *Hengst.*
John's office was to confirm the testimony of other Evangelists. *Bengel.* Refers
to many miracles wrought after His return to Judæa. *Temple.* Their preference of miracles above teaching a sign of unbelief. *Chrys.*

ὄχλος. No evidence of their being on their way to the Passover. *Hengst.*
Some think otherwise. *J. A. Alexander.*

---

3. And Jesus went up into a mountain, and there he sat with his disciples.

Jesus went. From retirement, and found the multitudes gathered.

He did not summon them, but received them graciously.

Mountain. The place more exactly designated Luke ix. 10.

Mountains convey the ideas of elevation, magnitude, permanency.

Our Lord often withdrew to those grand temples to worship.

On them the ancients believed men could approach nearer to the
Gods. John iv. 20.

Temples to the deities generally open-roofed, first erected on mountains, and often became *asylums* for men.

At times they were turned into *fortresses* for the weak. The superstitious believed demons there met and conversed with men.

Hindoos believe that *Meru* is a mountain 600,000 miles high,
265,000 at the top.

The greater gods are supposed to have palaces in different parts,
and reside there.

Salvation expected in vain from mountains, because *heathen* altars
  were built on them. Jer. ii. 20 ; 2 Kings xvii. 10.
Terraces for vines often covered them. " Mountains shall drop
  with wine." Joel iii. 18.   [Ezek. xxxvi. 8.
" But ye, O mountains of Israel, ye shall shoot forth your branches."
Moses, while Israel fought with Amalek, ascended with Aaron and
  Hur a mountain, to pray.
Mountains symbols of a pure elevated mind, Psa. xxx. 7, and of
  God's unchangeableness. Isa. liv. 10.
Kingdom of Christ is likened to and called a mountain. Isa. ii. 2 ;
  Dan. ii. 35.
Ararat a memorial of the deluge, of man's sin, and God's justice.
Sinai, of the solemn majesty and binding perpetuity of the law.
Hor of Aaron's, and *Nebo* of Moses' death. *Ebal* and *Gerizim* of
  the " curse " and the " blessing." Deut. xi. 29.
Carmel, of answer by fire. *Gilboa*, of death of Saul. *Lebanon*, of
  cedars.
Zion, of David. *Moriah*, of the Temple. *Tabor*, of the trans-
  figuration.
Calvary, of the crucifixion, and *Olivet*, of the ascension.
Millennial banquet will be held by Zion's King on a *mountain* side.
  Isa. xxv. 6.

τὸ ὄρος. Equivalent to a mountain. *Hengstenberg, Luther*. The only
portion of the Galilæan ministry related by John. *Alford*. Heathen believed
their prayers reached heaven more *surely* from mountains. *Lewis'* Heb. Ant.
Confirmed by Lucian. *Tacitus*. Some time must have elapsed before the multitude followed. *Hengstenberg*.

---

4. And the passover, a feast of the Jews, was nigh.

Passover. See on John i. 29, 36 ; ii. 13. Had not this feast been
  noted, no harmony of the Gospels could have been constructed.
This is the *third* recorded occurrence of this feast during His
  ministry, and the only one in which He did *not* go up to
  Jerusalem between His baptism and passion.
As the Jews threatened His life at the former passover, He declined attending this. John v. 16, 18.
One year after, " Christ our passover was sacrificed for us."
  1 Cor. v. 7.
" The living bread," which came down from heaven, was broken
  on the cross for the starving millions of our race.

Feast, &c.   See on John ii. 8, 9, 23.   John wrote among Gentiles, and hence his explanation of Jewish terms and customs.

He records the following miracle, that He may introduce the discourse founded on it, omitted by the other Evangelists.

This great feast accounts for the multitudes collected and directing their course to the central city of Judea.

πάσχα. No chronological importance, but simply an allusion to Christ being the true paschal Lamb. *Quesnel, Hengst.* Generally esteemed the key to the chronology of our Saviour's ministry. *Greswell.* Our Lord celebrated two passovers during His ministry. *Pearce.*

ἐγγὺς. Probably to account for the multitudes present. *Alford.*

---

5. When Jesus then lifted up his eyes, and saw a great company come unto him, he saith unto Philip, Whence shall we buy bread, that these may eat ?

Lifted.   Place was near Bethsaida.   Luke ix. 10.   There were two places of this name, this was on the eastern shore of the lake.   [wants.

He felt that the people for a moment had forgotten their earthly

Our Lord's compassion was not mere *mouth-mercy :* " Depart in peace," &c.   Jas. ii. 16.   [Mark ii. 5.

And saw.   He could see thoughts as well as material things.

This is the only miracle recorded and described by all the *four* Evangelists.

A great company.   Arrested by His fame as a Wonder-worker, on their way to Jerusalem.   [vi. 34.

He saw this great flock was without a shepherd or a fold.   Mark

Come.   Gr. *keep coming* or *increasing.*   Any one familiar with oriental character can understand this.   [preach.

Came to see Him who wrought such wonders, and to hear Him

Our fathers travelled fifty miles to hear a sermon, gave $ 50 for one religious book, a load of hay for a few chapters of St Paul.

Doubtless many had turned out of their course to gratify mere curiosity.

Philip.   See on John i. 43, 44.   For reasons known to Himself our Lord selected him.   Verse 6.   [designs.

A teacher wisely selects one who is the best fitted to carry out his

Whence ?   This question implies that He foresaw the sufferings those thousands would endure for lack of food.

Has He not similar forethought for all who seek to know His works and words ?

Already in His *purpose* He had prepared the entertainment about
to be given.   Verse 6.

Buy.   Gr. *as in a market*.   **Bread**.   John iv. 8, 31.

Eat.   Honey, butter, wheat, and vegetables eaten, flesh used on
festal occasions.

Water, sherbets, milk, and wine (see on John ii. 3) their drinks.

Hebrews carefully *washed* before meat. Matt. xv. 2.   Luxuriant
Greeks and Romans used *perfumed* water.

Two meals a day customary with Jews, Carthaginians, Romans,
and Greeks.

Dinner in the heat, at about 11 A.M., and supper, the principal
meal, at about 6 P.M., cool of the day.

No table used in more ancient times ; a skin was placed on the
floor, or a stool some ten inches high.

The introduction of the Persian couch led to use of tables.

Universal custom for guests to *recline*, not *sit*, at meals.

Hence John *reclined* or *leaned* on the bosom of the Lord at the last
supper.   John xiii. 25.

Jews practised hospitality and held it in the highest estimation.

At Feast of Pentecost widows and fatherless children were to be
invited.   Deut. xvi. 9, 11.   And slaves were welcomed during
Jubilee.   1 Kings iii. 15.

Feasts were held on particular occasions: Nuptials, John ii. 2;
birth-days, Matt. xiv. 6 ; funerals, Hos. ix. 4 ; sheep-shearing, 2 Sam. xiii. 23 ; arrival and departure of friends, Luke
xv. 23.

Guests received at or near the gate.   Those coming late were excluded.   Matt. xxv. 10.

Guests on entry were kissed by the host.   Luke vii. 45.

Heads, beards, hands, and often the raiment, perfumed with
ointment.   Oil in the lamps was often perfumed.   Psal.
xxiii. 5.

The festal dress among ancients was white.   Ecc. ix. 8.

Guests were presented with bouquets, and their heads were
wreathed with garlands.   Isa. xxviii. 1.

Places assigned to guests according to rank.   1 Sam. ix. 22.

A marriage feast lasted a number of days. Esth. ii. 18 ; John ii. 1.

Females at great feasts were excluded. Esth. i. 9.   At ordinary
feasts admitted.   John xii. 3.   Always excluded with Greeks,
except female slave waiters, whose attire was shameless to
the last degree.

Roman rule introduced riotings, Rom. xiii. 13 ; and revellings,
Gal. v. 21 ; 1 Pet. iv. 3.

Among Greeks, an altar always stood in the midst of the festal hall.

A solemn rebuke to *baptized* heathen, who eat and drink without
acknowledgment of God.

It was not so much *bread* the Lord sought from Philip as *faith.*

God often takes away our means, to test our trust in His Fatherly
care.   [for food.

Eat. They were so engrossed in His words, they took no thought

---

θεασάμενος. Not from the mountain, but after His descent. *Hengst.*
ἔρχεται, i. e. *keep coming.* Although the narratives of the Evangelists do
not agree in their mere letter, there is an inner and deeper accordance. *Augustine,
Alford.*
ἀγοράσωμεν. Kind of market at Jerusalem in Christ's time may be learned
from that held in Athens. It was an open space filled with booths, veils, shawls,
mantles, girdles, sandals, gold armlets, anklets, head circles, golden grasshoppers, seals, rings, brooches, cameos, and various gems. Jugs, vases,
tureens of bronze, ivory, &c. Food, apples, pears, quinces, pomegranates, dates,
plums, cherries, mulberries, grapes, oranges, citrons, figs, musk, melons,
caraway, roots, lettuce, beans, asparagus, radishes, turnips, garlic. Flower-
sellers' stands, droves of horses, mules and asses, and SLAVES FROM ALL PARTS
OF THE WORLD, OF ALL COLOURS. Men spent their money on arms, houses
and furniture, and women on dress. Auction stands, where all goods, even
libraries, went under the hammer. Hams, meats, lamp-wicks, fowls, ducks,
locusts, jackdaws, coots, hares, foxes, geese, moles, hedgehogs, cats, otters,
eels. Charcoal, corn, fish, oil. Pastry, sweetmeats, &c. *Xenophon, Aristoph.,
Theophrast., Lucian, Plutarch.* There were flower-girls, female flute-players,
dancing-girls, jugglers, cooks, parasites. These latter followed a servant who
purchased enough for a feast, and hung round, to get a meal *gratis. Julius
Pollux, Athenæus.* Pots, pans, and cooking utensils were lent out to those
about to make a feast. Idlers walked up and down, and many with wealth
crowded the perfumers' and barbers', armourers' and bridle-makers' shops.
There Socrates, Alcibiades, Critias, Plato, &c., went to converse with the
youth of Athens. Sophists in purple robes, embroidered vests, flowered
sandals and crowns upon their hats, were there also. *Athenæus.* Over all
these certain gods presided. Persons detected in cheating were beaten on the
spot by officers of police. Price of an ox, 4 drachmas or 72 cts, a sheep,
1 drachma or 18 cts. In Rome, an ox, 3 dollars, a sheep, 30 cts, farm horse,
12 dollars, yoke of mules, 20 dollars. ἄρτους. Females ought to be admitted
to the feasts, but were not. *Plato.* Etruscans admitted them. *St John's* Ant.
Gr. Perfumed waters and female slaves for the toilet of strangers. *Athenæus.*
Rich purple napkins were in use. *Sappho.* Used between each course.
Aristophanes. Hands and beards perfumed with incense. *Athenæus.* Before
any one· ate, food and drink were offered as an oblation to the gods. *Theo-
phrastus.* Musicians, female slaves, were at the market, to enliven the feasts,
waiting till some one should hire them. Matt. xx. 3. *Aristophanes.*

---

6. And this he said to prove him : for he himself knew what he would do.

He said to prove him. "*Tempt.*" John viii. 6. The word has
several meanings. Used here in the sense of *trial.*

Thus Abraham was "tempted," or *tried,* i.e. put to the test by
Jehovah. Gen. xxii. 1. [2 Cor. xiii. 5.

Why did our Lord apply this test to Philip, rather than the others?

He may have had charge of the food, as Judas of the bag ; or he
may have most urgently presented the people's hunger.

More probable, the Lord saw his faith was feeble, and He purposed
to strengthen it. [his answer.

Hence He begins by showing Philip his weakness as revealed in

Thus does the SEARCHER OF HEARTS often *prove* His people by
perplexing questions in Providence and in spiritual life.

1. He intends showing the tendency in believers to *cling* to things
of sense.

2. How *little faith* in God is in the best of men as a *habit !*

3. How prone Christians are to despair of aid when in straits. Ex.
xiv. 11. [unbelief.

Divided hearts measure the fulness of God by the short line of

The Samaritan nobleman unbelievingly said the windows of heaven
must open. 2 Kings vii. 2. [verified.

The windows of heaven were not opened, and yet God's word was

The disciples, yet carnal, looked on Him as Naaman on Jordan,
—with *Syrian eyes.*

To the question, What is in a man ? it may be answered that
which he is in temptation.

The Lord will refine His people, but this can only be done by the
fire. Isa. xlviii. 10.

David is anointed, and is hunted as a partridge in the wilderness.

Israel escapes Egyptian brick-kilns, and is pursued by Pharaoh.
Ex. xiv. 17. [him.

St Paul is exalted to heaven, and a messenger from *Satan* assaults

Philip seemed slow of heart, to recognize God Incarnate. John
xiv. 8, 9.

He Himself knew. Thus when the Lord would bestow a favour,
He prepares by His grace the receiver.

Abraham was *twenty-five years* préparing for the promised blessing.

Faithful as the patriarch was, the dross must be consumed and the
gold refined.

Knew. The Spirit thus vindicates our Lord from *the appearance
of asking advice.* [believers.

By this act He would establish His Messiahship in the hearts of

He knew that it would be *a sermon to the Church* in all coming
   time.

It would assure that the Creator of such supplies will never let
   His friends want.   [believe."

An inimitably Divine method of schooling those " slow of heart to

This proving of Philip has been a lesson to millions of feeble ones.

But this was the least part of the Lord's design. He would lay
   the foundations of His Church deep and strong as its enduring greatness and glory.

On this rock, broad as infinite love, millions of believers and
   martyrs should yet stand.

His law for unfolding *one* leaf controls the growth of all the leaves
   of the trees and forests of earth.

He intended to perform the miracle that He might exhibit Himself
   as the BREAD OF LIFE to the world.

πειράζων. Hebrew usage God tempts or proves. Heb. ii. 18.   Men tempt
God. Acts xv. 10.   Here the Lord shows him to himself. *Kuinoel.*   He proves
Philip as God did (Gen. xxii. 1) the patriarch. *Lampe.*   That men might learn
the secret of their own heart. Heb. xi. 17. *Hengst.* He would confirm his faith.
Cyril.   He was next our Lord seated on the grass. *Alford.*   He will show how
ignorant of themselves the disciples were. *Theophy.* He leads men to look up
to Him for strength. *Aug.*   He uses this rude multitude as a sermon to the
disciples. *Tittmann.*   Matthew, Mark, and Luke say the disciples came to our
Lord, after He had taught the multitude, asking Him to dismiss them, it being
evening. He said, Give ye them to eat. John simply *omits* that fact of the disciples
coming and their request, and adds that the Lord asked a question of Philip,
personally.   How any discrepancy can be seen (as in Alford) does not appear.
Author.

---

7. Philip answered him, Two hundred penny-worth of bread is not sufficient
for them, that every one of them may take a little.

Philip answered, &c.   John i. 43.   Human reason ever has an
   answer, whether right or wrong.   [success.

Worldly prudence impiously ignores that God is necessary to

Faith is deemed fanatical, because it rests on an arm of strength
   invisible to the eye of man.

Philip's mind was not only occupied with the people's want of
   bread, but their own want of money.   [a miracle."

He ought at once to have confessed, " They can alone be fed by

Hebrews of old looked back to the flesh-pots of Egypt, knowing
   not the heavens were full of *manna.*

Philip's faith was weak, notwithstanding all the wonders he had

already seen, viz. healing nobleman's son, John iv. 46 ;
draught of fishes, Luke v. 1 ; healing demoniac, Mark i. 21 ;
the leper, Matt. viii. 2 ; the paralytic, Luke v. 18 ; man at
Bethesda's pool, John v. 5 ; the withered hand, Matt. xii. 9 ;
centurion's servant, Luke vii. 2 ; raising widow's son at
Nain, Luke vii. 11.   [half.

Philip had been under our Saviour's instruction two years and a
What he learned then we, with myriads, need to learn now.
Our Lord's eye pierced his heart, and He put His finger on the
weak part, so that Philip first knew himself then.
Verily he and Thomas, and we know not how many others, must
have been slow of heart to believe.
Far less bread than Philip mentioned will be sufficient. He
whose power brings forth the harvest yearly will easily feed
a few thousands.   [sible to God."
Faith's motto, " The things that are impossible to men are pos-

---

ἀπεκρίθη. Philip looked for a miracle. *Bourgon.*

δηναρίων. See on John ii. 15. A Roman silver coin. The silver denarius
was at first equivalent to about 8½*d.* of English money, declining, under the
empire, to about 7½*d.*, and was therefore something less than the Greek δραχμή.
Smith's Dict. *Denarius*, from *deni*, ten, worth about 16 or 17 cents : so called
from the letter X upon it. *Webster.* Διακ. δηναρ. From 30 to 40 dollars,
American currency. *Krauth* in *Tholuck.*

αὐτῶν, omitted. *Tisch., Alf., Cod. Sinai.*

---

8. One of his disciples, Andrew, Simon Peter's brother, saith unto him,

Andrew. But very little is known of him. See on John i. 40.

Simon Peter. See on John i. 42. Older than Andrew, and
believed to have been older than our Lord.   [wrote.
Peter was better known than Andrew at the time, and where John

Saith. Andrew spoke for the twelve. He was one of the first
of our Lord's disciples. John i. 40. But evidently had no
more faith than Philip.

'Ανδρέας. Philip being unable to answer, one from the circle does. *Alford.*

---

9. There is a lad here, which hath five barley loaves, and two small fishes :
but what are they among so many ?

Lad. Gr. *a child* or *young person*, but used in Attic for persons
of all ages.

Not the first or last time a youth has been instrumentally
employed in the kingdom of God.

Barley. The same as used in America for manufacturing malt.

Used by poor Hebrews for bread. Mixed with wheat, beans,
lentiles, millet, &c., for their cakes. Ezek. iv. 12.

Harvest for barley in March, April, May, according to the land,
high or low.

Wheat one month later, hence mentioned as saved from the hail
in Egypt. Exod. ix. 31, 32.

Barley, not wheat, used for an offering in the case of trial for
jealousy. Num. v. 15.

Its coarseness (Hos. iii. 2) typified degeneration of character.

" Will ye pollute me among the people for handfuls of barley ? "
Ezek. xiii. 19.

Gives point to the dream. Judges vii. 15. *Gideon's* family were
poor in Manasseh.

The haughty Bedouin now ridicules enemies as " cakes of barley
meal."

A Roman soldier under disgrace was compelled to eat barley bread.

Greeks and Romans in early ages had it as regular rations.

Barley bread, although rough to the taste, nutritious, and used by
common people now.

An emblem of His own doctrine. Hard for the unrenewed, but
full of immortal life for the soul. Mark xii. 37. [*loaf.*

In the eye of the world sacramental bread, so simple, is but a *barley*

Yet to the believing soul, manna. Angels' food (Psal. lxxviii.
25) could not give so rich and rare a banquet. [viii. 7.

Small. 1. *Fish.* 2. *Small* fish. 3. A *few* small fishes. Mark

Each word *has* its weight. Small they were, or a lad could not
have carried them.

" Loaves and fishes," a phrase often used in derision of a *paid*
ministry in the Church. [of it.

But God hath ordained that those who preach the gospel shall live

" Irreverent application of Scripture a good man avoids for its
profanity, and witty men for its *vulgarity.*" *S. Johnson.*

In Matthew, Mark, and Luke, these loaves and fishes appear the
property of the disciples.

So they were, but not until they had *bought them for the company.*

An instructive instance of the way in which apparent *discrepancies*
arise. [likewise vanish.

Did we know *all the circumstances,* every Biblical difficulty would

Fishes. Gr. primarily anything eaten with bread or meat, to give it a *flavour* or *relish*.

In later times fish being the most common article of food, the word came to be applied to that alone or principally.

A jar lately found at Pompeii, has in it the roe of the tunny.

What are they? A deprecatory formula, like " Who are ye ? ' Acts xix. 15.

Unbelief ever looks at circumstances and no further, and as these are ever changing, the soul is tossed about like the troubled sea.

But faith looks at second causes, and looks through them to the ALMIGHTY, UNCHANGING GOD.

So many. A hungry crowd a sad and sorrowful sight at all times.

Were it not for man's own sins—idleness, intemperance, ambition, covetousness—there would be found enough for all.

Hunger of the soul is like hunger of the body, the result of sin also.

Man as first created could never have felt this *want*.

In forsaking the fountain of *living* waters, men thirst in the desert.

This gnawing hunger of the heart was felt by the prodigal amid his husks.

If Moses, Elijah, and Elisha were able miraculously to supply men's wants, surely the disciples might have hoped even for better things from their Master.

παιδάριον. A diminutive of παῖς. *Gesenius.* A baker's boy. *Bloomfield.* A young slave. *Zenophon.* παῖς anciently used especially in Attic as the French use *garçon* and we *post-boy. Liddell & Scott.* Word " boy " is used in Ireland describing men even advanced in life. *Petrie.*

κριθίνους. " A fine barley crop : " Tell that to the horses. *Talmud.* Servants are not to have luxuries, since the boy had nothing but barley loaves. *Coster.*

πέντε ἄρτους. Christ's superiority over the Mosaic law,—12 loaves of shew-bread a slender supper for the priests. Here a symbol of all the redeemed being fed. *Denton.* Out of " five " and " two " some derive Papal seven sacraments. *Tyrabosco.*

ὀψάρια. Anything cooked to be eaten with bread. *Gesenius, Liddell & Scott.* Was derived from ἕψω. *Trench.* Properly any relish made of flesh, olive, butter, &c. By degrees narrowed down to fish. *Plutarch, Suicer.* Because fish was the universal relish used by common people with food. *St John's Ant.* A kind of sturgeon still used by descendants of the Phocians at Marseilles. *Passard.* Eggs were made into a relish. *Plato.*

---

10. And Jesus said, Make the men sit down. Now there was much grass in the place. So the men sat down, in number about five thousand.

Sit down. See on verse 5. Gr. *recline,* a custom derived from Persians and perhaps Greeks.

Ancient Hebrews sat on the ground, or on skins, to eat. Gen. xxvii. 19 ; Judg. xix. 6 ; 1 Sam. xx. 24, 25.

Ancient Egyptian tables were about 20 inches high ; their couches were exceedingly elegant.

Each couch held three, and three couches nine, the ordinary number invited.

Jews hung their table (about 12 inches high) up by a ring, to avoid legal defilement.

They did not breakfast until sacrifice was offered, about nine o'clock.

A meal at mid-day, sparingly eaten, and a full meal at 5 or 6 P.M.

Oriental Jews now universally sit on the floor, like their Turkish masters.

The writer, in all his travels through Palestine, saw *no chair* in a private dwelling.

All Hebron could not furnish him with *one chair* or *one table*, although with a population of 5000.

The multitude sitting down, gave clear *evidence* of their strong *faith* in His power.

His *omnipotence* was the only means of supplying such a company.

Had He not been Almighty, the command was wicked folly, and their compliance mockery.

How calmly and deliberately He proceeds : proof that He who orders the courses of the heavens and the laws of nature wrought this miracle.

Much grass. Indicates spring-time in Palestine ; middle of February.

On that year the feast of Purim fell on the 19th of March. *Wieseler.*

The incidental remark as to the grass could only have been made by an eye-witness.

Grass. Gr. *an enclosed feeding-place*, then *grass* or *hay*.

These fertile spots skirted the edge of the wilderness. Matt. xiv. 15.

As the rainy season closes, grass fades rapidly under the Syrian sun.

An image of the fleeting nature of the honours and possessions of earth. [ix. 12.

" The glory of men is as the flower of grass." 1 Pet. i. 24 ; Job

Five thousand. The *men alone* were arranged in companies ; hence it is that any *account* was taken of them. Matthew (chap. xiv. 21) adds, " Beside women and children."

These, perhaps, not very numerous, were served promiscuously. *Alford.* [bless them.

Our Lord the first of all Israel's prophets who called *children* to

For although brought to worship, "the little ones" (Josh. viii. 35) were never specifically noticed by the prophets.

But the Redeemer opens the door of His kingdom to all, of every age, sex, and condition.

ἀνθρώπους. Here the men (not women and children) were arranged in ranks. Matt. xiv. 21. A touch of accuracy from an eye-witness. *Alford.*

χόρτος. A figure of the "green pastures" in which Jesus feeds His people. *Wordsworth.* As the people obeyed the apostles, so a flock will obey a good shepherd. *Stella.*

---

11. And Jesus took the loaves ; and when he had given thanks, he distributed to the disciples, and the disciples to them that were set down ; and likewise of the fishes as much as they would.

Took. To point out the object of the blessing about to be pronounced.

Thus He laid His hands on little children (Mark x. 16) and thus the Presbytery treated Timothy. 1 Tim. iv. 14.

Thus the apostles, by the laying on of hands, Heb. vi. 2, simply pointed out those blessed. Acts vi. 6.

He might have furnished supplies without the loaves, as in the primary act of creation.

But He makes use of what He had created, to prove all creatures good.

Bread and fish in this miracle prove Him Master of both land and sea.

He would also be more *readily comprehended in the mysterious act.* See on John ii. 7.

Had He not held and broken the loaves they might have suspected some *magic* had *deluded* their eyes.

But seeing part, they were impressed more *deeply* with that which they could *not see.*

There was no Divine virtue imparted to the loaves, nor to the hem of His garments, but the *invisible* power of God was made *visible* to mortal eyes.

Every harvest-field, whitening for the reaper, is the kind gift of His power.

Now a harvest rich and plentiful comes from a few grains. These loaves were seeds in His hands, not planted, but multiplied by the power that makes the seed of thousands of fields sown quicken and ripen.

The Lord thus warns us against despising the most common gifts.

He has exalted bread and wine into precious memorials of His love, instructing His people NEVER TO DISTRUST HIM !

" The eyes of all wait upon Thee, O Lord, and Thou givest them meat." Psa. civ. 28.

Yet He waits until the crowd are hungry and feel their need.

Only once He *seems* to have wrought a miracle without *first preparing the mind.* Luke xxii. 51.

He had shown His disciples their inability to supply food.

He often defers aid until we feel and confess, as Peter when sinking, " Lord, save," &c. [Ex. xvi. 12.

Israel must first hunger, and cry to heaven for food in the desert.

Relief from anguish of felt want confirms faith and kindles gratitude. [disciples.

He took from the hands of the lad, and put into the hands of the

That which none can do He does, but not that which others can do.

He never ignores or sets aside ordinary means, but sanctifies and uses them. [fanaticism.

Work without prayer is presumption, and prayer without work is

God alone knows the multitudes who have been cheered by this record to TOIL ON, TRUST ON, PRAY ON.

How marvellous must have been the growth, so rapid and abundant, *it eluded observation,* and *defied explanation.*

The crowning wonder,—*far more remained* than existed at *the first.* Prov. xi. 24.

We gaze on the works of God around us, and forget that every leaf is a *mystery* of power. [not of.

But that which is ordinary, although equally miraculous, we think

Thanks. As the Head of the apostolic household, He blessed it.

" He doth bless the sacrifice, and afterwards they eat that are bidden." 1 Sam. ix. 13. [16 ; xi. 24.

The same word occurs in the record of the Last Supper. 1 Cor. x.

Each sacramental feast looks back to these Godlike tables in the wilderness, and forward to the banquet to be spread in the New Jerusalem. Matt. viii. 11.

Before meals, even African heathen offer sacrifice to their unknown god to bless the food.

What condemnation in judgment on baptized millions who lived and died, but had no altar, nor thanks for their heavenly Benefactor !

He thus sanctified those loaves. " Man shall not live by bread alone." Matt. iv. 4.

Men, afraid to entrust their possessions to Him, find them lessen
instead of increase.

Looking up. Matt. xiv. 19 ; Mark vi. 41. The heart is not
where it *lives,* but where it *loves.*

Glorifying of His Father threefold : 1. He looked up with His
eyes. 2. He gave thanks with His *tongue.* 3. He blessed
with His *Spirit.*

Distributed. Matthew speaks of the disciples distributing. He
did it through them.

True to His Divine nature, He works by heavenly order.

Thus in making one grain of corn grow, He makes many things
co-operate. [to grow.

Air, moisture, light, heat, mould, gases, &c., help one little grain

These loaves *distributed, multiplied* by *division,* and *increased* by
subtraction.

The increase begins in His hands, and the miracle goes on in theirs.

He allots to the disciples their work in distributing, *He alone can
bless, and blesses.* [labour.

Though He giveth the increase, He wills that His ministers shall

His disciples had their faith confirmed, and " He is the same yesterday, to-day, and for ever." Heb. xiii. 8.

In His first miracle He changed water of earth into wine of heaven,
now bread of earth becomes bread of heaven.

The widow's oil does not increase *in* the cruise, but in *pouring.*
2 Kings iv. 4.

The grain bringeth no increase in the granary, but by *sowing*

The talent gained nothing in the napkin, but rust and a curse.

Graces improve, not by enjoying, but by *practising.* Eccl. xii. 9.

Macedonians found that by giving was the way to thrive. 2 Cor.
ix. 8. [xix. 8.

Never was Zacchæus so rich as when scattering his treasures. Luke

" What I have given to Christ *I have,* what I retained I have lost."
J. J. Gurney.

τοῖς μαθηταῖς, οἱ δὲ μαθηταί, omitted. *Cod. Sinai.* Cancelled. *Tisch.,
Alford, Hengst.*

ἔλαβε. Fontes panis erant in manibus Domini. *Aug.* If His " hem," how
much more His "hands," have virtue ! *Alb. Magnus.*

εὐχαριστήσας. This for the bread, εὐλογήσας, for the fishes. Mark viii.
7. *Luca Brug.*

εὐχαρίστησεν. *Cod. Sinai.* This word points out the exact moment the
miracle was wrought. *Grotius, Origen.*

ἄρτους. Bread symbol of legal observances, barren until they pass through His hands. *Aug.* So all good works in our own strength are fruitless. *Stella.*

ἀναβλέψας occurs in each of the other Evangelists. Four times at the Last Supper He lifted His eyes to heaven. *Hackett.*

διέδωκε τοῖς. The disciples thus became witnesses of this miracle. *Ferus, Maldon.* Figure of the consecration of the Last Supper. *Barradius.* Miracle continued in the hands of the apostles. *Chrys.* Completed in the hands of the. multitude. *Ambrose, Hilary.* Bishops the appointed channels for Divine gifts. *Bourgon.* All pastors are bishops. 1 Tim. iii. 1. *Author.*

---

12. When they were filled, he said unto his disciples, Gather up the fragments that remain, that nothing be lost.

Filled. A glorious earnest of the Redeemer's work for the soul.

The world, craving happiness, rushes hither and thither ever crying, " Give, give." Prov. xxx. 15. [Saviour.

Christ alone can give satisfaction to the heart. He is a " tried "

Surely if He has reserved a *crown* for His people, He will not refuse them a *crust.*

David said, " I have never seen the righteous forsaken, nor his seed," &c. Psa. xxxvii. 25.

Those leaving full tables at home and following Christ into the desert shall not want.

At the marriage-feast in Cana He gave a specimen of His kindness to His friends. [fishes went on.

So long as one child was hungry, the miracle on the loaves and

Should we not hope the *hearts* of thousands were fed also ? for only those whom God feeds will ever be " filled."

They came to hear Jesus, " taking no thought what they should eat." Psa. xxxvii. 3.

But then, as now, " seeking first the kingdom," all needful things were added. Matt. vi. 33. [modern Jews.

Gather. For each one's use. Defilement dreaded by ancient and

Like modern Hindoos, their food must be peculiarly sacred. See critical notes on John i. 24.

They could eat many things usually found among the Gentiles.

But their food polluted, they would fling it away, even if compelled to fast for some hours.

Gather. The Lord by a mere word made all this food, but none of it must be wasted. [Prov. xviii. 9.

" *Miser* " signifies *misery*, but he is " brother to a *great waster.*"

The Lord is lavish of His bounties, but at the same time careful of His gifts. [*Hume.*

" Providence has not provided sufficient for His creatures." *David*

In the amounts spent in unnecessary feasting and drinking, and on
houses, dress, furniture, theatres, operas, armies, fortresses,
navies, wars, &c., millions of God's treasures meant for man
are wasted, and *Hume's* impious charge answered.

He has satisfied those present, and He will show those absent that
the miracle was no mere imagining.

He will also teach His people that faith in God for temporal things
and frugality in use must go together.

Fragments. Divinely-appointed method of showing the greatness of the miracle.

God knows how to bring water out of a rock, honey from a carcase,
riches out of a widow's mite, and comfort from faith and tears.

Command here given of wide application : Gather up—1. *Fragments of* TIME. Our affairs prevent all our cares being given
to eternity.

But the ground-tone of our life must be a *heart love* fixed on Jesus.

As pilgrims have petty cares by the way, but one aim controls all.

Myriads waste hours, days, years, and find themselves beggars at
death.

2. *Fragments of* INFLUENCE. "No man liveth to himself." It
may be unconsciously exercised. [enemies.

He is watched unceasingly by children, servants, neighbours,

Like magnetism, it never slumbers ; like gravitation, it knows no
Sabbath.

It is ever drawing those around us to the Cross or to ruin.

3. *Fragments of* CONSCIENCE. Our sins weaken and scatter the
power Divine.

Some by a bold stroke benumb its energy, others flatter it by deceit.

But caressed or outraged, many at length ignore its authority.

Who loves his peace will treat it tenderly ; its voice is the voice
of God.

4. *Fragments of* FAITH. Objects of sense ever tend to weaken faith.

One in the labyrinth of the catacombs, losing his *thread*, goes back
and carefully looks,—his *life* depends upon it.

Cherish the faintest beams of faith, gather them up,—they lead to
heaven.

5. *Fragments of* LOVE. The bands uniting man to God were
broken at the fall.

Gather up every fragment of retiring lingering affection.

The Lord breaks not the bruised reed, and quenches not the
smoking flax.

6. *Fragments of* Consecration. As the needle always turns to the
   pole, so our life should centre in God.   [xvi. 12.

Remain. What we call our own is in reality another's. Luke
We are not masters of anything, but simply " stewards " of our
   Divine Lord.
Our God is ever providing for us " a table in the wilderness."
   Psa. lxxviii. 19.

Lost. God's blessings are not to be squandered. Luke xvi. 1.
Carefulness is a *sign* and *result* of *gratitude*.
Good *husbandry* is good *divinity*. Justice should be the *purveyor*
   of our goods, and temperance the *steward*.

Nothing lost. In all the vast processes of nature *nothing is lost*.
In the ravages of oceans, the flow of rivers, the crumbling of
   mountains, *nothing is lost*.

> " *Nothing is lost ;* the drop of dew
>   That trembles on the leaf or flower
> Is but exhaled to fall anew,
>   In summer thunder-shower."

Of all the countless forms of life that have flourished and died
   since the beginning *nothing is lost*.

> " The little drift of common dust,
>   By the March winds disturb'd and toss'd,
> Though scatter'd by the fitful gust,
>   Is changed, but *never lost*."

No work done for God, even the humblest effort, can ever *be lost*.
Sermons, prayers, contributions, sacrifices, *not one is lost*.
" My word shall not return unto me void; it shall accomplish," &c.
   Isa. lv. 11.   [Acts x. 4.
" Thy prayers and thine alms are come up for a memorial," &c.
" Even a cup of cold water given, &c., shall not lose its reward."
   Matt. x. 42.
What encouragement to parents, teachers, ministers, reformers, and
   all workers for God !

ἐνεπλήσθησαν, τροφῆς, understood. This use found alone in John. The
miracle lay more in the miraculous *frame of mind* than in increase of food.
Lange, Olsh. Our Lord's miracles differ from all attempted wonders of men
or demons, not being for His own glory. *Estius.* Exuberance of infinite
bounty does not silence cavils. Scepticism makes greater demands on credulity

than truth does on faith. *Author.* A mysterious interest in this miracle not yet studied out. *W. H. Mill.*

---

13. Therefore they gathered them together, and filled twelve baskets with the fragments of the five barley loaves, which remained over and above unto them that had eaten.

Baskets. Made of willow, and used by the Romans for carrying bread.

Some painted in the tomb of Rameses III., 1301 B.C., appear to have been made of gold.

Used to hold meat. Judg. vi. 19. Also for gathering grapes. Jer. vi. 9. Wicker baskets are used in Egypt.

Twelve. One for each of the twelve apostles, and symbols of a nobler banquet to which they would soon invite a hungry, perishing world.

More, doubtless, than Philip could have bought with 200 pence.

Doubtless the baskets were some of those *emptied* by pilgrims on their way to the passover.   [friends!

What royal bounties will our King in Zion scatter among His

All the four Evangelists particularize twelve here, and seven in the other miracle.

The remnant of the fishes is only mentioned by Mark, chap. vi. 43.

An equal wonder is found in Christ, feeding His followers *for* 1800 *years.*

Note—1. These twelve baskets remain as so many visible witnesses of Christ's power.

2. He did perform the deed in the name of the Almighty.

3. The lessons of economy here given are echoes of the same through all His works.

4. Unlike the manna, of which there was just enough for each.

"This MAN was counted worthy of more glory than Moses." Heb. iii. 3.

Gospel mercies dispensed by ministers are *limited.* Heb. iv. 7. But mercies imparted by Christ are without measure. John iii. 34.   [diminished.

Our Lord fed thousands, yet His supplies were not in the least

His miracles have a tongue, and they speak Him the WORD of God. See on John i. 1.   [rejoicings above!

If these be the festal days of earth, what will be the marriage

In the wilderness of life He provides for all the wants of pilgrims.

What variety and richness of outfit has He provided for His children!

Air, light, heat, refreshing shades, descending showers, distilling
dews, purifying winds, birds half-way between flowers and
angels, sea full of fish, forests abounding with game, trees
loaded with fruit, gardens adorned with herbs, flowers glowing with the colours of Paradise, fields waving with harvests,
mountains abounding with healing plants, coal, metals, gems,
&c., stored up in the earth, friends filled with sympathy and
love, all pledges of our heavenly Father's goodness, and men
still murmur.

This miracle is recorded out of historical order, as it is the ground
of the following wonderful discourse.

As stars have not all the same lustre, neither have all miracles
the same glory.   [prophets.

Yet this miracle advanced Him infinitely above Moses and all the

Our Lord on one occasion upbraids the disciples for not remembering it.   Matt. xvi. 9.   [See verse 14.

Multitudes enthusiastically cried, " This is of a truth *that* prophet."

κοφίνους. So universally did the Jews carry these large baskets, that a
Roman poet, 1300 miles from Palestine, called the Jews " *basket-carriers.*"
Martial. Juvenal also alludes to them. κοφίνος larger than σπυρίς, Matt.
xv. 37, a hand-basket for provisions. Used by gardeners to sleep in. *Greswell.* Used for baggage. *J. A. Alexander.* Whence obtained in the wilderness? *Lange.* Oriental caravans carry their valuables with them, as their
tents are not safe. *Author.*

κλασμάτων, broken pieces. Surplus fragments, showing the exuberance of
power. *J. A. Alexander.* Of a mountain of salt in Spain we read, " De quo
quantum demas tantum accrescit." *Trapp.*

ἄρτων. The government of the world is a far greater miracle than feeding
5000, but the *rarity* makes men wonder. *Aug.*

---

14. Then those men, when they had seen the miracle that Jesus did, said,
This is of a truth that prophet that should come into the world.

Had seen.   These eye-witnesses needed no further proof that God
was among them.

Yet our Lord has pronounced it more blessed to believe not
having seen.   John xx. 29.

Miracle.   See on John ii. 11, 23 ; iii. 2 ; iv. 48.   Performed in
a desert, similar to the miracle of the quails.   Num. xi. 17, &c.

It typifies the absolute helplessness of human nature.

Moses and the apostles thought it impossible to supply all the
people with food.

Human faith, in its feebleness, is ever prone to judge God by itself.

Jehovah resolved to put to shame the murmurers in the desert.
Moses cried, " Shall the flocks and herds be slain, to suffice ? "
For one month 600,000 footmen were fed on quails, Num. xi. 21,
    and for forty years on manna at the rate of 15,000,000 lbs. a
    week.   [Moses.
Our Lord takes the place of *Jehovah* to His disciples, not that of
" Yea, can God furnish a table in the wilderness ? "   Psa. lxxviii.
    19, 20.   [soul.
It showed—1. That He who feeds the body must also supply the
2. That in giving us food, He only under another name gives us
    Himself.
There can be no nutrition of soul or body without His power.
3. He ever supplies that great hunger of the heart in those looking
    to Him.   [iv. 19.
That prophet. See on John i. 21 (Critical Notes). Also on John
This miracle is the second seal of the Father to the Son.
Moses foretold that a great prophet should come.   Deut. xviii. 15.
Jews at the time of our Lord's nativity were in full expectation of
    Messiah.
Other nations were looking and longing for the coming of a Divine
    Teacher and Saviour.

σημεῖον. A greater miracle than Moses bringing bread down from heaven.
Here it was CREATED. No fragments remained of the manna, except that concealed in the ark. *Rosenm.* People led into the wilderness, that they might see
the greatness of miracles. *Chrys.*
  ὁ προφήτης. Deut. xviii. 15. This celebrated prediction fulfilled in Jesus.
Kurtz, Tholuck. The prophecy embraced others, but culminated in Jesus.
Ewald, Kiel. Refers exclusively to O.T. prophets. *Hoffmann.* A general prediction, like Gen. iii. 15. *Von Gerlach.* As was the first Redeemer, so shall be
the last Redeemer. *Huetius.* One who should be a lawgiver. *Wagenseil.* The
ground of so many false Christs among the Jews. *Rosenm.* Our Lord resembled Moses in giving bread in the wilderness, and in each case it was a type
of the TRUE BREAD. *Denton.*

---

15. When Jesus therefore perceived that they would come and take him by
force, to make him a king, he departed again into a mountain himself alone.

Perceived. Our Lord's omniscience, see on John i. 48 ; ii. 24, 25 ;
    iv. 18, 29.
Take by force. How like fallen nature, sliding down from the
    spiritual to the carnal.

With impetuous violence, they wished to crown Him.

This very violence proves they felt the honour would be unwelcome, and incompatible with His supremely holy and humble spirit.

Once in their grasp, they vainly dream that He will be compelled to do their pleasure.

Our Lord saw that His disciples, Jewish still in heart, were taken up with this scheme.

Hence the command for them at once to leave Him, and depart. Mark vi. 45.

A king. Jews would not accept a Messiah not having an earthly kingdom.

They believed Messiah would be not only greatest of all prophets, but mightiest of all kings. [king."

To exalt *the* PROPHET long expected they agree to make Him " a

As if an earthly crown would be attractive to Him who came to be a pattern of humility.

Doubtless selfish motives actuated them. He who had so wonderfully fed them could easily sustain Himself and them.

They had, in pride and wordliness of heart, wholly misapprehended prophecy.

Singular fact, the only time they ever sought to make Him king was after He had fed them.

Words and works of grace and love had failed to excite their loyalty.

It is so now. Men are ever ready to crown those who can help them to material prosperity. [Acts xiv. 13.

Lycaonians endeavoured to offer sacrifice to Paul and Barnabas.

Savages of Nova Albion insisted on sacrificing to *Sir Francis Drake.*

Like Joseph, He suffered for *the* very sin He so carefully avoided. Gen. xxxix. 8—14. [His trial.

The charge of *claiming to be king* was brought up against Him at

Yet while shunning the bauble of an earthly sceptre, He was " KING of KINGS," and will for ever wear " MANY CROWNS." Rev. xix. 12, 16.

To make Him King was of the Father, not of poor mortals. How low their ideas of Messiah's kingdom!

What had loaves and fishes multiplied to do with " THY THRONE, O GOD, IS FOR EVER AND EVER " ?

Departed. To His mind, how saddening such outbursts of carnal ambition and self-seeking!

He bears with their stupidity ; His only upbraiding is leaving them to their folly.

He went with His loving burden, and opened up His full heart.
Matt. xiv. 23. [xxiii. 15.

Some meet God like Balaam, as an unwelcome traveller. Num.

But others rejoice, as Jacob hailed the approaching band of angels.
Gen. xxxii. 1, 2.

Again. As was His wont, being glorified in His miracle, He retires
to commune with God.

If prayer is necessary in adversity, it is still more so in prosperity.

Popularity has often proved dangerous and injurious to ministers.

Our Lord's example of habitually returning to His Father should
be a minister's rule.

Mountain. John vi. 3. *Solitude* the banquet of grace, when improved by prayer. See on John v. 13.

Alone. Whenever escape is necessary, prayer is necessary also.
Mark vi. 46. [Father.

This proves His entire life was one continual sacrifice to His

The other Evangelists, although not stating the *reason*, relate the
fact of His departure.

Luke preserves a trace of the *motive* in the question, " Whom do
the people say that I, the Son of man, am ? " Luke ix. 18.

γνοὺς. Knowing. *Alford.*

ἁρπάζειν. Volebant Christum *rapere*, i.e. violenti impetu. *Calvin.* Would
expose Him to assassination or tumult. *Horsley.*

βασιλέα. The expectation of a universal sovereign was general among
oriental nations. *Virgil, Suetonius, Tacitus.* They believed, after this miracle,
He could feed a large army, and conquer like Gideon. *Hammond.* He may thus
have avoided Bethlehem, lest a crown should have been forced upon Him.
Bengel.

τὸ ὄρος. He went to pray. Mark vi. 46. He would arm His disciples for
the same temptation. *Hengst.* In prefiguration of His ascension. *Cyril, Aug.*

---

16. And when even was now come, his disciples went down unto the sea.

Even. Hebrews had two evenings,—first at 3 P.M. and second
at sunsetting.

Was come. A dangerous hour to embark on a treacherous lake.

He had left His disciples for wise reasons alone on the water.

He intended the storm should fall just where they were at that
time.

He will let them wait so long, and exercise their patience and faith.

Their fears would be enhanced by the darkness of the night.

As a skilful archer selects his arrows, so our Lord selects our trials.

Sea. For names and description of this sea, see on John vi. 1.

In Scripture, the sea is an emblem of the " *world*," Dan. vii., in
  its uneasiness and *unrest*, Isa. lvii. 20 ; Psa. xlvi. 3 ; and
  wild roaring. Psa. xciii. 3, 4.   [viii. 9.

Vessels on the sea typify the Church in times of persecution. Rev.

Some toil, others are passengers, but all are equally in peril.
  Psa. cvii. 23.

Its winds denote the fierce temptations of believers. Job ix. 17.

A believer must have on the ocean of life *Patience* for his tackling,
  Hope for his anchor, FAITH for his helm, BIBLE for his chart,
  CHRIST for his Captain, and the BREATH OF THE SPIRIT to fill
  his canvas. *Trapp*.   [turbing element.

In heaven " there shall be no more sea," Rev. xxi. 1, i. e. no dis-

Redeemed ones, with harps in their hands, appear in Apocalyptic
  vision standing " on the sea of glass." Rev. xv. 2.

Constrained. Mark vi. 45. Loth to leave such a Provider and
  Friend.

The presence of friends is so delightful, that death is called a
  " *departure*." 2 Tim. iv. 6.

The longer in Christ's company the stronger the ties ; and as He had
  dismissed them before, hence the gentle pressure necessary.

He sends them away, lest they should *join* the multitude who
  wanted to make Him king.   [xxxiv. 6.

The Lord often prevents sin by removing the temptation. Deut.

He did not *retire* until they had set sail, nor did He dismiss the
  multitude until the disciples had left.

A miniature map of His Providential government of the entire
  universe.

Not one of the countless millions of threads of warp or woof ever
  falls from His fingers.

In this world we see only the back of this tapestry, hereafter we
  shall see the glorious design in all its beautiful colours,
  divinely completed and perfected. *Bacon*.

ὀψία. Latter part of the evening. *Hengst*. Samaritans two evenings
between sunset and sunrise. *Alford*.

θαλάσσης. Like " *mare*," the sea as contrasted with land. *Trench*.
Psalm cvii. not applicable to ordinary mariners. Historically describes Israel's
perils and sorrows during the storm of Babylonian captivity. Having
wandered, hungry, thirsty, they came forth as from a storm at sea. *Hengst*.

κατέβησαν. The following miracle reassures His disciples, in prospect of
His strange discourse as to His body and blood. *Alford*.

17. And entered into a ship, and went over the sea toward Capernaum. And it was now dark, and Jesus was not come to them.

Entered. Without the Lord's consent, the storm might have resembled Jonah's. [from peril.

Believers, even certainly on their Master's errands, are not free
The assurance that *He will be with them,* Isa. xliii. 2, enables them to glorify God.

Ship. In our Lord's time a large population dwelt round this sea.

Hence there was always a great number of fishing and pleasure boats.

Boat-building was an active trade on its shores.

Modern travellers report that only one rickety boat is now to be seen on its waters. [ix. 1.

Capernaum. See on John ii. 12. Called "His own city." Matt.

Now dark. In Christian life it is always dark before Jesus comes.

His absence made night a double darkness to them.

At His nativity midnight became midday round Bethlehem.

At His death midday became midnight around Calvary.

When the LIGHT OF THE WORLD is present midnight is turned into mid-noon.

Morning dawn the natural type of salvation, as night is of danger.

Night an emblem of ignorance, Eph. iv. 18 ; of unbelief, Rom. xiii. 12 : time of robbery and plunder, Job xxiv. 14 ; of corrupt deeds, Eph. v. 11; of revelling, 1 Thess. v. 7; of Satanic mischief, Eph. vi. 12 ; of Divine visions, Gen. xlvi. 2 ; Job iv. 13 ; of trial, Psa. xvii. 3.

Israel saved at the Red Sea in the *morning.* Resurrection of our Lord in the *morning.*

" Weeping may endure for a night, but joy cometh in the morning." Psa. xxx. 5. [pillar.

Gloom of the desert to ancient Israel a background to the fiery
Thus the afflictions of Christians throw into bold relief the mercies of God.

Jesus not come. This was worse than the storm.

It was sad for Saul with his enemies upon him, but sadder still when God had forsaken him.

" I will not show you favour," was a worse doom than Israel's captivity. Jer. xvi. 13.

πλοῖον. This word and πλοιάριον seem to be used indifferently between verses 16—25. Term used by Josephus is sometimes πλοῖν, sometimes σκάφος.

Josephus in describing his own taking of Tiberias says that he collected all the boats on the lake, amounting to 230 in number, with four men in each. He states also incidentally that each boat had a "pilot" and an "anchor." *Smith's* Dict.

σκοτία. The nearer the end of the world approaches, the more errors will multiply. *Aug.*

-----

18. And the sea arose by reason of a great wind that blew.

Sea arose. This sea, surrounded by hills and mountains, was naturally liable to sudden storms.

And no Saviour within sight or call to these despairing souls.

In the fiery storm of persecution, the world wondered at martyrs singing in chains and death. Acts xvi. 25.

They saw Him by faith bending over them from His throne, and heard His voice saying, "Fear not." [them.

When the captives "hung their harps by the river" God cheered

When the world had come to its darkest hour the Lord sent His Son to be born at Bethlehem.

Christ was looking through that storm and watching over all.

There are far greater perils in our *doubts* than in God's storms.

Great wind. See on John iii. 8. Persians and others worshipped the winds. Hence the word in Amos iv. 13.

Wind described as a medium of Divine agency. Exod. xv. 10 ; Num. xi. 31.

"Sound as of a rushing mighty wind" typified the coming of the Spirit. Acts ii. 3.

"Wings of the wind" a figure representing great rapidity. 2 Sam. xxii. 11 ; Zech. v. 9. "Wind," violent but empty speech. Job viii. 2. Vain knowledge. Job xv. 2.

"Sowing to the wind" infatuation, "reaping the whirlwind" retribution. Hos. viii. 7.

"He stayeth His rough wind," &c., kindly interference of Providence. Isa. xxvii. 8.

Human life like a "wind that passeth away and cometh not again." Psa. lxxviii. 39.

A stormy wind a figure for Divine judgments. Ezek. xiii. 11, 13 ; Isa. lxiv. 6. [their aid.

Although He saw their distress and peril, He came not at once to

His interpositions are delayed till faith is tried, often sorely.

All the circumstances must show how hopeless it is to expect deliverance but from God.

Tossed. Matt. xiv. 24. " O thou afflicted and tossed with tempest." Isa. liv. 11.

How all unconscious were these tossed ones of the *presence* of the MASTER.

He saw. Mark vi. 48. Before He revealed His sympathy,—" I have seen thy afflictions." Exod. iii. 7.

As an eagle, however high her flight, ever keeps a watchful eye on her young, so our Lord on the mountain noticed every struggle of the disciples.

He once numbered the wanderings and tears of David. Psa. lvi. 8.

It is the seeing of omnipotent love, preparing and bringing help.

Now from His throne with sleepless love He observes the storms *outwardly* and *inwardly* of His saints, every *heart-storm* among His saints.

ἀνέμου. See critical notes on John iii. 8. εἶδεν. Mark vi. 48. A trait doubtless received by Mark from Peter, who received it from the Lord. *Hengst.* More probably revealed by the Spirit of God. *Author.*

---

19. So when they had rowed about five and twenty or thirty furlongs, they see Jesus walking on the sea, and drawing nigh unto the ship : and they were afraid.

When. The time is exactly stated as the " fourth watch." Matt. xiv. 25.

From dusk He had passed the time in prayer, leaving His disciples to toil through the storm, to test their faith.

How often has the cry gone forth, " Watchman, what of the night ? "

It was the " morning " or " fourth watch " when Jehovah " looked, &c., and troubled the Egyptians." Exod. xiv. 24.   [heaven.

Rowed. Against wind and wave, believers also must oft toil for

Here their faith, so tried, was being invigorated for trials in their ministry.

Not many days hence these disciples will see their Master in such circumstances that even *their* faith will break down.

Twenty-five furlongs. About four miles, according to our method of measurement.

The vessel had well nigh gone *half* the distance.

They were literally now " in the midst of the sea," Matt. xiv. 24, battling with the tempest.

Small progress and incessant labour is the rule of life to fallen men.

To encounter continual opposition, and patiently bear it, the rule of the Church.

How precious the assurance, His eyes are ever lovingly kept on His Church.

Or thirty. The inspiring Spirit could have given the *exact* distance on the sea. [men.

But He permits the record to go forth according to the manner of

If the Bible were not so thoroughly *human*, it would not be so evidently *divine*. [sea ?

Jesus. Why did He leave His place of prayer, and go forth on the

From the mountain He could as easily have hushed the storm and calmed their fears.

But He reads another lesson to His Church during all coming time.

These tempest-tossed disciples *saw* their prayer *answered* by a miracle.

Proving that all prayer offered in faith will be answered, whether we *see* it or not.

" He *would have passed by* them." Mark vi. 48. This was to draw out their cry for help.

" Pass not away, I pray thee, from thy servant." Gen. xviii. 3. "I will not let thee go." Gen. xxxii. 26. [angel.

" I pray thee, let us detain thee." Judg. xiii. 15. Manoah to the

" He made as though He would have gone further." Luke xxiv. 28.

He desires to be detained by loving entreaty, else *He will pass by*.

What amazing condescension: the Creator appears to yield to the prayers of the creature.

Walking. Herein He reveals Himself as Jehovah, " Thy way is in the sea." Psa. lxxvii. 19.

Willing or unwilling, all earth's powers are under the feet of Jesus.

" The Lord is mightier than the mighty waves of the sea." Psa. xciii. 4 ; Job ix. 8.

Afraid. Probably He was surrounded with a lustre which rendered Him visible during the midnight storm.

Innocent man knew no fear: fear not named nor felt until the fall. Gen. iii. 10.

Conscience arraigns and sentences, while fear awaits execution.

Dread follows sin, as the ground swell does the ocean storm.

Combined with filial confidence, fear is the *jealousy* of *love*, but "*perfect love casteth out fear.*" 1 John iv. 18 ; Rom. viii. 15.

Sad thoughts of the displeasure of Heaven are often aroused by a storm.

Fear was deified by pagans. A temple to Fear was built at Sparta
by the Ephori.
Tullus Hostilius introduced the worship of this deity at Rome.
Apparitions were to Jews, heralds of impending doom. Judg.
xiii. 22.
Peter, who drew his sword on Malchus, trembles here before an ima-
ginary spirit.
Delusion of sense oft converts friends into foes, and aid into harm.
The presence for which they prayed, coming in an unknown way,
fills them with terror.
Our Saviour sometimes comes to us in " strange apparel."
As a King, He has a large ward-robe, and often changes His robes.
Bunyan. [salvation.
That which seems to threaten with ruin, is oft a harbinger of
Thus winds and waves, and One above the storm, carry lessons to
these men and to all generations.

ἐληλακότες. Cum promovissent. *Vulgate.* Rendered by a passive. *Beza.*
ὡς. Characteristic. *Hengst.*
περιπατοῦντα. Symbolical and prophetic of the ascendancy of the spiritual
body above material laws and forces after the resurrection. *Lange.* John
intended to relate a miracle, that there should be no doubt about that miracle,
no chance of a mistake as to what they saw. *Alford.*
ἐφοβήθησαν. Fear of spirits a proof of the fallen state of man. *R. Hall.*
Human nature in this life cannot endure *spirit* presence. God in mercy has
drawn the veil between us and the spirit world. All attempts to force aside
that veil are wicked. So called "*spirit*" manifestations have caused madness
in hundreds in America and Europe. *Author.* Fear has its seat in the entrance
to Hell. *Virgil.* Among the furies in the retinue of Proserpine. *Ovid.*

---

20. But he saith unto them, It is I ; be not afraid.

It is I. Gr. I AM. Nine times in John He claims this JEHOVAH
NAME.
The same words, John xviii. 6, which terrified His foes, cheered
His friends.
Now it instantly calms all their fears, as to a supernatural being.
It is the language of home ; known well by all His children.
Knowing the meaning of this word, we enter into one of the deepest
truths of God.
It is learned by the affections, the way by which God leads us
farthest into Himself. [their hearts.
Jesus appeals to His own identity as supplying the true calm to

The ANGEL JEHOVAH had before been a light to His Church in the sea.   Exod. xiv. 20.

The Egyptians saw the Presence of God clothed in gloom and dread.

The sinner's death-bed often the gate-way of mourning and despair.

The believer's dying couch, a triumphant car, angel-drawn, bearing him home.   Luke xvi. 22.

A child folded in a loving father's arms, fears no danger or foes.

"I have got the victory!" shouted the good old Rutherford on his death-bed.   "Christ, my Saviour, is holding out both His arms to embrace me."

"Do you know Jesus?"   The question was put to a pious young wife, who, having been suddenly stricken down by typhus fever, was dying, unconscious of every loving friend by whom she was surrounded.   She responded, whilst the radiance of the coming glory beamed on her brow, and a bright smile played upon her lips, "Jesus—Jesus! Oh yes, I do know Jesus!   Why, He has long been my dearest Friend!   Know Jesus?   Why, He is close to me now, close here, quite close." *Power's* Breviates.

> " Thus love undying still abides,
>   When life is waning low :
> As sap in wither'd branches hides,
>   As moss beneath the snow."

Be not afraid.   After rowing six hours, they had not yet made more than four miles.

The sea is only eight miles wide anywhere from shore to shore.

They had ceased to look for aid, amid the overwhelming tempest.

He "constrained them" to start, and faithfully they had obeyed.   Mark vi. 45.

How differently they must have felt had they gone of their *own will!*

Whatever terror the storm brought, it brought not the remorse of rebellion.

Storms will come in the way of duty, but the peace of a good conscience is too deep for disturbance.

When the storm *without* and *within* was past, they had learned of a Divine KINGHOOD, meeting all the cravings of the soul.

Scribes and Pharisees heard not the words,—" IT IS I, BE NOT AFRAID."

They were heard only by humble fishermen, in a midnight storm.
By tempest tossed believers they have been heard ever since!

---

21. Then they willingly received him into the ship : and immediately the ship was at the land whither they went.

Willingly. Gr. *wished.* It was that they desired above all things. This is one of the chief benefits of trial : Christ's presence is hailed with joy.
Received. The immediate calm following Christ's approach, a peculiar revelation of His glory.
Every new necessity of the Christian a new manifestation of Christ's glory.
" He maketh the storm a calm, so that the waves thereof are still," &c. Psa. cvii. 29, 30.   [people.
This Psalm is prophetic of the encouragement Christ gives His
A universal and complete victory is promised, but not *immediate.*
The conflict may be long ; the battle may be continued till death.
No sin, no temptation, carried by prayer under the cross, can *long* survive.
" They cry unto the Lord in their trouble, and He bringeth them out of distress." Psa. cvii. 28.
The ship. Good and wicked sail over same sea and encounter similar storms.   [lxxiii. 1—10.
But oft the Lord permits His foes to sail o'er a calm sea. Psa.
If the Lord is with us in the ship, no matter what the storm, all will be well.   [miracle.
Immediately. Another miracle. Our Lord's life teemed with
The four remaining miles might have been reached by the oar, but when God begins a work, He stops not till it is completed. Phil. i. 6.
He had fed 5000 by a word, He had stilled the wind.
He had walked on the waves, and now He annihilates distance.
He will soon demand faith, which the same Power must create.
He will never find a knot He cannot untie. Ver. 53.
He will loose the cords of the grave,—death cannot hold when Jesus calls.   [ix. 28.
Some days after, Tabor will become radiant with His glory. Luke
The land. The other Evangelists note the calming of the sea, but John sweeps on to the end of their voyage.
When the believer has Christ, he is always close to land.

Any moment the storms of life may cease, and the spirit enter " the
desired haven."
Christ in the heart is the pledge and foretaste of future glory.
Christ the sea-king ; He, not Mary, the true *Stella Maris.*

ἤθελον. If there was "but" instead of "and" a contrast might be made
out against the synoptists. *Hengst.* Received different accounts. *Chrys.*
Wished to receive Him, but did not. *Bleek.* Received Him with willingness.
Beza, Tholuck, Winer, Trench.
οὖν. They were willing therefore to receive, but their hearts were reassured
by His voice. *Alford.*
εὐθέως. A new miracle. *Bengel.* No other miracle besides calming the
wind. The vessel traversed the remaining distance. *Hengst., Tholuck.*
Comparatively in a short time, or perhaps by a *miracle. Alford.* A miraculous gliding of the ship. *Luthardt, Andrews, Webster & Wilkinson.*

---

22. The day following, when the people which stood on the other side of the
sea saw that there was none other boat there, save that one whereinto his disciples were entered, and that Jesus went not with his disciples into the boat, but
that his disciples were gone away alone.

Day following. Day after miracle of loaves and fishes, and the
stormy night.
Day on which our Lord landed on the western side of the lake.
People. A remnant of the crowd who were fed the day previous
on the eastern shore.
In eastern lands many are always on the verge of famine.
He and His disciples repose after the tempest.
The other side, i. e. from the east coast. Our Lord was now at
Capernaum.
That one. It seems the crowd narrowly watched His move-
ments.
They saw that in " that one " boat the disciples alone had crossed
over the lake.
These minute particulars are characteristic of the Evangelist John.
How fearlessly those speaking truth may relate the slightest
details.

ὄχλος. People seeing the disciples embark *without* Jesus, were induced to
remain, and desired or determined to make Him king. A far larger part understood the miracle, and left for the passover feast at Jerusalem. *Hengst.*

23. Howbeit there came other boats from Tiberias nigh unto the place where they did eat bread, after that the Lord had given thanks.

Other boats. Driven by the storm to find harbour on the north-east side of the lake.

The crowd still lingered on the eastern shore, in hope of seeing the Lord return.

Tiberias. A city of Galilee, in the most beautiful part of it, on the western shore of the lake.

Named by Herod Antipas in honour of the Emperor Tiberius. See Sugg. Comm., Luke iii. 1.

From its origin it was the capital of the province until the reign of Herod Agrippa II.

Many of the inhabitants were Greeks and Romans, and hence foreign customs prevailed.

Our Lord, who spent so much of His time in Galilee, appears to have never visited this city.

Probably because Herod, the murderer of John the Baptist, chiefly resided in it.

After the dissolution of the state, it was for several centuries the seat of a renowned Jewish school and one of the four sacred cities.

Here the Mishna was compiled, A.D. 190, by the great Rabbi Judah Hakkodesh, and the Masorah originated in a great measure at Tiberias. [times.

The place. Perhaps a spot where merchandise was landed at The astounding reports of the miracle aroused all the country.

The crowd press to gaze on both the spot and the WONDER-WORKER.

Given thanks. See on ver. 11. Paul writes, " Men eat to God when they give thanks." Rom. xiv. 6.

To whom do they eat who refuse from day to day to offer a petition ?

ἐκ Τιβεριάδος. Coins of the city of Tiberias are still extant, which are referred to the times of Tiberius, Trajan, and Hadrian. The ancient name has survived in that of the modern *Tubarieh*, which occupies unquestionably the original site. Near *Tubarieh* are the celebrated warm baths, which the Roman writers reckoned among the greatest known curiosities of the world. The intermediate space between these baths and the town abounds with the traces of ruins. Population at present between 3000 and 4000. *Smith's* Dict. The present town " the most mean and miserable place in Palestine ; a picture of disgusting filth and frightful wretchedness." *Robinson.* This verse in parenthesis. *Markland.*

24. When the people therefore saw that Jesus was not there, neither His disciples, they also took shipping, and came to Capernaum, seeking for Jesus.

People. From Tiberias, to see the place and proofs of the miracle. Perhaps they hoped to share in the fragments that remained, but more probably to satisfy curiosity in looking at Jesus.

Capernaum. See on John ii. 12. They sought the Lord in the place of His residence.   [sake.

Seeking. Seeking Jesus with importunity, but not for His own

ὄχλος. Same crowd He had fed by miracle. *Aug.*

ζητοῦντες. Not 5000, for a fleet could not instantly be gathered. *Stier.* There were many vessels crowding the sea, to the number of 230. *Josephus.* Those of the crowd resolved to crown Him. *Grotius.* The most persistent of the Chiliasts. *Lange.* Intense curiosity to find out how He crossed the sea. *Brandt.* They follow the Lord for the sake of pleasure. *Augustine.*

καὶ, " *also*," omitted. *Tisch., Alf., Tregelles.*

---

25. And when they found him on the other side of the sea, they said unto him, Rabbi, when camest thou hither?

Found Him. They found the great Prophet. But they neither sought nor found Him who came to *save*.   [Judge.

All seeking Him with similar motives will find, not Jesus, but a

Other side. Western side of the lake, in the synagogue of Capernaum. Verse 59.

Rabbi. See on John i. 38, 49. A title of respect given to their doctors and teachers.

Not known to have been used before the reign of Herod the Great.

Thought to have taken its rise about the time of the disputes between the rival schools of Hillel and Shammai.

Before that period prophets and great men of the synagogue were simply called by their proper names.

When? They do not say " How? " although they wished especially to know *how* He had crossed.

Camest. Probably they had begun to think that a secret miracle had been performed.

His disciples could have answered the question, but such liberty it seems they never dared to assume.   [swered.

Lust after miracles is rebuked. He leaves their question *unan-*

It was not for *them* as a sign. It would be throwing diamonds before a herd.

In the next verse He shows them their low views and sensual spirit.

They thought the wind during the night would not permit a boat to cross.

They knew *not* that wind and waves are His servants.

They knew not they were speaking to Him " *Whose way is in the sea,* and whose paths are in the great waters." Psa. lxxvii. 19.

The Scriptures encourage earnest humble investigation. " Search " is the word. John v. 39. [Acts xvii. 11.

The Bereans for such searching are described as " *more noble.*"

But unholy curiosity is ever rebuked. Dwellers in Bethshemesh perished for prying into the ARK. 1 Sam. vi. 19.

That token of His presence left to all generations a *terrible sermon* on His MAJESTY. Exod. xix. 21 ; Prov. xxv. 2.

" Secret things belong unto the Lord our God." Deut. xxix. 29.

There is an unfathomable " DEPTH " in His counsels. Rom. xi. 33.

God's counsels, though secret, are just, and must prevail. " Pry not, lest ye perish." *Augustine.*

They recognized not the Divine sign in the first miracle, and hence their ignorance now.

εὑρόντες. At the synagogue ; they seem to have landed away from the village. *D. Brown.* Some interpolate this fact between the 41st and 43rd verses. The discourse may have been preceded by the reading of the law and prayer. *Doddridge.*

ὧδε γέγονας. Since when art thou here ? *Stier.* The people saw the disciples *alone* depart for Capernaum. In the night it blew a tempest from the west. *Blunt, Greenleaf.* Not to *learn,* but make a show of what they knew. *Trapp.* A warning against unhallowed curiosity. *Lightfoot.* Carnal ones flatter themselves they must comprehend ere they believe. *Hooker.* Many seem to live and die under this delusion. *Author.*

---

26. Jesus answered them and said, Verily, verily, I say unto you, Ye seek me, not because ye saw the miracles, but because ye did eat of the loaves, and were filled.

Answered. YESTERDAY He fled from an offered crown and kingdom.

He left their *question* unanswered, but rebuked their *impertinence.*

If the Lord of Glory so meekly and patiently replied to these *selfish seekers,* how rebuked ought we to feel when wearied with such toil.

Discouraged by the Hindoos at Dinapore coming only for rice, this verse came to *Henry Martyn's* mind, and he felt cheered in his work.

He might have put a counter-question, " Why seek ye ME ? "

They certainly could not have said, because " Thou art the BREAD of LIFE." Verse 48.

By His silence He admits He crossed in a *miraculous* manner.

Said. Having satisfied their *bodily* wants, He would now satisfy their *souls.*

Verily, verily. No mere repetition, a solemn summoning of the attention of all men.

Unto you. His miraculous power was not wasted; some did believe, although the large majority remained in unbelief.

Pearls had been cast, and in longing souls grace had created the desire for them.

He has come to the central point in His ministry, and He will now, by an allusion to His passion, make a *selection* of followers.   [hearers.

By a thousand methods since His Providence is ever sifting gospel

Some are attracted by the splendour of miracles, some by the low wish for food.   [Rome.

Ye seek me. To crown Him as their leader against imperial

Who ever before or since refused a crown offered in sincerity, nay, it was *pressed on Him* ?

Not because. They did not understand the true drift of the miracle. John vi. 29.

Their attempt to take Him by *force* and make Him a king proves no fault in the promised SHILOH.

They were *wilfully* blind to the spiritual glory of His character and work.

Miracles. See on John iii. 2. They were signs of mighty import, rightly understood.

He could feed thousands with bread created by His *power ;* could He not save myriads by His *grace ?*

He clearly hints that these outward signs point to boundless inward treasures.

Loaves. They thought that He who could create such supplies could easily support an army.

That He who could control the waves could also compel His enemies to submit.

As He showed the woman of Samaria that *other water*, He shows these that *other bread.*

Filled. The gratification of their bodily appetite was all they could comprehend.

Yesterday they had eaten without *faith*, and to-day they are hungry for another miracle under a BREAD-KING !

Eden, with half the glories of heaven, did not satisfy our first

parents ; neither could a throne and crown satisfy David.
Psa. lv. 6.
" THOU hast made us for THYSELF, and we can only be happy in
THEE." *Augustine.*   [Messiah's reign.
They thought this banquet *only* the *beginning* of the *good times* of
But He will show them that those loaves multiplied were a deep
mystery of eternal moment.
As the water to the Samaritan, so was the bread to these people,
sermons, such as Rabbis had never preached.
Mark God's sovereignty. He never spake of this bread to the
proud oligarchs and doctors in Jerusalem !
They had no heart even to *wish* to find in Him the promised
SHILOH.
From their low motive He advances as from a text, and publishes
to the world, the DIVINE SCHEME of SALVATION !
With inimitable wisdom He reveals man's wants and the fulness
of grace.

'Απεκρίθη. This narrative, questioned by neologists and infidels, bears the
unmistakable stamp of historical truth. *B. Crusius.* His expressions are
classical Greek. *Stier.*
ἐχορτάσθητε. Yet some think the miracle largely consisted in their own
spiritual ecstasy. *Lange.* They estimated it simply for its utility. *Grotius.*

---

27. Labour not for the meat which perisheth, but for that meat which endureth unto everlasting life, which the Son of man shall give unto you : for
him hath God the Father sealed.

Labour not for. Gr. *Busy not yourselves about.* God's answer to
spiritual wants, not questions.
This discourse might have been delivered by the wayside, but it
was the day of worship in the synagogue, and there He spake.
Verse 59.
This verse contains a double paradox : 1. That they should not
labour for the perishable food. which is the very thing they
must get by working. 2. That they should labour for the
heavenly food, which is not to be earned by labour. *Lange.*
" Labour " corresponds to the thrice-repeated, " Come, buy without money." Isa. lv. 1.
A fulfilment of the curse pronounced after the fall. Gen. iii. 19.
In vain do men think that *their* watching can preserve the city.
Equally vain the trust that God will preserve the city *without*
watching.

The husbandman dare not leave off his ploughing, sowing, &c.

Nor the merchant neglect his calling, without forfeiting God's promise.

God is sovereign, yet Abraham must *work* as well as *believe*.

If we would *reap* in joy, we must first *sow* in righteousness.

Othniel must conquer a city before he could be Caleb's son-in-law.

David must slay an hundred Philistines to call Saul father.

The pilot's hand must be on the prow, as well as his eye on the needle.   [*ence.*

Promises abound encouraging our *weakness*, not one for our *indol-*

He addresses them as though they were exhausted toiling for bread, although for once they ate it without toil.

Faith is no pillow for idleness. It needs more energy than good works.   [*working.*

Jacob's wrestling proves faith inseparable from struggling and

Labouring for mere things of sense is labour for a *world lost*.

Empty-handed love has long since been banished from God's kingdom.

David dealt kindly with Jonathan's son for his *friend's sake*.

He that loves a man for his bread loves the bread more than his friend.   [*mysteries.*

Their ever-deepening contradictions urge Him to ever-deepening

There will be shortly a sifting among even the narrow circle of disciples.

His words appear to undervalue His own gifts. Daily mercies often prove a snare. Psa. xlix.

Every *feast* ought to be the *sacrifice* of an adoring humble heart.

Meat. So it is first called, then *bread,* then FLESH and BLOOD of JESUS CHRIST.

As with her of Samaria, He passes over from earthly to eternal good.

He will not name the spiritual without alluding to the sensible gift.

Perisheth. Gr. *spoils, corrupts.* " Meats for the belly, and the belly for meats: but God shall destroy both." 1 Cor. vi. 13.

Earthly good goes to destruction, and with it the man who seeks his life in it.

Science, wealth, power, dignity, fame, and pleasure, must pass away.

Endureth. Has eternal sufficiency, eternal freshness, eternal durability. This world's glories are pictures of splendour drawn on ice.

Men come to this world's schemes as to a lottery, full of *hopes.*

They return with their heart and purse full of *blanks.*

Bread is not provided without patient persevering toil, delicacies
never.

A fable tells how cities came into a king's possession while he *slept*.

" But the kingdom of heaven suffereth *violence,* and the violent take
it by force." Matt. xi. 12.

First, thing *forbidden,*—making bodily wants the object of life.

Second, thing *commanded,*—aim at obtaining food for the soul's wants.

Third, thing *promised,*—Son of man will supply us with this food.

Fourth, thing *declared,*—this Saviour has been set apart for this
very work.

Everlasting. See notes. John iii. 15, 16 ; v. 24. Viewed in
the main as an outward object, but including the internal
operations of it.

Son of man. See on John i. 51 ; v. 27. Seen and known as man,
but referring to His Incarnate Godhead.

His lowly form as a servant (Phil. ii. 7) is in sharp contrast with
His being the BESTOWER of EVERLASTING LIFE.

As God-man, He gives His flesh for the life of the world. John
vi. 51.

Give. Neither merited nor earned. " The gift of God is eternal
life." Rom. vi. 23.

How these Jews must have looked with wonder at one *apparently*
a *man*, claiming to bestow life,—LIFE ETERNAL in HEAVEN !

God the Father. See on John i. 1, 2, 14, 18. When I speak of
my FATHER hear it aright, He is GOD.

He hath sent ME to give life to the world. What a God-like errand !

Father. How could Pharisaism, with its heartlessness, ever receive
such a truth ? [eternal study.

To understand the first sentence in our Lord's prayer will require

These labourers secretly sighed for a king, who was yet a *brother*.

Half their wild acts were struggles to find such an one.

Their yearnings after *rest* taught them there must be a *good God*.

One worthy the trust their fathers had put in Him.

A Being associated with the graves of loved ones and their children's faces. [dreams.

To hear Him called a " FATHER " was an echo to their own happy

There is an *unwritten* theology which exists wherever a soul is
found. [Luke xii. 57.

To this our Saviour appeals, " Wherefore judge ye not the right ? "

Sealed. John iii. 33 pointed out by this very miracle.

The genuine is thus approved and the spurious is rejected.

Seal is used—1. To confirm by testimony. 2. To distinguish as property.

Israel's high-priest wore the Divine signet engraved, "HOLINESS TO THE LORD." Exod. xxviii. 36.

In profane imitation, the Hindoo priests wear a well-known *mark.*

God the Father seals everlastingly by His Son the words He spake "at sundry times and in divers places" by the prophets. Heb. i. 1.   [heart.

Jesus Himself is that *seal.* He affixes His *image* on each believer's All other seals will be finally rejected as forgeries and impostures.

Coming as an angel of light, *Satan* counterfeits our Lord's signature. 2 Cor. xi. 14.   .[works.

Sealed. The stamp of Divinity is placed upon all His words and We seal the deed which is our own, and by which we will stand.

The Father seals—1. The Son of Mary as HIS ETERNAL SON. 2. Endorses and confirms His claims to SUPREME DIVINITY. 3. Places His Divine approval on THE ERRAND OF HIS SON TO EARTH. 4. Shows His perfect pleasure at the FULFILMENT OF THAT PLAN by His death, resurrection, and ascension. John iii. 33.

He placed his seal upon Him at the Jordan, on Tabor, and in the temple. John xii. 28.   [to men.

This Divine Saviour thus constituted, becomes the BREAD of LIFE The Father thus ATTESTS HIS SON, and the Son is the WITNESS of THE FATHER. Rev. i. 5.

It is this ground-tone of all our Lord's miracles that causes sceptics so passionately and so frantically to contend against the inspiration of John's Gospel.

ἐργάζεσθε. "Labour," an inexact translation. "Weary not yourselves." They had not toiled. "Busy not," &c. *Alford.* To gain by labour. *Xenophon.* To acquire by diligence. *Demosthenes.* Seeking to get. *Stier.* Produce. *Luther.* Work out. *De Wette.* Trouble yourselves. *Van Ess.* Work that earns or acquires. *Lampe.* All the pleasures of earth looked for by Jews in their Messiah. *Wetstein.*

μὴ ἀλλὰ. Supposed to forbid working for daily bread held in the time of *Epiphanius.* "Da mihi cor tuum, et sufficit" hath the essence of theology. *Andrews.* Basil, when tempted by high offers, replied, "Gloriam da quæ semper floreat." *Trapp.* The missionary Dr Carey was offered £1000 a year by the E. India Company to act as interpreter. Refusing it, they offered as much as £5000. But the man of God would not leave his work. *Choules'* Hist. Miss. Those who shared the miracle were partakers of spiritual bread. *Olsh.*

ἀπολλυμένην. Meat, whose nourishing power passes away. *De Wette.*

δώσει. The Son of man had not yet died. *Alford.*

ὁ πατὴρ ὁ Θεός. The Father, God. ἐσφράγισεν, χαρακτὴρ, Heb. i. 3. See critical notes on John i. 2. To seal up. Stamped. *Euripides.* A seal placed on a servant, a soldier, or a victim for the altar. *Lampe, Doddridge.* Not stamped, but by testimony. *Alford.* The Son's essential equality with the Father. *Hilary.*

---

28. Then said they unto him, What shall we do, that we might work the works of God?

Said they. Question probably *inspired*, to open way for answer of *eternal moment!*

Shall we do? They desired to earn heaven without faith in God. The jailer also clung to this broken hope of a lost Paradise, " What shall I do ? " Acts xvi. 30.

The human heart loves to weave a web of its own righteousness.

Work. Our Lord reduces the multiform works of the law to *one* —FAITH !

Of God. They do not say *for* God. Their word is far more accurate than their knowledge or intention. Who can benefit God ?

From God's Spirit must proceed all works which He will accept.

" A man is justified by works, and not by faith *only*." Jas. ii. 24.

That is, a man is justified by faith, which *ever works by love.*

As the cause to the effect, so is faith to good works. Matt. xxv. 34—46.

Faith invisible, seen only by God ; good works the fruit, seen by men. Matt. vii. 20.

Hence the philanthropy of infidels is worthless, because *without* faith. " For whatever is not of faith is sin." Rom. xiv. 23.

Faith is the source of all that is *peculiar* to Christian character. Heb. xi. [virtuous.

No religion but that of the Bible ever has made or will make men

Philosophy never made a man virtuous, its disciples being judges. *Cicero.*

As a rule, infidels of all classes have been indifferent to holiness.

The strongest motive " to work the works of God " is that of Christ's *atonement.*

LOVE moved Christ to fulfil the law for us, and the same LOVE *constrains* (Gr. *shuts up*) all His followers. 2 Cor. v. 14.

The spiritual law in the universal experience of believers is, " He died for all, that they should not live unto themselves." 2 Cor. v. 15.

Good works are like our Lord's sacrifice—1. By the Divine will.

2. By Divine love. 3. For the Church of God. 4. For the Divine glory. Psa. li. 19 ; Eph. v. 1, 2.

πoιοῦμεν. Bare presumption to trust His sovereignty while neglecting His rules. *Hammond.* "I would swim through a sea of brimstone if I could reach heaven," cried one under remorse. *Trapp.* Those wishing to be saved by good works are the devil's martyrs. *Luther.*
ἔργα τοῦ Θεοῦ. Such as God alone should work. *Stolz.* That which God alone could do. *Pfenninger, Hess.* A Divine task. *Schlier., Meyer.* This we must leave to God. *Herder.* How can we procure that which is God's prerogative ? *Schneider.* Their devotional works. *Stier.* Works of the law. *Lücke.* They see Him as a Lawgiver, not as a Saviour. *Lange.* Spiritual understanding alone satisfies the context. *Olsh.* The work resembles *our* work, as specifically the sacrifices,—*our* sacrifices in Psalm li. 19. *Hengst.* Work which He alloweth. *Sumner.* Jas. ii. 24, alludes to justification in the sight of man only. *Pres. Edwards.*

---

29. Jesus answered and said unto them, This is the work of God, that ye believe on him whom he hath sent.

Answered. He condescends to their weakness by using their own expression.   [God.
The very " contradictions of sinners " tend to bring more light from
Said. His Spirit was even then stirring and rousing their consciences.
He was calling them to trust and follow their King and their Friend.
Work of God. Saving faith is not of ourselves, " it is the gift of God." Eph. ii. 8.   [believe.
Faith has the DIVINE side,—God's work ; and the HUMAN side,—*Endeavouring* to believe will be found as difficult as *keeping* the Law.
Believe. See on John i. 7. This lies at the threshold of all acceptable obedience.   [be had.
Faith is the *unchanging* and *absolute* condition on which Life is to
It is confidence in the Almighty power, that Christ *can* save.
It is trust in sovereign grace, that He is *willing* to save.
It is that which neither gold nor sacrifice can purchase.
It is not found by ascending up to heaven or sinking down to hell.
It is known and felt by all who really " believe " Him to be " the gift of God."
It is not trusting to any human morality, virtue, or act of penance.
It consists not with taking aught of *all* the praise, power, and glory from God.
Faith in its *results* is a great work. John xiv. 12.

To comply with this word the Jew had to break away from all
the traditions of his Church.
From all his most dearly cherished hopes as to the expected Messiah.
From all the authorities highly seated, and honoured by his nation.
From public opinion, from his own fleshly lusts, and from family
interests.
From all ambitious prospects of honour and wealth among men.
From all confidence in his own virtue.   This was the final death-
blow.   [John xvi. 2.
For a Jew to believe was to lose fellowship with his kindred.
He gave up his dearest possessions—friends, himself. Luke xiv. 26.
To a Jewish mind all the one thousand burdens imposed by the
Pharisees weigh lighter than a feather when put against this
ONE WORD of Christ ! *Hengstenberg.*
Faith was ordained the way of life, by God, before Creation.
John xiv. 6.   [especially so.
Our Lord here calls it, " *The work of God* " prominently and
Faith, embracing the Christian's life, is the evangelized LAW.
Works without faith are arrows shot by the blind at random.
No better than a withered tree, neither leaves, nor bloom, nor fruit.
All *vital* power is a mystery, and plainly *the work of God.* Eph. i. 19.
So is faith, which is the "*mighty power* of God unto salvation." Rom.
i. 16.   [xiii. 23, 27.
"Faith is the *substance* of things hoped for."   Heb. xi. 1 ; Num.
It brings heaven so near us, that we can taste its joy.

ἔργον τοῦ Θεοῦ. God, the Author of faith. Eph. ii. 8. *Calvin, Luther.*
Singular opposed to plural significant. *Stier.* Denied. *Luthardt.* The root of
all religious life. *Schlier.*   The true God-appointed work. *Nitzch.* A work
of man free *in, through,* and *for* God. *Lange.* Faith the *instrument,* salvation
the *gift. Stier.* Wrought by God through faith. *Hess.* Faith not here the
sole work of God, because wrought by Him. *Lampe.* The *germ* of all apostolic teaching as to faith and works. *Alford.*
πιστεύσητε. Law of work puffs up, but faith removes all boasting for
ever. *Quesnel.* It is no easy matter to believe, and this *will-worship* hinders
the spirit. *Usher.* We believe with much *conflict. Dike.* No less difficult to
wish to believe than to be willing to die. *Beza.*

---

30. They said therefore unto him, What sign shewest thou then, that we
may see, and believe thee ? what dost thou work ?

What sign ? John ii. 11 ; iii. 2 ; iv. 48.   Why ask a sign after
yesterday's wonder ?

Doubtless the same fickle multitude who yesterday would *crown Him.*

They resolved to lay Him under obligation by their kindness.

The more the Lord gratifies their thirst of miracles the more *insatiable* they are.   [27.

They seem fully to comprehend the word, "Labour not," &c. Verse

"If you make so great demands on us, you must give greater signs."

"You ask much more than Moses, and yet he did greater works."

"Feeding five thousand cannot compare with his feeding a million."

They deemed this demand decisive, but they forgot that all Christ's miracles were only PROOFS OF HIS CLAIMS, SUCH AS MOSES NEVER MADE, TO BE THE SON OF GOD.

They indirectly request Christ to outdo the miracle of manna.

It was a concealed plea that He should be a temporal monarch and Messiah.

Give us freedom and bread for the body, and let spiritual life go.

Give us thunderings, lightnings, and smoke, as at Mount Sinai.

Give us a pillar of fire, such as led Israel from the Sea to Canaan.

Give us bread dropping down out of heaven like rain.

Give us quails, that shall prove Thee from God, as Moses.

Give us rock-water such as flowed forty years in the desert sand.

Proofs enough already had He given of His OMNIPOTENCE and LOVE.

They must have had a face like brass to ask such a BEING for miracles merely as prodigies to *amuse* their curiosity.

Had He given them another rain of manna, they might have asked Him to bring down from heaven a *legion of angels.*

They have had so many miracles already, "they can't see the wood for the trees."

As those living underground in darkness may come to doubt whether the sun shines, so these practical atheists ask for proof of our Lord's Godhead at the very time when devils 'confessed and trembled before Him. Jas. ii. 19 ; Matt. viii. 29.

Shewest Thou. " THOU " is emphatic, a challenge to equal Moses.

May see. That Thou art sent by God. Did Christ's miracles mean nothing ?

Believe. John i. 7. His claims on their faith as the *" sent of God"* were such as they never conceived of.

Five thousand miraculously fed did not remove their stubborn unbelief.

Six hundred thousand similarly fed did not convince their *fathers*.
That miracle was repeated *daily* during *forty* years.
Still they *murmured* against God, *rejected* Moses, and *perished*.
" As your fathers did, so do ye : ye do always resist the Holy
     Ghost." Acts vii. 51.
They were in double error about the manna. First, it did not
     come from heaven, but only from the air. Second, not Moses,
     but *the Lord* who made the heavens, gave it.
Thou work. Thou dost bid us work. What work wilt Thou do
     Thyself ?
This was rude and insolent, characteristic of unbelief in every age.
Infidels of the highest genius have been coarse in the extreme,
     e.g. Voltaire, Paine, Byron, Frederick the Great, &c.
Religion, ever true to its God, follows " *whatsoever things are*
     LOVELY."

ποιεῖς. A retort to our Lord's question. *Meyer.* From those who wished
to crown Him. *Stier.* From others, strangers. *Neander.* An undertone
request for the everlasting bread. Then we will follow Thee. *Ebrard.* He
must provide fully for them as Moses did for their fathers. *Lange.* A miraculous deliverance from Rome would have brought the entire nation to His feet,
shouting Hallelujahs. *Author.* Others, " We see not the sealing you speak of."
So dull and audacious is man. *Ber. Bib.*
τί εργάζῃ. σὺ is wanting to justify this emphasis. *Brückner.* The specious
plea founded on hardness of heart. *Klenker.*
" *Thou* " not in the Greek, but emphatic. *Alford.* What dost Thou produce ? Ironically pointed at His demand that they should work, *Lange.* They
were confounded by our Lord's *novel* claims. *D. Brown.* They want a
proof of His sealing. *Alford.* The Jews desire our Lord to define His plan.
Grotius. Hesitating between better and worse, they at last sink into unbelief.
Stier.

---

31. Our fathers did eat manna in the desert ; as it is written, He gave them
bread from heaven to eat.

Our fathers. Were murmurers and stiff-necked, and perished.
     1 Cor. x. 10 ; Acts vii. 51.
Of such miserable ancestry no good man would ever boast, espe-
     cially as the *manna* was the *occasion* of their *unbelief*.
Manna. Miraculous food given to Israel for forty years. Ex. xvi.
It fell first in the desert of Sin, and continued until they ate old
     corn. Josh. v. 12.
Its taste was like that of coriander seed, mixed with honey and
     fresh olive-oil.
It fell on the dew to keep it from the dust. Exod. xvi. 13.

It seems to have resembled a large frozen drop of dew. Num. xi. 7.
It fell daily, and became rancid if kept over the Sabbath.
A remarkable proof of the Sabbath having been constituted at
    Creation.
Fifteen million pounds were required each week for their daily food.
No one market on earth ever furnished such an amount of food.
Heaven's answer to the question, "Can God spread a table in the
    wilderness ? "
The number *alleged* to have followed Xerxes could not have been
    fed even with the aid of railroads.
An omer (three quarts) was to be gathered by each man.
He who had gathered little had no lack, and he who gathered
    much had none over.   [Sabbath.
A double quantity fell on the *sixth* day, and was gathered for the
That ungathered was dissolved by the sun, and disappeared.
It was reduced to meal and dough, and baked in the oven.
We learn provident industry,—if God *gives*, we must *gather*.
Divine bounty always leaves room for man's daily duty.
Two millions might sweetly sleep in humble, grateful, adoring faith.
Though they had no bread in their tents, God will not *fail*.
It was surer and safer in God's storehouse than in their own power.
The choicest treasures may turn to "rust," and highest honours
    become "disgrace." Hos. iv. 7 ; Jas. v. 3.
That is ever the *worst wasted* which we covetously have *spared*.
Gathered before sunrise. Man must not be idle, even in Paradise.
    Gen. ii. 15.
An omer was laid up in the ark in a vessel of gold as a memorial.
The Lord will not leave the memory of so great a miracle to die
    out.
Rabbis fabled that all kinds of *precious stones* fell with the manna.
THE MANNA OF THE WILDERNESS A TYPE OF CHRIST :
1. Both miraculous in their origin,—came down from heaven.
2. Covered with dew,—word of grace, *hid* from the unrenewed.
    2 Cor. iv. 3.
3. Small to the eye,—Christ a *root* out of dry ground. Isa. liii. 2.
4. Both mysterious,—" Who shall declare His generation ? " Isa.
    liii. 8.   [xvi. 21.
5. Daily,—Christ's grace used *continually* by all believers. Ex.
" Give us this day " is founded on this repeated miracle. *J. A.
    Alexander.*
6. Gathered by man, but given by God. Human and Divine meet

in conversion, John vi. 44 ; and Divine bounty never supersedes man's industry.

7. All gathering had enough. *Sincerity of faith*, not the *degree*
avails. Exod. xvi. 18.

8. All the twelve tribes welcome to share. Christ to be had without money or price. Isa. lv. 1.

9. Offered to murmurers. Christ invites His enemies to a banquet.
" God commendeth His love to us, since Christ dieth for His *enemies*."
Rom. v. 8. [Acts iv. 12.

10. Manna for a season the *only* food. Christ the only Saviour.

11. Manna was ground. Christ was " bruised for our iniquities."
Isa. liii. 5.

12. Furnished in a wilderness. Psa. lxxviii. 19. Christ, a banquet in the world under a *curse*. Heb. vi. 8.

13. Its early gathering,— the *first* promise given our first parents.
But it failed to impart immortality, therefore unlike this Bread of
Heaven.

" If a man eat of this bread, he shall live for ever." John vi. 51.

It was confined to Jews. *This* Bread is for all the world.

Manna of *Commerce* is a gum mostly from Calabria and Sicily.

Gathered in June and July,— drops from a leaf punctured by an
insect.

Written. Two hundred and forty distinct passages are quoted
by the Lord and His apostles from the Old Testament.

Gave. All the mercies of God are *gifts*, which sinners seem to
stumble on by chance.

Heaven. John i. 51. Contrasts with the earthly bread of the
late miracle.

These men, " wise in their own conceits," knew not what they said.
Prov. xxvi. 12. [heaven.

Our Lord refers *seven* times in this chapter to His *coming from*

Their request a virtual denial of the Bread of Heaven being in
their midst.

Thus the insane man wanted proofs at noon-day that the sun shone.

Atheists deny God amid a blaze of His Divine *daily* wonders.

The daring demand made of Him was nothing less than that He
should always support them, as He had here begun.

They were of the earth, and utterly estranged from the life, power,
and love of the Messiah. " What concord hath Christ with
Belial ? " 2 Cor. vi. 15. [*selves*.

Deceived as to their *fathers*, they are willing to be deceived *them-*

554 / Gospel of John

They believed the Messiah would bring with Him banquets of
richest, rarest delicacies without measure and without end.
Freedom and empire that would put all nations under their feet.
A kind of *worldly millennium*, in which *labour, care,* and the *curse*
would cease.

μάννα. MAN HU. Heb. word the neuter interrogative pronoun. " What
is this ? " Jews considered the manna greatest of miracles. *Schöttgen.*
θεῖον καὶ παράδοξον βρῶμα. *Josephus.* A natural phenomenon miraculously increased by the power of God for a special purpose. *Lange.* Wholly
miraculous, and not in any respect a product of nature. *Smith's* Dict.
κρυστάλλου. Sept. A crystal. *Reyland.* Beryl, gold-colour or crystal.
Wahl. A resinous product of Arabia. *Aquila, Pliny.* Persian pearls.
Bochart, Gesenius. False myrrh of India. *Royle.* Produced by the Arabian
tamarisk. *Ehrenberg.* Arabs use it like honey. *Burckhardt.* It lies like meal
on the leaves in Mesopotamia. *Niebuhr.* Jews believe they will eat manna in
Eden with the Messiah. *Lightfoot.* Its taste different to each appetite. *Bechai.*
It had no moisture, but dried away. *Lewes.* Daily amount 94,466 bushels for
40 years, amounting to thirteen hundred millions of bushels. *Frey.* Jews
despised it, preferring eating meat. *Stier.*
ἐκ τοῦ οὐρανοῦ. Antithetical to the earthly bread, eaten yesterday. *Hengst.*

---

32. Then Jesus said unto them, Verily, verily, I say unto you, Moses gave
you not that bread from heaven ; but my Father giveth you the true bread from
heaven.

Said. He patiently endured the contradiction of sinners. Heb. xii. 3.
He will make their " manna " the ground of a sermon, and thus
  should pastors make the complaints of their flocks new
  themes for instruction and warning.
Verily. Solemnly repeated, partakes of the nature of an oath.
  Heb. vi. 18.
He opposes the fulness of His own dignity to their " It is written."
Moses. See on John i. 17. The Lord's miracle suggested to
  them a comparison between Him and Moses.
He answered—1. Moses did not give them the manna, but GOD.
  Psa. lxxviii. 24. 25. 2. He calmly and gently denies it to be
  THE TRUE BREAD of HEAVEN. 3. His miracles were wrought
  by His own inherent omnipotence. Moses never claimed this.
My. He claims the everlasting Jehovah as His Father, an echo of
  " My beloved Son." Matt. iii. 17.
That manna could not detain for a moment the fleeting spirit of man.
But *this* BREAD imparted immortality, like the TREE of LIFE. Gen.
  iii. 22.   [heavens.
That manna was from the air, *this* BREAD from the *real* heaven of

That nourished the body, *this* the undying soul.

The *miraculous* food left the thousands fed, after a few hours, hungry still.

Neither Moses' law nor Moses' manna imparted *living power.*

Men still experienced that " death was the wages of sin." Rom. vi. 23.   [to reveal.

Father.   He pronounces the higher name, the new name He came

It was He who gave the bread in the wilderness to their fathers.

Their idolatry of Moses proved they needed some one to bring God nearer to them.

Giveth.   The present clearly named. *Now* and *always* is the GIFT OF HEAVENLY BREAD.

" I, the SON of GOD, am able, willing, and prepared to give it."

1. It *came*—was not rained down from heaven. Psa. lxxviii. 23—25.

2. It conveyed to the recipient the *gift* of *eternal life.*

3. It was not only intended for Jews, but for *the world of Gentiles.*

Manna but the type, JESUS INCARNATE was *the* REALITY.

True.   *Genuine, veritable, essential,* as opposed to derived, borrowed, imperfect.   If any man will taste this bread he will ask for no sign.

That taste is at once the *test* and *pledge* of all heart can wish.

Bread.   Contrasted with the perishable bread of the field and miracle.

Soul, in the Old and New Testament, is that which constitutes the man.   Gen. ii. 7 ; xlix. 6.

That which nourishes it can alone deserve the name of *bread.*

He had before called Himself the " WATER," now the " BREAD of LIFE."

οὐ Μωσῆς. The question is of the *real, true* manna. *Lange.* The negation to be taken relatively, not absolutely. *Tholuck.*

τὸν ἄρτον, illum panem. *Erasmus.* Bread from the *lower,* not highest heaven—not the *true* bread. An emphatic denial of each particular. *D. Brown.* It was from heaven, but not *the* bread. *Alford.*

οὐρανοῦ. The words " from heaven" in both cases (and in verse 31) relate not to the bread, but to δέδωκεν and δίδωσιν. *Meyer.* But the nature of the bread is described with the source of it, Psa. lxxxviii. 24. *Lange.* Some think the manna a production of the earth. *Bardht.* The sap of an Arabian plant miraculously increased. *Tholuck.* What did it signify to lay it up in the ark ? *Stier.* This corn grew in heaven and was prepared by angels. *Aben Ezra, R. Bechai.* Those fed by the food of the gods by Greeks called " *Saturn's nurslings.*" *Proclus* in *Plato.*

δίδωσι, instead of δέδωκε, which is said of Moses. *Lange.* Jam aderat panis. *Bengel.* Feeding pertains to the present. *Hengst.*

33. For the bread of God is he which cometh down from heaven, and giveth life unto the world.

The Bread. This verse is best left in its own transparent grandeur. *D. Brown.*

This DIVINE, SPIRITUAL, ETERNAL BREAD is CHRIST.

He claims openly and unequivocally to be the *World's Saviour !*

All infidels denying His Divinity profess great "faith in humanity,"
    i. e. faith in *depravity, desperate depravity.* Jer. xvii. 9.

Bread of God. The manna was a significant type of Christ. Verse 31.   [GOD."

Meat, producing *immortality*, alone worthy the name " BREAD OF " Bread of the mighty," that is, from the region of angels. Psa. lxxviii. 25.

Having this, one seeks no further sign,—he has been *satisfied.*

But those Jews had never so much as even *tasted* it.

This spiritual **Bread** shadowed forth by the LAST SUPPER.

Receiving Him by faith we drink in ONE SPIRIT.

This is that ROCK which cheered the host of Israel for 40 years. Exod. xvi. 35.   [xiv. 27.

Revives every Jonathan who spiritually tastes of this honey. 1 Sam.

This is the " barley loaf" striking down the Midianitish tent of Satan. Judg. vii. 13.

The angelic morsel which sustained Elijah 40 days in the wilderness. 1 Kings xix. 6.

The " TREE OF LIFE " in the paradise of God, whose fruit is sent down to those " hungering and thirsting after RIGHTEOUSNESS"! Jer. xxiii. 6.

Is He. An inexact translation, " *Bread of God is that,*" &c.

Cometh down. First mark of the bread of God : It must come down (not fall down) from heaven.

It must be spirit life, personal life, Divine life.

Anew to every believing heart, turning from earth and sense.

All unrenewed are lying in spiritual death, fulfilling the primal curse. Gen. ii. 17.   [i. 4.

"In Him was life " is a prophetic pledge to every disciple. John

As Christ is the life-giving BREAD, so there was a death-yielding *fruit.* Gen. iii. 3.

" What *fruit* had ye in those things whereof ye are *ashamed ?* the end of those things is *death.*" Rom. vi. 21.

Sodom's apples are fair to the eye, but full of *ashes* and *death* to the taste.

World. Second mark of the bread of God: It must give life to
the world. Awaken, sustain, and renew personal life for ever.
Jewish bigotry confined all blessings to their narrow race.
They boasted in the manna as exclusively a national miracle.
Our Lord rends these claims of fanaticism and spreads out His
promises as far as the wants of a ruined world, the true
horizon of every Christian.

καταβαίνων. Belongs to ἄρτος. *Stier.* The subject of the proposition.
Gerlach, Olsh. Questioned. *Lücke.* " Myself am the bread of Heaven" lies
in the background. He never says, ἐγω καταβαίνω. *Hoffmann.* Does not
refer directly to Christ, but bread. *Hengst.* Manna to carnal-minded ones
had no element of heaven in it. Thus faithless Jews at length disdained the
quails and manna. *Author.* He speaks not of a person. *Campbell.*

τῷ κόσμῳ. Non modo uni populo, uni ætati, ut manna cibavit unum po-
pulum unius ætatis. *Bengel.*

---

34. Then said they unto him, Lord, evermore give us this bread.

Lord. A good beginning, reverential and faintly expressing faith.
It was that expression of hunger, which every fallen soul feels.
Consciously or unconsciously " the Desire of all nations " is Christ.
Hag. ii. 7.
His splendid miracles actually began to arouse a feeling of hope,
that after all there might be something in His claims.
Hence they speak with a tone of seeming earnestness, but the
petition is sensuous. [ary bread.
Evermore. Supposing He meant food somewhat better than ordin-
To be constantly supplied they say "evermore," i. e. "Give us
daily this bread."
In contrast with the abundant but transient supply by the miracle.
Resemblance to the answer to the Samaritan woman proves the
same Divine hand was on the keys of the heart.
Not till *He roused the desire* did He tell them His relation to it.
Give us. Unbelief void of the sense of *heart-want* can ask for
more signs.
Many millions of our race are conscious of wants, but ignorant of
their real *nature.*
All efforts to quiet the cravings of the soul, instead of quenching,
only make them grow.
Most certainly these petitioners did not mean spiritual supplies.
But what they did really need they cared not to know.

They had far less sincerity than the Samaritan woman, "Sir, give me
this water." [the *body*.

This bread. They are dreaming that He is offering them food for

---

δὸς ἡμῖν. Dim suspicion of the higher gift. *Lücke, Tholuck.* They
think the bread something material, separate from Christ. *De Wette, Meyer.*
Some take the prayer as irony, but not warranted. *Schaff.* Thou dost promise
great things, but dost never give us bread of heaven. *Calvin.* The Fathers
held this view. *Lampe.* Questioned. *B. Crusius.* Decidedly in earnest,
nothing of mockery. *Doddridge, Hengst.* Spoken by the ignorant rabble.
Bloomfield.

ἄρτου. Some unknown food rendering men immortal. Rev. ii. 17.

---

35. And Jesus said unto them, I am the bread of life: he that cometh to me
shall never hunger; and he that believeth on me shall never thirst.

I. This grand truth seems to defy exposition, as no added light
could make the sun more glorious : and yet the Gospels are
as full of such sayings as the skies are full of stars.

I. Transition from the indirect to the direct form of speech.

Answer to the request just made, and indication how to obtain it.

" I am the Bread, and faith is the work or means of getting it."

With the strong emphasis, opposed to manna and all other food.

I and **me** limit the following declaration, being used some thirty-
five times.

I am. Sublime saying in full harmony with all His life and words.

I am the Bread of Heaven to all that seek Me.   I offer myself at
once.

Words to be written on the heart in letters of gold. *Luther.*

Bread. Amongst all nations the symbol of the universal sustainer
of life.

Life. 1. Indicates He *is*.   2. He giveth *life* to all who have it.
3. He giveth life that is worth the name—*Well-living.*

Christ the Bread of Life—1. In His Person and history. 2. In His
" flesh and blood," or His giving Himself a sacrifice.   3. In
believing participation in and communion with Him.

Joys of the Messianic kingdom shadowed forth by a feast.   Isa.
xxv. 6.   [of fat things."

" In this mountain shall the Lord of Hosts make to all people a feast

An invitation of the Father, Son, and Holy Spirit to a starving race.

This food alone can satisfy the hunger and thirst of the soul.   Isa.
xlix. 10.

Cometh to Me. To obtain what the soul craves as the only source
of joy.
If coming on their feet is meant, they had done it already.
If acknowledging Him as a prophet was coming, they had done it.
Their hunger, instead of being satisfied, is only intensified.
How the crowd pressed around Him, yet never " came unto Him."
    Luke viii. 45.   [unto Me."
" Here is this bread before you, and all you have to do is to come
" But you must first recognize that I am *personally* this ' BREAD
    OF LIFE ! ' "
Those who come not starve in sight of a celestial banquet.
" *Behold,* ye *despisers, wonder* and *perish.*" Acts xiii. 41 ; Hab. i. 5.
To Me. We must know and believe in a physician's skill before
    we go to him.
Pre-eminently it is reliance on the ATONEMENT as *the* WAY of peace,
    and implicit submission to His AUTHORITY as a TEACHER.
" Coming to Christ," " Receiving Christ," " Looking to Christ,"
    " Fleeing to Christ," " Laying hold on Christ," " Eating His
    flesh," express different states of the human mind seeking
    soul food and life.
Believing in Christ precedes coming to Him. This last is the
    fruit.   [Heb. xi. 6.
" He that cometh to God must believe (first) that He is," &c.
Hunger. This soul craving indicates the greatness and misery
    of man.   [can satisfy him.
Made *for* God, he is wretched separated *from* God. God alone
This explains all the strange discords and contradictions in man.
Bread of earth, however plentifully or frequently eaten, leaves the
    soul hungry still.
But once partake of THIS BREAD, and its Divine power, ever im-
    parting strength, will prove a life-long feast, and an immor-
    tal source of strength.   [full, for ever.
From this banquet the soul will never retire, but feel at home, and
From his own heart, or rather Christ in his heart, his supply
    abounds.
Among many wonders in eternity, *man's way* of supplying a
    hungry soul will be among the strangest.
Believeth. John i. 7. Vital distinction between believing Christ
    and believing *in* Christ.
The former is simply an intellectual assent to an historical fact,
    and may be ascribed to demons.

The latter implies vital union with Him ; a work of Divine grace,
and the highest work of man.

Lazarus among the dogs *within* had a *feast* kings might envy.

Thirst. One of the most painful sensations to which the human
body is liable. It soon produces fever, delirium, and death.

Thirst of the soul much more distressing than thirst of the body.

Pleasure-seekers have often testified to the intensity of this thirst
by their wretchedness : " Vanity of vanities, all is vanity ! "

Manna allayed hunger of Israelites, but excited thirst. Ex. xvii. 3.

As faith is the ground and sole condition, Christ becomes " all in
all." Col. iii. 11.

As faith is developed, it brings not only the impartation and sustenance of spiritual life, but deepest spiritual satisfaction.

As our Lord teaches His essential *unity* with the Father (Chap. v.).
Here He teaches His proper *Divinity*.

" I AM THE BREAD OF LIFE." " Whoso eateth My flesh hath
ETERNAL LIFE."

Great words, which would be impious and even blasphemous from
any one but God Himself.

He taught the same great doctrine to the Samaritan woman, and
in the streets of Jerusalem.

δὲ omitted. *Tisch., Alf., Tregelles.*

ὁ ἐρχόμενος. Same as believing, although strictly the effect of faith. *Calvin.*

διψήσῃ. Reference to the converse with the woman. *Braune.* Bread
and wine of the sacrament. *Stier.* Not to prove the divinity of His doctrine,
but Divine commission. *Rosenm.*

πώποτε graciously responds to their πάντοτε. *Stier.*

---

36. But I said unto you, That ye also have seen me, and believe not.

Seen Me. ME, the personal Christ. A MIRACLE a thousandfold
greater than manna.

But the present God seen nightly in the desert in pillar of fire
was a far greater miracle than manna.

Yet thousands gazed at it, wondered at it, admired it, and yet
perished as murmuring rebels.

Many stood by and saw dead Lazarus revive, and yet believed not.

Seen Me. Not His bodily presence merely, but the Majesty of
HIS LIFE, HIS TEACHING, HIS WORK.

The spiritual glory of such a Being outshone all miracles.

This *seeing* Him as a Divine Teacher, Physician, Redeemer, alone
avails.
Scribes and Pharisees *saw* Him, yet remained such still.
Caiaphas saw Him and rent his clothes, yet remained a scoffer
still.
Judas saw Him in daily private life for three years, and yet
hardened into *the* traitor
Believe not. John i. 7 ; vii. 38. Their knowledge had not
pierced the miracle of His Person.
So near were they to salvation, but lacked *faith.* Heb. iv. 1, 2, 11.

ἀλλ' εἶπον. But I wish to tell you. *Meyer.* Rather He refers to some
expressions in the present conversation. *Hengst.* Something said, but not recorded. John x. 26 ; xii. 34. *Euthymius, Alford, Lampe.* I have told you
(reprovingly) often times of this. *Bloomfield.* Allusion to verses 26—29. *Stier.*
Related to John v. 37, 38. *Lücke.* Ye have *both* seen me, &c. *Bourgon.*
Other occasions prove your unbelief. *Kuinoel.*

---

37. All that the Father giveth me shall come to me ; and him that cometh
to me I will in no wise cast out.

All. *Neuter.* The strongest expression of totality, as in chap. iii. 6.
The Father hath given to the Son, as it were, the *whole* man.
A singular word in Greek, embracing all in our or in other worlds.
A remote hint, perhaps, at the mysterious relations the Incarna-
tion may bear to the universe.   [tion.
Each He receives as a gift, an earnest of the reward of His humilia-
Those who have *faith,* the distinctive characteristic of God's people.
Prophetic of call of Gentiles ; unbelief, and consequent rejection
of Jews implied.
Father giveth. The same as whom the Father *draws.* Verse 44.
In man's salvation, as in all His other works, God will ever be
sovereign.   [Father.
All attraction toward Christ presupposes the operation of the
This Divine attraction or drawing is resisted by the unbeliever.
But our Lord consoles Himself with the fact that some will come
to Him. John xvii. 6.   [come."
Shall come. He does not say *do* come, or *may* come, but " *shall*
Each one given " *shall* come," though not by compulsion. " Thy
 · people shall be willing." Psa. cx. 3.
Not driven, but led ; not dragged, but " drawn by cords of a man."
Hos. xi. 4 ; Jer. xxxi. 3.
Seeing and *feeling* their depravity, misery, and danger, they come.

Each congregation seems like the Athenians before Paul. Acts xvii. 32, 34.

1. Some, daring and defiant in their guilt and shame, " mocked."
2. Some procrastinated. " We will hear thee again of this matter."
3. Some believed. " Certain clave unto him, as Dionysius and Damaris."

Coming to Christ the infallible evidence the Father hath given us.
Any other view of election is perversion of Scripture to personal ruin.

Jesus invites all who are weary and heavy laden to come unto Him.
It is with this free and loving invitation all seekers after the Saviour have to do.

None condemned because not elected. " Ye will not come unto me that ye might have life." John v. 40.

" In the wounds of Christ alone is predestination found and understood." *Luther.*

God having an eternal PLAN for such a sacrifice, will see to the rest.

Our Saviour taught subjection to a Divinely holy and benevolent SOVEREIGN.

" I thank thee, Father, Lord of heaven and earth, for so it seemed good in Thy sight." Matt. xi. 25, 26.

Him that cometh. Every one who *comes* to Him is *welcome.*

Only criterion coming or not coming ; no matter what previous guilt. [fulfil.

Coming bespeaks the Father's will which it is Christ's office to

Though some will not come, the promise is to *all.*

We have not to do with God's *purpose*, but with our *duty* to believe the promise.

If we only obey Him in time we may TRUST we were elected from eternity. *Beveridge.* [25.

The gates of the golden city are not shut day or night. Rev. xxi.

They face the four cardinal points,—symbol of universality. Rev. xxi. 13.

This doctrine has ever been a mighty spur to obedience. *Augustine.*

Master of the house will never rise to *shut the door* until the Spirit is finally grieved. Luke xiii. 25. [hand ?

Cometh. What creature could hold the hearts of all men in his

None but God certain that any, still more *all would* come.

His invitations are addressed to a " stiff-necked people."

Yet His eye pierces the future, and His heart is cheered with the salvation of the elect. Isa. xlix. 3, 6.

I will. This majestic " I " sweeps Eternity in its embrace and
promise.

I, the INFINITE, ETERNAL, UNCHANGEABLE JEHOVAH JESUS!

Shows that the will of the Son is identical with the will of the
FATHER.

The wicked fear Him as an angry judge with scourge and chain.

But He is a true Shepherd, a kind Teacher, an unfailing Friend.

No wise cast out. There is a stronger meaning than the words
literally convey.

Signifies not merely a first reception, but a lasting preservation.

Through all changes to the resurrection, the goal of all previous to it.

Expresses in a negative form more strongly Christ's readiness to
receive with open arms of love every one who comes to Him.

In no wise. For no reason or account that man or angel can
show.

Thus speaks the Maker, Redeemer, and Judge of all.   [open.

The faithful and true Witness, to whom all things are naked and

Greek words express a *double exclusion,* " No, I WILL NOT."

Unspeakable consolation : Proof of His Eternal Power and Godhead!

The *figure* represents an humble suppliant at the door of a palace,
who casts himself at the feet of the Prince, imploring protection.

The Lord bids him fear not,—His house and heart are large enough.

His arm is strong enough to receive and defend all who come.

What millions of aching hearts have found peace in this promise.

None will be refused, not even Pharisees, whose unbelief was then
saddening His heart.

For this word myriads now in glory have praised Redeeming Love.

They urged it with broken hearts, because of broken vows.

Burdened with guilt, pleading the greater burden of Infinite grace.

With their altar fires gone out, but love burning from the Cross.

With feeble step, bringing nothing but sin, nothing but a corrupt,
treacherous, backsliding heart!

Jesus receives such sinners, because the Father gives such to Him.

Amidst the fiercest assaults of tempting fiends *Bunyan* writes,
" Oh ! what did I see in that blessed sixth of John, verse 37,
' Him that,' &c.   Many a pull hath my heart had with Satan
for that blessed sixth of John."

" A *word,* a *word* to lean a weary soul upon, that it might not sink
for ever." *Sibbes.*

564 / Gospel of John

πᾶν. Neuter refers significantly back to κοσμος. Verse 33. *Stier.* All the elect. *Trapp.* An organic whole. "All that which" singular, "All who come" masculine plural. *Bengel.* The whole body of believers referred to John xvii. Here the whole mass of men (coming) to Christ. *Alford.* The whole as a unity which our Lord *evolves. D. Brown.*

δίδωσί. All whom the Father can give. Verse 44. *Stier.* The result, not procuring cause. *Watson.* Decretive act. *Hengst.* Father giveth to the well-disposed. *Euthymius, Grotius.* Refers to regeneration. *Calvin.* Not Divine purpose, but its execution. *J. Brown.* There will not want fruit of my labours, souls will be given me. *Kuinoel.* God gives faith to believers. Phil. iii. 13. *Olshausen.* Given as διδακτοὶ Θεοῦ, verse 45, metaphor from teaching children. *Hammond.* He draws the impenitent, but believers EFFECTU-ALLY. *Lampe.*

ἥξει. Must learn of Me as his Teacher. *Rosenm.* Our Lord never reveals His deepest mysteries to the public, but only to the inner band. *Bloomfield.*

ἐρχόμενον. Ever so creepingly. *Ber. Bib.* However long they may neglect coming, but when they do come He will not object. *Schlier.* How should I reject any one when this was my errand to earth? *Pfenninger.* It is not in me to reject any. *Richter.* Election a powerful motive to holiness. *Augustine, Beveridge.*

ἐκβάλω. Reference to the exclusion of others. *Tholuck, Lücke.* 1. To receiving. 2. Having received, never abandon. *J. Brown.* Figure from Matt. viii. 12, an enclosed community. *Olsh.* More than expressed. I will welcome them. *Bengel.*

ἔξω. A strong word. Greek, "I will not cast *out, out.*" *Trapp.* In John's style, apparently inaccurate, is a substratum of eloquence in itself Divine. *Bengel.*

---

38. For I came down from heaven, not to do mine own will, but the will of him that sent me.

I came. How could I cast out the penitent, since I am come only to do God's will in mercy?

From heaven. Special authority for the belief in His Divinity.

Thence originates an infallible proof of the inspiration of *the* gospel.

My own will. As a man He did His Father's will.

As God, His will is eternally *at one* with that of the Father's.

We have in Christ the only perfect instance of a will lost in God's.
Luke xii. 47.   [is powerless.

Knowledge of God's will merely avails not; like the winter's sun, it

Evidence of being one in will with God is the *doing* of God's will.

We judge not one's health by flush of face, but by beat of pulse.

A bitter persecutor writes, "Obedience of Christians to their Master makes their religion flourish." *Julian* to Arsatius.

Those refusing to obey His will cannot for an instant hinder its accomplishment. 1 Cor. x. 22.

Danger of opposing God's will,—Christ will come in flaming fire.
2 Thess. i. 7, 8.   [bark.

High honour to do God's will,—soldiers *proudly* rowed Cæsar's

Because it is God's will. Against flesh and blood Abraham obeyed
on Moriah. [willing mind."

Done freely. "And thou, Solomon, my son, serve God with a
Angels serve Him cheerfully, hence their harps are *in their hands.*
Rev. xv. 2. [xxvi. 39.

Some may do God's will in *tears ;* so did our suffering Lord. Matt.
Job in tears, and with rent mantle, bow*è*d to God under heavy
tidings.

His will is to be done *at any cost.* David's reproach broke his
heart. Psa. lxix. 20. [rebellion."

Elijah was called a "troubler of Israel," Luther a "trumpeter of
His will is just. "Shall not the Judge of all the earth do right ? "
Gen. xviii. 25.

" Smite, O Lord, where and when thou wilt, for my sins are
pardoned." *Luther.*

$\kappa \alpha \tau \alpha \beta \dot{\epsilon} \beta \eta \kappa \alpha$. They understood by this some mysterious or supernatural
origin of His humanity. *Stier.* He teaches clearly His miraculous conception.
Nitzch. Divine origin of His person, and celestial source of His doctrine.
Wetstein. His supreme and eternal Godhead. *Author.*

$\theta \dot{\epsilon} \lambda \eta \mu \alpha \tau o \tilde{v} \pi \dot{\epsilon} \mu \psi \alpha \nu \tau \delta s$. To Jews trying to erect a wall of separation be-
tween Him and the Father. *Stier.* An issue of the personal union with the
Father. *Bengel.* The doing God's will, as our will, a kind of idolatry.
Liguori.

---

39. And this is the Father's will which hath sent me, that of all which he
hath given me I should lose nothing, but should raise it up again at the last
day.

Will. With reference to the completion of the Divine purpose of
salvation.

God keeps His own counsel, except as found in the Scriptures.

All given. 1. In the Father's purpose. 2. Redeemed by His
blood. 3. Called by His Spirit. 4. Justified by His righteousness. 5. Sanctified by His grace. 6. Preserved by almighty
love unto eternal life. [from us here.

The two ends of this golden chain, election and glory, are hidden

That which we are concerned to know is that we come to Jesus
the Saviour.

We should pray as if all depended upon God, and watch and work
as if all depended upon ourselves.

Lose nothing. Our Lord pledges here His tenderest care and
solicitude.

566 / Gospel of John

The exquisite *pathos* of the *Greek* can scarcely be transferred.
Not only not a single saint, but nothing belonging to the saints.
Even their mouldering dust is guarded until the resurrection.
1 Thess. iv. 14.

Raise it up. Resurrection. See on John ii. 22 ; v. 29. This
world 's a vast Golgotha.

Resurrection alluded to often, since our Lord was to die and rise
again. [vii. 22.

Christ, under the arrest of death, was our glorious SURETY. Heb.

Having paid the debt, He was released from the grave.

Those who have wept tears of repentance shall " have all tears
wiped away." Rev. xxi. 4.

Those whose hands were lifted in trembling prayer shall hold
" palms " and " harps." Rev. vii. 9 ; xiv. 2.

Those whose feet were wearied in holy service shall " stand in the
presence of Jehovah." Rev. xiv. 1, 3.

If "gorgeous robes are worn in kings' palaces," what glittering
raiment shall they wear in the presence-chamber of the
eternal God ? Dan. x. 5, 6. [procured.

Resurrection not the whole, but the *completion* of the salvation Christ

After this aim of eternal mercy is accomplished, there can be no
more peril.

θέλημα. Is conditioned by faith, distinctive test of faith lies in the true
hearing. *Stier.*

πατρὸς. Omitted. *Cod. Sin., Tisch., Alf., Treg., Lach.*

πᾶν. Too deep for the mind to fathom. Neuter seems to include all
humanity, and all sharing man's destiny. *Maurice.*

ὅ δέδωκέ. Heathen can be saved as easily and freely. *Markland.*

ἀπολέσω. None perish *per me*, but quantum me, should live. *Kuinoel.*
None perish through my fault. *Euthymius.*

ἀναστήσω. Not only raise them up, but as saved without diminution.
Klenker. Present them fully in the glory of the resurrection. *Lücke.*
Resurrection presupposes death. *Hengst., Meyer.* All that are raised to be
given the Son. *Schlier.* You will all finally come to Me, for the Father hath
given Me all. *Müller.* Verse 37 is limited by their coming. *Stier.* Believers'
life always tainted with death, until risen from the dead. *Calvin.*

ἐσχάτῃ ἡμέρᾳ. New Messianic era. *B. Crusius.* The last day of each
believer. *Reuss.* He hints Himself to be the Restorer of the *entire man. Olsh.*
Glorified corporeity of the Resurrection as the goal of each believer. *Stier.*
From Christ's flesh our raised bodies receive their life. *Hooker.*

---

40. And this is the will of him that sent me, that every one which seeth the
Son, and believeth on him, may have everlasting life : and I will raise him up
at the last day.

Will of Him. Far back in eternity this WILL was ever unfolding God's thoughts.

As a vast *stream* it flowed on, bearing suns, systems, universes,
with their teeming myriads, and will unfold the Divine mind
for ever.

Nothing can, nothing has, nothing ever will be able to arrest it.

Seeth. Gr. " *beholding*," refers to a particular object, is *more* than
seeing.

Addressed to all who witnessed Christ's stupendous miracles.

To each one enlightened by the WORD, as He came into the world.

To each ignorant peasant, to each dweller in alley and lane.

To each one vainly tempted by wealth, philosophy, pleasure, superstition, hypocrisy, to satisfy their hunger of soul.

The Son. A stronger declaration of God's will in its final purpose.

Hebrews looked on the brazen serpent with *eyes of the soul.*

Nought else in the universe beside can afford hope to the sinner.

But these Jews could not rise to the grandeur of His *Nature.*

All the wisdom and glory of our earth must be laid at the feet of
Christ as their SOURCE.

Many speak of Him as the " all and in all," yet believe not to
salvation.

How many, like these Jews with *open eyes*, perish *blind.* Acts xiii. 41.

Hungering and thirsting in the presence of the " Bread of heaven,"
yet " *starve.*"

A wonderful fact in heathendom, that not a sage or philosopher
ever suspected the true *cause* of man's *misery.* Supposed to
spring from disease, or fate, or blind chance, anything but
depraved hearts.

Seneca, on the height of human wisdom, dying, said, " I am neither
sick nor well."   [Rev. v. 6.

This *seeing* the Son on earth is a pledge of the vision of John in

Believeth. John i. 7 ; vii. 38. Greek and Roman sages attributed all love to beauty.

But our Lord, infinitely *lovely* in Himself, is repelled and hated by
some of the most cultured minds.

If believing in Christ be the only door of heaven, whither must
those go who do not believe ?

DIVINE *side* of *man's salvation.* Verses 37, 39, " All that the
Father giveth Me shall come to Me. Of all that He hath
given Me I should lose nothing."

HUMAN *side* of *salvation.* Verses 37, 40, " Him that cometh to

Me I will in no wise cast out. Every one that seeth the Son,
and believeth on Him, may have everlasting life."
No human system of theology perfect. Pendulum like, they swung
past the Divine centre of truth.

Everlasting life. Makes the resurrection infinitely desirable.
This hope has its foretaste this side the grave, and gives life all
its charms. [1 Cor. xv. 19.
" Those having hope in this life only are of all men *most miserable.*"
In chap. iv. we have the refreshing of the soul by the "water of life."
Here the body, despite death itself, is a partaker of the "bread of life."

Raise them. See on John ii. 22 ; v. 29. In defiance of the great
" murderer," and fears of the grave. John viii. 44.
For our strong consolation against the last enemy, the Lord repeats
these words four times in this chapter, with the clear note of
triumph.

γὰρ. Instead of δέ. *Lach., Tisch., Alf., Cod. Sin.* The Lord's discourse
might here close, but He is forced to continue it. *Stier.*
For πέμψαντός με read τοῦ πατρός μου. *Cod. Sin., Lach., Tisch., Alf.,
Treg.*
θεωρῶν. The precondition of faith : faith not the necessary result of seeing.
Hengst.
ἀναστήσω. The future WILL of THE LORD is *emphatic.* The "coming ones"
of the second clause are the "given ones" of the first. He speaks with sublime certainty. *D. Brown.* In Christ's glorified body we have pledge of glory
of saints hereafter. *Stier.*

---

41. The Jews then murmured at him, because he said, I am the bread which
came down from heaven.

Jews. See on John i. 19. Here doubtless the rulers of Capernaum
synagogue.

Murmured. Perhaps not audibly to Him, but He heard their
hearts and answered.
Murmured because He called Himself the Bread of Life, but especi-
ally because He claimed to have descended from heaven.
To listen to cavils is to regard Satan more than the Redeemer.
When supplies fail, our faith, alas ! is soon gone too. *Luther.*
They now first perceive He means a *spiritual* Messiah.
Their wish was for Him to raise armies, fight battles, win victories,
take cities, drive out the Romans, erect the throne of David,
and restore the kingdom to Israel.
Such bread, although heavenly, as a poor despised Galilean could
bring they did not want.

Our Lord claims to be the Bread from heaven, on the ground of sharing personally in the DIVINE GLORY!

His claims to be a heaven-sent Prophet they might have tolerated on account of His works.

But His claims to be VERY GOD, ETERNAL, ALMIGHTY, OMNISCIENT, they resented as blasphemy.

They thought Him the son of Joseph, of earthly origin.

Because. This declaration transcending their idea of the Messiah, they rejected it.

Especially were they offended at the thought of a suffering or self-sacrificing Messiah.

Reason and faith are like the eye and the telescope. *Locke.*

Where the former fails the latter comes in and opens up glories of eternal truth.

Faith rises far above reason, "evidence of things not seen," but never contradicts the testimony of the lower faculty.

Putting reason against revelation is the result either of pride or ignorance.

Reason finds its true strength and glory in yielding unqualified submission to the word of God.

The profoundest thinkers the world has ever seen have loved to sit at Jesus' feet.

Not knowledge, but ignorance; not thought, but presumption, makes men infidels.

Plotinus the philosophic heathen said, "A good man differs from God only in age."

So these Jews, like many so-called "liberals," thought themselves as wise as the Lord.

He said. He had not used these very words, but His hearers rightly connected verses 35 and 33.

Came down, &c. By this the Jews understood He claimed supreme *Divinity.*

He refers not to His doctrine so much as to His own person.

Not His miraculous conception, but His personal pre-existence.

Who of the prophets ever dared claim that "he came down from heaven?"

ἐγόγγυξον. According to Greek usage a murmuring of disdain. *Tholuck.* Murmuring here is the expression of fault-finding. *Lange.* To "whisper." John vii. 32. Everywhere else in New Testament "murmur." *Hengot.* Because reason is silenced, scoffers persist in their infidelity. *Trapp.*

'Ιουδαῖοι. A portion had left the multitude. A Pharisaic party. *Lange.* Synonymous in John with the enemies of Christ. *Stier.*

περὶ αὐτοῦ. Masculine. *Bengel, D. Wette, Lampe.* They murmured *concerning Him. Ber. Bib.*

---

42. And they said, Is not this Jesus, the son of Joseph, whose father and mother we know? how is it then that he saith, I came down from heaven?

Is not this Jesus? The pronoun " this " is strongly demonstrative. The same person, of whom we know that He sprang from Nazareth. This is the person who pretends to have come down from heaven! The old and ever new offence at Christ :—1. Because He is of Nazareth He cannot be from heaven. 2. Because He is Son of man He cannot be Son of God.

Joseph. The son of Jacob, his lineage traced through David to Abraham. Matt. i. [Luke iii.

According to Luke son of Heli, and his lineage traced to Adam.

Last Evangelist uses word " supposed," i. e. so accounted in law, enrolled.

Matthew is believed to give Joseph's, Luke to give Mary's, lineage.

The two lines descended from *Solomon* and *Nathan,* David's sons.

They *unite in Salathiel,* and again *in Christ.*

Mary the blood-descendant, Joseph the legal descendant, of David.

Thus our Lord was heir to David's throne both by *law* and *blood.* Acts ii. 30.

Joseph was by trade a carpenter (word may mean artificer of any kind). Matt. xiii. 55 ; Mark vi. 3. [youth.

Even the chief citizens in Jerusalem were taught some trade in

Joseph dwelt in Nazareth and went with Mary to Bethlehem to be enrolled. [Egypt.

Joseph, warned by an angel, took his wife and Jesus and fled into

He took Jesus at twelve years of age to the temple during pass-- over, and he returned to Nazareth the reputed father of Jesus.

He acted as guardian for Mary during the childhood of Jesus, and that being ended, he is dismissed from our view.

We know. These people think they know Him because they know His parents. [father.

They think they know His origin because they know His reputed

They think they know His mother because they know her poverty and lowliness.

A picture of the world's condemnation of itself in its sundering of the Divine and human natures in Christ.

The drawing of partisan spirit a drawing of the earth, and against the drawing of the Father from heaven.

How is it? Wretched men dare reprehend what they can't comprehend.

What possible relish for such spiritual sublimities could such men have!

They certainly knew not the mystery of His Divine Incarnation.

And if they had, He was not the kind of a Messiah they wanted.

Heaven. John i. 51. Scribes talked learnedly about the heavens, but knew nothing.

Our Lord revealed it as the HOME of the pure, humble, holy children of God.

The Scriptures do not cheat us with words wanting realities.

They do not, like men, give us stones when we ask for bread.

οὗτός. This fellow. Greeks always used it contemptuously, like "iste." A name of a character. *Bentley.*

οἴδαμεν. Hints Joseph to be yet alive. *Meyer.* Not necessarily confined to personal knowledge. *Alford.* Implies that the Jews considered both (whom they once *knew*) to be His parents. *Lange.* For οὖν read νῦν. *Tisch., Alf., Treg.*

---

43. Jesus therefore answered and said unto them, Murmur not among yourselves.

Answered. Not their question. The mystery of the Incarnation must not yet be unfolded.

All their debates brought them no nearer heaven or preparation for it. [ways.

Murmur. The traitorous heart ever repines at God's words and Israel habitually murmured in the wilderness. Typical of all murmurers. [verse 37.

Their murmuring proved that they had not come to Jesus. See

Those holding their views of the Lord's person never have come to Him for salvation.

Deniers of His Divinity neither believe in the guilt of sin nor in the need of atonement.

"Liberals" denying these great doctrines, whatever their profession, unchristianize themselves.

οὖν omitted. *Tisch., Alf., Tregelles.*

44. No man can come to me, except the Father which hath sent me draw him : and I will raise him up at the last day.

No man can come. Greek, "*reach* ME," in particular : reach an understanding of MY nature.

Apprehend the Spirit in the flesh, Deity in humanity, the Son of God in the Son of man.

Our Lord plainly asserts men are under a moral incapacity, which Divine grace alone can remove.

He places their salvation in the *sovereignty* of God the Father.

Yet one who has squandered his means will find his "*cannot*" no excuse, but an aggravation of his inability to pay his debt.

Like the prodigal, man has wasted his powers, and now *will* not, and therefore *cannot* come. Those in verse 35 are drawn by the Spirit. Deut. xxix. 4.

Our Lord's Divinity comes out here in its uncreated radiance.

To come to the *Fountain* of LIFE and find LIFE is the work of works.

But if Christ be not God, why come to Him any more than to Moses or the prophets ?

How could we be sure He *knew* when we did come, or would *hear* when we cry, or could *aid* when we needed Almighty grace ?

If a mere creature, what a heartless mockery were such a promise, and what blasphemy such a claim in any but Jehovah !

Jews had no cause of murmuring, since God ever gives a right heart to those who ask it.

Hath sent me. As the Father *sends* the Redeemer, so He *leads* believers.

Draw. A beautiful term, denoting the secret work of Divine love in the heart.

Persons can be drawn only according to the laws of personal life.

Man is like a piece of metal, lost amid the rubbish of a world.

A *magnet* is presented, and by an invisible, but powerful attraction, draws that lost piece forth to light.

That any one, under the power of evil habit and love of the world, should apart from the Almighty Spirit change and love the Saviour, is *against all experience.*

Although this scheme is with Divine skill adapted to the soul, yet it is too spiritual for a carnal heart, too humbling for a proud one, too holy for the willing slave of Satan, too heavenly for the earthly-minded.

How can the moralist believe one sin counterbalances all his virtue ?

How can the spiritually *blind* see the beauty of the Holy and Just One ?

We know absolutely nothing of the way the mind acts on the body. How, then, can we know the way "God worketh in us both to will and to do ? " Phil. ii. 13.

The method is inscrutably hid from the human understanding.

The chains of habit are so strong, fetters of sin so binding, that rhetoric, however persuasive, cannot release the soul.

Logic, however powerful, cannot unbind the bonds of evil.

No angel could persuade an unrenewed heart to repent.

A low voice within the door is heard better than one shouting without.   1 Kings xix. 13.

Grace is irresistible, and yet no one ever came *unwillingly*.

> " 'Twas the same Love that spread the feast
> That sweetly *forced* me in." *Watts.*

The Father " drawing " denotes the efficacy of Divine Grace working strongly.   [sweetly.

The man " coming " denotes the efficacy of Divine Grace working

Our Lord's voice called Zacchæus, but the " drawing " was of the Father.

The young ruler went away sad,—the Father did *not* draw him.

1. The sinner's inability is the doctrine of the Bible.   Eph. ii. 1.

Man never begins with God, God must always begin with man.

2. This doctrine underlies all evangelical confessions of faith.

3. It is the doctrine of all eminently holy persons whose witness is recorded.

The responsibility of man is still as complete as Adam's in Paradise.

The offer of salvation must be made without *limit*, as it is God's work to " draw," and ours to press the offer.

The absolutely essential proof of being " drawn " by God is faith in Christ and love.

This drawing is through means.   God will honour the word and ordinances.

Seeking other evidence that we are " drawn " is trifling with God's promises.

" IF YE LOVE ME, KEEP MY COMMANDMENTS."   John xiv. 15.

Men may doubt their love, but no one ordinarily can doubt when he " keeps God's commandments."   See on John vii. 17.

One may doubt his own perfect honesty, but he cannot mistake the sincere, unalterable desire and resolve to live honest.

Men may neglect this " drawing." We may feel it to-day, but to-
morrow it may be weaker, and the day after we may feel it
no more. Heb. iv. 7. [proving.

" He that hath to him shall be given." God adds to those im-
Obstinate resistance cannot long go on, for God leaves him alone.

King Agrippa was once drawn, but resisting, he was left. Acts
xxvi. 28.

Divine love is powerful, Divine wrath is irresistible. *Luther.*

Infinite grace draws the broken-hearted to the mercy-seat.

Infinite justice draws the felon from his cell to the gallows.

These and a thousand other mysteries await the light of the upper
world.

" Secret things belong to the Lord our God, but things revealed to
us and to our children." Deut. xxix. 29.

See, 1. The plainness of God's oracles. 2. The reasonableness of
their doctrine. 3. The justice of their precepts. 4. The simplicity of their ordinances. 5. The abundance of their truthfulness. 6. The kindness of their spirit. 7. Their universal
usefulness.

Heaven must be filled with wonder that the entire race do not rush
into the kingdom.

If we perish it is our own *choice*, if saved it is *alone* God's grace.

We cannot compel the winds to blow, neither can we compel the
Spirit's drawings. See on John iii. 8. [Jas. i. 5.

" But we can ask wisdom of God, who giveth to all liberally."

We know there is a treasury infinite and inexhaustible, and He who
owns it said, " ASK, AND YE SHALL RECEIVE." Luke xi. 9.

No change of mental organization, no new faculty is required, but
a radical change of heart and will.

Men do not believe against their will, but being unwilling, are
made willing. *Augustine.* [Isa. xlix. 4.

Our Lord thus cheers His aching heart, amid the scorn of men.

The Father's designs of mercy will secure the fruits of all His toil.
Isa. liii. 11.

δύναται. Adam's will was created *free*, but at the fall it was paralyzed,
hence the bondage of the will. *Luther.* Freedom of the will held. *Pelagius.*
Jer. Taylor, Erasmus, Whitby, Limborch, Hamilton, &c. Bondage of will.
Augustine, Luther, Howe, Leighton, Beza, Calvin, Edwards, Pascal, &c.
Four kinds of grace : 1. Gratia præveniens. 2. Gratia operans. 3. Gratia
co-operans. 4. Gratia irresistibilis. *Augustine.* Evil created by the devil.
Julian of *Eclanum.* Evil created by an evil Being. *Manichæans.* Infants

need salvation, on account of an evil bias. *Augustine.* Saved by Christ's righteousness imputed. Rom. v. 12. *Calvin.*

ἑλκύσῃ. Mode of the διδόναι, an internal pressing and leading to Christ by the operation of Divine grace, though not impairing human freedom. *Meyer.* Ex nolentibus volentes facit. *Trapp.* As a teacher leads a pupil. *Meyer.* By the *law* through the Spirit. *Ebrard.* Not necessity but pleasure. Green pasture shown the sheep attracts them. *Augustine.* Influence used by a Divine Teacher. *Lampe.* Any tinge of predestination questioned. *Stier.* Drawing connected with subjective conditions, such as realizing one's misery, and stretching out the beseeching hand. *Hengst.* New understanding, a new perception, are requisite. *Calvin.* The individual will must be turned to Christ by the Father. *Alford.* It involves our *willingness*, but that is the result of Divine agency. *Doddridge.* No one would desire to come unless led by the Spirit. *Beza*, and all *Calvinists.* To human arguments the soul replies, " Non persuadebis, etiam si persuaseris." *Leighton.* A magnet finds nothing in *wood* or *leaves*, but only in metal, something to draw. *Theophylact.* A figurative vital constraint, subduing by the bias of want, of desire, of hope, of mind. *Lange.*

---

45. It is written in the prophets, And they shall be all taught of God. Every man therefore that hath heard, and hath learned of the Father, cometh unto me.

Prophets. See on John i. 21, 45 ; iv. 19. Our Lord lived, laboured, and died with the WORD on His lips.

All. " And all thy children shall be taught of the Lord." Isa. liv. 13.

Taught. To be taught one must *hear* and *learn* as the condition, and be willing to follow " the old paths " which were trodden by the patriarchs, apostles, and martyrs.

Well taught are those scholars having Christ as their great Teacher.

As one must first be a believer to become a true disciple of God, so must one be first taught of God to become a believer.

Hearing, learning of the Father, and coming, are intimately joined together.

Christ's word is our *lesson*, the Holy Spirit is our *Master*, and we are taught not only by external *revelation*, but internal *illumination.*

Hence the necessity of prayer which the impenitent sinner refuses. " Who is the Lord, that I should obey His voice ? " Ex. v. 2.

Proud man feels it beneath him to bend the knee, and ask teaching from God.

An infidel senator 50 years of age boasted " his knee had never yet bowed to his Maker," but his death-bed was a sad commentary on his impiety.

Of God. Taught *by* God ; the genitive with the participle denoting the agent.

Promises of universal illumination in the time of the Messiah.

Point in the passage quoted lies in the "**all**" in contrast with the isolated enlightenment under the Old Test.

Learned. Paul obeyed the moment he felt the drawing. Gal. i. 16.

Believers' whole life a continued experience of this Divine drawing.

There are some states of mind more than others favourable to repentance.

They who frequent the place of *worship* rather than the *theatre*.

They who daily kneel in *prayer* rather than spend time in *cards*.

They who daily peruse the *Scriptures* rather than devote themselves to *novels*.

All by nature are ignorant. No *human* teaching can remove it.

Perverse resistance of men to God's truth light and love distinctly foretold. "To the Jews a stumbling-block," &c. 1 Cor. i. 23, 24.

Father. The beginning the Father draweth, the progress he who is drawn hears, the end he **cometh** to Christ.

The reference is of course to the whole discipline of the Father.

Unto Me. As soon as a person has *learned* as one *taught* of God, he comes to Christ.

Dreams, visions, raptures, ecstasies, voices, may be the work of Satan transforming himself " into an angel of light."

But to COME TO CHRIST is evidence unmistakable of a DIVINE WORK in the soul.   [Person.

The Lord gives prominence to the Divine Majesty of His own

He now shows He has been, and will ever be THE LIGHT of *the world!* John i. 9.

That to Him all dispensations pointed : that He is the fulfilment of law and prophecy.   [the *sign*.

That He is the BREAD OF LIFE of which the ancient *manna* was but

These words ring out a timely warning in these days of pretended spirit manifestations.

Every spirit that testifieth not that Jesus is THE CHRIST, THE ONLY SAVIOUR, is of the devil. John iv. 1—3.

γεγραμμένον. Refers to Jer. xxxi. 33, 34. *Schlier*. To Isa. liv. 13. *Stier*.

πάντες. Promise is universal, all are without excuse. *Meyer*. All who actually *become* disciples. *Muchmeyer*. Not all who are taught accept the teaching. *Stier*. The prophets speak with one mouth, hence their harmony. *Ber. Bib*. The fulfilling of the prophecies is the Lydian stone, testing them. *Lampe*. The children of the covenant, baptized infants. *Trapp*.

διδακτοί. Inward teaching. *Stier.* Subject to the Divine voice in man, preaching that faith which leads to Christ. *Neander.* Docti a Deo. *Erasmus.* Dr. Franklin refused to examine Christ's claim to Divinity, as he would know after death, without the trouble of investigation. Letter to Dr. Styles, *Smith's* Messiah, vol. i.

οὖν omitted. *Lach., Tisch., Alf., Treg.*

---

46. Not that any man hath seen the Father, save he which is of God, he hath seen the Father.

Not that. Implies that the Father is seen when the Son appears, and the Father is heard when the Son speaks.
Is of God. Equivalent to "God's own Son." The full Divine nature is necessary to the full view of God. John i. 12.
Being the Son, He is in His perfect vision of God absolute prophet.
Hath seen. "No man shall *see* Me and live." Ex. xxxiii. 20 ; 1 Tim. i. 17 ; vi. 16.   [Bible.
The same Trinitarian fundamental thought pervades the entire
No man, not even Moses, hath ever seen the ABSOLUTE DIVINITY.
The Godhead is essentially invisible to sense. John i. 18.
Let no one confound this Divine teaching (ver. 55) with immediate vision such as the Son enjoys.
Our Lord would give a reason for His clear and wonderful assertion.
Even those taught of God in the Messianic age will still have need of the Messiah.

οὐχ ὅτι. The Lord would contrast His true seeing of God with that of Moses. *Cyril, Erasmus.* He would forestall the spiritualistic view, that the inward manifestation of God supersedes the historical Christ. *Calovius, Lampe.* He would mark a difference in degree and kind of revelation. *Bengel, Tholuck.*
πατέρα. Son seeing the Father places Him above all beings. *Theodoret.* Angels behold God veiled. Christ alone as in essence. *Cyril.* Intimate communion with the Father. *Kuinoel.*

---

47. Verily, verily, I say unto you, He that believeth on me hath everlasting life.

Verily, verily. A species of *oath*, confirming His word. One of the "immutable things." Heb. vi. 18.
The threefold repetition used in the Old Testament benediction a clear allusion to the *Trinity*. Num. vi. 25.
The three gradations unfolded the blessing with ever-increasing emphasis.
Believeth on Me. See on John i. 7 ; vii. 38.   1. Historical

knowledge. 2. Hearty assent. 3. Trusting. 4. Personal appropriation.   [*around* Him.

Believers' life continually proceeds *from* Christ, *towards* Christ, and

Out of all fear of death and all claims of death the believer will
come forth to life and light.

No one but the Infinite God could honestly utter these words.

Had our Lord been only human, instead of adoring Him as DIVINE,
men would have shunned Him as *insane*.

But in harmony with His incarnation, foretold for 4000 years, His
birth-song sung by *angels*, His stupendous miracles, His matchless instructions, His spotless life, this GREAT WORD became
Him.

WE FEEL THAT HE HAD A RIGHT TO SAY IT AND ABILITY TO FULFIL IT !

Hath. Mark the present tense *hath*, not *shall* have. Not only
promised as a *future* possession, but *present* enjoyment.

Eternal life is ours as soon as we lay hold of Christ, who IS ETERNAL
LIFE HIMSELF.

Everlasting life. 1. In Christ's purchase. 2. In God's promise.
3. In the firstfruits of the Spirit.

Without faith in Christ there is no salvation for *any* sinner : this
is the *exclusiveness* of the gospel.

But with faith there is salvation for *all :* this is its *charity*.

εἰς ἐμὲ omitted. *Cod. Sin., Tisch.*

---

48. I am that bread of life.

I am. Since he that believeth on ME hath everlasting life.

Bread is the symbol of *all natural life* enjoyed by mankind.

Our Lord shared as Bread becomes symbol of *all spiritual life.*

That bread. Refers back to a previous announcement. You
were right. You did not misunderstand My solemn claim.
I repeat,   [who share it.

" I AM THAT BREAD OF LIFE " which confers life everlasting on all

Bread. That is, I am able and willing to nourish all coming to Me.

His constant characteristics express His spiritual nature.

His voice was an echo of the purity and salvation from God.

As the LIGHT of the world, all nature became a mirror of His Spirit.

The birds and lilies became through Him thoughts of God.

As the BREAD of life, all our blessings became a Father's gifts.

As the WATER of life, our hopes became streams of salvation.

In sacred, solemn earnestness, He consecrated the place where He
stood, and the whole *world* was transformed into a sanctuary
of God. [tion.
By His living energy passing events became symbols of Redemp-
He transfigured the earth into the stepping-stone to heaven.
The LIGHT, LIFE, and JOY of the New Jerusalem, He brought
down to earth all the elements that form its glory.
Bread *sustains* life. THIS BREAD *begets* life as well.
Of life. " He that believeth on Me hath everlasting life," and of
that spiritual life I am the everlasting SOURCE and SUSTENANCE.
By eating of the forbidden tree death fell upon humanity.
Through eating the Bread of life life and immortality are restored.
As the WORD created all life at the beginning, John i. 3, so He
renews the lost, the perishing, as His prerogative.
To the patriarchs Christ came as *bloom*, under the Levitical dis-
pensation as corn in the *ear*, and at His incarnation as corn
in the BREAD. *Bernard.*
Bread of (the) life. Not merely the bread which has the quality
of life, but the life which is bread. The life existing and
offered in the form of bread, and operating as bread.

---

49. Your fathers did eat manna in the wilderness, and are dead.

Your. He carefully avoids saying " *our* " fathers.
Our Lord, though *a Jew*, was no descendant of the " fathers."
They saw He claimed a higher origin than they could boast.
Fathers. Your *unbelieving* fathers, whose genuine children ye are.
Sadly enough they approved the spirit and deeds of their fathers.
Matt. xxiii. 31.
Yes, they did eat manna in the wilderness,—" bread of heaven."
Ex. xvi. 32.
But you forget they were never *brought out* of the wilderness.
The manna I speak of imparts *everlasting life* to all who share it.
Manna. See on verse 31. It gave no abiding life, because it was
not essential life.
Are dead. Gr. " *they died ;* " implies they died in the wilderness
in their sins. John viii. 24 ; 1 Cor. x. 3, 5.
Manna, " angels' food," had not saved *them*, could not save *these*.
Psa. lxxviii. 25. [1 Thess. iv. 13.
Christians, sharing the bread from heaven, " sleep," but never die.
Ancient Greeks made Ambrosia *immortalize* their wretched deities.

Ancient Hebrews fed upon *daily sacraments,* and perished too. 1 Cor. x. 3, 5.

A man may " *die* " eternally, though he has eaten " the bread " and drunk " the wine " of the Eucharist.

Salvation by " sacraments " a delusion, a mockery, and a snare.

Dead. There is no *resurrection* power in the wilderness manna.

There is *death* also in all the chosen joys and hopes of the worldling.

The *bread* of *earth,* that cannot even keep the body from death, men think sufficient for the soul also.

Paracelsus boasted that his *Catholicon* would render men immortal. But he was found dead, with his elixir in his grasp, in the hospital of Salsburgh.

The BREAD of HEAVEN alone hath the power to impart life, and to change the grave into a gate of glory.

μάννα. Sacraments do not work, whether men are asleep or awake, ex opere operato, *sed* ex opere operantis. *Trapp.*

ἀπέθανον. Death through unbelief. *Alford.* Papists claim that the host, changed into Christ's blood, body, soul, and Divinity, is a greater miracle than manna. *Rheimish* notes.

---

50. This is the bread which cometh down from heaven, that a man may eat thereof, and not die.

This is the bread. Perhaps pointing, but certainly referring, to Himself.

He defines the true bread by its origin, its design, and its effects.

1. It cometh down from heaven. 2. That men may eat of it. 3. That he who eateth may not die.

From heaven. Notice how He strikes mightily on this key.

This errand from heaven was not for honours, wealth, pleasure, but to impart everlasting life to all who receive Him.

Eat thereof. A plain figure. Christ must become our *own.*

As our food becomes thoroughly ours, entering into the *whole* man.

We may purchase bread, look at it, handle it, taste it, talk about it, still it will not nourish us unless we *eat it.*

Myriads *hear* about Christ, *speak* about Him, *think* about Him, *dispute* about Him, *contribute* to the cause of His gospel, *contend* for Him, yet perish from the house of God and very gate of heaven !

Not die. Men universally *long* after immortality. Hence the

angel guard over the tree of life: "Lest he put forth his
hand, take of the fruit, and *live for ever!* " Gen. iii. 22.
Adam and Eve would doubtless have attempted it unless prevented.
Fable of Prometheus and fable of men riding with the gods round
heaven, falling to earth, breaking their wings, and becoming
mortal, show the longing for immortality.
Traditions of a *"golden age"* amongst all people indicate the same
fond desire. [same.
Cravings of the heart, inscribed on myriads of tombs, reveal the
Neither cruel laws, nor iron walls of caste, nor oppressions of
tyranny, nor priestcraft, nor dark and bloody superstitions,
nor rack, nor cross, nor torture, have been able to rob the
soul of this longing.
Among even the most enlightened heathen it was but a *mere hope.*
But a hope which no "power could ever *wrest* from the aching
heart." *Cicero.*

οὗτός. Our Lord pointed to Himself. *Beza, Lampe, Ryle.*
φάγῃ. Desire is satisfied, because this faith he enjoys. *Roos.*

---

51. I am the living bread which came down from heaven : if any man eat
of this bread, he shall live for ever : and the bread that I will give is my flesh,
which I will give for the life of the world.

Living. Participle increases the force, i. e. " Life-imparting bread."
He speaks allegorically as to " bread," but literally as to " flesh
and blood." [vealed.
Bread. *Prophetically points* to the Lord's supper as still unre-
Our Lord's words here, as often elsewhere, have a heavenly as well
as an earthly echo. [*believing.*
Our Lord *sustains* all as *Great First Cause,* but He is the LIFE of all
And this BREAD OF LIFE will find a symbol in the last supper.
In verse 35 the reason is obscurely given, " He that cometh to ME
shall never hunger."
In verse 47, plainly, " He that believeth on ME hath eternal life."
Here, " I AM THE LIVING BREAD," feeding the soul and raising
the dead. [Divinity !
It is now added, " I WILL GIVE." How majestically He claims
Living bread, i. e. not only lives in and of itself, but is LIFE-
GIVING to all believing.
" The last Adam was made a *quickening spirit.*" 1 Cor. xv. 45.

Live for ever. The sad truth found in the converse follows this promise.

If one eat *not* this bread his life is but a " *masked death* " here, and will prove a " *living death* " hereafter.   [speak.

The bread. THE BREAD (MYSELF) of which I now emphatically

I will give. Corresponds to sacramental formula : " My body which is given." Luke xxii. 19.

It is the nature of a loving personality to give itself.

As He stood among the people He was the BREAD OF LIFE.

Performing glorious miracles, they felt it to be so. But proud unbelief could not comprehend *how*.

Apostles wondering and adoring cried, " Thou hast the words of eternal life ! "

Refusing to believe spiritual truths because of *mystery* indicates depravity of heart, for our common life is full of mystery, and yet men believe and act.

Are the changes of grass into hair on the ox, into bristles on the swine, into wool on the sheep, or into feathers on the goose, less mysterious than the changes of grace or the miracles of love ? *Trapp.*

Jews were scandalized that a *mere man* should make such demands.

An eternal stumbling-block to human pride, which ever resists the claims of the Son of God.   [life.

He who will not receive His Divinity and atonement cannot have

All salvation is involved in the historical God-man.

All spiritual life proceeds from absolute self-surrender to His demands.   [or perish.

The wisest and greatest must come as mere beggars to this BREAD,

But as yet this word was a dark and mysterious utterance.

The writing they could read *when* light from the cross was thrown upon it. See on John ii. 22.   [Lord.

This text gives deep and eternal significance to the table of the

Yet by its radiance as an act of REDEMPTION it conceals the table itself.   [the glory.

Like as our Lord on Tabor was concealed by the effulgence of

John, in the clear light of the Spirit, understood all this when he wrote.

He dwells on the passover, but records not the last supper, though he shows the eternal law on which the last supper is founded.

I will give. Here we learn how one may become a member of Christ's family, and what the golden chain which binds that

family in one, and by which nations beyond that circle are
to be brought into ONE CHURCH.   [HEAVEN.

Is My flesh. Understand it is of MYSELF I speak as the BREAD OF
Here for the first time in this wondrous sermon our Lord speaks
of His SACRIFICIAL DEATH.

It is that element which imparts to Him a life-giving virtue !
Henceforth in this discourse we hear no more of bread.   THE
    REALITY IS HERE !   [coming ages.

Flesh.   This points to a festal board of sorrow and joy for all
Eating of the Paschal Lamb was not the *sacrifice*, but a feasting
    on it.   [Sacrifice.
Thus it is with the Lord's supper,—it is a *feast*, the *result* of the
Birth-hour of the soul is celebrated at the festal board of Christ,
    and spreads through our spiritual life.   Thus the Israelites'
    national life began at the passover.
Passover freedom spread its privileges over all the life of Israel.
The bread, angel-provided, sustained Elijah forty days. 1 Kings xix.
This flesh, Christ-provided, sustains the believer up to the mount of
    God.
1. He looks to Christ alone for *wisdom* to guide amid all his doubts.
2. He looks to Christ's *righteousness* alone to justify him.
3. He looks to Christ's *strength* alone to sustain him in life, death,
    and eternity.   [20.
He who looketh to any other source " feedeth on ashes." Isa. xliv.
Moses had given the people flesh as well as bread.   Psa. lxxviii.
Isaiah spake of the atoning work of Christ more than 700 years
    before His advent.   Isa. liii.
The Baptist cried, " Behold the Lamb of God, which taketh away
    the sin of the world."
All this discourse was spoken when the passover was nigh.
Paul calls Him " Our Passover ; " Peter, " a Lamb without blemish."
    1 Cor. v. 7 ; 1 Pet. i. 19.   [resurrection.
He procured for our body a new power of life fully seen in His
Thus the Lord's supper, by an adorable *mystery*, becomes an ever-
    repeated miracle of love.   [slain.
Flesh. In the midst of the throne He appears as the Lamb newly
Thus in the Divine order of salvation His blood is ever presented
    as the ground of pardon.
He is at the same time our Mediator and our PHYSICIAN.
Life. Communion with God the highest kind of life possible to
    man.

Some see no reference to the Lord's supper, only the *great truth* underlying it. (See critical notes.)

Had He spoken more plainly a thousand prejudices would have been aroused. [stood.

His sayings were so framed that they could not at once be under-

Nor could they ever be forgotten, but have been unfolding age after age.

Thus countless mysteries around us are one by one being revealed as full of the *wisdom*, *power*, and *love* of God.

Life. 1. He would give up His body to die upon the cross. 2. He gives a real, hidden, divine life. 3. The world *receiving* Him would not perish.

All other that men cherish as life is *death* in seed and in fruit.

God by His Son's death offers to all men a share in His life.

Spiritual life, which is consummated in the resurrection to glory everlasting.

ὁ ζῶν. Living nature peculiar to Jehovah, Jesus claims for Himself. *Hengst.* When did our Lord become a quickening Spirit? Some say, at His incarnation, others at His resurrection. *Macknight.* Others, ascension. *Newcombe.* Quickening nature at Creation. *Lightfoot.* By communicating His spirit. *Deodati.* From eternity. *Author.*

φάγῃ. Three interpretations have been given : 1. The discourse has no bearing either direct or indirect on the sacrament of the Lord's supper. *Tert.*, *Clem. of Alex.*, *Origen*, *Basil*, *Cajetan*, *Ferus*, *Jansen*, *Luther*, *Melancthon*, *Lücke*, *Calvin*, &c. 2. It refers, by prophetic anticipation, directly and exclusively to the Lord's supper. *Chrys.*, *Cyril*, *Theoph.*, The *Schoolmen*, and *Romanist* expositors generally, *Zinzendorf*, *Scheibel*, *Knapp*, *Wordsworth*, &c. 3. It refers directly to the spiritual life-union of the soul with the Saviour by faith, and inferentially to the sacramental celebration of this union in the Lord's supper. *Aug.*, *Bengel*, *Doddr.*, *Kling*, *Olsh.*, *Stier*, *Lange*, *Luthardt*, *Alford*, *Godet.*

ζήσεται. Communicants alone thought to be saved, led to the putting of the sacrament in the mouth of infants and of the dying. *Trapp.*

The second ἣν ἐγὼ δώσω omitted. *Hengst.*, *Lach.*, *Tisch.*, *Treg.*, *Alford*, *Vulgate, Cod. Sin.*

σάρξ. Faith not necessary to the Lord's supper. Cardinal *Camperus*. Profession alone needed. *Bellarmine.* Origen's commentary opposing transubstantiation is cancelled by Papists. *Luther.* A life communicated has a medium,—bread can be used only when broken. Christ must die. *Khanis.* The Evangelist has nothing new to add, since at the time he wrote it was adopted in all the Churches. *Maurice.*

First, βρῶσις, then ἄρτος, then σάρξ, and αἷμα must be something beyond spiritual. *Stier.* Absence of the article proves His flesh must be different from ours. *Scheibel.* This Bread was our Lord's teaching. *Grotius*, and " *Liberals* " generally.

κόσμου, whole world of believers. *Doddridge*, *Stier*, *Calvin*. The entire world absorbs Christ. *Lange.*

52. The Jews therefore strove among themselves, saying, How can this man give us his flesh to eat?

Strove. The announcement of giving flesh for food sounded very strange.

Not only murmuring (verse 41), but contended among themselves.

Men have resisted, and still resist, every truth urged by the gospel.

A true picture of the fiercely contending theories of *earthly* philosophy.

Tumultuously they contradicted, murmured, rebelled.

None whispered their cavils in the ear of our Lord.   But He knew all.

How?   As usual, the sceptics and cavillers lead the way.

They take it literally, and thus charge His word with an offensive meaning.

Our first lesson at the cross is to bind our shallow reason to the altar of faith.

" How can a man be born again ? " asked the venerable Nicodemus.

This man.   Among Greeks a contemptuous term.   See verse 42.

This scornful temper closed their minds to the entrance of life.

The prophet foretold the Messiah would spread a feast.   Isa. xxv. 6 ; lv. 1, 3.

THIS MAN, who had not where to lay His head, claims to put His image on every soul as essential to life eternal.

Give.   As though He who had *nothing* could give ALL THINGS, like GOD !

His flesh.   The offence was not in the idea of death, but that His death should involve *so much*.   [1 Cor. i. 24.

A CRUCIFIED ONE, claiming to be the *wisdom* and POWER of God !

The heavenly nutrition of the souls of unborn millions.

The Jews were familiar with figurative terms.   Psa. xxxiv. 8.

" Come, eat of my bread, and drink of the wine which I have mingled." Prov. ix. 5.

Fear of alienating or offending had not influenced Him : He had neither retracted nor softened His word.

He moved on serenely as the sun amid cloud and storm.

This strife, begun in Capernaum, has spread through the world, and will continue until the millennium dawns.

Some maintain that His words were a mere metaphor.   But has an imaginary *feast* ever brought peace to the souls of men ?

It will not do for man to live and die by a mere figure of speech.

The clamorous crowd felt real hunger, and wanted BREAD.

No less clamorous, their hungry souls cried after peace.
Weightiest and highest truths, which most quicken and comfort
believers, confound unbelievers.

πῶς. Curet quomodo are deadly words. *Luther*.
οὗτος. Contemptuously, "fellow." *Xenophon, Euripides*.
δοῦναι. Jew Trypho asks scoffingly, If a second God is to be set with
Jehovah? *Grabe*. D'Alembert and Voltaire boast that they will defend God's
rights from the claims of Christ or any other pretender. *Smith's* Messiah.
φαγεῖν. The right word, but misunderstood by the Jews. His flesh is His
Resurrection body. His blood is the life He gave up for the remission of
sins. *Alford*.

53. Then Jesus said unto them, Verily, verily, I say unto you, Except ye
eat the flesh of the Son of man, and drink his blood, ye have no life in you.

Verily, &c. This sacred affirmation of our Lord has all the
validity of an oath. [" He hath said."
Disciples of the philosopher Pythagoras silenced cavillers with
It was not understanding they wanted, but *humility*. They were
wilfully blind.
I say. Yet He recedes not for the offence, but proceeds to enlarge
the great mystery.
Unto you. His hearers, and through them to *us* and all mankind
to the end of time. [or hell.
This great truth received or rejected decides our destiny for heaven
No other truth has had a thousandth part of the *opposition, hate*, and
scorn of mankind. [perish.
They who obey in faith are saved, they who despise or neglect
Except. Jews contemptuously asked, How can? our Lord replies,
It is absolutely necessary.
The tongues of earth in their poverty fail to set forth spiritual truth.
Hence the Lord's words have a *celestial echo ;* they ring of heaven.
Ye eat. Christianity the truth, and the true sanctification of
eating.
1. Making faith an eating. 2. Making eating faith. Verse 36.
Food eaten becomes an integral part of ourselves, and thus
nourishes us.
" **Eating** " implies personal union of the believer with Christ, and
a living appropriation of His atoning sacrifice.
The flesh. Men may share the Lord's supper, and not eat His
flesh, &c. [supper.
Men may also eat His flesh, &c., and yet not share in the Lord's

Sacraments apart from faith are mockery. The state of the heart
 is all.
There are many in heaven who never communed, and it is to be
 feared many in hell who often did.
The highest claim any prophet had ever made was " obedience to
 his message." [of salvation.
But Jesus demands a sharing in His flesh and blood as the term
With the future present, He speaks as if the last supper *were spread.*
Blood. As though He had added " which I will pour out for the
 world." [science.
Blood described in Scripture as " the life," established by modern
From Noah's day eating blood a forbidden abomination. Lev. xvii.
This a new offence to Jewish ears. The penalty was being cut
 off. Deut. xii. 16.
The Lord will provide for His entire Church a new Paschal meal.
By it the Levitical covenant will be abolished because fulfilled.
Blood definitely separated from *flesh* intimates a *perfect death.*
Flesh and blood another name for mortal human life. 1 Cor. xv. 50.
How the sacramental bread and wine nourish the *soul* is a blessed
 mystery. [supper.
Certainly nothing *corporeal* enters into the soul's food at the Lord's
The word *blood,* apart from *flesh,* in the N. T. always refers to
 violent death.
This violent death was the necessary FOUNDATION of salvation itself.
This was the harshest word He had yet uttered in their ears.
Son of man. Title of condescension and humility identifying
 Him with the whole race. John v. 27.
Claiming this, He claims to be the promised MESSIAH. Dan. vii. 13.
No life. Spiritual life flows only from communion with God,
 and this can never be reached except by union with Christ.
This is decisive that He could not have made reference here to
 temporal life.
The entire teaching was certainly confounding, and meant to be
 so, to the carnal.
The Lord's supper to this very hour is *just as perplexing* to unre-
 newed philosophers and statesmen as it was to our Lord's
 hearers.
As the miracle of the loaves gave Him the ear of the thoughtful,
 He seizes the moment to announce for all time a most profound truth.
He is aware of the disgust of the proud and the wilfully ignorant.

He knew the deep prejudice even of sincere ones among His disciples.

It is simply a repetition of verse 51. HIS DEATH MUST GIVE LIFE !

His death gives all the value of these truths to us sinners.

Hence the New Testament scheme of mercy is openly FOUNDED ON THE DEATH OF THIS NAZARENE ! whoever He might be.

If this Nazarene was not the Son of God, His death was worthless.

If His death provides not for our salvation, then our lost race is left *without hope.*

Flesh and blood. The peculiar descent and nature of Christ in historical manifestation : the historical Christ.

They ask, " How is it possible to eat His flesh and drink His blood ? " and He answers, IT IS INDISPENSABLE !

Flesh and blood of Christ really the food and drink of man :

1. His sacrifice alone the means of escape from death, and way to spiritual life.

2. Only full reception of the historical Christ can effect communion with Him.   [cation).

Believers dwell in Him (justification) and He in them (sanctifi-

3. He that eats takes the nutriment of eternal life, which works in him to resurrection.   [have none.

4. He that takes not this nourishment has no true life, and can

---

σάρκα. For various interpretations, see critical notes on verse 51. God-pervaded flesh. *Besser.* Iron heated is no longer cold, but burning as fire. *Luther.*

αἷμα. Definite separation of flesh and blood only secures perfect death. *Stier.* Living organism denoted, Gal. i. 16 ; Eph. vi. 12. *Hengst.* So use Christ's death as meat and drink. *Cajetan.* Mere expansion of eating His flesh. *De Wette.* Means His body now in heaven. *Alford.* Neither human life, nor Divinity, but a union of both. *Stier.* The elements of the sacrament nourish without corporal matter. *Zwingle, Calvin.* Christ's body is consubstantially present. *Luther.* All Christ's *acts, sufferings,* and *teachings* become food to the believing soul. *Hezel.* A symbolical form of the eternal, ideal, communion beginning with Christian life. *Lange.* What became of His blood shed ? Lost in the soil of Gethsemane and Golgotha. *Muenscher.* Shared in His glorification, and is now retained separate in heaven. His *bones* are kept. Psa. xxxiv. 20. *Flesh* kept. Psa. xvi. 9. *Blood* of sprinkling. Heb. xii. 24. *Beck, Stier, Oetinger.* Preserved, but not distinct. *Bengel.* A strange exegesis. *Lücke.* Fellowship of the Spirit. *Irenæus.* Blood forbidden, because used in atonement. *Cudworth.* Baptism begins spiritual food, and the Lord's supper continues it. *Hooker.* God may, but man never can, dispense with sacraments. *Hugo.* But the dying thief never shared either sacrament, and yet was saved. *Author.*

φάγητε. Courage to die for our enemies, like Christ, is to eat, &c. *Hammond.*

ζωήν. Nothing exhausts its meaning but the Resurrection. *Stier.* John

alludes to baptism chap. iii. 6, and to the Lord's supper chap. vi. *Von Gerlach.*
To their visible instrumentalities. *Meyer.* A higher enjoyment of fellowship
in receiving σάρξ, than in receiving simply Christ. *Khanis.* All life-giving
power connected with receiving His flesh, &c. *Hengst.*

---

54. Whoso eateth my flesh, and drinketh my blood, hath eternal life ; and
I will raise him up at the last day.

Eateth. Faith in His atonement symbolized by partaking of
  the Lord's supper.
Doubtless He had that feast in mind, for its wilful neglect or its
  worthy participation fulfils all that is here implied.
The blessings to be received are purely spiritual and God-imparted.
The state of the partaker must correspond to receive these blessings.
The benefit of the passover was confined to the " pure in heart."
The blessings of the Eucharist are received by true believers alone.
This sacred rite conceals its meaning from all but humble, loving hearts.
" It is the Spirit that quickeneth ; the flesh profiteth nothing."
  John vi. 63.
By the sacramental cup the believer learns of his future glory.
Hath. Eternal life not identical with resurrection life, although
  it issues in it.
Our Lord gives prominence to the resurrection as consummating
  man's redemption, seldom given it in our days.
The simple sharing in the symbols of the Eucharist cannot save.
  Luke xiii. 26.
Many who never sat at the table of the Lord, like the dying thief,
  will share the kingdom.
Life. The Father a symbol of POWER, the Spirit of LOVE, the Son
  of LIFE.   [life in both.
So vitally connected are the branch and vine, that life in one is
Saints' life, having root in God, can no more perish than God Himself.
The great truth in this verse is enforced four different times in four
  different forms.

ὁ τρώγων. To gnaw, used of animals, refers to *raw* food, not dressed. *Homer,*
Herod. From the root τρώω, to wound. *Lid. & Scott.* Instead of φαγεῖν, intensifies the meaning. *Lange, Stier.* The Lord peremptorily and pertinaciously
pushes the figure to its uttermost extreme. *Luther.* Our Lord now gives first
to His figure its finish. *Hess.* Papists hold that the bread is changed during the
Mass into the body, blood, soul, and Divinity of Christ. *Decrees of Council of*
Trent. Lutherans hold consubstantiation, though they reject the term.
Gerhardt. Others hold a middle ground. Elements receive such a *Divine*
virtue from the Holy Ghost, as to convey all the benefits of Christ's sacrifice.

Laud, Wake, Poiret, Andrews, Bull, Patrick, Bingham, Jos. Meade, &c. A spiritual communion. *Hoadly,* and all the *Puritans.* Others, a feast on the one sacrifice. *Cudworth, Warburton, Law of Chester.* A spiritual feast only taught. *Tholuck.* A moral union proved by verse 63. *J. V. Müller.* This blood the antidote to death. *Tholuck, Ignatius.* Figures here used familiar to the Jews. *Lightfoot.*

ἀναστήσω. As the αἷμα becomes the sacrament, so our bodies become fit for heaven. *Irenæus.*

---

55. For my flesh is meat indeed, and my blood is drink indeed.

My flesh, My blood. The *historical* Christ in His *entire* connection with God and man made by His death (shedding of His blood) the life-giving meal of the world.

His whole human life as offered on the cross for the sins of the world. [become one.

As meat is changed into the eater's substance, so believers and Christ

By feeding on Him (believing) there follows a mutual inhabitation.

Meat indeed, drink indeed. Life of man proceeds only from life of Christ completed in death.

Christ's actual person the especial vital element of mankind.

The nourishment and refreshment of the real life of man.

Ground of life (His atonement), power of life (His Spirit), character of life (His image), issue of life (eternal glory with Him). *Hall.* [now.

He conveys the *virtue* of His body and blood to those communing As He did His *grace* when BREATHING on His disciples. John xx. 22.

Or as when "*virtue* went out of Him, and healed them all," *body* and *soul.* Luke vi. 19.

ἀληθῶς. Received text. *Hengst., Cod. Sinai.* Vere. *Vulgate, Lücke.*

ἀληθής. *Lach., Tisch., Alford.* The adverb falls short of the depth of the adjective. *Alford.* Question enters deeper into the corporeity of Christ than either side has hitherto done. *Nitzsch.* My flesh and blood being truly bread and drink, I am no other than a personal living *bread. Stier.* He did not give His Divinity, but concealed Himself in flesh and blood. *Luther.* To eat and drink is the believing appropriation of His theanthropic humanity. *Hengst.* Satan tempts man to decry the sacred symbols. *Latimer.* Christ's body in ours the cause of immortality. *Hooker.* He is present in the symbols as in the water at baptism. *Cranmer.*

---

56. He that eateth my flesh, and drinketh my blood, dwelleth in me, and I in him.

Eateth. He that eateth and that which is eaten come into the closest union.

That is, by faith we share the merit of His passion and death.

As the sun is the source of order, harmony, light, and heat to the planets, so all doctrines, precepts, privileges, hopes of the gospel, stand related to the cross.   [i. 30.

The believer vitally appropriates the whole person of Christ. 1 Cor.

How we are not careful to answer,—when the Spirit of God is silent we dare not speak.   [and body.

This sublime truth is no greater mystery than the union of soul

It is true modesty to confess our ignorance when " angels *desire* to look into " these things.

We *know* that the bread is THE COMMUNION OF HIS BODY and the wine THE COMMUNION OF HIS BLOOD.   1 Cor. x. 16.

" Let us be content to *adore* while others *dispute.*" *Augustine.*

Dwelleth in Me.   A phrase characteristic of this evangelist, chap. xv. 4 ; xvii. 23 ; 1 John iii. 24 ; iv. 16.

Denotes personal community of life with Christ in its true fundamental forms.   [Gal. ii. 20.

We in Christ, is the first. Gal. ii. 17.   Christ in us, is the second.

The sinner must give up his own nature and take Christ's.

Humility, meekness, forgiveness, benevolence, justice, purity, self-sacrifice.

The union between the Christian and Christ is that living union, mysterious, but strong, between *branch and vine.* John xv. 1.

We have seen fruit *tied* to branches, but, like hypocrites at the Lord's table, the connection was a mockery of life.

Conceive of a *dead* branch becoming vitally connected with the vine, and we have the dead sinner quickened, and spiritually united with Christ.

He who dwells in Christ and Christ in him, stands at the very source of eternal youth.

τρώγων. Adam found a positive sacrament in Paradise, Noah on his deliverance from the flood in a rainbow, Abraham in the stars and sand, Israel in the *Passover*, and the Church in the Lord's *supper*. *Lange.*

---

57. As the living Father hath sent me, and I live by the Father : so he that eateth me, even he shall live by me.

Living Father.   The FOUNTAIN of ALL LIFE,—LIFE ABSOLUTE, PURE LIFE.

Thus in a lower sense all created life lives in and by the Son.

Sent Me. Subordination of the Son to the Father in the great
work of man's salvation.

I live. Christ has His own life by the Father's living in Him.

Perhaps a glance at the mystery of His eternal Sonship, " begotten,
not made." John i. 1, 2, 14, 18, 34, 49.

As He possesses life from the life-giving Father, so those partaking
of His life are through HIM (THE FATHER) upheld IN LIFE.

By the Father. His life and mine are one, though I am SON and
He FATHER.   [lievers.

As possessing *infinite life*, so He gladly imparts spiritual life to be-

The living Father must cease to live before I cease to be able to
save.   [POWER !

IN ME ARE ALL THE EXHAUSTLESS RESOURCES OF INFINITE GRACE AND

The full conception of these words will only be grasped in heaven,
if then.   [*Milton.*

Like many radiant truths, this is " dark by excessive brightness."

Live by Me. See on John i. 1—4. Those without faith in Christ
only *seem* to live !

In God's judgment they are no better than *walking sepulchres.*

Their life hath only the likeness of life,—in truth, is *masked death.*

Christ is the only Principle and Prince of life in the universe.

His people are the only " heirs of the grace of life." 1 Pet. iii. 7.

" The Head of every man is Christ, as the Head of Christ is God."
1 Cor. xi. 3.

All of body and soul apart from Christ will perish eternally.

As our natural life exists only by union of soul and body, so our
spiritual life exists only by union of our souls with Christ.

κἀγὼ ζῶ διὰ. I live for His sake. *Schaultless.* By means of. *Wetstein.*
For the Father. *Lange.* Denotes the entire purpose and direction rather than
ground or cause. *Schaff.* " I am as much to Him as He is to Me." *Silesius.*
Propter. *Vulgate.* On account of. *Winer.* The ground of life. *Beck.*

τρώγων με comprehends τὴν σάρκα μοι in one. *Stier.* Our Lord drops πίνων
τὸ αἷμα. *Brückner* in *De Wette.*

ζήσεται. Attain to felicity through My intercession. *Kuinoel.*

---

58. This is that bread which came down from heaven: not as your fathers
did eat manna, and are dead: he that eateth of this bread shall live for ever.

Bread. Apostles, at times, celebrated the Lord's supper every
Lord's day.   [propriety

In *great awakenings* such a course might be renewed with evident

From heaven. Seven times in this discourse He repeats this truth.
He now speaks of THE BREAD, not which He *presents* or *gives*, but
which HE HIMSELF IS.   [ever.
The eternal Christ, by the eternal feeding upon whom we live for
These words show the folly of the doctrine of transubstantiation.
His flesh and blood did not literally descend from heaven : " He
was made of a woman." Gal. iv. 4.
As the " meat and drink " of the soul, the life-giving Saviour, " He
came down from heaven."   [perceive it.
But Jews, blinded with materialism and pride of heart, could not
Manna. See on verse 49 for account of the miracle in the
wilderness, and lessons taught by it.
Are dead. Manna was no elixir of immortality ; it could not
prolong life an hour.
King of terrors entered Hebrew tents under the very pillar of cloud,
and claimed his subjects according to the law, " Dust thou
art," &c. Num. xiv. 29.
In the early Church certain fanatics affirmed Christ a mere *emana-
tion* from God.   [died.
They denied the Word was made flesh, or that He actually had
Men of learning and power endorsed it, but it came to nought,
having no root in truth.
They fiercely contended for His spiritual nature, but *fed not on Him !*
As billow follows billow on a tempestuous ocean, heresies came and
went.
Men fought for creeds under the *cross* with the spirit of *wolves.*
But the *true Church* of *Christ had no part or lot in these battles.*
That body of Christ still lived, a " little flock," but known to God
through all " Dark Ages."
Its bond was the unity of every true disciple to the Master.
Each humble communion-table strengthened the saints of God.
Sometimes in *caves,* or in *catacombs,* or in *tombs,* they met around
the table of the Lord, and fed on " His flesh and blood."
A quickening, divine power,—girded millions for " the *baptism* of
blood," under Rome, Pagan and Papal !
The Church without Christ, its life, was as the " dry bones in the
valley." Ezek. xxxvii. 2.   [limities.
This bread. Our Lord would not modify these figurative sub-
He leaves the great truths of redemption in these chosen metaphors.
Not to bring down His truths, but to *lift* up our minds to them, is
our privilege.

After His ascension and the descent of the Spirit it all became transparent.

Live for ever. All who lived only under the law and in symbols have eaten manna and are dead.   [eternal.

Life of Adam in self was lost : " life hid with Christ in God " is When HE shall appear, who is our LIFE, we shall appear WITH HIM in GLORY. Col. iii. 4.

" I shall not in the grave remain, since Thou death's bonds hast
    sever'd ;
But hope with Thee to rise again, from fear of death deliver'd.
I'll come to Thee, where'er Thou art, live with Thee, from Thee
    ne'er part ;
                Therefore to die is rapture.

" And so to Jesus Christ I'll go, my longing arms extending ;
    So fall asleep in slumber deep, slumber that knows no ending,
Till Jesus Christ, God's only Son, opens the gates of bliss—leads on
                To heaven, to life eternal."

But to proud sceptics His words were "hard sayings," and are so
    still.   [hearts.
Heaven's golden gates, *high* and *wide*, are too narrow for proud

---

οὗτός ἐστιν. Five times He said My flesh, four times My blood, now twice again after speaking of bread nine times. As coming from heaven seven times. *Stier.* If it be " daily bread," how is it that some receive it but once a year ? *Ambrose.*

τὸν ἄρτον. Romish priests here pretend to find authority for withholding the cup from the people. *Rhemish Notes.*

ὑμῶν omitted. *Tisch., Lach., Alf., Treg.*

τὸ μάννα omitted. *Cod. Sin., Tisch., Alf., Treg.*

---

59. These things said he in the synagogue, as he taught in Capernaum.

These things. 1. The *occasion* of this wonderful REVELATION TO THE CHURCH :

The desire of the Jews to have the miracle of manna repeated.

Those of larger views may have had the supply of an *army* in thought.

2. The *design* was to quench for ever all such vain ambition.

If you desire a warrior leader, I am not of that kind.

3. The *manner*—showed man's true peace lay not in things of sense.

His errand was to bestow blessings spiritual on all mankind.
To do this He must die as a vicarious sacrifice, and faith in this
sacrifice is the *sole condition* of benefit.
Further, that being paralyzed by sin, Divine aid is needed.
The discourse is a complete *résumé* of the entire gospel-plan of sal-
vation.

He taught. Wisest sages of the heathen world felt and confessed
the need of a DIVINE TEACHER.
CHRIST THE GREAT TEACHER. Distinguishing characteristics: I.
THOSE WHICH CANNOT BE IMITATED: 1. His originality. 2.
His miraculousness. 3. His authority. II. THOSE WHICH
MUST NOT BE IMITATED: 1. His positiveness. 2. His self-
assurance. 3. His self-representation. III. THOSE WHICH
SHOULD BE IMITATED: 1. His naturalness. 2. His simpli-
city. 3. His variety. 4. His suggestiveness. 5. His defi-
niteness. 6. His catholicity. 7. His spirituality. 8. His
tenderness. 9. His faithfulness. 10. His consistency. 11.
His devoutness. *Thomas's* Genius of the Gospel.

Capernaum. John vi. 24. An historical note to fix the locality
of this discourse.
Hence a sensuous construction of eating the body of Christ called
a *Capernaitic* eating.

συναγωγη. Openly, publicly. *Rosenm.*
διδάσκων. See *Harris'* "GREAT TEACHER." Depth of Divine humility seen
in these dialogues between Christ and unbelieving Jews. *Doddr.*

---

60. Many therefore of his disciples, when they had heard this, said, This
is an hard saying; who can hear it?

Disciples. Not the twelve. His old adherents and followers in
Capernaum.
Heard. With various results. Verse 64. See parable of the sower.
Matt. xiii. 3; Luke viii. 5.
Hard saying. Gr. *harsh, stern, rigorous,* hard to *solve,* hard to *do,*
hard to *bear.* [evil hearts.
The hardness was not in the word of Incarnate Love, but in their
Jews stumbled at His doctrine of Incarnation, at His humility, at
His declaration of His supreme Godhead and oneness with
the Father, at His doctrine of the Lord's supper, at His per-
fect spirituality, at His being Lord of the Sabbath, Author of

the resurrection and supreme Judge, at His being older than Abraham, at His Messiahship and death, at His giving His flesh and blood as meat and drink, &c.

It is hard for the self-righteous to feel he deserves eternal punishment.

It is hard for the Laodicean, increased in goods, to feel that he is a beggar.

It is hard for the wise and prudent to believe that he is a fool, or for the man of pleasure that he is selling his soul for ashes.

But the hardest of all truths revealed is that man must owe his eternal redemption to the blood of a crucified Galilean.

Thousands have declared that no "*man of sense*" can believe it, and no "*man of spirit*" can submit to such a creed.

But HIS RESURRECTION removed all doubts and lifted the veil.

Christ's high demands were then all sealed and justified.

Many repented, and, ashamed, believed and died as *witnesses*.

One such martyr's death was equal TO TEN THOUSAND SERMONS.

And a stake and burning victim for Christ's sake in our day in London or New York would be a powerful plea for the gospel.

A large experience in the Christian ministry convinces us that men's objection to the Bible is not so much on account of the *hard things*, as the things EASILY understood.

No one will ever be condemned for not grasping *mysteries*.

Religion made a *science* is the most difficult of things, but when a state of heart (trusting and loving) nothing is more simple.

God's truth, as it relates to us, is *plain*,—" the wayfarer, though a fool, need not err." Isa. xxxv. 8.

" It would be strange indeed if God required of us, depraved beings, only to believe such things as were *agreeable* to us." *Bacon.*

Should men aspire to comprehend the *Divine* nature, when they cannot comprehend their own ?

Are there not secret things in nature as well as in Scripture ?

In every age men have tried to make our Lord's words an *easy saying.* [of speech.

Some explain away all, affirming that they are only oriental figures

Others, that the bread and wine are changed into a kind of *medicine* in the *Mass.* [*substantiation.*

The darkest veil ever thrown over the cross is the doctrine of *tran-*

Millions of Romanists, despairing of reaching Christ, have fled for shelter under the shadow of the VIRGIN'S INTERCESSION !

Some would extract from the Bible that which God never put in it.

As Orestes saw his own image in everything, so some see their
own conceits in God's word, and call them " inspiration."
A *tortured* text is like a *suborned* witness, " Men will wrest it."
2 Pet. iii. 16.
To know all things belongs to Christ ; to us, the grace of believing.
The peril of our age is lowering the authority of Scripture. Patron-
izing sceptics say, " We accept the Bible."
As preposterous as if a drowning man were to cry to him who
flings a rope, " I accept the means of safety."
Man's grasp of truth at the best is a weak thing. It is the grasp
of the truth on us that saves.   [cross.
We must deny ourselves chiefly our pride of mind, and take up our
To become as " a little child " in heart is the demand which excites
the world's hatred.
The wicked call God's sayings *hard* because they are *holy*, and try
to shut out His threatenings because He is *stronger* than they !

μαθητῶν. The seventy disciples, *Euthymius*. In the wider sense, followers
in general. *Tholuck, Lange*.
σκληρός. Designates a rough, and therefore disagreeable, word. *Tholuck.*
Impiety not obscurity. *Lampe.* Our Lord had placed Himself above Moses.
Schleier. Had claimed descent from heaven. *Lange.* His impending death
contradicting their Messianic idea. *Ebrard, Hase.* They understood that His
body literally was to be eaten. *Aug., Grotius, Lücke.* Because to this eating
He attached eternal life. *Pfenniger.* A *dying* Messiah laid all their earth-born
plans in the dust. *Hengst.* Not the difficulty, but its strangeness. *Alford.*
Consubstantiation is offensive to the carnal reason, therefore Christ's. *Besser.*
Is the *spiritual* view any less offensive ? *Author.*

---

61. When Jesus knew in himself that his disciples murmured at it, he said
unto them, Doth this offend you ?

Knew in Himself. Probably there were indications of aversion.
But He also knew how to interpret their thoughts as the SEARCHER
of hearts. John ii. 24, 25.   [and scorn.
Murmured. Gr. *whispered.* Mutterings of discontent, dislike,
They scarcely knew what was the point when the arrow pierced.
More wisely to have honestly opened their mind and their diffi-
culties.   [Ezek. xxxiii. 30.
Evil hearts talk against the truth " by the walls of their houses."
Offend. Are my words inconsistent with *your* ideas of the
Messiah ?
Do they appear to contradict your reason, or wisdom, or wishes ?
Even then I cannot retract or change a single syllable.

You must henceforth learn to distrust your own wisdom.
And more and more lean by faith on the testimony and will of God.
You need a far different Messiah from that desired by your nation.
Thus He repelled individuals hastening to Him by word of
rigid test. [iii. 12.
He is ever sifting His disciples as wheat is sifted from chaff. Matt.
This life is ever developing character, revealing ourselves to our-
selves.
The idea of DEATH offended them when applied to the Messiah.
Wilfully they ignored the revelation of a suffering Messiah in the
prophets. [ant and glorious.
They also wholly misunderstood the revelation of Messiah triumph-
Worldliness had so darkened their minds that they thought God
like to themselves.
The Cross at which men still stumble is to the believer "the power
and wisdom of God." [to *do*.
1. A certain test of what is good, that which the unrenewed *hate*
2. A certain test of what is true, that which the unrenewed *hate*
to *hear*. [*hate* to *become*.
3. A certain test of what is heavenly, that which the unrenewed
Ministers who faithfully preach the cross must expect the offence
of the cross. *Luther*. [plaud. *Howe*.
A minister has reason to suspect his preaching if worldlings ap-

σκανδαλίζει, σκάνδαλον. A snare laid for an enemy. In N.T. a stumbling-block, a scandal. *Liddell & Scott*. Will ye not then *much more* be offended? *Ols.*, *Tholuck*. Will ye altogether be in error concerning Me? *Schleier*. If you here in My presence adhere to your old delusion, how will you succeed when I am gone? *B. Crusius*. Doth My death offend you? *Meyer*, *De Wette*, *Ebrard*. The Messiah of the carnal Sanhedrists must never die. *Hengst*. Was it His death or His flesh being food which offended them? His *answer* is the *key*. *Lange*. This assurance removed at once the veil from the offence and the offence itself. *Lücke*. I confess to the same disease of our first parents, viz. a desire to know more than I need. *J. Hales*.

62. What and if ye shall see the Son of man ascend up where he was before?

What and if? Spoken not so much to *bring back* those already offended as for the sake of those who hereafter should *believe*.
If what I have said seems "*hard*," how can you accept another word?
You need not marvel at this, for ye will see greater wonders

The Lord repeatedly had said "HE CAME DOWN FROM HEAVEN." "He came from the Father." John xvi. 28. Now He foretells HIS RETURN.

Ascend. John xx. 17. John does not record the fact; Luke twice alludes to it. [iii. 13.

But John's utterances fully bear testimony to the reality. John The Holy Ghost would assure all who had the faith required. Acts ii. 33. [doubt.

He comforts them in that His actual ascension would remove all As the angel of the Covenant, He ascended under the Old Test. dispensation, from the flame of Manoah's sacrifice. Judges xiii. 20.

"God is gone up with a shout, the Lord with the sound of a trumpet." Psa. xlvii. 5.

These were types of the ascension of our Lord to that heaven where He was before.

They need not wonder at His command to "eat His body and blood," for this VERY BODY, *visible to all*, would ascend into heaven, whence He came.

This confounded them far more than anything they had yet heard.

They knew that if He ascended, the miracle would be seen by many.

They knew there could be no doubt of its immense importance, A SEAL TO ALL HIS CLAIMS!

The disciples, doubtless, with the Jews, believed "Messiah would abide for ever." John xii. 34.

At this word, all their prospects of a *worldly* glorious kingdom became "vanishing visions." [eat?

They must no longer ask, How can this man give us His flesh to Mary, approaching to touch His knees, was forbidden,—"for I am not yet ascended to my Father." John xx. 17.

He could not actually show them His descent.

But His ascension was a demonstration so grand and glorious, so Godlike, so full of the final resurrection and future judgment, that they had not even dared to *think* of such a proof.

A grander test than even they could propose was now first offered.

The ASCENSION was the *keynote* of 50,000,000 of martyrs for Jesus.

He was before. This does not refer to His humanity, but to His Divine nature.

The Spirit transfers to one nature what belonged to another.

Christ's pre-existence seen from John i. 14: "The WORD became flesh." See also on John i. 1, 2.

" The days of His flesh," Heb. v. 7, implies He had *other* days.

" God sent His own Son in the likeness of sinful flesh." Rom. viii. 3. His Son had other " *likeness.*" Gal. iv. 4 ; Phil. ii. 6.

" He *became poor,*" &c., 2 Cor. viii. 9, which could not have been unless He was once rich.

" He emptied Himself, taking the form of a servant," Phil. ii. 6, 7, who had infinite " fulness."

When you see the one you will acknowledge the other, and not wonder at My doctrine, but your own dulness.

ἐὰν οὖν. Form of the broken sentence completed by τί ἐρεῖτε. *Euthym., Kuinoel, Lange.* Disputed by *Meyer.* Will ye not *much more be ?* &c. *Stier, Ols., Lücke.* Then will ye err concerning Me. *Schleier.* If ye err in My presence, how when I am gone ? *B. Crusius.* Doth foretelling My death offend you ? what when it is accomplished ? *Meyer, De Wette, Ebrard.*

θεωρῆτε. Christ may have here addressed some of the apostles. *Schaff.* Witnesses of the resurrection were representatives of all the disciples. *Hengst.* Some present who probably would see that event. *Lampe.* Such assurance as though they actually had seen it. *Stier.* Not literally but morally to be interpreted. *Kling.* Nothing to lessen but rather increase the offence. *Calvin, Grotius, Khanis.* The faithful only understood the Lord's supper after the ascension. *Stier.* Many now have very crude conceptions of it. *Author.* Then you will be much more offended. *Maldonatus.* George of Saxony liked the reformation had not Luther wrought it. *Trapp.*

ἀναβαίνοντα. Denotes the dying of Jesus. *Beza, Semler, De Wette, Meyer.* His hearers could not have understood Him in this sense. *Schaff.* Denotes His ascension, chap. xx. 17. *Ancient Expositors, Alf., Ols., Hengst., Godet.* Then will a deeper insight into the φαγεῖν τὴν σάρκα come. *Aug.* Then will the offence at His sensuous manifestation be done away. *Calvin.* Glorification of His flesh and blood will then be provided for. *Lyser.* The glorified state will take the place of the fleshly. *Luthardt.* Ascent is more difficult than descent; if therefore, &c. *Wetstein.*

πρότερον. His Divine nature, not human. *Calvin.* Christ's pre-existence is clearly taught here and elsewhere. *Dorner.* Irreconcileable if He had no pre-existence. *Semler.*

---

63. It is the spirit that quickeneth ; the flesh profiteth nothing : the words that I speak unto you, they are spirit, and they are life.

Spirit. See on John i. 33 ; iii. 8. Holy Ghost the third person in the Trinity.

The Almighty Spirit, the Agent of Life proceeding from Christ, a fundamental truth of the Bible.

Saints sharing this Spirit become partakers of the Divine nature. 2 Pet. i. 4.

Hence our Lord is called the *Anointed,* as possessing the Spirit without measure. John iii. 34.

Quickeneth. Jesus Himself is called the " Prince of Life." Acts iii. 15.

" The last Adam (referring to our Lord) was made a quickening spirit." 1 Cor. xv. 45.

Flesh. Human soul destitute of the Spirit, or Christ's humanity without Divinity.

A communion of nature does not imply a communion in grace.

Profiteth nothing. Must not be understood to conflict with the preceding words concerning His flesh.

Flesh without THE SPIRIT, or flesh as *mere* matter, and materially eaten, is *worthless*.

His bodily ascension to heaven He has just announced.

This teaches that even if they could receive His body as food, it would avail nothing.

The same Spirit that will quicken the dead in their graves must impart spiritual life to the soul.

The words, &c. My words (not alone My body and blood) are Spirit and life.

Spirit there is in Divine truth, never *congealed* into *ink*, and it cannot be transferred to paper, but passes from THE SPIRIT.

This transforming power surpasses that *secret chemistry* which transmutes the dull mould into the plant with the bloom and beauty of Paradise.

The words. Revelation, in all its *shades* of *thought* and *doctrine*, FACTS WITH GOD.

Are spirit. Although ye cannot share My blood proper, yet under the emblems of My death believers shall partake of My flesh and blood.

It is a solemn *protest* against all the carnal interpretations of men.

He teaches the *soul* needs food appropriate to a *spirit*.

Life. As the spirit during life vitalizes every part of our flesh, and as a portion of flesh separated ceases to have life, so each soul in union with Christ, through the Spirit, *lives*, but apart from Him is *dead*.

Men feel the fetters of sin galling them amid all their boastings.

The Lord offers a higher, purer liberty in this new life.

But *who* or *where* is he who of his *own accord* seeks this life ?

That mighty drawing of which this chapter is so full is needed.

The offer of a *quickening* Spirit, boundless in mercy and power, is here announced.

For 1800 years every believer, living or dying, is a *sermon* on, and *monument* of, Christ's truth.

For λαλῶ read λελάληκα. *Cod. Sin., Bengel, Lach., Tisch., Alf.*

---

64. But there are some of you that believe not. For Jesus knew from the beginning who they were that believed not, and who should betray him.

Some. Words directed to those about to withdraw from Him.

It might have been " many," but it was only " some."

Believe not. See on John i. 7 ; vii. 38. Not My presumption, but your *unbelief*, is the cause of offence.

This is the true source of countless heresies and fatal errors.

Unbelief wilfully rejects the remedy, and frustrates the means of mercy.   [Heb. iii. 12.

It leaves the soul covered with pollution, and under condemnation.

Condemnation two-fold : 1. As judged and convicted by the law.
    2. From deliberate refusal of the remedy,—Christ's blood. Zech. xiii. 1.

" It matters little to some of you in what sense I speak."

Probably He saw some act of *levity* or *scorn* in some high in office.

Others think His eye rested at that moment on the cold features of *Judas*.   [true reason.

Or knowing that some were about to forsake Him, He gives the

Knew from the beginning. His Spirit could not be deceived by any *mask*.

The Holy Ghost here explains how it was He was not surprised.

Being God, with Him is neither past nor future, but ONE ETERNAL NOW (see chap. i. 1—3).

He could not have been the LOGOS without omniscience.

Peter saith unto Him, " Lord, Thou knowest all things." John xxi. 17.

" All things are delivered unto Me of My Father." Matt. xi. 27.

Solomon in the Dedication prayer, " Thou knowest the hearts of all." 1 Kings viii. 39.   [ii. 23.

Christ says, " I am He who searcheth the reins and heart." Rev.

" He did not commit Himself because He knew all." See on John ii. 24.

" Jesus knowing their thoughts " is asserted most clearly on six occasions. Matt. ix. 4 ; xii. 25 ; Luke v. 22 ; vi. 8 ; ix. 47 ; xi. 17.

Note the folly of "Liberals" and other infidels. Can any but an
INFINITE BEING know the thoughts of men ? [i. 48.
He read the heart of Nathanael when under the figtree. John
Betray Him. Gr. *deliver Him up.* See on verse 71.
He never was imposed on. When He called Judas He knew he
would be a traitor.
His course towards Judas was that towards all gospel despisers.
At that moment He saw treason, like a cold viper, coiled round
the traitor's heart.
The Evangelist writing *after* the betrayal, shows his marked
aversion for the traitor.
God foreknows all things, yet in mysterious mercy He permits evil.
The traitor's testimony (Matt. xxvii. 4) proved Jesus' *sinlessness.*
The circle of apostles would not represent the Church if Judas had
not been in it.
What a *beacon* to all followers of Christ to the end of time !
A disciple, daily listening to His words and seeing His works,
betrayed Him !
Our Lord warned Him repeatedly, so that He sinned *wilfully.*
Had Judas repented his first welcome would have been given by
Christ.
No iron links of fate bound him. Mercy's gate was ever open to him.
Yet he was chosen with the foresight that *he* would refuse to enter.
How this sheds light on our Lord's wondrous patience !
He clearly foresaw all His suffering, even the treachery of His
disciple.
How unspeakable the folly of hypocrites ! How can they hope to
deceive the omniscient God ?
But how cheering to believers: The world knows them not, but
Christ "knoweth them that are His." 2 Tim. ii. 19.
Case of Judas one out of many showing how the finger of God
touches the secret springs of thought and action.
This event was most certainly defined, appointed, and foretold.
Psa. xli. 9 ; Acts ii. 23. [known.
And yet his motives and act were his own as fully as if not fore-
Thus also is the eternal weal or woe of every man known to the
Judge. [judges."
Yet will "He be justified when He speaks, and clear when He
The fact of Judas's remorse proves he felt the sin to be his alone.
Thus conscience will at last witness for God in spite of all delu-
sions and excuses.

ἀλλ'. A new theme. *Stier.* An apparent ineffectual influence of communing is here hinted at. *Khanis.* Some followed for temporal advantages. *Kuinoel.* One may as well preach to rocks as to men without the Spirit. *Bede.* Spoken to the inner circle of hearers. *D. Brown.*

ᾔδει ὁ παραδώσων. Impossible to apply the ordinary rules of moral treatment. Why did He then continue him as an apostle, or entrust him with a bag? *De Wette.* Problem of Divine knowledge and man's free-will insoluble. *Alford.* To distribute punishments demands omniscience. Matt. iii. 11. *Michaelis.* He must know the inmost recesses of the mind. *Rosenm.* His knowledge is perfect, accurate, universal. Rev. ii. 23. To act as final Judge requires omniscience. Matt. xxv. 31—46. It implies also perfect intuition of all the wants of all believers in every land. Matt. xxviii. 20. *Pye Smith.* Committing the bag to him presupposes his avarice and a psychological (?) piercing of his character. *Hengst.* Omniscience can dispense with psychology. An eagle needs no crutches. *Author.* Link of connection between Divine and human operations will probably never be reached on earth, if ever in heaven. *D. Brown.* God-man did not act immediately from omniscience. *Neander.* With human hope He trusted to win him. *Lange.* Like a wolf, led about by a superior will, that the flock be not scattered too soon. *Lange.*

ἐξ αρχῆς. Metaphysically, from the beginning of all things. *Theoph.* From the beginning of His acquaintance with each one. *Stier, De Wette, Tholuck.* From the beginning of His Messianic ministry. *Alf., Meyer.* Beginning of murmuring. *Chrys., Bengel.* Beginning of first secret germs of unbelief. *Lange.* Judas from his tone of mind might become His traitor. *Tholuck.*

---

65. And he said, Therefore said I unto you, that no man can come unto me, except it were given unto him of my Father.

Therefore. As though they would have Him retract His words.

Explains that He had spoken that sentence with reference to faith or unbelief towards Him then forming in particular persons.

Said I. He repeats as it were the solemn truth, involving everlasting interest.

Men's unbelief did not astonish Him nor change His words.

God was merciful, Christ condescending, the Spirit gracious.

If men perished, God *foreknew* that they would sin on incorrigibly and perish WILFULLY !

" All that hate ME love death." Prov. viii. 36. And yet no sinner believes this God-spoken truth.

God's omniscience never interferes with man's responsibility.

No man can. See on verse 44. Unbelief fruit of a hard heart, a Divine judgment.

An old and long-agitated question, Whence the *first desire* of salvation ?

On man's unbelief He places *all* the guilt of rejecting mercy.

" Ye WILL *not come unto* ME, *that ye might have life.*" John v. 40.

1. *Faith* was once in man's *power*, but he forfeited it by the fall.

2. No unbeliever *desires* to believe. If he did, he would pray for faith.

3. *Unbelief* is in man's *power*, and he willingly chooses it.

His *obstinacy* is his pride ; his *boast*, and becomes his eternal ruin.

When prejudice, passion, love of the world are removed, " EVERY MOUTH WILL BE STOPPED ! " No murmuring will be heard then. Rom. iii. 19.

Testimony of the lost and saved through eternity : " *Just and true are Thy ways, Thou King of saints.*" Rev. xv. 3.

Given unto him. An efficacious and Divine operation, " Father's drawing." Verse 44.

God's holy *sovereignty* and man's *responsibility* are here taught.

God's sovereignty is ever disliked by the unrenewed heart.

Doctrines of Christ's Divinity and atonement, and man's depravity, are also hated and opposed.

Many boldly affirm they would rather be *Atheists* than receive such doctrines.

What folly to try to render such truths *acceptable* to such persons.

Chance, luck, fortune, casualty, contingency, mishap, are *pagan* words.   [by plan.

God's infinite wisdom presupposes that He governs the universe

John (Rev. v.) saw a book, sealed, in the right hand of Him upon the throne.

Symbol of wise and holy purposes incomprehensible to all creatures.

" There is not a fly whose destination is not of God." *Young.*

His foreknowledge in harmony with second causes and man's acts, though all was known of *necessity* from eternity.

He would never have permitted evil had He not intended to bring good out of that evil. *Augustine.*

His Sovereignty is even now a stumbling-block to many disciples.

Paul exclaims, " O the depth of the riches both of the wisdom," &c. Rom. xi. 33.

To reason is to darken counsel, &c. Job xxxviii. 2.   To believe is to enter into rest.   Heb. iv. 3.   [Psa. cx. 3.

Nothing but *grace* can *prepare* for grace : " We are *made willing.*"

ὑμῖν. Applies to a narrower circle. *Stier.*

δύναται. See on verse 44. δεδομένον. Had been given. *D. Brown.* Nothing is done but what God wills, either efficiently or permissively. *Augustine.* It mightily burdens natural reason that God should leave some to harden their hearts. *Luther.* The intense hatred of Christ's Divinity and God's sovereignty by cavillers a strong proof of their truth. *David Nelson.* Grant two things, God's true freedom to do good and man's true freedom in doing evil. *Jackson.* As to Divine power and the human will, I never was so happy as to find one who understood it. *Baxter.* There is no *meritum ex congruo. Trapp.*

---

66. From that time many of his disciples went back, and walked no more with him.

From that. On account of this discourse so opposed to carnal Messianic hopes.

Many. " Broad is the road that leads to destruction, and MANY," &c. Matt. vii. 13. [find it."

" Narrow is the way that leadeth unto life, and FEW there be that Pastors should not be surprised when similar desertions happen to them.

A preacher may lose his hearers through no fault of his own.

A promiscuous multitude is not so important as sincerity.

We may silence men's objections, but cannot impart faith.

Disciples. Not spiritually such : followers actuated by temporal motives chiefly.

They hung on the skirts of His band like the fringe of a garment, and were easily detached by persecution or temptations.

Went back. Many of them had been drawn by the miracle of loaves and fishes. [Him.

Externally numbered as disciples, but *internally* never were with Note the unchangeableness of God's love, and instability of man's attachments. [king.

Those are the very men who would have made Him their *earthly* Those are they who prayed, " Lord, evermore give us this bread."

Now, however, they show that His offers of " Bread from heaven " were not to their *taste.*

The saddest final parting from Christ at the day of judgment will be those who once went *half way.*

So many leaving rendered those desiring to remain *fainthearted.*

In burning our own homes we endanger all the dwellings around us.

Thus the dragon, falling, " drew the third part of the stars down also." Rev. viii. 12.

Thus tall pines falling, crush many an undergrowth.

" No man liveth unto himself." Hymenæus and Philetus falling away, " the foundations seem to shake." 2 Tim. ii. 19.

Many went back whence they came, to the manna their hearts had never left.

Some may have long followed Him, but now they finally give Him
up.
What was our Lord's offence ?   Had He not offered life to the
dead ?
They could believe in tradition, and in tithing mint and anise, &c. ;
in defrauding parents by a corban, in adulteries and hypo-
crisies, and in a thousand false things, but *not* in the WORD
OF LIFE !
History repeats itself : Christendom at present abounds with those
who believe men, spirits, devils, but not the word of the
Eternal God.
Marks of a reprobate mind quarrelling with God's word.   Mal. i.
13.   Replying against it.   Rom. ix. 20.   Reproaching.   Jer.
xx. 8, 9.   Blaspheming.   Acts xiii. 45.   Making unrighteous
inferences from.   Rom. iii. 8.
Those thus returning to the world "draw back to perdition."
Heb. x. 39.
Christ is none the poorer for losing what He never really had.
The " star " which falls never was a star, nothing more than inflam-
mable gas.
Walked.   Hebraism for the *tenor of one's life.*   Rom. viii. 1.
Why forsake Him who could feed thousands by His word, still a
tempest, heal the sick, and raise the dead ?
No more.   They could not reconcile their hopes with a *dying
Messiah.*
They saw He was not the Master they wished for, and certainly
they were not the disciples He wished for.
In this very place (Capernaum) where His mightiest works were
done, and He had remained the longest, this sifting began.
Ever true, " His fan is in His hand, and He will throughly purge
His floor."   Matt. iii. 12.   [them," &c.
Prelude and prophecy of final sifting—" Then shall He separate
No more.   How mysterious this dark and terrible power of will
by which man separates himself from God !   [ME."
To such the Judge, JESUS, will say at the last day, " Depart from
Chosen separation from Christ on earth will issue in banishment
from Him in eternity.
With Him.   God's presence is energetic, gracious, vital to be-
lievers' hopes.
The sight of spotless virtue is *tormenting* to the wicked mind.
The sad secret ground of *all persecution* in every age of the Church.

Strangest sight on earth, a wretched sinner flying from the wisest, mightiest, best, and only FRIEND in the universe.

A poor creature in an ocean of dangers spurning the only plank of hope.

As the Lord unkindly rejects none, so He will forcibly retain none.

We see here the sifting power of truth : The sin of backsliding.

Stages of apostasy : 1. Retention of earthly mind in discipleship. Matt. xiii. 5. 2. Development of unbelief, of rupture with Christ. 3. Actual apostasy itself.

The first apostasy from Christ in its typical import : 1. Its motives. 2. Its extent. 3. Its consequences.

Total view of the mournful thing : 1. Its main features in gospel history. 2. Its preludes in Old Test. history. 3. Its development in the history of the Christian Church. 4. Its final form as depicted in the prophecies of the Bible. *Lange.*

ἐκ τούτου. From this moment. *Lücke, De Wette.* On account of His teaching. *Meyer.*

ἀπῆλθον. Shows they had been led to the Lord by no inward sense of ɴeed. *Tholuck.* The turning back refers to Jehovah. Isa. i. 4 ; Psa. xliv. 18. *Hengst.*

μαθητῶν. Nominal followers. *Cyril.* Expectants of the Shiloh's glory. *Chrys.*

---

67. Then said Jesus unto the twelve, Will ye also go away ?

Twelve. The first time they are so called by this Evangelist.

A clear proof He takes for granted a general knowledge of gospel history.

Twelve tribes—the " signature of the covenant people," showing that the Church of the New Test. is the Divinely ordained continuation of Old Test. Israel.

Will ? Expressing confidence mingled with a warning in reference to the traitor.

Will ye, or *any one* among you, prove unfaithful also ?

He saw the commotion in the *wheat,* as the wind scattered the *chaff.*

Not greatness of *number,* but *purity* of His followers, was sought.

How weak is human faith that even after the last miracle, such a question should be necessary.

As angels followed Lucifer, so it was possible the twelve might follow Judas.

His object was to test faithfulness, elicit confession, and promote
closer attachment to Himself.
The eternal responsibility of deciding He throws on man.
No compulsion will be used to *dragoon* men into His kingdom.
The Father will not use force in *drawing* nor force in *detaining*.
Yet infinite love seems to hold them, although free to go away.
Were the gospel history *mythical* such a question as this would
not have been found in it.   [circle.
No *doubts* of fidelity would have been permitted among their inner
His majestic calmness visible through His grief: He begs not,
flatters not, makes no terms.   He is sure of Himself and of
His word.
Christ needed none, but no one can do without Him.
The Lord's words reveal wounded feeling, and a consciousness of
deserving sacred fidelity.
This proclamation was made at the Olympic games in Greece, " If
you are well trained and in good heart, *enter !*   But if there
be one unprepared, let him *retire !* "
None in Christ's service will ever be held by chains.   Jude ver. 6.
Ye also.   Literally, " But *ye* will not go away, will ye ? "   *Lange.*
There is an unfathomable depth of sadness in the question.
Who can reckon the sacrifice made for the ransomed soul !   Psa.
xlix. 8.
How can we listen to any temptation not *equal* to or beyond that
price ?
That matchless love that refused to come down from the cross
should bind the soul with an ever-increasing bond.
He had in a special manner chosen *the* twelve as *fast friends.*
Undoubtedly the first disaffection now formed itself in the mind of
Judas.
The Lord's words must have shown him that his glowing expect-
ations were vanity.   [it.
Peter's protestation shows how little the disciples in general noticed
Of the eleven who remained, " He made them *willing* in the day of
His power."   Psa. cx. 3.
Else all left to their own hearts would have forsaken Him for ever.
" Choose ye this day whom you will serve."   Josh. xxiv. 15.
This question was the mightiest appeal possible to their hearts.
Virtually, He bids those departing farewell, and commences *sifting*
the remaining disciples.
" Many are called, but few are chosen."   Matt. xx. 16.

Many went away, and, it is feared, never returned. THEY ARE
 GOING AWAY STILL!
"Depart," Matt. xxv. 41, sadly shows they will continue *going*
 FROM GOD FOR EVER!   [sliding.
Will ye? The Lord's appeal to all His disciples against back-
Ye who know anything of His grace and love, will ye, can ye,
 forsake Him?

Mὴ. The interrogative μὴ looks to a negative answer. Comp. vii. 31; xxi. 5.
Winer, Schaff.
θέλετε. No hint of a decree of reprobation. *Stier.* But His mercy alone
retained those abiding. Rom. ix. 16. *Author.* Freedom of will proved.
Bourgon. A mistake to suppose that responsibility implies free-will. *Author.*
In the mystery of His humanity, at such a moment of desertion He might seek
comfort in the faith and attachment of His chosen ones. *Alford.* How can
this be when He knew the future treason of Judas and foresaw also the faithfulness of the eleven? *Schaff.*
ὑπάγειν. No appeal of sorrow demanding consolation. *Stier.*

---

68. Then Simon Peter answered him, Lord, to whom shall we go? thou hast
the words of eternal life.

Simon. See on John i. 42. Two turning-points in this apostle's
 life,—a *question*, and a *look* of Jesus.
Here, a firm decision to *remain;* there, a weeping, broken-hearted
 desire to *return.*
Answered. Quickly, resolutely, and emphatically, He speaks in
 the name of the twelve.   [apostles.
His pre-eminence lies in this, that He is the mouthpiece of the
This gives him a certain primacy and priority, down to the day of
 Pentecost.   [of the Pope.
Romish Church turns this into a permanent and official supremacy
Peter's noble reply was grateful to our Lord's loving heart.
He could not deny they had been shaken on seeing so many depart.
Their own weak faith had been severely tried by the Lord's words
 that day.   [Thee?"
To whom? Lit. "To whom shall we go over, go away from
1. Shall we go back to the lifeless formalism and wretched traditions of the elders?
2. Shall we go back to the darkness and sadness of Judaism?
3. Shall we go to the superstitions and idolatries of the heathen
 world?   [philosophy?
4. Shall we go to the systems of a cold morality or of a cheerless
Peter's declaration in its light and shade. We must continue with

Jesus because—(1.) No other Christ will come. (2.) No one will bring a better word. (3.) There remains no other faith. (4.) There remains no brighter knowledge.

To find firm footing on the ROCK of AGES is unspeakable relief.

There is repose even in ignorance, if we only feel that *God knows all.*

Shall the children of earth be wiser than the children of light?

Do *they* ignore the facts of nature because they are *incomprehensible ?*

It needs courage to trust oneself to Christ and let the world go.

But the Lord gives believing courage to those who ask.

Shall we ? Peter indiscreetly, but with honest heart, answers for all, including Judas.

Malignant silence of Judas a bad sign. Contrast between Peter's happy confession and Judas's unhappy reserve.

Christians ought to attach themselves more fervently to Jesus in times of apostasy. [triumph.

Although unable to understand, and even perplexed faith should

Assured there is a bright light on the cloud, and that the wind will come and cleanse it. Job xxxvii. 21. [fidence.

Experience of the Lord's truth and grace justifies unbounded con-

Judas went out of the school of Christ far worse than he went in.

He went out "into the night," then to the *priests,* then to the *halter,* and then to " *his own place* " in eternity.

Thou hast. One truth concerning the Messiah after another they learned.

How long they stumbled and murmured at the idea of His dying.

How hard to comprehend that He had nothing for their bright visions.

He had many things to tell them, but, alas ! faith was too weak.

Words. Words which proceed from, possess, and lead to eternal life. [ance.

They felt assured He had something better than temporal deliver-

Thus much is clear, whatever else may be obscure.

Religion to the curious and profane is full of mystery, and dark as eternity. [all truth.

But to the believer is promised the presence of One who guides into

Roman law permitted deserters to be slain wherever found.

But those remaining faithful to the flag ofttimes returned home victors.

Those forsaking the living oracles perish. Eternal life, if we cling to the cross, is ours.

Christ's word had pierced the heart of Peter. Now with exultant
voice he gives back the echo.

Eternal life. See on John iii. 15 ; v. 24. In the essential sense
as life from God.

Not simply the eternity of duration, and of the world to come.

The Divine life, or the spiritual, embraces the depth and breadth
of eternity.

Eternal life, beginning with the new life of faith and love in the
Spirit, and completing itself in the glory of the resurrection.

ἀπελευσόμεθα, future, ever go away. *Meyer.* Denying the future possibility. *Schaff.*

---

69. And we believe and are sure that thou art that Christ, the Son of the
living God.

We. The disciples seem to have kept apart from the crowd.

Believe. See on John i. 7 ; vii. 38. Profane philosophers called
Christians " CREDENTES," *believers,* as a term of reproach, because they took what was written in the Bible on trust without argument. Just as on account of their pure lives
Christians were named *Cathari,* or *Puritans.*

" Let them jeer at us for our *faith,* we will believe notwithstanding." *Augustine.* [1 Pet. i. 7.

Christian faith one day will be found to bring "honour and glory."

Whatever others may think, **we believe** and are **sure** that none
but GOD could do such things.

This has been the answer of 50,000,000 of martyrs amid the flames
and agonies of martyrdom !

This faith was unquestionably *the inspiration of the Holy Spirit.*

Believe and are sure. Hints that the believing, child-like state of
mind must precede the attainment of knowledge.

Although faith itself is an intellectual as well as a moral and
spiritual act.

" Faith comes by hearing," but we must believe to obtain a saving
knowledge of Christ. [we *know.*

In science we first *know,* then *believe.* In religion we *believe,* then

Faith precedes obedience. " *Taste* and see that the Lord is good."
Psa. xxxiv. 8.

Perhaps in eternity the law will be reversed. Knowledge may
there precede faith.

To train us in humility, faith, and love, the special end of all God's
revelations here in nature, in Providence, and in the Bible.

Are sure. Indicates an *intelligent* creed : God accepts not blind
faith.

Christianity challenges ALL THE LIGHT and SCIENCE in the universe.

A false creed can live in Rome, where " *ignorance is the mother of
devotion.*" [battlements.

God does not demand rigorously concerning every stone in the

It availeth for salvation if we are on the true FOUNDATION, Christ
the Lord.

The doctrines of salvation have been the meat and drink of the
greatest intellects that ever existed.

Experimental evidence the best : " He that believeth hath the
witness," &c. [star."

Miracles and prophecy a " lamp ; " Christ in the heart " the day

The Christ. See on John i. 20, 41. Prelude to the confession of
Peter, Matt. xvi. 16.

The Son. That very SON the promised and looked-for Messiah.

Christ had clearly and distinctly called God His Father, implying
Divinity.

After all the fierce envyings and contentious blasphemies of the
Jews, we expect a glad, triumphant confession of His Deity.

If it be " no light thing to be son-in-law to the king," 1 Sam.
xviii. 18, what is it to be the SON of the Eternal Jehovah ?

Son of God. See on John i. 18, 34, 49. This title, THE SON OF
GOD, is never applied to any one but Christ.

This one grand comprehensive truth silences many scruples.

It implies all the *peculiar* doctrines of Christian theology.

Living God. This would *strengthen* his own faith and that of his
brethren against the effect of the Lord's words which had
caused some inward strugglings.

πεπιστ. καὶ ἐγνώκ. The perfect expresses completed action and permanent
result. *Lange.* Fides præcedit intellectum. *Aug., Anselm, Schleier., Bengel.*
But the reverse maxim : *Intellectus præcedit fidem (Abelard)* is also true,
though not in a rationalistic sense, and is supported by the order, John x. 38 ;
1 John v. 13. *Schaff.* God does not require faith in every capillary vein of
theological truth, upon pain of damnation. *J. Hall.* A hedge was set around
them. *Bourgon.* Yes, God's Almighty arms, else they too had fallen. *Author.*
  For ὁ Χριστος, ὁ υἱὸς read ὁ ἅγιος. *Cod. Sinai,* and four other *Codices,
Lach., Tisch., Treg., Alf.* The ONE consecrated by and for God. *Lange.*
  τοῦ ζῶντος omitted. *Cod. Sin.,* &c. Coincidence of original text with
testimony of demoniacs (Mark i. 24) is remarkable. *Schaff.* Thou art the
Son of God, and not of Joseph. *Grotius.*

70. Jesus answered them, Have not I chosen you twelve, and one ot you is a devil?

Answered. Peter replied in behalf of all the twelve. But our Lord saw their *hearts.*

"Well said, Simon Barjona, but thy '*we*' does not embrace you all."

Our Lord's joy at Peter's grand confession was saddened, for not all remaining were true-hearted.

Another sifting of the wheat will reveal more chaff. Matt. iii. 12.

Though depravity germinates slowly, it ripens rapidly to judgment.

Have I not? The words of this question are a more definite exposition of verse 67.

Not the language of reflection, but of sudden pain in contrast with Peter's joyful confession. *Meyer.*

Distribution of emphasis most significant—"I" first, then "you," then "the twelve."

I, as the Holy One of God, have chosen you to the highest honours.

Human gentleness and tone of soft complaint combined with the *severest* utterances of His lips.   [supper.

Their warning severity and force were only surpassed at the last

"One of you will *betray* me!" The question hints—*Beware how you stand !*

Chosen. See on verse 64. **I have chosen.** This majestic allusion to His Divine Sovereignty in electing the twelve mingles with the sad emotions of His human heart.

As though He said, even this Divine selection is not enough.

There is an election (to office or privilege) from which one may fall away.

There is another (to salvation) where one may fall *in* grace, but never *from* grace.

This is clearly affirmed John x. 28; 2 Thess. ii. 13 ; 1 Pet. i. 2 ; Rom. viii. 29, 30.   [saved.

1. Neither nations, communities, nor organized Churches are *all*

2. Those saved are chosen to salvation " through *sanctification*," &c. Eph. i. 4 ; 1 Pet. i. 2.

3. Those thus chosen are always addressed as *individuals.* John vi. 37 ; xiii. 18 ; xvii. 2.

Exhortations and warnings touching " shipwreck," &c., should promote in the chosen all *energy, watchfulness,* and *prayer,* as though they actually *wrought out their own salvation.* Phil. ii. 12.

Our Lord refers to the external election to apostleship,—Judas had
    none other.   John xiii. 18.
Our Lord mournfully sets against His kindness Judas' defiant will.
Twelve. The history of the Passion had impressed this word
    deep in John's heart.
Such boundless Love seeking to save, and seeking *in vain*, wrung
    from our Saviour's heart anguish we cannot comprehend.
Incomprehensible Love *created* Satan an archangel, knowing he
    would become Prince of *devils!*
So incomprehensible Love strove to *win* Judas, knowing he *would*
    not be won.   [Son of God.
Terrible omen : from among the twelve arose the betrayer of the
Alas ! even now for motives which are of the EARTH EARTHY, some
    attach themselves to the Church, and even give Jesus *a kiss.*
This word had in the end a sad significance—*only* twelve !
In that *small* band, chosen from all the thousands of Israel, could
    any one have imagined a *traitor* would be found ?
You believe all but true disciples are departed : alas ! it is not so.
Fearful contrast : chosen to a higher service than angels, and yet
    a devil !
One of you. It is evident the disciples had no definite idea as to
    whom the Lord meant.
Least of all do they seem to have fixed on Judas, who, on the con-
    trary (see the account of the anointing at Bethany in Matt.
    and Mark), appears to have enjoyed their confidence.
Hypocritical evil-doers conceal themselves because we are so *blind.*
Our Lord's words, perplexing as they must have been, gave them
    continuous warning.   [apostles.
He speaks as if the sin of the one rested on the whole circle of
This gives fearful emphasis to the piercing repetition " ONE OF
    YOU ! "
Believers though you are, be all humble, prayerful, watchful.
It is not *enough* to remain with Me, while others depart.
Had not Almighty grace *retained*, all would have forsaken Him.
" By grace are ye saved through faith, and that NOT of YOURSELVES."
    Eph. ii. 8.   [a *devil !*
A warning to all professors—one *apostle* of Jesus Christ became
In an earthquake, *temples* and *arches* sometimes *fall to the earth.*
" Let him that thinketh he standeth take heed lest he fall." 1
    Cor. x. 12.   [dish !
JESUS and Judas sat at the same table and dipped into the same

The dove and the raven, the clean and the unclean, were in the
same ark.   [mate.
The checks, hints, and warnings of God exceed in number our esti-
Christ bearing with Judas ; the hardest test of His love.
Devil.   Gr. *adversary, slanderer*.   See on John vii. 20.   Denotes
an actual traducer instigated by the devil.
A remarkable word spoken more than a whole year before His death.
The germ of apostasy, at that moment in the heart of Judas, con-
tained the black fruit, which in time it bore.
This word proves how deeply He was oppressed by the presence
of this miserable man in the apostolic circle.
Our Lord would put to shame Peter's confidence in going security
for *all*.   [xxvi. 21.
He pursued the same course of warning at the last supper.   Matt.
Wondrously searching word.   Each asks, "Lord, is it I ?"   Matt.
xxvi. 22.
During a terrible uncertainty, each one *distrusts himself*.
And yet none was allowed long to suspect his neighbour of such a
crime.
The heart being deceitful and desperately wicked, each Christian
should continuously pray, " Create in me a clean heart, O God."
Psa. li. 10.   [of death."
Indifference upon this subject a sure proof of peril : it is " the sleep
The wicked are called by the Son of God the " children of the devil."
John viii. 44.
Paul calls Elymas the magician " *child of the devil*."   Acts xiii. 10.
They who eat Christ's flesh *assimilate* to His nature.   John vi. 53.
They who are in sympathy with Satan *assume* his nature.
After Judas had given lodgment to the Satanic suggestion, Satan
himself entered him.   John xiii. 2, 27.
Thus men giving way to temptation invite the tempter to take
possession of them.
Judas, as a devil, was securing his own ruin, and *perilling others*.
A strange madness that prompts the diseased one to *infect others*.
Stranger still, infidels of all kinds are not willing to perish alone.
Num. xvi. 19.   [xxii. 20.
They go about to instil their poisonous errors in others.   Joshua
A heathen could say, " Any one self-ruined madly tries to ruin his
neighbours too." *Seneca*.   [also.
They will not be persuaded that if they are *safe*, Christians are safe
Either Christ or Satan will be finally *formed* in each soul.

When Peter, the leading disciple, errs, the word is, " Get thee behind me, Satan." Matt. xvi. 23.
Peter called " Satan " for his human weakness; Judas, a " devil " for his lurking treason.
Christ's wisdom and mercy in withholding the name of Judas while giving him a clear hint of his danger. [heart.
But hypocrisy, presumption, pride, and avarice had hardened his
In accordance with his dark spirit, he gives no sign that he is hit, but remains in malignant silence.
None stand in such peril as those who try to hide wickedness under the garb of religion. [agent.
Solemn and awful fact that Satan finds in the twelve his willing
Satan is never more truly himself than in the form " of an angel of light." 2 Cor. xi. 14.
Of all devils, none are so bad as a preaching or a praying devil.
Christ the true prophet of the heart : He alone knows and can reveal its secrets.

ὁ 'Ιησοῦς omitted. *Tisch.*
ἀπεκρίθη. To disciples generally, but primarily to Peter. *Hengst.*
ἐξελεξάμην. There is an election of the lost ; Satan's very creation was chosen by omniscience. *Stier.* Judas attracted by the Lord's personality, and all that was poetical in word or work. *Weisse.* The sentence affirmative. *Beza.* Nonne hæc ita se habent. *Lampe.* Interrogatively. *Euthymius.* Choosing him as an apostle not the eternal election of the Father. *Schaff.* Judas' defection traced to this discourse. *Maurice.*
διάβολός. An informer. *Theoph., De Wette.* An adversary or betrayer. *Kuinoel, Lücke.* Devil, devilish, of a diabolical nature. *Meyer, Alford, Hengst.* Christ had in view the treason of Judas inspired by the devil. *Schaff, Lange.*
δαίμων, *not* διάβολος, is always applied to one of the demons or agents of Satan, although both are confusedly rendered "devil" in our Auth. Ver. *Prescott, Gesenius.* Representative of the devil. *Gill.* Judas possessed the heart of an enemy. *Neander.* Homo diabolo similis. *Schottgen.* Secret traducer. *Euthymius.* Denotes the office of a fiend. *Stier.* Paul uses it always of a calumniator. Our Lord does not proclaim His Messiahship, and Judas accused Him of rebellion against the Romans. *Locke.* May be rendered a spy. *Campbell.* Equivalent to enemy or false accuser. Judas, here first learning Christ's kingdom was purely spiritual, conceives his treason. *J. Brown.* He suppressed the name of the traitor to arouse his conscience. *Kuinoel.*

---

71. He spake of Judas Iscariot the son of Simon : for he it was that should betray him, being one of the twelve.

Judas. See on verses 64, 70. We at length come *directly* to the dark mysterious form of Judas.

No one more stupid, more obstinate than the confirmed hypocrite.

Compared to the deadly adder, who closes his ear to the charmer.
Psa. lviii. 5.   [kingdom.

The Lord offered to His future betrayer all the blessings of His

In self-sacrificing love He held intercourse with him to change his
heart.

" How often would I have gathered you, BUT YE WOULD NOT ! "
Matt. xxiii. 37.

Iscariot.   Probably of *Kerioth*, son of Simon, always named last.

A surname to distinguish him from Judas son of Alphæus.

In the three lists of apostles it is added that he was " the betrayer."

John describes the successive steps of his sin.   John xii. 4 ; xiii.
2, 27.

He heard the most solemn and tender warnings about God and
Mammon.   Matt. vi. 19—34.

By a gradual hardening in worldliness and unbelief, his sympathies
froze out.   Mark xiv. 3—9.

Under plea for the poor he tries to conceal his avaricious malignity.

At Bethany he saw that intensely instructive parable enacted.
Mark xi. 20, 21.

His feet were washed by our Lord—" ye are clean, but not *all*."

His case an illustration that tares will be found with wheat till
the end.   Matt. xiii. 30.

The evidence that he was *present* at the last supper is very strong.

He asked the question, " Is it I ? " as a *veil* to conscious guilt.   Matt.
xxvi. 25.   [John xiii. 26.

John and Peter alone of the twelve understood by a sign who it was.

The Lord's words seemed to have irritated him to desperation.
John xiii. 27, 30.   [xviii. 2.

He well knew our Lord's custom to retire to Gethsemane.   John

Christ's apprehension and condemnation procured, Conscience began
her terrible vengeance.   [soul.

His pieces of silver commenced to burn, like red-hot coals in his

He hurls the accursed money past the first and second court, *into
the sanctuary* (ναός).

Pharisees, like the heartless world, *sneer at the tool* of their guilt.

One of the laws of the twelve tables punished the traitor with the
doom of the parricide.

On Judas descends the deep darkness that precedes self-murder !

He departed and " hanged himself," Matt. xxvii. 5, " and went
to his own place," Acts i. 25.

Can Satan instil a more fatal delusion into the mind than that of *refuge in suicide?*

Judas was a man of energy, and the fact of his being appointed treasurer points to administrative ability.

As he possessed the confidence of his fellow-disciples, it is probable he sought to inveigle them into participation in his guilt.

In his power of outward self-control he exhibits the strength of a demon.

The withering words, aimed at him, do not move *him in the least.*

In the synoptical Gospels his name is *last.* In the list in Acts i. 13 it *disappears* for ever.

Notwithstanding his guilt, he was involuntarily, through the overruling power and wisdom of God, an instrument for the greatest good.

Simon. His father's name, omitted by Matthew, Mark, Luke, is inserted by John.

Zebedee had two sons, apostles and saints. Simon had one son, an apostle by *name* but by sin a *devil.*

How fearfully important the warning—" Rejoice with *trembling.*"

To all ages and generations he stands out a fearful and solemn example.

Not of one given over at the first to the powers of evil.

Monsters do not exist. The best things perverted—that is the history of great crimes.

Judas sank deeper and deeper, casting from him the cords of love, and resisting the influences of the Spirit.

The twelve. Showing the diabolical character of Judas' infidelity and treason.

The only comment of the Evangelist is the traitor's deep crime.

The absence of *any expression of human judgment* in the Gospels a proof of their inspiration.

None but those on whose minds the hand of God rested could have manifested such impassiveness.

Ἰσκαριώτην. A man of lies. Prov. xix. 5. *Hengst.*
Ἰσκαριώτου. *Lach., Tisch.* Judas and his father both named Iscariot. *Alf.*
From Kartha in Galilee. *Ewald.* From Kerioth in the tribe of Judah. *Winer.*
He did not bear the name Iscariot until the betrayal. *Hengst.* Whether Judas was a *partaker* of the Lord's supper is a question encompassed with many difficulties. The general consensus of patristic commentators answers affirmatively. Most modern critics think he did not. *Plumptre* in *Smith's Dict.* Anciently men, women, and children communed. *Buxtorf.*

ἤμελλεν. Betrayal germinated in him from this time forth. *Lange.* Betrayal the Divinely-appointed result. *Meyer.* The mere future. *Alf.* More than this, it represents the future as an accomplished fact. *Schaff.*

παραδιδόναι. See on verse 64. The question why Christ called and received Judas admits of three answers, none of which is entirely satisfactory. 1. Christ elected Judas an apostle that through his treason, as an *incidental* condition or a necessary means, Scripture might be fulfilled and redemption accomplished. Objection : Though this view contains an element of truth, it seems to involve our Lord in some kind of responsibility for the darkest crime ever committed. 2. Jesus foresaw the financial and administrative abilities of Judas, which might have become of great use to the apostolic Church, but not his thievish and treacherous tendencies, and He elected him solely for the former. Objection : This is incompatible with the foresight of Christ and the express statement in verses 64, 70, 71. 3. Jesus knew the whole original character of Judas from the beginning, and elected him in hope that the good qualities and tendencies would, under the influence of His teaching, ultimately acquire mastery over the bad. Objection : This implies our Lord was mistaken or at least disappointed, a notion inconsistent with his perfect knowledge of the heart. *Schaff* in *Lange,* Amer. edition. An inscrutable mystery. *Calvin, Alf., Prescott.* Disappointed because our Lord's plans were all spiritual. *Ewald.* Thought our Lord might be sold, but could not be harmed. *Light., Winer.* A subtle plan to precipitate Christ's advance, and amid the triumphs of the Messianic king, he hopes for pardon. *Paulus, Whately, Neander.* Despairing of pardon on earth, he hastens by suicide to meet his Lord in the under-world to confess his guilt and ask His pardon. *Origen.*

ἀπήγξατο. Matt. xxvii. 5 includes death by some sudden spasm of suffocation such as might be caused by fearful remorse, and then he fell as described in Acts. *Suicer, Grotius, Hammond, Light., Gill.* The halter broke, and hence the result as given in Acts. *Papias, Œcum., Theoph.* Hung himself over an abyss, seeking a double death. *Lange.* In a paroxysm of insanity. *Plumptre* in *Smith's Dict.*

αἴδιος τόπος. Acts i. 25. Probably a dark region in Gehenna. *Light., Gill.* This explanation rejected by *Meyer, Hammond,* and other *Commentators.*

John 7

1. AFTER these things Jesus walked in Galilee : for he would not walk in Jewry, because the Jews sought to kill him.

After. A new general date succeeding the events and discourses of chap. vi.—He had remained in Galilee a whole year between the passovers of chaps. v. and vi.—The complete history of this period is recorded in Matt. xv.—xviii.

Galilee. John i. 43. Men of great abilities and piety are often found in obscure places.—Jon. Edwards while a missionary to the Stockbridge Indians wrote his " Essay on the Will."
Jesus quietly walking in Galilee a token of His prudence, His fore-sight, His wisdom, in His spirit of self-sacrifice.

Would not. Angels know no fear, neither did our Lord. " Per-fect love casteth out fear."—He was ready in due time to die, but He must first do His work.—When we cannot do all we would we must do what we can.—He might have overwhelmed His foes by His Almighty resources, but He has given us an example that we are not to be ashamed to retire, when not to do so would be tempting God. *Augustine.*

Jews. Members of the Sanhedrim and other ecclesiastical leaders
Kill. Points to chap. v. 16—18. Pretended zeal for God's honour the ground of this wicked purpose.—Fanatics may believe them-selves right : " I verily thought," &c. Acts xxvi. 9.
A course of hardening will produce such moral blindness.
They could neither pardon nor forget His Sabbath work recorded in chap. v.—But for His wise reserve His life would probably have fallen in the first year of His ministry.—A contrast with the many apparently premature sacrifices in Church history.

μετὰ ταῦτα. Chronology not preserved. These memoirs selected for their higher spiritual import. *Alford.* Selected by the Holy Ghost alone. *Author.* We are indebted solely to John for our Lord's fifth journey. *Lampe.* He went immediately. *Grotius.* Some weeks elapsed. *Rosenm.* Six months. *Besser.*
περιεπάτει. Roman rule in battle was, neither fly from nor seek danger. Christian motto,—Nec temere, nec timide. *Trapp.*
Γαλιλαίᾳ. An important statement, as we thus learn He did not attend the

passover of chap. vi. 4. *D. Brown.* Proximate period of walking in Galilee is from feast of Purim to feast of Tabernacles of the year 782 (A.D. 29), from month Adar to month Tisri (from 19th March to about 12th Oct.). *Wieseler.* "There are lands where now our enemies would devour us, but in Wittenberg they cannot come." *Luther.*

ἀποκτεῖναι. This proves His absence from the passover. John vi. 4. *Robinson.* The third of His ministry. *D. Brown, Wieseler.*

---

2. Now the Jews' feast of tabernacles was at hand.

Now. It was autumn, the time of the ingathering of first-fruits.

Feast. John ii. 23 ; vii. 37. Feasts of Jews must shortly be abolished.—Divine truth never grows old. Air and sunlight are as pleasant now as in Eden.—FEASTS : 1. PASSOVER. John i. 29, 36 ; ii. 13. The greatest of all their national feasts.—2. PENTECOST. Next in importance. Thanksgiving for first-fruits. Also commemorated giving of the law on Sinai.—3. DEDICATION. Commemorated restoration of the temple service after Antiochus, 173 B.C.—4. PURIM. In memory of the great deliverance from the plot of Haman, 509 B.C.—5. TRUMPETS. Beginning of the year was thus ushered in. Lev. xxiii. 24.—6. EXPIATION. Great penitential feast. Lev. xxiii. 7. Pointed to Christ. Heb. ix. 11.— 7. SABBATH JUBILEE. Held every 49 years. Slaves liberated and land returned to its original owner. Isa. lxi. 2 ; Luke xiv. 17, 21.— 8. TABERNACLES. Third of the great festivals. Lev. xxiii. 42, 44. Commemorated 40 years' tenting in the wilderness. It began 15th Tisri (October), and continued eight days. Lev. xxiii. 42. Eighth day (23rd Tisri) was kept as the feast of the joy of the law. Feast of Tabernacles distinguished by its grand offerings and joyful tone.—Intended to remind them Jehovah was the defence and strength of their nation.—In booths or tents they were safe from all enemies, for God was with them.

In stone houses and with strongest fortifications they fell before their foes, for "the glory had departed."—This feast one of the three when all the males went to Jerusalem.—People lived in te ts formed of live branches of trees, on roofs, in streets, and in open places.—They carried branches of palm in their hands and boughs of noble fruit, and made merry banquets.

Josephus calls it "the holiest and greatest of the feasts."

The great day of atonement had five days before been celebrated.

A priest with a golden pitcher each morning went down to the fountain of Siloam and drew water.—He met the procession at the water-gate, which was saluted with the sound of trumpets.

The water was poured on the altar, and the multitude shouted *Hallelujah !*—A commemoration of the miraculous supply from the rock. Ex. xvii.—Prayers were offered for rain during the coming season.—An illumination on the evening of the first day reminded them of the PILLAR OF FIRE in the wilderness.

From the court of the women two golden candlesticks shed light far round the temple mount.—Festivals of human authority cannot *bind* the Church of God.—The only ordinances established by our Lord are the two sacraments.—To a religious mind every morning's awaking is a festal *resurrection.*—True devotion makes daily meals feasts, and each feast a *sacrifice.*—Christians still celebrate *their* feast of tabernacles when they heartily praise God for His shelter and defence.

ἑορτή. Can it be possible, as Nehemiah hints (viii. 17), that during the palmiest days of the Jewish commonwealth this feast, divinely and solemnly appointed, should have been suspended for nearly 1000 years ? *Mede.* Impossible so flagrant a disregard of law could have been tolerated by Samuel, David, and other pious rulers. Its observance is indicated 1 Kings viii. 2, 65 ; 2 Chron. vii. 9, and expressly recorded Ezra iii. 4. *D. Brown.* This feast had so joyous an appearance that *Plutarch* thought it a feast of Bacchus. *Lange.* Water libations might be borrowed from Greeks. Illuminations took place on the evening of the first day. *Winer.* Lawgivers instituted festivals to cheer men in their toil. *Seneca.* Providence, to keep alive gratitude. *Augustine.* Had the Jews known WHO was in their land they would have borne Him in triumph to their feast. *Besser.* Very doubtful. We only know they would not have slain Him. 1 Cor. ii. 8. *Author.*

---

3. His brethren therefore said unto him, Depart hence, and go into Judæa, that thy disciples also may see the works that thou doest.

Brethren. John ii. 12. Sons of Joseph and Mary. Sisters also are named. Matt. xiii. 56.—On several occasions they showed a disposition to act as guardians or advisers of Jesus.

Cousins would never thus have presumed to meddle with His offices. Names of His brethren, James, Simon, and Judas one of the apostles. These brothers had a *worldly* faith in the future greatness of Christ. They admired His miracles, but were impatient with His prudence.

Depart, &c. The scene of this incident was probably at Nazareth. He had not gone to Jerusalem either to the passover or pentecost. Galilee was His field, and Capernaum had been His Jerusalem. They are at a loss to understand His conduct, and familiarly press Him.—Family vanity impels them to utter the challenge.

Bold in their ignorance, they address Him in an unqualified imperative.—None but those brought up with Him would have dared to use such terms.—His brethren do not imply that He was *legally bound* to go to the feast.—They recognize the fact that He was *above* the restrictions *binding* others.

They trust the dignity of His person in the centre of the nation will secure His acknowledgment.—These brethren assumed what His apostles never ventured to attempt.—Even Mary was checked as she presumed to dictate to her Son.—But many thus in prayer seem to urge *their advice* upon Jehovah.—How flippant is ignorance and how weak is vanity ! Amongst ears of wheat, the emptiest carry their heads the highest.—Religion in our day has more fuss, but less depth, than is becoming.—A sad prayer to Christ, " Depart ; " a far better, " Abide with us, for the day is far spent." Luke xxiv. 29.—The Sun of Righteousness can enlighten both hemispheres at once.—It ought to have been, " Depart not hence ; go to them without leaving us."

Into Judæa. They were right in assuming Messiah could not complete His work outside Jerusalem.—But wrong, 1. In beginning to think lightly of His quiet work in Galilee. 2. In still hoping that His public appearance in Jerusalem would carry the nation with Him. 3. In not submitting to His wisdom. Herein chiefly lay their unbelief.—Enthusiastic zeal is often characterized by want of the spirit of true obedience.

Self-love may prompt a minister to action that God neither requires nor approves of.—Love to God makes all depend on the will and indication of God only.—God does everything exactly at the right time ; but even good men do much out of season.

Disciples. His many adherents and followers in Judea and Jerusalem.—They hint that Galilean friends would be influenced by the capital.—So full were they of carnal notions about Messiah, that they despise Galilee.—They pledge their homage if He will only prove His claims before the great.—This counsel was very *natural* to relatives, filled with exalted expectations.

Another prophecy accomplished : " I am become a stranger unto my brethren," &c. Psa. lxix. 8.

See. Perhaps reference to the desertion of Him by some of His followers.—Or a hint of persistent and increasing enmity towards Him.—But none, not even His brethren, can comprehend Him or His hour.—They show that their zeal, such as it is, is of the earth, earthy.—They think that Galilee, an obscure corner, should

not hold Him.—They imagined He retarded His mission as
Messiah by secrecy.—With intense *curiosity*, as well as family
vanity, they longed for Him to sustain *publicly* His claims as
Messiah.—Admitting their principle to be right, they were
wrong in urging *their* time.—They trusted He would vanquish
all enmity, and be recognized as the Messiah.—In this world's
estimate their advice was good. If His object was to win the
Jews by miracles, He must show His power in Jerusalem.

His brethren, human in their *infirmities, vanity, conceit, ambition,*
desire their Brother of miraculous birth to show Himself in
His power, and become famous, and make the family renowned.
Relatives often throw more obstacles in the way of God's children
than strangers.—None but an *inspired* writer would have recorded
this circumstance.

ἀδελφὸς. See critical notes to chap. ii. 12. 1. A brother uterine. 2. A
fellow-countryman or neighbour. Matt. v. 47. 3. One of equal rank. Matt.
xxiii. 8. 4. A disciple. Matt. xxv. 40. 5. One of the same faith. Acts ix. 30.
6. An associate in office. 1 Cor. i. 1. 7. One of the same nature. Matt. v. 22.
8. One beloved. Acts ii. 29. ἀδελφοί. This passage one of the strongest
arguments in favour of the view that the " brothers " of Jesus were really
members of the holy family and under the care of Joseph and Mary, in whose
company they constantly appear. *Meyer, Godet, Lightfoot, Alford.* 1. It is
perfectly plain that John here distinguishes the " brothers " of Christ from the
apostles. 2. John represents the "brothers" as *unbelievers.* 3. Our Lord
characterizes His " brothers " as men of the world, &c. Ver. 7. *Schaff* in *Lange.*

Μετάβηθι. Disapproving of His course, they counted Him neither a prophet nor the Messiah. *Lampe.* Spectators of His miracles, Jew-like, they
thought Him ambitious. *Kuinoel.* Their course very strange, but blinded by
hopes of a Messiah. *Doddr.*

ὕπαγε. Tauntingly. *Stier.* A scoffing spirit. *Alford.* Anxious the Sanhedrim should approve Him. *Grotius.* The language of prejudice rather than
of unbelief. *D. Brown.*

μαθηταί. Generally. *Hengst.* All His adherents in Judea, chiefly the influential ones in Jerusalem. *Lange.* Galilean followers who might see Him do
wonders before the Sanhedrim. *Whitby.* His earliest followers. *Lampe.*

θεωρήσωσι. Every act of our Lord is full of significance, pervaded by a
typical reference. *Stier.*

---

4. For there is no man that doeth any thing in secret, and he himself seeketh
to be known openly. If thou do these things, shew thyself to the world.

In secret. They thus describe His work in Galilee, and His withdrawal to the Phœnician borders.—They cannot understand His
proposing to be Messiah with a *secret* ministry.—Their principle
was right, Messiah must be at the Temple.—Jerusalem, *mother*
of saints, must be the *altar* of their Redeemer.

To this day Christ and His work is a stumbling-block to the unbeliever.—So also is the work of the Holy Spirit in the soul of
the Christian.

If Thou do. That is, have a constant power of doing these
wonders.—They do not intend to throw doubt on the works :
it denotes the premise.

Shew Thyself. How true to human nature ! " All glorious deeds
desire to place themselves before the world." *Cicero.*

If thou seekest to be anything thou must boldly advance.

Like human restlessness : these " brothers," who lately would
have withheld Him through fear (Mark iii. ; Matt. xii.), now
recklessly seek to press Him forward.—They desire their mysterious relative brilliant success.—They have no trust of heart
nor any apprehension of the Divine in Him.—With a concealed
taunt they challenge Him publicly to prove His claims.

Doubtless they secretly hoped to rise with His rising glories.

If Thou wilt be the Light of the world (John viii. 12 ; ix. 5), shine
forth.—But prudence and humility wait God's time : then faith
goes joyously forward.—These worldlings would precipitate
Messiah's work. John v. 19.—They care little for " the honour
that cometh from God only." John v. 44.—And they know
little of His mission to seek and to save lost sinners.

As the " show " was their motive, so it now leads myriads to the
house of God.—A good appearance before men on the Sabbath
satisfies many a conscience.—The world still cries : Show thyself,
come out, make thyself known.—Those forward with *outward*
worship often the farthest from that which God seeks.

The world. From their point of view Jerusalem was " the world."

Judas Lebbæus recurs to this favourable idea of " the world."
Chap. xiv. 22.—Brothers of Jesus vaguely see a " world " ready
to receive Jesus with open arms.—To His eye " the world " is
rising up against Him, plotting and purposing His death.

Public virtue is a candle carried aloft, exposed to every breath of
passion.—Private virtue, the candle carried in a *lantern.*

Former gives more light, latter is in less danger of being blown
out.—Their advice was presumptuous, for it showed they did
not think Him competent to guide.—Some suppose they desired
to have His miracles tested by the Sanhedrim.

Others that they were weary of His holy company, and longed to
be rid of Him.—More probable, their motives were selfish : in
the splendour of His works they hoped as His kindred " *to make*

a fair show in the flesh."—They insinuate He had neglected confirming the faith of His disciples in Judea.—Or that He lacked the spirit to appear before great men in the metropolis. A Christian desires not glory for himself : the more secret he is the happier.

πάρρησία. With authority. *Hesychius.* They accuse Him of timidity. *Chrys.* They urge Him to become more honourable. *Hammond.*
    εἰ. Has an undertone of derision or of doubt. *Stier.* If Thou be the Light of the world ? *Lücke.* John implies miracles by ταῦτα. *Stier.*
    φανέρωσον. Play a public part. *Hezel.* Arguing *à priori* what God ought to do or say. *Shirley.*
    τῷ κόσμῳ. His brothers by this imitate the tone of disciples. *Kling.* But in a blind ironical manner. *Stier.*

---

5. For neither did his brethren believe in him.

Neither. Gr. *even* His brethren did not believe. See on John iv. 44.

Brethren. Ver. 3 ; John ii. 12. *Spiritual* light does not come from *natural* relationship.—Even the chosen twelve were " slow of heart to believe," though living in the full blaze of His personal purity, His words and His works.—Peter was addressed as " Satan : " to be avoided as an offence. Matt. xvi. 23. The sons of Zebedee contended for honour on the eve of the Last Supper. Matt. xx. 20.—They showed a worldly, proud, unkind, and inconsiderate spirit.—The steady service of genuine love is clothed in deep humility.—The highest moral heroism is always retiring in spirit.—Though an exalted honour to be of Christ's kindred, it cannot save the soul.—It is almost certain these " brothers" were not *converted* till after the resurrection. Paul refers to them as married, and as well-known disciples. 1 Cor. ix. 5.

Believe. John i. 7 ; vii. 38. Not unbelieving in the same sense as Caiaphas and the Jews.—They lacked the perfect yielding of a believing obedience.—" I am become a stranger unto my brethren." Psa. lxix. 8, literally fulfilled.—Jews still apply this word with bitter scorn to the Crucified One.

He seems to have wrought no special miracle to convince His mother's family.—He gave them the *same* warnings and teachings as *others.*—Relatives of Mahomet, won by worldly attractions, closely attached themselves to the " prophet."

It is a strong proof of His Divine mission that His " brothers did
not believe in Him."—Even after His resurrection the apostles
found it hard to receive His Messiahship in a *spiritual* sense.
Acts i. 6.

οὐδὲ γὰρ. Emphatic evidence of their being the real brothers of Christ.
Alford.

ἀδελφοὶ. See critical notes on ver. 3, and on John ii. 12. Mary's dignity
more compromised in being married to a widower with a number of children, as
Romanists and Romanisers affirm, than in her own subsequent fruitfulness.
Stier. Some suppose them our Lord's cousins, children of Alphæus and Mary,
sister of Mary His mother. But who ever heard of two sisters in one family of
the same name ? *Wieseler.* Mary having borne other children, casts no imputation on His miraculous conception. Her previous virginity an entirely and
essentially distinct fact. *Alford.*

ἐπίστευον. Germs of unbelief in the minds of the apostles themselves,
softened down to imperfections. *Hengst.* Their faith imperfect, had to contend
with unbelief. *Heumann.* Questioning whether His works were really Messianic. Not so high a type of faith. *W. H. Mill.* They had a kind of belief
in His Messianic character but of the lowest sort. Impossible to modify ἐπίστ.
so as to suppose they may have been of the twelve. *Alford, Lücke.* Jews to
this day deride Christ's pretensions on the strength of this text. *Trapp.*

---

6. Then Jesus said unto them, My time is not yet come : but your time is
alway ready.

Said. His answer gentle ; but often the milder the reply the
deeper it cuts.

My time. The time ordained and appointed to Him by God for
His public appearance.—In distinction from the hours arbitrarily
chosen by other men. John ii. 4.—It is the peculiar glory of
believers also, that in all their actions God's time is theirs.

He will not anticipate the greetings and Hosannahs of His followers.—His enemies cannot lay their hands upon Him without
God's will.—To sinners on earth time affords space for repentance, and is their FRIEND.—There is a time when we should
not only number our *days*, but *hours*.—" MILLIONS FOR ANOTHER
WEEK," the dying lament of Elizabeth, Queen of England.

Time a divine loan here for which eternity will demand account.

Nothing which the wicked spend so lavishly, nothing which they
will hereafter mourn over more bitterly.—Many tax their minds
how " to lash the lingering moments into speed."—The expression " killing time " reveals sadly the fallen character of man.

Step by step Jesus went on with His Father's design of mercy.

He would not incur the hatred of the world until the moment came.

No one is prematurely to squander His life: every one should, in the best sense, " sell it at the highest price."—His time was God's time, His brethren's time the world's time.—It mattered nothing to them when they went if the world was pleased.

Their time agreed not with His. Believers are also " a peculiar people."

Not come. When it came, He hastened to it, so that His disciples wondered. Mark x. 32.—" He steadfastly set His face to go to Jerusalem." Luke ix. 51.—His first public entrance was the entrance in the procession with palms.—By that He showed Himself to the world, and by that also brought on His death.

With heavenly precaution He guards His life that He may sacrifice it fully at the right hour.—A ministry of three years in Pharisaic Judea could have been secured only by such Divine wisdom.—Servants of the Lord, doing their duty, cannot always be masters of their own time.—Fetters of toil are far better for us than the liberty of idleness, the sin of Sodom. Ezek. xvi. 49.—All their plans of future ambition with their brother are dashed for ever.

Your time. The free arbitrary disposal of times which sinful men make.—A clear intimation of their want of decided faith.

Not at feast of tabernacles, but at the following passover He would die.—He discriminates as to their aims. They had no desire for God's glory.—Their desire was to stand well with the world, and this blinded their minds, and hardened their hearts.

They had volunteered allegiance, if He would " show Himself to the world."—But He repels them from Him with earnest, deep sorrow.—His words imply, " We, in reality, have now nothing in common.—No interests of infinite and world-wide moment rest on you.—You do not like me stand in full and pure antagonism to the world.—I, in respect to time and place, am under the control of my Father."—Thus was every point of His time a point of eternity: thus His being in every place a being in heaven.—It is also the peculiar glory of His people, that in all their actions God's time is theirs.

λέγει. Chaps. vii.—x. the conflict with unbelief. *Luthardt.*

καιρὸς ὁ ἐμὸς. 1. The time for Me to go to the feast. *Jansen, Lightfoot.* 2. The time to show Myself openly to the world (as they had demanded in ver. 4). *Rosenm., Lücke, Alford.* 3. The time of My passion. *Chrys., Euthym.* His going to Jerusalem was unsafe, therefore improper. *Doddr.* Opportune occasion. *Wetstein.* After the passion and ascension. *Grotius.*

7. The world cannot hate you; but me it hateth, because I testify of it, that the works thereof are evil.

The world. Considered as unbelieving, in its antagonism to the Lord.—Its rulers and myriads are by nature foes to my cause.

Cannot hate you. Ye are its fast friends ; as such, it has no controversy with you.—A word of keen condemnation to every class of *worldly* professors.—The world *cannot* hate you, for you leave it in peace.—The law is unchangeable, " The world will ever love its own." John xv. 19.—His yearning heart doubtless ached, thus to speak to His brethren.—The world has ever hated, and will continue to hate, " The Light of the world." John iii. 20.—Yet His testimony will be given until He yields to the world's hate on the Cross.—Truth condemns their sins, so they hate it and its Author.—An infallible proof that " Madness is in their heart while they live." Eccl. ix. 3.

The world repays fraternal fidelity with ill-will and hate. Lev. xix. 17.—Yet it is not cruelty, but charity, that restrains the madman.—We love that friend who *violently* snatches us from a burning home.—" To preach the truth with fearless fidelity is to arm the whole world against you." *Luther.*

Worldlings have a *union*, not of love, but of ambition with ambition, of envy with envy, of lust with lust, a marvellous union of the world's princes against truth. Psa. ii. 2 ; Luke xi. 18.

Christians who will attain to the honour of *persecution* must be holy.—Of Churches undisturbed by evil men, or evil spirits, the world says, " They are of us."—" There is no devil so dangerous to a minister as a *quiet* devil." *Whitefield.*

He proffered a *test* these worldly ones could not stand.

Their own principles laid them under condemnation.

Instead of reforming their practices, they assailed their Saviour.

A demonstration that these worldlings were not apostles.

The moment Christians renounce the world the world renounces them.—The laws of worldlings truth pronounces a fiction.

Earth's joys are the believer's snares, earth's gain the believer's loss.

Earth's honours the believer's stains, earth's crowns the believer's cross.—Whenever the apostles and the world meet it is as foes.

But Me. The Son of God coming into the world has affected the history of the whole race.—His death was the greatest shock ever experienced by mankind.—Jews and infidels generally deny there is any allusion to a *suffering Messiah* in the Old Testament. " Liberals " and other unbelievers in every age have tried to lessen its importance, but there it stands!—Shafts of hostile criticism can no more affect it than a word can level the Alps or put out the sun. It is a question whether persecutors have not done as much to advance Christianity as all the missionaries that ever lived.

It hateth. The entire antagonism brought forth by His testimony against the world.—The world's hatred comes out completely only in opposition to that which is Divine.—He tore the mask from pretended honesty and humility.—He showed the cruel hypocrisy of Pharisees and other ecclesiastics.—He laid bare the hollow-hearted worship of these whited sepulchres.

Of course those who honoured them detested and dreaded Him.

To believers remembrance of Christ is a continual festival.

To unbelievers an invisible *Nemesis*, awakening fears and destroying their peace.—Hence the avidity with which unbelievers receive accounts that science or historical criticism is opposed to the Bible.—The wish that it should be found untrue is father to the thought.—Perhaps never was the world's hate against Christ so strong as now.—Nero published a decree, " Let Christians be put to death wherever found, as the convicted enemies of mankind."—Christ's presence haunts the wicked. " We can't ignore Christ," said a modern sceptic.—Neither could the chief priests and Pilate as they signed His death-warrant.

The world gave Him a cradle, but it was a manger ; a throne, but it was a cross ; a crown, but it was thorns ; a sceptre, but it was a reed ; homage, but it was derisive mockery and bitter scorn ; companions, but they were crucified criminals; a kingdom, but it was a grave.—" Whosoever will be a friend of the world is the enemy of God." Jas. iv. 4.

I testify. " Truth begets hate." This is the testimony of the great comic author *Terence*.—Had He flattered the pride of the Pharisees, their highest honours would have been His.

But He pronounced blessings on " the poor in spirit, the meek, the merciful," &c.—This struck a fatal blow at their pretended holiness of character.—He urged men to lay up treasures in heaven, while they idolized the world.—He made religion to consist of spiritual excellency, "justice, mercy, faith." This destroyed their ritualism.—His life was a living exposition of the law of God. This condemned their hypocrisy.—" They who are after the flesh persecute those who are after the spirit." Gal. iv. 29; v. 17.

Ahab of Micaiah : " I hate him because he does not prophesy good concerning me, but evil." 1 Kings xxii. 8.

Paul to the Galatians, "Am I become your enemy because I tell you the truth?" Chap. iv. 16.—The only physician who will be tolerated *in the end* is he who is faithful.—Mountebanks deceive until their pretence and ignorance are unmasked.

"Liberals" and other unbelievers may get a hearing while men are in health, but when death thunders at the door they are seen in their true light.—A young scholar having been seduced by Voltaire's writings, on his death-bed cried, "Curse you, Voltaire!" *Jay* of Bath.—Jesus testified not only by His preaching and miracles, but pre-eminently by His *holy Life*.

A holy life in the humblest Christian is a silent but eloquent and powerful sermon.—A young man riding by a wood heard the sound of a human voice, and dismounting, crept through the hedge and saw an aged saint at prayer.—For thirty years the memory of that secret prayer held him like an invisible thread, until it drew him to the Cross, and he devoted himself and much wealth to Christ.

Works. Works are the full, strong, unmistakable expression of spirit, principles, and purpose.

Are evil. Evil in their origin, evil in their nature, evil in their issues and end.—"The heart of the sons of men is fully set in them to do evil." Eccl. viii. 11.—Wicked men denounce the world's deeds as evil, but each takes pains to except himself from the rule.

$\mu\iota\sigma\epsilon\hat{\iota}$ $\dot{\epsilon}\mu\dot{\epsilon}$. The universal hatred encountered by Christ and His followers for ages. *Grotius.* Voltaire and D'Alembert proclaimed themselves "Defenders of God," while their watchword was "Crush the wretch," referring to Jesus. *Smith's* Messiah. Treatment of our Lord by *Tacitus* and *Suetonius*, and by *Josephus*, indicates hostility to Christ. The two former had no motive to malign Him, but a conscience ill at ease. The latter notoriously pandered to Roman pride. *Author.* Rationalists can't find Christ in the O. T. *Ullmann.* Others can't discover Him in the New. *Lange.* "If I tell the Pope he has squandered the Church's goods with villains and harlots I do not offend him; but if I say that Papists are hypocrites he is angry, and would fain kill me." *Luther.*

---

8. Go ye up unto this feast: I go not up yet unto this feast; for my time is not yet full come.

Go ye. His unbelieving brethren, doubtless, went with the crowd of pilgrims.—You have no great plans in life, your moments are unimportant.—The world has no contest with you, but I denounce its hypocrisy and sins.

I go not yet. Our Lord followed His apostles in a private manner. Ver. 10.—With designed indefiniteness He repels His brethren.—He assigns a reason for sending them on their way alone.—I go not *as* the multitude to join in the celebration of the rites.—At a proper time I will go as a *stranger*, a mere visitor or spectator.—Our Lord's way of humility was chosen to prepare the way for His exaltation.—Others He enjoined to honour the rites of the Temple: "Go, show," &c., Matt. viii. 4.—Had He set a time His brethren might have thought they had influenced Him.

This was His last journey to Jerusalem until He went up *to die.*

My time. Our Lord, never through His career, made a confidant of any.—Men often wish to get the start of God, and enjoy in *their* time what He reserves for them in *His* time.

He who would too rapidly hasten his cure often makes death sure.

Some supposed He changed His purpose, and quote the case of the Syro-Phœnician. Matt. xv. 26.—But His purpose was no more changed there than here.—He would unfold their character, and He did it.

Not come. There is a sense of loneliness, even of sadness, in these words.—Misunderstood by His kindred, He was carrying out a work of LOVE, which those who were to be blessed by it would abhor.—He was straitened by the consciousness of having a message of mercy, and yet that He must undergo a baptism of blood.—All this for a world created by Him, but which knew Him not, and which longed to rid itself of His Presence.

The bearing of guilty men toward the Saviour excites wonder in heaven and probably among the lost. Isa. i. 2 ; xiv. 9.

τὴν ἑορτήν. That is, He intends to go up to some future feast. *Meyer.*
ταύτην omitted. *Tisch., Alf.* Retained. *Cod. Sin.*
For οὔπω read οὐκ. *Cod. Sin., Cod. Camb., Epiph., Cyril, Chrys., Tisch., Bengel, Stier, Lücke, Alf., Treg., Meyer, Lange. Porphyry* found οὐκ in *Jerome*, and drew from it the charge of fickleness against Jesus. Just to avoid this offence, οὔπω was introduced. *Meyer.*
οὔπω retained. *Lach., Westcott & Hort.* The only charge of the want of veracity against our Lord ever made fails if οὐκ be the true reading. *Rothe.* He did design unconditionally to refuse His brethren's request as they understood it. *Stier.* He who was not present on the first day of the feast was not held to have observed it. *Bengel.* He at first did not intend going, but afterwards changed out of regard to His Father's will. *Sepp, Meyer.* How can this view be reconciled with Malachi iii. 6, I AM THE LORD, I CHANGE NOT? *Author.* He certainly did intend at His own time to go up. *Lange.* He did not intend to go up to join in their religious ceremonies. *Cyril, Lampe.* I am not (at present) going up. *Alford.* Not with the caravan. *Ewald, Luthardt.* He took no part ritually in the festal train or scenes. *Ebrard.*

καιὼòs· He had no need to make them share His secret. *Hengst.*

πεπλήρωται. Intimates He will presently follow. *Lange.* Questioned, since the brethren must not be able to herald His coming. *Stier.* Our Lord's subsequent appearance at this feast an act of consummate psychological mastery. *Lange.*

---

9. When he had said these words unto them, he abode still in Galilee.

Abode still. He let the train pass on its way, and probably His brothers with it.—How calm and Godlike as He pursues His Father's counsels.—He never for a moment swerved from the path He chose. As the sun pursues his course through cloud and storm, so from the moment of His incarnation until He cried, "It is finished," not a single shadow of turning or variableness can be detected. Jas. i. 17.

Galilee. John i. 43. The scene of the greater part of our Lord's private life and public acts.

For αὐτοῖς read αὐτòs. *Cod. Sin., Tisch.*

---

10. But when his brethren were gone up, then went he also up unto the feast, not openly, but as it were in secret.

Then went He. Our acts of devotion, not the measured seasons, make life.—The good Samaritan numbered his days by acts of sacrifice and kindness.—He alone is happy whose clear conscience and finished duties mark his *calendar.*—Our Lord measured His ministry by labours of love and miracles of grace.

Thus it is presumed alternate seasons of praise will mark the cycle of life in heaven.—Most of His hearers had forsaken Him, now He seeks others.—He would not go with those refusing to believe in Him.—No reference to the Old Testament law. As Son, He was free.

Feast. John vii. 2. An exalted spirit characterized Israel's ancient theocracy.

Not openly. i. e. not with the caravans constantly passing.

Not in the festal train, not as a festal pilgrim.—With His apostles, who seem never to have been long absent from Him.

Twelve men would have been unnoticed amid the gathering thousands.

As it were. Qualifies the secrecy. He crossed the midnight lake in secret.—Perhaps He remained at Bethany for a short time before He appeared at the feast.

Secret. That is, as a private person, a spectator, not a participant. His personal movements, though marked by every sign of humanity, frequently resemble the glidings of a spirit. Mark ix. 15.

It is uncertain whether His appearance or movement amazed them most.—Jews, fearing hostility of Samaritans, went up to Jerusalem by way of Perea.—It would have been beneath the dignity of our Lord to travel with any display.

He must suppress all idea that He intends to establish an earthly kingdom.—His departure from Galilee now was private : His final departure took place under a great convoy. Matt. xix. 1, 2.

It was a judgment on the Jewish Church, that their King *was* not known by them.

ἀνέβησαν. He left His brethren behind. *Hengst.* No evidence of this. *Author.*

ἐν κρυπτῷ. His twelve apostles could not fail to excite attention. *Hengst.* A visit to Jerusalem amid the surging crowds of pilgrims during the passover would correct this mistake. *Author.*

---

11. Then the Jews sought him at the feast, and said, Where is he ?

Jews. The leaders, implacable in hatred and reckless as to results. His brothers desire His exaltation. His enemies desire to arrest and destroy Him.

Sought. With a fixed resolve to crush Him. Even now sinners hate their best FRIEND.—How diverse the motives with which men sought Jesus : the magi to adore Him : Herod to crush a rival prince ; Greeks to gratify curiosity ; Jews to see miracles, or to crown Him a king to promote their carnal interests : only a few hungry souls sought Him as the BREAD OF LIFE.

Some seek Him to find ground of objection to His mission into the world.—They would take from Him His name,—" ATONING LAMB ! "—They would strip Him of the brightest of the many crowns which adorn His brows.—How many frequent the Church and her ordinances, but never *seek* Jesus !—To how many of earth's feasters would He prove an unwelcome guest !

Where is He ? *Where is that man ?* They do not mention the hated name.—Every one knew to whom they referred.—It shows how well He was known by the people.

Joseph's brethren called him not Joseph, but, by way of scorn, the
"*Dreamer.*"—Saul asked not for David, but for the "son of
Jesse."—Papal Rome ordered that wherever the name of *Calvin*
occurred it should be erased.

Where is He ? Can there be a feast in the true sense without
Him ?—Earth's feasts are mockeries, where the soul " feeds on
ashes."

'Ιουδαῖοι. Sanhedrim. *Tholuck.* Dwellers in Judea. *Stier.* People, including the rulers. *Hengst.*

ἐζήτουν. Sent spies to take Him. *Hezel.*

ἐκεῖνος. Was too well known to be named. *Stier.* Used scornfully.
Grotius. They would enviously lessen the splendour of His word and works.
Gualter. The celebrated one. *Buttmann.* The illustrious one. *Hengst.*

---

12. And there was much murmuring among the people concerning him : for
some said, He is a good man : others said, Nay ; but he deceiveth the people.

Murmuring. Such excitement was awakened in all classes touching Him.—The multitude feared to say anything against Him,
lest the rulers should change their minds.—And if they spoke
for Christ, they would be excommunicated.—These are proofs of
the wide impression made by His miracles and teachings.

Some censured Him for neglecting their national feasts. Deut. xiii. 5.

People. Gr. *crowds.* An unconscious allusion to the hosts
gathered there.—At this day multitudes tent within and without
the city during the passover.—Some of the common people
hung upon His words. Luke xix. 48.—Many heard Him gladly.
Mark xii. 37. Others " came early in the morning." John viii. 2.

These appear to have been from Galilee, as next verse speaks of
Jews.

Good man. His friends timidly whispered His defence. But
" He seduceth the people" was sounded out aloud.

It was saying but little, but as a protest it was much.

Or perhaps they were hypocrites sounding the sentiments of the
people.—He who healed the sick, who had sight for the blind,
bread for the hungry, joy for the mourner, who had peace for the
tempest-tossed and life for the dead, must have been a GOOD
MAN indeed !

Deceiveth. This was a preliminary step to charging Him with
crimes.—They had to blacken His character before the mob would
say, " CRUCIFY." — Papists covered Jerome of Prague with

pictures of devils while taking him to the stake. The Sanhedrists first resolved to put our Lord out of the way, and then sought accusations to *justify* their *murderous* plan.

Verily, the race of " *impious Jews* " is not yet dead.

Satan is on his throne, not yet chained or in prison. Rev. xx. 1.

These wicked rulers taught men to call Him " deceiver." Matt. xxvii. 42, 63.

The people. Probably they alluded to His feeding the crowd, and also to His discourse, in which He required them to eat His flesh and drink His blood as a test of obedience.

γογγυσμὸς. Muttering. *Bloomfield.* Whispering. *Campbell.* Secret disputation. *Schleusner.* The effect of this unfriendly search. *Lampe.* A picture of things in Jerusalem. *Stier.* They think His absence a contempt of their feast. *Kuinoel.*

ἀγαθός. In O. T. used oft for well-disposed. 1 Sam. ii. 26. Righteous. Prov. ii. 20. Opposed to sinners. Eccl. ix. 2. *Hengst.* A well-wisher of the people. *B. Crusius.* An honourable true man. *Meyer.*

πλανᾷ. Seducers were to be capitally punished, since they murdered souls. *Lampe.*

13. Howbeit no man spake openly of him for fear of the Jews.

No man. None of His friends. Alas! how often fear seals the mouths of His professed followers.—His enemies might proclaim their scorn of His birth, His life, His deeds, His claims.

Openly. This was only true of those who spake kindly of Him.

As usual, a depraved world tolerates all kinds of wickedness.

MEN HAVE NEVER BEEN PERSECUTED FOR THEIR ILL TREATMENT OF GOD.—For all manner of crimes against Jehovah they have no law.—But fifty millions of Christian martyrs witness to this strange fact, PERSECUTED TO DEATH FOR LOVING GOD.

Bondage of soul was such that no one dared fully to utter his thoughts till the hierarchy had spoken.

Fear. John vi. 19. " Fear of man bringeth a snare." Prov. xxix. 25 ; but " perfect love casteth out fear." 1 John iv. 18.

On this rock faith, honour, integrity are often shipwrecked.

How many duties and principles are sacrificed to cowardly compliance.—Men often sin rather from fear of scorn than from love of evil.—Concession is often the *bane* of good, and the *policy* of bad men.—An old prophet from Judah once tried it, and was slain by a lion. 1 Kings xiii. 24.—Jehu tried it, and failed, and his posterity reaped the bitter fruit. Hosea i. 4.

638 / Gospel of John

Pilate tried it, and was despised by both Jews and Gentiles.
Caiaphas fell into this snare, and even Peter fell into a similar
temptation.

Jews. John i. 19. John generally refers to their rulers.

The Pharisees were the *soul* of this mass of corrupt humanity.

They even overawed Joseph of Arimathæa (John xix. 38) and
others. John xii. 42.—They persecuted or befriended, bound
or loosed, just as they chose.—" Fear of the Jews," or despotism
of the letter, an ancient and modern hindrance to faith and
knowledge.—A type of the whole spirit of hierarchy in the Church
and absolutism in the State.—Under such systems, enemies of
truth always speak rather more boldly than its friends.

The Papacy and despotism go together. The Bible promotes
liberty intellectual and political.—Mental indolence of Papists
upholds mental tyranny of their hierarchy.

παρρησίᾳ. Explains γογγυσμὸς, only as the unsuppressed feeling of the
heart. *Stier.* A most culpable weakness in the people around our Lord.
Schleier. Jerusalem ruled the domain of religious belief, and the Pharisees
ruled her. *Josephus.*

ἐλάλει. Even the hostile ones were afraid because the hierarchy had not
yet *officially* decided. *Meyer.* At Dola, Burgundy, Jesuits forbade men to speak
of God, either good or bad. *Trapp.* They suppress even Bellarmine's defence
of Rome, because he *names the Protestant doctrines* to refute them. *Author.*

---

14. Now about the midst of the feast Jesus went up into the temple, and
taught.

Midst. Feast lasted eight days (Num. xxix. 13), and as three or
four days were now past, it was evident He did not intend to
take part in it.—His unexpected presence, showing the utmost
confidence, secured for Him the protection of the people.

His wisdom neither courts danger nor shows undignified timidity.

It is thought the *Sabbath* occurred in the midst of the feast.

Went up. The temple was on Mount Moriah, and many massive
steps of marble led up on every side. Neh. xii. 37 ; 1 Kings x. 5.

Some fear to soil their devotion by mingling with the crowd.
Acts x. 22.—Highest piety is to imitate Him whose chosen
walks were among the poor, the diseased, the blind, the leprous, &c.

Temple. John ii. 14, 20 ; v. 14. He seems to pass from extreme
caution to extreme boldness.—But He proves Himself by this
step the great Master in the knowledge of men.

He relies on the utmost publicity against the secret plottings of
party spirit.—The lion-like spirit of the Lord, 1. Proved, by
this incident. 2. By His previous going into the wilderness.
3. By His subsequent surrender to the council.

Proved also in the life of His apostles and in the course of His
Church.—Apostles in Jerusalem, Peter in Babylon, Paul at
Rome, missions to heathen.—When did a " Liberal " or other
infidel peril his life or liberty for his opinions?

He chose the temple for its sacredness and because of the crowds
gathered.—Greek philosophers also lectured in temples, as there
the multitude resorted.—They found a shade from the burning
sun, and quiet repose from the forum or from the market.

Taught. Gr. *continued,* i. e. in a formal manner, not by snatches
of time.—This was the *fourth time* His voice was heard in the
temple.—1. When He was twelve years of age. Luke ii. 42.
2. When He drove out the traders. John ii. 15. 3. When He
delivered His first discourse, John v. 17 ; and now six months
before His death.—We may suppose that His teaching related
to the feast of tabernacles.—So in chap. ii. His teaching referred
to the symbolical import of the temple.—He always availed
Himself of surrounding circumstances to find texts for His discourses.—His life-labours were spent almost wholly outside of
Jerusalem. Why? His every act, like those of Providence,
has a voice which speaks through all ages.—This treatment of
the leading minds of the Church and nation was a *judgment.*
Luke xiii. 34.—He seemed to pause for the multitude to become
quiet ; never before had He found minds so excited.

The entire nation knew He claimed to be their *Messiah.* Mark i. 37.

An apostate Church groaning under the oppression of heathen
Rome, expected far *more* from the *Messiah* than from their *God.*

Our Lord's posture was equivalent to a public declaration of His
claims.—His miraculous power as well as His prestige *awed*
the Pharisees from taking sudden vengeance.—He who could
command legions of angels could easily control His enemies.

These hearers unconsciously felt as we all shall in the day of
judgment.—From His burning, searching glance even then men
could not flee.

ἑορτῆς μεσούσης. Days following the feast when some work was done.
Pococke. Not necessarily the fourth day. *Stier.* His appearance miraculous,
His change from Galilee so sudden. *Fikenscher.* A crisis waited for by our

Lord with longing patience. *Quesnel.* Sacrifices lessening, the people had
more time to hear. *Grotius.* Between the first and seventh. *Wetstein.* Probably on the Sabbath. *Bengel, Alford.*

 ἐδίδασκεν. Continued to teach. *D. Brown.*

---

15. And the Jews marvelled, saying, How knoweth this man letters, having
never learned ?

Jews. John i. 19. Judging from their expressions, scribes and
Pharisees.—Wisdom of Christ's teaching has proved a *hard problem* to infidels for 1800 years.—To this day it stands above the
efforts of the mightiest and most trained minds.

Marvelled. They had never seen such light with such irresistible
power.—Thus He opened the eyes of the two disciples as they
sat at meat. Luke xxiv. 31.—Not only were the rulers unable
thus to speak, but they could not *comprehend* Him.

They feared far more than they were willing to own.

Their surprise at *what* He says is lost in wonder at *how* He knows
it.—Wicked men are angry that Christians should be able to
know and publish truth. Acts iv. 2.—When men of learning
are withheld, God anoints the lips of the untaught to feed His
flock and fold His lambs.—Such was the son of Jesse, such the
herdsman of Tekoa (Amos i. 1), and such the fishermen of
Galilee.

How knoweth ? That a man cannot learn but from *man* is a
favourite dogma of priests.—That He had no education in the
schools a very important testimony from His enemies.

What transparent proof in His teachings that He derived nothing
from books!—His exposition of truth shows an unrivalled faculty
and depth. Matt. v.—Not having training they questioned His
right to teach publicly.—He made no pretence to the character
of a Rabbi.—They insinuated He was a self-made man, in
a bad sense.—All Jerusalem must have *known* Himself and
Joseph to have been *mechanics.*—Though no journals are published in Palestine, information travels marvellously fast.

Letters. John v. 47. As in the English phrase, a man of
letters.—Here it means chiefly *Scripture learning*, for it was almost
the only kind known to the Jews.—In this He displayed matchless penetration and comprehension.

Never learned. This passage shows the folly of all attempts,
ancient and modern, to trace the wisdom of Jesus to human
education.—No doubt He learned from His mother, and He

went to the synagogue.—He heard and read the Scriptures : He
studied nature and man.—The Holy Ghost descended on Him
at Jordan, yet the secret fountain of His knowledge must be
sought for in His mysterious relation to the Father.
Derived from direct intuition of the eternal source of truth in God.
" The only begotten Son in the bosom of the Father." From that
centre He shed light over the whole world of man and nature.
He taught the world as one who had learned nothing from it; as
one who not only *knows* truth, but IS TRUTH.—He was neither
school-taught, nor *self*-taught, nor even *God*-taught, like the prophets.—" In Him (HIMSELF) are hid all the treasures of wisdom
and knowledge." Col. ii. 3.—Humanly speaking uneducated,
He towers infinitely above all educated.—His thoughts, like
God's works in the natural world, clearly show their Divine
source.—" Increasing in wisdom," Luke ii. 52, describes the
development of His human mind.—His teaching opened an entirely new field of thought.—As though He had created a *new
sun* in the heavens for *astronomers.*—Human learning in our
Saviour's day was the handmaid of idolatry.—A man might
deliberately commit any sin, provided he knew what sacrifice
would atone for it.—Among the Greeks their very *devotions* were
screens for sensuality and crime.—Language, too, was a means
of concealing one's true thoughts. *Chesterfield* endorses this.
It was an age of falsehood when truth " had fallen into the streets."
Isa. lix. 14.—Words had lost their authority as media of living
truths.—A heartless age when men sacrificed to sense while
Jehovah was an UNKNOWN GOD. Acts xvii. 23.—That such a
Teacher should have arisen in such an age is THE MIRACLE of
miracles.

ἐθαύμαζον. Esteeming it presumption, they contested His right. *Lange.*
He had never taught in the temple before. *Lampe.* Not being trained, a new
way of rousing enmity to Jesus. *Brückner.*
γράμματα. Without ἱερά (2 Tim. iii. 15) denotes not the Scriptures
(ἡ γραφή), but literature, the field of learning. *Lange, Lücke.* Litteræ. *Vulgate.*
Without the article, learning. *Kypke.* The Scriptures. *Luther, Grotius.*
Science. *Fikenscher.* Jewish erudition. *Wetstein.* They had no books but
the O.T. *Alford.* Invention of letters ascribed to Adam, Seth, Enoch, Noah.
Hepburn. John calls Moses' works γράμματα. John v. 47. Our Lord was
instructed in the common rudiments. *Meyer.* Understood neither Hebrew nor
Greek. *Origen.* Illustrations then in vogue among Rabbis. *Doddr.*
μὴ μεμαθηκώς. Decisive words of foes as to His deriving anything from
human fountains. *Meyer.* He never refers to secular history, poetry, rhetoric,
mathematics, astronomy, foreign languages, natural sciences, or any of those

branches of knowledge which make up human learning or literature. *Schaff* in *Lange.*

---

16. Jesus answered them, and said, My doctrine is not mine, but his that sent me.

Answered. Their thoughts, since they could not have spoken in His hearing.

My doctrine. The religious instruction found in His discourses, parables, and miracles.—" Liberals " ignore this, stating that Jesus taught no doctrines.—But the great CENTRAL DOCTRINE and FOUNDATION of all others He clearly taught. John x. 11.

They imply His wisdom was the result of study, so that in their sense it was not His, but God's.—He·Himself the Alpha and Omega of His doctrine.—" He expounded to them in all the Scriptures the things concerning HIMSELF." Luke xxiv. 27.

Heathen philosophers find in Him no solution of their *vain* questions.—Yet every ray of light, of tradition, of philosophy, of science, came from Him and led to Him. John i. 10.

Not only does He reveal what none but the Son of God could have declared, but He embraces in His teaching all previously known spiritual and moral truth.—Whatever ground of truth Judaism or heathenism contained, finds in Christ its certainty and its completion.—Thus as THE TEACHER sent from God, He was to an unconscious world "THE DESIRE OF ALL NATIONS."

CHRIST is the GOAL of all really sincere devout thinking and striving.—His kingdom is the embodiment of all true knowledge, and all previous prophets were imperfect types of this GREATEST of PROPHETS.—His LIFE WAS HIS DOCTRINE, a fulfilling of the entire Old Testament, and a grand prophecy of all coming time.

Not Mine. I am no *self*-taught man in such a sense as to be an upstart or pretender.—There is another in whose school I have regularly advanced.—He sets off HIS TEACHING against *their* Rabbinical teaching, both as to form and matter.

He sets off HIS AUTHORITY, the FATHER against *their* authority.

He claimed to be a messenger of God, sent from heaven to earth.

They saw the form and heard the voice of a man, but such an one as they *supposed* Him to be was not the Author of this doctrine.

" If, however, you wish to ascertain whence this doctrine springs, begin by living My precepts, and you will know its nature and source."—" I do not derive it from study, nor is it wrought out by the understanding."—No learning to be had in schools can

ever teach that which the Father revealeth unto babes. Matt.
xi. 25.

Sent. Therefore not only the doctrine of God, but the direct
message of God to you.—A doctrine revealing the ground, means,
and issues of eternal life.—This word clearly distinguishes between the Son as sent and the Father sending.—The whole
Catholic Church has since the beginning held the great fundamental doctrine of Three Persons in one God. John i. 1, 2.

Our Lord solemnly protests against the *sufficiency* of mere human
learning.—All knowledge and speculations apart from this
doctrine are ineffectual.—As the noonday sun needs no star or
moon to reveal it, so our Saviour's doctrine needed no ornament
or illustration.—Earnest longing souls need but behold His
word and works to believe and adore.—Hence the Spirit gives
us no demonstration of Christ's Divinity, but *rebukes* atheists as
fools (Psa. liii. 1) and deniers of the Son as liars. 1 John v. 10.

His that sent Me. 1. Because it contains the whole counsel of
the Father. 2. Because it was one with Moses and the prophets
through whom the Father had spoken. 3. Because Christ was
filled with the Spirit of the Father. 4. Because His doctrine
aimed at the glory of the Father. *Starke* in *Lange*.

Test of orthodox teachers. 1. Taking their doctrine not from their
own reason, but from the holy revealed word of God. 2. Seeking not their own glory, but the glory of God.

διδαχή. Doctrine in our times a word of limited meaning, being simply
opposed to practical. But in Scripture it means *teaching:* anything taught is
doctrine. *Robertson.*

οὖν added by *Lach.*, *Tisch.*, *Alf.*, *Tregelles.* Places Himself modestly on
a level with other Διδάσκαλοι. *Stier.* His *Plan of Redemption* circle of all
wisdom worth the name. *Deitlein.* "To lay it all on the conscience" a sentiment scorned by *Schiller.* Right evidence must spring from moral experience,
where alone is the veritatis cum *pietate* vinculum. *Stier.* That we can only
firmly trust that which we can prove by science (*Huxley*) is "wisdom" which
God distinctly pronounces "VAIN." Col. ii. 8. *Author.*

οὐκ ἐμή, i. e. unauthorized. I am here by Divine commission, either the
sense of the Scriptures, or the teachings themselves. *Alford* prefers the
latter.

ἀλλά. Absolutely exclusive. *Meyer.* Hardly "absolutely," but only so
far as His person is regarded in its human aspect. *Lange.* His human personality is viewed abstractedly by itself, as in chap. v. 31 ; viii. 16. *Tholuck.*
He yields so far to their idea of an independent human person distinct from
God. *Lange.*

πέμψαντος. From the FATHER, by the SON, through the SPIRIT, but how
surpasses human power to conceive. *Hooker.*

17. If any man will do his will, he shall know of the doctrine, whether it be of God, or whether I speak of myself.

Will. Gr. *is willing to do,* or *wishes to do,* desires to do.

This is the key to that state of heart implied in the words, " *All that the Father giveth Me.*" John vi. 37. " *Father drawing.*" John vi. 44.—While many boast of being " willing," they make thăt very "*will*" the excuse for *persecuting* God's people.

This "*will*" with the Jesuits has been their authority for *all crimes!* —This is our Lord's famous test, which has never been superseded.—The indispensable condition for understanding the doctrine of Christ.—We must be truly turned *towards* God to recognize the *divine* from God.—Our *willingness* to do God's WILL is the alone condition for knowing Christ.—Without longing for God and salvation, no conviction of the truth of the gospel, no faith in Christ, is possible.

Do His will. Blind submission never leads to true knowledge, but faith leading to obedience *illumines* the mind, for Christ's law is " a reasonable service." Rom. xii. 1.—Men generally, however ignorant, think they *know* and are *able* to do their duty.

Socrates was one among millions who acknowledged the need of a Divine Teacher.—We must be earnestly bent on the divine in *practice* if we would know it as *doctrine.*—Without the earnestness of *doing* there can be no truth in our *knowing.*

Like cannot know like without a like bent of soul.

Willing to do is the beginning of that *doing* which developes into the love of God.—Many learn geometry, but never measure a field ; so many read God's word who never *intend* obeying it.

Bible duties always involve a knowledge of Bible doctrines.

The duties of the Christian are as *few* and *simple* as those of *life.* 1. To believe what God says because He says it. 2. To do what God commands because He commands it.—As the heart of every human being demands but one kind of blood and the lungs but one kind of air, so the renewed mind demands but one repentance, one faith, one love.—Zacharias walked in *all* the ordinances of the Lord blameless. Luke i. 6.

" Love and serve the Lord with all thy heart and all thy soul." Deut. x. 12.—To do the will of God is ever the joy of all holy hearts. Psa. cxix.—Sin prevents men from knowing when their will is not one with God's.—Cornelius followed a few rays of light, and they led him to the Sun of Righteousness.

Men *disguise* their perverse will with many pleas, slaves of vice

gild their chains, and boast of freedom.—Pride transforms man's
misery into ground of rejoicing.—We *plume* ourselves on our
raiment, while it is a memorial of our *shame.* Gen. iii. 7.
Christ, the living ideal of holiness, must be dear to those willing to
do His will.—Once convicted of our blindness and peril, we fly
to some one to lead us.—Hence the law showing us our sin as
a schoolmaster leads to Christ.—The " natural " man will ever
contend against the doctrine of the new birth. John iii. 4.
The wicked are not *content* with despising the gospel ; they hate
and persecute those doing God's will.—*Morality,* clung to, turns
virtues into so many *shining sins.*—No one trying to obey God's
law will doubt his *utter inability* to succeed. 1 Kings viii. 46.
He who regards sin as mere infirmity, or vice as mere tricks, will
never believe in our Lord's atonement.—No one doing His will
thinks loathing evil to be hypocrisy, or sensitiveness to duty
pedantry, or practising secret prayer formalism, or acts of self-
sacrifice ostentation.—If any one will refuse to eat until he
understands the mysteries of nutrition he will starve.
So will he perish who refuses to obey until he knows his final acceptance.—It is not the atmosphere merely, but our breathing it
which sustains life.—So it is not the *extent* of our knowledge,
but the *practice* which avails.—Yet is Divine goodness not
limited. God reserves His right of sovereignty.
" I am found of them that sought Me not." Isa. lxv. 1.
" He will have mercy on whom He will have mercy." Rom. ix. 15.
The patriarch testifies, " He giveth not account of any of His
matters." Job xxxiii. 13.—No one ever was or ever will be
passed over by Mercy, *willing* to do His will.—His feebleness
shall become strength, his ignorance shall become wisdom.
If, with the Bereans, any *will* search the Scriptures, like the Bereans,
they will believe.—The secret of the Magi and of Cornelius was,
they improved the light they had.—"Then shall we know if we
follow on to know the Lord." Hos. vi. 3.—Ignorance is a crime
only in those who " *love a lie*," i. e. persist in error. Rev. xxii. 15.
He does not say, " ye *have* not," but " ye *would* not." John v. 40.
They had neither the *heart* to love nor the *desire* for the heart.
Shall know. The " *know* " is emphatic. He shall have not only
assurance of faith, but living certainty of discernment.
Obedience to Jesus leads to experience of the Divine power of His
doctrine.—This experience corresponds to the three principal
faculties in man : power to enlighten (mind), to sanctify (will),

to bless (heart). *Pascal.*—If any one will try to imitate God's works, he will soon *know* that the wing of a fly is for ever beyond his skill—But those seeking to do God's will shall *know*, because God will make them *know*. It is no " experiment," as the Quietists maintained.—" Liberals " boast that men will become virtuous as they are cultured.—The Bible *reverses* this, as also nearly all other maxims of infidelity.

With God the heart goes before the head in His kingdom. Prov. xxiii. 26.—A terrible warning.—Rejecting Christ's Divine teachings proves a *bad heart.*—Christ's rejecters seem to wander " into a far country," where the wing of Almighty love does not extend.

A wide gulf now and for ever separates lovers of the Redeemer from rejecters.—These Jews came with a long array of stately arguments against Christ, but our Lord pronounces them all hypocrisy.

Even a heathen taught that vice weakens the mind. *Aristotle.*

Eyes must be healthy to find light pleasant and to judge rightly of colours.—Our Lord shows *sin* to be the source of all errors of head and heart.—A principle in God's kingdom. He who hath a willing heart and desires to glorify God will find an *open door* to all truth.

Seek not to know in order to believe, but seek to believe in order to know. *Augustine.*—Our Lord proposes three tests of the Divine origin of His deeds and doctrines :—1. Their inherent excellence, wisdom, and usefulness.—2. That they were not uttered to advance His honour among men.—3. These very doctrines would cause all His shame, pain, and death.—Respecting spiritual knowledge, some now rely on authority and some on a cultivated mind.—In opposition to both these extremes stands the teaching of Christ.—1. Christian knowledge—" shall know." 2. Its object—" the doctrine." 3. Its degree, certainty—" shall *know*." *Robertson.*

Doctrine. Indefinitely of every sort of religious doctrine, whether and how far from God.—In divine and spiritual things we must believe no one absolutely.—We must try every doctrine by the infallible standard of truth.—A heavenly disposition will enable us to know heavenly things.

Speak of Myself. From the preceding law this immediately follows.—He shall know whether Jesus only speaks on His own authority as an uncalled, self-taught person, or whether, on the contrary, His word be not absolutely from God.

The proposition here laid down is universal in its application : " If *any* man."—Sincerity of will the mark of a genuine witness of God.—Purity of doctrine dependent on purity of the mind in its endeavours.—Condition or law of a peaceful life, submission to the spirit of meekness.—Condition or law of the Beatific vision, a pure heart and life.—Condition or law of God's presence, obedience to the law of love.—Condition or law of spiritual wisdom and certainty in truth, obedience to the will of God.

θέλη. The rendering of the A. V. unhappy; not the bare performance of God's commands, but the subjection of the will to God. *Alford.* If a man desires to be learned in Divine things, the beginning is to believe the Word of God. *Tholuck.*

θέλημα αὐτοῦ. 1. The Old Testament revelation. *Chrys.*, &c. 2. The demand of faith in Christ. *Aug., Luther*, &c. 3. In His doctrine. *Semler*, &c. 4. Willing obedience to God in general. *Lücke, Meyer,* &c. Men should seek to do first what He says. *Ebrard.* The testimony of immediate intuition. *Theremin.* Voluntas Dei est lex fidei. *Lampe.* Believing as an experiment. *M. Guyon.* Men never pray or follow Christ as an experiment. *Stier.* It is difficult for ordinary minds to discriminate the *line* between *faith* in and *trial* of God's word. *Author.* If a man will obey as far as he knows God's will. *Roos.* This will is revealed in the law and in our conscience. *Von Gerlach.*

γνώσεται. Refers not merely to believers in revelation : has in view a universal revelation of God's will, therefore holds good even for the heathen. *Lange.* Understanding is the wages of faith. *Chrysostom.* Not the *doing* but the *willing* is crowned with the ability to perform. *Albertine.* The way to the testimony of the Holy Ghost, not its fulness. *Richter.* He who would cultivate the γνῶσις must amend his θέλειν. *Anton.* Our Lord discloses a secret perverseness of their minds. *Calvin.* The will of the Father and Son being one, obeying one we bow to the other also. *Bengel.* The will renewed is sanctification begun. *Lampe.* Every honest man sees the Divinity of the Scriptures. *Doddr.* One true to conscience the gods enlighten. *Plato.* These things we learn by doing them. *Aristotle.*

---

18. He that speaketh of himself seeketh his own glory: but he that seeketh his glory that sent him, the same is true, and no unrighteousness is in him.

Speaketh. The connection is between a right aim and a right result.—He only, willing to do the will of God in *humility*, will apprehend the *lowliness* of the Son of God.—Those Pharisees, deceiving themselves, impute deception to the Lord.
The licentious Jews would gather credit from the licentious. John viii. 3.

Of Himself. He alone, of all the sons of men, was free from every taint of vanity, the ineffaceable and incontrovertible seal of purity.—*Inward* seeking to do Christ's will brings eternal conviction of His humility.—Had there been any other path than one of shame and woe, our Lord would have chosen it, being free from all passion for martyrdom.—What flesh undertakes for

its honour ends in contempt.—Christ begins with the cross and
shame, and ends in a THRONE in HEAVEN!—The mark of one
who speaks from himself is ambition. " The nearest heretic has
his seat in the heart." *Wottersdorf.*

Own glory. Wishes to shine by himself, in himself, and for himself.—In times of apostasy this self-seeking is a fearful wasting
disease.—His enemies testified that He was free from this.
" Master, we know that Thou art true, *neither carest Thou for any
man.*"—Had our Lord acted differently the Jews would never
have put Him to death.—" We speak not as pleasing men, but
God," Gal. i. 10, therefore they were *martyred.*

So millions of saints have been put to death, but not a single
hypocrite has ever suffered willingly. John vii. 7.

Some make God their pretence, but in reality men are their idols.

Is true. He who speaks in God's name speaks worthy of God.

Such was Christ. He neither sought His own nor His friends'
glory.—He well knew His doctrines would lead to a shameful
death.

No unrighteousness. The sinlessness of Jesus a doctrine clearly
revealed. John viii. 46.—No error in knowledge, no sin in
will, aim, or deed, was ever found in Christ.—His holiness is its
own witness ; like SUNLIGHT, it is seen by its own radiance.

His miracles were so many *seals* put on Him by God.

Sabbath healing at once proves His Divinity and truthfulness.

Difference between a false Messiah and the true—the motive of
the false is self-glorification ; that of Christ, glorification of the
Father, to whom He attributes all He says and does.

Ambition betrays a calling not Divine, sign of a self-commissioned
prophet.

δόξαν. Omnis hereticus est animæ gloriæ. *Jerome.* The holiness of the
apostles was no distinctive criterion of the truth of their doctrines. *Neander.*
Vanity prompted the Jews to hold Jehovah beholden to them for their sanctity.
This feeling Paul ignores. 2 Cor. iv. 5. *Jackson.* External test of Christ's
Divinity. He never sought human praise, but the Father's. *Kuinoel.* These
words give the reason why he who *wishes* to do God's will will know of the
teaching of Christ, viz. because both are seeking one aim—the glory of God,
Alford.

---

19. Did not Moses give you the law, and yet none of you keepeth the law ?
Why go ye about to kill me ?

Moses. Here He quotes their highest authority. See on John
i. 17.

Give you the law. John i. 17. The law in general, for he who breaks one precept transgresses the whole.—Originally and pre-eminently the ten commandments.—Singular testimony of a heathen at Rome to the value of this law. " The Jews, though the lowest of people, have the best laws, and give laws to all the world." *Seneca,* quoted by *Blackstone.*

None of you keepeth. Our Lord suddenly passes from the defensive to the offensive.—He knew their intentions. He to whom the secrets of all hearts are open. Psa. xliv. 21.

He knew also the cause of their hate, and reveals their very thoughts. Ver. 21.—To the spirit and intent of that law ye are perfect strangers.—Those seeking refuge from the law's high claims by mere subterfuges cannot see its beauty or power.

The Lord formally meets their charge with a counter-charge.

Their guilt was in a most proper sense a national one.

None so loud in condemning treason as Athaliah the traitor.

None so complain of persecution as Papists, who burn heretics.

Because there is in you no true striving to do God's will, ye cannot know My divine mission.—How truly this is the case appears from the fact that ye seek to kill Me.—People idolized their law even to a bloody *fanaticism.* Acts vii. 53.

His solemn warnings became tender lamentations of LOVE !

A fatal paradox,—Man, the only rational being in the world, acts contrary to his own interests.—" We know the right, and yet the wrong pursue." *Horace.*

Kill me. John viii. 59. He unveils the fearful thought of murder against the Messiah.—It is even now germinating in their minds, while yet they themselves think not of it.

The people are unconsciously implicated, because the high-handed conduct of the rulers finds support in their mental indolence.

They must know He is " hated and persecuted without a cause."

Our Lord's doctrines ultimately compel men to take a side,—there can be no neutrality.—Condemnation of Christ's *despisers* is heavier than that of Christ's *crucifiers.* 1 Cor. ii. 8.

The stroke aimed at Christ fell on that very law of which they boasted.—Our LORD, the LIVING EMBODIMENT of that law, stood before them,—Boldly yet simply He speaks, and in majesty and meekness He condemns.—He brings out to light what was crouching in darkness.—" He that hateth his brother is a murderer." 1 John iii. 15.—The sinner would slay God Himself. Psa. xiv. 1.

Israel's resolution to oppose Christ was a clear conspiracy against

Moses.—" Whosoever will not obey the words He shall speak in My name, I will require it of him." Deut. xviii. 19.

In their killing the Lord of life was summed up all their transgression of God's law.—It was the greatest proof that could be given of their total ignorance of and rebellion against the law.

τὸν νόμον was the εὕρημα τοῦ Θεοῦ, the invention of god. *Demosthenes.* The twelve tables (mainly derived from the ten commands) excelled all the libraries in the empire. *Cicero.* The law was read during this feast. *Bengel, Alford.* Entire law read through during our Lord's ministry. *Sepp.*

τί emphasized keenly pierces their conscience. *Stier.*

ζητεῖτε. Why seek ye ? *D. Brown.*

ἀποκτεῖναι. Moses' law refers to murder, but ye keep not that law. *Chrys.* Violation of the entire law in spirit. *Lampe.*

---

20. The people answered and said, Thou hast a devil : who goeth about to kill thee ?

People. The crowd, as yet unconscious of the murderous intentions of the leaders.

Devil. Gr. *demon,* a figurative term drawn from belief in demoniacal possession.—Probably a proverbial expression to denote gloom, melancholy, brooding suspicion, or jealousy.

So it was said of John the Baptist, "He hath a demon." Matt. xi. 18. Not said to our Lord in pity, John viii. 48 ; x. 20, but in malignant scorn.—DEVIL, Gr. *diabolos.* See on John vi. 70.

His existence suspected, but not known by reason.—God's natural *supremacy* in goodness held by the deepest instincts of the heart.—By Divine permission alone, for inscrutable reasons, evil exists. Prov. xvi. 4 ; Isa. xlv. 7 ; Amos iii. 6 ; Rom. ix. 22, 23.—The conquest of evil began in the promised atonement. Gen. iii. 15.—It was effected on the Cross, and will be completed at the Judgment.—Existence and agency of Satan gradually revealed. Temptation first referred to a *serpent.*

Something *more* than mere *animal* agency seems indicated. Gen. iii. 1.—At length it is clearly revealed, " Old serpent, called the Devil." Rev. xii. 9 ; xx. 2.—Satan in O. T. first revealed in Job as among the " sons of God." Job i.—Revelation of the " strong man armed " not given till " the stronger than He," &c.

In our Lord's temptation Satan suddenly comes forth clearly.

The words, " Your father the devil," John viii. 44, settles for ever his personality.—HIS NATURE : a being of angelic order, created

holy, as are all beings in a *normal* state.—Called a spirit. Eph.
ii. 2. Prince of demons. Matt. xii. 24. Having subjects. Matt.
xxv. 41 ; Rev. xii. 7.—Zealously maintains his dark empire.
A number of angels, it seems, were seduced by him, and fell with
him. Rev. xii. 4.—Superhuman in wisdom, power, energy,
craft, with 6000 years' experience.—" Michael and his angels
fought with the dragon and his angels." Rev. xii. 7, 9.
" They are reserved in chains of darkness unto judgment." 2 Pet.
ii. 4.—Under guard, yet " going about as a roaring lion." 1
Pet. v. 8.—" I beheld Satan fall as lightning " hints at Christ's
victory. Luke x. 18.—"A murderer from the beginning,"
ruining our first parents. John viii. 44.—Pride the condemning sin. 1 Tim. iii. 6. Satan's by analogy.—Desire to be " as
gods " the subtlest and most deadly temptation. Gen. iii. 5.
Scripture *reticence* rebukes our vain speculation on these things.
Hatred and falsehood make up Satan's character. John viii. 44 ;
1 John iii. 10, 11.—Restless activity, impurity, craft, intense
desire to ruin, fill out the features of the fiend.—HIS POWER. 1.
Negative. Seen in the parable of the sower. Matt. xiii. 19.
2. *Positive,* seen in the parable of the wheat and tares. Matt. xiii.
39.—His power antagonistic to God in the world. Col. i. 13.
Excommunication " delivers over the evil person to Satan." 1 Cor.
v. 5.—Unbelievers called the " synagogue of Satan." Rev. ii. 9.
Secret false doctrines, " Depths of Satan." Rev. ii. 24. His
" seat." Rev. ii. 13.—Satan's influence over the soul a terrible
certainty. Rom. xvi. 20 ; 2 Cor. ii. 11 ; 1 Thess. ii. 18 ; 2
Thess. ii. 9 ; 1 Tim. v. 15.—He cannot tempt without consent
of his victim. Eph. iv. 27.—The means he employs are
" wiles." Eph. vi. 11. " Devices." 2 Cor. ii. 11. " Snares." 1
Tim. vi. 9. Vigilance against him enjoined. 1 Pet. v. 8.
Divine armour provided. Eph. vi. 10—17.—God's children, however tempted and tried by Him, in no *final* peril. 1 John v. 18.
Satan, a leader of a host, " principalities, powers, rulers," &c.
Eph. vi. 12.—Called the " prince of this world." John xii. 31.
" god of this world." 2 Cor. iv. 4. Has influence over nature,
" spirit of infirmity," &c. Luke xiii. 16. Paul's " thorn in the
flesh." 2 Cor. xii. 7.—HIS WORK. Through his malignity
mankind innocent became guilty.—The happy became miserable,
the immortal became liable to death.—His grand aim is to
counterwork the plans of God's kindness.—He is THE SLAN-
DERER : slanders God to man (Gen. iii.) and man to God. Job i.

The counter-claim of the blood of the Lamb alone can overcome
Satan.—Each fiery dart is thus quenched by the shield of faith.
Eph. vi. 16.—Each sin committed *enslaves* the mind to further
sin.   John viii. 34 ; Rom. vi. 16.—Each outward sin tends to
lead the inner man into *captivity*. Rom. vii. 14, 24.

If we yield without repentance, we become reprobate. Rom. i. 28.

"Thou hast a devil" was the chorus of Jews when a flash of His
omniscience had pierced their conscience.—Thus Pharaoh and
his host were *troubled* when pursued by Jehovah.

Kill thee.   They imagine He must be in league with a demon to
think this.—In verse 25 they condemn themselves as false, and
their rulers as murderers.—Preachers being faithful find their
apologies only new offences.—For sceptics to ridicule what they
cannot answer is Satan's ancient lesson.

ὄχλος.   Not the rulers. *Alford.*   Multitude were not in the bloody secret.
D. *Brown.*
καὶ εἶπε omitted.   *Lach., Tisch., Alf., Treg.*
Δαιμόνιον.   See critical notes on John vi. 70. Demons assumed the goat
form. *Hales, Selden, Vossius.* All allusions to demons denied. *Van Dale.* Jews
made them " souls of the wicked." *Justin Martyr.*   Fallen spirits. *Tertullian.*
Greeks, souls of those dying violent deaths.
ἀποκτεῖναι.   A hint that He feared being assassinated. *Lange.*

----

21. Jesus answered and said unto them, I have done one work, and ye all
marvel.

Answered.   Conscious innocence dreads no insult.   He replies
with Divine dignity.—He ever turns His replies into increasing,
advancing testimony.—Sincerity throws off slanders as Paul did
the viper.—He takes no notice of their coarse remarks ; some
knew well what He meant.

One work.   Strange that He should refer to a work done a year
and a half since.—He does not mean that He has done only one
miracle in Jerusalem. John iii. 2.—It is not the miracle but the
work that is here emphasized.—Proof of their morbid condition
making an ado over one act of a man whose life abounded with
Divine works.

Marvel.   The " one work " was healing the man infirm for 38
years. John v. 9.—Not *wonder* at the miracle, but surprise and
indignation that it was done on the Sabbath.—Men plotting
murder profess to be concerned for the sanctity of the Sabbath !

All His many kind acts are forgotten the moment *one* work offends
them.—All His other acts, by their silent admission, were unim-
peachable.—You pretend to be jealous of the Sabbath, but what
think ye of My works, proving Me to be Lord of the Sabbath?

ἀπεκρίθη. He shows them the cause of those murderous designs. *Lampe.*
And ignores their interruption. *Hengst.*
ἓν ἔργον. He alludes to His as a trifling violation compared with theirs.
Fikenscher.
ἐποίησα involves a gentle kind of irony. *Stier.*
θαυμάζετε. Present tense,—You enrage yourselves. *Bourgon.* Being offended. *Klee, Lampe.* Ye all wondered until some hinted at the breaking of
the Sabbath. *Tisch.* Our Lord alludes to some other miracle than the Bethesda
cure. *Olsh.* An unrecorded cure. *Trench.* An angry astonishment, merely
assumed. *Hengst.*

---

22. Moses therefore gave unto you circumcision ; (not because it is of Moses,
but of the fathers ;) and ye on the sabbath day circumcise a man.

Moses, &c. John i. 17. Our Lord proceeds to justify His miracle
of healing from their own law.—Moses *ordained* circumcision for
them : "And in the eighth day," &c. Lev. xii. 3.
Yet circumcision, strictly speaking, was not introduced by Moses.
It had come down from the fathers and was confirmed by Moses.
It was a fundamental law of the covenant of promise made with
Abraham. Gen. xvii.—It so outweighs the Sabbath law, that it
must be performed when the eighth day falls on a Sabbath.
Reason of this higher superiority to be found in the design of cir-
cumcision.
Circumcise. *Origin* of this rite, like origin of *sacrifice,* evidently
Divine.—No conceivable motive could prompt a human being
to originate either.—All that is solemn, beautiful, or instructive in
heathen ritual taken from the Hebrews.—Every male child was
to be circumcised at eight days, on pain of death. Lev. xii. 3.
Moses omitting this duty, the Lord sought to kill him. Ex. iv. 24.
Slaves, bought or home-born, were to receive this seal. Gen. xvii.
12, 13.—Foreigners before receiving the passover must submit
to this rite. Ex. xii. 48.—Usually a name was given at the performance of this rite. Luke i. 59.—Nubians, Arabians, Egyptians, practised it ; Abyssinians and Moslems continue it.
" I passed and saw thee in thy blood (circumcision), and said,
'Live.'" Ezek. xvi. 6.—This was the distinctive sign of the

Jews' relation to Jehovah.—Neglecting it implied exclusion from God's favour and the privileges of His people.

Not merely social degradation as heathenish, but treason to Jehovah. The sad and fearful mark of apostasy and final reprobation.

A similar guilt follows *wilful* neglect of the sacraments of the Church.—Christianity has substituted baptism for this ancient Jewish rite.—Both point to spiritual purification : " Circumcision is that of the heart," &c. Rom. ii. 29. " Washing of regeneration " &c. Titus iii. 5.

διὰ τοῦτο omitted. *Cod. Sin.* Refers to the preceding clause, θαυμάζετε. *Theoph., Lücke, Olsh., Stier,* &c. Refers to the clause following. *Chrys., Luther, Bengel, Meyer, Alford,* &c. Placed usually at the beginning of a sentence in John. *Schaff.*

οὐκ ὅτι. Undervaluation of circumcision as a mere tradition of the Fathers. *B. Crusius.* Antiquity and dignity of circumcision declared. *Bengel.* This sacred sign of the covenant was appointed by God Himself. *Stier.* Our Lord compares not persons, but prerogatives of dispensations, the Mosaic with the patriarchal. *Lampe.* He corrects the inexact popular expression following popular usage. *Küng.* From Abraham, as an hereditary custom. *Hezel.* Sabbath law of Moses and law of circumcision came in collision. *Luther.* Circumcision as older, takes precedence over the Sabbath. *Bengel.* Appears to have forgotten that the Sabbath was instituted in Paradise. Gen. ii. 3. *Author.* Precedent as to its comparative value. *Lange.*

περιτέμνετε. God borrowed no heathen rites. *Lewis'* Heb. Ant. It was performed by a sharp stone or knife of flint. Ex. iv. 25 ; Josh. v. 2, 3. O.T. rite referred only to σάρξ. *Olsh.*

---

23. If a man on the sabbath day receive circumcision, that the law of Moses should not be broken ; are ye angry at me, because I have made a man every whit whole on the sabbath day ?

Sabbath. John v. 10. **Law**. John i. 17. **Moses**. John i. 17. **Broken**. Gr. *loosened*, opposed to a binding or enacting law.

A seeming *collision* between law of circumcision and law of the Sabbath.—These Jews held that the law of mercy violated the fourth command.—They changed GOD's day into *their* day, but *their* sabbath was *not known* to the fourth command or to its AUTHOR. Alas ! that practical *atheists* should pretend to honour God.—Power of sin and power of conscience,—mankind will neither live with God nor without God.

Angry. Angry at their Maker for an act of mercy,—what depravity!—Yet pretend to honour a precept, as if God's commands could ever counteract His acts. — These miserable deceivers went further,—they professed to be wounded in heart

by Christ's want of piety, while their plans were maturing to
murder the Holy One of God !—Many now are zealous for ritual
who hate worship of God in spirit and in truth.

Many now are fierce adherents of creeds and dogmas who hate
judgment, mercy, and faith.—Many now talk loudly of the
gospel who hate salvation by grace, the substance of the gospel.

Many now make loud lamentation over the execution of a murderer
who strike at the Divine glory of our Lord and blaspheme His
Godhead.—This hatred of the good exists under a thousand
forms in our day.—Hereafter the *existence* of such *malice* will be
the WONDER OF ETERNITY!

Every whit. Gr. *entirely.* Not one daring to deny the reality of
the miracle.—As they saw his body was healed, here we see his
soul was also.—If it be right to apply healing to the wound of
circumcision, can it be wrong to heal the entire man ?

As usual, error weakens the intellect as well as corrupts the heart.
Every law of man's being is purified and invigorated by a holy life.
The moral law in the conscience is as unchangeably binding as any
written law.—It is older than the law given at Sinai by many
centuries.—" I will have mercy, and not sacrifice," saith Jehovah.
Matt. ix. 13.—But those " Liberals " of that age, rather than
Jesus should prove His Divinity, would prefer that the wretched
suffer on.—Divine goodness pervades all God's laws. A hired
servant was not to be oppressed. The deaf was not to be cursed ;
the blind not to be treated cruelly. Lev. xix. 14.

A stray beast was to be returned,—a fallen beast was to be helped.
Exod. xxiii. 5.—The Creator and Ruler of all worlds stoops to
legislate concerning the inmates of a bird's nest : " Ye shall not
take the little ones from the nest with the mother." Deut. xxii. 6.

Greeks and Romans muzzled their oxen treading out corn. This
God forbids.

ἵνα μὴ λυθῇ. Violating the Sabbath without circumcising. *Bengel.*

ὅλον ἄνθρωπον. Emphasis laid on ὑγιῆ ; some contemplate circumcision
in its merely external form. *Kling.* A man's entire body whole. *D. Brown.*
Refers to body and soul. *Aug., Olsh.* Healing of one member contrasted with
the healing of the entire man. *Lampe.* The well-known conversion of the
healed sinner emphatically includes his restored soundness of body. *Stier.*
Too subtle a meaning for the Jews. *Alford.* A mere juxtaposition of two
Sabbath works. *Gerlach.* The healing at least as important as the circumcising of a child. *Brandt.* A parallel drawn between its medical use and the
miraculous healing. *Winer.* A sign of the covenant. *Michaelis.* Circumcision esteemed a partial healing. *Lange.* Theocratic soundness and purity.
Meyer.

24. Judge not according to the appearance, but judge righteous judgment.

Judge not. The Corinthians were keenly rebuked by Paul for censoriousness. 1 Cor. iv. 3. — Faithful or unfaithful, Paul's responsibility was not to man.—Corinthians had not sent Paul, nor Jews, our Lord.—They were not stewards accountable to any self-constituted tribunals.—Our Saviour desires, not deprecates, a righteous decision.—Conscience is perverted in a partial or unenlightened judge. *Anaxagoras.*—How many now justify themselves whom God will condemn!

Appearance. Gr. *countenance.* " Ye shall hear the small as well as the great. Thou shalt not respect the person of the poor, nor honour the person of the mighty. In righteousness shalt thou judge thy neighbour." Deut. i. 17. Lev. xix. 13.

Men speaking ill of things they know not indicates a weak head and bad heart.—" Answering a matter before it is heard " is unreasonable. Prov. xviii. 13.—Judging according to the letter a judging by exterior looks.

Righteous. Not according to the outward form of the work, but its motive. *Melancthon.*—According to the fact, and not according to the person. *Augustine.*—An answer humbly sought by prayer will ever be a righteous verdict. Jas. i. 5.—Many come to a decision from self, then look for light, but not in prayer

Judgment. All men by nature are Pharisees, for without charity we are without humility.—Unprincipled persons do not wish to judge righteously, but to condemn efficiently.

The Lawgiver Himself by-and-by will be Judge,—guilty man can never be *assessor with Jehovah.*—A righteous judgment can only be given by us, while we ourselves hope to be forgiven.

τὴν δικαίαν. τὴν merely expression of habit,—Let your judgment be a just one. *Alford.* Shows the righteous is the only judgment. *Bengel.* The people cared not for the law. Their zeal was a mask to parry the blows from conscience. *Anton.* " I suppose some will find that in my works which I never conceived." *Aug.*

---

25. Then said some of them of Jerusalem, Is not this he, whom they seek to kill?

Some of them. Who better knew the rulers' mind than the crowd? Jerusalemites, in opposition to those of the provinces ignorant of the bloody design.

Jerusalem. See on John v. 1.—Topography and Geography. It stands on the site of ancient Salem. Gen. xiv. 18.

Shechem, Shiloh, Gibeah, Nob, Gibeon, were *capitals* before Jerusalem.—" I have set Jerusalem in the midst of the nations round about her." Ezek. v. 5.—It stands 2600 feet *above* the Mediterranean.—Jericho, in the valley of the Jordan, 18 miles distant, 900 feet *below* the sea.—Ramleh, in plain of Sharon, 25 miles distant, 2274 feet below Jerusalem.—Its exalted location was cause of constant exultation. Psa. xxxiii. 14 ; lxxxix. 27.

Jerusalem stands on a mountain ridge which extends from the plain of Esdraelon to the south as far as the end of the Dead Sea.

The site is an *inland promontory* with deep valleys on three sides ; in a military sense, an inland Gibraltar with trenches on three sides 500 feet deep, in the valleys of Kedron, Hinnom, and Siloam.

" The sides of the north " (Psa. xlviii. 2) are a high level widening into a noble table-land, where the sepulchres of the kings are found.—North portion called Bezetha, or new city.

Moriah, on the east. Temple stood there. 106 feet lower than Zion, the city and tomb of David.—Akra, or lower city, lies between Zion and Bezetha.—Zion, separated from Moriah and Ophel by Tyropœan valley.—Mount of Olives is 300 feet higher than Moriah or Temple hill.—Olives, Scopus, Mount of offence, and Viri Galilaei, are mountains round about Jerusalem.

Two main roads to Jerusalem : 1. From the Jordan valley by Jericho and Mount of Olives. 2. From the great maritime plain of Philistia and Sharon.

Twenty-four names of gates in the walls of Jerusalem are found in Scripture.—Some of the gates might have had double names.

Ancient Thebes in Egypt had one hundred gates. *Homer.*

Principal cemetery has ever been between Moriah and Kedron.

Millions there rest waiting the resurrection. John xi. 38.

Water Pools. Upper and lower reservoirs of Gihon.

Pool of Hezekiah near Jaffa gate.—Pool of Bethesda near St. Stephen's gate.—Pool of Siloam or Shiloh foot of the mount in the valley of Kedron.—It unites with Fountain of the Virgin by a winding passage cut through the rock.—The city is supplied with water brought about seven miles from the pools of Solomon beyond Bethlehem. John v. 2.—Streets. Six are named : East Street. 2 Chron. xxix. 4. Of the city. 2 Chron. xxxii. 6. Of the house of God. Ezra x. 9. Water gate. Neh. viii. 1, 3. Of Ephraim. Neh. viii. 16. Bakers' Street. Jer. xxxvii. 21.

The Jews were the leaders among the crowd at this feast of
tabernacles.—Larger multitudes came to the tabernacle feast
than to the passover.—Sin in capital cities soon becomes centred
and early matures.

To kill. Rulers had not the audacity to deny this.

τινὲς. These Jews were mainly from Jerusalem during the whole scene.
Hengst.
Ἱεροσόλυμα. Salem of Melchisedec, Gen. xiv. 18, identical with that of
Psa. lxxvi. 2. *Josephus, Eusebius.* Melchisedec built the first temple and
changed the name from Salem to Hierosoluma. *Josephus.* Salem was near
Scythopolis. *Jerome.* A rabbinical authority. *Winer.* Jerusalem identical
with Cadytis, a large city of Syria. *Herodotus.* Questioned by *Rawlinson.*
Kendrick. Hierosolymus, son of Typhon, founded it. *Tacitus, Plutarch.* Its
central location, umbilicus terræ. *Jerome, Leland.* The most celebrated of all
the cities of the east. *Pliny.* Altars and sanctuaries in tribe of Benjamin,
courts of the temple in Benjamin. *Lightfoot, Blunt, Stanley.*

---

26. But, lo, he speaketh boldly, and they say nothing unto him. Do the
rulers know indeed that this is the very Christ?

Boldly. A picture of the *Divine* majesty of His presence!
A hint that flashes of Divinity were sometimes felt by those hearing His voice.—His enemies, silenced, seem awestruck as conscious the MESSIAH stood before them.—The innocent may feel
safe anywhere under a God of justice.—A merchant darkens
his windows when his goods are *defective.*—But honest wares
may be held up to the sun fearless of fault.—The righteous are
bold as a lion. Prov. xxviii. 1.—The wicked skulk in the dark.
Gen. iii. 8.—The bravery of the wicked is oft a *mask* which
falls amid actual perils.—But the righteous sit secure, as Noah
amid the flood.—They know that " neither life, nor death, things
present," &c., can ruin them. Rom. viii. 38.—Daniel prefers to
meet the lions in their den, rather than conscience violated.
Ancient Romans called this *obstinacy* in Christians, and wondered
that fire could not subdue it.

Say nothing. God oft restrains men, puts a bit into their
mouths. Psa. xxxii. 9.

ἀληθῶς. Actually. Indicates the thing scarcely credible. *Hengst.*
Second ἀληθῶς omitted. *Cod. Sin.* Cancelled. *Tisch., Alford.*
ἔγνωσαν. Have they come to know indeed? *D. Brown.*

27. Howbeit we know this man whence he is : but when Christ cometh, no man knoweth whence he is.

Howbeit. The ineffable self-complacency of spiritual ignorance and pride.

We know. Although His miracles had made Him famous, yet they did not know or desire to know His real nature.
1. Knowing God's *power*, they would not have *resisted* His Son.—
2. Knowing God's *justice*, they would not have *rejected* His warnings.—3. Knowing God's *mercy*, they would not have grieved His Spirit.—4. Knowing God's *wisdom*, they would not have trusted their folly.—So far from knowing, they had never carefully inquired into His life and birth.—Indeed, they did not know that Jesus was born at Bethlehem.—Worldly maxims prove the diverging path leading *from* the WAY OF LIFE.

Had they known Him they would not have chosen the market as a place of prayer, nor have assumed the mask of a sad countenance while fasting in sin.—Nor have garnished the sepulchres of men, whom living they would have murdered.

Had they known Him, would they have felt angry at Sabbath healing, or murmured because He permitted publicans and sinners to come to Him ?

This man whence. Refers both to despised Nazareth and the carpenter's family.—Proud dwellers in the capital contemned His Galilæan origin.—With sinful conceit they presume no one could give them any information as to this person claiming to be the Messiah.—In their minds a groundless notion outweighs the works of Omnipotence.—What doth it avail to the blind, though suns were added to the blaze of noonday ?

Sinners are made up of *contradictions* to truth, to reason, and to God.

No man knoweth, &c. They may allude to Isa. liii. 8.

Mystery enveloped the origin of Messiah.—A clear admission that besides His historic origin and life, Messiah must have a supernatural manner of existence.—" WONDERFUL, COUNSELLOR, EVERLASTING FATHER, MIGHTY GOD, PRINCE OF PEACE." Isa. ix. 6.

" The crying mystery of the Incarnation had been wrought in the silence of God." *Ignatius.*—His *concealment* was as certainly foretold as His coming.—He could only be found by the heart desiring salvation. — " If thou seek the Lord with all thy *heart*, and with all thy *soul*, thou shalt find Him." Deut. iv. 29.

Thus God conceals Himself in nature, to be found by seekers after

Him.—These Jerusalemites rejected Jesus on account of His humble origin.—A singular instance of national ignorance with Bible in hand.—Elias they thought would with sudden splendour usher in Messiah's reign.—They heard the striking of the prophetic clock, but counted not the strokes. Micah v. 2.

True hearts will *listen* to the oracles of God, and *adoringly believe.* As Elijah could hear from afar the approach of the burning wheels of the angel-drawn chariot. 2 Kings ii. 1—11.

οὐδεὶς. According to *Justin Martyr* the Jews held that Messiah should be unknown even to Himself, until Elijah should have anointed Him. Probably they refer to this idea. *Lightfoot, Lücke, Alford.* From Dan. vii. 13, they expected a sudden *heavenly* manifestation of Messiah. *Tholuck.* One of the popular notions that He lived in a secret place, or in Paradise. *Targum Jonathan.* Born of a virgin, and the parentage unknown. *Grotius.* Jews believed in a preternatural birth. *Wetstein.* Matt. i. 22. Some that He would appear as an adult. *Lampe.*

---

28. Then cried Jesus in the temple as he taught, saying, Ye both know me, and ye know whence I am : and I am not come of myself, but he that sent me is true, whom ye know not.

Cried. He *cried out* very seldom. Matt. xii. 19. Weighty reasons existed when He did so.—Probably a *loud* lament over their obstinate prejudice and unbelief.—They deemed Him the carpenter's son, and despised His humble origin and surroundings.

He had no army, no victories, no courtiers, no flatterers, no throne, no palace.—His miracles, " like the body of heaven in clearness," were cold to their carnal minds. Ex. xxiv. 10.

Divine patience and mercy seemed roused by their infatuation !

That same voice will be heard by the universe from the judgment throne.—Men may stop their ears *now,* but they will listen *hereafter.*—No one will be dull of hearing when the last trumpet sounds.

Ye know Me. They knew the time and place of His birth, parents, occupation, features, trade, brothers, sisters. *Augustine.*

The upstart loses confidence when his origin is spoken of.

Our Lord acted openly and without the least reserve upon the subject.—He never disclaimed human relationship, affected nothing singular.—The God of their honoured temple, of Sinai, of the rock, was His Father.—They speak of the man Jesus ! He speaks of the same now.—But the Incarnate WORD in Jesus they had not faith to see.—" Ye neither know ME, nor My FATHER." John viii. 19 ; xvi. 3.

Whence I am. He here makes a difference between *Himself* and His *origin.*—The latter implied in *their* view utmost meanness; in *His*, supreme dignity.

Not come of Myself. Brief designation of His higher nature which they know not.—Introduces the declaration of His descent from God : He is come, and not of Himself.

Sent Me. The Father is never said to be *sent*, but is ever the SENDER.

Ye know not. " *Ye* " is very emphatic. Their ignorance was *total*, and would continue so. Psa. l. 21.—The glass must not be *coloured* to show the landscape as it is.—The truth of Scripture concerning God must come to *honest* minds.—*Judaism* and " *Liberalism* " have tried to hold on to God and let Christ go.

But together they have gone down from Deism to Pantheism, and in many cases to practical atheism.—Apart from living faith in the Divine Redeemer, men have JEHOVAH TO BE GOD NO MORE ! Two classes are in peril of final impenitence : 1. Hypocrites. 2. The wise in their own conceits.

κἀμέ οἴδατε. Interrogatively : " Know ye Me ? " *Grotius, Lampe, Doddr.* Ironically. *Calvin, Lücke, Stier, Lange.* But our Lord nowhere uses irony. *Bengel.* He charges them with certainly knowing His Divine person and origin, and yet denying them. *Chrys., Theoph.* A concession : the people really had this knowledge. *Meyer, De Wette, Alf.*

ἀληθινὸς. Equivalent to *verus. Luther, Grotius.* True in His prediction. *Elsley.* A reliable person. *Chrys., Lampe.* Used absolutely for the true, essential God. *Olsh., Kling.* The real living God. *Lange.* A real genuine person, fulfilling the idea. *Thol., Lücke, Alford.* Living, but hidden God. *Brandt.* Only real sender of any one. *D. Brown.*

πέμψας. The brightness and warmth do not send forth the fire, but the fire them. Thus the Father is never sent. *Augustine.*

οὐκ. We can't know God without knowing Christ. *Hengst.*

---

29. But I know him : for I am from him, and he hath sent me.

But I know Him. In intense contrast to their ignorance. 1. By descent from Him. 2. By commission from Him.

Before this assurance of consciousness of Deity all clouds of ignorance, deceit, and doubt vanish for ever.—In the mouth of Abraham, David, Isaiah, Paul, John, or even Gabriel, these words would sound presumptuous and shocking.—Why is that word " I KNOW GOD " perfectly natural to Jesus Christ ?

If He who healed lepers, cast out devils, stilled storms, created bread, raised the dead, had said, " *I know not God,*" we should have felt a revulsion as though the cloudless noonday were to say, " *I know not the sun.*"

I am from Him. Essentially, eternally, mysteriously, ONE GOD. See on John i. 1—3.—Hence the Church of God of every age has triumphantly confessed Him to be " GOD of GOD, LIGHT of LIGHT, VERY GOD of VERY GOD." *Nicene Council.*

Fifty millions have dared as martyrs to rest their eternal well-being on His Divinity.—Has a single martyr of intelligence and holiness ever died denying His supreme Godhead ?

δὲ cancelled. *Tisch., Alf.* Retained. *Cod. Sin.* Without it the expression would be still more direct and positive. *Stier.*

---

30. Then they sought to take him : but no man laid hands on him, because his hour was not yet come.

They sought. The rulers, who were made very uneasy by the remarks of the people, verses 25, 26.—Had their opportunity been equal to their will, His blood, like that of the son of Barachias, would have stained the temple pavement. Matt. xxiii. 35.—He had actually denied God to be *their* God, and had claimed God to be HIS Father !—The Sanhedrim sat in council close by the court of the Gentiles in the temple.

They must have sent officers to arrest Him, and bring Him as a prisoner.—But He knew well their plan, and that of their emissaries.—His omniscient glance doubtless rested on them, as they approached.—Before that burning eye their dark hearts were laid bare.—They might as well have thought of binding the lightning or arresting the sun.

No man. Such a spell did His majesty throw over their minds. They dared not lift a finger against Him, so bound were they by unseen chains.—Why did they not inquire as to this *strange, charmed life ?*—Why did they not ask if this *angelic armour* was not God's gift ?

Hour. The set time for His death, as the atoning sacrifice foretold Isa. liii. 3—12. — How constantly inspired writers note the hand of Providence.—God's hour is defined by His wisdom, and infallibly secured by His power.

Words full of comfort to all the afflicted servants of God.

Not come. The ultimate and highest reason why they could not take Him. Secondary causes, fear of the people and political

considerations, not mentioned.—When His work was finished
He "let them alone." Hos. iv. 17.—God's children are immortal as angels, until their work is done. *Whitefield.*

---

31. And many of the people believed on him, and said, When Christ cometh,
will he do more miracles than these which this man hath done ?

Many of the people. Gr. *common people.* Many of the crowd,
with crushed heart and hope, hailed the offer of mercy, and
hastened to the blessed cry, "Come unto me, all ye that are
wearied."—Some faithful pastors only preach men into hell.
Trapp.

Believed. John i. 7 ; vii. 38. Their faith was timid, depending
on miracles.—Yet was it faith in Him as MESSIAH, and not
merely as a prophet.—Over a burning waste of unbelief, malice,
and scorn, there came from God a refreshing breath of humble,
childlike faith. Ezek. xxxvii. 9.—The very first strivings of
life in the soul are accepted of God. Eph. ii. 1.
He blesseth the buddings of faith, hope, and love. Isa. xliv. 5.

Christ cometh, &c. Gr. *the* Christ. What can He do when He
cometh that has not been anticipated by the Son of Mary ?

Miracles. See on John ii. 11 ; iii. 2 ; iv. 48 ; vi. 30. They were
satisfied that He had done MANY GREAT MIRACLES.
His miracles, if Divine, settled for ever His claims as Messiah.
This shows *why* He wrought no miracles, until he began to preach
These *signs* were the seals of the Almighty to all His claims.

ὄχλου. Humiles et pauperes.—*Augustine.*
ὅταν ἔλθῃ. Implies their belief that the Christ had come. *Alford.*

---

32. The Pharisees heard that the people murmured such things concerning
him ; and the Pharisees and the chief priests sent officers to take him.

Pharisees. John i. 24. The bad impulse came from them, and
the chief priests join them.—These were the blind guides whom
He had rebuked with such severity. Matt. xxiii. 14.

Heard. The hall of the Sanhedrim was near by the crowd in the
Temple.—They heard how the people were inclining to acknowledge Jesus as Messiah.—They vainly resolve to stop further influence as ruinous to their power.—But until God draws the
bolt neither man nor angel can force the door.

Murmured. These murmurs seemed directed against the hierarchs at Jerusalem.—All these questionings sounded dangerous, and must be suppressed.

Chief priests. John i. 19. Priest, a Hebrew of the Hebrews, of the tribe of Levi, circumcised. Ezek. xliv. 9.

Moses' descendants, though Levites, never were advanced to the priesthood.—Priests required to be free from all bodily infirmities. Lev. xxi. 17.—If afflicted, the law forbad them officiating until they were healed.—Presuming to act as a priest without regular induction exposed to death.—Uzziah, king of Judah, was smitten with *leprosy.* 2 Chron. xxvi. 19.

Hebrew prophets were at times *inspired* to officiate as priests. 1 Sam. vii. 9.—At the age of thirty they were clothed in white, which typified spotless purity.—All their garments were of Divine pattern. Attempting sacrifices without these garments they forfeited life.—These garments being taken from Aaron, denoted he was about to die.—Stript of these while in health denoted degradation from office.—They might not wear these garments outside the tabernacle or temple. *Josephus.*

They could only marry a certain class of females. Lev. xxi.

They could not mourn for the dead, as that disqualified them for duty. Lev. xxi. 10, 12.—A priest must not rend his clothes, nor drink wine while in office.—They ministered without sandals, Exod. iii. 5 ; and hence Brahmins and Moslems still enter mosques *barefooted.*—Priests *stood* during time of officiating. None but kings dare sit in the temple in Jerusalem. *Targum.*—Chief priests possessed authority to issue hierarchal warrants.

Sent. The first messengers *formally* sent by the Sanhedrim to take Him.—The foreshadowing of an arrest, which would be made at another feast.

Officers. The Sanhedrim had a body of police under Roman rulers.—Rabbis trace it (the Sanhedrim) to the seventy elders associated with Moses. Num. xi. 16.—Consisted of chief priests, the heads of the 24 classes, scribes, or lawyers.

They had *lictors,* corresponding to our constables, referred to in the text.—They acted as a court trying idolaters, false prophets, &c. John xi. 47.—Jurisdiction extended beyond Palestine, Stephen was slain by a *mob.*

φαρισαῖοι. This occurred on the following day. *Stier.* They were the Jesuits of their day. *Author.*

ἀρχιερεῖς. Disqualifications, idolatry, defect of ancestry, clothed in black and dismissed. *Outram.* Priests in Grecian temples and priestesses, uttering their oracles, were without shoes. *Justin Martyr.*

ὑπηρέτας. At first under-rowers, servants, Latin ministri. Sanhedrim formed under Moses. *Selden.* Ceased on entering Palestine, and the Sanhedrim formed after Macedonia conquered Judæa. *Winer.* It is supposed by some there were 72 members. *Prideaux.* Presbyterian government is said to be formed after the Jewish model. *J. A. Alexander.* 1 Tim. iv. 14.

---

33. Then said Jesus unto them, Yet a little while am I with you, and then I go unto him that sent me.

Said. Our Lord calmly proceeds in His Divine work.
The stormy assaults of men or demons never ruffle his mind.

A little while. He is standing at the door of the nation, ready to depart.—So is it still : to one He is graciously entering ; from another He is departing for ever.—Our privileges are not always co-extensive with our years.—He has accurately numbered His days of toil and hours of pain.—" All your attempts to seize Me are vain. I shall abide here a little while."—" Having filled the appointment of God, I will return to Him in heaven."

I am with you. Words whose tenderness make the strong man as a little child.—This plea, He so often made, lies nearest to human tears.—He well knew the INFINITE VALUE of His presence and pleading to them.—He well knew the LOSS ETERNAL they would suffer when He left. Rev. xx. 10.

I am with you. Speaks of a day of grace not yet expired.
These golden sands of patience Divine are fast being numbered.
In sad vision the Son of God beholds their final rejection.
His heart mournfully anticipates the saddest requiem ever uttered by Love. Luke xiii. 34.—They will yet painfully, but vainly, long for one day of His merciful return.

I go. A solemn warning that with Him the grieved Spirit would go also.—His going not because they would thrust Him out by fierce hate, but because of His own free-will, He chooses to depart.—But, alas ! how supremely indifferent were they to words so full of meaning.—With what anguish will they yet " look on Him pierced " by their mocking words. Zech. xii. 10 ; Rev. i. 7.—" Behold, *your* house (it was once God's !) is left unto you desolate."—They never dreamt of His ascending to His Father in heaven.—" Your desire to be rid of Me will soon be fulfilled. In a little while we part company, and I go home

to God."—But these utterances of Love Incarnate they heard
in bitter mockery.

εἶπεν. To the officers. *Euthym.*, *Lange.* To those Pharisees who gave
the information. *Tholuck.* To the whole assembly, but chief priests mainly in
view. *Meyer.* Not to officers, but to the Jews representing the mass. *Hengst.*
αὐτοῖς cancelled. *Tisch.*, *Alf.*, *Stier.* Omitted. *Cod. Sin.* Verses 33,
34 a fragment of a long discourse. *Kuinoel.*

ὑπάγω. I go to render an account of my message to you rebels. *Grotius.*
Said as to their folly in trying to arrest Him before His time. *Alford.* Rather
to warn them. *Author.*

---

34. Ye shall seek me, and shall not find me : and where I am, thither ye
cannot come.

Ye shall seek—a refuge from ruin, but shall not find one.
In the depth of their fierce and passionate rejection of the Lamb.
When their woes come as a flood, then will they long for " one of
the days of the Son of man." Luke xvii. 22.—Even in judgment, they will rush to the gate of heaven in haste, crying,
" Lord, Lord, open to us."—Jews have incessantly sought their
Messiah, but—1. In another person. 2. In a secular majesty.
3. In the spirit of legal religion. 4. With earthly, political,
revolutionary prospects. *Lange.*
Me. Whom you now behold and despise with ever-increasing
guilt.—In righteous judgment *hardening* follows *blinding.*
Bereft of faith and light, they grope in the dark and can find
nothing.—To this day hardened Jew and Gentile perversely
seek in their own way for such a Redeemer as they will never
find.—" Ephraim is joined to idols " is its prophetic under-tone.
" It shall come to pass when they shall be hungry, they shall fret
themselves, and curse their king and their God." Isa. viii. 21 ;
Amos viii. 11, 12.—Some might, like Judas, say, " I have sinned
against innocent blood." Matt. xxvii. 4.
Not find. Points to the *false* seeking Israel has continued in ever
since.—None so much at a loss in trouble as those without God.
The wisdom they need only cometh from God, but to Him they
are *strangers.*—The surprising folly of sin,—men seek happiness,
but reject wisdom !—They abhor the *medicine*, but passionately,
nay, frantically, call for the *cure !*—To feel the pain but not the
guilt of sin shows one judicially hardened.—To feel both pain
and guilt without hope of mercy is to be lost.—A lifetime of

wilful gospel-despising forfeits mercy.—Successive sins inflame
the reckoning, and the sum advances mightily.

Where I am. As a man, He could be in but one place at a
time.—As Jehovah, He filled heaven and earth with His
presence.—Allusion may be made to the incommunicable name
of God.—"Say unto the children of Israel, I AM hath sent you."
Exod. iii. 14.—He is now about to withdraw, and specially show
Himself to His people.—In the many mansions a banquet is
spread, which is *not* for His foes.—"If I go my way, ye shall
seek me and die in your sins."—"Dreadful words! I do not
like to read them." *Luther.*

Ye cannot. Man cannot force his way with Christ into God's
presence.

Come. Neither discover nor reach Me.—How unlike a mere man
is the Lord's entire course.—Jews would gladly crown a king;
He flies from a throne.—He declares Himself the Messiah, then
"He will go away."—They lay snares for His life, He escapes
from their malice.—In the presence of His foes, in the temple,
near the council-chamber, He makes bold pretensions, yet no
man dare arrest Him.—His superiority over officers, judges, &c.,
points Him out as the Son of God.—These words have also a
background of prophetic meaning.—From that time the Jews
unconsciously have sought, but never found Him.

Their guilty blindness cannot recognize His throne, though *near*
unto them.—Here we learn the only way to God is through
faith in Jesus Christ.—When *that* Way is closed, the door of
hope is shut for ever.—"Ye cannot come." These words take
hold on eternity.—WHERE WILL THEY GO who do not enter
heaven *with* Jesus? John iii. 36.

ζητήσετέ. Even after His resurrection they will desire in craft to surprise
Him as Lazarus. John x. 12. *Origen.* As though He said, Your enmity can
touch Me no more. *Maldon.* You shall seek Me in your distress. *Grotius.*
Jews would actually cry to Him whom they had crucified after Jerusalem
was in ruins. *Chrys., Theoph., Euthym.* Brought to repentance by miracles
wrought by apostles. *Aug., Bede, Olsh., Stier.* Despised wisdom, in danger's
hour, will be sought in vain. *Ewald.* Will seek the Messiah too late. *Thol.*
Seek civil liberty. *Michaelis.* With all your seeking ye will not find Me. *De
Wette.* An amplified formula of the evangelist. *Lücke.* It has a reference to
the Messiah. *Alford.* Zion refused to admit the heavenly spouse until He
was gone. She seeks, but it is too late. But watchmen (ministers of vengeance)
find her. *Lampe.*. After murdering, they will vainly wish Him back again.
Meyer. With a false, Esau-like repentance. *Calvin.*

εἰμί used in a solemn sense John i. 18, signifies essential truth. *Alford.*

οὐ ἐλθεῖν. Amounts to exclusion from heaven. *Lampe.* Not all, but to many of them a terrible warning. *Wetstein.* I shall be personally in a place inaccessible to you. Ye cannot as ye are *now* enter there. *Alford.*

---

35. Then said the Jews among themselves, Whither will he go, that we shall not find him ? will he go unto the dispersed among the Gentiles, and teach the Gentiles ?

Whither? This was said probably in the mockery of malice.

Not find Him. His charity, sealed by stupendous miracles, had already broken down the barriers between Galileans, Samaritans, and Jews, and they wonder what next He will attempt?

Will He go? This reveals their increasing malignity, and also hints strongly at the depth and intensity of our Lord's zeal.

Unconsciously they give the key-note of all the future work of the Church, by exultingly noting that the Master Himself would be a MISSIONARY TO THE HEATHEN.

Dispersed. Jews, emigrated, after the Babylonian captivity, to various countries.—Still paid the temple tax, and looked for beacon fires, the date of feasts.—1. A large number of the wealthy Jews never left Babylon.—There was a jealousy between the poor who did leave, and those remaining.—Assyria, Media, Persia, all their thousands called "*Babylonian dispersion.*"—Favoured by Alexander and Antiochus, but hated by their neighbours.—2. Important part called Egyptians, first begun under Solomon. 2 Kings xviii. 21, 24.—Some of them were carried captive to Babylon by Nebuchadnezzar.—They had a temple at Leontopolis, and translated the Hebrew Bible into Greek.—About half the population (250,000) of Alexandria were Jews.—They became enamoured with Greek philosophy, mixing it with Revelation.—Cyrene Jews became so numerous, they essayed to subdue the people.—3. Antioch had also many Jews. — People rose up to destroy them under Vespasian.—Jews fled into Phrygia and Lydia, Ephesus, Sardis, Laodicea. — 4. The Greek dispersion extended into Macedonia, and had synagogues and oratories.—5. Rome had many Jews who were expelled under Tiberius and Claudius.

It is remarkable how many decrees of emperors aimed to protect them.—As clearly foretold, Deut. xxviii. 37 ; Jer. xxiv. 9, wherever they went they *excited the hatred* of the people.

Gentiles. In the original HELLENES, in N. T. always the Greeks scattered everywhere.—Men of all nations then used the *Greek* language, as now in the old world they use *French.*

Will He go to the Jews scattered among the Greeks, and teach
the Greeks?—They felt as if the words implied some grave
mystery as to themselves.—They affected to *despise* Him, yet
were continually cowering before Him.—Greeks and Hebrews
first met at a slave market, 800 B.C.   Joel iii. 6.

Greeks bartered their brazen vessels for Jewish slaves.   Ezek.
xxvii. 13.—A prophetic notice of Greece found Dan. viii. 21.

Alexander the Great's career is rapidly sketched, and his presence
and artful conduct at Jerusalem.   *Josephus.*—Greeks were eminently given to *religion,* as *they* understood it.   Acts xvii. 22.

To their feasts they invited by incense and prayer their deities;
hence the saying, " *I have feasted with the gods.*"

With strong social feelings was strangely blended a passionate
fondness for war.—They loved the sensation of hearing news,
and in its absence often invented it.   Acts xvii. 21.

An altar was found standing in every festal hall.—They began a
journey, approached a meal, or commenced a battle with *sacrifice.*

Even their *daily theatre* was opened by a *sacrifice.*

The author saw in the Parthenon *stains* of golden shields on the
marble, hung there by *pious Greeks,* as votive offerings to the gods.

Unlike many now, daily prayer was offered by Athenians.

Temple of Erechtheus, and altar of Jupiter, were never stained
by blood or wine.—On the 10th day infants were consecrated
to Hestia, by the nurse and friends.—Characterized by filial
piety, the mother's authority was supreme.—Cleobis and Biton
drew their mother's chariot 45 stadia, to Juno's temple, and
amid the shouts of the multitude they both fell dead from exhaustion.—The Argives raised a statue at Delphi to their undying *filial affection.*—The Erinyes, implacable furies, punished
undutiful sons.—These social duties made the house of the Greek
not unlike the Christian *home.*—No sacrifice is more pleasing
to the gods than a family living in unison.   *Dioscorides.*

They prayed facing the west, believing the gods had their dwelling-place near the *setting sun;* and buried their dead facing the
west.   Arabs face the east.—Immortality, the keystone of
responsibility, was held by the Greeks.—The soul was given to
watch over the body, as a guardian angel.—Romish priests
derive their doctrine of *Purgatory* from the creed of Pagan
Greece.—They held that tears shed in secret, and acts of devotion, appeased the gods.—At the door of each temple holy
water from a ewer was sprinkled on the worshippers; hence a

similar practice in Papal churches.—Merchants, when successful,
dedicated one-tenth to the gods.—Jews dwelling in Judea
treated those in foreign lands with *scorn*.—A holy land, a sacred
city, carefully performed rites, filled these fierce fanatics with
insolence.—Their question an unconscious prophecy pointing to
their own judicial rejection.

Teach the Gentiles. This was derisively said, but a blessed truth.
They saw the missionary spirit of Christianity kindling on the dying
embers of Jewish faith. — A Caiaphas prophecy, "The
kingdom was indeed to be taken away."—Their exalted privileges were all to be transferred to others.—A sadder note was
never heard than "*Let us go hence.*" Gen. vi. 3.

Jewish scorn for heathen can hardly be understood by us who have
dwelt so long under the love-beaming cross of Jesus.

διασπορὰν. Jews among Greeks speaking their tongue. *Gesenius.* Jews
scattered among heathen. *Meyer, Lücke, Tholuck.* A presentiment that His
doctrines were to be taught world-wide tended greatly to exasperate them.
Neander.

Ἑλληνες in the N. T. ever distinguished from Jews. *Stier.* Jews called
all nations beyond the sea "*Greeks.*" But the "*dispersed*" refers to Jews
scattered among those tribes. *Calvin.* Perchance mockingly—will He fix His
throne among the (Gentiles) Greeks ? *Alford.*

διδάσκειν. Caiaphas scornfully prophesies of the atonement, and these
mockers foreshadow their own doom. *Grau.*

---

36. What manner of saying is this that he said, Ye shall seek me, and shall
not find me : and where I am, thither ye cannot come ?

Manner. Its poetic rhythm helped them to remember it.

They *seem* to treat His sayings as contradictory and absurd.

Yet it is evident they cannot get away from His words.

Their dark fearful mystery alarms them, but they try to persuade
themselves He has spoken unintelligibly.—Men now often
tremble in their heart at the Word of God, but, like the Jews,
endeavour to cast off their terrors by professing to regard the
Bible as incomprehensible.—Their verdicts on Him were ever
judgments on themselves.

Ye shall seek. "Will God hear his cry when trouble cometh
upon him ? " Job xxvii. 9.—"When ye make many prayers, I
will not hear." Isa. i. 15 ; Prov. i. 24—33.—"Though they
cry in mine ears with a loud voice, I will not hear." Ezek. viii. 18.

To seek salvation and not find it is the lot of a world lost in vanity.

To seek and not find Messiah is the lot of unhappy Israel, sunk in the vanity of the letter and worldliness. *Lange.*

They transfer their bitter prejudices against the heathen to one who threatens, they think, to go and dwell among the heathen.

---

37. In the last day, that great day of the feast, Jesus stood and cried, saying, If any man thirst, let him come unto me, and drink.

Last day. See on ver. 2. The feast had continued seven days.

The *last* day of this feast was an high day, being not only the close of the feast, but of the festal season of the year.

Being a Sabbath also, the people assembled according to the law.

The longest feast of earth must end. But there is a banquet that never will cease.

Feast. Our Lord Himself condescended to found His sermon on a national custom, which Israel celebrated as a carnal, thankless festivity.

Stood. That all might *see* and *hear* THE SON OF GOD!

Hitherto Jesus had not so openly presented Himself as the personal Saviour.—How inexpressibly solemn and sublime that attitude and scene.

Cried. God's *herald*, making a proclamation from the throne of Jehovah!—The voice of boundless love is heard coming also from His throne. Rev. xxii. 17.—" Wisdom crieth in the chief place of concourse," &c. Prov. i. 20.—What He whispered to the Samaritan (John iv. 13) at the beginning of His ministry, He publishes to the world at its close.

If any man. The invitation embraces all the human race who *thirst.*

Thirst. John iv. 14. Hunger is less urgent, and not so keen a want, as thirst.—God does not force any man to thirst, but He has so created the soul that it must thirst until satisfied by Him. Luke xvi. 24.—There is a stream which will allay for ever all thirstings. Isa. viii. 6.—" Filled with all the fulness of God," they become springs to others' thirsting.—The stream following Israel forty years was a type of Christ. 1 Cor. x. 4.

1. A whole host were crying for water amid a sandy waste. Exod. xvii. 6 ; Num. xx. 2.—2. Christ's words are life-giving, as the water was to the travelling Hebrews.—3. The gospel's stream now issues from Christ, as that did from the smitten rock.—4. Divine power and grace started the stream of love from the

cross. It was *not* Moses' rod that brought water in the desert.—
5. Christ's mercy is ample and free for all. Millions shared the
stream in the desert.—6. Christ provides for present and *future*
supplies. Thus the stream followed Israel.—7. He, through
His ministry, *tells* the world where the streams for them flow.

If any man can be found *without* this "*thirst*" he is not invited.

Those trying to keep the law feel that they are unable to appease
their own conscience.—Yet the class that sigh after peace with
God delight in the law after the inner man.—Many thirst for
that which, instead of quenching, only inflames the thirst.

1. Man has a *mind*, by nature void of knowledge. Christ is made
unto us Wisdom.—2. Man has a *conscience*, responsible, guilty,
needs pardon. Christ is Righteousness.—3. Man has a *heart*,
restless without an object to love. Christ is worthy of supreme
Trust.—4. Man is *depraved*. Christ is made unto us Sanctification.—5. Man is *weak*. "Christ's strength is made perfect in
weakness."—6. Man is *mortal*. Christ is the Resurrection to all
the believing.—7. Man is *immortal*, and as a sinner doomed to
endless woes. "I give My Life for My sheep."

A man must thirst before he will come to Christ, and his coming
tests his earnestness.—No one, unless by *coming* to the Fountain,
can ever *drink* thereof.—All who came to drink from the festal
bowls of this great feast went away thirsting.—All the cere-
monials of the feast were prophetic of a nobler banquet.

Our Lord had already drawn the eyes of the thousands assembled
at the feast by His miracle.—He never during His ministry had
so large or expectant an assembly.—He who created all hearts
knew how, when, and where to command attention.

Above the sounding of the silver trumpet might have been heard
the voice of the world's Saviour !—He will and must ever impart
that thirst which He enjoins.—Here is desire without impatience,
ambition without envy, love without jealousy, coveting fulness
without anxiety.

Drink. The oriental figure for receiving any one's doctrine.

Here the grand idea is He Himself is the Source of peace to a
restless world.—To an humble workman of Galilee all the
heavy laden of earth are invited, yet who can appease these
wants but God Himself ?—Coming to Jesus relieves from doubt
and ignorance,—*Christ a Prophet ;* from guilt and its fruit,—
Christ a Priest ; from spiritual foes,—*Christ a King.*

Those that come may expect happiness without measure or end.

It shall be seen. The spring is known by the flowing streams and
flowery banks.—They become blessings to others ; all bodies
shone on become luminous to others.—Andrew brings Peter, and
Philip brings Nathanael to our Lord.

δέ after ἐν is not without force, and should not have been omitted in A. V.
Schaff.
ἐσχάτη. The eighth day. *Meyer, Bengel, Lange.* Seventh day. *Vitringa.*
God determined that day how much rain would fall that year. *Rabbis.* Water
poured out on the eighth day. *R. Juda, Lücke, Lightfoot.* Eighth day all
work ceased. Num. xxix. 35. *Hengst.*
μεγάλη. *Plutarch,* mistaking this for the feast of Bacchus, corrected by
Tacitus. Eighth day a separate feast. *Rabbis, Lücke.* Failing to contribute
to this festal joy contracted guilt. *Maimonides.*

---

38. He that believeth on me, as the scripture hath said, out of his belly shall
flow rivers of living water.

Believeth. John i. 7. This explains invitation in preceding text.
On Me. A great word, which none but JEHOVAH dare utter.
" He that believeth on the SON hath everlasting life." John iii.
36.—1. Faith has God as its object. Abraham believed God, &c.
Gen. xv. 6.—" He that believeth on Him that sent Me hath
everlasting life." John v. 24.—2. Gospel faith has Christ for
its object. " Believe God, believe also in ME." John xiv. 1.—
3. It contemplates Christ as the Son of God. John vi. 69.—" He
that believeth not the Son shall not see life, but the wrath of
God abideth on Him." John iii. 36.—4. Gospel faith rests on
Christ as a *Priest.*—" Whom God hath set forth, to be a propitiation through faith in His blood." Rom. iii. 25.—Those
" that were baptized into Jesus Christ were baptized into His
death." Rom. vi. 3.—5. On Christ as a *Prophet.* " If ye continue in My words, ye are My disciples." John viii. 31.—6.
On Christ as a *King.* " No man can say that Jesus is the Lord,
but by the Holy Ghost." 1 Cor. xii. 3 ; xv. 25.
Faith involves the heart. " With the heart man believeth unto
righteousness." Rom. x. 10. — Faith is confidence in God's
character, in Christ's power, word, love. " Though He slay me,
yet will I trust in Him." Job xiii. 15.—Faith, the ground of
justification, being a dispensation of grace only.
Its fruits, obedience, gratitude, honouring of Christ as Saviour.
His belly. Orientalism for from His wisdom or from His love.
Isa. lxiii. 15.—The *heart,* seat of sympathy, swelling with joy,

or contracting with grief. Also source of courage and understanding.—That very feast was opened by this prophecy being
read, Zech. xiv.

Flow. Water flowing from the temple a type of exalted spiritual
mercies. Ezek. xlvii. 1—12.—" Living waters shall go out from
Jerusalem." Zech. xiv. 8.—The Spirit's streams of life flowed as
never in the Old Test. times.—Three thousand souls dying of
thirst received water of life at Pentecost.—Reference is made to
the Church in its final perfection. Isa. ii. 2, 3.

Rivers. *Copiousness* and diffusiveness prove its Author the Creator
who pours the rivers and holds in His hand the oceans of earth.

The smitten Rock in the wilderness sent a stream for 40 years to
cheer Israel.—The smitten Saviour's love gushed forth upon a
thirsty land.—The Church of Christ is a glorious river, cheering
the millions of the redeemed.—Her prayers, her hymns, her
sermons, are precious streams, witnesses of her faith.

In due time they shall heal the world's dark and polluted waters.
Ezek. xlvii. 8.—Christ received the Spirit without measure, and
it overflowed on the Church. Isa. xi. 2.—Believers have the
fulness of a *vessel*, Christ the fulness of a *fountain*.

Living water. A flowing spring contrasted with cistern supplies.
Fountains being so rare in Judea, represent the transcendent value
of the stream.—Of course the vessel of itself yields no stream of
living water.—But this is the miracle of the new life, that when
received it becomes to the believer a flowing fountain of living
water.—Miracle at Cana, conversation with Nicodemus and
Samaritan woman, pouring out at Tabernacle feast, pool at
Bethesda, washing disciples' feet, water and blood at crucifixion,
connect WATER with DIVINE *blessings*.—Many graces here typified, as water in flowers, white in the lily, red in the rose,
purple in the violet, &c.—It springs up here in a palm, there in
a vine, yonder in a cedar, &c.—Thus there is ONE SPIRIT, but
diverse operations.—Moses mighty in *miracle*, Isaiah glorious
in *prophecy*, Apollos convincing in *eloquence*, Paul powerful in
reasoning. A Howard for *benevolence*. A Luther for *reformation*.
A Calvin for *theology*. A Huss and Jerome for *martyrs*. No
place having *one believer* is without a *living well*.

ὁ πιστεύων, an emphatic absolute nominative. *Schaff.*
ἡ γραφή. Lost book of inspiration. *Semler, Schulz.* Dixerunt Scripturæ.
Syriac version. This savours of a gloss. *Bloomfield.* A lost passage. *Whiston.*

Passages concerning faith. *Euthym.*, *Chrys.* Isa. lviii. 11. Accommodated. *Kuinoel.* Reference to the spirit of many passages. *Maldon.*, *Calvin*, *Beza.* Not their syllables, but sense. *Lampe.* To passages touching the efficiency of the Spirit. *Doddr.* Two texts. Isa. lv. 1; lviii. 11. *Campbell*, *Richter.* Isa. xliii. 20; xliv. 3; lv. 1. *Stier.*

ποταμοί. Secret treasures of waters under the temple mount. *Sepp.* Ezek. xlvii. 1, 2. *Alford.* Plausible, but unnatural. *Muchmeyer.* Reservoir of a spring. *Hezel.* Of the mountain. *Gerlach*, *Olsh.* Rock in the wilderness. *Meyer.* A thing hidden in the depths of nature. *Klee.* Word of Christ, not Scripture. *Euthym.*, *Erasmus.*

κοιλίας. Properly means *belly*, *abdomen*, *bowels*, *stomach*, as the receptacle of food, but in Hellenistic usage the *inward parts*, the *inner man*, the *heart*. *Schaff.* Even the corporeal nature was to be an abode of the Spirit. *Luthardt.* The new human nature. *Lange.* Allusion to jars of wide girth. *Bengel.* Church advancing to perfection. *Stier.* Sending forth streams to gladden others. *Luther.* Hill on which the temple stood. *Gesler.* Let him drink thereof who believeth on Me! as the Scripture (concerning Me) promises. *Roos*, *Stier.* A great promise and its undertone, the influence of one Christian on another. *Jul. Müller.* From the moment of believing waters begin flowing. *Lücke.* Benevolence, seeking another's good. *Aug.* His soul will ever receive refreshment and consolation. *B. Crusius.*

ῥεύσουσιν. Divine flows from the human in Christ. *Swedenborg.*

ζῶντος. The Holy Ghost opens in the soul a fountain of new life. *D. Brown.* Recent discoveries have brought to light that there was a living spring beneath the altar of the temple, from which all the fountains of Jerusalem were fed. *Schaff.*

---

39. (But this spake he of the Spirit, which they that believe on him should receive: for the Holy Ghost was not yet given; because that Jesus was not yet glorified.)

Spirit. An explanatory remark of the Evangelist similar to chap. ii. 21.—Spirit's influence compared to water for its properties of cooling, cleansing, quenching thirst, fertilizing and refreshing the earth and its dwellers.—By this Divine Agent dwelling in the soul those living fountains are opened.

Receive. Princes, being crowned, often receive splendid gifts. When Christ was inaugurated as Messiah at the Jordan and Tabor, He received glorious gifts from His Father. Eph. iv. 8.

Thus at the new creation the soul receives the lost gift of the image of God.—The nearer the sun to earth, the colder. In summer, when he is farthest, his beams are warmest. Thus our Lord's best gifts were to be bestowed after leaving our earth and returning to His Father. John xvi. 7.—Each vessel is filled, whatever be its size, which we bring to the Fountain.

Holy Ghost. Third person in the Trinity. See on John i. 1—3. Personality of the Spirit clearly taught. Always spoken of as a person. Personal feelings, acts, character ascribed to Him. Names, attributes, and works of God attributed to Him. United with the Father and the Son in baptismal formula and apostolic benediction.—Christ completes the law, the Spirit came to fulfil the Gospel.—Christ redeems the Church, the Spirit teaches the Church.—Christ to shed His blood, the Spirit to wash in His blood.—Christ to ransom the captives, the Spirit to strike off the fetters.—Christ's entire Passion and Resurrection are good news sealed up.—Spirit teaches us to know Him in the power of His resurrection. Phil. iii. 10.—The Holy Ghost, a gift springing from the gift of the Lamb of God.—The foundation of the *New Covenant* laid in the Trinity. John xvii. 3.—All *communion* with God must be through fellowship of the Spirit. 2 Cor. xiii. 14.

Not yet given, i. e. in Pentecostal fulness and power, since even in the O. T. the Spirit inspired the prophets, and was the principle of religious life in the Church.—Evident allusion to the Pentecost. The Spirit's dispensation not begun.

The waters of Life would not flow till the ROCK was smitten.

In this manner John alludes to baptism. John iii. The Eucharist. John vi. His ascension. John vi. 62.

Glorified. Christ's ascension and Spirit's descent were connected. John xvi. 7.—His absolute exaltation *above* the world the condition of His sinking *within* the world. This first brought into *full* manifestation the glory of the Holy Ghost as the third form of Divine personality. Christ must be first the Lord of Glory before He can glorify Himself through the Spirit in all hearts. When the manifestation of the Father was completed, it was followed by the manifestation of the Son. When that was finished, it was followed by the manifestation of the Spirit. And this itself is a glorifying of the Son, and the Father through Him. *Lange.*—" *Glorified* " referred to when our Lord prays that they may behold it. John xvii. 24.—Here Incarnate, it was veiled during His life on earth.—But the sun, under eclipse, loses nothing of his light or glory.—His humanity, soul and body, is glorified on the throne.—Believers glorified will be made partakers of this glory.—His glory as *Mediator* is absolutely and incommunicably His own.—Abraham had a gladdening, but glimmering view of this glory.—The Lord's glorified Body the temple from under whose threshold the Spirit flows forth to us. *Alford.*

ἔμελλον. Were about to receive. *D. Brown.*
ἅγιον omitted. *Cod. Sin.* Cancelled. *Lach., Tisch., Alf.* Found in *Codd.*
Vat. & Cant.
δεδόμενον omitted. *Cod. Sin., Tisch., Alf.* Inserted. *Lach.* The right
supplement. *D. Brown.* Operative. *Lange.* Had ceased since Malachi.
Lightfoot. Power to work miracles given before Christ ascended. *Eichhorn.*
Extraordinary effusion of the Spirit. *Euthym.* Presence and *working* of the
Spirit as the Spirit of CHRIST with the fulness of the accomplished redemption
in the Church. *Schaff.*

---

40. Many of the people therefore, when they heard this saying, said, Of a
truth this is the Prophet.

Many. Thus the separating and sifting work began, and is ever
going on.—Those who thirsted came and found all the soul
longed for in Him.—Others, offended, proudly scorned the offer,
and left hungry and thirsty.

People. The humbler ranks of men are often more *honest* than
their leaders.—They seem to have contended earnestly for our
Lord.—This popularity among them only sharpened the enmity
of the rulers.

Of a truth. They who thirst after truth must cry after knowledge,
Prov. ii. 1—6, " seek for it as for silver," and their feet should
wear the threshold of God's house.

The Prophet. John i. 21 ; iv. 19. Allusion to Deut. xviii. 18.
The prophet to be raised up like unto Moses was Jesus.—Our Lord
had perhaps thrown light upon certain truths and into unsatisfied
minds.—This glorious feast day had awakened longings in *true-
hearted* Hebrews.—The people generally expected a prophet to
come before Messiah.—This was well, but it was not all.

The wing of the fowl only lifts him from the earth, it cannot bear
him toward heaven.—Carnal minds never see aught spiritual in
any prediction, so long as they can wrest any other meaning
from the word.

πολλοί omitted. *Tisch., Alford.*
For τὸν λόγον, τῶν λόγων. *Codd. Sin., Vat., & Cant., Tisch., Alf.*
ὁ προφήτης clearly distinguished from ὁ Χριστός. *Alford.* In whose day
should take place the effusion foretold Joel ii. 28. *Grotius.* Jews anticipated
a forerunner to the Messiah. *Lampe.*

---

41. Others said, This is the Christ. But some said, Shall Christ come out
of Galilee?

Christ. John i. 41.—This rightly said is by the aid of the Holy

Ghost. 1 Cor. xii. 3.—He shows Himself to be a sealed, anointed Saviour, appointed by the Father.

Come out. Some ever stifle the yearnings of faith by misquoting Scripture.—Knowing so much, yet actually " perishing for lack of knowledge." Hos. iv. 6.—Cavillers often esteem it a title to heaven to tie a knot in religious talk which nobody can untie.

Galilee. John i. 43. Said with bitter scorn for a despised province.—It is evident His birth in Bethlehem was unknown to them.—He was to be born in Bethlehem, but reared in Galilee.

Satan, the cunning sophist, confesses Christ's Divinity, yet calls Him Jesus of Nazareth to encourage the unbelief of the people. Mark i. 24.—Galilee was made, by Christ dwelling there, to rank above Greece or Italy.—He was not ashamed to identify Incarnate Deity with humble Nazareth. Acts xxii. 8.

The fact that " not many mighty, &c., are called," operates still to the unbelief and ruin of thousands. 1 Cor. i. 26. " God hath chosen the weak things," &c. 1 Cor. i. 27—29.

Divine glory beams in the lowliness of Christ and His Church.

Doctrine of the cross still proves a stumbling-block to millions.

Χριστός. Isa. xlii. refers to Cyrus. Modern *Jews.* To Jesus Christ. *Umbreit, Dorner, J. A. Alexander, Henderson, Keil & Delitzsch.* To Isaiah. *Grotius.* Prophets as a class. *De Wette, Gesenius.*

---

42. Hath not the scripture said, That Christ cometh of the seed of David, and out of the town of Bethlehem, where David was?

Scripture. Reference to Isa. xi. 1 ; Jer. xxiii. 5 ; Micah v. 2. For SCRIPTURE, see on John v. 39.

Seed. Were there a shadow of doubt resting on the Redeemer's descent from David's line, none could accept Him.

Descendants of Mary and Joseph were summoned to Rome by Domitian the Emperor.—Mischievous persons had roused the jealousy of the tyrant as to a *king.* Finding them in humble circumstances, he dismissed them in peace. *Hegesippus* in *Eusebius.*—But it did not seem generally known that Mary was of the line of David.—David, Heb. *beloved ;* youngest son of Jesse, mother's name unknown, his grandmother Ruth.

Of Judah, born in Bethlehem, 1085 B. C.—Stature short, hair auburn, eyes bright and comely. 1 Sam. xvi. 12, 18.

Strength great, agility wonderful.—Only allusion to David's life in the N.T. Matt. xii. 3; Luke vi. 3.—Psalms lvii., lxiii., cxlii. composed in a cave.—Reigned in Hebron 7½ years. Took Jerusalem, made it the capital, called henceforth the city of David. Isa. xxix. 1.—The ark brought to the palace on Mount Zion. Great day of his life.—Psa. xxix. describes a thunderstorm during the removal of the ark.—Psalms xxx., xv., ci., lxviii., xxiv. also celebrate this splendid festival.—David's kingdom, enlarged and prosperous, became an Oriental empire.—" I have made unto thee a great name like the great ones of the earth," &c. Absalom and Adonijah possessed the beauty of their father. 2 Sam. xiv. 25.—Solomon alone had the higher qualities of the mind of David.—Gad and Nathan were the prophetic counsellors of the throne.—A prophet and psalmist, yet he acted as priest. 2 Sam. vi. 14, 17, 18.—Wore the priestly dress, offered sacrifices, and gave priestly blessings.—In 10 years reduced the Philistines, Moabites, Syrians, Edomites, and Ammonites. Psalms li., lii., record his bitter repentance after his fearful fall. Psalms xlii., lv., lxix., cix. written during his exile beyond Jordan. Died aged 70, buried on Zion. " His sepulchre is with us unto this day." Acts ii. 29.—CHARACTER. Passionately tender, generous, fierce, and brave.—Poet, soldier, shepherd, statesman, priest, prophet, king.—A romantic friend, chivalrous leader, devoted father.—Christ is not called son of Abraham, Jacob, or Moses, but Son of David.—" City of David, House of David, Throne of David, Seed of David, Oath to David," are inspired terms. His writings eminently reveal love of nature, sense of sin, tender, ardent faith, and high communion with God.—None but scoffers, void of holiness, sneer at the faithful record of David's sins and penitence.

Bethlehem. Hebrew, *house of bread.* Its history extends back 3000 years.—In sacred interest only second to Jerusalem. One the birth-place, the other the death-place, of the Son of God. Earliest name, Ephrath. Gen. xxxv. 16 ; xlviii. 7.—Life of Ruth, a descendant of Lot, a chapter in the domestic history of Bethlehem.—That devoted Moabitess is one of the links in the chain of the Saviour's genealogy.—Boaz here dwelt, and Jesse and his son David were born here.—Rachel's grave is 5 miles south of Jerusalem, on the mountain road to Hebron.—Bethlehem has now 500 houses, streets crooked, arched, and narrow. Two loaded camels can pass each other with difficulty. On the eastern ridge the church stands, erected 325 A. D. by the Empress Helena. It resembles a huge, grim baronial castle.

Here is a cave hewn in the rock 38 ft long, and the words, " H IC DE VIRGINE MARIA JESUS CHRISTUS."—A silver star in the marble pavement shows the spot of nativity.—The Basilica, erected by Helen, mother of Constantine, is a noble temple.

The oldest monument of Christian architecture on earth.

Has four rows of Corinthian columns, 48 in number, of finely-wrought light-brown marble, that which forms the mountains around Jerusalem. 170 feet in length, and 80 in breadth.

The Mosaic pavement has been trod by pilgrims for 1500 years.

Scenery bordering on the Dead Sea is full of solitary grandeur.

Here, amid the desolation of the wilderness, David strung his harp.

On these plains angels announced Christ's birth to watching shepherds.—Here the magi came from the east with gifts.

Here Herod slew the babes, and " Rama sent forth a wailing." Matt. ii. 18.—Bethlehem is named by Justin Martyr, A. D. 150.

Jerome, A. D. 399, here translated the Hebrew Bible into Latin, the *Vulgate.*—A. D. 1100, Crusaders captured it. Baldwin I. made it a see of the Church.—From the roof of the convent the Dead Sea is plainly visible.—There is no pasture in all these regions on the 25th of Dec., hence the birth-time of our Lord must have been in the fall, or spring.—In 1837 many houses were ruined, and many perished, in an earthquake.—Fragments of ancient pillars are wrought into the modern houses.—1600 Latins, 1200 Greeks, 200 Armenians, 300 Moslems dwell there.

Sacred relics of mother of pearl and selenite, asphaltum from the Dead Sea, cups from the black fig-tree wood, and trinkets from black coral are their sole manufactures.

Where David was. 1 Sam. xvi. Discriminates this village from Bethlehem in Zebulun. Jos. xix. 15. They maintain He must not only be from Bethlehem, but *not* from Galilee.

They entirely overlook the fact that Isaiah was supplemented by Micah v. 1.—Galilee, from the lowest depths, was to be elevated by the Lord's presence. Matt. iv. 15.—How unintentional was this testimony of His bitter foes.—God thus ever can raise witnesses at will.

Δαβίδ. Two heathen historians notice him,—*Nicolaus* of Damascus and *Eupolemus.* His birth and conception immaculate. *Rabbis.* Moslems call Abraham the *Friend,* Mahomet the *Apostle,* and David the *Prophet* of God. *Weil.*

Βηθλεείμ. Arabic, *house of flesh.* The Abbey, erected by Justinian the Emperor, A. D. 520. Early writers make no allusion to such a cave. *Eusebius,*

Origen, Socrates, Cyprian, Nicephorus. Jerome dwelt here 30 years in a cave excavated by his own hands. *Ritter.* Some taught Christ must go forth from Bethlehem to *teach*, as well as be *born* there. *Hengst.*

43. So there was a division among the people because of him.

Division. Thorough inquiry would have solved doubt and discord.—Authors of schism are generally swelling smatterers who have no true knowledge of Scripture. *Lange.*
The world is ever dividing from the visible Church, but the Church is one.—Ceasing to *defend* is equivalent to *betraying* the truth.
It is a false love of peace to suffer open enemies of truth in the Church.—It is far better to die pure than live polluted.
Neglected discipline is a reproach to Christ's people.
Heresies are but the furnace, making truth shine more clearly.
Storms make the roots of trees strike deeper.—When Satan rages most his time is shortest.—Enemies of truth have now and then won in a battle, but never in a war.—The hour may be theirs, but the day is ours. 1 Cor. xi. 19.—Nothing unites more closely or separates more widely than the gospel.—The truth being one, all under its light should be under one banner.
Sects in Christ's Church seem to have rent the seamless garment.
All believers are " sons of peace," and never grasp a sword save to secure or defend PEACE.

Σχίσμα. Jews did not discriminate between Messiah and Prophet. *Hengst.* A violent dissension. *Alford.*

44. And some of them would have taken him ; but no man laid hands on him.

Would have. Were minded to take Him.—Men will have to account for sins of the heart, having the *will* but not the *power*.
They were invisibly restrained. Psa. cv. 15.—Rage as they may, no one shall hinder God's plans.
But no man. We have not so much to fear from men's evil will as from our own.
Laid hands. Because God's hand overruled the hands of Christ's foes. 1. A hand of omnipotence. 2. A hand of wisdom. 3. A hand of faithfulness. 4. A hand of triumph.—He who is in the hand of God no fleshly hand can hurt.

45. Then came the officers to the chief priests and Pharisees ; and they said unto them, Why have ye not brought him ?

Officers. Greek word, a military term, an under-rower in a war-galley.—Then any strong workman, then one who attends on a superior.—Mark was thus *minister* or officer to Paul and Barnabas. Acts xiii. 5.—Our Lord Himself assumed the form of a " slave." Phil. ii. 7.—Officers were messengers of the courts to take charge of prisoners, to carry out the decisions of the court.—Lictors of Rome and constables of America similar in duties.

Why ? In the pride of their brief authority, they cannot conceive what should hinder.—" The Lord knoweth how to deliver the godly." 2 Pet. ii. 9.—" In the thing wherein they dealt proudly He is above them." Exod. xviii. 11.

Not brought. Already thirsting for His blood, and thinking it easy to take Him. Had they known His supreme Godhead the crucifixion could never have taken place.

Ahaziah's messengers found a grave instead of a victim.

When men interfere with His plans He reasons with them by thunderbolts. 2 Kings i. His words to " fools " are *rods.* Prov. xvii. 10.

ὑπηρέται and δοῦλοι in same verse—John xviii. 18. Former an humble waiter on a superior officer in an army, the latter a slave, opposed to ἐλεύθερος. Rev. xiii. 16. *Trench.* Translated "ministers and servants."

---

46. The officers answered, Never man spake like this man.

Never. With a marvellous mixture of fear and courage they speak.—Thus the Centurion, under pressure, said,—" Truly this was the Son of God."

Spake. John vi. 59. At times the Spirit coerces even a Balaam to utter true prophecies.—There was an honest kindness of heart among these hirelings.—Their integrity, perilling their employers' confidence and pay, contrasts with the cruelty of the Pharisees.—Highly they honour Christ's preaching, and joyfully confess His name.—They doubtless knew their masters desired to put Him to death. John vii. 25.—They imply that even their learned rulers had not spoken so well.

As the *sand* of the hour-glass to the flowing *fountain,* so are the words of human wisdom to the teachings of Jesus.

How pure His precepts. They point with radiant finger to heaven. His rewards and promises are suited to the wants of the soul. His golden rule between men, how exact and universally binding. With vehemence He rebukes hypocrisy, and tenderly treats the bruised reed and smoking flax.—He invites with earnestness and embraces with love all penitent sinners.—He instructs with mildness and bears with patience His own disciples.

His majestic authority commanded reverence where it did not secure love.—His words were *oracles*, all had an *after-echo* of heavenly significance.—" His words were thunder, His life was lightning." *Augustine.*—1. No one sharing in the counsels of God ever before came to earth as a Teacher. Eternity without a curtain seemed to stand before Him.—No one ever dared make himself the OBJECT and FOUNTAIN of FAITH.—2. Such majesty, originality, freedom, grace, power!—3. Such *effects*. No prejudice could resist. No threats could over-awe. No authority could make Him swerve.—Efforts age after age to arrest His kingdom have been like those of the madman who would chain the winds or prevent the sun.—Ocean's tides and the orbs of heaven seem guided by the same Almighty, unseen energy, as His Church.

Like this man. " This carried great authority in His sayings. His nature was so sweet, His manners so humble, His words so wise, so composed, His learning so grave and winning, His answers so seasonable, His questions so deep, His reproofs so severe and charitable, His pity so great and merciful, His preaching so full of reason and holiness, of weight and authority, His conversation so useful and beneficent, His poverty so touching, yet His alms frequent, His life so holy, His employment so profitable, His meekness so incomparable, His passions without change, save where zeal or pity carried Him on to worthy and apt expressions. Who never laughed, but often wept at the calamities of others. Who loved every man and hated no man. Who gave counsel to the doubting, instruction to the ignorant. Who bound up the broken hearts. Who strengthened the feeble knees. Who relieved the poor, and converted sinners. Who despised none who came to Him for relief, and as for those who did not, He went to them.

" He embraced all occasions of mercy offered to Him, and went abroad to seek more.—He spent His days in preaching and healing, and His nights in prayer and communion with God.—

He was obedient to the laws and subject to princes ; though He was PRINCE of Judea in right of His royal line, and of ALL THE WORLD by right of the FATHER !—The people followed Him, but He made no gatherings.—And when they were made, He suffered no tumult.—When they would make Him King, He withdrew Himself.—When He knew they would put Him to death, He offered Himself.—He knew men's thoughts, and answered them, thus preventing their questions.

" He would work a miracle rather than give offence, and yet suffer every offence rather than see God His Father dishonoured.

" He kept the Mosaic law with exactness, to which He came to put an end.—He honoured their Sabbath by healing their sick, a charity done by them to their beasts, and yet men were angry at His deed.—In all His life He was innocent as an angel of light. When, by the greatness of His worth, severity of His doctrine, charity of His miracles, applause of the people, authority of His sermons, reproof of hypocrisy, discovery of their false doctrines and weak traditions, He had branded the reputation of their vicious rulers, they resolved to put Him to death, they had no charge against Him but *truth*, and no crime but His *office*. No competent judge could be found to condemn Him until threatened with Cæsar's revenge. He made no reply to their murderous assault but silent innocence. He needed no more argument than the sun needs an advocate to prove it is the *brightest star in the firmament*." *Jeremy Taylor.*

" His history is matchless. In all literature nothing approaches it. To have it *written*, it must first be *lived*. He walked amid all the elements of nature, diseases of men and death itself, amid the secrets of the human heart, the rulers of darkness in the world, in all their number, subtilty, and malignity, not only as their conscious LORD, but as though they felt conscious of His resistless WILL." *D. Brown.*—Doctrine unearthly, eloquence convincing, aspect awful, manner Divine.

This was the noble testimony of plain honest men.

They were strangers, doubtless, to the full intent of our Lord's words, but the mysterious grandeur, transparent purity, and enchanting grace, led them captive against their own interest.

Had not the Spirit of God touched their hearts, could they have been so bold ?—They prefer braving the anger of their masters to the sacrilege of touching such a Being.

For a moment they became apostles, and began in the *Sanhedrim*

to preach Christ.—Some of the early Fathers held these officers
were *really converted*, and some by their death may have been
witnesses for Jesus.

ἀπεκρίθησαν. Unless urged by conscience, even this would not have been
said. *Anton.* It was a strong word they spake in their humility. *Luther.*
With my knowledge of men and books, I find no book like the Bible for
excellent wisdom, learning, and use. *Chief Justice Hale.* I have surveyed
most of the learning found among the sons of men, but I can stay my soul
on none of them but the Bible. *Selden.* No songs like those of Zion, no
orations like the Prophets, no politics like those of the Scriptures. *Milton.*
See Sugg. Comm. on Romans, vol. i. pp. 17, 18. Involuntary witnesses of
the innocence or even Divinity of Christ, and the truth of the gospel: Pilate
and his wife, the Centurion at the cross, Judas Iscariot, Tacitus in his Account
of the Neronian persecution, Celsus, Lucian, Porphyry, Rousseau, Napoleon,
Strauss, Renan, &c. See *Schaff's* Person of Christ. Marius sent soldiers to
arrest Mark Antony, but his *eloquence* disarmed them. *Plutarch.*

---

47. Then answered them the Pharisees, Are ye also deceived?

Pharisees. History and character. John i. 24.
Deceived. Not deceived, but enlightened, and we trust converted.
Our Lord's eye was upon their hearts, although they knew it not.
Unconsciously they were under the *arrest* of the SPIRIT of TRUTH
standing before them.—They admit their own officers were *cap-
tivated* by Him they were sent to seize.—They thus unwittingly
ratify the judgment given by their servants.
The serpent came forth to sting, but its fangs had lost their poison.
Jer. viii. 17.—Papists sent chaplains to catch the words of Henry
Zutphen of Bremen, but the arrows of the Divine Archer pierced
and converted them.—What truth is uttered, by its connection,
false ones make *untruth.*—If infidel lecturers were to speak truth
they would soon empty their halls of folly.—Testimony of the
officers: 1. As their own excuse. 2. As an accusation against
their superiors. 3. As a glorification of our Lord's superhuman
innocence. *Lange.*

οὖν omitted. *Cod. Sin., Tisch., Alford.*
πεπλάνησθε. Luther called an apostate, answered, "Yes, I am apostate
from the devil." Proper words from those calling Him πλάνος. καὶ hints at
a great number already deceived. *Lampe.* Severity would have driven these
men at once to join the disciples. *Lampe.*

48. Have any of the rulers or of the Pharisees believed on him ?

Rulers. They would oppress by authority, having no argument. Force has ever been the last resource of *tyranny* in theology, as in government.—Many *wise* are resolved to perish rather than acknowledge their folly. Isa. v. 21.—This infatuation is distinctly foretold. " God hides things from the wise," &c. Matt. xi. 25.—Secret disciples, like Nicodemus and Joseph, must have been stung to the quick if they heard this question.

Men wanting in moral courage, in every age, have sacrificed truth. Psa. cxvi. 11.—Woolston, Tindall, and other infidels, justified deceiving others.—It is the boast of Jesuits, that they have a right to deceive for the greater glory of God. *Steinmetz's Hist.*

His warnings, like the thundering voices of the Apocalypse, reach every generation. " Whosoever shall be ashamed of Me and of My words." Luke ix. 26.—Those denying Christ before men will be denied before the angels of God. Luke xii. 9.

Sin will ever be folly, and perseverance therein madness. Eccl. ix. 3.

Ancient Romans on the death of a great man sacrificed *human victims.* So when teachers apostatize, like the dragon, they draw down some stars with them. Rev. xii. 4.—The pope offered to confirm the English liturgy if Elizabeth would only join the Papal cause, and he offered Luther a cardinalship with its riches and honours, if he would return to Papal allegiance.

The sins of teachers are the teachers of sin.—The power of example extends to brutes.—A flock of sheep passing a ferry at Detroit lately, one sprang into the river and all followed and perished.

Pharisees. John i. 24. Added as if out of an evil conscience.

As much as to say, See how the whole great orthodox, aristocratic Jewish party is against Him. *Lange.*

Believed. For the sad privilege of continuing in unbelief, under what frail hiding-places men take refuge.—No more fatal delusion than trusting a depraved heart to guide to eternal truth.

Had these rulers become disciples, that moment their *influence* would have gone.—Yet one man with God on his side is stronger than any majority. *Schaff.*

ἀρχόντων. Sapientes sapienter in infernum descendunt. *Trapp.* Celsus wrote scornfully of Christians, " Wool-workers, cobblers, leather-dressers, and illiterate, mere preachers to children and women." *Origen.* Sadducees were more teachable than others. *Doddr.*

49. But this people who knoweth not the law are cursed.

People. Gr. *multitude.* In every age ecclesiastical demagogues have flattered the masses they despised.

Knoweth not. More shame to them for leaving the people in ignorance.—He who increases his knowledge increases responsibility also.—Many contend far more for science than for eternal life.—Hereafter it will avail more to have subdued one lust than to comprehend all mysteries.—Why did not these proud doctors examine Him of whom their own officers testified that He " spake as never man spake " ?—" *Light from Galilee was no light for them.*" Philip of Spain declared, " He would prefer his kingdom to be without subjects rather than that they should be Protestants." Charles II. said, " Presbyterianism was no religion for gentlemen."

Law. John i. 17 ; vii. 19. They used the term as we " the Bible." The more *false* a man's religion, the more *fierce* he is in maintaining it.—The worse the lot of goods some merchants own, the more earnestly do they praise them.

Cursed. Greek form intensifies the meaning, they literally *cursed* them.—The hierarchial insolence and theological self-conceit here bear a genuine historical character. The common people were called *vermin. Tholuck.*—Their purpose was to excommunicate all Jesus' friends.—They were evidently astonished at the number of His followers, for " the world had gone after Him." John xii. 19.—The reaction would have been too violent to carry out their plans.—This outburst of passion was an expression of their impotent rage.—The dialectics of unbelief are generally traceable to *passion.*—All forms of " Liberalism " are to hide some bosom sin.—A spirit of lying was permitted to enter the prophets of Ahab.—Servants of God have been cursed ever since Shimei cursed David.—Council of Trent utters one hundred and twenty-eight anathemas.—But from Antichrist these curses become blessings.—Greeks and Romans were accounted by the Jews as " *things that are not.*" 1 Cor. i. 28.—They had no desire to enlighten, or heart to sacrifice or pray for, the humbler classes.—One of the greatest wonders the disciples had to tell John, " THE POOR HAVE THE GOSPEL," &c. Luke vii. 22. Officers might reply, Are we to derive our faith from you, learned in the law ?—" Have the rulers *died* for us ? " " Have the Pharisees *borne our sins ?* " *Brienz.*—No tribunals have pro-

ceeded more unrighteously than spiritual tribunals. *Heubner.*
Theological passions are the deepest and strongest, as *religious* wars
are the fiercest. *Schaff.*

ὁ ὄχλος. "But only this rabble who know nothing of the law (believe in
Him); cursed are they!" *Lange.* Three classes. 1. Rabbis, Scribes. 2.
Scholars or wise men. 3. Illiterate. *Elsley.* The ignorant rabble, not "the
people." Greek notices these distinctions. *D. Brown.*

ἐπάρατοι. "The illiterate man is not godly." *Pirke Aboth.* "None but
the learned will rise from the dead." *Talmud* in *Lücke.* Pharisees spurned the
idea of eating with those they called "brute herd." *Wetstein.* Anathematized,
i. e. excommunicated. *Kuinoel.* Not a formula of excommunication, but an
intimation that the ban is impending, which in chap. ix. 22 is hypothetically
decreed against the followers of Jesus. *Lange.* A passionate outburst of the
rabbinical *rabies theologica. Schaff.* Denounced. *Lampe.* Rabbis called the
people "worms." *Lightfoot.* The Spirit of the Lord was never known to rest
upon a poor man. *Rabbis.* "Odi profanum vulgus et arceo." *Horace.*

---

50. Nicodemus saith unto them, (he that came to Jesus by night, being one
of them,)

Nicodemus. 1. A timid but honest inquirer after truth. Chap. iii.
2. A calm but decided advocate of justice. Chap. vii. 3. A
heroic confessor of the Lord bringing his grateful offerings.
Lange.

There is one ruler at least who dares to speak for Jesus.

The fire of love kindled in the heart will sooner or later burn and
shine.—A son of Crœsus *dumb*, seeing his father slain, broke
forth in *words* of grief.—Nicodemus, hitherto a night-bird, is now
heard in the morning.—He was a *slow scholar.* Judas, a *forward
preacher.* But at last Judas betrays in the night, Nicodemus
professes in the day.—"Not many noble are called." 1 Cor. i.
26. But there are *some* will choose life.

Saith. Those most timid before courts have proved bravest at
the stake.

Came to Jesus. Though a member of their Christ-hating body.

Different ways to Christ.—Contrasts his former timidity with his
present courage.—His colleagues seemed to *suspect* the source
of his friendship for the Lord.

Night. Having but little faith, he could do but little.

As his knowledge of Christ grew, he grew in grace and courage.

An invalid ventures not out in a storm, but becoming hardy, braves
the tempest.—It must have fallen like a thunder-clap upon these

Sanhedrists, that *one* of their *number* should interpose on behalf of the hated one.—What a word of cheer to the brow-beaten officers.—Even in high places Christ has friends of whom we know nothing. *Schaff.*

νυκτὸς. Πρότερον, according to B. L. T. and others. *Lach.*, *Alford.* But *Tisch.*, ed. viii., with *Cod. Sin.*, omits the clause ὁ ἐλθὼν νυκτὸς πρὸς αὐτὸν πρότερον, and reads simply, λέγει Νικόδημος πρὸς αὐτούς. *Lach.*, *Alf.*, *Meyer* retain the clause with the exception of νυκτὸς. *Schaff.* in *Lange.* The Evangelist intimates his timidity, still lingering, as the reason for his faint vindication of the Lord. *Calvin, Grotius.* Naturally a prudent, cautious mind. *Hengst.*

---

51. Doth our law judge any man, before it hear him, and know what he doeth ?

Law. The question proves the cautious timidity of the lawyer, The law itself is described as the authority in the case.
It looks as if he felt afraid of being openly classed with the followers of the Lord.

Judge. Gr. *after careful investigation, to give a righteous decree.*
They were guilty of a palpable violation of the law in the Sanhedrim. Exod. xxiii. 1.—In the gentlest manner and only indirectly he reproves their course.—But even this protest, uttered with extreme prudence, was much too strong for their passionate vehemence.—They saw he would be His disciple too, if he had the courage.—Sanhedrim was selected from the judges of their lower courts.—To fill the places of deceased judges, a school was formed for youth.—Their law all being in the Scriptures, they were students of the Bible.—They were laymen of the tribe of Levi, called FOUNDATIONS OF THE LAW.—Sanhedrim had 70 members, six of whom being selected from each tribe.
A President of the Council. His assistant was called the Father of the Council.—They had the power of life and death over priests and kings. Psa. cxlix. 8.

Before. Gr. *except it first hear from him.* A rather tame protest.
He was doubtless pressed by conscience, not designing to decide the case.—He denies that the officers were to be willing tools of cruelty.—Often have the decrees of insane rulers been arrested by the refusal of the army to enforce them.

Hear. Romans gloried in never condemning a man before having heard him in his own defence.—A party clothed sumptuously must change it for a *plain attire.*—Nor could one party *sit* while the other *stood* in court.—Nor must the *seat* of one party be any *higher* than the other. *Selden.*—But how long did the prisoner lie in durance before this hearing came ?

The *Habeas Corpus* is an outgrowth of Christian civilization alone. The simple protest was used by Jehovah to turn the tide of anger. Lamps within broken pitchers once scattered the enemies of God and of Gideon.—Thus Nicodemus meets their boasts : 1. That no ruler believes in Jesus. 2. That they were zealous for the law. *Lange.*

κρίνει. Not to hear one party, without the other's presence. *A. Levi* of Barcelona. Hence the Greeks took their law, not to condemn on hearsay evidence. *Philo.* Attic law required witnesses. *Selden.* Jurors swore to hear alike accuser and defender. *Solon's* Laws. A Sanhedrim existed in Babylon during captivity. *Gemara.* Also in Alexandria, in Egypt. *Lewis'* Heb. Ant. Three judges sat as court in villages after the manner of consistories. *Reland.*

---

52. They answered and said unto him, Art thou also of Galilee ? Search, and look : for out of Galilee ariseth no prophet.

Answered. Contradiction only inflames our love of our own counsels.

Art thou also ? Art thou determined to side with Him ?—A man's *party*, often against the remonstrance of conscience, *compels* him to sacrifice principle.—Yet perceiving their *cause* wrong, he must abandon them *first.*—To stand *alone* tests faith as truly as the stake.—Soon the friendship or enmity of the world will be to us no more than the wind that breathes over our graves.—It will be no regret then to have been called a " Galilean " on earth.—Nicodemus now rejoices that he sacrificed the honours of the Sanhedrim for Jesus.—He received a prophet in the name of a prophet, and the reward also. Matt. x. 41.

The giver of a cup of cold water in the name of Christ will be above kings. Mark ix. 41.

Of Galilee. Scoffingly, Art thou of that *faction*, believing in this Galilean ?—An insinuation that Christ had no followers save rustic Galileans.—The enemies of Jesus have never respected personal *integrity.*—Ridicule is a weapon of fearful power and influence with the unprincipled.—They thought to mock Him out of his religion, as many are in every age.

Superficial graces and flashing assurance often adorn the character of the successful libertine.—Virtue, awkward and homespun, is made the butt of wit and mirth.—Modesty is derided as a weakness, a troublesome companion.—Vice assumes a charming effrontery, the gilded pathway to licentiousness.

Hospitality and private friendship are gaily sacrificed to fill the audience with delight.—Julian the Apostate in the 4th century contemptuously called Christ "the Galilean," and Christians "Galileans." *Schaff.*

Search. Because he had *searched,* therefore he had found that out of Galilee the greatest prophet came.—Had they searched also, they too would have found Jesus.—Some go to the Bible as an arsenal, for arms against the *truth.*—As *Herostratus* took fire from the temple altar to burn the glory of Ephesus.

Look. That is, thou shalt easily see, they challenge him to search.—"Search the Scriptures," said the Redeemer, but for the way to *Eternal Life.*—Why not rather answer the protest against a bloody decree?—A mere caution to pause and consider was, to their fanaticism, *treason.*

Galilee. John i. 43. As though none but Galileans were His followers.—An opprobrious epithet, as *Huguenot, Puritan, Methodist, Quaker, Hussite,* &c., a mark for the shaft of ignorance and intolerance.—Galileans constantly linked with the despised Gentiles. Isa. ix. 1 ; Matt. iv. 15.

Had our Saviour confined His labours to Galilee, the Pharisees might have had cause to say Judea and Jerusalem, centres of religious hopes, had been despised.—But it was the dense darkness of their region which contrasts with His light. Matt. iv. 15.

Ariseth. It is nowhere foretold that the Prophet is to come out of Galilee.—They well knew that Elijah and Elisha, Jonah, Amos, and Hosea, Nahum and Habakkuk, were all from Galilee. Prejudice and pride blind the heart.—They hid by false reasoning, like fig-leaves, the rebellion rooted in their hearts.

Prophet. John iv. 19. Jonah of Gath-hepher was from Galilee. 2 Kings xiv. 25.—But as he was among the minor prophets, they did not note him.—They doubtless meant none were *illustrious* enough to make it probable.—Falsification of historical facts a favourite trick of priests.—Witness the *forged* decretals of Pseudo-Isodorus, A.D. 795, by Adrian I.—For 600 years these were the UNQUESTIONED BULWARK of the PAPACY !

In crushing the truth, they must trample the Scripture in the dust.

It was their frail defence : No prophet could come from Galilee.
And yet the *greatest Prophet did come* from the same despised
 Galilee. But rage is blind, and fanaticism distorts all that a
 person really knows —It seems they were afraid to lose Nicodemus, from their reasoning with him.—Men, unjust in little or
 great things, just so far are *tyrants.*—They browbeat their
 children, if parents ; and if rulers, they crush their subjects into
 slaves.—Hence among heathen, husbands are generally tyrants,
 and chiefs the plunderers of their unfortunate subjects.

ἐκ τῆς. Ridicule among the Greeks and Romans embraced as their objects
murder, parricide, ingratitude, perfidy, adultery. The last, to the disgrace
of civilization, is the principal source of sport in our *modern theatres. Jeremy
Collier*, Essays on the Stage.
προφήτης. The Messiah. *Pearce.* Sanhedrists referred not to the *time*
when the Messiah was expected. *Semler.* Jonah and Elijah were both from
Galilee. *Alford.* Had Jonah been named they would have quoted some such
proverb as—" One swallow does not make a summer." *Hengst.* Others make
Elijah a Galilean. *D. Brown.* Nahum is assigned to Galilee. *Jerome.* Also
Hosea. *Lücke.* Galilee not yet in contrast with Judea. *Ebrard.* Under
passionate excitement they uttered a reckless untruth. *Lange.* Mistake due
to the heat of passion rendering them forgetful. *Doddr.* In Tiberias a
seminary was afterwards founded in which were renowned Rabbins. The
Talmud also came from that quarter, so that the Jews now are ashamed of this
proverb. *Olearius.*
ἐγήγερται seems not sufficiently accredited. *Lange.*
ἐγείρεται. *Cod. Sin., Lach., Tisch., Alf.* These words should end this
chapter. *Blackwall.*

---

53. And every man went unto his own house.

Every man. Nicodemus's timely word arrests their bloody design.
A marvellous and strong combination melts away like the waves
 of the sea, broken by their own impetuosity. We recognize
 God's hand. He remains ever like Himself.—Passion in high
 councils proves *weakness*, as fever in sickness.
Went. They went up to the temple to triumph, but came down
 humbled. Our Lord ascended meekly, but came down in power
 and glory.—How Nehemiah firmly, but triumphantly, stood at
 Jerusalem.—How Paphnutius stood up for truth at the Nicene
 Council.—How Athanasius and Augustine contended valiantly
 for the faith.—Anselm and Aquinas, Luther and Calvin, heroes
 all in the sacramental host of God's elect !—Wickliff and Huss,

Cranmer and Ridley, were the lights in their day of darkness, rebuke, blasphemy, and blood.

His own. Our Lord had no home in Jerusalem, nor anywhere else on earth.

House. Materials were anciently of mud, brick, stone, wood, marble, porphyry and granite, chalk, mortar, asphaltum, ivory. 1 Kings xxii. 39 ; Amos iii. 15.—Doors, floors, were made of shittim and acacia, sycamore, cedar, algum, and cypress.

Houses for jewels, although temples were generally treasure-houses.

Houses for arms and all kinds of weapons of war. 2 Kings xx. 13.

Dwellings as tents, palaces, citadels, tombs, caves. Gen. xix. 30.

Hebrews dwelt in tents until after they left Egypt. Gen. xlvii. 3.

Private houses of the Assyrians and Babylonians have perished.

Houses mainly at present in Egypt, Syria, Arabia, Persia, are mere *mud-huts.*—Thousands of them are roofless and without furniture.

Scores of families dwell in the tombs in the mountains at Thebes in Egypt.—In many the oxen occupy the same dwelling, not even divided by a curtain.—Many dwellings in Palestine have the floors and roof of stone.—Timber being exceedingly scarce, the roofs are made by arches of masonry.—Not a chimney is visible, the houses of Judea, like those of Pompeii, are but one story, the walls on the street are without windows.

Doorways often bear an inscribed verse from the *Koran.*

Israelites directed to write passages of the law over their doorways. Deut. vi. 9.—Most large houses have one to seven courts. In the passage is a stone seat for the porter.—Called by the Romans *Impluvium,* generally paved with marble.—An awning is at times drawn to screen from sun and rain.—A raised divan of stone or carpets surrounded the chambers.—Ceilings of large dwellings are panelled and ornamented. Jer. xxii. 14.

A gallery runs round the inside of the court.—This court covering or roof was removed for the paralytic. Luke v. 18.

Roofs of many are covered with mortar of tar, ashes, and sand.

Those having domes have also large flat portions. Jerusalem from Mount of Olives presents thousands of white domes crowning the three summits of the city.—Rollers keep the flat parts solid, grass springs in the cracks. Psa. cxxix. 6 ; Isa. xxxvii. 27.

On them corn and clothes are dried, figs and raisins are prepared.

Dwellers sleep there. 2 Sam. xi. 2.—Moslems often pray on their roofs. Jer. xxxii. 29.—The writer often witnessed them on their knees, to be seen praying by strangers. Matt. vi. 5. From their

694 / Gospel of John

morals it seems their prayers cease when spectators withdraw.
Roofs had booths built for retirement.   Neh. viii. 16.
Mourners went on the roof to wail.   Isa. xv. 3.

ἐπορεύθη. One word scatters them. Sadducees, ever opposing Pharisees,
might prevent a vote by sustaining Nicodemus. *Grotius*. Meeting broken up
and nothing done. *Lampe*. By the time of evening service. *Lightfoot*. Sanhedrim sat until that hour. *Cocceius*. No abruptness indicated. *Doddridge*.

εἰς τὸν οἶκον. Not Johannean. Some Codices τὰ ἴδια. Some private dwellings of stone still survive in Bashan, in the land of the Moabites, beyond Jordan.
Porter. Roman houses lacked the battlements which Moses demanded.
Lewis' Ant. They had no chimneys. Modern Jews leave a cubit unplastered,
a memento of the temple ruins. *Lewis'* Ant. Their tradition is no house was ever
" To LET " in ancient Jerusalem. Other nations derived the custom of writing
sentences over door-posts, as Persians and Arabs. *Huetius*. They were forbidden to imitate any part of the temple or furniture in their houses. *Maimonides*.

John 8

1. JESUS went unto the mount of Olives.

Jesus. John i. 17, 41. Word. John i. 1—8. Son. John i. 18, 34.

Went. He generally left the brilliant misery of the city every night, that in quiet He might compose His sorrowful and interceding heart.—He preferred Bethany or Mount of Olives as His resting-place.—These spots were consecrated by many preparatory prayers,—knowing His deepest humiliation and highest exaltation would be here.—Faith must *interline* these hints of the Spirit, or we shall lose many radiating suggestions.

Our Saviour, the Creator of worlds, a homeless pilgrim here, a manger the first resting-place of the Lord of Angels.

Then a Fugitive, seeking rest among aliens in a strange land.

We then hear of Him in a midnight storm, a solitary voyager on the waves.—He retires to a desert place, and there spends the long night on the cold mountain. Luke vi. 12.

The birds and beasts have coverts, but the Redeemer is without a home.—Even an angel dwelling among sinners must feel *alone*.

Mount of Olives. A well-known mountain east of Jerusalem.

Christ's usual oratory ; name only occurs once in O.T. Zech. xiv. 4.

We never read of the Lord lodging in Jerusalem, or passing the night there.—The distance from Jerusalem was a Sabbath day's journey, 2000 cubits, or half a mile.—It rises so as to shut out all the view of the east.—It is one of many crowns of a mountain ridge in Central Judea, Zion, Moriah, Scopus, Gibeah, Ramah, Mizpeh.—Olivet is 150 feet higher than any other. Approaching the city from Joppa, Olivet is seen just beyond the castle of David and buildings of Zion.—It droops to the right, revealing 24 miles distant the pale blue mountains of Moab beyond the Jordan.

Its apparent nearness is owing to the clear atmosphere, and one in Jerusalem sees Olivet *joining* Mount Moriah, though the vale of Kedron, 500 feet below, is between.—Olivet, in grey terraced slopes, white limestone crags, rises 700 feet.—At the base of the Mount of Offence is Siloam,—From the central summit the Church of the Ascension arises.—The descent through the wilder-

ness of Judea to the valley of Sodom, some 18 miles distant, is
3700 feet.—The sides show patches of wheat, barley, straggling
vines, palms, pine, myrtle, fig-trees, and many olive-trees,
old, gnarled, and a few propped because of decay.

Both hill-sides of Kedron contain *countless graves* of the sons of
Abraham.—Here the Rabbis say the *Last Judgment* will be held.

Except Bethany, and three or four huts on the summit, Mount of
Olives is forsaken of dwellings.—Opposite St. Stephen's gate, at
the foot of 'Olivet, is Gethsemane, and two paths leave this gate,
one ascends and winds round the southern shoulder to Bethany.

The caravan road for thousands of years to Jericho winds around
it, the scene of the triumphant entry of our Lord.

Another path the left of Gethsemane, taken by David barefoot,
fleeing before Absalom.—"The glory of the Lord stood on the
mount east of the city."—"His feet shall stand in that day upon
the Mount of Olives, and the Mount of Olives shall cleave in the
midst thereof." Zech. xiv. 4. Millenarians believe this will be
literally fulfilled.—Pilgrims still tent out in the fields and groves
of Olivet for privacy, prayer, and poverty.—In the east, spots
whence the sanctuary is visible are *sacred*.—Our Lord visited
the temple for the last time, and predicted its utter ruin. Mark
xiii. 1.—After the institution of the Supper He went over Kedron
to the Mount of Olives. Matt. xxvi. 30.—The *ascension* took
place on the ridge extending over a mile from the summit of
the Mount of Olives to Bethany. "As He drew nigh unto
Bethany." Luke xxiv. 50.—Empress Helena, mother of Constantine, built a church there A.D. 325.—At the base of Olivet is
the chapel of the Virgin. The tomb is first named A.D. 600.

Olive trees are associated with the history of civilization; first
named Gen. viii. 11.—Connected with the reign of peace by
Greek and Roman poets.—Greeks and others hung enemies'
spoils upon olive trees.—Pilgrims halted by them as temples,
and left memorials on them as *votive offerings* to the gods.

The author saw a number of these suspended on acacia and olive
trees in the Orient.—Oak was sacred to Jove, laurel to Apollo,
olive to Minerva, myrtle to Venus.—Men thought the solemn
silence of a grove equal to a temple. *Pliny.*—Emblem of Divine
prosperity, "green olive-tree in the house of God." Psa. lii. 8.

Children of the righteous: "Olive plants round about his table."
Psa. cxxviii. 3.—Every village has its olive grove for *oil*, by
which *tax is paid.*—Solomon gave Hiram "20,000 baths of oil."

2 Chron. ii. 10.—Emblem of sovereignty, as it was used at the
coronation of kings. 1 Sam. x. 1.—It was mingled with sacrifices. Lev. ii. 1. " Pure olive oil beaten for sanctuary lamps."
Exod. xxvii. 20.—Used on the hair and skin. Psa. xxiii. 5.
Anointing the sick. James v. 14.—The wood is hard, solid, fine
grain, with a pleasing yellowish tint.—Wind easily blasted the
fruit while in bloom. Job xv. 33 ; Hab. iii. 17.
Its stature is low, trunk gnarled. Its foliage is grey, hence visitors
are disappointed, as the *hoary* leaves of the olive give a dull forsaken view to the landscape.

'Ιησοῦς δὲ. " *But* Jesus." This verse should have formed the last verse
of chap. vii. *D. Brown.* Some, rejecting the following incident as genuine,
admit the first and second verses. *Wieseler.*

ὄρος. Rabbis say the Shechinah remained 3½ years on this mount, calling,
" Return unto Me, and I will return unto you." *Reland.* The ascension was
from the summit. *Eusebius, Baronius, Williams, Ellicott.* Nearer Bethany.
Stanley. A ridge from Olivet to Bethany, extending about two miles, was
the place. *Author.* Others think it took place in Galilee. *Reland.* Monks
point out where the two angels appeared. *Willibald.* Here the olive leaf was
plucked by the dove from the ark. *Targum.*

2. And early in the morning he came again into the temple, and all the people
came unto him ; and he sat down, and taught them.

Early. Contrast the early visit of the Holy Jesus with the slothful sinner.—How can the " sweet hour of prime " be better spent
than in devotion ?
Morning. He determines to oppose His enemies persistently.
As the Light of the world, in His own way He will instruct to the
end.—Their hour to *hear* is not past ; His to *suffer* is not yet
come.
Temple. John ii. 14 ; v. 14.
All the people. Probably the whole remaining mass of festal
pilgrims.—Publicans and sinners, miserable aliens and outcasts,
often made up His congregation.
Taught. John vi. 59.—He seemed to divide His time between
preaching and praying.—He never, so far as we know, took a
pen in hand, but He was living a life that should make history.
Thousands of volumes have been written concerning Him and the
kingdom He founded.

Λαὸς instead of ὄχλος hints at a *diminishing* throng. *Stier.*

3. And the scribes and Pharisees brought unto him a woman taken in adultery ; and when they had set her in the midst,

Scribes. In earlier Hebrew writings, one skilled as a clerk. Exod. v. 6, &c.—In the time of the Judges, a herald or secretary of state. 2 Sam. viii. 17 ; xx. 25.—After the captivity, one skilled in Jewish law. Ezra vii. 6 ; 1 Chron. xxvii. 32.

In New Testament times, expounders and preservers of sacred books.

They counted the letters of each section of the entire Old Test. They were the school teachers of the youth.—During the 70 years captivity office of Scribe became more prominent.

Ezra's true glory was, not being a priest, but a " *Scribe* of the law." Ezra vii. 12.—The first " commentary " (margin) on the Scriptures was written by the prophet Iddo. 2 Chron. xiii. 22.

Comments of the Scribes : 1. The Mishna, i. e. " repetition." 2. The Gemara, i. e. " completeness." 3. Talmud, i. e. " instruction."—It was a proverb, " These men would purify the sun itself."—Prominent above all the Scribes stand the names of *Hillel* (born about 75 B.C.) and *Shammai*, his contemporary.

Former was surnamed the *Reaper*, latter the *Binder*.

They appeared in public in garments gorgeously decorated with gold.—To this sumptuous attire our Saviour may allude, Luke vii. 25 ; Matt. xi. 8.—They dreaded the touch of Gentiles, as pollution. Mark vii. 1—4.—Elder scribes in teaching occupied chairs ; elder pupils sat on benches ; younger sat on the floor.

Hence Paul was brought up at *the feet* of Gamaliel. Acts xxii. 3.

They were admitted to office at 30 by an oath.—They prepared phylacteries, drew contracts and covenants of espousal, and bills of repudiation.—The great Hillel wrought with his hands for support. Paul made tents. Our Lord was a carpenter.

This was in harmony with their highest idea of a *Rabbi*.

Proud, ambitious, and hypocritical, the deadly enemies of Jesus.

Pharisees. John i. 24.—They laid a snare to entrap the Saviour before the people.

Brought. His omniscient glance saw their crafty malignancy.

He knew their inability under Rome to carry out even the Mosaic law, " Thou shalt in any wise rebuke thy neighbour, and not suffer," &c. Lev. xix. 17.

Woman. This incident is omitted by many manuscripts.

Probably through the prevalence of an ascetic spirit.

Yet it bears the same relation to revelation as a ray of light does

to the sun.—Its *internal evidence* proves its inspiration.—Its consummate knowledge of the human heart.—Its masterly harmonizing of the demands of the Mosaic law with the gospel.
Its triumphant turning of the tables in the presence of insolent foes.
Its matchless teachings of mercy, mingled with the sternest rebuke to sin.—Its complete and glorious victory, in their terrible defeat and shame : All point out and prove the HANDWRITING of GOD.
As light is its own witness, and is known by its own manifestation.
God's WORD is a great fact in the moral world, as the Alps are in the natural.—A fragment of granite taken from the Alps proves God its Creator quite as fully as the mountain-range.

Set her, &c.   All the godliness some seem to possess is to find out others' sins.—Many hunt after these, not to *mourn* over, but to *expose* them.—Men ensnare their victims, and conceal their faults while they minister to their pleasure ; afterwards they thrust them away, with unfeeling cruelty.

γραμματεῖς. To the common people our Lord was a *scribe. Schoettgen.*
γραμματεὺς. With Greeks a registrar. Keeper of public documents.
Kirjath-sepher, Josh. xv. 15 : City of books. *Ewald.* Of princes. *Buxtorf.*
Of writers. *Gesenius.* Of Hillel it was said, " The Shechinah rested upon him.
If the heavens were parchment, they could not contain all his wisdom." *Geiger.*
Sanhedrim condemning Christ was irregular and decree vitiated. *Jost.*
Φαρισαῖοι The question was, whether they should publicly prosecute the criminal. *Ebrard.* Some deny the Pharisees would suppose Christ a theocratic judge, while the Sanhedrim was in session. *Lange.*
γυναῖκα. This narrative is wanting in the four oldest MSS., *Cod. Sin., Alex., Vatic., Ephraem.,* and in some of the most important ancient versions. It is not mentioned by *Cyprian, Cyril, Chrys., Origen, Tertullian, Theoph., Nonnus.*
An interpolation, but not untrue. *Erasmus, Grotius, Wetstein, Semler, Thol., Olsh., Davidson, Bleek, De Wette, Tisch., Lach., Griesbach, Hitzig, Neander, Luthardt, B. Crusius. Treg.* and *Alford* print in small type. Genuine work of John. *Ambrose, Bengel, Wolf, Mill, Fabricius, Maldonat., Michaelis, Kninoel, Heumann, Matthai, Selden, Ebrard, Niemeyer, Weisse, Lange, Webster & Wilkinson, Wieseler, Beza, D. Brown, Lampe, Ebrard, Stier, Storr, Horne, Hug.* Received by the Western, rejected by the Eastern Church.
Internal evidence : 1. Its evident divine originality. 2. Its every allusion to the morals of that age is true. 3. Its lofty position of the Redeemer, seemingly shielding the guilty, but actually crushing *hypocrites.* 4. Its tendency to *purity.* That book is pure that makes men pure. 5. Its grandeur in dealing with cunning foes. 6. Its utter annihilation of the snare laid so artfully.
Its matchless *wisdom* proves the footprints of a Divine Being. *Author.*
Could not be invented, and bears the mind and Spirit of Christ. *Hezel.* A symbolical fiction. *Hengst.* A tradition of the apostolic age, and not unworthy of the apostolic spirit. *Calvin.* Easy to account for its omission, but impossible for its existence. *Klee.* Quoted by *Jerome,* A.D. 340. Some older critics supposed that it is the same story as that which *Papias* (perhaps from the mouth of John) related of a " woman taken in many sins " (*Euseb.*) and contained in " the Gospel of the Hebrews." *Schaff* in *Lange.* A consoling

record to wounded consciences. *Lyser.* Genuine, but not John's. *Meyer,*
Ellicott. Out of its proper place. *Alford.* Added by John in a second edition
of his Gospel. *Scrivener.* Originally in St. John's Gospel. Removed by
jealousy of its morality, in the 4th century. *Aug., Lücke.* Mentioned by
Tatian A.D. 150, or 60 years after John's death.

---

4. They say unto him, Master, this woman was taken in adultery, in the
very act.

Master. Gr. *Teacher.* Courteously addressing Him as an instructor.

Adultery. Athenian and Roman law (time of Christ) permitted
the husband to kill his adulterous wife and the adulterer.

Nothing proves the terrible corruption of the theatre more than
the ridicule which virtue receives when overcome.

One of the proofs of deep depravity when vice becomes merely an
object of sport.—In the dark ages men converted Satan and evil
spirits into merely mischievous elves.—Certain sins, like a
thunderbolt, kill the soul at a blow. *Augustine.*

As God's *authority*, like a golden thread, runs through all commands, he that breaks *one* becomes guilty of *all.* James ii. 10 ;
Ezek. xviii. 10.

μοιχευομένῃ. Such sins apt to occur at the time of feasts. *Bengel.* Among
Greeks at one time, they put out the eyes of the guilty one. *Plato.* But Greeks
could satisfy the law by a heavy fine in some states. Augustus, by the Julian
law, made its penalty death by the husband. *Dionysius, Suetonius.*

ἐπαυτοφώρῳ. Some think her falsely accused. *Kuinoel.* But her silence
admits her guilt. *Bloomfield.* The man, who was likewise liable to death (Lev.
xx. 10 ; Deut. xxii. 24), might have escaped. *Meyer.*

---

5. Now Moses in the law commanded us, that such should be stoned : but
what sayest thou ?

Moses. John i. 17.—He was quoted merely as a foil to their concealed malice.—How often in sport or earnest is the Bible profanely made a *veil* for sin.

Law. John vii. 19.—Men may be zealous for the Divine law
with evil hearts.—Under the pretence of honouring the law they
sought to murder the Lord.—Deceitfulness of the hearts of hypocrites unfathomable and incorrigible.

Us. Yes, He had commanded Israel. But is this mob the judge ?

Deluded men ! God's word was to law-keepers, and not to law-
breakers.

Such should be. Poor heathen complained the gods had given them no power to see their own faults.—Men *mask* themselves with virtue to indulge their passions.—" Envy has no holiday." *Bacon.*—Masses are said for the *dead* to fill the coffers of *living* priests.—The inverted telescope shows objects to be very small. Pharisees anxious to crush the tempted with the thunders of the law. His eye was upon and His judgment was *for them.*

Stoned. See on verse 59.—A traditional command doubtless, as it is not found in the Scriptures.

Sayest Thou ? They knew His clemency, and expected He would show it.—A noble testimony from His enemies to His well-known *mercy.*—He had hinted that publicans and harlots might find forgiveness. Matt. xxi. 31.—They hoped that He, professing to be Messiah, would contradict Moses.—They knew that Messiah was bound to sustain Moses' law.—If He bade them stone her, He would give twofold offence.—1. He would condemn a laxity of morals sadly and widely prevalent.—2. He would infringe on Roman authority, and offend the rulers ; as Jews had no longer the right of capital punishment.—They challenged Him to carry out a law which prevailing license had rendered a dead letter.—They expected a very favourable decision from the past. Luke vii. 47 ; Matt. xi. 28 ; Luke xv. 11.—Thus the trap was cunningly laid.—If He say the law must be faithfully executed, the Roman authorities would object.—If that the law must be waived, then Moses would be sacrificed.

λιθοβολεῖσθαι. Did Moses leave such a law ? No. *Kimschi.* Yes. *Michaelis.* Intimated by τοιαύτας. *Lampe.* All kinds thus punished. *Macknight.* Begun after the captivity. *Grotius.* If betrothed, stoned ; if a wife, strangled. *Lightfoot.* Lev. xx. 10 and Deut. xxii. 22 signifies strangling. *Rabbis* in *Selden.* " I can find no authority for stoning in any Hebrew work." *Buxtorf.* Roman law had forbidden this crime to be punished capitally. *Hitzig.*

λέγεις. What now sayest Thou ? Even the waters of jealousy had been abolished, because of abounding licentiousness. *Sepp, Josephus.* Corrupt minds ever sympathetic with criminals. *Ebrard.* Solon and Lycurgus legislated in favour of fornication. *St. John's Gr. Ant.* The city of Rome, when under Papal rule, licensed houses of prostitution, but banished Protestant Churches. *Nitzsch.* This belongs to the last days of our Lord's ministry. *Alford.* Had He said " Stone," they would have cried out " Lynch law." *Besser.*

---

6. This they said, tempting him, that they might have to accuse him. But Jesus stooped down, and with his finger wrote upon the ground, as though he heard them not.

Tempting. Had He consented to have been really their Judge, His omnipotent justice might have blasted them with a word.

If He had condemned her, they would have said, Where is that mercy which the world accords to Thee?—If He had refused, Thou art opposing Moses' law, and therefore the God of Moses.

He sounds the depths of their hearts, and then utters the burning words.

Tempting. John vi. 6. 1. Proving. 2. Testing character. 3. Enticing to sin.—As storms of the ocean nerve the mariner, so temptations drive the believer to the mercy-seat.

Vine-like in his weakness, he clings more closely to the cross.

"The messenger of Satan buffeting Paul," kindled a higher flame of love.—Fierce assaults made Luther's heroism rise sublimely before all Europe.—Breaking his fetters, Cranmer rises to a far nobler martyrdom.—Our Lord was VICTOR in His first, and VICTOR in His last conflict.

Accuse Him. It reveals a remarkable idea of the Lord's *clemency.*

If not, why should they think He would *not* say, " Let the law be executed " ?—They bring this case, to find cause for PUNISHING HIS VERY GOODNESS.—But in the same net spread for Him are their feet taken. Psa. ix. 15.

But. He alone is qualified to speak who has learned to be silent.

Most persons speak, because they know not *how* to be silent.

Jesus. John i. 17—41.—The hour, place, occupation were all solemn.—The holy season must have partaken of Sabbath silence and awe.—Scribes and Pharisees rush in with their rude followers and disturb the Saviour's heavenly teachings with a filthy tale.

Stooped. In sublime repose, He was *sitting* at that time.

He opposes a silent but eloquent reply to their impetuosity.

Their thoughts and consciences begin their accusing revenge Rom. ii. 15.—As He sat, He bends and writes in the dust, on the pavement of the temple.—He acts as if He would prefer making no immediate reply.—He shrank within himself, as one ashamed of their *loud* effrontery.—The lesson is " Turn away mine eyes, lest they behold vanity." Psa. cxix. 37.

Finger. God's wisdom in the *hand.* A powerful and delicate organ peculiar to man.

Wrote. John v. 47.—"O earth, earth, earth, hear the word of the Lord." Jer. xxii. 29.—The Lord writes our sins on the sand *here*, as a warning in time.—After death impenitent sinners

will find them written in *immortal* characters on their souls.
Jer. xvii. 1.—A philosopher avoiding answer to a question wrote
on the wall. *Aelian.*—The spirit of the men bringing the guilty
woman presents a wide contrast between the atmosphere of
heaven and that of the pit!—Jehovah once wrote with His
finger the Ten Commands.—Jesus, the great Teacher of men,
wrote but one line, and that in the dust.—Yet He is the cause of
more writing, more study, more books, more learning, than all
other teachers of our world!—The Second Person in the
Trinity, whom infidels affirm to be a *mere man*, has been the
subject of far more controversy than God the Father.

He wrote as though He had said, You have the Law of Moses ;
what further rule of life can you expect ? Luke x. 26.

He ever referred His enemies and friends to the Scriptures. Mark
x. 3.—Or, Who made Me a judge or a divider over you ? Luke
xii. 14.—Or, They were not worthy of answer, this was out of
their province.—Or, To bring the woman before My bar, not
knowing or believing, that thus you and all men will appear
before ME!—Some find reference to the judgment records of
Rev. xx. 12.—Others, If the floor of this temple, and this entire
land, could speak, you would not be found bringing this culprit
hither.—" Those who depart from Me shall be written *upon the
earth.*" Jer. xvii. 13.—Remaining such, their names will never
be written *in heaven.* Heb. xii. 23.—Ye scribes write against
others. I write against *you.*—Your sins are written in your
hearts, and your names in the dust. Jer. xvii. 13.

A state of perishableness, having a place here, but no citizenship
in heaven. Phil. iii. 20.—He wrote not *her* legal sentence, as
those miserable ones desired, but *their* certain doom, unless they
repented.—These mute hieroglyphics taught them of an unwritten law.—Also of a law written out—but its statutes
neglected.—Of a day coming when the earth would not conceal
their sins. Isa. xxvi. 21.

As though, &c. Not found in the Greek, nor needed in any manner.—Our translators impute a motive to our Lord of which neither
they nor we could know anything. Our Lord never dissembled.
He wished to show them He heard, but despised their errand.

πειράζοντες. Well-meaning desire to get information. *Olshausen.* 1. Law
had become obsolete, and they thought He would not enforce it. But He said
He came to fulfil the law. 2. A political trap to produce collision with Ro-

mans. (*a.*) Romans allowed Jews to put persons to death, e.g. Stephen. (*b.*) Our Lord might have avoided all allusion to it. (*c.*) The accusers would involve themselves rather than Him. An unsolved matter. *Alford.* A difficulty raised, certainly not found in the text. *Author.* Our Lord treats it as a civil matter. *Lücke.*

δακτύλῳ. Gesture of supreme indifference with Greeks. *Aristophanes.* Repulsion, when asked an unseasonable question. *Euthymius, Calvin.* He must first reflect. *Meyer.* Asked by those unauthorized. *Tholuck.* The answer given in verse 7. *Sepp, Bede.* To avoid a snare. *Kypke.* He indicates bitter scorn for the accusers. *Hengst.* A minute instance, strong proof of authority. *Alford.* Go to your law you just named. *Lampe, Michaelis.* I also can write even as Moses. *J. Rupert.* How much could I reveal, but must bury in silence. *B. Crusius.* I will not act on this judicially. *Stier.* Appearing as if he heard not. *B. Crusius.* Ye scribes can write judgments against others, I can write them against you. *Bengel.* Such power in that writing, they knew He was recording their sins. *Bonaventura.* Recorded their names. *Augustine.*

"As though," &c. E. V. Our translators are inexact as to the Saviour's motive. *D. Brown.* Far too great a liberty by translators in their use of Italics. *Author.*

---

7. So when they continued asking him, he lifted up himself, and said unto them, He that is without sin among you, let him first cast a stone at her.

Continued. None are so pertinacious in intruding as those filled with ignorance and conceit.—They fondly dreamed they had entangled Him with the law.

Lifted. With a majesty of mien, which those men will *again* recognize, when the same person sits on the judgment throne. Matt. xxv. 31.

He said. If there be one, and but one, sinless, let him begin, and let the others follow.—What miscreants! even then they may have been gloating with adulterous eyes!

Without sin. Not absolutely sinless, but *such* heart sins. Matt. v. 28.—Free from *the sin* for which they desired her to be put to death.—The woman, with darkened mind, for a moment must have looked for a stoning, and must have tasted the bitterness of death. 1 Sam. xv. 32.—The veriest cowards are ever the most malignant and cruel tyrants.—Persecutors have ever been the trembling slaves of superstition!—Crœsus, the severest against avarice, was a covetous man himself.—Moses had said, "The witnesses shall begin the punishment." Deut. xvii. 7.

I say unto you, let those begin whose hands and hearts are clean.

Common law now requires one seeking divorce to come with clean record.

First. Principal accusers must fling the first stone. Deut. xiii. 9.

He draws the question out of law, in which they placed it, and answers it as one of eternal morality !—From the standpoint of law the character of the judge is not considered.

But from the standpoint of morality, one conscious of sin, while condemning another, pronounces his own sentence.

Our Lord's is a full reply, THAT SIN MUST AND WILL BE PUNISHED.

Now begin at home, and then you will work more consistently.

Why the partiality, discriminating between her and the equally guilty condemning her?—If you intend punishing guilt wherever found, begin with the most guilty, viz. YOURSELVES.

His reply to them was a lightning bolt from a clear sky.

The same breath that kindled the flames unquenchable blazed forth in a storm-fire through their souls.—He made them feel one pang of the undying worm.—If they thought His silence implied He could not solve their problem, what a tremendous surprise ! such as death is to the wicked !—Their minds were full of a seeming triumph with their net.—With one stroke of His word He reads and scatters their snares.—He oft put His foes to confusion, but never with such a bolt as this !—The toils of that same law, which they trusted would take Him, He gathers and envelopes them in its fiery folds.—They see the flashings of Sinai.—They hear the seventh command thundered anew in their souls.—Their own historian, Josephus, deliberately records the charge:—" MY NATION ARE AS CORRUPT AS THE CITIES of SODOM and GOMORRAH " !—This apostasy of the priesthood clearly foretold by Mal. ii. 14—17 ; iii. 1—15.—They had said " such should be stoned."—The Holy One asks with a gentle piercing cry, Are not *ye* actually *such ?*—Let her be stoned, but not by *such* a wicked herd as ye.—He that rears an altar must bring clean hands and a pure heart.—Thus He wrings the consciences of those censorious, supercilious hypocrites.—He points here at one of the common sins of the favoured people.

His ineffable wisdom eludes their malice, sustains Moses' law, and leaves the prerogative of the Romans untouched.

He had severely touched the judges themselves.

A moment since they rushed tumultuously and triumphantly into His presence.—Now they are neither witnesses nor judges, but *arraigned* and *convicted* culprits at the bar of conscience.

He does not diminish aught of the binding of the law of Moses.

But rather points and tempers its sanctions as divine.

He draws direct from the depths of man's consciousness of right.

No other prophet, for 6000 years, had uttered so simple and sublime
a rule.—He disclaims all earthly judicial functions, yet men felt
Him to be a SEARCHER of HEARTS and the future JUDGE of all.

Struck with dumb surprise, they justify His terrible rebuke.

Abashed they retire, confessing each one his own guilt by that act.

To question the Divine authenticity of this record one might as
well question the Divine origin of the sun in the heavens.

Our Lord seemed to take great risk against Roman law.

It forbade capital punishment of such persons, and He enjoined it.

How well, as its Creator, He knew the tremendous power of conscience !—Its warnings are the checks and chains of the Almighty
laid on the soul.—Faithfully hold up the mirror of the law to
conscience, God will take care of the rest.—No preacher of
righteousness ever failed to have an *aid* in each bosom, let men
deny and deride as they may.—He that would cleanse a blot,
only spreads it, without care. Psa. l. 16, 17.—The infinite wisdom
of God is transparent in this answer.—It is tempered TO BE
NEITHER AGAINST THE LAW NOR INCONSISTENT WITH MERCY.

Stone. He gives His solemn sanction to the law of Moses. Deut.
xxii. 21.—In all the boundless benevolence of One on the road to
the cross,—He still confirms Moses' laws and their penalties as
just and *kind*,—Though infidels, in their malignity and ignorance,
insist that they are *cruel*.—Our Saviour proved, by His unselfish
life and death, the infinite benevolence of their Author.

A solemn warning is here given, that there is a way of condemning
crime, which is sin.—A flippant exultant spirit, in pronouncing
the doom of sinners in the sacred desk, is as unworthy of the
pastor as it is a sign of fearful self-ignorance.

The motive must be *kind* as well as *pure*. Psa. cxix. 136.

It was seen when Pharisees upbraided our Lord for associating
with sinners.—A great truth here revealed was the character
of the judgment.—All the condemned will know, feel, and
add to their doom as just, a silent but approving AMEN.

Note the awful *stillness* of the storm raging in each guilty bosom.

No human eye saw those sins which burned within unseen.

To hush the struggling secret were to silence the thunder above.

The wicked will need no witnesses at the bar of God but
themselves !—This is the *greatest* miracle performed by the Saviour. *Jerome.* He thereby so omnipotently pressed conscience
as to show He was worthy to be Judge of all men.

ἀναμάρτητος. Not absolutely sinless, but free from this sin. *Whitby.* Possibly ironical. They had said τὰς τοιαύτας. It may be some of *you* actually do *such* things. *Stier.* Any sin whatever. *Grotius.* He intrudes on the domain of earthly judges. *Olshausen.* An infinite remove from all earthly decisions. *Author.* The mere reply, seemingly a shield for the life of the criminal, is a harsh sentence of death. *Rieger.* A judge living in impurity is bound to punish adultery. *Le Clerc, Hengst.* These Jews hated the *virum*, not *vitium. Trapp.* Natural equity of a judge not condemning, while doing the same, illustrated by *Cicero, Xenophon, Seneca, Pliny.* No community could exist where judges were equally guilty with the criminal. *Doddridge.*

τὸν λίθον. One might draw an inference tending to subvert justice. *Hengst.* Article inexact in A.V., *the* stone fatal, one first flung. He may have pointed to the stones in the hands of witnesses. *Schmid, Wolfius, Doddr.* But the temple was not the place of execution. *Lampe.* Allusion to the *first* stone thrown by witnesses. Deut. xvii. 7. *Alford.*

---

8. And again he stooped down, and wrote on the ground.

Again. His answer had a twofold object, to confound their device and to send home an arrow of conviction.—No conceivable answer would have humbled them more.—That ominous silence in the Temple made them hear the thunderings of conscience, as Israel at Sinai when the trumpet waxed louder and louder. Exod. xix. 19.

Stooped. He gave them an opportunity to slink away unnoticed. He had not expressly or personally accused any one of them.

That silent movement of His Spirit was writing a sermon read during the last 1800 years by millions of sinners.

God's greatest works on earth generally are performed in silence. He unbars the gates of the morning, and causes the sun to come forth, but we hear not the sound of its golden chariot-wheels.

The spring covers mountains and valleys with verdure in perfect silence.—The dews descend, and the entire system of sun and stars move more silently than a delicate watch.

The soul-creation (a transcendent change) takes place silently.

Wrote. Our Lord deals with sin here in *judicial* severity, though concealed.—Its condemnation is as *severe* as though He said she must die.—While He wrote, their consciences were recording a judgment also.—While Cranmer the martyr testified, the enemy's pen was moving behind the curtain.—Silently our words, thoughts, and deeds are recorded above. Mal. iii. 16.

Ground. Letters in the *sand* symbols of vanishing pleasures and honours.—Letters in *marble* the signs of enduring memories of the grateful heart.—The letters silently written on the palace

walls made the king's knees smite together with fear. Dan. **v.** 6.
Thus Christ's deeds always preach.—If He sleep on the boat, it will
be a sermon to all storm-tossed saints to the end of time.

If He eat a piece of honeycomb, a blessed proof of His resurrection.—If He weep on the mount of Olives, all the world shall
know the infinite treasures of His compassion.

His very depth of poverty a pledge of boundless wealth for His
friends.—His blood-drops in the garden the price of everlasting
songs for His saints.

πάλιν. Why? that the guilty creatures might pass out without confusion.
Jerome, Maldonatus. This is inconsistent with ver. 6. *Lange.* He wrote the
sins of each on the ground. So one MS. *Alford.*

---

9. And they which heard it, being convicted by their own conscience, went
out one by one, beginning at the eldest, even unto the last : and Jesus was left
alone, and the woman standing in the midst.

Convicted. While the penitent was washing His feet Christ was
forgiving her sin.—While our Lord was far from Jericho He
was bringing Bartimæus thither.—While Lazarus was starving
He was sending a convoy of angels to bring him home.

While listening to Moses' prayer God was arming the fiery serpents
to sting rebellious Israel.—He chastened their *pride* to save
their souls.—He cursed the fig-tree, being innocent for *our*
fruitlessness.—As Persians, when their great ones sinned,
chastised their garments.—When the Creator of the soul is
thundering and lightening at one's door, it is not in the power of
the mind to keep calm.—They were impatient to have the
woman convicted, their question answered, and our Lord compromised.—But their question is not answered at all, yet their
malice is defeated.—*They*, instead of the adulteress, *are condemned*, not of Him, but of *themselves.*—Never were enemies so
suddenly and utterly routed.—He has condemned her crime,
but not absolved her from punishment.

Conscience. See on John i. 9. The soul feeling and deciding
what ought or ought not to be.—A different faculty of the
mind from the mere understanding. *M'Cosh.*—Intellect and
conscience one and indivisible. *Butler.*—Conscience is the
mind, anticipating the decisions of the final judgment.

In the dark embers fire smoulders, but the wind must awaken

it.—In the seed slumbers the flower, the skyey influences bring
it out.—In the mine the diamond is the same as when set, but
it flashes not until the sun shines on it.—God's witness in every
man's bosom is a self-registering power.—" A preserver of the
court rolls of heaven." *Jeremy Taylor.*—" I have made thee a
god unto Pharaoh." Exod. vii. 1.—Called Household Guardian,
Angel of the heart, God's watchman.—It is not God, therefore
it is obscured ; it is from God, therefore immortal.

A perpetual pulse, which is sometimes benumbed, but which
will beat during immortality.—It may be trodden on and crushed,
but in the finally impenitent it becomes "a worm that never
dies."—Peter wept in response to the accusations of his conscience. Mark xiv. 72.—David mourned when his conscience
charged home his sins. Psa. li.—Judas was strangled by his
evil conscience. *Chrysostom.*—Dying, Antiochus, persecutor of
the Jews, cried, " I remember the evil I did."

Of Pashur, " Thy name shall be called Magor-missabib, for I will
make thee a *terror to thyself.*" Jer. xx. 3, 4.

What other men say of us is no more than what they dream of us.
Gregory.—A good conscience a perpetual comfort here and an
eternal crown hereafter. *Bernard.*—A man oft feels some one
abusing and denouncing him in solitude.—In Arkansas, 1870,
a murderer, after six years of unspeakable torment, confessed his
bloody deed, and begged the court to execute him, if perchance
he might find peace in the grave.—Conscience an avenging
judge, that never absolves the guilty. *Juvenal.*

Went out. Under a *supernatural* pressure of Christ's power.

The guilty are at times betrayed by a blush, but the incorrigible
become shameless in their degradation.—As they felt His burning eye, they must have hastened their steps.

Alas ! " Whither can they go from His presence?" Psa. cxxxix. 7.

These minor facts—the filling up of the canvas show the touch of
a Divine Master.—In the ten thousand volumes of human
writings not one such scene can be found.—Though our Lord
never wrote a line, He is the INSPIRER of all genius on earth and
of all the adoring songs of cherubim and seraphim.

Verse 5 they said " such women ; " He gives back the echo, " SUCH
MEN ! "—They had stood there, in all the air and prestige of a
holy company.—They had entered the Temple, jealous for the
dishonoured law.—They professed to have the right to sweep
impiety from the sacred land.—When men would do holy work

they must come with holy hands.—Where now is their lofty carriage, their haughty bearing ?—They were *fugitives* from an avenging deity in their conscience.—Thus at death scoffers will be suddenly silenced for ever.—Pleasure-seekers, praising the guilty sports of earth, will praise no more.—The loud cryings of men, having the " accursed thirst of gold," will be still.

We *double our sins* for the most part, by the very *apologies* we make. A patch poorly covering a rent is worse than the rent itself.

Hardened Pharisees, sunk in the styes of lust, quail when God lays His hand on the soul.—Neither Caiaphas nor Judas can withstand the pressure.—They must have felt the warm PRESENCE of DIVINE MAJESTY !—As Elijah, when fifty soldiers fell by a *flash* of God's vengeance.—His *stooping* proved He took *no* pleasure in their humiliation.—He was rather *grieved* at their impertinence, forcing from Him this tremendous revelation !

But all their daring and bravery are gone.—A proud answer given Him might bring a second and more dreadful thunderstroke !—How many courts and juries would be scattered by a rigid self-application of the above rules !

Eldest. A Divine hand was pressing the keys of their heart, in order.—He who bears the key of David can at will open heart and conscience. Isa. xxii. 22.—That finger-writing *on the sand* they dare not face.—The elders bearing office left first, having the weightiest burden on their souls.

Standing. Her accusers' weapons have spared her, but she moves not.—Pharisees convicted fly from Jesus, the woman convicted, *remains.*—The former fear to uncover their felt guilt, she surrenders to have the burden removed.—The malignity of these men only serves to drive a lost sheep to the fold.

" There is mercy with Thee, that Thou mayest be feared." Psa. cxxx. 4.—*Misery and mercy*, the pitiable one and He that is PITY itself.—A fearful sentence, to stand before Him *to be forgiven.*

Alone. The patient and Physician, mighty misery and mighty mercy.—Her accusers had left. The disciples saw her and Jesus left alone.—They waited silently and curiously to hear the sentence of the Lord.

συνειδήσεως. σύν and δέω. Its binding nature. *Epictetus.* Conscience is a god unto us. *Menander.* Speculum sine maculà Dei Magistratus. *Bernard.* " Would that my conscience let me eat thy very flesh." Achilles to Hector. *Homer.* Conscience is a theatre, in which virtues and vices will be seen. *Cicero*,

Tuscus. God has made it a righteous judge. *Hierocles.* Index, judex, vindex. *Trapp.* Though others keep silence, there is one that will not. *Isocrates.* The wicked ever live miserably. *Seneca.* Conscience lives immortal, until repentance kills it. *Juvenal.* Injustice breeds perpetual fear. *Chilon* in *Laertius.* The guilty ever dreads the revealing of his act. *Epicurus.* Amid the false fires, one cannot see the turpitude of a deed. *Virgil.* We think our crimes concealed from man, but we have something within proclaiming them. *Lucretius.* If I were sure the gods could forgive, yet could I not forgive myself. *Plato.* Our Lord uses inveterate sinners to save corrigible ones. *Brückner.* The unusual tenderness of conscience betrayed by Pharisees casts a shade on its authenticity. *Hengst.* The critic mistakes the lashings of remorse for sensibility. *Author.* Is it credible that all who brought her were adulterers? *Le Clerc.* The text affirms no such thing, but they saw their *heart-sins* more vividly than ever. *Author.*

ἐλεγχόμενοι. It is historically attested that at that time many prominent Rabbins were living in adultery. *Wagensail.* Pharisaic pride would have repelled the imputation with indignation. *Hengst.* Did Saul repel all fear when the ghost of Samuel came? Did Esau outbrave his remorse? Did Judas play the hero when conscience fastened its fangs upon him? *Author.*

πρεσβυτέρων. From the *elders*, the *presbyters* of the synagogue. *Schaff.* In the Gospels always a designation of dignity. *Hengst.* If the older consciences had heavier burdens, the younger were more tender. *Alford.* The record is there, and the *Spirit* knew the *leaders* in this shameful work. *Author.*

ἕως τῶν ἐσχάτων. From first to last. *Tholuck.* Departure of the whole crowd. *Fikenscher.* Only the accusers. *Stier.*

---

10. When Jesus had lifted up himself, and saw none but the woman, he said unto her, Woman, where are those thine accusers? hath no man condemned thee?

Jesus. Had His omniscient eye gazed long on their guilt, a bolt of vengeance, instead of a withering rebuke, might have fallen.

Lifted. He looks to see His enemies scattered by a mere *word.* The same look troubled the proud host of Pharaoh at the Red Sea. Exod. xiv. 25.—A "wave of His hand" will scatter His foes into eternal confusion. Isa. xxv. 11.—How will they be driven like summer chaff, when He lifts His *arm!* Psa. lxxxix. 10.

None. Another hour is coming, when the accusers of the saints will be wanting.

Woman. The adulteress remaining, instead of stealing away with the accusers, hints at the rising of *penitential* feelings. Could she have been chained to the spot by the Spirit's power? or was she assured that a depraved crowd would not let her escape until released?

Woman. Our Lord's word pre-supposes some *sorrow* as well as shame.—The anguish of death is past, but conscience has a more bitter cup.—Judas could face the Sanhedrin, shameless as had the traitor become.—But he could not steadfastly look at his own character under the light of conscience.

Where? As though He had said, " Behold the power of conscience ! "

Accusers. Depraved hearts are ever accusing both guilty and innocent.—Satan, the great accuser (Rev. xii. 10) of the brethren, is the father of such. John viii. 44.—This wretched adulteress doubtless knew that some of her accusers were as bad as herself. Fear not the judgment of men : thou art answerable to another.

No man. Hereafter the question will be different.

Hath conscience, or the Holy Scriptures, or the Sacred Spirit, condemned thee ?—" It is a small thing that I should be judged of you." 1 Cor. iv. 3.

Condemned. He asked, that He might not interfere with any magistrate's decision.—Had they adjudged her to undergo the legal penalty, viz., *stoning ?*—The renewed heart, sensitive to the least sin, is ever condemning itself that it may not be condemned. 1 Cor. xi. 31.

πού εἰσιν. Their leaving not expected by the Lord. *Stier.* He certainly foreknew, and therefore aimed to produce precisely *this* result. *Author.*

κατέκρινεν. Proceeded to punish. *Elsey.* Condemned to death. *Gesenius.* Judged thee worthy of stoning. *Lampe.* Their retiring left her free and uncondemned. *Euthymius.*

---

11. She said, No man, Lord. And Jesus said unto her, Neither do I condemn thee : go, and sin no more.

No man. Not one of her accusers was qualified to execute her.
Our Lord, who was SINLESS, would not.—He came to *save.*
1. He had, in her spirit, executed the sentence of the law upon her.
2. The process was nullified by the accusers not coming with evidence.—No man being able to prove a charge is by no means an acquittal.—Many think to go to heaven because their neighbours esteem them good.—A good *name* avails among men, but a good *conscience* before God.—Afflictions do not render one holy : *ploughing* will not produce a *harvest.*—Hence the delay of *mercy* is to recall the mind to repentance.—The Redeemer's compassion is slandered, if it be made to license the faintest tinge of evil.

Lord. She feels the majesty of Jesus, and this implies that she

condemns herself. Matt. xxi. 31.—Deliverance from the hand of
civil justice is not yet deliverance from the hand of the holy Lord.
He, with His meekness, showed greater judicial earnestness than
the severest condemnation to death can express *Braune.*

Neither. At His invisible tribunal she had been arraigned and
judged.

I. The sinless One, the only One who could, do not !
He might have flung the first stone, and not one in the universe
could have said, " What doest Thou ? " Dan. iv. 35.
Even the Lord sentenced not the *woman*, but her *sin.*
This is a negative absolution at the tribunal of Christ in the flesh,
mildly and graciously concealing His Divine Majesty from her.
He retains the hold on her *conscience*, but lets her depart.
She left Him with an arrow " fastened by the Master of Assemblies." Eccl. xii. 11.—Never could she forget that beam of mercy
in His eye, as He said, " SIN NO MORE."—With that word we
trust the Spirit kindled repentance unto everlasting life.
Who can tell how many penitent Magdalenes will be found among
the redeemed ?—The fearful falls of David and Peter were overruled to a holier life and greater usefulness.—We have here
doubtless another instance of sovereign grace converting a soul.
It is thought that all healed of *bodily* diseases were also renewed
in *mind* by His Spirit.

Condemn. Here equivalent to adjudge one as guilty and deserving
sentence.—His withholding of moral condemnation is no withholding of moral judgment.—Although the power of life and
death had been taken from the Jews, yet their Rabbis made it a
question whether it could be taken.—He uses the word in a different sense from that of the accusers.—His holy law cannot but
eternally condemn all iniquity.—But He has come to earth to
preach repentance and pardon.—What inimitable tenderness and
grace !—Consciously guilty, her enemies scattered, she will now
listen reverently and adoringly.—Many are by the terrible emblems of law led to penitence. Psa. cxix.
Even persecutions often prove " God's arrows in Satan's hands."
When one avails not, then come the second and third woes. Rev.
viii. 13.—Had the law condemned her our Lord would not have
interfered.—He pronounces no *pardon*, but only refuses to *sentence* her.—He being the great Author of law, can never relax
its demands, but can delay its execution. Gen. iv. 15 ; Deut.

xxii. 22, 24.—What sinner could survive, if the penalty followed as the thunderbolt the flash ?

Go. His word is "Go," but His hand held her heart-strings,—His loving heart is *winning* her from the way of death.

With whom, except Judas and Pilate, did our Lord commune, and yet leave them in their self-chosen desperate course ?

In the deep vale of humility we would reverently interpret His doings, nor ever presume to sit in judgment on His mysterious ways. Rom. ix. 20.—Our Lord's dismissal of one guilty refers back to the accusers.—He had actually arraigned and condemned them by His wisdom.—The miserable creature has been chapter and text for this purpose.—It was none of His seeking that she was brought hither.—Human laws, having no mediator, cannot exhibit mercy.—Moses' law knew of no mercy, hence the Lord's superiority to Moses.—To illustrate this is one of the essential designs of John's Gospel.

Sin no more. This was at once the deepest accusation and the most awful warning.—Our Lord's mission was exclusively moral, not judicial.—In telling her she had sinned, He guards His leniency against the slightest shadow of misconception.

This arrest was laid on her conscience by the hand of her Judge Himself.—It meant she had exposed herself infinitely more than to be *stoned.*—Her day of mercy was extended. "Spare this year, or else the AXE."—Her after life of penitence and faith not recorded, but we know its fruits. Gal. v. 22, 23.

You inquire if it rained in the night ? See if the dust be laid.

He who restores the sinner to penitence does *more* than he who punishes him.—It is a higher display of Divinity to illustrate *mercy* than *justice.*—He could not act as judge here among men without anticipating final judgment. Matt. xxv.

This solemn word to a lonely woman rings a warning through all time to the Church.—He doth not say, " *in peace;* " nor, " *thy sins be forgiven thee;* " only, " *sin no more.*"—In that " sin no more " is heard a threatening, prophetic, and foreshadowing a coming judgment !—Learn—1. A warning against sinners condemning sinners. 2. Encouragement for sinners never to despair of mercy. 3. The condition of mercy is to go and sin no more. 4. To imitate our Master, and show *mercy* rather than *judgment.*

There are law-worshippers, as there are rite-worshippers.

Law-worshippers are often law-breakers, and rigorous ritualists are frequently heartless formalists.—In the ratio of the light unimproved will be the doom incurred.—1. Their hypocritical homage He meets with calm Messianic majesty. (He stooped down, &c.)—2. Their tempting of His Spirit He meets with the searching of their conscience.—3. Their Pharisaic question He meets with the question concerning the innocent judge.—4. Their judgment was to work death and damnation. His, aims at deliverance and salvation.—5. They come as accusers and judges ; they go as condemned.—6. They intended to destroy a Holy One ; He rescues a lost sinner. *Lange.*

οὐδεὶς. A good sign that she does not *exult* over her *accusers*. *Lange.* The solemn judgment-feeling doubtless oppressed all present. *Author.*

κατακρίνω. Not a sentence of *forgiveness*, like Matt. ix. 2; Luke vii. 48 ; nor yet a mere *refusal of jurisdiction;* but a *reversal of the condemnation* in the consciousness of His Messianic mission, which was not to condemn, but to seek and to save the lost. *Meyer.* A sinner absolved (1 Cor. vi. 11) is bound to deliver himself up. *Stier.*

μηκέτι. Punished more by this gracious discipline than had she, *murmuring* at the cruelty of her fate, submitted to stoning. *Stier. Cod. D.* has ἀπὸ τοῦ νῦν, which is more forcible. *Schaff.*

---

12. Then spake Jesus again unto them, saying, I am the light of the world : he that followeth me shall not walk in darkness, but shall have the light of life.

Spake. Our Lord stands not among the noisy crowd to preach. Heathen did not build temples in crowded streets, but in retirement.

Jesus. John i. 17, 41. WORD. John i. 1. SON. John i. 18, 34.

Again. Allusion to their peculiar customs shows the festivities of the Tabernacle feast were just over.—It may have been about sunrise when our Lord entered the temple.—The marble, and gold, and furniture of the temple are in a blaze of splendour. The temple lamps, courts, and the entire streets of Jerusalem, illumined by the sun.—The preceding evening the entire city had been illuminated by lamps.

I am. This great word implies :—The whole world lies in darkness.—The gloom of Satan's rebellion was wrapping the race in " the shadow of death."—Sage and hero, like blind Ajax, were frantically calling for light.—At midday, with an unclouded sun, Saul of Tarsus was in *darkness.*

Light. John i. 4 ; iii. 20.—Our Lord now stood in the court of the women, or treasury. Ver. 20.—Two colossal golden lamps, with steps for lighting them, were before Him.

These were doubtless among the spoils of the temple, rescued by the Romans, and now carved on the Arch of Titus, still standing in the city of Rome.—The old and the young rejoiced merrily around these lights. John v. 35.—Each one held a torch, and mingled gaily with the sacred minstrelsy.—The prophet hints at this lighting, " At even it shall be light." Zech. xiv. 7.

The Sabbath *drew on.* Luke xxiii. 54. Gr. " *was dawning.*"

His reference to the extinguished lights of the feast connects Messianic promises.—As the water poured from golden pitchers reminds them of the smitten rock, so these lamps remind them of the pillar of fire.—Light, Scriptural emblem of —1. Knowledge. 2. Holiness. 3. Happiness.—As the sun is the source of light, heat, health, and beauty, so Jesus is the author of all wisdom, pardon, sanctification, and joy.—He was expected by selfish Pharisees to be the light of Israel only.

But God gave Him also to be a Light for the Gentiles. Luke ii. 32.—As Christ was so deeply despised, this word seemed so much more arrogant.—He hints they were all blind fools walking in darkness, and that He alone had light.

Far more, they must all actually come to Him for light !

He claims unconditionally before the universe to be the source of SALVATION.—" If any man thirst " was said amid the thousands of Israel gathered at the waters of Siloam.—" I am the light," alluding to the blaze of ten thousand lamps, or, more probably, the glory of the rising sun.—In polar regions, they sow in the *morning*, and reap in the *evening*.—But the reaping time for the saints is not promised on earth.—John was a mere " lamp," burning and shining indeed, but not *the* True Light. John i. 8, 9.—No other prophet ever advanced such a claim.

The sun must shine, despite and above storm, cloud, and change.

Our Lord's light, unlike the sun, never is eclipsed.

Midnight of persecution, or dark frowns of hell, cannot come between Jesus and His people.—A believer cannot conceal his light if he would, any more than the sun, yet vanity or self-righteousness displaying it are sure to *put it out.*

Sin obscures the soul's avenues; " Darkness was upon the face of the deep." Gen. i. 2.—Self-love begets ignorance, hence the soul is full of darkness and pollution. Eph. iv. 18.

Christ the Sun of Righteousness. Mal. iv. 2.—Scatters Levitical shadows, and Gentile superstitions.—Day breaks and shadows

flee away.   Cant. ii. 17.—" Christ is the Light of the Gentiles,
and glory of His people Israel."   Luke ii. 34.

As dust in a chamber cannot be seen until light is *let in*, so no man
can know himself until this Light reveals himself to himself.

The sun reveals its existence by its own light, so does each truth
in Scripture.—" Light is *sown* for the upright."—A harvest
time is coming.—On the wicked are chains of darkness ; many
become " *everlasting chains.*"—Science cannot tell of this Light,
except as cold and sickly.—The pale light of a glow-worm only
reveals the darkness.—One beam of the sun is of more strength
than ten thousand torches.—The latter may scorch, but cannot
quicken or cheer into life.—Light being so very common, misleads us as to its value.—A house standing in noonday all closed,
has night within, until opened.—A man asleep, noonday is
midnight to him ; but to be delivered from darkness, is only to
be delivered from one's self.

The world.   The world (κόσμος, John xvii.) of humanity in its
obscuration.—Jews are reminded that the Messiah was to be
sent to the Gentiles.   Isa. xlii. 6.

Followeth.   Not once repenting, but habitually pursuing a chosen
path.—As Christ was in the pillar of fire, and their fathers
followed Him 40 years.—Not enough to look and gaze, we must
follow it, for it is a light to our feet, not our eyes only. *Henry.*

The illumination of the understanding inseparably connected with
the sanctification of the will. *Lange.*

Me.   The true Light which enlightens the human night.

The Light in John i. 4 is a Light illuminating all.

Here the same is a detecting Light, and making manifest all.

A prophetic Light, hinting that He will overcome the darkness.

Not walk.   Hebraism.—Course of life.   1 John i. 6.

There's a walk by faith.   2 Cor. v. 7.—A walk after the flesh.   2
Cor. x. 3.—A walk after the Spirit.   Rom. viii. 1.—A walk
through the fire.   Isa. xliii.—Could one unrenewed, on angel
wing, follow the sun day by day, still he would dwell in thick
darkness.—His Church is a *Goshen*, amid a universe of evil and
gloom.—*Fear* and *doubt* becloud every soul away from this Light.

Sin is the penalty of sin.—As love binds to God, sin drives the
soul further from Him and from peace and life.

Hence those words of fearful import, " Dimness of Anguish "

(Heb. *Dizziness from despair*). Isa. viii. 22.—The testimony of eye-witnesses is, that heathen often die from *fear*.

Christ's imparted light never dims before disease or the grave. Psa. iv. 7.—Following Christ who has healing in His wings, i.e. rays, Mal. iv. 2, the believer will dwell in light, as a globe of glass hanging in the sunlight.

Darkness. John vi. 17.—Ignorance, error, guilt, pollution, misery, death! Continued, it becomes " the blackness of darkness for ever." Jude 13.—A terrible delusion! All unrenewed dwell where " the light is as darkness," Job x. 22, and, alas! they know it not.—He opened the blind eyes; a *prophetic sermon* of His future course.

Light of life. As darkness is in the soul, so light must take its place.—Here He announces Himself the LIGHT. In Matt. xi. 28, the REST of the world.—He invites all those who have *exhausted* the plans and pleasures of earth.—Those whose disquietude of conscience allows the guilty no *peace*.—He stands in the midst of an entire race *worn out* by Satan.

Light of life. That which gives, secures, and sustains the TRUE LIFE.—He SHALL HAVE it for a sure possession of his own. The life turning into light, and the light turning into life, as the water which He gives becomes a fountain within. John iv. 14.—The true Light and the true Life are one. Christ the true pillar of fire to His people.—He now in boundless compassion says, " Come ; " hereafter it will be, " Depart."

πάλιν. The discourse of last chapter continued. *Lampe.* Had Pharisees mixed with bystanders, the fact would have been noted. *Kuinoel.* This occurs several days after the last incident. *Lücke.* Immediately. *Stier.*

ἐλάλησε. He does not preach amid the turmoil of the festival. *Lücke.*

φῶς. The illumination repeated after the second, every evening of the festival. *Maimonides.* Lamps prepared, but not lighted, when our Lord spoke. *Tischendorf.* When the feast had ended, and all was silent. *Lücke.* The turrets of gold and marble lit up by the sun. *Lange.*

Φῶς, &c. Compared with φῶς ἐθνῶν. Isa. xlii. 6. He was preaching in the treasury, where strangers could come. *Grotius.* I am the key to all the world's mysteries. *J. Müller.* Pillar of fire a type to Gentiles. *Lampe.*

ἀκολουθῶν. Allusion to the adulteress. *Bengel.* Improbable. *Alford.* While He did not condemn her, no one without holiness can follow Him. *Stier.*

---

13. The Pharisees therefore said unto him, Thou bearest record of thyself; thy record is not true.

Pharisees. John i. 24. No blindness like theirs.

Said. Evidently with a bitter feeling.

Bearest. Finding, after the keenest search, no fault in our Lord. Dan. vi. 4.—Their reckless anger degenerated into mere personal abuse.—He is calm, but all proves the illimitable distance existing between His mind and theirs.—The groundtone of the last verse was, " All men by nature lie in darkness."—The great truths, *darkness* and *death* (Gen. ii. 17), ever *force* themselves on the mind.—The utter madness (Ecc. ix. 3) of the heart risks the doom of darkness, rather than seek light from the CROSS.—Believing Christ to be a mere man, but a very mysterious character, they would ask the *ground* of all these high claims.—True greatness has ever been humble. " Moses was meek." Num. xii. 3.—Paul declared himself " less than the least of all saints." Eph. iii. 8.

Record. So does the *sun* bear witness of itself. Psa. xix.— But these daring men resolve no half-way solution shall satisfy. —They knew He had wrought some miracles : they must probe thoroughly His claims.—He spake of a Father, who would show whether He was His Son.—It was not Jesus of Nazareth saying, " I am Christ," but the Father, by every miracle, " THIS IS MY BELOVED SON."

Not true. One may bear *true* testimony of himself, but among men it is not esteemed as *valid*.—Their denial was a reckless falsehood.

οὖν. Contest becomes more vehement. *Anton.*
μαρτυρεῖς. Illogical to transfer a principle of law into the domain of morals. *Ullmann.* This maxim is gathered from the darkest experience of human depravity, inapplicable to the King of Truth. *Hase.*
μαρτυρία. Firmitas and Veritas are but *one* word in Hebrew. *Trapp.*

14. Jesus answered and said unto them, Though I bear record of myself, yet my record is true : for I know whence I came, and whither I go ; but ye connot tell whence I come, and whither I go.

Answered. He is ever ready with the right reply.—The Pharisees, like all sceptics, had perverted His isolated word.—His Father had borne record to Him in chapter v.

I bear record. Gr. *witness.*—Like a burning lamp, the Bible is its *own witness.*—Spotless Truth here confronts a world full of lying and guilt.

My record. See on John v. 31.—Here he proceeds on a higher principle, in which Divinity alone is competent to be its own witness.—"He is the Amen, the faithful and true witness." Rev. iii. 14; Isa. lxv. 16.

I know. The pre-eminence of His knowledge gave value to His testimony.—Hence testimony applicable to men, when applied to God, was folly.—The consciousness of Christ is the star of night, the sun of day. His Divine self-consciousness is the starting-point of all Divine certitude. *Lange.*—A light shows itself as well as other things. Men do not light a lamp to look for a burning lamp. *Aug.*

Whence. Refers to His conscious existence during past eternity. —Man is absolutely ignorant of either his *beginning* or *mode* of being.—But He was to Himself, beyond all clouds, illusion, or dimness.—As if the sun were to speak, " I am the sun, self-witnessing are my beams."—" Nay," saith the Atheist, " thou mayest be the *night,* because thou bearest witness of thyself." *Berlin Bibel.*—The denial of the Jews was thus robbed of all its force.—No created being knows his own history.—Every moment of the infinite Past and boundless Future lay before Him.

Whither I go. He is sure of his origin (from the Father), of His destination (to the Father), and of His way (with the Father), and can therefore offer Himself with absolute confidence as the LIGHT OF LIFE. *Lange.*

But ye know not, &c. And yet from His teaching, miracles, and life, they might have inferred His origin. Although they intended to put Him to death, they did not know that by the sacrifice of His life in death He would arise to glory. *Lange.*

κἄν. Conditionally said. *Grotius.* Absolutely. *Stier.*

μαρτυρῶ. The question was as to His own consciousness, of which He only could bear witness. *Lange.* Even though I bear witness. *Grotius.* No such supposition in the Greek: it allows the fact. *Alford.*

οἶδα. Consciousness attested by conscience is the basis of all certitude. *Luther, Descartes, Kant, Schleier.*

πόθεν. Divine mission in two aspects. *De Wette.* His Incarnation and glorifying of His humanity. *Stier.* Ye cannot know my whence, and whither, unless I reveal them. *Kuinoel.*

καὶ ποῦ. Cod. Sin., Codd. D. K. T., and many others, read ἢ ποῦ. *Schaff.* Gives keenness to the reproach. *Lange.*

---

15. Ye judge after the flesh; I judge no man.

Judge. Witnessing always leads to judgment, and is the end of testimony.—He had just declared Himself *the* " Light of the world." Ver. 12.—That implied clearly all the world to be in a state of darkness.

The flesh. According to mere outward appearance, and mere finite standards.—Ye judge after passion and prejudice, fruit of lust and pride.—All the envious Pharisees saw was the man Jesus, the fringes of His unapproachable Self.

" Is not this the carpenter's son ? is not His mother called Mary ? " Matt. xiii. 55.—The very question implied that He was a wonderful person for the son of a mechanic.—The Lord said unto Samuel, " Look not on his countenance, nor," &c. 1 Sam. xvi. 7.

I judge. I pass sentence on no man, not being a judge, but a prophet.—Doubtless includes a reference to the preceding narrative. His office was not only not to judge, but to deliver and save.—" God sent not His Son into the world to condemn the world." John iii. 17.—Our Lord's repeated *warnings* are *anticipated* but infallible judgments.

No man. Humanly, capriciously, prematurely, proudly.—As ye do. His " neither do I condemn thee " is the mightiest judgment against sin.—Light being let in, reproves the works of darkness. Eph. v. 13, 14.—Contrast the bitter censoriousness of the Pharisees with the affectionate out-beaming of TRUTH amid such *perverseness.*—The way of the good is *heavenward.* " The way of life " is *above,* to the wise. Prov. xv. 24.

τὴν σάρκα. Seeing only the man, they persecute unconsciously the present Deity. *Aug.* After your prejudices. *Grotius.* Hopes of a temporal Messiah. *Elsley.* Article sanctions the objective noun. *Lücke.* The Lord would not attribute to Himself an external species. *B. Crusius.* Carnally, after the appearance and in human passion. *Meyer.* Denotes the passions and appetites of the soul, as opposed to πνεῦμα. *Campbell.* You judge Me as a mere man ; I came not to condemn. *Schöttgen.*

κρίνω. Not for the present. *Aug.* Such a limitation inappropriate. *Stier.* Not untrue to the sense, but superfluous. *Lange.* I have no pleasure in judging. *De Wette.*

οὐδένα. Not man substantially, but the caricature of man, made thus by sin. *Lange.* Perhaps a passing allusion to the scene in the Temple just closed. Ver. 3. I judge not, since My errand is teaching. *Lampe.* I judge not after mere appearance, neither ought you. *Kuinoel.*

---

16. And yet if I judge, my judgment is true : for I am not alone, but I and the Father that sent me.

My judgment. Of fearful moment, because one with the Father !

Since the destroying stroke must inevitably follow His sentence,
all human sentences are as mere " beating the air." Dan. iii. 27.

Is true. Real, essential estimation of persons ; discrimination of
sinner and sin ; separation of believer and unbeliever.

A threefold difference between His and man's judgment.

1. Man according to outward appearance ; His by the actual
moral state.—2. Man judges visible acts ; He the inner being.—
3. Man in haste ; He waiteth for the Father's disposal of the end.

Not alone. The Father unites with His judging and testimony.

Believers see the *Father* in all the works and words of His *Son*.

So the incarnation and crucifixion are deep revelations of the
FATHER.

I and the Father. A counterpart of " The WORD was with God "
in John i. 1.—From eternity the Son was with the Father : in
time the Father is with the Son.—Doctrine of the essential,
eternal trinity of the Godhead in these words. *E. D. Y.* in *Lange.*

Sent. A name of the Messiah among the Jews. John ix. 7.

Note the manifold modes He took to point out His Divine origin.

These mysterious utterances, linked with His splendid miracles,
would command the grave attention of all thinking minds, in
any age.—But the Jews were so fierce in their fanaticism, they
became frantic.

ἀληθής. *Cod. Sin., Wetstein.*
ἀληθίνη, suggests a more apposite idea. *Cod. Bezæ, Lach., Tisch., Alford.*
μόνος. I am not alone He who judgeth. *Stoltz, De Wette.* His testimony
is of God and of God's Son ; and His judgment is of man. *Bengel.*

---

17. It is also written in your law, that the testimony of two men is true.

Written. John v. 47.

Your law. Possibly ironical ; your much boasted but disregarded law.—" *Your* law."—He is *above* law.

Although calling it " theirs." He still holds it binding on all His
followers. Matt. v. 17.—They had proudly said, " Moses commanded *us*." Ver. 5.—That law was to Him a constant rule and
authority. Matt. xviii. 16.

Testimony. A judge brings no decision from home, but as the
testimony leans, so he decides.

Two men. " At the mouth of *two* or *three* witnesses, shall the
matter be established." Deut. xix. 15.—One *faithful* witness.

Aristotle.—A sad emphasis pertains to this, amid the wide-spread falsehood and treachery so universal where no Bible truth has gone.—Being the absolute Truth, He is exempt from the obligation of being challenged as a witness.—Human rules binding *sinful* man, have no claim on the Son of God.
Simple and fallible mortals wisely distrust individual testimony.

ὑμετέρῳ. To Him, the law was a thing to be fulfilled to the smallest iota. *Stier.* I am the Legate of God, the Father uniting with Me. *Kuinoel.*
ἀνθρώπων. Equivalent to personalities. *Olsh.* Paul thus argued with the Gentiles. Acts xiv. *Ambrose.*
μαρτυρία. Credit of testimony depends—1. Upon honesty. 2. Ability. 3. Number and consistency of witnesses. 4. Conformity of testimony with experience. 5. Coincidence of testimony with collateral circumstances. *Greenleaf.*

---

18. I am one that bear witness of myself, and the Father that sent me beareth witness of me.

I am one. The calm majestic reply to all their cavils and scorns. His peaceful yet sublime answers are altogether *superhuman* ; His stupendous miracles ; His incomparable parables ; His majesty ; His Divine energy ; His sinless life ; His boundless benevolence ; His reading and answering their *secret* envious thoughts ; His uncovering their cunningly laid nets, and rending them to pieces ; His unruffled repose when having every cause for alarm ; His instructions, embodying such consummate wisdom ; His gentleness ; His pure unselfish love ; His inimitable patience ; His unequalled humility, and burning devotion.—No such being had ever been seen before among men.—To all His claims to Divinity add the seals of Almighty God.—This Divine sanction by miracle, made the claims of the Saviour so troublesome to His enemies.—They did not hate or crucify the Lord for His miracles, but for His transcendently lofty claims proved by signs or miracles.—Divine logic is ever perplexing to unbelief.
Bear witness. "The works I do in My Father's name, bear witness of Me."—But deeply and desperately they resolved to resist all proof.—As though they said, " We do not believe in Thee, nor do we wish to accept Thee, as the Messiah."
What more splendid signs and proofs could *their* ideal Messiah have shown ?
Father. John i. 1, 2. His every word received a new seal from the Creator of worlds, as each miracle was performed.

Beareth witness. He produces two significant witnesses : *His own consciousness*, and the power of THE FATHER working with Him.—God in the miracles of Christ and His word in O. T. agree with the word of Jesus. A harmony of testimonies which is unanswerable. *Lange.*—Of the Redeemer it is true, as it was of Samuel, " The Lord let *none* of His words fall to the ground. And all Israel *knew*," &c. 1 Sam. iii. 19, 20.

ἐγώ. Not only the Eternal Son, but Incarnate Redeemer. *Stier.* Eutyches of Constantinople, A.D. 448, denied Christ's two natures after the Incarnation. Nestorians of the 5th century held two natures and two persons under one aspect. *Neander.*

μαρτυρῶν. The irony of lowly love is different from that of wrath. *Stier.* His simple testimony did seem to the Jews of much greater weight than that of any other man. *Lyser.*

19. Then said they unto him, Where is thy Father? Jesus answered, Ye neither know me, nor my Father: if ye had known me, ye should have known my Father also.

Where is? This question indicates assumed ignorance of His meaning.—Idolatrous pagans must have a god they can see or handle.—Primitive Christians were called *Atheists*, because they could not show their god.—At Polycarp's martyrdom at Smyrna, A. D. 167, the crowd cried, " Away with the Atheist."
Pagans and Jews hastened to bring wood to burn the holy man.
In every age, the sneering challenge is repeated to the bleeding martyrs.—At Orleans, the Papists asked their victims, the Huguenots, in the flames, " Where is now your God? " Psa. cxv. 2; xlii. 3.—*Mary* Queen of Scots, by French mercenaries having forced Protestants into desert hills, cried scoffingly, " Where is now John Knox's God? "—In Fotheringay Castle she had time to answer her own question.—Philistines thought Israel had lost their God when the ark was taken.
Romans (pagan) trusted the Church would die, if the pastors were martyred.—Rome (papal) hoped by the Inquisition to prove God had left His people.—Millions of saints lost their Bibles, liberties, lives, but never their God.—Believers know where to find Him, when losing all for His sake. 1 John iv. 20.
But when a change came, and Papists were afflicted, the Jesuits cried, " Jesus Christ has turned Lutheran."—" Where was your religion before the time of Luther? " asked scoffing Papists. Martyrs replied, " In the Bible, where yours never was."

Thy Father. That a poor common artisan should oppose the entire learning and authority of the seventy-two members of the Sanhedrim.—They do not put the question in the child-like simplicity of Philip, John xiv. 8, but a scornful fling at His ever imagining that God was His Father.—Where, then, does God, Thy Father, testify of Thee ?—Their earth-born idea, " If *You* are visible, can't we see something of *Thy* Father too ? "
All such frivolous questions are passed over in silence.
They ask about the Father, He replies as to Himself ; and when asked about Himself, He (verses 25—27) replies concerning the Father.

Ye neither. Had they clear faith in the Son, with His proofs of Divinity, their question would have been " *Show us sunlight at noonday.*"—*Not knowing*, was their heaviest condemnation. John iii. 19.

Nor My Father. This delicate and devoted appeal to His Father left no favourable impression.—If we love not, nor know not, a brother *seen*, how can we love God whom we have not seen ? 1 John iv. 20.

If ye had. If He had spoken blasphemy before, far more so now.
It was a bolder assertion than " My Father worketh hitherto."
He implies, if they wish to know the Father, they must *begin* with the Son.—They had resolutely and defiantly chosen to remain blind in the very blaze of the Sun of Righteousness !
Now they learn as from a voice from the opening heavens, " *Ye can never know God without knowing Me !* "—As they *would not* perceive the Divine Spirit in His words and life, they were blind to that Spirit in His miracles, and to the Father's testimony in Scripture. *Lange.*

πού ἐστιν. This petulant interrogation refers to a *human* father. *Augustine.* In derision of His pretensions. *L. Brug, Kuinoel.* The question was scornful and malicious as to claiming God as a parent. *Alford, Stier.* Pharisees held it an idle phantasy. *Hengst.* Sarcastic allusion to His supposed illegitimate birth. *Cyril, Theoph.* No such allusion in the N. T. *Lampe.* That bold blasphemy was left to Voltaire and his compeers. *J. P. Smith.* They would have Him avow His heavenly parentage, so that they might accuse Him of blasphemy. *Chrys.*
οὔτε ἐμέ. Your question is malignant ; you neither know nor care to know. *Lampe.*

---

20. These words spake Jesus in the treasury, as he taught in the temple : and no man laid hands on him ; for his hour was not yet come.

These words. Of severe and decisive condemnation of unbelief.
It is implied that He would have been stoned by the Jews, had
not the sanctity of the place prevented the outrage.

It was evidently the most direct claim to the Godhead yet made.

Jesus. Only an eye-witness would connect the address with the
place.

Treasury. A crowd was usually found there gathered. Mark
xii. 41—44.—Ancients having no Banks, placed their treasures
in temples, guarded by their priests, but supposed to be especially under the protection of the gods whom they adored.

These treasures consisted both of personal deposits and votive
offerings.—The treasury had 13 brass chests of trumpet-shape,
two of which received the half-shekel, paid yearly by every
Israelite.—Eleven received money for sacrifices and other
oblations, and the gold and silver vessels were kept here also.

It was as ancient as the sanctuary in Israel. Exod. xxx. 13.

Temple of Jerusalem was renowned through the world for its
immense treasures. *Tacitus.*—Herod the Great presented the
gold vine, a wonder of wealth and beauty. Luke xxi. 5.

Pompey, Augustus, and Agrippa enriched it with costly gifts.

Taught. John vi. 59. Our Lord—1. The *only* TEACHER, as
highest in dignity, in power, in authority.—2. The *true*
TEACHER, as sent from God. John vii. 29. As the TRUTH, teaching nothing but the TRUTH.—3. The *Good* TEACHER, apt to teach.
John vii. 46 ; 2 Tim. ii. 24.—His teaching led to God.

He taught by *parables*, and by *miracles*, but above all by HIS LIFE.

His life has wrought the deepest and widest *revolution* known in
history.—He taught with patience, gentleness, kindness.

Temple. John ii. 14 ; v. 14.—Why does the Apostle particularize the very spot of this discourse ? There it is supposed
the Pharisees had their proudest triumphs.—He charged them
publicly and plainly that they knew not God.

Before the people, they claimed *all* knowledge of their Creator.

For the *third* time, He was about openly to resist all their cunning,
and escape from their power.

Hour. They could neither hasten it nor prevent it.

No one has power over the life of another.—" My times are in
Thy hand." Psa. xxxi. 15.—God works by plan. Predestination is an eternal law of the universe. *D. Thomas.*

ὁ Ἰησοῦς. Omitted. *Lach., Tisch., Alford.*

γαζοφυλακίῳ. Ancients placed ἀναθήματα in the treasury of a temple. First locks of hair, tablets with description of recovery, escape, &c. Costly garments, lofty tripods, bearing vases, craters, cups, candelabras, pictures, statues of marble, bronze, silver, gold. *St. John's* Gr. Ant. The Evangelist names this place because it was the most public. *Lange.*

ἡ ὥρα. The refrain of the history with an air of triumph. *Meyer.*

---

21. Then said Jesus again unto them, I go my way, and ye shall seek me, and shall die in your sins: whither I go, ye cannot come.

Then. Doubtless on the same day that the snare was laid by the Pharisees.

Said. As He had said before, chap. vii. 33, 34.

Jesus. Moved at the thought of leaving them hardening under the tenderest entreaties and most solemn warnings.

About to leave the Temple; He would have made it the sanctuary of His love.

Again. This was His most vigorous conflict with the Jews.

He once more confronts children of the *liar* and *murderer.* John viii. 44.—He must continue to testify until the end.

I go my way. Their mockery is a new signal of His approaching death.—To those scoffers these were idle words, like Lot's to his sons.—But eternity alone can unfold all that is implied.

"Woe also to them when I depart from them!" Hos. ix. 12.

Tears of hell are not enough to bewail this loss of the vision of God.—Moanings of Cain exiled from God were like those of a lost spirit.—Saul's sad cry, "God is departed from me," 1 Sam. xxviii. 15, and Micah's, "Ye have taken away my gods," &c., Judg. xviii. 24, sound as the first notes of a lost soul.

He seems reluctant to surrender the sons of faithful Abraham.

The ground-tone of this sad lament is *their*, not *His*, death.

It will yet wring another wail from His breaking heart. Luke xxiii. 28.—Our enjoyment of the means of grace has its day, and "the night cometh."

Seek me. Denotes the seeking of Messiah amidst impending judgments.—Not a penitent seeking of the Redeemer, but a fanatical chiliastic seeking of a political deliverer. *Lange.*

Continue seeking me includes "Ye shall not find me." A hint that a deliverer from *death* cannot always be found.

Men, in constant *unrest*, have in all time sought for *peace.*

In the long night at the poles men long for the coming day.

So in the long dark night of heathenism, with its oracles and priests, its lawgivers and founders of religion, nations waited for Him, "THE DESIRE OF ALL NATIONS." Haggai ii. 7.

What tribe or people have not sighed and prayed for a Deliverer? But there is a class whose longings and prayers will not be answered. Job xxvii. 9 ; Psa. xviii. 41 ; Isa. i. 15; Zech. vii. 13.—The secret of this refusal is *disobedience.* Prayer at such a time is an abomination. Prov. xxviii. 9.—Some prayers *are* answered, but answered in wrath. Hos. xiii. 11.

" Go and cry unto the gods ye have chosen, let them deliver you." Judg. x. 14.—His *words* are sharper than arrows, what will be His *wrath ?*—The storming of Jerusalem revealed this in dreadful distinctness.—In spirit He sees their Temple, so idolatrously beloved, in flames.—Frantic myriads of starving Jews filling the heavens with shrieks.—Thousands in despair, refusing to survive this centre of their hopes, and in dread of Roman slavery, madly dying by their own hands.

The time is sure to come when men shall know those through whom God would have saved them. *Heubner.*

Die. John iv. 47 ; v. 24.—Death the enemy of our race. 1 Cor. xv. 26.—" Death reigned." Rom. v. 14.—Defines the separation of body and spirit. 1 John v. 16.—Has " gates," implying the authority to which one then submits. Job xxxviii. 17 ; Psa. ix. 13.

Die. 1. A resolute persisting in sin against conscience.—2. Eternal equity of their doom will be acknowledged by the universe.—3. Infallible certainty of the judgment here announced.—All men die, but the wicked are " *killed with death.*" Rev. ii. 23.—Death of the sinner has elements of terror.—1. Its terrible certainty.—2. Tokens of Divine displeasure.—Without sin, each would die, as the angel parted from Abraham in the plains of Mamre.—3. The plunge into an unknown state.—4. Remorse which seems the flashing up of the world of woe !—Annihilation is a dread and terrible dream of the practical atheist.—Not finding Christ is positively a dying in sin.

Your sins. The peculiar sin of the Pharisees was rejecting Christ as Deliverer, while their consciences approved all His miracles and words and deeds of LOVE !—The sin and death of the nation as a body are without limit.

Your. Emphatic.—Adam's sin involves our race. Rom. v. 12.

But God will hold us responsible for our *own* sins. Ezek. xviii.

20.—They had silently, but eloquently, confessed they were sinners. Verses 7.—9.—At the foundation was *unbelief.* It is " *Sin* " (singular) in the Greek.—The ruin is one and complete, since all sins spring from it.—"*In sin, shall ye die,*" i. e. " carrying it with you to judgment."

Whither I go, &c. This plainly extends their condemnation into the future world.—*Now* they could not reach Him spiritually : *Hereafter* even as suppliants they could not reach Him in heaven. *Lange.*

οὖν. No stress must be laid upon it as connected with ver. 20; it is only the accustomed carrying forward by the Evangelist of the great self-manifestation of Jesus. *Alford.* Expresses the result of their not having laid hands upon him. *Stier.*

πάλιν. Same day. *Stier.* Indicates a breaking off of the former discourse. *Klee.*

ὁ 'Ιησοῦς. Omitted. *Lach., Tisch., Alf.*

ὑπάγω. Symbol of His final departure from the nation. *Lange.* Remained in Jerusalem till the Dedication. *Stier.* " Plot as you list, in proper time, by death, I will go to my Father, and take my gospel blessing with me." *Lyser.*

ζητήσετε. You shall seek the assistance of the Messiah in vain, as you cannot fetch me from heaven. *Kuinoel.*

ἐν. Propter. *Stier.* Emphatic, referring to a particular sin, obstinate unbelief. *Lampe.* This your sin. *Beza, Doddridge.*

ἁμαρτία. The great sin of rejecting the only Redeemer. *Beza.* Emphasis falls on *sin ;* in the repetition, on *dying. Bengel.*

ἀποθανεῖσθε. Destruction by Rome. Individual perdition. *Alford.* Temporal and eternal death. *Grotius, Lampe.* Had Judas been annihilated, our Saviour's word would lose all force, Mark xiv. 21. *Author.*

---

22. Then said the Jews, Will he kill himself ? because he saith, Whither I go, ye cannot come.

Said. To one another, but meant for the crowd. The first time, it seems, the rulers deliberately misinterpreted His word.—How true to the human heart.—Instead of repenting at these terrible warnings, they began to speculate curiously as to Christ's future course.—If it were possible to *conceal* the life of Jesus, *advocates* without number would rise. If some Voltaire, or Strauss, or Renan, cast a shadow over the Truth, many rise : when the sun sets myriads of stars flash out from the clear sky.

Kill Himself. They had no conception of a voluntary departure in the violence of death.—Jews held suicides went to the lowest

730 / Gospel of John

hell.—They hint that possibly in despair He would thus escape
execution.—A worker of miracles, aided by Jehovah, turning
self-murderer !—Their question is full of scorn and malice.
Greeks said the gods place all men as soldiers on duty; it is
cowardice to desert one's post. *Pythagoras.*—Romans, on the
contrary, said, " The *best thing* the gods have left us is our
power to avoid trouble by taking away our lives," *Plutarch.*
As they think He has set Himself above them (ver. 21), they take
revenge by suggesting that He will sink far below them. *Lange.*
" These (suicides) herd together,
The common damned shun their society,
And look upon themselves as fiends less foul." *Blair.*
Saul, Ahithophel, and Judas, were suicides.—Cato, Brutus, Cassius,
and other Romans.—Thebes forbade by law that the memory
of suicides should be honoured.—Athens required the hand to
be cut off, and burnt apart from the body.
Milesian virgins committed suicide, and could not be prevented,
until by law their bodies were exposed. *Plutarch.*
Justinian confiscated the property of all committing suicide.
During the dark ages no mass was celebrated, or service at their
burial.—Scandinavians not permitted to perish in battle com-
mitted suicide in the Hall of Valhalla, Hall of Suicides.
During the voluptuous reign of *Louis XV.* many through mere
ennui, enjoying wealth, health, and youth, committed suicide.
It is practised in India by the sacred council of Brahmins.
Whither. I go to My Father, and you go to your father.
Ye cannot. Not the cause, as absolute decree, but infallible *result.*
Refusing to repent, the sinner closes the door of mercy.
" As certain as I ascend to My Father in heaven (if He were *your*
Father ye might bear Me company), so in due time, if incor-
rigible, you shall descend to yours in woe ! "

ἀποκτενεῖ. This eighth chapter the beginning of His passion. *Besser.*
Jews held suicide as the final doom of one given up by his Guardian Angel.
Josephus. These blind rulers never supposed that their cruelty could be over-
ruled for the highest purposes of mercy. *Hengst.* Suicides sunk to the lowest
Hades. *Lücke.* Pharisees assigned to them the darkest corner in hell. *Wetstein.*

---

23. And he said unto them, Ye are from beneath; I am from above: ye are
of this world; I am not of this world.

Said. Our Lord answers not the question in ver. 22.
He meets their mockery with a calm assertion which turns the
point of it against themselves.—They could only think of
the *grave* for Christ at death. They had no idea of *ascent* as the
home of the person standing by them.—On a former occasion
He yielded to their violence. But now He speaks the more
plainly.—He will not at this feast permit scoffers or murderers
to silence Him. Psa. xl. 9.

Beneath. Verse 44 seems to invest this word with a terrible
emphasis.—Denotes the diabolical nature which they have
shown, and which proves they belong to the dark nether world.
Wicked are called "inhabitants of the earth and of the sea."
Rev. xii. 12.—Righteous dwell in "new Jerusalem which is
above." Gal. iv. 26.—Lately He contrasted Himself with
earth-born messengers of God. John iii. 31.

I am. Allusion to the name of Jehovah revealed at the bush.
Ex. iii. 2.—They understood Him to claim no less than full and
perfect Godhead.

From above. He lived and moved in a different world from
such ungodly ones.—His motives were pure, honest, kind,
self-sacrificing.—His joys were holy, spiritual, expanding,
enduring, divine.—He had *heaven* in His soul, and they had
hell begun in theirs.—A gulf impassable between them, except
by *repentance.*—One must *think* with Christ, *will* with Him, *toil*
with Him, *endure* with Him, and *die* with Him, so as to *dwell*
with Him for ever.

Not of this world. The more obscure first sentence He explains
by this second.—In spirit and in life He belonged to the new
and higher world.—These words furnish a proof that there is
another world.

εἶπεν. What ye say troubles Me not. *Tisch.* The Lord calmly pursues His
former discourse. *Schleier.*
ἄνω refers to heaven. κάτω must refer to hell. *Stier.* Ex terra. *Bengel.*
Ab inferno. *Erasmus.* Earthly-minded, of the world. *Meyer.* If the Greek
allowed, I think it means "from hell." *Fikenscher.* Eph. iv. 9 refers to
Hades. *Koppe.* Christ's incarnation. *Rosenm., Doddr.* "Above," to heaven;
"beneath," to earth. *Hengst.* They saw the earth a comfortless void of finite
objects. He saw it a holy building of everlasting realities. *Lange.* Former
refers to His *Divine* excellence; latter to His perfect holiness. *Lampe.*
τοῦ κόσμου. Implying that a great gulf and impassable was between
them. *Anton.* Your desires, tastes, longings are not pure, spiritual, heavenly.
Grotius.

24. I said therefore unto you, that ye shall die in your sins: for if ye believe not that I am he, ye shall die in your sins.

I said. Meek repetition of these truths implies great *patience* and boundless condescension.

Ye shall die. John iv. 47 ; v. 24.—Solemn assurance of this was no iron-handed fate.—If ye believe not.—" Behold I set before you life and death."—Sin involves great misery ; its distractions tear, its inordinate desires torment, its lusts inflame.

Not that these men were ignorant, rude, cruel, or impure.

No ; they were the guardians of a nation's religion, high in social refinements, education, learning, the patrons of fine arts, and proud of Jerusalem's glory. — But underneath this gilded national magnificence, dwellers in Jerusalem were faithless, godless, polluted to the last degree.—They would banish all earnest efforts for reformation as public evils !

Believe not. John i. 7 ; vii. 38.—This solemn warning was repeated as He ascended to heaven. Mark xvi. 16.

A deep gulf lay between them and Him, and but one plank to cross it.—That plank was the cross of the Lord they crucified.

Soon they would find that plank gone, and His hand withdrawn.

I am. 1. I am HE in whom salvation is found.—The Messiah.

2. I am HE who has come from above, not sprung from earth.

3. I am HE who is not alone,—" I and My Father that is with Me."

4. I am HE who is the eternal Son of God " manifest in the flesh."

5. I am HE who is " the Light of the world."—Whoever believes not in HIM believes not in anything ! Matt. xvi. 16.

6. I am HE who *only* can save. There was but *one* ark. Acts iv. 12.—*Unbelief,*—1. Is a sin heavy with the burden of *ingratitude.* Luke xvii. 17.—2. It is a sin heavy with the burden of a *broken* law. Gal. iii. 10.—3. It is a sin heavy with impending *wrath of God.* John iii. 36.—4. It is a sin crimsoned with *blood.* Isa. i. 18 ; Heb. x. 26 ; Hos. i. 2.

I am. "He" of the A.V. is not in the original.—I AM what for 4000 years prophecy has declared ME. Gen. iii.; Isa. xviii. ; Deut. xxxiii. ; Isa. xlii., &c.—Similar mode of speech Jehovah uses in that grand old hymn, Deut. xxxii. 39.—How the *Divine reticence* (among men it is called modesty) is here seen.

He claims Jehovah's title " I AM." Ex. iii. 14 ; Deut. xxxii. 39 ; Isa. xliii. 10.—He is absolute being, and all forms of the word "Jehovah" is one perfect name.—Many shall come in My name,

saying, "I AM." "Christ" is not in the Greek, and ought not to
be in the translation. Mark xiii. 6.—God's words are always
perfect; Judaism had attached a wrong meaning to the term
Messias.—I AM THE REDEEMER from the guilt and doom of
dying in sin. Acts xiii. 25; John xiii. 19.—"Neither is there
salvation," &c. Acts iv. 12.—In the background of this
reserved expression He reveals His Supreme Godhead. None
but Jehovah could, without impious folly, say unconditionally,
"I AM." Deut. xxxii. 39; Isa. xxxiv. 16, 17; Jer. xiv. 22;
Psa. cii. 28; Isa. xliii. 10—13.

Ye shall die. Alluding to their destruction by Rome as a nation
as typical of their second death.—The Good Shepherd is commissioned to "feed the flock of the *slaughter.*" Zech. xi. 4.

Our Lord proclaimed the *Gospel* in love, amid flashes of Divine
wrath,—" LOVE *in flames.*"

ἀποθανεῖσθε. As objections are ever repeated, so opposing principles of
unchanging truth must be also. *Ebrard.* A nail by repeated strokes is fixed
in their hearts, not their understandings. *Stier.*

'Εγώ εἰμι. A disclosure of His *innermost* Being. *Storr.* Of His Messiahship. *Grotius.* Ex. iii. 14. One only, the Great and Only One, is He who is
as He is and because He is. All perfections are only exponents of His Being.
Stier. Describing the existence and attributes of Jehovah. *Hengst.* Some
insert "Messias." *Lücke.* Their conception of the Messiah a dread one.
De Wette.

εἰμι. What I was foretold. *Augustine, Bede, Maldonat.* Jehovah's
peculiar name. *Lampe.* I am what I profess, the Messiah. *Euthymius, Beza,
Hammond.*

---

25. Then said they unto him, Who art thou? And Jesus saith unto them,
Even the same that I said unto you from the beginning.

Who art thou ? A question of insolence and sneering sarcasm.

A bitter reply to His "I am He."—Their question proves they
don't intend to believe His answer.—Who art Thou that speakest
so loftily of Thyself, and threatens us also ?—Angrily and im-
petuously they press upon Him to say, "I AM CHRIST."

They defiantly challenge Him to prove His pretensions.

Thou. Now, as then, all sceptical controversy rages around the
person of Christ.

Saith. He makes no direct reply, but advances in His discourse.

He might have said, "They had no faith to hear such a word of
truth."—In fierce fanaticism they only desire vantage-ground
for the contest.—" Who art *thou?* " Another way of denying His

pretensions to any special dignity.—The crowning evidence of His Messiahship was now to be foretold :—" When ye have lifted up the Son of man, then shall ye know." Verse 28.

He would not say Messiah, for their ideal of the Messiah was a political caricature.—Had He uttered the great truth they would have misunderstood Him and only raged more and more, and the hour for that word, which would issue in death, had not come.

The same. These sublime and mysterious words are the best comment on the " I AM " of the preceding verse.

His undisturbed serenity stands out in perfect contrast with the tumultuous excitement of His foes.—His profound undertone is, " I AM THE WORD." John i. 1.—If you were deeply anxious for God's glory you could easily find out His Son.

In all Christ's discourses, miracles, parables, His Divine nature is *understood.*—As the sun rising, though still behind some alpine mountain, yet bathes the heavens above, and the landscape far and near, in an ocean of light, so Christ's supreme Godhead, though unseen, illumines the world for eighteen hundred years with all that exalts and blesses mankind.

Beginning. See on John i. 1, 2.—Before all "I AM."—What I speak is *Revelation.*—" I AM " the Revealer of Him who alone ESSENTIALLY IS.—In the O. T. Christ is everywhere, where Jehovah is, and His Angel.—Equivalent to " All things were made by Him, and without Him," &c. John i. 3.—Jews well understood from the O. T. that the " Angel of Jehovah " would appear as the Messiah. Isa. ix. 6 ; Micah v. 1, 3 ; Dan. vii. 13, 14.

That word " Beginning " was the specific *sting* to the mind of His enemies.—They must have *felt* His invisible power would end in their utter ruin.—His life was one that was without beginning, and one His enemies could never end.—As He is the ALPHA, so must He also be the OMEGA.

Σύ. No question, but simply indignation. *Koecher.* A formula used of those we despise. *Wetstein.* Indicating profound ignorance. *Lampe.* They desired no answer. Who art Thou, then, daring to use such words ? *Baumlein.* Τὴν ἀρχήν. The Alpha of Rev. i. 8. *Gnostics* and some *Fathers.* Beginning of my office. *Beza.* Used adverbially "originally." *Buttmann.* Principium. *Vulgate.* The beginning of all things. *Cyril, Lampe.* In very deed, that same which I speak unto you. *Alford.* (Do ye ask) that which I also say unto you from the beginning? *Meyer.* Synonymous with ἀμήν. *Lücke.* Before all that which I tell you. *Schleier.* I am that which I have *earlier* told you. *Tholuck.* I am the very same word, &c. *Trapp.* Ask not after *what I*

am ; learn from My sayings who I am. *De Wette.* " I am your Preacher; if
ve first believe this, ye will also know," &c. *Luther.* First of all, before My
name, I am that which I also speak to you. *Von Gerlach.* Not only the spirit
of His doctrine, but *declarations* concerning Himself. *Lange.* What I have
been saying all along. *Bourgon.* Angel of Jehovah to appear as Messiah, was
widely diffused among Jews. *Hengst.* I am altogether He whom I tell you,
namely, *the* Messiah. *Doddr.* For opinions on this *crux interpretum,* see *Lange,*
Amer. Edit.

---

26. I have many things to say and to judge of you : but he that sent me is true;
and I speak to the world those things which I have heard of him.

I have.   Majestically He demands the ear of the whole world.

And at a fitting moment will speak to the Church for all time.

Many things.   Many warnings for many sins : many promises to
cheer the believing.—Had He directed the lightning glance of
His Divinity against Roman masters, with triumphant joy the
Jews would have admitted ALL HIS HIGH CLAIMS.

His real offence was demanding deep genuine repentance of sin.

They fought against His Divinity, because as a fire it consumed
their sins.

To say.   His authority to demand hearing was in the Divine seals
given Him.—He might have said many more things but would
not.

Judge.   Unbelief and disobedience ever wrung His heart.

Our Lord seems here to answer the sneer on their lips.

His judgment would enter their hearts, making thorough work.

He had this infinite superiority over all teachers, that He alone
could always answer the deepest thoughts of men's hearts, and
compel them to feel the truth !—He appears for judgment
and salvation.   Luke ii. 34 ; John xvi. 8.—Those refusing to
tremble in *hearing,* will be ground to pieces in *feeling.* *Bradford* the Martyr.—At that moment His omniscient glance took
in their life, deeds, and thoughts.—Verily " many things " must
have pressed His mind, as they culminated in the sorrows of
Gethsemane.

Of you.   Emphatic.—This is the reason why He cannot go on to
the final, decisive declaration concerning Himself.

Men are pleased to speculate curiously concerning the Divine existence, but hate the truth that pierces the heart with conviction of
sin.—"Hast thou found me, O mine enemy? " is the thought which
inspires hatred to the Bible in millions.—Till repentance and faith
have done their blessed work there is no time for other things.

Many *while away* the season of grace in vain attempts to comprehend such doctrines as the Trinity, Predestination, &c.

But. Those refusing to hear the *word*, must hear the *rod*. Micah vi. 9.

He that sent me is true. Implies it grieves Him He has so much to judge of them ; yet it must be so ; God who hath sent Him is *true*. *Lange*.

To the world. Here we find why He reiterates these warnings. Beams of Divine light must not, cannot be entirely lost.

" My word shall not return unto Me void, but accomplish that," &c. Isa. lv. 11.—Words spoken in replies to blaspheming Jews nearly 2000 years since now outshine the stars.

It matters not that truth is scorned when spoken. 2 Cor. xiii. 8. It must run its course for all ages. It is Eternal as its Author.

Those things. Such as, " I AM THE LIGHT OF THE WORLD," &c. " Come unto Me, all ye that are weary," &c. " Except a man be born again," &c. " I am the resurrection and the life," &c.

Heard of Him. God judges in act according to truth. Christ, the interpreter of God, must do the same in word. *Lange*.

Thus faithfully and perfectly He discharges His commission.

------

27. They understood not that he spake to them of the Father.

Understood not. The Evangelist thus expresses his surprise at their blindness and unbelief.—Worldly conceptions and hopes as to Messiah have rendered them wholly incapable of perceiving His meaning.

The Father. Had they known the Father they would have known, without having to ask, who Jesus was, ver. 25. *Bengel*.

Men who can think of God as Creator, Upholder, Judge, &c., yet fail to apprehend Him as Father.—He can alone be apprehended and realized by and through Christ. *Luther*.

------

28. Then said Jesus unto them, When ye have lifted up the Son of man, then shall ye know that I am he, and that I do nothing of myself; but as my Father hath taught me, I speak these things.

When. He intimates that when His appointed hour is come, He will be " lifted up."—But not even then, though forsaken by His disciples, rejected by Israel, disowned by the world, will His Father forsake Him.

Lifted up. That is, on the cross. See on chap. iii. 14.

A two-fold meaning :—As instruments, they would lift Him to the cross ; as the result, He will ascend to His throne.

In inscrutable wisdom, His *murderers* will help to raise Him to His throne.—Jews, as representatives of the unbelieving world, will crucify Him ; thus will the world know Him to be *the* Messiah.—The first plain hint as to whom, and by what means He should die.

Then. And not till *then.*—Such small words are *lines* of *mercy* or *vengeance.*—Hereafter men will wonder, not that God hath done *so little,* but that He hath done *so much* for desperate rebels.

Shall ye know. Were the Sanhedrim *convinced* after the crucifixion ?—This distinctly announces the fact, although the fulfilment is unrecorded. — Either by the Spirit's mission of grace, or by judgments in wrath.—This clearly defined prophecy cannot be nullified by their denial.—It may imply that, convicted of their guilt, they would repent and join the witnesses for Christ.—When men read the title, " King of the Jews," many believed.—Especially at the Pentecostal revival the Church grew rapidly.—Amid the ruins and deep desolation of their city and nation many first saw that Christ was Messiah.—Individuals repented, but the nation filled up its cup, and fell under their doom.—Their fathers falling by tens of thousands in the desert for their rebellion, fulfilled Num. xiv. 29.—" Ye shall know that I am Jehovah."—" Ye shall fall by the sword, and shall know that I am the Lord." Ezek. xi. 10.

Our Lord evidently refers to these predictions, and thus identifies Himself with the JEHOVAH of the O. T.

That I am He. The promised Messiah, is the plain undertone. Verse 24.—And one day they will know it.—The grandeur of God on the throne will scarcely amaze the finally impenitent as much as their own *unbelief.*

Nothing of Myself. I do not of my own will or ambition claim to be Messiah.—By and by words, mocked by them now, will be found terrible truths.—His words, full of Divine majesty, proved God was with Him.—This and the 29th verse were spoken with such heavenly grace and power, that some of our Lord's hearers responded by faith and obedience.

My Father. " Our Father," He taught *us* to say, but never used it Himself.

Taught me. He manifests and conceals Himself as the Father instructs Him.

αὐτοῖς. Omitted. *Lach., Tisch., Alf.*

ὑψώσητε. Crucifixion, since the Lord would not use an unintelligible expression. *De Wette, Schleier.* They understood elevation to the Messiah's throne. *Lange.* Utterly unintelligible must such a thought be here. *Stier.* Universal proclamation and glorification of our Lord. *Meyer.* The shameful lifting up would be the means of His real exaltation. *Calvin.*

γνώσεσθε. Known by *fact*, which you will not believe by *word. Bengel.* Refers to parallel Old Test. passages, as the "stones," Luke xix. 40, refer to the "stones crying," Hab. ii. 11. *Hengst.*

μου. Omitted. *Cod. Sin., Lach., Tisch., Alf.*

---

29. And he that sent me is with me : the Father hath not left me alone ; for I do always those things that please him.

Is with Me. 1. Unity of essence. 2. Communion of spirit. 3. Consciousness of favour. 4. Present help. 5. One in eternal plans.—Jehovah was ever at His right hand in might, in majesty, and in love.—Hints at the foretold victory He should win in death.—To be with God, is to have light without darkness, truth without falsehood, power without weakness, love without limit.

Hath. Past tense implies He never had left Him.

Points to the help of God which He has hitherto received.

Left Me. He well knew that Peter would deny Him, the apostles forsake Him, all Israel reject Him, the world disown Him.

To you conspiring, and longing to crush Me for ever, I seem alone and unfriended. But I have friends you know not of.

I have the arm of the Almighty around Me, for " I always please Him."

Alone. See on John i. 1, 2.—Jesus' true Divinity can never be separated from the Father.—A sunbeam cannot be left alone, amid the dust of this world.—As soon think it possible the sun could forsake the world he enlightens, as God abandon the incarnate WORD, as a poor orphan thing.—The sunbeams spread their golden wings over us, and yet abide with the sun from whence they flow.—He who sent His Son into the world was so with Him, that He shared, so to speak, all the opprobrium and enmity with which His mission was met. In the same manner is Christ with all His people. Matt. xxv. 40.

Always. Eternally, past, present, and future.—At all times, everywhere, in all ways He requires from all, and teaches all those things which please God.—Of whom, but the eternal SON and SPIRIT, can this be said ?

Please Him.   This obedience of the Son, though strictly predicable of Him in His Messianic office, proceeds from His essential unity with the Father. *Olsh.*—Assistance of the Father is to be distinguished from the essential unity of the Father and the Son, and reciprocates the obedience of Jesus.—In His unconditional obedience He has the seal of His unconditional confidence. *Lange.*—No higher reward can a being desire than pleasing God.

πέμψας.   Besides sending me, He also granted me (up to this time) His constant help. *Winer.*

μετ᾽ ἐμοῦ ἐστιν.   Affording assistance. *Rosenm.*

ἀφῆκέ.   Not confined to Incarnation period, but embraces an indefinite future. *Stier.*   Aorist actually a convincing præterite. *Lyser.*

ὁ πατήρ.   Omitted. *Lach., Tisch., Alf.*   Retained. *Cod. Sin.*

---

30. As he spake these words, many believed on him.

He spake.   Gracefully, meekly, and confidingly, but irresistibly.

Many.   A similar crowd saw the face of Stephen, as the face of an angel. Acts vi. 15.—So it is possible that a heavenly radiance illumined the face of the Son of God.—It is never said they *all* believed ; some will resist, even although the Son of God Himself is *the Preacher.*—Doubtless some trembled, like Felix, but others mocked.—" Wisdom will," through time and eternity, " be justified of her children."—The Gospel will prove " a savour of death " where it is not " a savour of life."

Believed.   John i. 7 ; vii. 38.—Truth sent home by the Spirit. Faith wrought by hearing, deeper and stronger than the effect of miracles.—A slight clue as to the kind of truth that overcomes men.—The Son of God delighting the Father, and always pleasing Him, attracts the heart.—" If ye continue," in the next verse, proves they *confessed* their faith.

The flower, turning to the sun, silently confesses the source of its life.—" Stand forth." Mark iii. 3.   The man with the withered hand obeyed.—His standing was a *profession of faith* in Christ's Divinity.   For he well knew no created being could of himself work a miracle.—" Follow Me." Matt. iv. 19.   The two disciples *professed* their faith, *obeying.*—The young ruler (Matt. xix. 21) was invited to profess his faith in Christ.

All ashamed to profess their faith in Christ will be disowned hereafter. Mark viii. 38.—How much of ignorance or infirmity is
consistent with faith God alone knoweth.—However little faith
may be, it will lead, if followed, to *full* knowledge.
Knowledge *grows* with fidelity in religion. Hosea vi. 3.

ἐπίστευσαν. They stand upon the footing of the disciples mentioned in
chap. vi. 66; hence μένειν is required of them. *Tholuck.* In the simplest historical sense: Became disciples. *Lange.* Our Lord was conscious of the infinitely small impression made by His words. Isa. liii. 1. *Stier.* These
followers were not encouraged. Our Lord never avails Himself of *mistakes.*
D. Brown. No one under mistake would have been called a *believer* by the inspired penman. *Author.* Some knowledge must precede faith. *Ber. Bib.*

---

31. Then said Jesus to those Jews which believed on him, If ye continue in
my word, then are ye my disciples indeed.

Then. Gr. *therefore.* Implying why He specially addressed this
   class.—It indicates gracious earnestness and loving solicitude.
He would make a permanent lodgment for His truth in the heart.
Believed. John i. 7 ; vii. 38. Faith admits of degrees.
If. The Lord warns these half-converts not to be satisfied with a
   passing excitement of feeling.—By .heavenly uprightness. He
   gradually enchains true disciples and alienates false ones. *Lange.*
" **If** " is sadly abused in the popular theology of our day.
The admission into the kingdom is with multitudes the signal
   for folding their arms.—They make the fearful mistake of
   esteeming the *starting* place the *goal* of Christian life.
Continue. In classical Gr., *abiding* by a contract, solemnly
   entered.—The perils they feared began the moment they took
   their stand.—Temptations were not long in coming ; not to be
   despised. Luke viii. 13.—Not twenty-four hours elapsed between
   Peter's warning and Peter's fall.—Our Lord here tends the flock
   after bringing home the lost sheep. Isa. xl. 11.
" Perseverance of saints " means *preservation.* " They shall never
   perish." John x. 28.—A true believer to-day cannot be a reprobate to-morrow. 1 Sam. iii. 12.—It follows from their election,
   " called, chosen, faithful." Rev. xvii. 14.—Christ's intercession
   cannot possibly be frustrated. John xvii. 20.
Joy of angels over converts cannot be false. No error is found
   in heaven.—Heaven's dwellers cannot be tantalized by a good

they will never realize.—The promises of God secure it :—" He that believeth shall not come into condemnation." John v. 24. " Him that cometh to Me, I will in no wise cast out." John vi. 37. " I give unto them ETERNAL LIFE, neither shall any pluck them out of My hand." John x. 28.—They are also in His Father's hand. Ver. 29.—Believers are members of Christ : how can His members perish ?—" Predestinated" are " called;" "called" are "justified ; " "justified " are " glorified." Rom. viii. 30. Still the only evidence of conversion is CONTINUANCE IN OBEDIENCE. A graft must abide, nay, form a *vital* union with the stock. The word of truth lies on many minds as the dust driven by the wind.—Coming to Christ is not a solitary act, done once, but is a life-habit.—Not the plan or labour, but the *end* defines the Christian.—A thing almost done, is not done. *Basil.* The evening crowns the labours of the day.—Sudden flashings of zeal, like a land flood, soon come to nothing.

In My word. Obeying His teachings.—Not so deep as " Abide in Me." John xv. 7.

Disciples. Gr. *learners*, at first confined to the twelve apostles. Jewish youth were taught concerning the passover. Exod. xii. 26. " Teach them diligently (Heb. *Sharpen*), that they forget not." Deut. vi. 7.—No youth's principles can be trusted without such teaching. Deut. vi. 20.—Not only sons, but daughters, were to be indoctrinated. Deut. xi. 19.—Samuel was sent to Eli to school at Ramah. 1 Sam. xix. 19.—Bethel, Jericho, Gilgal, had schools in which the Law and Music were taught. 1 Sam. x. 5. Monthly meetings were held. 2 Kings iv. 23.—It was one thing to believe in Jesus, quite another to be disciples, *learners.* True discipleship the only condition and guarantee of knowing the truth.

Indeed. Experimental knowledge alone avails.—" Oh, taste and see." Psa. xxxiv. 8.

οὖν. Hints at the relation of His words to their faith. *Stier.* He saw some visible movement. He presses them to persevere. *D. Brown.*

μείνητε. Remaining pre-supposes already being in the truth. *Kling.* The Spirit imparts to believers a sense of acceptance. *Pearson.* A co-operation between God and the will. *Stier.* If ye hold firm to My teaching. *Schleier.* If ye continue in My doctrine. *De Wette.*

λόγῳ. Every single word involves the entire revealed will of God in its completeness. *Stier.* Perseverance of saints evinced—1. From the immutability of God's love. Jer. xxxi. 3 ; Mal. iii. 6 ; Rom. viii. 38, 39 ; xi. 29. 2. From Scripture. Isa. liv. 10 ; 1 John ii. 19 ; Isa. lv. 3 ; Matt. xxiv. 24 ; Rom.

v. 1, &c.   3. From the Covenant of Grace. Jer. xxxii. 40.   4. From Christ's *merits*,—Christ being assured of a seed. Heb. xi. 12; x. 14.   5. From His intercession. John xvii. 11—20; xiv. 16.   6. From the intimate union between. 1 Cor. xii. 12.   7. From prayers of believers.   8. From continued influences of the Spirit. 1 Cor. vi. 19; Eph. i. 13.   9. From joy of angels at the time of conversion. *Patterson*.

μου. Omitted. *Cod. Sin.*

ἐστέ. Then shall ye deserve to be, &c. *Hess.*

---

32. And ye shall know the truth, and the truth shall make you free.

And ye. Of all who ever preached, Christ alone knew the *effect* of His sermons.—He intentionally gave this blow to their prejudices, in infinite wisdom.

Know. Answers to feeding on Christ in heart, a felt trust in Him. Not theoretical, but practical, influential, heart-experience.

Truth. Equivalent to, Do not look for temporal deliverance from Rome.—Follow Me, and your eternal freedom will be secured. This offer, instead of being gratefully received, was scorned.

A miser, bound with fetters of solid gold, would cry out against the cruelty.—Alas! he knows not that fetters stronger far than metal bind him.—Had the Jews all been made *kings*, they would have been slaves still.—Had Tiberius at Rome by *proclamation* announced Judæa *free*, still they would have been in bondage.—Freedom, truth, and wisdom pass as great words among men.—That which is truth, pure, absolute, unchanging truth, men have, in all ages, persistently and presumptuously rejected.—" I AM THE WAY, THE TRUTH, AND THE LIFE." John xiv. 6.—"Faith cometh by hearing, and hearing by the word of God " (i. e. by the Truth).—True theology is a Divine *life*, as well as Divine *knowledge*.—In heaven we *see*, then love ; on earth we *love*, then see.   John vii. 17.

It surprised them that the *lords of the world* were to be made free by a Galilean.—This one word roused the Jews to a frenzy of madness.—Verily the Gospel cannot always be gently preached. Stiff-necked enemies must be met with the fire and hammer of truth.—Christ calls Himself THE *Truth*.   Incarnate Truth. John xiv. 6.—The types and shadows of the Law all pointed to Him as their end.—All the promises God made the Fathers were fulfilled in Him.

Free. This freedom exempts the sons of God from all *adverse* power.—Truth and liberty are inseparable companions.—The worst bondage, where chains cut deep into the very soul, is *unseen.*—No tortures of prison, rack, wheel, cross, or flame, can loosen these *invisible chains.*—6000 years of suffering have not relaxed Satan's fetters.—" Everlasting " may be seen impressed upon each fiery link. Jude 6.—Suffering begets sorrow, but not producing repentance it becomes remorse.—Esau wept bitterly that he had *lost*, not that he had *sold*, his blessing.

Men confess freely their errors, but stoutly deny they are bondmen. " His servants ye are, whom ye obey." Rom. vi. 16.

Truth and Freedom men earnestly and passionately profess to pursue.—This inextinguishable right has cost oceans of treasure and blood.—All freedom based on delusion is a most shameful servitude.—None are altogether free but those altogether sinless.

Faith producing filial love frees one from " fear bringing a snare ; " from the cutting chains of human dogmas and ordinances ; from all sensual ritualistic fopperies, memorials of the dark ages. The " *liberty of the sons of God* " is a holy, blessed *captivity*.

No man complains of the binding of his head with a jewelled crown.

The yoke and burden of Christ, like the plumage of the bird, bear the soul upwards to heaven.—But to be free to sin, is an unmitigated bondage.—" I will walk at liberty, for I seek thy precepts." Psa. xxxi. 9 ; cxix. 45.—Martyrs bound to the stake were free.—Paul and Silas, Luther and Bunyan, in prison, were free.—" Life is good, but eternal life is better. Death is bitter, but eternal death more bitter." *Hooper's* words in the flames.

The fear of death, a terrible yoke. Heb. ii. 15.—To know it to be certain, and yet keep it out of sight, is a chain the gayest worldling drags to the ball-room and theatre.

Physicians and friends dare not say, " this sickness is unto death."

Man is only free when he moves in harmony with the mind and will of God as his proper element. *Schaff.*—To gain liberty men have tried—1. Force. 2. Legislative enactments. 3. Civilization.—Truth of Christ alone liberates—1. Truth as to God. 2. As to man. 3. As to immortality.—Nature of the liberty truth gives—1. Political freedom. 2. Mental independence. 3. Superiority to temptation. 4. Superiority to fear.—Inferences—1. Cultivate the love of Truth. 2. See what a Christian is. *Robertson.*

ἀλήθειαν. See on John i. 14. λόγος only when completely known first becomes the truth. *Stier.*

λόγος in ver. 31 includes submission to Christ's authority, as well as embracing Him as Messiah. *Author*. Refers to John xiv. 6. *Chrys.*, *Euthymius*. Freedom and knowledge co-ordinates. *Lampe*. Sin cannot be overcome by mere knowledge. *J. Müller*. Means the objective truth of God. *Stier*. The true religion. *Wetstein*. Christ Himself here meant. *Theophylact*. A deeper and deeper knowing of Christ who is the truth. *Hengst*.

ἐλευθερώσει (manumit) not alone freedom from the bondage of sin. *Stier*.

------

33. They answered him, We be Abraham's seed, and were never in bondage to any man: how sayest thou, Ye shall be made free?

They answered. Not believers (ver. 37). A rude portion, the crowd and rulers.

Abraham. Heb. *Father of a multitude.*—Son of Terah.—Born in Ur, of Chaldea.—Site of Ur unknown.—He lived B. C. 2153.—At the age of 70 called of God to Sichem, the modern Nablous.—Here he erected his first altar.—Famine drove him to Egypt.—Through fear he denied to Pharaoh that Sarah was his wife.—On his return, Lot and he separated their flocks and interests.—Henceforth he dwelt in Mamre or Hebron.

Defeats Chedorlaomer.—Meets Melchisedeck, king of Salem, to whom Abraham paid tithes.—The birth of an heir announced, from whom He should come who was to bless all nations.

The Lord enters into a covenant with him by the sign of circumcision.—With two angels visits him and announces the doom of Sodom.—Sarah, at the birth of Isaac, demands the expulsion of Ishmael and Hagar.—After 25 years, goes to offer up Isaac on mount Moriah.—Bought Sarah's grave at Machpelah.

The Mosque of Hebron, according to tradition, covers this cave. The present building was erected before the time of Christ. *Josephus*.

Marries Keturah. Her six sons sent away.—Abram dies, aged 175; buried at Hebron.—He is called " Father of the faithful." Rom. iv. 11.—Integrity, hospitality, devotion, and strong faith his characteristics.—His descendants were—1. Israelites. 2. Some tribes of Arabs. 3. Midianites. 4. Ammonites and Moabites.—His name and Joseph's are familiar all over Asia at this day.

Seed. Not the posterity of Ishmael.—This proud Jewish pride in our day gives place to *faith* in humanity.

Infidels of a thousand opinions ask us to have *"faith in man."*

Never. Their pride was roused, and they utter a bold falsehood. The fiery sting of the Lord's word was its TRUTH.

Jehovah had assigned them unquestionably a real theocratic
eminence.—This charge annihilated their long-boasted pretensions, and reduced them to the level of Gentiles.

Our Lord had not spoken of any freedom a slave might not enjoy.

Holy things *corrupted* are the hardest to be *healed.*

" Ye are the (dear) children of the Lord your God." Deut. xiv. 1.

Israel was His first-born. They thought God alone cared for them.

The prophecy foretold Abraham's seed " shall serve." Gen. xv. 13.

Yet the true seed of Abraham, though in exile, ever a KINGDOM.
Exod. xix. 6.—The *true* CHURCH OF GOD has never been, and
never can be, enslaved.—Israel under all circumstances is a
" princess among the provinces." Lam. i. 1.

Moses, son of a slave, was yet Pharaoh's master and conqueror.

Daniel, a slave, was nevertheless Nebuchadnezzar's lord and judge.
Dan. iv. 27.—In all moral conflicts, it will be found that
" wisdom is better than weapons of war." Eccl. ix. 18.

Were not these the people who made bricks under the Egyptian lash ?

Were they not under the Babylonian master by the side of the
river Euphrates ?—Were they not at this very time paying
tribute to Cæsar ?—In truth they were scarcely ever *out of
bondage* to some master.—Alas ! another slavery they denied.

In truth they dreaded the liberty which Christ offered.

In mad contradiction they cried, " We have no king but Cæsar."
" No king " meant Jesus.—All the boasted freedom of " Liberals "
and the revelry of the impenitent resemble only the colours of
the portrait.—They come not from *flowing life-blood within,* but
from the pencil without.—In their mad blindness, Jews saw not
a tyrant who sat nearer than Rome.—Even now he was robbing
them of Abraham's blessing.—Chains, stronger than tyranny
ever forged of metal, fetters that no earthly king can ever
strike off, were their sad ornaments. Jude 6.

Myriads of Christ's redeemed freemen have gone to their graves
with bodies scarred and blasted by the taskmaster's lash and
chain.

Made free. As apostate children of Abraham, they were serfs,
not children of God.—The unrenewed soul has as many tyrants
as lusts.—All the senses of the wicked are handmaids to sin.

The eye watches for it, the ear, the tongue, the heart, all plead for
it.—Fancy paints it, memory records its secrets, the will is its
charioteer.—The passions are the providers, hunting for prey.
Thornton.

ἀπεκρίθησαν. Objected: Pharisees present. *Markland.* Some of the crowd not believers. *Lampe, Tholuck.* Not the slightest trace of faith in their answering. *Hengst.* Those believers to whom He ascribes the sins of their race. *Alford.* Believers join with others. *Maurice.*

'Αβραάμ. Native place, Ur. 1. *Orfah*, called by Greeks, Edessa. *Pocock.* 2. According to a Talmud tradition, *Warka.* Now called *Huruk.* 3. *Mugheir* on right bank of Euphrates. *Rawlinson.* 125 miles from the sea. A large Chaldean temple dedicated to *Hurki*, the moon god. Dead brought here from far and near for 1800 years. *Smith's* Dict.

οὐδενί. Never yet at any time, embraces the whole interval. Perhaps here an unintentional misunderstanding of our Lord's meaning. *Alford.*

δεδουλεύκαμεν. We are free de jure, and are also de facto. *Lampe.* Not political freedom. *Hengst.* Delusions of sin. *Stier.* They attached to bondage some technical meaning. *Alf., Tisch.* Refers to their entire political history. *Kling.* We at least were never in such bondage to any power as our fathers. *Bengel.* They hint that being Abraham's seed rendered slavery impossible. *Stier.* Stand convicted of impotent lying. *Augustine.* They had not felt the degradation of perfect slavery. *Stier.* They did not acknowledge the temporal authority of Rome over their spiritual privileges. *Lange.* Spaniards and Jews pre-eminent boasters amid national misery. *Alsted.* Their proud bluster seems ludicrous. *D. Brown.* Jews understood Christ rightly of spiritual bondage. *Macknight.* They only refer to their own age. *Kuinoel.* "Meanest labourer who is of the seed of Abraham is like a king." *Talmud.*

---

34. Jesus answered them, Verily, verily, I say unto you, Whosoever committeth sin is the servant of sin.

Verily. See on John i. 51; iii. 3.—Almost with the solemnity of an oath, found only in John.—He intensifies His word, seeing the Jews would bitterly resist it.

Whosoever. Exalted mercies only deepen responsibility.

Abraham's sons, chosen of God, having the higher calling of men. If such become slaves, how terrible the degradation!

Committeth. Gr. *doeth.* Liveth in the commission of it, 1 John iii. 8, whose tendency and habit it is.—Not one merely " overtaken in a fault; " but one in whom it is a " *law* of his *mind.*"

The " gnats," small sins, prepare for the "camels," larger sins.

Not the smallness of the *law*, but the greatness of the *law-giver*, binds the chains so fast.—Men do not distinguish between good and evil, hence vices are indulged under the mask of virtues.

Uzzah was with the ark,—a sign he loved it. He feared to see it rock by the stumbling oxen, and grasps its sacred staves. Into this chorus of good thoughts Satan infused one, which brought down the bolt of wrath.—Our Lord might have pointed to the " receipt of custom " as proof of His charge : but He teaches that though Rome's yoke might be shattered, *their* bondage would not cease.—Myriads are pitiable slaves who never paid tax to a foreign lord.

Sin. The violation of the law of God, rending of holy bonds.

The guilt of sin lies more in what it tears from, than leads to,—holy influences resisted, pure motives rejected, sacred laws violated, priceless privileges contemned, blessed heights of joy and peace abandoned, eternal friendship of God and angels forfeited.

Jews wore the livery of Satan in the house of Abraham's God.

There can be no more hopeless bondage than when we feel not our chains.

Servant. Gr. *slave.* 2 Pet. ii. 19.—The slave was the absolute property of his master, who held the power of life and death in his hands for centuries.—Sin the worst of tyrants ; its work, pollution ; its wages, death. Rom. vi. 23.—This service David deprecates : " Let it not have dominion over me." Psa. xix. 13.

The usurper of the house had parted them from the lord of the house.—Rome conquered kingdoms, and was overcome by her own vices. *Plutarch.*

Of sin. Gr. *the* sin, not occasional transgression of law, but the wilfully and persistently surrendering one's soul to a reigning lust.—Against the law and conscience, and warnings as to its ruinous results.—One who habitually lives in direct contradiction to himself.—The dominion of sin over the soul costs high in exchange.—Ten tribes " *sold* themselves to do evil in the sight of the Lord." 2 Kings xvii. 17.—Philosophers spake much of this slavery, but knew little of its *strength* and *depth.*

" Slavery of sin can *easily* be shaken off." *Seneca.*

How wide from truth was this eloquent Roman !

'Aμήν. Antithetical between truth and delusion, sincerity and hypocrisy, temporal and eternal things. *Besser.*

τὴν ἁμαρτίαν. The article of strong significance. *Stier.*

δοῦλός. Slavery to sin, not brought out clearly in the O. T. *Lücke.* Dream not of freedom while under the mastery of your desires. *Plato.* No one committing deeds of wickedness can be free. *Arrian.* Guilt may bear the name of virtue, but it is base bondage. *Epictetus.* Persian monarchs ruled empires, and yet were slaves to their wives and concubines. *Trapp.* Roma victrix gentium, captiva vitiorum. *Augustine.*

τῆς ἁμαρτίας. A gloss. *Klee, Neander.* Omitted. *Mill, Tholuck.* Authentic. *Cod. Sinai, Stier, Brüchner.*

---

35. And the servant abideth not in the house for ever: but the Son abideth ever.

Servant. Gr. *slave.* John iv. 51.—Slave by position, and servile in heart.—Even an Israelite as such cannot be a servant of God's house.

Abideth not. Has no natural rights nor tie, but is at the master's mercy.—A compulsory dismissal may be here alluded to.

Hebrews were bound to set a slave free at the end of seven years. Exod. xxi. 2.—Also at the Jubilee. Lev. xxv. 40 ; Deut. xv. 12.—If preferring bondage, he must submit to a rite, Deut. xv. 17, and he became a servant for ever.—Seldom was the slave compelled to retire, and find another home.—Jews had boasted of Abraham as father.—Here are two kinds of seed,—the *son*, properly so called, and the *slave.*—Ishmael and Hagar were driven out into the wilderness, because *he* showed a slavish mind. Gen. xxi. 10.—O. T. saints were never entirely free from a servile spirit.—While servants of Satan, we cannot abide in God's house.—There are " many mansions," but none for the voluntary servants of an *alien* master.

House. John vii. 53.—O. T. constantly typified the kingdom of God by a *house.*—" One thing have I desired ; to dwell in the house of the Lord." Psa. xxvii. 4.—The tent being so common, and their ordinary homes so humble, made the word house synonymous for a palatial residence.—This form of speech is just as significant to-day among the dwellers of the East.

Overcoming, the saints will be made a " pillar in the temple of God." Rev. iii. 12.

For ever. Allusion to the Jubilee, occurring every forty-ninth year.

The Son. He is by blood one with the house, and also its heir.

This point of law, is also a similitude, expressing the perpetual dwelling and ruling of Christ in God's kingdom. The Son of the house, the real FREEMAN, also the true LIBERATOR. *Lange.*

The natural rights of sons are here alluded to.—Men had power of life and death over their slaves, and fathers over their children, as now in many Oriental lands.—God's command to Abraham hints at this inherent power.—Parents had the right to *sell* their children for debt. 2 Kings iv. 1.—This custom passed from Jews to Athenians and Romans.—As slaves to sin, Jews had no *right* to remain in the house of God's privileges.

As slaves, they will certainly in due time be cast out for ever.

But adopted children will remain the everlasting heirs of His Son.

" As many as received Him, to them gave He power to become

sons." John i. 12.—As Abraham's seed, they held to being *of
the Church.*—Fearful delusion! Our Lord replies, This will not
avail you.—Matt. xxv. 10, " Door was shut."—Those having
the spirit of slaves have no right there, hence " Depart! "
God's sons bear His likeness, that being the centre of moral being.
Samuel was far more Eli's son than his own children. 1 Sam. iii.
6.—False hearts among Israelites were called " sons of Amorites." Ezek. xvi. 3.

Abideth. As the Son hath an eternal inheritance in reserve, so
hath God charged Christ with the safe keeping of every saint.
John vi. 39.—Hence all who abide in the Father's house must
be adopted as manumitted slaves were in Rome.—The bond-
woman's son could not be heir of Abraham with Isaac. Gal.
iv. 22, 30.

δοῦλος. Refers to Moses, in contrast with Christ. *Euthym., Cyril, Chrys.,
Theoph.* Ishmael and Isaac, the bond and the free. *Stier, Alf.*
μένει. To the legal time of securing freedom in the Sabbatical year or
Jubilee. *Lücke.* The question is concerning Abraham and his spiritual or
natural seed. *Calvin, Cocceius, Lampe, Bengel.* A compulsory casting out was
at the master's pleasure. *Hengst., Hezel.*
τῇ οἰκίᾳ. A slave still in the Lord's house, serving the enemy. *Stier.* A
casting out is here referred to. Gen. xxi. 10 ; Gal. iv. *Hengst.* Many servile
in heart præsumendo sperare, et sperando perire. *Trapp.*
ὁ υἱὸς. Article before υἱὸς as before δοῦλος renders it generic also. *Kling.*
Christ only and absolutely intended. *Lampe.* One spiritually related to the
Father by adoption. *Hengst.* This whole clause ὁ υἱὸς—αἰῶνα is wanting in
Cod. Sin., otherwise it is unquestioned.

36. If the Son therefore shall make you free, ye shall be free indeed.

Son. A new legal principle is here again pre-supposed.
No slave can liberate another slave.—As " He who rules o'er freemen should himself be free," so he who would free another
must himself be free.—The chains of the emancipated slave are
alone melted by the breath of DIVINE LOVE.—This LOVE becomes the law of the soul's life, like Aaron's rod, swallowing up
all other laws.—While love leads to the purest freedom, it is
also a constraining law.—Sin, like another Pharaoh, sets task-
masters over us, who compel us to make brick without straw,
to find peace where God says it cannot be found. Jer. vi. 14.
Sons, as a rule, wish to be sole heirs.—But this SON, with rare love
and self-sacrifice, desires *slaves* to be *freed,* and to *share the in-*

heritance !—Allusion to Ishmael being cast out to make way for Isaac.—" We are not the children of the bond-woman, but of the free." Gal. iv. 31.—Not bondage of law, but of sin, is here the theme.

Make you free. See on ver. 32.—Allusion to Greek custom, in which a *son* had the right to adopt *brothers* to share with him his inheritance ; or to Roman custom, whereby the son at his father's death could liberate all born slaves in his father's house. Elijah flinging his mantle over Elisha, thus adopted him. The father thus re-adopts the prodigal son, *alienated* by his guilty course. Luke xv.—Moslems take off their girdle, and bind it round the adopted one.—The Lord said, " I will clothe the son of Hilkiah with thy robe." Isa. xxii. 21.—Duty in our liberty is found consistent with liberty in our duty.—All other freedom is only to wander in the images of our own folly.

Free indeed. *Spiritually* free, not seemingly, like libertines. 2 Pet. ii. 19.—Jews can alone become free through Him of whom Isaac was a type.—This freedom opposed to their visionary, fanatical efforts.—Without the *real* freedom they could neither attain, nor maintain, nor enjoy *outward* freedom.—Paul was unconscious of his bondage until the Law came with THOU SHALT NOT !—Then he cried, " *Who shall deliver me ?* " One can no more release himself than a harp can retune its strings.—" I thank God through Jesus Christ ! " HE can do what I cannot.—But chains once severed, are for ever *broken* chains in Christ's household.—Sin is an enemy, but a conquered enemy.—It may harass, rebel, persecute, but never wholly subdue or destroy the redeemed.—This freedom from the power of sin Paul calls " *glorious liberty*." Rom. viii. 21.

> " This is a liberty, unsung
> By poets, and by senators unpraised,
> Which monarchs cannot grant, nor all the powers
> Of earth and hell confederate take away.
> God's other gifts
> All bear the royal stamp that speaks them His,
> And are august, but this transcends them all."—*Cowper.*

οὖν. Inferential, proves υἱὸς the same in both texts. *Kling.* Identifies the υἱὸς in both clauses. *Stier.*

ὁ υἱὸς. Alone has authority to emancipate the δοῦλος. *Kling.* Slaves born in a father's house freed by the son among Romans. *Elsley.* Greek law allowed a slave, adopted and freed and made heir, to adopt brothers, and make them co-heirs to his inheritance. *Grotius.*

ἐλεύθεροι. Man has ever had free will. *Rhemish Notes.* Adam's will was free. *Fallen* man is in slavery. *Author.* See *Luther*, and *Edward's* on the Will.

---

37. I know that ye are Abraham's seed; but ye seek to kill me, because my word hath no place in you.

I know. Heathens by their sacrifices, Jews by their relation to Abraham, sought to quiet conscience.—With what success the prophet has told us plainly. No peace to the wicked, Isa. xlviii. 22.—If the Jew is first in *privilege*, Rom. ii. 9, so is he first in *punishment.*—What comfort is it now to Dives to be called " Abraham's son " ?—What to Judas to have been once called Jesus' *"friend"?*—Jews were called " God's people ; " also " people of His curse." Isa. xxxiv. 5.—They would find the poor *Ethiopians* preferred before them. Amos ix. 7.

Abraham's seed. According to the flesh, but not by faith.
By gracious election He admits they are in the house.
" In thy seed shall all the nations of the earth be blest." Gen. xii. 3 ; Isa. lxi. 6.

But. Literally, not so *but otherwise.*—Not sons, but *rebels* in heart.—Changes the force of admission : It may be thus, but that avails not now.—Unrenewed Jews called " Canaanites in the house of the Lord."—Wicked Jewish nobles, " Princes of *Sodom.*" Isa. i. 10.—The Baptist, Luke iii. 8, and Paul, Rom. ii. 17, warned them of the folly of this trust.—Your eyes flashing murder show Abraham would disown you.
A holy friendship *must* exist between God's children and those of Abraham.—They would rid themselves of a reprover,—put out a light shining in their hearts.—They would destroy their King, that each one might be his own king.—They would blot out all the witnesses of God's love and truth.—In a word, they must have the *whole* " *inheritance* " at any cost.—Allegiance to God's Son they owe not,—*He* must be slain.

Ye. Those who had often blasphemously insulted Him.
The few who " believed " (verse 30) had passed over among His disciples.

Seek. My life.—Abraham entertained *strangers*, and believed their word ; ye refuse *God's* testimony.—Abraham was just ; ye are robbers of widows.—Abraham honoured Melchisedec, priest of God ; ye stone the prophets.—Abraham interceded for Sodom ; ye shut the kingdom against men.

Kill. His cross, with all its tremendous issues, is ever before
Him.—Hatred of a brother without cause is murder *begun.* 1
John iii. 15.

Me. The love of God manifested in the Angel of the Covenant.

My word. Did ever any prophet call the word of the Lord
" MY WORD "?—Jesus places HIS word on the same level with
that of JEHOVAH.

Hath no place. Gr. *Progresses not* in your souls. 2 Thess. iii.
1.—The fault is not in the truth, for there is nothing more
penetrating. Heb. iv. 12.—He boldly repeats the charge of
their being murderers in purpose.

ἀποκτεῖναι. Those who had previously believed on Him. *Stier.* Decidedly others. *Thol.* Exasperated enemies. *Hengst.* All through our Lord
carries His life on every word, going to Jerusalem. The end shows Him right.
Herder.

οὐ χωρεῖ. To make way, go through, encompass. Metaphorically, to come
to something, to succeed, to make progress. *Lange.* Same sense as 2 Thess.
iii. 1. His word had encountered hindrances which stifled its progress.
Hengst. Gaineth no ground. *Alford.* Embraces the idea of movement.
Kling. Taketh not in you. *Wicklif.* Since it does not find the entrance it
should. *Lücke.* Hindrances lying in the inner life of the Jews. *B. Crusius.*
Does not plant its roots within them. *Schleier.* Idea of motion ending in rest.
Olsh. "Continue," verse 31, and "hath place," are correlatives. *Bengel.*
The word is within, but does not pierce the heart. *Klee.* My living word
seizes you not. *Stier.*

---

38. I speak that which I have seen with my Father : and ye do that which
ye have seen with your father.

I speak. At each turn the discourse becomes more profound
and awful.— For 4000 years He had pleaded with their
fathers.—By patriarchs, kings, prophets, and Providence, He
had spoken.

Seen. He alludes to the habit of children imitating their
parents.

Father. In sublime severity of truth, He triumphs over the
opposing lie.—As you and I are unlike, so are *your* father and
My Father.—Your thoughts are formed after those of the prince
of darkness.—The terrible height of wickedness reached by the
Jews of this age is witnessed to by *Josephus.*

And ye do. The harmony once existing between man and God
is broken.—Abraham was the friend of God, and rejoiced to see

Christ's day.—But these Jews his children hate Christ with
a murderous design.—They knew these things, and that HE
knew them very well also.

That. This *alien power* in the depraved, the root of all evil
under the sun.—Health and life cannot come from disease and
death.

Your Father. Means " spiritual model," on whom character is
fashioned.—A remarkable antithesis. " The things which I
have seen with *My* Father." " The things which you have seen
(heard) from *your* father."—The irresistible inference is your
father *must* be opposed to My Father.—Your father cannot be
Abraham, a lofty type of a saint.—A mere possibility of the
soul's being Satan's, would fling one into an agony if the soul
was not DEAD in sin.—" *Your father* " marks His great tenderness. He will not at once plainly say, " your father is *the
devil.*"—Verse 40 shows this forbearance.

μου and ὑμῶν are probably exegetical interpretations. *Schaff.* Omitted.
Meyer, Lach., Alf., Tisch. Retained. *Cod. Sin.* Expression becomes keener,
but no advantage. *Hengst.*

καὶ ὑμεῖς οὖν. And ye accordingly (by the same rule). *Alford.* And just
so ye, &c., bitterly ironical. *Meyer.* We each follow our father, but assuredly
not the same,—Irony. *Stier.*

ἑωράκατε. *Cod. Sin., Tisch., Stier.* ἠκούσατε. *Alford, Lach., Treg.,
Cod. Vat.* The variation of the smallest critical value. *Author.*

πατρί. Satan their father might have been named in reply to δεδουλεύκαμεν, but here is merely hinted at. *Stier.*

ποιεῖτε. Their murderous designs. *Euthym.* The desperate crimes of
the Jews of that age prove this no undue severity. *Doddridge.*

---

39. They answered and said unto him, Abraham is our father. Jesus saith
unto them, If ye were Abraham's children, ye would do the works of
Abraham.

Answered. How prompt are the unrenewed to answer in *passion*,
and how slow in *devotion!*

Abraham. Ver. 33. As though they would ask Him, Have you
two fathers ?—They seem to admit children are like their
father. Abraham is ours. Who is yours ?—They would be left
alone. In mercy He will not do so. Hos. iv. 17.

A Jew had a birthright in the Covenant, a pledge of better things,
and if renewed, a share in the gifts and graces of Abraham's
God.

Our father. Admitting He was a Jew they imply His having a different father.—They would provoke Him to learn who the other father was.—It implies since *our* father is Abraham, if there is discord between us, see to it, Who is *Thy* father ?

A terrible delusion—the Temple, a sanctuary for those profaning it, the horns of the altar would screen those, while the blood upon the altar called for vengeance.

If ye were. "For they are not all Israel which are of Israel." Rom. ix. 6.

Children. Who emphatically bear a strong resemblance to their father.—He had said—verse 37—they were Abraham's children, as to the *flesh.*

Would do. "Neither, because they are the seed of Abraham, are they all children." Rom. ix. 7.

Works. Works of faith, above all *the* work of faith.—Abraham longed for the coming of Christ. Ver. 56.—Works avail to reveal the *reality* of GRACE in the heart.—Our Lord, with the Apostle Paul, elevates *faith*, and with James, *works.*

God had called Abraham "*My friend ;* " Heb. "*My lover.*" Isa. xli. 8.—Abraham received Jesus, the ANGEL of Jehovah, by bowing down to the earth. Gen. xviii. 2.

'Ο πατὴρ ἡμῶν. Jews here enter keenly into disputation. *Lange.* They care not who His father is, only their father is Abraham. *B. Crusius.* Speaking in passionate obstinacy, they would insist on the outward relation to the patriarch. *Stier.* A Jew should have a double status to the covenant,—jus ad rem, a birth-right, and jus in re, a share in the spirit of Abraham. *Lake.* Augustus called his children tres vomicas, tria carcinoniata. *Trapp.* One of America's most eminent statesmen said, "He had no reason to thank God for his children." *Author.*

Εἰ τέκνα. τέκνα distinguished from σπέρμα. *Origen, Kling, Olsh.* If genuine children like the father. *Stier.*

ἔργα and τέκνα are correlative. *Schaff.* Gen. xviii. 2. Prostration, an act of courtesy. *Patrick.* Of adoration. *Kiel* and *Delitzsch.* He did not recognize them. Heb. xiii. 2. *Diodati.*

---

40. But now ye seek to kill me, a man that hath told you the truth, which I have heard of God: this did not Abraham.

Kill me. 1. They would *kill a man.* 2. For *telling the truth.* 3. TRUTH FROM GOD.—You arm yourselves with the name of the Church, and yet are against the Church.

Ye desire to destroy a true prophet, Abraham did not.

He rejoiced to see My Day, but ye rejoice not. Ye cannot be his sons.

A man. Implies all that is essential to our nature. It occurs nowhere else, but instead of it the frequent title THE SON OF MAN, which at the same time, with the definite article, elevates Him above the *ordinary* level of humanity. *Schaff.*

Told. He assigns the reason of their malignity. He had told the truth.—Killing those telling it is as near as they can come to striking at its Author.—Hence to kill such is an insanely malicious effort to strike God dead. *Luther.*—Murderous striking at God's image in man ever deserves death at the hand of society through the magistrate.

The truth. Precious truth of infinite and eternal value, but detested by you.—Christians might have escaped the fiery baptism of martyrdom, but the TRUTH they preached and lived condemned the sensual.— The only *sad repose* infidels and demons find, is while battling with Truth.—In seducing our first parents Satan tried to *crush out* all Truth from the earth. Cain's hatred of the Truth would *blot* out a brother living the Truth.—Truth places powder under the homes of the wicked, so they cannot rest in peace.—Truth hangs a dark thundercloud of WRATH DIVINE over each wicked spirit. John iii. 36. Hence in every age Persecution has followed TRUTH as the shadow the dial.—" Art THOU come hither to *torment* us before the time ? " Matt. viii. 29.—*Incarnate Love* is charged with being a *Tormentor* of demons.—Depravity becomes more active the nearer it is brought to the Source of Truth.

This did not. If children are like their parents, Abraham is not *your* father.—Twice is *their* father left *unmentioned,* to arouse their mind.—The counterpart is Abraham with his benevolent spirit in general, with his homage for Melchizedek, and with his sparing of Isaac when God interposed. *Lange.*

The Patriarch *exemplified* virtues, which even philosophers barely imagined.

ἀλήθειαν. Hatred of truth invariably glides into hatred of those bringing it. *Schleier.* John i. 14. " He preaching the truth shall never prosper by living it." *Sir Walter Raleigh.*

οὐκ ἐποίησεν. A reference to Abraham's treatment of the Angel of Jehovah. Gen. xviii. *Lampe, Hengst.* This is not clear. *Schaff.* Seven sages of Greece fully illustrated by Abraham. *Ambrose.*

41. Ye do the deeds of your father. Then said they to him, We be not born of fornication ; we have one Father, even God.

Ye do the deeds. *Their* father, in respect of moral character, is exactly the opposite of Abraham.—They do the bidding and the deeds of *that* father.—So many called *Christians* do the deeds of the devil.—Seeds reveal character as fruit shows the kind of tree.

Your father. He had admitted them to have been Abraham's seed. Ver. 37.—But Zion by her treachery and adultery had begotten strange children. Hos. v. 7.—This tended to arouse the inquiry, Who is the father, of whom He speaks ?

Born of fornication. As much as to say : We are not bastards. We are not like the heathen, born of whoredom, in apostasy from God. Hos. ii. 4.—We are children of Abraham, and therefore children of God.—Their genuine descent from Abraham they proudly assume involves their having God for their Father in the spiritual sense. *Lange.*—They had ages before been called the " seed of adultery." Isa. lvii. 3.

Spiritual fornication is charged time and again on Israel. Ezek. xxiii.

One Father. *One* emphatic. As opposed to heathen who had many gods for their spiritual fathers.—Probably also includes a fling against the Samaritans.—The claim that God was their Father is in no opposition to the paternity of Abraham.—In appealing to the Divine Fatherhood it is evident they sought to force Jesus from His position.—Worldlings flippantly say, " We are all God's children."—Many men oft attach as little significance to *Creation* as to *Fatherhood.*—In childhood we are taught " Our Father," &c., but in riper years the sense becomes clouded by the world's mists, until it fades away.

Alas! what a claim, with all their sins to call God *their* Father !

They could not learn that God's children must love God's Son.

Men, the greater their guilt, the more anxious often to claim relation to the good.—Those who deny Christ's Godhead, still call themselves Christians.—Those ignoring the Divinity of the Holy Ghost, still dream of being friends of the Bible.

Scribes and Pharisees, enemies of *all* righteousness, still cried, " We are the sons of the Covenant."—And even Dives in torment cries, " FATHER *Abraham !* "

Even God. He led them to name God, that He might have

ground to tell the whole truth.—The sinner who is for ever
vindicating himself does but entangle himself the more.
God was not in their heads. Ps. x. 4.   Nor hearts. Ps. xiv. 1.
Nor words. Ps. xii. 4.   Nor ways. Titus i. 16.—He who loves
not Jesus is not of God, but of the devil.—Alas! none more
forward to call God Father in our day than those who *would*
wrest the crown from His Son.   Jer. iii. 4, 5.
Yet those who have no part in the SON, never can do the works of
the FATHER.

πατρὸς.   He is not named until the Jews presume to call God their Father.
Bengel.
πορνείας.   Intended an allusion to the birth of Jesus. *Wetstein.*   This is
doubtful. *Lange.*   Reference to Ishmael. *Euthym. Zig.*, but they justify that
concubinage. *Alford.*   They evade the spiritual argument no longer. *Klee.*
Spiritual paternity. *Stier.*   Allusion to the Samaritans, that spurious race.
Theodore, Theoph., Klee.   Not one father with Thee, but we all have one
father. *B. Crusius.*   We are not idolaters. *Grotius, Lampe, Lücke.*   No
reference to idolatry. *Meyer.*

---

42. Jesus said unto them, If God were your Father, ye would love me: for
I proceeded forth and came from God; neither came I of myself, but he
sent me.

God.   Claimed to be the Father of murderers!   This must have
awakened strange thoughts in Jesus' mind.
Your Father.   Piety to God while rejecting Christ's Divinity, is
like trying to use our lungs without air.
Love me.   Because kindred in spirit and life with God.
Not loving Him, the Beloved of the Father, He can infer with
certainty their ungodly character.—" He that denieth the Father and the SON is Antichrist."   1 John ii. 22.—" Who is a
LIAR but he that denieth Jesus is the CHRIST ? "—Professing to
worship God, and refusing it to Christ, proves that worship a
lie; for the revelation of the FATHER is the revelation of the
SON.—Wresting the evidences of the Son's Divinity from Scripture tears away that of the Father also.—There is no other road
to the Father's house, but by way of the Cross.—To climb up to
heaven apart from the Son, would be to force one's way up
Mount Sinai, amid the thunderings and lightnings and clangor
of the trump of God.—To Jesus, on whose shoulders rests the
key of heaven, must we apply.   Isa. ix. 6.—" If any man

love not the Lord Jesus Christ, let him be Anathema Maran-atha."
1 Cor. xvi. 22.—To worldlings He is an object of dislike, for
faith in Him implies they are sinners, whereas they deny any
such thing.—" To believers He is precious ; " *precious* in Himself, and *precious* in all His work for them and relations to
them.

Proceeded. See on John i. 1, 2, 18, 34.—This is the proof of
what He has just affirmed. His consciousness is the clear
mirror, the true standard.—So by all His miracles (John iii. 2)
the Father set His eternal seal that Jesus was the SON OF GOD !

From God. In His essence and personality, and in His appearance and mission amongst them.

Of Myself. He knew Himself free from all selfish motives.

The history of the temptation (see Sugg. Comm., Luke iv. 1—13)
fully proves this : He was conscious of being actuated by Divine motives.—Nothing but this is conceivable ; either from
Himself, or from God (chap. vii. 18, 28) ; no third origin is
supposable. *Lange.*

ἠγαπᾶτε. Insult or honour done our representative, is done to us. *Quesnel.*
Locus notandus est, there is no piety where Christ is rejected. *Calvin.* No one
could be intimate with Cæsar, without Sejanus. *Tacitus.* No favour from
God, save through Christ. *Author.*

ἐξῆλθον. Refers to His incarnation, and ἥκω to His presence. *Meyer.* It
is the result, and still belonging to ἐκ τοῦ θεοῦ. *Schaff.*

---

43. Why do ye not understand my speech ? even because ye cannot hear my
word.

Why ? This question, the overflow of His passionate loving to
save.—The deep feeling of mercy, repelled and often scorned.

Knowledge brings with it a painful sense of responsibility.

A terrible truth,—some wilfully withdraw from the light, *lest their
guilt be increased !* John iii. 19.

Understand. The emphatic clause of the entire verse.

They could neither understand nor hear, because they had no
moral likeness to the patriarch.—He speaks as in an unknown
tongue to Abraham's boasting sons.

My speech. The tone of love in the Shepherd-voice of Christ.

Ye understand not the *mother-tongue* of God's children.

Babel-builders, estranged by a guilty ambition from God, in one hour ceased to understand their fathers' dialect.—Hearts renewed hear, the Spirit speaking in His *own* tongue.

Pentecostal miracle of tongues was Babel to the unbelieving.

All is unintelligent to " the *Canaanite* in the promised land."

Essential truths rejected, it is blasphemy to call God our Father.

Sin and Grace are the centre of all Christ's words and works as Redeemer.—His words no human lexicon can expound or simplify.—Alas! those words are a strange tongue to many bearing His name.—*Fashionable* religion takes not its form from the robes of His righteousness.—" *Our religion*," Acts xxvi. 5, is too often diverse from Bible religion.

Ye cannot. To be understood ethically, not in a fatalistic sense.

They *could* not because they *would* do their father's deeds.

The Fall paralyzed man's moral affections, and renders prayer absolutely necessary.—Jews were proud of being free from serving false gods.—But the moment they confronted the True God, they hated Him.—" *Can* not," John vi. 44, in Bible language means " *will* not," have no heart to.—The ground on which the fearful charge of utter *deafness* of the soul is based.

John and Paul trace the result to the same cause. John xii. 39 ; Rom. viii. 7 ; 1 Cor. ii. 14.—Heaven's language, as well as joys, are a mystery to worldlings.—Gradually men become hardened into final incorrigibility. Isa. vi. 9.—Upon all such, grieving the Holy Spirit, a *ban* rests in judgment.—Christ's crucifixion proves His terrible earnestness in instructing Israel.

Closing their eyes and stopping their ears proves them *incorrigible*.—Joseph's brethren " *could not* speak peaceably unto him." Gen. xxxvii. 4.—Jews could not see that our Lord had any *authority* to warn them.—The key of knowledge was hidden, and the prophets were a sealed book.—Thus the Lord's hearers were fast becoming " children of the devil." 1 John iii. 10.—Truths, clear and loud as God's voice at Sinai, were knocking at their hearts, but they bolted and barred the door against heaven itself!—They had to all intents become " devil-worshippers." 1 Cor. x. 21.

Hear. Diminished sense from *understanding*. They could not even *hear*.—They are incapable of even *listening* to His words with a pure spiritual ear.—The instinct of *true* Love will catch more from a single *gesture*, than cold respect will from an entire chapter.

λαλιάν. In distinction from λόγος ; the personal language, the mode of speech, the familiar tone and sound of the words, in distinction from their meaning. Comp. Phil. i. 14; Heb. xiii. 7. *Lange.* They fail to hear λόγος, therefore understand not λαλιά. *Trench.* The former the sentiment, the latter the form. *Lücke.*

γινώσκετε. He who censures the word cannot be one with Jesus' mind. *Braune.*

ὅτι. Carried over to verse 44, to avoid tautology. *Hezel.* Included in the question. *De Wette.*

δύνασθε. Final transition to the last charge. *Stier.* Ye will not give heed to Me now, nor let Me finish My words. *Ber. Bib.* Final resisting of all appeals proved them incapable of instruction. *Hoffmann.* As operations of God in Nature veil His presence, and Atheists are willingly deceived, so parables conceal Christ from the profane. *Lange.*

---

44. Ye are of your father the devil, and the lusts of your father ye will do. He was a murderer from the beginning, and abode not in the truth, because there is no truth in him. When he speaketh a lie, he speaketh of his own : for he is a liar, and the father of it.

Ye are. Now He gives forth a word of thunder.

One of the most fearful passages in the entire compass of revelation.

Your father. He speaks of spiritual or moral paternity.

" You claim God, but in fact the devil is your father."

Implies the Jews had renounced all dependence on God.

They denied His ownership, and surrendered themselves to an alien.

Not " God's peculiar people," but *self-sold* slaves to the devil.

Pharisees were plants not planted by the heavenly Father. Matt. xv. 13.—Satan put certain thoughts into the mind of Judas. John xiii. 2.—Spirits of devils work miracles among the kings of the earth. Rev. xvi. 14.—A seed of godly children, and also of the devil, divide mankind. 1 John iii. 9.—The wicked are called the " seed of the serpent." Gen. iii. 15.

The devil. See on John vi. 70 ; vii. 20.—The article denotes the chief, the leader of those " who kept not," &c. Jude 6.

Most decisive testimony—1. As to the objective personality of the devil. 2. As to his agency in the fall of man, and his connection with the whole history of sin. 3. As to the devil's apostasy from a previous blessed state in which he was created. 4. As to the connection of bad men with him. *Schaff.*

In so solemn an appeal no metaphor could possibly be used.

The devil *absolutely* loves darkness, *absolutely* hates light.

His being is death, because a " godless existence is not life."

Since he could not hold Christ in death, he would slay all His followers.—If Satan had had his way, the stone would *never* have been rolled from Christ's tomb.—Since he failed then, he now daily *seeks to* " crucify Him afresh." Heb. vi. 6.

Lusts. Of three main classes (Matt. iv.),—love of pleasure, love of honour, love of power.—To devils " evil is their good." *Milton.* They live to increase vice, error, and misery.—*The plural* shows the endless unrest, the measureless impulses of this central, living, immortal principle of iniquity !—When Satan hath fed his birds he snares them, and destroys. *Trapp.*

Ye will do. Gr. your *will* is to do. You *love* to do the lusts of your father.—The Apostle confesses he did that which he did not *will*. Rom. vii. 19.—How sharply defined is the *line* between sin in the renewed and in the unrenewed.—A Christian does that which he *hates*. Rom. vii. 15. The sinner the same thing for *love*.—It is a terrible *will* and a frightful *must*, governing the ungodly.—Sin has ever " beset,"—has ever clung as a " weight." Heb. xii. 1.—Our Lord expresses the absolute responsibility of one who is the slave of Satan.—Resisting all restraint, the depraved become more Satanic still.—This vile bondage of sin, these self-deluded ones style *liberty*.—They *will* what Satan *wills*, whether it come to acts or no.—Satan cannot *induce*, much less *force*, us to sin without our will.—He may strike fire till he wearies *in vain*, unless there be tinder in our corrupt hearts.

Murderer. Implies *taking life*, whether of the *body* or of the *soul!* As the life of the soul is infinitely more valuable than the body, the guilt rises in the same ratio.—Satan hated Adam's *happiness* much, his *holiness* more.—Cain hated God's *image* on Abel's heart more than he hated Adam's son.—Now Satan tries to sever every human being from his proper life.

As a liar, he tries to persuade men God is not all good.

Myriads listen to him, believe him, and thus become *his children*.

The implication is, *all sinners* have the spirit of *hate*, i. e. murder.

" Hating a brother without cause " makes one " a murderer." Matt. v. 22.—Persecutors at judgment will not put in the Jesuit plea that they murdered the saints of God "*for the greater glory of God*."—Jesuits have ever made the moral law bend to their selfish evil purposes.—Satan, in seducing our race, infused the spirit of *hate* in all mankind.—As Satan aimed at murdering the father of our race, so these Jews aimed to kill Him who brought life to the race.—As he used falsehoods to ruin Adam, so he used frauds to destroy Jesus.

Beginning. Not of his existence, but of human history.
Satan lusted after the ruin of men from the first.
The sentence threatened embraced DEATH of the *body* and SOUL.
Gen. ii. 17.—At the fall that doom began to *issue* in its terrible
fulfilment.—The revelation of redemption does not change the
historic fact,—Wide is the way to death eternal, and MANY GO
IN THEREAT! Matt. vii. 13.—Broad as the wide world. All
paths converge into this.—A narrow, insignificant, mountain
path leads to life, *Tholuck;* "and few there be that find it."
Matt. vii. 14.

Abode. Gr. *And doth not stand.* He is perpetually in the act of
apostasy from the truth. *Lücke.*—Falsehood is the sphere in
which he stands : in it he has his station. *Meyer.*
There is a life of truth to stand in or *revolt* from. Matt. xii. 25.
By Divine power unfallen angels stood firm in truth in the house
of Infinite Love.—This passage does not directly teach the fall
of the devil, but it pre-supposes it.—**Abode not** has the force of
the present, and indicate the permanent character of the devil,
but this status is the result of a previous apostasy.—God made
all things through His LOGOS (chap. i. 3), and made the rational
beings, both angels and men, pure and sinless, yet liable to
temptation and fall. *Schaff.*—Scripture gives no information as
to the time of the creation and fall of Satan and his angels.

No truth in him. Void of all holy transparent rectitude originally possessed.—His habitual character is false, his delight is in
fraud.—His great lie of lies is, that peace can be found apart
from God. Isa. li. 21.—Our Lord implies Jews bore his image
in falsehood as in malignity.

Speaketh. An old proverb, "Satan speaking the truth, the greatest
lie."—His abiding, systematic, sole manner of acting is here
affirmed.—Essentially a liar, he cannot and will not do otherwise.

A lie. Not only a wilful falsehood, but ERROR itself. Rom. i. 25 ;
2 Thess. ii. 9.

His own. Out of his own *nature;* out of his own *resources.*
Lies originate from his *own will.*—His vernacular tongue, and that
of all his family, is falsehood.

Liar. Scripture gives a profounder idea of a lie than philosophers.
What men often call honest conviction, tested by Divine light will
be found to conceal many a falsehood.—Falsehood of Jews two-
fold: first, hypocritically claiming God as Father; and secondly,
denying that they intended to kill Him.—Lying begets hatred,

and hatred begets persecution to the death.—A lie is the cowardice of selfishness, hatred its proud overflow.

Hatred springs from lying, as needful to carry out its plans. Under a fiery passion for falsehood, the seared heart loses all *sense* of truth. As the hand, roughly used, becomes callous and insensible to touch.—The deceiving heart becomes thus liable to be duped by others.—No one is so terribly deceived as he who tries to deceive others.—Satan began his dark empire by lies, and by them upholds it still.—Created by a God of truth,— " *he abode not in the truth.*"—His nature has become a *lie*, and he is thoroughly *alien* from the truth of God.—As his deeds bring death everywhere, so his words breathe out lying.

" The world is an inn, over whose doors we read ' *lying* and *murder.*' To ruin body and soul is the work of this hostelry." *Luther.*—A liar is ever mean and base ; himself a deceiver, he fears all others.—Cowards are ever cruel ; all tyrants are of this class.—Nero, a bloody persecutor, trembled whenever it *thundered.*—True bravery is found alone in honest, noble hearts.

Father. He, by one lie, caused the being of all liars since born. A contrast between the sons of God and the sons of the devil,—a liar is a child of the devil.—The rule is to utter falsehood under the mask of the semblance of truth.—As all forgers select a solvent bank, so the wicked counterfeit truth.—No one forges on a broken bank. No one deceives under the mask of sin.

What a compelled tribute do the wicked thus pay to virtue !

All wicked ones, living or dead, belong to the empire of " the Black Prince."—But there is " a Stronger than he," Who overcomes him. Luke xi. 22.

Of it. More literal, *thereof.* Father of all liars, especially of these Jews.

πατρὸς. Of a father who is the devil. *Meyer.* The idea clearly confined to ethical fatherhood by the placing of *father* first. *Lange.* Not by birth, but imitation. *Augustine.*

θέλετε ποιεῖν. Emphatically *ye will*,—are *determined* to do. *Winer.* It implies freedom of the will. *Alford.* Rather man's perfect *responsibility.* Adam's will, *before the fall*, was free. *Author.*

ἀνθρωποκτόνος. 1. A murderer as the author of the fall of Adam, by which death came on man. *Orig., Chrys., Aug., Theoph., Luther, Calvin, Lampe, Olsh., Meyer, D. Brown, Alf., Luth., Gerlach, Wordsworth.* 2. As the instigator of Cain's murder of Abel. *Cyril, Nitzsch, Lücke, De Wette, Kling.* 3. Generally described as a murderer without any special reference. *B. Crusius, Brückner.* 4. The murderous work of Satan in all history. *Theod., Heracleon, Euthym.* The chief stress plainly lies on the temptation of Adam. *Lange.*

ἀπ' ἀρχῆς. Beginning of the Creation. *Lampe.* Foundation of the world. *Nonnus.* From the time that there were for him men to murder. *Stier.* Satan fell immediately at his creation. *Aug.* The origin of evil is a mystery. Freedom of will an inseparable attribute of a responsible being,—this implies a possibility of choosing evil. *W. H. Mill.* This is only true of *sinless* beings. *Author.*

ἕστηκεν. Primitive meaning to take one's stand. *Ernesti, Alford.* Attained not a fixedness. *Bengel.* Finds no resting place in truth. *Gerlach.* Did not establish himself in the truth of life. *Beck.* Implies his fall as a continuous, not isolated event. *Olsh.* Relation of an eternal, centrifugal repulsion. *Klee.* Present tense implies a continual aberration. *D. Brown.*

ὅτι. Not *although*, but "*because.*" *D. Brown.* Truth is not to be sought in him. *Hezel.*

ἀλήθεια. In the second clause, objective truth of God. *Stier.*

τὸ ψεῦδος. The nominative,—the lie,—i. e. antichrist. *Origen.* Latent ψεῦδος, found in the concrete ψεύστης. *Winer.*

τῶν ἰδίων. Out of his own "treasures." Matt. xii. 35. *Alford.* In his proper kind. *De Wette.* Not tempted, purely self-begotten sin. *D. Brown.*

ψεύστης. All falsehood on earth owes its existence to him. *D. Brown.* An habitual liar. *Sophocles.*

ὁ πατήρ. Father of *the* lie. Refers to the first lie recorded in history by which the devil seduced Eve. *Origen, Euthym., Lücke.* Christ speaks not merely of the father of the *lie*, but of the *liars*. *Lange.* Father of the *liar*. *Bengel, B. Crusius, Meyer, Tholuck, Stier, Alford.*

αὐτοῦ. "*Thereof.*" A.V. inexact. *Thol., Alf.* Greek language has no word for "author." *Beza.* Very important testimony to the inspiration of Genesis and the account of the apostasy. *Braune.*

---

45. And because I tell you the truth, ye believe me not.

Because. Had·He been false, they would have hailed Him as king.—Not to believe Him, is wilful treason against the Father. The very utterance of the truth made them reject and hate the Lord of glory.—When light is despised because *it is light*, then darkness is loved for its own sake.

I. He opposes majestically all the false sayings of Satan.

I, whose birth was foretold four thousand years since.

I, whose nativity was heralded by the Angel of God in holy song.

I, whose stupendous miracles none can work without God's aid.

I, whose sinless life challenges any one to point out a single spot.

Tell the truth. Could man's moral nature be more completely ruined?—They refuse to believe the Son of God simply *because* He tells the *truth*.—Could Satan himself have cried more bitterly, "Away with Him?"—Their foundations of being were so *saturated* with falsehood, that truth, instead of being a recommendation, was a hindrance.—Hence "liberals" and infidels of all kinds embrace a delusion for the very reason why they ought to reject it.

Believe not. If I were to falsify, then would ye believe Me!

Then would I speak what is peculiar to your father the devil.
Is it possible that men can *disbelieve* a thing simply because it is
true? Our Lord boldly answers, Yes.—Truths of the natural
world involve no change of life or heart.—But belief in the
Atonement, implies all mankind have sinned, and are exposed to
eternal punishment.—Because the doctrine of Atonement is
truth, therefore men hate it, and deny it is found in Scripture,
and affirm it contradicts God's nature.—Prejudice, alienation
from integrity, and above all a chosen course of vice, will cause
the mind to hate the truth, as owls do light.

ἐγὼ δὲ forcibly put first. In opposition to the devil. *Thol., Meyer.*
Opposition to the Jews as the spiritual children of the devil. *Lange.* As far as
regards Me. *Bloomfield.* An elegant emphasis strengthening the contrast.
Lampe.
δὲ ὅτι. A charge of wilfully resisting truth. *Alford.* If I had spoken
false, ye would believe Me. *Euthymius.*

---

46. Which of you convinceth me of sin? And if I say the truth, why do ye
not believe me?

Which? Gr. *Who?* A bold challenge to the world.
Let any one on earth testify against Me.—Of none of Adam's race
can it be said, " *He knew no sin.*" 2 Cor. v. 21.
Convinceth. Gr. *Convicteth.* HE NEVER PRAYED FOR PARDON.
Our Lord had shown falsehood and sin to be linked together.
His soul, ever overshadowed by the Divine, could not be deceived
by the tempter.—No trace of guilt without, no trace of evil
within.—A common but reckless saying,—" My own conscience
is clear." " I care not what all the world says."
Here Christ had respect to what the Scribes and Pharisees said.
Acts xxi. 20, 24.—Secure first, peace with God, then, if possible,
with the world.—With Christ alone Righteousness was *vertical,*
casting no *shadow.*—Among all the malice and blasphemy of
earth, no one ever doubted HIS PIETY.—He who reproves the
world, must be such that the world can't reprove.—Even " the
snuffers " of the sanctuary were made of pure gold. Exod.
xxxvii. 23.
Of sin. If I am without sin—and none of you can prove the contrary—I am also without error.—He here presents Himself as
THE LIVING IMPERSONATION of holiness and truth in inseparable
union.—He claims MORAL PERFECTION to HIMSELF.

He had claimed *supreme Divinity* as the Son of God.

He speaks this great truth *absolutely, definitely, solemnly.*

Scripture testifies to His sinlessness. " He is the Holy and Just One." Acts iii. 14. " Tempted, yet without sin." Heb. iv. 15. " Holy, harmless, undefiled." Heb. vii. 26. " He knew no sin." 2 Cor. v. 21. 'A lamb without blemish and without spot." 1 Pet. i. 19. " And in Him is no sin." 1 John iii. 5.

His majesty of moral character is placed before us in vivid reality.

His world-embracing love, did the noblest things, and stooped to the humblest.—He never confessed a sin, and never asked forgiveness.—He allowed Himself to be baptized *solely* to obey an ordinance.—By deepest suffering " He learned obedience." Heb. ii. 10.—Such a challenge flung to foes cunning and fierce is a claim to *absolute sinlessness.*—He acted as the PARDONER of sin, promising *peace* to the soul.—Nay, as JEHOVAH HIMSELF, He authorizes His disciples to " remit sins." John xx. 22, 23.

There is a distance between Him and us which none can traverse.

The idea of forming a society, embracing the whole human family, never before entered the minds of sages or lawgivers, or founders of empires.—By His union with God, He offers to bring God into union with *men.* The holiest high priest himself needed to be cleansed from sin. Heb. vii. 27.

He is THE FOUNTAIN in which all must be cleansed from sin.

He is THE JUDGE, and must be sinless, or else He will *condemn* Himself. Rom. ii. 1.—His very *servants* must shake off the dust of sin from their feet.—The bells on the priest's clean and white linen garments denoted *Righteousness.* Rev. xix. 8.

Even *Josephus* the accomplished Pharisee names Jesus with respect and good feeling.—His enemies, after the most venomous efforts, could never cast a stain on His apostles' character.

Pilate, a thorough worldling, was irresistibly impressed by His dignity and innocence.—And by a dream his wife testified that He was " a just man."—The Roman centurion and the thief unite in saying He was a righteous man.—Judas could not find aught by which to quiet his conscience, and died honouring Christ in *despair*, as martyrs died honouring Him in *love.*

The historical idea of sinlessness never arose before, and never since attached itself to any human being.—The Greeks and Romans never conceived of *a sinless God* in their Pantheon.

They had no *word* for the idea,—" Ever to excel others "

(*Homer*) is the nearest approach.—Christ's source of greatness was Divine *condescension.*—He professed no special calling, neither prophet, priest, nor king.—His repose was not the silence of ice-bound seas, but of warm, deep, Divine goodness.
In His woes He never betrays personal irritation.
He had no national peculiarity. He embraced the circle of the human race, and for it He sought to live and dared to die.
His obedience was not to law, but the living personal Author of law.
His love was a preventing love, a pitying love, a transforming love.
His ceaseless activity betrayed no excitement, ever working, yet calm in majesty.—For the idea of such a character, one would be willing to be broken on the wheel, or burnt to ashes at the stake. *Ullmann.*—Even an infidel was compelled to say the " Inventor of the character of Christ is more wonderful than the hero." *Rousseau.*—His answer at 12 years of age prepares us for all His coming glory. Luke ii. 49.—He accepted as proper the profound homage of John, knowing it was due to God alone.
Who ever before offered to men pardon, or the gift of the Holy Ghost?
The character of *Socrates* as drawn by his disciples Plato and Xenophon was an effort to paint a perfect philosopher.
Homer's *Ulysses;* Virgil's *Æneas;* Milton's *Adam;* Voltaire's *Henry;* and Fénélon's *Telemachus,* are efforts to paint perfect characters, but they come infinitely short of the portrait drawn by fishermen.—He never did an imprudent thing, always acted with Divine wisdom.—He lived His matchless sermons as well as preached them.—What ineffable humility as He stands rebuked by miserable sinners !—As the Holy One of Israel, He awaits patiently their condemnation.—We may suppose a sublime *pause* here intervenes.—He has put the question, and is silent ; *they are silent also.*—But once in the world's history did a man, from its countless millions, produce the impression, that a character was unfolding of *perfect purity* and *sinless holiness.* *Ullmann.*

The truth. Had they *dared,* they would boldly have denied that He did.—But with miracles blazing all around them, they were silent.—With thousands of healed bodies,—so many living, moving, eloquent witnesses.—Could they have detected a single slip of the tongue, a solitary burst of passion, would they have kept silence ?—Nineteen centuries of keen-eyed scepticism have detected *no flaw* in His words, works, life.

Why? Convict Me of sin and reject Me.—If ye cannot, why resist?

Believe. John i. 7; vii. 38. His question is redoubled. If not a sinner, wherefore believe ye not My word? A glorious dilemma!—" Who hath bewitched you, that you will not obey the truth?" Gal. iii. 1.—The answer is,—" Rebellion is as the sin of witchcraft, and stubbornness as idolatry." 1 Sam. xv. 23. " Because thou hast rejected the word of the Lord, He hath rejected thee." 1 Sam. xv. 23.—Many accepted His miracles, but rejected His doctrines.—Thus, many now believe firmly in *the* Christ, but reject the REDEEMER.

ἐλέγχει. " To put to shame." *Homer.* " Convince," obsolete for " convict." We may *convict* one of sin without *convincing* him. *J. Brown.*

περὶ ἁμαρτίας. 1. Means here error or intellectual defeat. *Orig., Cyril, Erasmus.* 2. Sin in speech, *untruth, falsehood. Melancth., Hoffmann.* False doctrine. *Calvin.* 3. Sin, the *moral* offence. *Lücke, Stier, Luth., Meyer, Alf., Web. & Wilk.* This is the uniform usage of ἁμαρτία in the N. T. *Schaff.* He is Redeemer, not as not being able to sin, but as not having sinned. *Stendel.* Old Test. taught His sinlessness. Isa. liii. 7. *Umbriet.* It involved His Divine mission. *Alford.* They would not be bound to believe Him if they could convict Him of error. *Kling.* Sin within the sphere of His office as Messiah. *Bengel, Tholuck.* A question of self-consciousness, not fearing contradiction. *De Wette.* This does not assert directly the absolute sinlessness of Christ, since none but God could see the heart. *Stier.* But it does affirm His conscience free from guilt, His inner life unstained. *Lücke.* By ὑμεῖς He excludes Himself from sinful men. *Weber.* If groundless, we must believe Him the victim of self-delusion. *Ullmann.* Ancient philosophers, Plato, Xenophon, Demosthenes, &c., denied that any one could live without sin. *Luthardt.* Plato draws a picture of a perfect man, but he is a sufferer, and will be bound, scourged, tortured, blinded, and at last hanged. *De Republica.* Christ's Divinity inferred, since He was perfect. *Wolf.* This " Who?" is a *challenge* to all beings! His Divine doctrine made a proof of a sinless life. *Tisch.* His sinlessness proved by His resurrection. *Fritzsche.* His baptism is mere compliance to law. *Neander.* Our Saviour's birth from a virgin, the keynote of His sinlessness, placing Him above that secured by regeneration. *Mastricht, Witsius.*

δὲ. Omitted. *Tisch., Alf., Treg.*

πιστεύετέ. If free from sin, then free from falsehood, trustworthy. *Meyer.* Knowledge of truth rests on purity of the will. *De Wette.* John makes this knowledge intuitive. *Meyer.* His being immaculate, a proof of His knowledge. *Ullmann.*

---

47. He that is of God heareth God's words: ye therefore hear them not, because ye are not of God.

He that. Since ye have answered the first question by silence, I will answer the second,—Those alone who are " of God, hear

the words *of God.*" Ye, as *aliens* from God, " hear them not."
John iii. 31.

Is of God. Describes a person as the peculiar property of another.—The Jews, Samaritans, all nations, in this sense, are
God's property.—Those born " not of the will of the flesh, but
of God," are here meant. John i. 13.

Heareth. 1. Attention of the body. 2. Intention of the mind.
3. Retention of the memory.—Equivalent to listen, attend, believe, obey ; to be *one* with Christ.—His servants simply say,
" Speak, Lord." 1 Sam. iii. 9.—They leave issues with Him.
" Every one that is of the truth, heareth My voice,"—a lover and
doer. John xviii. 37.—Men are not wicked by compulsion, but
wilfully reject God's counsels. Luke vii. 30.—We cannot think
rightly of God, unless we somewhat resemble Him.
Alexander kept the Iliad under his pillow, to become like its heroes.
How carefully does He draw the line of awful separation between
those *of God* and those *not of* God.—The sting of this truth in
their hearts is measured by their scorn. Verse 48.—A son
prizes and studies an absent father's message.—But " gold and
the honeycomb " express believers' love of truth. 1 John iv. 6.

Hear not. Hebraism for not approving, embracing, obeying.
A drum brings the tiger out of its den in a rage.—So the truth
arouses the tiger in every unrenewed heart.—No surer sign of
a *reprobate* than anger at the Gospel of peace.—1. Some defiantly refuse to come *where* they may hear.—2. Others *intend*
to disregard, loving the present world. 2 Tim. iv. 10.
3. Others with tears of joy receive the truth, but, tempted, abide
not to the end.—" Ye did run well (that is, for a time) ; who
did hinder you ? " (from winning the victory). Gal. v. 7.
Truth and its lot upon earth : 1. It is rejected, but does not keep
silence. 2. It is reviled, but wearies not. 3. It is persecuted,
but does not succumb. *Rautenberg.*

ἐκ τοῦ θεοῦ. Of *Divine essence and origin*, in dualistic, Manichean sense
of two originally different classes of men. *Hilgenfeld.* Elect, predestinated.
Aug., Piscator. Born again. *Luther* and *Evangelical Commentators.* Non
natura, sed fide; non ore, sed amore. *Ludolph.* Words apply to the adopted
sons of God. *Lampe.* Imply imitating God. *Euthymius.*
ἀκούετε. Yet many after the Crucifixion did hear and obey. *Cor. à Lapide.*

---

48. Then answered the Jews, and said unto him, Say we not well that thou
art a Samaritan, and hast a devil?

Answered. Proud malignants, they dreaded to have their vileness unveiled.—They shrank back from the mirror, and would have dashed it to pieces.—Rallying all their fierce fanaticism, they revile and blaspheme.—Bereft of truth, they become shameless in their guilt.—For depravity, long persisted in, renders the heart both rude and hard.—Our Lord meets with passionate " contradiction of sinners." Heb. xii. 3.

Say we not well ? A self-complacent reply : *Are we not right?* Form of the expression shows they do not utter these words for the first time.—To His reproaches they oppose insults, hoping to silence Him.

Samaritan. John iv. 9.—Doubtless the designation of a *heretic.* Includes also the accusation of a spurious origin, and an adversary of orthodox Judaism. *Meyer.*—A hard name is easier than a hard argument.—As' much as to say, Thou art an alien, estranged from the true God and true Israel.—A term of the most intense contempt known to ancient Jews.—Who but a sworn foe of the holy nation could call us slaves ?—It needed the ignorance and impudence of a Samaritan to forge it.—1. Because with Samaritans He rejected the traditions of the elders.—2. Because He had intercourse with Samaritans, and preached to them. Luke xvii. 16.—3. Because in His famous parable He had set up *one* for Jews' imitation. Luke x. 33.—4. Nazareth, near to Samaria, was His birthplace, and much despised.

They would exclude Him from Israel's promises, and Israel's God. Samaritans and slaves could not testify in Jewish courts of justice. The intensity of their malice measures the depth of their *troubled conscience.*—While Stephen's face became radiant as an *angel's*, they gnashed their teeth. Acts vi. 15 ; vii. 54.

Malice is reckless whether it wound or kill.

Devil. See on John vi. 70 ; vii. 20. Gr. *Demon.* "Devil" an inexact translation.—Christians were called Atheists, Galileans, &c.—Elisha, a "mad fellow." 2 Kings ix. 11.—Luther, a trumpeter of rebellion.—1. He was charged with working miracles through Beelzebub.—2. The devil sought to make himself equal with God,—so did He.—3. That the folly of His words, and blasphemy of His pretences, were inspired by Satan.

When the wicked cannot crush, they persecute, "which, if not victory, is still revenge." *Milton.*—What boundless patience in Jehovah ! "The riches of His long-suffering !" Rom. ii. 4.

But His *heavenly tranquillity* remained undisturbed by all their rage.—The depths of His compassion were moved, and He only pitied them.

οὐ καλῶς. Betrays some fear in the bold blasphemy. *Bengel.*
Σαμαρείτης. One pretending to believe in Judaism, and being a Samaritan. *Origen.* Because Christ taught a new religion. *Jewel.* A desertion from the law. *Hammond.* One corrupting the law and despising tradition. *Author.* A mongrel, pretending to be partly Jew, but in reality a heathen. *Trench.*
δαιμόνιον. See Critical Notes on John vi. 70; vii. 20. Not the same charge as He had made. His reply is,—No under spirit actuated Him. *Maurice.* Each one more or less is under demoniac influence. *Origen.* Because He claims perfect sinlessness. Verse 46. *Chrys.* Implies aggravated madness. *Alford.*

---

49. Jesus answered, I have not a devil; but I honour my Father, and ye do dishonour me.

Answered. Exhibits wonderful proof of our Lord's self-command, patience, and freedom of spirit; His frankness, His prudence, His wisdom, His incorruptibleness, His love.—"When reviled, He reviled not again." 1 Pet. ii. 23.—"Our answer to their reason is, No!—to their scoffs, nothing." *Hooker.*—He ever opposed the highest excitement of passion with the deepest tranquillity.—Compare the calm repose of Stephen with the tumultuous Caiaphas.—The quiet of our Redeemer with the restless, guilty Pilate.—The grand serenity of Milton with the volcanic passion of Byron.—The heavenly, humble trust of the martyr Rogers with the remorseful death of Elizabeth.—The righteous "fall asleep," Acts vii. 60, but "A tempest steals away (the wicked) in the night." Job xxvii. 20.

I have not a devil. I is emphatic. "Whoever is under Satan's power, not **I**."—He does not say, "I am not a Samaritan." With sublime self-control and calmness He ignores the first reproach.—He will not recognize the name of *Samaritan* either as a title of abuse or a verdict of rejection.—He had already believers amongst Samaritans, and in His parable had represented Himself as "THE GOOD SAMARITAN." *Lampe.*—It was infinitely preferable to be a believing Samaritan than an unbelieving Jew.

I honour. By honouring His authority and obeying His commands.—He well knew one word of flattery would set the whole

nation in a blaze of enthusiasm for placing Him on the throne.
His Father sent Him on another errand, and nothing could divert
Him.—A " no ! " would have provoked a passionate reply.
He condescendingly opposes blasphemies, if so He can *win* them.
1. I honour Him by my sinless life,—" Who convinceth me of
sin ? "—2. By condemning the works of the devil, as murder
and lying.—3. By giving all the glory of my deeds to God,—
Satan cannot do this.

My Father. Their insults of the Son reached the Father through
Him.—This reply furnishes counter-proof that He is no Sa-
maritan, and has no demon.—He proves by word and life that
God is His Father, therefore He is no Samaritan.
He is not possessed of a *dark spirit*, but full of the Spirit of the
Father, and glorifying Him. *Lange.*

Ye dishonour Me. They insult in Him the living representative
of God's glory, therefore GOD HIMSELF.—How far will this apply
to " Liberals " and others who *now* deny His supreme Godhead ?
The depth of His emotion is shown by the short, pregnant sentences.—If a *wise* man slander thee, endure him ; if a fool,
pardon him.—" For Thy sake I have borne reproach I am a
stranger to my mother's children."—Psa. lxix. 7—9.

ἀπεκρίθη. "Luther calls me a devil; I will honour and love him as a
servant of God." *Calvin.*
οὐκ ἔχω. No retort in the emphatic. *Cyril, Lücke.* Simply contrast of
the parties. *Alford.*
τιμῶ. I announce only His truth. *Lücke.* The present tense hints, "I
must testify in My own behalf." *Stier.* His adhering to Jewish customs, a
sufficient reply. *Roos.* I justify Myself only against invective. *B. Crusius.*
The Father's interests are identical with those of the Son. *Luther.*
καί. Belongs to the consummate peacefulness and mildness of the word of
His victorious benignity. *Stier.*

---

50. And I seek not mine own glory : there is one that seeketh and judgeth.

I seek not. Our Lord's true motive was obedience to His Father
at any price to self.—The end was that glory adorns His brow
with " many crowns." Heb. xii. 2 ; Rev. xix. 12.

Own glory. Load Him with reproaches as they will, He will not
vindicate Himself.—In the deepest abasement He came, hiding
His majesty.—Not honour, but their salvation, He earnestly

and perseveringly sought.—Our Lord well knew many would
perish through despising Him.—He knew myriads would have
followed Him if He had flattered them.—Yet He never tried to
be great as a means to attract souls.—If God trust His honour
in our poor hands, can we not trust ours in His ?

Men making their own glory their aim, usurp the rights of their
Creator.

Seeketh. Supply " my glory " after " seeketh," but not after
" judgeth."—He will one day demand it of those now refusing
it.—" To Him every knee *shall* bow, and every tongue shall
confess." Phil. ii. 10.—With Him I seek to rescue you from
the grasp of a " liar and a murderer." Ver. 44.

Judgeth. This warning points to a coming day of retribution.

My Father will judge between Me and all those rejecting Me.
Psa. xliii. 1.—All public and secret dishonour to THE SON will
be made known.—At the judgment day, nothing will so amaze
Gospel-despisers as the number and degree of their sins against
CHRIST !—Unbelief is the sin that dyes the very soul with crimson
hues. Isa. i. 18.—" Whosoever shall not hearken to My words,
which He shall speak in My name, I will require it,"—Deut.
xviii. 19,—i. e. surely punish him. Acts iii. 23.

A flash of omniscience over the dreadful *future* of all Gospel-despisers.

---

51. Verily, verily, I say unto you, If a man keep my saying, he shall never
see death.

Verily. John i. 51 ; iii. 3.—After the doctrine then follows the
application.—He had unfolded their terrible relations to the devil.

He tells them how to cease to be children of the evil one, and become sons of God.—As if with a loud cry of warning, He
would rescue them from the flames of judgment.

No unmeaning tautology ; it has all the solemnity of an oath.
Heb. vi. 18.—He was never wearied in His work of salvation :

Bound, He preached with His loving eyes.   Luke xxii. 61.

Silent, He preached with His flowing tears.   John xi. 35.

Dying, He preached with His atoning blood.   Zech. xii. 10.

If a man. Judgment is His strange work.   Isa. xxviii. 21.

From it, He turns away to the work of mercy, i. e. preaching the
Gospel.—If ever among such daring blasphemers as you *any
one*, &c.—Here we find an epitome of the whole Covenant of

Grace.—This great Gospel reverberates far into that judgment
now begun.—The solemn future, with its joys and woes, stood
before His mind.—1. A system so benign in itself and in its
results, must be from God.—2. These Gospel offers are proposed
to those who calumniate Him.—3. The true deliverance of the
mind from doubts is faith in truth.

Keep. Reference to the standing formula,—salvation hangs on
obedience. Exod. xv. 26.—Signifies much more than hearing.

A man may lose knowledge utterly, but the habit of obedience remains.—The keeping of faith is only proved by holiness.

Kept (James i. 25) as the seed of Divine life, until it bears fruit.

" Keep " corresponds to " continue " (ver. 31), a living, permanent
principle.—1. Believing what He says. 2. Hoping for what
He promises. 3. Obeying what He commands.

My saying. Our translators unhappily change " word " into
" saying." The latter is used as that entering the " ear," the
former as that entering the " heart."—If a man cling to " My
word " he lives ; if he part from it, he dies.—The majestic
" **My** " indicates His lofty claims as Lord of the Kingdom.

As a flash of lightning is its own evidence, so Christ's words oft
affect the mind with the consciousness of present Deity.

But even to His revilers He holds out the sceptre of mercy.

Never see. The most naked statement of a very glorious truth.

See death. Orientalism for dying.—" Seeing death " here first
occurs, it is *to know* death, as such.—Expiring, the believer first
begins fully and perfectly to live!—Believers die, fearing nothing,
being " filled with THE FULNESS of GOD." Eph. iii. 19.

As one walking towards the sun, sees not his shadow behind him.

Christ tells them of a life to gain,—He warns them of a death to
shun.—He unconditionally claims LIFE for His disciples, BECAUSE
THEY ARE HIS.—To them death, having become the GATE OF
LIFE, is no more to be called death.—His hearers think He
alludes to temporal death, Rev. ii. 11 ; but in Scripture, death
is not merely ceasing to breathe, nor life merely the beating of
the heart.—His word will carry believers, not only safely
through, but beyond judgment and death.—Christians really
experienced this at the destruction of Jerusalem.

Life " hid with Christ " shall pass entirely safe through the whole
succession of judgments, and will not see death even in the final
judgment. *Lange.*

"In Christ I live! In Christ I draw the breath
Of the true life!—Let then earth, sea, and sky
Make war against me! On my front I show
Their mighty Master's seal. In vain they try
To end my life, that can but end its woe.—
Is that a death-bed where a Christian lies?—
Yes! but not his—'tis Death itself there dies." *Coleridge.*

ἀμήν. Turning from enemies, these words are limited to believers. *Calvin, Tisch.* Incorrect to assume this. The thought of the terrible judgment always awakened in Him an impulse of pity and mercy. *Lange.* Addressed to those whom He had just described as children of the devil. *Alford.* The Gospel is to be preached even at the mouth of the pit. *Bunyan.*

θάνατον. Emphatic. *Stier.* So little fellowship have I with Satan, that he murders, and I give life. *Aug., Beza.* Here the national spiritual life, sharing in God's immortality. Even all family and national feeling have their root in God. *Maurice.* An argument against the annihilation of the soul. *Bengel.* They supposed a material kingdom and death. *Chemnitz.*

θεωρήσῃ. He shall mori vitaliter, i. e. live though he die. *Trappe.* "Dum spiro, spero," Epicure would say. "Dum exspiro, spero," Christian replies. *Leighton.*

---

52. Then said the Jews unto him, Now we know that thou hast a devil. Abraham is dead, and the prophets; and thou sayest, If a man keep my saying, he shall never taste of death.

Said. The answer of blind bigotry and malice to His enticing call of mercy.—They fasten upon His word of compassionate love, as heresy.—How malice ever tries to make others as vile as itself.

Now we know. As much as to say, There can be no doubt now this man is mad, insane by pride.—At last we know positively what we have before accused you of.—Whether He pipe or mourn, they complain. Luke vii. 32.—Neither judgment nor mercy will please "reprobate minds." Rom. i. 28.

The more the wicked hear, the more incorrigible do they become.

First they *thought,* then they *said,* and at last they *knew* He had a devil!—Depraved minds are ever seeking for some colour of pretence to justify their hatred of the godly.

Devil. Gr. *Demon.* See on John vi. 70; vii. 20.

Abraham. See on John viii. 33.—Their misunderstanding has malice for its ground-tone, but now theocratic pride unites with carnal sensuousness.

Is dead. These carnal-hearted Jews had no conception of life, but bodily.—No idea of the higher life binding Him to patri-

arch and prophet.—The patriarch was living the higher form
of life at that moment.—If He could guarantee His disciples
from death, then surely He Himself must be above the power
of death.—Thus He exalts Himself above Abraham.

" What man liveth (Heb. *What hero ?*) and shall not see death ? "
Psal. lxxxix. 48.—This question finds its answer *only* in Christ.
" The patriarchs kept God's sayings, and are dead.   Are Thy say-
ings more than God's ? "—They speak like the Samaritan woman.
John iv. 12.

Prophets.   John iv. 19.—Pre-eminently honoured of God,—as
heralds of His laws—as expounders of His will—as announcers
of His judgments—as comforters of His people—as leaders of
His hosts—as guardians of His glory—and as recruiters of His
kingdom,—yet they all are dead.—They argue : He who promises to others bodily immortality, must Himself possess it in
a still higher degree.   But since Abraham and the prophets
died, it is a demoniacal self-exaltation if you claim freedom from
death. *Lange.*

Taste.   Makes prominent the special *bitterness* of death.
Ancients gave to persons doomed to die a cup of poison.
They cannot, it seems, lift their mind above the regions of sense.
Our Lord spake of *seeing*, they of *tasting*, death.—The wicked
draw only poison from the fairest flowers of the Divine Word.
Lampe.

οὖν.   Omitted. *Cod. Sinai., Lach., Tisch., Alford.*   Retained. *Stier.*
γεύσεται instead of θεωρήσῃ.   A perversion of His meaning. *Luca. Brug.*
A usual expression among the Rabbins. *Wetstein.   Not to see death*, denotes
the *objective* side of the believer's experience, according to which death is
changed into a metamorphosis of life : *not to taste death*, means the *subjective*
emancipation from the guilty sinner's dread and horror of death. *Lange.*

---

53. Art thou greater than our father Abraham, which is dead ? and the prophets are dead : whom makest thou thyself ?

Greater.   Inasmuch as our Lord pledges eternal life to one keeping His word.   *This*, great as were Abraham and the prophets,
they had never proposed.—Instead of rebuking His Divine
claims, they try to reason them away.—He not only was
greater, but claimed to be from everlasting infinitely greater.
Did Abraham ever call God " My Father," or ever raise the
dead ?—Did he ever " make Himself equal with God ? "   John

v. 18.—The Jews had for ages acknowledged Messiah would be far above Moses, Abraham, or angels.—They believed He would raise the dead and judge the world even in the carnal, literal sense.—Hence, not receiving Him as Messiah, their professed astonishment at His language.—Bitter enmity prompted their treatment of His words, and utter contempt is visible in their reply. *Gerlach.*—Being Messiah, He claims all they and their fathers admitted.

Abraham and the prophets. John viii. 33.—Each claim and each word of our Lord were endorsed by the Father in His miracles.

Dead. They cannot rise toward spiritual life, being themselves carnal.

Whom? With more than half-feigned shudder at the word of self-exaltation He is about to utter. Yet with a demoniacal curiosity to know this last word. *Lange.*—" Liberals " and others still raise this question, often with ill-suppressed malignity, although Scripture and the whole *Catholic* Church bears but one witness. John i. 1—3.—What are the limits of Thy pretensions, or have they any?

---

54. Jesus answered, If I honour myself, my honour is nothing: it is my Father that honoureth me; of whom ye say, that he is your God.

If I honour. Gr. *glorify.* A protest against the reproach of self-exaltation.—He makes nothing of Himself from His own will.

It is My Father. Christianity is the *outgrowth* of the prophetic Scriptures of the Old Testament. Same Author, same Spirit, same plan, same fallen race, same precious offers of mercy, same Church, same warfare, same foes, same victories, same everlasting rest!—But Jewish perverting of the truth caused a constant conflict.—The self-styled orthodox Pharisees, in the name of the O. T. Jehovah, crucified the Messiah. " Ye do always *resist* the Holy Ghost." Acts vii. 51.—Revelation of sin and death in the O. T. the essential preparation for Redemption.—Our Lord's words, verse 51, ought to have been hailed by every true Israelite with Simeon's joy.

From Job to Malachi, RUIN and REDEMPTION are " the burden " of the prophets.

Honoureth Me. Gr. *glorifieth Me.* The fruit of self-humiliation and perfect patience. Phil. ii. 6. See on John vi. 27.
"Them that honour Me I will honour." 1 Sam. ii. 30. A contract of the Lord's own devising.—Christ's glorification went on unceasingly, but blind unbelief could not see it; just as their fathers could not see the wonders of old. Deut. xxix. 3.—Because they understood not the O. T. they neither received nor honoured Christ.

Ye say. You claim Him as your God *only*, i. e. the God of Israel in the O. T.—He distinctly asserts, that the Being He claims as FATHER, is the same as the JEHOVAH of the O. T.

Your God. Ironically said,—they were cherishing a lying, atheistical temper.—Their claim was unjust, as they did not even know Him.—Abraham well called Him THE JUDGE OF ALL THE EARTH. Gen. xviii. 25.—The promise to Abraham embraced all the families of the earth. Gen. xii. 3, &c.—This covenant by no means abolished in the N. T. Acts iii. 25, 26.

Our Lord meant, that He was greater than Abraham and the prophets.—"I am Divinely authorized to promise what they were not."—"I am able to do what they could not."—"My FATHER hath exalted Me far above Abraham."—"I am His Messenger."—"My credentials are all signed and sealed BY HIM you call *your* God."

ἐάν. Implies, It will one day come to light that Christ is the Son of God. *Hengst.*
δοξάζω. δοξάσω. *Cod. Sin.* Familiar word to John. *Schleusner.* Glorify oneself. *Wetstein.*
πατήρ μου. The main contrast seems to lie between the Jews' ignorance and Christ's knowledge of God. *Yeoman* in *Lange.*
ὑμῶν. *Cod. Sin.* ἡμῶν. *Tisch., Alf., Bengel.*

55. Yet ye have not known him; but I know him: and if I should say, I know him not, I shall be a liar like unto you: but I know him, and keep his saying.

Yet ye. They boasted no other nation did know Him but themselves.

Not known Him. That is, not thoroughly and truly,—a severe reproach, and a sad lamentation.—Ye know not His Son whom ye have seen, now how then can you know the invisible Father?

1. They knew Him not in His infinite and boundless mercy.

2. They knew Him to be the Creator of the world, but not the
Father of all mankind.—3. They knew Him not as related to
the Son and Spirit in the mystery of the Trinity.
4. They knew Him not by obedience to His laws.
5. They knew Him not in His word, therefore they knew not His
Son, revealed and reflected in promises.—Their lying was,
declaring they knew God, while their every act refuted it.
Hence their terrible blindness, and terrible rejection as a race.
" His blood be upon us, and on our children,"—an imprecation most
fearfully fulfilled. Matt. xxvii. 25.

I know Him. Contrast between " *Ye have not known* " and the
threefold " I know."—1. Having the same nature, and coming
forth from the bosom of the Father.—2. As a man, he had learned
the Father from His Divine nature, and from the Spirit.
3. By His perfect obedience to all the Father's will and pleasure.
He knew and taught the counsels of the Father faithfully and
tenderly.—But they neither knew them, nor desired to be taught
them.—Obedience to God's commands, a proof that we know
Him.

If I should. A child-like expression of sublime self-consciousness. *Lange.*—Let it not surprise you, that I avow myself before
you what I am.—Thus, almost in tones of *entreaty*, HE ASSERTS
HIMSELF DIVINE.—Such pure TRUTH condemns such deceivers.
If to avoid threatened death, or to make friends with you, I should
deny my exalted claims, I should be as false as you, when you
claim Jehovah for your God.

A liar. Either not to be what we profess to be, or refuse to profess what we are.—They boasted Abraham as their father, while
defiantly rejecting Abraham's God.—Had He through cowardly
modesty denied His peculiar and constant experience of God as
His Father, He would have become a liar like them.
They were false and hypocrites pretending to know God: He
would fall into the opposite kind of hypocrisy if He denied His
consciousness. *Lange.*—Christians should humbly and faithfully
testify for God against the world.—" Ye are my witnesses, saith
the Lord." Isa. xliii. 10.

Keep. Our Saviour both *knows* and *keeps* God's sayings. Hosea vi. 3.
We are always to *keep* whether we *know* or not. " We walk by
faith," &c. 2 Cor. v. 7.—When parental character is good, the
mere command should be sufficient for the child. *Gurnall.*
Faith simply asks, "Lord, what wilt Thou have me to do?" and the

780 / Gospel of John

darker the circumstances, the more faith triumphs. *Sir T. Brown.*
Yield everything as it regards self—nothing, absolutely nothing of
God's.—The reformer Melancthon asked till morning to consider
a point. Dr Eck the Papist replied, " This is not for your
honour, Philip." " We have not NOW to do with OUR honour,
but GOD's," was the reply.—Never let thy mouth be stopped for
Christ, till they take up stones. This is a high art, learned only
on the knees. *Luther.*—Disclosure of His Divine glory He will
await from the Father.

I know Him and keep His word. A declaration of war against
whole hell.—The word of God confided to Him, which is one
with His own consciousness, He will not permit to be torn out
of His heart by the storm of the cross. *Lange.*

οἶδα. In Triune nature. *Bede.* Far transcends the sense of any ἐγνώ-
κατε. Our Lord says first οἶδα, then τηρῶ. *Bengel.* They had no vision as
the Lord had. *Aug.* Not through obedience. *Euthym.*
ὅμοιος. "Then should I be of your kind." *Bengel.* "Like you, a liar."
De Wette.
τὸν λόγον—τηρῶ. " Keep" sounds somewhat Socinian in its tone, suggests
to carry out the command of God. *Olshausen.*

---

56. Your father Abraham rejoiced to see my day : and he saw it, and was
glad.

Your father. Our Lord admits Abraham has degenerate sons.
" Your " according to the flesh, but strangers to his faith and
spirit.
Abraham. John viii. 33.—You ask if I am greater than
Abraham ? Let him answer.—You say he is dead. I say
Abraham liveth, although dead.—Our Lord intends to link
Abraham's joy and destiny with His own.—The patriarch is
immortal, through the words of Christ.—His faith living, and
reward dying, are due to his *relation* to the Saviour.
Rejoiced. Gr. *He leaped forward with joy* that he should see.
His belief in the word of promise was the cause of his joy. Gen.
xv. 4 ; xvii. 17 ; xviii. 10.—The word translated "*rejoiced*"
occurs 270 times ; and in 200 applies to believers *alone.*
The unrenewed and unbelieving, are under God's abiding wrath.
John iii. 36.—Their revelry is unseemly, as the dancing of the
insane. Eccl. vii. 6.—It is not true joy, but hollow, a mere
mockery of the soul.—A wide contrast between the patriarch

and these Jews : He *rejoiced* in the promise, that his spiritual
" seed should be as the stars."—He *rejoiced* that God established
His covenant with him.—He *rejoiced* that " in his seed all the
nations of the earth should be blessed."—He *rejoiced* to inquire
" what manner of time the Spirit of Christ did signify."

To see. Not a revelation merely, but as an actual eye-witness.
" Abraham, then, has not seen death, but lives through My word ! "
At once He breaks through their thoughts entangled by *time*.

The **Word** Who created man, and is the Light of men, conversed
with Abraham. Abraham heard His voice, and saw His light.

Some think the vision occurred when God first called him at Ur ;
others, with more probability, that it took place at the close of the
memorable trial on Mount Moriah.—That would appear the more
fitting moment for the vision of THE LAMB God had provided.
Gen. xxii. 8 ; John i. 29.—The 11th of Hebrews reveals a clear
view of God's spiritual empire. Especially as that history is
interpreted by the Redeemer Himself. Matt. xxii. 32.

If the mere dawn kindled such joys, what the noon-day ?

He saw the glory of the Redeemer, and may have heard His birth-
song too.—If Moses and Elijah on Tabor rejoiced under the
splendour of Jesus, why should not Abraham in bright vision be
glad also ?—If the telegraph lines belting our globe annihilate
time, shall it be thought strange that God's " lines " (Psa. xix. 4)
of sympathizing LOVE should reach the humble circles of earth as
well as the loftier circles of heaven.—John, amid Patmos' rocks
and billows, heard " a new song " as it came breaking over the
crystal walls of the New Jerusalem. Rev. xiv. 3.

The angels began it at Bethlehem, and saints redeemed took up the
chorus.

My day. Our Lord often causes the veil between us and the
eternal world to tremble as though about to part.

He stood in both worlds all the while He was here. John iii. 13.
The whole record of His life is bathed in heavenly light and love.
We cannot open a page but out flashes " His excellent glory."

Day of the Messiah, a Jewish term of solemnity, used to express
the appearing of Christ. Luke xvii. 22.—*Day* of the Lord used
to express His appearing in glory at His second coming.

Day of Christ is the whole time of the N. T. as it reaches beyond
the last day to the eternal day of His glory. *Lange.*

Abraham was *persuaded* of the promise and *embraced* it. Heb. xi.
13.—His hope of the *inheritance* was based on the appearing of

the Divine Heir, who includes all other heirs and the whole inheritance.—Jews understood the Lord *rightly*, that Abraham had *actually* seen Him.—In ver. 25 He clearly hints His personal identity with "the Angel of Jehovah," and in ver. 58 declares He *existed* before Abraham.

He was glad. But these unbelieving Jews were *sorry* to hear of any *honour* to Jesus.—Note the 'unity of spirit of O. T. saints with those of the N. T.—All the faithful of former times *waited* for Christ. 1 Pet. i. 10, 12.—In answering their question He asserts : 1. Abraham did not die in their cheerless sense of death. 2. He did not raise Himself above Abraham, but Abraham subordinated himself to Him ; comp. the parallel word on David. Matt. xxii. 45. *Lange.*—As Giver of life, Abraham had joyfully expected and received life from Him. *B. Crusius.*

ἴδη τὴν ἡμέραν. 1. He foresaw the day of Christ in faith on the ground of the Messianic promises made to him during his earthly life. *Calvin, Melancthon,* &c. 2. He saw it in types : the three angels (one of them being the Logos. *Hengst.*) ; especially the sacrifice of Isaac. *Chrys., Theoph., Eras., Grotius,* &c. 3. In prophetical vision. *Jerome* and all the more *ancient expositors.* Similar to Isaiah's vision of the glory of Christ. Chap. xii. 41. *Olsh.* 4. In the celebration of the birth and meaning of Isaac (*laughing*). *Hofmann, Wordsworth.* 5. As one living in Paradise in the spirit world. *Origen, Lampe, Lücke, Meyer, Stier, Godet, Luthardt, Alford,* &c. The proper sense. *Lange.* As the angels who sang the anthem over the plains of Bethlehem. *Schaff.* See *Lange,* Amer. Edit. As the angels desire to look into the mystery of redemption, 1 Pet. i. 12, or as Moses and Elias spake with the Lord of His decease at Jerusalem. Luke ix. 31. *Tholuck.*

ἠγαλλιάσατο. Indication of changes in the realm of death, wrought by the appearing of Christ. The calm joy of the blessed, ἐχάρη, in opposition to the excited joy of anxious desire in ἠγαλλ. *Lange.*

---

57. Then said the Jews unto him, Thou art not yet fifty years old, and hast thou seen Abraham ?

Said. They seek in these strange utterances new proof of His insanity.—As though He could have been contemporaneous with one who had been in his grave 1800 years.

Their malicious misunderstanding of His words grows more and more in its folly.—They saw the chasm, at this moment, between them and Christ, very wide.—His reply was from the lofty, far-off distance of Abraham's vision.

Fifty. Thou hast not seen *half* a century, much less *twenty* cen-

turies.—*Fifty* was with the ancient Jews the full age of a man.
They *magnanimously* grant more than could be demanded in order
to give the appearance of greater absurdity to His words.
Braune —Abraham was born 1996 before Christ, 20 centuries
lacking four years.—The *early* Fathers inferred that our Lord's
person was clothed with supernatural beauty. Psa. xlv. 2.
Others, that His mental conflicts and agonies had marred His face,
and made Him look prematurely old. Isa. liii. 2.
These hypocritical pretenders to *spiritual* life were plunged in *sense*.
A gulf of nineteen centuries divided them, and confronted His claim.
Had He been much younger, He would have been charged with
presumption as a public teacher. His unwearied zeal would
have been named youthful *enthusiasm*.—Had He been aged, His
piety would have been called the fruit of *necessity*.
He had survived the passions of youth, and having forgotten its
perils, made no allowance for others.—Even His crucifixion
would have lost much of its impressiveness, if by age He had
been on the verge of the grave.

Seen ? The next verse proves the Jews had *perfectly* understood
Him.—Habitually given to prevarication, they even twist His
very words in His presence.—He had said Abraham had " seen "
His day. Now He is about to claim eternity as God.

πεντήκοντα—τεσσαράκοντα. *Chrys.* Merely an exegetical reading. *Lange.*
They intended something like mockery. *Hengst.* Premature old age from
mental agitation. *Clem.*, *Euth.*, *Eras.*, *Lampe*, *Heumann.* His solemnity of
spiritual devotion rendered His age greater. He was actually above forty.
Irenæus. Sufferings had not marred His visage. Heb. i. 9. *Bengel.* Fox
wrote "Martyrology" in 11 years,—his friends did not know him, so lean he
had become. *Trapp.* Moses at 120 had all his natural energy. *Hengst.*
Inborn æsthetical spotlessness reflected in Christ's exalted beauty of person.
Psa. xlv. 2. *Vitringa*, *Weisse.* Isa. liii. 2. His anguish would render Him
an object of pity to behold. *Munster.* Dazzling beauty not inferable, but
majesty, dignity, and grace, with calmness, may be assumed. *Ullmann.* Unlimited perfection and unapproachable dignity. *Stapfer.* Fifty the age when
Levites were pronounced emeriti. *Lightfoot.* Pharisees concede more than
usual. *Beza.* No clear inference as to our Lord's age can be drawn from this
indefinite estimate of the Jews, and *Irenæus* was influenced by a dogmatic consideration, viz. that Christ must have passed through all the stages of human
life, including old age, in order to redeem them all. *Schaff* in *Lange*, Amer. Edit.
TRADITIONARY DESCRIPTION OF OUR LORD'S PERSON.
Tall, comely, reverend countenance, to be loved and feared. Hair of the
colour of a ripe filbert, somewhat curling about His shoulders ; forehead plain
and delicate ; face without spot or wrinkle ; beard thick and short. His eyes
grey, clear and quick ; in reproving, awful ; in admonishing, courteous ; in
speaking, modest. No one ever saw Him laugh, but often weep. A man for
beauty surpassing the children of men. *Proconsul Lentulus.*

58. Jesus said unto them, Verily, verily, I say unto you, Before Abraham was, I am.

Verily. John i. 51 ; iii. 3.—These repetitions of our Lord are of the character of the ancient oracles, uttered from the PILLAR OF FIRE, or from BETWEEN THE CHERUBIM.—This stupendous declaration is deliberately uttered with all the solemnity of an oath.

Before. JESUS CHRIST THE SAME YESTERDAY, TO-DAY, AND FOR EVER. Heb. xiii. 8.—John places our Lord's pre-existence (see on John i. 1—3) in the forefront of His gospel.

This refutes the Jews' denial of Abraham having seen Christ's day.—" So far from My existence having begun later than his, I existed before he was created."—In brief, " I existed before his birth, and after his death,"—virtually, " I AM ETERNAL ! "

He sends forth a sudden flash of revelation from the depths of His eternal consciousness.—We wonder that He was so long reticent before the wretched mockers.—This gives to "*greater than Abraham,*" ver. 53, an appropriate and transcendently sufficient answer.—His eternal Divinity appears the original fount of all creation and revelation.—Honour of the Father not invaded, but the mystery of the Trinity affirmed, by " I AND MY FATHER ARE ONE " (John x. 30), therefore ETERNAL.—He gives of HIS OWN, in giving " life everlasting."—As a man, He was *after* Abraham, but He was more than man.—" Before Abraham " implies ETERNAL, ESSENTIAL EXISTENCE !

Was. Gr. implies *Creation.* "**Am**" implies *Existence,* i. e. I was **existing,** before Abraham was *created.*—Abraham's existence presupposes MINE, not Mine that of Abraham. He depends for his very existence on ME, not I on him.

I am. All interpretations denying His essential pre-existence are dishonest quibbles.—The different Greek verbs not noted in the English translation.—It is, " Before Abraham was brought into being—I EXIST !"—Denotes His perpetual Divine existence before all time. *Schaff.*—The identical name given to Moses at the bush,—" JEHOVAH." Exod. iii. 14.—Here the Saviour claims with a double " Amen," THE INCOMMUNICABLE NAME. Exod. iii. 14.—It embraces and signifies UNCHANGEABLE ESSENCE and EVERLASTING DURATION.—This is the NAME which for centuries Jews had not dared to utter.—Silently they had read it, used another in its stead, revered and adored it. Now the humble Nazarene openly assumes and claims it !

Discern the creature in Jesus; adore the Creator in CHRIST!
1. He was with God *before* all time.—2. "I am" implies perpetual presence running through all time.—3. Resting in God, He ever existed without regard to time.—As the ETERNAL LOGOS, all things were upheld by Him, Abraham among them.
God's memorable word to Moses implies the giving a full definition of this NAME to be *impossible*.—Or that finite creatures could not comprehend it, if given.—He does not say, "I am their Light, Life, Guide, Strength, or Tower."—He sets His hand to a *blank*, that *faith* may write her *prayer*.—Are believers weary? I am their strength. Poor? I am their riches. In trouble? I am their comfort? Sick? I am their health. Dying? I am their life. I am justice and mercy. I am grace and goodness. I am glory, beauty, holiness, perfection,—all-sufficient through eternity,—Jehovah!—1. As being *born*, He is our BROTHER.—2. Eating with us, He became our BREAD.
3. Dying, He became our RANSOM.—4. Reigning, He became our REWARD.—It is inconceivable that one so holy could have used such words, being consciously a creature only!—This verse clearly implies His eternal Godhead, and so the Jews understood Him.

'Aμὴν—ἀμὴν. Warns the reckless hearers to ponder earnestly. *Anton.* "Truli, truli, I seie to you, bifore that Abraham should be, I am." *Wickliff.*

γενέσθαι. The E. V. (Before Abraham WAS, *I am*) obliterates the important distinction between γενέσθαι, *to become, to begin to be, to be born, to be made*, which can be said of creatures only, and εἶναι, *to be*, which applies to the uncreated God as well. This distinction clearly appears in the Prologue where the Evang. predicates the ἐστί and ἦν of the Eternal existence of the LOGOS, ἐγένετο of the man John. *Schaff* in *Lange*, Amer. Edit. Should be made—"fieret,"—Before Abraham was made, and he could not be, but by Me, I AM. *Aug.* Pre-existence in Divine appointment,—Before Abraham became Abraham, i. e. father of Israel. *Socinus, Artemon.* Before Abraham was born, I was the destined Messiah. *Norton.* i. e. My mission was settled. *Wakefield.* Men who would deal with a neighbour's will as Socinians ("Liberals") deal with the Bible, would not be admitted into the society of honourable, upright persons. *Coleridge.* I was virtually already in being. *B. Crusius.* Pre-existence in an ideal sense. *De Wette.* Before Abraham lived I was the centre of all Divine promise. *Schleier.* Pre-existence clearly unfolded in John and Paul, and not wanting in the synoptics. *Dorner.* Refers not to pre-existent purposes, but to personal pre-existence. *Hengst.* He distinguishes between Himself and Abraham as between Creator and creature. *Lyser.* Jews inquire concerning the personal pre-existence of the Lord, He solemnly prefixes His reply with an oath. *Lampe.* Jews believed in the pre-existence of the soul, also that the Messiah existed before Creation. *Kuinoel.*

εἰμι. Present often includes the past. *Artemon* (Unitarian). With modest assurance, he calls this a "barbarism." *Bengel.* He claims the name Jehovah

or Jahovah. *McWhorter*. Jahvah. *Calvin*. "I AM" was before Abraham.
J. Brown. Not "*I was.*" Points the unchangeable character of the Godhead. *Hengst*. From Creation to the day of doom the same. *Calvin*. He does
not say "*I was*," but "I AM,"—the eternally existent Being. *Euthy*. Essential
existence ; used by Him, as a Divine Being. *Alford*. Eἶ was inscribed on the
temple at Delphi, i. e. the most perfect Name of God. *Ammonius* in *Plutarch*.
A Being that is always, having no beginning. *Plato*. That which is eternal,
steadfast, invariable. *Numenius*, a Pythagorean. Before I became a Christian,
this sublime name attracted me. *Hilary*. πρὶν sets forth the past. εἰμι embraces eternity, the past, the present, the future. *Gregory*. "Liberals" hold
that Christ came into existence before Abraham. The Lord declares He never
came into existence at all. *D. Brown*. Honest exposition cannot deny He
claims here essential pre-existence. *Lücke*.

---

59. Then took they up stones to cast at him : but Jesus hid himself, and
went out of the temple, going through the midst of them, and so passed by.

Took up. See on John v. 18.—Our Lord's words led the Jews
to a natural and correct inference.—He had claimed not merely
pre-existence, but ETERNAL EXISTENCE.

Stones. John iii. 24.—Stoning was the punishment due to all
blasphemers. Lev. xxiv. 16.—Had He been merely a *man*,
they had a *right* to stone Him. Lev. xxiv. 16.

He claimed *absolutely* and *definitely* nothing less than *to be* GOD !

They were compelled to choose between *worshipping* and *stoning*
Him.—As many workmen were engaged on Herod's Temple, it
was not necessary to tear up the splendid pavement as sceptics
suppose.—Stones of the visible Temple cast at the CORNER-
STONE of the Temple of God.—No want of means for good or
evil where there is a *will*.—Even the sacredness of the Temple,
where human blood was pollution, could not protect Him.

These are the wages the world pays the friends of God, for whom
alone the world exists.—Satan's kingdom has four instruments
of support : 1. Railing. 2. Hypocrisy. 3. Sophistry. 4. Tyranny or Persecution.—Jews from the beginning applauded this
work of blood. *Milman*.—Heathen philosophers sneered at
Christians sacrificing their lives for a CRUCIFIED ONE.

" Madness makes some, *custom* makes Galileans martyrs." *Epictetus*.

"These wretches (holy martyrs) despise death, thinking to *live
for ever.*" *Lucian*.—This slander only proves that the witnesses
of Jesus would rather *die* than *sin*.—Let us, with Stephen, look
up to heaven through a cloud of stones.—Jews punished capitally by stoning for *eighteen* different crimes.

Most culprits stoned to death were then hung up as warnings.
Greeks stoned persons for blaspheming their vain gods. *Pindar.*
Considering the frequent attempts of the Jews to stone Jesus, it
must appear the more providential that He died on the cross.
Evidence of His Divinity also that He foresaw this end from the
first. *Lange.*
1. The solemn introduction proves He claims Eternal Godhead.
2. The Evangelist aims thus to confute those denying His pre-
existence.—3. It is in perfect harmony with Abraham's seeing
His day.—4. The crowd so understood it, and took up stones
in a rage.—5. It removes all ambiguity in His words and
works.—6. The " *Ego* " " **I** " limits the personality to the Lord
Jesus Christ.—7. Nothing is said or hinted to limit the august
claims of the Son of God.—8. His reply was to the question,
Whether He had personally seen Abraham ?

Hid.   No concealment.—His retreat was prudent, humble, instructive.—Secured His safety by His Majesty, breaking through
the midst of His foes.—He did not refuse to die at the proper
time, for the proof of His Divinity.

Went out of the temple.   He came to be a sacrifice, not for
the Jews only, but for the whole world.—He required a *new*
altar, a new *place* of sacrifice, whereon He might be offered up
in sight of all the world.—Neither the avarice of Judas, nor the
wrath of the Sanhedrim, nor the will of Pilate, could determine
the time.—He Himself was a direct stupendous miracle, by day
and by night.—His claims in last verse, sustained by such
wonders, a miracle.—His leaving took all worth living for, or
praying for, with Him.—As the Divine Son of God departed
Satan entered.—What a fearful state for a Church, where Jesus
must hide Himself, and give way to blind zeal, pride, ambition,
falsehood, selfishness. *Gossner.*

" *Let us go hence!* " was the mysterious warning heard for months
at midnight over Jerusalem. *Josephus.*—The bands of government, the girdle of confidence, all loosed.—Foundations of society heaving, like billows in a storm.—All passions of anger,
wrath, malice, revenge, despair, kindled, burned, raged, devoured, as though demons held high carnival.—He did not take
refuge behind a pillar through fear, nor did He make Himself
invisible to His enemies.   He hid Himself in a cloud of glory.
By His omnipotence He disarmed their rage and malice.

Thus Christ always passes gloriously through the midst of His enemies.—Although in the end they crucified Him, they only contributed to His Eternal glorification. *Lange.*

For a moment a number yielding and believing, threw a celestial radiance around the Temple of Herod, but in these details we see the thickening crisis and the gathering storm.

TRUTH is hated : 1. Because it sees too deeply. 2. Because it speaks too plainly. 3. Because it judges too severely. *Schnur.*

ʼΗραν οὖν. Amid the blind rage of shouting, pushing, running hither and thither, Jesus escaped. *Tisch.* Jews, bigoted fanatics as they were, understood Christ far better than modern sciolists. *Hengst.*

ἐκρύβη. Vanished out of sight. *Aug., Luthardt, Wordsworth.* To become invisible is not a withdrawal, a hiding. Hid Himself amongst His adherents. *Lange, Lightfoot, Alford.* He showed boundless patience. *Bengel.* His mercy seen in absenting Himself from our sinful course. *Fonesca.* He abandons the temple of our hearts if we sin on. *Stapfer.* From those despising His words the truth is hidden. *Gregory.* Hid Himself in the secret depths of His invisible Godhead. *Hopgood.* He sought refuge in some house favourably disposed. *Lücke.* Miraculous. *Winer.* The words from διελθών to the end are wanting in *Cod. Sin., B. D., Vulgate.* They seem to have been transferred from Luke iv. 30 by way of exegesis. *Lange.* Omitted. *Tisch., Lach., Alf., Tregelles.* The addition occasioned by the idea that His departure was *miraculous,* which ἐκρύβη excludes. *Meyer.* Implies Providential protection. *Tholuck.*

John 9

1. AND as Jesus passed by, he saw a man which was blind from his birth.

Jesus. In this Gospel John gives the last public testimony of the Saviour as to His person.

Passed. This incident probably occurred at the close of the Feast of Tabernacles: the disciples doubtless had gathered round the Lord after the tumult.—The Gr. shows He did not *seek*, but the occasion for a miracle presented itself.—Our Lord, though deeply grieved, was not embittered.—He had not lost a moment. His profound unbroken repose is seen in contrast with the angry crowd.

His enemies, restless and malignant, oppose Him step by step, and in every attempt to obscure, only add to His increasing glory.

Our Lord may have taken His seat where beggars died deserted.

How all unconscious the poor blind man was of the presence of the " LIGHT of THE WORLD "!—Jews saw and heard of this stupendous miracle, but who was led to the Redeemer, save the one healed ? John ix. 38.

Saw. With a look of mercy,—compassion ever reigned in His soul.—With a similar look Zacchæus felt his heart aroused to Christ.—His loving, significant gaze was meant to attract the disciples.—They may have been disappointed at their Master's sad reception, and humbled at being thus driven by violence from the Temple.—A miracle, proving that Master almighty, would cheer them.

Man. He well knew that He would meet the poor miserable creature.—Particular Providence, bitterly opposed by infidels, because it brings His dreaded Eye on each particular heart-sin.

To *manifest* the works of God, that beggar must be there then.

By mercy, *he* would be more readily won than hardened enemies.

He was a well-known beggar in Jerusalem, and for an entire age had begged.—That this man was *born* blind was a fact familiar to many. Verse 8.

Blind. See on John v. 3.—No sense opens up so many sources of pleasure as sight.—No loss is productive of calamities so multiform or so bitter.—Sight gives body, form, and colour to all

our mental acts, even the most abstract.—The blind are unconscious of any space, except that they occupy themselves.
Some can tell the height of a person entering the room, by the
angle of his voice.—Others can distinguish the red rays of the
prism, by a delicate sense of feeling.—They apprehend danger
from every object which they approach, and are dependent on
others for every comfort.—They are considered rather prisoners
at large, than citizens of earth.—A fearful curse God pronounces
on those unkind to this class. Deut. xxvii. 18.
They are the *saddest* among the many afflicted children of men.
Sin-blinded ones have no peace, though they try hard to be merry.
Isa. xlviii. 22.—" I will have peace, though I add drunkenness
to thirst." Deut. xxix. 19.—Afflictions are sent : 1. To unfold
some concealed grace : Abraham's temptation.—2. To purify
the soul of vanity, pride, or ambition : Paul's thorn.—3. To
chastise into learning some hard lesson : Dives and Lazarus.
4. To illustrate the glory of our Redeemer and Creator : This
blind man.—5. To stimulate others to self-sacrifice for God's
glory : Martyrs.—6. To lessen our responsibilities preparatory
to the Judgment.
From his birth. Makes the miracle all the greater : places it
beyond the reach of an extraordinary medical cure.

καὶ. Hints a general relation between the last and present section. *Lange.*
παράγων. Departing. *Lampe.* Leaving the temple, He met the blind
man. *Stier, Meyer.* On the following day—being so calm after the conflict.
De Wette, Lücke, Alford. It was the Sabbath. *Lange.* Same day as the
discourse which, beginning at chap. vii. 34, reaches to the end of chap. x.
Trench.
εἶδεν. The Evangelist was himself present. *D. Brown.*

---

2. And his disciples asked him, saying, Master, who did sin, this man, or his
parents, that he was born blind?

Disciples. Believed with reason, parents' sins are visited on
children. Exod. xx. 5.
Master. A collision by the angered rabble had been just passed.
And now He quietly proceeds as though all had been peaceful.
Note how His calm repose passed into the minds of His disciples.
An ancient question, " Wherefore is light given to him in
misery ? " Job iii. 20.—A metaphysical doubt has here occurred
to fishermen.—The themes agitating schools and philosophers

for long ages meet us in our daily walks, assuming living practical forms.

Who? Pythagorean idea of the Metempsychosis, or transmigration of souls, held by a few Jews.—Doubtful that the disciples alluded to this ancient dogma.—A possible hint that he was born blind on account of sins he *would* commit in the *future.*

Did sin. A profound problem,—the relation between sin and suffering.

Asked. A clear proof that His disciples believed Him OMNISCIENT. On the ground that all suffering is punishment, saints' sorrows are disciplinary rather than penal.—Our Redeemer *suffered* for us, but can we say He was *punished ?*—A far more fit inquiry would be, " Is it not of God's mercy that we are not blind also ? "

Their Master is calmly and sympathizingly contemplating the wretched case.—A common impression children suffer with criminal parents.—This law carried out in the case of Achan. Josh. vii. 24.—Jehovah never professed to reveal the. secrets of His government. "It is the glory of God to *conceal* a thing." Prov. xxv. 2.—Job was told that God exacteth less than one's iniquity deserveth. Job xi. 6.—God's sovereignty implies He is not bound to bestow all mercies.—The disciples, true to depraved nature, inquire as to the *evil ;* our Lord speaks of the *good* to come out of it.—Here is our only key to that great question, the " ORIGIN OF EVIL."—Why was evil permitted ? BECAUSE GOD IS GLORIFIED IN ITS REMOVAL.—Why did He permit man to fall ? THAT HE MIGHT SAVE HIM.

Why does the body die? THAT HIS POWER MAY BE SEEN IN RAISING IT.—Unbelievers often discuss this theme with the desire to embarrass others.—Believers, too frequently with the hope of solving the problem that is generally considered insoluble.

This man. The warning given the paralytic might indicate the man's guilt, John v. 14, and that he was afflicted by Providence in anticipation of evil he would certainly do.

A common saying, "If he was not afflicted, he would do much worse."

Parents. Jews held that thus a kind of atonement was paid for parental guilt. An ancient opinion that sin must be punished here. Luke xiii. 1—5.—Sailors (Jonah i.) attributed storms to the wrath of the gods.—Hence an error held by Job's friends, but corrected by young Elihu.—This error forbids the duty of " weeping

with those who weep."—Seeing a neighbour under heavy affliction it cries, "*He deserves all.*"—The looker-on flatters himself he
is much better than his neighbour.—The Maltese, seeing Paul
bitten by a viper, made the same inference. Acts xxviii. 4.

All suffering is " creation groaning," and ever uttering the word
"Sin ! "—In the way of *natural law*, but not *moral guilt*, children
suffer on account of parental sins.

Born blind. His label on his breast revealed the melancholy fact.
Where God sets up an altar, let us be ready with our sacrifice.

We must ever acknowledge God's hand, though we can't learn
God's purpose.—More miracles were recorded as to the blind
than any other disease. *One* of palsy, *one* of dropsy, *two* of
leprosy, *two* of fever. *Three* dead were raised, but *four* blind
were restored to sight. Some writers extend the number to *six*.
Matt. xii. 22. Isaiah alludes oftener to curing the blind than
to the removal of any other form of misery.—This miracle strikes
us with greater power,—the only one *born blind*. John ix. 32.

We do not find that He ever left an object of suffering unhealed.
Healing seems not to have been thought of by His disciples.

The apostles inquired not about sin in general, but about the terrible mysterious nature of *that* sin.—Their piety was too pure
and simple to think of impeaching God's goodness.

Nor would a great crime by the parents make a man deserve such woe.
The all-pervading teaching of Scripture is, " Each suffers for his
own guilt." Ezek. xxxiii. 9.—The disciples' question asserts
nothing—even if it did it would not bind us.—Parents' sins are
visited on their children *only* when following in their steps.
Exod. xx. 5.—Christ's answer to curiosity refers alone to the
object to be accomplished.—The walls, mountain high, have
not, and cannot be passed by mortals.—We feel the shock that
drives us back from things unrevealed.—The *cause* is often
hidden, but God's *object* plain.

ἠρώτησαν. Thus they might have spoken—Judas : " His parents must
have sinned grievously." Thomas : " God foresaw great sin here." John :
" I know not what to think." Peter : " Master, tell me who ? " *Pfenniger*.
Disciples, terrified at the late danger, warn their Master to have nothing to do
with this child of sin. *Lange*. Had heard the word, " Lest a worse thing," &c.
John v. 13. *Sumner*. Disciples were acquainted with him. *Kuinoel*.

ἥμαρτεν. That sin must be *somewhere* to cause this calamity,—a loose inference. *D. Brown*. Jews held Transmigration of Pythagoras and Buddhists.
Beza, Hammond, Doddr. Statement without authority. *Lampe, Olsh.* Jews

held *good* souls passed into other bodies. *Lightfoot.* Possibly *antenatal* sin. *Lücke, Meyer.* Sin foreseen would be committed. *Gerlach, Tholuck.* Not predestinated. *Alford.* This man, or, since that is out of the question, his parents. *Stier.* A general question for solution. *Trench.* Romans held calamities proofs of Divine vengeance. Quo numine læso. *Virgil.* Disciples hint at the doctrine of original sin. *Lampe.* Belief in pre-existence of souls implied. *Lightfoot, Kuinoel.* Later Jews held that children did not deserve punishment for fathers' sins. *Rotheram.*

τυφλὸς. Our Saviour may have often passed by and seen him begging. *Schleier.* Known as a believer. *Hengst.*

γεννηθῇ. Some hold that souls had sinned in a pre-existent state. *Origen, Cyril of Alex., Beecher.* All men fell with Adam's *sin. Augustine.* Each soul created as to its final destiny. *Jerome, Tertullian. Augustine.* Gnostics held evil to have been created. *Enfield.* If neither parents' nor son's sin the cause, the problem in the background, still more difficult. *Hammond.*

---

3. Jesus answered, Neither hath this man sinned, nor his parents: but that the works of God should be made manifest in him.

Answered. Our Lord answers His disciples more plainly than He would hopeless sceptics.—God will yet answer all doubts, and solve all problems.—Our Lord rebukes evil surmises concerning the secrets of others' lives.—Job's friends held that extraordinary suffering proved extraordinary sinning.

Neither. Human reason delights to infer special sins from special suffering. So *fixedly* does the mind determine each crime deserves punishment.—An abiding truth—Sin is the cause of all evil. Though sufferers are not necessarily more guilty than others. Luke xiii. 2.—This idea lies deep in the universal consciousness of the heathen.—Yet God protests against the perversion of this principle, as though it dispensed with all reference to personal guilt. Ezek. xviii. 19, 20.

Parents are by no means released from much of their children's sufferings.—Curse of *parental* guilt lies heavily on children. Exod. xx. 5.—He clearly denied any *particular* sin caused this misfortune.—How we may suppose this man listened, on hearing these strange words!

Sinned. Our Lord never disturbed that great principle in God's empire, suffering involves sin, either personal or imputed. Job xiv. 4.—He teaches that these parents had sinned no *more* than those parents whose children see.—The holiest of men seem to have suffered most. Heb. xi.—He answers their question :—No particular sin of parents or son caused blindness in this case.

His earnest decision shows superhuman penetration.

But. Their question did not lead to the true solution.

He does not deduce general principles, as usual, from specific cases. He says God's design in this particular case is to glorify God. The man is to be an illustrious witness of Christ as THE LIGHT OF THE WORLD.—He who had cast out *devils* by the finger of God, here casts out *darkness*.—He speaks in the hearing of the unhappy man, and turns the answer at once into a promise of help.

He implies, the Restorer of the *defective* is the Creator of all bodily members.—" Good men view evil, as they do fire begun in their own house. The question is not so much how it caught, but how to put it out." *Cecil.*

But that. By a transcendent miracle of Love He will ring the great bell of the universe, and summon men to hear the Gospel.

Thus Lazarus' sickness was not unto death.—That voice, " I AM THE RESURRECTION, AND THE LIFE " (John xi. 25), heard in the tomb of Bethany, has been echoing from age to age ; and has cheered millions, once in tears, now in glory.

This suffering, sightless wretch is changed in a few hours into an *Apostle* and *confessor* of Christ.—His eyeballs healed have preached to myriads of the great LIGHT-GIVER of our blind race.

Works of God. Primarily His own miracles of healing and deliverance.—One work of God fully known gives us the *key* to them all.—Our Lord rebukes all who would be " wise above what is written."—Our finite minds cannot explore those deep abysses of good and evil.—Their high lessons are for the scholars and light of the *upper world.*—Our duty is to look forward in waiting hope, to the sin-removing works of God.

Our studies and prayers should seek how to ameliorate or remove evil.—Affliction has often led to thought and penitence. Psa. xxxi. 7.—Uncharitable judgments of the suffering are here rebuked.

No one can ever want an object for whom to take up his cross. Mark xiv. 7. So universally are His creatures " groaning " under the curse. Rom. viii. 22.—Nor are those seemingly the most afflicted the most unfortunate.—Countless multitudes will for ever adore Him for parental chastisement. Heb. xii. 6. " It is good for me that I have been afflicted." Psa. cxix. 67, 71.

Made manifest. Are we taught that *all* afflictions illustrate God's glory ?—Sight restored to this blind man, was actually no greater act than God daily giving sight to infants born.

But these two blind eyes healed have been manifesting God's glory for eighteen centuries.—It will be manifest before all heaven, when this scheme ends.—In heaven God's *strokes* seem all

lost in His boundless *compassion.*—The work of creation is here
before many-witnesses to be repeated!—The disciples shall see
the almighty power of God's *word,* " Let there be light," Gen. i.
3, as the angels on the morning of creation.—The HAND of
Christ in creation as the WORD, is here set forth.   See on John
i. 3.—A double miracle at creation : first the *body,* then the *soul*
of Adam.—So now, first this man's sight *is* created, and then
his soul is born again. Ver. 39.—Had he been born with vision,
he might have lived and died a Pharisee.—This rod chastened
his mind to the humility of faith in the Messiah.
He, as *subject* and *instrument* to others, unfolded God's glory.
Evil is evil, though Stoics and Pantheists deny it.
The glory of our Lord has been reflected from this blind beggar
for eighteen centuries.

οὔτε.   Our Lord's remark confined to this case.   *Strauss.*   Parents still responsible for their offspring's sufferings. *Rieger.*
οἱ γονεῖς.   Had violated the law. Lev. xx. 18. *Grotius.*   They did not sin
so as to cause this blindness. *Chrys.*   Not more than parents having seeing
children. *Beck.*   He repels all ground for the dream of Pythagoras or the
Brahmins. *Schubert.* In the plan of Providence, this among others, &c. *Alford.*
Denied as to any *general* application. *De Wette.*   His answer would prevent
the disciples hurrying on, and dissuading Him from attending to the case.
Lange.   Not precisely had they sinned, but *so* sinned as to, &c. *Glassius.*
φανερωθῇ.   God can use any creature for any of His designs. *Anton,*
Leibnitz.   My mind reposes before the fact of God's sovereignty, as quietly as
before a truth explained. *Arnold.*   He *concentrates* extraordinary penalties
that He may evolve extraordinary grace and glory. *Trench.*
ἔργα.   Miracles. *Stier.*   Works of Providence. *Hengst,*   The Son's works.
Theophylact.

---

4. I must work the works of him that sent me, while it is day : the night
cometh, when no man can work.

Must.   He felt " straitened till it be accomplished." Luke xii. 50.
In the obligation and counsel of pitying love, He *must* pour Light
upon the darkness of this victim.—Even for *him* Christ had left
His throne ; He came to illumine that soul.
One of the lost sheep, the Good Shepherd had sought and found.
Work.   The unceasing energy and activity of God are here seen.
1. Our Lord had a *definite* work all arranged for Him on earth.
2. That work was *doing good.*   3. He had a definite *time* and
place for each work.
Works.   Of healing and of salvation which accompanied it.

796 / Gospel of John

God had said " *Let there be light.*" Christ says " Let there be light."
The same motive that created the sun, creates sight here.
Every such work was a REVELATION,—it showed God's mind.
It showed a Will, absolutely good—a Light, that loved no darkness.
Day.   No one can say *his* day will have twelve hours in it.
Night is the time for receiving wages, not for doing work.
Some here find reference to the fact that it was the Sabbath.
  Chap. v. 16.   Others, that the time for accomplishing His mission
  was almost ended.—What Christ left undone, He did not return
  to earth to finish.   Eccles. ix. 10.—But what He began, at
  death He cried " IT IS FINISHED."—" Day " refers to His three
  and a half years' ministry on earth, and " night " to His passion.
God's sovereignty is seen in selecting this poor beggar, while
  scores of blind Pharisees were passed by.
" Ye are the light of the world ; " an implied command—" *Let that
  light shine.*"—Though evening comes to earth, no night ever
  overtakes the sun.—Thus, no night can overtake HIM who said
  " Let there be light."
Night.   Christ departing, night comes.   Gloom is only the *absence*
  of the sun.—As night ends man's labour, so death ended His
  toils.—He found our world a spiritual *Egypt :* He made it a
  Goshen.—He enters darkness, it becomes day ; He enters death,
  it becomes life.—Some although they die young live a long life,
  as Josiah.—"That life is long that answers life's great end."
  Young.—But the sinner of a *hundred* years shall die accursed.
  Isa. lxv. 20.—Our brief span but faintly shows what Master we
  serve, and for what world we live.
No man.   Gr. *No one.*   Every man has for his day's work his one
  day.   So too must the Lord perform His great, single, historical
  day's work.—With Him we should be attentive to the signal and
  purpose of God in His service, that we may neglect nothing.
Grasp time and opportunity to do good : defer not till to-morrow.
To every man God has appointed the limit of his activity and
  labour: this goal is soon attained.

ἔργα. Especially those relating to His mission. *Lampe.*
ἡμέρα. The great working day of Christ during His incarnation. *Stier.*
John often represents our Lord speaking indefinitely of things, in their nature
limited. *Bengel.* Time of Christ's presence in the world : *night*, time of His
absence. *Luthardt.* His bright day was still secure ; He can fearlessly tarry
and heal them. *Lange.*

δεῖ ἐργάζεσθαι. Having received such power, I must work. *Hammond.*
However I may rouse the malice of Jews, I must, &c. *Kuinoel.*

νύξ. The day of My great work is declining. *Gerlach.* Resurrection
issues, since only after death His spiritual power was shown. *B. Crusius.* He
began His work in the under-world, in opening the prison door to the dead.
Zeller, Stier. Period from His death to His return. *Nitzsch.* νύξ here corresponds to the Heb. parallelism of *Sheol* in Eccl. ix. 10. *Hengst.* Contrast
between salvation times, and the season of the dark powers. *B. Crusius.* Night
is when one cannot do *his own* work. *Trench.*

---

5. As long as I am in the world, I am the light of the world.

As long. This sadly refers back to their murderous designs and
forward to the cross.—The light for a time will be quenched.
This is a glimpse of the sacred secrets of the Sacred Sufferer.
The sorrowful words take the colouring of the Heart, whence they
came.—In the Son of man alone, can we ever know the Son of
God.

In the world. His mission was threefold, and faith provides us
with a *key* :—At His birth the sun went forth like a rejoicing
bridegroom. Ps. xix. 5. At His death it was night. At His
resurrection it beamed forth again. At His ascension He
finished His day's work of suffering.

I am the light. John i. 4, 5, 7, 8, 9.—He had spoken of His
day which Abraham rejoiced to see.—The Lord's day bounded
by His ministry casts its splendour far into the coming eternity.
The deepest truths relating to both worlds are the *commonest.*
Christ here compares Himself to the sun, the light of day, as in
chap. viii. to the pillar of fire, the light of the night.
The sun was created, but Christ is uncreated light.
The sun's rays become less intense the more distant from the
source; but Christ's retain all their power, despite distance or
time.—The sun's rays leave objects still dark in themselves ; but
Christ has healing in His wings (Heb. *beams*), which makes
believers luminous like Himself :—Moses. Exod. xxxiv. 29.
Elijah. 2 Kings ii. 11. Stephen. Acts vi. 15.
Velocity of the sun's rays computed, but not the movement of the
love of Christ.—Beams of the sun falling are *absorbed*—Christ's
light is *quickening.* The sun's are *reflected* from polished surface—
Christ's from holy life. Isa. xliii. 10. *A ll* the colours found
in each beam— all graces spring from Christ.
All the *beauty* of the world due to light—the glory of man due to
Christ.—The sun the fountain of all *fertility*, all *health*, all

comfort—so is Christ to the soul.—The sun rose on Zoar to bless, while lightning blazed over Sodom.

Light, the first object of sight—Christ is God over all.

All things are seen by means of light—Christ illuminates Nature, Providence, the Bible, and the soul.—None ignorant that there *is* light, but none know *what* it is. Job xxxviii. 19; Isa. liii. 8.—Light infinitely and absolutely *pure*—Christ sinless and holy. Heb. vii. 26.—Light of the sun not diminished by imparting its living splendour.—The sun unbinds the fetters of winter, and decks the earth as Eden.—Christ comes to a soul ruined by sin, and repairs all its desolations. Isa. lv. 12; Cant. ii. 10—13.—Darkness flees before light; thus shadows and types flee before Christ.—All the refined morality and science of man cannot illumine the soul.—All the stars with the moon cannot make it day on earth.—As the sun *gladdens* as well as *glorifies* creation, so does Christ the world.—Without Christ, darkness broods over all forms of government, all systems of philosophy, all results of science. Psa. xxxvi. 9.

We have only to open our eye, and sunlight enters.

It ceases when the sun becomes invisible—Christ's light is bright in the darkest night.—The sun cannot pierce the eye of the blind, but Christ can make the *blind* to see.—The sun shines on in majesty, *unfailing*, though all close their eyes.

The sun has spots marring its glory, but Christ has none.

The sun is superior to all the celestial bodies—Christ Lord of Angels.—There is but *one* sun—" THERE IS BUT ONE MEDIATOR." Heb. viii. 6.—The sun at times under clouds—thus Christ is veiled to His people.—The sun rising heralded by the morning star—thus Christ by John the Baptist.—One following the sun never will have night—one following Christ will never be left in darkness.—Christ is the sun of heaven : " there shall be no night there." Rev. xxi. 25.

Of the world. Not that He would cease to be its Light after death.

Before raising Lazarus, He named Himself " THE RESURRECTION, AND THE LIFE "—now He proclaims Himself, THE SOURCE of *spiritual and natural* LIGHT.—The poor man hearing of " THE LIGHT OF THE WORLD " must have trembled with joy.

ὅταν. As long as. *Kling, Stier.* Whilst. *Lücke.*

φῶς. Logos identified with, or typified by, the sun. *Philo.*

6. When he had thus spoken, he spat on the ground, and made clay of the spittle, and he anointed the eyes of the blind man with the clay.

Spoken. Intentionally in the hearing of the blind man.
Kindest friends have often nothing but *words* for the wretched.
But our Lord's power was ever co-equal with His love.
A believer's *words* can never satisfy his energetic *benevolence.*
Good deeds go hand in hand with good words, in the life of faith.
On all other occasions our Lord was *solicited* to help the blind.
Here it was unasked, as in the case of Malchus, an *enemy.* Luke
 xxii. 51.—This miracle and that at Bethany the last drops in
 the cup of Pharisaic jealousy.

He spat. It had no *conceivable* relation to the cure. Mark vii. 33.
But a *blind* man must be reached by the sense of feeling.
When the clay *touched* his eyes, he knew something was *attempted.*
A touch healed a woman. Luke viii. 44. A leper. Matt. viii. 3.
 The blind. Matt. ix. 20, 27, 29.—Washing in the pool only
 commanded *once*—various methods were chosen.
It proves no sacramental sign did the healing, but faith in His word.
Our Lord *ever veiled* the glory of His Divinity in working His
 miracles. Mark vii. 33, &c.—His *nature-side* is seen in permitting
 the woman to touch His garment.

Clay. Apparent *channel* by which creatures might approximately
 understand it.—As there was no *physical* reason, hence it tended
 to excite the blind man's faith.—We see God working by clay
 and spittle, which are useless in themselves.—We see the man
 arising, and step by step going to the pool. Yet there was *no*
 virtue in his going, aside from the state of his mind.
Thus the Saviour's POWER which heals, and the man's FAITH which
 secures it, are both hidden from the eye of man.
" *Clay* " hints at the use of *earthen vessels* in the Gospel ministry.
Some are a little more glazed than others, but earthy, fragile still.
The Creator, *the* LOGOS, had " formed man of the dust of the earth."
 Gen. ii. 7.—Here the works of the Creator are revived, and the
 Son works as the Father.—Clay is the unconscious conductor of
 light to his eye, as the Almighty's breath conveyed life to Adam's
 dust at creation.—The clay a type of the world's power in
 blinding its victims.—The water, like the Gospel, washes away
 the defilement for ever.

Anointed. Reason might sneer at the means chosen.
The man might say, " I can see no connection between a cure and
 such a remedy." Equal folly is shown by infidels in cavilling

at the *plan* of Redemption.—*Faith*, the condition, is humbling
to the pride of philosophy and to self-righteousness.
What HE offers as eye-salve, will heal us, though it be clay!
Kings, blending vanity with superstition, pretended to heal by a
touch.—Note the simplicity of the means God chooses here and
in His Church.—He chose *water* for the sacrament of baptism,
and *bread* for the Lord's supper—visible signs of invisible grace.
Yet the benefits sealed on the soul are *enduring* and *immortal.*
God purposely selects the most *unlikely* means, for all the *glory* is
His.—Sounding of horns at fall of Jericho : Naaman's washing
in Jordan : The brazen serpent : The lanterns of Gideon, &c.

πτύσματος. Used because no water was near. *Grotius.* A common
operation with Jewish physicians. *Dophé.* Cures attempted among Roman
practitioners. *Suetonius, Tacitus.* Saliva recommended as an eye-salve. *Pliny.*
A mere fancy. *Wetstein.* Our Lord made it to assert the right of doing work
on the Sabbath. *Hess, Bauer.*

ἐπέχρισε. The man, to permit this, must have known Jesus. *Hengst.*
Superstition led men to anoint the eyes of catechumens with clay. *Bingham.*

πηλὸν. Dust in Egypt supposed cause of the ophthalmia, now prevailing
there. *Author.* Used by Samonicus, physician in the time of Caracalla, and
here actual medium of cure. *Trench.* Symbolical as being sent to the pool.
Hengst. A parallel to the creation of Adam. *Irenæus.* Notion of Prometheus
stealing fire from heaven, to vitalize the body he had made, derived from
Genesis. *Beza.*

---

7. And said unto him, Go, wash in the pool of Siloam, (which is by interpretation, Sent.) He went his way therefore, and washed, and came seeing.

Go. Meant as a strong trial of his faith. Another's faith thus
tested. 2 Kings v. 10.—Being totally blind, some kind by-
stander must lead him.

Wash. Thus Elisha sent Naaman a journey of faith to Jordan.
2 Kings v. 10.—As Elisha referred the Syrian *away* from his
hand to God's power, so also does Christ.—Each step of God is
seen, and obeyed by the man.—Our Lord enjoins *one*, Elisha
commands *seven* washings.—With more child-like faith than
Naaman, this man obeys and is healed.—Go, sinner, wash in
the Fountain opened for sin in the house of David. Zech. xiii. 1.
Go where the Law broken has been triumphantly vindicated.
Go where "righteousness and peace embrace each other."
Go where the fire and thunder of Sinai are merged in the "Father
forgive" of Calvary.—Go where the "weary and heavy laden"

alone can ever find rest."—Go where the " Lord God is a sun and
shield, and will give grace and glory."—Go " ask of Jesus, and
ye shall receive ; seek, and ye shall find," &c.
Pool. Gr. *bath.* See on John v. 2.—Sheltered by porticoes. John
v. 2.—The *spring* mentioned, Isa. viii. 6 ; the *pool,* Neh. iii. 15.
As multitudes at all hours frequented these places of luxury, our
Lord knew the miracle would be witnessed by a crowd.
Water, exceedingly scarce, was carefully husbanded.
Springs were pre-eminently regarded as " messengers of the gods."
There are but few wells in Palestine, and none in Egypt.
The ancients wore no linen, hence the necessity of frequent bathing.
Greeks used fresh and salt baths : warm baths were a later luxury.
Taken after exercise, and previous to the principal meal.
Steam baths used by Romans.—Baths opened at sunrise and
closed at sunset.—After bathing, the body was anointed by
perfumed oils. Ruth iii. 3.—Nobles put perfume in the baths ;
others scattered it on the walls of baths.—The public were hon-
oured at times by a free permission to bathe by Emperors.
A quarter of a penny was ordinarily charged for admission.
At Pompeii, this box (with the money still there) was lately dis-
covered.—Stupendous baths, whose ruins still cover many acres,
and are the wonder of the traveller, were erected by Nero, Titus,
Trajan, Caracalla, Diocletian.—Caracalla's bath had 200 marble
columns, 1600 marble seats.—There were 856 public baths in
Rome according to *Fabricius.*—Agrippa, son-in-law of Augustus,
built 60 baths for *free* use of the Romans.
Bathing was endorsed by the Divine Law with rules. Lev. xiv. 8.
Egyptians, Hindoos, and Moslems bathe as an act of *worship.*
Private baths made of wood, stone, bronze, glass, or green marble.
Luxurious Romans bathed from *three* to *eight* times a day.
Hebrew females, in the absence of water, used *bran,* as Moslems
do *sand.*—High priest bathed at his inauguration, *hence baptism.*
Warm climate made bathing essential to health as well as pleasure.
Siloam. Heb. *Sent.* A name given to it ages before, showing the
wide embrace of God's plan.—Confounded with the well of the
Virgin by a few scholars.—Recent discoveries show that they
were connected by a channel cut through the mountain 4 feet high,
and 550 yards in length.—Drs Robinson and Barclay crept
through the entire length.—One of the few undisputed localities in
Palestine.—It lies in the valley of Kedron, 500 feet below Mount
Moriah.—Its waters belong to intermittent springs, rising and

falling 6 inches about 3 P. M. daily. The pool is 53 feet long, 18 broad, and 19 deep.—Several broken columns, *remains of porches*, are still in the water.—The sides of the pool are lined with large hewn stones.—It was built probably before the days of Solomon.

All the waters of Siloam are derived from the Virgin's well.

In 1479, the arches and buttresses were supported by marble pillars.—The water is sweeter in winter than summer, then slightly brackish.

Interpretation rolls away the stone, and provides a bucket for the well of Jacob.—It parts the curtain, that we may look into the holy place.—"Read this, I pray thee : I cannot ; for it is sealed." Isa. xxix. 11.

Sent. It bears testimony to Him who was SENT OF GOD. 1 Tim. ii. 4 ; Phil. ii. 13.—This humble stream, making glad the city of God, shows a present Deity.—He would make this pool, whose risings and fallings are a *mystery* (Robinson), a perpetual preacher of His overflowing POWER and LOVE.

In John v. our Lord is a BETHESDA (House of Mercy); here a SILOAM (The Sent).

Went. He did not look upon Siloam as Naaman did upon Jordan.

His obedience full proof of faith imparted by the grace of Christ.

Had he paused to reason he might have asked, How could the pool heal ?—Has any one ever been healed, while thousands of sick have bathed ?—Would not a failure expose him to the bitter sport of His companions ?

Came seeing. A double miracle. 1. Sight restored. 2. In all its perfection in an instant.—A fever leaves one feeble, but Simon's wife's mother went forth strong. Mark i. 31.

The storm was hushed, and even the never-failing ground-swell also. Matt. viii. 26.—At sight of the universe around, what a shout of joy must have gone up from the man.

Emotions of adoring love and wonder would contend for mastery !

The crowd witnessing the miracle must have exulted in triumph also !

Seeing. Singular enough, at the moment sight was given him he saw not Jesus his benefactor.—Christ can heal afar off as well as at hand. Jer. xxiii. 23 ; Matt. viii. 9, 10.—This miracle was foretold 789 years before it actually occurred. Isa. xxxv. 5.

Our Lord draws aside for a moment the veil showing the hand of God at work in the processes of life.—God has stored all nature with instruments of healing.—Physicians would conceal their remedies ; God puts honour on earth and water.

In Lazarus' case, one of His greatest miracles, nothing was created.

But here the Lord becomes Creator : sight had *never* been here before.—While the disciples were inquiring into the cause of one being born blind, our Lord cries, " I AM THE LIGHT OF THE WORLD," and illustrates it by a miracle.—This long night had settled on this man, to provide a text and sermon for the Church in all time.—His ministers are to turn the nations " from darkness to light." Acts xxvi. 18.—Our Lord and he did not meet until he was expelled from the synagogue.

To the Jewish nation, he was a living parable, touching our Lord's advent.—Like the beggar, they were actually blind, wretched, and miserable. Rev. iii. 17.—But, unlike him, they " knew not the day of their visitation." Luke xix. 44 ; John ix. 39.

God knows how to make use of our infirmities for the glory of His name.—The more speedily we grasp the word of Christ, the more quickly and powerfully we experience His help.

Do not ponder over the origin of evil : work with helpful, Divine love.

νίψαι. πλύνω, νίπτω, λούω. Our language in its poverty has but one word, "to wash," with which to render these three; although the three have each a propriety of its own, and one which the inspired writers always observe. Thus πλύνειν is always to wash inanimate *things*, as distinguished from living objects or persons. νίπτειν and λούειν, on the other hand, express the washing of living persons ; although with this difference, that νίπτειν almost always means washing a *part* of the body. *Trench.*

κολυμβήθραν. See critical note, John v. 2.

Σιλωάμ. Probably with reference to the fact that the temple-mount sends forth its spring-water. *Lange, Ewald.* Type of Christ THE SENT ONE. *Hengst., Aug., Theophy., Eras., Calvin, Ebrard, Luthardt, Godet, Trench, Alf., Wordsworth.* Christ the Sender of the Apostles. *Olsh.* Blind man *sent* thither. *Meyer.* Type of the Spirit. *Stier.* Built by Hezekiah. *Kraft.* Before Solomon's time. *Ritter.* Being intermittent, ascribed by Arabs to hidden dragon. Present pool probably work of Crusaders, or Saladin. *Bailey* in Smith's Dict.

ἀπῆλθεν. A faint dawning of light had already begun. *Lange.* He had a guide. *Neander.* Was *led* to the pool. *Tholuck.* An unnecessary conjecture ; blind beggars generally have a guide. Yet blind men can often find their way without aid to a locality. *Schaff* in *Lange.*

ἐνίψατο. Typical of baptism. *Ambrose, Jerome, Trench.* Unsuitable. *Schaff.*

ἦλθε. To his own house. *Lange, Trench.* Rather to the temple. *Lyser.*

8. The neighbours therefore, and they which before had seen him that he was blind, said, Is not this he that sat and begged ?

Neighbours. They crowded to see the man who had returned cured.—He hastens first to announce to his friends at home the glorious work, and then returns to the temple to offer thanks, and seek his Benefactor.

Is not this? Change of countenance from the *utter blank* of one blind, was great. So the change produced by the Holy Ghost in the soul : even the acquaintances and friends of the converted do not *know* him.—The actions of God are more widely and better known through men's speeches and opinions concerning them.

Sat. He dare not trust himself to stand amid the jostling crowd.

Begged. Their form of asking alms was, " *Do thyself good by me.*" The blind only, as a rule, were beggars.—Belisarius, a general of world-wide fame, dishonoured, humbled by misfortune, sat in blindness at the gate of Constantinople and begged.

The world is a hard master. To-day it cries, " Live for ever," and to-morrow hisses them out of sight.—When a man is delivered from spiritual blindness, people say : Is not this he who formerly did so and so ? In this way they testify to his conversion.

τυφλὸς. The true reading is προσαίτης. *Cod. Sin., Lach., Tisch., Treg., Alf., Schaff.*

---

9. Some said, This is he : others said, He is like him : but he said, I am he.

Some said. How minute, distinct, and true to life is this narration !

This is he. They saw a resemblance to the man's former self.

How strangely are one's opinions, habits, tastes, changed by grace ! What a difference between Saul of Tarsus *praying* and the blood-thirsty persecutor ! Acts ix. 13. The drunken, swearing tinker, Bunyan, and the author of " The Pilgrim's Progress " ! The captain of the slave ship and the evangelical preacher and poet, John Newton !

Like him. Human reason will conjecture anything rather than admit a miracle.—Unbelievers are against the Bible because the Bible is against them.—In their own eyes unbelievers are always the wisest and most sharp-sighted, though blinder than

bats.—The Bible is not simply *wisdom*, but the *wisdom of God*,
and that *in a mystery*. 1 Cor. ii. 7.

I am he. This settles for ever the question of his personal
identity.—He is too full of gratitude to suppress the truth.

The *doubts* of his neighbours are made to *confirm* the reality and
splendour of the miracle.

ὅτι. Read οὐχί ἀλλ'. *Cod. Sin, Tisch., Treg., Alf.*

---

10. Therefore said they unto him, How were thine eyes opened

How? Christ's work in creation, providence, and grace, a *Divine*
work.—The more examined, the more God's power is illustrated.

It is inconceivable before conversion what a believer enjoys of
comfort after it. *Augustine.*—*Cyprian* of Carthage made the same
admission before he was martyred.

---

11. He answered and said, A man that is called Jesus made clay, and anointed
mine eyes, and said unto me, Go to the pool of Siloam, and wash: and I went
and washed, and I received sight.

A man. He knew well the power of the Galilean Wonder-worker,
although not acquainted with His Messianic character.

His testimony adheres strictly to what he knew and had felt.

Jesus. John i. 17, 41.—He had noticed the significant Name, and
emphasizes it.—That he had learned something about Jesus is
quite certain.—How many things the sacred writers must have
passed over in silence!—Prompt obedience proved his implicit
triumphant faith.

Made clay. Having seen nothing of the process, he carefully
avoids the *how*.—He could *feel* the clay put on after it was made.

The world, as judge, would pronounce this act of our Lord folly.

Clay on eyes, already sealed in night, will make him doubly blind.

God is His own Designer as well as His own Interpreter.

Human reason is not the measure or model of His plans of mercy.

Thus when trials come believers suffer first in shame or slander.

He seems, unlike men, to show His friends neither face nor favour.

Life eternal is hidden under mysteries and miseries.

Go. God's mercies always bring with them command and duty.

To some, " Go, show yourselves to the priest ; " to another, " Give

God praise ; " to another, " Sin no more ; " to another, " Tell
no man."

I washed. He obeyed without hesitation, or captious questioning.
To the soul, the body will by and by be transparent as glass.

Received. Gr. to *look up*, to *see again*. As sight is natural, it is
spoken of as *recovery*.

ἀπεκρίθη. So vivid is the narration, John may have received it from the
beggar. *Meyer.* Better still to have received it from the Holy Spirit. *Author.*

ἀνέβλεψα. Didymus, the last distinguished teacher of the Alexandrian
School of theology, a follower of Origen, was blind. He wrote several commentaries, and an able work on the Holy Ghost. St Anthony, the father of
monks, once told him : Do not mourn over the loss of those eyes with which
even flies can see, but rejoice in the possession of those spiritual eyes with which
angels in heaven see the mysteries of God. *Schaff* in *Lange.*

καὶ εἶπεν. Omitted. *Tisch., Treg., Alford.*

τὴν κολυμβήθραν. Omitted. τὸν Σιλωάμ. *Cod. Sin., Lach., Tisch., Treg.,
Alford.* Text. recept. is explanatory. *Schaff.*

---

12. Then said they unto him, Where is he ? He said, I know not.

Where is he ? Where He will prove His Divinity, grant remission of sins, show to all Gospel-despisers their folly, and crown
His friends as kings, &c.

I know not. Note how terse, concise, and pertinent the man's
replies.—While the beggar went to Siloam, our Lord went on
His way.—" It is the glory of God to conceal a thing : "—thus
at the miracle, John v. 13.—Our Lord's life is stamped with
matchless majesty and condescension.—His power was mingled
with pity, compassion, and transforming grace.

In deep humility He shrank from the gaze of idle curiosity.

Thus the grand changes of the seasons and heavens are wrought
by His secret hand.—The excessive lustre of His Divinity shows
the brighter by His ever veiling His transcendent virtue. *Ullmann.*—Our Lord had no special home, He was much alone,
while the disciples dwelt in their respective houses.

οὐκ οἶδα. Our Lord withdrew as He did John v. 13. *Hengst.* Not deemed
prudent to appear publicly after their attempts to stone Him. *D. Brown.* He
had no fear of hindrance—" I *must* work." *Author.*

---

13. They brought to the Pharisees him that aforetime was blind.

Brought. This untiring zeal and enmity a rebuke to the indolence of believers.—Doubtless the man was under regular legal arrest for Sabbath-breaking.—His parents were also summoned as witnesses. Ver. 18.—In their simplicity they had long confided in the learned rulers.—But the work of the Creator, like the sun, is its own witness.—The harvest field of grain demands no learning to judge of its value.—We need no physician's skill to inform us of the reality and worth of health.—The feeblest person could relish the bread multiplied by His power.

The humblest toiler of the sea could value His word, " Peace, be still."—Thus with Bible-truths—The unity of the Godhead, our ruin by the fall, redemption through Christ, and regeneration by the Spirit, stand out like the Alps and Andes.

Pharisees. John i. 24.—Most numerous, influential, and bitter enemies ; in ver. 18 called " Jews."—The Sanhedrim mainly composed of such, although Caiaphas was a Sadducee.

" The LIGHT of the world " was again pursuing these lovers of darkness.—This inexorable brightness flashes on them, causing bewilderment peculiar to those under the fascinations of Satan.

They expect the blind man to refute the impression made by Jesus.—Those judges chosen by the people were *stone blind* still. And wilfully resisting, they turned the light itself into darkness.—Thus George, Duke of Saxony, condemned the Reformation without listening to its claims ; and Philip of Spain said he would rather reign over a *desert* than Lutheran subjects.

The Redeemer's foes unwittingly made themselves the heralds of His power and glory, although they would rather the blind man were not cured than that Jesus should have the praise.

ἄγουσιν. Their motive may have been envy. A Sabbath was broken. *D. Brown.* Well disposed, but under their rulers. *Trench.*
φαρισαίους. The Sanhedrim. *Hengst.*

---

14. And it was the sabbath day when Jesus made the clay, and opened his eyes.

Sabbath. John v. 10.—He had of set purpose *chosen* that time to perform the miracle.—He foreknew all that followed, and the offence taken by them.

When. The specific reason *why* they bring the affair before the Pharisees.—This miracle tended to overthrow all their super-

stitions concerning that day, but especially all their power and prestige in *taxing* the nation.—Their Sabbath superstition and the Sanhedrim will stand or fall together.—Our Lord desired to establish a Sabbath in their heart first. Prov. xxiii. 26.
Those *loving* Sabbath solemnities, never violate its outward proprieties.—Their exaggerated severities in externals were an insult to their God.—He called their " oblations *vain*," and " their sacrifice a *weariness*." Isa. i. 13, 14.—" Obeying the voice of the Lord is better than sacrifice, to hearken," &c. 1 Sam. xv. 22.—Our Lord did not contend against Moses' Sabbath, but its *caricature.*—It was to be a day of rest as to self, but a day of toil in blessing others.—He knew that His miracles on the Sabbath would strengthen the infatuation of the Pharisees.
But the interests of an everlasting kingdom, as well as justice to His foes, are embraced in His plans.

σάββατον. A rabbinical statute specially prohibits the spreading of saliva on the eyes on the Sabbath. *Maimonides.* If this ordinance was not yet extant or sanctioned, still the general law was in force which forbade all healing on the Sabbath, except in cases where life was imperilled. *Schöttgen, Wetstein, Meyer* (quoted in *Lange,* Amer. Edit.). For ὅτε: ἐν ᾗ ἡμέρᾳ. *Cod. Sin., Lach., Tisch., Treg., Alford.*

---

15. Then again the Pharisees also asked him how he had received his sight. He said unto them, He put clay upon mine eyes, and I washed, and do see.

Again. His neighbours first (ver. 10), Pharisees next interrogate him.—They hoped he would yield to pressure, and change his answer.—Ermined judges, who were high in office on earth, will experience a fearful change of condition with some they sentenced.—The most daring stroke that the wicked can make at the LORD, is to smite His followers.—" Your brethren that cast you out for MY *name's sake.*" Isa. lxvi. 5.
Papists always began the sentence of martyrs, " IN NOMINE DOMINI." A martyr once replied, You begin your work of Satan " In the name of the Lord ! "—Persecution—1. The chosen baptism of the Redeemer. " Partakers of Christ's sufferings." 1 Pet. iv. 13. 2. It belongs to the lot of believers. " No strange thing." 1 Pet. iv. 12. 3. Cause of rejoicing. They shall share Christ's glory. 1 Pet. iv. 14. 4. Reward in eternity. " Blessed are ye when men shall hate you." Luke vi. 22.—Christians are persecuted simply because Christ loves them. John xv. 19.

Our Lord forewarns all who will follow Him. 2 Tim. iii. 12 ; Matt.
v. 10.—*White robes* given the martyrs, *kingly* insignia, *coronation robes.* Rev. ii. 10 ; vi. 11. (See on Luke xii. 27.)

No follower of Christ escapes bearing the badge and burden of his
Lord. Matt. xvi. 24.—" As soon hope to quench one's thirst by
fire, as for Christians to escape persecution " (Dying words of a
martyr).—The very *holiness* of Christians roused Roman envy to
cry, ' CHRISTIANOS AD LEONES ! "—Their not only hating the
light, but the *faint reflexion* of it, proves their malignancy.

Saints called " Sons of peace," but alas ! they kindle a fire on the
earth. Matt. x. 34.—An eminent physician saw an only daughter
become a Christian ; deeply enraged, he had her placed in an
Insane Asylum.—Light of love becomes a fire scorching conscience.—Men rejoiced (Gr. *caroused,* Rev. xi. 10) around the
ashes of the martyrs of Christ.—Bishop Gardiner would not dine
till news came of the martyrs burning. *Neal's* Hist. of the
Puritans.—Martyrs have by their victorious patience kindled
the faith of Christ in others.—Like their Lord they conquer
dying. Heathen cried, " COME, LET US DIE WITH THEM ! "

Pharisees. John i. 24.—May have been sitting in council.

How. They pass over the miracle *itself,* and inquire at once as
to the *manner,* because the latter is the point to which the charge
of heresy against Jesus must attach itself. *Lange.*

Thus infidels, unable to deny the *fact* of conversion, prefer to
stumble at the *how.*

Received. Gr. *recovered.* Malice detracts where for shame it
cannot deny.—An ungodly " man diggeth up evil." Prov. xvi.
27. He ploughs the ground, and then sows the seed in every
furrow.

Put clay. Three instances of outward application are on record.

Indicates the minutest accuracy. He names not the saliva. He
relates only what he felt—he saw nothing.—His senses were
impressed, and he could *connect* his cure with *the act.*

Thus the grounds of this man's assurance enabled him to silence
the captious Pharisees.—The brief exclamation of joy of a heart
full of gratitude.—Thus the renewed must try the truth as the
eye tries colours.—God's truth shall be established for ever ;
" the humble shall hear and be glad." Psa. xxxiv. 2.

Hypocrites, ever shunning the light, seem to hide under a *mask.*

πῶς. Presupposes he had received his sight. *Stier.*

ἀνέβλεψεν. Recovered, to lessen the miracle. *Trapp.* As though he once had seen. *Gesenius, Robinson.*

---

16. Therefore said some of the Pharisees, This man is not of God, because he keepeth not the sabbath day. Others said, How can a man that is a sinner do such miracles ? And there was a division among them.

Therefore. Thoroughly perplexed by the miracle, the man's deposition placed them in a fearful dilemma.

This man. Said scornfully, feigning unacquaintance with *Jesus.* Many try to mask their wickedness under the veil of defending morality.—Conscience *must* be satisfied, the Divine law in man *will be heard.*

Not of God. Antichrist nevertheless wrought miracles by God's permission. 2 Thess. ii. 9.—Was a falsehood doing violence to their own conviction.—They spake truly, if He *wilfully* despised and broke the Sabbath.—A holy Sabbath kept, has ever been a standing warning to men.—Heathen conscience could not be flattered into silence.—Either the Sabbath, or those that devotedly keep it, must be put down.—" Hast thou kept the Sabbath ? " a query put to primitive Christians. Answering " *yes*," they were led to the *lions* or the *flames* as martyrs for Christ.—Thus the *Waldenses* preserved the TRUTH from the primitive Christians. *Allix.*—While the Church lives, the world will stand ; but removed to heaven, it cannot endure. When Lot left Sodom, the fire-storm descended.

Because. To interpret a good deed as evil is Satan's custom. Many would prefer to detect a fault rather than commend a virtue. The wicked have ever a conscious approval of the holiness they hate ! Rom. ii. 14, 15.—The law written in the heart will in eternity vindicate the awful sentence. Matt. xxv. 41.

Keepeth not. He might have cured him on the morrow. But He saw the nation fanatically clinging to an empty form. His errand to earth was to re-instate the Law in its sacred binding nature.—He knew this miracle and Lazarus' resurrection would lead to His own arrest and crucifixion.—He therefore directed His course to meet this beggar on the Sabbath. It was part of the preparation for Gethsemane and Calvary.

The Sabbath. John v. 9, 10.—Not indeed the Pharisees', but He did keep God's Sabbath.

Others. These things were drifting the nation fast to their doom.

But a few honest spirits, " Abdiel-like," dared to lift their voice for TRUTH. Nicodemus and Joseph of Arimathæa were representatives of this party.

How can? This sounds very much like the question of Nicodemus.

Sinner. These words, " of God " and " sinner," describe all mankind.—A timid protest of fearful ones against cruelty of aim. In the end, they are silenced by daringly wicked adversaries.

Division. " I came not to send peace on earth, but a sword." Matt. x. 34.—This was He who in the beginning divided the light from the darkness.—The inevitable fruit of revived affection and truth by the Spirit.—The seed of the serpent will wage an exterminating war with believers.—The result of this conflict of ages has been clearly foretold. Rev. xx. 10. Cain and Abel could not sacrifice together on the same earth. " Brethren " alone can " dwell together in unity." Psa. cxxxiii. 1. 1. Diverse principles: benevolence, selfishness.—2. Diverse affections : meekness, forgiveness, pride, revenge.—3. Diverse plans : these reach to eternity, those end in the dust.—4. Diverse means : right and truth, fraud and deceit.

---

17. They say unto the blind man again, What sayest thou of him, that he hath opened thine eyes ? He said, He is a prophet.

Again. Gladly would they have the poor man's blindness back again.—Faith in the *Prophet* led him rapidly to faith in the Son of God. Ver. 35.—But the Pharisees, like modern " Liberals," say in their heart, " We *will not* see."—*Voltaire* declared " If a miracle were done in the market, in presence of 1000, I would rather disbelieve those 2000 eyes than believe in a miracle." Thus the owl in the fable affirmed *sunlight was of small account.*

What sayest? What hast *thou* to say ?—They would entrap him to his condemnation.—He might suspect that Jesus used magical arts in the work. But they find him an honest, prudent, strong-minded, spirited man.

A prophet. John iv. 19.—The blind man doubtless had heard Him pray (verse 31), hence the word.—He held a firm belief that his Healer belonged " to God."—Harassing persecutions shook off his trust in and care for man.—His faith rises higher at each assault made upon his gratitude and integrity. He knew from his parents that *the* question was, " Is this the Christ?" A deep under-current in favour of our Lord among the people arouses these wicked men.—He claims for Jesus the glory, and wists not that the same Jesus *inspires his answer*.

How intense the malignity, that would make him betray his Benefactor !—Their questions prove they care not for the beggar or his cure, but that out of him they hope to make accusation against the Lord.

λέγεις. Refers to breaking the Sabbath. *Lampe*. To his judgment as to His person. *Cyril, Chrys*.

προφήτης. He adjudged Him a Divine person. *Euthym*. The Messiah. *Wolfius*.

---

18. But the Jews did not believe concerning him, that he had been blind, and received his sight, until they called the parents of him that had received his sight.

Jews. John i. 19.—Here the Pharisees (verse 16), who affirmed that they were *the* Jews by way of eminence.

Not believe. John i. 7 ; vii. 38.—That is, they *pretended* not to credit the evidence, which was overwhelming.

Unbelief here assumes the mask of honest inquiry.

How seldom do such persons anything, without *masking* their sin under a *virtue*.—*Renan* affirms this miracle was " invented " to show Jesus to be THE LIGHT OF THE WORLD ! Yet he declares if a committee should examine and decide that a miracle had been performed, he would believe. Condescending indeed ! If a committee should unanimously decide it is light when the sun rises, he will believe it.—This history, as in holy irony, had fulfilled this arbitrary demand centuries before it was made.

The investigation was conducted by hostile judges—with hostile witnesses:—opinions were heard and possibilities weighed against one another, and the result is, that while the miracle itself is not comprehended, the evidence as to the fact is overwhelming.

Need we wonder that the guilty but candid *Rousseau*, tormented by remorse, cried, " Take away from me these miracles ! "

Been blind. This questioning arose from the *resolve* not to admit the Divinity of Jesus.—They laboured hard to prove that the man was not *born* blind. Then to make him confess that Jesus was not the *healer*.—How much pains the wicked take to silence an *honest* conscience, or to show that wrong is right. Prov. xiii. 15.

Parents. Were they so infatuated as to trust to entrap *them* in a lie ? or that they would deny their son's blindness from his birth ?—They act as though they could put out a brilliant star with a breath.

γονεῖς. Necessarily aged beggars themselves. *Ebrard.* Questioned by *Stier.*

---

19. And they asked them, saying, Is this your son, who ye say was born blind ? how then doth he now see ?

Asked. The evidence is taken by judges the most prejudiced and captious.—These men oppose their senseless NO to the clear YES of the work of God.—In the same way they opposed evidence as to the lame man. Acts iii. 4.—Having removed the son from court (verse 24), they question the parents, doubtless very poor, and perhaps dependent on these very rulers.

Threats of excommunication also make the parents very guarded.

They try to *elude* the truth, rather than speak that which might endanger themselves.

Is this ? How God checked the wiles of Sennacherib, Naaman, and Herod.—These men intend to *obscure*, but they will only *exalt* the miracle.—" God taketh the wise in their own craftiness." 1 Cor. iii. 19.—"The Lord knoweth the thoughts of the wise that they are vain."

Your son ? What a mockery of justice !—The courts of earth, by torture, have wrung out confessions of crime never committed.

Examination of witnesses has often *any other* object than truth even among ourselves.

Ye say. A clear insinuation of *fraud* on the part of the parents.

That is, " whom ye pretend to say was born blind." " How then has he recovered his sight ? " (said sarcastically).

Yet these men in Moses' seat doubtless cherished the hope of entering *heaven* at last.—Who need not tremble, while the heart is so *treacherous* with its delusions ? Jer. xvii. 9.

---

20. His parents answered them and said, We know that this is our son, and that he was born blind.

Parents. Saw the cunning trap laid by which to catch them.

Answered. They felt they had to deal with dangerous rulers on the bench.—With extreme caution they point to the subject of the miracle.—Confident of their son's honest sagacity, and filled with joy at his wonderful cure, they are willing to trust the affair to him.—Truth, like fire, burns the more brightly by the very efforts to put it out.

Our son. The argument that some of the neighbours doubted his identity is nullified by the introduction of the parents themselves.

αὐτοῖς. Omitted. *Tisch., Treg., Alf.*

---

21. But by what means he now seeth, we know not ; or who hath opened his eyes, we know not : he is of age ; ask him : he shall speak for himself.

But. The questions " Is this your son ? " and " Was he born blind ? " they answer affirmatively. But the third question, " How did he recover his sight ? " they evade.

Though careful as to committing themselves, their son might tell.

The reply shows honesty and sense with timidity and selfish caution.—Many parents now are willing their children should enter the ark, while the love of the world, or the pride of life, makes themselves linger.—" Whosoever shall be ashamed of Me, of him shall the Son of man," &c. Luke ix. 26.

An unnatural evasion ! To put their son in peril to save themselves.—Cruelty belongs to cowards, the more base, the more cruel.—Having such teachers, we need not wonder at the depravity of the Jewish people.

Of age. Arabians at eighteen, Greek and Roman males at twenty-five, females never—always subject to guardianship.

---

22. These words spake his parents, because they feared the Jews : for the Jews had agreed already, that if any man did confess that he was Christ, he should be put out of the synagogue.

Feared. " The fear of man bringeth a snare." Prov. xxix. 25.

Abraham denies his wife. Gen. xii. 12. David timidly flies to Achish. 1 Sam. xxvii. 1.—Peter denies his Lord before a little maid, Matt. xxvi. 69, and also dissembles, Gal. ii. 12.

On the roll of judgment, the first are the " fearful." Rev. xxi. 8.

Jews. John i. 19.—Report of a decree which they intended to pass terrified simple ones.

Agreed. They *had* sent officers to arrest Him ; now, to be consistent, they must warn the people against Him.

Confess. He was THE CHRIST. That is, they would punish for

speaking *the truth.*—Worship may be offered to God, yet false in
fact, and ruinous to the soul.—He abhors more deeply Jews worshipping Him in a heathen way than the idolatry of the heathen.
Isa. i.—Upon this circumcised sacrilege our Lord's woes descend
like the seven Apocalyptic thunders. Matt. xxiii. 33.

Put out. 1. For thirty days : he could not approach a synagogue
within four cubits.—2. If he refused to repent, they heaped
anathemas on him, forbidding his friends to transact business
with him.—3. Banished him among the heathen. This delivered
him to Satan. 1 Cor. v. 5.—Instead, the Jews themselves for
1800 years have been cut off to this day.—How terribly holy
and exact is God's retributive Justice.

Synagogue. Gr. *a gathering,* an *assembly.* An institution of the
later phase of Judaism.—It influenced the people's religious
character more than the temple itself.—Moses and the prophets
read, fostered far and wide the hope of the Messiah.

Our Lord in youth worshipped, and during His Messianic life
preached, in them.—Synagogue worship He recognized, though,
like the temple, it was doomed. He wrought miracles in them.
Mark i. 23 ; Matt. xii. 9.—"Synagogues," Psa. lxxiv. 8, Heb.
"*Meeting Places of God,*" no reference to the Synagogue proper.
"Sanctuary," Ezek. xi. 16, referred to the synagogue by many
scholars.—"Proseuchæ," or place of prayer, Acts xvi. 13, name
given to synagogues.—Synagogues silently prepared the way
for the *abolition* of priest, altar, and temple.—Always had a copy
of the law. Reading the main thing. Teachers sent by Jehoshaphat took a copy with them. 2 Chron. xvii. 9. A copy
found by Hilkiah surprised Josiah, showing how rare they were.
It seems as if they had *never seen a copy before.*

Synagogues located, like temples, on the hills ; a pole over it, the
origin of steeples.—Worshippers, seated, must face the temple.
They were located with *that view.*—Sometimes built by a proselyte. Luke vii. 5. Sometimes by a benevolent Jew.

At the Jerusalem end stood the ark, containing the Book of the
Law, the highest seat. Matt. xxiii. 6.—An eight-branched lamp,
one ever burning, a chest for the Scriptures, a box for alms, and
notice board, completed the furniture.—Synagogue, place of
trial, Luke xxi. 12 ; stranger still, of punishment. Matt. x. 17.

Officers : Elders, Minister, Deacon, Trustees.—Hours for worship in
N.T. times, 3rd, 6th, 9th hours, i. e. 9, 12, 3 o'clock.

Modern Jews preserve a copy of the *Law* in a coffer in imitation

of the ark, and all kiss it each time it is brought forth. *Lewis'*
Heb. Ant.

συνετέθειντο. A party agreement. *Hengst.* A formal decree. *Lücke.*
First and mildest discipline. *Buxtorf.* They anticipated the decision of the
Sanhedrim as to Christ's claims. *Trench.* Sanhedrim placed the person under
anathema. *Meyer, Stanley.* Delivered him over to Satan. 1 Cor. v. 5. Bodies
of men were supernaturally afflicted by Satan. Acts v. 11; xiii. 9—11; 2 Cor.
x. 8; xiii. 10. *Theoph., Irenæus, Rosenm., Hodge.* Ordinary ecclesiastical
discipline. *Aug., Beza.* Not excommunication. *Lightfoot.* Only one form of
discipline named in N.T. *Hengst.* Mishna alludes to but one. *Vitringa,
Winer.*

συναγωγή (σύν and ἄγω, *to bring together*). A synonym of ἐκκλησία. A
lawful assembly in a free Greek city. Summoned by the crier at Athens.
Hence Christians' "high calling," or being summoned from on high. Phil.
iii. 14. *Flaccius.*

---

23. Therefore said his parents, He is of age; ask him.

Therefore. The carnal mind has a "*therefore*" for every sin.
Cain envied Abel's favour with God, "*therefore*" he murdered him.
Ahithophel coveted the honours of state, "*therefore*" he rebelled
against the king.—Haman cherished revenge against Mordecai,
"*therefore*" he would destroy a nation.—In trials God's children
are known from Satan's servants.

---

24. Then again called they the man that was blind, and said unto him, Give
God the praise : we know that this man is a sinner.

Again. Gr. *second time.* "That of which Paulus regretted the
absence in the tale of the miracles, a *thorough investigation*, is in
this instance present in the form of a judicial examination on
the part of the most embittered antagonists." *Tholuck.*
Baffled in council, they resolve to break down the testimony for
Christ.—A clear hint to the healed man that now they fully
understood the *fraud*, and that he would be guilty of great
sin if he persisted in refusing to confess.—Alas ! how often have
courts of justice been instruments of cruelty.
Give God. It seems to have been the form of an oath in that
day. Josh. vii. 19 ; 1 Sam. vi. 5.—Devils also adjured Christ by
God NOT to cast them out. Mark v. 7.—They mean, Confess a
fraud between yourself and the man called Jesus.
A lie is a denial of the omniscience, holiness, truth, and justice of
God.—In the dark ages, in Europe, men swore over the *Corpus*

Christi, now upon the Bible.—Greeks made perjury a crime punished by furies after death.—Glaucus, a Spartan, for even asking an oracle if he might break his oath, was destroyed with all his family.—Carthaginians were proverbial for perjury, hence " *Punic faith.*"—Greeks and Romans took an oath *standing,* with *hands lifted to heaven.*—Roman officers could, at will, *execute* a soldier.—His *oath* to be faithful was called *sacramentum.* Hence the name *sacrament* given to the Lord's Supper and Baptism.—Ancients laid their hand on the victims, hence to " swear by the altar." Matt. xxiii. 18.—In early ages perjury with Romans was as rare as in later times it was common.

God the praise. They imply the cure was good, but the instrument evil.—They dare not assault our Lord—cruelty and cowardice go together. Rev. xii. 12.—Pretending to urge the man to truth, they actually desire him to blaspheme.

We know. They were silent as the grave when He challenged them " to convict Him."—Now *they know,* and intended the healed man to give his assent.—*This* the miserable hypocrites styled " *Giving glory to God !* "—Millions in the very act of robbing the Son, like these Pharisees, pretend it is for the glory of God.—*Is it possible to find an infidel, professedly honouring God, who does not* HATE *Jesus ?*—Men of spotless integrity are ever known by *modesty* of speech.

This man. The only man among all earth's millions who was *not* a sinner. See on John viii. 46.—His spotless innocence appears with no apparent diminution of His *sublimity.*

His terrible denunciations of Pharisees would ill become our sinful lips.—In driving out the money-changers no vestige of *passion* can be seen.—In tempest and thunder the God of nature shows nothing but *Goodness.*—Pilate, confessing His innocence, in vain washes his trembling hands.—Jesus neither felt the necessity, nor offered prayer for forgiveness.—Piety without one tear, or one word of contrition, would among men inspire *derision.* Men would call it a most *impudent conceit.*—A character of model grace and perfect moral beauty has commanded the admiration of the world for eighteen centuries.—So far from one of earth's millions ever *living* such a life—no one could even so much as *conceive it,* until it was lived and recorded.

Δὸς δόξαν. Hebrew formula. *Beza, Lampe.* Not strictly adjuration.

Maldonat. Simply an adjuration to speak the truth. *Trench.* Acknowledge some error. *Stier.*

 ἁμαρτωλός. An impostor. *Kuinoel.* Opposed to παρὰ θεοῦ, verse 16. *Cremer.*

---

25. He answered and said, Whether he be a sinner or no, I know not: one thing I know, that, whereas I was blind, now I see.

A sinner. Used ironically. You may say of Him what you will. He is what He is.—If He be a sinner, I do not know it. He never admitted such a charge.

I know not. He opposes to their *knowing* his knowing *not.*

His *opinion* he well knew would be *with them* utterly ignored.

He stands a type of the future Church in the presence of the world.

He modestly evades their malice, and points to an undeniable fact.

Truth is an ever-present guest, always consistent with itself.

Renewed, we *feel* those things true we only *thought* were so before.

One thing. He would speak of a *fact* before these unprincipled inquisitors.

I know. To their " we know " he opposes the fearless " I know " too.—Their bold effrontery and falsehood daunt him not in the least.—He will not be argued out of his actual experience.

Nothing frets dishonest men so much as such unbending honesty.

The rulers showed their irritation by vainly repeating the question.

Now I see. The manner was to him just as much a mystery as that of *conversion.*—Our Lord clearly taught Nicodemus that clouds and darkness rest on the mode. John iii. 8.

As the *how* is not revealed, so often the precise *when* is also concealed.—The blooming of Aaron's rod proved God was imparting life.—Not the " anointing," but his actual use of his eyes, proved his sight restored.—Mere feeling and emotion have often deceived, and may again deceive.—*Love, joy, peace, long-suffering,* the Spirit's fruits, never deceive.—*Gentleness, goodness, faith, meekness, temperance,* are never fruit of sin.—Blessed victory of personal, spiritual experience over traditional ordinance.

The Christian feels the change, and no argument can touch it.

Thus he did " give God the glory," and with a martyr's fidelity braved their wrath.

καὶ εἶπεν. Omitted. *Cod. Sin., Lach., Tisch., Alf., Tregelles.*
οὐκ οἶδα. Some see dissimulation in the healed man. *Chrys., Theophylact.*

His words carry a sarcasm. *Euthymius.* Not so much that *he* knows, as
wonders why *they* do not know. *Bloomfield.* Brevity of reply shows he knew
the cunning of the Pharisees.
ἕν οἶδα implies special knowledge. *Wetstein.*

---

26. Then said they to him again, What did he to thee? how opened he thine
eyes.

Again. They seek not for light, nor conviction, but for evidence
to condemn.—Objections are multiform, captious, endless, and
lead to error.—Honest hearts who seek to know the *truth*, sooner
or later find it in *peace.*
What did? They were, as the schoolmen used to say, "Question
sick."—ENVY would, like the enraged viper, fain fasten her fangs
on Christ.—They fiercely hope to make the man contradict
himself, or to get him in their snares.
How? They return again to the *how.*—Why did they not ask, *How*
the sun gives light? *How* food nourishes the body? *How* the
blood is kept warm? These questions could not *then*, and cannot
now be solved.—Is it wise to admit, God performs one mystery
and not another?—He that gave virtue to the clay to restore
sight to the blind, can give virtue to bread and wine, to restore
strength to the soul.—How strangely these men torment themselves,—"What"? "How?"—So many deceptions have been
practised on men, that they are bound to sift well all wonders.
But amid much pretence and fraud, the TRUTH itself is in great
danger of being rejected.

πάλιν. Omitted. *Cod. Sin., Lach., Tisch., Alf., Tregelles.*
Τί ἐποίησέ σοι. Dogs losing their scent, go back to start another. *Chrys.*

---

27. He answered them, I have told you already, and ye did not hear: wherefore would ye hear it again? will ye also be his disciples?

Answered. With words perhaps *inspired;* certainly sustained by
the Spirit. Luke xxi. 15.—Had he received all the culture of
the favoured Pharisees, could he have more thoroughly foiled
them?—This young man seems certainly more than a match for
these rulers.
Already. The impertinent can ask a question in three lines,
requiring learning in thirty pages to answer. *Horne.*

Having done this, the same question will be asked next year.
Depraved minds prefer short objections to long answers.
God has revealed enough to save our souls, if not to solve our
doubts.—Some evidence, like the sunlight, would leave no room
for *faith*.

Hear it. No weapon known to TRUTH can pierce the seven-fold
shield of bigotry.—*Fire* alone can enter the fortified conscience
of a fanatic.—Indicates he despised all their windings and
twistings.—Browbeaten by these unprincipled rulers, he becomes
defiant.

Will ye also? Thus he confesses his desire to become Christ's
follower.—In a vein of keen irony, he treats them as " *anxious*
inquirers."—" What means all this tedious investigation as to so
plain a miracle ? "—" Do you wish to learn what a glorious work
has been done for me, that *you* as well as myself may become
His disciples ? "—He plainly foresees they will excommunicate
him, and he grows more resolute, just as *the fire* seemed to NERVE
the martyrs!—At last, as he despised their craftiness, so he
spurned their malice.—As they cannot resist the arrow he sent,
they disgrace their office by descending to use vulgar abuse.

Disciples. Followers of this great Wonder-Worker from Galilee.
Are you willing to renounce your terrible prejudices, and listen to
reason ?—Men who close their eyes cannot see " the light of
seven days." Isa. xxx. 26.—If he thought them honest inquirers, the bare supposition must have been a stinging word to
their proud hearts.

ἀπεκρίθη. Proudly and bitterly. *Lücke.* Some condemn the severity of
his answer. *Braune.* After such inquisitorial arrogance, his keen replies were
proper. *Stier.*
ὑμεῖς. A hint that he intends to be a disciple. *Chrysostom.*
μαθηταί. How many know the right, yet fear to do it. Father Paul being
asked " How could he remain with Rome ? " replied, " Deus non dedit mihi
spiritum Lutheri." *Bayle.* A latent reproof. *Hengst.* A gentle irony. *Bengel.*
He affects to regard them as earnest inquirers. *Trench.*

---

28. Then they reviled him, and said, Thou art his disciple; but we are
Moses' disciples.

Reviled. Their *reviling* was under God an actual *blessing*.
They aimed it at the grateful creature in whose glorious vision

they should have rejoiced, but the insult was intended for our Lord.—By it they say, "Depart from us, we desire not a knowledge of Thy ways."—The man is impatient at their falsehoods, but, unlike them, he is courteous still.—In the spirit of Jesus, " being reviled, he reviled not again." Psa. xxxv. 15.

Moses'. See on John i. 17. They of Capernaum also fled to Moses. But Moses cried out against their fathers' *similar* sins. So far from being Moses's disciples, they did not even *believe* him. 1. Moses was the *first*, as Jesus was the *last*, great Prophet. 2. Moses, like our Lord, was a great Law-giver ; Mount Sinai and our Lord's sermon on the Mount suggest parallels. 3. Moses and our Lord were prophets " from among their brethren." Two of the Gospels open with His strict Jewish genealogy. " Of the Israelites as concerning the flesh, Christ came." Rom. ix. 5. 4. Moses and our Lord both opened new dispensations. Heb. iii. 1—19. 5. Both were Guides, Rulers, Shepherds of the flock of God.—The friends of Moses never can be the foes of Jesus.—The most wonderful delusion of the human mind for believers of the O. T. to reject the Divine claims of Jesus Christ.—Many aided in building the ark who yet perished in the flood.—Sin comes clothed in the robe of reason. " Adam was not deceived." 1 Tim. ii. 14.—The jar of the chemist may have a gilded title, but poisonous contents.—How many, like the insane, mistake their shadow on the stream for a bridge.

Disciples. The antithesis : *Jesus' disciple, Moses' disciple*, relates here to the pretended violation of the Sabbath. *Lange.*—Pharisees to this day cling to the form and reject Him for whose sake the form is, and to whom it is to lead. They hold to the letter, and with it and the form strike dead the life of the Spirit. *Braune.* What a mockery to the meekest of saints were such disciples !

οὖν. Omitted. *Lach., Tisch., Alf., Tregelles.*

---

29. We know that God spake unto Moses : as for this fellow, we know not from whence he is.

We, i. e. We who stand by God's revelation to Moses.
Know. Alas! under what terrible delusion did these haters of the Lord live.—Scripture was to them a dead letter, as to its

Author, its aim, its spirit, and its fruits.—Least of all had they any acquaintance with the MESSIAH it foretold.

God. Had they *known* GOD the FATHER, they would have *known* and *loved* HIS SON.—The sun shines high in the heavens, but the blind never see its glory.

Moses. These Pharisees pretended that honours to Jesus were insults to Moses.—They crucified Him who had the very spirit of Moses.

This. A derisive pronoun among the Greeks. Matt. ix. 3 ; Mark vi. 2 ; Luke v. 21.—The name " Jesus," so gracious and significant, they never took on their lips.—They had blasphemously called Him a *sinner* (John ix. 16), now they pretend profound ignorance of Him.—As the sun sets the stars arise, but not thus with God's prophets.—The nearer the planets approach the sun, the less they are visible.—God's saints the nearer the Saviour the more sunlike they become.—In Joseph's dream, the sun, moon, and stars were all shining at the same time.

We know not. This confession of utter ignorance of such a Wonder-Worker emboldens the man still further.

Lately they pretended to know all about Him (John vii. 27), now they profess to know nothing.—Here note their base falsehood: Rejecters of Christ reject TRUTH also.—They knew that Herod had aimed to strike the incarnate BABE at Bethlehem.

They had heard Him call God " MY FATHER " in the Temple. Luke ii. 49.—They had heard of Siloam, but saw in it no power of the Divine SHILOH.—They had heard of the lame and the deaf being restored, but had refused to see their Messiah in one who could raise the dead.—Alas! they deliberately utter a falsehood. They knew Him well.—They had hounded Him from place to place, from miracle to miracle.—They had tracked Him wherever He went by their spies.—Even devils knew Him—" We know Thee who Thou art ; the Holy One of God." Luke iv. 34.

And the day will come when these very men will " look on Him whom they pierced." Zech. xii. 10.—" These things were not (could not be) done in a corner." Acts xxvi. 26.

The healed man standing among them knew his Redeemer.

Darkness is the result of misused light : obduracy, of perverted awakening.—Falsehood turns light into blindness : sincerity, blindness into the beginning of sight.—When the morning comes, birds of *day* obtain sight : on the other hand, *night* birds become blind. The former have light enough to see and hate the darkness; to long for and love the light, and to see in it : the latter have light enough to see the light, to hate it, and to be blinded by it. *Lange.*

Whence He. That is, He has no commission as a prophet.

They could not deny that from some quarter He possessed extraordinary power. His dealings with the blind man proved this.

Now if this power was not from God, the healed man would be distressed to think that He had been cured by demoniacal agency.—Thus Satan and His emissaries still tempt Christians to question or doubt Divine grace in their salvation, and when they cannot do this, will ridicule them.

τοῦτον. Classically thus used. *Xenophon.* And in Acts vii. 40 ; 1 Cor. v. 2, 3. *Gesenius.*

οὐκ οἴδαμεν. Miracles are from a Divine or a demoniacal source. *Beza, Grotius.*

---

30. The man answered and said unto them, Why herein is a marvellous thing, that ye know not from whence he is, and yet he hath opened mine eyes.

Answered. As the rulers put no question he volunteered this word.—Inspired with true Christian heroism he waxed bolder in defence of Christ.—He virtually charges them with uttering falsehood. They said, " We know not."—All Judea for more than two years had *resounded* with the Galilean's wonders !

Marvellous. Gr. *wonderful.* The irony implies they had deliberately told a lie.—Their not knowing would have been a far greater wonder than the healing.—These very works of love and power doubtless convinced them.—They knew as well as the beggar a great Prophet was in their midst.

But His warnings, doctrines, parables, miracles, and HOLINESS all *condemned* them.—A strange thing indeed that the fathers in Israel knew Him not, and yet He was a Prophet, and had opened this man's eyes.

Ye—is very emphatic. *Ye* pretending to discriminate between true and false.

Ye know not. Ye knowing ones, great divines, illustrious rabbis.

He must have been well acquainted with what was passing.

His views of natural religion were remarkably clear and full.

His use of logic in his humble way quite baffled these rulers.

His intrepid spirit and generous nature shine out nobly, and contrast with the crooked policy of his persecutors.

Opened, &c. Foretold as a sign of the coming Shiloh. Isa. xxxv.
4, 5.—To the same glorious task Paul also was commissioned.
Acts xxvi. 18.—Such a seal from God proves the work Divine.
Jer. xxiii. 22 ; 1 Cor. ix. 2, 3.

γὰρ hints at the motive of the answer. Equivalent to, "I must contradict
you." *Hengstenberg.*

ἐν τούτῳ. In respect to this one. *Lange.* Probably the true reading is
ἐν γὰρ τοῦτο, &c., this one thing is marvellous. *Masson.* The answerer first
of all makes reference to the words of the Pharisees in verse 29 (ἄρα), and
then adds an asseveration, *in this, then, there is certainly,—truly it is indeed
wonderful.* *Winer.*

θαυμαστόν. Referring to their ignorance. So wonderful as to be incredible. *Lampe.*

---

31. Now we know that God heareth not sinners : but if any man be a worshipper of God, and doeth his will, him he heareth.

Now. He appeals to their common creed. Job xxvii. 9 ; xxxv.
13 ; Psa. cix. 7 ; Prov. xv. 9 ; Isa. i. 15.

We. Not members of the Sanhedrim, still with humble sense
" *we* " know.

We know. Note the wondrous illuminating power of *truth.*

" He who walketh with the wise will become wise," &c. Prov.
xiii. 20.—" They took knowledge of them that they had been
with Jesus." Acts iv. 13.

Heareth not. He took for granted that Christ's prayer had been
heard.—" Will God hear his cry (the hypocrite's) when trouble
cometh upon him ? " Job xxvii. 9.—Far from the wicked, the
Lord heareth the prayer of the righteous. Isa. i. 15.

A common sense inference, for a miracle is a hearing of prayer
(chap. xi. 41 ; Mark vii. 34), consequently Jesus must be free
from their reproach.

Not sinners. Not *as such ;* but as *penitents* pleading, He will
always hear. Psa. lxvi. 18 ; Isa. i. 15.—No music to the ear of
the Father sweeter than that prayer, " God be merciful to me a
(*the*) sinner." Luke xviii. 13.—" The eyes of God are over the
righteous, and His ears are open to their cry." 1 Pet. iii. 12.

The leper's lips should be covered, according to law. Lev. xiii. 45.
The wicked compass God with lies. Hos. xi. 12. Their incense

is an abomination. Isa. i. 13.—" *Your* sacrifices " (Isa. i. 11),
not " *Mine*," saith Jehovah to the rulers —" The sacrifice of the
wicked is an abomination to the Lord." Prov. xv. 8 ; Jer. vi.
20 ; Amos v. 21.—This deep impression Satan can never erase
from the mind.—A good word from a foul mouth falls like hail
to the ground.—" Some indeed preach Christ even of envy and
strife." Phil. i. 15.—Moslems pray five times a day, and yet live
in loathsome licentiousness.—Romanists repeat many *Pater
Nosters* and *Ave Marias.*—Wild coasters and wreckers are said
to pray for success in their plunder.—Brigands in Greece and
Italy diligently attend mass preparatory to robbery and murder.
Prayers of the wicked are likened, by the Spirit, to "the howling
of dogs." Hos. vii. 14.

If any man, &c. God having heard Jesus, He is of necessity no
sinner, but in favour with God.—God does the will of any praying man who doeth His will. *Bengel.*—This is the healed man's
testimony to the innocence and piety of Jesus.

δὲ. Omitted. *Lach.*, *Tisch.*, *Alf.*, *Tregelles.*
ἁμαρτωλῶν. Men in their sins, and not desiring to be delivered out of
them. Isa. xxxiii. 14; Gal. ii. 15. *Trench.*
θεοσεβής. *One who fears God,* and therefore avoids evil, *God-fearing.*
Cremer.
ἁμαρτωλός. *Sinful*—only in Bibl. and Eccl. Greek. *Cremer.* 1. Each
child of Adam. 2. One more than usually guilty. 3. One content in sin. 4.
A worker or leader in sin. *Author.* A contemner of God. *Tholuck.*

---

32. Since the world began was it not heard that any man opened the eyes of
one that was born blind.

Since the world began. An enthusiastic testimony to the un-
approached prophetic glory of Jesus.—The healed man elevates
Him above all the prophets, and even above Abraham and
Moses, whom they had exalted as His judges.

Not heard. At that time it was a thing unattempted by surgical
science or skill.—It would *now* be just as stupendous a miracle
to be instantaneously cured.

Opened the eyes. Jews predicted just such miracles of the coming
Messiah. A miracle, such as was never wrought by a prophet,
looked for from Shiloh. Isa. xlii. 7.—Wonders of this kind reserved to the times of Christ's incarnation. Isa. xxxv.

What else could have mixed the clay but the finger of Him who

first created the eye and the ear ?—To this belief he gradually
came, until he *worshipped* Him as GOD.

Born blind. The eye of the body once put out can never be restored but by the Creator.—So neither can the spiritual eye,
save by the Almighty Spirit.

ἐκ τοῦ αἰῶνος. A reminiscence of the O.T. *Hengst.* From eternity.
Lange. Neither Moses nor any prophet ever restored sight to the blind. Psa.
cxlvi. 8. *Grotius.* In Greek classics it means from the beginning of the world.
Wetstein.

---

33. If this man were not of God, he could do nothing.

Of God. As much as to say, Why did God impart to Him the
power of working miracles, but to confirm His teachings and
endorse His claims ?—A strange process had been going on in
the mind of the healed man. A world of beauty had opened to
him : faces of parents and friends looked lovingly upon him ; and
all shone in the light of Him who had opened his eyes.

He saw a light in sun and star which came from that Higher
LIGHT.—He felt assured that LIGHT would follow him, if cast
out of a thousand synagogues.

Nothing, i. e. of this supernatural character ; no sign of a Divine
commission.—Satan's " signs " are " lying wonders."

This young man illustrates the Christian hero :—1. The *courage*
of a heart consciously *reposing* on the arm of God. 2. The
strength of spirit shown by a helpless one under Divine promises.
3. The *wisdom* imparted by the Spirit in answer to prayer.
Luke xxi. 15. 4. The *meekness* with which believers should
sustain persecution.—The relations between the speaking beggar
and the proud Pharisees change. The beggar becomes *teacher*,
and the Pharisees unwilling listeners.—They stood convicted of
hypocrisy, malice, and falsehood.—The most solemn hour in the
life of David Hume was, when *a child on his lap* asked him
about God !

εἰ μὴ, &c., imperfect in both clauses. Were He not from God, He would
be able to do nothing. *Winer.*
παρὰ θεοῦ. Tiberius would enroll Jesus among the gods. Servius worshipped Him in secret with his idol gods. Hadrian proposed to erect temples

without images ; showing that they looked upon Him as an extraordinary
Person. *Horneck.*

οὐδέν. See on John iv. 48, and critical notes. Miracles of Satan ut
plurimum, sunt præstigiæ, imposturæ, phantasmata, ludibria. *Bucholcer.*

---

34. They answered and said unto him, Thou wast altogether born in sins,
and dost thou teach us ?   And they cast him out.

Answered.   Intense Pharisaism now rose to fiery fanaticism.
No hatred on earth so deadly as that toward pure holiness.
The *secret* of the murder by Rome, Pagan and Papal, of 50,000,000
   of martyrs.—Had this miserable victim of blindness done aught
   to harm them ?—Had our Lord wounded their feelings, or
   robbed them of their treasures ?   Had He not simply and
   solely healed a poor man helpless from birth, whom all the world
   by *skill, science,* or *treasure,* could not aid ?—What did Nero
   bring against the primitive martyrs, of whom was St Paul ?
What charge did the King and Court bring against the Huguenots,
   Puritans of France ?—Who can doubt or deny the necessity of
   future retribution after seeing such crimes ?—As a confessor of
   Christ, he first fully learned what *such* men were.
Thou.   Base-born, *sin-marked,* presumptuous youth.
Altogether.   They assume from the first that his blindness was a
   punishment of sin.—Now they hint that, as a heretic, his soul
   shared the defects of his body.
Born in sin.   To what depths must these rabbis have sunk to
   cast his affliction in his teeth.—No wonder thou art wicked
   thyself, and a friend of this sinner.—Their revilings now contradict their denial that he had been blind.—They forgot their
   previous charges.—How hard to harmonize falsehood.
That he had entered life with the brand of sin upon him was a
   blasphemous fling against Providence.—If blindness was the
   sign of sin, then to remove the penalty *demonstrated* Almighty
   power ; but they ignored the logical inference of their words.
What cared such reckless ones if they did " reproach their Maker."
   Prov. xvii. 5.—" Who maketh the dumb, the deaf, or the blind ?
   Have not I, saith the Lord ? "   Exod. iv. 11.
But they had indulged their temper, and now look for *revenge.*
Dost thou teach ? With arrogant emphasis : *thou,* born *thus, thou*
   wilt *teach* us ?—One humble in heart is willing to be taught by
   any one.—Learned Apollos was better instructed by a couple
   of tent-makers.

Cast him out. Excommunication under cruel priests proved a
terrible ban.—When the curse was begun, candles were lighted;
at the close, they were put out; as if he was deprived of the
light of heaven.—His goods were confiscated, his children were
not to be circumcised.—If dying and not repenting, a stone was
cast on his coffin.—None dare mourn for him, being denied a
decent burial.—" Blessed are ye when men shall cast out your
name as evil." Luke vi. 22.—They excommunicated him, yet
he had not owned Jesus.—He was the first CONFESSOR, as John
the Baptist was the first MARTYR.—Characteristics of the hierarchical spirit of persecution :—1. Malevolent examination.
2. Hypocritical exhortation. 3. Anathematization.
How impotent when exposed to the bravery of a faithful soul. *Lange.*
He who condemns believers, condemns not them, but himself.
Braune.—Their cursing is before God nought but blessing.
Besser.—*Diocletian* struck a medal to commemorate the ruin of
Christianity, and *Voltaire* boasted that what twelve men were
required to plant, one would root up.—The peace of the healed
man was to leave such company for higher, the synagogue for the
church.—Blessed excommunication that separates us from blind
and malicious men, and brings us nearer to Christ.

ὅλος. From his being begotten. *Theoph.* Soul and body at birth. *Stier.*
Parents and child at his birth both under *a ban.* ——. An allusion to Psa. li.,
but hinting at an aggravated form of original sin. *Hengst.* Sinner from infancy. *Chrys.* Referred to original sin—doctrine held by Pharisees. *Lampe.*
That before his birth he was a sinner. *Calvin, Chemnitz, Bucer, Beza.* Punished for his parents' sins. Exod. xx. 5. *Le Clerc.* They cast his misfortune
in his face. *Bengel.* They continually insult him, as if he was born with this
mark of sin. *Calvin.* Sin in utero. *Lightfoot.*
ἐξέβαλον. Excommunicated from the synagogue. *Stier, De Wette, Olsh.,
Thol., D. Brown.* Although the man had not yet confessed Christ. *Blee.* Not
excommunicated, for even the disciples were not yet cast out. *Hengst.* Hurled
him out of the council hall. *Grotius.* They put in force sentence of excommunication. *Lampe, Vitringa.* Violence in expelling him from the temple. *Calvin,
Maldonat., Cocceius.* Forbade his communion with his friends at home. *Cor.
à Lapide.* So frequent does the pope anathematize, that it was a proverb formerly, In nomine Domini incipit omne malum. Bonner, the bloody prelate,
thus began to read the sentence of Robert Smith, the martyr. He replied, " You
begin in the wrong name." *Trapp.* Louis XII., anathematized by the pope,
replied, " He was placed there to bless, not to curse." *Firron.*

---

35. Jesus heard that they had cast him out; and when he had found him,
he said unto him, Dost thou believe on the Son of God ?

Jesus heard. " The Lord hearkened, and heard." Mal. iii. 16. The great Listener.—Omniscience is often distinctly predicated of our Lord. John ii. 25. " All things are delivered unto Me of My Father." Matt. xi. 27. " I am He which searcheth the hearts and reins." Rev. ii. 23. " And Jesus knowing their thoughts." Matt. ix. 4. " He knew all men." John ii. 24.—A truth full of comfort to the believer, and of terror to the unbeliever.

Cast him out. Our Lord saw how violent the tide that was setting against Himself.—He sympathized with one suffering for His sake, although as yet a stranger to his Lord.

They, who for confession of the truth are rejected and accursed by the world, are graciously looked upon by Christ, and blessed by Him with a larger measure of Divine light. *Zeisius.*

He found. He who knoweth all things, knoweth where to find him.—Being excommunicated, he dare not enter the temple.

The interval was enough to mature, by the Spirit, his faith and gratitude.—Did the healed man *recognize* his Benefactor?

Probably something in our Lord's appearance may have arrested him, and doubtless the spiritual light, which was now irradiating his soul, would clothe Jesus with a mysterious interest in his eyes. At all events, as soon as He spoke, the well-remembered voice would thrill through his heart.—Religion will never prove a loss.—Rejected by wicked Sanhedrists, he is found and cheered by the SON of the LIVING GOD.—The Jews cast him out of the temple, but the Lord of the temple found him.

Not surely by chance. His eye watched him from the moment of cure.—The Good Shepherd seeks His poor sheep, cast out into the wilderness, and brings him to a Fold into which *such* cruel Pharisees cannot enter.—What a pattern for all under-shepherds. John xxi. 16, 17.—Judgment is God's *strange* work, as though it came with a struggle. Hos. xi. 8.—His mercy turns to wrath. " The Lord shall make the rain of thy land powder and dust." Deut. xxviii. 24. " I will go and return to My place, till they acknowledge their offence." Hos. v. 15.—A human foe strikes secretly, that he may destroy effectually. God *threatens* that He may not *chasten,* and chastens that He may *save.* If a *word* will correct His chosen, He never uses the rod. Prov. xviii. 6. He calls heaven and earth to hear His complaint against rebellious children. Isa. i. 2.—If His people are thrown into a furnace, it is only to refine them. Mal. iii. 3.

The loss of means, credit, friends, all necessary to drive the prodigal back to his father.—" Come, let us return : HE hath torn,
HE hath smitten ! " Hos. vi. 1. Not a word of the instruments,
Nebuchadnezzar or Shalmanezer.—How intensely must the
healed man have longed to see his Benefactor.

Said unto. Against the whole host of Pharisees He rejoices over
him.—A poor *mendicant* kindles far deeper interest in the Son
of God than all the proud Sanhedrists.—At the proper time He
will ever reveal Himself to His chosen.

Dost thou ? After such persecution from men, dost thou believe
on the Son of God?—The exceptional use of the pronoun (in
the Greek) makes it like an affirmation. *Bengel.*

Believe. John i. 7 ; vii. 38.—Our Saviour knew his mind, and
the means necessary to build up his faith.—The mendicant was
satisfied a " prophet " had healed his life-long malady.

But one step more was required to say, " Thou art the Son of God."
Son of God. (See critical note.) John i. 1, 2, 14, 18, 49.
A question intended to arouse the utmost earnestness.
John the Baptist had greatly cleared the people's minds.
The O.T. sayings had made the nation familiar with the Messiah.
The poor healed man must have had very feeble ideas of his De-
liverer.—The Holy Ghost leads sincere hearts far beyond them-
selves.—He who brought him out of a lifetime darkness had
a right to question.—Besides, the beggar must confess the Lord
before men. Luke xii. 8.

ἤκουσεν : on the day following. *Stier.*
εὑρών : on Mount Olivet. *Stanley.* This lacks evidence. *Author.* His
tumultuous joy had so filled his mind with amazement that he could not find
the way among strange objects. *Stier.* A private interview. *Doddridge.*
πιστεύεις. An affirmative : a true Israelite thou seemest, believing in the
Messiah. *Hess, Tisch.* An interrogative. *Stier.* Jesus assumes that the man
has confessed the Messiah before the tribunal, and this conclusion is virtually
correct. *Meyer.* The Lord only assumes that he has believingly recognized the
living God in *His* miraculous deed, and has maintained this belief in temptation, without being aware of what faith nominally comprehends. *Lange.*
υἱὸν τοῦ θεοῦ. What did the man understand by this term ? Jews now
have the idea of a future Messiah. Popular sense of Messiah. *Lücke.* Not
the metaphysical, but solely the theocratical, signification of *the Son of God* is
to be understood. *Meyer.* The theocratical signification was not exclusive ;
its background was formed by the " metaphysical " acceptation of the title.
Lange. For υἱὸν τοῦ θεοῦ Codd. B. D. and the *Ethiopian translation* read :
τοῦ ἀνθρώπου, because Jesus was wont thus to designate Himself. This
reading is also sustained by *Cod. Sin.*, and adopted by *Tisch., Westcott &
Hort. Schaff* in *Lange*, Amer. Edit.

36. He answered and said, Who is he, Lord, that I might believe on him ?

Answered. The question evidently found him still musing over his change. But true to his *self-possessed* character, he asks for information.—It is not presumptuous to think that his answers to Pharisees and friends, and even to the Redeemer, were fulfilments of the promise, " The Holy Ghost shall teach you what to say." Luke xii. 12.—The answer is the method by which the Lord's gracious design is to be accomplished.

Who is he ? He is quite ready and willing to take Jesus' word for it. The germ of his faith is in Jesus.—He seems to have a presentiment of the issue of the question and vividly enters into it. The animated response shows the depth of interest aroused by the inquiry.—He held Him to be a *man* of God, soon he will receive Him as Son of God.—Improving what light he has, he will surely receive more. Rev. ii. 25.—" A great door and effectual" will ever be opened to sincere and humble hearts. Rev. iii. 8.

Lord. (See critical note on κύριος, John xx. 28.) He seems to recognize the title as belonging to the " *Promised* One," but he knew not that any one claimed to be the Son of God.

Believe. John i. 7 ; vii. 38.—His answer involves, *believing* by anticipation, he had a *heart* of faith. Rom. x. 10.

The amount of ignorance in the minds of believers is only known to God.—Their sincerity rests on *what* they know, while it may be exceedingly small.—Some seek *repose ;* God in sovereign mercy sends new trials and perplexities. Some seek for an *assurance ;* He sends new clouds, and bids them *walk* by *faith.*

ἀπεκρίθη. His dogmatic knowledge did not come up to this question. *Stier.*
καί. A lively impulse to a prompt answer to the questions. Luke x. 29. *Hengstenberg.*
Τίς ἐστι. I wish to know this in order that, &c. *Winer.* καί before Τίς. *Tisch., Alf., Lange.*
κύριε. He must have known Him by the tones of His voice. *Lange.*

---

37. And Jesus said unto him, Thou hast both seen him, and it is he that talketh with thee.

Thou hast. Not only the great *dignity* of the Person, but the great *favour.*—The animated question is promptly followed by an animated reply from Jesus.

Seen him. He never had the joy of seeing his Benefactor and Redeemer *before*, although doubtless with all haste he returned to the temple.—Doubtless the *seeing* involved spiritual vision also. John vi. 40.—Sunlight and salvation seemed to have visited him at once.—His grateful emotions may be conceived, but not expressed.—How few of our entire race had ever *such* a cause for thanks!—Hagar was glad when she saw the fountain to save her son's life.—Abraham was glad when he saw the victim a substitute for Isaac.—Our thirst is far deeper and more continuous than Hagar's.—Our danger is far greater than Isaac's, without the Lamb of God.—A similar revelation our Lord made only once before to her of Sychar. John iv. 26.

Those suffering most for Christ here, will stand nearest His throne hereafter.

Talketh. If this were all of our Lord's discourse to him, there must have gone forth Divine power with the word.

" The words that I speak unto you, they are SPIRIT, and THEY ARE LIFE ! " John vi. 63.—In the times of Henry VIII. many were converted by a few words spoken by a neighbour. *Fox's* Martyrs.

How intensely did his new-born sight gaze on the " LIGHT OF THE WORLD ! "

δὲ. Omitted. *Lach.*, *Tisch.*, *Alf.*, *Tregelles.*

ἑώρακας. Perfect tense: Thou hast seen Him and dost see Him now. *Lange.* Thou hast already beheld Him in His power to heal. *Tisch.* Recognized Him in his implicit obedience when told to go. *Stier.* With reference to experience, namely, even to their first meeting. *Thol.* Refers to the present seeing. *Meyer.* Alludes also to spiritual receiving of sight. *Lücke.* Present tense. *Rosenm.*, *Kuinoel.*

καὶ—καὶ, not only—but also, implying the dignity of the Healer, &c. *Hengstenberg.*

---

38. And he said, Lord, I believe. And he worshipped him.

Lord. (See critical note, John xx. 28.) " *Lord* " in a loftier sense here than in ver. 36. *Bengel.*

I believe. How clear and bold is simple child-like faith.

How crooked, tortuous, suspicious, cold and cheerless, is unbelief.

Believe. John i. 7 ; vii. 38.—" Lord, I believe ; help thou mine unbelief." Mark ix. 24. " We believe and are sure that thou art that Christ." John vi. 69.

Worshipped. *Adoring worship.* Our Lord often received, but

never demanded worship of any one.—He worshipped Him as
the Son of God, who as God had healed him. The Apostle John
never uses this word in any other sense.—That our Lord feared
to receive this honour in the temple, and that He retired to some
private place, has no authority whatever.—His disciples doubtless were present, and were addressed in verses 39, 40, 41.
Would you see what kind of a person he believed Him to be?
He prostrated himself on the pavement and worshipped Him. Maldo-
natus.—This man risked all and gained all.—The experience of
millions of believers proves the worship of Christ as God to be
no mockery. (See critical notes on John i. 2.)
Development of the blind man's faith instructs us as to the
nature of true faith : 1. The heart before the head. 2. Trust
before knowledge. 3. The thing before the name. 4. Acting and confessing before worshipping. *Lange.*
Calamities of others, are sermons to us, concerning the same helping Saviour.—To heathen sages, this world *an enigma,* is solved by
Christ.—Martyrs risked their lives, and found a martyr's crown
in Paradise.—The farmer risks his ploughing, sowing, time,
labour, patience, in *faith.*—The merchant risks his treasures,
toil, and often his all at sea, in *faith.*—Of all the millions who
have trusted their well-being to the Redeemer, did a solitary one
ever *renounce in death* that trust?—He sums up the incident in
one deep sentence as to judgment.—How like Jehovah! a solemn
comment on the entire chapter.—The miracle is *interpreted* as
in the light of the judgment morn.

προσεκύνησεν. Our Saviour received this homage in private. Its religious
significance was indubitable. *Stier.* Not that yet he comprehended clearly the
glorious Personage near him. Christ was worshipped as God's representative.
Rev. xix. 10. *Hengstenberg.* Not that even now we need suppose him to have
known all which that title, "Son of God," contained, nor that, "*worshipping*"
the Lord, he intended to render Him that supreme adoration, which is indeed
due to Christ, but only due to Him because He is one with the Father. For
"God manifest in the flesh " is a mystery far too transcendent for any man
to embrace in an instant. *Trench.*

---

39. And Jesus said, For judgment I am come into this world, that they
which see not might see ; and that they which see might be made blind.

And Jesus. This act He made a text as a solemn warning to the
false church.

Said. He addressed all present as well as His disciples.

Relentless foes lurk around to catch at His words.

Though put down and silenced, they seem resolved never to quit Him.—Had they taken half the pains to *obtain light* they did to *destroy* it, what a change in their history!—The wonder at judgment and through eternity will be, how men with Bibles in their hands could fight so fiercely against Divine Truth and Love.

Blind Pharisaism will not look at the Truth until it reads it in the flames of hell.—Of all *evil spirits*, there is none so incorrigible and none so cruel as the *spirit* of proud, self-righteous orthodoxy.

The Lord sees in this incident the consequence of His mission to earth.—He well foreknew the offence His words would give.

His primary design in His Incarnation is alluded to in John iii. 19. Here His saving work precedes His condemning work.

Judgment. Not so much for condemnation, as *discrimination*.

It does not condemn us for being dark, but not *owning* our darkness.—Our eyes are not formed for creating light, but receiving it.—The dividing line begun was *invisible* to man, but plain to Jesus.—Christ was " set for the *fall* and *rising* of many in Israel." Luke ii. 34.—Some would build on the *stone*, others be broken by it.—The thoughts of many hearts would, through Christ, be revealed. Luke ii. 35.—" Loving darkness rather than light " was "*judgment*" begun. John iii. 18.—Prophecy foretold Him to be a " refiner's fire," separating the gold from the dross. Mal. iii. 2.—He was thus engaged before—" Dividing the light from the darkness." Gen. i. 4.—*Each one may anticipate his own final sentence at yonder Bar.*—Our Lord's first advent was typical of the work of the great and terrible day.

Judgment, not so much a judicial, but a disciplinary separation between those who are in need of light and those who shun it.

Men's love and hate have been unfolding wonderfully ever since. John iii. 19—21.—He proves in every age (like John, with fan in hand), a DIVIDER.—Many that promised a glorious harvest, will prove mere chaff.—Christ is a rock on which some build, against which some stumble.—The sun matures the golden grain, but kills the rootless stalks.

Come. He distinctly alludes to a preceding glorious existence.

The setting up of His cross, the banner of the Redeemer, has (under the reign of the Spirit) *compelled* all to arrange themselves either under it, or Satan's.

That. The sad result of rejected light, and chosen darkness.

Still the original design shows that the Light of the world was to guide, and would blind none.

See not. The traveller without bread must feel his hunger before he seeks food.—This poor man did not in proud conceit close his heart, but said, " *I believe.*"—His judges had all their lives been learning, and yet knew nothing.

Who see, i. e. Who know the truth, but through pride their sight becomes blindness.—Vain pretenders to virtue and boasters of knowledge.—Proud, presumptuous persons who, " mad on their idols," wilfully resist and blaspheme the Holy Ghost.

The Sun of Righteousness blinds those who " *see,*" and enlightens the " *blind.*"—He saves the self-convicted sinner, and condemns the self-righteous.—Those who are lowly He exalts, but humbles the proud.

Made blind. Spiritually by nature we are all born blind. Rom. xi. 7.—Confessing our blindness is our first seeing.

The same Sovereign Goodness which reveals the truth to " *babes,*" at the same time hides that truth from the " *wise.*" Matt. xi. 25.

The children of earth are wiser in their generation than believers. *Owls* can see further than *eagles—in the dark.*

Our Lord *gratefully* set His seal to this arrangement of His Father's good pleasure. Matt. xi. 25.—The *seers* in Jerusalem had advantage *far above* all the world beside.—They boasted of their knowledge, Rom. ii. 18—20, but shut out God's light.

Assumed the position of *judges,* when they ought to have been *learners.*—Antichristian Judaistic bigotry was intense and desperate. It invited a consummate judgment and a fearful doom.—The Gospel was published and rejected years before these results were seen. Isa. vi. 10.—A similar judgment is still going on in Christendom, and will end in a similar but more awful crisis.—" He that hath ears to hear, let him hear what the Spirit saith to the Churches."

$\varepsilon\tilde{\iota}\pi\varepsilon\nu$. Addressed to His disciples. *Stier.* Addressed particularly to the blind man ; but also loudly and solemnly uttered for the disciples, and all that were about Him. *Lange.*

$\kappa\rho\iota\mu\alpha$. In the N. T., as in later Greek, this word always denotes a judgment *unfavourable* to those concerned, a punitive judgment, involving punishment as a matter of course. *Cremer. Here* used with a distinctive emphasis, better felt than expressed. *Stier.* A judgment of damnation. *Euthym., Olsh.* Not so, for it refers also to the blind who obtain sight. *Lange.* Not merely *distinction,* but judgment ; the following out of the Divine $\varepsilon\tilde{\upsilon}\delta o\kappa\iota\alpha$. Matt. xi. 25, 26. *Alford.*

ἵνα. A result foreseen. *Stier.* Indicates the event indirectly following Christ's coming. *Bloomfield.*

οἱ βλέποντες. Flatter themselves as seeing, but do not, and *appear* blind. *Kuinoel.* Wilfully see only through prejudice and self-conceit. *Clarke.* A relative goodness, still excluding regeneration. *Hengst.* Beneath the *plus* there is concealed a sad *minus. Anton.* A blind boy, a convert, came to Hooper for baptism. The martyr bishop said, "God hath taken thy sight, but hath given thee vision above thousands." *Fox's* Martyrs. The Church of Christ hath children seven years old able to confute the errors of Papacy, and the learned Pharisees from the University. *Beza.*

γίνωνται. Partly ironical for remaining blind. *Stier.* Antithetical; either in their own eyes, when conscious of their blindness, *or* becoming more blind. *Tholuck.*

---

40. And some of the Pharisees which were with him heard these words, and said unto him, Are we blind also?

Pharisees. John i. 24.—"Thou blind Pharisee," said our Lord. Matt. xxiii. 26. "Ye blind guides." Matt. xxiii. 24. "Ye fools and blind." Matt. xxiii. 17; and yet they then passed for the wise.—As the body dies from bleeding, so the soul of inward pride.

With Him. Implies they were prowling after His steps. Luke vi. 2.—Their official dignity was offended, hence the question.

Are we? "We"? the successors of Moses and the prophets; "*We*"? leaders of Israel!—A question asked with indignant irony.

Blind also? A number of Pharisees boastingly called themselves "*open-eyed,*" as if all mankind but themselves were wilfully blind.—Our Lord makes this terrible charge—"*Ye fools and* BLIND!" Matt. xxiii. 17. As much as to say, "Let them alone; you may provoke them, but never convince them."

David warmly denounced the supposed wrong-doer in Nathan's parable till "Thou art the man" pierced his conscience.

The most timid bird fears not the falcon, as long as he is high in the air.—The Corinthians were self-complacent until Paul said, "And such were some of you."—A sad condition of the Church, when no one thinks himself ignorant.—Ignorance itself is no sin, only when we mistake it for wisdom.—If we know more than others, we have more reason to be humble, for we are more accountable.—Our knowledge, as a lamp, helps to direct our way *out* of ignorance.—"It is impossible for one to improve, who knows everything." *Chrysostom.*—Their official pride is irritated: "We have sight as clear as we need, for which we are under no debt to Thee. Dost thou mean us?"

" Must we become Thy disciples before we learn to see ? "
They well understood the saying was a challenge, and meant for
them.—" Wilt thou put out the eyes of these men ? " Korah's
band to Moses. Num. xvi. 14.—Here the Light of the world
shone with His brightest effulgence. The last, and undeniably
the greatest, sign before their eyes. Yet they inquire why they
cannot see ? " Behold, ye despisers, and wonder, and perish."
Acts xiii. 41.—The very manifestation of the Messiah blinded,
i. e. revealed their blindness.—This roused all the fierceness of
their enmity.—This very tumult of their passion, proved the
charge well founded.—A sign of their blindness, *not to know* that
they were blind. " And KNOWEST NOT *that thou art blind*," &c.
Rev. iii. 17.—" Have we not Abraham for our Father ? " Rom.
ii. 17, 18.—" Have we not been instructed out of the Law, and
make our boast of God ? "—One of the many illustrations of our
Lord's omniscience *in action.* He could always touch the right
key in the mysteries of the heart.—All this proves that He *who
first created the soul* was now moving among men.
To their arrogant question our Lord replies that they *were* blind.

καὶ. Omitted. *Tisch., Alf., Lange, Tregelles.*
φαρισαίων. They met Him descending Mount of Olives. *Maurice.* A
very unlikely spot. It was doubtless outside the Temple where the crowd
was passing. *Author.*
καὶ ἡμεῖς. The application of general rules to particular persons causes all
the strife. *Epictetus.*
τυφλοί. Supposing that Jesus spake of physical blindness. *Chrys.,
Fikenscher.* Are we become blind in Thy light ? *Stier.* They suppose themselves in need of no further light. *Hengst.* They assail the principle laid down
by the Lord, and establish a third class, consisting of men originally possessing sight, and ever becoming more clear-sighted. This attack upon His antithesis calls forth the piercing words of the next verse. *Lange.*

---

41. Jesus said unto them, If ye were blind, ye should have no sin : but now
ye say, We see ; therefore your sin remaineth.

If ye, &c. If you felt your moral blindness you would, with this
poor beggar, long to be healed.—If ye were unable to discern
My claims, then ye would have excuse.—The natural blindness
of the human heart was guilt, but not such as they now had.
Relatively, their sin without Christ's signs and teachings was *no
sin.*—" *If I had not come* and spoken unto them, &c., they had
not had sin." John xv. 22.—This, like the text, is a paradox,

found often in our Saviour's teaching.—Men were sinners before Christ came, and are so now.   But compared with the guilt of impenitence under the noon-day of the Gospel He calls it *no sin*.—There is hope of those who *see* and frankly *own* their errors ; but those who *see* and yet are too *proud* to confess, of such, He solemnly hints, there is but little hope.

Self-blinding results in self-hardening on the part of the intellect. Their eyes were in some faint degree illuminated, but just sufficiently to render them entirely blind. *Lange.*

No sin.   No flagrant, God-defying, abiding, unpardonable sin.

THE SIN of man, like that of these Pharisees, is *Despising the Gospel.* John iii. 19.—There is no sin like it, so daring, so insulting to Jehovah Jesus.—Like one being led to the gallows and yet tearing in pieces the pardon offered him, or one firing a ship at sea without a plank of hope being left.

We see.   You boast your privileges which exalt you to heaven. Luke x. 13.—Your intelligent claim to understand all my deeds and words seals your guilt.—A clear decision of the Searcher of hearts that Gospel-rejecters sin against their solemn convictions.

Your sin, added to all former guilt, hinders forgiveness, because God has promised pardon *only* on the ground of repentance and faith.

Remaineth.   Providence contrasts unavoidable ignorance with proud knowledge.—These rulers did know much of Scripture, far *too much* to leave them guiltless.—Infatuation and obstinacy quenches the Spirit.—Deliberately and defiantly the sinner retires beyond the reach of mercy or hope.—These and all Gospel-despisers, calmly counting the cost of rejecting Christ, close the door of hope. Luke xii. 10.—They *perfect their blindness* by closing more firmly their own eyes, and fiercely endeavouring to prevent those who *would* from seeing.   Matt. xv. 14.

The Sanhedrim, in their treatment of this blind man, prove all here charged against them.—They first sought to seduce him into telling a lie, and then excommunicated him because he resists their temptations.—Resolved to resist to the last, they sign and seal their own eternal condemnation.

The very greatness of the light produces a more absolute darkness. The Jews an awful example of the truth, that by the very power of light they who see may become blind.—" The earth which drinketh in the rain bringeth forth herbs." Heb. vi. 7.   But

the same earth, under the same sun and showers, " bringeth
forth thorns."—How many will in the judgment morn have
their eyes opened for the first time.

Εἰ, &c., cannot imply that they had now the power to see. *Cyril.* Since ye
have confessed it yourselves. *Hezel.* If ye were simple and honest. *Beza.* If
ye wanted capacity to know the Divine. *Olshausen. If ye considered yourselves blind.* Thus with reference to the "ye say, We see." *Aug., Calvin,
Meyer, Kuinoel.* The words recognize a certain superiority. *Chrys., Lücke,
Neander, Alford.* If ye were ignorant, erring, with the accessory idea of
susceptibility. *De Wette.* Christ here attributes to them a certain degree of
sight. It is the gleam of a better objective Old Test. knowledge, which they
are consciously converting into a false, unbelieving knowledge, i. e. into the
blindness of self-infatuation. *Lange.* They had a certain degree of sight, but,
in a higher sense, were blind. *Von Gerlach.* If you could only confess your
blindness, then would you be saved from lying and unbelief. *Stier.* Questioned,
since ἁμαρτία would then be only their sinful condition. *De Wette.* Had they
not known Moses and the prophets, they would have had no sin of infidelity for
which to be condemned. *Prescott.* Their unbelief, as an impenetrable veil, is
drawn more and more closely around them. *Tittmann.*

ἁμαρτία. Denotes primarily, not *sin* considered as an action, but sin considered as the *quality* of action, that is, sin generally. *Cremer.*

οὖν. Omitted. *Tisch., Alf., Cod. Sin.*

John 10

1. Verily, verily, I say unto you, He that entereth not by the door into the sheepfold, but climbeth up some other way, the same is a thief and a robber.

Verily, verily. See on John i. 51 ; iii. 3. No unmeaning pleonasm, but half an oath in our Lord's discourse.—Either a truth of transcendent importance to our race, or one the human heart is strongly prejudiced against.—Addressed to those who cast out the blind man from the synagogue; who declared that Jesus was not the Messiah. John ix. 22.—And that His confessors, should have neither part nor lot in the Church.—They charged the Lord Himself with being "a sinner." John ix. 24.—By rejecting Him, they proved they knew not where the door was.

I. The utterance of a Majesty that becomes no created being.— Yet in the Redeemer, it seems natural; it is becoming His Divinity.

Say unto. This allegory is noted for its exquisite simplicity and imagery—true to nature.—For its unfolding the tenderest relations between Christ and His people.—It teaches that Christianity is essentially the discipleship of the heart.

He that. The Lord would graciously awaken some disposed to self-knowledge, and having a craving for true spiritual sight.

Entereth not. This cannot imply that the Jewish rulers were not *lawfully* such, but to their want of a call of far more value, a seal of Heaven.—Those now assuming to be spiritual guides, without this, are *intruders* in God's house.—I have not sent these prophets, yet they run. Jer. xxiii. 21.—These false prophets prophesy out of their own hearts. Ezek. xiii. 2.—Pharisees, without a Divine vocation, set themselves up as Teachers.—No legal knowledge, nor ceremonial observances avail to admit.

By the door. Gr. *through* the door.

Door or gate. Made of wood, stone, brass, or iron, two-leaved, plated and locked.—Near the town gate was an open space, where business was transacted. Ruth iv. 1.—A place for news. 2 Sam. xv. 2.—People sat to converse. 1 Kings xvii. 10.—The traveller now finds this in every town in Egypt and Palestine.— A place of public audience. Ezek. xi. 1.—Of the administration of justice. Est. iv. 2.—Equivalent to Government. Matt. xvi. 18.—Hence " Porte," Turkey's sovereignty.—Of public markets which still are held at Oriental gates. 2 Kings vii. 17.—Altars for sacrifice usually stood near the gates. Acts xiv. 13.—Gates of cities guarded carefully at nightfall. Deut. iii. 5.—Among Romans, porters were often chained there to be always present to open them.—At the destruction of Pompeii, some of these porters perished in their chains.—Chambers over the gateways used by sentinels. 2 Sam. xviii. 33.—And by Priests in Egypt.—Private gates often highly ornamented, sentences written over them.—In Egypt locked with wooden or iron keys, or sealed with clay. Job xxxviii. 14.—Gates of Palace at Ispahan, sanctuary for criminals. *Chardin.*—Solomon covered his gates of the Holy place of olive wood with pure gold.—The gates of the temple were of fir. Herod covered the gates of the temple with gold or silver.— The " Beautiful Gate " was made entirely of Corinthian brass.— As Christ entered on His work by the door appointed by the Father, so pastors must not take this honour on themselves. Heb. v. 4.—Pastors must enter through the authorities of the church.—To adopt the calling simply as a *trade*, is not to enter through the door.—He who waits at God's altar must love the service *above* all other callings.

Sheepfold. Church in Old Test. often noted under the word " flock ; " " and ye are My flock, the flock of My pasture, and I am your God." Ezek. xxxiv. 31.—" He shall feed His flock like a shepherd," &c. Isa. xl. 11.—" The Lord Jesus, that great shepherd of the sheep." Heb. xiii. 20.—The universal church the fold, Israel the peculiar fold.—Possibility of there being " other folds " alluded to in verse 16.

Sheepfold. Some think He stood near where the sacrificial sheep were kept, others, where the tinkling bells were sounding from the folded herd.—Israel was the sheep of God's pasture, and the Church His fold.—The Scribes and Pharisees, such as they were,

were shepherds.—Here described as intruders; ignoring Christ, they were wrong in everything. ALL HANGS ON HIM.—*Sheepfolds*, in our country, are loose rails or hurdles put slightly together. In the East, they are strong substantial stone buildings with gates.—Wild beasts, as the bear, the lion, the jackall, found in Palestine.—From time of autumnal rains to the vernal equinox, no flocks left in the fields.—*Succoth* proves Jacob built *houses* for himself and flocks. Gen. xxxiii. 17.—Pharaoh's pious servants drove their flocks into houses. Ex. ix. 20.—Hezekiah provided out of royal bounty cotes for the flocks. 2 Chron. xxxii. 28.— The idea of a fold is inseparable from that of a flock.—Each member of the flock bears relations to the entire Church of Christ.

Climbeth. Those not related to Christ as believers, "climb up," &c., cannot lead a flock.—There is but ONE door to the fold, all others are closed.—The enemy pretends to show other doors, but they lead to *death.*—A thousand broad ways lead *from* heaven, but only one "narrow way" *to* it.—Usurping it for attaining ease, or a living, or social position, or preferment full of peril.— False doctrines draw myriads away from the chief shepherd, and those under Him.—He who nullifies truth, deadens conscience, and murders the soul. John viii. 44.

Thief. A *secret* stealing—asks not for the door—cares not if it is shut.

Robber. An *open* plunderer; in contrast with *thief*, one spoiling the innocent in *secret.*—Pharisee shepherds entered without faith in His name; they were not ministers of Messiah, not preparers of His way.—They were followers of a false god and a false messiah.— Pride, prejudice, fanaticism make the worst of thieves. Souls immortal are their spoils, treasures of heaven are lost.—" As troops of robbers wait for a man, so the company of priests murder," &c. Hos. vi. 9.—" Causing men to stumble at the law " robs them of their best portion. Mal. ii. 8.—Our Lord testifies that these guardians of the fold are to be removed.—In turn they denied His miracles, rejected His claims as Messiah.—Paul, a true undershepherd desired to know nothing save Jesus Christ.

'Αμὴν. This occurred at Jerusalem at the feast of dedication. *Robinson.* Chap. x. ought to begin at chap. ix. 35. *Meyer, Lücke.* First twenty-two verses spoken at another time. *Schulz.* The more this gospel is studied, the more the connection appears. *Alford.* Uttered on Olivet. *Stanley.* With sheep grazing in sight. *Maurice.* Could not our Lord utter a parable in the Temple Court, about sowing seed, or tending flocks? *Author.*
'Αμὴν. Haters of the Bible by their passions, point out those truths peculiar to the Gospel plan. *Nelson.* With this high assurance our Lord never begins a dis-

course. *Heumann.* Connected with John ix. 40. &c., *Hengst.* Implied double assurance. *Trapp.* This comparison an allegory. *Trench.* Not a parable. *Lange.* A prophetic allegory. *Greswell.* Not a history. *Meyer.* This only parable in John the deepest, the solidest, sweetest, serenest, surest view of spiritual christianity. *Knox.*

ἡμεῖς τυφλοί—of official pride connects this with the last chapter. *Stier.*

λεγω. Verses 1—6, all referred to Christ. *Neander.* In part. *Schleier.* His answer to the accusation of the Pharisees. *Lampe.* They called Him ἁμαρτωλός. He describes them as wolves prowling round the fold. *Bloomfield.*

ὑμῖν. His hearers must have thought themselves meant. *Stier.* This allegory surpasses any work of human genius in its exquisite simplicity, its truth to nature, its vivacity and clearness of thought, its elegance and purity of style. *Greswell.*

θύρας. The scriptures. *Chrys., Theoph.*

αὐλήν. The bounded inheritance of Israel under the Theocracy, not the narrow penfold a church. *Stier.* Door and porter have no distinctive import in the fable. *Lücke.* Members, the sheep, αὐλὴν the kingdom, and θύρα the Divine calling. The door of the sheep, not the sheepfold. *Hengstenberg.*

κλέπτης. Secret fraud.

λῃστής. Open fraud by violence. *Grotius.* Matt. xxi. 13, den of robbers not "thieves." Luke xxiii. 42: the penitent "robber" *Trench.* All not ordained by Romish bishops are thieves and murderers, as Arius, Calvin, Luther.—*Rheimish Notes.*

---

2. But he that entereth in by the door is the shepherd of the sheep.

Door. Implies he is the owner and has a personal knowledge of the sheep.—He enters in an open, regular and peaceable manner as the master.—But these intruders, wicked rulers, sat in Moses' seat, but were strangers to Moses' spirit.—A divine call, as well as the "laying on the hands of the presbytery," is necessary to qualify for the ministry.—Christ's under-shepherds must bear a direct commission from Him, and endorsed by the Holy Ghost if they would do God's work.—1. An immediate call by the Head accompanied always by the necessary gifts. 2. A mediate call: —(1.) A sincere love to God and the work of Christ.—Peter expressing this *love* heard the command, "Feed my sheep." (2.) An overcoming desire to preach the Gospel. 1 Tim. iii. 1. (3.) An inward call sustained by corresponding efforts to qualify oneself.—Minister or pastor ought to be : 1. A man of piety. 2. Of wisdom, 3. Of knowledge. 4. Of prayer. 5. Of self-denial. 6. Of heavenly mindedness. 7. Of heavenly conversation. 8. Of exemplary life. 9. Of meekness. 10. Of zeal and diligence. 11. Of intense love for his flock. 12. Of sensibility. 13. Of faithfulness in declaring the whole counsel of God. 14. Of simplicity of speech and manners. 15. Anxious about success. 16. Faithful in pastoral duties. 17. Sustaining discipline. 18. Careful of the religion of his own family. 19. Studious.—*Smith* on "The Sacred Office."

Shepherd. See verse 11. "The" is wanting in the Greek : the word denotes a number of shepherds.—Our Lord is called a shepherd as bearing a relation to His sheep.—A door as

He introduces us to the Father.—This word, a sermon on the duties of each pastor.—Jacob and Joseph call Christ "The Shepherd," Gen. xlix 24.—Moses is styled the shepherd of the flock of God. Isa. lxiii. 11.—Messiah is set forth as having the gentlest attributes of a shepherd.—Kings were generally described under the pastoral character. **Jer.** xii. 10.; Micah. v. 5.; Nahum, iii. 18; Zech. x. 3.—The undertone is " I AM THE TRUE SHEPHERD.—I entered the door and am sent to the lost sheep of the house of Israel."—Door is lowly, as our Lord stooped to the depth of humiliation to enter.—Anyone now exalting himself climbs up some other way.—No man can be such a shepherd, except through Christ.—As one torch kindles another, so human pastors receive from Christ all the gifts of office: 1. Able to rule. 2. Apt to teach. 3. Gentle, both learned and loving.—A shepherd must feed the lambs, as well as the sheep.—A pastor that has no capacity of interesting the young, loses about *two-thirds* his opportunity of being useful.—Our risen Lord to Peter : " Feed my lambs:"—Children form a large portion of congregations.—They are far more accessible, far more docile and hopeful than adults.—Pastors unconsciously stand before children as *transparent as glass.*—It is a serious mistake that to teach a youthful mind, but slender abilities are needed.—The deeper the darkness, the greater the need of light. —The Sanhedrim were called of God to be shepherds of His flock. Matt. xxiii. 3.—But they withheld food both from the lambs and the sheep.—They offered chaff or stubble instead of healthy nourishing pasture.—The flock was starved, and the cry of the famishing came up to the Throne.—Thus, there are many *lawfully* called to the ministry, but barrenness and spiritual death are the only results of their labours.—" Woe to the shepherds of Israel that do feed themselves, but feed not the flock." Ezek. xxxiv. 2, 4.—Without faith, humility, love, self-denial, sad will be their account.

Sheep. Its name in Hindoo is the " timid one," prone to wander. —Sheep, though silly, yet quick to detect their shepherd's voice, and clever enough to cling to him, as long as they are able to follow.—Well-known as harmless, trustful, helpless, patient, feeble, yet docile.—By its very nature, it seems to require the protection of a shepherd.—The wolf, leopard, lion, &c., are made to *win* their food and fight their own battle.—They who hear not the shepherd's voice are goats not sheep.—Sheep have been necessary to man in every land and people.—They have never become *wild*, like most other domestic animals.—Their relation is one of absolute dependence, balanced by reciprocal benefits. **With Christ's flock their confiding helplessness begets a**

mutual endearment.—As sheep are perfectly dependent, the *rights* of the shepherd are *complete.*—Sheep are relatively inferior, the shepherd superior.—Constant defence and support are needed by the flock.—Unremitting care, vigilance, and protection are due from the shepherd.—Affection of the sheep, tenderness of the shepherd.—The shepherd has no mercenary trust, nor is he of a doubtful affection.—He will love his flock as he loves himself, and their welfare as his own.—1. They are *wandering* in their nature. Instinct leads many animals to go back to their home, but true to their nature, sheep seldom return. Sinners never, unless *brought back* by the Good Shepherd. 2. All *agree* to wander, though they differ in everything else. Sinners differ, contend even to blood, but all agree to forsake the path of life. 3. Sheep are *content* in their wandering though exposed constantly to destruction. Sinners flatter themselves *all is well.* 4. Various paths of danger all end in one at last—eternal RUIN. Truth is one. One Ark, one Bible, one Saviour, one Faith, one Heaven.

ποιμήν. A shepherd, article is wanting. *Greswell.* One asking, Do you think I am called to the ministry? I answer, No, if your conscience will permit you to do anything else. *Breckenridge.* "I fear I am hiding my talents," said one. " The more you *keep* them hidden, the better for the Church." *Rowland Hill.* I have shaken your napkin, and I find no talent *there.* *R. Hall.* A legitimate aiming at God's glory, salvation of men, and perfect consecration to His service. *Quesnel.*

εἰσερχόμενος. Shepherds always enter by the door. *Campbell.* He entering by the door is especially the shepherd. *Bloomfield.* He who reaches the flock by Me, is an authorized teacher *Kuinoel.* Questioned as to this *usus loquendi. Tittmann.*

θύρας. A door of liberty, of grace, of truth, of freedom, of purity. *Alb. Magnus.*

προβάτων. Domestic sheep, a legacy of paradise, none of them like other beasts ever lapsed into wildness. *Wagner.* No similitude in nature, so descriptive of the dependence and helplessness of man. *Steinmeyer.* Not the good and the bad in the visible church, but real believers. *Alford.*

---

3. To him the porter openeth; and the sheep hear his voice: and he calleth his own sheep by name, and leadeth them out.

Porter. An Oriental picture of surpassing beauty and fitness.— In the evening the flock is gathered into the fold, an open walled place.—Wealthy Hebrews kept a porter. Ezek. xliv. 11. Greeks had a freedman.—A porter stands in close relation to the shepherd himself, and having care of the flock in the pasture and fold, spritually represents under-shepherds, each *representing* the chief shepherd.

Openeth. The shepherd is known to the porter because *with* the flock.—The sheep also know there own shepherd, as well as he knoweth their cry.—" No man can come to Me, except the Father draw him." John vi. 44.—God opened a door of faith unto the

Gentiles. Acts xiv. 27.—Every good gift is finally traced up to the Father as its origin. Jas. i. 17.—God generally owns the faithful pastor's labours, although he is not always permitted to see results.

The sheep. See on John ii. 15. The faithful who *are* what all the fold *should* be.

Hear his voice. Gr. *give heed to. Lange.* A Hebraism for obeyi still used in the East.—Ministers by the pulpit give the call, preaching finds its completion in the pastoral care of soul Why do some hear, and others refuse to regard mercy's call? the former it is the Spirit of God *who worketh in them both to* WI and to DO. Phil. ii. 13.—The reckless and wicked care not to ask even for the *hearing ear*, or obedient will.—Some seem resolved to perish, if they can *find* a hell in the universe.—They are bent on closing every crevice, through which light can enter.—Resolved to insult the Spirit, each time He would call.—Determined to defy the Son, each time He would knock at their hearts.—Even when " His locks are wet with the drops of the night." Cant. v. 2.

Calleth. Shepherds either whistle or call by a pipe to the flock.— " Who hath saved us, and *called us with an holy calling*." 2 Tim. i. 9.

His own. Redeemed, regenerated, sealed, elect. Rom. viii. 28. —An orientalism for a complete and minute knowledge of their hearts.—This tender relation differs from that of the *hireling* :—1. By Creation. 2. By Redemption. 3. By Regeneration.—Israel has ever been the Angel Jehovah's " peculiar people." Deut. xiv. 2. " A chosen generation." 1 Pet. ii. 9.—" For all the earth is mine." Ex. xix. 5.—A king, having many possessions, yet prefers one above all others.—Our Lord out of all believers chose twelve, out of twelve, chose three. Matt. xvii. 1.—Our King has myriads of beings, but chooses a number for Himself.—" Children of the promise," are by the new birth of one *land*, one *law*, one *hope*, one *home*. Gal. iv. 28.—They are a " royal priesthood, being washed in His blood." 1 Pet. ii. 9 ; Rev. i. 5.—The *world* accounts saints the humblest and lowest of mankind.—The Eternal God esteems them His SONS, FRIENDS, PRIESTS, and KINGS. Rev. i. 5.

By name. In oriental lands sheep, as well as children have names. —*Daughters* among the *heathen* Chinese, are 1st, 2nd, 3rd, &c., nameless as our herds.—Soldiers and slaves have been called as " things " by number.—But a name implies a person.—When the the Lord called "*Mary*," He summoned up all the *devotion* and *love* of that believer.—He called John, Cephas, Zacchæus, Cornelius, and others.—Isaiah represents the Almighty Creator as leading out the starry heavens, as a shepherd leadeth his flock.—The

humblest may hope that He will write his name in the Eternal
Register of Heaven.—Christ hol ls a particular relation to individual persons.—He knows them, loves them, watches for them
and leads them individually.—Our Saviour alludes to a pastoral
scene of touching beauty and interest, a flock of sheep, not driven
by violence, nor harassed by pursuing dogs, but slowly moving
along, following their shepherd. he, perhaps, with a lamb in his
arms.—For a while they linger to graze or partake of the clear
stream, still he makes progress towards the fold of safety for the
night.—Are any missing as one by one " called by name," they
enter ? He goeth out into the wilderness to seek the lost one.
Ezek. xxxiv.—All the volumes of classical literature have nothing
that approaches this picture of a *Teacher of religion* leading his
disciples through an unfriendly world, to the fold of peace.—
The twenty-third psalm, that Divine pastoral has for 2500 years
been a source of consolation to myriads of weary, care-worn,
heavy-laden believers.—In the protection of the Divine Shepherd
"they shall neither hunger nor thirst."—"The Sun shall not
smite them" &c. Isa. xlix. 10.—"The Lamb which is in the
midst of the throne shall feed them, and shall lead them unto
living fountains of waters." Rev. vii. 17.—To call by one's name
indicates a loving regard of one, the reflection of the name.—" I
know thee by name," Ex. xxxiii., same as, "Thou hast found
grace in my sight."—"I will give them an everlasting name that
shall not be cut off." Isa. lvi. 5.

Leadeth.—In our land they are driven, in Oriental lands they are
led.—The author in Palestine saw a shepherd and a flock of sheep
and goats following.—Several dogs kept the stragglers from
straying away.—A secret allusion to His leading the blind man
out from the snares of the Pharisees. *Chrysostom.*—The pillar of
cloud *led* the thousands of Israel through the desert.—God
present, ever leading.—"He led them on safely and they feared
not." Psalm lxxviii. 53.—"Give ear, O shepherd, thou that
leadest Joseph like a flock." Psa. lxxx. 1.—"He shall lead them,
even by the springs of water shall he guide them." Isa. xlix. 10.
—"I will feed them upon the mountains of Israel by the
rivers." Ezek. xxxiv. 11, 16.—Leading those trusting Him,
excludes the unbelieving world.—1. He leadeth them in a
way where is no *uncertainty.* 2. In a way of *safety.* 3. In a
way of *peace.* 4. In a way of *joy.*—But of false shepherds He
saith, "My soul loathed them." Zech. xi. 8.

Leadeth. He does not drive them on before as a herd of *unwilling*
disciples. He goes before Himself, leading them into paths that
He has trod, and dangers He has met, and sacrifices He has borne
Himself, calling them after Him, and to be only followers.

Bushnell.—What a mistake to regard the Christian life as a legal or constrained service.

θυρωρὸς. Romans had a eunuch or slave chained to the post. *Suetonius.* Jesus, the Door, Porter, Shepherd, all within Himself. *Fikenscher.* God the Father, opening an entrance for Christ. *Bengel, Hengst.* Holy Ghost, the Porter. *Weisse.* Such a ministry inappropriate to the Lord of the flock. *Tholuck.* Moses as an author of scripture. *Chrys.* John the Baptist, supposed by some to be the Porter. Holy Spirit openeth the Scripture door to those knocking. *Origen, Theoph., Alford,* The Porter—he to whom the sheep belong. Exegesis ought not to be more specific. *Calvin, Meyer, Luthardt, D. Brown.* Christ is His own Porter. *Cyril.*
ἀνοίγει. Right of free access. *Calvin, Meyer, Luthardt.*
φωνῆς. A whistle, as the bird's note, and cock's crowing, is thus called. *Bloomfield.*
ἴδια. Put for αὐτοῦ. *Rosenm.* Christ, the alone shepherd who led the Church from the Old Test. to the New. *Lampe.*
ἴδια. Elect, beloved ones. *Lampe. Omnes sunt propriœ. Bengel, Stier.* High Priest's attire shadowed the three-fold office of Christ. The Crown, His kingly. The Urim, His prophetical. The twelve names on the Ephod, His Priestly Office. *Godwyn.* Distinction between "sheep" and "own sheep," gives rise to mistakes. *Alford.*
καλεῖ. φωνεῖ *Cod. Sin., Lach., Tisch.* φωνεῖ better corresponds with the figure. The sheep, as sheep, are not influenced by an understanding of the call, but by its warm, accustomed tone. *Lange.*
καλεῖ. Whom He draws, He calls, and *vice versa. H. Charo.*
κατ᾽ὄνομα Gives His people a name, *e. g.,* Israel. *Schleier.* Sheep, goats, horses anciently had names. *Callimachus.* Different folds under many shepherds. *Lücke, Crusius.* "Known thee by name." Ex. xxxiii. 12, *i. e.,* chosen thee to do My will. *Oehler.* A specific personal relation. *Keil.* Parallel with: Thou hast found grace in My sight. *Hengst.* In Germany a shepherd in charge of three or four hundred sheep can call at will by name those belonging to a family. *Blackley.*
ἐξάγει. Formerly the Syrian shepherd with a low humming voice preceded the flock. *Salmeron.* An old English law required farmers not to irritate beasts at work, but with pleasant musical sounds to encourage them. *Selaen,* in *Denton.*

---

4. And when he putteth forth his own sheep, he goeth before them, and the sheep follow him: for they know his voice.

Putteth forth. Illustrates the energetic mode of "leading them out." Appropriate to the employment of a shepherd who "turns out" the sheep to pasture.—It implies that the sheep hesitate and linger behind.—He frees them from the burden of their sins, as Israel was freed from the tyranny of Pharaoh.—Sin has imprisoned by bolt and bar the guilty race of Adam. Zech. ix. 12.

Goeth before. As He led them by the Pillar of fire in the desert forty years.

Follow. See on verse 3. Sheep are social and affectionate to those kind to them.—In the Old Test. no allusion is ever made to *driving* the flock.—The custom alluded to is common to this day in Palestine and on the Downs of England.—The Moors' descendants in Spain still lead their *Merino* flocks.—Twice *literally* the Saviour walked in *advance* of His disciples. Matt. xxvi. 32;

Mark x. 32. Not as an intrepid leader, but as a faithful and loving shepherd.—In the garden He took the lead to confirm and protect them. John xviii. 4.—By His crucifixion, He precedes each believer through the ga*es of death.—Ambition prompts proud prelates to walk in advance of Christ's ministry.—Christ's followers eye their shepherd's steps, and listen for His voice.— "These are they who follow the Lamb whithersoever He goeth." Rev. xiv. 4.

Know. This reveals the fact of acquaintance. Job xxii. 21.—The sheep know the voice of every *true* shepherd; honest minds generally discriminate truth from error; hence, believers soon forsake preachers who become heretics.—The hungry soul finds false doctrines, as bitter ashes to the taste.—When the pulpit becomes a fountain of heresy, a sad sifting is going on among the people of God.—"Tasting the good word of God," shows His previous working. Heb. v. 14.

His voice. Truth is like light: visible in itself. Christ came with truth, and the true recognise it as true. In all matters of eternal truth, the heart is before the head. You know truth by being true. You recognise God by being like Him. *Robertson.*— They know His voice so well, that an angel from heaven must expect no welcome, if he bring another gospel. Gal. i. 8.

ἐκβάλη and ἐξάγει the same sense. *Grotius, Rosenmuller.*
ἐκβάλη. Not necessarily violence. *Wakefield.*
τὰ ἴδια πρόβατα πάντα. All his own. *Lach., Tisch.* A more expressive reading than the received text, in accordance with B. D. L. X. etc. *Schaff, Tregelles.* His favourite sheep, and the rest of the flock follow. *Lange.*
ἀκολουθεῖ. "The Lord led, and the sheep followed." Book of Enoch. *Lawrence's* Translation. Allusions are found in *Ignatius, Clemens Alex., Chrys.* The Corsican shepherds led their flocks. *Polybius.* Believers not to be treated as driven beasts. *Maldonatus.* His voice has an agreement with their higher reason. *Albertus Magnus.* Goeth before in temptations. *Dion. Carth.* He walked before His disciples, Mark x. 32, as a bold commander. *Grotius.* He advanced to protect them. *Bengel.*
οἴδασι. The shepherd's voice is self-evidencing. *Stier.*
φωνήν. A harp stood in a room, when a clock at midnight in a neighbouring belfry struck one. One solitary chord out of many vibrated, one note sounded, for but one chord was in *harmony. Author.* It cannot be fundamentally understood, without something resembling itself. *Stier.*

---

5. And a stranger will they not follow, but will flee from him: for they know not the voice of strangers

A stranger. The Jews are thus reproached with more obstinacy than beasts.—They must discern between good and evil. Heb. v. 14.—A spirit of discerning. 1 Cor. x. 12.—Mind of Christ. 1 Cor. ii. 16.—Reasonable service. Rom. xii. 1.—

Obedience by faith. Rom. xvi. 26.—1. *A stranger* to the deceitfulness of his own heart. 2. *A stranger* to the utter poverty of all his promises and schemes. 3. *A stranger* to the fulness of the grace of God. 4. *A stranger* to the Divine shepherd whose flock he appears to tend.—So infatuated and hardened were the Pharisees that they never, for an instant, doubted that they were genuine shepherds.—The intruder is called a thief, he leads others to the pit, not to the fold.—Some under *judicial blindness*, may be unconscious of their state.—One holding the key of knowledge should be a man of prayer and should exercise self-denial, meekness, diligence, zeal, heavenly-mindedness.—They are "set for the fall and rise of many in Israel." Luke ii. 34.—Emperor Julian subjoined on all the Pagan priests of the Roman empire to be sober-minded and pure in converse, to avoid all shows, and to excel all in virtue.—" I never knew him say an idle word, or that which did not tend to edify." *Burnet*, of Leighton.—People and minister are sometimes one in guilt, and one in punishment.— " Mine anger was kindled against the shepherds, and I punished the goats." Zech. x. 3 ; Lam. iv. 13.—Prayer pre-eminently aids the faithful shepherd, as feathers, the eagle.—Strip him of his plumage, and you fix him to the earth.—Those who persecute, prove themselves strangers to the flock of God.—That which hath horns to push is Anti-christ, whatever be their office. Rev. xvii. 3.—When Chrysostom, the faithful minister, was banished from Constantinople, the people said, " It had been better that the sun itself had been darkened."—The magnet drawn through the earth's rubbish, only attracts the iron : our Lord only draws those hearts seeking Him.

Follow. The true flock of God have a voice as to the choice of their under-shepherd.—The Great Head of the Church here assigns them a Charter for their liberty of conscience ; each believer will be held responsible for his influence, but the supreme Arbiter in all these things is the Great Shepherd.—The true call draws the flock of God to the green pastures. Psa. xxiii.— Since the flock have an ear and a heart, to heed His voice, those shepherds whose voice the flock regard not, may well doubt their call.

Know not. Sheep are called silly, but they never confound their shepherd's voice with that of strangers.—This world supposed to be the *night* in which Christ leads His flock, and amid the *darkness* of our life, we walk by *faith* not by *sight*. 2 Cor. v. 7.—True Christians are taught by the Spirit and the word to know the voice of the stranger, and to flee from it as *perilous*.—False leaders in worldly churches call this refusal *pride, obstinacy*, &c., for the true church has always been "a *little flock*." Luke xii. 32.

Flee. Not only *not* follow, but *flee* from him, as from a pestilence. —"Their word doth eat as a canker." 2 Tim. ii. 17.—Error is often incurable; like a plague, it is exceedingly infectious and frequently mortal.—Like leprosy, when it begins, the diseased one is looked upon as beyond hope.—"Jealousy, insanity, and heresy are curable only by God." *Italian Proverb.*—Fleeing is all the flock may do to the intruder.—No weapons of carnal temper are to be used.—Their appeal is to the Great Shepherd, and they must wait till He investigates.—This is the record of the Church of God in all past ages, and must be the rule to the end of time.

Voice. There is often much seductive melody in the words of false teachers.—For the Apostle hints their *eloquence* at times may be *angelic*. Gal. i. 8.—"They are oft as a pleasant voice playing skilfully on the harp." Ezek. xxxiii. 32.—Their doctrines please the carnal and promise peace to the troubled, and their paths are thornless, and full of goodly prospect.—While prophesying peace, the pit of woe is yawning at their feet, but concealed by flowers.—Their "voice is the voice of Jacob, but their hands are the hands of Esau."—The bringing in of strange doctrines, either drives the sheep to the right fold, or scatters them.—The Churches of Philippi, Corinth, Ephesus, Thessalonica, Corinth, Rome, the boasted "seals of Paul's apostleship" are now scattered. Rev. ii. 5.—Such flocks must first cease to be a flock of God, and they cease to be such, whenever they prefer *thieves* and *robbers* to true pastors.—The hungry soul will sooner or later find food that can satisfy it.—Our Lord the TRUE SHEPHERD: 1. He was sent by the Father. 2. Commissioned by the Spirit. 3. He knows the individual wants of each particular sheep. 4. His whole care was for His flock 5. The sheep hear and know His voice. 6. He was an example to the flock. 7. His life and death draw all to Him.

ἀλλοτρίῳ. Only the false prophets can here be understood, until the time of the pseudo-Messiahs. *Lange.* Note the deep laid principles of the apostolical church. The flock must be asked—"Wilt thou have this shepherd?" *Stier.* The stranger, not a shepherd of another section of the flock, but a robber. *Alford. Dr. Samuel Johnson* declined a Rectory in youth with, "I cannot in conscience shear the sheep, which I am unable to feed." A great scholar of Rotterdam complained that ministers in his day were—"adoloscentes leves, indocti." *Erasmus.*

ἀκολουθήσωσιν. *Cod. Sinai.* ἀκολουθήσουσιν A. B. D. *Lach., Lange, Schaff.* They will not indeed follow, but certainly flee. *Lücke.* A faithful pastor need not fear, the flock *will* follow him. *Alex. Natalis.*

ἀλλοτρίων Judas. *Chrysostom.* Antichrist. *Theophylact.* A flock will never forsake a faithful pastor. *Quesnel.* Provided the flock are the followers of the true Shepherd. Sheep would be ill off if they could not discern the true marks of Christ's shepherds. *Anton.* The whole picture of verses 4 and 5 is drawn from real life, and is to this day illustrated every day on the hills and plains of Syria and Palestine. *Thompson.* Mr. McCheyne when in Palestine, induced two shepherds to change clothes, but the sheep knew the voice of their own shepherd, in each case, and could not be deceived.

6. This parable spake Jesus unto them: but they understood not what things they were which he spake unto them.

Parable. Gr. *A similitude*, embracing a *narrative*, diverging from the common way of speech; here an allegory.—A condescension to the ignorance and stupidity of the human mind.—Our Lord, during the first of His ministry uttered no parables.—His teachings in Galilee and Jerusalem were met with scorn.—The question of the disciples, Matt. xiii. 10, intimates their astonishment.—Scriptural truths are uninviting to the unrenewed heart.—A *penal* character is hinted at by our Lord: " So then it is not given." Matt. xiii. 10—15.—Men set themselves against the truth, hence it was *hid* from them.—So the inner circle was led to know the mysteries of the kingdom.—Parables attract, and are sure to be remembered by the sincere.—The careless and reckless hear, but carry away no instruction.—Yet the Saviour's parables are infinitely more full of wisdom than all the teachings of men.—Many parables were uttered by Him which are not recorded. Matt. xiii. 34 ; Mark iv. 33.—Their ground tone implies the existence of Satan, the soul's immortality, man's responsibility, future judgment.—Their conciseness, candour, and charity are preeminent traits.—An exact decorum pervades them, nothing common or vulgar is seen.—They are so natural, that they seem almost histories, and a peculiarity is, His *own person* is so often introduced—He seems never to have premeditated or studied them. All is ORIGINAL,—Their profound depth and far reaching truths have occupied and *exhausted* the mightiest intellects for 1800 years, and still they are as fresh and exhaustless, as the ever flowing *fountains of sunlight*.—No man, before nor since, has been able to teach in this way.—The human mind delights in discovering unseen resemblances.—Pastoral life has ever proved a fruitful and pleasant source of analogy.—Parables of our Lord:—1. The sower. Matt. xiii. 2. The wheat and tares. Matt. xiii. 3. The mustard seed. Mark iv. 4. Seed in the ground. Mark iv. 5. The leaven. Matt. xiii. 6. The hid treasure. Matt. xiii. 7. The pearl of great price. Matt. xiii. 8. The net cast into the sea. Matt. xiii. After several months these answer various questions. 9. The two debtors. Luke vii. 10. The merciless servant. Matt. xviii. 11. The good Samaritan. Luke x. 12. The friend at midnight. Luke xi. 13. The rich fool. Luke xii. 14. The lower seats Luke xiv. 15. The fig tree. Luke xiii.. 16. The great supper. Luke 14. 17. The lost sheep. Matt. xviii. 18. The piece of money. Luke xv. 19. The prodigal son. Luke xv. 20. The unjust steward. Luke xvi. 21. The rich man and Lazarus. Luke xvi. 22. The unjust judge. Luke xviii. 23. The pharisee and publican.

Luke xviii. 24. The labourers in the vineyard. Matt. xx. As the Lord enters Jerusalem for the last time they become prophetic. 25. The pounds. Luke xix. 26. The two sons. Matt. xxi. 27. The vineyard. Mark xii. 28. The marriage feast. Matt. xxii. 29. The wise and foolish virgins. Matt. xxv. 30. The talents. Matt. xxv. 31. The sheep and goats. Matt. xxv. —The truths they enshrine, have never before, nor since, been so illustrated.—They are inimitable and unapproachable in majesty, simplicity, and significance. — No human writing can get the "image and superscription" of the Son of God.—For their wonderful clearness, yet profound depth of meaning, for their earthly and heavenly echoes, they stand alone among all the works of our race : yet He never wrote a line, as far as we know of, but the one in the Temple, on the dust of the floor with His divine finger.—Apochryphal gospels contain no parables.—Like the Egyptian priests, their authors here confess THIS IS THE FINGER OF GOD. Ex. viii. 19.

Understood not. A mournful fact : their boasted love of Scripture was a mockery. They were sealed up against the truth. Their sensuality had destroyed all spiritual feeling and knowledge of Scripture.—For the Old Testament is the book of shepherds— Abraham, Moses, David, Christ.—Shepherd emblems abound in Hebrew poetry ; in Isaiah, as oft as in Homer.—What cared the cold, cruel, carnal Pharisees, and sensual Sadducees for such exquisite lines as—" THE LORD IS MY SHEPHERD, I SHALL NOT WANT."— The faith, that God's wisdom beams in each blade of grass, and in every dew drop, had disappeared from Israel.—Men walked not the earth, as a holy place, full of God's presence as the heavens are full of sunlight.—The book of Nature written by the finger of God, like the two Tables, had been written over and over by the *daring hand* of *Mammon !*—Now Jesus comes to interpret these words blotted and blurred.—No wonder earth's wayfarers, in dust and care, fainted for lack of wisdom.—Madly resolved to cling to darkness rather than light, Pharisees *wilfully*, and *wickedly* perish.—They pronounce there own sentence, " Are we blind also ? " And thus prove that they were given over to strong delusions to believe a lie. 2 Thess. ii. 11.

παροιμίαν. Heb. Mâshâl, a similitude, a way-side saying, corresponds to our bye-word. *Bengel.* A single proverb from οἴμη. *Passow.* Used by the LXX. frequently, and by John instead of παραβολή. *Trench.*

παραβολή. Latter generally is in a narrative, and herein differs from a proverb. 1. Differs from fable, excluding animals. 2. Higher ethical import. It differs from allegory, since this personifies ideas, &c. *Quintilian, Erasmus.* A Parabolic allegory. *Alford, Meyer.* Number of Parables, twenty-seven. *Greswell.* Thirty. *Trench.* Fifty, according to others, including similes and illustrations. *Smith's Dict.* The noblest allegory in modern times is the " Pilgrim's Progress." The Pharisee and Publican an historic reality. *Greswell.*

οὐκ ἔγνωσαν. They resisted all the light of miracle and prophecy. *Hengst.* They persisted in rejecting the Messiah's claims and perished. *Augustine.* Our Lord had been giving a portrait of Himself in the first five verses. *Lampe, Stier.* They understood the word, but not the application. *Lampe.* They suspected they were glanced at, and they pretended not to understand. *Kuinoel.* It was *difficult* for them to understand the force of the comparison. *Tittmann.*

---

7. Then said Jesus unto them again, Verily, verily, I say unto you, I am the door of the sheep.

Verily. See on John i. 51. Jews needed this solemn confirmation.—They believed being Abraham's seed, the fold, the door and heaven were sure.—He saw some signs of *unbelief,* or contempt, or perhaps scorn.—The record indicates the result of His Omniscience searching their hearts.—It is the one foundation of all the faith, all the hope, all the comfort of saints.—All schemes not embracing the atoning Redeemer, afford no peace, leave the trusters miserable, and without hope in death.

I say. First five verses spoken of shepherds generally.—But they go in and out of the fold by the same door as the sheep.—Christ is that door, DOOR OF THE SHEEP into the fold of God.

I say. Here begins the interpretation of the allegory.

I say unto you. The second time He utters this truth not understood by them.—He will make the judgment of their blindness more complete.—There must have been some present, illumined and drawn by the Spirit.—Moreover these words were spoken to all coming ages in the Church.

I am the. The undertone of which is " ye Pharisees *are not,*"— He places himself in contrast with the presuming Pharisees.— They had for ages claimed to be the door and to carry the key. Luke xi. 52.—Nor were these proud, self-righteous Pharisees the only rivals of the Redeemer.—Each self-confident heart in its own worth, claims to be the door of the kingdom.

The door. In a similar manner He calls Himself "The Way."— He does not say of the fold, but of the sheep.—We, through Him as our sacrifice, our advocate, offer up our petitions to the Father. Through Him we enter the Church, and at last through Him reach Heaven.—Our Lord's words seem to *ring with a celestial echo* in their depth of meaning.

Door. John x. 1. The hearers, not understanding the similitude to us so plain, He terms Himself, not *a* door—one of many—but THE DOOR.—Entrance and office into that fold from the beginning was through Him *alone.*—" There is no other NAME given &c., whereby we can be saved." Acts iv. 12.—" Chief Shepherd" of His people, and " Son over His house." 1 Peter v. 4; Heb. iii. 6.—1. None can enter without the *permission* of Christ.

2. Without the *knowledge* of Christ. 3. Without the *image* of Christ. 4. Without *faith* in the blood of Christ. 5. Without sharing in the *blessedness* of Christ.—The door of heaven by *good works*, finally closed by the Fall. Gen. iii. 24.—1. The door of the chamber of suffering and sorrow *shunned* by all. 2. The door of the grave *feared* by all who are incorrigibly impenitent. 3. The door of perdition *entered* by all who reject the offers of mercy.—Our Lord is the *door*, both to the shepherds and to the sheep.—Each true pastor must first be a sheep of the fold of Christ.—He must receive light from Christ, before he imparts it to others.—Bigotry dreams of having exclusive access to *the only door* open to sinners.—Before Christ came, this fold was the Church of God among the Jews.—Because of His *humanity* our Lord is called a *sheep*. Acts viii. 32.—On account of His loving-kindness and His God-head, a SHEPHERD. Isaiah xl. 11.

Door. Christ is the door to a right understanding of nature, of providence, of history, of the Bible.—Through Christ " we have access by one Spirit, unto the Father." Eph. ii. 18.—He is the only way of admission into God's fold on earth and in heaven.—Hence rejecting Christ's atonement, excludes all such from seeing God.

εἰμι. Not an exposition but expansion of the allegory. *Alford.* By a new discourse, He would tell them who He was. *Heumann.* He would place Himself in opposition to Pharisees. *Hengst.* The allegory is repeated, the imagery retained. *Rosenm.* An explanation. *Tittmann.*

θύρα Door to the sheep. *Tholuck, De Wette, Meyer.* Our Lord discriminates between the door of the fold, that through which the shepherd enters, and door of the sheep, through which they enter. The shepherd comes as Messiah, with all the duties, responsibilities of the anointed one. While His fold contains many flocks : "Other sheep have I, not of this fold." *Greswell.* There is no other entrance for pastor or sheep, except through this door. *Hess.* In verse 1, the door of the shepherd, *i. e.* their divine calling, here the door of the sheep. *Hengst.* Pastor and sheep enter by one door. *Maldonatus.* Door is Christ. *Alford.*

τῶν προβάτων. For the sheep. *Nonus, Chrys., Aug., Mald., Lampe.* The indirect meaning. *Tholuck.* Christ the door to glory. *Steinmeyer.* θύρα, in a two-fold sense, door for the shepherd and sheep. *Neander.* This is obscurity. *De Wette.* Nay, but profundity. *Stier.* Christians are never called goats ; name sheep never applied to unrenewed. Ez. xxxiv. 17. *Hitzig.*

---

8. All that ever came before me are thieves and robbers; but the sheep did not hear them.

All that, &c. Condemnation is passed not on *persons* but on *character.*—Their climbing up by another way, their strange voice and ungodly teachings, point out all those wearing the livery of Christ, but serving Satan.

Came. They were not sent, their credentials not signed by the Holy Ghost.

Before me. Pretending to be leaders without Divine sanction.— As turning Israel from the paths of truth and from trust in God.—Moses and the prophets came not so much *before* as *with* Christ.—Breathing deeply His spirit, and following His lead, they trusted in Him and called on men, to trust in His mercy.

Are. Their essential nature belongs to, and is of the Evil One.

Thieves. Ver. 1. Under the guise of religion, worldly-minded sons of earth.—Secretly they steal the strength and life of the Church's power.—Opposed to the " hirelings " or hired keepers, established orders of ministry.—There was such a ministry before Christ, in the Jewish Church, and there has been such an order since in the Christian Church.—" The devil was the first thief, who climbed into God's fold." *Milton.*—All his followers, sharing his spirit, have followed his steps.—He was the first who " before " Christ sadly succeeded in misleading our race.—He enters intrusively, clandestinely, under the *mask* of religion.—The shepherd hired a hireling in a way open, regular and peaceable.—Thieves are labourers from mercenary motives in Christ's employ.—But they seek to feed *ambition, covetousness, pleasure, ease.*—False Messiahs and pretending teachers mock the soul's hungering after food.— " Ravening wolves " expresses another phase of character. Matt. vii. 15.

Robbers. Ver. 1. Open, violent persecutors, plunderers and avaricious, ambitious pretenders "lording it over God's heritage." 1 Peter v. 3.—Pharisees boldly assumed as their own the Messianic position.—In the properly spiritual domain, there was no room left for Christ.—In utter caprice, they opened and shut the kingdom of God. Matt. xxiii. 13.—Not as servants ; they bore themselves as irresponsible masters.—The Temple was the centre of the Church to them, *sacrifices* under them were a fraud, and their atoning virtue ignored and forgotten.—They resisted Christ as resolutely and defiantly as Rome did afterwards for centuries.— The being of Christ's church was threatened, and it was a conflict of life and death.—The thief, when revealed, proves to be half-hireling, half-wolf.—" Woe unto the pastors that destroy the sheep of my pasture." Jer. xxiii. 1.—" Woe to the shepherds of Israel, that do feed *themselves*." Ezek. xxxiv. 2.—Pharisaism, before the Temple was destroyed, became a bare-faced robbery.— They did indeed sit in Moses' seat, but left the church to utter ruin.—Who but thieves " devoured widows' houses," changed the temple into a warehouse ?—Who but thieves " robbed God of tithes and offerings ? " Mal. iii. 8, 9.—No title is too sacred for these false shepherds to claim.—The sheep know them not.—In our Lord's day, they preferred the words of the carpenter of

Nazareth, to those sitting in Moses' seat, clothed in long robes and wearing phylacteries.—In our day, they prefer the earnest, sincere words of plain men to the enticing errors of rank, though in a church or cathedral, time-honored and with a gorgeous ritual.

Sheep. Ver. 2. Not Jews in general, but the few Simeons, Annas, Elizabeths, &c. 1 Peter i. 11.—Believers with divinely taught hearts, are not often led astray.

Not hear them. Not absolutely, but did not listen, so as in the end to become disciples.—Those who hear and follow such, never belonged to the *true flock*.—A sad truth: In every age thieves and robbers have dared to enter the church, and call upon the children of God to follow their pernicious errors.—The nearer to heaven Capernaum was exalted, the deeper the fall. Luke x. 15. —Hophni and Phineas only increased their guilt by assuming the priestly robes.

ἦλθον Frequentative aorist, equal to the present. *Greswell.* In Hebrew prophecies, the past tense constantly used for the future. Matt. xxiii., xxv. Here πρὸ instead of αντί, used by *Eurip., Arist., Esch.* The sheep shall not hear them. *Greswell.* Came before the time of Christ. *Hengst.*

πρὸ ἐμοῦ. Omitted. *Cod. Sin., Tisch.* Retained. *Alf., Westcott, Hort.* Omitted from fear of Gnostic and Manichæan misuse of the passage against the Old Test. *De Wette, Meyer, Lange.* Before me, instead of me, without regard to me. *Schaff.* Before the Incarnation. *Theoph., Mald., Schoettgen.* As sent without authority. *Menochius.* In opposition to me. *Aug.* Teachers of another doctrine. *Calvin.* As opposed to διά ἐμοῦ in the next verse. *Stier.* An entire supplanting is implied. *Lange.* Those immediately before our Lord. *Bengel.* All pretenders to be the Messiah, or the true shepherd. Not false Messiahs, but perverters of the people. *Olsh., D. Brown.*

κλέπται. Those claiming Messiahship. *Chrys., Cyril, Grotius.* No Messiahs certainly before Christ. *Lampe, Lightfoot.* They broke in precipitately and prematurely before they had time to find the door. *Von Gerlach.* Not waiting for Me; rush before they come to the door. *Luther, Stier, Besser.* Verses 7 and 9 having ἐγώ εἰμι, hint at false Messiahs. *Anton.* Herod's pretences were to fulfil Haggai ii. 7, and set himself against the hopes of the people. *Hengst.* Applied to Moses and Pharisees. *Manichæans.* Pharisees only *Meyer.*

λῃσταί. All that ever came at variance with me. *Aug.* All prophets before Him, actually were thieves, &c. *Gnostics.* All seeking to open a door πρὸ except the Lord. *Lampe, Elsner.* False Christs and teachers after Christ. Our Lord would not thus designate Sanhedrists. *Tittmann.* Discourse refers to the future of the Church. *Herder.* The Lord rejects all the teachers who went before Him. *Marcion.* Emphasize ἦλθον, a self authorised coming. *Jerome, Theoph.* To come *before* Jesus, is in their own name, *after* Him, is to testify of Him. *Steinmeyer.* True or false pastors. Jesus, the first of his time, who cared for the common people. *Ebrard.* The false Messiahs were not numerous enough for πάντες ὅσοι. *Stier, Wolf.* Those who came not as my forerunners, but as superseding me in the fold. *Lange.* Preferring their own person to His. *Luthardt.* This meaning of πρὸ abundantly refuted. *Olshausen.*

ἤκουσαν. Have not heard with a relish. *Doddr.* People susceptible to the voice of the Lord. *Lücke.* Jews did not avoid Pharisees. *Stier.*

πρόβατα. Citizens of the kingdom. *Rosenm.* The true man in us, *i. e.*, conscience that was ever bleating after a better shepherd; that detected the thief in the shepherd's dress. *Maurice.*

9. I am the door: by me if any man enter in, he shall be saved, and shall go in and out, and find pasture.

I am the door. Kings, priests, prophets, teachers, had led men to light, just so far as they glorified God.—Rulers, claiming to be their *own* masters, were the robbers and tyrants of earth.—Monarchs, witnesses to the invisible, brought strength to the nation and joy to the people.—Every monarch exalting himself, brought slavery, or superstition and ruin.—An equally grand test of all the rulers of ancient and modern empires.—Every priest, pope, king, or philosopher, so far as he went not to the Fountain of Light, has been a *thief, caring for nothing but to steal.*—Christ is at the same time sole shepherd of all pastors and flocks.—He would call again and again for His wandering sheep to return.—Those Pharisees not the door, though pretending to be. The door's double object to protect the enclosed flock from danger, and an opening to lead the flock out to pasture.—The great truth : No salvation, but by and through Jesus Christ.

If any man. By Me, both the folded flock and shepherd must enter. Each under-shepherd must, as a sheep himself, lead the flock.—As he enters through the Door he must go as *one of the flock.*

By Me. Knock at the door through faith in the blood of the Lamb of God.

Enter in. We are not born within the fold, but " children of wrath." Eph. ii. 3.—" We have access by one Spirit unto the Father." Eph. ii. 18.—Persian kings proudly kept their best friends at a distance: not so with God. Day and night the pearly gates are open. Rev. xxi. 25.

Saved. From the guilt and curse of sin.—The fence of the fold saves from destruction ; so also does entrance into the church through Christ. *Lange.*

Go in and out. Each day's duties and joys, the cares and rest of life. Acts i. 21.—Live securely, feed daily and daintily while God reigns.—Freedom from the thraldrom of sin points to the only true liberty of the soul; all other promises are merely the boastings of slaves to sin.—To all earth's myriads in bondage to Satan, habit and passion, He says: " Believe in Me, continue in My flock, and the truth shall make you free."—Our Lord is the true Jehovah to His chosen ones. Num. xxvii. 16, 17.—The true David. 1 Sam. xviii. 16.—The true Solomon. 2 Chron. i. 10.

Find. " In dusky lane, and crowded mart," believers may find comfort of which the world knows not.

Pasture. This embraces the privileges of the tended flock of God. —It implies " they shall have life, and life more abundantly."—

"I will feed them in good pasture." Ez. xxxiv. 14 ; Isa. xl. 11. Worldling's fare hard. Luke xv. 14.—A perpetuity of bliss is bliss. *Young.*—The perfect security of the saints' reserved inheritance, is here pledged.—Grace on earth possessed, and glory in the world to come.—The " green pastures and the still waters " shadow forth this privilege.—In another state, all believers will be led by " the Lamb to fountains of living waters." Rev. vii. 17.— In Christ's flock, believers find all that enlightens, purifies, confirms, exhilarates and soothes the mind.—This pasture finds its richest verdure, and virtue, from heaven's dew.—All the truth suited to the hunger and thirst of the soul is of Christ alone.— Blessed is that shepherd, who feeds in the same pasture, where he leads the flock of God.—He who goes out through the door, shall reach the true pasturage of faith, knowledge, peace.— Whosoever brings not the flock to Christ's pastures, robs them of their food.—Whoso *starves* the *soul*, is a *murderer* before heaven. John viii. 44.—What a terrible word of warning to those who *pretend* to *preach salvation.*

Ἐγώ εἰμι. This verse refers to the shepherds of preceding verses. *Müller, Kuinoel.* Only relates to the sheep. *Lampe.* Both shepherds and sheep. *Doddr., Tittmann.*
ἡ θύρα. No safe entrance to the church, for shepherd or sheep, but Christ. *Erasmus.* For shepherd only. *Meyer.* Any pastor having authority to guard the flock, must be one of the sheep of the pasture. *Maldon.* We must enter by the sacrament? deriving its virtue from Christ. *Wigandus.*
σωθήσεται Official blessing. *Lücke.* In order to be saved. *Tittmann.* Feeling trust and security through delivery from bondage. *Sylveira.* Shall be fed by the bounty of His providence. *Montanus.* Going in and out: means the actions of life. *Toletus.* Shall be preserved. *Pearce.* Perfect safety amid life's temptations. *Tittmann.* Not leaving and entering the fold, but within the fold we need aid. *Maldon.*
εἰσελεύσεται Hints at prosperity in one's business. Num. xxvii. 17, Deut. xxviii. 8. *Tittmann.* "Go in and out." Hebraism—most perfect intimacy of the shepherd and master. Num. xxvii. 17. "Go in," *i. e.*, in the truth of the Old Test. he shall subordinate himself to the Law. "Go out," *i. e.*, he shall find in the fulfilment of the Old Test., in Christ, the liberty of the New Test.—faith. *Lange*

---

10. The thief cometh not, but for to steal, and to kill, and to destroy: I am come that they might have life, and that they might have it more abundantly.

The thief. A change from the plural to the singular : *the thief*— "Satan."—As all the under-shepherds are represented by the *One* Good Shepherd, so the one type of many thieves and murderers, is the devil.—He stole the crown and sceptre from our first parents by guile.—Stealing, killing. destroying body and soul, his constant study and work for 6000 years.—Heretics show such zeal for error, as "to compass sea and land." Matt. xxiii. 15.— When certain tradesmen wish to get rid of a lot of bad goods, they are continually and eloquently talking them up to others.—

A conscience deceived, demands these efforts of infidel zeal, otherwise it would be intolerable.—" Cunning craftiness," Eph. iv. 14, is the serpent stinging, without the hiss.

Steal and kill, &c. He robs Gods of His honor and glory, being at heart a *thief*.—He taketh the life of the soul, hence he is a *murderer*. He takes away all foundations for *peace*, hence a *destroyer*.—He *wastes* the hopes, the joys, the peace, the whole treasures of grace.—Not content with the wool and milk, he will also slay and eat. "Ye kill them that are fed : but feed not the flock." Ezek. xxxiv. 3.—The wolfish mind of the thief finds pleasure in selfish gratification, and that which it cannot share it ruins. — The terrible purpose of a faithless shepherd is to secure his own gain, reckless of its issue in the ruin of the souls of his flock.—History ever reproduces this melancholy result, until the scheme of Antichrist has induced millions of our race to barter their hopes for the protection of wolves in sheeps' clothing.

I am come. Our Lord's church is likened to a ship, Himself the pilot ; to a vine, Himself the stay ; to a flock, Himself the shepherd.—In this passage to be for ever known, honoured and loved as the " GOOD SHEPHERD."—I am come in mercy and power to secure life for My people.—When Christ comes, woe to the thieves wasting His flock !—The world's history ever shows traces of His iron rod, or shepherd's staff.—Yet His *main* interest of grace is to give life in abundance.

Life. John i. 4. ONE only hath essential LIFE to bring or give.— "Life" and "abundantly" include all the fulness of good in Christ Jesus. Phil. iv. 19. — Implied where the Lord is shepherd : "I shall want nothing." Psa. xxiii.—Our Lord claims here all-sufficiency to Himself which alone belongs to God.

Abundantly. Old prophets proved their celestial birthright, by giving life for the people.—When Jesus pledges Himself to His beloved flock, He guarantees they shall not lack : "I shall not want." Psa. xxiii. 1.—It has been His triumphant challenge to His trusting flock in every age : "Lacked ye anything ?" Luke xxii. 35.—David answers, "My cup runneth over." Psa. xxiii. 5. —Seeking *first* the kingdom, all things shall be added. Matt. vi. 33.—They who seek it *first* shall not want for anything.—His mission was not to preserve, but *impart* life to the spiritually dead. What a claim ! A repetition of His sermon in Capernaum, and an echo of all His teaching as to the *bread* and *water* of life.— Such assertions prove Jesus to have been either the greatest impostor and most impious of men, or VERY and ETERNAL GOD.

The article ὁ κλέπτης, points to one thief Satan. *Stier*. The Pharisees. *Hengst*. Spondanus epitomized Baronius, and made his poisonous error resemble the very bread of heaven. *Trapp*. Socrates thus gilds the errors of Novatian, until they appear truth from God. *Billius*.

θύσῃ καὶ ἀπολέσῃ. To kill and murder. *Stier*. To butcher as *Papal Rome* by the martyrdom of millions of saints. An *auto de fé* was a *holiday* for the young Spaniards. "*Sta ferme Moyse*" the mob cried, fearing lest a young Jew would renounce his faith and the crowd lose their sport. *Milman*.

ἀπολέσῃ. Destruction of pasturage. *Bengel*. They kill only for the sake of gain and love of killing. *B. Crusius*.

ἐγὼ ἦλθον. An impressive antithesis to all false shepherds. *Stier*.

περισσὸν ἔχωσιν. A fuller share of the *means* of grace after, than before Incarnation. *Lampe*. Boundless felicity in addition to immortality. *Alex. Natalis*. He arrogates to Himself Divine powers and all-sufficiency. *Luther*. Sealed by their prosperity in this life. *Euth., Theoph.* Sheep to thrive, need a variety and exuberance of pasture. *Grotius*.

---

11. I am the good shepherd: the good shepherd giveth his life for the sheep.

I am. That is, ever was, and ever will be the shepherd, Ex. iii. 14, whom prophets foretold.—Assures us of His Divine unchangeable care over His beloved flock.

I am. "The first and last." Isa. xli. 4.—"Alpha and Omega." Rev. i. 8.—With an eternal emphasis THE Good Shepherd.—The only one chosen of the Father. Isa. xl. 11.

Good Shepherd. Foretold centuries before the Incarnation. Isa. xl. 11; Ez. xxxiv. 23.—As here used, implies, both *instructor* and *ruler.*—Isaiah alludes to the authority of the shepherd. Isa. xl. 11. —Christ the GOOD SHEPHERD :—1. His *knowledge* of all the wants of the flock is perfect. 2. His *wisdom* to provide is infinite. 3. His *power* enables Him to carry out all His will. 4. His *kindness* amid all their waywardness. 5. His *faithfulness* will never forsake those He has chosen. 6. His undying *interest* forgets nothing and omits nothing for their good.—Christ the ACTIVE SHEPHERD :—1. He rescues His sheep from the great robber. 2. Brings them into His own fold. 3. Provides them with all the nourishment needed. 4. Gives them refreshing repose amid the cares and toils of life. 5. Guards them from all danger. 6. Guides them in their perplexity. 7. Heals all their diseases. 8. Reclaims them from all their wanderings. 9. Folds them at last in heaven.—JESUS CHRIST is the GOOD SHEPHERD :— 1. He provides and secures all the blessings His people need. 2. He has obtained them at an immense cost to Himself. 3. He brings them into vital and most intimate union with Himself. (*a*) He *distinguishes* them from those alien to His flock : "The Lord knoweth them that are His." 2 Tim. ii. 19. (*b.*) He is intimately *acquainted* with all their wants. (*c.*) He acknowledges them as His "peculiar treasure."—The rightful owner and true lover of the flock is ever a foe to the robber.—The *Door* becomes the

Shepherd: all enter *through* Christ and *under* Christ.—Our Lord here alludes to one of the great mysteries of our world.—He illustrates His own pastoral love for His saints by bringing out the *mutual* affection between man and brutes.—Christ "is the Shepherd and Bishop of our souls." 1 Pet. ii. 25.—"The Great Shepherd." Heb. xiii. 20.—Peter is charged "to tend the sheep and feed the lambs." John xxi. 16.

Good. Contrasts with all kinds of faithless shepherds, down to him who feeds his flock *in the grave.* Heb. *in Hell.* Psa. xlix. 14. —Prophetic allusions, Isa. xl. 10.—To His vicarious death on the cross; "Awake, O sword, against MY SHEPHERD," &c., Zech. xiii. 7. —To His reign as king, "He brought Him to feed Jacob His people, and Israel His inheritance." Psa. lxxviii. 71.—"And He shall stand and feed in the strength of the Lord." Micah. v. 4.— This is one of the most gracious among the many names of Jesus. —Amid all the folly and weakness of His people, He is their wisdom and strength.—In the darkness of earth, He is "Brightness of the Father's glory." Heb. i. 3.—Surrounded by foes, He leads them to victory, "Captain of their salvation." Heb. ii. 10.—Human shepherds are overcome by strong foes—but the Good Shepherd is the Almighty.—Amid their countless perils from temptation, His tenderness is exhaustless.—Not one of all the myriads of His flock will ever fail to reach the heavenly fold.—They hear His voice even in the grave, for He is THE RESURRECTION and THE LIFE.—A shepherd never *domineers* over or oppresses his flock. 1 Pet. v. 3.— It is the standing duty of the pastor to *feed*, not to *please* the flock of God.—"Had I some of the blood poured out on the cross, how carefully would I carry it! Ought I not be as careful of those souls for whom it was shed?" *Bernard.*— The sword of truth, however jewelled, should ever be of celestial temper, and with it, the faithful shepherd watches his flock with unslumbering diligence.—Like David, he encounters "the lion and the bear."

Giveth. Rather, *layeth down.* Same Greek word, verses 15—17.— If words are here honestly used, this implies a SACRIFICE!—If Christ did not die for His sheep, this text cannot be true, for His death was not for *Himself!*—Also that the death of the shepherd, will be the *salvation* of the sheep.—Also that He died *voluntarily,* under no possible constraint.—He proved by many *miracles,* that, if desirable, He could have prevented it.—"Who was delivered (to die) for our sins, and raised (to life) for," &c. Rom. iv. 25.— Highest expression of self-devotion, conceivable by the human mind.—What a contrast to the malicious, destructive course of others, verse 10.—Strangers may *call* like the true shepherd, but not *die* like Him.—Some may give their bodies to be burned, through a fierce ambition, yet their blood is shed against, not for the sheep. *Augustine.*—Those in famine, pestilence, or war, forsaking their flocks are *hirelings.*—Martyrs may die for their flocks, but none can *redeem* but Christ.—The Greek poets tell us the pelican, in want of food, opened her breast and fed her young with her life blood; but it is no *fable* that the Good Shepherd feeds His chosen flock with His heart's blood. John vi. 51.— "He calleth His own sheep by name."—a call never resisted. John x. 3.—He alone accompanies His flock through the valley of death. Psa. xxiii. 4.—Because He loved His flock, *therefore* His foes sought His life.—He enjoins nothing on His pastors, but that He first endured.—*Good* Shepherd, *true* Light, *true* Bread, *true* Vine, all others are mere shadows.

His life. He stands forward as the champion of His flock in the hour of danger.—He defends His flock even to the laying down of His own life.—If there is no other way of escape, but by the shepherd's death (as there was none for *man*), He will sacrifice His life.—Some infidels sneer at "vicarious sacrifice and imputed merit" as not found in the scriptures.—But "Christians" were in the land, long before the name was given. Acts xi. 26.— This is the first of four prophecies of His own death.—Disciples breathe the same spirit, else martyrs would have been fewer. —A shepherd, it is said, once saw a hungry lion coming, and sacrificed himself to save his flock. 1 John iii. 16.

ὁ ποιμὴν ὁ καλός. The shepherd, *the* good one. *Greswell.* καλός equivalent almost to αληθίνος. *Stier. Fair, beautiful,* often in the moral sense *good. Schaff.* A name shared with created pastors. *Aug.* Populariter for teachers. *Grotius, Rosenm.* Never denotes teachers. *Bloomfield.* Shepherd of this verse confounded with θύρα, verse 9, by mystics. He that was the *Door* is now the Shepherd. *Lücke.*
τίθησιν. Analogical to laying aside a garment. *Lücke, De Wette.* Staking or venturing life. *Stier.* In parable a hireling left the sheep, while Moses offers himself for their life. Ex. xxxii. 32. *Dopke.*
τίθησιν. Occurs independently in N. T., not found in profane authors, nor familiar in Hellenistic usage. Refers to Isa. liii. 10. *Hengst.* "Laying down," occurs five times in this discourse. He gives His life, by gathering the flock during the ministry. *Grotius.* Giving His mortal, that we might have immortality. Equivalent to *profundere vitam. Lampe.* Duty of ancient shepherds to defend their flock with their lives. Allusion to the fact is made by Homer. *Bochart.* Not a prophecy but declaration. *Alford.*
ὑπέρ. For, to the advantage of. *Hengst.* Isa. liii. 10. A voluntary oblation. *Vitringa.* Generic term for sacrifice. *Alexander.* In the stead of, in place of. *Winer, Passow, Gesenius, Robinson.* No human shepherd intends to die for his flock. *Maurice.*

---

12. But he that is an hireling, and not the shepherd, whose own the sheep are not, seeth the wolf coming, and leaveth the sheep, and fleeth: and the wolf catcheth them and scattereth the sheep.

Hireling. Wolf and Good Shepherd are characters ever recurring in history.—The wolf, an undisguised enemy of all that love God.

—Hireling, one indifferent, serving his own pampered lusts, at the expense of his employer or his trust.—His error is not that he receives wages; for faithful shepherds do also.—But he leaveth his sheep at the approach of danger.—THE REWARD coveted by the faithful shepherd is the approval of God.—The hireling is characterised by two things: 1. He is not a real shepherd to the sheep, but a hired servant; he has no affection for the sheep. 2. The sheep are not his own, are not united to him, and cannot confide in him. The inner vital bond is wanting on both sides. Characteristic of the Pharisaic leaders of the people. *Lange.* —He sees here prophetically, the long list of those selfish teachers who make merchandise of the ministry for filthy lucre and hate the cross, from the Apostolic age down to the present. Gal. vi. 12; Phil. iii. 18. *Schaff.*—In Judea, where much of the wealth consists in flocks, hired persons are a common and necessary class.—Under ordinary circumstances they faithfully protect the flock.—They might defend them as faithfully and valiantly as the shepherd.—There are some hirelings labouring for, and others now receiving the rewards of eternity.—"How many hired servants (hirelings) of my father have bread!" Luke xv. 17.—Sheep, believers, are entrusted to the hireling.—David-like we must face the lion, and bear, and trust in God for victory. 1 Sam. xvii. 35.—Very often the sin of secularised ministers lies at the door of their covetous flocks.— Pastors have a right to a competent support to free them from care.—The people able, but unwilling to sustain them, cannot be innocent.—A sad sign that God's Spirit is departing, when the candlestick is removed, and the pulpit is silent and desolate.

Whose own. The hireling does not own the sheep: they are not his.—Our Lord claims what in Old Test. is given to God alone.

The wolf. A wild beast, marked for its *daring* and savage fierceness.—Natives of all parts of the earth, they have great strength, and associate in packs.—"Cruel as death, and hungry as the grave: burning for blood, bony, gaunt and grim." *Milton.*— Cowardly, a characteristic of all cruel men, mistrustful, suspicious.—As long as a reindeer is tied, he fears him as a decoy.— The moment he is loosed, he hastes, howling for his blood.— When famished, their courage becomes desperate.—Old Saxons believed him possesed, calling him "*were wolf.*"—King Edgar pardoned criminals, on condition of their killing a number of wolves.—A Welsh prince was to bring him annually 300 skins of wolves.

He seeth the wolf. He seems to tend the flock until the wolf comes.—The fearful but *well-known* wolf-howl, *tests* his fidelity.— The timid sheep, pursued and afraid, fly to the hireling for safety.

—But unfaithful and selfish, he prefers to sacrifice the sheep to himself.—He leaveth the sheep at last to the *robber* of the fold.— Wolves are named here, but *men* are meant. Zeph. iii. 3.—Every wolf is a thief, and every thief is a wolf.—A wolf's ferocity leads him to tear many sheep to death, before he begins to eat.—Three classes of false prophets : 1. The hireling lawfully ordained, but neglecting the flock. 2. The thief who steals into the fold to seduce men from truth. 3. The robber who enters to destroy within the fold. Papal and other persecutors.—Paul knew "grievous wolves would enter, not sparing the flock." Acts xx. 29.—Our Lord warned, " Beware of false prophets, for they are ravening wolves." Matt. vii. 15.—Satan under the figure of a wolf : 1. His attacks are deadly. 2. His surprises are crafty. 3. His hatred of Christ is implacable. 4. His hunger to devour is insatiable. 5. He attacks under darkness.—Satan scatters the flock by tempting them to luxury, avarice and sensuality.—Filling their minds with pride, envy, anger, deceit or malice.—At times, Christ sends His sheep in the midst of wolves.—By the wolf's appearing, the true spirit of the hireling is revealed.—This world, a wilderness, hath *lions* in it, with claws to tear, and teeth to devour. 1 Peter v. 8.—It hath *wolves*, oppressors of Christ's flock, in authority. Matt. vii. 15.—It hath *foxes*, false teachers, seducing spirits. Cant. ii. 15.—It hath *wild boars*, tyrants rooting up the Lord's vineyard. Psa. lxxx. 13.—It hath *serpents*, insinuating the poison of error in the soul. 2 Cor. xi. 3.—Noah's ark held the voracious *raven* as well as the *dove*.

Fleeth. When he is silent amid abounding errors, for the true shepherd is the natural defender of his flock.—He does not abide merely for convenience, but from principle.—As a faithful guardian he tenderly loves his charge ; others, devoid of affection, desert them in danger.—A hireling need not flee to come under the curse.—He withholds consolation from the afflicted children of God. Isaiah xl. 1.—He neglects, through fear of men, to rebuke those living in sin. Lev. xix. 17.—Certain doctors of the mint, love the image of Cæsar, more than that of God. *Farindon*.—The face of Mammon on their heart, is visible also in their lives.—Shepherds, false to their vows, may hear at judgment Eliab's question (1 Sam. xvii. 28) : " With whom hast thou left those few poor sheep in the wilderness ?"—But Jacob, Moses, and David, three eminent types of Christ, were devoted shepherds.

Scattereth. What are not devoured are scattered, and the flock ceases to be as such.—The Good Shepherd may ask some silent ones on that day, " Where is thy flock, thy beautiful flock?" Jer. xiii. 20.—Two-fold misery : Individual souls are destroyed, and the flock as a whole, the Church, is confused and scattered.

μισθωτὸς. Hired keeper. *Greswell.* One who without evil intention, but without any, love tends the flock. *B. Crusius.* Those open mouthed for gain and human honours. *Aug.* Spoken to Pharisees, looking for man's, not God's praise. *Toletus, Lampe, Kuinoel.* Even a shepherd, legally introduced, may be a mercenery. *Lyserus.* λύκον. Satan distinctively. *Euthymius,* and other *Fathers, Olsh., Stier, Alf.* Heretics. *Aug.* and others. Every Anti-theocratic power. *Lücke.* Every Anti-Messianic power, whose ruling principle, however, as such, is contained in the devil. *Meyer.* In any case the instrument of Satan. *Lange.* The last τὰ πρόβατα omitted. *Cod. Sin., Tisch., Westcott* and *Hort.* Bracketed. *Lach., Alf.* Defended by *Lange, Meyer.*

---

13. The hireling fleeth, because he is an hireling, and careth not for the sheep.

Hireling. Our Lord is not only the *Door*, but *Guardian* of those within.—The hireling is a shepherd on wages, with special duties to the flock.—Void of self-sacrificing love, not willing to peril his safety for the sake of his charge: "Whoso loveth *life itself*, more than Me, is not worthy of Me." Luke xiv. 26.—There is no necessity *that we should live here.* Dan. iii. 18.—But it is necessary we should be faithful to our covenant vow. Dan. iii. 18; Acts vii. 58.—Loyalty is infinitely more valuable than life.—Lazarus seems to have starved, but to die was gain to him.—We may, even if we have no bread, like this beggar, reach a destiny far more glorious than "Abraham's bosom"—THE BOSOM OF JESUS.— "They all look to their own way, every one for his own gain." Isa. lvi. 11.—"Woe to the shepherds of Israel that feed themselves." Ezek. xxxiv. 2.

Fleeth. He loves his life above all things, and dreads death, for which he is unprepared.—From whom does the hireling expect to receive his wages? Assuredly not from God.

Careth not. The doctrines preached are to *please*, *not* to *save.*— A thousand pulpits there are, in which no Redeemer is found.— Yea, there are cases (Phil. i. 16) where Christ is even preached "through contention."—But the *true* preacher preaches Christ through love to Him, and the souls He has redeemed.—Cowards and apostates are the two classes of shepherds to be found when destruction overtakes a church. *Lange.*

Sheep. These sheep are not the property of the hireling.—They are Christ's: 1. By creation. 2. By redemption, John xxi. 16. 3. By free and loving surrender of their hearts to Him through the work of the Holy Spirit. Psa. cx. 3; John vi. 44.—Our Lord said not to Peter "Feed *thy* sheep;" but, "FEED MY SHEEP."—Instead of living *on* the flock, faithful shepherds live *for* the flock. —Although they may never be called to follow the Good Shepherd, by laying down their lives for the sheep, yet they never flee at the approach of danger.—"I am ready not only to be bound, but to die at Jerusalem." Acts xxi. 13.

ὁ δὲ μισθωτὸς φεύγει, might appear to be a superfluous repitition, or might be omitted; on this account they are wanting in *B. D. L.* and *Cod. Sin., Tisch.* They, however, serve as an introduction to the characterization of the hireling. *Lange.*

---

14. I am the good shepherd, and know my sheep, and am known of mine.

Good. Gr. *The* shepherd, the *good* one. Rightful owner and true lover of the sheep.

Shepherd. The flock being related to their Shepherd, and bound up in Him, the excellence of their Head flows to the members.

Know. Orientalism for approve : "The Lord knoweth (approveth) the way of the righteous." Psa. i. 6.—The Father in His Love knows the Son, and the Son feels Himself recognised by Him and follows his drawing. Thus the Son "knoweth them that are His" (2 Tim. ii. 19), and the result is we know him. Gal. iv. 9.—"I know in whom I have believed." 2 Tim. i. 12.— This secret is carried like a river underground till death.—Let him that died for my soul see to the salvation of it. *Luther.*—A child, having a jewel, to secure it, commits it to his father's care. —"We love Him, because He first loved us." 1 John iv. 19.— Satan would winnow, but Christ prays. Luke xxii. 31.—Those known in heaven, are humble and often unknown among men.— In brief but eternally emphatic response, Christ cries, "I KNOW MY SHEEP."—Mutual knowledge : a bond of love between sheep and shepherd.—"You only have I known, of all the families of the earth." Amos iii. 2.—"If any man love God, the same is known (loved) of Him." 1 Cor. viii. 3.—"Thou hast known my soul in adversity." Psa. xxxi. -7.—Not merely an intellectual perception, but friendly recognition.—Consciousness of being loved by Christ, awakens love in believers.—His knowledge of them intuitive, entire, perfect, all comprehensive.—Theirs of Him, imparted, intimate, direct, personal, both bound by LOVE ! —Of the foolish virgins, Jesus says, "I know you not." Matt. xxv. 12.—To the self-righteous He says, "I never knew you." Matt. vii. 23.—He knows all the strivings of His people after holiness, and shields them in trials.—However unknown to the world, His heart and eye are on them.—The fire of this love and knowledge is kindled in their bosoms. 1 John iv. 19.—He sadly intimates : *Not all in His fold here, are His sheep.*—But He can, and will soon point out all bearing His secret marks.

My sheep. No other Pastor has such *proprietorship* as Jesus.— His by Creation, but doubly so by Redemption, and the Spirit's work.—Apostles and martyrs laid down their lives, not for the church, but for Christ.—They were dying men ; death inevitable ; only came a little earlier.—Martyrs benefit themselves, but Christ dies only for others.—Men are in the dark as to the result of their sacrifices, but Christ knew all from the beginning.

Am known. A rebuke of those doubters, who, in voluntary humility, refuse to be sure of their salvation. *Besser.*—" Known," not indeed by the hearing of the ear, or the seeing of the eye.— A father, at a distance, educating and supporting a son at home : the son knows the father and feels him to be near, without seeing him.—"Whom not having seen ye love ; in whom, though now ye see Him not," &c. 1 Peter i. 8.—Knowing has no reference to dreams, visions, or ecstasies of men.—But as a child knows his parents, or a soldier his commander.—By sin, this world no longer affords pasture for the flock of Christ.—In this parched, barren wilderness a fold is still found, and all classes, from the monarch to the slave, are here on a level.—Over this flock the Shepherd watches, who is known by having given His life for His people.— Because He knows them, *therefore* they know Him, and soon we shall know Him, even as we are known. 1 Cor. xiii. 12.—He knows their infirmities as well as their virtues, and provides grace for them.—A shepherd marks his flock, and believers bear Christ's mark.—Some professors, confident of final acceptance, will be disappointed : "Their spot is not the spot of my children." Deut. xxxii. 5.—Eminent saints have enjoyed wonderful communion with God. —" I called you friends, for all things I have heard of My Father I have made known to you." John xv. 15.—They " know the love of Christ which passeth knowledge."—He feeleth wonderful things, seeth great things, and uttereth unheard of things, whose soul is filled with Christ. *Hooker.*—There is an intimate communion with God, whose joy is unutterable. *Marriott.*—To suffer patiently and live in peace, *because* of the pattern He set.— He knows us perfectly, but we know Him imperfectly.—Still He exhorts us to love the bretheren, *because* we bear His image.— Such a flock, though small, Jesus had already gained in Israel.

Am known. " My beloved is mine, and I am His." Cant. ii. 16, —To that the soul anchors : it is not *satisfied* until it knows that Christ is attached to it, and it to Christ.—This *thirsting after righteousness* is a more scriptural evidence of conversion, than a simple *feeling* that one is a Christian.—The very best assurance of faith is hungering, rather than saying, " I have already attained it." Phil. iii. 12.—To be *without* this hungering shows a state of spiritual disease.—Where there is health of soul there is *appetite* as in health of body : diseased and dying persons have no *craving* for food.

I know. He knows all we suffer and that which words cannot utter.—Every temptation from riches or poverty, from solitude or society.—From learning or ignorance, from gladness or dreariness.—From the waxing or waning of affection, from the anguish of doubt, or the dulness of indifference.—From the whirlwind of passion or the calm that follows.—From fleshly appetites, or the darker suggestions of the corrupt will.—His sympathies are never with our *foes*, but with *us.*—BELIEVERS and their SHEPHERD : 1. They can *distinguish* Him from all others : " None but Jesus " is their watchword. 2. They *intimately* know Him and follow on to know to Him. 3. They know Him *experimentally* : " His flesh is meat indeed," &c. 4. They *acknowledge* Him as their Shepherd, and with the mouth make confession, &c. Rom. x. 10.

Of mine. Allusion to the soul's response to the efficacious call of the Holy Ghost.—The first hint in the parable of there being false *sheep*, as well as false *shepherds.*—Their knowledge of the Son is not barren, but fruitful in living active love.—As water mingles with water, so Christ's and believer's love flow together.

γινώσκω. Caring, protecting. *Stier.* Predestination hangs on our obedience, not our obedience on predestination. *Faber, Denton.* Both hang on the grace of God. *Author.* More than knowing, omniscience. *D. Brown.* An emphatic expression, by which a loving knowledge is implied. *Lange.*

γινώσκομαι : instead of γινώσκομαι ὑπὸ τῶν ἐμῶν (Text. rec.). *B. D. L. Cod. Sin., etc.,* read γινώσκουσίν με τα ἐμά, *Lach., Tisch., Lange.* This active turn is in conformation to the following. *Meyer, De Wette.* He knows all His Father will give through coming time. *Calvin.* The Redeemer knowing, an *active* element infusing life into the soul ; believer knowing, the *passive* reception of His life. *Olsh.*

---

15. As the Father knoweth me, even so know I the Father; and I lay down my life for the sheep.

As. This belongs to the preceding verse. The E. V. wrongly treats this as an independent sentence. *Schaff.*—" As " describes similarity of manner, as also of kind.—Such reciprocal knowledge, none dare claim but Himself.—The believer's relation to Christ is often learned by the Son's to the Father.

Father. John i. 1, iv. 23. The infinite, eternal love of the Father for the Son, is the *source* of the Son's love for man, and man's love for his God.—Our Saviour had often spoken of Himself as " The Son of man."—Lest His disciples should think His *knowledge* man's knowledge, He here boldly claims Omniscience ; and therefore His love is perfect, unchanging, everlasting.

Even so know I. Gr. *and I know.* Cognition of the Father, the foundation for the corresponding cognition of Christ. Comp. chap. xiv. 20 ; xv. 10 ; xvii. 8, 21.

And. Expression and measure of the strength of His love towards His people.—Hereby the sheep know how *good* the shepherd is

I lay down. Repeated solemnly THREE TIMES, expressive of the will of the TRINITY.—Prophetically spoken to His enemies foreseeing what they would do.—How loftily this sounds after *such claims* as just expressed.— It embraces the DUST of His humanity, and the ETERNAL THRONE of His Godhead.—Here we find either His *vicarious* death for His church, or boundless presumption!—Christ's death was a voluntary sacrifice to *Law* and *Love*.—With a clear eye He saw a little flock, exposed and helpless round Him. —He saw those among the Gentiles, who would enter His fold.—He saw the death in His path, by which they were to be purchased.—He thus openly claims the *despised Gentiles* as His *followers*.—His death would remove for ever the partition wall.—Where else is that shepherd, who fed his flock with *his blood?* Acts xx. 28; Isa. xlix. 15. 1. Christ a *universal* Shepherd. Sheep of earth and of other worlds; verse 16. 2. Christ a *wise* Shepherd. He knows all the flock. 3. Christ a *self-sacrificing* Shepherd. Dies for His flock. 4. Christ an *almighty* Shepherd. Jehovah, "mighty to save." Isa. lxiii. 1.—Jacob's unslumbering care could not prevent some from being stolen. Gen. xxxi. 39.— "Of the sheep Thou gavest Me, none of them is lost." John xvii. 12.—Christ's whole life on earth, a journey to death: not "*am going to,*" but, "*am continually doing it.*"

I lay down. The vicarious sacrifice of Christ, the key-stone of our faith.—Sin transferable from man to a beast, taught first in scripture.—Idea of the sacrifice of an innocent lamb, for the guilt of a sinful man, *abhorrent* to every well-balanced mind, and perfectly *unnatural.*—Conception of God being placated by the death of another, could only arise in the mind of Jehovah Himself.—With all the light of revelation on the Cross, we can see no *possible relation* between sacrifice and satisfaction, save in the SOVEREIGN WILL OF GOD!—DIVINE ORIGIN OF SACRIFICE, inferred from these facts: 1. Sacrifice being universal, points to one source. 2. That it is pleasing to God, seems unnatural and profane. 3. Inconceivable that the Lord would incorporate in Divine service a bloody right of heathenism. 4. Cain's thank-offering rejected, as being no offering for *sin*. 5. Abel's *faith* (Heb. xi. 4.) implies a Divine warrant.—A sacrifice is a "federal feast," God the HOST and man the *guest*.—Meat consumed, called God's "fire-offerings." Lev. iii. 11, 16; Num. xxviii. 2.—Each head of a family in primitive times was his own priest.—Human sacrifices were offered by many heathen nations, in order to increase and strengthen their claims on their deities.—Carthaginians at one time sacrificed three hundred children of the first families! Three hundred citizens at the same time volunteered to die, and were sacrificed with the babes!—Childless parents *purchased* babes to pay the cursed tribute.—Israel, after the abominations of the Canaanites, did the same thing. Psa. cvi. 37, 38.—But their sacrifices merely calmed their spirits, and were utterly unable to remove the guilty cause.—Yet our Lord saw we would feel sore, therefore He would suffer sore. *Bradford.*—Judas betrayed Him, and the Romans crucified Him; yet His death was a free and loving sacrifice.—He *surrendered* His spirit into the hands of His Father.—He well lays down his life, who lays down all love of it.—Our Lord gave His life (1 Tim. ii. 6.) a *ransom* for all. *Ransom* is money or sacrifice in behalf of another.—It frees those thus ransomed from peril of punishment for sin.—It is sufficient, without the paying of any other price.—This was the crowning proof of His being the *Good Shepherd.*

My life. The life of one, who was Son of Man and yet Son of God.—" Feed the Church of God, which He hath purchased with His own blood." Acts xx. 28.—The redeemed in heaven pay Divine honours to Him who shed His blood. Rev. i. 5, 6.—Union of Divinity with the humanity rendered His life of infinite value.— The good shepherd becomes a lamb for the sacrifice: " The Lamb of God, which taketh away the sin of the world." John i. 29.— " He bore our sins in His own body, and was made sin for us." 2 Cor. v. 21.—" We have redemption through His blood, even the remission of our sins." Matt. xxvi. 28.—" He hath reconciled us to His Father in His Cross." 2 Cor. v. 18.—" By His own blood He entered once into the holy place." Heb. ix. 12.—" Once in the end of the world hath He appeared to put away sin by the sacrifice of Himself." Heb. ix. 26.—" We are sanctified by the offering of the body of Christ once for all." Heb. x. 10.—" The precious blood of Christ as of a lamb without blemish." 1 Peter i. 19.—" I beheld a Lamb as it had been slain." Rev. v. 6.—This Divine sacrifice, most effectually proves the infinite guilt of sin.—It demonstrates the depth of the Divine hatred of sin.—No honest, unprejudiced person can read the Bible without finding vicarious sacrifice for sin.—They who flatter themselves God can fling pardons from His throne, without regard to the demand of justice, cannot be Christians, whatever they may profess.—In infinite wisdom God chose a plan, in which an atonement would be absolutely necessary.—A gospel without the atonement is like a day without the sun, no light, no warmth, no beauty, no life.—Whatever Unitarianism and its kindred forms of " Rationalism," may be, most assuredly none of them can lay claim to the name of Christianity.— They are no better than heathenism under the mask of words stolen from the New Testament.—But while we cannot fathom the reasons of the Divine course, we can *humbly adore* the DEPTH of the RICHES of His WISDOM and LOVE. Rom. xi. 33. See also in John i. 29, 36.

His sheep. Foreseen as His sheep, for whom alone His death effectually avails.—While sufficient for the sins of all mankind, its application is limited to those believing. In another sense, **He** died for all the straying sheep. Isa. liii. 6.

καθὼς. Is not a sentence by itself, but a sequel to verse 14. *Alford.* Verses 14 and 15 should be read : " I am the good Shepherd, and know my sheep, and am known of mine, as the Father knoweth me, and as I know the Father ; and I lay down my life for the sheep." *Robertson, Lange, Bengel.*

γινώσκω. Curare. Can the Son be said to care for the Father? *Stier.* He cares for the Father's honour. *Hezel.* Man's love all traced to the mysterious love of the sacred Trinity. *Corn. à Lapide.* Perfect knowledge absolutely necessary for the highest love. *Hugo de St. Charo.*

τίθημι. Valentinians, 150 A.D., denied that Christ died. Basilides, that an innocent person could suffer without sin. *Shedd.* Marcion, that a spectral body was crucified. Ebionites denied any connection between God and man in Christ. Mohammed denied Christ's death, affirming that He escaped from His murderers, and a Jew was sacrificed in His stead. *Burnet.* Sacrifice of human origin, consciousness of sin the cause. *Spencer, Grotius, Warburton, Maimonides., &c.* Invented by Egyptians. *Herodotus, Porphyry.* From " *hostia*," some infer that war first introduced sacrifices. *Ovid.* They were followed by invoking a curse on those breaking federal rites. *Herod., Livy.* Phœnicians, to bribe the Gods, offered their children. *Sanchoniathon in Eusebius.* Cretans, Arabians, and Persians practised it. *Amestris,* wife of Xerxes, entombed twelve persons alive for her soul's good. Dwellers on the Tauric Chersonesus, offered upon the altar of Diana, strangers thrown on their coast. Pelasgi promised in a famine to offer up every tenth child born for food. Caius Marius, Jethro like, offered his daughter a sacrifice to the Dii Averunci, after marching against the Cimbri. *Dorotheus* in *Clemens.* A law under Lentulus and Crassus, Consuls, forbade human sacrifices. B.C. 97. *Pliny.* Yet Augustus Cæsar offered 300 human victims to the manes of Julius Cæsar. Heliogabalus offered them to a Syrian deity. Scandinavians, on the Baltic, offered human victims to Woden and Thor. Harold slew two sons to propitiate the Gods. Another king slew nine sons to prolong his own life. Israelites following the Canaanites, offered up human victims. Passing through the fire, (Lev. xx. 2.), signifies actual burning. *Aben Ezra.* The mode is described. *Jalkut* in *Paulus, Fagius.* Only as a purification. not harming them. *Kimchi, Maimonides.*

τίθημι. Present, *i.e.*, a near and certain future. *Meyer.* His whole life was a going forth to death. *Bengel.* One offering sacrifice without *salt*, or with honey or leaven, was to be castigated. *Selden.* Sacrifices in no wise to be changed because ordered by the Gods. *Plato.* Whether sacrifice was enjoined by an external command, or whether it was based on the sense of sin and lost communion with God, which is stamped by His hand on the heart of man, does not affect the authority and the meaning of the rite itself. *Barry* in *Smith's Dict.* Sacrifices needed, even if man had not fallen. *Bellarmine. Gregory.* There might have been a Messiah, without making an atonement for sin. *Cassianus.* Such statements are unwarrantable. *Author.* A perfect man, should he ever appear, will be bound, scourged, tortured, and after enduring many evils, will be hanged. *Plato.* ὑπέρ. In this particle lies the great doctrine of vicarious sacrifice. Vicarious sacrifice, a general law : Motherhood, Friendship, Patriotism. vicarious. *Bushnell.*

προβάτων Not for *all*, that however true, is not the point here. In the depth of the Divine Counsel, for those who are His sheep. *Alford.* His death *was sufficient* for all, but *efficient* for those who believe. *Calvin.*

---

16. And other sheep I have, which are not of this fold : them also I must bring, and they shall hear my voice ; and there shall be one fold, and one shepherd.

Other. Gentiles *already* His in the loving purpose of the Father.— There being no future, but one eternal *now* with God, He sees all whom He intends to call, as redeemed, tended, folded in Heaven.

Sheep. Sheep for whom I, the Shepherd, must die beside the children of Abraham.—That Pharisaism is the worst of devils, is seen by the fact that the Jews were actually willing that all the millions of Gentiles should be excluded from heaven.—The solemn record of the Spirit is " *they despised others.*" Luke xviii. 9.—The boundless grace of Divine sovereignty is seen in calling Gentiles, as yet wandering in the paths of death, " *My sheep* "— " Whom he did fore-know," &c. Rom. viii. 29.—All the race is Christ's.—Jews unconsciously for ages worshipped the Messiah.— Of the Gentiles, it is said, " Ask of Me, and I will give thee the heathen for thy inheritance." Psa. ii. 8.—He will encourage the Gentiles to come to Him—He shews that the God of the O. T. is the God of the New.—Apostles were His servants, but Christ alone *brought* them in.—When the great light shines around Saul, he hears nothing but Christ's *voice.*—The cock may crow, but the *eye* of the Lord arouses Peter.—They are already His, given to Him by the Father's counsel.—" *I have* much people in this city," *i.e.*, country. Acts xviii. 10.—Then they were heathen. They were scattered abroad ; but " them also I *must* bring."

I have. Note this word. Neither *Past* nor *Future* with the Eternal.

This fold. Gr. *flock.* His prophetic eye glances forward to a wider range.—He sees the long lost tribes with the " fulness of the Gentiles " coming in. Rom. xi. 25.—Note the majestic clearness and fulness of this comprehensive parable.—How the thoughts flow forth from the depths of His Shepherd Heart.—Little did those envious Jews dream of the myriads of Gentiles yet to be gathered.—He was far richer than they conceived. " HEATHEN HIS INHERITANCE." Psa. ii. 8.—" Though Israel be not gathered, yet shall I be glorified." Isa. xlix. 5.—" I will also give thee for a light to the Gentiles, that thou mayest," &c. Isa. xlix. 6.— Gentiles were to be " brought nigh by the blood of Christ." Eph. ii. 13.—Malicious mockers might say : " Alas ! what a little company this band of Galilæans ! "—The Lord, in His dignity, anticipates and answers these profane thoughts.—His expansive benevolence demolishes for ever all bigoted claims of Jews.—They who unchurch those who love the Lord, prove themselves *anti-christ.*—This great word " other sheep " embraces ALL who trust His blood.—It for ever cries: " THEM ALSO I MUST BRING IN." He is speaking mainly to embittered enemies, flaunting their unbelief.—They feel sure of baffling His schemes ; but He foreknows His countless victories. Isa. liii. 10 to 12.—The Gentiles by His death, have access to the hitherto guarded treasure of infinite mercy.—Not sheep of another fold, but other sheep, not of this fold.—There is but *one* shepherd, *one* pasture, *one* entrance, *one* rest, *one* fold.—They shall come from the east and the west, and sit down with Abraham, &c. Matt. viii. 11.

I must bring. The eternal purpose of mercy is the Father's command.—Love : 1. Everlasting.—2. Free and sovereign.—3. Gracious.—4. Precious.—The consuming fire of redeeming and saving love urges Him on.—Neither worldly power, nor human wisdom, nor angelic zeal, can bring to pass this yearning desire, this holy purpose of God.—What His apostles and ministers are permitted to do, is as if done by Himself.—The Gospel preached, is no other than His voice, His plan of Mercy.—This great missionary promise may be pleaded by all His servants.—"Many are called but few chosen." Calling and choosing, both *sovereign* acts.—Even among Gentile professors, some will, alas ! be without the wedding garment.—He brings : He does not compel. He *dragoons* none into His kingdom.—"He *gathers* in one the children of God who are scattered abroad." John xi. 52.

Hear. They only hear Christ, who listen with the *heart* as well as ear.—Not mere foresight, but an expression of His Purpose to draw them to Himself.—They who hear and obey the voice of His ministers are included.—"He that heareth you, heareth Me," a fact which the world will find true too late.—In every age He has been gathering the flock, and will gather until the last one is safe.

My voice. Though erring, sinful men speak, yet it is Christ's voice.—The vessel may be *earthen*, but the treasure is of great value.—Alas ! how many are charmed with the voice of the world, the flesh, the devil.

One fold. Gr. *one flock*, not " one fold," as in our translation.—Christians now are divided into a number of folds through different opinions.—These folds keep not the world out, but effectually keep Christians apart.—Instead of "one flock " into which none but the blood-washed can ever enter.—The walls around the gardens are so high as to *cast a shade* on the beds.—There is but *one* olive tree into which Gentiles are grafted. Rom xi. 17.—There is but *one* commonwealth into which believers are admitted. Eph. ii. 12.—There is but *one* Zion, the birth-place of many nations. Psa. lxxxvii.—There is but *one* language of Canaan, in which all babbling dialects shall be lost at last. Rev. vii. 10.—There is but *one* house of our Father to which myriads of ransomed come. Micah iv. 2.—But *one* Jew with whom is salvation. Zech. viii. 23.—The only different marks the sheep now bear are not of *grace.*—Language, government, customs, colour may make differences, but all bear *one image*, love *one Saviour*, surround *one table*, have to encounter common *foes*, and travel towards *one home*. Eph. iv. 5.—The elect will be gathered from the four winds, through trials of fire and blooḍ. Rev. vii. 1.—The scattered sheep, harassed by a thousand temptations, will gather close to their shepherd.—" I will make them one nation in the land, upon the mountains of Israel." Ez. xxxvii. 22.—The *spirit* of all believers is to *union*, that of Satan to *disunion*.—To rend asunder the Church, the marks of a *bigot*.—We have never been born again, if we are not *drawn* towards believers.—" One Lord, one faith, one baptism "impresses on every heart the same image of humility, faith, hope, and charity. —This is that light which we cannot, if we would, conceal; our Lord commands us to "let it shine," though it is ever shadowed by meekness. Matt. v. 16.—If all are of one Family, under one Head, going to one Home, then THEY LOVE ONE ANOTHER; if not, they are *aliens from* God.—All saints pray, " Gather into oneness of faith all the nations of the earth."—Sects and parties in the Church only contend, through ignorance or lack of piety.—All the peace ever enjoyed, was, is, and shall be through HIS BLOOD!—" He will draw all men to Himself." A bond shall bind them. Eph. ii. 13.—That bond is the atoning merit and intercessory prayer of Christ. John xvii. 22.—" The beautiful flock " (Jer. xiii. 20) shall have an eternal fold, on the high mountains of the heavenly Canaan.—" They shall hunger no more, neither shall they thirst any more." Rev. vii. 16.—Then the grand hallelujah chorus shall rise, " Unto Him that loved us, and washed us," &c. Rev. i. 5, 6.

One shepherd. " I will set up one Shepherd over them." Ezek. xxxiv. 23.—" He hath made both (Jew and Gentile) one." Eph. ii. 14.—Those claiming to be the only church (Romanists) are headed by Anti-christ. 2 Thess. ii.—The ONE REDEEMER of ONE CHURCH, militant below, and glorified above.—He who hath said these words hath the power also to fulfil them, and will.—" In that day there shall be one Lord, and His name one." Zech. xiv. 9.

ἄλλα. Gentiles dimly shadowed forth by the uncircumcised trees. Lev. xix. 23, 25. *Trapp.* The Gentiles already His, because foreseen. *Bengel.* All mankind have universal salvation. *Schleier.* What means the prayer? John xvii. 9, " I pray *not* for the world ? " His chosen ones from every kindred. Ezek. xxxiv. 30, 31. *Stier.*

πρόβατα. Such of the Gentiles, as would embrace the gospel. *Grotius.* Not inherent excellence, but divine election. *Aug., Hengst.* He does not call them another fold. *Sylveira.* Jews dwelling abroad amongst Gentiles. *Wolfius. Paulus.*

τῆς αὐλῆς. Not out of another fold. *Bengel.* In the night time of the Old Test. there was a fold; in the day of the New Test. only a flock. *Lampe.* The New Test. has also discipline and fellowship, a church, and a fold. *Stier.* A testimony against exclusiveness or bigotry of sectarianism. *Munchmeyer.* He intimates His relations to Gentiles whether they believed it or not. *Deutz.* He bases the bringing in the Gentiles to the kingdom solely on His death. *Hengst.*

δεῖ. "Must," points to the divine counsel. *Hengst.* The decree of His Father's love and His own love. *Lange.* ἀγαγεῖν. συναγαγεῖν. *Theop.* προσαγεῖν. *Glassius.* Rightly supplemented "through my death." *Bengel.* συναγαγεῖν. His death the bond of unity between the two kinds. *Thol.* Ministers are the instrument, Jesus is the real agent. *Jansen.* Not "lead out" nor "bring in," but simply "bring." The Gentiles are folded wherever Christ renews them. *Bengel.*

ἀγαγεῖν. Certainly indicates that the imminent *manifest* leading of these sheep is a continuation of a *secret* leading, previously begun (*gratia prævveniens*). *Lange.* A Jewish parable: A shepherd had a flock, and a goat from the wilderness joined it. He gave it food and drink, and loved it much. A stranger wondering, asked why he loved it more than the flock? He answered, much pains have I bestowed on my flock, but this goat from the desert *voluntarily* joined it, and for this reason I love it. Thus Jehovah trained, fed, watched, cultured Israel, that they might be my children, but this stranger proselyte unbidden came and joined my people, and he equally with Israel shares my regard. *Jalkut Simeon.* μία ποίμνη, εἷς ποιμήν, not μία αὐλή as *characteristically, but erroneously rendered in the E.V.*, not *one fold*, but *one flock*; no one exclusive enclosure of an outward Church,—but one flock all knowing the one Shepherd, and known of Him. *Alford.* The E. V. followed the Vulgate, Cranmer's, and the Geneva Bible. *Schaff.* Silences for ever the error of there being anything in the New Test. opposed to the Old. *Theoph.* Not external union, since many sects are in Christ's Church *Tittmann.* This oneness of fold, &c., began when the Good Shepherd laid down His life. John xi. 52. *Bengel.* As Israel and Judah were to become one, so the chosen among the Gentiles and Jews. Ezek. xxxvii. 22. *Hengst.* One corner stone will unite all the living stones. 1 Peter ii. 5. *Bengel.* The two flocks become one flock by means of the one Shepherd, in Him; not by entrance into the αὐλή of the Jews. *Lange.* This word of Jesus progresses and will only be complete with Rom. xi. 25. *Meyer.*

---

17. Therefore doth my Father love me, because I lay down my life, that I might take it again.

Therefore. On this account, for this reason. *Lange.*—What humility! On our account He wishes to be loved by the Father, viz.,—because He died for us.—The deepest ground of His love, is His relation to the Father.—The majesty and humility of Christ here gloriously blend.—His authority and power to gather untold millions into one flock, had just been asserted. Now He speaks of his obedience unto death.—At once child in Bethlehem, and Messiah, the Prince, at once servant and Lord; Dying, yet Immortal. One with God, and yet obedient to the Father.—Allegory laid aside, He now speaks plainly of the mystery of the Father's love to the Son.—He had humbled Himself to earn the crown of the Cross. Phil. ii. 8, 9.

My Father. See on John i. 1, 2, 18, 34. As the Son's sacrifice of Himself was the highest possible act of love, so the Father's love reached its consummation when the Son died.

Love Me. In His compassion in not sparing His Son for the world.—The infinite depth and height of the Father's love, is only equalled by the height and depth of the Saviour's humility and love in death!—What a fearful error for Jews to make His death a sign of God's wrath. Isa. liii. 4.—"Blind unbelief is sure to err." *Cowper.*—Dying, He rendered a sacrificial obedience whose principle and motive was boundless trust in his Father. *Lange.*

Because. The flock of Christ seems here the *reward* of His sacrifice.—"Wherefore God hath also highly exalted Him." Isa. liii.

878 / Gospel of John

11, 12.; Phil ii. 9.—Jesus dies not merely in order to die, but to found a kingdom.

I lay down. Redemption is replete with *wonders* and *mysteries.*— Human wisdom is offended at God the Son becoming a babe.— Human science sees no value in the sacrifice on Calvary.—Christ returns to the central idea of His Shepherd love.—Herein lie the divine power and dignity of this dying Man that He alone "yielded up;" all else of mankind have life *wrested* from them.— The Father took no pleasure in the death of His Son, as death, but as voluntarily and lovingly suffered for such a glorious end! —This idea, that no *created* power could take His life, He repeats again and again. This gives value to His death.—His sufferings were willingly, freely, patiently, piously undergone.—His death before that of the thieves was doubtless a miracle. *Aug.*

My Life. Dying, yet immortal to quicken, save and glorify the countless myriads of the elect.—Without the conscious design of overcoming Death, Christ's death had not been permissible or possible.—The angel having the power of life and death, had none over him. Rev. xiii. 15.—The entire attributes of the Godhead stand pledged to shield every innocent being in the universe. James v. 6.—He yields because He is in perfect harmony with "the counsel and the foreknowledge of God" which had appointed it. Yet those who put him to death were held accountable, and punished for the dreadful crime. "By wicked hands ye have taken," &c. Acts ii. 23.

Take it again. A very remarkable utterance as to His resurrection.—Lest His Divinity should be overlooked, He affirms His death to be of His own choice, "delivered for our offences, and raised for our justification." Rom. iv. 25.—He proves that God's plans never interfere with man's responsibility.—Any pastor might die for his flock, but who can *retake* life?—Life and death were the absolute *servants* of Christ.—In His victorious reliance on the new life in death contained in His sacrifice, Christ is the delight of the Father. In a similar spirit, the Christian is well-pleasing to God in Christ. Isa. liii. 12; Luke ii. 14; Matt. iii. 17; John xii. 28; xvii. 1. *Lange.*—His resurrection life essential to His securing the results of His death. "I fall into the ground like a grain of wheat, in order to bear much fruit." *Lange.*

Διά. As to this διά, note the word, "The pleasure of the Lord," &c. Isa. liii. 10. Because of this offering. *Anton.*

ἀγαπᾶ. Christ suffered under the *anger* of the Father. *Aquinas. Origen.* Father's love to us, seen in Christ's passion, not the result of avenging severity. *Bengel*

ἐγὼ τίθημι. "I lay it down." Let not the Jews glory. To rage they were able, but to have power they were unable. *Aug* On no other scheme Christ's atoning death were possible, or awful *Stier.* Not mere sufferings, but voluntary pangs. *Brownrig.*

ἵνα. Not end but event. Not casual, but declaration of the future. *Euthymius.*

18. No man taketh it from me, but I lay it down of myself. I have power to lay it down, and I have power to take it again. This commandment have I received of my Father.

No man. A terrible delusion seems to have infatuated the Jewish leaders, that He who could heal the *sick*, and raise the *dead*, could not protect His own life.—They vainly dreamed that they had Him in their power ; but He tells them they were only instruments of His own will.—His death He fore-announces as a *voluntary sacrifice* for the salvation of the world.—Its voluntariness proves it was not the effect of personal sin.—So far from interfering, it flowed from His *relation* to the Father. Pilate ignorantly boasted, " I *have power* to crucify," &c. John xix. 10.—He proved that He had *power* to live. John xviii. 6.—The church finds a further proof in His last dying words. John xix. 30; Luke xxiii. 46. —Twelve legions of angels were ready to fly as lightning to His aid. Matt. xxvi. 53.—His resurrection was an act of *His own* supreme Godhead, one with the Father.

Taketh. No language could better express the *absolute voluntariness* of Christ's death.

Taketh it, *i.e.* Against His will : although God's decree rendered it necessary, it was based on the Son's consenting. Acts ii. 23.— Neither a compulsory decree of the Father, nor the power of the evil one occasioned the death of the Son.—It resulted only from the inward impulse of the love of Christ. *Olsh.*—This answers the objection of some, that the Father appears *unjust* to the Son.—All He suffered was the spontaneous, free out-going of INFINITE LOVE ! —His death was independent of every law of mortality, known in God's universe. It was the pure effluence of boundless endless love, displaying its very essence in the sublimest form. *Olsh.*

To take it again. His resurrection, though frequently ascribed to the Father was, nevertheless, His assertion of *His own right to life*, when His work was finished.—The power to rise from the dead, illustrates the word, "I AM THE RESURRECTION and the LIFE." John xi. 25.—His dying was the freest possible self-surrender of His life.—Martyrs suffering for Christ were sustained by this hope of rising again.—Our Lord at His resurrection, was discharged from the alliance with dust. His covenant of atonement, even to humiliation was completed.

Commandment. Christ has never but *one* law of life, for holy life is perfect simplicity.—His death was at once by " command " of His Father and by such voluntary obedience as proved Him infinitely worthy of His Fathers's love.—All the sad steps from that hour to the sepulchre are implied.—Deepest humiliation and greatness infinite, are here plainly affirmed.—Christ's life being His own, He had a right to give it for us at the command, and in covenant with the Father. Freedom in the self-sacrifice of Christ:

1. As a power of love; 2. As a power of life; 3. As a power of hope. The mark of genuine pious submission unto death, is the hope of resurrection.—True joyfulness in sacrifice is always at the same time an assurance of resurrection.—The death of Christ, the consummation of the good-will of God to mankind in Him. *Lange.*

οὐδεὶς αἴρει. Not the intrinsic, physical necessity of death that is denied, but the compulsive force of circumstances. *Tho'uck.* Refutes the blasphemy of Socinians asserting God's injustice towards His Son. *Rosenmuller.*

ἐξουσίαν. Not *by* the flesh, 1 Peter iii. 18, but *in* the flesh, not *by* the spirit, but *in* the spirit.—Implies the inherent energy of Christ in dying and rising. *Beck.* It is immediately connected with ἀπ' ἐμαυτοῦ. *Hengst.*

ἐντολὴν· Commission. *Greswell.* Refers merely to dying. *Chrys.* Simply a promise of new life. *Many of the Ancients.* Embraces both considerations, their indissoluble connexion being precisely the main point. *Lange.* He undertook with His Father's WILL.. *Chrys.* The God-man suffered by reason of His will to suffer. *Hilary.*

---

19. There was a division therefore again among the Jews for these sayings.

Division. *Schism.* The fore-token of approaching final separations. The followers of Christ are a *united band.*—As the Spirit of Christ ever unites His followers, these schismatics were not of His fold.—Variety of names or denominations never keeps true believers *apart.*—Following same *shepherd,* animated by same *spirit,* beset by same *foes,* ruled by *same law,* bearing *same image,* travelling to *same* HOME!—The seamless garment of the Lord by prophetic word was not divided.—The Church of Christ is one loving, united, devoted band.—The dove *will not* battle, the lambs and sheep of Christ *cannot.*—Those bearing the name of Christ, and yet of a *contentious* spirit are *enemies* of the Gospel.—No Christian can by habit be given to *strife.*

Jews. Members of the Sanhedrim.—Pharisaic hearers with whom the Lord's last discussion was. John ix. 40. *Lange.*

These sayings. These interchanges between the Persons of the Trinity had filled some of His hearers with silent and adoring wonder.—But our Lord foresaw that His words would rather increase the guilt of the Jews than lead them to repentance, yet He spake them.—Faithful ministers will preach the whole counsel of God whether men will hear or forbear.—The children of God must be served with the bread of life even although the devil should put pins into it to choke hypocrites. *Bunyan.*

Σχίσμα. Not because He had used terms unknown in Israelitish Theology, but because in their proud rebelliousness, they knew them not. *Anton.* To this σχίσμα our Lord makes no allusion. *Tittmann.* Those witnessing such a miracle, then slan-

dering Him, were beneath a reply. *Euthymius.* Ignorance of Christ's personality the cause. *B.ngel.* Depraved hearts refusing such a Saviour. *Author.*
'Ιουδαίοις. Dominant parties with the πολλοί from Galilee. *Neander.* Not limited to Pharisees. *Hengst.*
πάλιν. Points back to John ix. 16. *Hengst.*
οὖν omitted. *Lach., Tisch., Treg., Alford.*

---

20. And many of them said, He hath a devil, and is mad; why hear ye him?

Devil. See on John vi. 70 (and critical note) ; vii. 20.—Our Lord's allusion to Gentiles as other sheep of His fold, and His assumed power of laying down or taking up His life had angered them.— It is impossible that a holy God should please unholy men.—Light and darkness cannot dwell together.—Malice delights ever to misinterpret the words of the wise and good.—The amount of *violence done to conscience* by cavillers, will be a source of wonder in eternity.—Sceptics get credit for *honesty of heart (!)* with the depraved world, but God sees through their hypocrisy, and by-and-by will reveal their true character to the universe.

Mad. True to their moral fatherhood, they *slander* the innocent. John viii. 44.—The devil was first a liar, then a murderer.—Persecutors have always first slandered, then murdered saints.—Slander is murder of character, and it paves the way for shedding blood. " He that hateth his brother without a cause is a murderer." Thus fifty millions of martyrs were first hated, then slandered, then put to death.—Need we wonder if men affirm that the Son of God was "mad," when they will, even now, blacken the humblest of His servants?—"They set their mouths against heaven, and their tongue walketh through the earth." Psalm lxxiii. 9. For such "the arrows of the Almighty and coals of juniper" are prepared. Psalm cxx. 4.

Why hear? The most remarkable feature of human depravity is that men resolved to reject all the calls of grace, are not willing to perish ALONE! This dragging others down to ruin, the habit of all infidels, seems an element of hell.—He meekly listens and remains silent under these charges.—He will yet speak from His throne to these men.

δαιμόνιον. See critical notes on St. John vii. 20. μαίνεται. Not synonymous with δαιμόνιον ἔχειν. *Stier.* They meant possessed with a devil. *Hengst.* A common reproach to honest persons speaking unseasonably. *Lampe.* Neither the words nor the works of one possessed. *Markland.*

---

21. Others said, These are not the words of him that hath a devil. Can a devil open the eyes of the blind ?

Others. Thus the dividing line had begun before He reached the cross.—A wider gulf even now exists between those who believe and those who reject.

Words. An appeal to the calm, collected, composed testimony of the WORD. — "Wisdom will ever be justified of her children." Luke vii. 35.

Demon. John vii. 20.—His enemies had proposed to treat Him as a madman, and pay no more attention to Him, but a friendly minority are evidently powerfully affected by his words.—Possessed ones do strange things, but never works of kindness.

Open. The miracle seemed too great to be performed by such agency.—God's works demonstrate His *power, wisdom* and *goodness.* —All things must be traced to God, their Great First Cause. No plant grows except from seed. Whence did the first seed come ?—The oak springs from the acorn. Whence came the first acorn ?—Some articles attract each other, others repel. Whence came these *laws* of attraction and repulsion ?—Electricity, gravitation, light, motion, have some CAUSE unseen by us.—Matter being inert, all motion either organic or inorganic must have a CAUSE.—No man of sane mind can believe that bodies are moved *causelessly.*—The harmony between various parts of the creation prove ONE intelligent author.—The air adapted to the lungs ; light to the eye, ear to sounds, the earth to seed, the sun to plants, the dew to vegetation, &c.—Earth with its vast and varied furniture is a work of Divine art. The *skill, power, benevolence,* of the Divine artist shine out everywhere.—Hume and other scoffers dare question God's benevolence, but they confound nature under the curse of sin, with its normal state, when pronounced by its Maker "very good."—Teeth are not made to ache, as a sickle is not made to wound the hand.—The veins are not made to be inflamed with fever. Nor are the glands made to secrete poisons in the system.—He might have made each ray of light an *arrow* from the sun ; each breath of air, a *sigh ;* each odour, *offensive ;* each taste, *bitter ;* each touch, a *sting ;* each thing of beauty, a *stain ;* each sound, a *discord ;* and each step a *pang.*—The human body is "fearfully and wonderfully made ;" but the soul with its intelligence, self-consciousness, personality, sense of moral law, and will, is a greater work than the material universe with all its vastness and minuteness.

Open the eyes. Our Lord takes no notice of this internal dispute. —Persons who obstinately shut their eyes at mid-day and cry out there is no light, are not worthy of reply.—Christ is still opening the eyes of the blind.—A gracious experience of His salvation in the soul is the best answer to cavillers, and the most powerful safeguard against every form of infidelity. *Chalmers.*—Pharisees and false teachers endeavour to keep men in blindness. Christ gives light,

and His followers love light and walk in it.—That Popery is
antichristian is proved from its fear of a free and open Bible, and
its hatred to all education save that which its priests dare allow.—
As all light comes from heaven, the Christian welcomes every
beam.—History, science, scripture, are lights leading up to and
revealing the Eternal Light.

δαιμόνιον. From Matt. xii. 24, it appears that in former times even beneficent
miracles may have been ascribed to demons. *Lange.* δύναται. Not the power but
the mind. Being essentially malevolent, all the devil's acts of power are for evil and
not good. *Olshausen.*

22. ¶ And it was at Jerusalem the feast of the dedication, and it was winter.

It was at. Time, place, circumstances, witnesses, prove the authenticity of the Bible.—Impostors never introduce these tests, if they
can possibly avoid them.

Jerusalem. See on John v. 1 ; vii. 25.—"The conflict thickens,
the issue looms up with certainty, the great hour approaches
swiftly." *Lücke.*—That recorded from the 7th chapter to the 21st
verse of the 10th chapter occurred at the Feast of Tabernacles.
The following incident occurred at the Feast of Dedication. Our
Lord's position and plans, during these ten weeks are unrevealed.
He remained here from the Feast of Tabernacles to that of Dedication.

Feast. See on John ii. 8, 9, 23. Established by Judas Maccabæus,
165 B.C., 1 Mac. iv. 36 ; 2 Mac. x. 6.—It commemorated the
purifications from the profanations of Antiochus, and its re-dedi-
cation to the service of Jehovah. Held on Kislev or Chisleu,
Middle of December (25 ?), lasted eight days.

Dedication. For *three* years Antiochus Epiphanes persecuted the
Jews. For three years he polluted the Temple, and attempted to
change their religion. He was the fifth of the name, the son of
Seleucus, a vulgar and cruel tyrant. He reigned 175 B.C. He
conquered Egypt, but fearing Rome, released his hold. He
plundered Jerusalem, slaying 80,000 Jews, because they rejoiced
at a rumour of his death. Book of Daniel, ii. 21, notes his
"flatteries." He spent his treasure in bribes. He forbade the
Jews to use circumcision, and burnt their books. He visited Persia
intending to rob the temple of Elymais. Hearing Maccabæus had
defeated his armies, he was filled with rage. Falling from his
chariot, he died under a terrible plague from God. His remorse
on account of his crimes, especially murdering innocent Jews, was
terrible.—Conscience, "the worm that never dies."—All fasts and
mourning were strictly forbidden during this festival.—All houses

were illuminated, and it was called "FEAST OF LIGHTS," a type of the liberated nation. *Josephus.*—A three-fold benediction pronounced during the festival; a hint of the Trinity, Num. vi. 24.—Purim and Dedication feasts might be kept by the Jews at *home.*—The second temple was dedicated at the Feast of Tabernacles. Ezra vi. 16.—The Jews, in our Lord's time, continued their shadowy semblance of devotion, while their spiritual life declined daily into apostacy and unbelief.—Church of God also hath her rejoicing festivals for the glorious Reformation.—The new Jerusalem is built of all excellent things, finest gold, precious stones, pearls, &c. Rev. iii. 12.—Our Lord went to the feast doubtless to preach to the crowds there assembled.—Church dedication an old but abused custom.—*The life of Christ, the ideal realization of Maccabaean, heroism and of the new Dedication of the Temple. Lange.*

Winter. For seasons in Palestine, see on John iv. 35.—December to February were winter months. This was added for readers unacquainted with the climate of Palestine.—Mount Hermon's peaks are nearly always covered with snow.—The writer, in May, at Beyrout, felt extreme heat, although winter snow-drifts were then whirling round the summit of Lebanon. Snow falls nearly every winter.—In 1857 it fell eight inches, and lasted two weeks.—One-fourth of the houses of Damascus were injured and many ruined.—In the valley of Sharon, on the coast of Palestine, and along the bed of Jordan, snow is unknown.—Round the Dead Sea the climate is that of Thebes in Egypt.—The atmosphere is fœtid and dangerous to tourists from Europe and America.—Palms flourish at Gaza, Joppa, Kaifar, and as far as Beyrout.—The heat is dangerous during the Sirocco from the East.—The Divine pilgrim takes shelter from those inclement changes of the seasons His own power had brought about.—*Winter* typifies the cold malicious hearts of His persecutors. *Gregory.*

ἐγκαίνια. The Karaites do not observe this festival because there is no divine authority. *Alexander* in *Kitto's Dict.* The cleansing of the Temple and restoration of the altar. Macc. iv. 52. *Hengst.* During eight days it was unlawful to fast or weep. The festival was called "Lights." *Josephus.* In the Temple at Jerusalem the "Hallel." was sung every day of the feast. *Lightfoot.* In the Gemara a story is related that when the Jews entered the Temple after driving out the Syrians, they found there only one bottle of oil which had not been polluted. and that this was miraculously increased so as to feed the lamps of the sanctuary for eight days. Hence the custom of illuminating each house with one candle on the first day of the feast, two on the second day, three on the third, and so on. *Maimonides.* χειμών. Not the season only the stormy weather. *Lange, Lampe,* and *others.* Christ must still have tarried at Jerusalem. *Neander.* His proximity to Jerusalem brings Him to the feast. *Liebst.* Three great feasts must be kept in Jerusalem alone, but this might be kept anywhere. *Lightfoot.* He remained from the feast of Tabernacles to the Dedication. *Tholuck, Bengel. Olsh., Lücke, Schleier.* John explains, for Gentiles, that the feast occurred during winter, and why he sought protection under the porico. *Stier, Alford.* The record seems to imply that our Lord preferred preaching under the open sky. *Hengst.*

Which was undoubtedly the fact. *Author.* 25 Chisleu or 20 Dec. *Wieseler.* 15 Dec., added for tho e ignorant of the season. *Bengel.* 25 of Chisleu, same as Dec. 25. *Alford.* *καὶ*, omitted, *Tisch., Treg., Alford.*

---

23. And Jesus walked in the temple in Solomon's porch.

Jesus. He was there to preach the Gospel, and work miracles of mercy.—His presence is no evidence that He countenanced this feast.—The church of God is not *bound* to anything which is not of Divine command.

Walked. A short time since, enemies had taken up stones to kill Him.—Fearless, He returns and proclaims the *same* Gospel truth. —Walking alone among Orientals, who seldom move, indicates deep meditation.—Isaac walked at even-tide.—David walked to the house of God. Psalm lv. 14.—Greek philosophers, especially stoics, walked during their lectures.—The Good Shepherd, Lord of the Temple soon to be desolate, remained there, waiting to find any strayed sheep or lamb. As though He would say, "Behold, I am with you yet."—He might have descended in thunder and flame, as on Sinai and on Sodom.—It denotes *familiarity.* He might have come on the wings of the wind. Psalm xviii. 10. —It denotes *deliberation.* He is not in haste, but slow to anger. Neh. ix. 17.—It denotes *friendliness.* Enemies rush on as a whirlwind. Isa. v. 28.

Temple. See on John ii. 14, 20; v. 14.—The centre of all their glory.

Solomon. Heb.—*peaceful.* Son of David and Bathsheba, B. C. 1033. —Called Jedidiah, "Beloved of the Lord," by Nathan the prophet. 2 Sam. xii. 25.—He was a child of promise. 1 Chron. xxii. 9, 10. Crowned at 18.—Adonijah, his brother, by his usurpation, hastened Solomon's reign.—Absalom slain when Solomon was ten years of age.—He is trained by Bathsheba, a mother whose piety was of a low type.—Adonijah put to death, and Joab slain for the crimes of the past.—Marries daughter of Pharaoh, and she brings, as dower, city of Gaza.—He commences the Temple with materials his father David had gathered.—Hiram of Tyre (having an Israelitish mother) aids him in the building.—His ships visit Spain (Tarshish), Ophir and Sheba (India and Ceylon).— He built Tadmor of the wilderness, Tirzah, Millo, Hazor, Megiddo, two Beth-Horons, a palace grander than David's, another for his queen, stately gardens (Heb. *paradises*) at Etham; (Ecc. ii. 4—9), ivory palaces, ivory towers, ascent to the Temple, &c.— Temple work was not interrupted by sound of hammer. "Like some tall palm, the noiseless fabric grew."—He built aqueducts and fortifications, pools and palaces.—He reduced many strangers

in the land to *servitude*.—In seven and a half years he completed
the Temple.—Psa. cxxxii. composed by Solomon for the Dedication
Service.—Temples to Baal, Ashtaroth, Chemosh, he built on the
Mount of Offence.—Queen of Sheba visited him, alluded to by our
Saviour. Matt. xii. 42.—Is there any hope that he repented ? The
Spirit drops a vail as a warning !—The Church can find no penitential wail from the son like the father's fifty-first Psalm.—Scripture sheds no light on the parting hour of those who forget God.
(Yet many have thought the book of Ecclesiastes to be the Confessions of Solomon after his repentance. That Solomon was the
author was received by the Rabbinic commentators, and the
whole series of Patristic writers. " Did not Solomon, King of
Israel, sin by these things? Yet among many nations was there
no king like him, who was beloved by his God." Nehem. xiii. 26.
Six hundred years after Solomon had been sleeping in earthly
dust, Nehemiah thus summarises his chalacter. He speaks of him
as a saint, imperfect, tempted, fallen; but still ranked among
those whom God's love had pre-eminently distinguished. Compare
with this the prophecy uttered by Nathan before Solomon was
born : " I will be his father, and he shall be my son, if he commit
iniquity. . . . But my mercy shall not depart from him, as I took
it from Saul." In this we have a distinct covenant made prophetically. If God foretold Solomon's terrible apostasy, did he
not with it also foretell his restoration ?)

Solomon's Porch. Arcade, colonnade.—According to tradition a
remnant of the first Temple left by the Babylonian destroyer,
and incorporated into the new Temple buildings. It was situated
on the eastern side of the Temple-porch. *Josephus.*—Herod
Agrippa, under Claudius, petitioned to rebuild the Porch, and
thus employ the 18,000 men dismissed after the Temple's completion.—But its ancient glory, or his penuriousness caused him to
refuse.—It was 400 feet long, facing the Mount of Olives.—The
grandeur of Herod's Temple rendered it the noblest work of any
age.—Herod's Porch was 600 feet in length, supported by 162
Corinthian columns, arranged in four rows, forty in each row,
and each fifty feet high.—The centre columns were 100 feet in
height; the material seems to have been of pure white marble,
for the entire structure of the Temple " resembled a mountain of
snow." *Josephus.*—These porches formed the chief splendour of all
Greek temples as well as Egyptian.—The colonnade of St. Peter's,
at Rome, is the grandest in the world.—Near Tarsus a magnificent
remnant of a colonnade rises from the sea, built during Pompey's
rule of Rome.—During showers, the people fled from the rain to
these porches.—They were not only attached to temples, but to
theatres also.—Orientals live much in the open air, and desire

shelter from sun and rain.—Porticoes were first plain, then of marble and adorned with statues, &c.—Some had seats, not only for loungers, but scholars and teachers.—*Stoic* philosophers were so called from the *Stoa* or Porch.—Senate was held, law-suits conducted, and sales made at them in Rome.—People were accustomed to gather there and gossip.—They had no journals, from which to gather the news of the day.—In this place the Jews reject the Lord of Glory. John x. 39.—Under the same porch, the apostles proclaimed His Godhead to people gladly accepting the Gospel. Acts iii. 11.

περιεπάτει. Our Lord observed, without superstition, a humanly devised festivity. *White.* Not a shadow of evidence for this assertion. *Author.* A Christian may, with a good conscience, observe those festivities which, though instituted by men, have a single aim to the glory of God and the edification of the Church. *Zeisius.* The Passion, Resurrection, and Ascension, and the coming of the Holy Ghost may be celebrated without any revealed injunction. *Augustine.* Σολομῶντος. His name given because David saw many wars. *Plumptree. Smith.* Solomon carefully trained by David. *Ewald.* Personal appearance given in Canticle v. 10. *Bossuet, Lowth.* Solomon's main works were in natural history. *Ewald.* Moral sayings. *Renan.* Treasures left by David amounted to £833,000,000. *Prideaux.* στοᾷ. Temple of Theseus at Athens is circular, and has a porch all round it. *Ferguson.* Porch, called after Solomon, by Herod, who partly by ambition, and partly to please the Jews, rebuilt it. *Beza.* But they hated him nevertheless. *Trapp.* Not built by Solomon, but stood where his stood. *Tittmann.*

---

24. Then came the Jews round about him, and said unto him, How long dost thou make us to doubt? If thou be the Christ, tell us plainly.

Jews. John i. 18.—They promptly take advantage of the absence of his adherents.—He had however His reasons for permitting their arrival at this moment.—Here again their most secret thoughts are laid bare : " All things are naked and open " to the WORD. 1 John i. 2.

Came round. Gr. *encircled Him*—in a pretended friendly way.—He had by many things awakened a widely extended hope.—How cheering to Him had they come inquiring, with sincerity, how to return to God ! " Shall I crucify your king ? " By this question Pilate hoped to impress their hearts.

How long ? Truth often becomes a burden, that conscience cannot fling off—perverse man blames his Creator for his own rebellion.—They charge our Lord with keeping back that which they ought to have known.—He had again and again told them that very thing they now demand.—He claimed in the Temple that He was THE SHEPHERD and THE DOOR ! More than that, He had *proved* by His *work* that He was the CHRIST !

Doubt. (See on the character and conduct of Thomas, and the Lord's treatment of him. John xx.)—Gr., *raise our minds,* i.e.

wear our lives out with suspense.—How long dost thou agitate our soul? *Lange.*—Unhappy men! They were wearing out their own lives, and knew it not.—Now they bring themselves under the *grinding* of the ROCK OF AGES.—" On whomsoever He shall fall, He will grind him to powder." Matt. xxi. 44.—Their question was hypocritical.—Our Lord well knew what these words meant.—They pretend to seek for information : He saw a cunning snare for Himself.—His stupendous miracles had raised the hopes of the nation, but His holy, self-denying doctrines had dashed those hopes : hence their manifold storms of passionate excitement.—They could not have had a vestige of doubt as to His *professions.*—But one so spiritual, so humble, and so holy, they could not admit to be the *Messiah.*—Often and often they had heard Him claim to be THE SON OF GOD.—Although they did desire that one who could perform such wonders, would prove Himself equal to their expected Shiloh.—Paul affirms they *did not know* Him to be the Lord of Glory. 1 Cor. ii. 8.—They saw Him wield a tremendous power over men and things.—The festival vividly reminds them of Judas Maccabæus, *the Hammer.*—They sing their songs, wondering if another HERO PATRIOT will rise.—Alas! they shut the windows to keep out the light.—Their imputation is false : His words and works proclaim Him the Christ.—But not such a Christ as their earth-born hopes demanded.—They *ask* for evidence of His Messiahship, while what they really desired was some ground for rejecting Him.—Such doubt comes not but from ignorance, prejudice, and dislike to truth.—That we see not the sun, is not because it is not clothed *in robes of light*, but through our short-sightedness or blindness.

If thou be, &c. There is a visionary longing as well as a fanatical irony in their question.—Hypocrisy certainly is at work, but only inasmuch as they feel He will not answer their worldly cravings. *Lange.*

Tell us. As though he had not told them again and again, perhaps, even with tears. Luke xix. 41.

Plainly. Gr. *openly, roundly.*—No evidence will satisfy wilful, wicked, unbelief.—By calling Himself the GOOD SHEPHERD, He had claimed Messiahship. Ezek. xxxiv. 7—16.—Affirming Himself the LIGHT of the WORLD, He had made a similar demand.—David Hume denied that a revelation to Isaiah or Paul, was one to him.—So sceptics generally demand that God shall speak to them, as they will not regard the word written.—It is a proof that men were on the out-look for the Messiah, when they hint that the impression of the people was that He was the Messiah.—But it was a false inference they intended Him to draw, that if He would only *say the word, they* would receive Him as such.—The words imply a dark insinuation : that He knows He was not Messiah, yet, would willingly pass for Him.—True He had not *publicly* proclaimed Himself the Messiah.—He never did so until solemnly adjured to do so. Matt. xxvi. 63.—But the Father's seal was visible on every claim He made.—As the Baptist explicitly *denied*, so Jesus explicitly *confessed* that He was the Christ.—Only to the twelve, the Samaritan woman, and the blind man had He told the secret. —It is not for us to teach God *how* He should teach us.—In judgment the question will not be, *could we resist the evidence?* —But had we enough to lead us into the way of life?—If the heathen are without excuse, Rom. i. 20, what will be the guilt of those to whom " the light of the moon is as the light of the sun, and the light of the sun as the light of seven days?" Isa. xxx. 26.—It is not evidence unbelievers want, but an humble, teachable heart.—There is light for those who wish to see ; and darkness for those who desire to remain in blindness. *Pascal.*— Infidels demand to have objections removed, questions answered, and difficulties explained, all which have been done over and over again a thousand times. *Riddle.*

ἐκύκλωσαν. Parted Him from His disciples. *Lange.* With no friendly motive. *B. Crusius.*

ἔλεγον. A design to entrap the Lord by some word of imprudence. *Von Ammon.* Double feeling of weak inclination, combined with decided repugnance. *Hengst.* αἴρεις. Weary us to death. *E'sner, Wakefield.* Deceive us with vain hope. *Wetstein.* Tollis. *Vulgate.* Excite expectation. *De Witte.* Raise or agitate. *Tholuck.* Wear our lives out by suspense. *Bengel, Meyer.* Take away our life. *Fickenscher.* In *Josephus* ψυχὴν αἴρειν means *to uplift the soul, to raise the courage*, but it has also the more general sense *to excite the soul*, (μετεωρίζειν) which in this case was done by Messianic expectations. *Schaff.* People would persuade Him to be a Messiah in their sense, to release them from Roman rule. *Lange.* Hold us in suspense. *Hengst.* Used to violent pain, by *Sophocles.* The effect of eloquence. *Libanius.* Doubts, like all other evils, *test* our moral principle. *Butler.*

παῤῥησία. With boldness. *Gesenius.* Freedom or frankness in speaking ; fearless candour. *Cremer.*

---

25. Jesus answered them, I told you, and ye believed not: **the works that I do in my** Father's name, they bear witness of me.

Jesus. Heb. *Saviour.* John i. 17. *Word.* John i. 1. *Son of God.* John i. 18, 34.

Answered. Although He knew it was a *snare*, yet He replies. But questions of curiosity or malice were answered so as to disappoint, and at the same time convey a cutting reproof to consciences.

I told. Gr. *I have spoken.* Neither Hebrew, Greek, nor Latin has any word for our modern " yes."—His gracious and solemn reply, flings back the charge they had made.—" I have not, but your own hard hearts, have made you doubt."—He perceives their pertinacious unbelief, under their specious question.—The time was not fully come to say to them, " I am the Christ." Matt. xxvi. 64.—Had they been honest, His works would have convinced all.— But they were defiantly determined to believe nothing unless it *pleased* them ; no one is so utterly reckless, as the Christ-despiser.

Believed not. John i. 7 ; vii. 38.—They denied they had good ground to believe in Him.—Thus myriads have lived and gone to judgment with a lie in their right hand.—The frank confession has been made or recorded by a number of converted infidels, that it was their *heart* and not their *head* which needed to be convinced. —Ye believe not because ye are not my sheep.—Leave Me alone, we have no sympathy with one another.—Yet he had some timid ones who trusted it was He, &c. Luke xxiv. 21.—To these He will minister gracious aid and a weightier *promise.*—He will answer more than they asked, as to who He was.—Enmity shall not make Him falter in His pleadings with them.—Had He paused long, the storm would have burst forth again.—Neither oracle nor miracle could convince such incorrigible foes.—This stubborn malicious scorn, refusing overwhelming evidence, when every cavil is silenced, has been thought by some *the* sin against the Holy Ghost.— There is a class in gospel lands so exultant and heaven-defying in their malignant hate of Christ, that nothing save God's thunders can subdue—"Sharp arrows of the mighty, with coals of juniper " (Psa. cxx. 4). will bring down these haughty ones.—His glorious works and matchless teachings showed them *His* idea of the Christ, but all these begat no faith.—If casting out devils, healing the sick, raising the dead, &c., failed to convince ; so, to say " I am the Christ " would only have been " casting pearls before swine," a sneer or a curse would have been His reward, or He would have been reported as *traitor* to Cæsar.

The works. Miracles on man, nature, and the spirit world. See on John iii. 2. Trees, diseases, winds, waves, all were *subpœnaed* to testify for Him.—Heaven, earth, and sea, and even hell, gave their witness to His Divinity.—Sickness, health, death, and the grave declared Him God.—The darkened heavens, the trembling earth, the rent veil, the angels, the empty tomb, the rising saints, proclaimed Him Incarnate Deity.—That unbelief which could resist such proofs was simply incorrigible ; for unbelievers so hardened there could remain nothing but a "fearful looking for of judgment." Heb. x. 27.

εἶπον. Must not be translated : I have told you so; for that would be an unmistakable affirmative, and would at once present to them the alternative either of paying Him homage as Messiah, or of seizing and trying Him as a false prophet. *Lange.* Read, " I

said unto you, &c." *Campbell.* He had implied Himself to be the Messiah, bu not such as they expected. *Bloomfield.* Given you to understand, *Norton.*
πιστεύετε. Not to assent to our Lord's claim as Messiah. *Tittmann.*
ἔργα. Supernatural works. *Kuinoel. Tittmann.*
ἐν τῷ ὀνόματι. Father's authority. *Kuinoel.* He who has this, may claim **Divine** Commission. *Tittmann.*

---

26. But ye believe not, because ye are not of my sheep, as I said unto you.

Believe not. John i. 7 ; vii. 38.—They had seen the "signs" proving His Divinity.—They had heard His claims to be equal with the Father.—He nowhere had concealed His mighty works from witnesses.—These stupendous miracles could " not be done in a corner." Acts xxvi. 26.—All He had said or done, unbelief, like a wall of brass, resisted.—"What more could I have done for my vineyard?" Isa. v. 4.—Searing conscience grieves the Spirit, and renders the incorrigible reprobates. " It is impossible to renew them to repentance." Heb. vi. 6.—They hear the solemn appeals, share the sacraments and sin on.—Thus the girdled tree is marked by the woodman's axe.—Sun, dew, and rain descend on its outspread branches : but all these enriching and vitalizing elements avail not to stop death's work.—" Ephraim is joined to his idols : LET HIM ALONE !"—So far from believing in and following the Shepherd, they attempted to drive His flock into the wilderness to perish.

Not of my sheep. See on verse 2.—The phrase synonymous with not my believing disciples.—Ye do not recognize ME in MY word and work, and not knowing ME ye do not subordinate yourselves to me and trust in MY guidance. On the contrary ye desire a Messiah, that he may be the tool of your passions. *Lange.*—They longed for a king with a splendid victorious army to redeem them from Rome.—They did not know that this same Good Shepherd now calling them, was also a KING, whom the *armies of heaven* rejoice to obey. Heb. i. 6.—That His throne, unlike the tottering, tumbling one of Cæsar, was an everlasting throne.—These Jews did not want a Saviour dying to atone for their sins.—Like modern " Liberals," they did not believe their sins needed any atonement. —Their carnal Messiah must be immortal, mighty as an angel, and ambitious and victorious as Alexander.—They wanted no prophet from God to instruct them, being wise in their own eyes.—All are His sheep who believe in His words, works, and claims as Messiah. —They are not His sheep:—1. Who hear not the voice of the Good Shepherd. 2. Who know it not when they hear it. 3. Who are not known by Him. 4. Who follow strangers.—His voice, i.e., His truth makes no impression on them.—Believers are called sheep for their gentleness, meekness, patience.—Hence those *not innocent, not* useful, prove themselves *out* of Christ's fold.—Those

not of Christ's sheep, are enemies of Him, and His followers.—
They were unwilling to follow Him as their shepherd, not because
He was not the true shepherd, but because they were not His
sheep.

γάρ. Our Lord foresaw they were not elected. *Aug., Jansenius, Aquinas.* Non-
election is never the cause of unbelief. *D. Brown.*
καθὼς εἶπον ὑμῖν. A gloss. *Erasmus. Lange.* Omitted, *Cod. Sin., Tisch., Tregelles.*
Refers to the entire allegory; an obvious deduction, and its difficulty proves its
genuineness. *Alford,* As I said lately. *Stier.* It implies the conflict with the Jews
was renewed. *Meyer.* He would remind them, that truths disregarded are easily
forgotten. *Author.*

---

27. My sheep hear my voice, and I know them, and they follow me.

My sheep. See on verse 2. Equivalent to " Ye are not My *sheep,*
nor in My fold."—" The fold which I tend has no protection for
such as you."—How could these unbelievers dwell with Christ's
sheep whom they persecuted?—Their obstinate enmity against
the *Shepherd* is here noted.—All that are not Christ's sheep are
either goats or wolves. Matt. xxv. 33.—Between our Lord and
His followers a living, mutual relation exists.—In another parable
He points to the connection between the branch and the vine.
John xv. 5.—Separation ends in the certain death of the branch.
—As the body holds the limb with a living grasp, so Almighty
grace holds the believer.—Hence the promise: " None shall pluck
them out of my Father's hand." John x. 29.

Hear. Not dispute and question, but believe and obey.—It implies
they did not hear His voice, therefore they are *not* His sheep.—
Every word is of eternal import to each human being to whom the
Gospel comes.—How much momentou truth is here crowded into
a single line !

Hear my voice. They do not question and fret under His teachings.—One may give an *outward* hearing to the words, without
submitting to the voice of God.—But the sheep always *follow,*
when they "*hear*" His voice.—The regeneration of a soul a
greater miracle than raising the dead.—The Blood of the Lamb of
God alone could pay the price of a soul's salvation. Acts xx. 28.
—They hear Him, " Repent: for the kingdom of heaven is at hand."
—They hear Him, " Labor not for the meat that perisheth, but
for that," &c.—They hear Him, " Take my yoke upon you and
learn of Me," &c.—They find consolation in His words.—They
think of them, pray over them, prize them, live in them and die by
them.—" Open Thou mine eyes, that I may behold wondrous
things out of Thy Law."

I know them. Doubtless a vital connexion between these words and the sheep hearing His voice and following Him.—His *knowing,* an enlightening, disposing, drawing knowledge.

I know them. What a word of consolation to the persecuted blind man.—Christ's knowledge of His people is discriminating, tender, loving, helping like that of a wise and good mother for her children in every place, in every situation, in every duty, in every work, in every trial, in every affliction, in health and in sickness, in life and in death, in time and in eternity.—Thousands of martyrs, confessors, and faithful ones have been cheered by this ray of light, from the Good Shepherd.

They follow me. Christ's flock often addressed by the seductive voice of strangers.—Often they are promised the treasures, honours, and pleasures of the world.—Often they are told there are other and smoother ways of reaching heaven. *They follow* HIM: 1. In HOLINESS.—"Be ye holy for I am holy." 2. In LOVE.—"By this shall all men know that ye are my disciples, if ye have love one toward another." 3. In SELF-DENIAL.—"If any man will come after Me, let him deny himself, and take up His cross and follow me." 4. In MEEKNESS.—"This mind must be in you, which was also in Christ Jesus."—Their relish for spiritual joys is such, they slong not for those of the world.—His arm around them, nothing can ever separate from Him. Rom. viii. 39. His power within them, over all temptations, will finally prevail.—"It is not the will of my FATHER that one of these little ones should perish."

ἐμά. Not emphatic, but πρόβατα. *Stier.* A contrast between sheep who do, and do not follow *Lücke.* All that are *sheep* do hear and follow *Hengst.* Those refusing to follow, cannot be sheep, but goats *Author.* Here are five links in the golden chain of salvation: my sheep—*election.* Hear—*vocation.* I know—*justification.* Follow—*sanctification.* Eternal life—*glorification. Trapp.*

φωνῆς. The spiritually quickening influence of the word upon the heart. *Zeller.* Converting a soul a greater work than creation. *Greg.* Our Lord's miracles were great outgoings of divine power, but their *moral echoes* were more glorious displays of Divinity. *O.sh.*

---

28. And I give unto them eternal life; and they shall never perish, neither shall any man pluck them out of my hand.

I give. What majestic greatness and consciousness of Divinity.—I, the reputed son of a carpenter, the despised Galilean.

Give. "Not some future day, but *now;* I actually am giving."

I give eternal life. Their works cannot secure it, their sufferings cannot purchase it.—I GIVE it to all my sheep though they are now persecuted and scorned.—All that is implied in *Omnipotence, Om-*

niscience, and *infinite love* is here pledged to the believer.—If Jesus be the Son of God, all true Christians are eternally safe.

Eternal life. See on John iii. 15, 16, 36 ; v. 24.—Divine life in the soul embraces the depth and breadth of eternity.—Temporal health, ease, character, goods, nay life, may perish.—The people of God in every age, have been a *suffering* people Matt. v. 10, 11.

Never perish. Because "their life is hid with Christ in God.' Col. iii. 3.—Because He *knoweth* them as His, and therefore will defend them.—Because His purpose from eternity is to save them, and He is able to carry out His purpose.—Because Jesus has taken away the sting of death.—Because Christ the risen, ascended, and glorified Lord dwells in them by His Spirit, "the hope of glory."

Perish. Gr. *Cause themselves to perish.*—The sinner is his own destroyer.—Least of all can ye Pharisaic *robbers* shear sheep within MY fold.—Violently driving them out of your synagogue only drives them to Me.—"The Lord forsaketh not the saints, they are preserved for ever." Psa. xxxvii, 28.—"They that trust in the Lord shall be as Mount Zion, which abideth," &c. Psa. cxxv.l —"Israel shall be saved with an everlasting salvation." Isa. xlv. 17.—"Yea, I have loved thee with an everlasting love." Jer. xxxi. 3.—"And I will make an everlasting covenant with them." Jer. xxxii. 40.—"No weapon that is formed against thee, shall prosper." Isa. liv. 17.—"I will make with them a covenant of peace, and they shall dwell safely." Ezek. xxxiv. 25.—They are exposed to malignant and powerful foes with whom they cannot contend. But their Redeemer, "the mighty God," giveth them the victory ! "The gates of hell shall not prevail." Matt. xvi. 18. —"Those whom HE LOVES, He loves to the end." Zeph. iii. 17 ; John xiii. 1 ; Psa. ciii. 17.—"He who begins a good work will perform it unto the day of Jesus Christ." Phil. i. 6.—Perseverance, save in holiness, is anti-scriptural and mockery.—Only those who "hear His voice," and "follow Him" have any comfort in this truth.—The undertone of these words is, "ye unbelieving Jews shall perish."—Jews under the Romans certainly dreaded perishing as a nation ; even as far back as Moses' day warning notes of the coming ruin were heard, but now they were becoming muttered thunders. Deut. xxxii. 21.

Neither shall any man. "Man" is not in the Greek and should not have been inserted as it weakens the force.—"No one shall pluck" &c.—The words secure against all foes, temporal and spiritual.—Interrogatively, who shall pluck them ? Rom. viii. 33—35.—Jews were "robbers," and so are all opposing Christ's kingdom John x. 12.—The "Synagogue of Satan" was trying to suppress the Church of God. Rev. ii. 9.—A sad historic fact,

that Pagans ever found Jews willing helpers to burn, crucify,
torment, and murder the disciples of Jesus.—"There is none who
can deliver out of my hand." Job x. 7.—Such a statement had
been impious arrogance were Jesus not the Supreme God.—
Jehovah in giving His honour to Jesus does not give it "to another." Isa. xlii. 8.—Our Lord ascribes the same great work to
Himself as He does to the Father.

Pluck. That is, finally separate saints from God's protection.—
" Who shall *separate us* from the love *of Christ?*" *From His love
to us.* Rom. viii. 35.—All things are *of* the Father, *by* the Son,
through the Spirit.—Satan desired to pluck Peter out of God's
hand, but Christ's intercession secured salvation for the fallen
apostle. Luke xxii. 31, 32.—Had he " watched and prayed," he
might have escaped that unspeakable anguish.—Yet sovereign grace
overruled it for his spiritual good, and for the good of the Church
to the close of time.—The truth must *abide in us* and we in it, if
disciples.—The promise was to Paul, no one should perish in the
wreck: yet, " Except these abide in the ship, ye cannot be saved.
Acts xxvii. 31.—Our Lord's memorable prayer, " Keep them in Thy
name " (John xvii. 11), by no means implies we are to be careless
to keep ourselves.—Although the pillars of the earth have trembled, saints have been safe.—The sun may lose its light, but God's
sunlight never grows dim.—The moon may change, but no
change comes over Divine love.—The stars may fall, but His
promises shine on more gloriously for ever. The fire dare not
kindle on His chosen, though fiercely blown. Dan. iii. 27.—
The lions, keen with hunger, dare not touch the prophet. Dan.
vi. 23.

Pluck them. Believers may fall from grace ; alas ! they often
do, but the promise is against *final* falling ; falling into hell.—
Many are said to fall from grace who only fall from a profession,
they never were in grace.—" A great many of so-called *back*-
sliders of the Church never were *front*-sliders." *Berridge.* The
parable of the sower (Matt. xiii.) illustrates this truth.—As sheep,
believers are exposed to voracious wolves.—They have foes without and foes within.—These enemies would rob them of faith, of
joy, of peace, of life.—To overcome these " principalities and
powers" of darkness, one bringing weapons from the armoury of the
Almighty was needed.—Such an eternal, mighty friend Christ
claimed to be.—In this text He gives us a THREEFOLD PLEDGE of
His fidelity, and saints' safety.—Love, Truth, and Power, a threefold chain let down to earth to draw us up to heaven. *Bernard.*
—The FATHER! the SON! and the HOLY GHOST! condescended
to guarantee salvation to believers.—" I will NEVER, no NEVER, no
NEVER forsake thee." Heb. xiii. 5.

My hand. The human *hand* represents wisdom and strength. The hand of Christ represents His Divine wisdom and power.—True faith prompts to a sincere doing of God's will.—John vii. 17.— To such, eternal love promises forgiveness of all sins heartily repented of.—A shield against wilful presumptuous transgressions.— 1 Cor. x. 13.—A guarantee against all beyond mere human temptations.—It is *coid consolation* to say so long as they *remain* His sheep, they are safe.—*Above all other dangers believers desire a* GUARANTEE AGAINST THEMSELVES. — Jews are here taught that nothing could ever alienate His flock from Him : 1. He hath adopted believers in love.—" With an everlasting love," &c. **Jer. xxxi. 3.** 2. He is true in promise.—" Two immutable things in which it is impossible," &c., Heb. vi. 18.—3. He has POWER to fulfil all pledges.—" He is able to save to the uttermost," &c. Heb. vii. 25 ; (on this subject see Comm. on John viii. 31, also critical notes on same verse).

οὐ μὴ, &c., a formula, *never. Kuinoel.*
ἀπόλωνται, *shall not perish for ever.* In the future is included αἰώνιον. *Rosenm.* Middle voice in Greek, *Shall not destroy themselves. Bengel.*
εἰς. Embraces in itself all hostile powers. *Hengst.*
ἁρπάσει To tear. *Lange.* The freedom to fall away from grace, not taken away. *Thiersch.* God includes this freedom in His explicit promise. *Author.* Reference to spiritual powers which imperil the inner life. *Luthardt.* A species of godless shepherd exercising force or violence from without. *Stier.* There is none that can *deliver* out of my hand. Deut. xxxii. 39. *Knobel.* He makes His power equal with His Father's. His reason is They are One in essence and One in power. *Beveridge.* Nothing can happen in life, in death, or eternity, that can rob them of this life. *Titt.* The views known as Calvinism alone can honestly be found in Romans. *Gibbon,* the Historian.
χειρός μου· A Hebraism, but of classic authority. *Bloomfield.*

---

29. My Father, which gave them me, is greater than all ; and no man is able to pluck them out of my Father's hand.

My Father. Jesus stood before them as the Son of Man only.— The assertion in the last verse must have seemed vain boasting to them ; He now points to a power behind His own, that of His Father.—His Father gave the sheep to Him, and would defend their union with Him.

Gave them Me. Gr., *hath given.*—This act of the Father, the source of their salvation. In " the counsel of peace " between the Father and the Son, the elect were given as a reward of the Son's humiliation and death.—" He shall see his seed." Isaiah liii. 10. Zech. vi. 13.—Unity of the Son with the Father is here clearly taught. Those saints given to the Son, *still remain in the Father's hand.*

Greater than all. That is as Father : "The Head of Christ is God." 1 Cor. xi. 3.—Doctrine of the Trinity involves subordination of the Son, as Son, to the Father. 1 Cor. xv. 28.—Yet is the Son the Father's "fellow." Zech. xiii. 7.—He is "equal with God" (Phil. ii. 6), in nature, perfections and glory. See on John i. 2.—By the *Oneness* of Him and the Father the security of the flock is guaranteed.

No man. "Man," not in the Greek. The sentence is unlimited in application.—The words sweep the universe ; heaven, earth, and hell are comprehended. *Newton.*—"If God be for us, who can be against us?" Rom. viii. 31.—The closer God's friendship, so much deeper the malice of our foes.—"Spiritual powers" assaulting believers do by far overmatch them.—Fire often kindles in, and reduces, our homes to ashes. Job i. 16.—Storms mock our expected gains, and scatter our treasures. Job i. 19.—Sickness and death destroy those on whom we lean for aid. Ruth i. 3.—Sin stains our good works, and makes them filthy rags.—As Pharaoh and his army pursued redeemed Israel, so do sin and Satan pursue the redeemed soul.—Our safety is not in our wisdom, grace, or strength : "The LORD is my *Rock*, and my *Fortress*, and my *Deliverer.*" Psa. xviii. 2.

Can pluck. To attempt this were to make war on the Omnipotent. —Ancient impostors were quite as zealous for Satan as those of modern times. "They would thrust Israel out of the way." Deut. xiii. 5. Restless in their efforts, and earnest in pressing them to ruin.—"Neither death, nor life, nor things present, nor things to come, nor height, nor depth, nor any other creature, &c.," Rom. viii. 38 ; this is Paul's triumphant challenge and hymn of victory —Die we must, but like Antaeus, we receive new strength when we touch *the earth.*—Thus by falling in death, and being covered with earth, Christians overcome all enemies.—Assurance here follows promise, which secures the believer.—Still they are preserved through faith unto salvation. 1 Peter i. 5.—He that perseveres uses the divinely appointed means to that glorious end.

My Father's hand. Being eternally safe amid temptations is not owing to our *fidelity*, but solely to God's *power*. *Olsh.*—Characteristics of Christ's sheep: 1. *Subjective marks:* (a) "They hear My voice"; the receptive side, *faith.* (b) "They follow Me;" the active side, love, obedience. 2. *Objective marks:* (a) "I know them"; this knowledge implies recognition of the sheep by Christ, and corresponds to their faith. (b) "I give unto them eternal life," I am giving, even now in *this* world. This life is eternal both intensively and extensively.—"No one can tear MY sheep from the hand of MY Father, God Almighty : I and MY Father are one ; therefore no one can tear them out of MY hand."—*Schaff* in *Lange. Amer. Edit.*

μείζων. Neuter: Something greater, a greater power than all the opposing forces,
singly or combined. *Schaff*. Something unusual in the *neuter*, our Lord is speaking
of hostile persons, not powers. *Hengst*,

ἁρπάζειν. Can no more rescue them from MY power, than from MY Father's grasp.
Titt My Father will frustrate all designs to defeat MY will. *Kuinoel*. The form of
the sentence is a climax. *Alf*.

μου. Omitted. *Cod. Sin., Tisch., Alford*.

---

30. I and My Father are one.

I and My Father. For doctrines of Trinity and Christ's
Divinity see on John i. 1, 2. This great saying supplements
verse 16.—Divine unity not the solitariness of Deism or pseudo
" Unitarianism."—All Christians hold to the *Unity* of the Godhead,
who hold Christ's supreme divinity.—" Liberals " pretending to
singularity in holding divine unity found their name as well as
their *creed* upon a false assumption.—A " liberal " rallied Daniel
Webster for his faith in the Trinity as contradicting Unity. He
replied, "I do not understand the arithmetic of Heaven." " Whatever ' Unitarianism ' may be, most assuredly it is not Christianity." *Coleridge*, once a Unitarian preacher.

I and My Father. We would pity that folly that denied the
unity of humanity ; because body, soul, and spirit form it.—So we
would pity the ignorance that denied the unity of a sunbeam ;
because it consists of three distinct rays.—Father and Son are
same in essence, although distinct in *person*.—" Out of My Father's
hand," not as if His power was not enough, but because His
Father's hand and His are ONE Hand.

Are one. One in nature, one in will, one in love, one in the work of
salvation.—The eternal life which He puts in the hearts of His sheep
corresponds with the destiny prepared for them by the Father.—
The triumphant Church of Christ is the triumphant Kingdom of
the Father. *Lange.*—In verse 28 He had advanced claims far up
towards the throne of God.—In this verse He calmly takes His
seat upon the ETERNAL THRONE !—All the hopes of a redeemed
world rest *on this unity.*—That the Jews understood Him to claim
absolute equality with JEHOVAH is fully proved by their future
acts.—What sort of logic is it that repudiates these claims and
yet calls Him "a good man," and appropriates His name, and enjoins people "to follow His example." But this is the logic of
so-called " Unitarians " and other " Liberal " Christians !—This
claim justifies the word " none can pluck them out of MY HAND."
—He thus reveals in what sense He calls God His Father.—Israel
is often called a Son of God ; here He for ever shuts out all possible
misapprehension.—He well knew the Jews would accuse Him of
" making Himself *equal with God.*" John v. 18.—He well knew

how they and the future Christian Church would take these words.—He well knew how infidels would rail at His claims, cavil at his sacrifice. and deny His work.—Therefore He for ever settles the infinite value of His victorious death by affirming the equality of His *works*, and, therefore, the equality of His *power* with the Father —As all His works in nature are characterized by simplicity, as far as man can understand them, so He will never give any cause for the misinterpretation of His works in His Mediatorial Kingdom.—If men misapprehend Him, the fault lies *with themselves*.—His truth—His life—His teaching—His works prove Him Jehovah!—If He is not one with the Father, then all our Christian ancestors for eighteen hundred years have been, and we ourselves really *are* as much idolators as our pagan ancestors.—If His *Godhead is not supreme* why did He not correct their mistake?—Did He intentionally put stumbling-blocks before men, over which they have, age after age, fallen into idolatry?—The Jews refusing to believe in His divinity found in these words actual blasphemy: why did they understand Him better than the "Liberals" do now; —The whole Catholic Church since the beginning has sung, and will continue to sing to all eternity: "Thou art the King of glory, O Christ. Thou art the everlasting Son of the Father. For Thou only art holy ; Thou only art the Lord ; Thou only, O Christ, with the Holy Ghost, art Most High in the glory of God the Father." (On the subject of Divine worship paid to Christ by the Ante-Nicene Church see critical notes on John i. 2. See also on this subject Commentary on John v. 18, 23.)

ἐν ἐσμεν. Listen to both words "*are*" and "*one*." The word "*are*" delivers you from the heresy of Sabellius; the word "*one*" delivers you from that of Arius. *Aug , Bengel, Wordsworth.* Unity of counsel and work. *Erasmus, Calvin, Bucer.* Unity of will. *Novatian Tisch.* My works are His works. My authority, His authority. My sheep. His sheep. *Norton.* Unity of will and power. *Epiph.* What *I do* and what *God wills* is one. *B. Crusins.* Needing power to defend His sheep, the unity is one of authority. *Lücke.* Singular ἐν and plural ἐσμεν prove both the *unity* of nature and difference of person. *Theoph.* A *dynamic* union. or union of power. *Meyer, and others.* A *moral* union . *Arian and Socinian interpretation. Essential* union. *Orthodox writers, ancient and modern.* Relation of the Incarnate One to the Father. *Tholuck.* One in *essence* primarily, but, therefore, also one in *working*, and *power*, and in *will. Alford.* That the orthodox interpretation is correct will appear : 1. The *economical* Trinity of Revelation points back to the *ontological* Trinity of essence. 2. The Jews apprehend this expression *ontologically*, and hence accuse Christ of blasphemy against God. 3. Christ does not correct their *ontological* conception of His meaning, but favours it, and in conclusion, as they fully believe, confirms it, ver. 33. *Schaff in Lange*, Amer. Edit How absurd and blasphemous for any created being, angel or man, to say, I AM ONE WITH GOD. Doctrine of the Trinity (see on John i. 1), not dependent on a few proof texts. It is interwoven with the whole revelation of God. *Chalmers.* See a sermon, "Life, Salvation, and Comfort for man in the Divine Trinity,' by F. D. Huntington, D D, in his "Christian Believing and Living," Simpkin and Co., London. Dr. H was formerly a leading minister in the "Unitarian" denomination in America, and his testimony is remarkable.

31. Then the Jews took up stones again to stone Him.

Jews. They had urged Him to declare plainly His claims for their consideration.—He knew the truth would arouse their mad fanaticism, as it has always kindled the anger of scoffers in every age.—*Voltaire* and *D'Alembert* could not allude in social letters to Christ's divinity, without breaking out in blasphemy. —They deem him a usurper of divine honours, and determine He shall die.—They now throw the mask aside, anxious enquirers they pretend to be no more.—They shut their eyes to the fact that each of His stupendous miracles was the Father's solemn seal to the very claim.—And so they intend to murder the prophet of Galilee for declaring himself the I AM.—Their impious hands were before restrained by unseen power, and now the object of their vengeance again eludes them.—The sense in which they understood His words is abundantly testified by the whirlwind it raised among His enemies.

Took up stones. John viii. 59.—Jews did not intend to stone Him to death, for that would invade the rights of the rulers. Another kind of death was foreseen by Him and foretold from the first.—This is the reward given by the world to its faithful teacher.—Fidelity dare not hope that the servant will fare better than Christ.—Infidels confess they cannot find that He *claimed* to be God: against such dishonesty these very "stones" cry out *Maldonatus*—Their question—verse 24—was evidently intended as a trap.—He answers "plainly," and their murderous stones are their response.—Thus men still *insidiously* approach believers to betray them.—In a paroxysm of rage they seized the first stones at hand.—But patient divine love keeps pace with their malice.—If He was not supreme God, the Jews were only carrying out a divine law: "He that blasphemeth the name of the Lord, Israel shall stone him." Lev. xxiv. 16.—What a proof of the clearness of His teaching upon this subject.—Twice they recognized His *claiming* to be DIVINE by attempting to stone Him.—But the arms that threatened were held back by Almighty power.—His "hour had not yet come," and when it arrives it will be by a Roman and not a Jewish mode, although Jews will demand it.

ʼΕβαστασαν. Not Hellenistic, found in Aristophanes and Homer. *Rosenm* Indicates a more deliberate and earnest act than ἦραν. John viii 59. *Winer.* Literally *carried* large stones. *Bengel.* Lifted, act of moving. *Meyer* Both taking them up and a so holding them. *Ellicott.* Caught up stones and raised them high in air. *Lange.*

---

32. Jesus answered them, Many good works have I showed you from my Father; for which of those works do ye stone me?

Answered. He replied to their murderous attitude by words of gentle remonstrance.—His glorious miracles, Himself the greatest, had already *answered* to all honest minds —His words now did not lessen the claim, or correct the impression.—St. Paul at Lystra instantly corrected the mistake of the people with horror.—Those denying the Godhead of the Saviour, charge Him with a sin like that of the *impious Herod.* Acts xii. 23.—Had He known Himself *not* to be God, His answer was neither appropriate nor honest.

Many. Far beyond in number those recorded in the Gospels. John xxi. 25.

Good works. See on John iii. 2. " Good," Gr., *beautiful;* with the *grace* of Divine *truth* and *love.*—A sad undertone of despised mercy and unrequited kindness.—He did no other than works of *pure* benevolence. Acts x. 38.—He had given sight to their blind, hearing to their deaf, feet to their lame, voice to their dumb, life to their dead, health to their sick, wisdom to their teachers, food to their hungry, rescued those possessed from the power and rage of demons, &c.—His CLAIMS could not be sundered from His DIVINE WORKS, and for proof of His claims He appeals to the number and character of those works.—Opposing such Godlike works was to come under condemnation : " *Do ye thus requite the* LORD, O foolish people and unwise ? " Deut. xxxii. 6.—" O my people, what have I done unto thee ? Testify against me." Micah vi. 3.—" But they soon forgat His works." Psa. lxxviii. 11.— Jesus had given demonstrations of His divinity similar to those their fathers had witnessed and forgotten.

Shewed. They were "signs" of the KING, and of the KINGDOM. —The land of Palestine was illumined with His miracles.—All the craft and malice of His foes could not detect a flaw, nor is the boasted " criticism " of the present age more successful.—He might have " shewed" them His power, and dashed them into ruin. But instead of fiery bolts, He heaps coals_of LOVE on their heads. Rom. xii. 20.

My Father. Another claim to a union in NATURE with God. —Here are blended the *humility* and *majesty* of our Lord's character.

Stone me? The terrible assault on the Son of God is *already* committed in *their hearts.*—Every single miracle protested against their act.—His remonstrance implies He would submit to the law if they could show cause against Him in His works.—Have My works been so poor that ye stone Me ?—I intended them as acts of kindness, have I failed?—Although there is a holy irony in His words, a tone of lamenting sorrow and entreating humility pervades them.—"They have rewarded Me evil for good, hatred for My love." Psa. cix. 5.—Amid our persecutions let us remember. those of the Master. Heb. xii. 3.

ἔργα. The calmness of His answer must have arrested their arm. *Lange*. Rather it intensified their passions. *Author*. Doctrines as well as miracles. *Rosenm*. Mirac e: alone. *Kuinoel*. Both. *Titt*.

Καλὰ. Moral beauty. *Lange*. Honestum *Cicero*. Wo ks of love. *B. Crusius*. Excellent works. *Meyer*. Irreproachable works. *Luthardt*.

ἔδειξα. Exhibit, perform. *Wetstein*. Without doubt contains the idea of signgiving. *Lange*.

πατρός μου. Who is in ME, and from whom they proceed through Me. *Meyer*. Ejus auctoritate fretus. *Beza*. An answer to their charge of unwarrantable presumption. *Luthardt*.

μου. Omitted. *Cod., Sin , Vat , Tisch., Alford*.

ἐκ. By the aid of. *Titt*.

λιθάζετε. *Will*, not the *Act*. *Markland*. Are you going to stone? *Titt*. Execution should be preceded by a regular trial. *Lange*.

---

33. The Jews answered Him, saying For a good work we stone thee not; but for blasphemy; and because that thou, being a man, makest thyself God.

Answered. First the stones remain unused in their hands.— Then probably they lay them down in order to answer Him.

A good work. Force of conscience obliges them to admit His good works.—The world confesses kind deeds wrought by Christians in every age, but denies they are wrought of God. Primitive disciples were *kind* to the poor, but they were called *Atheists* by *Julian*.—Their harmless character admitted, but their superstition was pestilent. *Pliny's letter to Trajan*.—They were accounted as enemies of the gods, because they sacrificed not to idols. *Celsus*. —His enemies do not this time charge collusion with Beelzebub.

Blasphemy. They reproach Him with two things : first, that He places God on a par with Himself, and this they call blasphemy; secondly, that He makes Himself God, and in this they think they recognize the false prophet. *Lange*.—The legal punishment for blasphemy was stoning. Lev. xxiv. 11-16.—Jews blinded by worldliness and national pride were unprepared for the claims of Christ.—The incarnation of the Deity, a human manifestation of the Angel of the Covenant, was their abhorrence.—Pharisees separated things inseparable in their very nature.—His God-like words and claims, attested by the Divine works He wrought. Providence permits this incident to silence the enemies of His divinity.—The Jews here plainly and unequivocally charge the Redeemer with arrogating equality with Jehovah.—Persecutors have always pretended to act from regard for God's honour.

Being a man. They mean thou art no more than a mere man.— They long for a king like Cæsar (the Imperator) who should have super-angelic power.—But they had in Christ a KING of KINGS. His throne was in Heaven.—All the angelic hosts, His army, ready to obey His will. Heb. i. 6.—Eternity His life-time, the universe His dominion. Yet truly human and subject to all the infirmities and temptations of men.—He did not deny His manhood, but asserts His God-head.—Yea, He often reminded them of His humanity, lest amid the blaze of His miracles, they should forget He was "THE SON OF MAN."—Less than two centuries after our Lord's crucifixion and ascension, the Ebionites denied His *divinity*, and the Docetæ His *humanity*. Thus unbelievers and "liberals" unite in robbing us of our Saviour altogether.

Thyself God. The Jews contended against the idea of a God-man. Had some one arisen and freed them from the power of Rome, they would have accorded Him any *honors*.—But our Lord's humble birth, humble disciples, humble appearance, self-denying acts, humiliating doctrines, they would not tolerate.—No matter how glorious His miracles, or sublime His teaching, or holy His life, *such* a Messiah could never be *their* Messiah.

βλασφημία. Calumniation, abuse. It seems to denote the very worst kind of slander, especially *to revile God and divine things. Cremer.* From an O. T. stand-point, the assertion that a man was God, was metaphysically impossible. A corrupted Judaism could not discern the incarnate personality of Christ. *Dorner.* A golden thread concerning God and man becoming one, runs through the entire O. T. *Lange.* O. T. idea of God was the *germ* of the fulness of the Christian idea. *Liebner.* The O. T. labours earnestly to show this *becoming one* with man. *Stier.* Resolving that Christ neither was, nor could be *divine*, from their point of view they judge rightly as to the nature of the sin charged. *Calvin.*

θεόν. Without the article, generally, as God is opposite to Angel. In verse 18, with article, the supreme God. *Hengst.* The best truth uttered by men, mistaken for falsehood. *Quesnel.* Men contest Christ's divinity, not as enquirers, but *censurers.* *Basil.* A revealed mystery fitter for meditation on our knees, than controversy. *Jackson.* To conceive of God is difficult, to describe Him impossible. *Plato.*

---

34. Jesus answered them, Is it not written in your law, I said, Ye are gods?

Answered. He declines to "cast pearls before swine," Matt. vii. 6. —He vindicates His right to His name as being divinely commissioned.—He calmly replies to their stormy anger, but yields absolutely nothing.

Written. See on John v. 47, also critical notes on same verse.— About 200 quotations from the Old Testament are found in the New.

Law. See on John i. 17 ; vii. 19.—Our Lord's reference is to Psalm lxxxii. 6.—The Pentateuch has not the words, but the Jews called the Old Testament *the Law*.—The entire Psalm warns tyrants and unjust judges (not Gentiles only).—Our Lord asserts the authority of the *law* over the Jews, hence He would by it convict them.— Although He appeals to the words of this Psalm, the laws of Moses are in the background.—David's Psalms are called "The Prayers of David."—Psa. lxxii. 20.—Lyric Psalms express pain, grief, fear, hope, joy, trust, gratitude, submission.—Hebrews generally united music with all their poems.—"Selah," used seventy-three times in the Psalms, indicates a pause while instruments played.—Psalms cxx.–cxxxiv., called the "Songs of degrees," are thought to have been sung either ascending the temple steps, or by pilgrims going up to Jerusalem.—A thousand years intervene between the date of the first and last of the Psalms.—David wrote seventy-two Psalms ; these compositions are marked by sweetness, softness, grace, and sometimes sublimity. He collected the wild flowers from hill and valley, and planted them on Mount Zion. *Herder.*—In every age the Psalms have been used and extolled for their inspiring devotion. The authors seem steadily and constantly to seek intercourse with God. They appear to live in God. The lines glow with testimonies to His power, providence, love, faithfulness, holiness.—Sacrifice is seen to be the consecration of *personality* to God's service.

I said. This made *men* gods.—But Christ was not *made*, He is the ONLY-BEGOTTEN Son. See on John i. 1-3, 18.

Gods. Men called so as executors of God's particular commands, whether judicial or prophetic.—But pre-eminently applicable to one consecrated as God's messenger, the mediator of His perfected revelation.—It is never said of Christ "The word of the Lord came unto Him."—Ancient Greeks and Persians called their kings gods.—The emperors of Rome demanded sacrifice to be offered to themselves as gods.—Not a few Christians were *compelled* to be *martyrs* for this cause.—The general position that man is never called god is baseless. Ex. iv. 16. Paul in Athens: "we also are His offspring." Acts xvii. 28.—At creation man was constituted God's representative.—In honouring those in office we honour God who ordains them.—In honouring parents, children respect the authority of their Creator.—A command to reverence the aged (Lev. xix. 32) is based on this fact.—Under the human appearance, is reflected the majesty of Jehovah : "For in the image of God created He man." Gen. i. 27.—" Man is the image and glory of God." 1 Cor. xi. 7.—He who stands before the judgment seat, stands before God. Ex. xxi 6.—He concedes to these rulers Theocratical dignity, but predicts its loss in their punishment—"I have said ye are gods, but ye shall die like men." Psalm lxxxii. 6.—Our Lord's citations from Scripture often have an *undertone of warning.*—He had just solemnly declared that He could and would protect his followers even as the Father protects them, and if He will thus protect His friends, *what will become* of His foes ?—It is not the breaking of the law merely, that constitutes the burden of the warning, but the conscious contemning of the riches of grace. Mark xvi. 16 ; John iii. 15–18, 36 ; v. 24 ; xi. 25.

ἀπεκρίθη. He would show them that there existed no *Dualism*, but that the Incarnation was pretypified. *Hengst.*

ὑμῶν. Emphatic. *Lange.* Our Lord reckoned the law not binding on Himself. *Schweizer.* On the contrary, His ministry began, continued, and ended in, "*It is written.*" *Van Doren.*

νόμος. At first the Pentateuch, then applied to the rest of the O. T., because it was all to direct and rule the life. *Hengst. Law* in its widest scope, the O. T. *Alford.* Titles of Psa'ms received mainly. *Thol., Hengst, Delitzsch.* ɪerm, "Degrees," over 15 Psalms. Higher choir. *Luther, Thol.* Rising in paraliels or rhythm. *Gesenius De Wette.* Sung by pilgrims ascen ing to feast. *Herder, Ewald, Hengst.* "Maschil," 13 Psalms, skilful poems. *De Wette.* Didactic. *Gesenius, Thol., Hengst.* "Michrain," mystery. *Hengst.* A writing. *Rosenm.* Main portion of Psalms, dramatic odes. *Horsley.* Some question whether Moses wrote Psalm xc. *De Wette,* Psalms collected first for devotional purposes. *Ewald.* Christ names the law as *peculiar* to the Jews. *Röhe.*

'Εγὼ εἶπα Certain words in which rulers were specifically called *Elohim.* *Hengst.* θεοί. *Elohim.* Psa. lxxxii. 6. Heathen tyrants re erred to, as Egyptian kings. *Lampe.* Israel tish kings and magistrates *Bourgon.* Judges in Israel. *Stier.* Priests constituting the court. Deut. xix, 17. *Gesenius, De Wette.* All the people of Israel. *Ebrard.* Pious pers ns only beneficent like God. *Barhdt.* In loftv irony, Since your fathers in office are called gods, may not I? The id a of a communication of Divine majesty to humanity is not foreign to the O. T. *Neander.* God here (Psa. lxxxii. 6) would accustom men fi om the beginning to think of more than a shadowy office. *Ber. Bib.* Divinity is communicative to men, since at first man was made in God's image *Hengst.* In each magistrate was a shadow of Divine majestv. *Lampe.* His appeal to the law shows that not the mob, but Sanhedrists were in the foreground. *Lücke.* Application of the title "gods" to men: "I said," made them gods. 2. Every ruler claims this honour. 3. It is only for a while. Death removes it. 4. These gods are local. *Hacket.* Greeks, Persians, Egyptians called their monarchs gods. *Diodorus Siculus.*

---

35. If he called them gods, unto whom the word of God came, and the scripture cannot be broken.

Scripture. John ii. 22 ; v. 39.—Note here the idea of the unity of the Scriptures, the whole expression shows our Lord's boundless confidence in the Scriptures.—Nothing less than His knowledge of their inspiration by the Holy Spirit can explain this confidence. —Scripture, the immovable foundation of the faith of the Church of God.—Hence in all ages infidels have sought to overthrow this foundation ; but each attack has only more fully revealed its divine beauty and strength.—The canon of Scripture then received was the Old Test. as we have it now.

Cannot be broken. *Its words remain a law for ever* to all mankind.—Heaven and earth shall pass, but the word of the Lord remains for ever. Matt. v. 18.—The slightest *word* shall abide : it is here compared with the *universe*. Witness for the existence of a *God-man* is to be found in the *inmost* heart of the O. T.—Jews admitting the inspiration of their Scriptures could not evade the inference.—Doing so, would undermine the word, put themselves outside the Theocracy.—In verse 34 He has placed all Scripture on the basis of *the law*.—In quoting the Psalms, He pronounces their divine authority. Matt. v. 18.—The omniscient Lord assumes their inspiration, and declares their testimony in violable.—When sceptics cavil about the Geography or Chronology, &c., of Scripture, the cavils are mere feints to *mask* their hatred to more *vital* doctrines—A book which received such honour from the Divine LORD may well satisfy the disciples. To *Dr. Colenso, et hoc omne genus,* these words are all the answer a Christian need ever give.

πρὸς οὕς. All the people of Israel. *Ebrard.*

ἡ γραφή. The tι ought of *the* Scripture as a who'e, first appears in 2 Chron. xxx. 5, 18. Κατὰ τὴν γραφήν, LXX., "as it was wri'ten," A V, and is probably connected with the profound reverence for the Sacred Books whi·h led the earlier Scribes to confine their teaching to oral tradition, and gave therefore to "the Writing," a distinctive pre-eminence. With this meaning the word γραφή passed into the N. T. Used in the singular, it is applied chiefly to this or that passage quo'ed from the O T. (Mark xii, 10; John vii. 38. etc.) In the plural, as might be expected, the collective meaning is prominent. Sometimes we have simply αἱ γραφαί (Matt. xxi. 42, etc.), Sometimes πᾶσαι αἱ γραφαί (Luke xxiv. 27). The Epithets ἅγιοι (Rom. i 2), προφητικαί (Rom. xvi. 26), are some'imes joined with it. *Plumptre* in *Smith's* Dict.

λυθῆναι. This points to the strength of the argument. *Hengst.* Loosened, implying Scri·ture is binding. *Bourgon.* To deprive it of its authority—making it void by rejection. *Wetstein.* If you cannot explain away this expression, etc. *Alford.*

---

36. Say ye of him, whom the Father hath sanctified, and sent into the world, Thou blasphemest; because I said, I am the Son of God?

Say ye? *Ye,* in emphatic contrast with the authority of tLe *Scriptures.*

Of Him. *Him* is wanting in the Greek, rather of *Me.*

Father. He does not say God, but THE FATHER, that is HIS Father from all eternity. God did not then in sending Him, *first become* HIS FATHER.

Sanctified. Consecration to the Messianic office. Jer. i. 5.— Through whom the Father speaketh to the world the word of God. John i. 9.—Before and at His birth, sealed with the pure impress of holiness. John vi. 27.—Thus sealed, sent as the Holy One into an unholy world—A double anointing : 1. Set apart to the office of Mediator as the Son of God. 2. By effusion of the Spirit without measure as the holy oil was composed of many spices.

Sanctified. Set apart, selected as His minister, destined from creation for this work.—The meaning, according to the idea of sanctification is:—1. The Father has taken Him out from the world in order to appropriate Him to the world, *i.e.,* He has made Him the God-Man, the New Man, the wonder of the new life. 2. He has accredited Him by His sinlessness and miraculous works.—This is spoken in antithesis to the typical sanctification, or consecration to office, enjoyed by the O. T. Judges.—They were *consecrated* by men, by outward anointing or calling.—Jesus is consecrated by the Father, by the anointing of the Spirit and the attestation of works. *Lange.*

Sent into the world. This can only refer to our Lord's pre-existence.—It implies that before He was sent, *He was the Son of God in Heaven.* (See on John i. 1—3.)

Blasphemest. His argument is that when they knew His mighty miracles, which none but God could do; wisdom would suggest that they *enquire* before they condemn the utterance of certain words seeming strange to them.

I said. He had spoken of Himself in the third person; now He here passes over and adopts the first : " Am I not He? "—He *distinctly* ACCEPTS and appropriates the charge " Thou makest thyself God? " John v. 18.

Son of God. (See on John i. 18, 34, 49.) In Him, Being and office are one. He possesses all the Father's God-head. Col. i. 19 ; ii. 9.—If it was no blasphemy to call mere men " gods," how could it be so to name Him thus, being so manifestly more than man ?—Dignity lies in this, that whom " the Father sanctifies," IS THE SON.—He had said, " I and the Father are One." He discriminates between the Persons.—He said, " I am the Son of God," equal to " I am God."—He claims not to be the Father, but " the Son of God " : " The Father is in Me, and I in Him." John x. 38. —Relationship of Father and Son necessarily coeval. The material sun and its effulgence inseparable. It was no sun *till* it shone. It became a sun *when* it shone. Christ is the brightness of the Father's glory. *The effulgence of His Splendour.* The Father being eternal, the Son must be eternal also. *Watson.* (See critical notes on John i. 2.)—Had they attributed to Him more than He claimed, in the presence of Him who gives not His honour to another, He would instantly have uttered the most emphatic protest.—Even passing the limit one hair's breadth, is *here* blasphemy.—The zeal of the Jews would have been endorsed by the Spirit of God.—" In the beginning was the WORD, and the WORD was with God, and the WORD was God." " He is before all things, and by Him all things consist."—Name JEHOVAH often applied to the SON, implies necessary, independent, self-sufficient, infinite, eternal BEING (See Comm. on John viii. 58, and critical notes on same verse) ; He is therefore God absolutely ; not relatively or by virtue of office.

ἡγίασε. Eternal generation. *Aug. Beza.* Used of ministers unconsciously fulfilling their divine mission. Isa. xiii. 3. *Alexander.*

λέγετε. The argument is from the less to the greater. *A'ford.* From the less to the greater, because all prophets were sanctified, but more The SON of God. *Author.* In respect of the dignities He proceeds *a minori ad majus,* in respect of the title *a majore ad minus (gods,* SON OF GOD). *Lange.*

υἱὸς τοῦ θεοῦ. He substitutes for unity (verse 30), the idea of the Son of God. *De Wette.* He, called in Scripture the SON, the WORD, of the FATHER, must be of the essence of the Father. *Dis. Alex.*

εἰμι. That man and God being one, an idea not alien to Old Testament. *Alford.*

ἀπέστειλεν. Sent as one sealed as the "Son of God" before His birth in Bethlehem, therefore God. *Bengel.*

---

37. If I do not the works of my Father, believe me not.

If I do not. Setting aside the charge of blasphemy, He refers again to His works. Verse 32.—The Jews might answer to His claim of sanctification, "This is the very matter in question."— He has proved that Divinity and humanity are not necessarily opposites.—Now He shows that what was *possible* had become *an actual* fact.

Works of. (See on John iii. 2.)—*The very works* which ye admit are God the Father's works.—Moses always had a point in nature to start from. He, and other miracle-workers, claimed to be no more than *servants* of God.—Their miracles were *such* as to prove their being God's ministers. But Christ claims to be ONE WITH THE FATHER. John x. 30.—Each miracle is a *distinct* and *visible* seal of God to this truth.—All other prophets wrought in God's name: Christ in HIS OWN NAME.—His works are the outbeamings of His Person, and therefore a solid basis for faith.—Each miracle was God the Father's voice proclaiming from Heaven, "THIS IS MY-BELOVED SON!"—He would have them look away from Himself personally for a moment.—He allows they have a right to reject His claims, if not authenticated by the Father.—His miracles were confessedly works of the *Supremest Power and Mercy.* —For these acts they were solemnly bound to give the Father glory, even if they rejected Him.—If they would only study His works, they would soon find they were assaulting the richest display of grace of the Father Himself.—A COMMUNION of MIND and EQUALITY of POWER is here affirmed.

Believe me not. (See on John i. 7; vii. 38.)—Christ never demanded blind assent.—His miracles of benevolence were beyond any created being's power.—His claims, which they could not comprehend, were proved by works which they could not deny. —We are commanded "to try the spirits whether they are of God." 1 John iv. 1.—"I speak as to wise men; judge ye what I say." 1 Cor. x. 15.—Our Lord would have us test His claims by the same divine standard.—Through all this gospel there seems a grand chorus, like the music of heaven, in which similar strains are ever and anon recurring, with increasing and deepening symphony.

τὰ ἔργα Incarnate Divinity had not been shewn absolutely and independently an unimaginable thing. *Hengst.* The Pope demands belief without any evidence, thereby proving himself Antichrist. *Trapp.* "*I and my Father are one.*" In what sense? "*I do God's works.*" Therefore they are ONE IN POWER. *Titt.* If my works bear the imprimatur of the Father, though you hate me, yet trust the works and thence my unity with the Father. *Alford.*

μὴ πιστεύετε. A conditional absolution from belief; at once real and ironical. *Lange.*

---

38. But if I do, though ye believe not me, believe the works: that ye may know, and believe, that the Father is in me, and I in him.

Believe not me. A clear and loud condemnation for not believing Him.

Not me! His birth, teachings, sinlessness, holiness, miracles, His entire Personality, were the proper grounds of faith.—His appeal to miracles was only a concession to the infirmity of men.— "Since His incarnation there is such a unity that we neither think of the man apart from that which is God, nor of God without that which is man." *Leo.*—At this distance, we cannot well realize the drawbacks to their faith.—Our Lord had no historic prestige then as 1800 years have given Him.—His appearance was very humble, His parents and home the same.—His disciples were poor, and lowly in their occupation.

The works. Distinction of a gradation in faith. *Lange.*— "Works," miracles, sunlike, self-evidencing, resplendent with truth, majesty and love.—Those so *blind*, so *perverse* as not to see the glory of Himself should have seen the Divine in His works.

May know and believe. Proves that Christian faith is "a reasonable service." Rom. xii. 1.—True Christians ever stand up for the broadest scattering of truth.—Julian destroyed Christian summaries of learning, and dreaded gospel light.—Domitian ordered sacred books of Christians to be burnt.—Moslems gloried in burning all religious works except the Koran.—Papal Rome keeps millions in midnight darkness. Witness her relentless hatred of the Bible Society, and of all science and true progress.

Father. See on John i. 18 ; iv. 21-23.—Instead of receding from His claim of absolute Divinity, He repeats it with additional power and emphasis.

In me, &c. The living manifestation of His union with the Father in His works.—Thus He reiterates His essential oneness with the Father.—He *seemed* to soften down this claim ; but it was only that He might prepare their minds by a quotation from their *Law* for another affirmation of the same great truth.

γινώσκητε. *Meyer, Lach., Tisch.* Sense of received text, rich and pertinent *Lange.*

ἐν αὐτῷ. Instead of this, most ancient authorities have ἐν τῷ πατρί. *Schaff.* God is
in me, might be said by any holy man, but as Father, no one can. *Hengst.* The Jews
here did not understand an equality with the Father. *Hoffman.* This lower formula
not identical with that in verse 30. *Stier, Lange.*

---

39. Therefore they sought again to take him : but he escaped out of their hand.

Therefore. Jews saw that our Lord in no sense modified His claims
for which they charged Him with blasphemy.—Their unbelief
was rigidly set against all His words. They saw clearly He meant
to make Himself equal with God. John x. 33.

Again. They had a short time previously attempted to stone Him.
Verse 31.

Take him. Denotes a milder ebullition of rage in comparison with
their previous attempt. *Lange.*—They will not now stone, but
arrest Him for trial.—Persistent and infatuated, they resist all holy
influences.—Unable to take up His challenge as to His works, they
will silence Him in death.—This is the way so often taken to answer
lovers of truth.—Cain took up this line of argument in reply to
Abel.—Rome, pagan and papal, thus silenced millions of martyrs.
—"A faggot will silence you," said the persecutor to Hawks, the
martyr. " You can do no more than God permits you," was the
reply.—But "persecution dragged them into fame, and chased
them up to heaven." *Cowper.*—No one can ever take ("*apprehend*,"
Phil. iii. 12) Christ except by the hands of *faith.*—Those imagining
themselves near God, yet without faith, are farthest from Him.—
Athenians, rearing an altar to the UNKNOWN GOD (Acts xvii. 23),
were nearer God than these fanatical sons of Abraham —To perish
at sea with home in view, to die of thirst and water bubbling from
a fountain close at hand, can convey no idea of the hopelessness
of those who die rejecting Christ.

Escaped. Probably by a miracle similar to that in John viii. 59.—
His turning away from them, significant of their doom.—No circles
drawn around Christ or His followers, but sooner or later will be
broken.—"Believers are as immortal as angels, until their work
is done." *Whitfield.*—His day's work was not yet finished. He
escapes to Peræa, beyond Jordan. How often had their designs
of wrath been defeated, yet they begin again!—How often have
assaults of infidels on the Gospel been triumphantly repelled, and
yet, like these Jews of old, they return to the attack with the broken
weapons ; so persistent and deadly is the enmity of the unrenewed
heart to truth. *James.*—Truth is like its Lord : even if it should
appear to be slain and buried, it will rise again to greater might
and glory. *Beecher.*

ἐξῆλθεν. No miracle intimated. *Hengst., Meyer.* Slipping away. *D. Brown.* Possibly miraculous. *Alford* Without any effort. *Bengel.* Rescued Himself by a miracle. *B. Crusius, Luthardt.* John has just shown that our Lord was able to so to impress His enemies as to render them powerless, *Lange.*

40. And went away again beyond Jordan into the place where John at first baptised; and there he abode.

Went away. The Evangelist at the same moment records the futile wrath of His foes, and the influence of His words on distant believers.—Why does He depart from Jerusalem? Because He must die there, and the time was not yet arrived. The Passover had not come.

Jordan. The river of Palestine.—See on John i. 28.—The further He was from Jerusalem the safer He was, just then.—That city was at once the *mother* and *altar* of saints. Like Papal Rome, she was, for ages, a slaughter-house of God's servants.

The place. Generally believed to have been the "Bethabara" of John i. 28. (See Comm. on chap. i. 28, and critical notes on same verse.)—The scene of His first appearance on the banks of Jordan. There the Baptist pointed Him out to the multitude. John i. 36.— There the Testimony of the FATHER and of the HOLY GHOST took place. There the people heard, "This is My beloved Son, in whom I am well pleased." Matt. iii. 17.

ἀπῆλθε. He has not given up the people, but He withdraws into a region of greater susceptibility. *Lange.* He retired to Bethabara that His adherents might remember the miracle wrought at His baptism. *Euthymius.*

41. And many resorted unto him, and said, John did no miracle; but all things that John spake of this man were true,

Many. Surely the Spirit had prepared the minds of the people for this visit!

Resorted. How Providence meets those whoever and wherever longing for Jesus.—If there be a widow in Sarepta or a pilgrim from Ethiopia waiting for the truth, some Elijah or Philip will be sent with tidings of mercy.—To slaves who longed for redemption, Jubilee tones sounded sweetest.

John. See on chap. i. 6, 19.—The Baptist.—Gone from his work on earth to a martyr's crown.

No miracle. Said by the people, and probably correct; but not endorsed by the Spirit.—The sayings of the crowd sometimes repeated, although not always true. Acts xxviii. 4.—Evidence of miracles was not absolutely indispensable; although John himself was a miracle.—They honestly confessed the motive which brought them to Jesus.—They would either indulge their curiosity or *avail* themselves of His miraculous power.—The author of many miracles, He is Himself the greatest and the most constant miracle to all ages.

John spake. A fresh testimony of the people to the holy man whose memory lived among them; and corroboration of their previous statement.—How often the seed sown never springs until after the death of the sower.—Yet the toiler, who saw but little result, and was left to murderers, is not forgotten.—The prophet falls, but his words will live while the world stands.—See on John iv. 36, 38.

True. Approved themselves true, and so will every word of truth; whether men at the time acknowledge it or not.—The great delusion of Satan is to make men *believe* what they *desire.*—Thus our first parents were tempted to doubt the death-threatening; thus the antediluvians despised Noah's warning; thus Lot's sons disregarded the angels' message; and deluded by the same evil spirit thousands now will not believe in sin, or salvation, or judgment, or hell, or eternity.—They knew and here imply that John's testimony had been generally disregarded.—But like all faithful ministers, his " record was on high," and his " judgment with his God."—The Lord attests his words, and thus his testimony to Christ lives again, and continues to work to the furtherance of faith. *Lange.*—Meditation on the things that formerly occurred, often the Spirit's method of leading to repentance and faith. *Starke.*

σημεῖον οὐδέν. A contrast of John's many disciples without miracle. and Jesu's many wondrous works. *Luthardt.* Their motive was to honour John. *Hengst.* How came John with so much prestige? a very holy life. *Trapp.* His testimony to the Jews proved true. *Tittmann, Hengst.* Especially the witness borne at Ænon. John iii. 23. *Anton.* We believed John, working no miracle; why not Jesus, working many? *Euthymius.*

---

42. And many believed on him there.

Many. Our Lord spent here the last four months of his ministry. —The flights of Christ lay the foundation for the refuge of sinners.—The seed, long buried, now springs up in a harvest of life eternal.

Believed. See on John i. 7; vii. 38. Where the preaching of *repentance* has had success, there the preaching of Gospel grace is most likely to be prosperous. *Henry.*—Peacefully and calmly the

despised Galilæan builds up the work of His love.—Silently and
secretly are the living stones wrought into beauty and placed in
the spiritual temple. Eph. ii. 21.—As the sound of neither
hammer or axe was heard in the erection of Solomon's Temple.
The fact recorded in this verse is an encouraging illustration of
the way in which Divine sovereignty overrules the malice of earth
and hell for the extension of the kingdom and glory of Christ.

John 11

Now. Gr., *" But,"* conveys the reason why the Lord's retirement (see chap. x. 39) was broken in upon.—He was now near Jericho, about 18 miles east of Jerusalem.—Here follows the record of His grandest miracle. *Augustine.*—Simplicity of the style of the narrative : *But .here was a certain man sick, &c. Meyer.*—Delight rather than wonder should be our emotion, for why should we wonder at His raising one from the dead, when He CREATES so many every day ?—He creates all, yet raised few, but the raising of those few demonstrates, that He could have raised *all the dead.*—Our Lord's deeds are " signs " (see on John iii. 2), and as full of the *gospel* as His words.—Every believer is a Lazarus, he is morally raised from the dead.—Yet while millions dread to die as to the flesh, few dread the death of the *soul.*—This great miracle closes our Lord's testimony, and it seems to be a *résumé* of the evidence of His Supreme Godhead. The Holy Spirit, therefore, for the first time names the subject of the miracle, also the place, and the manner of His proceeding.—Had this record been written while Lazarus lived, the Jews might have sought His life.—Crowds coming to the great feast, would have thronged the house.—Their curiosity would have troubled him with queries about the unknown world. —Thus the silence of the three Evangelists (proof of Heavenly wisdom) threw a veil over the sisters at Bethany.—Thus the Spirit restrained their *naming* the woman who anointed the Lord. Matt. xxvi. 7. Mk. xiv. 3.—From John we learn the name of that person many years after her death.—Many particulars that would have gratified our curiosity have not been recorded.—Hand of God visible in the *silence* of the sacred writers as in the *record.*— Three were raised during His life, and *many* at His death. Matt. xxvii. 52.

Certain man. A household, such as is described in Ps. cxxxiii. 1., with one heart, one hope, one aim.

Lazarus. (See critical notes) Same as Eliazer, one whom God aids. It occurs about 30 times in the O.T.—No particulars of his person or character are given, apart from his sisters.

Was sick. 1, Fellowship of a believing family : to a relationship of blood and spirit ; 2, to a fellowship of suffering and triumph.—The distress of His people draws the Lord unto them.—The Church of Jesus resembles this family : it has Marys, clinging with ardent devotion to the Lord ; it has Marthas, active and fruitful in good works ; it has Lazaruses, sick or even dead (better : it has suffering and dying members), but who are healed and raised up by the word of Jesus.—Love and a cross; man cannot make the two rhyme, but it is thus that God always rhymes. *Gossner.*

Bethany. Named from the palm trees around the village, which have disappeared.—Residence of Lazarus, Mary and Martha.— About two miles from Jerusalem.—Our Lord often went out from the city, and lodged there.—No record of his spending a night *in* Jerusalem.—Alas! many families would esteem the Redeemer's company no special favour.—From Bethany, our Lord began His triumphant entry into Jerusalem.—Here the memorable supper was given by Simon the leper, when the woman anointed His feet. Luke vii. 36.—It lies at the end of a high narrow ridge, two-thirds of a mile from the Mount of Olives.—As He left the Mount of Olives, and drew nigh to Bethany He ascended to Heaven.—The very spot may almost be identified.—The identity of Bethany has never been disputed.—Like most Oriental towns it appears beautiful, at a distance, but entering it is found to be a wretched village of some twenty families.—The walk from Mount Olivet to Bethany with Jerusalem, the Dead Sea, the valley of the Jordan, &c., in view is, for depth of interest, unequalled on earth.

The town of. To distinguish it from the Bethany beyond Jordan. —Source of peace in this family, *faith* in and *love* to Jesus as the Redeemer.—They knew, and unlike Nicodemus, openly confessed Him as Messiah.—That nothing is recorded of them beyond their connection with Jesus, a proof that God held the hand of the writer.—Noteworthy that Bethany is not said to be "the town of" Lazarus.—The words might imply that the sisters owned the land on which the village stood.—Jewish law rendered the entire possession of a village impossible.—But Roman customs might have wrought great social changes.—The narrative presupposes the acquaintance of the readers with the family of Bethany.

Mary. The younger sister, but more illustrious from her higher devotion.—Placed thus in the foreground as the most prominent personality of the group.

Martha. Evidently the mistress of the house, probably older than Lazarus or Mary.—The three synoptists omit this miracle.—Their selections were of the Spirit. *Author.—Synoptists* not acquainted with it. *Lücke.*—It lay beyond the circle of their plan. *Meyer.*— Omitted from a prudential regard to the surviving family of Lazarus. *Herder, Lange, Olsh., Godet, Wordsworth.*—Such a supposition alien from the character and spirit of the Evangelists.

Alford.—Each gospel being a particular view of the Lord's life, the Evangelist in each case uses only such historical matter as suits its total. *Schaff.*—The same silence is observed of the earlier events in Judæa. *Hase, Neander.*—Neither Matthew nor Mark alludes to the raising at Nain. *Tholuck.*

Βηθανία. House of dates. *Lightfoot, Reland.* Now called El-Azariyeh, *Robinson.* El-Lazarieh, *Stanley.*

ἀσθενῶν. This miracle carries its own evidence to every fair and unprejudiced mind. But as the performance of it was a moral test to the Jews. so is its narrative to the readers and critics: a savour of life and a source of comfort to believers, a stumbling-block to unbelievers. There are four false theories opposed to the true one : 1. The *Rationalistic* view of a raising from a trance. *Paulus, Ammon, &c.* 2. The *Mythical* hypothesis of an unconscious poem of the primitive Christian fancy. *Strauss, &c.* 3. The theory of a conscious *symbolical* or *allegorical* representation of the death-conquering glory of Christ. *Baur, &c.* 4. The infamous hypothesis of a downright *Imposture. Renan.* All these theories owe their origin to disbelief in the supernatural. They neutralize each other and explain nothing. The historic truth is abundantly attest-d by the simplicity, vivacity, and circumstantiality of the narrative, the four days in the tomb, and the good sense and moral honesty—to say the very least—of Lazarus and his sisters, the Evangelist. and Christ Himself. *Schaff*, in *Lange*, American Edition. "I have been assured that *Spinoza* would say to his friends : If he could have convinced himself of the resurrection of Lazarus he would have dashed to pieces his entire system (of Pantheism) and embraced without repugnance the common faith of Christians." *Bayle.*

Λάζαρος, abridged from the Hebrew Eliazar, *God, a helper* The Ecclesiastical applications of the name, *Knights of St. Lazarus, lazaretto, lazar-house, lazzarone* are derived from the Lazarus of the parable. The *Lazarists*, a French Society of Missionary Priests, were named after Lazarus. of Bethany. *Schaff*, in *Lange.* According to tradition, Lazarus lived thirty years after his resurrection. and died sixty years old. *Epiph.* The Lazarus of Bethany, identical with the poor Lazarus of the parable. *Hengst., Wordsworth.* No foundation for this view. *Godet.* Possible that the Lazarus of John xi. was either a son or a brother-in-law of Simon the Pharisee. *Schaff.* The same as the young and rich ruler who came to Jesus. *Smith's Dict.* A conjecture without proof and contrary to the chronological order of events. *Schaff.* The traditions concerning the later life of Lazarus and his labours in Marseilles, where he is said to have founded a church and suffered martyrdom, are worthless. *Lange.* He seems to have been younger than the sisters, and to have held a subordinate place in the household. *Meyer.*

Μαρίας. Roman tradition since *Tertullian* identifies Mary of Bethany with Mary of Magdala, and the unnamed sinful woman who anointed the Lord's feet (Luke vii. 37), although *Irenæus, Origen,* and *Chrys.* clearly distinguish them. This view is now rightly opposed by several Romanist and nearly all Protestant divines. *Schaff*, in *Lange*, American Edition.

Μάρθας, wife of Simon the Leper. *Hengst.* She represents the active, practical. Mary, the contemplative, passive. type of piety. They are related to each other as Peter and John among the Apostles. Romish asceticism has perverted Mary into a Nun, and abused the eulogy of the Lord, Luke x. 42,. *Schaff.*

2, It was that Mary which anointed the Lord with ointment, and wiped his feet with her hair, whose brother Lazarus was sick.

That Mary. One act, virtuous or vicious, may render a person noted through all ages. 1 Kings xvi. 3.—The history of one devoted believer will be of interest in eternity.—It was *character* our Lord loved in these devoted sisters.—The conversion of a soul a greater event than the resurrection of Lazarus.—Mary risked neglecting other guests, and encountered the rebuke of her sister, that she might listen to the LIVING TRUTH.

Anointed. See on John i. 41.—Greek Tense implies, " who had anointed the Lord formerly."—Hence the origin under Divine grace of that holy friendship with those of Bethany.—This anointing is understood, for the other evangelists had already recorded it.—John alludes to it, although in the order of time it occurred after this miracle.—It shows that this gospel was written long after these things happened.—The Spirit selects this incident instead of her sitting at the feet of Jesus.—Our best in everything should be freely devoted to the Lord. An important question :—What am I willing to part with for HIM ?

Sick. No trace of lamentation, that one dear to the Son of God should be sick.—Sufferings of believers a proof of election. *Bunyan.*—Every shepherd has a peculiar mark for his sheep : Christ the Good Shepherd marks His sheep with the cross. *Flavel.*—Sickness not a sign of God's anger, but of fatherly love. Heb. xii. 6.—Sickness of loved ones a means of intensifying and strengthening the bonds of love.—Before God all the discord of suffering humanity is already melted into harmony. *Gossner.*

ἠσθέναι. It was a fever. *Nonus.*

3. Therefore his sisters sent unto him, saying, Lord, behold, he whom thou lovest is sick.

Sisters sent. What a comfort to have such a friend to whose sympathy they might appeal!—" Oh, tell thy woes to those beloved, for sorrows shared, are half removed."—Though God knows all our wants, He will know them *from us*, and is honoured by our laying them before Him.—These messengers may have spent at least two days on their errand, and in the meantime Lazarus died.—This explains the fact of his having lain in the grave *four* days.—Note the knowledge these sisters had of their Friend's hiding place.

Saying. They make no request that He would " come."—They do not say " Come down ere he die," or " Speak the word and he shall live," but simply remind Him of His love for their dying brother, and leave the rest to His wisdom.—They well knew the depth and tenderness of His heart.—It is enough for LOVE to know true love never forsakes.—Having received largely from a friend, we are slow to ask more, yet the more we have received from God the more our prayers increase.

Lord. To Christ the omnipotent Physician of soul and body should the sick first of all resort. Psalm cxxxiii. 1.—In distress and

misery let us despatch sighs and tears to Him, and remind Him of
our covenant that we have made with Him.—But we must not
limit the Lord in respect to time and method.—God's manner of
regarding sickness and prayer for the sick often differs materially
from that of praying relatives and friends. *Quesnel.*—He sometimes
denies a small favour that He may shew us a greater one. 2 Cor.
xii. 8, 9.

Thou lovest. Christ has not only perfect wisdom, power, and
holiness, but HE LOVES.—Man was made in God's image ; from
human love we therefore learn something of Divine love.—All
God's acts begin and end in love, however painful or perplexing to
us.—*Thou lovest.* A most womanly appeal to His known affection.
—They evidently leave the consequence to be inferred : " Come
and heal him."—God's boundless liberality offers both *measure* and
motive for the future. —As grace begins, so it ends, all good.—Nothing before but prayer, nothing after but thanks.—Afflictions are
Christ's love-tokens : " As many as I love I chasten." Rev. iii. 9.
—We pray well when we ground our petitions on Christ's love to
us, not on ours to Him.—Having loved His own that are in the
world He loves them to the end. John xiii. 1.

Sick. The request implies the illness was dangerous.—When grief
is deep and overwhelming it writes but short letters.—This message,
the first which directly appealed to the Lord's *personal* friendship.
—It called Him to help a friend because He was a friend.—Jesus
has all the qualities of a human friend in perfection, and yet is an
Almighty, omniscient Friend.—What an appeal to a loving, human
heart. How much more to Christ's.—They knew that *without* HIS
WILL their brother could not die.—When the storm of death shatters
all around us there is no shelter like this : " And they went and
told Jesus." Matt. xiv. 12.—Note 1. There are some followers
of Jesus for whom He hath a special kindness. John xiii. 23.—
2. It is no new thing for those whom He loves to be sick.—3. It is
a great blessing when we are sick to have those about us who will
pray for us.—4. There is great encouragement to prayer for the sick
when we have reason to believe they are those Christ loves. *Henry.*
—The love of the Lord a tabernacle of God among men. The
outer court (ver. 3), the Holy Place (ver. 4), the Holy of Holies
(ver. 5).—The way of Divine love : He acts in darkness, He walks
in light. *Schröder.*—The sisters' message, a confession of lofty faith :
Lord, whom *Thou* lovest *Thou* wilt never forsake.—Prayers recorded
in the New Testament are but a few words, but, how powerful !

ὃν φιλεῖς. These words are more solicitous of help than if they had mentioned his
name. *Schaff.* The *request* lay in the message itself, and the addition ὃν φιλεῖς supplied
the motive for its fulfilment. *Meyer.*
For difference between φιλέω and ἀγαπαώ see critical notes on John xxi. 15, 16, 17.

4. When Jesus heard that, he said, This sickness is not unto death, but for the glory of God, that the Son of God might be glorified thereby.

He said. Spoken generally in the hearing of those present, the messengers are the disciples.—Sufficient for the moment as a preparation both for the sisters and the disciples. *Meyer.*

This sickness. See on John iv. 46-52.—This proves He foresaw all from the first.—I know no greater blessing than health, except *sickness.* *Adams.*—Our losses, sickness, pains, and death are so many *stages* in Christian progress.—Thus Joseph, from field to slavery, from slavery to prison, from prison to court, and from court to chain of office and royal chariot, even next the throne.— Christ, the believer's physician, pain his medicine, Divine promises his support, grave his bed, and death an angel to release and carry him up to glory.—Although our Lord sent this answer as a comfort, yet like many other words it was not thoroughly understood until fulfilled.

Not unto death. See on John iv. 47. *It is not to have death for its result*, which does not mean : it is not *deadly*. *Meyer.*—He saw the result, and the sisters would soon see it.—In this case death was to end in a glorious *miracle* of re-awakening.—These words are like some of those dark Providences which perplex in the life of believers. " What I do (or say) thou knowest not now, but thou shalt know hereafter." John xiii. 9.—We must never attempt to judge of Christ's love to us by outward dispensations.

Glory of God, *i.e.*, for the *furtherance* of the honour of God. *Meyer.*—Sick or well, alive or dead, the believer glorifies God. " Whether we live we live unto the Lord, or whether we die," &c. Rom. xiv. 8.—Paul was in earnest expectation (Greek "*stretching his neck*") to learn how to live and die. Phil. i. 20.—This reply teaches the great truth that in Providence as in Grace He will maintain His sovereignty.

Son of God. See on John i. 18, 34. The emphatic and more definite explanation stating the kind and manner of the *Glory.* *Meyer.*—Glorification of the Son involves the glory of the Father. Implies the glorifying of Christ in Lazarus himself. Men not mere *tools* but temples of God. *Alford.*—Resurrection of Lazarus, the comprehensive concluding symbol of all the miracles exhibiting the glory of God in Christ. *Stier.*—In all the afflictions of saints the Son of God is glorified in His wisdom, power, and goodness : 1. In supporting ; 2. In relieving ; 3. In ordering all for their welfare.—Three resurrections : 1. The child on its death-bed ; 2. The youth on his bier ; 3. The man in his grave. Each in its order symbolical of the resurrection of the soul "from the death of sin to the life of righteousness," our Lord's most divine and glorious work. *Neander.*

920 / Gospel of John

θάνατον. Doubtless this message was delivered, although the hearts of the sisters were too heavy to understand its import. Grief often blinds the eyes to the bright light in the cloud. "No chastening for the present," &c. Heb. xii. 11. *Braune.* Hints at Christ's omniscience. *Grotius.* Jesus certainly knew by His higher knowledge that the death of Lazarus was *certain* and *near at hand.* The assumption of a second message is purely arbitrary. *Meyer.* δόξης. The spiritual good of the sisters also. *Olsh.* Through Lazarus himself in perfecting his spiritual being. *Trench.*
ἵνα δοξασθῇ. In these words the doctrinal design of the narrative is contained. *Meyer.* The performance of so striking a miracle before a great multitude and near to Jerusalem. *Lange.*

---

5. Now Jesus loved Martha, and her sister, and Lazarus.

Loved. Explains the motive impelling Him to open to them the consolatory prospect in verse 4. *Meyer.*—This is the key to all that follows, even to the great trial to their faith in His apparent indifference and delay.—"When Israel was a *child,* then I loved him." Hos. xi. 1.—Childhood is lovely: 1. For its guilelessness; 2. Innocence; 3. Faith; 4. Humility.—Entertaining a *stranger* in their house they have the ANGEL of the COVENANT as a guest.— It was at the hospitable table at Emmaus that Jesus revealed Himself.—The Christian host is willing to open his door to the wretched, as grace has opened heaven to him. Luke xvi. 9.— We should not too bitterly mourn the death of those whom Jesus loves.—Plato says the "Athenians were highly favoured for many things, but first and chiefly because they were *beloved of the gods.*"—"I love them that love Me; and they that seek Me early," &c. Prov. viii. 17.

ἡ γάπα, not ἐφίλει, describes the loftily severe conduct of the love of Christ. *Lange.* ἀγαπᾶν may be used of Divine love, but φιλεῖν expresses human love, and the personal relation of friendship. *Schaff.* An expression chosen with delicate tenderness. *Meyer.* Explanatory of verse 3, *De Wette;* of verse 4. *Meyer;* preparatory to verse 6, *B. Crusius.* Martha is named *first* as being the mistress of the house and the eldest. *Meyer.*

---

6. When he had heard therefore that he was sick, he abode two days still in the same place where he was.

Heard. He needed no messenger to tell Him of Lazarus' illness. See on John vi. 64.—He well knew the metal was in the fire, and the refining process going on.—He waits until it obtains purity and splendour.

Abode. Out of *pure love* He hastens not.—Urgent reasons would prevent His haste.—The disciple must not dictate to Him; that were to set the sun by our dial.—When beloved ones were hoping against hope it was then that He chose to remain away.—"The Lord will judge his people *when He seeth their power is gone.*" Deut. xxxii. 36.—To the sisters it was a mystery, to us it is plain

—*We* cannot tell why God permits sorrow to oppress, pain to afflict, temptation to incite and disquiet. The Psalmist asked, "Why go I mourning? Why hast thou forgotten me? They say unto me, ' Where is thy God? ' "—Our Lord by one word of His wisdom, explains it: It is for GOD'S GLORY.

Same place. What work His untiring love was performing we know not.—Some suppose a specially gracious activity at the Jordan.—This looks as though He did not respond, yet His inmost heart must have yearned to bring relief.—He makes no sign of moving towards Bethany.—Here His humanity is seen to be the medium of His divinity —Help is often delayed to make the deliverance all the more glorious.—It is not said, He loved them, and *yet* He lingered; but, He loved them and *therefore* He lingered.—He *lovingly* delayed: 1. That He might try the sisters and through trial, bless. 2. That He might have opportunity of doing more for Lazarus and his sisters than for any others.—God ever hath gracious intentions in seeming delays. Too often we never think of applying to our Lord until all other hopes have failed.

ἔμεινεν. The motive indicated, ver. 4: the glorification of God through the miracle. *Meyer, Alford.* Undoubtedly a final and supreme motive, *so fine an historical trait cannot have been invented. Lange.* He was detained in Peræa by important business. *Thol., Lücke, Neander.* He was not responsible as human beings. He took a circuitous route from Jordan to Bethany, making a week to elapse before He arrived. *Tittmann.* Jesus never designedly occasioned or magnified His own miracles, and hence it must have been something *external* that delayed Him. *De Wette.* To test the faith of the sisters. *Olshausen, and the ancient Commentators.* This motive too arbitrary. *Meyer.*

δύο ἡμέρας. He was to depart from a province in which there were many that believed on Him. *Lange.* He would not leave this region without saying farewell to His followers. *Schleiermacher.*

7. Then after that saith he to his disciples, Let us go into Judæa again.

After that. Awed by His mysterious words, the disciples waited for clearer light.

Let us go. Mark the *delay* and *haste* of Jesus. Only when the proper moment arrives will He proceed to His great work.— Christ ever arises to the help of His people when the *set time* is come.—The *worst* time with us is commonly His *set time*.—Man's extremity is God's opportunity.—" *Let us go:* " The distress of His people draws the Lord unto them: 1. Down from Heaven into human misery; 2. Over the Jordan into peril of death; 3. From the rest above into the conflict of earth; 4. From the throne of glory to the Judgment-seat. *Lange.*

Judæa. John iii. 22. He does not say to Bethany, but to Judæa, the land of unbelief and deadly hatred.—It was now for the last time, to be irradiated with the presence of the Sun of Righteousness.—Our Lord here blends Sovereignty with mercy : 1. From oppression, deliverance ; 2. Out of danger, a triumph ; 3. Out of temptation, a victory ; 4. Out of misery, redemption ; 5. Out of death, a festival of resurrection.

ἔπειτα. His disciples understood the promised miracle. *Ebrard.* Uncertain. *Stier.*

---

8. His disciples say unto him, Master, the Jews of late sought to stone thee ; and goest thou thither again?

Master. Their love for Lazarus would have led them to go also.— They doubtless thought there was no imminent danger to the sick, or that their Master might heal him at that distance. Luke xvii. 15.

Jews. John i. 19. Jews of power and position.

Late, &c. Gr., *were just about.*—Stoning was the ordinary method of capital punishment among the Jews. See on John iii. 24 ; viii. 59 ; x. 31.—Probably this explains the form of the message sent by the sisters. *Lange.* This and verse 16, show that the disciples were chiefly apprehensive for His safety.—They had forgotten that one "is immortal till his work be done."—"It is not in man that walketh to direct his steps."—Slow to believe in His supreme divinity ; hence their loving anxiety for His safety.

Goest thou thither? Yes, despite their warning, He will go again among His foes.—He will go in human form, but with the arm and voice of the ALMIGHTY !—He will go as a friend who will never forsake. Mothers have forgotten and forsaken the babe drawing its life from their bosom ; but, " I will not forsake thee, saith the Lord." Isaiah xlix. 15.—The ancients painted friendship as a young man with his bosom open and his heart bare, with the words *Longe prope, i.e.,* "a friend at home and a friend afar off : " under his feet Death and Life, *i.e.,* faithful in all changes.—Such friendship only to be found in " Jesus Christ the same yesterday, and to-day, and for ever." Heb. xiii. 8.—When God calls on a man to venture something, he must shun no danger.— They who seek to escape the cross, are never in want of an excuse.

νῦν. *Just now,* refers to the recent events, which, though past, seemed still to form part of the present. *Meyer.*

---

9. Jesus answered, Are there not twelve hours in the day? If any man walk in the day, he stumbleth not, because he seeth the light of this world.

Answered. He never failed to answer so as to *silence* the questioner.—He implied they had a higher law than mere safety.

Twelve hours. See on John i. 39 ; iv. 52. "In Palestine, where the days are of nearly equal duration, they are divided the whole year through into twelve hours." *Gerlach.*—Jesus probably uttered these words in the early morning in view of the rising sun. In like manner John ix. 4 was spoken in face of the setting sun.— "*Twelve*," emphatic, signifying life, rich, full, measured with its manifold appointments.

Day. See on John ix. 4, 5. Under this figure the idea of the *life-day* of man and the *day's work* appointed him is presented.—The Lord is referring to His own life-journey, but He employs general terms applicable to us all.—Daniel's entire arithmetic was in *Division*, giving each hour its duty. *Gurnall.*—Day, a picture of life, with its morning, noon, and evening.—Our Lord implies there are twelve full hours for work, and while that day continues He can safely do His Father's work.—He had now reached the eleventh hour of His day.—There is a span of life assigned to each of us also, and a work. "The night cometh when no man can work."

Walk. Orientalism for the course of one's life.—The living man a walker and worker, a pilgrim and workman of God.

Walk in the day. I have a set time to finish My work appointed by My Father ; during that time I am safe from My enemies ; I walk in His Light, as the traveller in the light of the sun, and ye are safe while walking in My Light.

Stumbleth not. As men run against objects at night.—He does not stumble upon an occasion of his death.—All apart from My Light stumble, and may perish.—"Whosoever shall follow the leadings of God may venture through the desert and seas unshod." But out of the path of duty we are not to ask, nor hope for His protection.

For he seeth. Light shines upon him, and he both sees and avoids stumbling-blocks that obstruct his way, even in day-time.—Our Lord would have us to see, in the light of our divine calling, dangers we should avoid without being obliged to abandon our vocation.—The twelve hours of the day, or life-time and life's duty in their indissoluble unity : 1. The certainty of life within the bounds of duty ; 2. The sacredness of duty within the bounds of life. *Lange.*—Day, life, for work ; night, death, for rest.

περιπατῇ. Blameless conduct. *Erasmus.* Fellowship with Christ. *De Wette.* Our Lord has a double meaning : First, He stands fraternally with men fulfilling His appointed work. Second, He refers to His higher dignity as the Spiritual Illuminator of the world, as the promoter of every thing good and beautiful on earth. Hence in presence of His LOVE and POWER they were safe. *Olsh.* The whole simile refers to

the disciples. *Chrys., Calvin, Lampe.* The first simile refers to Christ, the second to
the disciples. *Hengst.* So far as I have a *glimmering perception of the height and depth*
of His meaning, He refers to their unbelief. *Augustine.*
προόκόπτει. Literally for want of light. *Tisch.* A rule of Life for the disciples.
Danger of sin. *Lucke.* Murmuring against Providence. *Braune.* Open ministering of the truth. *De Wette.* I can walk in My own Light. *Meyer.* He walks
by day, men by night. *Stier.* ὧραι. These twelve hours are the twelve apostles. *Aug.*
Changing moods of men. *Luther.* His work on earth limited by earthly time. *Hess.*
Can work out His allotted time without peril. *Lange, Meyer.* John adopts the Asiatic
reckoning. *Towson.* Jewish time. *Alford.* Romans divided the day into twelve
parts, although it was not legal. *Lücke.* 'Day,' the time preceding the Passion; '*Night*,'
the Passion. *Theoph.* Idea of working predominates over walking. *Thol.* Day of
life, and day of duty. *Melancthon,*

---

10. But if a man walk in the night, he stumbleth, because there is no light in him.

But. He thus calms their fears.—They need not dread danger
while with Him.—No foe could spring up without His permission.
In the night. A rule which obtains in a still greater degree in the
moral life than in the physical.—No man should continue in a
work on which he cannot ask God's blessing.—Such a conscious
presence of Deity *lets in light* upon dark deeds.—A prayerless
spirit ends in night, as distance from the sun terminates in darkness.—Sin causes a darkness God never created.—Not one of the
myriads of the spiritually blind of earth stumbles because there
is *no* sun.—The impenitent, like Pharaoh, carry darkness with
them.—The night of sin is "the hour and power of darkness."
Luke xxii. 53.
Stumbleth. As Jesus never "walked in the night," this remark
applies to His disciples.—Thus Josiah went to battle with Pharaoh
and perished.—Thus, in the history of the Passion, the disciples
sleeping instead of watching and praying, *stumbled.*
Light is not in him. No daylight from heaven, no light in the
eyes or on the path.—The believer must not move until God
points out the way. Then like Luther going to Worms he feels
all is well.—Christ ever walked in *the day*, and so shall we if we
follow His steps.—The duty of the day is the day of the duty.

νυκτὶ Not of a night when none *can* work, but when none should walk. *Lücke*
Conscious of doing no sin, we need not fear. *Chrys.* ἐν αὐτῷ. An influence within
the man, *Lange.*

---

11. These things said he: and after that he saith unto them, Our friend Lazarus
sleepeth; but I go, that I may awake him out of sleep.

These things. The social interview is ended. A lesson has been
given to coming generations.—Having comforted them, He tells
them that He purposes to return to Bethany.—Not to dispute with
the Jews, but to awaken Lazarus from the sleep of death.

After that. As though they had forgotten their friend Lazarus.—Have ye no desire to see how My glory is to be revealed by his death?—Infidels profess to wonder that His disciples did not understand Him.—Had it been said they understood Him, these cavillers would have found some ground for objection; for nothing will please a heart hating truth.

Our friend. An expression of hearty love and fellowship in which they also share.—An instance of our Lord's kind condescension. *Bengel.*—Christ's disciples have the same sorrows, the same joys, the same friends as their Master.—Only *twice* more does our Lord call men by this endearing name; viz., the apostles, John xv. 14; Luke xii. 4.—Figuratively, John the Baptist called himself a friend of Christ (John iii. 29). Abraham is called "a friend of God" (James ii. 23; Isaiah xli. 8), but more in the passive sense—the favourite of God. *Schaff.*—It implies that the friendship expressed by our Lord was reciprocated.

Sleepeth. Gr., *hath fallen asleep.* Christ proclaims the kinship of death and natural sleep.—As sleep is the withdrawal of life inwards, for the gathering of new strength, so is death.—Christ has changed death into sleep; but as the death of His people is sleep, so the spiritual sleep of unbelievers is death. *Lange.*—This word hath a powerful charm to take away the bitterness of death.—Those dying in their sleep, angels kiss their breath away. *Rabbis.*—As mothers kiss their babes, and then lay them down to sleep. *Trapp.*—"Sleep, the sweet parenthesis of all griefs."—Ancient heathen poets spoke of death as a sleep, but it was in a half despairing tone.—Scripture alone describes death as a sleep from which the pious awake in the glorious morning of eternity.—The figure becomes a living blessed truth from the lips of the PRINCE of Life.—How often does the Spirit take an earthly word, and fill it with heaven.—Saints sleep in Jesus, hence, Greeks call graves Dormitories, "chambers of rest." Germans call graveyards "God's acre;" bodies are sown for the harvest.—Martyrs' epitaphs in the Catacombs of Rome, illustrate Christ's word.—"Sleep so much resembles death, I dare not enter on it without prayer." *Andrews.*—His words not fully understood at the time by the apostles, nor even by us.—Hints at the slender thread which separates sleep from death.—Hints at the *nearness every night* to heaven or hell!—Sleep, periodical death on earth; death, the final sleep of all.—Furnishes no basis for doctrine of unconscious condition of souls from death till resurrection.—Life-union with Christ cannot be suspended or lost in the darkness of unconsciousness. "For me to die is gain," saith Paul. Could this be affirmed of a merely unconscious state of existence?

I go. Mark the confidence Jesus had in His Divine mission and

power. The calm assurance of one *conscious* that He is LORD
of "hell (Hades) and death." Rev. i. 18. As if He said,
"Will ye not go with Me to see this blessed awaking?"
To the world Lazarus was dead; to our Lord, he was only sleeping.—To Jesus, and *in* Him, all the myriads of departed saints are
asleep. 1 Thess. iv. 13.—This word like all other prophecies can
only find interpretation in its fulfilment.—If Lazarus is at rest in
Paradise, why disturb him? some might have said. Because in
his resurrection God will be glorified and millions of believers to
the end of time confirmed and blest.—Instead of "I will go and
burst the bands of death," what "modesty" marks His words!
Even a child can awake its father, but to awaken from death demands the power of ALMIGHTY GOD.—He actually lessens rather
than exalts the greatness of the intended miracle.—A general
rebuke to that spirit of *exaggeration* universal in our race.—There
was in that sleep a deep profound rest unknown to the wicked.—
"They rest from their labours, and their works do follow them."
That is a blessed friendship that transfigures death into a sleep.—
Of every departed saint it may be said the Awakener is alrea*ᵈ*
on His way.—When Christ carries the torch before us and bids
us follow, we may courageously advance, even though menaced
on all sides by death. *Gossner.*

Out of sleep. Sleep, like other functions, is a mystery.—Silence
and darkness favour sleep.—Sleep is the torpor of the voluntary
organs, while the system is being renewed.—Plants sleep at night,
their leaves drooping: stimulus of light ceasing.—All languages
convey the same figure, but the N. T. introduces a new
idea.—It tells of an awakening which will be eternal.—Dives had
prayed for a certain departed spirit to return to earth, Lazarus by
name : a spirit from another world of that very name did come
back.—How Lazarus exhorted men to repent, we know not: but
each Christian should preach by his daily life as if angels had
sent him back from heaven to bring more souls to bear them
company.—Christ calls a believer, *friend;* a believer's death, *sleep.*
—Those whom Christ owns as *His* friends, all His disciples should
take as *theirs.*—Death does not break the bond of friendship. A
believer when he dies does but sleep : 1, rests from the labours of
the day : 2, is being refreshed for the morning. *Aug.*—He who
is asleep and dreaming, though not separated outwardly and
locally from the material world around him, is yet relatively "beyond or above the world;" the same is true of the dead. The
tendency of the disembodied spirit is not outward, but inward ; a
going into itself, a going back, not a going forth. *Martensen.*

κεκοίμηται. Separation of soul and body causes a certain depression of consciousness. The Bible knows of no purely spiritual immortality apart from the resurrection, and the interval is merely a state of transition. *Olsh.*—Calvin wrote his first theological treatise against the notion of the " sleep of the soul." Milton, and in later times Archbishop Whately, inclined to this notion, though chiefly on psychological grounds. Refuted by the Lord's words to the dying malefactor, the Parable of the Rich Man and Lazarus, the appearances at the Transfiguration, and many passages in the Epistles. The souls of martyrs under the altar cry " How long, O God, how long," &c., Rev. vi. 10.

---

12. Then said his disciples, Lord, if he sleep, he shall do well.

If he sleep. Heathen poets believed souls vanished into the air, and there was *no* resurrection.—Greeks held the soul passed from the domain of a celestial to that of an infernal god : gods attended men always, especially at death ; hence they feared not death.— The Greek expected a welcome from his parents in the Elysian fields.—Females crowded the death chamber to catch the parting breath of the dying.—Loving friends intensely desired the last commands.—Having washed and anointed and covered the corpse with costly garments, placing a crown of flowers upon it, they carried it to the vestibule, with the feet to the door, in token of its readiness for the last journey.—Vessels of perfumed waters stood around the bier, and those passing in and out sprinkled themselves.—Branches of laurel and acanthus with locks of hair of the dead were hung over the doorway.—Funerals in Athens took place before daybreak, with torches lighting up the melancholy way.

If he sleep. They think of real sleep in antithesis to the sleep of death.—Our Lord's words here, as often, an enigma to the disciples.

Do well. Gr., *be saved, i.e.,* recover by means of sleep as a health-bringing crisis.—If so, why run the risk of entering Judæa? Mark the child-like manner of these men : they take his words *literally.* " Beware of the leaven," &c. Matt. xvi. 6.—" I have meat to eat that ye," &c. John iv. 32. They would thus dissuade Him from going to Bethany.—Dread of the perils of a journey among fierce foes lies in the background.

For οἱ μαθηταὶ αὐτοῦ : αὐτῷ. *Tisch.*—σωθήσεται. He will be kept alive. *Homer.*— They seize on the least excuse to avoid the danger. *Calvin.*—Sleeping patients are not to be disturbed. They think our Lord has already effected a cure. *Ebrard.*—They think the sleep has been produced by Jesus while yet absent. *Bengel, Luthardt.*—The text affords no ground for either assumption. *Lange.*

---

13. Howbeit Jesus spake of his death : but they thought that he had spoken of taking of rest in sleep.

Jesus spake. How many words of God require to be *translated* on account of our unbelief and hardness of heart.—Through the same causes how many dealings of Providence need an *interpreter !* —" All these things are *against* me," Jacob to his sons. Translate *" for* me."—" One day I shall perish by the hand of Saul." Translate *" receive a crown* through Saul."—" All things work together for good to them that love God." Rom. viii. 28.—Ezekiel saw a wheel within a wheel, yet all went *forward.*

His death. A day of blessedness to Christ's friends. *Negative:* 1. Freedom from sin ; 2. From temptation ; 3. From suffering. *Positive :* 1. Admission to the presence of Christ ; 2. Enjoyment of perfect spiritual life ; 3. Complete holiness ; 4. Glorious expectations.

Death. A day of misery to the wicked: 1. Entrance into a world with which they have no sympathy—forced away from all their sinful pleasures ; 2. Cravings for things left behind for ever ; 3. Society of evil spirits and evil men ; 4. Fruitless grief for the loss of heaven ; 5. Sense of the wrath of God ; 6. Hopeless despair.

Thought. Our Lord used this word "sleep," knowing that at first they would not understand Him.—His words, like His works, are subjects of *study* for *all* coming generations.—He called death, " sleep ;" for He can raise the dead far easier than we can awake the sleeper.

---

14. Then said Jesus unto them plainly, Lazarus is dead.

Plainly. Gr., *free-spokenness, boldness.* Without circumlocution. *Lange.*

Dead. He who created the " golden bowl " and the " wheel at the cistern " had broken both.—When our Lord said " he sleepeth," He added, " I go to awake him."—But when He said, " he is dead," He made no such promise.—Lazarus is dead with respect to *you* but asleep with respect *to Me.*—The supposition that Jesus had received secret information of his death contradicted by verse 21.—Although not bodily present with Lazarus, He was with him in His divine presence.—Is with all His people, for "precious in the sight of the Lord is the death of His saints."—He has " the keys " of life and death ; and our " times are in His hand."

ἀπέθανε. He was not τέθνηκε as to Christ, therefore He says, " he died." *Wordsworth.* —Assurance of death: 1. Deliberate delay of Jesus ; 2. Foretelling his death ; 3. Multitude of witnesses ; 4. Faith of many on account of the miracle, and the perversity of the rest. *Bengel.*—He knew it by the inner power of His spirit. *Trench.*

---

15. And I am glad for your sakes that I was not there, to the intent ye may believe; nevertheless let us go unto him.

" *Dead* " and " *glad* " follow each other almost in the same breath.— " At evening-time it shall be light." Zech. xiv. 7.

Glad. Not at Lazarus's death ; but because the greater miracle, the raising of the dead, should take the place of the healing of the sick. *Lange.*—Although He was grieved, foreseeing the Jews would be hardened.—Disciples would soon have proof of His omniscience and omnipotence.—From Lazarus's tomb he would preach a sermon that would teach unborn millions.—He was rejoicing when others were weeping.—" *Glad,*" because through the miracle they will take a higher step in the life of faith. To strengthen their faith He rejoices.—Arriving, He groans and weeps to behold the ruin wrought by sin.—At one moment His human tenderness flows in tears ; at the next, His Godhead flashes over the grave and through the world of spirits.—This word confirms the word of the sisters that *had He been there,* LAZARUS HAD NOT DIED.—Into the presence of the PRINCE OF LIFE death dare not have intruded.

Believe. The subjective intent with regard to them : the objective being the glory of God. *Schaff.*—Refers to their still weak faith, and to the trials awaiting them. Every new step of faith is in measure a new believing. *Meyer.*—Their secret fear is put to shame by His foretelling of an increase of faith.—After the miracle at Cana, His disciples *believed* on Him. John ii. 11.— After the stilling of the tempest, His disciples *worshipped* Him. Matt. xiv. 33.—We cannot judge of Christ's love to us by outward dispensations.—The temporary pain of a *few* was ordained for the lasting benefit of *the whole Church.*—Our Lord's plans often appear strange and unwise to our poor and short-sighted minds.—We may not rejoice in the death of Christians, but we may rejoice in the circumstances attending, and the glory redounding to God, and the benefit accruing to believers.

Let us go. Note the difference between these words as used by Christ and used by Thomas in verse 16.

To him. Christ will assuredly arise in favour of His people when the *set time* is come.—The *worst* time, in man's estimation, is commonly the *set* time with Him.—Believers may be sure He will never bring them into peril without accompanying them in it.

---

16. Then said Thomas, which is called Didymus, unto his fellow disciples, Let us also go, that we may die with him.

Thomas. See on John xx. 24. He had three characteristics : 1. Slow to believe ; 2. Subject to despondency ; 3. Devoted love to his Master.—He judged of things from a *human* standpoint, rather than a *divine.*

Didymus. Gr. *Twin.*—Mentioned in the Gospels (Matt. x. 3; Mark iii. 18; Luke vi. 15) in connection with Matthew, in the Acts (ch. i. 13) with Philip. Probably a Galilean. John xxi. 22. Tradition has made him a veritable twin and named his sister Lysia.—His characteristics vividly portrayed in the sayings preserved by John.

Let us go. In exact harmony with Thomas's turn of mind, ever ready to look at the dark side.—But he determines to share the peril.—He has been called the "doubting apostle," from his hesitancy. John xx. 25.—In his statue by Thorwaldsen, he stands with a rule, meditating the measure of evidence.—Tradition states that he preached at Parthia and was buried at Edessa.—According to later authority, he made an apostolic journey to India and there suffered martyrdom.—The Christians of St. Thomas at Malibar are called after this apostle.

Die with Him. He believes Jesus is going to His death (verse 8) and is ready to die with Him.—Weak faith, strong affection. Mingled melancholy, resignation, and courage controlled by love to Christ.—Life without this *Divine* LIGHT would lose to him all its charm.—He represents the honest, earnest, noble sceptics who require tangible evidence before they believe, but who submit to the evidence when presented.—He who was now so weak, afterwards became the strongest.—A man may have notable weaknesses and yet be a disciple of Christ. Fruit before the time of ripening is often unpleasant to the taste. *Owen.*—Thomas's doubt: 1. As to the victory of life; 2. As to the way to heaven (chap. xiv.); 3. As to the certainty of the resurrection (chap. xx.)—Thomas's faith: 1. Prepared by his ardent love to Jesus and to the brethren (chap. xi.); 2. Introduced by his longing desire for a higher disclosure (chap. xiv.); 3. Decided by his joy at the manifestation of the risen one (chap. xx.). *Lange.*—1. Let us with Jesus go; 2. Let us with Jesus suffer; 3. Let us with Jesus die; 4. Let us with Jesus LIVE.—Thomas, here so bold, shamefully forsook the Lord in Gethsemane.—Let not him that putteth on the armour, boast as he that putteth it off.—Our Lord set His face steadily to go to Bethany, in perfect knowledge of what death He should die.

Θομᾶς. Born at Antioch according to tradition. Called Judas. *Eusebius.*—Despondent yet acute in sensibility. *Tholuck.*—His doubts the result of intense ea nestness. *Lange*—Had a bias towards the visible and comprehensible. *Winer*—Δίδυμος. Christ gave him this name to designate his double nature and vacillation between unbel ef and faith. *Hengst.*—Christ did not thus brand His disciples. *Schaff.*—συμμαθηταῖς. Used thus once in N.T. *Trench.*—μετ' αὐτοῦ refe s to Lazarus. *Bengel.*—Fellowship in dying. *Maldonatus.*—To Christ. *Stier, Alford, Meyer, Calvin, Lange.*—With Lazarus in Hades, they thought their hopes of a New Day were buried. *Luthardt.*—It intimates fear. *Chrys.*—Alloy of bitterness, *Drascke.*—Melancholy tenderness. *Hase.*—

He speaks candidly but sadly. *Roos.*—We would often prefer to die rather than struggle on. *Braune*—Spirit of murmuring. *Lampe.*

---

17. Then when Jesus came, he found that he had lain in the grave four days already.

Found. The Spirit tells us what our Lord *found* in Bethany: He must speak after the manner of men.—The dead had been buried, and now sad friends surround the sisters.—Miserable comforters of earth only aggravate our misery.

Four days. Lazarus must have died on the day the messenger was sent, and was buried that evening, according to Jewish custom.— In hot climates, burial of necessity must immediately follow death. —The message sent the sisters (verse 32) failed to cheer them.— Jesus, coming as a Saviour, never comes too late.—He always brings salvation with Him, though to us He often *seems* to tarry.

τέσσαρας. Peræa was ten hours distant from Bethany. *Meyer.*—The journey might be made in a single day *Trench*—It also might have occupied two days.—*Tholuck.* Speedy burial among Greeks was esteemed an honour, *St. John's Ant. Greek.*—ἤδη. Omitted. *Tisch.*—Retained. *Alf.*

---

18. Now Bethany was nigh unto Jerusalem, about fifteen furlongs off.

Bethany. (See on verse 1.) One of the humblest villages becomes a scene of glory, where the Resurrection morn dawns on the night of the grave.—On the Judgment morn how many reluctant witnesses will be assembled!—The walk from the Mount of Olives to Bethany is one of the finest natural promenades in the world. Jerusalem and its environs, the valley of Jordan, Jericho, and the Dead Sea, form the scene.

Furlongs. *Stadia.*—A stadium a distance of 125 paces: fifteen stadia about two miles. *Lange.*

σταδίων. Strictly, *that which stands fast*; hence. *a fixed standard of length, a stade.* 600 Greek, 606¾ English feet, about ⅛ of a Roman mile. Hence a *race course.* That of Olympia, so called because exactly a *stade* long. *Liddell & Scott.*—Tradition makes Hercules measure out the stadium with his own feet. *Plutarch.*

---

19. And many of the Jews came to Martha and Mary, to comfort them concerning their brother.

Many. The high social position of the sisters attracted citizens of Jerusalem.—Many went to comfort the mourners, and were present at the miracle.—When God wants witnesses, He never fails to bring them in time.

Martha and Mary. Possibly they wished to regain this family in His absence. *Lange.*—A crowd of the curious with a few mourners are met daily in our cemeteries.—But the sublime event about to take place has no parallel in history.—The heart is strained to the utmost by a few plain sentences.—The footstep of God is distinctly heard along these pages of John.—Like all the grand operations of Nature, it steals noiselessly upon us.

Comfort. Grace will keep sorrow from the *heart* (chap. xiv. 1), not from the *house.*—How weak is all human sympathy to a broken heart.—Oriental sympathy in general, then, as now, mere formalism. —The conventional condolences lasted seven days. *Lightfoot.*

Concerning their brother. Probably by speaking : 1. Of the good name he had left behind ; 2. Of the happy state to which he had gone.—Such condolences often sinful, because false and hypocritical.—For those who have fallen asleep in Jesus we may sorrow, but not as others who have no hope. 1 Thess. iv. 13—18.

Ιουδαίων   Jerusalemites. *Grotius, Tittmann.*—People of Pharisaic views. *Lange.*— Points to high social status of the sisters. *Meyer, Alford.*—Good reason to infer that the family was one of large hospitality and acquaintance. *Schaff.*—πρὸς τὰς. Those around Mary and Martha. *Tisch*—The sisters themselves and no others. *Winer.*— Properly, to the two sisters, with the persons about them. *Lange.*—Especial *decorum* in the expression, since those who came to them were men. *Meyer.*—Female mourners from Bethany came before those from Jerusalem. *Olsh. Lücke.*—παραμυθήσ. Some half complainingly, and others, perhaps, half sneeringly, would comment on the absence of Jesus. *Besser.*

---

20. Then Martha, as soon as she heard that Jesus was coming, went and met him : but Mary sat still in the house.

Martha. First to hear of the Lord's arrival.—She appears as mistress of the house, and receives the message.—She goes instantly to meet Jesus, not waiting to communicate the news to Mary.

Coming. As far more than a comforter.—In the end, He will ever surpass our prayers.—His name is CONSOLATION, and He also beareth the name of Conqueror.

Went and met. It shows her energy and activity.—Different conduct of the two sisters, as here depicted, in perfect agreement with their characters. Luke x. 38—42.—This accordance between Gospels so widely different strong proof of historical faithfulness. —Both loved the Lord, but Martha was more active, practical, demonstrative.—Mary contemplative, pensive, quiet, speaking less and feeling more.—Their different temperaments are displayed in their conduct upon this occasion.—Grace sanctifies, but does not change mental peculiarities.—The analogy precise between Peter and John.

Sat still. Perhaps musing on those mysterious words, "This sickness is not unto death."—There is a silent, wrestling spirit of faith and prayer that, like the precious balsam, when wounded, bleeds its life away for others.—Not a few murmur at the humble place assigned them by Providence, but it demands advanced grace to sit where and as long as God wills.

ἐκαθέζετο. Mary did not notice His first arrival. *Niemeyer.*--Remained through courtesy to her friends. *Schlier.*--Tidings, simply brought to Martha as mistress of the house. *Stier.*--A disciple hastened forward to tell Martha. *Drascke.*—Mary being *in* the house had not heard of His arrival. *De Wette.*—Condoling friends received by mourners sitting. *Braune.*--Sitting was a part of the mourning rites with the Greeks and Jews. *Geier.*—She was overwhelmed with grief. *Erasmus, Doddridge.*—Having a quieter disposition. *Tholuck.*

---

21. Then said Martha unto Jesus, Lord, if thou hadst been here, my brother had not died.

Lord. She makes no allusion to the message sent, verse 4th.—She, doubtless, had failed to comprehend it.—God's commands address our *faith*, not always our understanding.

If. Thus the poor man looks back with an "IF" on all his heavy trials.—" *If, if,*" is the universal cry of humanity. " *But, but,*" is the reply of Omnipotence.—She almost appears to hint a reproach, because He had not been there.—" IF." *Sinful,* when an expression of grief that will not be reconciled to the will of God. —" IF." *Warranted,* when an expression of pain investigating the causes of suffering.—" IF." *Salutary,* when an expression of humiliation before God on account of actual neglect. *Lange.*— We add to our troubles by fancying what might have been.

Brother. Neither said " our brother." They met the Lord singly. —Both sisters betrayed weak faith in the Power of Christ; one limited Him to *place*, the other to *time.*

Died. She hints that her brother might be raised, but dare not express so grand a hope, all unconscious that He was kindling that very hope.—The cause of His delay was *then* a dark mystery.— After *one hour,* sunshine breaks through the deep gloom.—They learned why the Lord tarried, and adored Him for tarrying.—Will not all believers' doubts be as gloriously resolved?—If those who sat at Jesu's feet encountered such temptations, how can we escape?—Martha evidences a strange mixture of emotions: 1. Reproachful passion; 2. Love; 3. Faith; 4. Unbelief.—To know

how much grace believers have, they must be seen in trouble.
Ryle.

---

it. Not the language of reproach, but of regret. *Schaff.*--"If Thou *wert* here," not abiding in distant Perea. *Meyer.*--But Bethany was not our Lord's permanent dwelling place. *Lange.*--A lamentation. *Luthardt.*--A complaint. *Lücke.*--Her faith still unshaken. *Brandt.*--Thy prayer in time might have saved him. *Fickenscher.*

---

22. But I know, that even now, whatsoever thou wilt ask of God, God will give it thee.

Even now. She seems to check herself from reproaching Him, by ascribing to Him high gifts.—A delicate hint of a hope of miraculous aid from the Lord.

Even now. Thus, on the darkest thunderstorm, faith discerns the bow of promise and the bright light upon the cloud.

Whatsoever. The sisters were acquainted with the raising of Jairus's daughter and the youth at Nain.—She knew that He could call back her brother if He would ask for it, but she shrank from the greatness of her own thought.

Thou wilt ask. This is the only place where this word, implying dependence and need, is used of Jesus as *praying* to God.—It is in keeping with Martha's deep excitement and her as yet imperfect knowledge of the essential divinity of Jesus.—She did not anticipate the coming miracle in its actual splendour.—Her mind appears vibrating between an inspired hope and doubting fear.—Her faith was not in Christ's inherent power, but in His prayer to God.—She had not yet learned that He and the Father are one.—He who could say, "I AM the RESURRECTION" was in no need of asking *a gift.*

God. Her repetition of the Divine Name implies her firm faith in the supernatural relation of Jesus.

Will give. An indirect expression of the boldest hope, but to which she dare not verbally give utterance: 1. Whatever *Thou* mayest ask; 2. God will give it to *Thee.* What Thou wilt do is for Thy judgment and not for my presumption to determine. *Augustine.*—When we know not what in *particular* to ask, let us in *general* refer ourselves to God. *Henry.*

Will give it Thee. When we know not what to pray for, the Great Intercessor knows and is never refused.—Him the Father heareth alway.—If David will hear Joab for Absalom, what may we not hope for from our Advocate?

αιτήσῃ. The only place where this word is used of our Lord praying, instead of ἐρωτᾶν, παρακαλεῖν, προσεύχεσθαι, δεῖσθαι, compare Luke xxii. 32; John xiv. 16; xvi. 26; xvii. 9, 15, 20. *Schaff.*--Verbum minus dignum. *Bengel.*--δώσει σοι. Takes precedence of the rest in the or'ginal. *Lange.*—Martha remembe¬ed the promise (verse 4) contained in the message of Jesus. *Tholuck, Meyer.*—That our Lord would implore consolation. *Rosenm.*—That Lazarus may not be cast away. *Euthymius.*

---

23. Jesus saith unto her, Thy brother shall rise again.

Jesus saith. No scene ever pictured by human genius approaches this in simple grandeur.—The comforting answer of Jesus directs Martha's thoughts to what *shall be.*

Thy brother. Death had not severed the relationship.—In the spirit world Lazarus was still *her brother.*

> "One family, we dwell in Him,
> One Church, above, beneath;
> Though now divide 1 by the stream,
> The narrow stream of death."— *Wesley.*

Rise again. Not, I will *now* raise him up.—A grand promise, corresponding to her indefinite hope, therefore indefinitely worded. —She might understand Him as referring to the general future resurrection.—Specific faith in the raising of the dead must proceed from such a general faith.—His words intentionally ambiguous for the trial and development of her faith. *Lange.*—The same hand that buried Moses and locked the treasure in the valley of Moab, kept the key, and on Mount Tabor brought him forth like an *angel* of God.—Glorious as was this promise, yet she was disappointed.—She wanted the quenched light of their home rekindled.

'Ἀναστήσεται. Used to lead on to the requisite faith in her mind. *Meyer* —Doubtful whether it *could* be used of a recall into human life. *Alford.*—Refers *mainly* to the final resurrection. *Hengst.*—He meant the *raising of Lazarus*, which *actually* afterwards took place, and which was the fulfilment of the ἐξυπνίζειν. *Nonnus.*—She would have received her brother raised at this stage as a mere *mortal.* She must be instructed so as to receive him in immortal union, *Olsh.*

---

24. Martha saith unto him, I know that he shall arise again in the resurrection at the last day.

Know. She seems to imply that she acquiesced in that, but had dared to hope for something more.—As much as to say I am aware of that, but does that avail me now?—The depth, tenderness, and purity of these sisters' love is the key to their message to Christ, and their sad regret at its result.—It unfolds the cause of the Lord's unusual interest in answering their prayer so gloriously in the end.

Resurrection. (John ii. 22 ; v. 29 ; vi. 39.)—Confession of human weakness, declining the consolation promised.—It was something on which to lean her faith, but not much for comfort.—Her inward yearning dare not express itself plainly : Canst Thou not raise my brother?—Is it not possible to set aside the ordinary

936 / Gospel of John

laws *now?*—He had not come for merely personal interests.—
Every word and act in its sweep embraced a world. Therefore
the truth He uttered in the following verse was not for *her alone,*
but for all to the end of time.

οἶδα. Expresses the res'gnation of disappointment; and yet is full of submission.
Meyer.--She is only feeling her way. *De Wette.*—ἀναστήσεται. Doubting, inquiring,
hoping. *Lange, Berlin Bible.*—Half susceptibly, half despondingly. *Stier.*—"I well
know this, but wish something else from Thy lips." *Neander.*

25. Jesus said unto her, I am the resurrection, and the life: he that believeth in me,
though he were dead, yet shall he live.

I. The central idea of the chapter and the glory of the revelation in
the miracle.—The most wonderful words ever heard by mortal
ears.—Star of heavenly hope and blessedness shining down on the
darkness of death and the grave.—Has been the solace and
stay of millions, and will be of millions more till the last trumpet
sounds.

"**I**" and no other: the resurrection is no impersonal event to take
place at a future time.—A personal effect proceeding from ME now
with you.—At this moment it is present and active in Me. *Lange.*
—He directs her attention to Himself as the EVER-LIVING and LIFE-
GIVING SAVIOUR.—The general resurrection only the outcoming of
the power of Him then standing before her.

I am. The name by which Jehovah revealed Himself to the
covenant people.—Appropriated by our Lord on a former occasion:
see on John viii. 58.—Implies self-existence, eternity, independence, unchangeableness.—Mysterious union of humiliation and
majesty, of human feelings and divine power and glory in this
miracle.—Mary had spoken of Him as obtaining whatever He
might ask of God; and now He assures her that He possesses all
in Himself for evermore.—In ME is victory over the grave, in ME
is life eternal.

The Resurrection and the Life. Resurrection put first, for in it
the power of death is overcome.—Resurrection is life in conflict
with. and victory over, death. It is the death of death, even to the
extent of "mortality being swallowed up of life."—Christ the
Life unto resurrection; the Resurrection unto life.—The promise
of the New Covenant: 1. What it is, for the *body,* a blessed
resurrection; for the *soul,* a blessed immortality; 2. To whom
made, *believers* in Him. *Henry.*—Christ, the PRINCIPLE of the
future resurrection: 1. *Foretokens:* miracles of transformation
and histories of raisings from the dead in the Old Testament and
by Jesus; 2. *Manifestation:* revivifying life and spiritual resurrection of Christ; 3. *Operations:* as seen in believers ti l the general

resurrect'on. *Lange.*—Christ's resurrection the revelation, pledge, power, and model of our resurrection.—Faith in Christ *embraces* the resurrection.

The Life. See on John i. 4.—All life *in* Him and flowing *from* Him as the eternal LOGOS or WORD.—This is the principle of the resurrection as well as its essence and result.—On His WILL, all the countless myriads of created beings in God's empire depended for life at that very moment.—From that Lord's *death* will all the *life* eternally flow through believers. Rom. v. 21.—Our Lord's *divine decorum* is seen here: He tells her Lazarus sha l rise—and, not comprehending her Lord, He then discloses to her His august majesty and almightiness.—He affirms an unbroken life union with Himself as Prince of Life.—In His life there can be no antagonism: death cannot claim aught of Him.—This elemental life-principle is imparted by faith to mortals.—The soul, long subject to death's claims, leaves that realm and goes where death never comes.—Hence physical death, so far from destroying the sanctified soul, merely strikes off a few shackles.—The Life of Christ is the author of the resurrection in a twofold sense: 1. It is the power which effects moral awakening, which raises the soul from the death of sin to the life of righteousness; 2. Because of this it is the root of the waking of the physically dead: see on John ii. 22; v. 29; vi. 39.—Mankind can scarcely realize the truth that the conversion of a soul is a greater work than the raising of the dead.—As the soul is more subtle, more valuable, more enduring, any change carries its own proof.—The changes that occurred to Christ's body will occur also to His people.—They rise spiritually and corporeally to the new life of the resurrection.—The miracle about to be performed, the promise and pledge of all.

He that, &c. *Whoso believeth in Me, even if he shall have died* (physically), *will live* (be a partaker of life, *uninterruptedly*, as prior to the resurrection, in Paradise; so, by means of the resurrection, *eternally*); *and every one who lives* (is still alive in time) *and believes in Me, will assuredly not die for ever, i.e.,* he will not lose his life in eternity, ch. viii. 51—a promise which, though not excluding physical death in itself, does exclude it as the negation of the true and eternal life, ch. vi. 50. Compare Rom. viii. 10. *Meyer.*

Believeth. Through faith, the believer receives Christ Himself.

In me. In Christ, he shares the immortality belonging to Him. 2 Cor. i. 21.—It will be proved before the world that " My conflict with death is a victory." In ME is victory over the grave, in ME is life eternal. In ME that becomes yours which makes death not to be death.

Dead. "Those dead in sins hath He quickened together with Christ." Eph. ii. 4, 5.—The Father in the parable sublimely intones His joy : "This my son was *dead*, and lives again ; was lost, and is found."

Shall he live. Bodily death, the fruit of sin, not abolished in appearance, but is in *results*.—The saint's death is no death, for the death of the body is the life of the soul.—A paradox, "he lives, even if he dies." Death touches not his inmost life : It only divests him of his body.—He lives an eternal and imperishable life, which death only perfects.—The mystery he reveals is, that this Resurrection is associated with Himself.—Martha knew that Abel had been no loser, that Enoch had gone to another life.— Here she learns that the key to life eternal is in Jesus Christ alone. —What unspeakable folly that men should speak of a happy future without the Redeemer.—They forget there is a sting in death which none but the Lord can take away.

ἡ ἀνάστασις, &c. Impossible here to separate the moral and the physical sense. *Godet.*—ἀποθάνῃ. Even if he have died. *Sepp.*—Former refers to believers dying before, and the latter to those dying after. *Bengel*—Verse 25, to life temporal; verse 26, to life eternal *Klee*—First sentence refers to the resurrection of the body, and the second to that of the spirit. *Lampe, Olsh., Stier.*—A view not tenable. *Lange.*

---

26. And whosoever liveth and believeth in me shall never die. Believest thou this?

Whosoever. Lit., *every one.*—The provisions of the Gospel are for all our race.—Every one that liveth through faith, or livingly believes.

Believeth. No allusion to Lazarus here.—He would raise the fainting faith of Martha to a far higher truth.—He turns her thought from her slumbering brother to Himself, the Giver of all life.— Reveals His consciousness of divinity.—All His words, acts, parables, miracles, point to HIMSELF, yet without the least shadow of egotism. —He claims from the living and dead here and through eternity all that Jehovah could possibly demand : yet it all appears right and becoming.—"I said unto thee" (v. 40), points back to these words.

In Me. This great word is like the sun among the planets. All other revealed truth revolves around it and depends on it.—Faith not in popes, or councils, or fathers, or churches, or dogmas, but IN ME.—A loving trust of the individual heart in the Personal Living Lord.

Never die. Faith has wrapped up in it the immortal principle found in angels.—How near the redeemed soul comes to angels, when sharing life with the Lord of angels!—The regeneration of a soul a great mystery, so is the resurrection of the body.—To believe what is above reason is FAITH; what we can analyze and comprehend is mere *philosophy*.

Die. The second death, the only death deserving the name.—The *dead* will live again, the *living* will never die.—An advance in the thought: Last verse, "though he were dead;" now the Lord will not admit it *possible* for the Christian *ever to die*.—As the hammer and chisel jar the limbs of the slave, when his fetters are broken, yet he calls not that pain *slavery*, but the *struggle into freedom*, so death is the transient agony of the soul *as it enters* HEAVEN!

Never die. The Law song was: "In the midst of life we are in death."—The Gospel song reverses it: "In the midst of death we begin to live." Luke xxiii. 43.—We now hear the prelude to our Lord's own resurrection.—Natural death is overlooked as unworthy of being noted in the eternal progress of being.—Death is a loss, the greatest known to unbelievers: but to the believer, God solemnly teaches us "*It is* GAIN!" Phil. i. 21.—1. Loss of worldly *substance:* gains an inheritance incorruptible, undefiled, and everlasting. 1 Peter i. 4. 2. Loss of *health:* gains immortal youth, and "no inhabitant shall ever say I am sick." Isaiah xxxiii. 24. 3. Loss of *friends:* gains a countless number—shall be as angels. Luke xx. 36; Cherubim and Seraphim will be friends. 4. *Loss of* LIFE: gains sweet peace and rest; blessed harmony of every power and full enjoyment of the vision of God.—"They serve Him day and night in His temple." Rev. vii. 15.

Believest? Her answer proves she *understood* His question, yet how many understand who feebly believe.—He would for ever pierce all such hearts by this word.—His own resurrection has now put the profoundest emphasis on His question.—We are left at the grave of our friends to wait for the last trump.—Yet in life-giving faith we experience the first fruits of this great word.—When the dead bury their dead the Gospel comes with no word of cheer.—When the living bury their living, nothing but resurrection joy is the theme.—From the Bush Jehovah proclaimed Himself the God of departed saints, but its full import only burst forth after a thousand years.—Here stands the same "*Angel of the Covenant*" in *the body* and on the way to the grave.—He asks us to REALIZE IN HIM all our grounds of immortality and all our longings for resurrection life.—"Were there no other, Christ is Providence." *Jean Paul.*—"Were there no other, Christ is Resurrection." *Stier.*—*Believest?* The mysteries of religion are only understood by believing.—Hence unbelief, blind, stumbles at those truths which to faith are a rejoicing and a glory.—How few admit the thought, this year, this day, I may die, and enter eternity!—How blessed to be able to say, "*I know in Whom I have believed.*"—A creed is a summary of truth or falsehood embraced by men.— Infidels have ever warred against Christian creeds.—These symbols of faith are lights in the spiritual heavens.—They cheered myriads while in the flesh who are now in glory.—Have been the joy and crown of millions of martyrs in their fiery baptism.— Countless death chambers have been made *radiant* by their presence.—Honest men are not ashamed to own what they believe.—It is a bad sign for a merchant to be afraid lest his balance-sheet shall see the light.—Men of integrity never move under an *alias;* their *names* and *principles are known.*—Our Lord here demands a confession of our faith. Rom. x. 10.— From Martha, before He raises her brother, from the disciples before the transfiguration, from the two blind men following Him, from the father of the lunatic child.

This. In substance that the RESURRECTION of the last day was then present in Christ.

ζῶν. Every person on earth. *Aug., Bengel, Alford.*—Surviving members of Lazarus's family. *Theoph., De Wette.*—If every person, then the believer cannot physically die. *Olsh.*—Physical life. *Alford.*—Spiritual life. *Lampe, Olsh., Stier.*—οὐ μή—εἰς τὸν αἰῶνα. This phrase is ambiguous, and may mean either *not for ever,* or *never.*—The first and literal rendering would give a plain sense: *He that liveth* (physically) *and believeth in ME, will not die* (physically) *for ever, i e.,* will be raised again. But in all other passages where the same phrase occurs, it is equivalent to *never.* We must then suppose that Christ either spoke of *spiritual* death, or overlooked *physical* death as a vanishing transition to real and eternal death. *Schaff.*

---

27. She saith unto him, Yea, Lord : I believe that thou art the Christ, the Son of God, which should come into the world.

She saith. His question is as to the Resurrection : she answers as to the Incarnation : "I, for my part, freely acknowledge all thy claims."

Yea, Lord. "Not that I understand all, but nevertheless I believe," &c.—Thus the blind man healed promised beforehand to believe on the Son of God.—Thus we believe *in eternal life;* yet, with all our light, how dimly!—How far short of all implied in that noble confession (Mark viii. 29) did the *apostle fall?*—She seems suddenly overpowered by the divine glory of His presence. —To shield herself from the oppressive splendour, she adoringly confesses her faith.—How plainly she discloses the hand of a Divine Instructor on her spirit!

Believe. Lit., *I have, and continue to believe*—*i.e.,* am thoroughly convinced.—What could Peter say more?—Damaris esteemed as much as Dionysius—Areopagites stand with God no higher than the humble.—No Areopagite ever left such a memorial as the humble maid of whom we read. Mark xiv. 9.

The Christ. She names the three well-known names of the Messiah.—As Quickener of the dead, she implies that He had spoken great things about Himself; but she knew not what they were.—Hence, when asked one thing, she replies to another.

The Son of God. See on John i. 18, 34, 49. She assumes that Christ has attributes of Jehovah.—No point of doctrine can be deduced from this simple confession: but our Saviour *received* this ascription of Divine attributes, and did *not* repel it as Paul and Barnabas did. Acts xiv. 15.—Martha's Creed: 1. The *guide* of her faith, the *Word* of Christ; 2. The *ground* of her faith, the *authority* of Christ; 3. The *matter* of her faith, that Jesus was THE CHRIST, the Son of God, the ONE who should come. *Henry.*

πεπίστευκα. I have and do believe. *Bengel.*—But yet she hesitated to use πατέρα instead of θεὸν. Verse 22. *S'ier.*—Hitherto she did not regard Jesus as the Messiah. *Hezel*—"I believe what the Church believes:" Queen Elizabeth's answer to the Jesuit sent to ensnare her. *Hume.*—When she believed Him the Son of God, then she believed Him to be the Resurrection and the Life. *Aug.*—ἐρχόμενος. The name by which the Messiah was known. "*Him that was to come.*"

---

28. A\d when she had so said, she went her way, and called Mary her sister secretly, saying, The Master is come, and calleth for thee.

She went. She cannot enjoy this revelation alone—Mary must hear it: it was for her, above all others.—The key is found in the fact that the Lord will gather an assembly to witness the miracle.

Secretly. That is, *privately,* on account of the Jews who were present.—He never made a parade of His miracles.—Remarkable harmony of human prudence with divine assurance. *Lange.*

Master. Gr., *Teacher.* Her sister had been a faithful pupil.

Is come. He had neither entered the house nor village, but had remained in the highway.

Calleth. His actual request is not recorded—"There is a time to weep," and there is a time to refrain from weeping.—A beautiful picture of domestic piety: one sister calling another to come to Jesus.—It is often better to preach Christ in secret than to proclaim Him publicly.

Thee. It is a question of personal relationship.—*Christ calleth for thee:* 1. By the admonitions of conscience; 2. By the strivings of His Spirit; 3. By strange and varied Providences, sometimes dashing our idols to pieces; 4. By the joys of heaven and the terrors of hell.

ἐφώνησέν. She does not say when, where, or how; but for brevity's sake, lets it be inferred. *Aug.*—The Lord had said, Call her. *Pfenninger.*—Evidently with hopes raised, though faint and indefinite. *Alford.*—λάθρα. To prevent His enemies from marring the interview. *Futhymius.*—By Christ's command. *Trapp*—He would remove His disciples from the influence of the Jews. *Lange.*—Ὁ διδάσκαλος. Their domestic name for the Saviour. *Bengel.*—Designates their chief friend. *Braune*—No reference spec ally to his teaching *Luthardt.*—φωνεῖ. The Lord had not *actually* asked for her. *Stier*—Mary's statement is decisive. *Alford.*—His words amounted to a call, she thought. *Besser.*

---

29. As soon as she heard that, she arose quickly, and came unto him.

Quickly. Where else could this mourner, stricken of God, go?— —The disciples of John buried their Master, and " *went and told Jesus.*" 1. The believer in *prosperity* hastens to Him for grace to bear it ; 2. In *adversity*, for grace to improve it ; 3. In *temptation*, for grace to overcome it ; 4. In a *friendless* world, for sympathy.— Lot's wife a warning against halting and lingering. The gracious *haste* of Mary: she did not consult 1, the decorum of her mourning ; 2, her neighbours. *Henry.*

---

30. Now Jesus was not yet come into the town, but was in that place where Martha met him.

Not yet come. Painful trial to faith: love lingering so long.— But all was ordained for the glory of God.—Comfort to us when Christ seems to keep at a distance.—He *will* have his disciples come out to Him to make their confession of faith.—Jerusalem had witnessed at least one glorious miracle in Bethesda. John v. 5.—Now her citizens visiting Bethany will view a still grander act of God.

---

31. The Jews then which were with her in the house, and comforted her, when they saw Mary, that she rose up hastily and went out, followed her, saying, She goe h unto the grave to weep there.

Comforted. The consolations of the world often, like frozen hail, chill the heart, yet those whose hearts are very heavy, and particularly those that are sorely tempted, should not be left alone. *Zeisius.*—Sympathising ones coming to comfort are themselves blessed.

Followed. Mourners are often persecuted by the curious gaze of pretended friends.—True grief prefers and seeks solitude, though too great isolation is to be avoided.—Mark the fathomless mystery of Providence: our Lord's eleventh hour was come.—The time for retiring for prayer in deserts and mountains was ended.—The last great miracle must issue in the decree of His death.—That act must have many witnesses, friends and foes.—Unconsciously they gather to behold a God-like work of love of One they would murder.—Link by link of the golden chain of Redemption is being wrought, and human responsibility is untouched.

To weep there. Tears are words known in all the tongues of our fallen race.—Without the Bible mourners know of no Divine sympathiser in the universe.—Ancients, to express their grief, " Sat among the ashes." Job ii. 8.—Rent their mantle and put dust on their heads. Job ii. 12.—Cut their flesh. Lev. xix. 28, &c.—Jews and Greeks accustomed to sit down and mourn by the graves of their dead.—Tears a merciful provision for relieving the oppressed heart.—Tears of penitence precious gems to angels: " There is joy," &c.

ἠκολούθ. " Let no man follow a woman in public, not even his own wife." *Rabbis.*— Either they were females who followed her, or if men, then at a great distance. *Lightfoot.*

---

32. Then when Mary was come where Jesus was, and saw him, she fell down at his feet, saying unto him, Lord, if thou hadst been here, my brother had not died.

Saw him. A delicate touch of nature.—She cared not how many witnessed her adoration of the Lord.—A stroke of character which at once distinguishes her from Martha.—Her kneeling posture and her tears far more eloquent than words.

Weeping. Verse 33.—Tears are the inheritance of the apostasy.— Either our sorrows or our sins call for them, and the dust of the grave alone will dry them.—He heard the secret sighings of her devoted heart.

Fell down. An instance of the deepest faith-begotten reverence.— She does not dare speak, until prostrate at His feet, the throne of grace to every true suppliant.—Note Mary's unchanging love: though He had seemed unkind in His delay, she takes it not amiss. —Like Job, " Though He slay me, yet will I trust in Him."

If Thou. The same words from both sisters, the key of their converse during the last four days. A coincidence proving its authenticity.

Had not died. Gr., *would not or could not have died.*—These words almost admit us into the dying chamber of their brother.—They had doubtless repeated this again and again until it filled their hearts.—Life is sweet, but if death alone be the gate to Paradise, is it wise to cling to earth?—These sisters were doubtless right, as we learn from verse 15.—What a revelation of the flight of diseases, demons, and death, wherever Jesus went.—The presence of an ALMIGHTY BEING living, moving, working wonders in their midst, sent a tremor through the hearts of men.—At this very hour every thoughtful pilgrim, touching the first soil of the Holy Land, feels here lived, toiled, suffered, and died my Creator, Redeemer, and Judge. He who walked these hills and valleys will pronounce over my soul, "Come!" or "Depart!" Matt. xxv. 34—41.—He entered the world to destroy him that had the power of death.—Of this astounding fact the sisters must have had some hints.

μου ὁ ἀδελφός. Martha had said, "My brother would not have been dead;" Mary says 'My brother (the position of the pronoun is more emphatic) would not have died." *Farrar.*

---

33. When Jesus therefore saw her weeping, and the Jews also weeping which came with her, he groaned in the spirit, and was troubled.

Weeping. The weeping of Mary and the weeping of the Jews: 1. In itself; the external similarity, the internal diversity; 2. In its signification: thus voices mingle in the songs of the sanctuary, tears in our houses, different spirits in the company of Jesus. *Lange.*

Groaned. The surroundings touched Him so deeply, that a strong effort of self-repression was needed.—The Greek words imply *indignation.*—Probable causes: 1. At the hypocrisy of the Jews when He saw them lamenting and professing by their tears of condolence to share Mary's feelings, whilst they were full of bitter hostility to Him and His; 2. At the unbelief of the disciples and others; 3. At the thought of the ruin wrought by sin.—"Jesus excites Himself to the conflict with Death, the enemy of mankind." *Hengst.*—All the world's sins and woes rose before His eye, all its mourners and graves.—It did not abate His sorrow, that Lazarus would rise, only to die again.—The tears he was about to staunch would flow when no comforter would be near.—His was a holy sympathy when he saw humble-hearted believers in such anguish. —His a life-long conflict with sin.—"By thine unknown agonies." *Greek Litany.*—In Bethany, Gethsemane, and Calvary we find these crises.—In the background is a wrath against the arch worker of all this ruin.—His earthly tabernacle trembled and shook under the power of His Godhead.—An echo of this groan rises in the hearts of millions daily as they look at the sad work of death.—Christ's groans are vicarious; "the whole creation groaneth," and He as the great High Priest of all collects those groans in Himself and utters them in one loud cry to God. *Novalis.*—Wretched folly in the Stoic's pride, as in the frantic grief which cursed the gods, because a friend had died.

He groaned. 1. A proof of divine power and love ; 2. A pledge of our resurrection ; 3. A model of the exercise of *human affections;* 4. An expression of holy anger against unbelief ; 5. A lesson not to mourn for the dead as those " without hope." 1 Thess. iv. 13.

In spirit. His feelings visible to spectators were only the outward sign of the deep and awful agony of His mind; of the divine storm which swept through His breast.—His " spirit," the seat of the religious emotions, as distinguished from His " soul," the seat of the natural ; compare Mark viii. 12 ; John xiii. 21, and John xii. 27. *Godet.*—God alone knew His feelings as CREATOR while incarnate; these we dare not attempt to fathom.

Troubled. Gr., " troubled Himself."—Expresses the external manifestation of the inward commotion by a voluntary act. *Lange.* —Christ's affections were not *passions,* but voluntary emotions, which He had entirely in His power.—Those here spoken of were therefore orderly, rational, full of dignity, and directed to proper ends. *Augustine, Bengel,* &c.—The twice-repeated convulsion of Jesus in spirit: 1. The occasion ; 2. The mood ; 3. The fruit.— The heart of Jesus in its full revelation : 1. Of its love ; 2. Of its holiness ; 3. Of its divine power. *Lange.*—Note our Lord's perfect participation in our natural feelings and His sympathy with our sorrows.—Also His perfect control over passion and grief. *Schaff.* —Strong emotion and perfect virtue not contradictory. *Rothe.*— He who cannot feel deeply at sight of wrong-doing and wickedness must have a very imperfect moral nature ; and he who cannot feel deeply at sight of human misery and woe must have a very hard heart. *Trench.*—What then must Christ have felt who was perfect purity and perfect love?—Seek not to dry the stream of sorrow, but keep it within the banks. *Leighton.*

ἐνεβριμήσατο, &c. A passage of exceeding difficulty.—The affection here depicted has been explained in three ways: 1. Of ANGER.—In respect of His divine nature, with His human spirit in its passionate emotion, *Origen, Chrys., Cyril,* &c.—At the power of sin and death. *Aug , Erasmus, Luthardt,* &c.—At the unbelief of the Jews. *Wordsworth,* &c.—At the unbelief of the sisters. *Lampe,* &c.— At the misconception of His foes and want of comprehension in His friends. *Bruckner, &c* —At the hypocritical tears of the Jews. *Meyer.*—That he was unable to avert the death of Lazarus. *De Wette.*—2. Of GRIEF. *Luther, Tholuck,* &c.—3. A GENERAL AFFECTION of the spirit. *Lange.*

---

34 And said, Where have ye laid him? They said unto him, Lord, come and see.

Where ? Omniscience need not ask for information.—A hint that

He is about to perform a God-like deed.—How modestly He fore-shadows a stupendous miracle.—How unlike man!—He would arrest attention as in the question to Moses : " What is in thine hand ? " Exodus iv. 2.—He would also avoid all appearance of collusion.

Laid him. He speaks of Lazarus in his *personality*, though the spirit was in Hades.—Spoken in the consciousness of an almighty conqueror.—His word is enough to snatch the spoil from death.—By-and-bye He will destroy that foe absolutely and eternally.— " O death ! I will be thy plague ;" " Neither shall there be any more death."

Come and see. Martha and Mary thus answer.—The grave a moving yet a salutary sight.—Our friends, deceased, not in the grave.—" Those who sleep in Jesus " (whom Jesus puts to sleep) " will God bring with Him."—Light of Christ's resurrection falls on their graves, and not only chases away the darkness, but gilds with a sure and certain hope of a glorious immortality.—Christ by the grave of Lazarus the pledge and promise of this.

---

35. Jesus wept.

Wept. This is the shortest text and the longest sermon in the Bible.

Wept. Gr., SHED SILENT TEARS.—In verse 33 it is *loud wailing.*—He wailed loudly over Jerusalem ; for the death of the body is nothing to the death of the soul.—When about to do almighty work, He first showed His humanity.—He awoke from sleep to speak in the voice of God and silence the storm.—He shed tears now as a mourner, while He is about to raise the dead as Jehovah.—As John records the loftiest, so he writes of the lowliest things done by our Lord.—Wonderful harmony of humanity and divinity through all His eventful life.—No instance wherein His words and acts do not perfectly agree with the great mystery, " God manifest in the flesh."—How could the human mind have produced the Gospels had not the LIFE of Christ been present to the writers?—It is in His LIFE that the key to this marvellous history is found.—Having " troubled Himself in spirit," He now permits the pent-up emotion to flow forth in tears.—Thus summer rain succeeds the thunderstorm.—The RESURRECTION and the LIFE on His way to the grave weeping.—Tears are now sanctified since Jesus wept. *Luther.*—Three times He wept : 1. At the grave of Lazarus, tears of *sympathy ;* 2. When he drew nigh unto Jerusalem. Luke xix. 41. *Prophetical* tears ; 3. During His passion. Heb. v. 7. *Atoning* tears.—The most sacred, most solemn spots to this hour in Palestine are those moistened with the Redeemer's tears.—Our Lord's life one of transcendent contrasts.—A babe in the manger.—Hosts of angels singing His birth-song.—His helpless infancy.—The midnight turned into midday.—His mother chiding her child ; yet knew not He had just cried MY FATHER ! of the Eternal God !—One moment hungering, the next creating food for thousands.—Now wearied by the side of a well, then imparting life to the dying and the dead. —Now hanging on the cross ; now opening the doors of Paradise ; now crying a solemn *death* cry ; now shaking the earth and darkening the sun.—God's saints in all ages have been men of tears, " Oh God," prayed Augustine, " give me the grace of tears." —These tears of Jesus would have been unnoticed in a mere man ; but GOD INCARNATE is touched with a feeling of our infirmity. Heb. iv. 15.—Such a thought never entered the mind of philosophy. —At dawn light and darkness seem contending : thus Christ's love and wrath in tears.—Stricken humanity finds a perfect type in the weeping Saviour.—The dark background of such sinless perfection in tears is the deep curse of sin causing all woe.

ἐδάκρυσεν, fleut non ploravit. Here at the grave, but He ἔκλαυσεν over Jerusalem. *Wordsworth.*—He wept lovingly. *Bengel.*—He wept for joy. *Chrysologus.*—He wept because the miracle would bring Lazarus back to the unrest of life. *Isodorus.*—This was the decision of the *Concilium Toletanum.*—All these explanations of the Fathers unnatural. *Heubner.*—The sympathising physician will sometimes weep with an afflicted family, though he knows he has the means of giving relief. *Neander.*—He wept merely as an example. *Basil.*

---

36. Then said the Jews, Behold how he loved him!

How he loved. They infer this from His weeping.—Our Lord's love for our departed friends far surpasses ours.—Even a mother's love is but a faint reflection of the love of Christ.—" In the palms of His hands hath He graven them."—Anciently the worshipper laid his written prayer on the altar or in the hand of the god.— Both the plea and the name are symbolised by the wounded palms of the Lord.—The spear was the key which opened the boundless treasures of His heart.—" We thank you, oh ye friends from Jerusalem ! for this testimony to His *human tenderness.*" *D. Brown.*—Of all graces, love most attracts and influences the opinion of the world.—From Christ's love we ascend to God's love : " He that hath seen ME hath seen the Father."—Love of Christ proceeds from Himself, is unchangeable in its nature, necessarily provides for and secures the eternal welfare of the loved ones.

---

37. And some of them said, Could not this man, which opened the eyes of the blind, have caused that even this man should not have died?

And some. Gr., *but some.*—Hints that two classes were present.—

The uniform result of the Lord's miracles to reveal character. Luke ii. 35.; John vii. 12, 40—43; ix. 16; x. 19—21.—He ever is separating light from darkness.

Could not? These Jews may have heard of the dead raised before in distant Galilee, but the stupendous miracle of giving sight to the blind man was still on every tongue.—No one ever dared *ask* Him to raise the dead, not even Mary and Martha.—Their question implied that while performing many wonders, this sickness was beyond His power.—They either reproach Him for His neglect, or mock Him for His weakness.—If He could not save this man, what are we to think of the alleged healing of the blind?—They threw in their hissings, as serpents leave their venom on the most beautiful flowers. *Tischendorf.*—There is a depth of truth in their question which they knew not of.—Yes, Jesus could have stayed the hand of death, but He answers not in *words*, His deeds will soon reply.—They will shortly see that He was the Lord of the issues of life and death.—This is the second time public testimony to the miracle (John ix.) is given. John x. 21.

Opened. An undesigned coincidence: these Jews referring to a miracle well known rather than to those in remote Galilee.

The blind. The blind *man*, referring to the particular case John ix.

This man. One in the prime of life, and dearly beloved by all. —Many of these witnesses, it is believed, died as martyrs for *this* very faith.

Not died. None seemed to dream of his ever being brought to life. —A strong proof from enemies to our Lord's former miracles.— They denied His divinity, yet wonder He does not act like God!— How delicate a touch—we also are prone to dictate to our Maker. —These words, not meant for Jesus, were still heard by Omniscience.

δέ. Seldom used as copula, rather as contrast, "but." *Alford.*—ἠδύνατο. Why did they not ask about earlier resurrections? the captious question of *Strauss.* They intimate His love was unseasonable, because He had the power but did not use it. *Erasmus.*—Their speech had malice in it. *Meyer, Alford, Godet, Luthardt.*—Well meant. *Lücke, Tholuck.* They would cast a doubt on the healing of the blind man. *Meyer.*

---

38. Jesus therefore again groaning in himself cometh to the grave. It was a cave, and a stone lay upon it.

Groaning. Gr., *shuddered.*—Stirred not only in spirit but in Himself. *Lange.*—This second emotion seems to have been provoked partly by the unbelief implied in verse 37. *Schaff.*—The third time our Lord's deep feeling is noticed.

Grave. Gr., *memorial:* implying that some inscription was there.—Immortality generally held.—In Greece death was passing from the domain of one god to that of another.—A cloud of celestial messengers hovered around the dying.—They hoped for a welcome to the Elysian fields from those departed.—Death was falling asleep in one place, and awaking in another.—Friends crowded around the dying, pressing the hand and catching the parting breath. Having washed and anointed the corpse, they covered it with costly garments. Placing flowers on the head, laid the feet toward the door, as its last journey; vessels of perfumed water stood beside, branches of laurel were hung at the door ; coffins of sycamore, cedar, or cypress, stone or marble; funerals at daybreak, preceded by persons carrying torches; mourners loudly wailing, mingled with musicians playing on flutes. At times they rode in chariots, special honour was paid by all going on foot. The dead faced the west—Moslems face Mecca, in the east; returning, they celebrated a funeral banquet, gave thanks for their friends' kindness.—Sacrifices were offered to the departed spirits and Uranian gods.—Black was the mourning dress, and hair half shorn proved their grief.—Corpse held as the deserted mansion of a friend ; neglect of burial an outrage : hence their land was adorned with monuments of exquisite beauty.—Athenians made war against Thebes for refusing burial to the fallen Argives.—If unburied, the ghost wandered a hundred years on the desolate shores of Orcus. —Persons about to perish at sea bound their jewels to their bodies to defray the expenses of sepulture.—Persons struck by lightning were believed enemies of the gods, and left unburied ; also those guilty of suicide, sacrilege, or treason.—Greek, Roman, and Jewish cemeteries lined the highways leading out of cities.—Spartans buried their dead around temples, as we around country churches. —Burying in churches arose from erecting small chapels over the martyr's tombs.—A law of Solon forbade luxurious expenditure on Athenian tombs.—Tomb of Mausoleus in Caria one of the seven wonders of the world.—Ancients tempted to plundering of graves by burying jewels with their dead.—The museums of Europe are enriched with their spoils—Coffins were seldom used by Jews, hence the "young men sat up." Luke xi. 7.—Jerusalem is surrounded by a vast cemetery thousands of years old.—The tombs are elaborately cut in the rock; those of the kings are splendid ruins.—Embalming was used to repair the appearance of bodies mangled in war.—In pestilence bodies were burned.—Egyptians preserved them to be reinhabited by the absent spirit.—None but the regal formerly were buried in the city, "the sepulchre of the kings."—They did not let the earth press heavily on the dead.— They built spacious chambers for the spirit's use, and placed a lamp to cheer the gloomy solitude.

Cave. Note this graphic touch from an eye-witness. Most tombs
were hewn out of the sides of hills and mountains, others sunk in
rocks, as in Egypt and Palestine.

Stone lay. Sepulchral vaults were entered either by a perpendicular opening with steps, or by an horizontal one : they were
closed either by a large stone or a door.—They exist in great
numbers down to this day.—The grave of Lazarus was of the first
kind, if the words be rendered *it lay upon it.* But they may also
mean : *it lay against it,* or *before it ;* and then the reference would be
to a grave with an horizontal entrance. No decision can be arrived
at. *Meyer.*—The one at present shown as the grave of Lazarus is
of the first kind. *Robinson.*—To own such a tomb indicates a good
social position and comparative wealth ; the poor were buried in
common places.—The large concourse of mourners from Jerusalem,
and the very costly ointment with which Mary anointed the
Lord's feet (xii. 3), point to the same conclusion. *Schaff.*—So
circumstantial an account refutes the absurd allegation of sceptical
critics that Lazarus was in a swoon.—*Renan* has the audacity to say
that the whole affair was "got up."—The credulity of unbelief is
boundless.

ἐμβριμώμενος. Grief and anger alternate. *Kleuker.*—At the unbelief of the Jews
present. *D. Brown,* &c.—μνημεῖον Jews held that Abraham's race, buried in foreign
lands, returned underground to Judea. *Rabbis.*—No person could build a house in
Thebes without providing a grave. *Plato.*

---

39. Jesus said, Take ye away the stone. Martha, the sister of him that was dead,
saith unto him, Lord, by this time he stinketh: for he hath been dead four days.

Take away. A heavy task ; at times requiring several strong men.
—No one must approach a grave within four cubits. *Rabbis.*—
Our Lord ignored at Nain and Bethany these absurd traditions.
—Virtue cannot be soiled by death's memorials ; sunlight remains
pure on a battle-field.—Our Lord made others do the work : thus
Elijah at Carmel prepared the victims, but others filled the trenches
with water.—How calmly and quietly He proceeds to work His
grandest miracle!—Thus we neither hear nor see the sunbeam
that quickens vegetable and animal life.—How majestic His composure now after those tumultuous emotions.—He might have
commanded the stone to roll away of itself, or have caused
Lazarus to come forth through the rock.—His act will now answer
those questions, What made Him weep? and whether He could
have cured His friend?—Martha thinks it only the desire of a
friend to look at the corpse.—The stone on the dead an image of
the sinner *under the law. Augustine.*—"Take ye away the stone,"

symbolical of the work of ministers: 1. Of Prejudice; 2. Of
Unbelief; 3. Of Pride; 4. Of Covetousness.—It is the work of
man to remove the stone; but God alone can raise the dead.—
Neither philosophy nor science can take away the stone from man's
heart, cannot give an account of our origin, cannot explain the
entrance of sin, cannot show how the curse may be removed.—
Scepticism leaves the mourner without consolation, the dying
without hope, the dead without a resurrection, the world without
beginning or end.—He who asked for the grave now requests the
friends to roll away the stone, to convince them the body was
there, and to prevent any dispute as to his identity.

Sister. Martha speaks as the sister of the dead, and not the
disciples.

He stinketh. The fearful reality of the grave disturbs her soul
and shakes her faith.—She thinks that a scandal may result from
the bursting forth of the odour of corruption and in presence of
so many people. *Lange.*—How little do even Christ's most
devoted friends know of His almighty power; and how often do
they "limit the Holy One."—She shudders at the thought of
seeing the face so beloved in a putrefying state, not perceiving
the glorious promise concealed in the command.

Four days. Lit., *he is now the fourth day, i.e.,* as a dead man.—A
proverb in the Talmud and the Targum, that corruption sets in
the third day after death. *Tholuck.*—Rabbis say that the soul
lingers around the corpse for three days, but, seeing the aspect
changed, it retires until the resurrection morn.—Her hope of
seeing him restored had evidently failed.—Job illustrates the
vacillations of the believing heart under trials.—Martha had no
idea that His mighty word could undo the work of death.—How
clearly every point was overruled to glorify God in the greatness
of the miracle: see on verse 4.—Before the grave of every sinner
buried in sin and death Christ stands in the promise, "Lo, I am
with you," therefore Take ye away the stone!

ὄζει. A corrupt body raised would make the miracle *monstrous. Olshausen.*—The
Lord had 'suspended the process of decay. *Lange, Luthardt, Trench.*—Judgment of
Martha a statement of a sensible *fact. Aug., Calvin, Owen, &c.*—No more monstrosity
in the raising of a decaying corpse than in the restoration of a withered hand. *Godet.*
—The high state of the family suggests embalming of the body. *De Wette.*—Could not
have taken place; otherwise Martha would never have come to such a conclusion. *Meyer.*
—Caves had merely a stone to protect from jackals. *Stier.*—First three days after
death spent in weeping, fourth in beating the breast, since there was no hope of his
reviving. *Lightfoot,* from the Rabbis.

---

40. Jesus saith unto her, Said I not unto thee, that, if thou wouldest believe, thou
shouldest see the glory of God?

Said. Although no record of it is left, He alludes to it as a fact.—

Refers, probably, to the whole of His sayings from verse 4.—Said graciously, yet with some slight rebuke for her weak faith.

Believe. Even amid the ruins of death, *faith* will have this sight.— *Unbelief* sees in the same place the woes of life and worse beyond. —The stone at the grave of human *hope* cannot be moved by *unbelief.*—Unbelief is so venomous, it poisons the hand of the soul. —So rooted is unbelief, that the Lord must shame and rouse faith by the word, "Did I not say unto thee?"

Shouldest see. Our Lord here affirms faith to be *the* condition of seeing His glory.—He knew many would see the *miracle* but not the *glory of God.*—All the claims made by the Redeemer as to His supreme divinity will be verified at Lazarus's tomb.—Martha will see Jesus Christ is *the* RESURRECTION and *the* LIFE!—The great law laid down in this particular case universal in its application.— No discovery of the divine glory but to faith: 1. In NATURE; hence the errors and absurdities of sceptical scientists; 2. In PROVIDENCE; hence the errors and absurdities of sceptical historians; 3. In REVELATION; hence the errors and absurdities of sceptical critics.—From "the wise and prudent" God conceals Himself; to "babes" He reveals the "secret of the Lord."

The glory. By faith alone can we now see through the ruin wrought by death the glory beyond.

εἰπόν. That which He had said in verse 4 was to be realized by means of the ἀναστ. promised in verse 23—promised in the sense present to Christ's mind. At the same time, the performance of the miracle was itself dependent on the fulfilment of the condition ἐὰν πιστεύς. *Meyer.*

---

41. Then they took away the stone from the place where the dead was laid. And Jesus lifted up his eyes, and said, Father, I thank thee that thou hast heard me.

Took away. An act either of faith or curiosity.

Lifted up. He turned from the crumbling mortality to heaven.— Jews shall see not only His miraculous power, but His connection with their God in the working of the miracle.—Hence the unreserved outpouring of the prayer. *Lange.*

Father, I thank. Words expressing confidence, and referring, probably, to earlier prayers. *Lange.*—The Greek signifies the wish of an *equal* rather than begging for a favour.—A DECLARATION TO THE PEOPLE of the relation between the Father and the Son.—The INTERPRETATION our Lord put on His divine deeds among men. **Verse 42.**—He prayed not for *what He wanted*, but thanked the Father for *what He had.*—On Carmel Elijah prayed "that the

people may know that THOU art GOD." 1 Kings xviii. 37.—
Humanity may be pictured as standing waiting at the grave of
Lazarus.—The question of the Saviour's supreme divinity must
here be decided.—Next verse furnishes the *key* to all the Father's
responses and the proof that their WILL is ONE !—Jews shall see a
miracle with the endorsement of Jehovah.—A radiance streams
back upon those first mysterious words, "This sickness is not
unto death, but for the glory of God."

ἦρε τοὺς. This prayer was not heard by the people. *Stier.*—A heaven enforcing
prayer. *Albertine.*—εὐχαριστῶ. Lazarus had come to life when this word was spoken.
Chrysostom, Lampe.—Highly improbable. *Alford.*—He was heard before He prayed,
hence He here gives thanks for it. *Origen*—Pre-supposes earlier prayer. *Meyer,
Alford.*—Petition and thanksgiving coincided. *Tholuck.*—In anticipation of the miracle.
Godet.—ἤκουσάς. When He prayed unknown—likely at Perea. *Alford.*—Thou hast
and will. *Tittman.*—οὗ ἦν ὁ τεθνηκὼς κείμενος. Omitted. *Scholz, Tisch.*

---

42. And I knew that thou hearest me always : but because of the people which stand
by I said it, that they may believe that thou hast sent me.

Always. In His oneness with the Father lay His uninterrupted
power of doing these mighty works. *Schaff.*—A testimony to the
Lord in the face of the unbelieving Jews present.—There was an
essential difference between His prayers and ours.

I knew. The mysterious relation between the Father and the Son
makes it impossible for us to comprehend these words ; we cannot
comprehend how one human mind can act on another.—How vain
to think of understanding *how spirits commune.*—He prayed not
because He wanted help, but the people wanted instruction.—
Thereby informed them that He raised the dead in His own
power.

Hearest. Shows intimate communion by His asking nothing, doing
nothing without His Father.

The people. Gr., *the multitude* who stand around.—Design of this
prayer that the people migh *hear this* claim and *see* the proof of it.
—"Not that I have been heard at one time and refused at another,
or had a doubt of Thy hearing Me, for I know that," &c.—Moses
obtained by wrestling prayer the privilege of doing God's work in
God's name.—Whereas "In Christ dwelt the fulness of the Godhead bodily."—In His own name and by His own authority He
commands, and nature and the spirit world obey His voice.—He
does not say "In my Father's name," but works as God.—His
words show deep HUMILITY, His deeds show POWER.—With a word
He created man, but with groanings, tears, and prayer He recalls
the dead to life.—Type of the whole creation groaning and waiting
for redemption.—God ordered it that this death should take place

in a family of distinction, in a village nigh to Jerusalem.—Bethany road along the summit was then, as now, much frequented by the citizens.—Doubtless many familiar with the Sanhedrim were there. —Only a few days after many of these people cried, "Crucify Him."—In His prayer every believer has a personal interest.—He was hungry that he might give thee the bread of life ; thirsty that He might give thee living water.—He embraced the earth in prayer that thou mightest sit upon a throne.—He was betrayed that thou mightest be free.—Travailed, that thou mightest not be weary. —Incarnate, that He might be under the curse.—He was called the Son of Man that he might call thee the son of God.—He took our miseries that we might be eternally blest.—He prayed that we might believe.—Died to make us immortal.—Descended into the grave that we might enter Paradise.

Believe. They knew no one but the Almighty could raise the dead, hence His direct appeal to heaven.—Unbelief, arising from pride and bigotry, prevented them trusting in Him as the Messiah.—To remove this He toiled for three sad years, making His path radiant with wonders of mercy until the conspiracy to murder Him reached its consummation.

ἐγὼ δὲ ᾔδειν. Said after a pause. *Bengel.*

---

43. And when he thus had spoken, he cried with a loud voice. Lazarus, come forth.

Loud voice. Gr., *shouting.*—That all the crowd might hear.—For the people a prelude to the call of the last day.—Sublimity of this call can only be surpassed by the call that will awake the dead. John v. 28.—This loud call in open day and in presence of a crowd in marked contrast with the mutterings of those who practise incantations, and with the pretended wonders of modern spiritualism.— Not like Elisha, who by intensity of prayer painfully called back the dead.—He shall not cry (Isaiah xlii. 2) refers to the noiseless progress of His kingdom.—When the winds rent the mountains, &c., God was in the still small voice.—The grain, the grass, the forest grow silently.—His last utterance on the cross was a "loud cry."—Lazarus must feel in the spirit-world the authority and weight of that divine voice, and all the people standing round must hear.—To restore life to one dead four days is the same as one dead 4000 years.—This evangelist witnessed a more tremendous scene: I SAW THE DEAD, BOTH SMALL AND GREAT, STAND BEFORE GOD.

Lazarus, come forth. Properly : *Lazarus, hither, forth.*—All His miracles proclaim His Godhead, viz. : "Damsel, arise ;" "Young man, arise;" "Stretch forth thy hand;" "Thy sins are forgiven thee;" "Peace, be still;" "Take up thy bed;" "I say unto thee come out of him;" "Be it unto thee;" "The Lord hath need of him;" "To-day shalt thou be with me in Paradise."

Come forth. In simple grandeur it resembles " Be light, and light was!"—The heaven-tone, the peal of love, and lightning-flash of life in the voice of Christ.—A royal command befitting the Infinite Majesty.—He speaks not as though Lazarus was dead, but only asleep, and He had said He would "awake him" (verse 11).—I WILL, BE CLEAN! (Gr. has but two words) and Nature obeys the voice of its Creator.—Lazarus comes forth instantly, and sound as he was before his sickness. —The scene can almost be realized as the pencil of the Holy Ghost has painted it.—These miracles among the dead were preludes to His own and the general Resurrection.—Sermons preached to all the countless multitudes who have heard and will hear this record until the end of time.—Whether Lazarus' soul had actually entered Paradise, the record is divinely silent.—God's design was not to lift the veil which His wisdom had dropped, but to show forth His Son's glory.—As to these mysteries he, like Paul, was of *necessity* silent. 2 Cor. xii. 4. —Thrice blessed shall they be who on that morn shall, like Lazarus, hear the voice of a FRIEND.—Like David they " will be satisfied when awaking in His likeness." Ps. xvii. 15.—The cave is opened; the Redeemer lifts His eyes, still suffused with tears; all have now fixed their eyes on Him.—They behold the wonder-worker in mysterious intercourse with God, whom He calls FATHER!—They hear an awful voice ringing through the silent air.—As the living at the Resurrection morn will hear the last trump, they doubtless heard Him.—He calls the dead by name, and all eyes are turned to the open cave.—A shrouded corpse, blinded by the napkin and bound hand and foot, moves out.—His summons had been heard in eternity; the departed spirits knew their Maker's call.—The powers of the unseen world had been shaken, and for the third time He had burst the gates of the grave.

δεῦρο ἔξω. The moment of awakening preceded the thanksgiving, and the call merely occasioned the forthcoming. *Origen, Chrys.*—Manifestly, the moment of awakening was that of the loud call. *Lange, Meyer, Alford, Trench.*—An old legend makes him thirty, and he lived thirty years afterwards. *Epiphanius.*—Not all the changes of death had passed on him. *Ebrard.*

---

44. And he that was dead came forth, bound hand and foot with grave-clothes: and his face was bound about with a napkin. Jesus saith unto them, Loose him, and let him go.

Came forth. It is uncertain whether the limbs were wrapped separately or together.—In Italy the bodies, simply wrapped in linen are laid in church crypts under the floor.—Ancient paintings represent Lazarus as gliding, not stepping forth.

Bound. This was the ancient custom with Greeks, Romans, and Egyptians.—He was laid like a pledge in the grave, bound for security.—They had questioned the identity of the blind man.— Here are the bands and wrappings of the corpse.—They cannot doubt that this is the very Lazarus who had died and whose funeral they had attended.—Some think his hands and feet being bound rendered movement impossible.—He whose POWER could raise the dead was at no loss to bring him forth.—Others hold that as embalming was to follow the binding was loose.—The appearance of the living man in the garments of the grave, a type of the new life of the Christian in the old vestments of death. *Lange.*— The relics of the grave still hang around the believer, and Christ hath appointed his ministers to remove them.

Napkin. Ancients used what we call handkerchiefs; but they were handed a napkin or towel whenever they ate or drank.—If Egyptian customs were in use the face was not covered.

Loose him. Awestruck by the flash of Almightiness, they seemed stunned for a moment.—The apparatus of death clinging to one who in full vigour of life is pressing forth from the tomb.—No human eye saw Jesus in His *grave clothes* at His resurrection.— That which was done in the Lord's grave by angels is here to be done by mortal hands.—How harmoniously the creature here works with the Creator.—Human hands had laid the great stone, and human love had bound the dead.—What a mockery the taking away the stone and the undoing of the bands had it not been the sleep of death.—*The act of giving life He reserves to Himself.*—The ministry must stand in the valley amid the bones and prophesy.— The Gospel must by human, not angelic instrumentality, be preached.—He could by the same word have undone the winding-sheet, but He would have them *handle* the person raised.—The hand of God is seen in the *veil drawn* over the scene which followed.—Not a syllable about the effect of this august deed is uttered.—The Spirit here drops the narrative, as no human authors would have done.—Bible mentions eight persons raised from death and two transported to heaven without dying: 1. Son of widow; 2. Son of Shunnannite; 3. Dead man cast in Elisha's grave; 4. Young man of Nain; 5. Daughter of Jairus; 6. Lazarus; 7. Tabitha; 8. Eutychus—How deep their adoring love, how high their rapture and gratitude, all untold; joy was theirs alone among the mourners of all lands and times

> "Who to the verge have followed those they love,
> And on the insuperable threshold stand,
> With cherished names its speechless calm reprove
> And stretch in the abyss their ungrasped hand."—*Trench.*

Touching Lazarus, history is silent.

Let him go. That is, independent of aid.—He was not only restored to life, but, like Peter's mother-in-law, to perfect health. Mark i. 31.—How the adoring amazement of the Evangelist is lost in silence; how Christ gives Lazarus full vital strength; how He diverts attention from Himself to him raised up. *Lange.*—These "powers of the world to come" were to try their strength in retaining the Lord Himself, who had just shown His right over the grave.—The general Resurrection is called a "Revelation of the Son of God," an unveiling of the sons of God in Him, a "gathering together in Him of all things in heaven and earth."—All creation is groaning and travailing, and our Saviour's groan was His sympathy with the bursting groan of creation.—His sorrows through life show the same path for the Shepherd and the sheep, to victory and rest.

δεδεμένος. Jews bound them as Egyptians did their mummies. *Tacitus.*—Their limbs were bound separately. *Olshausen, De Wette.*—Wrapped from head to foot so closely that his freedom of motion was not impeded. *Lücke, Meyer, Trench.*—A miracle within a miracle that Lazarus was able to go forth in spite of his wrappings. *Basilius. Chrys., Aug, Lampe, Stier.*—Windings seem to have been partial. *Lange.*—The corpse had not been embalmed. *Alford*—Walking on his knees. *Pearce.*—Mummies were wrapped in fine linen in Egypt, so fine that the warp consists of 270 and woof of 170 threads to the square inch. *Wilkinson.*—ἄφετε has a triumphant tone, like the order to the cripple: "Take up thy bed," &c. *Godet.*—Rome finds authority here for priestly absolution, falsely quoting Cyril. *Rheimish Notes.*—At the very moment Jesus issued the summons Lazarus might have been conversing with the soul of some departed saint. *Bourgon.*—*Tennyson's* lines are too beautiful to be omitted:—

> "When Lazarus left his charnel-cave,
> And home to Mary's house returned,
> Was this demanded—if he yearned
> To hear her weeping by the grave?
>
> 'Where wert thou, brother, those four days?'
> There lives no record of reply,
> Which telling what it is to die
> Had surely added praise to praise.
>
> From every house the neighbours met,
> The streets were fill'd with joyful sound,
> A solemn gladness even crown'd
> The purple brows of Olivet.
>
> Behold a man raised up by Christ!
> The rest remaineth unrevealed;
> He told it not; or something sealed
> The lips of that Evangelist."—*In Memoriam.*

---

45. Then many of the Jews which came to Mary, and had seen the things which Jesus did, believed on him.

Many Jews. *Death* itself yielded more rapidly to Christ than UNBELIEF.—Demonstration that the most stupendous miracles are useless where the heart is opposed to truth.—Those believing were, doubtless, pious friends of the family from Jerusalem.—The second great spiritual miracle connected with the raising of Lazarus.

Came to Mary. The anointing alluded to (verse 2) shows her heart had reached an exalted state.—The "ointment of precious spikenard" may have been prepared for her brother.—It was reserved for Him who raised her brother, as a thank-offering of love.

Believed. Doubtless "some" believed and yet trembled with rage and fear.—Even the new life of Lazarus became a savour of death unto death. Thus every important awakening is an offence to those who love not the truth. *Lange.*—How perfectly unlike all human composition is this verse.—An angel could not write in a more completely passionless style!—Not a syllable about one of the most stupendous works ever wrought.—Not a solitary allusion to the emotions of the risen brother.—No gleam from the eternal world of the things experienced there.—Such reserve and silence evidence of the divine inspiration of Scripture.—The miracles of the blind man and Lazarus the two most noted, and Providence provided for their attestation both by friends and foes.

ἐπίστευσαν. This miracle has been t eated as an allegory of spiritual things by *Jerome, Augustine,* and others.— Obviously without historical foundation. *Heubner.*

---

46. But some of them went their ways to the Pharisees, and told them what things Jesus had done.

But. Implies not all, *some* with malice went.

Pharisees. See on John i. 24.—All knew their deadly enmity towards Jesus.—Had those who went been friends, their witness would have been noticed.—Precursors of Judas, and in a general sense types of apostates.—Treachery a mainspring of unbelief. *Lange.*—Like many a council, Pharisees sat like a "spread-out net." Hosea v. 1.—Some rulers so wicked they would stop the sun from shining had they power equal to their malice, but God maketh the wrath of man to praise Him, and the remainder of wrath He restrains.—We can do nothing against the truth but for the truth.—Devils and wicked men are, unconsciously, instruments in furthering the kingdom of Christ.—Strange that persons who went to comfort should show such malice ; but human "goodness" and divine grace are wholly distinct things.—Sterne wept over a dying ass and left his aged mother on parish charity.—Thousands

weep on Good Friday at dramatic representations of the sufferings of Christ, who "crucify him afresh" daily in their lives.—
Many weep at the imaginary trials and sorrows of a stage hero or
heroine or of a novel, who never show any sympathy with the woes
and miseries of real life.—Excitability of emotional feeling often
found in persons with much frivolity, **hardness of heart, and
capability of great cruelty.**

Had done. The *fact* could not be questioned any more than the
sun at midday. But both it and the facts could be misrepresented
and defamed.—Thus the cause of Christ, and thus His servants,
have always been treated.—What great spiritual awakening has
ever taken place but it and the instruments have been maligned
and persecuted! *Heumann.*—What Jesus "had done" could not
be denied, but He could be charged with seeking to draw away
the nation, and thus provoking the wrath of the Roman Government.—Rome, pagan and papal, and all other persecuting powers
and persons, have always endeavoured first to blacken and then to
destroy.—"But there will be a resurrection of names and reputa-
tions one day, as well as of bodies." *Milton.*

τινές. Not believers. *Stier, Alford*—Denounced Him as a sorcerer. *Euthymius.*—
As sacrilegious. *Theophylact.*—As dangerous. *Lange*—Friends of Jesus, whose intentions were good. *Origen.*—Accused Him as an impostor or magician. *Kuinoel.*—Their
motives unknown. *Tittman.*—δέ. This particle shows hostile intent. *Alford.*

---

47. Then gathered the chief priests and the Pharisees a council, and said, What do
we? for this man doeth many miracles.

Chief Priests. See on John i. 13.—A class always ready to
combine against those questioning or opposing their assumptions.—
History shows that generally they have been enemies of liberty and
progress.—Epistle to the Hebrews lays in the dust all sacerdotal
claims and pretensions now.—Believers are "a royal priesthood,"
&c. 1 Peter ii. 5, 9.

Council. Gr., "*Sanhedrim.*"—The supreme spiritual court of the
Jews, composed of seventy-one members, priests, elders, and
scribes.—Pharisees and Sadducees the parties—Caiaphas of the
latter.—The high priest its president.—Its sessions were held in
the Temple.—Its jurisdiction embraced matters of tribes, war, false
prophets, blasphemy, &c.—Its power formerly extended to capital
punishment; latterly, to excommunication.—Tradition traced it
to Moses; first named in the time of Antipater.—Enemies of Christ
have testified to the power of His doctrines in every age.

What do we? *What are we to do?*—They feel that matters cannot
stand as they are; something *must* be done.—Like Bible "fools"

(Ps. xiv. 1) they are more energetic in ruining themselves than escaping.—Not a solitary thought touching faith in this Worker of wonders.—Not a word to show that they were open to conviction or desired to know the truth.—History witnesses how the selfish fear of ecclesiastics brings on the very trouble they would avert by arbitrary acts.—They felt His claims like chains of fire; but their cry was, " Let us break his bands asunder." Ps. ii. 3.

This man. From their lips a term of contempt.—Indicates implacable hatred.

Many miracles. See on John ii. 11, 23 ; iii. 2.—Might have been said to obliterate the recognition of the miracle just wrought or to lessen its importance, or might have been an expression of fear that He would perform yet other miracles. *Lange.*—These wonders of LOVE and POWER press on their consciences (John x. 32), and will press for ever.—What testimony from enemies, who never dreamed it would be given to the world.—Note the beginning of that stream of Divine Power which bore away Levitical customs, Jewish rites, Greek philosophy, and the gorgeous splendours of heathen superstitions.—The success of the Gospel ever fills its adversaries with dread.—" Art thou come to torment us before our time ?" a common feeling and a common cry.

συνέδριον. A sitting together, an assembly.—*Sanhedrim*, more accurate form. *Schaff.*—ποιοῦμεν· What shall we do ? *Beza.*—What are we doing ? *Dodd., Alford.*—What must we do ? *Lightfoot, Bourgon.*—ὅτι. Something must be done. *Tholuck.*—σημεία. Not true miracles, but wonders. *Kuinoel.*

---

48. If we let him thus alone, all men will believe on him; and the Romans shall come and take away both our place and nation.

Let him alone. They feel that either He or they must fall.—Theirs a kingdom of darkness and falsehood.—His of light and truth.—The handwriting on the wall appals them as Belshazzar of old.

All men, &c. The wicked habitually charge the results of their crime on the innocent.—Thus *Tertullian* tells us if the Tiber overflow its banks, or the Nile fails to produce a harvest, or if earthquake, pestilence, or famine ruin the hopes of men, straightway the cry is heard, " CHRISTIANOS AD LEONES."—The wicked rulers of the earth have usually left God out of their reckoning.—Here the fear is that the people would accept Him as King and Messiah, and then *their* " craft " would come to an end.—Forty years after those who BELIEVED on Christ escaped the avenging fury of the Romans.—Josephus notes an unaccountable suspension of the siege by Titus, so that the Christians left Jerusalem and fled to

Pella.—The rulers by these very acts brought down the ruin which by them they intended to avert.—A *wicked* and *empty* fear that all will believe on Him.—A *wicked* and *empty* fear that this would cause the Romans to invade them.—A *wicked* and *empty* fear that they would then put an end to the Jewish common-wealth. *Lange.*—In all these charges there was a false assumption, and they knew it.—Their course was defiantly *Jesuitical*, doing evil that good might come.—Thus Rome charged the Reformers, and now charges Protestantism with the guilt of socialism, communism, anti-Christianity, and all those other forms of evil and unbelief of which she herself has been and still is the fruitful parent.

Place. Among nations; their national existence among earthly powers.

Nation. Not only subdued, but as individuals reduced to abject slavery.—Both these things literally happened to them.—Thus awakening the fears of the people they hoped to stir them up against the Lord.—The policy of cowardice a policy of intimidation and terrorism.—The false Church of those days, as ever since, cruel and bloodthirsty.

ἀφῶμεν. That left alone and making Himself king, &c. *Alford.*—All would believe and become *peaceful*, and refuse to join to fight the Romans. *Aug.*—All this fear was feigned; they were conspiring against the Romish yoke, but, because they could not use Jesus, they would put him out of the way, yet instead of perishing for receiving they were ruined for rejecting Him. *Kuinoel.*—Or that the Pharisees really believed Him to be the *Messiah*, but, so opposed to all their hopes, they would rather have no Messiah than such a one. *Markland.*—ἀροῦσιν. Annihilate. *Tholuck.*—Will wrest from us; this is more in accordance with their egotistical sentiment. *Nonnus, Lange.*—τὸν τόπον. Variously constructed: 1. As the *Temple*, as the central sanctuary. *Origen, Lücke, De Wette, Hengst.*—2. As the country. *Luther.*—Country and people. *Bengel, Luthardt, Alford.*—3. As the holy city, the seat of the Sanhedrim and hierarchy. *Chrys., Meyer.*—The expression an unconscious prophecy. *Lange.*

---

49. And one of them, named Caiaphas, being the high priest that same year, said unto them, Ye know nothing at all.

Caiaphas. High Priest under Tiberius; said by Josephus, who calls him Joseph Caiaphas, to have obtained the office by a bribe. —Appointed by the Procurator Valerius Gratus A.D. 25; son-in-law of Annas.—He held the office under Pontius Pilate, and was deposed by Proconsul Vitellius, A.D. 36.—Was succeeded by Jonathan, son of Annas.—Caiaphas was a Sadducee (Acts v. 17), and this party had already begun to show decided hostility to Jesus.—Their active enmity is doubtless excited by the resurrection of Lazarus.—Now, in the person of Caiaphas, they take the foremost place in the persecution; for a time they exceeded the

Pharisees in bitterness against the Christian Church. Acts iv. 1,
2. *Lange.*—He unconsciously acted as though that year might
end his office, as it did.—He was the high priest who ignorantly
sacrificed the Lamb of God.

That same year. That *memorable* year, the *death year* of the Lord
of Life!—It was the chiefest of the seventy weeks of Daniel the
prophet.—The fortieth year before Jerusalem was destroyed.

Said, Blinded by bigotry, he felt no guilt, saw no need of an
atonement, though he sat on the high priest's throne, wearing the
sacred vestments of Aaron, and his duty was to pronounce the
blessing upon the completion of the sacrifice.—It was the power
of God that constrained him to become an involuntary witness of
the true Sacrifice!

Ye know nothing. It seems their counsels were divided.—
Evidently a few opposed any violent measures.—The protests of
Joseph and Nicodemus were doubtless heard.—He well knew their
minds, hence his pretence of a righteous indignation.—A powerful
leader here, as too often, carries the multitude with him.—In
eternity many who now task their mightiest energies to sway
others will wish they had less influence to give account for.—With
a proud dictatorial tone he forces them to face the issue.—As we
all wish to get rid of this man, *Let Him die!* our course is so plain and
the urgency of the case so great that discussion is useless.—Here
is the disturber of our power, let us destroy Him and we will have
peace.

Nothing. Ye lack the kind of knowledge, the *state-craft* that is
now demanded.—Persecutors have always found it harder to
silence conscience than to destroy life.

καϊάφας. Tradition makes him a convert to Christianity. *Assemani.*—Annas and
Caiaphas are coupled by Luke, and some suppose they acted in turn.—Others that
Caiaphas was called high priest and Annas was *ex* high priest.—Others that Annas was
vicar. *Kuinoel.*—This deputy might enter the holy of holies. *Lightfoot.*—Some think
that some had proposed to forbid Him preaching (Acts iv. 8). *Pearce.*—Our Lord had
given no just cause for legal proceeding, hence Caiaphas feared their hearts might
fail.—He concedes no crime could be pleaded, and they were left to expediency.
Campbell.—Their fierce contests for honour ended in having several who served in
turn. *Augustine*—The key of his words is found in his being a Sadducee; the priests
were generally of the same sect. *Maurice.*—ἐνιαυτοῦ ἐκείνου. The year of Christ's
death.—The Evangelist deemed it superfluous to add a reference to the duration of the
office. *Meyer, Alford.*—An intimation also that the office was debased at that time by
frequent alterations. *Lange.*

---

50. Nor consider that it is expedient for us, that one man should die for the people,
and that the whole nation perish not.

Expedient. This word is often used now to represent *policy* rather
than *principle.* But the Greek means that which is *profitable,* and

is consistent with moral integrity. " Expediency," in the sense
of Caiaphas, has been carried to its extreme limits by the Jesuits.
—For the "GREATER GLORY OF GOD" every crime in the Decalogue has been committed. *Steinmetz.*—A strange scene, the high
priest of a holy, merciful God, in his official character advocating
the murder of a guiltless man as the means of preserving the
nation! He virtually decides that their victim, *innocent* or guilty,
must be put to death. Of what consequence is a *single* man? it is
the *many* to whom regard is due. The world cares nothing for
the small ones. What if they be unjustly dealt with so long as the
others are satisfied? *Gossner.* What is *morally wrong* can never
be *ecclesiastically* or *politically right.* The ostensible ground in
this case was patriotism, public zeal, loyalty. The motive on which
a deed of sin is done is not that which a man allows to others, or
whispers to himself. Better perish the whole nation than slay the
innocent.—Eternity alone will reveal all the deeds of wickedness
perpetrated both in Church and State under the maxim here laid
down.—But that very calamity which they sought to escape by
committing a crime that crime brought upon them.—" His blood be
upon us and upon our children," the most fearful prayer ever heard
under heaven, was answered in the most fearful ruin ever known.—
A warning spectacle, the Covenant people relapsing into the worst
heathenism.—Following the counsel of Caiaphas, they became in
intention votaries of Moloch.—After Jerusalem was destroyed they
fell into the suicidal despair of Hinduism.—In their Talmud, into
a mythology more odious than that of Greece or Rome.—Thus,
too, in Christian times Romanism has relapsed into the most abominable heathenism. *Lange.*

Die for the people. The idea of expiatory sacrifice common to all
nations—*Altars, victims, sacrifices, temples,* and *priests,* have
absorbed treasure by millions in every age.—The dearer the
victim and the more costly the more prevailing with the gods.—
Hecatombs of *animals* as well as *men* were offered.—In the heroic
ages princes and kings slew the victim to add solemnity to the
scene.—Wine, incense, prayer, and music accompanied the offering.
The remarkable point in this Judgment of Caiaphas is that it
contains the central doctrine of the New Testament, the necessity
of the innocent suffering for the guilty.—He has stated it in words
John could have adopted. But what a difference between holy
love and heartless tyrannical policy.—He unintentionally and
unconsciously utters the great word ATONEMENT!—In God's purposes of mercy, death is the way to life: shame the path to glory:
the weakness of the Cross power unto salvation.—The high priest
was the interpreter of the Urim and Thummim, and, like Balaam
of old, he is made to declare JEHOVAH's *purpose.*—Willing to curse,

he must pronounce a blessing on the true Israel.—Unconsciously he confirms the prediction of the law and the prophets.—Similar instances of involuntary witnessing to truth we have in Pharaoh, Saul, Nebuchadnezzar, Pilate.—God uses bad men as well as good for His own ends.—He can speak wisdom even through the mouth of an ass.—The title over the Cross, though put up in scorn and contempt, was a veritable prophecy.—The irony of Providence exercised over human perversity.—He, believing in neither angel nor spirit, is compelled to speak under spiritual influence.—Caiaphas and Pilate both condemned Jesus, yet both testified to His innocence.—Both as witnesses used terms whose meaning far transcended their own ideas.—Caiaphas testifies to Christ as HIGH PRIEST.—Pilate as KING.—How often we do the very things which we vainly try to defeat.—There is scarcely a doubt that Caiaphas assigned a reason which was not his or *their reason.*—The influence of Jesus and the power of the Sanhedrim could not long co-exist.

People. Usual term for the chosen race; they regarded themselves as favourites of heaven, as having a monopoly in God.—Privileges abused always produce greater depravity : " If the light that is in thee become darkness," &c.

Whole nation perish not. Jesus shall be a *guiltless* and *involuntary* sacrifice to secure the good of " the whole mass of the people ! "—Truth perfected in the *mouth;* falsehood perfected in the *heart.*—Blasphemy in words of prayer; prophecy in words of diabolical policy.—They would kill Him because He made alive.—Unconsciously and unwillingly the Jewish priesthood expired with a prophecy of Christ's atoning death, which it typically foreshadowed. *Lange.*

διαλογίζεσθε. What terrible instruments are words, more terrible than rifles or swords.—How often are we unconscious proclaimers of the Divine purposes. *Maurice.*—συμφέρει. When Farel entered Geneva, Papists cried, "Better he perish than the town be disturbed ;" the reformer replied, "Speak not the words of Caiaphas, but God's truth." *Trapp.*—The custom of human sacrifice is endorsed even by *Cicero.*

---

51. And this spake he not of himself; but being high priest that year, he prophesied that Jesus should die for that nation.

And this. This verse and next added to explain the singular fact. —A note characteristic of John, but clearly of the inspiration of the Spirit.—The human, the organ for the divine, in revelation.—Hence the wonderful variety of Scripture.—Each writer has stamped his production with his own mental peculiarities, and yet in all there is a unity that knows no discord and a faithfulness that

knows no error.—The Bible a standing miracle in the Church and
to the world.

Not of himself. By the Spirit he uttered that which he did not
understand.

High Priest. He was eleven years in office under Pontius Pilate.

That year. See on verse 49.—According to Levitical Law this
office was *for life* and confined to Aaron's family.—Through
sacrilegious ambition it had even been put up *for sale.*

He prophesied. Prophecy in the mouth no infallible evidence of
grace in the heart.—The wicked decree, as *he* apprehended it, had
the force of an official prediction.—The fearful double meaning of
his speech : 1. With regard to his intention ; 2. With regard to
the meaning of the Spirit.—Man, master of his intention, but not
of the full import of his words and acts.—Tne false high priest a
prophet of the true High Priest and His sacrifice.—Involuntarily,
while uttering the counsel of depravity, he uttered the counsel of
eternal wisdom and love.—Romanists apply this to popes : " Popes
though wicked may still be the organs of truth." *Stolberg.*—As a
hallowed charm still lingers over the ruins of Palestine, so God had
not yet quite deserted the wreck of the Jewish Church.—When
the veil of the Temple was rent, and Christ uttered " It is finished,"
the glory finally departed.—The enemies of Christ have ever, and
must ever, advance the very cause they hate.—Even a statue
often holds a torch to light the living on their way.—Not everyone doing a just act is a just man, nor one that prophesies a
prophet.—Even devils were constrained at times to act as *confessors.*
Luke iv. 34.—He who made the dumb brute rebuke the madness
of another prophet, made this man the organ, unconsciously, of
declaring the great mystery hidden for ages from the sons of men.

Should die. See on verse 50.—Gr., *was about to die.*—Declaratory
of the purpose of God and of the action of Providence which
caused the wicked decree to be so worded that it expresses the
doctrine of Redemption.

That nation. In the sense of Caiaphas, if Christ die, the Jewish
nation lives, in the ordinary sense ; in the higher sense, if Christ
die, the nation lives as a redeemed people ; and thus a *great nation*
is formed from the scattered children of God. *Gerlach.*—This
proposition of Caiaphas, from his point of view, a violation of the
law of nations.—But the Cross, the intended instrument of death,
was to be a message of love to all nations.—The appointed punishment for rebels and slaves is to bind man in one common bond of
family life.

ἐνιαυτοῦ. A greater, a universal sacrifice should be offered. *Tholuck.*—Final year of the Levitical priesthood. *Stier.*—Some official distinction from Annas—now lost. *Alford.*—Alludes to circumstances not recorded. *Bourgon.*—προεφήτευσεν. In accordance with the appointment of the high priest to prophesy by the 'Urim and Thummim, *i.e*, to utter the decision assignable to divine causality. *Lange, Alford, Meyer.*—But that oracle had long since been lost. *De Wette.*—A grand *irony of Providence* making the retiring priesthood foretell the true sin offering. *Stier.*—Although shorn of its glory in later times, the people still had faith in the office. *Meyer.*—A blessing was attached to it which brought deliverance to the pious. *Schöttgen.*

---

52. And not for that nation only, but also that he should gather together in one the children of God, that were scattered abroad.

That nation only. " He is the propitiation for our sins ; not for ours only, but also for the sins of the whole world." 1 John ii. 2.—" He, by the grace of God, should taste death for everyone." Heb. ii. 9.

Gather. See on John vi. 35.—Jews regarded Christ's work as a scattering and destroying of the ancient people of God.—Instead of that, it is the creation of a new and real people of God, gathered from abroad. *Lange.*—Prophecy had foretold the calling of the Gentiles; here it is repeated.—Not the LAW which the Jews boasted in as bond of union, but the *Death of Christ* ignoring this bond.—The Jews repelled all hope of union with Gentiles.—This work of " gathering " shall go on till the last of the " scattered " has been brought home.—A work that none can hinder or frustrate, for it is secured by the will and word of Omnipotence. —It is the assurance of this divine work of " gathering " which supplies the preacher of the Gospel with confidence and hope — " They shall come from the east and from the west," &c.—The Spirit sees these " kings and priests " in exile, and calmly contemplates that day when Christ shall be " the Firstborn among many brethren."

In one. Into *one nation ;* an antithesis to the " nation " of Caiaphas. —There can be no perfect oneness save by living fellowship with Christ.—Councils may decree unity and rulers attempt to enforce it, but the love of Christ alone can bind mankind in immortal brotherhood.—" That they all may call on the name of the Lord and serve him with one consent." Zeph. iii. 9.—" That they all may be one ; as thou, Father, art in me, and I in thee." John xvii. 21.—Not agreement in creeds or ritual or Church order merely, but life flowing into the soul from THE RESURRECTION AND THE LIFE.—All societies on earth but the Church of Christ are founded in selfishness.

Children of God. See on John vi. 44, 64, 70.—The Spirit regards their sonship as now existing.—He reads the names of the " scattered " ones as already written in God's heart.—Election is of

grace, not works: "It is not of him that willeth," &c. Rom. ix.
16.—Neither philosophy nor learning ever led men to heaven:
"They who glory, glory in the Lord." 1 Cor. i. 26—31.—God
predestined believers to be His sons; chosen in Christ before the
creation of the world. Eph. i. 4—6.—Predestination implies foreknowledge, and that implies calling, justifying, glorifying. Rom.
viii. 29, 30.—The objection that such sovereign acts are unjust is
answered in Rom. ix. 21.—Election to eternal life implies election
to holiness.—Faith and repentance are God's gifts.—Salvation is
by grace; grace is love, not such as He has for angels, but for
enemies.—Other doctrines imply election.—Regeneration is not
effected save by the "mighty power of God."—"Of his own will
begat he us," &c.—Our Lord chose to raise some from the dead
while in the flesh and not others.—Paul was not the first preacher
of this doctrine, for our Lord Himself refers to it. Matt. xi. 25,
26; Luke iv. 25—27.—This doctrine also conforms to the experience
of all Christians.—"*Unto him,*" &c. Rev. i. 5.—The theology of
the heart is the same among all believers, although their views
differ.—"By the grace of God I am what I am;" "He worketh all
things after the counsel of his own will." Eph. i. 11.—"He doeth
according to his will in the armies of heaven." Dan. iv. 35.—
God's will is necessarily good; it is not that He wills and *therefore*
the thing is right; but He wills *because* it is right.—Relation of the
finite to the infinite, the conditioned to the absolute, must ever be
a mystery to us.—No difficulty emerges in theology which has not
first appeared in philosophy. *Hamilton.*—God's government of the
universe both in Nature and Providence is in harmony with the
doctrine of election.—It is full of comfort, for if men were left to
their own courses all would remain in sin, and perish.—Had not
Christ by His almighty word healed some, not a leper would have
been cured.—The *practical* effect of this doctrine should be to lead
each sinner in his *helplessness* to the throne of grace to ask for
mercy.—Thus the blind man, desperate in his misery, urged his
plea on Jesus.—No soul was ever rejected that came in the same
spirit to Christ.—We know not who are elected, but we know
whether we have come to Christ for salvation.—This is the important question to each and all: "Dost thou believe on the Son of
God?"—Election is in the divine mind, and being unrevealed as to its
objects, is no rule of duty; but we are commanded to believe, and
he who believeth shall be saved.—"Him that cometh to ME I will
in no wise cast out." See on John vi. 37.—Had not our Lord
loved Lazarus, He never would have raised him from the dead.—
Did He not love the sinner, He never would send the Spirit to
convert him.

Scattered. Our Lord had spoken of "other sheep, not of this

fold." John x. 6.—His arms extended on the cross symbolize the
wide embrace of His mercy and His gathering His elect from afar.
—Note the enlargement of the Spirit on Caiaphas's prophecy,
teaching—1, *for whom* Christ died, (1) the Jews, (2) *the children*
of God scattered abroad, (*a*) then living, (*b*) throughout all
time ; 2, *the purpose* of His death concerning these, *to gather them
together in one.*—Christ's dying is, 1, the great *attractive* of our
hearts ; 2, the great *centre* of our unity ; (1) by the merit of His
death recommending all in *one* to the favour of God, (2) by the
motive of His death drawing each to the love of every other.
Henry.

τὰ τέκνα τοῦ θεοῦ. All the future children of God. *Meyer, Alford, Trench.*—Among
the heathen. *Euthym.*—In a ιredestinarian sense. *Calvin, Meyer.*—Children of God
who are longing for Christ. *Tholuck, Godet, Luthardt*—The children of God generally
among the Jews. *Lange.*—συναγάγῃ. *To lead or bring together.*—Implies *power* : " Thy
people shall be willing," &c. *Gossner.*

53. Then from that day forth they took counsel together for to put him to death.

Took counsel. They long had sought to kill Him, now they begin
to bring out their designs.—The question is how they shall put
Him to death ; He had long been under their ban.—Evil men confirm themselves and one another in evil practices by conferences.
—What one or two would shrink from, a " committee " or
" council " will perpetrate.—But that which their wickedness
determined against Him He turned to purposes of mercy.—
Although their malice resolves to kill Him, a thousand "councils"
could not have accomplished it.—His death a free, loving, laying
down of His life for His sheep. John x. 17, 18.—Wonderful how
the cruelty of man and the cunning of hell were overruled for the
fulfilment of type and prophecy, for the execution of God's decree,
for providing the means of mercy to a lost world, and for the
highest manifestation of the Divine glory the universe has ever
witnessed.—A lesson to faith to the end of time.—Human actions
and God's purposes are ever in view in Scripture.

To death. Before this they had secretly but informally plotted.—
They had resisted and persecuted Him and had excommunicated
His disciples.—They would have formally excommunicated Him
from the synagogue, but they feared the people.—His friends,
Joseph and Nicodemus, if present, were compelled to silence, else
they might have been condemned and murdered too.—Little did
they think that His death would give life to the world ; that He
would rise again and found a Church against which " the gates of
hell shall not prevail ;" that His crown of thorns would become a

rich diadem, and His Cross a throne of eternal glory. So **man** *proposes* but God *disposes.*

---

54. Jesus therefore walked no more openly among the Jews; but went thence unto a country near to the wilderness, into a city called Ephraim, and there continued with his disciples.

Openly. He would not tempt them to persecute the "Lord's anointed."—He will not expose Himself to the danger of being prematurely sacrificed: His "hour had not yet come."—Neither will He abridge their day of grace, now fast drawing to a close.— "Grace alone can teach us when to fight and when to fly." *Luther.*—Probable allusion to these trials; " Ye have continued with me in my temptations." Luke xxii. 28.—His brethren at the Feast of Tabernacles desired Him to manifest His glory. John vii. 4.—He revealed His Divinity, and the rulers hated Him for it.—Now hell and earth arm for the final assault to chase Him out of the world.—The disciples saw approaching that *hour* of which they had often heard.—He would teach them that it is not at all times the duty of Christians to be martyrs: "If they persecute you in one city, flee ye into another."—But when the alternative is to deny their Lord or die, millions of witnesses reply : " Be it known unto thee, O king, WE WILL NOT SERVE THY GODS !" Dan. iii. 18.— Had He told them that He claimed to be Jehovah, they would have stoned Him.—Retiring, He leaves this miracle to tell them who He is.—The rich man in Hades thought his brethren would repent if Lazarus or one from the dead went to them.—Here a Lazarus does come forth from the dead, and instead of repenting, the Jews, who had Moses and the prophets, conspire to murder both Him who raised and him who was raised.

Wilderness. See on John i. 25.—Sometimes covered with very thin grass during February and March.—If followed, He can easily escape amid its countless hills.—Christ in the wilderness at the beginning and the end of His ministry.—The Son of David, the Messiah, the Hope of Israel, outlawed and banished!—"Many causes made Him obnoxious to the rulers, although the immediate occasion of this persecution was the fame of the resurrection of Lazarus. If His teaching were once received, their reign was over: a teaching which abolished the pretensions of a priesthood, by making every man his own priest, to offer spiritual sacrifices to God; which identified Religion with Goodness, making spiritual excellence, not ritual regularity, the righteousness which God accepts ; which brought God within the reach of the sinner and the fallen ; which simplified the whole matter by making Religion a thing of the heart, and not of rabbinical learning or theology ;

such teaching swept away all the exclusive pretensions of Pharisaism, made the life which they had been building up with so much
toil for years, time wasted, and reduced their whole existence to a
lie. This was the ground of their hatred to the Son of Man ; but
this was not the ground they put forward." *Robertson.*

Ephraim. The location of this place is utterly unknown at present.
—Some make it identical with Ophrah (Josh. xviii. 23), others
with Ephron, eight miles north of Jerusalem.—The sites of several
cities standing in our Lord's day have not yet been identified.

Continued. Gr., *tarried.*—Just after the splendour of His miracle
many must have wondered to see Him shrink away into the
wilderness.—No human being ever did or ever would act thus :
" This is the finger of God." Exodus viii. 19.—A strange
contrast to us, but must have been far greater to His disciples.—
Yesterday, the dead obeying His voice ; to-day, He flees like a
timid bird.—His ways, though mysterious, are directed by Divine
wisdom and love.—If Jerusalem *loses* His presence, Ephraim *gains.*
—Doubtless there are those in heaven with Him who will bless
God to all eternity for that visit.—If we do not avoid our persecutor, when we can do so without sin, we make ourselves
responsible for his offence. *Origen.*

ἀπῆλθεν. The tumultuous crowd of believers compel Him to leave. *Stier.*—He went
to Ephraim, twenty miles distant from Jerusalem. *Jerome.*—Others eight miles.
Eusebius.—ἐρήμου. A kind of thin pasture land without settlers or water. *Porter.*—A
uniform desert tract between Jerusalem or the hill country of Judea and the valley of
the Jordan. *Lange.*—'Εφραὶμ. The Ophrah of Joshua xviii. 23.—Same as Taiyibeh of
our day, twenty Roman miles from Jerusalem. *Robinson, Stanley, Van De Velde.*—
Unknown. *Alford.*—The family at Bethany would find it unsafe to remain, and
followed the Lord to Galilee, of which they were natives. *Greswell.*—διετριβε. The
place fitted for a temporary sojourn. *Lange.*

---

55. And the Jews' passover was nigh at hand : and many went out of the country up
to Jerusalem before the passover, to purify themselves.

Passover. See on John ii. 13.—The time was in March and April.
—The fourth Passover, according to the ordinary chronology.—At
this feast He became " OUR PASSOVER." 1 Cor. v. 7.—*Theirs* was
the shadow, *ours* the substance.—Their door-posts marked with
the blood of an animal, our souls sprinkled with the blood of
Christ.—They went up to Jerusalem to be purified, we to the
throne of the heavenly grace.

Country. Judea generally, not Peræa, the country last spoken of.

Up. To the metropolis it is always *up ;* but specially so as Jerusalem
stands on the mountains of Judea, and it is an ascent from every
side.—Heaven is gained by toil ; no one is converted by chance.

—The " Hill of God " can only be ascended by earnest prayer, faith that triumphs over difficulties, and self-denial that stumbles not at the greatness of the sacrifice. *Flavel.*

Purify. See on John ii. 6 ; iii. 25.—Jewish law demanded cleansing according to the sin, from one to six days.—While engaged in *purifications* they were plotting the Lord's death.—So Romanists and others show zeal, even to slaying, for the rites and ceremonies of their church, while they are breaking each law of the Decalogue. —They will readily wink at the violation of every commandment of God if men will only take their yoke.—The religion which expends itself in zeal for outward formalities is worthless ; and it is always *intolerant, persecuting,* and *cruel.* *Owen.*

χώρας. Simply that region. *Bengel.—Country,* in contrast to Jerusalem. *Lange —* ἀγνίσωσιν. The washing of disciples' feet connected with the Passover. *Besser.*--From ceremonial uncleanness. *Lightfoot.*—Those who failed to celebrate the Passover at the right time. being unable to do it, might do it a month later, according to the exact rules, at the right place. *Ewald.*

---

56. Then sought they for Jesus, and spake among themselves, as they stood in the temple, What think ye, that he will not come to the feast ?

Sought. Indicates how eagerly all the people were expecting His presence.—Doubtless many were seeking Him with bad intent.— Our Lord never acted *recklessly,* nor in *bravado,* nor in the spirit of one *seeking martyrdom.*—It would have been better for His Church had His followers been more careful to follow His example. —He hid Himself from danger when duty did not require exposure. *Lange.*—Note, Christ *retires* Himself for a season before His last great work.—It is well to be alone and still before undertaking any great work for God, more especially if it is likely, as in His case, to bring sorrow and suffering.—Often have the enemies of Christianity " sought " Him since in the *sins* of His followers, to gratify their malice against the Master.—But the day will come when the eternal destiny of all men will be decided by their relation to Jesus of Nazareth.—Sins, faults, and infirmities will be nothing in that day in comparison with, " Ye did it unto ME."— Virtue, lofty character, and what the world calls " honourable and noble actions," will fade away before the fact, " Ye did it not to ME."

What think ye ? Singular, they do not converse about their rites and ceremonies, but about Christ.—A sort of betting whether He will come or not. *Lange.*—His enemies *cannot* banish the thought of Him from their minds, and His friends *will not.*—How often since have ecclesiastical powers, though supported by the arm of

state authority, quailed at the name of some *Luther* or *Knox!*—
It is a sad state of things when a man's religious duties are
squared by a neighbour's opinions.—"It is a part of a great
mind to smile at insults." *Erasmus.*—The habit of self-torment-
ing, on account of what others may think or say, is despicable.

Will he not? Some infer from the condition of things He will not
come; others question this.—The splendour of the recent miracle
had filled the land.—The multitude, with their minds full of the
wonder at Bethany, anxiously inquire.—Hints the *rulers* were the
enemies, and the people the friends, of a Reformer.—How little any
of them know of the eternal will which underlies his movements —
With Him is neither rashness nor fear; calmly and steadfastly He
fulfils the purposes of God.—His servants, like Himself, are immortal' till their work be done. *Whitfield.*

Τί δοκεῖ. Some make two instead of one question. *Campbell.*—ὅτι οὐ μὴ λθη. That
He will not come. *Meyer.*—Has not come. *Vulgate.*

---

57. Now both the chief priests and the Pharisees had given a commandment, that, if
any man knew where he were, he should shew it, that they might take him.

Commandment. Explains the questioning of the preceding verse.
—Doubtless spread abroad throughout the land by special orders
of the rulers.—Carried all the force and effect of a decree of excommunication.—During the ages of Romish ascendancy such an
interdict embittered life in all its relations.—The victim's property
was taken by the priests or transferred to his friends.—His death,
civil and religious, was declared, and the funeral celebrated.—
How this edict accomplished the reverse of their design.—An
obedient son of the devil was Judas, who obeyed this decree and
delivered the Lord into their hands.—He would plead, "The
Church hath commanded it."—Under the same plea what crimes
known and unknown have been perpetrated!

Any man. Probably this was specially aimed at the Bethany
family (chap. xii. 10).

Show it. All the world, friends and enemies, fulfil this edict.—He
soon gives information concerning Himself, for, knowing all their
plans, He willingly comes forth.—There is a PLAN which they can
neither hinder nor accelerate.—Unconscious instruments all, in
working out the eternal ordination of heaven. Acts ii. 23.—They
anticipated a festive joy, and to do God a service by slaying His
Son at the Passover! *Gossner.*—But the event was at hand to
which all dispensations and revelations pointed, the centre of

History, the solution of all problems in Nature and Providence, the wonder of heaven, the despair of hell, the joy and glory of earth.—The slain Lamb in the midst of the throne is alone able and worthy to open the sealed book and expound its contents, and to Him shall ever ascend the praises of the universe. Rev. v.

καὶ. Omitted. *Lach.*, *Tisch.*, and many *Codices.*—Recommended by *Cod. D.*, and others *Lange.*—ἐντολὴν. Must be set aside for the plural ἐντολάς, *orders,* on the authority of *Cod. Sin.* and *B.*, &c. *Schaff.*—The High Priest had issued the arrest, and yet in all Ephraim there was not a traitor.--On this decree of arrest Judas acted, and may have silenced his conscience by pretending obedience to the church. *Hengstenberg.*

John 12

1. Then Jesus six days before the passover came to Bethany, where Lazarus was which had been dead, whom he raised from the dead.

Then Jesus six days. Gr., *Then Jesus, therefore, six days, &c.* The οὖν, *therefore*, designed merely to resume the story of Jesus. *Meyer.*—Declares simply that He went consciously and freely to meet death. *Luthardt.*—Preparatory to the fact that He showed Himself to the Sanhedrists in the most public manner. The edict concerning the *hidden* Jesus is answered by Him with the palm-entry. *Lange.*—Though He gives place for a time to the rage of His foes, He returns, in accordance with His Divine vocation. Duty must not be abandoned by a preacher or by any Christian on account of danger.—Love spares no cost.

Six days. Until the death of Jesus.—The six days of our Lord's great toil and labour—Passion-days. Isaiah lxiii. 1.—The number *six* is symbolical of work, toil, and need.

Passover. See on chapter i. 29, 36, and chapter ii. 13.

Bethany. See on chapter xi. 1, Our Lord's earthly *home*.

Lazarus was. See on chapter xi. 1.—A continual living sign of the glory of Jesus; a motive: 1, for the anointing of Mary; 2, for the palm-entry ; 3, for the hatred of the Sanhedrim.

Had been dead. See note. For proof of death see on chap. xi. 39.

Whom He raised. See on chapter xi.—Three different meetings with the Lord: 1, the visit of Jesus: Lazarus probably at his business, Martha serving, Mary learning at Jesus' feet (Luke x.) ; 2, the return of Jesus: Lazarus in the grave, Martha busy about the grave, Mary with her tears at the feet of Jesus (John xi.) ; 3, the departure of Jesus: Lazarus at the table, participating in the feast, Martha, the festive hostess, Mary, with the costly ointment, at Jesus' feet (John xii. 3). Or; 1, the school of the word; 2, the battle-ground of distress; 3, the feast of salvation. *Schaff.*

ἐξ ἡμερῶν. The 15th of Nisan was the dying day of Jesus, a Friday; six days before, therefore, was the Sabbath (the 9th of Nisa). We learn here that a day intervened between the departure of Jesus from Ephraim (and Jericho) and the palm-entry on Sunday; this day is passed over by the Synoptists, who place the palm-entry in immediate connection with the departure from Jericho. In accordance with the more exact statement of John, we must suppose that Jesus left Jericho on Friday, in company with the festive caravan, and arrived in the neighbourhood of the Mount of Olives. Here they rested during the Sabbath. On the evening of that day after the legal Sabbath time, the meal was prepared for Him, at which the anointing occurred. *Lange.*—The supper at Bethany was probably on the Sabbath before His death. It was on a Sabbath—*the* Sabbath before *that great* Sabbath, on which He *rested* in the grave and fulfilled the Sabbath and prepared the grave as a place of rest for all who pass from this life in His faith and fear. *Wordsworth* —ὁ τεθνηκὼς. Wanting in *Cod. Sin, B. L. X.*—Bracketed. *Lach., Alford.*—Omitted. *T.sch., Westcott and Hort.*—Probably this purposely significant term was employed as expressive of the fact that a man who lately had been dead did, by means of the miracle of Christ, appear as one of the guests at the feast. It is, however, superfluous, the fact being sufficiently indicated without it. *Schaff.*—ἤγειρεν. Add ὁ Ἰησοῦς. *Cod. Sin., A. B. D. E. G. Tisch, Alford, &c.*

---

2. There they made him a supper; and Martha served : but Lazarus was one of them that sat at the table with him.

Supper. Matt. xxvi. 6; Mark xiv. 3. *Dinner* or *feast.* It was the chief meal of the Jews, as also the Greeks and Romans, taken after the work and heat of the day, early in the evening, and often prolonged into the night. *Schaff.*—The Jews were fond of giving entertainments at the close of the Sabbath.—Even in extreme persecution, God does not leave His own without comfort and refreshment.—A friend of Jesus should make any sacrifice, even to the choicest of his possessions, to show his love to his Saviour. *Cramer.*—This festive celebration a symbol of the feasts of the living communion in the Church, and of the heavenly feast. *Lange.*—All Christ's friends, when they have been awakened by Him, sup with Him in the Kingdom of Grace (Rev. iii. 20), and when He shall have aroused them from bodily death at the last day, they shall sit with Him at His table in the Kingdom of Glory. Luke xiv. 15; xxii. 30.

Martha. See on chapter xi. 1. See also on Luke x. 38-41.

Served. She was formerly reproved for being *troubled with much serving;* but she did not, therefore, leave off all *serving*, like some, who, being reproved, rush from one extreme to another. *Henry.*—Martha *serveth,* whenever a believing soul devotes itself to the worship of the Lord. *Alcuin* —Better a *waiter* at Christ's table than a *guest* at the table of a prince.

Lazarus . . . sat at the table. Gr, *reclined.*—This meal a physical proof of his resurrection, as afterwards, in the case of our Lord Himself. Luke xxiv. 41-43.—He who had lain in the tomb four days, alive and sitting at the side of Jesus! This calls forth from Mary the anointing which testifies to her gratitude and love.—Those whom Christ has *raised up* to a spiritual life, are made *to sit together with Him.* Ephesians ii. 6.—" Lazarus is one of them that sit at table when those who have been raised from the death of sin rejoice together with the righteous, in the presence of truth, and are fed with the gifts of heavenly grace." *Alcuin.*—The presence of Lazarus at the festal board points to the glorious consummation of faith and hope, when all Christ's *raised ones* shall sit at "the marriage supper of the Lamb." Rev. xix. 9.

διηκόνει. The tense of this verb differs from that of the others in the verse, and implies the continued act of serving, whilst "made a feast" is the statement of the fact as the whole. *Ellicott.*

---

3. Then took Mary a pound of ointment of spikenard, very cost'y, and anointed the feet of Jesus, and wiped his feet with her hair: and the house was filled with the odour of the ointment.

Mary. See on chapter xi. 1.—John alone gives the name.—Matthew and Mark say "a woman."

A pound, &c. Precise statements characteristic of John. Chap. xix. 39; xxi. 11.—"An alabaster box of very precious ointment." Matt. xxvi. 7.—"An alabaster box of ointment of spikenard very precious." Mark xiv. 3.—This unwonted measure of ointment an expression of love. *Olshausen.*

Anointed. Here is a table spread before Him in the presence of His enemies, and His head is anointed with oil. Psalm xxiii. 5.—God's *Anointed* should be our *Anointed*—with the ointment of our best affection and service.

The feet. According to Matthew, she anoints the head of Jesus; likewise, according to Mark, breaking the flask, however. According to Matthew, she pours it on His head; so, too, according to Mark; John gives prominence to the fact that she anointed His feet and dried them with her hair. Manifestly this latter item does not exclude the former ones. In John, however, this strong expression of adoration and devotion is the main point. *Lange.*

Wiped. Gr., *wiped off, wiped dry.* A similar act to that of the woman who was "a sinner." Luke vii. 37.—From this coincidence, as well as from the name of Simon in Luke, some have, without ground, identified this history with hers (see note, chapter xi. 1).

House was filled, &c. Peculiar to John.—The ointment was imported from the East in sealed flasks, which, being broken, the perfume escaped and so spread through the house. So should the odour of our love fill the House of God with the sweet perfume of praise. *Braune.*—So shall the odour of His people's love one day fill the universe. Mal. i. 11.—The anointing of the Messiah, the Anointed One: (1) By whom anointed? The Christ, by a grateful, presageful Christian woman. (2) Wherewith anointed? With flowing ointment, with precious balm, the offering of devoted love. (3) How anointed? On the head and feet. The hair which adorned the head of His disciple appropriated to His service. (4) Whereunto anointed? To His high-priestly sacrificial death as the completion of His life-work.—The anointing in its signification: 1, the expression of the most heartfelt gratitude; 2, of the most solemn veneration and homage; 3, of the deepest humility; 4, of the most devoted love; 5, of the holiest sorrow; 6, of the boldest confidence. *Lange.*—Christ at the table with the leper He had cleansed (Matt. xxvi 6), and with the dead man whom He had raised to life—a figure of His Church, when he who is cleansed and he who is raised from the death of sin sit with Christ and eat and drink in His Kingdom, which is filled with the odour of His death. *Williams.*

λίτραν. The Roman *libra* was divided into 12 ounces. and was equivalent to nearly 12 ounces avoirdupois. *Schaff.*—μύρου. *Aromatic juice which distils from trees; ointment, unguent,* usually perfumed.—νάρδου. A species of aromatic plant with grassy leaves and a fibrous root, of which the best and strongest grows in India; in N. T. *oil of spikenard,* an oil extracted from the plan, which was highly prized and used as an ointment either pure or mixed with other substances. *Robinson.*- πόδας. "The anointing of the *head* at feasts was a customary thing, and might have been passed over by the Evangelist, in order to mention the unusual demonstration of love for which the remainder of the ointment might be employed. To wash the feet with tepid water, and then to anoint them with costly oil, as mentioned in the Talmud as a duty of maidservants." *Tholuck.*— The anointing of the feet particularly noticeable to John, since he reclined by the side of Jesus, and the anointing of the feet took place behind him. *Braune.*

---

4. Then saith one of his disciples, Judas Iscariot, Simon's son, which should betray him.

One of His disciples. One of their number, but not one of their nature. *Henry.*—The Spirit's explanation is that by transgression he fell from the Apostleship. Acts i. 25.—Herein the warning and the lesson to all professing Christians.

Judas Iscariot. See on John vi. 71.—Was of a different country from the rest of the Apostles. This may account for his want of fellow-feeling with them.—Together with moral causes, it contributed to his gradual alienation from them.—John throws light upon the character of Judas—His sin against love would naturally raise a feeling of abhorrence in the mind of the disciple of love. John, therefore, dwells much on moral contrasts in character.

Simon's son. See on John vi. 71.—*Son* not in Gr.—The form of expression may mean Simon's *brother*.—But the other Judas had, probably, a brother named Simon. Matt. xiii. 55.—*Son* of Simon is, therefore, likely to be the description intended, as more accurately to distinguish *this* Judas.—We do not know who this Simon was.—Mentioned again in John xiii. 2, 26.

Saith. All hearts not full of sweet odour, as Mary's.—In the Apostolic circle murmuring ought not to be heard.—The selfish have no sympathy with works of kindness and love: they but obstruct others.—The presence of goodness, when it does not stir up to imitation, sometimes develops the evil of the heart.—There are occasions on which the *inward* man becomes revealed by the words of the mouth.—The conduct of men towards Christ and those who love Him, a test of character.

Betray Him. Gr., *was about to betray Him.*—Matthew and Mark next relate that Judas went to the Chief Priests to betray his Master.—Treachery was already in his heart—his cold and cynical words give signs of it.—One base passion was gathering strength within him every day, and would increase in power till bold enough for the utmost villainy.—A constant force acting upon a body already in motion generates a high velocity: so temptation, acting upon a soul accustomed to yield, plunges it with fearful haste into the depths of destruction.—"Very gross hypocrites may be near to Christ in outward profession, and may be entrusted in eminent employments." *Hutcheson.*—Judas was already a thief, and followed the Lord in *body*, not in *heart*. *Augustine.*

'Ἰούδας. John. as in chapter vi. 8. names the person who actually spoke, or was most forward in speaking.—Σίμωνος. Of Simon—leaving the exact relationship to be supplied.—Appears doubtful, having now become superfluous. *Lange.*—Omitted. *Cod. Sin., Tisch., Alf., Westcott and Hort.*

---

5. Why was not this ointment sold for three hundred pence, and given to the poor?

Why? Matthew says that His *disciples* had indignation, saying, "To what purpose is this waste?" But Mark simply, that "there were *some* that had indignation within themselves, and said," &c.—Mark speaks thus, as not being an eye-witness, nor one of the twelve.—*Both* imply that the Apostles, as a body, censured this action. *They* did so from regard to the duty of almsgiving, but *Judas* from avarice and love of unjust gain.— "This one trait of Judas unlocks his soul to a glance, which renders clear all that follows." *Tholuck.*—The rest of the Apostles were excited by his language, and adopted his sentiment without reflection.—Judas was, therefore, the originator of this murmuring.—An evil man possessing great force of character can thus influence those who are too simple to perceive the depth of his design—The presence of such a nature may be said to act inductively upon others. Their better nature is rendered captive and constrained under such an influence.—Those who have but feeble moral power and perception are easily deceived by baseness assuming a virtue.—There is a point at which even the worst examples cease to be contagious ; but to this Judas had not yet come.—His influence was, therefore, most dangerous at this stage.—By-and-bye, his evil would assume a shape which could only spread abhorrence and dismay.—Could we know the origin of many judgments we echo—the Judas hearts from which they spring—how would we recoil!—Long had the honours bestowed on Christ been insufferable to *him*.—He preferred money in his purse to the Saviour in his heart: and now such costly perfume wasted on the Master's feet!—He might impute the blame to Mary's excessive love of display.—Mary must have been deeply absorbed in her heart-work for the Lord.—This outburst of prudential formality brought a cloud upon her soul.

Three hundred pence. Only Mark and John mention a definite sum.—Judas reckons it up quickly—"yes, three hundred pence."— It may be doubted whether they could have accurately estimated its value.—It is a phrase resembling an adage. *Bengel.*—Strange conduct to raise an objection on the ground of economy in the presence of Him who emptied Himself of all for man's sake. 2 Cor. viii. 9.—There was the appearance of reason in this question ; for the principle was right to sacrifice luxury for the sake of the poor.—Still, the loving heart must also have its luxuries.—This action involved a question of moral beauty, not of mere utility.—The great Artificer of Nature has contrived the universe with a view to ornament as well as use.—The Greeks and Romans used the words κόσμος and *mundus*—which signify *order* and elegance—to designate the universe.—This external beauty is one of the many ways by which God speaks to mind.— The beauty of moral actions addresses itself to answering minds. —As love cannot be estimated by weight, so it has no equivalent in coin.—"Three hundred pence" was all that Judas could say for this action: Jesus valued it as so much love—Judas was accustomed to estimate every action by its money value, or by some sordid idea of utility.—Such a standard must not be applied to science, nor to religion.—To demand, in advance, an assurance of utility would put an end to the sublimest efforts of the human mind.—"The question *cui bono*, to what practical end and advantage do your researches tend? is one which the speculative philosopher who loves knowledge for its own sake . . . can seldom hear without a sense of humiliation. He feels that there is a lofty and disinterested pleasure in his speculations which ought to exempt them from such questioning." *Herschel.*—The great minds of the past, who thought and laboured for pure truth, did not trammel themselves by the question of utility; yet many of the truths they discovered have, in after ages, found a use, and contributed even to man's material progress.—Our Lord's commendation of this action is a bequest of truth and principle to the Church.—It has a potency to generate many such noble deeds.—There are sublime uses of moral actions which cannot be reckoned by the coin of earth.—Heaven has willed it that the heart must be free from the tyranny of maxims and narrow rules.—The airs and graces of love require nobility of nature to recognise and interpret them ; they are wasted upon the unloving and selfish.—Christian thought, feeling, and effort must be contemplated upon the broadest basis.

To the poor. Philip considered that 200 pennyworth of bread might stay the hunger of 5000 men. John vi. 7.—This sum of money bestowed in charity would have supplied the temporary needs of many.—But it has flowed to us as wealth of sublimer value.—Our Lord had enjoined kindness to the poor.—It was a high praise that Christianity received from one of its bitterest foes when Julian, the Apostate, bade the heathen to imitate the conduct of the Christians towards the poor.—Judas would reason thus: How thoughtless towards the poor is this woman! How many wretches in Bethany or Jerusalem who might be aided by this seeming waste! This pious enthusiast ought to have been wiser for her good.—But our Lord saw far beyond the passing needs of men, and the praise of economists and calculators.—The basest designs have often been concealed under the pretence of philanthropy.—Thus even the worst natures are compelled to pay homage to virtue.

ἐπράθη. Judas concealed his murmuring behind the others. *Dräscke.*—The other disciples knew not as yet the power of love. *Meyer.*—He was vehement in condemning Mary. *Tischendorf.*—She felt that now being blamed she deserved their censures.

Stier —Three hundred pence—δηναρίων —The sum is about £9 16s. of our money. *Alford.*— πτωχοῖς. The destitute—those who obtain their living by begging. Distinguished from πένης, one who has a scanty livelihood.

6. This he said, not that he cared for the poor; but because he was a thief, and had the bag, and bare what was put therein.

Not that he cared. He thus glossed over his hypocrisy as with a mask.—" It is hypocrisy when one thing is said while another thing is cared for. Avarice makes the poor its pretext, and that in serious earnest at times, for it hates even genuine munificence." *Bengel.*—Of all sinners encountered by Christ, hypocrites received the heaviest doom.—" As Christ knoweth the naughtiness of every heart, so He will, in due time, discover what is within men ; for here the veil is taken off Judas." *Hutcheson.*—" Thus some warmly contend for the *power* of the Church, as others for its *purity*, when perhaps it may be said, not that they care for the Church, it is all one to them whether its *true interests* sink or swim, but under the umbrage of this they are advancing themselves." *Henry.*

Thief. A saddening expression—*a disciple yet a thief.* Verse 4.— To the eye of God he stood revealed in his true character ; now shortly to be revealed to men.—Rank and place in the Church, even when personally assigned by the Lord himself, did not confer reality of spiritual life.—Judas, so hypocritical as to present himself in the presence of Jesus, and wish to seem the friend of the poor at the very time he was robbing the poor.—The question arises, why did Jesus, knowing him to be such, still own him as His disciple?—It may be answered that Jesus received him on the ground of his *profession*, content with the justification of outward appearances.—Jesus received him on the same principle as the Church should act on now.—His life would be no genuine or possible example for us, had He acted in all things according to His infinite knowledge.—We are thus taught that the actual Church is not identical with the real Church.—Taking human nature as it is, subject to the tremendous power of evil, there seems to be a sad necessity that offences must arise.—The Church must accept the evils arising from the special moral risks of individuals.—The love of gain has been a terrible factor in the corruptions of the Church, both in doctrine and manners.—Other forms of idolatry have been exterminated by Christian truth, but this idolatry remains—.Even where it stops short of crime, it yet impairs the delicacy of conscience, and is the root of countless evils.—The ointment, if turned into money, would only have been more convenient for the covetousness of Judas.

Bag. This was the treasury of the Apostolic band, and was likely to have been empty at that time.—" What was put there'n :" the same word is used for giving in alms. Mark xii. 41-44. Luke xxi. 1-4.—Jesus, during the course of His ministry, cast Himself upon the love of others.—He wrought no miracle to supply His own wants; and while bestowing freely the greatest gifts, was yet ready to receive the lowest, as if He needed them. —How little outward glory had Christ, when this scanty and precarious store was all that He possessed!—Women ministered unto Him of their substance. Luke viii. 3.—He who was Lord of all had nothing that deserved the name of property.—Such majesty in such low estate!—" Riches and the bag are not in such esteem with Christ but that the basest of His followers may have them in keeping, and under their power." *Hutcheson.*—The trial of virtue is real and serious: Providence does net deny opportunities to the covetous.

And bare. Gr., expresses continual action: *"used to bear."*—The word, probably, has the force of *bearing away, i.e.,* " he pilfered." —To have the bag in possession would be bearing it; the expression is, therefore, unnecessary, unless it is intended to convey the idea of little pilferings from time to time.—The same word is used in the sense of *bearing away.* John xx. 15.—" This is certain that He has left a solemn warning to all on the trial of pecuniary trust and possessions.—He has also thus bequeathed to us an example of patience and forbearance.—We may not forsake the communion of the Church even though a sacrilegious Judas ministers therein." *Wordsworth.*—Our Lord suffered from the hands of sinners of every kind.—The cross, designed as it was to atone for all guilt, gathered around it every type of human iniquity.—" Judas, that betrayed his trust, soon after betrayed his Master." *Henry.*—Christ did not *force* men to be virtuous by any special constraints of moral government.—How awful is this gift of moral freedom to man, when one of the Apostles of Christ could steal!

κλέπτης. *A thief.*—A curious question is raised by some; how came John to *know* Judas was a thief? *Stier.*—How came he to know that the Λόγος was in the beginning with God? *Author.*—The word signifies one who steals by fraud, and in secret, as distinguished from ληστής, a *robber*—one who steals by means of violence, and openly. —γλωσσόκομον. Originally a wooden box, in which pipers placed their mouth-pieces; then any casket for holding money. - βαλλόμενα Not all given but all put in. *Kuinoel.*—What was offered. *Titmann.*—The word is used for depositin gmoney. Mark xii. 41. ἐβάσταζεν.—He used to bear (away), *i.e.,* to steal.—It gives a reason for the heavy charge. *Lampe.*

7. Then said Jesus, Let her alone: against the day of my burying hath she kept this.

Jesus. It was fitting that He should vindicate Mary's self-denying love, since the action was done to Himself. He stood forward to defend one too simple to be aware of the strength of her cause; too humble to be conscious of the beauty of her deed.—Jesus is the champion of all who are misunderstood, or unfairly judged.— He will yet vindicate all whose righteousness is clouded and obscured here. Ps. xxxvii. 6.—Jesus is the fulfilment of the vague longings and prophetic instincts of the heart.—The Gospels present the picture of the Teacher surrounded by His scholars.— He has not only to teach them truth, but also to protect their minds from the evil influence of other minds.—He is a Saviour to save man from *error* as well as *sin;* from all that is false, both in *feeling* and in *thought.*

Let her alone. Observe Christ's words : He does not condemn Judas, but praises and encourages Mary. *Aug.*—Addressed to Judas as the originator of the rebuke. The others might concur, but without his malicious intention—as Malchus and other servants might help to arrest the Lord, only in obedience to their masters.—Cease these words, they please me not, why trouble ye the woman?—As one who had authority, He utters calmly a dignified final decision.—But He speaks for all generations in coming ages, and assigns a reason.—He does not say " *Me,*" though He might have felt aggrieved that they thought such honours too much—the anointing too precious for Him. But He is wounded by the imputation cast on her, and makes her cause His.—Thus His calm joy is embittered by the folly of one who professed himself a friend.—This quiet feast cannot end without trouble.—The keener and deeper the wound, the more warmly does the Lord vindicate her.—Love must be allowed to show itself in its own way.—The majesty of love sanctions its refusal to be measured by the standards of utility.—In the service of God, love alone gives a real and permanent value to actions. — Like genius, love marks out a path for itself, and disdains the formal precepts of a short-sighted policy.—Jesus would not allow that dark, cynical spirit to overshadow Mary in this solemn hour of her joy.—He shields the tender plant of love from those rude blasts that might wither it.—There are ornaments and graces of soul that cannot be judged by the utilitarian standard. — The cultivation of those thoughts and feelings that raise man above the dull level of his week-day life are sanctioned by the spirit and aim of the Gospel. Hence wealth employed in art for the service of religion may be in accordance with the mind of Christ.—

" Christ would not have them censured or discouraged that sincerely design to please Him, though, in their honest endeavours, there be not all the discretion that may be." Rom. xiv. 3. *Henry.*

My burying. Includes all the varied rites of shrouding, anointing, and sepulture.—She has, in truth, paid me this last honour, for death is before Me.—On Tabor, amid the effulgence of the throne, visitors from Paradise speak of His death.—Here, during a royal anointing, He thinks of death.—Amid these festal joys, He sees the cross and the stony, cold sepulchre.—He saw what Mary did not —she did it to the living, He meant it for the dead.—To what a depth of human and Divine consciousness does this touching utterance point?—Mary has no thought of His death or embalmment, but *He* interprets its *providential significance*, just as He interprets Scripture prophecies by their fulfilment.—He elevates and glorifies her simple act of love into a *prophetic deed.*—Mary had no suspicion that the death of her Lord was near : the mention of it would touch her heart with unspeakable sorrow.— She had not bought this ointment on purpose for His burial. But He extends the deed beyond the reaches of her thought, even to its sublime issue.—He seizes the tendency of it, He knows to what it will grow.—The loving heart has depths which itself cannot explore.—Mary did not know the mysterious depths of her own heart.—True love has something of the nature of the gift of prophecy—its insight becomes foresight.—It is akin to genius, which differs from mere talent, in that it utters more than it consciously knows.—Every believer has something of the poet in his nature ; he has mysterious suggestions of that which is above and beyond life.—The loving heart is inspired, and knows not half its wealth.—Like the prophets who foretold the grandeur of Messiah's reign, it knows not the full meaning of the message with which it is charged.—Christ completes the vague, prophetic yearnings of pious hearts.—He is the fulfilment of all the unutterable feelings of pure and holy souls.—The simplest beginnings of love may lead to the highest acts of service and adoration.—He who was love incarnate makes all love great by assimilating it with his own nature.—There is something impressive and affecting in His reference to the day of His burial, because, probably, it took place on the day-week before His rest in the grave. *Wordsworth.* —"She hath wrought a good work on me." Gr., a *noble* work. Mark xiv. 6 ; Matt. xxvi. 10.—Judas implicates her as performing a bad work for display.—The disciples seem to have imputed vanity to her in her charity.—Our Lord implies that Mary never thought of her *own* reputation.—As men cannot read the heart,

let them know that an ignorant charge is a malicious slander.—
Note God's estimate of the nature of human deeds—*infallible*.—
Elsewhere He marks the value of faith and love.—He corrects a
thousand human errors of judgment regarding the acts of others.
—He shows that their real value in the eye of heaven depends
upon the state of mind and heart.—They need not be *great*, not
necessarily *useful*, as men call it.—What the world calls a waste,
He commends.—" Christ Himself, who was never sumptuous,
allows costly ointment on His burial, to testify how highly He
prized and loved to lay down His life for His people." *Hutcheson.*
Mary and Judas in their participation in the death of Jesus.—
Self-denial in its heavenly brilliance, over against selfishness, in
hellish darkness.—How the secrets of hell come to light, face to
face with the secrets of heaven.—The Lord's defence of Mary in
its eternal significance : 1, a defence of a festive spirit in opposition to hypocritical sadness ; 2, of great love-offerings in opposition to a hypocritical reckoning ; 3, of holy spending (prodigality)
in opposition to a hypocritical pauperism. *Lange.*

Αφες. The singular points to Judas alone. *Stier* —Vindicates a lawful luxury.
Rothe.—To gratify our æsthetic tastes is right. *Schleiermacher.*—A social and religious
act of the heart. *Stier.*—ἡμέραν. This very day—this ἐνταφιασμοῦ, *preparation* for
the sepulchre. *Bengel.*—The latter word signifies, not the commital of the body to
the sepulchre, but the preparation of the body for it. Matthew and Mark add a little
more than John. τετήρηκεν. Not wasted but well bestowed. *Titmann* —At the same
time Judas is warned; for his treachery waxed stronger and stronger, until it eventuated in the Saviour's death. *Bengel.*—Instead of τετήρηκεν τηρήσῃ. *Cod. Sin., Tisch.,
Lach., Alford.*

---

8. For the poor always ye have with you; but me ye have not always.

The poor. Gr., signifies *the poverty of utter destitution*, or *that
which subsists on alms.*—Plato would have such banished from his
ideal State.—Alms not the only kindness to be shown to the
poor.—" I would rather be denied a favour kindly than be
obliged insultingly." *Chesterfield.*—Charity, destitute of self-
sacrifice, can never win the heart of the wretched.

Always. Sorrowfully He speaks of the sad continuance of poverty.
—" For the poor shall never cease out of the land." Deut. xv. 11.
—A surprising fact, for it might have been supposed that riches
would be on the side of strength and numbers.—Perfect equality
in the earthly condition of men is evidently no part of the plan of
Providence.—Poverty included in the primal curse.—Sin made

the battle for subsistence necessary.—In that struggle it is to be
expected that many shall fare ill.—This condition has some com-
pensations derived from religion.—Upon the improvement of it,
multitudes will receive a better portion.—"And whensoever ye
will ye may do them good." Mark xiv. 7.—Intimates a reproach
to Judas, and perhaps an allusion to the fact that it was *his* office
to give to the poor. *Alford.*—The relief of the poor had taken a
well-assured place among the duties of good men.—We, like
Mary, anoint *Him* in blessing the poor.

Me—not always. The opportunity for honouring Him in person
would soon be past.—His spiritual presence would remain, but
His bodily presence would be removed. John xvi. 7.—His influence over them must soon cast off the limitations of time and
space.—As the hour was drawing near, our Lord takes every occasion of referring to His departure.—He had been with His disciples long enough to make evident the reality of His human nature
and to lay the foundations of the new religion in the verities of
history.—They would think of their omissions of duty to their
Master when He was gone.—We know not how soon we may have
to perform duties to others for the last time.—To follow the instincts of the loving heart is always right, and will be justified
by the event.—We also have opportunities for serving Christ
which will pass away with life.—There was work which even *He*
could do only in this world.—In this respect His mortal day, as
ours, was rounded by that night when work was no longer possible.—There are constant duties, but there are special summonses
of the heart to action which must be at once obeyed; for the opportunity is passing. "Opportunities are to be improved, and
those opportunities first and most vigorously which are likely to
be of the shortest continuance and which we see most speedily
hastening away." *Henry.*—"When Christ calls for anything we
have, no other thing should come into competition with Him."
Hutcheson.

πτωχοὺς. Luke vi. 20 Not mendicants, as *Beza*, but suffering saints, as a rule. *J.
A. Alexander.* No Lex Agraria ever has or can abolish poverty. *Stier.* This verse is
wanting in *Codd.* Retained, *Tisch., Alf., Westcott* and *Hort.* The complete preponderance of *Codd.* is alone decisive in its favour. *Schaff.*

---

9. Much people of the Jews therefore knew that he was there; and they came not
for Jesus' sake only, but that they might see Lazarus also, whom he had raised from
the dead.

Much people. These were Jerusalem Jews, and are to be distinguished from the multitude of ver. 12, which was composed of provincial people. "The odour of the ointment, and the fame of the anointing, might have supplied them with the information." *Bengel.* The warm climate encourages the people to live out of doors, or in open tents.—The poorest among the spectators would greedily devour the remnants of the feast.—"The more because He had lately absconded, and now broke out as the sun from behind a dark cloud." *Henry.*

Jews. See on chap. i. 19. Not the people but the leaders and persons of repute. *Alford.*—Their visit to Bethany was on the day of the supper in Simon's house.—These had everything to fear from the decree of the chief priests and Pharisees. Chap. xi. 57.

Not for Jesus' sake only. The interest in Jesus was deepening through His last great miracle.—Many followed Him from no better principle than the love of the wonderful.—Such a motive may draw towards Jesus, but cannot put the soul in possession of Him unless it improves to pure spiritual desire.—Many stop at mere admiration for what Christ has said or done, and do not proceed to the true knowledge and desire of Himself.—Christ has much to show to those who look for the miraculous, but more to the eye of faith and love.—"It is the sin of many that they choose rather to gaze upon His works than fall in love with the worker." *Hutcheson.*—These Jews came rather to see a prodigy than to hear the truth.

Lazarus. See on chap. xi. 1. From his high social position he would be an object of intense curiosity.—The people wished to see this trophy of the Redeemer's power.—"Who is there that would not seek Bethany for the sake of seeing him?" *Bengel.*—"Lazarus served for a *show* these holydays to men who, like the Athenians, spent their time in telling and hearing new things." *Henry.*

Raised from the dead. See on chap xi. The fact was unquestionable.—The most violent enemies of Jesus admitted it, even in their ecclesiastical council. John xi. 47.—Lazarus was a persistent proof of one of the mightiest deeds which Jesus wrought.—Here was veritable spoil rescued from the enemy.—The power of the Conqueror was placed beyond a doubt.—Christ the Resurrection and the Life: this miracle one of the proofs and issues of it.

---

10. But the chief priests consulted that they might put Lazarus also to death.

Chief Priests. See on chap. i. 13, and xi. 47.—They were men of ritual—precedent—prescription.—Their love of power and place, and their deeply-rooted prejudices, could resist the most overwhelming evidence.

Consulted. This was on the day of the supper in Simon's house.—They soon framed their evil design.—The movement of the people in this new direction filled them with perplexity, and drove them to new devices.—The public mind was beginning to be agitated by ideas dangerous to the priestly caste.—These men of hoary, immovable traditions were now roused up in spite of themselves.

To death. Lazarus was an awkward fact, and calculated to establish the claims of a man suspected of heresy.—The case was now desperate, as he was sitting beside Him who had raised him from the dead.—The priests must needs use the only argument they had left, an appeal to brute force.—This is the logic of prejudice and error.—Men are slow to learn that they can do nothing against the truth.—They sought to destroy the proofs of the power of Jesus; but what if that power were exerted again?—" There was one doctrine and one miracle which occasioned their killing Jesus: the doctrine was that of Jesus being the Son of God; the miracle, the raising again of Lazarus." *Bengel.*—The fact was the foundation of the doctrine, and no human power could destroy either.—" The high priests named here, and in chap. xi. 57, were of the sect of the Sadducees, and therefore disbelieving the fact of the raising of Lazarus." *Alford.*—The power of the mind to resist the strongest evidence for moral truths one of the saddest proofs of the bondage of sin, as seen in the perversion of the noblest faculties of man.—" See the blindness of their rage; as if Christ could raise one who was dead, and not raise one who was killed.—He did both—He who raised Lazarus raised Himself." *Wordsworth.*—" None are so malicious and bitter enemies to Christ as corrupt Churchmen; for it is the chief priests who are so cruel as to conspire to kill a man for being the harmless occasion of drawing men to Christ." *Hutcheson.*—The rich man in Hades exclaimed, " Nay, Father Abraham; but if one went unto them from the dead, they will repent ! "—Here is a case in point : One appears amongst them who has come back from the dead, and instead of repenting they conspire to murder him.—No miracle will win those whose hearts are opposed to the truth.—" If they believe not Moses and the prophets," &c.—What a striking illustration of the truth of these words. Luke xvi. 30, 31.

11. Because that by reason of him many of the Jews went away, and believed on Jesus.

By reason of him. Gr. *For on his account.* The resurrection of a soul from the death of sin to the life of righteousness the most powerful witness to the truth of the gospel.—Every one converted increases the force of the testimony.—Thus the humblest believer may glorify God and help to extend the Redeemer's kingdom in the world.—Experimental knowledge of the things of God and a corresponding holy life the best of all preaching.

Went away. Gr. *Were going off,* or *getting away.*—They kept continually going from Jerusalem to Bethany to see this living miracle.—The love of the marvellous not the noblest motive, but may lead to it.—Curiosity may at length improve to reverence, faith, and devotion.—As the spiritual building approaches perfecfection, the scaffolding can be taken away.—Religion uses all the faculties of our nature, and guides them to their best issues.—The chief priests were enraged at this new movement in the public mind, and felt as if the people were leaving *them.*—They had no consciousness of resting upon the deep foundations of truth, and therefore were easily disturbed.

Believed. See on chap i. 7 ; vii. 38. Gr. *Were believing,* or *becoming believers on.*—This new teacher was achieving the only true success in any teacher or writer—the production of belief.—This is the strongest force in human history.—He who brings the souls of men into subjection is the true sovereign of the race.—These Jews saw the proof of mighty power, but they rested upon the Divine Worker.—Belief in Christ has generated a society united by the strongest bonds.—Forces powerful enough to overwhelm mighty empires could not destroy the organization of the Church. —The development of religion was advancing now to a new stage. —The chief priests were the guardians of a system which, though Divinely inspired, they only knew by rote.—Now all religious thought and feeling were to centre in a living Person.—This gave a new life and interest to godliness, making devotion more easy and grateful to our nature.—The truth of heaven was to be embodied not merely in venerable rites, prophetic voices, or formal teaching, but in a *life.*—Thus the depth and fulness of truth were made apparent to the minds of men ; for who can exhaust a life?

On Jesus. See on chap. i. 17 ; and on Matt. i. 16, 21, 25.—This is the true and permanent foundation for a living faith.—Something more than a mere belief in the doctrine of Christ is implied. —In the belief of His doctrine the *intellect* only may be concerned.—Genuine faith trusts *Himself.*—We may believe a man's statement upon sufficient evidence, quite independent of his character.—But when we have confidence in his character, we trust *himself;* we believe *in* him.—Thus when the fact of personality and character is considered the *moral element* is introduced.—Faith trusts CHRIST *Himself,* and reposes upon HIM.—The fame of truth may lead to the belief of it; and further still, to heartfelt confidence in its author.—The perfection of faith is to rest on Christ—to settle down upon Him as an everlasting foundation.

---

12 On the next day much people that were come to the feast, when they heard that Jesus was coming to Jerusalem,

Next day. Probably the first day of the week—our Sunday.—This day stretches down to verse 50.—How many events are crowded into it!—Jesus shows no fear of His enemies, but is ready to encounter them at once.—" When they are vexed with hearing of the confluence at Bethany, even the next day they see Him more glorified coming to Jerusalem."—*Hutcheson.*

Much people. Gr., *great multitude* or *crowd.*—They were people from the provinces, not from Jerusalem, as in verse 9.—Believing pilgrims, who had come to the feast. *Lange.*—The more regard men have to God and religion in general, the better disposed they will be to entertain Christ. *Henry.*

The feast. The Passover: see chap. i. 29, 36.—The solemn proclamation of Jesus as the Messiah originates with these festal pilgrims.—Jerusalem herself seems to receive the Lord as her King.

When they heard. Doubtless they were anxiously *waiting* to learn of His movements.—Such a state of mind a happy preparation for the news that *He is coming.*—Jesus is *always coming* to those who are seeking their Lord.—Tidings of His approach and His Kingdom should awaken us to consider the work of *the day,* that it may be done in the day. *Henry.*

Coming to Jerusalem. He was now on His way to the City.—It is probable that some of those who had gone to see Jesus at Bethany had returned, and announced the intention of His coming.—These are now informed that He is approaching.—Jesus might have chosen to enter Jerusalem unobserved: hitherto He had avoided publicity.—But by a blessed necessity He could not altogether conceal His native dignity.—Even in a state of humiliation the Lord must preserve His rights of sovereignty.—The people desired to do Him homage; not from any deep veneration, but in the passing excitement of the hour.—Yet He does not borrow misery from the future, nor allow the fickleness of the multitude, nor the shadow of approaching calamity to disturb Him.—In this journey Jesus knew what dreadful consequences He had to accept.—But He was conscious that the will of Heaven was being accomplished.—In the gathering of this crowd, the sudden generation of enthusiasm, and the mischievous plotting of His enemies, ordinary observers could only discern mere accident.—Even the most thoughtful could only rise to the conception of the natural tendency of things in history.—It was well known that some of the greatest teachers of mankind, who had won popular applause, had died a martyr's death.—In the life of Christ there was an extraordinary purpose ; therefore it is not to be judged by the philosophy of common history.—All things now, however varied and discordant among themselves, were precipitating the event to which the history of mankind was really tending.

ὄχλος πολύς. John menti ns that part of the Palm-procession which issues from Jerusalem, whi'e Matt, Mark, and Luke give prominence to tha portion accompanying Jesus. *i.e.,* the Ga'ilean.—John's account supplementary to theirs.—The Synoptists themse ves, however, distinguish between a part of ihe procession that preceded Jesus and a part that fol'owed Him.—By the former those seem to be meant who set out from Jerusalem, intending to bring Jesus in'o the city.—John also dis'inguishes between two divisions (verses 17 and 18)—citizens of Jerusalem and festal pilgrims already in Jerusalem. *Lange.*

---

13. Took branches of palm trees, and went forth to meet him, and cried, Hosanna: Blessed is the King of Israel that cometh in the name of the Lord.

Took branches. See on Luke xix, 37, 38.—They took, in the sense of assuming them as the symbol of victory. Rev. vii. 9.— They were not afraid of the commandment of the chief priests and Pharisees. Chap. xi. 57.—*The* branches of *the* palms which grew there. *Wordsworth.*—The people were ready to acknowledge Jesus as the Messiah, and expected that He would vindicate His claim by assuming temporal sovereignty.

Palm trees. John alone mentions that the branches were those of the *palm* tree.—The symbol of joy in all ages, in which use they were well known to the Jews. Lev. xxiii. 40.—" The palm, which *crescit sub pondere,* is emblematic of victory, and especially such a victory as that of Christ, which was made more glorious by the *weight of suffering* for the sins of the world laid upon Him, who, from the lowest depths of sorrow and humility, and from the pit of the grave, raised Himself, and ascended on the clouds to the right hand of God." *Wordsworth.*—It was reserved for St. John to see the palm-branches in the hands of a more glorious assembly. Rev. vii. 9, 10.—These people were ignorant of the full glory and surpassing claims of Him whom they were thus honouring.—Most of them probably were sincere, to the extent of their knowledge, but lacking solidity and depth therein, were inconstant and fickle.—Even the best can but imperfectly celebrate the praises of Christ here.—When His people are directly conscious of the victory He has won, they will praise Him with a sublimer and surer joy.—Jesus will then have no coming disasters to perplex and endanger weak faith.—Many still flock after Christ rather out of *curiosity* than *conscience*.

Hosanna. A word of prayer and worship—"*Save us.*" They are inspired to recognize Christ as greater than a prophet; Christ is God, for *salvation* is from God alone. *Chrys., Aug., Theoph.*— Luke omits this term, as unknown to *his* readers; Matthew and Mark add "in the highest."—From the frequent utterance of the word, the branches carried about at the Feast of Tabernacles were named *Hosanna.*—"It is the duty of all such as love Christ heartily to wish and pray for the prosperity of His kingdom; for they cried Hosanna, as wishing safety and success to Him and His kingdom." *Hutcheson.*

Blessed. Taken from the song of triumph, Ps. cxviii. 26.—The Jews applied this Psalm to the Messiah, and our Lord applies it to Himself. Matt. xxi. 42.—St. Peter and St. Paul quote it as a prophecy of Christ. Acts. iv. 11; Eph. ii. 20; 1 Pet. ii. 6.—This Psalm was sung at the feast of Tabernacles, and in the great Hallel at the Passover.—To ascribe blessedness to Jesus was to acknowledge His righteous claims, for only that which is founded upon right is worthy of benediction.—This was a King in whom "all the families of the earth" shall be "blessed." Gen. xxii. 18.

King of Israel. The people were now prepared to hail Him as the Messiah.—They thought that He was about to establish a temporal sovereignty.—Some minds seem capable of dealing only with the lowest side of spiritual truth.—The material setting of the ancient prophecies was taken for the principal thing intended. —This mistake of the Jews should be a lesson to those who interpret yet unfulfilled prophecies of the Messiah in a somewhat gross and material sense.—Earthly monarchies are but a feeble type of the office and condition of this highest of Princes.—In His reign over His subjects, Christ alone realizes the true ideal of a Kingdom, for they are bound together by love.—This is the only enduring fellowship ; a nation of brothers is strong.—In Mark xi. 10, " Kingdom " and " our father David " are connected together. Isa. ix. 7.—Christ has the throne of David. Luke i. 32. —That throne was but a representative, and not a portion, of the royal dignity of Messiah.—The people considered, and, indeed, such was the reality, that the presence of the *King* was the setting up of His *Kingdom.*—They were permitted thus to honour Christ, so that it might afterwards be seen that they rejected Him whom they acknowledged to be their *King.*—Thus men may seize spiritual truths and ideas, but only so far as to condemn themselves.—In a far wider and truer sense than they dreamt of Christ was the King of Israel.—"Though He went now in poverty and disgrace, yet, contrary to the notions their Scribes had given them of their Messiah, they own Him to be *a King,* which speaks both His dignity and honour which we must adore, and His dominion and power, which we must submit to." *Henry.* —For Christ to be King of Israel was a condescension, not an elevation ; a sign of His pity, not an increase of His power. *Augustine.*

In the name of the Lord. See on Matt. i. 21, 22, 23.—These words should be construed with *blessed* : " Blessed in the name of the Lord," &c.—Blessing in *the* NAME of God is full of the wealth of His nature ; for *His name* signifies all HE *is* to man.—" Christ was not the King of Israel to exact tribute and command armies, but to direct souls and bring them to the Kingdom of heaven " *Augustine.*—" This is what more than any thing made men believe in Christ, *viz.,* the assurance that He was not opposed to God, that he came from the Father." *Chrysostom.*

Baía, from Baíos, *little ;* the flexible light twig of the tree. *Webster.*—τῶν φοινίκων. The article which is omitted in the E. V. indicates that the palm trees were on the road. *Lange, Meyer.*– Perhaps the custom was usual at such festivities. *Alford.*— ὑπάντησιν. Said of those who had been to Bethany, and now having returned, announced His intention of coming. ἔκραζον. *They kept crying out.* Ὡσαννά, Hosanna, Heb. for " *save now,*" " *be now propitious.*"—Part of Fsa. cxviii. 25, 26, was probably part of the hymnal and church services of the Passover.—In John, the Hosanna precedes the mention of the ass's colt, while in the Synoptists it is subsequent to that.— Naturally, because the Hosanna with which, as with the watchword of the day, the festal pilgrims from Jerusalem approach, is not communicated until later to the festal train from Galilee and Persæa. In this the new disciples are in advance of the old ones ; hence, too, more rapturous. *Lange.*

---

14. And Jesus, when he had found a young ass, sat thereon ; as it is written,

Had found. After sending in quest of—*procured.*—Jesus was too poor even to make so humble a pretence to property.—John does not mention every minute circumstance, but only so much as is necessary to serve his main doctrinal purpose.—As the ass was brought from a village opposite to where He was (Bethany), it was probably procured from Bethphage.—Providence was preparing the way for accomplishing the purposes of the Messiah.—It is probable that the owners of the ass were friends of Jesus.—When the decrees of God require the distinct and hearty co-operation of men, they are made willing.—God has mysterious ways of access to men.—The disposal of persons and events in remarkable crises of Providence indicates (like miracles) the distinct working of a will.—"Albeit, Christ became poor for us, yet He wanted not anything as He needed it, that so He might teach His people what care He will have of them." *Hutcheson.*

Young ass. Rationalists have sneered at the idea of *both* animals being brought, forgetting that the foal had never left the side of the dam.—Where there is not the disposition to believe, the truth may be ridiculed upon the slenderest grounds.—Matthew only makes mention of *two* animals, as exactly fulfilling the prophecy. Zechariah ix. 9.—Mark and Luke only allude to the *colt*, on which no one had ever ridden.—*Both* were brought: the mother may have followed, or may have been led behind.—"The young ass was one on which no one had ever sat, and was emblematic of the Gentile world, which had never been broken in, and was about to submit to Christ; together with the ass, its mother, the elder Church of the Israel of God." *Aug., Chrys.*—The bringing of the ass is described by Mark with fuller detail, after his manner; he even describes the way in which it was tied.—The ass was used in time of peace; the horse reserved for war. Hosea xiv. 4; Prov. xxi. 31; Jer. xvii. 25.—Persons of distinction rode on asses, but not *warriors.* Judges v. 10; x. 4; xii. 14.—In submitting thus to encourage the political hopes of the people, Jesus showed that He could have reigned by force had He so willed it.—He consents to enter Jerusalem with the circumstance, and seeming to cherish the ambition, of an earthly king; but He does so assuming the symbols of peace.—Though the people were possessed with merely political ideas, Jesus would even then remind them that His kingdom was not erected on the basis of *force.*—It is by meekness that Christ and His people shall conquer the world.—This Heavenly Monarch reigns and triumphs by principles which all men feel to be right.—He constrains by love, not by force.—Men have always felt that the power which binds all hearts together must be *spiritual.*—"If He would have made a public entry, according to the state of a man of high degree, He should

have rode in a chariot like that of Solomon's, Cant. iii. 3, 9, 10.—
His kingdom was not of this world, and therefore came not with
outward pomp." *Henry.*—" Christ's kingdom is so great a
stranger to carnal glory and pomp that any mean splendour is
very much unlike it ; for this also takes off the ignominy that this
was much glory and state to Him who never used to ride before."
Hutcheson.

Written. Zech. ix. 9.—" John does not often quote the Heb.
Scriptures, and gives the substance rather than the letter."
Wordsworth.—The deep lessons and impressions of Divine truth
are of more importance than the vehicle in which it is conveyed.
—That upon which the Evangelist alone lays stress is the contrast between the homage paid to Jesus, and His humble equipment, and the prediction concerning this fact. *Lange.*

εὑρὼν. *Having procured.* A suitable word for a writer to use who knew all the circumstances of the transaction but did not judge it necessary to narrate them. *Webster.*
—ὀνάριον. *A young ass.* Is not so much opposed in this passage to an ass of ordinary
size as to the fiery horse, which our Lord did not use. *Bengel.*—γεγραμμένον. It has
been, and still stands, written. The usual word of reference to the O.T. Scriptures.

---

15. Fear not, daughter of Zion: behold, thy King cometh, sitting on an ass's colt.

Fear not. Quoted from the prophecy, Zech. ix. 9.—The recorded
vision issues at length in a fact.—The LXX. and Hebrew have
" Rejoice greatly."—The two ideas are in essence the same, for
to be delivered from dread is to clear the ground for joy.—
Neither Matt. nor John quotes the O. T. prediction literally.—
Matt. lays chief stress upon the *meekness* of the King.—The
phrase, "Tell ye the daughter of Zion," seems to have been
added from Isa. lxii. 11.—The inspired writers do not foster the
worship of the mere letter.—There was a spirit in the words of
those ancient prophets which could make itself felt through many
changes and varieties of expression.—The presence of a King,
who is both meek and bringing salvation, quiets fear, and kindles
the fervours of joy.—"Though He comes but slowly, an ass is
slow-paced, yet He comes surely, and with such expressions of
humility and condescension as greatly encourage the expectations and addresses of His loyal subjects.—Humble supplicants
may reach to speak with Him." *Henry.*

Daughter of Zion. Jerusalem was regarded as the centre of the spiritual kingdom.—The Jew could point to an outward kingdom which had realized, though imperfectly, God's ideal.—The City of God ennobles, cherishes, and comforts all her children.

Thy King. Christ is the true Sovereign of all the spiritual Israel. —" Not like most of thy kings, proud and cruel, but meek; and not leading an army, but on the colt of an ass." *Chrys.*—With this King the hard outlines of law melt away, and are lost in the light of His love.—His Kingdom is the true fellowship of souls; it is a nation of brothers, and is therefore the strongest of all.— Earthly kings reign over strictly defined regions, but this King has subjects in all realms and worlds.—His kingdom has no seeds of decay, and shall increase for ever.—This King comes to sit upon the throne of the heart, not to displace earthly sovereignties. —He claims the strongest and nearest internal relationship to men.—He who feels that Christ is the sovereign of His soul is a true citizen of Zion.

Ass's colt. John gives the true meaning of the Hebrew idiom, " An ass, and a colt the foal of an ass."—Another example, Ps. viii. 4.—*Two* animals were brought, but Jesus only rode upon the *colt.* Matt. xxi. 7.—" Christ in His kingdom and glory is adorned with meekness and lowliness; and this is the comfort of His subjects that they have to do with such an one." *Hutcheson.*

Μὴ φοβοῦ. . . . Both this quotation and that in Matt. xxi. 5 differ from the LXX. and from the Heb.

---

16. These things understood not his disciples at the first: but when Jesus was glorified, then remembered they that these things were written of him, and that they had done these things unto him.

These things. Highly emphatic!—Thrice repeated in this verse. —The significance of His entry, and of the circumstances attenaing it, and the prediction thereby fulfilled.

Understood not. John includes himself in this ignorance.—He did not understand this passage till after the Lord was glorified. —" Observe the modesty of the Evangelist: he is not ashamed to confess their former ignorance." *Chrys.*—" An evidence of truth." *Wordsworth.*—Other instances, Mark viii. 17; John ii. 17, 22; viii. 28; xiii. 7; xvi. 12, 13.—Men may be in the midst of the most distinct preparations of Providence, and themselves even be the chief actors, yet they may be ignorant of the Divine purpose therein.—The reasons of God's words and ways are usually hidden, or greatly obscured, in the beginning ; they take time to work themselves into clearness.—As a teacher, Jesus uttered words whose deep meaning could not be understood at the time.—He could afford to cast Himself upon the future, for He spake to the ages.—He addressed a far wider audience than the few who were gathered around Him.—It is the duty of faith to receive what God offers in the present ; to make great ventures, and to wait for strength and light —How often in the ways of God to us does the present need the light of the future.— On some human lives there is such a shadow cast as can only be dispelled by the light of another world.—Some of the truths of Scripture await the comment of events, or vary the wealth of their meaning to the growing needs and expansions of the human mind.—Thus the Epistles of Paul were brought out from their obscurity. and b gan to declare their significance, at the Reformation —Men's spiritual needs, when they are truly felt, become the interpreters of Scripture.—It should not be a fatal obstacle to belief that any portion of Scripture is obscure; it shall be vindicated in due time.—The Bible needs continual interpretation.— The history of mankind, the lessons of experience, are ever throwing fresh light upon it.—Many other things the Apostles understood not till afterwards, such as, that Jesus would be separated from them, to be more essentially present by His Spirit ; that the Jewish ecclesiastical system would be broken up ; that all nations would be equal in the favour of God, and equally share Gospel blessings ; and the full knowledge of the Divine nature of Christ.—Yet all these truths were *in germ* in the teaching of Jesus.—" It well becomes the disciples of Christ, when they are grown up to maturity in knowledge, frequently to reflect upon the follies and weaknesses of their first beginning, that free grace may have the glory of their proficiency, and that they may have compassion on the ignorant." *Henry.*

At the first. During the time that they were disciples—before they had attained to any maturity in spiritual knowledge.— Beginners in all sciences have to receive much which they do not fully understand at the time.—God's revelation may be limited, not so much by itself, as by our capacity.—Discipleship implies faith in the teacher.—The need for faith is stronger when *spiritual* truths have to be conveyed ; we venture more upon the result.

Was glorified.   See on John vii. 39.—Refers by way of eminence to His Resurrection and Ascension, but spoken also of some other actions of His life.—Christ, when He had reached His Throne, would shed the glory He had obtained upon His disciples.—

Jesus resigned His glory at His incarnation. Phil. ii. 6, 7.—
There was a glory belonging to Christ from the commencement
of all time. John xvii. 5.—This was the glory of His Divine
eternal Sonship.—It is not said that the Son of God was glorified,
but the *Son of Man.*—This accession of glory was only proper and
suitable to His human nature.—When His work was done, as
God manifest in the flesh, He appeared in Heaven with new
honours won in this world.—Jesus was too familiar and too near
to shine in His full glory when He was with His disciples in
the flesh.—This grand picture needed distance and perspective.—
The Apostles could not have borne the full revelation of so great
a Being while He was with them in their homes and in the
common ways of life.—Christ must conquer death and share His
great reward before He can be all to man.—" Hereby is kept a
due proportion between the Head and His members, that He shall
be first exalted before they get their full allowance ; and hereby,
also, Christ being exalted, giveth evidence that He remembers
His people." *Hutcheson.*

Then remembered. The past was revived, but transfigured by
new light.—It is always difficult to estimate the true proportions
and discern the full meaning of what lies immediately before us.—
The aid of memory is needed to bring past impressions to their
fruition.—The disciples were partakers of the glorification of
Jesus, whose splendour reached them and threw light upon all
life —An advanced revelation is not so much the presentation of
new truth as the bringing out the full significance and power of
the old.—The vague and rudimentary forms of great truths are a
prophecy of their expansion and fulfilment.—The future gradually
revealing the meaning of the past is God's way of leading us on.—
However slowly our knowledge may have been attained, we can
rapidly glance backwards over it.—There are moments in human
life when a flash of light seems to come, suddenly revealing the
past.—The power of memory enables us to attain the only image
we can have of the Sovereign Intellect.—Memory gives a permanence to what *has* been, gives man a kind of property in the
universe itself.—The remembrance of the impressions of events
and truths is necessary to the very existence of our moral life.—
Without this, we could have no gratitude or love for what is
good.—Some of our purest thoughts and feelings have their
distant springs in the events of the past.—Spiritual men are going
forward to that light which will not only revive, but irradiate the
past.

These things. A repetition intended to show the strict harmony
between the prophecy and the event.

Were written. The Church's history brings out the significance of her records.—The varied dealings of Providence summon the attention of men to successive portions of revealed truth.—The Bible receives the light of illustration from all ages : history becomes an interpreter.—If we wait with patience, in humble dependence upon the teaching of the Spirit, we shall see the reason why many things in the Bible were written.

Of him. Christ is the theme of prophecy.—All the prophecies either point directly to Him, or determine something which has a definite relation to Him.—" The testimony of Jesus is the spirit of prophecy." Rev. xix. 10.—Human history is either looking out for Christ, or working out His principles either by obedience or opposition.

They had done. Both the disciples and the people, in hailing Him as king.—" Such an admirable harmony there is between the word and works of God, that the remembrance of what is *written* will enable us to understand what is *done;* and the observation of what is done will help us to understand what is written. *As we have heard, so have we seen.* The Scripture is every day in the fulfilling." *Henry.*—" When the Spirit of God is most amply poured out, He will still lead men to the Scriptures to discern of Christ, and compare their own actings by it." *Hutcheson.* A superior light is needed to understand ourselves and the true intent of our actions.

ταῦτα. *These things.* This His entry, of so momentous importance, and His prediction. *Bengel.*—ἔγνωσαν. They saw nothing in them beyond an impression of joy and honour, and of belief that Jesus was the Messiah. *Webster.*—ἐποίησαν. *They did.* John omits the ὅτι before this word. He considered the prediction and the fulfilment so linked together that *both* were remembered and understood.

17. The people therefore that was with him when he called Lazarus out of his grave and raised him from the dead, bare record.

People. Gr, *crowd.*—These were the unsophisticated multitude.— They had not, like the Scribes and Pharisees, any supreme interest in the persistent maintenance of venerable errors.—The miracles of Jesus were not wrought before the select few, but before multitudes, which strengthens our confidence in their reality.— The people have ever been the truth's safest guardians and most reliable witnesses.—Heresies and the various corruptions of religion have mostly arisen from professed ecclesiastics.

Therefore. Gr., *then.*—Resuming the narrative from verse 11, and looking forward to the statement in verse 19.

When he called Lazarus. See on chapter xi. 43.—Some MSS. read, "*that* He called," &c., which would mean that the people bore witness to that fact.—These demonstrations expressed the convictions of the people that the miracle was real.—"Their hosannas were a public proof of the miracle." *Wordsworth.*—The miracle was not lacking in proof, though it be not mentioned by the other evangelists.—This stupendous miracle is referred to with matchless simplicity of language.—Ordinary writers would have been tempted to heighten their description of such wonders by word-painting.—But this evangelist had grown familiar with these signs of power, and makes the recital of the most wonderful deeds subordinate to his great ethical purpose.—"Called Lazarus." We are reminded here of the Voice that spake at Creation.—With God, *thought, word,* and *act* are in essence the same.—He speaks, and the world is summoned into His presence.—In that powerful word, spoken at the tomb of Lazarus, Jesus gave proof of His dominion over the grave.—The Voice that called was that of One with whom power and will were commensurate.—The miracles of Christ are virtually prophecies of what He will do hereafter on a more extensive scale, and with more permanent results.—"It is recorded what was the seen cause (for the unseen was the overruling hand of God) moving the multitude to come out and convey Him in state—to wit—some of the people's testimony concerning the miracle wrought on Lazarus." *Hutcheson.*

Bare record. Gr., *bore witness.*—They testified to the miracle.— "They who wish well to Christ's kingdom should be forward to proclaim what they know that may redound to His honour." *Henry.*—The spectacle of the raising of Lazarus rendered homage to the worker of so great a deed most easy.—The people showed the sincerity of their testimony to the miracle by exalting Jesus as their Messiah-King.—From such an exhibition of power and authority as they had seen, it was not hard to pass to the idea of a king and kingdom.—Their enthusiasm, though short-lived and imperfect, reposed upon a great truth; for devotion to a Person, with all the instinct and simplicity of love, is the genius of the Christian Religion.—This King of Zion derives glory from the testimony of His subjects.

ὁ ὄχλος . . . ὅτε. If we read ὅτι, as the Syr. version, the *people* would mean those who had been in Our Lord's company, and had been at Bethany, and had seen

Lazarus, bore witness to this fact. *Schaff.*—ἐμαρτύρει. *Bare record* as to the miracle at which they were present. *Bengel.*

---

18. For this cause the people also met him, for that they heard that he had done this miracle.

For this cause. Some of the spectators of the miracle went before to the city and told others, who, in consequence, came to meet the triumphal procession.—These latter had not seen, but they believed upon testimony.—Such is our position; we believe first upon report, then we verify by experiment.—We cannot be exactly in the same position as those who witnessed the putting forth of Divine power in Jesus, but we can attain to as full an assurance that such deeds were wrought.

People met him. "Many a good sermon He had preached in Jerusalem which drew not such crowds after Him as this one miracle did." *Henry.*—Great changes in human thought and feeling come after long preparations of Providence.—"It is the duty of them who hear anything of Christ's commendation to go and seek Him and do homage to Him." *Hutcheson.*

Miracle. See on chapters ii. 11, 23; iii. 2; iv. 8; vi. 30.—Gr., *sign :* St. John mostly uses this word.—To translate it by *miracle* robs the word of its full bearing and significance, and frequently does manifest injury to the sense (see chapters iii. 2; vii. 31; x. 41); there is a remarkable instance in chapter vi. 26.—This word shows more than any other the ethical end of the miracle.— These mighty works of Christ were *signs* of Divine power and *seals* of His mission.—The amazement produced by those signs of power should improve to veneration, faith, love, and obedience.

ὄχλος. The people who were hearers being informed by the people who were spectators.—Matt. and Mk. call the former, *those that went before;* the latter *those that followed. Bengel.*

---

19. The Pharisees therefore said among themselves, Perceive ye how ye prevail nothing? behold, the world is gone after him.

The Pharisees. See on chapter i. 24.—Ready to take alarm at the least sign that threatened danger to their class.—They depended upon mere visionary sources of greatness, not upon realities.— Such fashions of thought and feeling as they relied on pass away ;

they are in constant danger.—He who possesses eternal truths need take no alarm nor bend his invention to strategems.

Said. They might be considered as muttering, "Ye see that Caiaphas was right : your half-measures are useless. Follow the counsel of our prudent High Priest, and all will be well."

Among themselves. They would not confess their fears publicly : it would not be fitting to show signs of alarm before the multitude.—They had a different order of phrases for the uninitiated.

Perceive ye? Better rendered indicatively, *ye perceive*.—Compare Acts xxi. 20.

Prevail nothing. Suggesting, perhaps, that something new must be tried.—They considered that they could not vanquish Him nor His cause by the command they had just given, chap. xi. 57. —They had shown the same spirit on previous occasions, chap. vii. 45.—Now they take counsel, as in chap. xi. 47.—They were forced by the course of events to confess the inherent weakness of their cause.—In the mad rage of opposition to the truth, there are lucid moments when men fairly see the hopelessness of the conflict.—To this confession all the enemies of the truth must come at last.—" They could not with all their insinuations alienate the peoples' affections from Him, nor with all their menaces restrain them from showing their affection to Him." *Henry.*

The world. A hyperbolical expression; as we say, *everybody*.— This was a confession that *they* were completely deserted.—They exaggerated, through mere vexation, the popularity of this new teacher.—Yet here they give an unconscious prophecy of what has been, and will be more fully accomplished.—Such was the prophecy of Caiaphas, chap. xi. 50.—Also Pilate's unconscious testimony to the Kingship of Jesus in his inscription on the cross, chap. xix. 19.—The old world was now breaking up, and humanity was looking forward towards a new object of hope and desire.— A new enthusiasm was to be introduced into religion, generating a devotion, zeal, and courage hitherto unknown.—Men were to be attracted and united in the strongest of all fellowships by the power of a living Name.—In the complaint of these Pharisees there was a truth quite beyond their intention.—In the perplexities of thought and feeling men sometimes utter truths beyond the reach of their souls.—There was a new centre of attraction now ; it was a stable centre, for it acted upon the highest and best principles of human nature.—When science discovered the true centre of the Solar System, the idea of all its motions was simplified : instead of the endless epicycles of the ancients, all its revolutions were seen to be regular and harmonious.—Christ was the living centre of souls, and in Him were exalted and simplified the relations between God and man.

Gone after him. They felt that *they* could no longer retain the people.—Now their sovereignty over the minds and consciences of men is threatened.—The time for blind, ignorant, helpless dependence upon mere authority was now passing away.—A teacher had now appeared who took truth for authority, and not authority for truth.

κόσμος. Some ascribe the words to the Sanhedrim.—Taken as a question. *Lampe.* —The popular formula for numerous followers. *Wetstein.*—ὠφελεῖτε. The bold cheering up the timid. *Stier.*—Helpless wretches angrily mocking one another. *Lange.*

---

20. And there were certain Greeks among them that came up to worship at the feast

Greeks. Proselytes from heathenism who had conformed to the whole Jewish law, *i.e.*, " proselytes of righteousness."—Such was the Ethiopian eunuch. Acts viii. 27.—They were not Greek-speaking Jews, for such were described by a different name.— They were not pagans, for they came to *worship*.—The ancient Greeks were supreme in intellectual power, culture, and skill.— In *Arts*, the world has never surpassed their works in marble.— In *Philosophy*, no nation has ever equalled them in their taste for speculation.—In *Literature*, they have left for all ages their deep impress upon the literature of the world.—" Wherever literature consoles sorrow or assuages pain—wherever it brings gladness to eyes which fail with wakefulness and tears, and ache for the dark house and the long sleep—there is exhibited, in its noblest form, the immortal influence of Athens." *Macaulay.*—Greek language was the tongue of all civilized nations, as French at present.—The New Testament comes to us, not in the Aramaic, which the Apostles spoke, but in Greek.—It is the richest and most delicate in flexibility and clearness of expression.—Restless in mental and bodily activity as seen in their subtle disputations and games.— Remarkable for love of the beautiful, quickness of perception, and unwearied investigation.—Their religion, a fanciful poetic mythology, without any influence on their morals.—A thousand objects of worship, with endless contradiction of attributes.— Their deities often personifications of human passions.—Festivals and sacrifices, so obscene that they often polluted even heathen

1004 / Gospel of John

temples.—Their demons, through famous oracles, gave great power to their priests.—Life was a gay frolic, a mockery of the earnest wants of their souls.—In great calamities they sacrificed to "unknown gods," in hope of relief. Acts xvii. 23.—Their poets were the nation's teachers: " Homer " was their Bible.

Came. The word signifies that they were *wont to come* up to worship.—That these Greeks thus joined the throng of regular worshippers was significant of a new tendency in the human mind. —The Kingdom of God was about to come to other nations.— Illustrious persons from Greece and Rome came to Jerusalem to worship. Even members of the family of the Cæsars did thus, as Suetonius writes.—Some came to seek a better kind of religion than their own. *Philo.*—" My house shall be called the house of prayer *for all nations* " was surely now in process of fulfilment.

Worship. There was a slender ground for the idea of worshipping with the Jews.—The classic Greeks and Romans, as at every feast at home, worshipped on general principles, caring little what or whom.—"Their gods differed from men only in age." *Photinus.* —Many Greeks in the time of our Lord had an inward yearning for the truth, and found a refuge for mind and heart in the purer theology of Judaism.—Here was to be found the grandest solution of the deepest moral problems, the way of reconciliation for the ease of the troubled conscience, the presentation to the mind of the most sublime conceptions of the Divine nature.—The deity of Greek philosophy, such as Plato conceived, was a cold and heartless abstraction, when compared with the living God of Israel.—" These Greeks belonged to the Church invisible, to the children of God scattered among the heathen (chapters x. 16 ; xi. 52), and were the forerunners of the Gentile converts." *Schaff.*

The Feast. The Passover.—See on chapters xi. 55 and ii. 13.

Ἕλληνες. Jews who spoke Greek. *Calvin, Ewald, Semler.*—Contradicted by the name; compare chap. vii. 35, the whole scene and the deduction of Christ, verses 23 and 32—the reference to the extension of His ministry. *Lange.*—A prelude herein is given of the kingdom of God being about to pass over from the Jews to the Gentiles. *Bengel.*—ἀναβαινόντων. The present indicates *habitual* pilgrimage to Jerusalem. *Schaff.*—προσκυνήσωσιν. The incident took place on the same day as the entry. *Neander.*—On Monday. *Lange.*—ἑορτῇ. The Passover, mentioned in ch. xi. 55.

---

21. The same came therefore to Philip, which was of Bethsaida of Galilee, and desired him, saying, Sir, we would see Jesus.

Philip. See on chap. i. 43, 44.—Both he and Andrew were either known to some of their friends or were expectants of the special glories of His kingdom.—Our Lord's answer seems to confirm this opinion.—He will show them that His future glories lie along the path of suffering.—Philip was the only Apostle who had a purely Greek name.—He may have been brought up, or have been a resident in one of the Hellenistic cities of Asia Minor, Syria, or Egypt.—Thus it was, perhaps, natural that these Greeks should go to *him*.—It may be their reverence for Christ imposed reserve upon their conduct, and forbade their approaching Him directly.—They sought the mediation of those who were nearer to Christ than they.—Christ Himself satisfies this felt want of minds spiritually awakened.—To go at once to Him is to reach and to know God.—" It is a great mistake, and an injury done to Christ, to think that He will keep a state and distance from sinners who sincerely seek Him." *Hutcheson.*

Bethsaida of Galilee. See on chap. i. 44.—" Galilee of the Gentiles, and therefore a very fit person to bring *them* to Christ." *Wordsworth.*—These Greeks having a desire to see Christ were industrious to use the proper means: they that would have the knowledge of God must seek it.—They made their application to one of the disciples: they that would see Christ by faith should apply themselves to His ministers.—It is good to know those who know the Lord. *Henry.*

Sir. Not in the higher sense, yet with reverence. *Lange.*—A title of respect, chiefly used by those who had no intimate knowledge of each other ; acquaintances were usually addressed by name.— " They call him ' Sir,' though a fisherman, as being the civil compellation of these times, given even to mean persons," chap. xx. 15. *Hutcheson.*

We would see. See on Matt. ii. 1.—Gr., *we wish*, &c.—The word implies *desire*.—This longing desire of the Gentiles stands contrasted with the prevailing unbelief of the Jews.—Thinking men of all nations were now looking out with vague longings for something greater and better.—The great institutions of the world seemed to be wearing out, and men were looking towards some living Director and Restorer, who would bring in a better time.—In the deep spiritual desires of men there is an appeal to Heaven.—Perplexed and needy children are looking imploringly to the Father.—The desire of these Greeks was not mere curiosity, else Jesus would not have gratified it.—There was in that desire something of a prophetic yearning for the days of the Son of Man.—" It was John's privilege to change the denunciations of the Synoptists into this joyful outlook for the very Pagans whose tongue he had used." *Herder.*—"These men from the West, at the end of His life, set forth the same as the Magi from the East, at its beginning; but they come to the *cross* of the King, as those to His *cradle.*" *Stier.*

See Jesus. A literal fulfilment of the prediction of the prophets, especially of Isa. lx.—A fulfilment of the type contained in the history of the wise men from the East. (See on Matt. ii. 1.)—A foretoken of the ensuing conversion of the proselytes of the gate, then of the Gentile world itself. *Lange.*—See on chap. i. 29.—To see Him privately, so as to be in His company.—They were, probably, unable to get near to Him on account of the crowd.—Another difficulty was, that Greeks were not admitted into that part of the Temple where Jesus was now teaching. The time had not yet come for Jesus to speak much with the Gentiles.—He had limited His ministry to the chosen nation, for the Kingdom of Heaven was only "at hand:"—To see Jesus was the prophetic longing of all earnest spirits since the world began.—Such a desire has enabled many to live above and beyond the spirit of the age.—Many longed for Christ with vague desire, who could not shape His name into syllables.—John does not mention that Jesus addressed any words to these Greeks personally.—His chief purpose was to show the great principle involved in the words given in answer to this request.—The Evangelists are satisfied if they give us enough of detail to infix great principles upon our minds.—These suffice to show us what were the underlying facts of Gospel History.—As proselytes of the gate, these Greeks shared Israel's hope, and the enthusiastic feeling of the people.—The expression of their desire is threefold:—1. The solicitation; 2, the respectful manner of addressing even the disciple of the celebrated Master; 3, the strong yet modest expression of the wish. *Lange.*—With us, to see Jesus by the eye of faith is to have perfect satisfaction for the *heart, conscience, intellect.*—"In our attendance upon holy ordinances, and particularly the Gospel Passover, the great desire of our souls should be to *see Jesus.*" *Henry.*

Φιλίππῳ. They address Philip because from Bethsaida, or because he understood Greek. *Stier.*—ἰδεῖν. *To see, i.e,* to have an interview.—Uncertain if the wish were gratified. *Titmann.*—Time and place unsuitable. *Lampe.*—The request granted from the appropriate answer. *Hammond.*

---

22. Philip cometh and telleth Andrew: and again Andrew and Philip tell Jesus.

Telleth Andrew. See on chap. i. 40.—Andrew was a name of

Greek origin; this may account for Philip's application to him.—
An instance of the respectful manner in which the Apostles
behaved, even on ordinary occasions, to their Divine Master.
Mark ix. 32. *Webster.*—The request may have been regarded as
extraordinary, and therefore requiring consultation.—Neither of
these Apostles was prepared for the extension of Gospel privileges to the Gentiles.—They were like men who felt the oppression of a new truth, and therefore required time for deliberation.
—Heaven regards with patience all honest delays in the search
after the Divine will.

Andrew and Philip. " One would not come alone, a proof of the
reverence for Jesus after the stupendous miracle He had just
wrought." *Wordsworth.*—He felt it expedient to divide the burden
of his perplexity with another.—Both faith and courage are
strengthened by companionship.—Mediation is the great law of
life.—We derive through others our knowledge of Jesus.—
" Christ's ministers should be helpful to one another, and concur
in helping souls to Him." *Henry.*—The Apostles are still the
sources of our knowledge of Christ; they give us those facts and
truths upon which our faith in Him is founded.

Tell Jesus. He alone can answer every question, and solve every
difficulty.—In all perplexities and cares, hopes and fears, joys
and sorrows, temptations and sins, we should " tell Jesus."—The
beginning, the middle, and the end of faith is personal union
with Him.—He who does not know the blessedness of the habit
of telling Jesus everything, has yet to learn the nature of true
Christian prayer.

Instead of καὶ πάλιν, &c. (Text rec.), read ἔρχεται Ἀνδρέας καὶ Φίλιππος, καὶ λέγουσιν.
Cod. Sin., A. B. L., Lach., Tisch.

23. And Jesus answered them, saying, The hour is come, that the Son of man
should be glorified.

Answered. The answer wears the appearance of a refusal.—Jesus
was accustomed to enter at once upon subjects that seemed not
to touch the questions addressed to him.—Truth from His lips
was sudden light, and developed the thoughts of men to sublimer
issues.—Christ gives essential and real answers to all the solemn
questions of the soul.—The solemn hour upon which He is now
entering will furnish the answer to many seekers after God in the

Gentile world.—Whether or not these words were delivered in the presence of the Greeks, their request obtained a real answer.

The hour. Of this hour there is frequent mention afterwards. Verse 27, chaps. xiii. 1; xvi. 32; xvii. 1; xvii. 5.—" From the visit of the Gentiles, He deduces the preparation of His mission for the Gentiles, *i.e.*, His resurrection.—From the nearness of the period when the bounds that have encompassed Him shall be removed, and His ministry be rendered a universal one, He infers His imminent death.—Universalness and resurrection are for Him reciprocal terms.—Universalness and preceding death are for Him inseparably connected. Chaps. x. 15, 16; xvii." *Lange.*—There are periods in history when the past seems to be summed up into one point, and all things take a new beginning.—There may be long ages of preparation for one important hour.—God appears in the hour of His special working, when men have felt their need through long years of sore experience.—This was the hour when Jesus would rise from His deepest trouble to fresh and ever-during honours.—It was the hour towards which history was working, and from which it works.—His hour of glorification coincides with the conversion of the Gentiles.

Is come. It was so near now that the conflict was as good as won. —Through the slow ages of time the vast preparations were being made, and now the long-looked for event is about to be precipitated.—The time has come when the plan of the Redeemer's mission must be enlarged, in harmony with His benevolent purpose and triumph.—At an earlier stage He had commanded His Apostles, " Go not into the way of the Gentiles." Matt. x. 5. —Now He is about to give them a commission to preach to the Gentiles.—The awe-inspiring events of that " hour " would decide many waverers.—It was part of the joy which Jesus set before Him that the Gentiles would believe.—" Do the Gentiles begin to enquire after me?—Doth the Morning Star appear to them, and that blessed *day spring* which knows its place, and time too, doth that begin to *take hold of the ends of the earth?*—Then the hour is come for the *glorifying of the Son of Man.*" *Henry.*—Not, however, His hour of death by itself, but that together with the hour of His departure out of the world.—The two are comprehended in one, as in the idea of exaltation in verses 32, 34, and in chap. iii. 14.—The decisive hour when He will surrender Himself to full communion with the Greeks is at hand.—The future of the believing Gentile world, the future of its access to Him, is before Him, in its nearest representatives, as an incipient present. Compare chap. xiii. 31. *Lange.*

Son of man. See on chaps. i. 51 ; **v.** 27.—Implies that He was also the " Son of God."—Because He was Divine, it was appropriate to insist upon His humanity.—It was as the *Son of Man* that Jesus was glorified.—" The glorification of the Son of man is the exaltation of Christ in His human nature above death (a transit from the first stage of human life to the second) ; above the limits of the servant to the boundless liberty of the lord ; above a qualified working by individual words and signs, to unqualified activity through the Spirit.—It is a development of His inner wealth, according to verse 24 ; a personal lifting up, according to verse 32 ; a local, but at the same time, an universal one, according to verse 33." *Lange.*

Glorified. See on chaps. vii. 39 ; xi. 4.—Jesus emptied Himself of His glory at His incarnation. Phil. ii. 6, 7.—His glory had long been hidden in human weakness and dependence.—It was humility, being such as He was, to have lived so long in obscurity, not saying or doing anything great ; to submit to be poor and despised ; to witness how men doubted the validity of His claims, or the success of His mission.—The glory of Jesus was the acknowledgment of Him in the world.—That glory can only be recognised when we know Christ for all He really is.—The greatness of Christ sheds a lustre upon all who receive Him.—" The heavens *declare* the Glory of God," but man can *ascribe* Glory to God.—It was a glorification of Jesus to be entirely trusted in by many hearts ; to be believed on in the world.—The glory of Christ becomes reflected, and therefore multiplied in many souls. —Man cannot add anything to the glory of the Divine Nature : therefore to " glorify God " must signify to extol or praise Him. —By the liberty given to the intellectual and responsible creature, God has so far tied Himself to conditions that He can receive praise from man.—To give glory to Christ is to give glory to God.—" Such as get open eyes to discern the glory of the cross and the glory that abides on Christ and His followers after their suffering, will not care nor relish worldly pomp and glory, or carnal respect from men." *Hutcheson.*

ἀπεκρίνατο. It is implied that Jesus granted the request, and uttered these words when the Greeks were presented to Him. *Webster.*—αὐτοῖς. Refers to Andrew and Philip. *Alford.*—The apostles and Greeks together. *Stier.*—ἵνα δοξα θῇ. When the Son of Man shall be glorified.—ἵνα has this force in ch. xvi. 2.—He referred to his resurrection, ascension, and atonement. *Lampe.*—*Glorified* with the Father. Ch. xvii, 5. *Bengel.*

24. Verily, verily, I say unto you, Except a corn of wheat fall into the ground and die, it abideth alone: but if it die, it bringeth forth much fruit.

Verily. See on chap. i. 51. Gr., *Amen.*—Matthew, Mark, and Luke are accustomed to set down "verily" (amen) in the speeches of Jesus *once*, but John *twice.*—Everything He uttered was faithful and true, for He was such Himself.—True in *substance*, true in *words*, true in the Father, in Himself, in the nature of God, and in the nature of man.—In the time of John it was appropriate to use the double formula, to remind men of the solemnity of the words of the Lord Jesus.—This was His usual preface to all His weighty sayings.—It is a word whose office is to calm and solemnize the mind before the presence of a great truth.—By that one word He indicated the sum of His mysterious verities, as if He said, "What I am going to utter is eternal truth."—The words thus emphatically introduced are delivered for the advantage of these inquiring Greeks, as the substance of the Gospel. —The death, resurrection, and exaltation of Christ are the chief facts of the Christian creed. 1 Timothy iii. 16.

Say. His not appealing to the Prophets seems to imply that He was addressing the Greeks.—The Prophets so clearly foretold His death that some infidel scholars say these things happened first.—But dumb nature shall now prophesy secretly, but by Christ, publicly, through all time.—The Greeks had profoundly observed, but could not interpret this prediction.—In their dreams they perceived dim traces of a redeeming death.—Death they saw everywhere, but now will read in it the wages of sin.

Corn of wheat. Gr., *grain*, same Greek word used 1 Cor. xv. 37. —Our Lord will now preach to Jew and Greek a brief sermon— a single grain of wheat is His text: the cross His theme.—The Great Teacher recognized the symbolism of Nature.—Nature is an expression of the thoughts of God, a part of His Revelation, and a parable of better things.—We find through several ages and countries the same metaphors used to illustrate the same ideas.— This universality can only arise from the aptitude which comes of truth.—Nature is animated by the breath of the Eternal, and needs but spiritual insight to discover therein a wondrous volume of Divine truth.—Oriental Mysticism has a profound reflection in a similar strain—

> "Widely sow the wheat deep in the lap of earth,
> Soon the golden, rich, large ears of grain have birth;
> When again the flail shall smite the ears in twain
> From the beaten ears comes bread to nourish man."

Die. The change in the dissolution of the seed is such that the

Creator calls it *death.*—The ordinance of heaven makes the fruit spring from the dying seed—a primitive prophecy of the mystery of the Atonement.—The death of our Lord causes fruit of salvation to spring forth.—The covenant of seed-time and harvest was firmly established; so was His counsel respecting the death of Christ and life of the Redeemed.—In this faith seed is sown, and increase from the Divine law arises.—The great truth covered by this parable the Greeks cannot perceive. But when the Cross proclaimed SALVATION, all was plain.—Even the Apostles continued dreaming until the Spirit aroused them.—Had this seedcorn died simply as a martyr, His life, His energy, His wisdom, His benevolence above the entire race were *alone.*—Now, a multitude that no man can number are the fruit.—This word "die" seemed to forbid the idea of a near glorification.—The mention of it might well prove a stumbling-block to the Greeks, but for the indication of the sublime results that are to follow.—Jesus enclosed within Him mysterious germs of a sublime future for man.—He put off all that was mortal and suited to the things of passing time, that He might manifest to the world the power of a more plentiful and enduring life.—The Greeks could not see Jesus, in the reality and fulness of His nature, before His death. —They must wait until the time when He is on high, and yet near to all believing souls.—His glorification after death would give Him a perpetual presence, and do away for ever with the disadvantage of all that was merely local and temporary.—In like manner eternal youth, beauty, and glory in the new world are attained by the Christian only through death.

Abideth alone. "As the death of the seed is absolutely necessary to its springing, so my death is the only way by which I can be glorified and men saved."—This reply to the Greeks gave them a key to unlock all the mysteries of His miracles after they heard of His resurrection.—The death of Christ was necessary to the life of the world.—Had He not died to rise again, humanity must have been left without a remedy.—His path to glory was through the obscurity and humiliation of the tomb.—The grave was but the place where He was laid awhile, that He might come forth without the signs of weakness in all the attributes of a more plentiful life.—There are strong necessities in the spiritual as well as in the natural worlds.—God, in His wisdom, has seen fit to make laws which appear to have the effect of binding and limiting Himself.—There was a needs be that Christ should suffer these things. —"It had been no prejudice to Him, only His love could not be without us, nor had it been manifested unless He had brought many sons unto glory, but all the loss had been ours." *Hutcheson.*

—"All the chief moments in the life of Christ are prefigured in the history of the grain of wheat: Christmas, Good Friday, Easter, Ascension, Whitsuntide." *Lange.*

Much fruit. The death was but for a moment: the life proceeding thence, and the blessed fruits of it, remain.—Jesus had confidence in the triumph of His cause and large hope for man. —Christ multiplies Himself in human souls by communicating to them the energy and spirit of His life.—The fruits of His dying are thus diffused through all nations and ages.—The glorification of Christ, through His rising from the dead, has elevated and ennobled every power and condition of man.—It has produced *intellectual* fruit—the mind has been quickened to higher conceptions of truth.—New regions of contemplation have been laid open.—If we examine the intellectual store of the poorest and most uninstructed Christian man, we find that all his greatest and noblest ideas have been derived from the teaching of Christ.— The death of Christ has generated an enthusiasm of love for Himself, hitherto unknown: hence have sprung the most precious fruits of charity to man.—By His death and subsequent glorification, Christ has imparted to man the energy of His life, truth, and example.—By the triumph of Christ over death, our hope of immortality is placed upon the only sure foundation, for it reposes upon an accomplished *fact*; hence the precious fruits of hope.— "Hereby the Father and the Son are glorified, the Church replenished, the mystical body kept up, and will at length be completed." *Henry.*—The history of all that is best and truest and noblest in the life of eighteen centuries is the fulfilment of our Lord's words.—Hearts hardened, sinful, dead, have been led to think of His death, and have felt germs of life springing up and bursting the husks of their former prison, and growing up into living powers, which have changed their whole being—this is the individual fulfilment that has come to many, and may come to all. *Plumptre.*—The saying concerning the grain of wheat and the succeeding sayings: 1, a sermon on salvation, as a word concerning Christ; 2, a sermon on repentance, as a word for us; 3, a sermon of consolation, as a word concerning suffering and dying Christians. *Lange.*

κόκκος. Some cannot see the relation of this figure to the Greeks.—The Greeks sought riches and honours from an earthly kingdom.—Our Lord points them to His death and spiritual results.—πεσὼν When it has fallen.—ἀποθάνῃ. It is only the outward husk that dies; the germ does not perish.—How life is contained in and developed and multip ied from the grain, remains still a profound mystery.—αὐτὸς μόνος. By itself alone. Christ, even though He had not died for us, yet could have been in

Himself the same that He now is. *Bengel.*—καρπὸν. Some confine the fruit to His glorified humanity as expanded into the church. *Luthardt.*—These words of our Lord were evidently intended to correct the Greek view of the world, just as those contained in chapter xviii. 36 are applicable to the ideas entertained by the Romans.— Human nature does not attain in this world a true and essentially beautiful appearance by the aid of pretty and art; but it arrives at the true and the beautiful by passing through death into a new life (1 John iii. 2).—The grain of wheat here symbolizes the new life which must proceed from death in order to appear in its richness, its fruit." *Lange.*—ὁ κόκκος. *The grain. Lange.*—μόνος. *Isolated*, by itself alone. *Schaff.*

---

25. He that loveth his life shall lose it; and he that hateth his life in this world shall keep it unto life eternal.

Loveth. Hebraism for excessive love of life, or morbid fear of death —To love life is the law impressed on all conscious being.— Our Lord in His humanity dreaded death, and shrunk from the bitter cup.—That He yielded Himself to death in obeying the will of His Father, teaches us that the natural impulse to preserve our physical life must be modified by higher claims.—To love our *outer* life more than Christ, is to reject Him as the sovereign of our *inner* life.—To love supremely that portion of life which belongs only to time is vilely to cast away our birthright.—The love of what is highest of all must regulate every other love.— "This is the watchword of Christ, and it should be that of His people also." *Lange.*

Life. The animal soul in us, "self"; for the *self* is the *life.*—The N. T. uses "self" and "life" with the same force of meaning.— Even life, in the lowest sense of the word, has more absolute value than the whole world, for our possession of, and interest in the world depend upon it.—There is another world, and a higher life, possessing a real and a permanent value.—Man touches both worlds in his complete nature : the lower element in it must give place to the higher.

Lose it. He who held to his wheat, refusing to sow, never reaped.—Such shall lose life spiritual—the happiness of the world to come — They shall fail of the only true life.—He loses not a mere physical and transitory life, but that which alone is worthy of the name.—Our way to dominion is through self-denial and sacrifice.—To lose the life of God hereafter is the only real calamity.—"Many a man hugs himself to death, and loses his life by overloving it. He that so loves his animal life as to indulge his appetite, shall lose the life he is so fond of, and another infinitely better." *Henry.*

Hateth. Hebraism for *not loving*, or *loving less.*—Self-renouncing, self-sacrificing resignation, leads to the higher life.—To gain eternal life involves some real sacrifice : Christ imposes the law of His own life upon all His followers.—To live in the spirit of sacrifice and absorbing devotion to the will of God is to commence already the life of triumph and everlasting joy.

This world. The place where our physical life is manifested, and by which it is bounded.—As far as we are concerned this world is a vanishing scene.—"The person is snatched away, the things remain."—The very desire for the things of the world, causing us to sin through temptation, passes away before the world itself.—The troubles of those who yield themselves in the spirit of self-sacrifice to God will go out entirely with this life.

Keep it. Oriental mysticism conceived of man's highest bliss as consisting of absorption into God, as a drop returning to its ocean fount.—The outward form of life was to be destroyed, and the soul mingle with the infinite sea of being.—In the Christian system, man's individuality is not destroyed, but he himself is transfigured.—The spiritual man will enjoy the presence of God; his soul does not perish by diffusion throughout the soul of the universe.—God will never invade the heritage of the soul's individuality.—The immortal essence of man's nature will be preserved; only that which was vanishing and temporary shall pass away.— A man is already ennobled when he aims at the highest life, and counts all things but loss to attain it.—By laying down self upon God's altar, a man procures a sanctuary for his soul, and places it beyond the reach of accident.—To put our real life in the hands of God is the surest way of keeping it ourselves.—The only "true riches," are those which run parallel with our immortal life.

Life eternal. Chapters iii. 15, 16, 17, v. 24. This is the life of God, which He lives—the expression of His existence pervading all space and time.—Life eternal is something more than endless existence ; it is the partaking of the Life of the ever Blessed One.— When God communicates His nature to the soul, there is imparted that intimate knowledge of Him which is eternal life.—The sharing of a nature is the only means of knowing that nature.—The basis of this "eternal life," the knowledge and participation of God, is only to be attained through that love which is ready to give up all for Him.—"Such as live by faith must renounce the principles of carnal sense and reason, and be content to walk on grounds contrary to these, especially in times of trial; for they must learn that love and keeping of life is loss, and hatred and losing of it is keeping of it." *Hutcheson.*

τὴν ψυχὴν αὐτοῦ. *His own soul* That ψυχη must here mean *soul* in our conception of the word does not result (as *Meyer* maintain) from the distinction made between ψυχή and ζωή (αἰώνιος) ; for the latter is expressive not simply of an endless duration of natural life, but of divine life. *Lange* – ψυχή means " self," as well as "life." *Tholuck.*—Should be distinguished here from ζωή and be translated as in verse 27. *Schaff.*—The word *soul* (or, *life*) is not really in a double sense; as the wheat corn retains its identity, though it die, so the soul; so that the two senses are in their depth but one. Notice that the *soul* involves the *life* in both cases, and must not be taken in the present acceptation of that term. *Alford.*

---

26. If any man serve me let him follow me; and where I am, there shall also my servant be: if any man serve me, him will my Father honour.

If any man. Gr., *any one would.* Chap. vii. 17.

Serve me. Gr., signifies the service of a personal attendant, not that of a bond-servant. Such service implies action, waiting, reverence.—" They also serve who only stand and wait." *Milton.* Those who serve this King of Zion, by that fact itself attain rank. —"They *serve* Christ who seek not their own things but the things of Christ, *i.e.*, who follow Him—love Him for His own sake, and think it a rich reward to be with Him." *Augustine.*

Follow me. By the form of the expression this condition is bound up with the idea of necessary realization, as if He said, "in my service you must follow Me."—These words look towards the glorification of the Redeemer.—Christ was to be an example on a broader and grander scale than the limitations of His earthly life would permit.—The Gospels present the picture of a Rabbi surrounded by his disciples.—Afterwards (as in the Acts) the local centre of religion is removed on high, and Christ becomes the inspiring life of the world for all time.—These Greeks, being strangers, could not join the number of Christ's literal followers.— Had the Redeemer continued on earth, they must needs go out of the reach of His direct influence.—We are in their position, and the same provision suits our case.—The Centre of Christianity is raised on high to bless all regions and all ages.—Privilege is no longer to be determined by relation to some earthly centre of light and influence.—They were to follow Christ by professing His name, receiving His truth, catching the spirit of the law of His life, taking up their cross and following Him.—Such service rises in dignity above the idea of obedience to external command, simply because it is commanded.—This is the service of adoration, love, and personal attachment.—It is like that of the angels, " All for love, and nothing for reward."—It is thought, action, and the resulting character, all being formed through the communication of a life.—To reproduce the character of Christ by means of love, is the true, and the only noble idea of service.—Such a following

of Christ implies a readiness to sacrifice all to the will of God.—
These Greeks were not deceived by concealing the difficulties of
duty; they were warned that the path lay through suffering, and
the scorn and contempt of the world.—" Let him make an open
and public profession of his relation to me by following me, as
the servant owns his master by following him in the streets."
Henry.

Where I am. Chapters vii. 34; viii. 58. This is implied in the
idea of following.—In the bewilderment of our outlook upon the
future this gives a fixity to contemplation and a place of repose
for our heart.—In the vague sublimity of the hereafter the loving
thought of Christ makes the soul feel at home.

Servant be. It is enough for the servant that he share the glory
of his Lord.—This view of heaven has for us more practical importance than any minute descriptions of that happy state.—The
mention of Him with whom we are to live for ever becomes the
force which forms our spiritual character.—This promise includes
the idea of being with Christ after death; with Him in the
triumph of His eternal reign.—There is a like necessity that after
believers shall have suffered these things, they too shall enter into
their glory.—Christ is the fixed point to which our eternal hope is
directed.—He who is crucified with Christ to the world and sin,
shall share His glorious victory.—The life of the Church is but a
repetition throughout history of the life of her Lord.—The Christian
idea of future reward contemplates no mysterious absorption into
God—believers shall be with Christ, yet for ever distinctly themselves.

Him. Emphatic.—He is the fellow-heir of Christ, the Son.—
" That He might be the firstborn among many brethren."
Rom. viii. 29.

Father. Chapters ii. 16; iv. 21, 23.—Honour bestowed alone
upon the servants of His Son.—Christ constantly refers to the
Fountain of the Godhead as the source of all to man.—" The
Father Himself will esteem him as a personality connected with
Himself, and exalted above death." *Lange.*

Honour. First, promise unto life eternal (verse 25); second,
being where Jesus is; third, honoured by the Father.—Many
have toiled hard to secure from their fellows their verdict of
approbation.—The honour of men was the great ambition of
the Scribes and Pharisees.—Such honour is brief and uncertain,
but that which comes from God is ever-during and sure.—
It comes from the highest source, and is approved of by the
purest and highest creatures.—Such honour confers the only

nobility worth the name.—To honour God demands a constant, deep, and painful sacrifice.—Can any created mind conceive what the King of kings has in reserve for His guests?—Our spirits sink under the burden of glory in store for those whom the Father will delight to honour for His Son's sake.—" Christ as Mediator is so accepted of the Father, that He will put marks of favour and honour upon all His servants.—The Greeks desired to *see Jesus*: He lets them know that it was not enough to *see* Him, they must *serve* Him.—Christ fixes for His servants both their *work* and their *wages*: 1. Their *work*, to attend—(1) *His motions*—let him follow Me; (2) *His repose*—where I am, let my servant be; (*a*) in the *assemblies of the saints*, (*b*) in *heaven*—in thought and affection.—2. Their *wages*, they shall be (1) happy with Him; (2) honoured by His Father." *Henry.*

ὅπου εἰμὶ ἐγώ. The same road. *Luthardt.*—The Parousia. *Meyer.*—First, in the state of humiliation, of death, then in the state and land of δόξα, beyond death—the idea of the raising of the servant being thus involved. *Lange.*—The ministering to, or intimate union with, Christ (the position of Philip and Andrew and the rest, and that into which these Greeks seemed desirous to enter) implies *following* Him; and that, through tribulation to glory.—εἰμὶ—the *essential* present—in My true place, *i.e.* (chap. xvii. 24) in the glory of the Father. *Alford.*

---

27. Now is my soul troubled; and what shall I say? Father, save me from this hour: but for this cause came I unto this hour.

Now. Occurs also verse 31.—The agitation of soul experienced by Jesus, introduced by the whole train of thought from verse 24. —Primarily, He fixed His eye upon the great goal of the death-road; now the road itself engages His attention.—The Greeks must learn by His example neither to be fanatically enthusiastic about the conditions of death, nor to turn away from them in cowardly dread.—He therefore gives free utterance to His emotion.—This change of mood not unlooked for in the life of the Lord.—In the perfect life of the spirit the most blissful moods pass, in the sublimest transition of feeling, into the saddest.— Thus in the Palm-entry (Luke xix. 4); thus here; thus after the High-priestly prayer; thus at the Supper (chap. xiii. 31).—On the other hand, the saddest moods likewise pass into the most blissful. —Thus at the departure from Galilee (Matt. xi. 25); thus at the Supper (chap. xiii. 31); thus in Gethsemane (John xviii. 15ff.); thus on the Cross (Luke xii. 49, 50). *Lange.*—The shadow of death touches His soul, and He makes this natural exclamation.

Soul. Same word as that rendered " life " in verse 25.—His human

soul—the life of man that was in Him.—Jesus took all the consequences of being "made in the likeness of sinful flesh."—"As
He draws near to the Cross His human nature appears.—That
nature was free from *sin*, but not from natural infirmities."
Chrysostom.

Troubled. His assumption of our humanity and sad inheritance
was no figure of speech.—Christ did not *act* this scene of man,
He truly felt our human woes.—This was a premonitory pang of
that mental anguish which was intensified in Gethsemane.—Jesus
confessed to a human shrinking from "the cup" of suffering.—
The evangelists write this sacred biography with all the simplicity of nature.—They do not paint their hero beyond the life.—
An evidence of reality and a proof of their inspiration.—A natural
feeling is here struggling with a strong and obedient will.—By a
few delicate strokes, the sacred writer represents the condition of
one who was mysteriously Divine, yet bound by this terrible
necessity of suffering.—A perfect picture is thus given of a truth
which yet contains unknown depths of mystery.—Jesus did not
hold the stoical theory of life; He felt, and yielded to the impressions of pain and sorrow.—His experience teaches us that we
may feel all the sorrow of the present, though supported by truth
and the prospect of ultimate triumph.—"This may also discover
unto us what difficulty there was in the work of our redemption,
that it put the Son of God to such pressures and perplexities to
carry it through." *Hutcheson.*

What shall I say? These words are to be taken rather as an
exclamation than as expressing a perplexity of choice.—Such
sentences impress us with the reality of His human nature.—
There are times when feeling seems to overwhelm thought, and
to use language to relieve the heart rather than the mind.—His
human horror of death and His divine love of unfaltering obedience, in keen conflict.—Human language unequal to express
His mighty emotions, as a drop of water to reflect the glory and
grandeur of the starry heavens.—"Christ speaks like one at a loss,
as if what He should choose He wot not. There was a struggle
between the *work* He had taken upon Him which required sufferings, and the *nature* He had taken upon Him which dreaded
them." *Henry.*—"By thy *unknown* sufferings, good Lord, deliver
us." *Litany of the Greek Church.*

Father. The Fatherhood of God the strongest refuge of the soul
in calamity.—The Son of God has taught His brethren that they
too can feel that a Divine Fatherhood is a pledge of love and
guardianship, a foundation for hope and succour.—In the darkest

dispensation of suffering, the righteous soul feels that this truth remains, that he is God's child.—Christ's whole life, down to the latest moment, one act of glorifying His Father.

Save me. In these words, sorrow is allowed to express itself with the true touches of nature.—The human sense of distress and the strength of faith are thus briefly signified.—A similar prayer, Matt. xxvi. 29.—This prayer had an element of that momentary sense of desertion on the Cross. Matt. xxvii. 46.—This is all that man can cry when about to be engulfed in a great calamity. —" Were our distress and perplexities never so great, yet it is our duty to believe the power of God, that He is able to deliver us out of them all." *Hutcheson.*

This hour. " The hour of suffering is made present to His mind as if He had actually entered into it." *Meyer.*—The expression relates not to certain moments of intense agony, but to the whole period of His sufferings.—He knew the components of that bitter cup which was preparing.—This was a critical juncture in the history of mankind; He alone knew its solemn significance, and felt its awful weight.—" The time of His suffering was (1) *A set time,* set to an hour, and He knew it.—It was said twice before that His hour was not yet come, but now it was so near that He might say it was come.—(2) *A short time.* An hour is soon over, so were Christ's sufferings.—He could see through them to ' the joy set before Him.' " *Henry.*

For this cause. The purpose of suffering to redeem man.—The sense of duty soon emerges strong from the conflict, and rises superior to suffering and sorrow.—The merciful purpose of Heaven and His submission thereto stand out clearly amidst the terrible perplexities of this " hour."—The recognition of a Divine purpose in our work is the true impulse of courage.—The will of God which Jesus was commissioned to work out was founded upon a sufficient reason: it was determined by the " counsel " of God. —The vicarious nature of His passion, by which He bore the sins of the whole world, can alone explain His deep commotion on this occasion and in Gethsemane.—Some have wondered that John passes over the agony in the garden, but it is here, and the very words of Matt. xxvi. 39 are echoed.—Some have wondered too, that in the life of the Son of Man a struggle such as this could have had even a moment's place.—Not a few, indeed, would at any cost read the words otherwise ; but they *cannot,* either on the written page or in the hearts of men.—That troubled soul asked, " What shall I say ? "—Blessed reality !—In that struggle humanity struggled, and in that victory humanity won. *Watkins.*—

Innocent nature got the *first word*, but divine wisdom and love got the *last*.—Reference is here had to the divine counsels concerning His sufferings. *Henry.*—He knows: (1) That grief itself has its holy aim; (2) that the humiliation in His grief, like every one of His humiliations, is connected with a glorification, to the glory of His Father.—And because in His grief He has now sacrificed Himself to the Father He can pray as follows. *Lange.*

ἡ ψυχή μου τετάρακται. An affection of suffering inflicted upon Him by the objective situation.—The horror of death which its contemplation brings upon the inward life of feeling.—The *soul* may and must be thus troubled—prepared, as it were, for its death; but not so the καρδία (chap. xiv 1, 27).—It is the antithesis of passive and actual consciousness, or of the life of feeling and the will. *Lange.*—The ψυχη is the seat of the natural feelings and emotions, and as the fatal hour approaches, our Lord is in that region of His human life troubled. *Watkins.*—"Concurrebat horror mortis et ardor obedientiæ" *Bengel.*—πάτερ, σῶσόν με To be taken *interrogatively*, as a reflective monologue, instead of an address to the Father. *Chrys., Lampe, Tholuck, Ewald, Godet, Lange.*—In this case a colon must be put after *say*, and an interrogation mark after *hour. Lachmann.*—A veritable prayer which corresponds to the prayer in Gethsemane, and the Messianic prayers in the Psalms (Ps. vi. 3 4; xxv. 17; xl. 12, 13; lxix. 1). *Meyer, Alford, Schoff, Lücke* – Unc rtain whether the words are a prayer or a question.—In the latter case the meaning would be. "What shall I sa ? Shall I say, Father save me from this hour? But no: for this cause came I unto this hour. I cannot shrink back or seek to be delivered from it."—As a prayer the meaning would be, "Father, save me from this hour; but for this cause, that I may be saved from it, came I unto this hour. The moment of agony is the moment of victory."—The real difficulty of the verse lies in the words "for this cause; " for which a meaning must be sought in the context —No interpretation of them is free from objection, but that which seems most probable, understands them as referring to the words which follow, and reads the clause, "Father, glorify Thy name," as part of this verse.—The sense of the whole passage would therefore be, "Father, save me from this hour; but Thy will, not mine, be done; for this cause came I unto this hour, that Thy name be glorified; Father, glorify Thy name." *Watkins* in Comm., edited by *Ellicott.*

---

28. Father, glorify thy name. Then came there a voice from **heaven**, saying, I have both glorified it, and will glorify it again.

Father. The address again repeated.—In those moments of the greatest rapture and intensity of devotion, He appeals to the same Father who heard Him in the time of His overwhelming sorrow.—Filial love is the very life of zeal for God's glory.

Glorify thy name. See on Matt. i. 21, 22, 23.—The Name of God signifies all that He *is*, and especially what He is to *us*.—The office of our human science is to affix true names to things, which set forth their properties and relations.—The practical recognition of the Name of God is the sum and substance of our duty, our eternal life.—The *manifestation* of God's Name is His glory.—We know something of nature around us by observation, but we can only know a *person* when he is pleased to reveal himself.—

Nature is but an imperfect revelation of God; quite insufficient for *us.*—It has no heart, no message of kindness and love.—God's glory is seen most of all in the work of Christ for the salvation of man.—It is here that the lovingkindness of our God appears, and the infinite treasures of plenteous mercy which lie in His Name stand revealed.—Jesus knew the cost to Himself involved in this petition.—In the best natures the highest and noblest principles are always triumphant.—Belief in the rightness of God's purpose is the stay of the soul.—Job but imperfectly realized this; in the Son of Man it was completely realized.—" Submission unto the will of God is a real outgate from trouble, and a special victory over it; for hereby Christ gets an issue of His agony and perplexities." *Hutcheson.*

Voice from Heaven. Three times this voice was heard; at His baptism, on the Mount of Transfiguration, in the Temple.—Each time in relation to His Incarnation, and His destiny of death.— First, when our Lord solemnly commenced His office, in the presence of the Baptist.—Second, when in the presence of the Law-giver and Old Testament prophet.—Now, in the Tabernacle of God.— Again the thunder voice resounds, and the Father acredits His Son.—This last voice was the response to His petition.—It was not some ordinary sound fancifully interpreted, but a distinct and special Divine utterance for the purpose of attesting His mission. —It was the penetration of this natural world by the spiritual.— The meaning of such is only clear to the spiritual ear.—Earnest men have heard such voices; they have seen in nature around the reflection of their own internal states.—Augustine, in an anxious mood of thought, heard a voice like that of a child, saying, " Take and read! Take and read!"—Since the *people* heard this voice, it could not have been subjective.—How near is the spiritual world. (See on Matt. ii. 13.)—We are surrounded on all sides by mysterious powers.—Sometimes they are forced upon the attention of men in great crises of spiritual life.—Paul at his conversion heard the voice of his Lord.—Those who believe in the existence of the spiritual world have no difficulty in believing such statements.—" There is no true comfort against soul-trouble but what comes from God, and is spoken by Him from heaven; for this comforts Christ." *Hutcheson.*

I have glorified. That name was glorified in the incarnation, teaching, and works of Christ. (See on Matt. vi. 9.)—Every word and act of Jesus was a fresh revelation of God.—Whenever God reveals Himself, His glory appears more and more.—Nature had proclaimed the being and attributes of God to all mankind.—

The Name of God had been revealed through the symbolic worship of Judaism; more fully by the utterance of psalm and prophecy. —The heart of God, which is the inmost glory of His nature, was now being revealed in His Son.—" When we pray, as we are taught, Our Father; hallowed be thy name, this is a comfort to us, that it is an *answered* prayer, answered to Christ here, and in Him to all true believers." *Henry.*

Will glorify. By His death, resurrection, and ascension.—By these Jesus was raised to that position where He could accomplish all things.—He could thus fill up the outlines of the Divine plan concerning the redemption of mankind.—God's gracious favours in the past are the pledges of more to come.

φωνή, *Resembling thunder,* so that the precise words sounding through these tones were unperceived by the insusceptible. *Meyer.*— *Of an angelic nature.* mediated by angelic ministry. *Hofmann. A spiritual and celestial, yet audible voice,* which was understood more or less according to the corresponding frame of mind.—*So the Ancients;* and *Olsh , Kling, Stier, Lange, Tholuck, Godet, Alford,* &c.—Natural thunder which was identical with "the voice from heaven," and through which God spoke to Christ. *Hengstenberg.*—But then it could not have been mistaken by some for the voice of an angel.—It was clearly a supernatural phenomenon, a spiritual manifestation from the spiritual world, clothed in a symbolic form, an articulate sound from heaven, miraculously uttered, heard by all, but variously interpreted according to the degree of spiritual susceptibility *Schaff.*—πάλιν No mere repetition, but an intensification of the glorification.—The consummated glorification of the name of God refers to His revelation in Israel, closing in the labours of Christ, and the new glorification of His name to the impending revelation of God in the Gentile world, this being conditioned by the death and resurrection of Jesus. *Lange.*—The first sentence of the voice refers to the works of Jesus hitherto, the second to the impending glorification through death to δόξα. *Meyer.*

---

29. The people therefore, that stood by, and heard it, said that it thundered; others said, An angel spake to him.

Heard. All heard some voice or sound, but the greater part heard no distinct words.—The majority failed to recognise God's testimony to His Son.—When the spiritual faculty is dormant, men hear, and yet do not hear, the words of God.—They feel that they are in the solemn presence of the mysterious, yet become possessed of no distinct idea.—The message of the Gospel makes some impression upon the mass of those who hear it.—To many, that message is a mere voice or sound; its solemn meaning is not appreciated; the importance of its requirements are unheeded.— Many mistake the outward voice of truth for spiritual knowledge. —Some day they will wake up to find that they have deceived themselves.—They have never he rd God with the inward ear, nor seen Him with the inward eye. Job xlii. 5, 6.

Thundered. There was evidently a voice like thunder, for such was the general impression on the minds of the crowd.—It is certain that an intelligible voice was uttered, having a distinct message for the people. Verse 30.—Thus the *same* manifestations of God work different effects in different minds.—The external universe, with all its grand revelations of God, is to each man as his own mind is.—All Divine revelations require some answering faculty in the recipient.—What to some may be an unintelligible sound, to others is as the voice of an ange.—This was the spring-time, and thunder was frequent.—Destructive criticism has taken advantage of this fact by resolving the accounts of such Divine manifestations into superstitions, based upon natural phenomena. —When men postulate the impossibility of the spiritual and supernatural, it becomes easy to explain away the whole force and teaching of the Gospel history —This narrative bears internal marks of reality ; a writer of fiction would have invented a voice which all understood.

An angel. See on chapter i. 51, and on Matt. i. 20; ii. 13.—These were much nearer the truth ; they recognised the element of personality.—Men who feel and know that there are living powers beneath external nature, have attained to higher truth and noble-ness of view than those who only discern matter and force.—Is it not possible that by these others the Greek proselytes are meant ? —Such a thing is not positively expressed, yet it is these very men whom Jesus seems to answer in the subsequent speech.—At all events, their attitude towards the people is that of a more susceptible minority. *Lange.*

Spake unto him. Gr. implies *hath spoken and is still speaking.*— Here is the recognition of the utterance of an intelligible thought. —"Before men will hear and believe in God they will resort to all kinds of imaginations of thunders and angels." *Hamann.*

---

30. Jesus answered and said, This voice came not because of me, but for your sakes.

This voice. He calls it a *voice*, implying that it had a distinct message for the people.—There was a distinct manifestation of mind and will.

Came not. Was not audibly uttered.

Because of me. Gr., *for my sake.*—Jesus wanted no assurance for Himself of the Divine source and approval of His mission.—He and the Father were one. Chap. x. 30.—The higher the nature, the less the occasion for special manifestations of God.—The dulness of men to observe the ordinary ways and customs of heaven has rendered miracles necessary.—To Jesus no miracle could be a "wonder;" He possessed a power to which each exertion was alike easy.—There is much that happens to good men, not for their own sakes, or for their own consolation or comfort, but for the sake of others.—Je us does not deny that the assurance given by that Voice would invigorate Him for the baptism of blood.—Yet it was not *necessary* for Himself to have such assured consolation.—Had He not prayed? And wherein did it fail of being an answer?—The Divine Petitioner finds in it a publicity and solemnity worthy of note.—He corrects their mistake as to the thunder, but says nothing as to an angel.—The splendour of the miracle was the same, whether the voice was that of an angel or of God.—The VOICE *itself* is to be distinguished from its *purport.*—The Voice, in the abstract, was a glorification of the Father and the Son. *Lange.*

Your sakes. "The disciples were really no longer in need of this attestation of Jesus. Neither was it needed by that portion of the people that believed on Him on account of the raising of Lazarus.—From the words immediately following, it seems to be spoken with special reference to the Greeks." *Lange.*—All the wonders, as well as the words of Jesus and His works were for our sakes.—Essentially and supremely all things are for the Father's sake; the Redemption as well as the Creation and Preservation of the world.—But since Creation, no being had ever offered such a prayer as that in verse 27.—No prophet, or apostle, or even angel of God's throne had a right to pray thus.—We may well believe that no such answer had been heard from heaven.—He thus prayed, knowing that all must honour the Son as they do the Father.—Hence no one can serve God without first knowing His Son.—"Thou Father in me, and I in thee" (chap. xvii. 21), inter-communion of love and work.—Here is the Key of Redemption's plan, Redemption's fruit and glory.—The great expense to which heaven was put can thus be explained and justified.—Hence we learn that giving up all for the sake of others is that which is most God-like in man.—Infinite love does not seek its own; cannot be moved by motives of profit or advantage; only delights in spending itself.—"That you, my disciples, who are to follow me in sufferings, may therein be comforted with the same comforts that carry me on." *Henry.*—"They are curiously debating what this should mean, when Christ tells them that they should study for whose sake it came." *Hutcheson.*

31. Now is the judgment of this world: now shall the prince of this world be cast out.

Now. The work of Redemption to dethrone Satan and exalt God. —The Cross involves the reconciliation of the world to God, the slaying of sin and the flesh, the abolition of death, and the breaking down of Satan's power.—It is the victory complete and everlasting over *all* opposed to man.—This word marks an important crisis; there are such moments in history and in the individual life.—There are solemn hours which seem to condense into themselves the gathering forces of years.—"*Now* for that glorious achievement; *now* that great work is to be done which has been so long *thought* of in the Divine counsels; so long talked of in the written Word, which has been so much the hope of saints, and the dread of devils." *Henry.*

The judgment. *Concerning* this world, as to who is to be its rightful possessor.—The Cross was a complete triumph over all enemies. Col. ii. 15.—When Christ died for man's sin, and rose again for his justification, all the powers of evil were *judged*— doomed to failure and loss.—Our Lord now speaks as one who sees the end from the beginning.—He knew what His death would accomplish.—He could discern to what this dying seed of corn would grow.—Men shall no longer have cause to think that the world is in the hands of an Evil Power.—"The sick and diseased world is now upon the turning point; this is the critical day upon which the trembling scale will turn *for life or death* to all mankind." *Henry.*—The death of Jesus a judgment, glorified by the Spirit. (See chap. xvi. 1.)—1. The foundation and beginning of the separation between Satan and the world.—2. The foundation and beginning of the separation between believers and unbelievers. —3. The foundation and beginning of the union of all the godly. *Lange.*

Prince. See on Luke iv. 2.—This appellation is found in chapters xiv. 30; xvi. 11.—It signifies that Satan is the author of evil; that he is the master whom the mass of mankind obey.—St. Paul uses the expression, "the god of this world." 2 Cor. iv. 4.— The terrible reality and power of evil must be acknowledged; our consolation is that it shall be overcome by the superior strength of a Righteous Power.—Satan and his work come out clearly in the N. T.—Our Lord made no effort to conceal the dark malignant fiend.—Before the Greek strangers, Apostles, and crowd, He proclaims this fact.—" Satan never possessed the Kingdom itself, which was given to Christ on high, but he from time to time entered its limits and borders, from which he is doomed ultimately to be cast out." *Bengel.*—"The devil never ceases to tempt believers; but it is one thing to *reign within,* another to *lay siege from without.*"—*Augustine.*

This world. The world of mankind.—Wherever man was found there were the bitter fruits of Satan's power.

Cast out. This contains the promise of a final and complete victory, when Christ shall have subdued all things. 1 Cor. xv. 28. —That work was virtually effected when Christ died for sin.— From that point the purpose of God to overthrow all evil was to be wrought out through the long ages of time.—The idea of a kingdom in which God should rule, and from which shall be excluded every element of rebellion, is the underlying thought of the teaching of Christ.—These words are not the records of a past which is dead and gone; they have an ever-living force and significance.—There are causes now in existence which are continually tending to bring about the complete victory of the Gospel.—As there are silent and unheeded forces of nature that culminate suddenly in some terrible convulsion, in like manner, sudden and unexpected, are some of the victories of the Gospel.— Every victory of truth over error is a dethronement of Satan: one more lie is rendered ineffectual.—Christ revealed as "The Truth" will cast out the "father of lies."—Each time a sinner is converted there is a casting out of Satan.—The evil one must be separated from the community of all the pure and holy.—This is the destiny of all evil, to be cast out for ever from God's sight.—The separation of evil from its accidental contact with the good in them is the glorious destiny of redeemed man.—The belief that goodness shall triumph, and be for ever set free from all hostile invasion, is our strong consolation amidst the present disorder.—The expulsion of the evil spirits who had bound the children of Abraham was a fall of Satan. Luke x. 18.—"Christ reconciling the world to God by the merit of His death broke the *power of death,* and cast out Satan as a destroyer; Christ *reducing* the world to God by the doctrine of His cross broke the *power of sin* and cast out Satan as a *deceiver.*" *Henry.*—These words are explanatory of the heavenly voice: *I will glorify it again.*

κρίσις. There is a judgment, not of *condemnation* but of *selection,* which is the one here meant—the *selection* of His own redeemed. *Augustine.*—τοῦ κόσμου τούτου. The old pre-Messianic and non-Messianic world—with special reference to the Gentile world whose highest *cosmical* formation is the very Hellenism that is confronting Him. *Lange.*—ὁ ἄρχων τοῦ κόσμοῦ τούτου. S. Paul calls Satan—ὁ ἄρχων τῆς ἐξουσίας τοῦ ἀέρος. Ephes. ii. 2.—Satan's empire over the world is shattered with the death and resurrection of Jesus.—He is indeed still tarrying and working over the earth; here he retains his 'Εξω, the air and wind regions of the human world as far as it is not yet spiritual, whence he reacts upon the Church of Christ.—Subsequen ly he is cast upon *tne earth* (Rev. xii. 9), *i e.,* he possesses himself of tradi ional, anci nt or finances, now deadened—lif less.—But in time to come he is also cast out of the earth into tne bottomless pit. (Rev. xx)—Thus this saying opens up a perspective of the final judgment. *Lange.*

---

32. And I, if I be lifted up from the earth, will draw all men unto me.

And I. The majestic I, claiming Divine power over all the race of men.—He now turns to Himself as the ruler of the powers of goodness; He had before spoken of the ruler of the powers of evil.—The humility of Christ did not involve any disguise of His authority.—Such words of self-assertion imply a claim of Divinity.

Lifted up. See chapters iii. 14 ; viii. 28.—"If I," &c., conditional in form, but not expressing any doubtfulness.—The certainty of the event depending upon it is implied, as if He had said, "As sure as I am lifted up, I will draw," &c.—He who has in His hands the ages to come can well afford to make such a supposition.—The local reference is to death by crucifixion, verse 33.—But His removal from the world, and glorification in Heaven are also implied.—"In the very Cross there was already something that tended towards glory." *Bengel.*—The Cross the place where He had won His victory ; His native Heaven the place where He would enjoy it for ever.—The return of the living and triumphant Christ to Heaven is the crowning miracle. Chap. iii. 14.—The deepest humiliation of Christ is at the same time His highest exaltation: His crown of thorns is His crown of glory.—The Saviour crucified is in fact the Saviour glorified ; so that the exalting to God's right hand is set forth by that uplifting on the Cross.

Will draw. See on chapter vi. 44.—In Greek, the *milder* word is used ; no idea of irresistible force is conveyed.—The will is incapable of force.—The word signifies the exertion of a spiritual power towards conversion.—This is not a force of that kind which makes a man a mere machine.—Christ draws men by the sweet attraction of His love.—The heart which fiercely and defiantly closes itself to the threat of terror opens freely to the gracious power of love.—The power of the Cross is that of attraction ; it operates by a sweet constraint.—The realization of a living and exalted Christ lifts the soul heavenward.—The power arising from the love of Christ is the strongest force acting upon humanity.—It has given birth to an enthusiasm of devotion such as the world had never seen before. —Christ has ability to satisfy and eng ge the noblest faculties of man.—He has truth to persuade the reason, and goodness to win the heart.—His love generates belief, not merely *about* Him, but *in* Him ; a perfect trust in His heart.—To obey from love is Heaven begun on earth.—" I will draw," He says, as if men were in the grasp of some tyrant, from whom they could not extricate themselves. *Chrysostom.*—Christ *all in all* in the conversion of a soul.—1. It is Christ who draws.—2. It is to Christ we are drawn. —He does not *drive*, but *draws.*—*Drawing* is no *enforcement. Henry. Before* the glorification of Christ, the Father draws to the Son; *afterwards* the *Son Himself* draws immediately.—" All men are not *effectually* drawn to Christ, but by the preaching of the Gospel they are so drawn as to render those who do not come inexcusable." *Burkitt.*

All men. See on Luke xv. 2.—The force operates upon all, but some resist.—Here is the answer to the request, " We would see Jesus."—The universal power of the Cross is intended; no rank or race is excluded.—Implies also persons of every order of mind, and every shade of character.—The Cross is the test and discriminator of the responsible character and final destiny of the race.— The *Cross* becomes a throne of Judgment. *Whedon*—" The passion of Christ began to draw souls at once, as in the case of the penitent thief and the centurion."—*Euthymius.*

Unto me. Gr., *unto* MYSELF.—Not to an idea, or system, but to a *person.*—Hence there is afforded for the affections a definite and stable centre.—To know that the Son of Man is there, invests Heaven with a grateful attractiveness for the soul.—The believer feels that he is not altogether a stranger to that unknown world. —To be with Christ implies a partaking of His character, for He will have no one near Him but those who are like Him.—The energy of Divine love to draw and assimilate all things to itself is the great law of Heaven.—That which in the physical universe is attraction, in the spiritual universe is love.—All things in Heaven and earth gathered together in one to Christ, is the central idea of Scripture.—Christ is now raised to Heaven, and though we are ignorant of the full glory of that blessed state, yet we know the *direction* in which our hearts' affections should move.—In things spiritual, to be like another is to be near, and to be with him.— The true rest of faithful souls is to be with Christ.—In their best estate here they are still uneasy and confined from home.—The double effect of Christ's death: 1. The judgment of this world ; 2. The drawing all men unto Him.—Christ's *dying* as consistent

with His *abiding for ever*, as an eclipse of the sun with its perpetuity.

ὑψωθῶ. The lifting up upon the cross and the lifting up upon the heavenly throne;
in this place, pre-eminently the latter.—The double meaning of the word is in keeping
with John, comp. ii. 19; iii. 13; iv. 10; xi. 51. *Tholuck, Alford, Lange.*—The ἐκ τῆς γῆς
conflicts with the interpretation that refers to the crucifixion. *Meyer.*—Refers to the
crucifixion (verse 33).—So *the Fathers* and most of *the ancients*; also *Kling, Frommann,
&c.*—πάντας. Refers to the antithesis of Jews and Gentiles, after chap. x. 16. *Chrys.,
Cyril, Calvin, Lampe.*—All who hear the Gospel and do not resist the drawing of Christ,
Lutheran Theologians.—The elect. *Reformed Theologians.*—Without restriction. *Meyer.*
—Indicative of the totality of the nations in antithesis to the firstlings of the Greeks
who have here inquired after Him. *Lange.*—Some infer from these words the *apocata-
stasis* or final restoration of all men.— But in all such passages *all* must be explained in
accordance with other passages where *faith* is expressly laid down as the indispensable
condition of salvation. *Schaff.*—ἑλκύσω. By the diffusion of the Spirit in the Church;
manifested in the preaching of the word mediately, and the pleading of the Spirit
immediately. *Alford.*—An intimation of deliverance from the chains of Satan. *Chrys*
—Implies the strong and irresistible power of Christ's love. *Schaff.*—A drawing without moral compulsion because it is a drawing of love calling unto freedom. *Lange.*
πρὸς ἐμαυτόν. To the state of dominion and glory to which He was raised. *Owen.*—
The emphasis (comp. chap. xix. 3) signifies *to Myself.*—They will not stay with Philip
or Andrew, or require the mediation of a Jewish or priestly church. *Lange.*—Any
system, whether called Catholic or Protestant, that interposes forms, dogmas, or priestly
acts *between* Christ and the soul is Anti-Christian. *Pressensé.*—The true Church is known
by this that in everything it seeks to exalt Christ and to lead souls to Him. *Nitzch.*

---

33. This he said, signifying what death he should die.

This. Referring to the words, " If I be lifted up."

Signifying. The evangelist adds a brief explanation.—He wrote
his Gospel late, when the words of Jesus were not quite so fresh in
the minds of men, and is therefore desirous of bringing his readers
into the position of those who heard them.—He may have used
the expression in the sense of pointing to a certain event in the
future.—" Christ's words ought not only to be reverently heard,
but should be marked and pondered till they be understood."
Hutcheson.

What death. Gr., *what kind of death.*—The people would understand the words in their ordinary sense of crucifixion.—Yet as
employed by Jesus, the full meaning could only be satisfied
by His glorification.—John may have regarded the Cross as a
symbol, a rallying point for humanity. Isa. xi. 10.—The Cross
suggested and implied all the glory that followed it.—To be lifted
up between Heaven and earth—as unworthy of both—was regarded by the popular mind as the utmost disgrace.—But since
Christ died on the Cross, that word is associated with different
ideas.—The mention of it awakens touching and hallowed recol-

lections.—Thus words become transfigured and ennobled by the touch of the Divine thought.—The Lamb slain, even in Heaven, has for us a fulness of meaning beyond the simple words — " They that put Christ to that ignominious death thought thereby to drive all men from Him ; but the devil was outshot in his own bow." *Henry.*—The glorification of the Son of Man comprehends three things : 1. The perfection of His obedience in the sacrifice of His love ; 2. Exaltation to the glory proper to Him ; 3. The exhibition of His name as that of the Saviour of mankind, the gathering of a holy Church, the outpouring of the Holy Spirit. *Besser.*

ἔλεγε. A Johannean interpretation. *Meyer.*—A mere hint. *Tholuck.*—The death of the cross was not only objectively the condition of the lifting up of Christ; it is also subjectively the strongest and the single decisive attraction to the exalted Christ. *Lange* —ποίῳ θανάτῳ. Comprehensively expresses all that our Lord had said concerning the *significance*, the *power*, and the *fruit* of His death. *Stier.*

---

34. The people answered him, We have heard out of the law that Christ abideth for ever : and how sayest thou, The Son of man must be lifted up? who is this Son of man?

We. Emphatic.—" *We*, for our part, have heard something quite different ; but *you* are wiser."—There is an ironical imputation of superior authority.

Heard. They were acquainted with the O.T. chiefly through having heard it read. Matt. v. 21.—Books were only written on skins, lead, leaves, stone, or brass; they were therefore very few.— Hearing was their chief method of getting knowledge.— In our day the people would have said, " We have read."—Should it be said, " We have heard," a different idea would be conveyed.

The law. Referring to the O.T. generally.—They thought, probably, of such passages as Psa. cx. 4 ; Dan. vii. 14 ; Psa. xlv. 6 ; lxii. 5 ; Isa. liii. 8.—But these passages contemplate a sublime result to be reached through humiliation and death.—They did not know that it was only through death that Jesus could conquer death.

Christ. Gr., *the Christ.*—Therefore they understood Him to claim the Messiahship.—As the years of Jewish history flowed on, the idea was getting clearer that the Messiah would occupy the throne of David.—The idea of " the Christ " had by this time taken a definite shape in the minds of the people.

Abideth for ever. The people cannot reconcile His dying with the

assured continuance of the Messiah's reign.—However perplexed
they might be, they were clear concerning His claims.—Their
consciences were stricken with terrible remorse after His death.—
Their utter madness in rushing to a suicidal grave during the
war proves that their ruined city, power, glory, temple, were not
ALL THEIR WOE!—They fastened upon one idea, but forgot what
led up to it, and those great truths to which it was related.—
Exclusive attention to half-truths may lead men into great errors.
—These people made the basis of Messiah's kingdom too narrow.
—They forgot that an earthly centre of government was inconsistent with the Messiah's sovereignty through all time, and in
every place.—The spiritual and essential truths of Scripture are
as things utterly strange to those who are the slaves of the letter.
—" In the doctrine of Christ there are paradoxes, which to men
of corrupt minds are stones of stumbling." *Henry.*

Son of man. See on chapters i. 51 ; v. 27.—They do not accurately
repeat the words Jesus had spoken, verse 32.—We can scarcely
suppose that they adopted this expression as an equivalent to
what had just been uttered.—They had not sufficient ability to
frame and fit so fair a phrase.—But we find the words almost
exactly the same as those to Nicodemus in chap. iii. 14.—It is
probable that Jesus (verse 32) had really repeated those words,
but John does not record them.—Jesus was in the habit of
repeating important things, chap. xiii. 20 ; Matt. x. 40 ; Luke ix.
48 : Matt. ix. 13 ; xii. 7.—The Evangelist may therefore have
given a mere outline and suggestion of words so well known.

Lifted up. See on verse 32.—" Are the bright hopes thus raised
by the Prophets doomed to disappointment ? "—The people possessed a fragment of the truth, but they lacked those comple-
mentary truths by means of which they could survey the subject
as a whole.—No one fact connected with the manifestation of
Christ can be considered by itself ; its true significance can only
be seen by its position in the whole scheme.

Who is this Son of Man? They could not understand such a
Son of Man, whose course was thus to end disgracefully.—The
Christ they thought of was superior to the necessity of dying.—
The Apostles abandoned the expression " Son of Man," after the
exaltation of Jesus; His divinity was then fully established.

ὁ ὄχλος A people is spoken of that recognises the Christ in Jesus. *Lange.*—μένει
εἰς τὸν αἰῶνα. The people, as also the disciples, lack as yet all discrimination betwe n
the first and the second coming of Christ. *Lange* —τίς ἐστιν Who is this Anti-
Scriptural Son of Man who is not to abide in accordance with Daniel, but is to be lifted

up from the earth? *Meyer, Tholuck* —But in that case they would not ask, Who is this Son of Man? but how does that agree with the Son of Man?—The first offence, namely, at His being lifted up, concerns the *spiritual* and *heavenly* side of the Messianic picture set up by Christ; the second concerns that universality in the idea of the *Son of Man,* which they doubtless feel.—The Greeks, evidently, have again excited their Jewish jealousy —Their carnal Messianic hopes prevent them having the slightest suspicion of what is impending over the Messiah, and hence also over them in their relation to Him during the next few days. *Lange.*

---

35. Then Jesus said unto them, Yet a little while is the light with you. Walk while ye have the light, lest darkness come upon you: for he that walketh in darkness knoweth not whither he goeth.

Said. Not an answer to their words, but one to their needs. Disputings avail not now; work, now or never, must be done.—The people could answer the question for themselves by attending to the true meaning of the Prophets.—But the question was too wide and intricate to treat at this time in the presence of ignorant and prejudiced men.—The question was, probably, proposed in the spirit of scorn.—They had made up their minds that Jesus was not the Messiah.—Our Lord attacks their unbelief from another direction, by representing Himself in another character.—In this also He asserts His Messiahship.—"Instead of answering these fools according to their folly, He gives them a serious caution to take heed of trifling away their opportunities in such vain and fruitless cavils as these." *Henry.*

A little while. They thought that the Messiah, when once He had come, would never remove from them.—They did not reflect that a local centre of religion would be incompatible with the universality of the Messiah's kingdom.—The world had no fitting place for the Son of God in all His glory.—Had He remained on earth, then the privileges of religion would be local and exclusive. —Short was the opportunity of the people for acknowledging Him in His humiliation.

The light. See on chapters i. 4; viii. 12.—Christ speaks of Himself as a light of native splendour; not an artificial, short-lived light, such as the Baptist. Chap. v. 35.—He was the light given for man to work by.—Had they allowed themselves to be cheered, invigorated, and summoned to diligence by that light, the proof of His Messiahship would soon be clear.—Like the sun, Christ is His own evidence.—This light requires a spiritual eye in man; though surrounded by it the soul may yet be dark.

With you. Gr., *in you,* a more correct reading; meaning, according to the Hebrew usage, *among you.*—The light was then over their nation, but did not shine in their hearts.

Walk. Implies using effort which tends to progress.—They were not to dispute, or curiously to enquire, but to act.—In the Kingdom of God it is not by study but by action that we obtain an assured knowledge of the truth.—The light of faith and love summons to labour.

While ye have. In what sense do the impenitent enjoy the Gospel?—1. They have the mind as well as ears to comprehend and hear the terms of life.—2. They have a conscience to decide the facts of their ruin and the remedy.—3. They have the Spirit's power, which will leave them without excuse.—There are times when belief and action are comparatively easy.

Darkness come upon you. Gr., *Lay hold upon you.*—Darkness would fall upon them unexpectedly.—At that time they had the opportunity of obtaining knowledge and guidance in spiritual matters.—Sin and ignorance paralyse the moral energies.

Knoweth not whither. Without the light of truth and goodness men must suffer the natural penalties of ignorance and sin.—If we reject the light which Christ gives, life becomes deprived of a worthy end, or satisfactory prospect.—Uncertainty and fear ever accompany darkness.—Spiritual darkness consists in not knowing what is the true end of life.—Men who reject the teaching of Christ, have, in the depth of their being, no principle which gives unity to life; they are divided over endless speculations and pursuits.

Instead of μεθ' ὑμῶν read ἐν ὑμῖν. *Lach., Tisch., Schaff, Cod. Sin.*—ἕως. The reading ὥς has overwhelming authority in its favour. *Lach., Tisch., Alford, Schaff.*—" Walk, according to your present state of privilege in possessing light: which indeed can only be done *while it is with you.*" *Alford.*—σκοτία. The great night of temptation came upon them on the day of crucifixion, and to those who confronted it unsuspiciously. with their outward Messianic hope, it likewise became an inward night of apostasy and ruin.—περιπατῶν. Expressive of the fault by which outward darkness is converted into inward obscurity.—οὐκ οἶδε ποῦ ὑπάγει. Strikingly demonstrative of the fate of the Jews.—They knew not whither they went—into perdition. into dispersion to the ends of the world, into the curse of judgment till the end of time.—Antithesis of Christ's going to the sure goal of glory. *Lange.*

---

36. While ye have light, believe in the light, that ye may be the children of light. These things spake Jesus, and departed, and did hide himself from them.

Believe. See on chapters i. 7; vii. 38.—He passes from metaphor to precept.—Faith, which works by love, gives that certainty and confidence which a man has when he walks in the light.—Belief in One who is able to enlighten, save, and defend is the stay of the soul.

That ye may be. Gr., *That ye may become.*—They must pass into another state of spiritual existence.—Believing in the light would transform them into its image.

Be the children of light. Gr., *may become sons of light.* A Heb. form of expression, like "Son of peace," &c., denoting their dependence upon light as a child upon its mother.—Light was to nourish and guide them, and under its sweet influences they were to live.—As children, they would hold a perpetual relationship to that light.—The believer maintains a relation of perpetual dependence upon Christ.—The children of the light know the light not by demonstration but by its manifestation to the soul.— They that believe in the light shall be children of light : 1. Sons of God, Who is *Light;* 2. Heirs of heaven, which is *Light.*—Most fitting that these should be the last words of Christ to the believing portion of the people.—Nothing but trust in that light which had risen upon them in Him could lead them safely through the fearful night of trial. *Lange.*

Departed. A significant act, threatening the removal of the light. —Their precious opportunity would depart.—" Christ justly removes the means of grace from those that quarrel with them, and *hides his face* from a *froward generation."* *Henry.*

Did hide himself. An intimation that He withdrew Himself from His public labours.—He retired to Bethany, or perhaps to the gardens and woods of the Mount of Olives.—The time that remains is to be spent with His friends.—He will only speak to the *initiated* the deep things of His kingdom.

ἀπελθών. This moment coincides, as regards the main point, with the departure from the temple described by the Synoptists. *Lange.*—ἐκρύβη. Probably to Bethany (Luke xxi. 37), in order to spend the last days of His life, before the coming of His hour, in the circle of His disciples.—These last days amounted at the utmost to two.— On Tuesday evening He left the temple ; on Thursday, towards evening, He returned to Jerusalem to celebrate the Passover. *Alford, Meyer, Lange.*

---

37. But though he had done so many miracles before them, yet they believed not on him.

But. From verse 37 to verse 43 is a passage by way of comment and observation, a usual practice with this evangelist.—The public work of Jesus had now ended, and the writer is passing it under review.—Before he treats upon the history of the Passion and the subsequent triumph, he pauses to take account of the effect of Christ's teaching and miracles.—The Apostle of Love would feel keenly the ingratitude and distrust of men.

So many. Jesus was in the habit of working miracles all the time of His ministry, yet this did not produce the habit of belief among the people.—The number of miracles gave increasing strength to their evidence, so that the fact of them could not be denied.— They gave indications of His unexhausted power.

Miracles. See on chapters ii. 11, 23 ; iii. 2 ; iv. 8 ; vi. 30.—The divinity of His works corresponded with His Supreme Godhead. —This had been seen in spirit and foretold by the Prophet Isaiah. —Faith in miracles is nothing without some claim to be confirmed. —A seal upon a letter is nothing unless there is something within.—His miracles were far in advance of those wrought under Moses and Elijah.—They indicated a Supreme Authority over the trees of the field, over the fish of the sea, over the wild winds when roused, over the elements of the harvest field, over the vines in their fruitfulness, over the diseases of mankind, over the brute creation, over the demons who had left their prison, over the bodies slumbering in the tomb, and over the spirits in the Paradise of God.—These were wrought by a mere word of command, without a touch.—At His death the earth trembled, and the sun was veiled in night.

Before them. The miracles were wrought in their very sight ; they had not to depend upon any hearsay evidence.—Not in secret, and before a few spectators, were they performed, but in the centre of the crowds at their great festivals.—In the presence of eminent jurists, rulers, senators, divines.—Despite their rage, His fame increased the more they tried to crush Him.—They essayed to quench in blood the infant faith of the church.—But martyrs multiplied faster than their crosses and their stakes.—Each funeral pile became a mightier miracle of love than ten thousand pulpits. —At length, the gorgeous ritual of myriads of pagan priests gave way.—Their temples, the ruins of which are the wonder of men, were deserted.—Their oracles, by which millions had been swayed, were silent.—As Julian, the apostate Emperor of Rome, testified, " O, GALILEAN, THOU HAST CONQUERED ! "

Believed not. In disobedience to the purpose of God in the "signs," and to the divine attestation of Jesus.—If there is not the moral disposition to believe, the strongest evidence may be resisted.—This the statement of the fact in bare terms, the moral cause of it is stated in verses 38, 39.—The Jews rejecting the noonday evidence of Christianity for 1800 years is no more strange than the impenitence of many in our own circles.—The facts of Christ's miracles were admitted, but were attributed to magic, or the power of Satan.—Unless there is a moral disposition towards the truth, the strongest evidence is unavailing.—" Darkness does not blind men so much as light, unless God renews the mind by His Spirit." *Rollock.*—The *yet* of unbelievers and the *yet* of believers, Ps. lxxiii. 1: 1. An antithesis, in which the reality of human freedom is expressed; 2. The glory of divine judgment and divine grace; 3. Decision for eternity; 4. A contrast, as betwixt heaven and hell.—How unbelief is changed from guilt to judgment: 1. Unwillingness to believe, as a crime demanding judgment; 2. Inability to believe, as the judgment upon the crime.—The fault contained in the unbelief of the Jews (fear of man) a warning to all times.—The curse of the fear of man, especially in matters of faith.—The ultimate and deepest cause of all evil, the want of a sense of God's glory. Rom. i. 21. *Lange.*

On him. Gr., *in Him.*—In the King of Heaven, now strangely disguised in mortal form, whose glory the Prophet saw. Verse 41. —Even the recognition of spiritual truth is not enough, unless it be known and felt " as the truth is in Jesus."

τοσαῦτα. *So great, such. Lücke, 'De Wette.—So many. Meyer, Alford, Tholuck.— Such. Lange.*—The generalness of the term indicative of *quality* as well as *quantity. Schaff.*

---

38. That the saying of Esaias the prophet might be fulfilled, which he spake, Lord, who hath believed our report? and to whom hath the arm of the Lord been revealed?

Esaias. See on chapter i. 23, and on Luke iii. 4.—The quotation (Isa. liii. 1) corresponds exactly with the LXX.

The prophet. See on chapters i. 21; iv. 19; and on Matt. i. 22.

Fulfilled. Their unbelief might be expected from what the prophet foresaw.—Their unbelief did not set aside the gracious *purpose* of God, nor cause the work of the Redeemer to fail.—The Divine plan is being accomplished, though men may resist.—Faith traces the supreme control of God amidst the mazes of appearances.— We may wonder at the unbelief of men, but there can be no surprise or amazement to the infinite mind.—Things do not come to pass because the prophets foretold them, but the prophets foretold them because they would come to pass.—This shows the Divine infallibility of prophecy.—" God predicted the unbelief of the Jews, but did not cause it: He does not compel men to sin because He knows they will sin." *Augustine.*—" The prophets had

predicted this very unbelief, and He came (amongst other intents)
that it might be made manifest.—*That* is expressive not of the
cause but of the event." *Chrysostom.*

Who hath believed. The prophet states the actual result of the
Messiah's preaching and miracles upon the masses of the people.
—Ministers of Christ, when mourning over the want of success,
should consider how small the success of our Lord's own ministry.
—The Gospel, in all ages, has met with more that rejected it than
have savingly embraced it.

Our report. What they hear from us.—They had heard words
descriptive of the reality of the Messiah's claims; words which demanded the assent of the understanding and heart.—Prophets can
only bear witness to the truth concerning Christ; they are but
the *voice* of which He is the inspiring *thought.*—" Many hear it,
but few heed it, and embrace it." *Henry.*

Arm of the Lord. A well-known Hebraism.—The Oriental robe
was so shaped that it usually concealed the arm, but when the
arm was stretched forth, it appeared naked and prominent.—
Heroes, when preparing for battle, uncovered their arms, and when
the leader gave orders, the bare arm was stretched forth.—Hence
the phrase "laid bare his arm," signified to address oneself in earnest
to a work.—The question points to an implied answer in the prophet's own times.—But it has the same sad answer in our Lord's
day, and down to our time.—How few know Him who is both the
power and the *wisdom* of God!—The power of God was manifested in Christ, in His miracles and teaching, and in the spirit of
His life.—God's power was thus brought close to man so as to
demand and win their attention.—That power was unregarded
and unrecognised in the ordinary manifestations of God.

Revealed. As a fact, the power of God in Christ was revealed to
all these unbelievers.—But it was not revealed to them inwardly,
so that they might feel and acknowledge it.—The light was clear
about them, but they had no inner eye to see.—He who can discern and feel the power of God in Christ is a true child of the
light.—The great forces of nature, which are also powers of God,
act whether men are willing or unwilling.—But moral forces have
regard to the freedom of man.—It is not the kingdom of God's
power that men oppose (for *that* could crush them), but the kingdom of His *righteousness.*—God by creating man such as he is has,
in a sense, bound Himself to accept the consequences of man's
freedom.

ὁ λόγος. "It is in the very presence of unbelief and of hindrances cast in the way of
the kingdom of God that both Jesus and the apostles most frequently appeal to the

1038 / Gospel of John

word of prophecy. For prophecy exhibits the divine ὡρισμένον (compare Luke xxii. 22, with Matt. xxvi. 24), while it demonstrates the fact that even these seeming contradictions in history must be co-included in the divine counsel (chap. xviii. 19: xvii. 2)." *Tholuck.*—Κύριε. Jesus addressing God. *Meyer.*—A lament of the evangelist and those like-minded with him. *Luth rdt.*—The lament of the prophet, in his own name and that of his colleagues, over his time.—But the emphasis is upon the words ἵνα πληρωθῇ, and thus the lament of the prophet becomes indirectly, and as a type, the lament of Christ (compare Ps. xxi. 1).—The saying is most significantly chosen from the beginning of the prophecy about the suffering Messiah (Isa. liii.) –The hardening began to be accomplished in the face of the sufferings of the prophets: its fulfilment is completed in the crucifixion of Christ on the part of the Jews and in the rejection of the Crucified and Risen One. *Lange.*

---

39. Therefore they could not believe, because that Esaias said again,

Therefore. Gr., *on this account*, or *for this cause.*—Another explanation is given which takes a severer form.

They could not. They had rendered themselves incapable of belief through their persistent rejection of Christ.—The gradual loss of power to receive goodness is one of the punishments of sin.—There is no necessity for explaining away such statements concerning man's moral inability.—It is a stern law of God's moral government that men are doomed to lose those talents which lie unemployed —"*First*, they do not believe, *as being refractory ; then* they cannot *believe. They are mistaken who suppose what is said to be in the inverse order :* they could not *believe ; therefore* they did not believe." *Bengel.*—"The fact that the guilt of the parties involved is not excluded in such an *actus judicialis Dei*, in the Scriptural sense, is most plainly set forth by the history of Pharaoh, in which it is said in six places, he hardened himself, and in six others, God hardened him." *Tholuck.*

διὰ τοῦτο ὅτι. Has reference to what has gone before, *i.e.* the saying of verse 38 contains the ground for the saying of verse 40. *Meyer.*—Is preparative ; it announces the cause, *i.e.* the inability to believe of verse 39, explains why they did not believe, according to verse 38. *Tholuck, Luthardt.*—Their divinely decreed destiny, as a judicial infliction, presupposes their guilt in voluntarily choosing unbelief. *Lange.*

---

40. He hath blinded their eyes, and hardened their heart: that they should not see with their eyes, nor understand with their heart, and be converted, and I should heal them.

Blinded. Isaiah vi. 10. Quoted in many places.—As the words differ from the Heb. and the LXX., the quotation may have been made from memory.—This blindness continued to St. Paul's time, and remains even to the present (2 Cor. iii. 14).—Such is God's judgment on those who *will* not see.—The eye to receive and appreciate the vital ray of truth becomes dim from disuse.—The results of laws spiritual can be predicted with the same certainty as those of laws natural.—God's spiritual laws are in favour of a man if he keeps them, but if he disobeys, they press upon and crush him.—" When men close their eyes *wilfully*, it is just with God to close their eyes *judicially*." *Burkitt.*—" Although God was the unwilling cause of their blindness, it was their wicked will that gave to the cause its effect." *Whedon.*

Hardened. Man has the faculty of *feeling* after the truth.— Spiritual things are apprehended through the heart : we must love in order to know.—The continued rejection of the truth impairs spiritual sensibility.—Their perverse will transformed His mercy into judgment: His means of softening into results of hardening. Thus does the same sun that melts the wax harden the clay. *Whedon.*—" God hardens and blinds a man by forsaking and not supporting him." *Augustine.*

Converted. Signifies the turning about and away from their whole state of blindness and sin to God.—This is the result of seeing with the spiritual eye and understanding with the heart.

Heal. A word frequently used in Scripture to denote God's renovation of the soul.—Sin is a departure from the standard of spiritual health.—It was the work of Christ to make men *whole*, so that all life and thought should be resolved into one purpose and expression.—In disease, some particular organ asserts its independent existence, so that a man feels that he is not *whole:* there is a want of harmony.—Such is the state of man by nature ; he is not at one with himself.—Christ heals men by speaking peace to the soul, giving " quietness and assurance for ever."

τετύφλωκεν. Not Christ, but God, is to be understood as the subject. *Meyer,* *Tholuck.*—The nation itself is the subject. *Morus.*—Christ is, in the sense of the evangelist, the speaker in Isaiah, God the hardener, while ἰάσομι has reference to Christ. *Meyer.*—Should be referred to God. *Tholuck.*—The whole refers to Christ. *Grotius, Luthardt, Lange.*—πεπώρωκεν. ἐπωρωσεν. *Cod. Sin., Tisch* —ἐπιστραφῶσι. στραφῶσιν. *Cod. Sin., Tisch., Alford, Schaff.*—ἰάσωμαι ἰάσομι. *Cod. Sin., Lach., Tisch., Schaff.*

---

41. These things said Esaias, when he saw his glory, and spake of him

Esaias—saw. By this word is vividly represented the spiritual insight of the prophets.—They dealt not in conjecture or vague hypothesis, but *saw* visions of God.—Hence their firm convictions and solemn earnestness.—Isaiah saw this vision "In the year that King Uzziah died," as though the prophet would place in contrast the King who reigns for ever, with frail and short-lived man.— The prophet realized the "substance of things hoped for:" to him the Redeemer of mankind was present.

His glory. The grandeur of the sun cannot be known without study.—When known, its power is seen through all the changes of our earth.—Were the sun blotted out, not a stream would flow, not a wind would blow, nothing would grow; all the signs of life would cease; earth's myriads of living creatures would die.—To the intelligent eye, the sun fills the heavens with its splendour, and the earth with its teeming millions of sensitive creatures.—Thus, to the eye of one studying Christ's character, the Eternal throne is filled with His Person, wearing many crowns.—By His word He created the sun, kindled the stars, made the earth, formed the ocean, built up the mountains, and clothes all nature in her robes of verdure and fruit, or of snow and ice.—By His word angels, cherubim, and seraphim were called into being.—These are some of the beams of glory seen by the prophet, rapt into future times, (Isa. vi. 1)—the King in His beauty, seated on a throne, His train filling the Heaven of Heavens.—"I saw no temple there, for the LAMB was the temple thereof." Rev. xxi. 22.—It was the glory of the Lord of Hosts that the prophet saw ; therefore Jesus is divine ; He fills all time and space.—Long before the time of the prophet, the Logos was the revealer of God, as speech is a revealer of the hidden thought of the mind.—It was only through the Logos that God spoke to men in O.T. times : " No man hath seen God at any time." See on chap. i. 1-18.

Spake of him. The prophecy, therefore, had reference to the Messiah and His times.—This was the beginning of Isaiah's mission, the solemn inauguration of his high call.—The vision of divine realities is the strength of every true prophet.—He took hence the true key-note of his whole theme.

ὅτε. ὅτι. *Cod. Sin.. Lach., Tisch., Alford, &c.*—δόξα. According to Isa. vi. i., it was indeed the glory of *God* that was seen by the prophet; in accordance with the idea of the Logos, however, the theophan∙es are appearances of the Logos. *Meyer.*—The Logos, who is about becoming incarnate, is Himself one with the δόξα of the Father, although this again in the abstract is distinguished from the δόξα of Christ (compare Heb. i. 3); and hence too the δόξα of God is one with the Angel of the Presence (see Luke ii. 9), although Christ again has also His divine-human δόξα.—His essential estate is the μορφὴ θεοῦ. *Lange* —Αὐτοῦ. *Of Christ.*—The evangelist is giving his judgment— having had his understanding opened (Luke xxiv. 45) to understand the Scriptures—

that the passage in Isaiah is spoken of Christ.—And indeed, strictly considered, the glory which Isaiah saw *could only be* that of the Son, who is the ἀπαύγασμα τῆσ δόξης of the Father, whom no eye hath seen. *Alford.*—The evangelist here says that Isaiah saw the g'ory o the *Son*.—St. Paul says (Acts xxviii. 25) 'hat he heard the words of the *Ho'y Spirit.*—There is one glory, therefore. of the Holy Trinity; and the glory of the Father is the glory o' the Son, and is the glory of the Holy Ghost. (*Theoph.*)— The g ory of the E.er-bless d *Trinity* appeared to Isaiah when he heard the Angelic *Holy, Holy, Holy* (Isa. vi. 3); and the glorv o' the Trinity is here called the glory of Christ, because Christ is G.d. (*Cyri'*).—There is a remarkab'e resemblance to this passige in Rev. iv. 8-11, compared with Rev. v. 12-14, where the glory ascribed to the *Holy Trinity*, and the worship paid, is ascribed and paid to Christ. *Wordsworth.*

---

42. Nevertheless among the chief rulers also many believed on him; but because of the Pharisees they did not confess him, lest they should be put out of the synagogue:

Nevertheless. *Yet however.*—Verses 38-40 speak of failure, this of partial success.—The picture of unbelief is not altogether dark.— The case of those is described who were impressed with the truth, but who had not the moral courage to confess it.—In the darkest times of the Church there is some bright spot for contemplation to rest upon.

Chief rulers. Such as Nicodemus, Joseph of Arimathæa, and the young ruler.—These are censured for that moral weakness which prevented them avowing their convictions.—Jairus and the noble-man of Capernaum were rulers, but they honourably professed their faith.

Also. There were others besides these, not to mention the common people.

Many believed. John will not exaggerate the unbelief of the Jews. —He eagerly notes any signs of the hope that they are not im-penetrable to spiritual .truth.—"There may be true faith and grace, where yet there is much infirmity to smother and bear it down." *Hutcheson.*

Because of the Pharisees. These kept the rulers in continual dread, holding over them the threat of ecclesiastical penalties.— By this means men of tradition, forms, prescriptions, have hindered the world's progress, lengthened the reign of superstition, and often injuriously complicated the affairs of state.

Did not confess. They were convinced, but hindered by the fear of man from a complete expression of their faith.—Moral courage is an essential ingredient of the Christian character; the "fearful" as well as the disobedient come under condemnation. Rev. xxi. 8. —Such secret disciples deprive the Church of her lawful accession of influence.—The Church should have the full advantage of her conquests over unbelief.—How strong is the verdict of society, that it can thus overbear the convictions of the mind and heart!

Put out of the synagogue. See on chapters vii. 13 ; ix. 22.—
There are times when the rulers of the Church may abuse her
ordinances by employing them to suppress the truth.—The corruption of the best things often leads to the worst evils.—Those
who administer Church discipline are not secured from those perversions which come of human infirmity, error, and evil.—The
hour may come in history when loyalty to the truth must be the
supreme devotion in us, and be stronger than reverence for
prescriptive authority.

ὅμως μέντοι This limits and explains the preceding sentence. *Lange.*—ἀρχόντων.
Such persons as Nicodemus and Joseph of Arimathæa. *Meyer.*—Cannot refer to these.
John distinguishes between the wider sense of the word "believe" (chap. viii. 30)
and its more limited sense (chaps. vii. 5; xx. 27).—Manifestly, it is belief in the
wider sense of the term, inward historical recognition ("almost faith"), that is here
meant. The evangelist then proceeds to explain how it happened that the great commotion and awakening in the nation did not ripen into a great conversion. *Lange.*

---

43. For they loved the praise of men more than the praise of God.

They loved. Gr. word signifies the love of esteem.—The feelings
derive their moral character from the objects on which they are
placed.—The Gospel does not destroy the essential properties of
our nature, but directs them to a proper end, and affords them
full satisfaction.

Praise of men. Gr., *glory.*—See on chapter v. 44.—Seeking the
approbation of men, as a supreme object, in order to advance
our worldly interests, is one of the chief dangers to our
spiritual life.—The praise of men is near, is an object of our
immediate perception ; that which comes from God seems distant,
and can only be discerned by the spiritual eye.—Hence some are
too weak to escape from the tyranny of the present.—These words
seem severe, when we consider that some who are thus censured
afterwards embraced the faith: Therefore they show God's displeasure against such conduct.—That belief lacks vigour and full
influence which does not enable the character to rise to moral
heroism.

More. The approbation of men is to be valued when it is just, and
does not come into conflict with that of God.—These weak and
timid believers refused a higher nobility than society could confer.
—With sublime thoughts within them, they had not sufficient
moral courage to pass the barrier that hid from them the clear
view of things spiritual.—" *Love of the praise of men, as a by-end*

in that which is *good*, will make a man a *hypocrite* when religion is in fashion, and credit is to be *got by it;* and, as a base principle in that which is evil, it will make a man an apostate when religion is in disgrace, and credit is to be *lost for it.*" *Henry.*

Praise of God. Gr., *the glory.*—God is the source of all true honour and nobility.—He despises the image of the wicked, though the world may yield them the respect due to outward grandeur and state.—Nothing that He despises can be truly great. —The praise which comes from God lives when all else is destroyed by the tooth of time, or is hidden in shame through the disclosure of the solemn realities of eternity.

δόξαν τῶν ἀνθρώπων. Excommunication seemed frightful to them because they loved honour among men better than any (ἤπερ emphatically) honour with God. This means in the first place objectively, the honour which men bestow by their recognition, in contrast to the honour given by God. Not exclusive of the subjective sense, however, in which we interpret that honour of men to be of a human kind, but the honour of God of a divine sort (Rom. iii. 23). *Lange.*

---

44. Jesus cried and said, He that believeth on me, believeth not on me, but on him that sent me.

Jesus cried. Gr., *cried aloud.*—He uttered His words with special emphasis and power, so as to be heard by the multitude.—He will assert His divine mission in strong and clear terms, so that there shall be no risk of mistaking the nature of His claims.—The older expositors taught that Jesus here resumed His public discourses, broken off in verse 36.—Chrysostom says that the signs, referred to in verse 37, were wrought during the interval.—The words are of the nature of proverbs : short and pithy sayings that do not naturally grow out of each other.—The evangelist was inspired to select these weighty sayings of Jesus, so that the unbelief of the Jews might be seen to be without excuse.—Whatever may be mysterious in the teaching of Jesus, the nature of His claims and our duty are sufficiently clear and emphatic.— " The raising of His voice and crying intimates (1) His *boldness* in speaking. If they were ashamed of His doctrine, He was not, but set His face as a flint (Isaiah l. 7) ; (2) His *earnestness* in speaking. He cried as one that was serious and importunate ; (3) His desire that all might take notice of it. This being the last time of the publication of His Gospel by Himself, He makes proclamation." *Henry.*

Not on me. It was not that their minds had a clear conception that the object of faith was God the Father.—Jesus teaches that belief in Himself is really a belief in God, because of His oneness with God.—He is preparing the world for the declaration of God in His Son.—The difficulties of devotion towards an invisible object of worship are to be removed by giving men the means of knowing God in Christ.—" It may encourage faith that believers do not fasten upon an infinite Deity, but do ascend up to God through Christ the Mediator." *Hutcheson.*

Him that sent me. Jesus always refers back to the authority of the Father.—All advances towards men arise from the gracious will of the Father.—To believe in the efficacy of the work of Christ is to believe in that Infinite Love which is the spring and fountain of it.—The words and works of Jesus were a fresh revelation of God.—The glory of the Sender and the Sent is the same ; that of the one is not diminished by employing such an expedient, nor the other by accepting the mission.—The Son claimed no position independent of the Father.—He was the representative of the Father, and those who believed in Him believed not in the representative as apart from, but in that He represented, the Sender.—The same thought occurs in Mark ix. 37.

ἔκραξε. Implies public teaching addressed to the multitude. and it may be inferred there was some such teaching after verse 36.—*Chrysostom and all the Ancients ; Kling, Watkins.*—A continuation of the remarks of the evangelist, from verse 36, substantiating them by the testimony of the Lord Himself.—The words are taken mostly, but not altogether, from discourses *already given* in this gospel. *Alford.*—An epilogue of the evangelist. *Lücke, Tholuck, Olshausen, Meyer.*—On His departure from the temple and in the very act of withdrawing from the Jews, He shouted out these words to them from afar. *Lampe, Bengel.*—Uttered in the presence of the disciples. *Luthardt, Besser.*—Reminiscences which grew under the hand of the evangelist into a regular discourse, though not delivered by Jesus. *De Wette.*—The whole is a *résumé en gros* of the life of Jesus, in which the account of the unbelief and obduracy of the great mass of the Jewish people and its rulers is contrasted with the account of Christ's holy testimony to Himself. *Lange.*

---

45. And he that seeth me seeth him that sent me.

Seeth me. Gr., *beholdeth.* Cannot mean His outward appearance as apprehended by the organ of vision.—The visible things of the life of Jesus were interpreted differently by different minds.—Some saw in Him a mere pretender to a Divine Mission, others a worker of wonders by magic or some evil power.—Those of a simple and better nature saw in Him a well-meaning but mistaken enthusiast.—Those who had faith (true spiritual perception) saw in Him the Christ of God.—Thus Jesus was to each man as the state of his own mind and heart.—Men bring what is in their own minds to the objects they see.—Nature herself speaks with different voices to different minds.—Everything in the outward world was the same to the eyes of Newton as to those of ordinary men ; yet his piercing intellect saw a glory in Nature unknown to the rest of mankind.—The eye of faith sees in Christ the Son of God, the true life of the soul, and the hope of salvation.

Him that sent me. The believing soul contemplates in Christ the manifested life of God.—Such know all that can be known of the Father.—Through God as revealed in Christ, devotion becomes easier for the intellect and heart.—" In eyeing Him as our Saviour, Prince, and Lord in the right of redemption, we see and eye the Father as our owner, ruler, benefactor in the right of creation, for God is pleased to deal with fallen man by proxy." *Henry.*

θεωρῶν. Means to see, in the sense of "behold, contemplate, gaze upon."—The form of the expression is different from that of the previous verse, passing from the negative to the positive, in accord with the difference of thought. He that beholdeth Christ doth behold Him, and in Him beholds the impression of the substance of God. *Watkins.*

---

46. I am come a light into the world, that whosoever believeth on me should not abide in darkness.

I am come. Gr., *I have come,* and therefore am here.—Christ's work among men was a real mission from another world.—Other teachers have arisen from among men ; they are of the earth, earthly ; this teacher came down from Heaven.—He came not to bring a philosophy, but a salvation.—He who came from on high must have forces within Him capable of raising the world into the life and light of God.

A light. See on chapters i. 4 ; iii. 20 ; viii. 12.—Light is the emblem of knowledge, purity, and joy.—These were the gifts of Christ to men.—The driving away of spiritual darkness was salvation.—To behold Christ by the eye of faith is to behold the light of life, and therefore to be transformed into its purity.—To live in that light is to be a partaker of the joy of God.—Light is necessary to the life of all things that live.—Even were all other conditions satisfied, but this wanting, every form of life would perish from the earth.—Christ is absolutely necessary to the real life of the soul.—" Christ is the discoverer of men's misery and of the true remedy thereof." *Hutcheson.*

Believeth on me. Natural light is an object of consciousness to those who see, and Christ is a felt truth in every believing heart. —Light always brings its own evidence, being so familiar that its presence is silently accepted, and doubt is impossible.—The true Christian sees the light of God; he dwells in that light, and wants no further proof.—To believe in Christ is something more than the intellectual acceptance of His teaching, or the facts of His history.—It is the belief of the *heart* that saves a man.—The *character* can only be transformed by the belief of the *heart*.— Intellectual belief may exist without having any influence upon the life.—To believe in Christ is to believe in a *Life* of infinite compassion and love.—No one can truly contemplate that life without being, by thus beholding it, transfigured as in the light of life.

Not abide in darkness. Chapter i. 5.—Therefore the world was in darkness when this light came.—There was the darkness of sin in all its sad variety of forms: error, ignorance, transgression of law, and moral helplessness.—This spiritual darkness was not merely the privation of the light of God; it was in itself a fearful condition, wherein men were distracted with the rage of evil, and filled with superstitious fears.—Belief in Christ is a light that shines amidst the darkness of sorrow and death.—" I know whom I have believed." 2 Tim. i. 12.—"They were without any true comfort, or joy, or hope, but do not *continue* in that condition; light is sown for them." *Henry.*

---

47. And if any man hear my words, and believe not, I judge him not: for I came not to judge the world, but to save the world.

Hear my words. Our Lord is speaking to those who then actually heard His voice, and putting their case by way of supposition.— These had the advantage of Christ's bodily presence, with all the vividness and impression of actual beholding and hearing.—We may be tempted to envy them these high advantages, and to suppose that had we been in their situation our conduct would have been different.—Yet we have not their inveterate prejudices to contend with; we have not the difficulty of freeing ourselves from the bonds of a system grown strong in its coherence by ages of prescription and authority.—To the Jews of His day, the out-ward conditions of Christ's earthly life were a difficulty in their way of receiving Him as divine.—It was hard to see the strength and glory of His kingdom under such limitations and disguise.— Distance in time is required to estimate the full grandeur of the character of Christ.—It is the safest rule of interpretation, first to

explain the words of our Lord as they apply to the circumstances
in which they were spoken, and then to judge of their application
to our own case.—In this way we elevate what appears only of
transient and local importance into universal principles.—Jesus
was not only speaking to the few around Him then, but for all
time.—His audience was the listening ages of the future.—" Those
shall not be condemned for their infidelity that never had or could
have the Gospel.—Every man shall be judged according to the
dispensation of light he was under.—But those that have heard,
or might have heard, and would not, lie open to this doom."
Henry.

Believe not. The words of truth are not irresistible; they are *able*
to produce belief, but they do not of necessity compel it.—Divine
truths must be loved and felt in order to be known.—Love is
spiritual intelligence.—"The Gospel contains threatenings against
despisers as terrible as any threatening of the law." *Hutcheson.*

I judge him not. Does not mean that He did not form in His
own mind a judgment of their real spiritual condition.—But He
would not then *decide* in their case.—He would not then assume
the office of judge.—He could afford to wait through all the
slow movements of the just ways of God.—Sin and unbelief, of
themselves, fix a man's spiritual position in the sight of God.—
" Christ did not strike those dumb or dead who contradicted
Him ; never made intercession against Israel as Elias did.—
Though He had authority to judge, He suspended the execution of
it, because He had work of another nature to do first." *Henry.*

Not to judge the world. See on chapters iii. 17, 18; v. 45;
viii. 15, 26.—He came not to denounce doom, to utter the harsh
voice of the law.—That love which impelled Him to His mission,
and supported Him through it, now swallows up all in its own
boundless charity.—Nothing must be allowed to come between
the Saviour and the sinner.—Moses was the channel of law to
mankind, but Christ was the fountain of grace and truth. (See
on chap. i. 17.)—The world was to be won by the power of a
mighty love.—Moses announced the law with fierce threatenings
against disobedience, but Christ sets a beatitude in front of each
spiritual condition and duty.—It was His to bring the law of
Heaven upon earth : the obedience of love.

To save the world. See on chapter iii. 17.—This object of the
Redeemer's mission must be considered in all the fulness of its
meaning.—This was the greatest idea that had ever been entertained in behalf of the race.—Some have laboured by social
reforms to benefit a small portion of mankind ; others have con-

tributed to the world's intellectual wealth, but they have only made these high and refined pleasures the property of the few.—No unaided human mind had conceived the idea of a possible salvation for the world.—But Jesus had such an idea, and this with a complete knowledge of the terrible facts of society, and the injuries which sin inflicts upon the soul.—He knew that the remedy was of infinite efficacy.—He cared for the highest and most lasting interests of men.

μὴ πιστεύσῃ. πῇφυλάξῃ. *Cod. Sin., Lach., Tisch., Alford, Westcott and Hort, Schaff.*—οὐ κρίνω. *I judge him not, i.e.,* not now; *now* is the time of *mercy, afterward* will be the time of *judgment. Augustine.*

---

48. He that rejecteth me, and receiveth not my words, hath one that judgeth him : the word that I have spoken, the same shall judge him in the last day.

Rejecteth me. To do this it was not necessary actually to oppose Christ and His cause.—To reject Himself, it was sufficient to set aside His claims by giving them no consideration.—This was not the rejection of an opinion, but of a real, personal power.—We cannot be unkind or ungrateful towards laws or principles, but we can be towards a living presence, the manifestation of all truth and goodness in a life.—" It notes a rejection with scorn and contempt. Where the banner of the Gospel is displayed, no neutrality is admitted ; every man is either a subject or an enemy." *Henry.*

Receiveth not my words. Not enough to receive them into the memory or the understanding ; they must be treasured up in the heart and conscience, and be a power to influence the whole life.—The soul must receive the words of Christ as the soil receives seed to nourish it into the strength and beauty of the plant.—The Christ of the Gospels is not some great personage moving in the stirring events of history, of whom scarcely any distinct utterance is recorded.—The Gospels not only give a clear delineation of our Lord's character, but also record many of His gracious *words.*—There are men who have made a great figure in history, and whose influence has been felt through ages, yet few or none of their sayings have been preserved.—The sublime grandeur of their lives still speaks to us, but they have transmitted no teaching in words.—Such lives, for the most part, were those of Enoch and Abraham.—The words of Jesus in the Gospels are fresh with the vigour of life from age to age.—It is necessary for the continuity of the Church's life that we should have preserved to us the words of Christ Himself.—What the Apostles have seen and heard they declare unto us (1 John i. 1-3).—Unlike human teachers, we feel no painful separation between the character of Christ and the truths which dropped from His lips.—He was Himself that model which He drew.—His words are lit up with the glory of His own character.—Yet Christ Himself is greater than His words, for human language cannot express the full grandeur of the divine thought.—As Christ is the light of His own words, we can only begin to receive them by loving Himself.—The barrier of sin is in our way; our sin must be removed, or the words of Christ will not be a living power in us.—We must learn to obey His words not merely for their truth and beauty, but for *His sake.* Christ and His words cannot be separated; to refuse to love Him is to reject His words.

Hath one that judgeth him. There is still a Judge though He appears not now.—What a man does is laid up for eternity and forms his portion when he is brought face to face with God.— Every human life is hastening towards a solemn crisis.—Every man is on his way to God; none can escape Him, or pass on one side of Him; for weal or woe, each must stand *before* the Judge.— While mercy spares, and the reign of grace lasts, the preparations for Judgment are making; they cannot be set aside.—The sinner must be warned by the stern realities of doom, as well as invited and encouraged by the mercy of the Gospel.

The word that I have spoken. The Gospel: His message and revelation to man.—Heb. ii. 2-4. Words, though they seem to die away with their uttered sounds, are yet the most potent things we know: if they represent eternal realities they can never die.— Man must meet again the truth he now despises or neglects.—The words of Jesus represent realities; they will assert themselves when the deluding things of this life are swept away.

The same. Gr., " *That is it which shall,*" *&c.*—"The pronoun looks a long way forward." *Bengel.*—The acceptance or rejection of an offered Gospel is the test by which men shall be tried, the method and warrant of judgment.—The rejected light of truth is the condemnation of men.—" Though all other witnesses against a wicked man were gone, yet the word preached will stand up against him as a witness and accuser. It shall be a witness of what was offered, and make up an accusation against him for his contempt, upon which Christ shall pronounce sentence.' *Hutcheson.*

Shall judge. The Word of Christ is so sure that it can determine the great issues of the hereafter.—That Word shall be powerful to justify as to condemn.—The position which men assume towards the words of Christ will determine their fate at the hands of God.

Last day. See on chapter v. 22, 23.—"To that day of judgment Christ here binds over all unbelievers to answer then for all the contempts they have put upon Him.—Divine justice has *appointed a day* and adjourns the sentence to that day." *Henry.*—All the days of time were made for this great day, which will gather up their issues in the solemn decisions of Divine judgment.

ἀθετῶν. This word, more correctly rendered *nullifieth*, occurs only here in St. John. *Watkins.*

---

49. For I have not spoken of myself; but the Father which sent me, he gave me a commandment, what I should say, and what I should speak.

For. Gr., *because.*—The reason is given why the Word shall judge the unbeliever.

Not spoken of myself. Christ did not speak of His own authority merely, but referred back to the Father.—Christ accepted His mission as THE SENT of God, and refers continually to the Divine Authority by which He acted.—The people had sufficient proof that the doctrine which Jesus preached was from God.—If they had believed in God thus speaking to them they would have believed in Jesus to the extent which He demanded.—"No Word but God's Word is sufficient to condemn men for disobedience; and if men cannot prove their doctrine to be divine, it is neither to be obeyed, nor are the terrors for the neglect thereof to be regarded." *Hutcheson.*

The Father which sent me. See on chapter xiv. 9.—The Son could only obey the commission of the Father, imitate His work, reveal His character, and manifest His thoughts concerning men. —God was now revealing Himself to men, becoming more intimate to their thought and feeling; and Christ was the appointed Way.—God from all eternity had contemplated Himself in another (His Divine Son), and now that Son stands as His representative before the world.

Gave me a commandment. See on chapter x. 18.—The reference is to the commission of His Messianic life.—Christ came to men with a formed and definite message.—The sum of Christ's doctrine was the Father's commandment: that commandment was concerned with the great question of eternal life.—"They were like those given to an ambassador, directing him not only what he *may* say but what he *must* say. The messenger of the covenant was entrusted with a message which he must deliver." *Henry.*

What I should say. In the way of a distinct and special enunciation of truths.—Jesus had distinct truths of God to announce.—These were not speculations or matters of curious enquiry.—They had all a bearing upon the practice of righteousness; for they were commandments of God.—The words of Christ were more than accurate representations of realities; they were life, the means by which the soul of man truly lives.

What I should speak. This word "speak" describes His general teaching.—The same spirit breathes through all the words of Christ.

τί εἴπω, &c, Our Lord intends a distinction between "saying" and "speaking."—We have had the same distinction in chapter viii. 43.—That which He should say was the matter of the revelation which He made; that which He should speak was rather the method in which He made it. *Watkins.*

---

50. And I know that his commandment is life everlasting: whatsoever I speak therefore, even as the Father said unto me, so I speak.

I know. The possession of this knowledge gave Him the right to deliver a personal testimony for God.—Jesus did not, like some great teachers of mankind, slowly feel His way towards the truth and gain some fragments of it through many failures; He came with a given portion of truth from God.—He brought to mankind that knowledge which saves.—Christ gave men spiritual *facts,* and not the uncertain conclusions of the speculative reason.

His commandment. The commission of the Messianic work.—The Son speaks not of Himself, but as executing this commission, which brings spiritual and eternal life to the world.—This commandment being eternal life, the whole teaching of the Messiah must simply be an utterance of it.

Life everlasting. See on chapter iii. 15.—Better, *eternal life.*—Not any particular commandment, but every commandment of God is eternal life.—All the words of Jesus were spoken under the authority of God; they are a spiritual power; they endure for ever; they are living.—In the teaching of Jesus we have the living utterance of God.—The "commandment" is not satisfied by merely legal obedience; it demands the living energy of faith and love.—Eternal life is conformity to the will of God which is the law of all who dwell for ever in His sight.—How few words of human wisdom we can trust ourselves upon in the hour of our saddest necessity, but we can venture the eternal interests of our souls upon the words of Christ.

As the Father said. By way of definite instruction.—Answers to " what I should say and what I should speak " in the last verse.

So I speak. He had expanded the instructions given Him by the Father in the course of His teaching.—As human necessity suggested it, and as the circumstances of life led the way, Jesus unfolded the truth of God.—" The external revelation is regarded as the work of the Son. That which the Father says is the truth revealed, and the matter and form are here identified." *Watkins*

John 13

1. Now before the feast of the passover, when Jesus knew that his hour was come that he should depart out of this world unto the Father, having loved his own which were in the world, he loved them unto the end.

Before. Immediately before the Feast of the Passover—the fourth day of the week—Wednesday.—During the interval from the close of the last chapter to the opening of this—from Sunday till Thursday—the several events took place which are related in Mark xi. 12; xiv. 2; Matt. xxi. 28; xxvi. 5; Luke xx. 1; xxii. 6. —This word indicates the *time*, and the rest of the verse the *subject* of our Lord's discourse.—This particle of time denotes the day on the evening of which the Supper and discourse occurred.

Feast of the Passover. See on chap. i. 29, 36; ii. 13.

Jesus knew. Gr., *Jesus knowing.*—That knowledge had spread a sadness over His whole life.—He waited for His baptism and His hour, but all the while the fatal oppression lay on Him.—Jesus did not make experiments, did not feel his way gradually until some reliable path should open up for Him : He had a well-defined purpose of life from the beginning.—"Christ was not surprised with His sufferings, nor were they carved out according to the will of enemies; but the time thereof was determined, and He knew of it beforehand." *Hutcheson.*

His hour was come. See on chap. ii. 4; xii. 23, 27.—The close of His troubled life.—The completion of His work, as far as this world was concerned.—He was drawing nigh to the confines of His mortal day.—There was an appointed day in which even the Son of Man must do the work given Him.—He had spoken shortly before of this "hour" (chapter xii. 27).—It was to the world the hour of seeming defeat, but to Himself the point of departure homewards to His native Heaven.

Depart out of this world. This expression is an euphemism for His death.—He often refers to that dread hour by such mild expressions (chap. xiv. 12; xvi. 10, 28; also in verse 3).—It was a world of pain, conflict, and sin; He was now about to pass into the kingdom of eternal peace.—Jesus regarded this world as a place in which duty had to be done: the painful task He had undertaken accomplished.—In His earthly life He was aiming at one great purpose; and, until that was fulfilled, a sad oppression lay upon Him.—When His life work was done, His reward was

ready.—This world had no fitting home for Him in the proper
majesty of His nature.—As He alone of all mankind consciously
and voluntarily came into the world, so He alone of His own will
departed from it.—Christ has taught His people to regard death
not as the extinction of light and joy, but as transition.—
Believers depart hence, and arrive at the presence of their Lord.
—The doctrine of man's immortality, as a being created in the
image of God, is everywhere assumed in revelation.

Unto the Father. See on chap. i. 14; iv. 21, 23.—The Logos,
which in the beginning "was with God," must return to that
glorious fellowship: "the only begotten Son who was in the
bosom of the Father" must go back to His natural home.—It
was fitting also that the love which gave the Redeemer for His
work should welcome Him to rest and honour when that work was
done.—The humiliation of the Son of God was necessary to our
salvation, but He must not be detained in that state.—Such
majesty as His must not remain long in disguise.—Christ could
not be held in any of the inferior conditions into which He entered
for our sakes.—He could not be held by poverty and suffering
here.—He could not be held by the bonds of the grave, or of the
invisible world.—The permanent condition of the Son of Man is
to dwell in full glory with the Father.—Jesus has thus opened up
the way for us to go to the bosom of our Father and our God.—
The Church copies the life of her Lord, passing through the stages
of suffering, humiliation, and glory.—The whole family of God
will be gathered home to Him at last: Christ will be ever calling
"many sons" to His side to share His own joy.—The loving
Father will not see His children always despised and troubled,
nor will He leave His image in the grave.—"This Gospel is
divided into three parts, of which the sum and substance is: *I
have come from the Father; I have been in the world; I go to the
Father.*" *Bengel.*

Loved His own. All who believed were His by peculiar right, by
likeness to Himself; such are opposed to those who had no disposition towards the truth, and who therefore could not recognize
its voice.—Jesus had finished His public ministry; and now He
turns to that little flock who were not ashamed to confess His
Name.—He whose love could embrace mankind had yet peculiar
satisfaction in those who were being conformed to His own image.
—Even the love of so great a Being has conditions laid upon it.—
The delights of God are not capricious, but rather a necessity of
His nature.

In the world. He knew the dangers to which they would be ex-

posed, yet His interest in them did not diminish ; they were still
held securely in His love.—While in the world, believers are
"absent from the Lord ; " but the consciousness of being loved is
the true solace of absence.—Spiritual life must commence under
the conditions of imperfection, trial, and danger, before it can pass
to the higher stages of eternal peace and security.—These words
apply to all "His own" who are now in the world.

Loved them unto the end. This signifies more than that He
loved them to the last ; as long as He lived.—Christ loved His own
to the full extent and consummation of loving.—Human friendship
is capable of much, has many resources of sympathy and kindness,
yet it is often powerless to help.—Jesus had an " end " to accomplish for His own, His *death*, in which the full effect of His love
for them was manifest.—He did not love merely whilst He was
man amongst men, but still loves with that love which takes
delight in His own.—The love of such a Being, and who showed
it in such a manner, is not to be measured by our notions of time,
but must be considered in all the dimensions of life, feeling, and
imagination.—The love of Christ "passeth knowledge ; " it is a
capacity embracing all possibilities, and extending beyond the
reaches of creaturely thought.—Christ's love to His people is unchangeable and closes them in on every side.—" Even to the death
He suffered for them, and in so doing He loved them perfectly,
as the word also will signify, proving that His love was a growing
love, in letting out such abundant effects at the last." *Hutcheson.*
—The love of Christ now is a pledge of future love, of all the
fulness belonging to that word.

'ελήλυθεν. ἦλθεν. *Codd.* **A. B. K.** *Sin., Lach., Tisch., Alford,* &c.—" The perfect
resulted from the recollection of chap. xii. 25." *Meyer.*—ἐις τέλος. The sense " unto
the end" is very rare, and the general meaning is, "in the fullest degree," "up to the
limit."—It thus answers exactly to our "extremely."—John thinks of the intensity of
our Lord's love, and speaks of it in the simple expressiveness of the old Hebrew
phrase, "Loving, He loved them with fulness of love." *Ellicott.*

---

2. And supper being ended, the devil having now put into the heart of Judas
Iscariot, Simon's son, to betray him.

Supper. John is writing to those to whom the chief incidents in
the life of Jesus were well known ; therefore, he omits details not
necessary to his main purpose.—The other evangelists relate the
preparations that were made for the Last Supper.—John gives
prominence to the significant act of the feet-washing and to the

deep discourse which Jesus pronounced to His chosen few at the table.—It may seem strange that the institution of the Last Supper is not related by this evangelist; but he is equally silent concerning the institution of Baptism.—It is a sufficient solution that he was writing for those who were acquainted with the externals of the Christian religion.—His design was to unfold the inner glories of the truth, using only those historical incidents which were necessary.—The other evangelists had sufficiently narrated the facts connected with the institution of the Last Supper.—It was only necessary to supply a few incidents they had omitted in order to complete the picture of Christ in the glory of His nature and offices.

Being ended. Gr., *when it was being made*, *i.e.*, when supper was served.—The washing of feet would therefore be at the *beginning* of the supper; evident also from verses 4, 12, 26-31.—This is in accordance with Jewish customs.

The devil. See on chap. vi. 70, and on Luke iv. 2.—Judas was called such by our Lord Himself, but the word as here employed describes a being distinct from the mind or purpose of Judas.— Jesus had just hinted His departure, and the terrible means by which it was to be effected must now be indicated.—In the conflict with evil, which is shortly to be described, it is necessary to bring the Prince of darkness, the great enemy of man, upon the scene.—The foe who had vanquished the first man now levels his attacks against the " second man, the Lord from Heaven."

Put into the heart. See on Luke xxii. 3.—The Greek expression is forcible, *having already cast it into the heart*, *i.e.*, having already *suggested*.—The purpose of Judas was then quite hidden.—Sin begins by taking possession of the heart; the act is but the revelation of a thought and purpose already formed.—Satan had an easy victory in gaining the throne of such a heart as that of Judas. —Some sins are so great that we feel bound to ascribe them to the immediate instigation of the devil.—The heart is the centre of man's personality.—*There* belief becomes faith, and the suggestion of sin becomes inclination and wrong doing.

Judas Iscariot. See on chapters vi. 70, 71; xii. 4; and on Luke vi. 16; xxii. 3.

To betray Him. The devilish thought had entered the heart of Judas and he had already made the agreement with the chief priests.—Sin has a natural course of development—the base idea put into the heart, the captivity of all the powers of the soul to that one evil thought, and then the finished transgression.—

" It was not a sin of human infirmity, but a devilish sin so to do. Such diabolical suggestions may be darted into the bosom of believers, and therefore they are warned to quench them (Eph. vi. 16) ; but the wicked do give way to them." *Hutcheson.*—How great the self-abasement of Jesus to wash the feet of one whom He well knew had framed this terrible purpose.—How great the sin of Judas to accept so loving and tender an office, all the while conscious of his baseness.—What a picture we have here of the humility of the Saviour, and the presumption of sin in His wretched disciple !—Even the power of Satan required great corruption on the part of Judas to make the temptation successful ; the spark would soon die out unless it falls upon combustible material.—The covetous nature of Judas had blunted all moral sensibility, and he was ready for any deed of shame.—Satan opposed the Son of God by inflaming the malice of His open enemies ; now he seeks to incite His friends to treachery.

γενομένου. γινομένου. *Codd. B. L. X. Sin., Tisch., Treg., Westcott and Hort.*—"Supper being served." *Noyes and Conant*—"When supper was begun." *Alford.*—The E. V. ("supper being ended") is inconsistent with verse 12, where Jesus placed Himself again at the table ; and with verse 26, where the meal is going on.—The aorist crept in as the more usual form in disregard of the chronology. *Schaff.*—The reading ἵνα παραδοῖ αὐτὸν Ἰούδας Σίμωνος Ἰσκαριώτης, in accordance with *B L. M. X. Sin., Copt., Arm., Vulgate,* etc., received by *Tischendorf,* affirmed by *Meyer* to be the correct one, is not entitled to prevail against the reading given by *A. D.,* etc., *Lachmann* [which is the text. rec. followed by the E. V.: εἰς τὴν καρδίαν Ἰούδα Σίμωνος Ἰσκαριώτου, ἵνα παραδῷ (*Lachm.* παραδοῖ) αὐτόν].—*Meyer* interprets the above reading : " When the devil had already made his plot (taken it into his own heart) that Judas should betray Him," and remarks that this reading was early (so early as Origen) misunderstood to be an account of the seduction of Judas by the devil.—Fear was, however, probably entertained that fatalism might find a support in the *Recepta,* and thus originated a conjecture which, however, without its being remarked, must necessarily have a far more fatalistic effect.—The preponderance of authority is in favour of the more difficult reading : εἰς τὴν καρδίαν ἵνα παραδοῖ αὐτὸν Ἰούδας Σ Ἰσκ., which is adopted by *Tregelles, Alford, Tischendorf, Westcott and Hort.*—The text. rec. looks like a rearrangement to escape the difficulty of construction.—The subjunctive form παραδοῖ is unusual in the New Test., but sustained by *Codd. Sin., B. D.*—The text. rec. reads παραδῷ. *Lange, Schaff.*

---

3. Jesus knowing that the Father had given all things into his hands, and that he was come from God, and went to God.

Jesus knowing. The force of the expression is, that inasmuch as He had perfect knowledge of all things, He did the lowly act recorded.—Jesus did not make ventures in hope as one to whom the issues of futurity were doubtful.—He knew what He would do ; how His words and actions would be received, and what would be the results of His great mission through time and eternity.—If the divinity of Jesus, and therefore His infinite knowledge, be accepted, this ought to explain any difficulties suggested by His conduct while amongst men.—His history can only be seen in its true harmony when we recognise the greatness of His nature. —To wash the feet of His disciples seemed to be beneath the dignity of our Lord's character.—Therefore, to disarm all prejudice, and to set aside all hasty reflections upon His actions, the evangelist prefaces this incident with a statement attributing to our Lord perfect knowledge of all things.—The words and deeds of such a Being are to be interpreted by what He was.

The Father. See on verse 1.—The Father of Jesus in a peculiar sense in which that relation can be claimed by no other being ; the evangelist had already used the expression, *His own Father.*—His oneness with God gave Him a sufficient foundation to assert the highest claims.—In the midst of His humiliation and apparent defeat Jesus was ever conscious who He was, and of His infinite treasures of power and knowledge.—God had ever contemplated Himself in His own Son, and though that Son is now on an errand of mercy, involving His deep abasement, yet His relation to the Highest remains unbroken.—The height of glory from which Jesus came imparts a depth to His humiliation.—To humanity, lying so low in sin and misery, that height is also an aspiration.— To be glorified together with Jesus is the privilege of all the sons of God (Rom. viii. 17).—" It is the duty of saints, in the time of their abasements and trials, not to dwell always on the thoughts of these, but to raise up their hearts in the consideration of their esteem with God through Christ." *Hutcheson.*

Given all things into his hands. See on chapter iii. 35.—All things, without any exception whatever.—To all other beings God gives by measure, but to His Son in infinite fulness.—Therefore Jesus is sufficient for our souls ; to Him our full obedience is due, and our faith and hope should be in Him.—The nearer our Lord approaches to His great sorrow, the brighter is His glory made to shine.—True believers in Christ can rely on eternal verities that become all the more glorious and strong in the time of deepest trial.—Of the " all things " given to Christ, some only were subdued to God, many were perverse and rebellious ; but Christ was to go forth and conquer until all had either submitted to love or were shut up in the impotence of rebellion.—" 1. Saints may sleep soundly, having such a friend at the helm of Providence. 2. However wicked enemies seem to rage at their pleasure against Christ and His followers, yet they are also given into His hands.

The most pernicious of His enemies are given through Him to the Church for her good. 3. Men are but great fools when, notwithstanding all their covetousness, they must be content with a few things, and yet all things might be theirs; for all things are His, and theirs in Him. 4. They are no less fools who make themselves slaves to anything, whereas in Christ they might be masters of al things." *Hutcheson.*

Come from God. He was with God, and one with Him in glory and dignity.—Christ did not slowly arrive at the consciousness of His pre-existence; the felt conviction of it was ever present with Him.—His humanity might have obscured the Divine glory in Him from others, but not from Himself.—His humiliation shows how He loved; His high origin shows that He was Divine who loved.—All benefits for men begin with God: He makes the first advances. Intelligent natures, whether fallen or unfallen, owe all to grace.—Jesus came from God to the poverty and evil of man's condition.—It is the highest glory of love to make cause with and become as the object loved.

Went to God. He was on His way to that glory from whence He came.—He was sure of His reward, and the full investiture with His ancient dignity.—Christ herein marked out the true path for His people and the pattern of their service.—Every child of God must return to Him and dwell with Him for ever.—Spiritual death consists in separation from God; eternal life consists in union with God.—" Christ suffered for sins, the just for the unjust, that he might *bring us to God*" (1 Peter iii. 18).—When He shall have accomplished His work as Mediator, "then shall the Son also himself be subject unto him that put all things under him, that God may be all in all" (1 Cor. xv. 28).

The words ὁ Ἰησοῦς are wanting in *Codd. B. D. L. X. Sin., etc.—Cod. A. and others* give them.—They might easily have been omitted, because they seemed unnecessary in the already involved sentence. *Schaff.*

---

4. He riseth from supper, and laid aside his garments ; and took a towel, and girded himself.

Riseth from supper. See on verse 2.—This is *consistent* with the opinion that the feet-washing occurred after or during the supper; yet the statement does not *require* that signification.—Jesus had taken his proper position as host at that supper, and now He quits that position to perform the work of a servant. The disciples had disputed about precedence, and the wounds of pride were still fresh in them.—They required a practical lesson in humility before they could commune together by the tokens of a meal presided over by such a host.—Believers require many a hard lesson before they are fit to sit down with Jesus and partake of the blessed refreshments of His kingdom.

Laid aside his garments. His upper or outer garments, which would have proved an incumbrance to Him in this act.—He became altogether as one that serveth, assuming the badges and observing the very forms of humility.—With what a graphic minuteness is the whole of this scene described!—The writer of this history has wrought and perfected a great picture with few strokes.—Thus the scenes of the Gospels ever live again, so intimate are they to Christian thought and feeling.—"Christ acts all the parts of a mean servant here; and He did this, being on earth, to give proof what mean necessities of ours He will stoop to take notice of, though He be absent in body." *Hutcheson.*

Girded himself. He fastened the towel about His person like a girdle.—All these minute circumstances impress the picture the more vividly upon our minds.—They open up to us something of our Lord's nature.—They show His sense of order, the dignity, the deliberation, and even the heartiness with which He could perform such a work.

τὰ ἐμάτια. May mean the outer and inner garments, or, as here, and often simply the outer garment, *mantle, pallium* (different from the tunic or χιτών, and worn over it), which was wrapt around the body or fastened about the shoulders, and was often laid aside; comp. Matt. xxi. 7, 8; Acts vii 58; xxii. 20.—There is no necessity to suppose that Jesus literally divested Himself as the basest of slaves. *Lange, Schaff.*

---

5. After that he poureth water into a bason, and began to wash the disciples' feet, and to wipe them with the towel wherewith he was girded.

After that. That is, after rising, referring to the next thing that He did.—His rising from the table at that time showed that He was bent upon some special design, and would put the disciples into a state of expectancy as to what He next would do.

Poureth water. In this act of condescension He takes upon Himself every duty of a servant, suffering no part to be performed by others.—The humiliation of the Son of Man was not a scene acted, it was humanly real in every part.—It was not an appearance but a reality that Christ was in the "form of a servant;" for this condition is opposed to the manner of His Divine existence, which was in the "form of God" (Phil. ii. 6-8).—All the service of Christ for men was a ministry; it was only in reference to God that He was a servant, bound by a solemn obligation.—He was δοῦλος του Θεοῦ, never δοῦλος ἀνθρώπων.

A bason. Gr., *the* basin.—The article is employed when only one thing of the kind was in use.—There was generally such a basin provided, made of metal or of wood.

Began to wash. Gr., *proceeded to.*—"The word paints the gradual course of the action; the wiping of the feet points to its completion." *Tholuck.*—"A new and marvellous 'beginning.' The word is rare in John." *Bengel.*

The disciples' feet. There is frequent mention of this practice in Scripture (Gen. xviii. 4; xix. 2; xxiv. 32).—It was regarded as a menial act, and was always performed by servants or slaves.— Jesus now stoops to this lowly office.—What a picture of humiliation was presented to the minds of the disciples when they saw the Master take upon Him such a service!—The highest can minister to the lowest without degradation or risk to moral purity, as the light can shine upon the most noisome things and yet remain pure and unstained.—No act of Christ's humility was unbecoming His true dignity, but every manifestation of it did but extend a surface from which His love was reflected.

To wipe them. He followed out this lowly service to the end.— The action recorded in this verse was not designed to end in itself. —It was not one of the sudden sallies of officious virtue, or an uncalled-for deed of humiliation.—The earthly things with which Jesus had to do were made both to represent and to deepen the impression of eternal realities.—By the light of the love of Christ, every deed He did becomes transfigured.—The significance of this feet-washing was two-fold: 1. It taught a *truth, the necessity of spiritual washing.*—Christ herein revealed the purpose of His mission, which was to make the souls of men clean.—2. He left an *example* of that humble duty and loving service which one disciple should render to another.

---

6 Then cometh he to Simon Peter: and Peter saith unto him, Lord, dost thou wash my feet?

Then. As if the evangelist said, "So in the course of this duty He comes to," &c.

Cometh to Simon Peter. It is probable that He performed the

office for some of the disciples before He came to Simon Peter.—
They accepted the service in silence and without opposition.—
But when He came to Peter, the silence was broken.—Most of the
disciples would fear to express the thought of their mind ; they
would be either perplexed or dumb with amazement.—The impetuous nature of Peter forbade such reserve.—The case of Peter
showed those disciples who had already received this service that
their silent acceptance was so far right.—Those who followed him
had sufficient warning that the action must not be opposed.

Lord. "Peter on this occasion speaks thrice ; in the first and third
instance he calls Him, *Lord ;* the second address is, as it were, a
continuance of the first." *Bengel.*—" Christ's abasing Himself
and condescending to His people ought not to obscure His
majesty, nor make them forget it ; for in the midst of this washing
He is to Peter Lord." *Hutcheson.*

Dost thou wash ? *Thou* is emphatic.—*Thou*, my Lord and Master !
—The question indicates amazement that He should stoop so low.
—It involves also a kind of suspicion that such an action would be
undignified in one to whom he was ever accustomed to look with
such deferential regard.—Peter assumes the office of guardian of
his Lord's dignity—But this was a zeal for Christ which was " not
according to knowledge."—Peter could only comprehend a small
part of Christ's character and work.—He forgot how poor his
Master must become that we might be rich, how low He must
stoop whose office it was to lift up man from the depths.—
He failed to recognize the truth that " the Son of Man came not
to be ministered unto, but to minister."—This forward disciple
did not reflect that whatever Christ does, *He* knows the reason
why.—Christ knew all the avenues to the human soul and how it
could be best affected for truth and righteousness.—Peter did not
wait to see wisdom cleared and justified.—" So characteristically
and so consonantly with the previous delineation of him is this
disciple here depicted, that it would involve gross blindness to
regard scenes like this as *fictitious.*" *Tholuck.*

My feet. *My feet,* the feet of one so poor and unworthy !—It
would be more becoming that I should wash thine.—So far, Peter
gave proof of his humility.—It was right that he should be filled
with a sense of his own unworthiness.—But there is a humility
which grows from the secret roots of pride, one so lost in self-
contemplation as to forget that *obedience* is of the first concern.
—It is not genuine humility to refuse what God offers so freely.
—When the Saviour bestows benefits, the sinner must forget himself, and be content to receive with all simplicity.—" Shall those

hands wash my feet, which with a touch have cleansed lepers, given sight to the blind, and raised the dead"? *Theophylact.*

---

7. Jesus answered and said unto him, What I do thou knowest not now; but thou shalt know hereafter.

Jesus answered. He will not turn upon His impulsive, unreflecting disciple with the language of censure, but condescends to reason with him.—Peter was near the true path, needing but the loving glance and beckoning hand to guide his feet into it.—He committed the faults of a hasty spirit in the time of perplexity: our Lord knew how to deal with such a nature.

What I do. The full significance of this action.—Peter knew what the outward fact would be, but was ignorant of the hidden truth it contained.—As in His *words*, Jesus says many things at once; so in His *acts*, there is more intended than appears at first sight.

Thou knowest not now. The sense of ignorance should have made this apostle cautious and reserved, willing to trust entirely in his Lord.—He ought to have known that Christ would do Himself no dishonour by any action, and that His purpose must ever be wise and merciful.—It was the duty of Peter to wait until his Lord had explained Himself.—The rash ventures of thought should not be mistaken for knowledge, or we may, without intending it, actually oppose the purposes of God.—These words contain a general principle.—There are many things of which we are ignorant in this present state.—Both the nature of God and the reasons of His dealings are hidden from us.—We see but parts of His ways, and do but catch here and there fragments of the discourse of Providence.—We cannot explain why evil came into the world, and why it is still permitted; nor can we render a full account of the reasons why we are tempted and tried as we are.—Infinite wisdom cannot be reviewed by those who are but of yesterday, and who, in the presence of the unexplored infinity around them, know nothing.—God's dealings with *ourselves* are full of mystery.—After we have allowed for what is necessary for moral discipline, there remains an unknown quantity of which we can give no further account.—"And no wonder we be in the dark here if we consider: 1. That the worker of these works is wonderful in counsel, and excellent in working, infinitely beyond politicians whose projects and purposes are oftimes hid from us, and therefore much more His.—2. That His way of working and bringing about His purposes is very strange and unperceivable, for He brings things out of nothing (Rom iv. 17), one contrary out of another, as light out of darkness (2 Cor. iv. 6); He brings meat out of the eater, and takes enemies in their own snares.—3. That His end in working is not to satisfy our sense and curiosity, but He chooseth such a way as may leave enemies to harden their hearts, and may try and humble His people. *Hutcheson.*—" What *I* do *thou* knowest not now; " both pronouns are emphatic, and convey a rebuke to Peter.

But thou shalt know hereafter. Gr., *after these things,* i.e., after the action of feet-washing was finished.—" What I do thou knowest not now; but thou shalt come to know presently "— Thus the promise of knowledge was near fulfilment.—The aw of spiritual life here is duty first and clear knowledge afterwards. —In this special instance "hereafter" means shortly, but the statement involves a principle of the widest application.—Either in this world, or in the next, God will make His ways plain.—The inheritance of the saints will be *in light*, and the righteous judgment of God *revealed.*—A life of faith would be impossible were all now made obvious and familiar.—The Bible is clear on every question of duty, but throws little light upon the *reasons* of God's dealings.—For this the saints must await the revelation of the future.—We now see but dimly; we are not favoured with the direct ray; a diminished light reaches our eyes.—Direct knowledge is the privilege of the future life.—We know in part now, but in the future we shall know completely.—A Christian cannot see the whole of his journey, nor the glory of the end.—He is content with seeing one step before him.—" Subsequent providences explain preceding ones; and we see afterwards what was the kind tendency of events that seemed most cross; and the way which we thought was *about* proved the *right* way." *Henry.*

---

8. Peter saith unto him, Thou shalt never wash my feet. Jesus answered him, If I wash thee not, thou hast no part with me.

Peter saith. He was rash thus to protest a second time.—He assumes a knowledge now which becomes ignorance and impiety through his self-will, because he is not content to wait for that knowledge which will be given at the right time.

Never wash my feet. The Greek is an emphatic form of forbidding an action.—Thus (1 Cor. viii. 13) the same expression is rendered *while the world standeth.*—It was the indignant protest of a well-meaning sense of reverence.—This apostle had one of the ingredients of moral heroism, but his character required tempering with meekness.—Peter ought to have been satisfied with the promise of his Lord, but he was hurried by his self-confidence into an attitude uncalled for and unjustifiable.—He did not see that he rejected the authority and did dishonour to the wisdom of his Lord.—It is not genuine humility to refuse what God offers, on the ground that the gift is too good or great.

If I wash thee not. Jesus does not take this apostle at his word, but disputes the point so as to shame his unbelief.—He does not say *"thy feet,"* but *"thee."*—The feet unclean defiled the whole body.—Christ Himself must cleanse the whole nature of the sinner.—Vague ideas of the provisions of mercy will not save us ; the Saviour must come with His cleansing virtue to each individual soul.

Thou hast no part with me. This phrase is a Hebrew thought in Greek dress; compare Matt. xxiv. 51, and Luke xii. 46.—It is frequent in the Old Testament (Deut. xii. 12).—The chief lesson which our Lord intended to teach by this action was *humility*.— He explains that such was His meaning (verses 12-17).—But the actions of Jesus can convey more than one kind of instruction.— This incidental lesson touches a deeper question than the main thing intended.—It was something to learn humility, yet humility must be based upon *purity*.—The soul must be cleansed, or there can be no fellowship with Christ.—Purity of heart is the perfection of all graces ; it leads to the clear vision of God and of all things in God.—Such spiritual knowledge is the strength of the soul.—"It is neither the goodness of our nature, nor legal purifications, or our own endeavours, that can either prove or make us clean ; but it is Christ alone who must wash us, that we may participate with Him, and who must apply the merit and efficacy of His blood for that end." *Hutcheson.*—Jesus in His humiliation still retains His dignity, and makes Himself the centre of man's spiritual life.—Peter is brought to this tremendous issue to have a part with Christ, or to be cut off from Him.—These are the issues of life or death.—"It is necessary to having a part in Christ that He *wash us.* All those whom Christ owns and saves He *justifies* and *sanctifies.* We cannot partake of His glory if we partake not of His merit and righteousness, and of His Spirit and grace." *Henry.*

---

9. Simon Peter saith unto him, Lord, not my feet only, but also my hands and my head.

Lord. Peter maintained his reverence through all his faults and weaknesses.—He sincerely loved his Lord, and this preserved his soul from fatal damage.—There was one superior force that ever brought him back in all his wanderings.—Nothing could tempt this disciple to give up his Master.

Not my feet only. Such an impetuous nature would be given to the greatest extremes in conduct.—Wherever there is great force in character, if it be checked in one direction, it is likely to rebound to the other.—The affections of the soul need the control of enlightened reason, else they degenerate into weakness or boisterous passion.

My hands and my head. Instead of refusing to be washed at all he is ready to go beyond his Lord's intent.—Such a spirit as his disdained to hold a middle way ; he refused duty through self-will, and now the same force carries him beyond it.—Peter's mind could not hover under an indifference, but must decide strongly. —His dread of separation from Him he loved brought him to this large desire.—The real wish of his heart was to share a better, greater, and fuller portion with his Lord.—Though this language exceeded the fact, it involved an important truth.— Sanctification must extend to all the powers and principles of man's nature.—The *mind* must submit to the teaching of Christ, be informed and guided by His truth.—The *affections* must be turned to Him and purified from every mean attachment.—The *will* must be guided by His pure and righteous will.—The *conscience* must be purged and made sensitive to pain at the touch of aught that displeases Him.—Christ requires the renewal of the whole man, for He has redeemed our entire nature.—Love gives up all to Christ, who returns that love by imparting the whole wealth of His nature.—In the survey of ourselves we discover our vileness everywhere ; we need cleansing throughout.

---

10. Jesus saith to him, He that is washed needeth not save to wash his feet, but is clean every whit: and ye are clean ,but not all.

He that is washed. The Greek word signifies the washing of the *whole body.*—The soul is cleansed in the one great act of justification.—We are only raised from the death of sin *once.*

Save to wash his feet. The bath, in which the whole body was immersed, was generally taken before the chief meal, at the close of the day.—It was not, therefore, necessary to repeat the process of complete washing.—Partial washing was sufficient, which should cleanse away the defilements afterwards contracted.—In walking about, the feet would be the only part likely to be soiled.

(Cant. v. 3).—It might be even necessary to wash them several times.—There is no need that the soul's great washing, in the act of justification, should be repeated.—It is sufficient that those defilements be removed which the believer contracts by his contact with the world.—Peter stated the doctrine of purity in an extreme form.—He was reminded that the cleansing of his whole nature had taken place before.—That great act need not be repeated, and in the nature of things, was incapable of repetition.—The justified man must still be cleansed from the errors and defilements of his daily life.—From the Cross, where the believer is cleansed, he starts on a journey to his heavenly home.—The road is rough and miry, and he will need to wash away the pollution which clings to him, and which interferes with his comfort, and is abhorrent to his soul.—The relation of the sinner to the Saviour is that of continual dependence.—The grace which started the soul in the new life is still necessary to maintain its energy.—The same fountain which cleansed at first is always open.—Our feet cannot walk with comfort in the ways of duty without this renewed cleansing.—"The evidence of a justified state may be clouded, and the comfort of it suspended, when yet the charter of it is not vacated or taken away.—Though we have occasion to repent daily, God's gifts and callings are without repentance." *Henry.*

Every whit. He is entirely clean when the *feet* have been washed. —His purity is maintained as at the first.—He still stands accepted in the sight of his Saviour.

Ye are clean. They were all cleansed by outward washing.—In the visible church all have access to the same means, all are holy by vocation and in the Divine intention.—The fact is sadly below this ideal.

But not all. They were but a small company, and yet one was a hypocrite.—Judas had not been washed in the sense intended.— Partial cleansing would not have sufficed for *him*, for he needed the complete renewal.—"Christ sees it necessary to let His disciples know that they are not all clean; that we may all be jealous over ourselves ; and that when hypocrites are discovered, it may be no surprise or stumbling to us." *Henry.*

Ο λελουμένος. They were clean in general through baptism. *Origen, Theodor, Mopsu., Augustine, Erasmus, Olshausen, Ewald, Hengst., Godet. Wordsworth.*—Clean by means of the *doctrine. Théod., Herak.*—Clean through the *Word* (chap. xv. 3); the washing of their feet signified that they had still to learn *humility. Chrysostom, Meyer* —The latter interpretation is doubtless the true one.—As disciples, they had received, in the fellowship and the Word of Christ, the principle of their general purification or regeneration; but they must, by the shaming example of their Lord and Master, be cleansed from ambition and other sins which had clung to their feet, their endeavourings, in their pilgrimage as disciples. *Lange.*—ἡ τοὺς πόδας. Omitted. *Origen, Tisch., Cod. Sin.*

---

11. For he knew who should betray him; therefore said he, Ye are not all clean.

He knew. Christ has reasons for all He says and does.—Possessing such knowledge as He did, the reticence of Christ as a Teacher shows that self-control which belongs to all exalted natures.—This knowledge brought sorrow to His soul, which would be still deeper when constrained to point out the betrayer (verse 18).

Betray him. Gr., *who was about to betray Him.*—The meaning is that he was meditating the act.—He had already made the agreement with the chief priests (see on verse 2).—There was hypocrisy in that little circle before it was made manifest, save to that eye which saw the hearts of all.—By keeping back the name of the betrayer till the last, each one was constrained solemnly to question himself.—" Were hypocrites and traitors in never so excellent a society, and never so like saints in outward appearance, yet they are not clean in Christ's account." *Hutcheson.*

Therefore he said. John notes every circumstance that brings out the dark features of the character of Judas.—The apostle of love would keenly feel such baseness.

---

12. So after he had washed their feet, and had taken his garments, and was set down again, he said unto them, Know ye what I have done to you?

After he had washed. Christ carried His purpose through, though Peter interrupted and the treachery of Judas was foreknown.—There was a calm composure and freedom from hurry in all the actions of the Son of Man.—Knowing His purpose and what was the end He awaited the solemn movements of Providence : He would not precipitate events.—The disciples must first be exercised in the duty of submission and then wait for light.—What Christ does to us in the course of His dealings we must humbly receive ; and be content that He knows the reason why, and will make all clear hereafter.—The *fact* is God's first revelation to man ; the *reason which lies behind it* is made known afterwards.—Our faith and obedience are tried when God withholds the reason of His ways.—The Spirit which enlightens man was not poured out until

the great facts of our redemption were completed (Luke xxiv. 46)
—We must feel our difficulty and need before God will grant
relief and satisfy our desire.

Taken his garments. He *assumed* them, after having laid them
aside.

Set down again. He took again the recumbent posture.—The
symbolic action was completed, and He now prepares to give
instruction.

Know ye what I have done? He asks a question to whet the
appetite for instruction.—All candidates for the heavenly knowledge which Christ imparts must be made to feel their ignorance.
—To those who are perplexed with difficulties, and yet who look to
Him, Jesus gives time to settle into the attitude of attention.—It
is the will of Christ that we should look beneath the outward
sign and discover the inner truth.—Christ is not content with an
ignorant and unreasoning devotion ; His gifts of knowledge to us
are only limited by our condition and capacity.—The discourse on
humility, recorded in Luke xxii. 25-27, was uttered together with
these words.

ἀναπεσὼν. καὶ ἀνέπεσεν. *Tisch., Codd. Sin., B.C.*

---

13. Ye call me Master and Lord : and ye say well; for so I am.

Ye call me. *Ye,* emphatic.—*Ye,* at least, are bound to stand by
that profession.

Master and Lord. In their salutations they used sometimes the
one, and sometimes the other.—*Master* indicates their relation to
Him as disciples, or learners ; *Lord* their obligation of perpetual
service.—Faith and duty are the elements of the spiritual life ;
submission of the understanding and conscience to the truth of
Christ, and the practice of His commands.—The Greek has the
article, *The* Master and *The* Lord, thus displacing all others
(Matt. xxiii. 8).—Christ does not demand blind obedience, but
teaches while He commands.—They who obey Christ feel that
they are doing reverence to truth.—To receive the instruction of
Christ is not sufficient; He must be Lord as well as Master.—
" If Christ be our Master and Lord, be so by our own consent,
and we have oft called Him so, we are bound in honour and
honesty to be observant of Him." *Henry.*—The great enlightener
of mankind has also the power to save and defend.

Ye say well. Our Lord and Master will be true to His character. —The *saying* such only requires the seal of obedience to render it the genuine utterance of the heart.

So I am. The facts of our Lord's nature remain ; we have but to realize them.—The self-assertion of Christ was consistent with His humility only on the ground of the reality of the high claims He put forth.

---

14. If I then, your Lord and Master, have washed your feet; ye also ought to wash one another's feet.

Lord and Master. " As you acknowledged me to be, and as indeed I am."—In the case of One whose nature was so exalted, there could be no doubt regarding the humility implied in the action. —The sacred relation which Christ holds to the believer is the strength and inspiration of his duty to others.

Have washed your feet. If the Master stooped so low as to perform this humble act, His disciples may surely do the same : the servant is not above his Lord.—In all His teaching, Christ was the great example which He drew.—He went before us in all things and led the way.—The truth in Him became living : His light was the life of men.

Wash one another's feet. As regarded the disciples, this command might be taken literally.—It was an ordinary custom of Eastern hospitality, being necessary wherever sandals were worn.— This command seems to have been obeyed in the Church of Apostolic times, as a token of those self-humbling services which Christians should render to each other (1 Tim. v. 10).—Afterwards it was observed as a symbolic rite, and connected with the ceremony of baptism.—After the fourth century, the feet of the newly-baptized were washed.—In later times, the Pope and Catholic Monarchs used to wash the feet of twelve poor, old men, on Maunday Thursday.—The literal copying of such an act may become an empty ceremony, from which the meaning has long ago vanished.—When the truth is hidden away and out of sight, to adore but the image of it is superstition.—We have here one of those precepts which, in the literal form, are only obligatory when required by the occasion.—Should the same circumstances again arise, this humble duty would be plain.—But in altered circumstances, to repeat this duty would argue a slavish devotion to the letter, and a mind and will incorrect to the truth.—The essential point to be laid hold of is the truth intended to be set forth and the duty thence arising.—

That *truth* was the necessity of spiritual purity, and that *duty* was the obligation of Christians to promote purity in themselves and others.—The desire to be pure and true would naturally spread itself out into acts of humility.—This feet-washing is a single act put for the whole circle of humble and self-denying duties.— The *spirit* of this lowly action should animate Christians in their services to one another.—In order to maintain our humility it may be necessary for us to keep the sharp and vivid outlines of this incident constantly before our eyes.—No *doctrine* of humility could so affect us as this touching history.—" *Washing the feet* after travel contributeth both to the *decency* of the person and to his *ease*, so that to wash one another's feet is to consult both the *credit* and *comfort* one of another; to do what we can both to advance our brethren's reputation and to make their minds easy (1 Cor. x. 24; Heb. vi. 10). The duty is *mutual;* we must both *accept* help from our brethren, and *afford* help to them." *Henry.*— "The Church doth then live in true peace when every one of her members becometh a servant to another." *Hutcheson.*

---

15. For I have given you an example, that ye should do as I have done to you.

An example. The refusal of this service of humility from his Lord was, on the side of Peter, an " example " of a proud self-will.—On the part of Christ, this action was an " example " of condescending love, which can stoop to the lowest service and yet retain its dignity; which, like the light, can shine everywhere and yet is incapable of being soiled.—It is not the outward form of the action but the tone of mind that is important.—The aimless deeds of men may have some interest as facts, but they teach no great moral truths; they impart no inspiration of life.—In the life of Christ, every action has some great moral end, and has virtue to stir up to imitation.—Humility is, of all lessons in Christian graces, the hardest to learn —Our Lord had exhorted to this grace by frequent precept; now He gives to this teaching the force and vividness of a special example.—This incident marked itself deeply on the minds of the disciples, and the same effect is repeated in the successive generations of Christians.—Such an incident must hold a permanent place in our memory and always retain the freshness and grace of life.—When we consider our imperfect condition here and the difficulties of virtue, we must be thankful that the Book, whose object is to teach us how to live, should for the most part itself consist of life.—" Christ teacheth by example as well as doctrine, and for that end came into this world and dwelt among us, that He might set us a copy of all those graces and duties which His holy religion teacheth, and it is a copy without one false stroke." *Henry.*

Should do as I have done. The actions of Christ are rather to be imitated in their spirit than in their outward form.—They were a mode of instruction portable for the memory, easy for the mind, and grateful to the heart.—When the Spirit was given the disciples would learn a great truth from this action of their Lord. —They would learn that it was their duty to point men to that fountain in Christ which cleanses from all impurity.—They would see that the dignity of their office would not be impaired by the most lowly service ; yea, that it would be enhanced by such service. —They would learn that charity which could make large allowances and "become all things to all men."

---

16. Verily, verily, I say unto you. The servant is not greater than his lord ; neither he that is sent greater than he that sent him.

Verily, verily. This solemn introduction has its principal bearing upon ver. 17.—The Great Teacher laid the chief stress upon right practice ; doctrines and principles were to find issue in life.

The servant. Gr., *the bond-servant*, one who is bound to another under a permanent obligation of servitude.

Not greater than his Lord. This was a proverbial saying, and was employed by our Lord with different applications (chap. xv. 20 ; Matt. x. 24 ; Luke vi. 40).—"Nor ought he to refuse to do the same things, and submit to the same things." *Bengel.*—The servants of Christ should be satisfied if they have no better treatment or portion than He had.—To be the servant of such a Master is a portion sufficiently rich and honourable for an immortal spirit.—"If the servant be not made less than his Lord, it is no reason that he should look to be greater." *Hutcheson.*— "When we see our Master serving, we cannot but see how ill it becomes us to be *domineering.*" *Henry.*—He who considers how low his Lord stooped will feel that pride was not made for man.

He that is sent. The same word employed from which the designation 'Apostle' is derived.—The word afterwards acquired a peculiar sense as applied to certain appointed messengers of Christ.—Every true believer is called by his Lord and appointed to the work of his mission.

Greater. Gospel ministers especially should keep this in mind.-- They should not require men to believe more than Christ required.

or force upon them those refinements of human systems which do but ill agree with the simplicity and living force of His teaching.— They should not lay greater burdens upon the human conscience than Christ imposed, thus multiplying the snares of the soul.— The want of this humility has been the chief bane of the Church. —Whenever the Church has forgotten what was the real source of greatness in Christ, and that it owed nothing to outward grandeur, she has become corrupted.

---

17. If ye know these things, happy are ye if ye do them.

If ye know. The actions of life which determine our moral character begin in thought.—That the actions may be right, it is necessary that the mind be in possession of the truth.—In the Sermon on the Mount, Christ laid down the principle that thought and action are in essence the same.—Eternal life, with all its possibilities and acts, is involved in the knowledge of Christ.—It is God's method to work from mind outwardly to actions.—The religion of Christ is no friend to ignorance, for every duty of it is founded upon a clear knowledge of His will.—The conduct of the disciples at this time was partly the result of their ignorance. —They had still carnal conceptions of the Messiah's kingdom.— Clear light is both the guide, the impulse, and the joy of duty.

These things. What He had done to them and the lessons thence arising.—The same principle extends to all the words and actions of Christ.

Happy. He speaks not in tones of threatening, as Moses, but is content with declaring the blessedness of duty.—Christ set forth a law of duty, but it was the law of love.—This was a law which, while it commanded, was itself the source of that strength by which it was obeyed.—When our whole nature is in sympathy with the external command we are happy in obedience.—Christ as the minister of the better covenant set a beatitude in front of every duty.

If ye do them. Speculation was not sufficient; there must be practice.—There is a knowledge of the truths of Christ which is consistent with a practical disregard of them; yet they can only truly be known by obedience.—Spiritual life will of necessity find an outward form of expression.—The disciples had known the truth and admired it.—They felt the force and beauty of the words and actions of Christ.—Still they lacked much of the strength and fulness of duty.—Christ had often spoken to them of humility, and He has just inculcated it by a significant action. —They were so slack in obedience that they needed repeated lessons.—Christ now had Judas in His mind, who sinned against the knowledge of the truth.—He thought of Peter, too, who made a distinct promise to be faithful and yet failed when the 'rial came. —He knew that all His disciples would shortly flee and leave Him alone.—He knew that *we* require this precept now, who know so much and perform so little.

---

18. I speak not of you all : I know whom I have chosen : but that the scripture may be fulfilled, He that eateth bread with me hath lifted up his heel against me.

Not of you all. Not of all the disciples as *happy* in the feeling of duty done : Judas was excepted.—Christ is satisfied with merely hinting at his treachery ; He will not point him out till almost the last moment.—Judas was now drawing near to the outer range of that whirlpool in whose fierce vortex he was soon to be swallowed up.—Christ would assure His disciples that He had not been deceived as to the real character of Judas.—Had they thought so, it might have proved a stumbling-block to them.—Therefore, He assures them that all is foreknown.—" Christ is loath to grieve or displease His meek followers by bringing forth what may displease or stumble them ; therefore doth He at first prepare their minds for these sad news with such general intimations and cautions." *Hutcheson.*—The most comfortable things can only be spoken with just reserves even to the choicest few.

I know. The pronoun is emphatic : "*I* know, though others do not."—Christ frequently reminded His disciples that there were supreme qualities of His nature, and ways of action, in which He could not be imitated.—The future and the hearts of all men to Him alone were known.

Whom I have chosen. See on chap vi. 64, 70.—It would seem that He referred to one of the apostles as not belonging to the chosen, but this is contrary to the statement, " Have I not chosen you twelve, and one of you is a devil "? (chap. vi. 70).—The inference that chosen to salvation is hereby signified is plausible.— Yet if this were so, why should the following statement be introduced with the word " *but* "?—Christ had truly chosen them all, but He was not ignorant of their true characters.

The scripture. The particular scripture is Psalm xli. 9, the quotation being slightly altered from the Hebrew.—That Psalm has its primary reference to David and his betrayer, Ahithophel.—Christ refers back to what is written to quiet the minds of His disciples, and to show them that the principles of human conduct fulfil themselves in many ways throughout the course of history.— Christ in taking humanity accepted all its sad experiences, and now that is about to happen to Him which had happened before to many a faithful friend.

May be fulfilled.   David was the type of Christ; his fortunes pre-figured those of his greater son.—The Son of Man gathers up in Himself all the scattered experiences of humanity throughout the ages.—Christ now shows His disciples that Providence cannot be surprised; that all concerning Himself was foreknown; that the history of others contained the rude sketch and outlines of His own.—There is no reason why prophecy should not take the form of a *fact* which looks to a future and a farther fulfilment.—" Let it not therefore be a stumbling-block to any; for though it do not at all lessen the offence of Judas, it may lessen our offence at it." *Henry.*

Eateth bread.   Judas was admitted into the closest familiarity with his Master; sat down at the same table, partook of the same fare.— He ate with Him when the meal was miraculous; when the loaves were multiplied.—He ate the Passover with Him.—Those eat with Christ who are admitted to share the outward privileges of the Gospel.

Lifted up his heel.   The image employed is that of an animal suddenly and treacherously kicking its owner.—A similar image is used in Gen. xlix. 17.—He who accepted friendship and observed the outward forms of it discovers himself to be false and an enemy.—In human friendship, such conduct is condemned as base ingratitude; in such friendship as Judas was admitted to, it was rebellion against Heaven.—The Church all the way through has suffered from false friends as well as open enemies.—To cherish enmity and dark purposes of betrayal while receiving open favours shows the utmost baseness of heart.—What more can be done for the sinner when the last and most gracious efforts of love have been tried upon him!—It is sad to go from the table of Christ to perdition!—" (1.) He *forsook* Him, turned his back upon Him, *went* out from the society of His disciples (ver. 30). (2.) He *despised Him*, shook off the dust of his feet against Him, in contempt of Him and His Gospel.   Nay (3.), He became an enemy to Him, spurred at Him, as wrestlers do at their adversaries whom they would overthrow." *Henry.*

ἐγὼ οἶδα οὓς ἐξελεξάμην.   "I have made the selection in the service of that divine destiny conformab y to which the Scripture had to be fulfilled." *Meyer.*—" It might be

supposed that this treachery has come upon Me unawares ; but it is not so : I know
who n I have selected ; but this has been done by the determinate counsel and foreknowledge of God, declared in the Scriptures." *Alford.*—"I know whom I have *really*
chosen. Thus in 1 John ii. 19, the signification is: ' Those who have fallen away from
us were, not *really* of us.'" *Tholuck.*—A distinction must be made, in this place, as in
chap. vi, 70, between the *eternal election of God* and the *historical election of Christ.*
Lange.—ἐπῆρεν, ἐπῆρκεν. *Cod. Sin.*

**19. Now I tell you before it come, that, when it is come to pass, ye may believe that
I am he.**

Now. The most emphatic particle is used, meaning ' at this particular point of time.'—From this moment they are to look out
for the accomplishment of the prophecy.—This is a summons to
the disciples to keep their attention awake, so that they might
learn that the purposes of God were being accomplished.

Before it come. His warnings were also prophecy ; the great
future was clear and manifest to Him.—The treachery of Judas
might prove a stumbling-block were it not announced beforehand.

When it is come to pass. When the prophecy concerning this
treachery shall be fulfilled.—They were not to stumble at the
event, but consider how it fitted in with the purposes of God.—
The great events in the life of our Lord are not to be taken as
isolated facts, but rather in their connection with the scheme of
redemption.

Ye may believe. See on chap. i. 7 ; vii. 38.—Prophecy is not intended simply to fill us with wonder, but to produce belief.—The
faith of the disciples would need confirmation at such a time, and
the fulfilment of this prophecy would contribute to that end.—
Even in the deep crime of Judas they could see the claims of
Jesus to the Messiahship strengthened.—Belief can exist in several
degrees ; it needs increasing and strengthening.—All that happened afterwards would force upon the disciples the remembrance
of the words of their Lord.—Full and sufficient proof would be
given of His claims as a prophet, and strong foundations laid for
higher claims.—The practical end of all God's revelation is that
we might believe.—Belief is the last refuge of the soul ; the time
must come when we can do nothing else but calmly rest upon
those eternal verities that cannot be shaken.

I am he. Gr., *I am.*—See on chap. viii. 58.—He was truly what
the prophets foretold, what His disciples expected, and what He
professed Himself to be.—To receive the claims of Christ and to
act accordingly is all that is necessary for man to know and do ;
the soul rests here because it hath the Son, and therefore hath

life.—"Christ rightly taken up will be believed to be matchless, singular, and inexpressible in His fulness and excellency: for this He aims at that 'ye may believe that I am'; to wit, that singular and inexpressible One." *Hutcheson.*

---

20. Verily, verily, I say unto you, He that receiveth whomsoever I send receiveth me; and he that receiveth me receiveth him that sent me.

Verily, verily. See on chap. i. 51.—This is our Lord's usual summons to attention when about to introduce important statements. —Owing to the weakness of our flesh we need the aid of these awakening, assuring words, that the spirit may give heed to truth and duty.—Such words excite the mind to give thoughtful, earnest audience to the truth.

Receiveth. Accepts His message and acts accordingly.—It is not enough to admire the messengers of God and commend their zeal; the truth they deliver must be appropriated and made a living power in us.

Whomsoever I send. The servants of Christ may not have outward splendour or rank, but they have sufficient dignity in tha they are commissioned by Him.—When a teacher is sent by Christ that fact should overcome every prejudice against his person.—Judas may desert Christ, but He will send others.—When the disciples of Christ feel most discouraged, they may be comforted by the thought that they are clothed with His authority.— If a preacher feels he has a Divine mission, this is the strongest consolation for himself and the best answer to those who may be tempted to despise him.

Receiveth me. He had given them a lesson in humility and now encourages them by the thought that they possess true dignity.— If the disciples of Christ share in His abasement they shall also share in His glory.—His servants can always refer to their Master as the fount of their authority, as the complement to what in them is imperfect.—"Such as would approve themselves to be Christ's scholars ought not to hearken unto nor receive those who run without a calling, but only those whom He sends; nor ought they to receive them who are sent upon any carnal respect." *Hutcheson.* —Due regard should be paid to the ministers of Christ, however humble their gifts may be, for the sake of Him who sends them.— Ministers can only have strong consolation and encouragement when they can refer all to Christ: motive, aim, authority, inspiration.

Him that sent me. Thus the servants of Christ refer to Him, and He refers to the Father.—They become linked to the Highest by means of a Mediator.—We ultimately ascend to God as the source and fountain of all.—Our union with God is accomplished through His servants and His Son, His servants making known to us His Son's office and power.

'Ο λαμβάνων, &c. A gloss derived from Matt. x. 40. *Kuinoel, Lücke.*—Should be annexed to verse 16. *Lampe, Hengst.*—The original fitness ef the saying in this place is confirmed by the preceding " Verily, verily." *Lange.*—A contrast between the future glory of His faithful ones and the traitor ; between those whom He has historically chosen and those, from among these, whom He will send in the might of the Spirit (between disciples and apostles). *Melanchthon, and others.*—The contrast between treason and apostolic worth. *Hilgenfeld.*—Christ means to say : The wickedness of some few, who are guilty of unworthy conduct in the apostolic office, does not impair the dignity of that office. *Calvin.*—He designs to dissuade the others from imitating the apostasy of Judas. *Zwingle.*—Connected with ἵνα πιστεύσετε, verse 19, *i.e.,* to confirm you in this faith, I say to you, &c. *Meyer.*—The words set forth the dignity of that office from which Judas was about to fall ; and the consideration of this dignity, as contrasted with the sad announcement just to be made, leads on to the ἐταράχθη τῷ πνεύματι of the next verse. *Alford.*

---

21. When Jesus had thus said, he was troubled in spirit, and testified, and said, Verily, verily, I say unto you, that one of you shall betray me.

Thus said. He was preparing them for the more particular announcement of the treachery of Judas.

Troubled in spirit. See on chap. xi. 33.—He was deeply agitated by the thought that He was about to become a victim to the base treachery of one of His own disciples.—To feel the dark shadow of such a soul was an exquisite distress to His sensitive spirit.— The manifestation of this feeling is in keeping with the character of Christ.—How deeply the Son of Man entered into the experience of our earthly sorrow when He suffered at the hands of a false friend !—The sins of disciples are always a great trouble to Christ ; they grieve His spirit.

Testified. He manifested the trouble of His soul by some outward signs or gesture.—This was the signal for His solemn words; He did not speak without strong necessity pressing from within.

One of you. Strong emphasis is placed upon the "*one of you.*"— You, My disciples whom I have called and sent, who have testified your allegiance to Me, and who have bound yourselves to maintain My cause at all risks !—As the time drew near He marks more minutely the circumstances of His betrayal.—From the vague suggestions of prophecy He proceeds to draw out the circle which it fills, and at length narrows this to the individual.—Such a definite announcement as this would serve to put each disciple on his guard.

Betray me. Therefore He bestowed confidence in them all, and admitted them to familiar intercourse.—To say the least, the betrayal was a sin against a most sacred and confiding friendship.— "This did not determine Judas to the sin by any *fatal* necessity; for, though the event did follow *according to* the prediction, yet not *from* the prediction." *Henry.*—The power of evil in Judas must have been great since he did not retreat from his design at such a warning.—The power of evil, when we encourage it to work, may take such possession of our souls as almost to have the force of fate.—The bonds of sin, at first slender, and easily snapped by conscience, may at length be changed to iron fetters.

---

22. Then the disciples looked one on another, doubting of whom he spake.

Looked one on another. John omits the enquiry they made, "Lord is it I"? and fastens upon the most graphic features of the incident.—It was for most the look of astonishment that any one of them should be capable of such a crime.—They may have tried to discover what face showed signs of conscious guilt.— There are times when the purest are put to these sore trials.— Judas had grown so hardened as to show no signs of guilt before the searching glances of others.

Doubting. The hypocrite had not yet been made manifest; he could bear up against all those dark suggestions of his sin.—The time of such doubt is the time for anxious search and self-examination.—"Judas in this business put on such a countenance as when they looked about they still doubted of whom He spake, and Peter and John are put to another shift to find them out." *Hutcheson.*—A good conscience is a safe refuge from such doubt.— In great moral perplexities we are cast upon ourselves and God.

---

23. Now there was leaning on Jesus' bosom one of his disciples, whom Jesus loved.

Leaning. Reclining at the table, so that his head would rest on the bosom of Jesus.—This was the place of honour.—The local nearness of this disciple to his Lord was a fitting symbol of his love.—

"They who lay themselves at *Christ's feet*, He will lay them in His bosom." *Henry.*

Whom Jesus loved. See chap. xix. 26; xxi. 7, 20.—Here, for the first time, this Evangelist thus designates himself.—He conceals his name, thinking it more honour to be loved by Jesus than to be marked out for fame.—He speaks not of his own love to Jesus, though that was strong : for him the consciousness that he was loved by his Lord was sufficient.—This disciple has told us more of the love of Jesus than any other.—He was fittest to interpret the overwhelming grace of his Lord.—He rises to higher strains than any in describing the Divine nature of Jesus, and at the same time reveals to us His tender human love.—"Such as are beloved of Christ will delight much in intimate familiarity with Him, and will be admitted thereto ; for it is John's choice and Christ's allowance that he leaned on Jesus' bosom." *Hutcheson.*

ἐν τῷ κόλπῳ τοῦ Ἰησοῦ. The bellying of the garment over the girdle (Luke vi. 38), the bosom, the lap ; ethically defined, the breast.—They reclined on divans or couches in a half-sitting posture, facing the low table, the left elbow resting upon the pillow, the feet outward (behind), and the right hand free, so that the person who sat to the right of another seemed to lean upon his breast. *Lange.*—ὃν ἠγάπα ὁ Ἰησοῦς. In a special sense : hence designative of friendship.—Here, for the first time, we meet with this nameless and yet so expressive self-designation, induced by the hallowed moment, never to be forgotten by him. *Meyer.*—A periphrase of the name: "Jehovah is merciful." *Bengel, Hengst., Godet.*—For this reason Jesus gave to John no new name, as He did to Peter. *Godet.*

---

24. Simon Peter therefore beckoned to him, that he should ask who it should be of whom he spake.

Simon Peter. See on chap. i. 40, 42, and on Luke vi. 14.—Always the first to speak ; the boldest in enterprise.—There was a close intimacy between this disciple and John.—When Mary Magdalene had found the tomb empty, she " cometh to *Simon Peter*, and to *the other disciple whom Jesus loved* " (chap. xx. 2).—They are associated together when Jesus appears to His disciples at the Sea of Tiberias ; John saith to John, " It is the Lord."—After the dinner which followed, Peter enquires concerning John, " Lord, and what shall this man do "? (chap. xxi. 7, 21).

Beckoned to him. He intimated by means of signs, using no words.—It would not have been convenient to the occasion to direct such an enquiry in audible language.—John only mentions himself that he might introduce the circumstances of Peter's question.—Peter was in a convenient position for making this significant sign to John. —He was reclining at the back of Jesus, while John was below Him.

That he should ask. John was conveniently situated for this purpose ; he could easily come sufficiently close to receive the faintest whisper.—Peter, bold enough at other times, will not speak out now ; he humbly seeks the aid of a more favoured disciple.—The man of activity gives place to the man of contemplation.—" Such as are most beloved of Christ will get most of His mind." *Hutcheson.*

Who it should be. Who among the disciples should be guilty of the base treachery which was hinted.—Peter's conscience did not accuse him of so foul an intent, yet he must needs obtain the approbation of his Lord.—Peter may have desired to know who the betrayer was, not only to clear his own conscience, but possibly to come to the aid of his Lord.—It would have been safe for Peter to have remained silent, content with the approbation of his own conscience.—Such an aspect of soul we must maintain now, for there is no infallible authority to point out to us who shall prove hypocrites and traitors.

Codd. Sin., *B.C.I.L X. Vulgate* and *Origen* read καὶ λέγει αὐτῷ. εἰπέ τίς ἐστιν, περὶ οὗ λέγει. —Adopted by *Treg.*, *Tisch.*, *Alf.*, *Westcott and Hort.*

---

25. He then lying on Jesus' breast saith unto him Lord, who is it?

Lying on Jesus' breast. Gr., *throwing himself back.*—He who was wont to recline on his Master's bosom now brings his head still nearer.—This was an unusual instance of familiarity, even for John. —Love admits of great boldness.—The loving heart always has the ear of Christ.

Lord. Though he made so bold, he still preserved the forms of reverence.—Our privilege of secret communion with Christ should not diminish our proper awe.

Who is it ? Christ alone could answer such a question.—Hypocrisy may be so hidden and disguised as not to be detected by the most saintly souls.—It is the office of Christ still to discover who are false ; the day will come when He will say to some, " I never knew you."

---

25. Omitted. *Cod. Sin.*, *Treg.*, *Tisch.*, *Alford.*

26. Jesus answered, He it is, to whom I shall give a sop, when I have dipped it. And when he had dipped the sop, he gave it to Judas Iscariot, the son of Simon.

Jesus answered. Gr., *answers*, the present tense being appropriate to vivid narration.—The answer was spoken into the ear of John, the rest of the disciples being entirely ignorant of it (verse 28).—"They are not mistaken who expect that much of Christ's mind will be revealed to such as are beloved of Him, and that in their familiar and reverent addresses they will be made welcome." *Hutcheson.*

He to whom I shall give a sop. Gr., *the morsel.*—It is probable that with the word Jesus took the "sop" into His hand.—Giving the morsel thus to Judas may have seemed to the rest as a favour conferred upon him.—Men may appear to enjoy the outward favours which Christ bestows in His church, and yet be far from Him.—Christ did not name the traitor to John but indicated him by a *sign.*—"The false brethren we are to stand on our guard against are not made known unto us by *words*, but by *signs;* they are made known to us by *their fruits*, by *their spirits*." *Henry.*—Judas, by taking this morsel from the hands of his Master, fulfilled the prophecy that the traitor should be one who had eaten bread with Him.—In the kindness of Jesus towards a known enemy we have an example of the tolerant spirit by which He was actuated.

Dipped. Soaked the morsel in the sauce.

Gave it to Judas. Gr., *gives.*—Such an act of tenderness might have won Judas back to repentance, yet he hardened himself.—How terrible is the case of those on whom the last efforts of love have been tried in vain!—How many opportunities had Judas to return to faith and goodness; but the power of evil was gaining upon him, the dark stain of covetousness was deepening and spreading over his soul!

ψωμίον. The original root of the word means "to rub."—Hence it is "anything rubbed or broken off."—It was often used for a mouthful, just like "morsel," which means literally *a little bite.*—As used here the word means any portion of food. *Ellicott.* —That Judas was not present at the Lord's Supper is now generally admitted by the best commentators.—In favour of this: (*a*) The destination of the love-feast, to purify the circle of disciples ; (*b*) the great contrast made by John between the celebration prior to the departure of Judas and after it ; (*c*) the account of Matthew and Mark. *Lange.*—The presence of the traitor would have most seriously disturbed that holy feast of love, and would cut off the right of discipline and excommunication so necessary for the purity and dignity of Christ's Church *Schaff.*

27. **And after the sop Satan entered into him.** Then said Jesus unto him, That thou doest, do quickly.

After the sop. After the morsel was given.—The Greek has a word denoting the point of time, *then.*—Before this fatal moment Judas may have wavered in his evil design, now it is fixed in his soul.—The first suggestions of evil often require time to ripen into sin (James i. 15).

Satan entered. At first the evil course was put into his heart by way of suggestion; now it overcomes and possesses his entire nature.—Satan first casts the evil thought into the soul to make way for his own indwelling.—The operations and effects of goodness are imitated in the powers of evil.—As the Spirit of God may enter into a man and possess him, so in like manner may Satan.—Judas on a former occasion was called a "devil" (see on chap. vi. 70).—He had been the son of perdition, but now Satan gains a more full possession of him.—There are sins that stand out like mountains on the scene of the world's guilt, and seem to imply that those who commit them are given over to the powers of evil. —Now that Satan has taken entire possession of him, Jesus can no longer endure his presence.—" Many are made worse by the gifts of Christ's bounty, and are confirmed in their impenitency by that which should have led them to repentance. The coals of fire heaped upon their head, instead of melting them, harden them." *Henry.*

Into him. Gr., " *into that (man).*"—" John already marks Judas by a pronoun that removes him to a distance." *Bengel.*

That thou doest. That terrible crime which he was about to commit.—" Judas might have perceived from this ray of the Lord's omniscience that he is known." *Bengel.*

Do quickly. Gr., " *get done more quickly.*"—This must not be understood as either commanding or approving sin, an act abhorrent to the nature of Christ.—Judas, now given over to the powers of evil, is simply permitted to ruin himself.—He had hardened himself against all access by love and goodness and must now take the consequences.—There is an accelerating force in evil which God permits to exert itself.—Christ, who knew the future, could speak thus without any imputation on His goodness.—He knew that the power of evil in Judas had attained to such a height that it must soon exert itself in outward acts.—Men who have attained to the utmost wickedness of heart are restless to execute mischief. —Therefore in these words, which seem so like a command, Jesus simply announced a *fact.*—It is possible that Jesus may have uttered the words as implying His readiness to suffer the worst at the hands of His enemies.—Judas might do his utmost now; it would but precipitate the event to which the Son of Man had been looking forward.—" Christ's willingness to suffer for His people made all attempts against Him to be nothing terrible ; He was willing to suffer, and therefore cared not how soon he would put Him to it." *Hutcheson.*

τότε. Marking with graphic power and pathos the horrible moment of Satan's entering into the heart of the traitor and taking full possession of him. When Satan entered *into* Judas, εἰσῆλθεν, Judas went *out*, ἐξῆλθεν, from the company of Christ into the darkness of crime and despair (see on verse 30). *Schaff* —Became an organ of Satan in consequence of perceiving that he was known and with the bestowal of the sop branded. *Tholuck.*—"Ο ποιεῖς. The command in all these judgments is never: Do quickly what thou art not yet intending to do, but invariably: *What thou wilt do,* what thou hast already begun to do, do *more speedily. Lange* —ποίησον. The imperative is permissive. *Grotius and others* —τάχιον. The comparative expresses the idea: *Hasten your deed. Meyer* —Jesus desired to be freed from the irksome proximity of the traitor. *Ambrose, Lücke.*—Jesus invoked the decision for his own sake also. *Lange.*—These words are not to be evaded as being *permissive,* or *dismissive (Chrys.)* —They are like the sayings of God to Balaam (Num. xxii 20), and of our Lord to the Pharisees (Matt. xxii. 32) —*The course of sinful action is presupposed.* and the command to go on is but the echo of that mysterious appointment by which the sinner, in the exercise of his own corrupted will, becomes the instrument of the purposes of God.—Thus it is, '*that which thou art doing,* hast just now fully determined to put in present action, *do more quickly* than thou seemest willing,' or perhaps better, 'than thou wouldest otherwise have done.' *Alford.*

28. Now no man at the table knew for what intent he spake this unto him.

No man. Gr., "*no one.*"—Jesus, John, and obviously Judas himself excepted.

Knew. There were two at that table who *must* know ; Jesus, for He knew all things ; Judas, for he knew his own terrible purpose.—There was one to whom the dreadful secret was communicated as the privilege of friendship.

For what intent. They did not know that Judas was a traitor, and therefore could not be aware of the exact application of the words.—They were slow to suspect evil ; a favourable quality of character and disposition.—It may be necessary for us that we should be ignorant of the meaning of many things which are spoken concerning the future acts of men ; in this way we are hindered from striving to prevent the high purposes of God.

29. For some of them thought, because Judas had the bag, that Jesus had said unto him, Buy those things that we have need of against the feast; or, that he should give something to the poor.

Because Judas had the bag. He was the treasurer of the household.—The disciples, therefore, thought that these words had some connexion with his office.—A knowledge of the internal state of Judas would have reversed their decision.—It is the soul which receives that puts meaning into words, whether for good or for evil.

Buy. The property of this little company was small, scarcely deserving the name; yet the use which was made of it teaches us a great principle.

Against the feast. For the purposes of the feast.—Some portion even of this little property must be spent in works of piety.— That discipline is a benefit by which the ordinances of religion are made so to press upon us as to draw out the spirit of sacrifice.— "That is to be reckoned well bestowed, which is laid out upon *those things we have need of* for the maintenance of God's ordinances among us." *Henry.*—It is highly probable that Jesus was celebrating the Passover at this time.—The command, "do quickly," would appear most natural on this supposition.—The necessary things must be purchased, or the feast would soon be over.—The Jews were permitted to prepare whatever was needful for the feast, though it was a Sabbatic season (Ex. xii. 16).—It was lawful to make purchases during the Passover (Mark xv. 46, xvi. 1).

Give something to the poor. Part of the offerings at the feast would consist of alms to the poor.—On the supposition that this was the Passover night, if any alms were to be given they must be given at once.—"The time of a religious feast was thought a proper time for works of charity. When we experience God's bounty to us, that should make us bountiful to the poor." *Henry.*

---

30. He then having received the sop went immediately out: and it was night.

He then. The pronoun emphatic: *that man.* Judas is now distinctly marked.

Went immediately out. He might possibly have dreaded the anger of the rest should his evil intent be discovered to them — He was no longer fit for such company, and to remain would but have increased his discomfort.—The character of Judas had all along shown tendencies towards this complete cutting himself off from the society of the pure and good.—Now the last checks are removed and Judas is ready to execute his evil design.—He could no longer feel himself one with that little company, or look his Master in the face.—He had gone forth like one who has crossed a river and destroyed the bridge behind him.—The wicked shall be separated from the righteous by the inevitable tendency of

things, and not by an arbitrary decree.—That separation from
man brought about by great sins points to a yet more terrible
separation from God.

It was night. An image of the gloom of his own dark and disturbed spirit.—A suitable time for the deeds of darkness.—" It
gave him the advantage of privacy and concealment. He was
not willing to be seen treating with the chief priests, and therefore chose the dark night as the fittest time." *Henry.*

ἦν δὲ νύξ. The δὲ, *but*, is indicative of an antithesis.—It was, indeed, rather late to
buy provisions for the feast or to give alms to the poor: night had stolen unobserved
upon the deeply-agitated circle; but still another truth is intimated, viz., that Judas
went out into a spiritual night to accomplish the work of darkness. *Origen, Olshausen,
Stier, &c.*—There is certainly something awful in this termination, and its brevity
makes it all the more impressive. *Meyer.*—The event had so deeply engraven itself on
the mind of John that be remembered the hour.—Similar indications of his retentive
memory see in chap. i. 40; vi. 59; viii. 20; x. 23.—The "night" does not imply that
Judas was present at the Lord's Supper (*Wordsworth*); the contrary may be inferred
from ἀγόρασον, verse 29.—The institution of the Eucharist took place *after* verse 30.
Meyer, Lange, Schaff. &c.

---

31. Therefore, when he was gone out, Jesus said, Now is the Son of man glorified,
and God is glorified in him.

When he was gone out. Judas had now left that community in
which he was no longer fit to dwell.—Morally, he was separated
from his fellows long before; now by his withdrawal, that isolation is complete.—The apostasy which begins in the heart reaches
at length to the very extremities of life, involving local as well as
moral separation.—God's moral government is ever tending to this
result, that " sinners shall not stand in the congregation of the
righteous " (Psalm i. 5).

Jesus said. This marks the commencement of a discourse which
lasts to the end of chap. xiv.—We come now to the Holy of Holies
of the evangelical history.—It was given to John to exhibit the
Divine grace of his Lord, to reveal the deeper glories of His nature;
the other Evangelists describe Him chiefly in the mournful
majesty of His humiliation.—The discourse commences in the form
of familiar conversation, then attains a higher strain, and at last
reaches ineffable heavenly sublimity and glory.

Now. This marks a period in the history of the Redeemer's sufferings.—Judas having gone, a disquieting element was removed
from that little society; the Son of Man felt relief and opened

His mind more freely.—Knowing also the purpose which the traitor went to execute He now felt that His *hour* was come (chap. xvii. 1).—That all-important *hour* concerning which He once said that He was straitened till it be accomplished (Luke xii. 50).— "Albeit hypocrites cannot pollute an ordinance of God to any but themselves, yet they are ofttimes such a burden and impediment to the society of God's people that the company will fare the better when they are out of it." *Hutcheson.*

The Son of Man.   See on chap. i. 51; v. 27.

Glorified.   For Him the triumph of the future filled the present hour.—It was as the *Son of Man* that He was glorified.—He came appointed to do a certain work and that work was now on the eve of completion.—The victory He was about to achieve on the Cross would bring Him endless glory as the crown of His redeeming work.—"Jesus regards His passion as a short journey, and looks forward to the goal." *Bengel.*—The Cross reveals the depth and power of His love to man and the completeness of His obedience to the Father.—He shrank from the Cross, for it was the instrument of suffering and degradation; but He embraced it in that it was to become the throne of an everlasting kingdom, the source of eternal honour and praise.—Both these emotions appear from time to time in the life of the Son of Man.

God is glorified in him.   The Son is the *true* glory, the full reflection of the Father.—The success of the Son's work in the world brings glory to the Father for it was the accomplishment of *His* purpose (chap. iii. 16).—Christ glorified the Father by personally revealing Him, by perfect obedience to His will, and by working out His gracious purposes towards man in a manner which eternally vindicates the majesty and excellence of His law.—The nature and character of God are in Christ, and in Christ alone, made manifest to men.—The glory of God had been revealed by His works, and by good men, but in Christ the eternal Heart of God is brought into full view before the adoring universe (1 Peter i. 12).—When the dark cloud passes from the Cross the awful Power which gave nature so mysterious a constitution and permitted sin and death to fall on man, is seen to present the personality and wear the face of an *all-wise, holy,* and *loving* FATHER,

---

ἐδοξάσθη.   A proleptical announcement on the approaching triumph. *Alford, Meyer.* —It is the celebration of an *actual* triumph. —*In spirit* He has already vanquished the king'om of darkness. *Lange.*

32. If God be glorified in him, God shall also glorify him in himself, and shall straightway glorify him.

If God be glorified. It was in His purely human nature that He, as the Son of Man, overcame Judas; but, as this Son of Man, He was also the instrument of God (chap. v. 19; 2 Cor. v. 19).—"It is effectual to the glory of God Himself that evil is overcome in so purely a human manner now, and that it shall henceforth be thus overcome throughout the world." *Lange*.

Glorify him in himself. Not by means of the Son, but in Him *personally*.—Glory shall fill and surround the sacred person of Christ who returns to Heaven (1 Tim. iii. 16).—The glory of Jesus was hidden while He was on earth; in Heaven it shone out again, and there He is hid in God.—When Christ glorifies Himself in us, our life too is hid with Him in God (Col. iii. 3, 4).

In himself. Note the distinction between God being "glorified in Him" and God "glorifying Him in Himself."—Whatever this glorifying may mean it is something which takes place *within* the Divine nature itself, and it is as Son of Man Jesus is thus glorified.

Straightway, Gr., *immediately*. This glory was at hand.—The glory which Christ had with the Father before the world was would shortly shine out undimmed.—"Christ and His followers' true glory may be so little delayed by clouds and sufferings, that it may be very near when they are engaging in the throng of afflictions." *Hutcheson*.

The words εἰ ὁ θεὸς ἐδοξάσθη ἐν αὐτῷ are wanting in some ancient MSS.—Omitted. *Westcott and Hort.*—Bracketed. *Alford.*—Retained. *Tischendorf, Lange, Schaff.*—ἐν ἑαυτῷ. He shall glorify the almighty spiritual power of the Son in His (the Father's) divine Prov dence, in His peculiar domain, the sphere, the revelation of the Father, and that especially in that world and from that world whither Christ is now returning. *Lange.*—By the return to the fellowship of God out of which He went forth. *Meyer.*—The thought is that the humiliation by which God is manifested to the world is the glory of God in the person of the Son of Man, and that this shall be followed by the glory of the Son of Man in the person of God, not simply and generally by His return to the glory of the pre-incarnate state, but by His return to it as the Son of Man. *Ellicott.*—εὐθὺς. This accounts for the present tense of the last verse.—The whole is present to His mind as occurring forthwith. *Ellicott.*

---

33. Little children, yet a little while I am with you. Ye shall seek me: and as I said unto the Jews, Whither I go, ye cannot come; so now I say to you.

Little children. This is the first time the Lord calls them such.—It is the only place where the term occurs in the gospels.—Such a title of endearment is a fitting preface to His words of consolation respecting the loneliness they would soon have to endure.—

"Affectingly express^s not only His brotherly, but fatherly love (Isa. ix. 6) for His own, and at the same time their immature and weak state, now about to be left without Him." *Alford.*—The same term of endearment is used once by Paul (Gal. iv. 19), and seven times by John, the disciple of love, in his Epistle.

A little while. They are thus gradually prepared for His final departure.

I am with you. "He designs teaching them not to set their hearts upon following Him to death now." *Lange.*

Ye shall seek me. Shall feel the want of My presence and shall look for Me.—Shortly they would realize a crushing sense of their desolation.—"To *seek* Jesus is to seek the Word, wisdom, righteousness, truth, all which is Christ." *Origen.*

Said unto the Jews. See on chap. viii. 21.—He did not apply to His disciples the whole of the expression he addressed to the Jews, nor in the same sense.—He did not say, "Ye shall not find Me, ye shall die in your sins."—The Jews would feel the want of Christ in the despair of neglected opportunity; the disciples would feel themselves deprived of a friend.—"The *seeking* of the unbelieving Jews is the vain looking for a deliverer after rejecting the true Messiah, the *seeking* of the disciples is the *seeking* of faith and love." *Schaff.*

Whither I go. The glory into which He was to be received.—Troubles for Him would soon end, and He would be at rest, but *they* would have to endure a while longer.

Ye cannot come. This is not to be understood absolutely, but as explained in ver. 36, they were not able to follow Him *then.*—Their work was not yet done, nor were their characters matured enough for this.—To the Jews, He spoke in the language of threatening; but to His disciples in that of love and hope.—This is an instance of the many sides which the sayings of our Lord exhibited.—"He was unwilling to say this to the disciples sooner; whereas to unbelievers He said it at an earlier period." *Bengel.*

Now. The Jews would never be able to follow Him, but the disciples were unable only for a little while.—What He says to them *now* is binding only *for the present.*—"From the two propositions: ye will miss Me; and, ye cannot follow Me now, the following (verse 34) results." *Lange.*

---

34. A new commandment I give unto you, That ye love one another; as I have loved you, that ye also love one another.

New commandment. "Ye will be left on earth, when I go to heaven: but, unlike the Jews, ye will seek Me and find Me in the way of love to Me and to one another, forming an united body, the Church, in which all will recognize My presence among you as My disciples." *Schaff, Stier, Alford.*—The law of love had long ago been inculcated upon the Jew (Lev. xix. 18). Yet the Jew narrowed its meaning, making it apply only to his countrymen or even to his friends.—Our Lord once referred to the Rabbinical rendering, "Thou shalt love thy neighbour and hate thine enemy." —Christ made the old commandment *new* by giving it the widest possible range, and making it capable of *new* applications.—Inventions lose not their claim to novelty because they are but the forms in which old and familiar principles exert themselves.— Christ gave the commandment of love a *new* place by making it both the impulse and measure of all duty.—Love is not a commandment impelling from without, but the very soul of duty, the health of our spiritual life.—In reality, there can be only one rule of life, and love is the original law of the universe.—Christ taught that to love as God loves is perfection (Matt. v. 48).— This command shall be *new* for ever, for love cannot fail in any world.—" And they sung as it were a *new* song before the throne " (Rev. xiv. 3).

Give I unto you. " Manifestly, the new Commandment is to supply His (visible) presence to them for a time, until they come to Him again." *Lange.*

Love one another. Gr., *in order that ye may love one another.* With a self-sacrificing love; not with the feeling which is fitful and uncertain.—The possession of the same truths, hopes, and emotions tends to draw the disciples of Christ closer together : any external command to love would only be an expression of a necessity of their nature.

As I have loved you. This marks the degree and measure of His love.—Christ gave all He had ; He gave His life.—" He saved others, Himself He cannot save," was the taunt of His enemies, yet it is a glorious truth.—So great was Christ's love that He submitted to endure the complicated penalties of our sin, even unto death.—We whose affections are so contracted in their range can never fully know that infinite love which embraced a world !— This love of Christ made the *old* law of the universe a *new* one, because in Him it was for the first time fully revealed —Before Christ came, love had never been fully manifested in ai 7 individual life.—That which was an abstract truth, in Him became a reality.—We depend no longer on the statement of a law, we *see* in Christ how God loves.—" Christ hath loved His disciples and followers, and so loved them as may well be a copy and pattern of all love." *Hutcheson.*

ἐντολὴν καινήν. The consideration that the commandment is not a *new* but an o'd one, has led some to ascribe an *intensive* sense to the adjective *new*, and o hers to take it in an *altered* sense.—The INTENSIVE sense (new in *degree*).—' ne is not to love his neighbour simply as himself, but more than himself. *Cyril, Theophyl., Theod. Mopsu., Euthym. Zigab, Knapp, &c.*—One should love his neighbour as Christ has loved His people. *Chrys., Tholuck, Wordsworth,*—It is the new commandment of Christian brotherly love as distinguished from a general love to our neighbour. *Grotius, Luthardt, Ebrard, Brückner, Hengst., Godet, Meyer.*—The principle of the new life brought by Christ. *De Wette.*—The removal of the bounds which in the Old Test. inclosed neighbourly love within national limits. *Köstlin, Hilgenfeld.*—ALTERED sense. *Preceptum illustre. Hackspan, Hammond, Wolf—Mandatum ultimum. Heumann.*—The most recent. *Nonnus*—One always new never growing old, ever fresh. *Olshausen.*—A renewed one. *Irenæus, Jansen, Calvin, Maldon., Schöttgen.*—A renewing (regenerating) one. *Augustine, Wordsworth.*—An unexpected one. *Semler.*—The newness consists in simplicity and unicity. *Alford, Owen.*—A new and different commandment by which His spiritual presence would be at once realized and proved. *Ellicott.*—The new commandment is indicative of the institution of the Lord's Supper.—The Lord's Supper is to be the chief channel for the conveyance of light, impulse, and strength, for such a brotherly love. *Lange.*—This view of Lange's is ingenious and plausible, and allows ἵνα its full force. *Schaff.*

---

35. By this shall all men know that ye are my disciples, if ye have love one to another.

All men know. Gr., *perceive.*—They shall have a convincing proof; knowledge founded upon observed facts.—Jesus was about to leave them; therefore it was necessary that they should draw closer together and be known among men by a distinctive mark.— Mutual brotherly love, the distinctive mark of Christians.—The heathen were wont to exclaim with astonishment: "Behold how these Christians love one another, and see how they are ready to die for one another."—"Christians love each other before knowing each other." *M. Felix.*—"Their lawgiver has persuaded them that they are all brethren." *Lucian.*

My disciples. The followers of a Master who manifested such love.—"Albeit, true saints should not be ostentatious, nor self-seekers, yet as they ought to assure their own hearts of their good condition before God, so they ought to shine and appear such as they are." *Hutcheson.*

If ye have love. Thus their distinguishing mark was not so much a common belief as the whole *effect* of that belief upon their minds and hearts.—The disciples of Christ are to be marked by that in which the children of the world most of all fail.—It is only in Christian societies that the purest love can exist, conforming itself to the loftiest ideal, and based upon the most sacred motives.— The most unselfish love is that which regards the eternal relations of souls to God.—The offences of professing Christians against the law of love have proved the greatest obstacle to the progress of religion.—The love of Christians to one another should not waste itself in emotion, but be embodied in acts of self-sacrifice, for these partake of the spirit of the cross of Christ.—The only way in which men can recognize the love of Christians to one another is by those acts which spring from it.

---

36. Simon Peter said unto him, Lord, whither goest thou? Jesus answered him, Whither I go, thou canst not follow me now ; but thou shalt follow me afterwards.

Simon Peter. See on chap. i. 42, and on Luke vi. 14. Always the first to speak: impulsive, self-confident, loving.

Whither goest thou? Characteristic of the bold and impetuous nature of Peter, of a mind intent rather upon immediate action than upon the contemplation of principles or duty.—Peter takes no notice of the teaching concerning brotherly love, but seeks to indulge his curiosity.—He takes up the statement in verse 33, as suggesting a more ambitious line of conduct in which his courage might distinguish itself.—We are more apt to admire duties which require great force and energy than those which belong to the meek and retiring graces of the Christian character.—Points of mere speculation and curiosity have more attraction for many than the plain principles of obedience.—The true corrective for such a disposition is to follow duty first, and then the designs of Providence will work themselves clear.

Jesus answered. Not giving an answer that would completely satisfy his enquiry, but directing attention to what was of *practical* importance.—Though not according to Peter's mind, yet it was a comforting and encouraging answer.

Not follow me now. Peter had a vague idea that the departure which Christ had spoken of was associated with danger (ver. 37). —He knew not his own weakness, nor those slow movements of Providence for which man must be content to wait.—Peter could not follow his Master into those depths of suffering which He was about to enter.—He would be one of those who would desert his Lord in those dread solitudes.—The Lord often mercifully postpones our severest contests and trials because of the immaturity of our spiritual character.—"The disciples were no more *ordained* to pass through death immediately with Christ than they were *ripe* for such a journey." *Lange.*

Follow me afterwards. The conflict was only delayed ; for Peter afterwards, like his Lord, closed his life by crucifixion.—This ever-forward disciple possessed some great capabilities of soul, which, when sanctified, would be adequate to the most severe duty.—Genuine honesty and an unfailing love for his Lord were ever manifest in the midst of all his infirmities.—The strength of believers is graduated by their necessity.—" Such as the Lord keeps for a time under much weakness, yea, and corrects their presumption with a fall, may yet be raised up and strengthened to suffer eminently for Christ." *Hutcheson.*

αὐτῷ. Omitted. *Tisch., Alford, Westcott and Hort, Lange.*—Retained. *Cod. Sin.*—μοι. Omitted. *Cod. Sin., Tisch., Alford, Westcott and Hort.*—The question of Peter. *D mine, quo vadis?* has furnished the name to a church outside the city of Rome on the spot where, according to the legend, Peter having from love of life escaped from prison, was confront d by the appearance of Christ, and asked Him, " Lord, whither goest Thou ? "—The Lord answered, " I go to Rome, to be crucified again," whereupon Peter returned to his prison and cheerfully suffered martyrdom on the Cross. *Schaff*

---

37. Peter said unto him, Lord, why cannot I follow thee now ? I will lay down my life for thy sake.

Why cannot I follow thee now? Peter is not content with the answer he had received.—He had not yet learned complete trust and submission, but is more desirous of distinguishing himself by an act of courage.—It was painful to such a nature tlat his love and constancy should fall even under the semblance of suspicion. —The betrayer was now gone out and Peter might well suppose that his Master had perfect confidence in all the rest.—" Men are not easily convinced of their presumption till their experience discover it." *Hutcheson.*

I will lay down my life. The resolve was sincere though it was the venture of inconsideration.—These confident words give rather the promise of what shall be than represent what he was then.— The man who could thus boldly speak soon learns to tremble at a damsel's voice.—The most efficient courage is that which is formed slowly through patience and meekness.—The annals of martyrdom show that the gentlest natures were capable of the most sublime courage.

For thy sake. Gr., *for Thee.*—This is the *one motive* of all Christian duty.—The moral heroism which the history of Christianity has shown could never have been produced by devotion to an idea : it could only arise from supreme devotion to a person.— " Nay, it was Jesus who would lay down His life for Peter's sake. ' *Bengel.*—" When Christ had died for Peter and redeemed him by His own blood, and had risen from the dead, then Peter was able to follow Christ, even to the Cross." *Augustine.*—" That Peter did not, in the exercise of faith and obedience, keep silence, was the *inward* beginning of his fall." *Richter.*

1094 / Gospel of John

38. Jesus answered him, Wilt thou lay down thy life for my sake? Verily, verily, I say unto thee, The cock shall not crow, till thou hast denied me thrice.

Wilt thou lay down? The language of gentle irony.—He might well speak in such language to one who professed a courage which he could not sustain in the hour of trial.—Peter had fainted in lesser trials, and how could he now expect to endure the greatest of all?—" It was an easy thing to lay down thy boats and nets to follow me, but not so easy to lay down thy life." *Henry.*

Verily, verily. See on chap. i. 51.—" It is incredible how contrary men's carriage, in a time of temptation, may be to their presumptuous resolutions; therefore Christ must confirm it with a ' Verily, verily.'" *Hutcheson.*

The cock shall not crow. Mark says, " Before the cock crow twice."—Matthew's statement is to the same effect as here.—The former statement implies that the cock crows twice, once at midnight, and again towards morning.—Therefore the morning watch was called *cock-crowing* (Mark xiii. 35).—The only one reckoned in the East was that at the dawn of day.—This denial was to take place in the night, before the ensuing morning : a most improbable circumstance in itself, and a clear instance of the prescience of Jesus.

Denied me thrice. This was worse than ceasing to follow Him; it was being ashamed of His cause.—The vaunting hero would soon become a coward.—" That he would do this not once only by a hasty slip of his tongue, but after he had paused would repeat it a second and third time ; and it proved too true." *Henry.* —" Comparison of Judas and Peter at this moment: 1. Similar features: the former, out in the night, prostitutes himself to the enemy in determined apostasy ; the latter, within the circle of disciples, lays claim to a fidelity for which he has not the strength. 2. The difference : In that case, embitterment; in this, love to the Lord ; yonder the utmost falseness, here sincerity and open outspokenness.—There is always a capability of redemption in the sincere man.—The sad certitude of Jesus touching the imminent denial of Peter, set in the calm assurance of the certain victory of grace." *Lange.*

ἀπεκρίθη. The best authorities read ἀποκρίνεται.—Φωνήσῃ, against Φωνήσει, has very strong authority.—It is so given in *Cod. Sin., and in the best critical editions.*— The reading ἀρνήσῃ decidedly preponderant. *Schaff.*

John 14

1. Let not your heart be troubled : ye believe in God, believe also in me.

Let not, &c. We now come to the *Holy of Holies* of the gospel history.—The Spirit anoints John alone to open this sanctuary.—It hath the last words of our Lord, with His heart all aglow.—Since the world began no man had heard such sublime truths.—They comprehended them not *fully*, nor will we on this side of heaven.—Millions in every age have been cheered by these words ; in cares, in sorrows, in agonies, in exile, and in the flames of martyrdom.

Troubled. Unaware of His speedy death by violence, yet they knew a separation was near.—Judas' treachery, Peter's denial, and our Lord's departure had saddened their spirits.—Sinners in Zion ought to tremble, but sons of Zion may be joyful in their king.—The Jews looked for a Messianic kingdom to be ushered in in all imaginable splendour.—Instead poverty, contempt, reproach, and persecution were theirs.—Now their Master was suddenly about to leave them with no hope of better.—Rabbis threatened one leaving the synagogue with being sent to hell forever.—The infinite mind of redeeming Love found for them an inexhaustible treasure of consolations, disclosures, predictions, promises.—His sweep of thought embraces His church through eternity.—His words may be compared to the blue vaults of heaven in their crystal clearness, and illimitable depths.—The longer we gaze and adore, the further they seem to recede in measureless grandeur.—Heart-felt consolations for all the woes of fallen humanity, their fulness and richness no created mind can wholly grasp.

Ye believe, &c. He opposes to trouble the sovereign remedy of infinite love, Faith.—The apostles had far loftier and clearer proof of the divine in Christ than the patriarchs had of God.—Here Christ makes Himself co-equal with God, in that He requires the same trust in Himself as in the Almighty Father.—If He were not the Supreme God such faith would be idolatry, and such a demand blasphemy.—As a mighty conqueror He calls "cheer up, never be dismayed ;" this is the key-note to the entire farewell discourse of the Redeemer.—"All things are yours ; and ye are Christ's ; and Christ is God's " (1 Cor. iii. 21-23)

Believe. A startling demand from a companion at the table.—But recalling His healing the sick, calming the storm, raising the dead, it seems *natural* to trust our eternal interests to such a Being.—Perfect peace has ever been the result of faith in Christ.—Our blessed Lord never gives mere *human* consolation.—Whether He awakes in a storm, or teaches, or works miracles, or agonizes in the garden, or dies, it is as A GOD!—No living or dying master ever before offered *such* comfort.—No sentimental comforting as man can only conceive.—All the myriads of earth are asked to take shelter under Christ's wings.

In me. As God in Providence, so Christ claims supremacy in administering grace.—Gather up your Israelite faith in God and in ME.

ἡ καρδία. The spirit, the soul, may be troubled (see chap. xi, 33; xiii. 21); not so the *heart*, as the organ and symbol of trust. *Lange.*—πιστεύετε εἰς τὸν θεὸν, &c. The sentence admits of four interpretations and translations.—πιστ. may be taken both times in the imperative, or both times in the indicative, or once in the imperative, and once in the indicative sense.—Hence: 1. " Believe in God, believe also in Me." *Cyril, Nonnus, Theophyl., Lampe, Bengel, Whitby, Dodd., Lücke, De Wette Stier, Meyer, Alford, Hengst., Godet.*—2. " *Ye* believe in God, *ye* believe also in Me." *Luther.*—3 " Believe in God and (th·n) *ye* will also believe in Me." *Olsh., Lange.*—4. " *Ye* believe in God, (therefore) believe also in Me." *Vulgate, Aug., Erasmus, Beza, Grotius.*—Both causes imperative. *Schaff.*

---

2. In my Father's house are many mansions: if it were not so, I would have told you. I go to prepare a place for you.

My Father's house. The holy familiarity with which He speaks of Jehovah and Heaven; as a prince might speak of the splendours of a palace to an astonished peasant.—This strange word had once resounded in the Temple (Luke ii. 49; John ii. 16).—*Fifty times* does our Lord call God by this endearing appellation.—*Heaven* He thus introduces as OUR FUTURE BLESSED HOME!—Passing through the valley of death, a glance is given at the golden city. —The universe is God's House, but not His dwelling-place; the essential, personal, peculiar unfolding of His glory requires this.—Heaven called: Paradise, Luke xxiii. 43; Light, Rev. xxi. 23; Building of God, A house not made with hands, 2 Cor. v. 1: A city God built, Heb. xi. 10; A better country, Heb. xi. 16; An Inheritance, Acts xx. 32; Kingdom, Matt. xxv. 34; A Crown, 2 Tim. iv. 8; Glory, Psa. lxxxiv 11; Joy of the Lord, Matt. xxv. 21; Rest, Heb. iv. 9; Peace, Isa. lvii. 2; Holy Jerusalem, Rev. xxi. 10; New Jerusalem, Rev. iii. 12; Bride, Rev. xxi. 9; Temple of My God, Rev. iii. 12; That within the veil, Heb. vi. 19; Mount Zion,

Heb. xii. 22; Tabernacle of God, Rev. xxi 3; Zion, Isa. xxxv. 10.
—Implied by Eden, Rev. ii. 7; If the noonday sun be His mere
shadow, what must His palace be?—The foundations twelve
varieties of precious stones, the walls of jasper, the gates of pearl,
the streets of pure gold transparent as glass.—The Lamb the
temple; no need of the sun, the Lamb is the light thereof, and
" there shall be no night there."—Heaven's glories exhaust all the
ideas of beauty, loveliness, and pleasure.—With spiritual bodies,
the redeemed bear the lineaments of Christ.—Heaven a home
where all the inmates dwell in blessed family love.

Many mansions. My Father and I are not content to dwell alone;
the Greek word gives the idea of *permanence.*—" Here we have no
continuing city."—The constant changes of Christ's pilgrims on
earth a contrast.—Riches " make themselves wings," (Prov xxiii.
5).—The glories of earth like pictures drawn on ice vanish while
gazing upon them.—" Many mansions; " enough for each and
all.—Hints also at degrees of dignity and blessedness corresponding to the degrees of perfection.—No envy or jealousy will arise
from disparity of glory, for the unity of love will reign in all.
Augustine.

If it were not so. Our Lord never raised a false hope.—He had
taught them to say " Our Father," but had there been no Father,
no home waiting for them, how bitter the disappointment, how
great the misery.—In all the boundless luxuriance of God's works,
no sham, no fiction can be found.—As if He had said : In leaving
your humble homes and following ME you were not deceived.
—Your faith in ME will be infinitely more than realized.—Christ
fed His disciples with no false hopes as did Mohammed and
other impostors.—He alone of all founders of religion discouraged
men from following Him.

I go to prepare a place for you. Heaven is a *prepared place* for
a *prepared people.*—Our heaven-born affections are God's chosen
harbingers in advance taking possession of our home.—As the
courier goes before and prepares accommodation for the traveller.—
By nature all men live in exile from the kingdom of God.—Creation amply shows how boundless His resources are.—Christ has
pledged His word to His people that there is a heavenly inheritance prepared for them.—He makes all things ready for the
heavenly life: 1. the place for His people; 2. His people for the
place.—In all one Father, one Son and Heir, one inheritance for
one throng of children.

οἰκίᾳ τοῦ πατρός. Mark the connection of these words with τεκνία (chap. xiii. 33);
the touching ideas of Father, house, home, peaceful and durable rest, room enough

for all 'n heaven. *Schaff*—The house of the Father is the real temple of God, as opposed to the typical temple or house of the Father (chap. ii. 16), which they are now cast out of, having taken their leave of it as Jews *Lange.*—Not heaven *in general*, but the particular *dwelling-place* of the divine δόξα in heaven, the place of His glorious throne, considered as the heavenly sanctuary, according to the analogy of the temple at Jerusalem as the οἶκος τοῦ πατρός on earth (chap. ii. 16) *Meyer.*—μοναί This term, which in the N T. occurs o ly here and verse 23, is derived from μένω, *to abide.* and hence implies the idea of abode, rest stability, home.—The E. V. *mansion*, from *mansio*, *manere* (introduced by Tyndale), here and in old English means dwe ling-house ; not, as in modern usage, manor-house, palace. Christ probably alludes to the temple, His Father s house on earth with its numerous chambers ; perhaps also to the vast Oriental palaces with apartments for all the princes and couriers. *Schaff.*—The universe is the dwelling-place of My Father : in that vast abode *earth* is one mansion, *heaven* is another; it should not be a matter o' grief when we are called to pass from one part of this vast habitation to another. I am about to leave you; but shall still be in the same habitation with you, performing an important work for you. *Barnes.*—πολλαί. The multiplicity of the μοναί indicates a diversity of grades. *The Fathers, Stier, Lange, Wordsworth.*—"If the devil with his tyrants hunt you out of the world, ye shall still have room enough." *Luther.*—Refers to the number. *Alford, Godet, Meyer.*—εἰ δὲ μή. "If it were not so, I would say to you : I go to prepare a place for you." *The Fathers, Eras., Luther, Bengel, Ebrard, &c.*—"If it were not so, would I have told you : I go to prepare a place for you"? *Lange*—"If it were not so, I would have told you." *Beza, Calvin, Lücke, Tho'uck, Grotius, Olsh., De Wette Meyer. Alf., Lach., Tisch.. Hengst., Godet*, so also the E. V. ὅτι before πορεύομαι. *Cod, Sin , Lach., Tisch., Alford, &c.*—ἑτοιμάσαι τόπον. Does not mean to create the place as a place, but : to arrange it as a habitable place.—Christ *prepared* a heavenly home for His disciples by H's atoning death, resurrection, and ascension. *Lange.*—Heaven is not only a *state*, but also a *place* from which Christ descended and to which he ascended — according to the Apocalypse. the many heavenly mansions here spoken of are after all not the final but the intermediate resting-places of the saints till the general resurrection when the Heavenly Jerusalem wil descend upon the new. glorified earth, and God will dwell with His people for ever (Rev. xxi 1; 2 Pet. iii. 13). *Schaff.*

———————

3. And if I go and prepare a place for you, I will come again, and receive you unto myself ; that where I am, there ye may be also.

If I go. *And though I go.* Lange.—He does not intend to indicate the *time* of His return, but the *consequence* of His departure.

And prepare. As the Ark of God went before the ancient Church to search out a resting place.—To prepare for them the place, He must first leave them.—The first preparation for Christ and ourselves is the Cross.—Though the world disowns you, My Father and I will befriend you.—This establishes the believer's claim through Christ to a home in the skies.—" For me to die is gain," proves Paul felt heaven to be sure.—" Lord remember me," showed that Christ has the keys of the golden city.—Stephen's last prayer, " Receive my spirit," intimates that he knew he was just entering his rest.—Christ has *disclosed* and *unclosed* heaven.—The heavenly mansions: 1. prepared from the beginning; 2. receiving additional preparation through the ascension of Christ ; 3. undergoing an eternal process of glorification. Lange.—Christ's appearing in the presence of God, through the offering of His blood in the Holy Place, or the presentation of the sufficient reconciliation made by Him, has purchased for us our re-adoption into heaven.—It is to Him we owe our heavenly citizenship. *Heubner.*

I will come again. Gr., *I am coming.*—Faith knows nothing of time, but fixes upon and is filled with the great event itself.—A mere "good night;" He will return again soon. *Henry.* —At death, and in the glory of His Second Advent, Christ Himself comes to take His children home.—We say it was fever, or consumption, or storm, or fire; but whatever the secondary cause, Christ is the Agent.—What consolation and what honour is this assurance!—At His Second Advent all His children will be openly gathered into eternal family blessedness and joy (2 Thess. ii. 1). —Many now are waiting for this consolation of Israel; in the words of Sisera's mother they exclaim, "Why is His chariot so long in coming"?—The answer is: "The Lord is not slack concerning His promise; but is long-suffering to us-ward, not willing that any should perish, but that all should come to repentance" (2 Peter iii. 9).—He is ever coming; the Judge is even now standing at the door.—Because of the uncertainty of His appearing as to *the time*, believers are to be always prepared to meet Him.—" In such an hour as ye think not the Son of Man cometh," therefore, " Be ye also ready."

And receive you unto myself. A majestic word absolutely unbecoming anyone but Jehovah.—"Thou hast made us for Thyself, and our hearts are restless till we find rest in Thee." *Augustine.* —The Father's House is the Son's to do its honours.—" Whom having not seen ye love," but then, " we shall be like him, for we shall see him as He is" (1 Peter i. 8; 1 John iii. 2).—Believers are His portion, His inheritance; and He is theirs.— " Heirs of God," because, " joint heirs with Christ."

Where I am. This promise, the grandest Jehovah Himself could make.—The presence of Jesus is here claimed to be the chief attraction and element in heaven's bliss.—The joy of the saints in glory is " the joy of their Lord."—" This day thou shalt be with me in Paradise."—" Absent from the body, present with the Lord."—As Christ is the great object of *faith* on *earth*, so He is the great object of *vision* in *heaven*.—" I saw no temple therein: for the Lord God Almighty and the Lamb are the temple of it" (Rev. xxi. 22).

Ye may be also. My home shall be your home, My power your shield.—" Him that overcometh will I make a pillar in the temple of my God, and he shall go no more out" (Rev. iii. 12).—Mansions and pillars imply permanence, stability, perpetuity.—" Your fruit shall remain" (chap. xv. 16).—An inheritance in substance in-

corruptible, in purity undefiled, in beauty unfading (1 Pet. i. 4).
—Our Lord counts not His glory full till all His people are
with Him ; as a father waits for all his children to come home.—
Heaven will be where Jesus is, this is enough to know.—Perfect
bliss is bound up in this truth: the unfolding will require the
ages of eternity.

πορ κ. έτοι. The antecedent facts which, once accomplished, result in the πάλιν
ἔρχομαι. The nearness or d's'ance of this return is left undecided by ἐάν. *Schaff.*
—πάλιν ἔρχομαι. Refers to the παρουσία of Christ at the last day. *Origen, Calvin,
Lampe, Meyer, Luthardt, Brückner, Ewald.*—Christ's coming again to His people,
through His Sp'rit, and their reception into the full and holy spiritual fellowship of the
glorified Christ, in accordance with verse 10. *Lücke, Neander, Godet. &c*—Indication of
a coming of Jesus for the purpose of receiving the disciples into heaven by means of
a blissful death. *Grotius, Knapp, B. Crusius, Nitzsch, Reuss, Tholuck, Hengst.*—Begun in
His resurrection; carried on in the spiritual life, the making them ready for the place
prepared ; further advanced when each by death is fetched away to be with Him ; fully
completed at His coming in glory, when they shall for ever be with Him in the perfected resurrection state. *Lange. S'ier, Alford, S'haff.*—The word (ἔρχομαι) is emp'oyed
to express every revelation of the Lord, every manifestation of His power. *Tholuck.*—
καί before ἐτοιμ. omitted. *Lachmann.*—Retained. *Tisch., Cod. Sin.*

---

4. And whither I go ye know, and the way ye know.

Wither I go. The " I " is emphatic.—After three years' intimate
converse how could they think of any other place but with His
Father !—His clearly confidential words make earth and heaven
one. *Herder.*

Ye know. The voice of cheer is often more arousing than
the voice of admonition.—This is not one of Jehovah's secrets
(Deut. xxix. 29).— It is easy to awaken doubt and anxiety, but
a word of encouragement and assurance is of great service at
times.—The disciples did not know that they knew the way.
Augustine.

The way ye know. Because ye know the way to the place to
which I am going, ye also know the goal. *Lange.*—The way should
be their guide to an inference concerning the goal.—As pilgrims
with an outlined route travel on by faith.—But after our re-union
our way will be eternally together.—To me the way can only be
by death and to you the same.—He would now, as oft before, excite
their curiosity and faith.—To follow the Man Jesus will assuredly
lead to God. Not only has he prepared the way but He is HIM-
SELF THE WAY (verse 6).—If we know the goal we may easily know
the way, for there is but one way, the " *new and living way* " (Heb.

x. 20).—Jesus is the beginning (*i.e.* elements of faith), the middle
(*i.e.* perfection of faith), and the end (*i.e.* blessedness in heaven).
Calvin.

οἴδατε τὴν ὁδόν instead of the text. rec. *Tisch, Meyer, Schaff. Alford, Westcott and Hort,
Cod. Sin.*—τὴν ὁδόν. 1. The passion and death of Christ. *Luther, Grotius, Luthardt.*—
The way of denial. *Tholuck.*—2. Christ Himself in accordance with verse 6. *De Wette,
Meyer.*—Christ most undoubtedly: Christ, however, in His motion; consequently
the view presented in No. 1 is equally to be held here, in accordance with verse 3
(*Tittmann, Knapp*).—Christ is the living way for Himself and His people to δόξα with
the Father. *Lange.*

5. Thomas saith unto him, Lord, we know not whither thou goest; and how can we
know the way?

Thomas. See on chap. xi. 16; and on Luke vi. 15.—Slow of faith but
full of love.—His sad heart timid, yet trusting, dreading separation
from Jesus.

We know not. The dust of earth oft blinds the eye of holiness.—They were dreaming of an earthly monarchy.—It was
among the last weaknesses clinging to their minds (Acts 1. 6).—
The same spirit prevails still, wherever the Church strives for
worldly pomp and power.—Thomas interrupts the Lord and seems
to offer rude contradiction.—He speaks not for himself merely,
but for all—" *We* know not."—But words of those confused or
perplexed must not be retorted on them as arrows.—Perhaps for the
moment, like Peter, "he knew not what he said" (Luke ix. 39).—
Adoring reverence for the Lord ever marked their course.—No mere
man could have commanded such profound homage.—Men are
often unconscious of what they do know.—Some truly converted
ones have no definite assurance of it.—Their prayer is, "Show us
a token for good."—But to ask Jehovah to enter the witness-box
is neither wise nor right.—We must not attempt to limit the Holy
One, or to define what the mode of His operation shall be.—Salvation comes by faith; perdition by unbelief.—The miner in the
dark walks by the light of his candle; he does not see.—The
worldling walks by what his eye, ear, hand, tongue, show him.—
The believer walks as "seeing Him who is invisible."

How can? To-morrow's sun may reveal to the pilgrim a path
now lost.—So the Spirit will unfold to us our duties, dangers, &c.
—This was an humble prayer for light.—With the light as of
seven days in our time, our unbelief is perilous.—The measure of
responsibility is not the light actually possessed, but the light
which might be obtained.—The honest though perplexed Thomas

asking in faith will find light.—" He that lacketh wisdom, let him ask of God" (James i. 5).—Whoever had Christian patience except by grace?—"Smite, Lord, smite on ; my sins are pardoned, all will be right." *Luther.*—A suffering saint said to those around him, "Don't pray for my ease but for patience."—The true Christian is ever known as one that waits. *Pascal.*—*How can we?* —"I can do all things through Christ who strengtheneth me" (Phil. iv. 13).—*How can we know?*—"No man can come to me except the Father who sent me draw him" (chap. vi. 44).—Our Saviour gives to them the key, the Holy Ghost, who is the only true expositor.—*How can we believe?*—"Lord increase our faith." —*How can we go in the way?*—"My presence shall go with thee, and I will give thee rest."—No one has ever proved the promise false : "Unto the upright there ariseth light in the darkness" (Psa. cxii. 4).—No one has ever perished who sincerely sought for mercy in God's way.—This question indicates an oppressive sense of obscurity, of uncertainty with regard to the goal, arising from imperfect apprehension of their Lord and Master.—To what a cheerless distance did Jesus seem to be receding.—*Where* shall they find Him?—*When* shall they learn all they need to know?— How ignorant often is even the wisest and holiest saint of God's ways.—To become a little child is the only way to peace and blessedness in the Kingdom of God.—To every question of unbelief or doubt, faith answers, "I know in whom I have believed." —The sweet experience of God's faithfulness and love in the past inspires him with trust and hope for the future.—"Though He slay me, yet will I trust Him."

δυνάμεθα τὴν ὁδὸν εἰδέναι (the text. rec.) : οἴδαμεν τὴν ὁδόν. *Lach., Tisch.*—The *text. rec.* is explanatory, and is sustained by *Cod. Sin. Schaff.*

6. Jesus saith unto him, I am the way, the truth, and the life : no man cometh unto the Father, but by me.

I am See on chap. viii. 58.—The same glorious name given to Moses (Ex. iii. 14).

The way. No part of the Bible unfolds more of the unwise questionings of frail humanity, yet our Lord makes these the occasions of some of His sublimest revelations.—The disciples could not harmonize His death with the predictions of the Old Testament; hence their perplexities and queries.— Carnal interpretations of Scripture are still the cause of unbelief and error in the Church.—As the Father's house is the goal so Christ is the way thither.—1. Christ leads the way to heaven ; 2.

Speaks the truth concerning heaven: 3. He gives Eternal life, which, through the fall, was lost.—As the WORD He is the source and sustainer of the life of the universe.—As the WORD He is the atoning Redeemer and fountain of salvation.—As the WORD He is the true light enlightening every man coming into the world (see on chap. i. 1-14).—Faith converts all creation into finger-boards, pointing to Christ.—There is only *one* way to the Father's house, and that is by faith in Him.—Sin made a chasm between God and man, but Christ is the bridge over that bottomless pit of ruin.—We march over that fatal cleft safely and securely by Christ.—Through His blood He entered the Holy Place, and we too must follow (Heb. ix. 22).—Not only the soul but the law itself is sprinkled with blood (Ex. xxiv. 6-8).—A *thousand* ways lead down to ruin, but only *one* way to blessedness.—" He hath consecrated for us a new and *living way* " (Heb. x. 20).—Who would be a bridge over a chasm with his body even for a King?—Yet the Lord of Glory made Himself a highway over *ruin* for wretched sinners!—His Cross has become our ladder from earth to glory.—Angels ascend and descend upon the Son of Man (chap. i. 51).—Jews dreamed of being saved *by* the law instead of *in* the law.—Coming to God by the law ceased in Paradise.—Being *in* the law is the unchangeable order of salvation.—This divine way like a stream both guides and bears to the goal.—Thomas desires *first* to know *where*, and secondly the way: our Lord shows first *the way*, and secondly *whither* it leads.—A germ truth : Present duty is ours, future results the Lord's.—Only get in the way and keep in it and the end will be gained.—" Through much tribulation " is a word that repels the worldling.—But as Christ is the way it follows we also by *cross-bearing* are to reach the goal.—As our FORERUNNER He endured the various trials we meet (Heb. vi. 19).—This way is so plain that "the wayfaring men, though fools, shall not err therein," and hereby we know it is of God.—What a contrast between this *way* and those which men have contrived !

The truth. Christ is the *truth* of this *way*, the clear manifestation of it, because He is, in general, the truth or manifestation of God.—His deeds and words are the system of saving truth. —Therefore, faith in Christ is faith in all He *was*, all He *became*, all He *spoke*, all He *suffered*, all He *accomplished*, and all He *continues* to do.—*The* Truth as opposed to types, as opposed to error, and as opposed to all deceit (1 Cor. i. 20).

The life. Christ is the *life* of this way, the animating motive power by which we come to the Father, because He is, in general, life.—" Our life is hid with Christ in God " as to its origin (Col. iii. 3).—As the life of a flower is hid during the wintry reign of death in the root.—"Hid " as to its source of nourishment, strength, and beauty.—1 Christ is the way, as the truth of the way; the living, personal motion to the Father because He is truth itself.—2. He is the way, as the life of the way; the victorious mover to the Father because He is life in general.—Christ the way in His divine-human personality: 1. God's way to man; therefore, 2. Man's way to God.—Christ's personality as a pledge of the heavenly home: 1. As the truth of the heavenly life ; 2. As the life of heavenly truth. *Lange.*—1. Christ is *Man*, the *way* which offers itself to all men ; 2. Christ is *God*, absolute, independent *truth;* 3. Christ is *God-man*, the life, that is the fountain of life springing from Him and received by us. *Stier.*

No man cometh. "I am the door of the sheep " (chap. x. 7).— "Through him we have access by one Spirit, unto the Father " (Eph. ii. 18).—Our Lord only expounds the first, *the way.*— Penance, the Romanist's boasted " second plank after shipwreck," is a mockery of the guilty soul.—An ocean of tears could not wash away the stains of sin.

But by me. "And so, when a man is saved, the Lord Christ must have a hand in the work." *Luther.*—A thousand saints avail nothing to intercede for us.—"There is no other name under heaven given among men, whereby we must be saved " (Acts iv. 12). —Our Lord here declares the central truth of Christianity.—The *human* side, " ye will not come unto me " (chap. v. 40).—The *divine* side, "no man can come unto me except the Father who sent me draw him " (chap. vi. 44).—The result of these two truths is, that salvation is by sovereign grace.—The utter helplessness of the sinner is clearly implied.—That man can of himself never bridge the chasm between God and the soul.—That men would ever resist the method of salvation by Christ.—Therefore, He arouses the entire energies of the apostolic band to the truth.—The whole revelation of God turns on this great fact as on a hinge.—Such as reject the terms of mercy claim to be wiser or holier than God.— Christ is the only way to God as the Father.—In Him and by Him alone can any soul of man ever realize the fatherhood of God.— Through Him we reach the heart of infinite love and find our rest. —Jesus is the Eternal Christ and High priest of humanity.— —" Walk by the *Man*, and thou wilt arrive at GOD." *Hilary.*

---

7. If ye had known me, ye should have known my Father also: and from henceforth ye know him, and have seen him.

If ye had known me. That is, had known Me aright.—Men read the Bible wrong.—Christ asked, "How readest thou?"—Men know God, but not as the true God.—Thousands saw Jesus and admired Him as a wonder-worker.—The wilful ignorance of unbelievers and the blindness of believers alike strange.—Under the prophets, the only veil was the unbelief of the Jewish heart.—In the Saviour's time the obscurity was doubled by the smoke of *tradition.*—Their Rabbis taught a scheme completely opposed to the Word of God, though they professed almost idolatrous reverence for the letter of Scripture.—This national blindness affected the minds of the disciples also.—They must have the Holy Spirit before they could rightly and fully know Christ.

My Father also. They had not as yet recognized in Him the living, heavenly image of the heavenly Father, an image coming from heaven and going to heaven.—"In a knowledge of the eternal, divine-human personality of Christ they would also have obtained a view of the personal Father and His love-kingdom in heaven, a kingdom elevated above all transitory things." *Lange.*—Christ is "the brightness of the Father's glory, the express image of his person" (Heb. i. 2).

From henceforth. From this time onwards, after the full declaration of Himself in verses 6 and 9, and those following.—The law of progressive revelation is the law of the kingdom of heaven, both in the Church and in the soul of the believer.

Ye have seen him. Said of the intuitive glance of faith.

εἰ ἐγνώκειτέ με. The emphasis is not upon "Me," but upon "known."—The English word "known" represents two Greek words in the better text which are not identical in meaning.—The former means, to know by observation, the latter to know by reflection. *Ellicott.*—ἐγνώκειτε ἄν is opposed to ἤδειτη ἄν by strong authorities. *Lange*—ἀπ' ἄρτι. Refers to the time of the communication of the Spirit. *Chrys., Lücke, Kuinoel.*—The words are hypothetical. *De Wette.*—Indicative of the beginning of appropriation (comp. chap. xv 3). *Tholuck.*—"After my having told you (verse 6) what I am." *Meyer.*—Denotes that method just now to be disclosed by Him, and which He desired sharply to define, by which they were to arrive at a knowledge of the Father and the Father's house, the method of faith.—Doubtless, however, the ἄρτι at the same time embraces the confirmation of this method by the whole grand period of Christ's death and resurrection, whereby, according to Rom. i. 4, He was demonstrated to be the Son of God, and thus at once made the Surety and the Heir of the Father in heaven. *Lange.*

---

8. Philip saith unto him, Lord, shew us the Father, and it sufficeth us.

Philip. See on chap. i. 42.—Like Thomas he looks for the confirmation of faith by sight (comp. chap. i. 46; vi. 5).—These apostles retained their distinctive mental characteristics all the way through.

—Grace sanctifies the man but does not alter constitutional peculiarities.

Shew us the Father. What a demand to address to one "in the likeness of sinful flesh."—As if He could then and there rend the heavens or take them up to heaven.—He declares his faith by assuming Jesus to be capable of producing such a vision.—But his failing to perceive the manifestation of the Father in Christ proves that faith to be but small.—Philip wants some *visible*, material display of God's glory.—"The Jews require a sign" (1 Cor. i. 22), a national characteristic.—They could not see a human soul, how much less the infinite Spirit.—Roman soldiers called Christians *Atheists*, because they had no gods to show.—The Father was being continuously manifested in Christ's life, words, and works.—"The light of the knowledge of the glory of God is seen in the face of Jesus" (2 Cor. iv. 6).—Unbelievers ever cry, "Show us! show us! Prove! prove!"—The love of the world repels the claims of Christ and hides His face from the soul.—Moses once earnestly desired to see the divine glory (Ex. xxxiii. 18).—The prayer was granted, but O, in what a God-like manner! —"I WILL MAKE ALL MY GOODNESS PASS BEFORE THEE."—The desire to see God has been so intense and overpowering that in some cases it has dethroned reason.—Hence the wisdom and goodness of the revelation of God in Christ.—On Him the mind can settle and rest.—"We have seen His glory, the glory as of the only-begotten of the Father full of grace and truth" (chap. i. 11).

Sufficeth us. David Hume said that if he could see a miracle in the market-place he would believe.—But there are no new doctrines to be taught.—Must God work new miracles to prove the former ones?—As well ask God to create a *new sun* to prove He created the *old one.*—Some will never believe till they see God grasping His thunderbolts.—There are no sceptics in hell, but, alas! faith there brings no peace.—"The devils also believe, and tremble" (James ii. 19).—Some raise such an uproar that they cannot hear God's voice; others shut out all light and Jehovah is "an unknown God" to them.—The very beauty and order covering nature become a *veil* over their hearts.—The sun dazzles and blinds those who endeavour to look at him with naked eye.—To unbelief, shadows are realities and phantoms are truths.—Robert Dale Owen rejected the revelation of Scripture, but became the victim of spirit impostors and cheats.—"There is light for those who love light, and darkness for those who love darkness." *Pascal.* —Philip in asking to see the Father had asked ineffable blessedness. —The "vision of God" was intensely longed for by all the Old Testament saints.—To "see God;" what a contrast to all mere ceremonies and rites!—The heart purified by the Spirit becomes a shining light.—" If we walk in the light," &c. (1 John i. 7.)—" I will behold thy face in righteousness: I shall be satisfied, when I awake, with thy likeness " (Psalm xvii. 15).—A soul with immortal and ever-growing capacities and yet *satisfied!*—It is the divine mark of the gospel of Christ that it *satisfies.*—" To the joy of beholding the Father's face nothing could be added." *Hilary.* —One such vision of the Father, Philip thinks, would remove all their doubts ; and satisfy the deepest yearnings of their hearts.

---

9. Jesus saith unto him, Have I been so long time with you, and yet hast thou not known me, Philip? he that hath seen me hath seen the Father ; and how sayest thou then, Shew us the Father?

So long time. Three years with the Lord ; a *long time.*—It was a *long time* also for the Lord Himself, tempted and tried in every possible way, and with the Cross constantly in view.—Long to be absent from the joys and glories of His Father's house.—The perception of the course of time depends upon one's state of mind; therefore, to the Lord, who was " a man of sorrows and afflicted with griefs," three years must have appeared *long.*—This, however, was not the worst: to dwell among sinners must have been unutterably painful to the Holy One of God.—Jesus thus gently reproves Philip for his request: some " ask amiss " (James iv. 3).

Not known me. For so long a time I have appeared among you and hast *thou* not *known* the nature of My appearing?—Not only from the " words and works," but from the whole personality of Jesus, Philip should have recognized His heavenly origin.—To how many might these words still be addressed?—Thousands hear the gospel and profess discipleship who nevertheless *know* not Jesus as their Lord and Saviour.

Hath seen me. The invisible soul of man is seen through its deeds.—The Father was seen through the works of the Son.— As a man is *in himself*, so are his works.—Thus the works of the Son are a revelation of the *nature* of the Father.—Spiritual eyes are required to see spiritual things.—" The natural (soul) man understandeth not the things of the Spirit; because they are spiritually discerned."—A man may be a learned scholar and critic, yea, a great theologian, and yet be ignorant of the divine glory of the Son of God.

Hath seen the Father. Christ is " the brightness of the Father's glory, and the express image of his person " (Heb. i. 2).—Jehovah, in the works of nature, is seen working miracles of power —His infinite knowledge is seen in prophecy: the Jewish people for example.—His holiness is seen in the law and the gospel; even Infidels are forced to acknowledge this.—His wisdom is seen in redemption : justice and mercy uniting in opening the door of grace to the sinner.—His Providence is seen in history, more especially in the propagation of the gospel and its preservation in the world.—In Jesus the moral attributes of God shine forth with matchless splendour.—In Him the eternal heart of God is revealed and the universe beholds that it is LOVE.—How sufficing is this to all the longings of the soul!—On the top of the great " world-stairs that slope through darkness up to God," Jesus is seen stand-ing, and He proclaims to all, " He that hath seen Me hath seen the Father."—This announcement from Him who is " the Faithful and true Witness," should banish all gloomy apprehensions and fears from our hearts.—What the Jesus of the Gospel IS, that the Creator and Ruler of the Universe IS.—God is therefore no longer " the unknown God."—Who is there that cannot trust the Jesus of the Gospel?—And if so, why not equally trust the invisible, awful Power behind, for that Power is the Father of Jesus and Jesus is His Son and image?—In the darkness and mystery of this sad life this should be our comfort that we are in the hands of a Being so like Jesus that he who hath seen the one hath seen the other.—All that saw Christ by faith saw the Father in Him ; *wisdom* in His doctrine ; *power* in His miracles ; *holiness* in His purity ; *grace* in His acts of grace.—Christ is the *visibility* of the *Invisible*, as far as, and in such a way as, He may be seen. *Stier.*— So sweet were the attractions of Christ's love that He drew to Himself those whom society and the Church had cast out for ever. —" The bruised reed *He* did not break, and the smoking flax *He* did not quench."—Little children are the best physiognomists in the world, and they went to Him without fear or distrust.—And ever as we think of that face that looks upon us from the page of gospel history, so full of tenderness, purity, and love, let us con-nect with it these words : " He that hath seen ME hath seen the Father."

How sayest thou? Let this be a warning to all against wasting time and strength in endeavouring to force their way into " the secret things that belong unto the Lord our God."

Shew us the Father? To this hour men look for God and Christ as *apart*.—In the entire life of Christ there is no question so great as this.—Faith alone provides the key that solves it.—In the revelation of the mystery of our Lord's person is given the revela-tion of the mystery of God. *Luthardt.*—Nature, Providence, and the Bible find their explanation, meaning, unity, and glory in the

God-man.—Heathenism in all its forms is a cry to see the Father.—
In Jesus *Himself* the Father is disclosed, and hence the words and
works of Jesus are the words and works of the Father.—How
near does this bring God to us.—We feel we are on holy ground
here, for in the beating heart of Jesus we hear the beating of the
heart of the Eternal One.

---

10. Believest thou not that I am in the Father, and the Father in me? the words that
I speak unto you I speak not of myself: but the Father that dwelleth in me, he doeth
the works.

Believest thou not? See on chap. i. 7.—Faith the *divinely-
ordained*, and therefore *the only ground* of personal salvation.—
Not because it is a *reasonable* mode of bestowing mercy.—Nor
yet because man is the *weaker* and God the stronger.—Nor yet
because it is *comprehensible* in its various parts.—It is utterly independent of man, and ignores his wishes, his ways, his works.—
Eternal life is associated with faith; eternal death with unbelief.
—From first to last, from the fall to the end of all things these are
the only alternatives offered.—"By grace ye are saved through
faith; and that not of yourselves: it is the gift of God" (Eph.
ii. 8).—This faith proved to be genuine by its fruits, love, joy,
peace, long-suffering, gentleness, goodness, charity; yet how
often have men, in their ignorance, charged the gospel with
ignoring morality?—"Talk they of morals, oh, thou bleeding
Love! the best morality is love of Thee." *Young.*—This method of
salvation humbles us to the dust, but it exalts us also to be sons
of God (chap. i. 12).

I am in the Father. See on chap. x. 38, where He had there
taught this truth to the Jews.—The order of the clauses is reversed here, because He is speaking of the knowledge of the
Father through the Son.—The Father is in Christ in virtue of
His Father-revelation in the works of Christ.—Christ is in the
Father in virtue of His Son-revelation in His words. *Lange.*—
Could any mere creature, however exalted, claim to have God
dwelling in him?—Has any one ever demanded faith in such a
claim by showing such works?

The words. He "was a prophet mighty in deed and word before
God and all the people" (Luke xxiv. 19).

Not of myself. See on chap. viii. 38.—Refers to the whole of His
manifestation of the character and attributes of God.—All His
words had been a revelation of the Father whom Philip had now
asked to see.—As the Son He speaks His words from the depths
of the Father.

Dwelleth in me. A real divine union.—No temple like Christ's body.—In Him dwelt the true Shekinah, "all the fulness of the Godhead" (Col. ii. 9).

The works. Embraces all the miracles He performed.—To Him they were mere every-day works on the humblest scale.—Not only are the words God's words, but the works also are God's works.—The words and the works are the property of both the Father and the Son.—The words, however, are pre-eminently and primarily the Son's, the works pre-eminently and primarily the Father's. *Lange.*—His *words* are no other than *works*, and His *works* are speaking and testifying *words.*—"*Believest thou?* That is still the *humbling* question of the Lord which rebukes the presumption of every aspiring Philip *in life*, as it is the *consoling* question which alleviates the sorrow of every downcast Martha at the *grave.*" *Stier.*

ὸ δὲ πατήρ, &c. The better reading is "*the Father, abiding in me, doeth His works,*" which is supported by *Codd. Sin., B. D.,* and adopted by *Tischendorf, Lange, Schaff, Ellicott,* &c.—ποιεῖ. As it respects His words the initiative lies within Himself, while for the works the initiative is in the Father who permanently dwells in Him. *Lange.*

---

11. Believe me that I am in the Father, and the Father in me: or else believe me for the very works' sake.

Believe me. See on chap i. 7.—Trust in Christ, the root of all other Christian graces.—A faith in *His Person*, the grand doctrine of the Atonement.—It implies a sense of guilt, personal guilt, and hence it is opposed by the carnal mind.—All true faith works by love, and by love is made manifest, as the sun is by its light.—"And the life which I now live in the flesh I live by the faith of the Son of God, who loved me, and gave Himself for me" (*Paul* in Gal. ii. 20).—Our Lord now addresses Himself to the whole body of the Apostles.—He claims from them a personal trust in Himself, which should accept His statement that He and the Father were immanent in each other. *Ellicott.*

The works' sake. See on chap. ii. 11, 23 ; iii. 2 ; iv. 48 ; vi. 30.—He takes lower ground with them.—He will place before them the evidence He placed before the Jews (chap. x. 38).—If they will not hear *Him* they ought to believe on account of His *Works* which they had seen.—As much as to say : Through a belief in the Divinity of My works, arrive at a belief in the divinity of My person.—The *works* wrought by the Gospel in the soul, and in the world, an ever-living witness of its heavenly origin.—Jesus still

maketh the blind to see, the lame to walk, the deaf to hear.—He
still cleanseth lepers, feeds multitudes, turns water into wine,
casts out devils, controls storms, gives peace, raises the dead.—By
the works wrought through His Word and Spirit He still appeals
to men and demands their faith.—These works will testify against
the unbeliever in the day of Judgment.—Before them he shall be
found "speechless," and as he would not receive the light the
outer darkness shall be his abode for ever.

---

12. Verily, verily, I say unto you. He that believeth on me, the works that I do
shall he do also; and greater works than these shall he do; because I go unto my
Father.

Verily, verily. See on chap. i. 51.—A formula that has the
solemnity and authority of an oath.

He that believeth. An act which the wisest scholar and the most
illiterate peasant can exercise. Every sane person has the faculty
of believing.—Unbelief of the Gospel is caused not by want of
power but want of will.—The heart (the affections) domineers
over the head (the intellect). *James.*—God's greatest gifts are the
easiest of access.—Faith in itself has no ground of merit, but God
honours it as the medium of His blessings.

On me. Faith not only leads to Christ but so unites the soul to
Him that He becomes all and in all.

The works that I do. Now follows a new series of consolations.—
Not only shall *they* be united to *Him*, but also He to them.
Tholuck.

He do also. Not to be limited to the disciples.—He that by faith
is one with the Son shall have the Son, and therefore also the
Father, dwelling in him.—He shall become an instrument through
which God, who dwelleth in him, shall accomplish His own works.
—He shall therefore do works of the same kind as those which the
Son Himself doeth.—The words express the essential relationship
between the works of believers and the works of Jesus.—They
proclaim the eternal progress of His wonder-works through the
world by means of His Church.

Greater works. Not in degree but in kind: spiritual works, under
the dispensation of the Spirit, soon to be ushered in.—Not as
separate from Him; but in Him, and by Him.—The work which
He did by Peter's sermon (Acts ii.) was one of these, the first
fruits of the unspeakable gift.—" He has sown, we reap; and the
harvest is greater than the seed-time." *Stier.*—He has in view the
greatness of the development of His wondrous works throughout

the Christian ages until the glorification of the world. *Lange.*— The conversion of sinners a greater miracle than the healing of the body. *Godet.*—Fulfilled in every great moral and spiritual victory. —Every revival of a truly religious spirit an instance of it.—Every mission-field a witness to it.—Every child of man brought to know the Father in Him is a work such as He did.—In the world-wide extent of Christianity there is a work greater even than any which He did in the flesh.—He left His kingdom as one of the smallest of the influences on the earth ; but it has grown up a mighty power, and all that is purest and best has found shelter in its branches. *Ellicott.*—The Church of Christ is the greatest miracle ever wrought on earth. *Lessing.*

Because I go unto my Father. This is the reason why the believer shall do the works that Christ does, and also why he shall do greater works.—Believers are His representatives on earth as He is their representative in Heaven.—He will be at the Father's right hand and will do whatsoever they ask in His name.

καὶ μείζονα. The καὶ is climactic : *And even. Lange* – 1. Greater in their numerical superiority ; 2, in their local extension beyond Judæa ; 3, in the more striking signs, such as the healing by the shadow of Peter (Acts v.). *Theod., Herak., Wordsworth.*— In the victories which believers obtain through faith over the world, the flesh, and the devil. *Origen.*—In the results of the preached word in the heathen world. *Augustine.* —" He took but a little corner for Himself, to preach and to work miracles in, and but a little time ; whereas the apostles and their followers have spread themselves through the whole world." *Luther.*—πορεύομαι. Forms the foundation for the idea that they are to do the miracles in His stead, because of His retirement from the scene. *Chrys., Theophylact, and many others.*—Because He goes *to the Father, i.e.,* to glory with the Father and will thence work in them in His might. *Luther, B. Crusius, Luthardt, and others.*—The two considerations are not to be sundered.—His going to the Father, as well as His being with the Father, is the reason for their doing greater miracles. *Grotius, Lücke, and others.*—Both items are more directly emphasized in chap. xvi. 7, in accordance with which our passage is to be explained. *Lange.*—μου. Omitted. *Codd. Sin., A. B. D., &c.*

---

13. And whatsoever ye shall ask in my name, that will I do, that the Father may be glorified in the Son.

Whatsoever ye ask. The matter of petition is limited only by the wants of the soul.—Prayer to the Son is the completion of a believing trust and love.—The " prayer-ladder" not so showy but far more useful than Jacob's.—Since all are lost by sin all are bound to pray.—It is not merely obedience to a divine precept, it is a felt necessity of the soul.—Prayer should be offered to God with a due sense of His Divine Majesty (1 Cor. xiv. 15, 19) ; with a sense of our deep unworthiness, and continual dependence

(Gen. xviii. 27) ; with adoring gratitude and penitential heart (Psa. li. 17) ; with unwavering faith (Heb. xi. 6) ; with perfect sincerity (Psa. cxlv. 18) ; with fervency (James v. 16) ; with love (1 Tim. ii. 8) ; with perseverance (Eph. vi. 18) ; with humble submission to God's holy will (Micah. vii. 7).—The end of prayer is neither to inform the Deity nor seek to change His mind.—He has ordained this *link* between His giving and our need.— Prayer can only be for things agreeable to the Divine will (1 John v. 14, 15).—We must prefer spiritual to temporal mercies (Matt vi. 33).

In my name. This explains His going to the Father, in reference to their power to work miracles.—Their power of prayer is to have no other limit than *His name.*—A name is objectively the *revelation* of any subject, subjectively, *experience of it ;* the *signature* of its consciousness stamped upon the consciousness of others. *Lange.*—Let your faith in My Person become prayer in My Name. —A mere mention in His Name will not avail.—We must *depend upon Him* in connection with the thing asked for.—We must ask for nothing but what is *according to His mind*, in *His interest.*—To pray in *His Name* implies an absolute self-sacrifice, and involves a request that our very prayers may not be answered, except so far as in accordance with God's will.—Thus petitions asked in ignorance may be most truly answered when they are not granted.— For a mere creature to speak in this manner would be the most impious folly ; but it is becoming in Jesus and fits in perfectly with His whole character, life, and claims.—How evident it is that to pray aright we need the influence of the Holy Spirit.

Will I do. A testimony to the consciousness of His divinity.—One of God's names, " O thou that hearest prayer " (Psa. lxv. 2).— When Jehovah answered Elijah's prayer, Israel cried out, " The Lord, he is the God " (1 Kings xviii. 39).—The history of Christ's Church is that of God's wisdom, goodness, and power.—His mercy is often shown not only in delay but in positive denial.—Every earnest, believing prayer is answered, but *in God's own way.*— I will do it as Prince and Saviour unto whom " all power " is committed " in heaven and on earth " (Matt. xxviii. 18).—We have the answer in the soul when complete submission to God's will is the result.—The most precious element in prayer is communion with God.—Better our homes should be without a roof than without an altar.—The only defence for the young exposed to life's perils is prayer.—Parents neglecting prayer seem to challenge Heaven to forsake their children - As all are alienated from God

a Mediator is indispensable.—Our sins are so clamorous for justice
that our prayers, otherwise, would be drowned.

That the Father, &c. See on chap. xi. 4 ; xii. 28 ; xiii. 31.—Glory,
the glory of the Father, the glory of the Father in the Son.

ἐν τῷ ὀνόματί μου. The formal invocation of the Name of Christ. *Chrys.*—In the
name of Him who is called *Salvator (non contra sa'utem nostram)*. *Augustine.*—Me
agnito. *Melanc.*—With faith in Me. *Luther*—Per meritum meum. *Calov.*—In gloriam
Christi. *Erasmus.*—In accordance with My mind and in My cause. *De Wette.*—In
submi sion to My will, and conducive to your own salvation and God's glory. *Wordsworth.*—In union with Me, as being Mine, manifesting forth Jesus as the Son of God.
Alford.—In faith, knowing and confessing Christ. *Lücke.*—Manifestly, the prevailing
thought is the end purposed; hence the predominance of the idea : *as ambassadors of
Christ, the Son of God,* by virtue of His δόξα. *Lange.*—τοῦτο. Stress falls upon this
word —He will do precisely that for which they pray and in such a manner, besides,
that *their* doing in the matter shall be vindicated, their believing, individual personality. *Lange.*

---

14. If ye shall ask any thing in my name, I will do it.

Any thing. An emphatic repetition of the width of the promise
and its condition.

In my name. See on verse 13.—The sum of personality. *Harless.*
—Jesus with all His exalted claims and blessed memories.—To
pray *in His Name* implies our full trust in Him as our great High-
Priest before God, and with a view to the interests of His kingdom.—The full substance of saving faith is confession of Christ.
—This is the element in which the believer's activity lives and
moves.—The *Name* specifically defines the mind of God and controls the praying soul.—To use His Name as if it were a mere
charm is a mockery ; the *spirit* of prayer is the all-important
requisite.— Prayer, as a rule, should be addressed *to* the Father
through the Son, although prayer to Christ is abundantly authorized.—Stephen offered the glorified Lord absolute Divine worship in its highest form, using the very words addressed by Jesus
Himself, on the Cross, to His Father.—Paul besought the Lord
(Jesus) that the thorn in his flesh might be taken away (2 Cor.
xii. 8).—That this was a common practice in the early Church is
evident from Acts ix. 14 ; 1 Cor. i. 2 (see on Matt. i. 22).—Jesus
claims attributes belonging only to Jehovah Himself.—1. He
claims to know all the prayers offered by the myriads of His
people.—2. He claims to know all the designs of the infinite
Father.—3. He claims to know the precise way in which all these
prayers ought to be answered.—4. He claims to know the proper

measure and time for the myriads of answers.—To assure the Church He solemnly reiterates "In My Name."—He knew also that millions would be tempted to idolatry (the Mariolatry and Saint worship of Rome), and hence this repetition which has all the force of a solemn warning.—Prayers to any mere creature must issue in another dreadful prayer, "Rocks and mountains fall on us, and hide us from the wrath of the Lamb" (Rev. vi. 16).

I will do it. "I (on My part) will do it."—In the parallel passages in chap. xv. 16, xvi. 23, the Father is spoken of as answering the prayer.—The transition from one to the other is natural, for the Father and the Son are one.—Who but God, omniscient and omnipresent, could know the prayers that are offered, and who but God omnipotent could answer?

This verse is wanting in X. and a few Minuscles and Versions.—Omitted probably on account of its similarity t·verse 13. *Schaff* — ἐγὼ ποιήσω. Prominence is to be given to the ἐγώ. *Bengel.*—Stress is laid upon the asking in the name of Jesus, the mind, the communion of spirit with Him, and, to correspond with this, upon His doing, as *His* doing. *Lange.*

---

15. If ye love me, keep my commandments.

If ye love me. See on chap. xiii. 34.—The condition, "in my name," includes willing obedience.—Our Lord explains more fully how they are to do greater works in His Name.—Love, an answering dependance of the heart, a principle of life.—It is the end of true prayer and the ground of true faith.—Anything desired must be embraced in His kingdom.—The prayer "Increase our faith" (Luke xvii. 5) becomes "Increase our love."—He promises through prayer the very *works* His law requires.—The law itself becomes a gospel to us through Jesus Christ.—All His commandments are promises to the loving heart.—To love God supremely, an eternal law which binds all beings in His kingdom. —Love ever increasing widens our obedience (Prov. vii. 8).—The law does not *drive* the believer, love *draws*. *Luther.*

Keep. Gr., *keep watch upon, guard*, as a precious treasure.

My commandments. "My" is emphatic.—Those you have received from Me.—"With John, love is no mere blissfulness of feeling; it is *oneness* of will with the beloved." *Tholuck.*—Our Lord exhorts to faith, then to love, then to obedience.—He is about, for the first time, to announce the coming of the Paraclete, and love alone can make them susceptible to His communication.—

Obedience is the fruit and proof of love.—Love is so acceptable to God that it is counted as the fulfilling of the law (Rom. xiii. 10). —Paul affirms that whatever gifts a man may possess without love he is nothing, for the end of the commandment is charity (love) (1 Cor. xiii. ; 1 Tim. i. 5).—Many seem to think they can love God and not keep His commandments; others, that they can keep His commandments and not love Him.—But love and obedience sustain the relation of cause and effect, and the one cannot exist without the other; a moral necessity binds them together in this and in all worlds.

---

16. And I will pray the Father, and he shall give you another Comforter, that he may abide with you for ever.

I will pray. See on chap. xvi. 23.—The pronoun is again emphatic.—"I have given you your part to do: I on my part will pray the Father."—The word used for "pray" implies more of nearness of approach and of familiarity than that rendered "ask" in verse 14.—It is the word John regularly uses when he speaks of our Lord as praying to the Father (chap. xvi. 26 ; xvii. 9, 15, 20). —Our Lord in the days of His flesh offered up "prayers and supplications with strong crying and tears" (Heb. v. 7).—At the grave of Lazarus He said, "Father, I thank thee thou hast heard me. And I know that thou hearest me always" (chap. xi. 41, 42).—The Son of God, the Maker of all things, engaging in prayer.—At one time receiving the honours due to the King of kings, at another a suppliant.—He pledges His all-powerful intercession as our exalted and glorified Lord.

Another. "Another," implying the advocacy of the second Person in the Trinity, as well as that of the third.

Comforter. Used of the Holy Spirit here, and in verse 26, and in chap. xv. 26 ; xvi. 7.—In each of these instances it is used by our Lord.—Found once again in the New Test., and is there applied by John to Christ Himself (1 John ii. 1).—In His office as Mediator He will obtain another Comforter for them.—This is the first distinct announcement of this "Comforter."—He had intimated that the Holy Spirit was one of the best gifts (Luke xi. 13). —Our Lord implies we need a Helper ; just such an one as Himself.—Though leaving the world He will continue His gracious help through another.—Ask thyself, reader, whether thou dost not need such a Helper.—The deeper their love for their departing Lord the greater their loss and the greater their need.—This is the grand promise of the New Test., as the Messiah was of the Old.

Abide. The acts of the three Persons in the Trinity, asking, giving, abiding.—Since the hour the Spirit was fully given, the Church has never been without His presence.—Even in the darkest times there were those who had not bowed the knee to the Baal of superstition.—Some Christians have so represented the work of the Spirit as to make man a mere machine.—In the Scriptures such extremes are ever avoided.—On the human side we are to work out our salvation with fear and trembling.—On the divine side, it is God that worketh in us to will and to do of His good pleasure (Phil. ii. 12, 13).—It is because of the latter that we are encouraged and commanded to do the former.—The thought of the *abiding* is opposed to the separation pending between them and their Lord.—He would come again to them in the person of the Comforter, and this spiritual presence should never be withdrawn. —It involves essentially eternal communion with God in Christ through the Spirit.—A divine gift of which God will never repent. —You shall never mourn His departure as you will do Mine.

ἐρωτήσω This word implies that he who asks stands on a certain equality with him from whom the boon is asked, as King with King (Luke xiv. 32), or, if not equality, on such a footing of familiarity as I nds autho it to the request. *Trench* (see note on chap. xvi. 23).—παρακλητον is according to classical Greek usage, one who is summoned to help; in particular. an *advocate*, one who manages another's cause or an intercessor. *Meyer.* —Must not be taken in the narrow sense of a legal advocate or pleader, but in the more general sense of *counsellor, helper, patron. Knapp.*—The idea of *Comforter* must be added to that of *advocate.*—A comforter is a *spiritual* Helper.—Unfortunately, we have no single word co-extensive in signification. *Schaff.*—One who performs all that which a *Counsel* or *Representative* being at the same time an *Adviser.* can perform for us. *Stier.*—Combines the idea of *help* and *strength* with that of *consolation.* Olshausen, *Alford*—Combines the id a of *He p r* with that of *Mediator:* a *Representative. Lange.* —The English rendering *Comforter* is derived rom Wickliff, who often used it in the sense of the Latin *comfortari,* so as to combine the idea of *help* and *strength* with that of *consolation. Hare*—Instead of μένῃ, read ῇ. *Cod. Sin., Lach., Tisch., Alford, Lange, Schaff.*

17. Even the Spirit of truth ; whom the world cannot receive, because it seeth him not, neither knoweth him : but ye know him ; for he dwelleth with you, and shall be in you

The Spirit of truth. Gr., " of *the* truth."—The Holy Ghost is the living, personal, divine unity of complete revelation.—It is His special office to bring home truth to the hearts of men.—The words of Christ Himself without this Spirit are dead, but become life-giving through Him.—He enlightens us to receive the truth, confirms our faith in it, and increases our love of it.—Without the Spirit the highest scholarship and the mightiest reason will fail to comprehend the truth.—Unhappily there is a love of falsehood and deceit in the heart of man.—Hence the necessity of regeneration by the Spirit of truth.—Guided by this Divine teacher the humblest Christian may enter the holiest of all and behold the face of God in truth.—The Spirit makes *objective* truth *subjective* in the believer, in order to the knowledge of truth.—He it is who applies the full truth of the perfect revelation of God in Christ.

The world cannot receive. He can be received only by those who have the spiritual faculty.—The world caring only for the things of sense has lost spiritual perception.—It has neither eyes to see nor heart to know the things of God.—All experience shows that devotion to the world shuts out heavenly truth from the soul.— With the promise of the Spirit the Lord clearly draws the line between the Church and the world.—Many in these days are trying to obliterate that line.—But the world will love its own and them only.—It will never be won by a half-and-half religion ; for, though it may smile, in its secret heart it regards all such professors with contempt and scorn.

It seeth him not, &c. In His manifestation, for it lacks the eye of faith.—It lacks experience of the Holy Ghost.—It does not even see the One God above the world, much less the oneness of His manifestation in the world.—*Seeing* in nature appropriates the beauty and glory of things.—"I am a part of all I have seen." *Tennyson.*—Men saw Christ raise the dead, and yet saw not His divine character.—Though in the world, to the world He remains unknown.

Ye know him. As opposed to the moral blindness of the world.— He speaks of the future as if present, inasmuch as they had commenced to recognize the Spirit in Christ.—They had already begun to have an experimental knowledge of Him.—They had in part received the Spirit, and by that were prepared for the fuller gift.—Every divine blessing is a pledge and foretaste of something greater.—As the bud contains in itself the flower and the fruit.

Dwelleth in you, &c. He was then, and should be in the future, a living power.—He will not relinquish His activity among them, until He comes in all His influences to abide in them.—"Since His abode is in the midst of them in the Christian Communion." *Meyer.*—The greatest wonder on earth this condescending love of God.—The Spirit dwells in the soul as the sap in the tree.—This ineffable gift, called "the hidden manna," and "the white stone" (Rev. ii. 17).—This the test of Christian character: Does the Spirit dwell in us, our light, our life, our comfort?

18. I will not leave you comfortless: I will come to you.

Comfortless. Gr., *orphans.*—Fatherless. *Wickliff.*—Believers are
the kindred of Christ: children of God in Him who is the eternal
Son.—Renouncing the world a wide gulf between them and it was
set.—For Christ's sake believers have left father and mother, &c.
—He is about to leave them in an unfriendly, evil world.—The
Greek word, in classic use, embraces every kind of destitution.—
Oft in sorrow yet never comfortless.—Not orphans even in Christ's
departure.—The Gospel abounds in tenderest consolation to
mourners.—To those like Mary, "They have taken away my Lord,
and I know not where they have laid Him."—No sorrow like that
which springs from a sense of the absence of Christ.—He sometimes withdraws His presence as a chastisement, but it is an
evidence of His love (Heb. xii.).

I will come to you. Gr., *I am coming.*—His spiritual presence in
the person of the Comforter.—He says *I am coming* lest they
should think the Spirit was exclusively to take His place.—It is
the Comforter's office to take of the things of Jesus and show
them to the believer (chap. xvi. 14).—By revealing Christ and
the Father in Him the Spirit comforts.—From the time the Spirit
was given, Christ lived in them, and His heart beat in them.—
Thus Christ is ever with His people, though while "in the body
they are absent from the Lord" (2 Cor. v. 6).—When friends
part it is said, "Let us hear often from you;" therefore this precious promise is given.—I go not away from you so as to leave
you orphans; on the contrary, it is now that I do really come
unto you.—The Apostolic writings and the history of the Church,
show how truly this was fulfilled.—His presence was bodily and
therefore local; but after His ascension it was spiritual and
universal.—Doubtless this glorious coming extends on to His
Second Advent, the consummation of all His comings.

ἔρχομαι. Christ's Parousia itself. *Aug., Bede, Luthardt, Hofmann.*—The manifestation subsequent to the resurrection. *Origen, Chrys., Rupert, Grotius, Ewald.*—Christ's
spiritual coming through the Paraclete. *Calvin, Lücke, Olsh., Thol., Godet, Meyer, &c.*—
Christ had in view both His spiritual and His corporeal return. *Luther, Beza, Lampe,
Hengst., Ebrard, De Wette, Lange, Schaff, &c.*

---

19. Yet a little while, and the world seeth me no more; but ye see me: because I live,
ye shall live also.

A little while. See on chap. xiii. 33.—From now until the moment
of His death less than twenty-four hours elapsed.

The world, &c. To the world the grave seemed the closing scene. —They thought of Him as dead.—He made no manifestation of Himself to the world after His resurrection.

Ye see me. They saw the Risen Lord with the bodily eye, and by the Spirit they saw Him in His Divine nature and glory.— " Faith is the substance of things hoped for ; the evidence of things not seen " (Heb. xi. 1).—By faith we see the crucified One enthroned as our King.—The promise, " Lo, I am with you," has been abundantly verified.—Saints living and dying have been more conscious of the presence of Jesus than of that of the dearest earthly friend.—The testimony of millions to this effect, including persons of every grade, age, clime and tongue, places the truth of the Gospel beyond all question and doubt.—Paul describes his own conversion as a revelation of the Son of God in him (Gal. i. 15, 16).—By faith we see Christ ever interceding for us before His Father.

Because I live. Gr., *for I live and ye shall live.*—Our Lord speaks of His own life in the present.—Essential life of which He is the source and which death cannot affect (see on chap. i. 4).—Expresses His Divine vital power, and is the reason of the preceding " Ye see me."—His death and burial, mere shadows passing over the Sun of Righteousness.—To John in Patmos: " I am He that liveth, and was dead ; and, behold, I am alive for evermore " (Rev. i. 18).

Ye shall live. Believers have even here this principle of life which no change can affect (see on chap. vi.).—His resurrection a pledge of blessed eternal life.—The highest state of spiritual life attainable here is not to be compared with the " fulness of life " to be enjoyed hereafter (1 Cor. ii. 9).—The vine imparts life to all the branches vitally united with it; a picture of the union between Christ and His people (see on chap. xv. 1).—In the eye of God believers never die ; what is called death is but a change of place and state.—All worth the name of life lives on, for it is Christ who lives in them both here and hereafter.—You shall share My life on to its eternal perfection in glory.—" Thou king of terrors, thou mayest slay my Lord Christ ; but thou must restore Him, and be destroyed by Him.—Thou mayest destroy me, but I live immortal in Him." *Luther.*—All other arguments for immortality are mere shadows compared with this living Word.—How this Word should wipe away our tears.

ὅτι ἐγὼ ζῶ. On these assuring words of Christ, Schleiermacher, in the touching funeral discourse on his only son, despairing of all philosophical arguments for the immortality of the soul, firmly placed his hope and trust for a future life. *Schaff.*

20. At that day ye shall know that I am in my Father, and ye in me, and I in you.

At that day. The day of the coming of Christ to them by the Spirit.—True also of every spiritual quickening, and of the final coming in the last day.

Ye shall know. A knowledge that is of the Spirit's operation by faith.—The *experience* of the truth gives a far deeper and more convincing *knowledge* than can be obtained by sense or the understanding.

I am in the Father. See on verses 10, 11, and on chap. x. 38.— The Spirit reveals the life of Christ to the heart, and the believer sees in it the manifestation of the Father.—Here again our Lord repeats the grand truth of His oneness with the Father.—This oneness gives to each promise and each act the character and glory of a divine reality.—Those worship not as Christians who do not worship the Father in Christ.—What salvation for a sinner without an atonement ?—What efficacy in an atonement if the Atoner be not Divine ?—As the bones sustain the body, so Doctrine is the strength of faith.—A faith which does not proceed from true Christian doctrine can never be a true, saving faith.

Ye in me. And, therefore, those who have received a new life.— They would feel that in and through the life of Christ their own spirit had communion with God.—They would seek no longer for a manifestation from without, for they would have Christ dwelling in them, " the hope of glory."—As if He had said : Your life is My life, your cause is Mine.—So if God takes care of me, He will take care of you.—The believer is spiritually one with Christ in all things ; in suffering and in glory (Rom. viii. 17).—Christ's life, ours ; Christ's death, ours ; Christ's resurrection, ours ; Christ's ascension, ours ; Christ's throne, ours (Rev. iii. 21).— Believers are in Christ through the Holy Ghost, because Christ is in them by means of the spirit of His glorified life. *Lange.*

ἐκείνῃ τῇ ἡμέρᾳ. Its historical fulfilment was the day of Pentecost. *Meyer.*—The day of the Parousia. *Luthardt.*—In that time. *De Wette.*—Reference to His resurrection. *Bengel.*—Spiritual experiences. *Alford, Tholuck, &c.*

---

21. He that hath my commandments, and keepeth them, he it is that loveth me : and he that loveth me shall be loved of my Father, and I will love him, and will manifest myself to him.

He that hath. Points out the degrees which led up to the full maniestaton of Christ.—*Hath,* as bread eaten becomes a part of ourselves—enters into our life.

My commandments. The moral law, which is summed up in the love of God and our neighbour, is binding for ever.—Christ came not to *destroy* the law but to *fulfil.*—He claims that the commands given in Sinai, with all the dread accompaniments described in Exodus xx., are *His.*

Keepeth them. The proof of *having* them as a living possession is the *keeping* of them.—And that shall be the mark of *love* to Jesus.—Ye think to show your love to me by sorrow for my departure; but keeping my commandments is a far greater proof of love.—Not those who give the most in gold and silver, in tears and words, but those who with the heart obey in self-sacrificing love. —Here lies the secret of the marvellous attainments of the earnest disciple of Jesus.—With Him as the Teacher, and the Holy Spirit as the Sanctifier, the humble soul makes wonderful progress in divine things.—This is the key to the victories of Christians in every age.—An obedient heart opens the door of heaven to the believer, he abides in the secret place of the Most High, and can do or suffer as his Lord ordains.

He it is that loveth me. *He,* and he only.—Love inspires delight in pleasing the loved one, while that which displeases gives keenest pain.—Here is the principle of Christian holiness in its highest form.—Wherever love to Jesus exists in a soul, that love will show itself in doing the things that are well-pleasing in His sight, and in this it finds its heaven.—And no grief, no pain on earth, not even that which comes from the loss of the nearest and dearest of kin, is so deep and poignant, as that which the thought of having sinned against the Lord causes to the loving soul.—The keeping of the commandments of Christ springs necessarily from love to Him, and love to Him necessarily produces this obedience. —It is a *law;* deep, universal, unalterable, eternal.

Loved of my Father. The Father loveth the Son, and loves all who love Him.—*We* love those who love our beloved.—Love to the Son is that whereupon experience of the Father's love depends.—As objects near to the sun become *sun-like,* so the Father's love transforms all loving His Son into that Son's image.

I will love him. The *special* love of the Son follows from the *special* love of the Father.

Manifest myself. And this manifestation through the Spirit will supply and overbalance the wonted, actual, and visible presence of Jesus.—In this great word the Lord promises " all the fulness of God " (Eph. ii. 19).—This singularly glorious reward of our love to Christ is our wealth (1 Cor. i. 5).—Beyond this, neither promise nor hope has anything higher or greater to offer or expect.

—But only souls born of God can receive these heavenly mysteries, and to them only are they "exceeding great and precious" (2 Pet. i. 4).

---

22. Judas saith unto him, not Iscariot, Lord, how is it that thou wilt manifest thyself unto us, and not unto the world?

Judas saith. Thaddæus or Lebbæus (Matt. x. 3; Luke vi. 16).
Not Iscariot. To distinguish him from all possibility of confusion with the traitor.—That wretch had gone out into the darkness, and was no longer of their number (chap. xiii. 30).—John brings into view the contrast between the malignant Judas who had despaired of his Master's cause, and this other Judas who is even now conceiving of his Lord as certain of victory over the world.—There is no record of Iscariot having ever asked Jesus a single question.
How is it? What has happened? what is the reason?—They thought that Messiah must manifest Himself to the whole world in His judicial glory.—Carnal expectations prevented them understanding the spiritual nature of our Lord's words.—They mistook the testimony of prophecy, and hence stumbled at what He had just said.—These questions were, however, overruled for good by our Lord taking occasion to make His answer a further unfolding of truth.
To us, *i.e.*, to a few persons only.—Doubtless also the idea of their low estate was in his mind.—Believers, sensible of their unworthiness, often ask, "Why was *I* made to hear Thy voice?"
And not to the world. Never before had He so plainly renounced the world.—His words had perplexed them; they were unable to reconcile them with the prevalent belief of Messiah's reign over the Gentiles, and the establishment of the Theocracy.—Yet Jesus is King of the world, and the world is to be subdued to His authority.—The *world* which is excluded from His manifestation is a world of spiritual darkness and unbelief, that will not come to the light, but hateth it.

---

23. Jesus answered and said unto him, If a man love me, he will keep my words: and my Father will love him, and we will come unto him, and make our abode with him.

Jesus answered. At first His answer seems to be a repetition of what had appeared so unintelligible.—Our Lord's answers, like

His words generally, have a meaning and a range far beyond the mere local application.

If a man love me. He reaffirms the condition on which the manifestation of God to a man is possible.—This is His answer to Judas; for the world in its rejection of His words, and destitute of the spirit of love, could not receive this manifestation.

He will keep my words. See on verse 21.—Love is faith in action. —Love and self-sacrifice are inseparable.—He might have said, He who loves Me. and therefore keeps My words, is the one who believes on Me.—The Word of God knows nothing of love without faith, and nothing of faith without love.—Faith works by love and purifies the heart (Acts xv. 9).—Faith is an act of trust, and love is the effect and evidence of this *unseen* relation of the soul.—Here we perceive the harmony between the teaching of Paul on the subject of *faith*, and the teaching of James on the subject of *works*.—Faith and theology are not the same ; for faith and love may co-exist with much ignorance of theology.—Faith has respect to Christ as a personal, living, loving Redeemer— "faith that is in ME" (Acts xxvi. 18).—"My *word*," the Greek is in the singular; "My *word*" in its wholeness and entirety.—The unity of revelation, an evidence of inspiration.—"The Scripture cannot be broken" (see on chap. x. 35).—Unbelievers, and especially those calling themselves "Liberals," *do* endeavour to break the Scripture—We are not to choose and pick as may please ourselves : "All Scripture is given by inspiration of God, and is profitable," etc. (2 Tim. iii. 16).—Much of the inconsistency and weakness of Christians in our day may be traced to their neglect of Scripture *as a whole.*—"*He will keep my word,*" implies personal appropriation and love.

My Father will love him. See on verse 21, where Jesus makes a similar declaration concerning those who keep His commandments.

We will come unto him. See on chap. x. 30.—The Father comes with the Son, by means of the Paraclete.—The manifestation of Christ is the glorification of the Father through the Son, and of the Son with the Father through the Spirit.—The Father will manifest Himself through the Son, the Son through the Holy Ghost.—" They *come* to us in that we *go* to Them ; They *come* by *succouring*, we *go* by *obeying;* They *come* by *enlightening*, we *go* by *contemplating;* They *come* by *filling*, we *go* by *holding:* so Their manifestation is not *external* but *inward*: Their abode is not *transitory* but *eternal.*" *Hilary.*

Make our abode. God dwelling in His sanctuary and among His people, a thought familiar to the disciples (Ex. xxv. 8; xxix. 45;

Lev. xxvi. 11; Ezek. xxxvii. 26).—" Despise not the meanest human being who loves Jesus; meet such with reverence; his soul is a dwelling-place of the Triune God." *Luther.*—They come to us; not as to a wedding or on a visit, but to dwell in us; and so we are the temple of God. *Cramer.*—The theocratic idea is realized in a glorious manner when God thus dwells among His people.—" I heard a great voice out of heaven saying, Behold the tabernacle of God is with men," &c. (Rev. xxi. 3.)

With him. Not merely *in* him; They found a community, a place where the Triune God manifests Himself and which forms a contrast to the world.—The Spirit is not only *in* the faithful, He is *with* them as well.—He forms a fellowship of believers, the Church.—This is the real Shekinah. *Lange.*

μονὴν παρ' αὐτῷ. "Since therefore God invisibly enters into the region of the soul, let us prepare that place, in the best way the case admits of, to be an abode worthy of God; for if we do not, He, without our being aware of it, will quit us and migrate to some other habitation which shall appear to Him more excellently provided." *Philo,* " *De Cherubim.*"

---

24. He that loveth me not keepeth not my sayings: and the word which ye hear is not mine, but the Father's which sent me.

Loveth me not. Characteristic of the world.—The world, as an ungodly world, loves itself.—This explains how there can be no manifestation to the world (see on verse 22).—The eternal unfitness of the heart, for Christ abiding, is here declared.—There is no sadder word in the Bible for a gospel hearer.—The great heart of Jesus seems to throb with sorrow as He utters it.—As He is altogether lovely and infinitely good, why does any one *not* love Him?—It is because a sense of guilt makes the sinner ever dread the thought of so holy a Being.—And this prevents the sinner from reflecting upon Christ's character and claims.—As at the first, He was in this world, but the world cared not to know Him, so it is now.

Keepeth not my sayings, &c. The world lacks the bond that should hold it and Christ together, the Spirit.—In failing to keep Christ's words it also fails to keep the Father's word.—Thus the condition to receive the manifestation of God is wanting.—He who rejects the love of the Father revealed in the Son has himself closed the channels of communion with God.—God cannot dwell with him, because there is nothing in such an one receptive of the Divine presence.—He who keeps not the word of Christ rejects not only the Son but the Father who sent Him.—There can be no obedience without love, and no love without obedience.

25. These things have I spoken unto you, being yet present with you.

Have I spoken. *I have spoken it*, it shall be certain.—He seems about to rise from the table and end His sayings. *Tholuck.*—He well knew they were slow of heart to understand.—With untiring patience, with line upon line, He goes on.—The exclusion of the world from Divine manifestation appeared to them a hard saying.—It is still a stumbling-block and an offence to many.—" *These things,*" *i.e.,* thus much ye can understand now through My words.—He had spoken of the heavenly life on earth as the sign of the heavenly home beyond this world.

Being yet present with you. *While abiding with you.*—He was about to depart from them.—He had been speaking words which they found it hard to understand.—But now He pauses to tell them of the Holy Spirit, the Divine Interpreter of His words.—At some future time the Paraclete would make all perfectly clear.

---

26. But the Comforter, which is the Holy Ghost, whom the Father will send in my name, he shall teach you all things, and bring all things to your remembrance, whatsoever I have said unto you.

But the Comforter, &c. See on verse 16, and on chap i. 33.—The different predicates are summed up together : The Paraclete—the Holy Ghost—whom the Father sends—in the Name of Jesus. *Lange.*

In my name. See on verse 13.—As My representative.—His NAME, the sphere of the Spirit's operations in the world.—A test by which to try all professed experiences and revelations.—All such that are *not* in the Name of Jesus, *i.e.,* which do not testify of Him according to the Word of God, are delusions of the evil one.—*His Name,* the only source of power with God, the only source of holy influence on Man. *Owen.*—Through the Spirit confession is made of *His Name* in the world.—" No man can say that Jesus is the Lord, but by the Holy Ghost " (1 Cor. xii. 3).—By the Spirit, all the issues of redemption proceed to perfect consummation and glory.—The object of God's intent and design is the Name of Jesus.—Here the emphatic words are : *In My name* and *what I have said unto you. Luther.*

Teach you all things. Proximately the reference is to the subject of the heavenly home, the heavenly goal ; but includes also all fulness of Christian knowledge regarding the whole plan of salvation.—" *All things* " here equal to " *all truth* " in the later passages.—The Apostles had *special* Divine Inspiration while it was needed.—Like God's works in all forms of life, this inspiration is a mystery.—As the spirit of man at the first came from the breath of God so this inspiration is a *Divine inbreathing* also (Gen ii. 7 ; 2 Tim. iii. 16).—Not *new* truths, or even *supplementary* ones ; still less not such as shall take the place of those taught by Christ, or correct or contradict them.—The Spirit's teaching consists in reminding of the word of Christ, and giving insight into its meaning.—The heart is closed against heavenly things till opened by the Spirit to receive them (Acts xvi. 14).—Even the Word of God is a dead letter till the quickening influence of the Spirit makes it a living power in the soul.

Remembrance. See on chap. ii. 17.—Every wholesome hint to *remember* is of the grace of the Spirit. *Augustine.*—Our weakness or our sinfulness makes it necessary that we should have such help.

Whatsoever I have said. This promise of the Lord to the Apostles is a guarantee of their inspiration, and of their sufficiency and authority as witnesses and expounders of the truth.—Abundantly testified by their writings, which carry in themelves their own best evidence ; as the shining sun proves his existence to all but the blind.—A complete answer to Romanists as to their claim of an additional and co-ordinate rule of faith in tradition.—Their modern dogmas of the Immaculate Conception of Mary and the Infallibility of the Pope, have not a shadow of foundation in the New Testament.—Of themselves the Apostles were altogether incapable of conceiving such heavenly, sublime truths as appear in their writings. —Till after the Day of Pentecost they were very imperfectly acquainted with Gospel facts and doctrines.—To reproduce and unfold the words of Jesus, according to *His* mind, demanded the agency of Him who " searcheth all things, yea, the deep things of God " (1 Cor. ii. 10).—The Gospel of John, with its full records of the words spoken by our Lord, is itself a commentary on this text.—For instances of the recurrence of words which have a fulness of new meaning revealed in them by the Spirit, comp. chap. ii. 22 ; xii. 16.

τῷ ὀνόματί μου. At My intercession. *Grotius, Lücke, &c.*—Instead of Me.—As the representative of Me in My character as Ambassador. *Euth. Zigabenus, &c.*—The name of Jesus is the sphere containing the divine purpose and will which are to be accomplished by the sending. *Meyer.*—Since the name is the subjective knowledge of an objective manifestation, the sense is : In the knowledge of Christ, perfected through the perfect manifestation of Christ. *Lange.*—πάντα. The first πάντα says that every one of Christ's words shall attain its full development ; hence it refers to the infinite import or capability of development belonging to His words.—The second πάντα declares that none of the words of Christ shall be lost, that they all, as items of His doctrine, shall become operative. *Lange.*—ἃ εἶπον ὑμῖν. This limitation is to be taken with this claim only, and is not to be extended to the words διδάξει πάντα. *Ellicott.*—He shall teach you all things, whilst He brings all things that I have told you, to your remembrance.—The καὶ is explicative. *Schaff.*

27. Peace I leave with you, my peace I give unto you: not as the world giveth, give to you. Let not your heart be troubled, neither let it be afraid.

Peace I leave with you. Like the common Oriental form of leave-taking (1 Sam. i. 17; Luke vii. 50; Acts xvi. 36).—The farewell greeting of Christ to His people. *Neander.*—Last words, as of one who, on the eve of departure, says good-night or invokes a blessing. *Luther.*—Has a deeper meaning; it is the peace of re-conciliation Jesus speaks of. *Tholuck.*—The Gospel blessing with all its immortal hopes.—This gift is the pledge of heavenly rest and blessedness.

My peace I give. He repeats it with the emphatic "My," and speaks of it as an actual possession which He imparts.—This is the Lord's legacy to His people.—He knew they dreaded the fierce trials which should follow His leaving them.—Hence He addresses Himself to calm their perturbed spirit.—Jehovah is often called "the God of peace."—"The Lord will bless His people with peace" (Psa. xxix. 11).—"The mountains shall bring peace" (Psa. lxxii. 3).—The end of the upright is peace (Psa. xxxvii. 37). —The closing word in the Aaronic blessing, "The Lord lift up His countenance upon thee and give thee peace" (Num. vi. 26). —The believer is the subject of the Prince of peace (Isa. ix. 6).— "Being justified by faith we have peace with God" (Rom. v. 1).— The *law* of Christ's kingdom ever works for peace.—"Peace on Earth;" the angels' song at his birth.—He pronounced, "Blessed are the peacemakers," &c.—He says of the officers of His king-dom, "I will make them peace" (Isa. lx. 17).—In the new earth there shall be "no more sea": the sea, the well-known emblem of restlessness and tumult (Rev. xxi. 1).—This legacy of peace infinitely more prized by myriads than crowns of gold.—His words fall upon the heart like morning sunshine after a night of dark-ness and tempest, or as the calm glory of the starry heavens when they look down upon the battlefields of earth.—"*My* peace," the peace of Jesus, *the peace* which He obtained by His blood.—By sin man is at war with himself, his neighbour, and his god.—The only peace therefore which sinful man can ever receive is that which flows from the Lord's death.—It is *the peace* which cost Jesus His agony and bloody sweat, His Cross and passion.—But it is *perfect peace;* for His mediatorial work is complete, finished, everlasting.—As the adopted children we are made partakers of peace similar to that which reigns in the breast of the Son of God, our Elder Brother.

Not as the world giveth. This is not the kind of legacy ordinarily left by the world, or desired by man.—He gives not land, or houses, or gold, yea, He often gives poverty; but He gives "the peace of God which passeth all understanding."—Outward circumstances may be perplexing ; the lot of the believer may be " great tribulation," but deeper and mightier than all troubles is the peace of God which rules his heart.—The world gives as it greets, in a vain and empty way.—" At the start the world with its greeting promises golden mountains ; coldly and heartlessly it takes leave of its servants, and prepares them an end full of terrors.—It fared literally thus with Judas.—*Christ makes a warm and comforting farewell greeting the forerunner of the beatific salutation which shall accompany the eternal meeting." Lange.*—The world's peace, like Satan's "kingdoms," a mockery (Matt. iv. 8).—It cries, " Peace! peace! when there is no peace " (Jer. vi. 14).—It heals the hurt of sin, as some parents try to hush a hurt child by offering sweetmeats.—It talks of serene skies even at the moment when the thundercloud of heaven's wrath is gathering.—Its teachers eulogise sinful pleasures and speak lightly of "the things of God."—Deluded into tranquillity, the foolish heart says, "Take thine ease ; eat, drink, and be merry," when God has said, "This night thy soul shall be required of thee."—The willingness of mankind to be deceived in respect to their immortal interests, an overwhelming proof that Satan is "the prince of the world."—Christ's peace is beyond the reach of the world, either to give or take away.—Its presence as certainly witnesses for the indwelling of God, as light witnesses to the sun.—It spreads a sweet and blessed sense of confidence and rest which never can be defined ; it must be felt.—Hence, "it passeth all understanding," for it is one of "the things of the Spirit," which can only be known by His grace working in the soul.—*Peace;* the whole *salvation* of man, his *re-establishment* into final perfect external and internal *well-being. Stier.*

Let not your heart be troubled. A repetition of the exhortation in verse 1 (see note).—Having His peace, having the Comforter, having the Father and the Son abiding with them, there is no ground for trouble even though He is about to leave them.

Neither let it be afraid. The Greek word rendered "be afraid " occurs nowhere else in the New Testament.—It points especially to the cowardice of fear.—Peter's fall an abiding warning against this kind of cowardice.—"If God be for us, who can be against us ? " (Rom. viii. 31).—Nevertheless, "Keep thy heart with all diligence ; for out of it are the issues of life " (Prov. iv. 23).

εἰρήνη. In the sense of *prosperity,* like the Hebrew *Shalom,* but so as to include the peace of redemption as the first essential element. *Meyer.*—A farewell salutation, but includes *peace of soul* likewise. *Lange.*—οὐ καθὼς. Refers to the *manner of giving*. *Alford, Godet.*—A reference to the empty formulas of worldly greeting entirely out of p'ace in the solemnity of this moment. *Meyer.*—δειλιάτω. He views the *trembling* as a natural emotion that might seize them at the thought of a hopeless parting, while in uttering the δειλιάτω His mind is contemplating the danger of a cowardly course of conduct proceeding from that emotion. *Lange.*—Though this is the only place this word occurs in the N.T., it is often met with in the Sept.—δειλός, *timid, fearful*, occurs Matt. viii. 26; Mark iv. 40; Rev. xxi. 8. *Schaff.*—It refers to the *extrinsic* fear, ταρασσ. to the *intrinsic. Bengel.*

---

28. Ye have heard how I said unto you, I go away, and come again unto you. If ye loved me, ye would rejoice, because I said, I go unto the Father: for my Father is greater than I.

Ye have heard, &c. See on verses 19, 20.—Gr., *Ye heard how I said unto you.*—A hint that they had not heard aright.

I go away, &c. Explanatory of the farewell just uttered : "Peace," &c.—" My peace," &c.—By going away I come to you more truly than ever.—As *man* He went, as God He remained with them in the power of the Spirit.

If ye loved me. True love seeks another's good, not its own.— Selfishness was at the root of their sorrow.—So is all sorrow for those who "die in the Lord," however little we may think it so.— He makes their love to *Him* a motive of comfort to *them.*

Rejoice. Had they loved Him more spiritually they would have rejoiced at the prospect of His abiding spiritual presence.—" Love begets joy, both of itself, and because it keeps the word of Christ, which opens up all the most joyful prospects." *Bengel.*—Our Lord does not mean that they would not be in the least affected with grief at His departure, but that the joy of faith would overcome it.—What they should chiefly think of is His triumphal return to His Father.—A caution against overmuch sorrow when our beloved ones go to be for ever with the Lord.—Their entire thought was fixed upon the loss they were soon to suffer.—His resurrection banishes all our dark forebodings about the grave.— His triumph over death changes the tomb into a place of glory.— He who now abides "in the midst of the throne" is our brother as well as our Lord.—It is our humanity that sits at the Father's right hand, wielding the sceptre of universal power and wearing the crown.

My Father is greater than I. How strange for any man, prophet, or apostle to say that God is greater than he!—We feel at once that He who really said these words claimed for Himself that He was *very God.*—Here, however, as elsewhere in the New Test., it is asserted that in the divine nature there is a subordination of the Son to the Father (verse 16 chap. xvii. 5; 1 Cor. iii. 23; xi. 3;

xv. 27,.28 ; Phil. ii. 9, 11).—We must remember also that our Lord speaks these words as the battling and suffering Messiah from His state of Humiliation, which was to cease with His departure to the Father (see note).

μείζων. Expresses the ἀγεννησία of the Father in antithesis to the begottenness or eternal generation of the Son. *Athanasius, Greg. Naz., Hilary, Euthym. Zigab., Olshausen.*—The superiority of the Father has reference to the *human* nature of Christ, because it is in this alone that He *goes* to the Father. *Hunnius, Gerhard, Webster and Wilkinson,*—Refers to Christ's state of humiliation. *Cyril, Luther, Wordsworth, Calvin, Melancthon, Beza, Bengel. De Wette. Luthardt, Brückner, Stier, Alford, Barnes, Owen, &c.*—We must grasp at once the theological import and the Christological one, for there is a good reason why the *Son* of God became man and humbled Himself—not the *Father.* —Theological y considered, the Father is greater than the Son, as the first principle, *in respect of order or succession,* by whom the Son was established both being perfectly equal in substance.—Hence it follows that He is greater in *substance* also than Christ in His human nature ; and, above all, greater in regard to the *rule* or *power* which He exercises, than is Christ in His humiliation.—And it is upon this latter circumstance that the stress here lies. *Lange, Meyer, Ellicott.*—The Father's *official* superiority. *Schaff.*—ἐχάρητε ἄν. On account of His exaltation to glory and blessedness. *Cyril, Olsh., Tholuck.*—On account of the more powerful protection He should thenceforth be able to bestow upon the disciples. *Theoph., Lücke, &c.*—On account of Jesus' exaltation to greater power and activity. *Meyer.*—Because the going away of Jesus was His own exaltation and was likewise of benefit to them. *Luther, Bengel, Lampe.*—Through His exaltation alone He should in very deed become their own. *Lange.* – εἶπον. Omitted. *Cod, Sin, &c.*

---

29. And now I have told you before it come to pass, that, when it is come to pass, ye might believe.

I have told you before. See on chap. xiii. 19 —He has told them the event before the accomplishment that it may strengthen their faith.—Prophecy is like miracles, a proof of the divine power and presence (Isa. xli. 22, 26).—A frequent custom with the Lord to tell His disciples such and such things beforehand.—Here not the mere announcement of His death, but of His exaltation by means of His death, resurrection, and ascension.—Includes also what He had told them of the coming of the Paraclete.—Prophecies fulfilled in the past confirm faith as to those still future.—Prophecy an everlasting witness to the truth of Scripture.

Believe. See on chap. i. 7 ; xiii. 19.—A faith not *new* but only enlarged ; a faith failing at His death, but renewed at His resurrection. *Augustine.*—Every word of the Lord is intended to establish our faith, as it is by faith we live.—In seasons of darkness we should call to mind " the days of the right hand of the Most High" (Psa. lxxvii. 10).—The remembrance of Divine faithfulness in the past should stimulate and strengthen our confidence· " For this God is our God for ever and ever : He will be our guide even unto death" (Psa. xlviii. 14).—Promises fulfilled become the soul's ladder to ascend to higher and greater things. *Flavel.*

---

30. Hereafter I will not talk much with you: for the prince of this world cometh, and hath nothing in me.

Hereafter, &c. A presentiment of departure.—The discourse is broken by the thought that the hour of conflict is at hand.

The prince of this world. See on chap. xii. 31.—A dark mysterious being would cross His path.—The entrance of evil into the universe an abyss of mystery none can fathom.—It still remains, and must for ever in this world remain, an insoluble problem.—Blessed be God! He has provided the means for its removal—What wonderful calmness the Lord manifests ; how unlike to our poor fallen humanity.—One moment serenely comforting His distressed disciples; the next, facing with undisturbed dignity the greatest foe in the universe.—He betrays not a shadow of doubt as to whom victory would crown.—He passes from the unclouded glory of heaven to the midnight of Satan's approach with the majesty of a God.—The disciples had fondly hoped that their Master would be "Prince of this world," and now they learn that there is another, and he a foe.—Satan has myriads of subjects now on earth ; but Christ will yet bind the usurper and cast him into the eternal darkness (Rev. xx. 1, 2, 10).—For He and He alone is the Prince of this world by right and inheritance and the eternal decree of the Father (Heb. i.).

Cometh. Gr., *is coming*, the approach is spoken of as then taking place.—He is working in and by Judas, who is carrying out his plans and doing his work (see on chap. vi. 70 ; xiii. 2, 27).—The Lord is well aware that His enemies are now making ready to advance against Him, led on by the traitor, into whom Satan had entered.—What a help and consolation to tempted and sorely buffeted believers, to be assured that Jesus knows every design and movement of the foe, and is able to deliver them.—That foe, whose malignant hatred of the Son of God follows all the Lord's children, is now gathering up his forces for a final assault.—But the powers of darkness in dashing against the Rock of Ages will be dashed to pieces.—A sublime scene! Jesus calmly going forth to encounter the combined forces of earth and hell.—By sin, Satan with the power of death lords it over man.—Wherever guilt is, there his dark dominion is established.—Flushed with victory over the first Adam and his posterity, he hoped to vanquish the Second Adam.—But the spotless Lamb of God is not a mere creature, and hence has no element of moral weakness

within.—His soul was at rest on the bosom of His Father ; therefore, though tempted in all points like as we are, it was without
sin (Heb. iv. 15).

Hath nothing in me. See on Matt. i. 20.—These words are to be
taken in their full and absolute meaning.—Here is the great distinction between Jesus and every son and daughter of Adam.—
The " prince of this world " never had even the faintest power
over Christ, for He, and He alone, was *perfectly sinless* in nature
and in life ; and not only so, but He, and He alone, was *perfectly
holy* in nature and in life.—It follows from this that His surrender
of Himself was altogether voluntary (see on chap. x. 18).—Alas !
the " prince of this world " *hath* something in us : even in the best
and holiest there remains something of the old corrupt nature.—
It is upon this the tempter works, and, too often, successfully.—
Not so with Jesus; and hence His confidence and peace.—Blessed
be God ! there will come a time when, through sovereign grace,
Christ's people shall be free from sin.—"Not having spot, or
wrinkle, or any such thing, but holy and without blemish," He
will present His Church to the Father (Eph. v. 27).—Meanwhile,
forewarned is forearmed.—Every believer ought carefully to consider what his easily besetting sin is, and should watch and pray
lest he enter into temptation.—Having a great High Priest who
was tempted as we are, and yet is the Holy One, " let us come
boldly unto the throne of grace," &c. (Heb. iv. 14-16.)

ἔρχεται. The ἐν ἐμοὶ antithesis to the prince of this world. – He comes as the prince
of this world's power, of this world's fear, of death and corruption, to claim a power
over Me (Heb. ii. 14). *Lange.*—καὶ ἐν ἐμοὶ,&c. *He can, or is able to, do nothing to Me ;
he cann t inflict death upon Me ; of My own free wi l I suffer it. Chrys., Kuinoel.—He
finds nothing in Me ; no accusation against Me. Origen &c.—He possesses nothing in
Me. Cyril, Augustine, &c.—In Me he possesses nothing as owning his sway. Meyer.—No
point of app ance wher on to fasten his attack. A ford.—He has no claim on Me.
Tho'uck, De Wette. Hofmann. &c.—The words certainly declare not only Jesus' sinlessness but also his freedom from death.—As Satan possesses nothing in Him morally, he
can have no power over Him physically. Lange.*

---

31. But that the world may know that I love the **Father** ; and as the **Father** gave me
commandment, even so I do. Arise, let us go hence.

But that the world, &c. Expresses His willingness to become a
sacrifice.—The very world over which Satan rules will see in this
self-sacrifice the love of the Father.—That love will deliver them
from the bondage of the usurper, and restore them to the freedom
of children.

1134 / Gospel of John

Gave me commandment. It was not Satan that secured the Redeemer's death.—Love for the Father, for His glory, induced Him to yield Himself a free and willing sacrifice.—The glory of the Father is manifested in His death, and in the salvation of man accruing by it.—As Christ's love to His Father constrained Him to the death of the Cross, our love to our Lord should bind us to unquestioning obedience.—The world knows that Divine love is stronger than death.—" In this free submission His high-priesthood is perfected : the Priest is the Sacrifice, and the Sacrifice is the Priest Himself." *Lange.*

Arise, &c. (See note).—The outgoing of His infinite heart of love nearing the goal.—He does not say, " I must go;" all was voluntary, and He calls His people to no trial that He has not had experience of.—Thus pre-eminently fitted to be the Captain of our salvation ; " made perfect by sufferings " (Heb. ii. 10).

ἐγείρεσθε, &c. Jesus, accompan'ed by the disciples, proceeds to a secure place, where He uttered chapters xv., xvi., xvii. *Chrys., Theoph., &c.*—Jesus had been outside of the city ; He was now about departing for Jerusalem to keep the Passover. *Bengel.*—Full of the matters still pressing upon His heart. He spoke chapters xv.-xvii.. still standing in the room where they had eaten the supper. *Knapp, Lücke, Meyer, Tholuck, Calvin, Bleek, Olsh., Brückner, Ewald, Alford, Owen, &c.*—The following chapters (xv.-xvii.) spoken by Him on the road to Gethsemane. *Luther, Grotius, Lampe, Ebrard, Barnes, Webster and Wilkinson, Wordsworth, Lange, Schaff. &c.*—A question which we cannot solve ; but the immediate connection of the opening words of the next chapter with the present verse naturally leads to the opinion that they were spoken in the same place, and, in the absence of any hint of a change, it is safe not to assume any. The words of chap. xviii. 1 are probably those which express the act to which the words our Lord has just spoken summon them. *Ellicott.*

John 15

1. I am the true vine, and my Father is the husbandman.

I am. Our Lord uses the word Jehovah gave to Moses at the Bush : " I AM hath sent me unto you " (Ex. iii. 12).—" Before Abraham was, I AM " (see on chap. viii. 58).

The true. Christ the reality of the idea figuratively represented in the natural vine.

Vine. See on verse 5.—Earthly things mere shadows and similitudes of heavenly realities.—The imagery here may have followed from some incident, or custom, or remark, now wholly unknown to us,—It was familiar to the disciples from the Old Testament, and would have come to their minds from any slight suggestion (Ps. lxxx. 8-19; Isa. v. 1 *et seq*; Jer. ii. 21; Ezek. xix. 10).— Expressed also in Rabbinic sayings : " Whoever dreameth of a vine-branch shall see the Messiah."—Christ the true, veritable, perfect Vine : 1. As distinguished from all mere symbols; 2. As opposed to all false Messiahs (see critical note).—Our Lord's parables, illustrations, teachings, like the flowers and sunlight, common every-day sights, but always fresh and pleasant.—Some think the vine was created to illustrate this relation between Christ and His Church.

My Father, &c. Matt. xxi. 33 ; Mark xii. 1; Luke xx. 9.—He is the owner of the vine, who Himself cultivates and trains it (see critical note).

ἡ ἄμπελος. The figure chosen presupposes a particular inducement to its selection. —Various opinions as to the inducement : suggested by the golden vine on the door of the temple. *Jerome, Rosenm., Lampe.*—The sight of the wine-cup at the Lord's Supper. *Grotius, Nösselt, Meyer, Trench, Ewald, Ellicott.*—A vine which, from the house, had shot its tendrils into the guest-chamber. *Knapp, Tholuck.*—The view of vineyards reposing outside in the full moon. *Storr.*—The mental recollection of the Old Test. figure. *Lücke, B. Crusius.*—This and the sight of the wine-cup at the Supper. *Alford, Hofmann.*—The walk down to Kedron through the vineyards. *Lange, Godet.*—The communion wine, the symbol of His blood, presented the nearest motive for this discourse on the closest union between Him and His people yet does not exclude an external occasion. *Schaff.*—ἡ ἀληθινή. The *essential* Vine. —That which the earthly vine is figuratively as a symbol, that which the people of Israel was as a type, Christ is in radical essentiality; He is the trunk-root and stem of the kingdom of love, of its invigorating and inspiriting fruit and effect. *Lange.*—An antithesis to the *unfruitful* vine of the Jewish theocracy. *Ebrard, Hengstenberg.*—Not a natural interpretation, since Christ represents Himself, and not His Church, as the true Vine.—The word means *true* in the sense of true to the idea, genuine, primitive, essential, as dist'nct from what is derived, copied, typical, shadowy, and more or less imperfect. *Schaff.*—ὁ γεωργός. The owner of the vineyard as well as the labourer.—King Uzziah ca led γεωργός (2 Chron. xxvi. 16), and the leaders of the Jewish theocracy γεωργοί (Matt. xxi. 33–41).— "He tills our hearts with the ploughshare of His Word, and scatters the seeds of His precepts there, and sends us the dew and rain of the S irit, that He may reap the fruit of holiness " *Wordsworth.*—God's rule over the world is a personal g vernment exercised upon Christ as the centre of the world and upon His disciples as His organs; a strict and wise government corresponding to the noble nature of the Vine. *Lange* — Arians used this passage as implying that the Son was a creature and entirely subordinated to the Father.—But Christ calls Himself the true Vine, not in His eternal Divine nature, but in His historical mediatorial character and work. *Schaff.*

---

2. Every branch in me that beareth not fruit he taketh away: and every branch hat beareth fruit, he purgeth it, that it may bring forth more fruit.

Branch. The union of the branch with the vine secures the *vital fluid.*—The union of the believer with Christ is *vital* and *mysterious.*

In me. In organic union.—Without this baptism, eucharist, profession, zeal, benevolence, self-sacrifices, fasting, prayers avail nothing.—Our life is hid with Christ in God (Col. iii. 3).—Hid as to its origin, its mode, its power, its true joy.—"All my springs are in thee" (Psa. lxxxvii. 7).

Beareth not fruit. Paradise had no trees that were barren (Gen. ii. 16).—The tree drinks its life from the air, light, heat, water.— These sources are from above, and similarly believers receive repentance, faith, love purity, from *above.*—"What fruit had ye in those things whereof ye are now ashamed?" (Rom vi. 21).— Barenness always the result of sin; shame and death the invariable fruit.—If heaven smile *not* on us, "The olive may cast his fruit" (Deut. xxviii. 40).—But the Lord blessing, "Our fruit shall shake like Lebanon" (Psa. lxxii. 16).—There are those who claim to be branches of the true Vine, and yet are fruitless.—The ground of unfruitfulness is declared in verse 4.

Taketh away. Equivalent to cutting down of the barren fig-tree (see on Luke xiii. 6-9).—The two chief duties of the vine-dresser, removing fruitless branches and pruning fruitful ones.— An illustration of the work of the Divine Husbandman.

Every branch, &c. Purging is applied without respect of person, sparing none, according to the vine-dressing rule which aims at fruit, and the utmost possible fruit.

Purgeth it. Gr., *purifieth.*—Seeming to attack *their* lives also by the knife.—The whole process of sanctification which includes temptations and afflictions.—Not accomplished without the internal operation of the Spirit.—Pruning neglected, the strength of the tree runs all to wood. -Shoots which waste the sap, and excrescences which hinder healthy growth must be removed.—A picture of the work of the Heavenly Husbandman in His Church.—The explanation of so much that is painful and severe in the life of the true Christian.—A reference to those Divine judgments such as overtook the disciples in the Passion-night.—"Whom the Lord loveth He chasteneth" (Heb. xii. 6).—Not that God takes pleasure in afflicting, but He looks to the end (Heb. xii. 10).—God had one Son without sin, but none without sorrow.—Iron to weld with iron must pass the fire, so we to be united with Christ.— Joseph looked sternly at his brethren while his steward was preparing to feast them.—As the storm followed Jonah so the rod our sins.—God's vines bear better for their bleeding by the knife. —His spices smell the sweeter for being under the pestle.—David acknowledged God's stripes healed his infirmities.—Men lift the flail when the wheat is to be threshed.—Ignatius flung to the lions cried, "Now I begin to be a Christian."

---

3. Now ye are clean through the word which I have spoken unto you

Now. Gr., *already are ye clean.*

Clean. See on chap. xiii. 10.—By being united to the true Vine, yet needing to be cleansed as branches (verse 2).—Clean by justification; in need of cleansing by sanctification.—Clean in respect of inward vitality, needing pruning as to outshoots, &c.

Through the word, &c. Embraces our Lord's whole teaching.— His word the revelation of God to them by which they had been cleansed.—The living word of Christ received by faith into the heart and dwelling there.—He had just before washed their feet, but the water was only a type of the word.—Baptism saves, not by the putting away of the filth of the flesh, but by the answer of a good conscience toward God (1 Peter iii. 21).—The purifying word must be supplemented from without by the Father's school of suffering.—This cannot give the principle of purity, but it cleanses and strengthens it.—Purification in the Father's school of suffering is rendered complete by abiding in Christ. *Lange.*— The principle of regeneration and purification is the word received into the heart by faith and kept there (chap. xvii. 17; James i. 18; 1 Pet. i. 23; Eph. v. 26).—"That which is clean bears fruit; that which bears fruit becomes also more clean." *Hiller.*

διὰ τὸν λόγον. It is not said *by reason of baptism*, for the apostles were not baptized, except with the preparatory baptism of John.—Augustine, who otherwise, as most of the Fathers, has an exaggerated view of the efficacy and necessity of water baptism, remarks: " Why did He not say, ' Ye are clean by baptism ? ' B'cause it is the word which cleanses in the water Take away the word, and what is the water? Add the word to the e'ement and it becomes a sacrament. Whence is this power of the water that it touches the body and the heart is cleansed? Whence, but because the word operates not merely in being spoken, but in being believed." *Schaff.*

---

4. Abide in me, and I in you. As the branch cannot bear fruit of itself, except it abide in the vine ; no more can ye, except ye abide in me.

Abide in me, and I in you. The clauses are connected as cause and effect.—He who abides in Christ has Christ abiding in him, and is a fruitful branch of the true Vine.—Abiding in Him is the condition of His abiding in them.—All is bound up with the maintenance of spiritual communion with Christ.—We abide in Him in the contemplation and experience of His love.—He abides in us, and therefore we abide in Him : we abide in Him, and therefore He abides in us.

As the branch, &c. The branch apart from the vine has not only no fruitfulness but no being, for it has no original source of life. —The branch of itself is lifeless, and only fulfils its functions by connection with the vine.—From the vine flows the vital sap to every part.—All the parts live, move, and have their being from and by the vine.—The vine receives nothing from the branches but gives them all.

No more can ye. As it is with the branch and the vine, so it is in the spiritual life.—The believer apart from Christ has no source of life and fruitfulness.—The question is not of the moral inability of man by nature, but of the simple spiritual dependence of the soul in Christ.—Nothing without Him, everything in connection with Him.—This is fulfilled in the branch, in organic vitality ; in the believer, in free personality. *Lange.*

Except ye abide in me. Abide as a living branch *in* the vine, not merely as a shoot *on* the vine.—The fruit of this union is love, joy, peace, long-suffering, gentleness, goodness, faith, meekness, temperance (Gal. v. 22, 23).—If we are fruitless, it is evidence we are not *in* the vine.—Christ lives in all His members, as the spirit animates and rules every part of the human body.—This command, like all the others, is a promise.—What the Lord enjoins the Lord will give grace to perform.—The experience of all real Christians testifies to the truth of these words ; and no less forcibly the condition of backsliders.—The fall that strikes consternation into the Church, and amazes even the worldly, was seen long before by the eye of God.—*Not abiding in Him,* we may deny

Him as Peter did, or even betray Him like Judas.—*Abiding in Him*, he that is feeble shall be as David, and David as the angel of the Lord (Zech. xii. 8).

μείνατε ἐν ἐμοί. Reference to the communion in which they had so recently shared. *Grotius, Knapp, Stier, Ebrard.*—It is singular that this "abiding" doctrine was delayed till after the Lord's Supper. *Roos.*

---

5. I am the vine, ye are the branches: He that abideth in me, and I in him, the same bringeth forth much fruit: for without me ye can do nothing.

I am the vine. See on verse 1.—This is repeated to bring out what follows.—He had not before directly stated that they are the branches.—It may be that there was a pause after verse 4, accompanied by a look at the disciples, or at that which suggested the imagery of the vine. *Ellicott.*—Our Lord's reference to *the Vine and its branches* is connected by a threefold foundation with the whole system of the sacred language of figures : 1. *Nature* in itself; 2. The *prophetic phraseology* which interprets nature; 3. The recently-instituted *Supper.*—As Christ gives His *life* to death for our spiritual nourishment, and in His *blood* makes us especially partakers thereof He is THE VINE.—In the profound phraseology of Scripture the juice of the grape is the *blood* and *life* of the Vine.—The vine an emblem of fertility (Deut. viii. 8); an emblem of peace (Micah iv. 4) ; an emblem of value (Jer ii. 21) ; an emblem of culture (Isa. v. 2) ; esteemed for its fruit alone (Ezek. xv. 3).—Its fruit an emblem of joyous communion and fellowship (Matt. xxvi. 29).—"Little foxes that spoil the vines" (Cant. ii. 15) emblematical of the injury done to Christian character by "little sins."—Christ the Vine and therefore the only principle and source of life to the Church.

Ye are the branches. Entirely conditional upon the Vine and dependent upon it.—The vital union between the vine and branches is maintained by the circulation of the sap.—The nature of this circulation, its cause and mode, remain a mystery.—A symbol of the mysterious union between Christ and His people.—The sun must shine upon the vine to draw up and circulate the sap, and so the Sun of Righteousness must shine upon the soul.—All the evidences of life, the bud, the leaf, the fruit, due to the vine, and so with the believer and his union with his Lord.—In proportion to the constancy and closeness of the union will be our beauty and fruitfulness.—This figure supplemented by the symbols of the Shepherd and the Flock, the Head and the Members, the Corner-stone and the Stones built upon it, the Bridegroom and the Bride.

Without me ye can do nothing. Gr., *separate from Me,* or, *apart from Me.*—Intended to show the fulness of the meaning of abiding in Christ.—He and he only who abides can bring forth fruit, for the man who is separate from Christ is necessarily fruitless.—Ye cannot be productive and creative as vine branches.—Christian vital activity is wholly dependent upon vital communion with the Lord.—" He doth not here speak of a natural or worldly life and conduct, but of fruits of the gospel." *Luther.*—It is only through fellowship with the Christ of gospel history that a man attains to Christ-like life.—The words mean not merely, " Ye can do nothing *until* ye are in Me and have My grace," but, "*After* ye are in Me, ye can even then accomplish nothing except ye draw life and strength from Me." *Trench.*—From first to last Christ must work in and through the believer.—" A warning to the regenerate man that he never seek to do aught of himself ; not a declaration that he is unable to do aught." *Schaff.*—Our Lord is not speaking to unconverted men but to Christians, and He declares that after conversion there is constant need of His grace.—Christ is the beginning, middle, and end of spiritual life.—" I can do all things through Christ which strengtheneth me" (Phil. iv. 13 ; 2 Cor. xii. 9, 10).

οὐ δύνασθε. These words have often been unduly pressed, to exclude all moral power apart from Christ, whereas the whole context limits them to the fruit-bearing of the Christian life.—The persons thought of all through this allegory are true and false Christians, and nothing is said of the influence on men of the wider teaching of God the Light of the Logos ever in the world.—A moral power outside the limits of Christianity is clearly recognized in the New Testament (compare Rom. ii, 14, 15). *Ellicott.* —Even such noble things as precede conversion are, so far as they are noble, done in the truth of the Logos. *Olshausen.*—Christ speaks here not of natural morality and civil righteousness, which has nothing to do with man's salvation, but of spiritual righteousness and fruits of the Gospel. *Schaff.*

---

6 If a man abide not in me, he is cast forth as a branch, and is withered; and men gather them, and cast them into the fire, and they are burned.

If a man, &c. Gr., *If any one shall not have abode.*—Our Lord passes from the fruitful to the sterile branch ; from the man who abideth to the man who will not abide.

He is cast forth. Gr., *cast out, viz.,* from the vineyard, that is, the true Church.—It shall not benefit by the care of the husbandman. —It can no longer be allowed to remain where life and fruitfulness are expected to be found.—This is no arbitrary act; it is the result of an unchangeable law.—The withered, dead branch is useless, and therefore is cast out as a worthless thing, fit only for fuel.—Separation from Christ must necessarily end in separation from *His*.—God's blasting is the end of barrenness.—Only those who *wilfully* forsake Christ can ever come to this; only apart from Him, this dreadful ruin must ensue.—It is not a case of common backsliding our Lord is speaking of, but of *complete apostasy*.

Men gather them. The lifeless branch is in company with other lifeless branches.—The law of classification is universal : Judas went "to his own place" (Acts i. 25).—Judgments manifold and fiery precede the last Judgment, and every trial is converted into a fiery judgment to him who has not stood the test (Mal. iii. 3 ; Matt. iii. 12).—When we see branches gathered together we know that these *were* withered because they were cut off, and they were cut off because they had not abode *in the vine*. *Lange.*—The tares shall be gathered into "bundles" (Matt. xiii. 30).—A vivid picture of the fearful history of those who are apart from Christ.

And they are burned. Gr., *and they burn*, more graphic and terrible than the E. V.—Like dry brush they flame up speedily and are quickly consumed.—Indicative of the rapid, conspicuous, and shocking ruin of apostates, or, in general, of dead Church members.—Our Lord's words demand rather to be trembled at than need to be expounded. *Trench.*

ἐβλήθη and ἐξηράνθη. Interpretations of the Aorists : 1. As is the custom. *Grotius.* —2. They have a future signification. *Kuinoel, B. Crusius.*—3. Expressive of what is immediately to happen. *Beza, Lücke, Winer, Tholuck, De Wette, Hengst., Luthardt, Wordsworth.*—4. The events described are things past as viewed in the presence of the Last Day.—The fire meaning the fire of the final judgment. *Meyer, Alford.*—The *fire* is a prelude to the fire of Gehenna and points towards it; and the *gatherers* are all divinely ordained instruments of judgment. *Lange.*

---

7. If ye abide in me, and my words abide in you, ye shall ask what ye will, and it shall be done unto you.

If ye abide in me. He does not say, "and I abide in you," as in verse 4, for His abiding in them necessarily accompanies their abiding in Him.—As a glass globe placed in sunlight is filled with light, so Christ's presence penetrates those abiding in Him.—It is no transient emotion of sympathy or affection, but the habit of life and character that is implied.

My words. This is the means by which, and the proof that they do abide in Him (see on chap. xiv. 15, 23, 24).

Ye shall ask. The promise is the same as that in chap. xiv. 13, 14 (see notes).—As if He had said, " Ye not only shall be preserved, but the most glorious gain shall accrue to you. But for this you must pray ; and in order to pray aright you must retain My words within you.—And for this end you must stedfastly continue in the true fellowship of love with Me " (1 John v. 14).

What ye will. In the way of God's will, and tending to much fruit.—In the way of love and of Christ's word.—In this direction (in His name) no request can be too great.—Those abiding in Christ can only pray in entire submission to His will, and for things which tend to His glory.

Shall be done. Such prayers cannot fail of being heard.—But God will hear according to His own wisdom and goodness, both as to time and manner.—Sometimes the substance of prayer is heard best by the denial of its form.—Paul's prayer for removal of " the thorn " answered by, " My grace is sufficient for thee."—Our Lord's prayer in Gethsemane, " Let this cup pass," answered by, " An angel from heaven to strengthen Him."

αἰτήσεσθε. The reading is not certain, but the first verb should probably be imperative, "Ask what ye will." *Ellicott*—The Aorist αἰτήσασθε, in accordance with *A. B. D*, &c., is adopted by *Lachmann, Tischendorf, Lange, &c.*—But *Codd. Sin., B. G. H., &c.*, agree with the *text. rec. Schaff.*

---

8. Herein is my Father glorified, that ye bear much fruit; so shall ye be my disciples.

Herein. Refers to the preceding words and means : " In this doing whatever ye ask, my Father is glorified, in order that ye may bear much fruit, and that ye may become my disciples." *Ellicott, Meyer, Lange.*

Father glorified. The one aim of our Lord's life was to glorify His Father.—This was the joy set before Him, for which He endured the cross, despising the shame (Heb. xii. 2).—The Father is eternally glorified in the work of the Son, and in all the blessings to mankind hence accruing.—The first object to be accomplished by granting the disciples' prayer is the glorification of the Father.

Ye bear much fruit. This is the result of the Father's glorification reacting upon the disciples.—" We are His workmanship (Gr., handiwork), created unto good works " (Eph. ii. 10).—" Elect according to the foreknowledge of God the Father, through sanctification of the Spirit, *unto obedience*," &c. (1 Pet. i. 2).—*Much*

fruit, evidence of the divine power and fulness of faith, and therefore, precious in the sight of God, and useful to men.

So shall, &c. Gr., *and may become My disciples.*—The pronoun
" My," is strongly emphatic.—Another result of the Father's glorification reacting upon them.—The bearing of much fruit not the
means of their entering into new discipleship.—So shall ye grow
up to be true disciples to Me.—Discipleship of Christ is the beginning and the end, the foundation and top of Christianity.
—Disciples worthy of Me, worthy of the name *Christians*,
followers and imitators of Christ.—Living union with Him, inspiring prayer in His name, prayer which He would answer, and
which produces fruit to God's glory, the mark of true discipleship.

ἐν τούτῳ. Relates not to the ἵνα following it, but to the verse preceding it. *Meyer,
Schaff Lange, Ellicott* —γενήσεσθε. *Codd. Sin.* and *A.*, text. rec., *Tisch., Meyer, &c.*—
γένησθε. *B. D., &c., Lach., Treg., Alf., Westcott and Hort, Schaff.*

---

9. As the Father hath loved me, so have I loved you: continue ye in my love.

As the Father, &c. Gr., *As the Father hath loved Me, I have also
loved you.*—He speaks now of the foundation of their union with
Him and with God.—The eternal love of the Father is ever going
forth to the Son, and from the Son ever going forth to His disciples.—The Father's love and presence was ever with the Son,
because the Son ever did those things pleasing to Him (chap. viii.
31).—The Son's love is ever present to the willing heart of the
disciple.—The Father's love to the Son appears in His glorification, and this reveals the measure of the Son's love, a love which
will also glorify them.—The Father loved the Son from eternity,
so has Christ loved His people.—The Father's love to the Son is
unchangeable, so is Christ's to His people.—The Father's love to
the Son is everlasting, so is Christ's to His people.

Continue ye in my love. Not love to Jesus is meant, but the
love of Jesus to them (verse 11).—Love to Jesus is here, as throughout the section, expressed by the *continuing in Him.*—" *Abide ye in
my love*, the word 'continue' misses the connection with the
context." *Ellicott.*—Not love to Me in your hearts, but *My* love
towards you, which will produce your love to *Me.*—" We love
him, because he first loved us " (1 John iv. 19).—They are to
abide in His love to them ; for this will preserve from apostasy
and secure " much fruit."—" Keep yourselves in the love of God "
(Jude 21), as one keeps himself in the sunlight.—Satan gains his

greatest victories by tempting believers to doubt Christ's love to them.—How grandly Paul triumphs, "For I am persuaded that neither," &c., "shall be able to separate us from the loveof God" (Rom. viii. 38, 39).

---

10. If ye keep my commandments, ye shall abide in my love; even as I have kept my Father's commandments, and abide in his love.

If ye keep, &c. See on chap. xiv. 21, 24.—Precepts, promises, instructions, consolations and warnings.—Fidelity is proved by obedience in little things as well as in great.—The keeping does not originate love, love yields obedience, and obedience opens up greater glories to the soul.—Love produces obedience, and obedience love, for in keeping His commandments there is great reward (Psa. xix. 11).—Our love which itself flows from Christ's love to us (verse 9) is the means by which we abide in His love.—While we cherish love for Him, our hearts are receptive of His love to us.— Our continuing in His love, and our obedience the effect of Divine grace.—However Christians may differ in their creeds upon this subject, they are one in their prayers and praises to God.— Arminians and Calvinists ask for grace and unite to ascribe salvation to grace.

Even as I have, &c. He was "obedient unto death, even the death of the cross" (Phil. ii. 8).—This obedience was the test and proof of His love to the Father.—He ordains the same course for us to show our love to Him.—Love to the Father was the great, impelling, sustaining principle of His life and sufferings.—Another appeal to His perfect holiness, and willing subordination as Son to the Father. —Not an arbitrary condition imposed upon Him by authority, but a necessary result of love itself.—*Because* He loved the Father ; He kept His commandments, and in this love abode in the Father's love.—*Because* we love Him we keep His commandments, and in this love we abide in His love.

---

11. These things have I spoken unto you, that my joy might remain in you, and that your joy might be full.

These things. He seems hastening on to the end of His day of toil.—He will now show them the joy which this new life of love and obedience brings.—What has been said upon the love of Christ was to be the means of developing joy within them.—"The fruit of the Spirit is *love, joy*," &c. (Gal. v. 22).

My joy. The joy experienced by Christ Himself, the joy of His own Spirit.—Christ communicates to His people that which He *possesses* in Himself.—Strange to find Him speaking of *His joy*, at this moment, when on His way to Gethsemane and the Cross.— His joy arose from the consciousness of His love to the Father, and the Father's love to Him, and was so deeply seated in His soul that outward circumstances, however appalling, could not disturb it.—Similarly, His people, conscious of His love to them, and theirs to Him, can rejoice evermore.—The brightness of that joy lit up the darkest hours of His life, and He wills that it shall light up ours.—No sorrow can overcome this joy, for it is the joy of Jehovah, and is our strength (Neh. viii. 10).—He had already bequeathed them the legacy of *Peace* (chap. xiv. 27), and now He tells them of the source of joy.

Your joy might be full. See on chap. iii. 29.—His joy of the same infinite fulness as His love.—To love God and to be loved of Him the ideal perfection of life.—This alone can satisfy all the deepest desires of our being.—By this all the soul's capacities are filled, and joy is perfect.—Through Christ's joy theirs shall be made complete.—Uplifted and ennobled to the extreme of their capability and satisfaction.—Yet the joy shall be *theirs*, existing under a peculiar phase in each one.—The dominion of Christ's personality in the hearts of His people quickens, develops and glorifies their own personality (1 John i. 4; 2 John, verse 12). *Lange.*—All clouds and darkness shall end in day; all sorrows shall end in joy.—" We know that all things work together for good to them that love God " (Rom. viii. 28).

ἡ χαρὰ ἡ ἐμή. My joy in you: the joy insp'red by His viewing their life as pictured in Divine predestination. *Aug., Lampe.*—That ye may be a cause and subject for My joy. *Luthardt.*—Your joy over Me; over Christ's merit. *Euth. Zig., Grotius, Piscator.*— That the joyfulness occasioned by Me may be in you. *Calvin, De Wette.*—The joy of Christ's own Spirit. *Cyril, Lücke, Meyer, Alford, Lange Schaff, Ellicott, &c.*—The holy joyfulness of Christ, the untrammelled, glad upsoaring of His soul in the midst of all His tribulations shall, through the Spirit, by means of the communication and awakening of love, devolve upon them (see chap. xvi 22; Phil. ii. 17; iv. 4; 1 John iii. 21; iv. 17, and many passages in Paul's epistles). *Lange.*—ᾖ instead of μείνῃ. *Tisch., Lach., Treg., Alford.*

12. This is my commandment, That ye love one another, as I have loved you.

My commandment. See on chap. xiii. 34.—" My," as if no other were His.—To love God supremely is the first, and love to one another is the invariable result.—Love to God is proved by our love to each other.—The two great commandments are really one:

"If a man love not his brother whom he hath seen, how can he love God whom he hath not seen?" (1 John iv. 20).—This is that vital law whose aim is the perfection of their joy.—It is grounded on His love and developed in mutual brotherly love.—The earthly heaven of the believer, with its heavenly joy, is to be revealed in this brotherly love.—All commandments are included in love, for "love is the fulfilling of the law" (Rom. xiii. 10).

As I have loved you. His love was self-sacrificing; "He gave Himself for us."—This elevates Christian love to the highest possible degree, and for ever distinguishes it from men's love to each other as men.—Christ's love for His people, both an *obligation* to brotherly love, and a *pattern* for it.

---

13. Greater love hath no man than this, that a man lay down his life for his friends.

Greater love, &c. Gr., *hath no one than this.*—It is impossible to conceive of anything greater in the thought of love.—He hints at what His love really was and what theirs should be also.—He leaves out of sight for a time the *atoning* character of His death.—"The Lord does not speak of the *redeeming* design of His death, but of that point in great love which we may recognise and imitate." *Richter.*

Lay down his life. See on chap. x. 11.—The self-sacrificing element in His love is the point upon which He would fix their minds.

For his friends. Those to whom He is speaking were His friends.—There is no opposition here to Romans v. 6, for dying for men who *have been* enemies, is a dying for men who *shall* be friends.—Christ dies in a *special* sense for sinners who have already become friends; in a *general* sense for friends who are still sinners. *Lange.* —He is speaking of His death under its *representative* form as a death of self-sacrificing friendly love.—The highest reach of love is the self-sacrifice which spares not life itself.

---

14. Ye are my friends, if ye do whatsoever I command you.

My friends, &c. He now applies what He has just said to His disciples.—What sacrifices men often make to secure the friendship of the great!—Yet the Lord of all condescends to call believers (often poor and despised) *His* friends.

I command you. I look upon you as friends for whom I die; but

ye must prove yourselves My friends by obedience, by loving one
another as I have loved you.—How honourable the title by which
He invites to keep His commandments.—He proclaims His cordial
and intimate connection with His people, thus supplying the
motive, the rule, and the reward of obedience.—But we are not
at liberty to pick and choose what we shall do; the word is, *"whatsoever I command you."*—As He can only be received as a *complete Saviour,* so He can only be served as a *complete Lord. Flavel.*

φίλοι. Not merely passive recipients of love: the word must always, from the
nature of the case, mean something more than that. *Lange.*

---

15. Henceforth I call you not servants; for the servant knoweth not what his lord
doeth: but I have called you friends; for all things that I have heard of my Father
I have made known unto you.

Henceforth. Gr., *no longer do I call you,* or, *I do not still call you.*
Servants. See on chap. xii. 26; xiii. 13.—Gr., *bond-servant, slave.*—
He had not officially called them servants before, but they were
such in the conception of discipleship; and at the feet-washing
He had expressly brought out the relation.—The word is used
again in verse 20, but with reference to an earlier saying.—He
will not apply this name to them, but it became the common title
which they applied to themselves (Rom. i. 1; James i. 1; 2 Pet.
i. 1; Rev. i. 1).—" We have not received the spirit of bondage
again to fear " (Rom. viii. 15).—This servile fear " perfect love
casteth out " (1 John iv. 18).—The holy fear which springs from
love is quite a different thing (1 Pet. i. 17; iii. 15).—Filial fear,
so important and necessary an element in religion that there can
be no genuine piety without it.—Christ's servants become friends,
but remain servants in work and reward (Matt. xxv. 21).—With
Christ all His servants are children and heirs (Rom. viii. 16, 17).
Knoweth not, &c. A servant executes the orders of his master,
but is not privy to the whole idea which forms his government.—
He obeys as under authority, without being in full unison with it,
because it is not imparted to him as a motive.—It is his master
that works through him.—He does not understand what his master
does personally, or through the instrumentality of others.—With
his unfree individual service, he does not know the free doings of
his master.—The part of the servant is mechanical obedience,
without any principle of love between his master and himself.—
He knows nothing of the purposes or aims of his master, even
though he sees the deeds that are done by the master's commands.

Friends. Their emancipation does not estrange them from Him.
—Though friends before they become such now in a far higher
sense.—Ceasing to be servants in a legal sense, in the sense of
free obedience they serve more devotedly than ever.—Just as He
Himself, the Son of God, was also the Servant of God.—The
friend is the confidant of the thoughts and purposes of his friend
and works in loving harmony with him.—All Christ's servants are
admitted to intimate communion with their Lord.—After His
resurrection He called them brethren (chap. xx. 17): the dignity
of believers is a growing dignity.—The longer any one follows
Jesus the higher and greater will be the privileges enjoyed.—The
proof of friendship is *open, confidential, unrestrained communion*,
the typical expressions of which are found in Abraham's case
(Gen. xviii. 17); that of Moses (Ex. xxxiii. 11), and of the pious
generally (Psa. xxv. 14; Prov. iii. 32). *Stier.*

All things, &c. No contradiction with chap. xvi. 12, for the cause
of His reticence was not on His part, but on theirs.—He had
acted towards them as friends, and had kept back no truth which
they could understand.—They could not then receive more, but
the Paraclete, whom He would send, would lead them into *all
truth.*—He had confided to them the grand secret of His life, His
sacrificial death in accordance with the purpose of the Father.—
By this confidence He would arouse them to a loving activity
which should rejoice in sacrifice.—They are initiated into His
personal kingdom of love and called to assist in its extension.—In
this respect He had made known to them all that He had heard
from the Father.—All, not *extensively*, but *intensively;* in the
Father's *counsel of love* all lies enfolded. *Lange.*—A great thought;
friendship with Jesus is copartnery in His self-sacrificing love.

πάντα. All that I have heard that was meant to be communicated to you. *Lücke.*—A
distinction between the will of salvation and the *further* instructions connected with
it. *Meyer.*—The distinction between a principle and its development is also intimated.
Lange.

---

16. Ye have not chosen me, but I have chosen you, and ordained you, that ye should
go and bring forth fruit, and that your fruit should remain : that whatsoever ye shall
ask of the Father in my name, he may give it you.

Not chosen me. See on chap. vi. 70; xiii. 18.—A wholesome
memento after the lofty things He had just said about the friendship they had been admitted to. *Brown.*—The principle of their
friendship is not resident in them, but in His love.—They owed
all to His election and gifts.—No room for boasting and no ground

for mutual jealousies.—Although primarily referring to their office as apostles, our Lord here asserts a general law of His Kingdom. —All believers are chosen ; else, left to themselves no human being would believe.—" Knowing, brethren beloved, your election of God " (1 Thess. i. 4). (See on chap. vi. 37, 44.)—A divine election is constantly seen in the course of Providence in the world, and in individual life.—" No difficulty emerges in theology which has not already appeared in philosophy." *Berkeley.*—The friendship between Christ and His people began with Him.

Ordained you. Gr., *appointed you* —Gives prominence to the idea of the apostolic calling.—I have set you in your place as ministers of My Kingdom.—Christ is Head over the Body the Church, and it is His prerogative to appoint His servants their work.—The blessedness of this certitude is more or less realized by every true minister.—Not only to appoint to office, but when, and where, and how, and how long.—And this is true of every servant of Christ from the highest to the lowest.

Ye should go, &c. Implies the activity of the apostles as distinct from that of the Lord Himself.—Each branch ever united to Him was to grow and to bring forth his *own* fruit.—Establishment in the *fellowship of His love* was to result in their going forth under *impulse of love,* and their bringing forth fruit, their *ministry of love.* —This applies to all the Lord's servants in their degree.

Remain. See on chap. iv. 36.—Their work founded and carried on in love would be imperishable.—His Church, built by them upon the eternal Rock, has survived the storms and tempests of the ages.—The little sapling which they planted has grown to be a great tree, and all that is good and noble in the world finds shelter in its branches.—In like manner the fruit of every true believer shall remain unto eternal life.

Whatsoever, &c. See on chap. xiv. 13, 14.—In verses 7, 8, the bearing of fruit is made dependent upon prayer, now the hearing of prayer is affirmed to be the fruit of holy activity.—Prayer must precede work ; and work again, must become the foundation for greater earnestness and power in prayer.—Thus He fortifies His servants for their work and fellowship of love, against all the opposing forces of the world.—He gives the believer liberty to draw upon the Bank of Heaven in His name, to any extent he pleases.—From prayer the Christian proceeds to work, and from work he goes back to prayer.—Prayer is cause, and work is effect ; work is cause, and prayer is effect.

17. These things I command you, that ye love one another.

These things. The things He has spoken from verse 1, but more especially from verses 12-16.

Love one another. See on chap. xiii. 34.—This was the beginning and the end of all His precepts, as it should be of all Christian teaching.—Unhappily, theological systems and sects have often promoted, rather than repressed, alienation and strife.—" Now the end of the commandment is charity (*love*) " (1 Tim. i. 5).—The decrees of the Church of Rome generally begin and end in curses. —Our Lord sums up in one great concluding utterance.—Everything He has told them of His perfect joy, His friendship, His election and their calling, is intended to become to them a vital law of brotherly love.—In this fellowship His disciples can confront the world and vanquish it. *Lange.*

---

18. If the world hate you, ye know that it hated me before it hated you.

The world. The children of *this* world as distinguished from the children of God.—Called *the world* as indicating their number, confederacy, and spirit.—Three characteristics : 1. Governed by sense ; 2. Living for the present ; 3. Ruled by the opinions and customs of men.

Hate you. Having spoken of their close union with Himself and their love to each other, He now proceeds to speak of their relation to the world.—What a contrast between the " love " in the last verse and the "hatred" in this.—Hence the more need for union amongst themselves and with their Lord.—The very pretension of Christianity to speak with authority from God armed *the world*, Jewish and Gentile, against it, and this is the explanation of the hatred it calls forth to this day.—Had it been a new sect, like that of the Pharisees and Sadducees, the Jews might have allowed it. —But it deposed Moses from his authority, and placed him beneath the prophet of Galilee, whom they execrated as the " carpenter's son."—Nay, more, it was a loss of rank and caste to themselves likewise.—" Christianity still lives in the same world that Christ did; and these two will be bitter enemies till the kingdom of darkness is entirely at an end (Gal. iv. 29 ; 2 Tim. iii. 12 ; 1 Pet. iv. 12-14)." *Law.*—An infidel age is no reproach upon the goodness of Providence.—His infinite patience magnifies His infinite mercy (2 Pet iii. 3-9). *Wilson.*

Hated me before. See on chap. xiii. 16.—*Me* as the first, in advance of you: *Before* (above) you all.—Together with its reference to time, the expression is indicative of causality and comparison : *Me* first, *Me* most; *Me* as the predecessor for whose sake it hateth you. *Lange.*—The superlative comprehends the comparative. *Tholuck.*—The most conscientious and tender Christian is the most likely to fall into the temptation of seeking the cause of the world's hatred solely in himself.—Of thinking that if he were perfect in goodness, love, humility, and meekness, the evil of the world must needs be overcome ; and this might lead to a false compliance.— Against *such* trouble and temptation the Lord arms us beforehand. —" If the most holy love upon earth found no better return, if He did not succeed, if He could not in His wisdom avoid hatred when it arose against Him, all the more fiercely as His pure love more brightly beamed upon it—how could *we* hope to escape this hatred ? or do we vainly imagine that *we* can surpass the love and patience of our Lord ? " *Dietz.*—The world *cannot* love you, it *must* hate you *as* it hates *Me !*—We cannot experience worse usage than our Master met with ; and we ought not to be offended or grow weary in well-doing, if we meet with no better.—As if He had said : I know it is a hard trial, but you will endure it for My sake.—Yea, this very hatred becomes a bond of union with our Lord, and this thought should supply strength to meet it, and joy when suffering from it (see on verse 11 ; compare 1 Pet. iv. 12, 13).

γινώσκετε—imperative, not indicative. *Tisch., Treg., Alford, Lange,* &c.

19. If ye were of the world, the world would love his own · but because ye are not of the world, but I have chosen you out of the world, therefore the world hateth you.

Of the world. 1. Their affections are set upon the world ; 2. Their conversations are conformed to the world ; 3. Their portion is allotted to them in this world.—Five times is the " world " mentioned in this verse.

Love his own. See on chap. vii. 7.—Indicates the utter selfishness of the world.—It would love not them, but that in them which was its own.—Any conformity to the world is hailed as a tribute to themselves ; especially when found amongst professors of the Christian name.—Such professors forget the solemn word, " Whosoever will be a friend of the world is the enemy of God " (James iv. 4).—Although worldly men often quarrel fiercely it is only about particular conflicting interests : *in the great essentials there is always a perfect accord amongst them. Lampe.*

I have chosen you. See on chap. xiii. 18.—The " I " has a twofold emphasis: as to the *world*, its hatred is reduced to hatred against Himself; as to the *disciples*, it is impressed upon them that He alone is the origin of their new life (see on verse 16).

Out of the world. The children of God are in this world as in a strange land, and are looked upon by it, as strangers, and are used by it accordingly.

Therefore, &c. The world hates Christianity because it condemns a worldly life and calls men to holiness.—Whom Christ blesseth the world curseth, therefore this curse becomes a sign of salvation.— Hence Christ's children ought rather to grieve if they were loved by the world.—Not that they are to seek the world's hatred, but when it comes, *then* they may comfort themselves with the thought that the love of the world would be a sad condemnation (Luke vi. 26; Gal. i. 10; James iv, 4).—When the *I have chosen you out of the world* is obtruded upon them in all its earnestness, then begins their exclusion, their ban, their rage.

---

20. Remember the word that I said unto you, The servant is not greater than his lord. If they have persecuted me, they will also persecute you ; if they have kept my saying, they will keep your's also.

Remember. See on chap. xii. 16.—In chap. xiii. 16, the saying is used in a different sense; and in Matt. x. 24, it occurs in the same connection as here.

If they have persecuted me. Expresses the certainty that Christ's disciples will experience the same treatment from the world which He Himself met with.—The members must be willing to endure with the Head.—"It belongs to the *perfection* of a disciple, who would be as his Master, that he should encounter the hatred of the world." *Braune.*—The *consolation* has an undertone of *demand*, that they should rejoice in being counted worthy to suffer as their Lord.

Kept my saying, &c. His disciples cannot expect to be better treated than He was in person and ministry.—"It is the great advantage of believers that Christ and they have the same common friends and enemies, and are embarked together in sufferings; therefore doth He parallel their case with His." *Hutcheson.*—Either we must not profess to be servants of Christ, or we must put up with His cross.—The fruit of the world's hatred : 1. Persecution; 2. Rejection of doctrine.—Yet the world's hatred is not to be a cause for keeping back Christ's word.—With that word *alone* His disciples are to oppose the world; for the rest they are to suffer patiently as He suffered.—Christ's word is to be *kept*; implying prayerful effort to understand it, firm, believing reception of it, and complete surrender of the life to its authority.

---

21. But all these things will they do unto you for my name's sake, because they know not him that sent me.

All these things. Refers chiefly to the warning as to persecution.
For my name's sake. All would be done to them as representing their Lord.—This the key to the world's hatred, and this the ground of the disciples' consolation.—The Acts of the Apostles and the Epistles supply a commentary on this fact.—The name of Christ is the confession of His disciples.—All the malice of earth and hell is aimed at the Son of God.—In crushing Christians the hope has been to crush *Him*.—Ministers and all others who stand for *His name*, in accordance with the full extent of its meaning, must expect hatred and opposition.—Popularity in the pulpit is often secured by withholding or obscuring that name.
Because, &c. This hatred is traced to its true source, ignorance of God.—Christ's name is odious to the world, for the author of it, the Father, is unknown to them.—The Apostles were sent by Christ, and He was the Apostle of the Father.—The world would hate His messengers and hate Himself because they know not God.—This ignorance reveals itself in practical persevering *unbelief.*—All opposition to the Gospel proceeds from ignorance of its true nature, and of God, and Christ, and the relation He sustains to the Father.—Many infidels have acknowledged that they had never even read the New Testament.—" Among all the number of malefactors whom you condemn, there is not a *Christian* to be found chargeable with any crime but his *name*. So much is the hatred of our *name* above all the advantages of virtue flowing from it. Setting aside all enquiry into the principle of our religion and of its Founder and all knowledge of them, the mere *name* is laid hold of; the *name* is attacked; and a word alone prejudges a sect unknown, and its Author also unknown, because they have a *name*, not because they are convicted." *Tertullian.*

---

22. If I had not come and spoken unto them, they had not had sin: but now they have no cloke for their sin.

If I had not come. Expresses the depth of His origin, the glory of His being, the holiness of His mission.—A position immeasurably higher than prophets and apostles is assumed.

Spoken unto them. Expresses the perfect familiarity, clearness, fulness, warmth, and condescension appertaining to the revelation He has made of Himself and of God. *Lange.*—Herein lies the guilt of the world's hatred, that it is in the face of His revelation by both word and work.

Not had sin. That is, in respect to this sin (unbelief) they would be relatively sinless, guiltless.—Unbelief is "the new and deeper fall" (see on chap. iii. 16).—Apart from this revelation, their sin would have belonged to the times of ignorance, which God overlooked (Acts xvii. 30, 31).—The *negative* evil of those who know not ; but now the *positive* evil of those who, knowing the truth, wilfully reject and oppose it.—Implies that all former rejections and oppositions would have been forgiven.—Unbelief of the Gospel, "the damning sin," for it is rebellion against the heart of eternal love, and involves in itself the germs of all iniquity.—It contains the substance of all possible enmity to God.—Sins of ignorance are, as it were, no sins, compared with those committed against light, and opposition to Christ is of awfully aggravated guilt, because He is the light of life.

No cloke. Gr., *no pretext or excuse.*—Every attempt at an apology comes to nought.—It vanishes in face of the revelations of Judgment.—The Gospel, when plainly set forth, takes away all excuse from sinners.—Ignorance would be otherwise an excuse, but *here* it is in the fullest sense *inexcusable.*—Hence the *speechlessness* of the man who had not on the wedding garment (see on Matt. xxii. 12).

πρόφασιν. This word occurs nowhere else in the N. T.—The idea in "cloke" is *to cover up, to hide as with a garment,* so that they may not be seen ; whereas, here the idea is of *excuse for manifest sin Ellicott.*—Had Jesus not come, or not yet come, they would still be under the πάρεσις (Rom. iii. 25) of the olden time; now their sin has become guilt, has become a new παράβασις.—It cannot be inferred from this that the heathen, to whom Christ has not yet spoken, are guiltless; such a supposition is the less tenable from the fact that the crucifixion pe petrated upon Christ by the Jews must be regarded as an act of the whole world.—What does result from the passage is, not that they incur a lesser punishment, but that decision in regard to them is still reserved until the time of their own decision. *Lange.*

---

23. He that hateth me hateth my Father also.

Hateth me, &c. See on chap. v. 23.—Our Lord pictures the world's hatred in its successive degrees of sin.—Hatred against His disciples is hatred against Himself whom they represent.—Hatred against Him, the Son, is hatred against the Father whom He represents.—Whatever excuse men may make for their rejection of the Gospel its secret source is hatred against God.—The living, personal God of the Bible, is the object of the hatred of both unbelieving Jew and Gentile.—One of the many consequences that result from the unity of the Father and the Son: " He that seeth Me, seeth the Father; he that believeth in Me, believeth in the Father ; he that loveth Me, loveth the Father; he that *hateth* Me, *hateth the Father.*"—He that can *hate* Jesus, the manifestation of God in the flesh, *must* bear in himself hatred to God. *Braune.*—How can those who hate the Truth, love the Father of Truth ? *Deists* are in effect *Atheists. Henry.*—Hatred of the Father !—There can be no greater darkness.—The guilt of sin, in this, reaches its consummation.—" God is love," and the heart that can hate love has hardened itself, and cannot be loved. *Ellicott.*

24. If I had not done among them the works which none other man did, they had not had sin : but now have they both seen and hated both me and my Father.

If I had not done, &c. See on chap. ii., 11, 23 ; iii. 2 ; v. 36 ; ix. 3, 4 ; x. 21, 37 ; xiv. 10.—Gradation of the guilt of unbelievers in accordance with the distinction of degrees of faith.—Our Lord's miracles far exceeded those of Moses, both in number and quality · not only so, His miracles were done among them, while those of Moses rested solely on the testimony of their fathers.—Yet hatred led them to ascribe the highest good to the power of evil ; for they said that He had a devil, and did His works by the power of the devil.—Such hearts are closed to every means by which truth and goodness can reach them (see on Matt. xii. 31, 32).—Though unbelievers protest that they are not enemies to God they put that name in practice in their works.—" My works, Me, and the Father, in them, to *see* and yet to *hate ;* these two irreconcilables are reconciled by a God-hating world." *Lücke.*—Miracles must be connected with a holy life and true words, to have any power and significancy as being from God.

πεποιηκεν. ἐποίησεν. *Cod. Sin., Lach., Treg., Tish., Alf., Lange.*

25. But this cometh to pass, that the word might be fufilled that is written in their law, They hated me without a cause.

In their law. See on chap. x. 34.—He constantly refers to Scripture as the infallible interpreter of God's will.—They habitually read the law and boasted of it (Romans ii. 17), but they read with

blinded eyes.—That same Scripture wherein they read has sketched
their portraits with a sure touch (see on chap. v. 45).—A judicial
appointment that their unbelief should issue in the fulfilment of
a prophecy which pointed them out as *haters of God!*—Already
the handwriting of doom is upon the wall, but they see it not.
They hated, &c. How minutely, and with what precision, He
points out the application of Scripture.—How exactly He shows
where and how they may see themselves depicted.—The words are
found Psalm xxxv. 19 ; lxix. 4 ; in neither case as a verbal prophecy,
but as a mental type.—"They have cast their hatred upon Me,
without a reason, without a cause."—As a judgment upon them,
there must be a fulfilling of what is written in their law.—They
had no reason for their unbelief, and therefore their hatred was
causeless.—These words were true of many earlier teachers, but
were only fulfilled in their completeness in the Great Teacher.—
" A hatred without cause is worse than idolatry or blood-guiltiness."
Talmud.—A man hates *without a cause* who seeks no advantage
from his hatred ; thus the ungodly hate God. *Aug.*—The last
solace which our Lord adduces, lies in the counsel of the Divine
wisdom which foretold all this.—As the hatred of Christ was
causeless, so is the hatred men still show against His Gospel and
His Church.—As He justified His claims to Messiahship by pointing
to the benevolent character of His work (see on Matt. xi. 4, 6), so
the believer can justify the claims of Christianity to be Divine.

---

26. But when the Comforter is come, whom I will send unto you from the Father,
even the Spirit of truth, which proceedeth from the Father, he shall testify of me.

The Comforter. See on chap. xiv. 16, 26.—From verse 18 our
Lord warns His disciples that they will have to encounter the
hatred of the world.—He now promises the Holy Ghost as the
strength of their martyrdom.—Left to themselves they must be
overcome, but by the power of the Spirit they would be enabled to
meet the world's hatred victoriously.—They would overcome it by
the Spirit of love.—*Comforting*, an important function of the Spirit's
office, though it constitutes but a small portion of His work as
Helper and Guardian of believers.—Repeated promise of the Holy
Ghost : He is first promised as the Spirit of faith, and of the
living knowledge of Christ (chap. xiv.).—Here as the Spirit of
stedfast testimony for Christ.—In chap. xvi. as the Spirit of the
world-overcoming strength of the gospel, and as the Spirit of
Christ's glorification and of the future until the consummation.
Lange.

I will send. It is declared in the promise (chap. xiv. 16) that the Son *asks* the Father, and the Father sends the Spirit.—Here the Son sends the Spirit who "proceedeth from the Father."—It is only through the intercession of the Son that the Spirit is given. —The sending by the Father in answer to the Son's prayer, the sending by the Father in the Son's name, and the sending by the Son Himself, are thought of as one sending.

The Spirit of truth. See on chap. xiv. 17.—In a world of illusions and falsehoods He would reveal eternal realities.

Which proceedeth from the Father. (See note).—This gives weight to the Spirit's testimony to the Son.—The words imply that the original abode of the Spirit was *with* God. *Owen.*—He is of the Father's essence, and therefore is very and eternal God.— He is sent, and cometh, and witnesseth, which things are proper to a person only.—His witness concerning the Son is the witness of the Father himself.

He shall testify of me. Gr., *He shall bear witness of me.*—He emphatically, as opposed to the world, which hates Christ.—Indicates the *personality* of the Holy Ghost, as distinct from a mere power or influence—His witness is personal, and distinguished from the personal witness of the disciples.—This word ("witness") is one of the key-notes of the Johannine writings recurring alike in the Gospel, the Epistle, and the Apocalypse.—Unhappily its force is partly hidden by the various renderings "record," "testimony," "witness," for the one Greek root.

Of me. "Of My Person, My work."—Of Him as the true Vine, the source of life to His people.—Of Him as the sum and substance of all revelation.—Of Him as "the Author and Finisher of faith."—The Holy Ghost *testifies* of Jesus, this is the beginning of His office in the world; He *glorifies* Jesus, that is the goal and end of His office in believers.—The Lord calls Him the *Spirit of Truth*, to show the perfect faith that is due to His testimony.—This verse furnishes decisive proof of the doctrine of the Trinity.—Both the essential identity and the personal distinction of the Father, of the Son, and of the Spirit, are clearly stated (compare also xiv. 16, 18, 26; xvi. 7, 13; xx. 22).

ἐκπορεύεται Refers to the œconomical Trinity, or the Trinity of revelation.—The words are to be understood *historically. Beza, Lampe, Luthardt, Alford, Webster and Wilkinson,* &c.—A *theological* reference to the Trinitarian relations of the Spirit. *Most of the Greek fathers and Lutheran exegetes, Lücke, Olshausen,* &c.—The first clause (ὃν ἐγὼ πέμψω) spoken of the office of the Spirit in the Church: the second clause (ἐκπορ.) refers to the essential relation of the Spirit to the Holy Trinity. *Stier.*—The noun ἐκπόρευσις, *processio,* nowhere occurs in the N. T., and belongs to the ecclesiastical language, but it is legitimately formed from the verb ἐκπορευομαι which is here (and here alone) used of the Holy Ghost and denotes the characteristic individuality (ἰδιότης, *proprietas*, *character hypostaticus*) of the person (not the essence, which is the same in all Persons) of the Holy Spirit, as Sonship or e ernal Generation is the propriety of the Son, unbegotten Paternity the propriety of the Father.—Christ speaks here no doubt mainly of the Trinity of *revelation* and of the *historic* mis ion of the Holy Ghost in the Christian Church and in believers.—Yet it is significant that while He speaks of His sending of the Spirit in the future tense (πέμψω), He speaks of the procession of the Spirit from the Father in the present (ἐκπορ.), as if he intended to intimate a *permanent* relation of the Spirit to the Father.—The effusion of the Spirit on the day of Pentecost is the historic manifestation of His eternal procession from the Father, and bears a similar relation to the latter as the incarnation of Christ does to the eternal generation.—At all events, we have a right to deduce the œconomical Trinity from the ontological or immanent Trinity : the former is the revelation of the latter; for God manifests Himself as He is. *Schaff, Lange, Godet. &c.*—The Eastern Church, from the days of Mopsuestia downwards, have claimed this text as proving the procession of the Holy Spirit from the Father only, and have quoted it as decisive against the addition of the "filioque clause" in the Nicene Creed.—The Western Church, comparing it with chap. xvi. 15, and such tex's as Rom. viii. 9; Gal. iv. 6; Phil. i. 9; 1 Pet. i. 11, have held that it includes the procession from the Son.—If it refers to the person of the Holy Spirit, it must be granted that the *ipsissima verba* of our Lord are in favour of the interpretation of the Greek Church: but if it refers, as with much greater probability it does, to the office of the Holy Ghost, then *these words* have no bearing on the doctrinal question at issue. *Watkins.*

---

27. And ye also shall bear witness, because ye have been with me from the beginning.

Ye also. Gr., *and ye also bear witness;* or, *and ye also are witnesses.* —The words point to their past and present experience, as the foundation of their future testimony.—" The witness is one and the same; the Spirit will witness in and by them." *Alford.*—Under the Spirit's influence they are to stand forth as personal witnesses in accordance with their own peculiar historical and spiritual experience.—The personality of the Spirit never converts believers into involuntary, mechanical organs.—Hence the beautiful *variety*, and yet the unbroken *unity*, of Apostolic teaching.—The Spirit by His testimony makes others testify.—He takes away fear from Christ's friends, and converts the opposition of enemies into love. —The Spirit's working is not to supersede, but to engage and encourage ours.

Because ye have been. Gr., *because ye are with Me.*—The present tense indicates the relation as continuing.

From the beginning. From the commencement of the Messianic teaching and works of which they were to be witnesses.—An important qualification of the apostles, which in Paul's case was made up by a direct call of the exalted Lord (compare Acts i. 21, 22 ; x. 40, 41 ; xiii. 31).—As witnesses for Christ the apostles were under the infallible guidance of the Holy Spirit.—Not speculative ideas, but *historical facts*, form the foundation of Christian faith, and the ground-work of the world's salvation.—" We (of

the present day) *first* livingly experience and receive, through the
New Testament Scriptures, the life, deeds, and sayings of our
Lord, as eye and ear witnesses of the second degree ; *then* we also
wait humbly for power from on high ; and *then* it is our obligation
and right to testify with power and success what *we* have seen
and heard in historical conviction and living experience." *Lange.*—
All friends of Jesus are laid under the mightiest of all obligations
to witness faithfully for Him.—" Ye are my witnesses, saith the
Lord " (Isa. xliii. 10).—They, and they only, are able to witness
for Christ who have themselves been *with Him.*—He who will
preach Christ must first learn Christ, and as God admits any of
us to know anything of Christ, we are bound to witness the same
in our places and stations.

καὶ ὑμεῖς, &c. The apostles themselves distinguished between their own witness of
things which had come within their own experience and the witness borne by the
power of the Spirit, of which the Day of Pentecost was the first great instance (Acts
v. 32). *Watkins.*—The Spirit shall testify by miracles, in particular by the Pentecostal
miracle. by the conversion of the masses ; the apostles by the word. *Theod., Mopsueste,
Gerhard,* &c.—The two sides of the testimony of the apostles are mentioned in company with one another. *Augustine.*—The testimony borne by the Holy Ghost within the
apostles and designed especially for them ; the testimony of the apostles through the
Holy Ghost, addressed to the world. *Luthardt.*—The *Divine* testimony through the
divine power of the Word, and the *historical* testimony founded upon the fact that the
apostles were eye-witnesses of Jesus. *Lücke.*—One testimony; with a distinction, however, in respect of its two actual factors. *Meyer.*—The Spirit's testimony, as distinguished from theirs, consisted in their inspired utterances concerning the nature,
office. and work of Christ, attested by the miracles which the Spirit enabled them to
perform ; also in His action upon others besides themselves.—Their additional testimony ("and moreover ye ") consisted in their attestation of the facts of His life, death,
and resurrection. *Webster and Wilkinson.*—The apostles are not mentioned as witnesses *separate from* and *working with* the Spirit.—The allusion is to the historical
witness which the Spirit in them should enable them to give, which forms the *human*
side of this great testimony of the Spirit of Truth, and OF WHICH OUR INSPIRED
GOSPELS ARE THE SUMMARY : the *Divine side* being, His own indwelling testimony in
the life and heart of every believer in all time.—But both the one and the other are
given *by the self-same* SPIRIT; neither of them inconsistent with, or superseding, the
other. *Alford*

John 16

1. These things have I spoken unto you, that ye should not be offended.

These things. See on chap. xv. 17.—Refers to what He has just said (verses 17-27).—He had foretold them of the world's hatred and the Spirit's witness.

Offended. Gr., *stumbled.*—See on chap. vi. 61.—In John, the word only occurs here and in vi. 61.—The world's motto is, "Overcome that you may not suffer."—The Lord's, "Suffer that ye may overcome: Die that you may live."—Through the world's persecution they might stumble and fall from the faith.—His glance pierces beyond the offence that they shall take at Him in the impending night (verse 32).—Hus, Jerome, Cranmer, "stumbled," but God's grace raised them up again, and they sealed the truth with their blood.—The Captain of the Lord's host never sends a soldier to the field unarmed.—He warned His disciples, as no false teacher ever did, of the trials they might expect.—Many now "stumble" at the claims and doctrines of Christianity.—That we must become as little children, to enter the kingdom of God.—That the gospel makes no distinctions in its announcement of salvation by grace.—That faith demands implicit acceptance of the Divine Word and unreserved submission to the Divine will.—Love calls for the consecration of all to God; avarice protests.—Troubles threaten our peace; cowardice dreads disturbance.—The world reviles our names; pride shrinks from reproach.—Death demands our loved ones; affection refuses to give them up.—The power of the Spirit necessary to us as it was to the first disciples.

---

2. They shall put you out of the synagogues: yea, the time cometh, that whosoever killeth you will think that he doeth God service.

Put you out, &c. See on chap. ix. 22, 34; xii. 42.—He now reveals the operations of the world's hatred.—First comes *excommunication.*—Jewish persecutions typical of all the persecutions directed against His followers.—The effect of excommunication was a kind of moral outlawry, like losing caste in India.—Fruit-bearing branches in the true Vine cast forth as if withered and dead.—Can only come to pass when the ecclesiastical organization, calling itself "the Church" has become a synagogue of Satan

(Rev. ii. 9).—This is the answer to the accusation that the Church has persecuted.—It was not the Church of Christ that did it, but the Church of Anti-Christ.

Synagogues. See on Matt. iv. 23 ; Luke iv. 15; John ix. 22.

An hour cometh. A form of expression designed to give exceeding prominence to what follows.—Introduces the contrast of a much more grievous persecution (2 Cor. i. 9 ; vii. 11 ; Phil. iii. 8). —They were to experience the *bloody* fanaticism of the world.— Jesus Himself fell a sacrifice to it, as also Stephen (Acts vi. 8).

Whosoever. Gr., *every one*, implying how widespread the hatred of the gospel.—Even to murder *one* saint *forty* conspirators bound themselves by an oath (Acts xxiii. 13).

Killeth you. Jews would destroy the temple of the Holy Ghost (1 Cor. vi. 19) to save the temple of stone.—This blindness was both their guilt and their punishment.—Those who have revealed truth and refuse to walk by it God judicially abandons to their destruction.—Pagan and Papal Rome have killed millions of Christ's followers.—The former chiefly on alleged grounds of care for the welfare of the State, the latter on alleged grounds of care for the welfare of the Church.—The injury done the State by the murder of its purest and best citizens cannot be computed.— France is suffering to this hour for the murder of the Hugenots. —A church that requires fire and sword to maintain its dogmas or its authority is the church of the devil.—Rome has persistently opposed every attempt at reformation.—Her garments are red with the blood of the saints of God.—And she is to-day what she has ever been : her boast is that she is unchanged and unchangeable.—Had she the power she has the will to use the fagot and the stake as in days of yore.—She has never been known to regret a single act of persecution she has committed.—The medal struck by the Pope to celebrate the murders of Bartholomew's Day is still in the Vatican.—Unhappily, Protestants are not free from the sin of persecution for religious opinions.—But while Romanists persecute in *accordance* with their principles, Protestants persecute in *violation* of theirs.—Yet Satan and his allies have gained no victory, for the blood of the martyrs has been the seed of the Church.—There are some kinds of Christianity the world does not hate but rather likes : a Christianity that gives up belief in supernaturalism ; or that accommodates its doctrines to the pride of human reason ; or that explains away the principles and precepts of Christ to please corrupt affections and tastes ; or that ignores spiritual worship and substitutes æsthetic forms ; or that devolves all personal responsibility upon the priest and makes him the way to heaven : the Christianity that combines devotion with

worldly gaieties and pleasures, the Church with the theatre, religious services with selfish gratifications, &c.—In short, any kind
of Christianity almost, except the *genuine one.*—It is the *thing
itself*, not the mere name or form, which the world ever hates.—
Thus the chief enemies of Christianity, in the end, are unbelieving, worldly-minded professors.—A Christian should know there
is something wrong if the foes of his Master flatter and caress him.
—Christ's disciples need never be ashamed of the scorn or hatred
of Christ's enemies.—Yea, rather should it be regarded as an
honour and a *glory*, for such it will appear in the Day of Judgment.

Will think, &c.   Gr., *will think that he offereth to God a sacrificial
service.* The word rendered "doeth" is the technical word for
offering service (Matt. v. 23 ; viii. 4).—The word rendered
"service" means the service of worship (Rom. ix. 4 ; xii. 1;
Heb. ix. 1, 6).—It is a Rabbinic comment on Num. xxv. 13,
"Whosoever sheddeth the blood of the wicked is as he who
offereth sacrifice."—A striking illustration of this is found in St.
Paul's account of himself as a persecutor (Acts xxvi. 9 ; Gal. i. 13).
The performance of the curse-sacrifice (*Cherem*), as the last and
highest form of excommunication, was looked upon as a religious
act. *Lange.*—The Gentile world also had the same idea, and
carried it out in sundry ways (1 Cor. iv. 12).—Thus religion, the
supreme good, has been made a cloke for malice and hate and
murder.—"As Cain persecuted Abel, so the false Church still
persecutes the true, so misbelievers still persecute true believers,
hypocrites and mouth Christians those who are Christians in sincerity" (Gal. iv. 29). *Zeisus.*—Unbelief becomes so blinded and
hardened that it seeks to justify even before God the most cruel
crimes.—The *hour*, when it is thought to be a species of religious
service to persecute the truth and its witnesses, shall only cease
with the end of the world.—At the head of the noble army of
martyrs is the Lord Himself.—Nearest in time to Him, and in the
beauty of his death stands Stephen.—A glorious host of every
rank and age followed.—The incessant stream of blood quenched
the fires, if not the rage of enemies.—Crowd after crowd came
forward until the axe fell from the exhausted arm of the executioner.—Owing to our weakness and the natural love of life the
martyr's death must ever be regarded as the crown of patience
and endurance.

ἀποσυναγώγους, A punishment involving the direst consequences, socially and
religiously.—It was, in fact, the lesser excommunication, whi h lasted thirty days,
but might be lengthened for continued impenitence, or curtailed by contrition.—It

shut a person utterly from the synagogue, for even if he entered it he was reckoned as not present ; no mourning for the dead, and no rite of circumcision. could take p'ace in his house ; and no one but his wife or chi d could come within four cubits of him. *Geikie.* (See also on Matt. xviii. 15, 18) - The excommunication and outlawry to which the worl l sentences the followers of Jesus : 1. In a secular form ; 2 In an ecclesiastical form ; 3. In a sectarian form. *Lange —* λατρείαν. Since the rise of the Spanish Inquisition, it has burnt, from the year 1481 to 1808, no less than 34,358 Christians in person, and 10,049 in effigy. *Gossner.*

---

3. And these things will they do unto you, because they have not known the Father, nor me.

These things, &c. Consolation for the disciples in regard to their persecutions : 1. These persecutions do not arise because of anything in their faith as Christians; 2. Their persecutors while parading their intelligence and zeal are grovelling in the most lamentable darkness.

Not known, &c. See on chap. xv. 21.—Ignorance of God revealed in Christ, the cause of the world's hatred and persecution.—A special force in the mention of this ignorance in connection with the preceding verse.—Those who think that in excommunication, curses, torments, deaths of men made like themselves in God's image, they are offering to Him an acceptable sacrifice, can know nothing of the true nature of the Father.—He is long-suffering, not willing that any should perish, but that all should come to repentance (2 Peter iii. 9).—They know nothing of the compassion of the Son of God, who came not to destroy men's lives, but to save them, and who pleaded even for His murderers, "Father, forgive them; for they know not what they do ! " (Luke xix. 56 ; xxiii. 34.)—" He that loveth not his brother whom he hath seen, how can he love God whom he hath not seen ? " (1 John iv. 20.)— Yet persecutors profess to serve a God whose *name* and *nature* is LOVE.—Often crying out while persecuting His saints, " Let the Lord be glorified " (Isa. lxvi. 5).—Doing the destroyer's work wearing the livery of the Saviour.—They think to silence conscience by slandering their victims.—Thus before murdering, persecutors have always calumniated and blackened God's saints. —Thus the agents of Rome preferred the most monstrous accusations against those they condemned to the stake.—Witness the charges which Romish and Ritualistic priests are now putting forth against God's servants the Reformers.—Children of lies they resemble him who was a liar and a murderer from the beginning (see on chap. viii. 44).—Rome says ignorance is the mother of devotion, and as is the parent so is the child.—Ignorance cannot relieve of responsibility when it is the result of wilful and wicked perversion of truth.—" Thou thoughtest that I was altogether such an one as thyself : but I will reprove thee, and set them in order before thine eyes " (Psalms l. 21).—Persecutors picture a God out of the blackness and malignity of their own hearts, and then blasphemously call Him " the true God."—And the crimes which these wretches commit are attributed by infidels to the religion of the Bible !

---

4. But these things have I told you, that when the time shall come, ye may remember that I told you of them. And these things I said not unto you at the beginning, because I was with you.

These things. See on chap. xiii. 19 ; xiv. 29.—Our Lord strengthens His disciples by forewarning them.

Time shall come, &c. In persecution they would remember His word, and find in it support of faith and assurance of His presence.—Thus even persecution will be among the "all things " which shall work together for *good* (Rom. viii. 28).—That is for *good*, in the highest sense, through which the believer realizes the truth of the divine word and the comfort of the divine presence, though it be brought about by sorrow and pain.—The Christian religion must be *lived* to be learned.—How poor a foundation for faith were not these the words of the Faithful and true Witness, the God of Truth.—Reproach, and scorn, and every other persecution are but so many evidences of the truth of the gospel.

I said not unto you, &c. While with them, He would spare them, as it was against Himself the hatred of His foes was directed.— He had it in His power to tell them, but had neither inclination nor need to do so too soon.—Now, however, being about to leave them He tells them, that they may not stumble at the sufferings of the coming of which He had forewarned them.—It was not necessary to anticipate : "Sufficient unto the day is the evil thereof."—Moreover, He always proportioned His teaching to their gradual development.—But the time is now at hand when they shall represent Him and stand in the foreground of the battle.— Christ is ever so tender of His disciples that He will not put the burden of suffering upon them till He has prepared them for it.

οὐκ εἶπον, &c. "Because I was with you," serve as an elucidation. *Lange.*—So that I could comfort you. *Aug., Lücke.*—The hatred of the world touched Me alone. *Chrys., Luther, Meyer.*—Because ye were then too weak to bear such sayings. *Erasmus, Calvin.* Because He now promises them the help of the Spirit. *Bengel, Tholuck.*—According to the Synoptists, Christ foretold such sufferings to the disciples at a much earlier time (Matt. v. 10; x. 16 ; xxiv. 9, &c.).—The passages are not, however, really incorsistent, for "these things" in this verse (compare verses 3 and 1, and chap. xv. 21) refers to the full account He has given them of the world's hatred and the principles lying at the bottom of it, and the manner in which it was to be met by the Spirit's witness and their witness of Him.—These things which the infant Church would have to meet, and meet without His bodily presence, He told them not at the beginning. *Ellicott.*—As a farewell word the revelation was a new one *Luthardt.*—He spoke in reference to his immediate departure. *Alford.* - He before spoke *minus aperte. Grotius, Bengel.*—Now He proclaims the cause of the world's hatred. *Lampe.*—Earlier intimations of a more general and less definite character are reported by the Synoptists in agreement with later and more definite ones. *Meyer.*—Those earlier predictions probably belong to the time when Jesus delivered his last discourses. *Beza, Maldonatus.*—Those utterances were of an isolated cast; Christ here more expressly declared the principal position of the disciples. *Tholuck.*

---

5 But now I go my way to him that sent me; and none of you asketh me, Whither goest thou?

I go my way, &c. See on chap. xiii. 1 ; xv. 12.—His mission was nearly accomplished, and He was about to return to Him who sent Him.—The words point to His death, resurrection, and ascension to glory.—This was the reason for His present enlightenment of them with regard to their future.—Together with what is said He will tell them the most gladdening things.—This departure was to Him matter of joy, and if they truly loved Him would be so to them also. —They ought to have thought of the future before Him, as He, in the fulness of His love, was then thinking of the future before them.

And none of you asketh, &c. This seems at variance with chap. xiii. 36, and xiv. 5.—Peter had asked this very question, and Thomas had implied it.—The meaning is : Ye give yourselves up to the sad thought that I go *away*, and make no inquiries as to the glad thought, *whither*, namely, to the Father. *Lange.*—None of you out of love for Me ask about the place whither I am going. —Your thoughts are not with Me.—Is it to you as nothing that I am returning to Him who sent Me ? *Ellicott.*—It seemed as if they still clung to the old hopes regarding Messiah's kingdom, and were afraid to embrace the new views of life to which He was calling them —So hard is it to emancipate ourselves from the bonds of early religious prejudice.—A lesson of patience and forbearance to missionaries and all those engaging in a similar work.—The Lord gently rebukes them for not seeking the required knowledge which He would readily have imparted.—Worldliness not only darkens the mind, and prevents us beholding the glory of Christ, but it restrains prayer likewise.—As His whole life had but one direction, one aim, one goal, so should ours.—"If ye then be risen with Christ, seek those things which are above, where Christ sitteth on the right hand of God" (Col. iii. 1).

6. But because I have said these things unto you, sorrow hath filled your heart.

Because I have said, &c. Explanatory of the mild reproach in verse 5.—The thought of their loss in His departure had so filled their hearts that there was no room for thoughts of the glory He was hastening to.—Under these words lies a gracious excuse for their remissness.—He mildly upbraids them for their silence, but hints that it was caused by excessive grief.—" He knoweth our frame ; he remembereth that we are dust. Like as a father pitieth his children, so the Lord pitieth them that fear him " (Psalm ciii. 13, 14).—With similar divine tenderness He made excuse for them in Gethsemane : " The spirit indeed is willing, but the flesh is weak " (Matt. xxvi. 41).—In this life sorrow often contends with faith and hope for the mastery.—Many weep, bearing their cross who fail to catch the consolations offered.—The state of the mind determines the power of outward circumstances, as a rule.—Dark prisons become light, and barren deserts bloom where Christ's presence is realized.—Our sins, not our afflictions, separate between us and our God.—" Whom the Lord loveth he chasteneth " (Heb. xii. 6).—As sorrow filled the hearts of the disciples and prevented them thinking of the glory their Lord was rising to, so it often happens upon the death of Christian friends.—However unwilling we may be to believe it there is much selfishness in our sorrow.—Our all-absorbing grief prevents us seeing that what is loss to us is infinite gain to them.—Love should rejoice in their deliverance from sin and suffering and their entrance upon eternal blessedness.

---

7. Nevertheless I tell you the truth; It is expedient for you that I go away: for if I go not away, the Comforter will not come unto you ; but if I depart, I will send him unto you.

Nevertheless. Refers to the sorrow in verse 6.—He is about to speak of the Holy Ghost as the source of their victory over the world.—This whole passage (7-12) incomprehensible to the carnal mind, but unspeakably precious to those knowing the things of God.—It touches on the deepest questions of doctrine, and on the practical discipline of our hearts and lives.—With a few great strokes our Lord depicts all and every part of the Spirit's ministry in the world, His operation on individuals as well as the mass, on believers and unbelievers alike. *Olshausen.*

I tell you. " *I myself*," in the consciousness of personal ability to remove their sorrow by sending the Comforter : " I, who know all."

The truth. He appeals to His own knowledge and candour in dealing with them (see on chap. xiv. 2).—They were overwhelmed with grief and needed this strong assurance and consolation.—The Lord condescends to the infirmities and fears of His children.

Expedient for you. For your advantage.—Expresses the divine necessity and intention.—Looks to the purposes destined to be accomplished by it.—Indicates that the dispensation of the Spirit is higher and more blessed than the dispensation of the Son in the state of His humiliation.—Christ's departure, without the coming of the Spirit, would have been the greatest of all calamities.—No communion upon earth could be compared with theirs with their Lord.—But they lived more in sight than in faith, and depended too much on His visible presence, like children upon the presence and form of parents.—They had to lose Christ as a mere man to find him again as God enthroned.—The book of Acts shows what they gained in independence and self-government, in strength and endurance of faith by the Lord's withdrawal of His visible presence.—It is the Spirit who makes us partakers of the whole fulness of Christ and His completed redemption..—The Church of Rome seems unable to recognise how expedient it was for Christ to go away : " She has never been content, unless she could get something *present*, a vicar, images, outward works, actual sacrifices, with priests to offer them up, real flesh and real blood. She chose rather to defy the evidence of the senses, than not to have an object of sense." *Hare.*—She has loved the Lord Jesus Christ as a man loves man, as the carnal loves the carnal, not as the spiritual loves true Majesty.

That I go away. See on chap. xiv. 16.—As if He had said : " There is no cause for the sorrow that fills your hearts."—It was for *their* welfare that *He*, as distinct from the Comforter, who was to come, should go away.—Yet it was a hard saying, and at the time must have seemed incomprehensible, that His departure should be for their benefit.—They had left all and followed Him ; their hopes were all centred in Him ; they had none to go to but Himself.— Like many other " hard " sayings of the Lord, it contained the promise of glorious blessings.—Often also He takes from us the desire of our hearts that He may bestow upon us far greater mercies.

If I go not. See on chap. vii. 39.—The coming of the Spirit as the Spirit of redemption and adoption presupposes the offering of the atoning sacrifice, the glorification of Christ's humanity and His exaltation to His Mediatorial throne.

The Comforter will not come. See on chap. xiv. 16, 26.—The Son was to be glorified before the Spirit was to be given.— Humanity was to ascend to heaven before the Spirit could be sent to humanity on earth.—The revelation of saving truth was to be complete before inspiration was to breathe it into man's soul.

I will send. The coming of the Spirit upon the day of Pentecost, the Father's seal upon every claim, word, work of Jesus.— Wherever the Spirit's power is manifested there is evidence of the resurrection, ascension, and glorification of Christ.—The Spirit in the heart is the witness of our Lord's exaltation and the pledge that where He is there His people shall also be.—The presence of the Holy Ghost *with* us is a greater comfort and advantage than the presence of Christ in the flesh *amongst* us.—Through the gift of the Spirit, the risen and glorified Lord is present to every believer at the same moment of time, in every part of the world.— The coming of the Spirit considered with reference to the riches of His names : 1. The (other) Mediator; 2. The (other) Helper; 3. The (other) Awakener; 4. The (other) Comforter.—The marvellous coming of the Comforter : 1. How it adds new sufferings to the old ones (the sufferings of the martyrs) ; 2. How it transforms the old sufferings together with the new ones into joy. *Lange.* (See also on chap. vii. 39.)

The E. V. reverses the distinction between ἀπέλθω, to *depart* (from earth) and πορεύομαι, to *go* (to heaven) —The one here signifies the starting-point, the other the goal of Christ's journey. *Schaff.*

---

8. And when he is come, he will reprove the world of sin, and of righteousness, and of judgment.

When he is come. Solemn and triumphant exaltation of spirit, and proclamation,—The witness of the Spirit (chap. xv. 26), a threefold *victory* over the world.

He will reprove the world. The disciples not mentioned : as bearers of the Spirit, they seem to vanish from sight in His glory. *Lange.*

Reprove. See on chap. viii. 46.—Gr., *convince*, or, *convict*.—" The Holy Ghost, as the Paraclete of the persecuted apostles, turns the table upon their adversaries."—He prosecutes the persecuting world, brings it to judgment, and, as sinner, convicts it.— Thus He executes an ideal judgment upon the whole world.—The Spirit's operation is never external but always internal.—His testimony is never addressed to the intellectual consciousness alone, but invariably to the moral consciousness, the conscience. —It is a revelation to the hearts of men of the character and work of Christ, and, therefore, a refutation of the evil in their hearts.—Some turn this conviction to belief, others harden themselves in unbelief.—Thus by convicting the world He occasions its separation into the two portions of the saved and the judged.—Men either accept this conviction, and are saved by it, or reject it and are condemned (see on chap. iii. 20 ; viii. 46).—The effect of Peter's sermon on the Day of Pentecost is the first great historical comment on this verse.—The whole history of the Church's work continues that comment.—The three steps in this conviction are defined in the three following verses.

ἐλέγξει. In Homer and earlier Greek authors the word means chiefly *to rebuke, to reprove, to reproach;* so also in Luke iii. 19; 1 Tim. v 20; Rev. iii. 19.—But in the phraseology of the courts of justice and of the schools, the verb expresses demonstration, conviction, and refutation of an opponent by fair and conclusive arguments.—The meaning of the word here is a *conviction,* by which the sinner is proved to be such, and becomes conscious of his sin and guilt, is "pricked to the heart" and "smitten in conscience" (Acts ii. 37), and brought to a crisis that he will either sincerely repent and be converted (1 Cor. xiv. 24), or harden his heart and bring upon him condemnation (Acts xxiv. 25; Rom. xi. 7).—The Divine intention of this convicting agency is the salvation of the sinner; for the Holy Spirit, like Christ Himself, was sent not to condemn the world, but to save it (compare iii 17). *Calvin, Beza, Lampe, B-ngel. Lücke, Olsh., Thol., Stier, Meyer, Alford, Hare, Schaff, &c.*—In ἐλεγχειν is always implied the refutation, the overcoming of an error, wrong, by the truth and the right *Lücke.*—They shall not do such things unreproved; on the contrary, sentence shall be passed upon them. *Chrys, Theophylact Erasmus Wetzel &c.*—The patristic interpretation *to reprove,* conveys a very inadequate descrip i n of the work of the Spirit, and gives no clear sense when applied to righteousness and judgment. *Schaff.*—τὸν κόσμον. Must not be confined to the Jews, or to the heathen, or to the ungodly, but be extended to all men (John iii. 16; xii. 31) who come under the influence of the Spirit and the preaching of the gospel. *Lange.*—The term *world* comprehends those who were to be truly converted to Christ, as well as hypocrites and reprobates. *Calvin.*

---

9. Of sin, because they believe not on me.

Of sin. That is, concerning, on the subject of, in respect to, *sin.*—Not the sin of unbelief only, but of sin generally ; unbelief is stated as the cause of sin.

They believe not on me. Sin consists in, is rooted in, in its different phases comprehended in, and finally, made manifest in, their not believing in Christ.—The rejection of Christ is the central appearance of all the sins of the world.—The world distinguishes between sin and unbelief, many considering the latter something praiseworthy.—Unbelief in its various forms of doubt, scepticism, &c., is looked upon as virtuous.—Where the Spirit convicts these false notions are subverted.—He shows that *the condemning sin* of the world is the want of a personal and living recognition of Jesus as the Lord (1 Cor. xii. 3).—The Spirit makes sin manifest, not in its outward character—this is the work of the Law (Rom. iii. 20)—

but in its inward deep root, unbelief, which is the parent of all
sinful actions.—And the most offensive and criminal form of this
unbelief is, unbelief in the Incarnate Christ.—The inability of
recognizing this purest manifestation of the Divinity reveals utter
blindness. *Olshausen.*—Sin is missing the aim of life, the dis-
ordered action of powers that have lost their controlling principle.
—Christ is the revelation to the world of the Father's love, and
by union with Him the soul finds the centre of its being, and its
rest.—By the Spirit's witness He convinces men of this, and shows
them their sin in not believing on Christ.—" Henceforth he who is
condemned must not complain of Adam and of inborn sin ; but
must cry out against himself for not having believed in Christ, the
devil's head-bruiser and sin-strangler." *Luther.*—He who is convicted of sin, passes over either to the righteousness of Christ, or
to the judgment of Satan. *Bengel.*

περὶ ἀμαρτίας. He will discover to them the sin they commit in not believing on
Me. *Euth. Zigab., Lücke.*—He will convince them that their unbelief is sin, is wrong.
Meyer, &c.—ὅτι. The triple ὅτι defines the substance and ground of the triple ἐλεγχος,
and is, *in that, inasmuch as. Lange.*– πιστεύουσιν. The point of view taken by Christ
in describing these events is that of the consummation of the things predicted : hence
He employs the Present tense. *Lange.*—That which was to be effected by His Spirit
in the Church during the whole course of ages down to the end of the world, He concentrates, as it were. into a single point of space, and a single moment of time ; even as
our eye, with the help of distance, concentrates a world into a star. *Hare.*

---

10. Of righteousness, because I go to my Father, and ye see me no more.

Of righteousness. The righteousness of Christ, not that of the
world.—The world pronounced the Lord a sinner (chap. ix. 24) ;
in His crucifixion it set Him forth as sin itself, and treated Him as
such.—By the convincing power of the Spirit these views will be
subverted, and, together with these, the world's views of the
righteousness of God and the human life itself. *Lange.*—Christ's
righteousness becomes *our* righteousness by *faith ;* He is *the Lord
our Righteousness.*—The conviction merely of God's righteousness, or of Christ's, could be of no benefit to us, we could no
more venture to look upon it than the naked eye could look upon
the sun.—It is the conviction that Christ's righteousness is the
righteousness which He purposes to bestow upon mankind that
fills us with joy and peace through believing.—The conviction of
Christ's righteousness necessarily precedes that of the soul's own
sin.—The light reveals the darkness, and the revelation of the
darkness shows the clearness of the light.

I go to my Father. This is the most certain demonstration of

Christ's righteousness.—By His triumphant exaltation to the right hand of the Father, He, who had been put to death as a " sinner," a blasphemer, and an impostor (chap. xviii. 30 ; ix. 24), was vindicated by God Himself and proved by the testimony of the Paraclete, through the apostles, to be *the* JUST ONE.—His return to His Father, therefore, was the Father's proclamation of His righteousness to the universe (Acts ii. 27, 31, 36, 37 ; iii. 14 ; vii. 52 ; 1 Pet. iii. 18 ; 1 John ii. 1, 29 ; iii. 7).

Ye see me no more. The word means "look upon " or "behold."—They should gaze upon His bodily presence no more.—This renders it easier for us to make His righteousness ours.—Were He still living upon earth it would not be so.—We should then live by sight, not by faith.—Sight, as belonging to the world of sense, partakes of its imperfections.—To put forth all its power, faith must be purely and wholly faith.—It is only when love springs from faith that it is transforming and abiding. *Hare.*—The Spirit's witness is a truer presence of the Lord than any which physical eye could see.—The eye of the spirit sees the reality ; the eye of the body only looks upon the appearance.—Christ's kingdom this side of eternity must be a kingdom of the cross, and the world can reach Him only through faith.—The full glory of righteousness is still in the hereafter with Christ, and not until the Last Day shall it *appear. Lange.*

περὶ δικαιοσύνης. The righteousness of Christ ("guiltlessness"). *Chrys., Beza, Lücke, Meyer.*—The *righteousness that comes of faith* in the Pauline sense. *Cyril, Aug., Calvin, Luther, Stier, Gerlach, Alford.*—The personal righteousness or absolute sinless perfection of Christ, and not justification by faith, although this of course rests upon the former : 1. δικαιοσύνη is plainly the opposite to ἁμαρτία, and *Christ* is the subject of "righteousness," as the *world* is the subject of "sin." 2. The explanatory ὅτι πρὸς τὸν πατέρα, &c., refers to *Christ.* not to us, and gives the proof of *His* righteousness, not ours.—3. John uses δικαιοσύνη always in its proper sense of *righteousness,* not of *justification,* which corresponds to the Greek δικαίωσις, a term unknown to John's vocabulary.—4. John expresses the Pauline idea of justification in opposition to condemnation not so much in its legal as in its moral aspects and in connection with its effects upon the soul by the familiar phrase, " He that believeth hath *eternal life.*" *Schaff, Lange.*—Christ's exaltation to the throne of glory is the central appearance of God's righteousness ; of God's righteousness in Christ, God's righteousness in His Providence, God's righteousness in believers, in the conscience of unbelievers even. *Lange.*

---

11. Of judgment, because the prince of this world is judged.

Of judgment, &c. See on chap. xii. 30, 31.—The Greek indicates the completion of the condemnation—" The prince of this world hath been and remaineth judged."—Christ's work of redemption, complet d bv the coming of the Paraclete, a condemnation of the prince of this world.—The conviction of this follows upon that of sin and upon that of righteousness.—The world made the cross a sign of reprobation, and success a sign of God's favour; but conviction by the Spirit's testimony of Christ, subverts this view.—The judgment of the prince of this world commenced in the victory over the tempter in the wilderness, and was consummated on the cross.—This judgment has been in process of development ever since, and shall become fully manifested in the Last Judgment.—The power of Satan is overcome by the opening of the kingdom of heaven to all believers.—The King of righteousness claims mankind whose nature He has redeemed from the power of the dark usurper.—Satan judged and cast out: 1. From the heathen world, when his oracles were silenced and his altars deserted; 2. From the bodies of men *in Christ's name;* 3. From men's souls by the grace of God working with the gospel; 4. As lightning from heaven. *Henry.*—The final act of this judgment upon the prince of this world is "the lake of fire and brimstone" (Rev. xx. 10).—With that he disappears for ever.—The convincing and convicting of the world: 1. In respect of its subject: *a.* Of the one sin in which all sins are embraced; *b.* Of the one righteousness wherein all righteousness is manifested and fulfilled; *c.* Of the one judgment in which all judgments are decided and grounded. 2. In respect of its effect: the convincement of men's opinions, minds, consciences, hearts. *Lange.*—The Spirit's great aim is to deliver man from his sin and from the judgment to come, and to make him partaker of the righteousness of Christ.—In the discourses of the Apostles recorded in Acts these three subjects most prominent: 1. Christ the only Saviour, and rejection of Him fatal and damning sin; 2. Righteousness or justification through the exaltation and intercession of Christ; 3. The kingdom of Christ, instead of Satan's, now, and to be perfected in the final judgment. *Webster and Wilkinson.*—In the three great words, *sin, righteousness, judgment,* the Lord names the three all-embracing, essential elements of truth and its whole procedure.—Not until the Spirit has explained these words does the world know what they are.—Yet the natural man has some slight perception of them, as is evident from the writings of the heathen, and the penal codes of all nations.—But the production of an experimental and perfect knowledge of them is the office of the *Spirit* alone, and that *as* Spirit.—Unfolding to the inner law of conscience, the higher law of God, especially the atoning sacrifice and divine-human glory of Christ, the Spirit leads to a living, practical knowledge and personal conviction of these three *facts.*

περὶ δὲ κρίσεως. The judgment executed upon the devil through the death and resurrection of Christ, is the central appearance of all God's judgments in the history of the world until the end of the world ; an appearance fully illuminated by means of the spiritual manifestation of the cross, or the accursed tree—to which Satan brought Christ—as the sign of victory. *Lange*

---

12. I have yet many things to say unto you, but ye cann't bear them now.

Many things to say. The *things* with regard to which the Spirit of Truth shall be their guide (verse 13).—Parts of the one revelation to be fully disclosed to them hereafter.—Would include the perfect emancipation of Christianity from Judaism, its promulgation to all nations, &c. ; and pre-eminently those revelations which appear in the Apocalypse, in the Epistles to the Thessalonians, and in Rom. viii. xi., &c.—Doubtless, the principles of these are contained in the communications already made, especially in His discourses respecting the "last things."—Yet the Apocalyptic revelations subsequently received by the Apostles exhibit views of the development of the kingdom of God never before presented with such distinctness and fulness.

Ye cannot bear them now. Intellectually incapable of comprehending them ; and morally incapable of supporting them.—He is ready to impart to them as friends all things that He had heard from the Father (chap. xv. 15).—But revelation can only be made to a mind capable of receiving it.—A mere formal statement of truth is not a revelation to those who do not perceive that truth.—Our Lord lays down a rule, which all who profess to teach in His name should remember.—Paul acted upon it: we find that he fed some with milk because they could not bear meat (1 Cor. iii. 3).—The teacher must take the lower ground of the pupil's knowledge, and from that lead up to his own.—Christ's truths must be taught as He Himself taught them, if they are to be taught successfully. —Prematurely to pour out to people the whole truth, is not only *useless*, but *it is also positively hurtful.*

πολλά. New articles of doctrine are intended.—Tradition and its dogmas. *Roman Catholic Exegetes.*—Sufferings to be endured by the apostles. *Luther.*—New forms of truth, in itself already familiar. *Aquinas.*—New developments and applications of truth already known. *Ancient Protestant Exegetes, Lücke, &c.*—The entire ecclesiastical development of doctrine. *Hegelian Exegetes.*—Apocalyptic disclosure of apostolic Christianity in its more developed stage. *Albertus Magnus, Tholuck, Schaff, Lange, &c.* —Would include the doctrinal system of the early Church, and would not exclude all the lessons which the spirit of God has taught the Church in every age. *Watkins.*

13. Howbeit when he, the Spirit of truth, is come, he will guide you into all truth: for he shall not speak of himself; but whatsoever he shall hear, that shall he speak: and he will shew you things to come.

The Spirit of truth. See on chap. xiv. 17.—He now refers to the Holy Ghost as the Spirit of the development of Christianity, and of the revelation of the future.

All truth. *The whole truth; the full truth.*—The full knowledge of living, practical truth as it is in *Christ* and as it relates to our soul's salvation.—The Bible is an infallible guide of religious faith and life; but not a universal encyclopædia of knowledge.—This important passage proves the sufficiency of Scripture both as a rule of faith and practice.—Moreover, in a certain sense, the Holy Spirit alone can lead us *into all truth*, even in temporal and human things.—For the love of truth is inseparable from the love of God, and the perfect knowledge of truth from the knowledge of God, and this can only come from the Spirit of God, the true illuminator of the human mind now darkened and distorted by sin.—Yet no promise of universal knowledge, nor of infallibility, is hereby conveyed.—The Spirit will guide them into the *fulness* of truth.— The word rendered "guide," occurs also in Matt. xv. 14 ; Luke vi. 39 ; Rev. vii. 17 ; and metaphorically, as here, in Acts viii. 31 ; and from comparison of these passages the meaning seems to be "to point out the way," "to lead one on his way."—The Holy Spirit will take them by the hand, and step by step, as they have strength to follow, will guide them into the *fulness* of truth.—The Spirit will *lead*, the believer must therefore *walk with* Him.—The words had a special meaning for our Lord's Apostles ; but they hold good for every disciple who seeks after truth.—It is thus some become scribes "instructed unto the kingdom of heaven ; bringing forth out of their treasures things new and old" (see on Matt. xiii. 52).

Not speak of himself. See on chap. v. 19 ; vii. 17, 18; xiv. 26.— Like the Son Himself, the Holy Spirit will represent to the world the eternal truth of God.—Contrast with this what is said in chap. viii. 44, where the essence of the lie is that the devil speaketh of *his own.*—"Thus He imposeth a limit and measure (a basis and principle) to the preaching of the Holy Ghost Himself ; He is to preach nothing new, nothing other than Christ and His Word ; to the end, that we might have a sure sign, a certain test, whereby to judge false spirits." *Luther.*—Thus the Spirit is conditioned by the Son, as the Son is by the Father. *Lange.*—"If the Holy Ghost may not speak of Himself, and out of Himself, O Preacher, how canst thou draw thy preaching out of *thyself*, out of *thine head*, or even *heart?*" *Gossner.*—No preaching or testimony should come from the mere impulse or will to preach ; the Spirit must teach and impel. *Braune.*—Self-love darkens the mind and renders it incapable of receiving and understanding "the deep things of the Spirit."

Shall hear. Such historical things as He, as the Spirit of believers, and of the Church, has heard from Christ, either directly or indirectly. *Lange.*—"Nor need you fear to trust Him less than you have trusted Me; for just as I have not spoken of Myself, but have only repeated what I have heard from My Father, He, the Spirit of Truth, will not speak for Himself, or of His own promptings, but will utter only what He has heard from God." *Geikie.*

Things to come. See on verse 12.—*Gr., He will announce to you the things to come.*—Especially the doctrine of "the last things," of which the Apocalypse of John is the most remarkable example.—"He will give you, my Apostles, the gift of prophecy, by which the future development of My Kingdom will be revealed to you, to fill you with comfort and triumph." *Geikie.*—The words also have their fulfilment in the Spirit's illumination in all ages.

For εἰς πᾶσαν τὴν ἀλήθειαν read εἰς τὴν ἀλήθειαν πᾶσαν. *Cod. Sin., Tisch., Treg., Lach.. Lange Alford. &c.*—ἀκούσῃ. ἀκούσει. *Treg., Alford. Westcott and Hort.*—ἀκούει. *Cod. Sin., Tisch.*—*Hath heard,* historical transmission. *Lange.*—Heard from Christ. *O'sh., Kling &c.*—Heard from the Father. *Meyer.*—Heard from both the Father and the Son. *Luthardt, Godet, Alford.*—A hearing from the Father on the part of the Spirit, a hearing independent of history, is no a clear idea at all; it would. moreover, set the revelation of the Spirit, as a separate one, by the side of that of the Son, *Lange.*

---

14. He shall glorify me: for he shall receive of mine, and shall shew it unto you.

He shall glorify me. *He* is emphatic, and clearly implies, as this whole discourse does, the personality of the Holy Spirit: *Me* is also emphatic.—The Son reveals and glorifies the Father, the Spirit reveals and glorifies the Son.—The sole aim of the Son to glorify the Father, the sole aim of the Spirit to glorify the Son.— A mysterious rivalry, so to speak, of Divine love, whose very essence is to do all for the beloved.—How much more should our sole aim and end be to glorify God.—Jesus would be glorified by the revelation of the "many things" concerning Himself which they were not then able to bear.—The testimony of Jesus is the kernel and spirit of all prophecy.—The Spirit *witnesses* for Jesus in the world; but He *glorifies* Jesus in believers.—The glorification of Jesus *before us* must coincide with the establishment of His image *in us.*—There is no other receiving of this glorifying light, than that which takes place according to 2 Cor. iii. 17, 18.—The Spirit alone gives us a living knowledge of Jesus as our Lord and Saviour, and makes us partakers of His life and His benefits.—As all that the Spirit reveals has reference to Christ, so in the fulness and clearness of His revelation is Christ glorified (2 Cor. iv. 6).

He shall take of mine, &c. This defines what the Spirit shall announce.—Everything that shall be revealed is not only actually enclosed in Christ, but also germinally contained in His Word.— This is the standard by which to try all professed revelations, or interpretations of Scripture.—"Every spirit that confesseth that Jesus Christ is come in the flesh is of God, and every spirit that confesseth not Jesus is not of God" (1 John iv. 1, 2).—The word of Christ is not an imperfect revelation to be afterward either supplemented or corrected by the Spirit.—His office is to illumine the mind and bring home to it *the things of Christ.*—" He will purify and enlighten your hitherto imperfect conceptions concerning Me, and, while thus fitting you to spread My Kingdom, will but develop, expand, and complete what I have taught you, and thus increase My glory." *Geikie.*—A warning to the Church against all pretended revelations subsequent to and besides Christ.—The Spirit declares *the things of Christ,* not anything new and beyond Him.—How the Holy Ghost leads the children of truth into all truth : 1. He leads them, not away *from* Christ, but *unto* Christ ; 2. He adheres to gospel words and facts and explains them ; 3. He unfolds what there is of a prophetic nature in Christian truth ; 4. He glorifies the Christ to come in the present of the Church's life.—The Holy Ghost conducts into the whole inheritance of God. *Lange.*

---

15. All things that the Father hath are mine : therefore said I, that he shall take of mine, and shew it unto you.

All things, &c. The Son is the Revealer of the Father, and the fulness of the truth is given unto Him (verse 13).—As in chap. xv. 26, there is here an incidental proof of the doctrine of the Trinity, both in its internal relation, and in its external, self-revealing action upon the world for its salvation.—The essential unity of Father, Son, and Spirit is implied, and the tri-personality clearly taught in the words employed.—Christ distinguishes Himself both from the Father and from the Spirit, and yet claims the whole fulness of the Father as His own, and communicates His fulness to the Spirit (Col. ii. 3).—The words vividly exhibit the *living, inter-existence* of Father, Son, and Spirit. *Olsh.*—"For being Three, and they all subsisting in the essence of one Deity, *from* the Father, *by* the Son, *through* the Spirit, all things are. That which the Son doth hear of the Father, and which the Spirit doth receive of the Father and the Son, the same we have at the hands of the Spirit as being the last, and therefore the nearest unto us in order, although in power the same with the second and the first." *Hooker.*—Our Lord has opened to us a glimpse into the living blessed bond of love in receiving and giving in the eternal ground of the triune essence of the Godhead. *Œtinger.*

Therefore said I, &c. Better, *He taketh of Mine, and shall declare it unto you.*—The present *(He taketh)* sets forth the unchanging relation of the Spirit to the Son.—As if our Lord had said, " I have a full right to designate the *divine* truth which the Spirit will reveal as My property, for all which the *Father* has, *i.e.,* according to the context, *the whole possession of the truth of the Father,* belongs to *Me* as the Son 'who was in intuitive communion with the Father (chap. i. 18), who came out from the Father (chap. viii. 42), who am consecrated (chap. x. 36), and sent to fulfil His work, who also continually live and move in the Father and the Father in Me (chap. xvii. 10)." *Meyer.*—These verses (14 and 15) teach the Divinity of the Son, the Personality of the Spirit, and the Trinity in Unity and Unity in Trinity.

For λήψεται read λαμβάνει. *Tisch., Lach., Treg., Alford, Lange, Schaff, Westcott and Hort.*

---

16. A little while, and ye shall not see me: and again, a little while, and ye shall see me, because I go to the Father.

A little while, &c. Gr., *and ye no longer behold Me* (see on chap. xiv. 18, 19).—Refers to the time between the moment of His speaking to them and His death.—After a brief space of mourning, His withdrawal, now at hand, will be followed with joyful effects.—The first " little while " reaches to His death upon the cross, about one day ; the second extends from that death to His resurrection, about another day. *Lange.*—The one and the other are symbolical of Good Friday and Easter periods in the Church. —Our spiritual life also is subject to vicissitudes.—The words, " a little while," contain much consolation for those in distress, pain, poverty, sickness, sorrow.—Impatience objects that it is not " a little while," but faith teaches the contrary.—In this saying lies the secret of many of God's dealings with His people.

Because I go to the Father. He goes to the realm, not of death,
but of life, and therefore can soon manifest Himself again.—They
should see Him continually and more thoroughly than they had
ever seen Him.—See Him with the eyes of the spirit and of living
knowledge.—Because with the Father in the kingdom of life, as
He that *liveth.*—Together with the resurrection it embraces the
entire manifestation of Christ until His coming.—A manifestation
whose principle is contained in His resurrection.—With the Holy
Ghost He Himself shall re-appear to them in His glory.—The
new day of Christ is but one day, and the eternal seeing of Him
again in faith essentially one seeing.—Partings among God's
people are but for a little time, and shall be followed by blessed
re-unions.—Yet the thought of future meetings is full of solemnity and warning.—For many a one the re-seeing of others will
be fearful.—Christians at death go to be with Christ, who is with
the Father.—Though no longer seen with the bodily eyes they
are seen with the eyes of spiritual love.—" When Christ, our life,
shall appear, we also shall appear with him in glory " (Col. iii. 4).
—This vision of " Him as he is " (1 John iii. 2) will take place at
His coming, and " our gathering together unto him " (2 Thess.
ii. 1).

μικρὸν. Before the Spirit can fulfil His blessed work a painful separation is necessary. *Olshausen.*—The promised coming of the Comforter with His disclosures of the
whole truth (verses 13-15) is near at hand. *Schaff.*—No real cessation between Him
and them. *Lücke.*—The mode of expression is (purposely) enigmatical, the θεωρεῖτε and
ὄψεσθε not being co-ordinate ; the first referring merely to physical, the second also to
spiritual, sight.—The ὄψεσθε began to be fulfilled at the resurrection; then received
its *main fulfilment* on the Day of Pentecost; and shall have its *final completion* at the
great return of the Lord hereafter.—In all these prophecies we have a perspective of
continually unfolding fulfilments presented to us. *Alford.*—In the transient return of
the Risen One they are to see a pledge of the Parousia. *Luthardt.*—The text reads οὐ ;
but οὐκέτι is supported by *Codd. Sin., B. D L., Origen, Vulgate, Syriac, &c.,* and adopted
by *Lach., Tisch., Treg., Alford, Lange, Westcott and Hort.*—ὅτι ἐγώ, &c. Omitted. *Cod.
Sin., B. D. L., Origen, Lach., Tisch., Alford, Treg.* Westcott and Hort.—Retained. *A.,
Lach., Lange.*—It looks as if they were inserted to suit verse 17. *Schaff.*

17, 18. Then said some of his disciples among themselves, What is this that he saith
unto us, A little while, and ye shall not see me: and again, a little while, and ye shall
see me: and, Because I go to the Father?—They said therefore, What is this that he
saith, A little while? we cannot tell what he saith.

Then said, &c. Gr., *therefore said.*—What He has said seems incomprehensible and even contradictory.—The word, " a little
while ": 1. An enigma to the disciples ; 2. A prophetic type in the
mouth of the Lord; 3. A blissful contemplation and experience

in the new life of the children of His Spirit.—Spiritual truth mysterious till Christ opens the understanding (Luke xxiv. 45).

Among themselves. Gr., *to one another.*—They draw aside and discuss the matter privately.—Divine truth, a stumbling-block "to the wise and prudent," is revealed unto " babes."—Not babes in understanding, but babes in heart.—The childlike spirit enters the kingdom of God.

What is this? They passed by the first mention of " a little while " without staggering (see on chap. xiv. 19).—They have forebodings of the greatest, the most mysterious changes, but are perplexed to hear that all is to happen in a short space.—It is here they stand still, and it is the purpose of the Lord that they should do so ; for He is now about to give them a new and consoling view of His death.

I go to the Father. In verse 7 He had spoken of them beholding Him no more because He goeth to the Father, whereas He now speaks of a little while after which they shall see Him.—These things are beyond them to reconcile, much more to understand.

We cannot tell. Gr., *we know not what He is speaking of.*—Whatever difficulties we meet with in Scripture, we must not reject Scripture because of them, but **pray and wait.**—Some are too proud to ask for light; others too busy with the world; others too full of desire to enjoy the fleeting hour.—The truth of the Bible must be *lived* to be understood.—Experience of the truth is the best teacher.—Our Lord's words were only fully comprehended after the Pentecostal gift.—Although pointing to exalted joy and blessedness, His words seemed to them the overthrow of their fondest hopes.—Thus do we all misunderstand God's words and works.—Revelation is purposely given in a way which makes earnest, prayerful searching necessary, and which severely tries and exercises faith. *Hall.*—Spiritual ignorance produces melancholy, and this darkens the mind still more, and oppresses the heart.—Mistakes cause grief, and griefs confirm mistakes.—But the Lord's love is mightier than all, and no soul looking to Him shall remain in darkness (Micah vii. 8, 9).

τουτο τι εστιν, &c. The disciples are perplexed by this μικρόν, as connected with what our Lord had before asserted in verse 10.—*That* seemed to them a long and hopeless withdrawal : how was it then to be reconciled with what He now said of a short absence? What was this τὸ μικρόν ? This connection not being observed has led to the insertion of ὅτι ἐγὼ, &c., in verse 16. *Alford.*—τοῦτο is very forcible here, *i.e.*, they had never understood anything less than this. *Bengel.*

19. Now Jesus knew that they were desirous to ask him, and said unto them, Do ye enquire among yourselves of that I said, A little while, and ye shall not see me : and again, a little while, and ye shall see me ?

Jesus knew. See on chap. ii. 25; vi. 6, 61.—He knew their thoughts, being divinely omniscient.—One of the greatest comforts to faith, *Jesus knows.*

Desirous to ask him. It was His purpose to lead them to this point.—The end for which He had uttered His dark saying was gained.—Their minds have been exercised and the desire for light excited.—Their doubts and difficulties became the occasion for further development of truth.—All perplexing and painful things designed to make us feel our need of the Lord and to draw us to Him in prayer.—The knots we cannot untie we must bring to Him.—Christ takes notice of pious desires even though they have not been expressed.—He will teach the humble who confess their ignorance, and the diligent who use the means they have. *Henry.* —He is so gracious a Master that He will not cast off even the dullest scholar who comes into His school to learn.—Those who love to entertain doubts, and who raise questions to give colour for unbelief, He will leave to their own perversity ; but those who desire to have their doubts resolved, that they may the more fully embrace the truth, He will mercifully visit with heavenly light. *Watson.*

Do ye enquire ? An indirect reproof for not applying at once to Him.—Why should we puzzle and distress ourselves with difficulties, which Jesus only can explain, and which He is ready and willing to explain ?

---

20. Verily, verily, I say unto you, That ye shall weep and lament, but the world shall rejoice : and ye shall be sorrowful, but your sorrow shall be turned into joy.

Verily, verily. See on chap. i. 51.—Intended to impress them with the magnitude and certainty of what is to follow.

I say. I, the faithful and true Witness.—Our Lord's personality, as God-man, the ground of Christian faith and trust.—The first part of His answer is concerned with the "little while," which was their real difficulty.—Afterward (verse 28) He addresses their thoughts about His going to the Father.—He gives light to lead on to higher things.—" The path of the just is as the shining light, that shineth more and more unto the perfect day " (Prov. iv. 18).

Ye shall. Gr., *ye will*, indicates their great contrast to the world.

Weep and lament. Vividly portrays the intensity of their anguish.—Because of the crucifixion of the Lord, together with the apparent downfall of their hopes as to the kingdom of Messiah and the redemption of Israel.—They would mourn for His as dead and the cause of God as lost.

The world shall (will) rejoice. Seen in the scoffs and scorn of those who witnessed the crucifixion.—God, in His Providence, allows the "world" their opportunities of rejoicing.—It exercises the faith of His afflicted people; it brings to light what is in men's hearts; it justifies His righteous judgment in their final discomfiture and overthrow.—The tears and the mockery in the scene at the Cross show how both parts of this prediction were fulfilled. —But the joy of the world is always brief, as the sufferings of Christians are also.—The world can only secure its joy by evading all thought of sin and death.—Hence the dissipation by which it tries to drown the voice of its inmost nature.—Therefore, its joy is *loud,* while *silent* joy is alone genuine and profound.—The dead Christ a subject for joy!—What heavier condemnation could be pronounced?

Ye shall be sorrowful. Emphatically: *plunged in sorrow.*—Goes deeper than the weeping and wailing before.—Not limited to the sorrow of the desolate disciples while the Lord was in the tomb.— Includes the grief continually manifesting itself in the course and conflict of the Christian.—Includes also the grief and widowhood of the Church during her present state.

Turned into joy. Gr., *changed into joy.*—Not merely that sadness shall be followed by joy; but that their joy will grow out of their sadness.—The very *matter* of their grief shall become the *matter* of their joy.—The bottomless depth of their grief the *measure* of their joy.—Christ's cross of shame has become the Christian's glory (Gal. vi. 14).—Dying with Christ is the condition of heavenly life with Him.—The sorrow of the believer is changed into joy by the advancing work of the Spirit of Christ (see on Matt. v. 3-6). —The sorrow of the Church will be turned into transport at the coming of her Lord.—All sorrows work for great and abiding joy to the friends of Christ.—Our greatest consolation is often concealed in our greatest cross.—"There is none whom the heavenly Father calleth *Benjamin* (son of my right hand), whom the Church, his mother, hath not first called *Benoni* (son of my sorrows)." *Gerhard.*

---

21. A woman when she is in travail hath sorrow, because her hour is come: but as soon as she is delivered of the child, she remembereth no more the anguish, for joy that a man is born into the world.

A woman. Gr., *the woman, the* woman in the illustration.—This figure is frequently met with in the prophets (Isa. xxi. 3; xxvi. 17, 18; lxvi. 7, 8; Jer. iv. 31; xxii. 23; xxx. 6; Hosea xiii. 13, 14; Micah. iv. 9, 10).

In travail. A touching proof of our Lord's sympathy in woman's deepest trial (Gen. iii. 16).

Hath sorrow. Gr., *hath pangs.*—Not alone physical pangs, but also mental pressure, anxiety, and anguish.

Her hour. Her appointed time; the destined hour of tribulation.

The child. The Greek word not necessarily masculine; indefinite.

She remembereth, &c. The anguish is forgotten; swallowed up in the joy.

A man is born. The Greek word is the general word for "*human being.*"—The child, whether male or female, is a human being, a mystery of personal life.—"Our Lord does not say, a *child;* He says, a *man* is born; a man, still undeveloped, yet present, with all his hopeful powers, dispositions and destinies, in the child." *Braune.*

Into the world. Not into the natural life only; into the Cosmos and for it, in order to the full development and moulding of it. *Lange.*—The joy of maternity absorbs the sorrows of childbirth. —She loses sight of the one in the fulness of the other.—This touching simile reveals the tender interest the God-man felt in mother-woes and mother-joys, a thought helpful and comforting to sensitive, pious mothers.—The natural birth of a man becomes a symbol of a higher life.—Thus the death-pangs of Jesus were birth-pangs into the high and glorious life of the spirit in heaven. —Thus those pangs might also be called an anguish of birth belonging to all humanity.—Through those pangs the *perfect man* was born into the world, and in this birth of the new man lies the spring of eternal joy.—Through Him and His power the renovation of the whole is rendered possible. *Olshausen.*—Christ, the Firstborn from the dead, the Firstborn for the kingdom of everlasting life.—When Christ died, the great work of God was finished; when He arose, the Eternal God-man was perfected.— With Him, the Church, the new mankind, was born. *Lange.*—The way from sorrow to joy for the disciples was as the pangs of birth for the outburst of resurrection gladness.—The child-bearing woman is also the Church through the Spirit within her.— Vigorous pangs an indication of vigorous birth; so also in spiritual things.—The true Christian passes through sorrow to joy, till "Christ be formed in him," in this birth of pain.—"The children of God have three kinds of birthdays: 1. The natural

one. Then they weep; their kinsmen rejoice; 2. The new birth.
Then, also, do they often weep piteously; the angels in heaven
rejoice; 3. The day of death (celebrated among the martyrs in
the ancient Church as a birthday). Their end is not without
tears and woe, but after that an eternal rejoicing begins." *Fenne-
berg.*—Even creation itself travails in birth-pangs, until "the
manifestation of the sons of God" (Rom. viii. 19-23; 2 Pet. iii.
11-13).—Then the new earth and the new heavens shall be born
into the universe (Rev. xxi. 1-5).

---

22 And ye now therefore have sorrow: but I will see you again, and your heart
shall rejoice, and your joy no man taketh from you.

Sorrow. Gr., *birth-pangs;* the same word is used as in verse 21.—
Our Lord explains the symbol to His disciples.—Ye are like the
travailing woman, in your sorrow, soon ye will also rejoice exceedingly.—"The death-hour of Jesus was for the disciples the
natal hour of new life." *Lücke.*—The hour of their birth-pangs
was near: but it would pass away, and fulness of joy would come
in the constant presence of their Lord.—Their sorrow, though
deep, would be but temporary: their joy great and abiding.—
Our spiritual life is an alternation of mourning and joy, as the
natural life is of joy and sorrow.—The natal hour of the natural
man a type of the natal hour of the kingdom of God: 1. Symbol
of the woman; 2. Symbol of the child.—Every human being a
token of the change between sadness and joy in God's kingdom:
1. With anguish expected and born; 2. Jubilantly received and
welcomed into life.—The winning of life from out the peril of
death: 1. In the natural life; 2. In the spiritual life. *Lange.*—In
the Cross of Christ every believer learns and experiences that
true sorrow which leads to heavenly joy.—By *dying* with Christ
we become capable of understanding His resurrection and of
rejoicing over it as we should.—Every affliction (religiously
applied) is a birth, in which the new man, or some gracious
addition to the new man, is born. *Braune.*

I will see you again. In verse 19 He had said, "Ye shall see."
—He will come to them again and see them as they shall see
Him.—How deep His sympathy with His disciples: He sees them
now in the depth of their sorrow and tenderly feels for them; He
will see them again in the time of their joy, and will rejoice with
them.—"I will see you again; at My resurrection, by My Spirit,
at My second Advent." *Alford.*

Your joy. The heaviest hour, the womb of the most glorious day.
—"As wine issues from grapes when they are pressed, and as
spices, when bruised, give forth a powerful odour, so the tribulation of believers beareth glorious fruit." *Hedinger.*—Though now
they seem forsaken, there is joy in store for all who sorrow on
account of the Lord's absence (see on Matt. v. 4).—Joy in the
heart, solid, secret, sweet, sure. *Henry.*—Joy that can only be
known by *experience;* being the joy of the Lord, it cannot be
described.—It is "a joy unspeakable and full of glory" (1 Pet.
i. 8).—Manifested in each believer according to spiritual capacity,
ability profitably to bear, &c., and therefore, "*your joy.*"

No man, &c. Better rendered indefinitely, *no one,* as in chap. x.
18 and 29.—No being or thing in the universe can rob the believer
of his joy.—The assertion sweeps the whole realm of possibilities.
—It is the beginning of the eternal life in the heavenly existence,
in which heaven and earth are intrinsically united. *Lange* —The
world is satisfied without satisfaction ; but the Christian loseth
not his heart's peace, no matter what may befall.—The root and
principle and strength of his joy cannot be touched whatever
may come.—His "life is hid with Christ in God," where no foe
can reach (Col. iii. 3).—The joy of the world is from circumstances without ; the believer's joy is in his heart.—The anchor of
his hope is cast within the veil (Heb. vi. 19).—Christian life a
deep, inscrutable mystery to the world.—The last fulfilment of
this promise reaches on to the final victory, and this joy of the
heart is the contrast of the world's joy turned into mourning
(Isa. lxv. 13, 14).

λύπην. The death of Christ is the agonizing travail of humanity, from which labou-
the God-Man issues, glorified, to the eternal joy of mankind. *Apollinaris, Chrys., Olsh,*
&c.—In a secondary and wider sense, the Church in this world is the woman in travail; she is in travail with souls for the new birth to grace and glory (Gal iv. 19).—
She groans in the pangs of parturition even to the great day of Regeneration, the day
of the glorious re-appearing of Christ, and the general resurrection and new birth to
immortality (Rom. viii. 22).—Then humanity will cast off its grave-clothes, and be
glorified for ever with Christ. *Augustine, Wordsworth, Luthardt.*—Man is perfectly born
into the world only in his second, heavenly state of existence, in the resurrection —
Before the resurrection of Christ no human being had been fully born into the world,
whilst with His resurrection, the birth of One Man into the world did at once make
manifest this new world, and involve the co-geniture of the new humanity for this new
world.—Thus again, He was born of the travail-pangs of the Theocracy, the whole of
the old humanity in its higher tendency, its longing for salvation ; these pangs truly
centred in His heart; at the same time however, they thrilled through the members
of believers and became the mortal agony of their old view of the world (see Isa. xxvi.
17 ; lxvi. 9 ; 1 Cor. xv. 47; Rev. xii. 1). *Lange.*—αἴρει, present indefinite, indicating the
quality and essence of the joy that it cannot be taken away. *Alford.*—The text. rec.
(αἴρει) is adopted by *Lange, Tisch.;* the future ἀρεῖ, is adopted by *Lach., Treg., Westcott*
and Hort.

20, 23.—Gr., *I find no crime in Him.*—" *I*," emphatically : opposed to " *ye*," who had found fault in Him.—" I find no ground for the legal charge (verse 33). Whatever He may be, there is no proof of treason against the majesty of Cæsar." *Ellicott.*—Pilate seems to have taken Jesus to be a good-natured but guiltless, perhaps rather tiresome, fanatic.—But notwithstanding this declaration, he was soon after entangled fatally in the net of a wretched policy.—Here follows the sending of Jesus to Herod Antipas, recorded by Luke (see on Luke xxiii. 12).—" Pilate mocks both, the Witness of the Truth and the haters of the Truth. His conduct presents a pitiable specimen of the moral weakness of that spirit of worldly power, which reached its culminating point in the Roman empire." *Alford.*—Pilate, like Judas, was compelled to acknowledge the innocency of Jesus (see on Matt. xxvii. 4).

Tί. Probably Pilate thought that Jesus professed only to add one more to the list of philosophies, or systems of ideas, and turned away from it in sickness of heart. *Grant.* —He has evidently no suspicion of subjective vital truth, and he understands, by truth, merely an objective school problem about which a practical man of business need not puzzle his wits. *Lange.*—αἰτίαν. John uses this word only in this place.—It is used by Matt. (xxvii. 37) for the technical "accusation written, This is Jesus, the King of the Jews," and this seems to be the sense here. *Ellicott.*—The word means, in a forensic sense, *an accusation of crime, a charge. Robinson* —At this place comes in Matt. xxvi. 12-14; the repeated accusation of Jesus by the chief priests and elders, to which He answered nothing ; and Luke xxiii. 5-17, the sending to Herod. and second proclamation of His innocence by Pilate, after which he adopts this method (verse 39) of procuring His release (Luke xxiii. 17). *Alford.*

---

39. But ye have a custom, that I should release unto you one at the passover : will ye therefore that I release unto you the King of the Jews ?

A custom. See on Matt. xxvii. 15 ; Luke xxiii. 17.—Supposed to have arisen from the paschal feast having been regarded as a time for reconciliation. *Tholuck.*—More probably a kind of dramatic Easter play, intended, perhaps, to illustrate the sparing of the Jewish first-born. *Lange.*

Will ye? Pilate thinks to outwit the Jews, but they outwit him. —He ought simply to have administered justice, and this would have compelled the release of Jesus.—Instead of this, he proposes to concede to them the power to release Him themselves, in consideration of their custom.—The consequence of this half-measure is ruinous to Pilate.—With the first deviation from rectitude, a man enters upon the road to calamity.

The king, &c. The mockery, implied in these words, is not at Jesus, but at the Jews.—" This is your king; such is your national subjection, that your king is bound, my prisoner: Shall I release this king?" *Ellicott.*

---

40. Then cried they all again, saying, Not this man, but Barabbas. Now Barabbas was a robber.

Again. John, though he has not mentioned any clamour before, evidently implies that recorded in Mark xv. 8, and in Luke xxiii. 5-10.—They cried this time, and that *en masse* or with one voice.

Barabbas. See on Matt. xxvii. 16, and on Luke xxiii. 18.—Probably was the son of a Rabbi, as Abba was a Rabbinic title of honour. *Ewald.*—Appears to have been a leader in the insurrection (Mark xv. 7) against Pilate, arising out of his misappropriation of a part of the Temple revenues to the construction of an aqueduct. *Josephus.*—This may explain the eagerness with which the Sanhedrim and the people demanded his release.—According to Matthew, Pilate placed Barabbas beside Jesus and bade the people choose, hoping thus to make the release of Jesus more sure (chap. xxvii. 21, 26).—" Pilate stands as a warning example of the consequence of endeavouring to satisfy God and the world. We meet with Pilate under various forms; many a one has placed himself, like him, in a situation in which he must either set Barabbas free, or give up the Saviour, because he was deficient in courage to brave every danger for Christ's sake. Many reckoning, like Pilate, on the instinctive moral feelings of the multitude, with whom they do not wish to be at variance, have cowardly asked, ' Which will you choose, right or wrong?' and the unexpected reply has been thundered back, 'We choose rebellion and treason.'" *Krummacher.* —" ' *Not this man:* ' Thus was Jesus the goat upon which the Lord's lot fell, to be offered for a sin-offering." *Luthardt.*—(See more fully on Matt. xxvii. 16.)

Robber. See on chap. x. 1.—The word implies unrestrained violence, which often leads to murder.—There is a solemn irony in the words of John—a *Robber!*

" Thou who condemnest Jewish hate,
        For choosing Barabbas, a murderer,

old Messianic hope.—They had not prayed in submission to the
name of Jesus and His work.—They had not yet received the
Paraclete.—By His presence their thoughts would become Christ's
thoughts, their will His, their prayers His.—After His resurrection
and ascension they would clearly understand His relation to the
Father and to mankind.—They could only pray in His name when
He had entered into His glory.—It is a fulness of joy characteristic
of the dispensation of the Spirit, to be able so to do (Eph. ii. 18).

Ask. Now, in the bright hope of that great day, *ask and pray as ye
have never done before.*—The future is thought of as already present.—The birth-pangs He had spoken of (verse 22) are passing
away and the fulness of joy is at hand.—Many only half pray ;
and therefore cannot afterward *receive* even what they have prayed
for.—True prayer obtains the hand which enables us to lay hold
of and receive the heavenly gifts.—Kant, the great philosopher,
would not pray ; but in his last hours folded his hands.—Spinoza
could not pray, and wept because he could not.—Ability to pray
a sure indication of the spiritual condition.—To learn to pray and
to pray in Christ's name, the commencement of a new era in the
life.

Joy may be full. See on chap. xv. 11.—Ultimate end of the life
of prayer, and glorious condition of the blessed spirit-life.—By
prayer Christian life becomes transformed from inquiries into experiences.—In that great day of New Testament spiritual life the
believer shall walk in the manifestation of heaven upon earth.—
Thus perfect joy and life in the Spirit are one.—The Holy Ghost
is the mediator of that joy which should be their portion in the
unanimity of love.—Unanimity of prayer (Acts ii.) is the yearning
of love.—Unanimity in the Holy Ghost is the fulfilling of love,
and that is heaven upon earth. *Lange.*—The final aim of all God's
dealings with Christians, especially of all experience in prayer, is
that "our joy may be perfected."—The highest joy is to enjoy
God, the Holy Trinity, in the image of Whom we are made.
Augustine.

---

25. These things have I spoken unto you in proverbs : but the time cometh, when I
shall no more speak unto you in proverbs, but I shall shew you plainly of the Father.

These things. Refers especially to what he had just said from
verse 16.

In proverbs. Gr., *in parables.*—So in the second clause of the verse
and in verse 29 (see on chap. x. 6).—The word implies generally
in Scripture and oriental usage something dark and enigmatical.—

This describes all our Lord's discourses before the Holy Spirit furnished the key to their meaning.—All human speech is but a " parable," only able to hint at, not to express fully, the things of God.—Our Lord contrasts this weak and insufficient medium with the inward teaching of the Spirit which is a real imparting of the divine nature and life.—To an unenlightened mind, every discourse, even one which in a direct manner presents ideas, becomes a *parabolic* speech.—To an enlightened mind, every discourse, even a *parabolic* one, becomes a clear word of revelation.—Law and symbol are the indivisible forms of revelation for those in a state of pupilage ; the law for the heart and conscience, the symbol for the understanding.—On the other hand, the Gospel and spiritual speech are the inseparable forms of revelation for the believer who has attained to maturity.—Life in the Spirit is a life in the everlasting Gospel. *Lange.*

The time cometh. Gr., *the hour.*—The same as that indicated in verses 16 and 23.—Not *one* hour exclusively, but the various stages of education and progression in spiritual knowledge.—There shall come an " hour " when the boundaries and wrappings of His revelation shall fall off.—This " hour " is inseparably connected with their praying in the name of Jesus.

Plainly. Gr., *openly*, without concealment ; freedom of speech, without reserve, with directness. — He would no longer speak in parables, such as that of the travailing woman, verse 21, but by the Spirit would reveal to their spirit the glorious truth of the Father.—" It is the comfort of saints that what measure of light and instruction they need and yet want at one time, it is but reserved for another ; for it sweetens their case to whom He had spoken in ' proverbs ' to hear that ' the time cometh ' when He would no more thus speak." *Hutcheson.*

---

26. At that day ye shall ask in my name : and I say not unto you, that I will pray the Father for you.

At that day, &c. See on verses 23, 24.—Under the influence of the Spirit their life would be wholly subject to His will, and they would pray in His name.—" The Spirit maketh intercession for the saints according to the will of God " (Rom. viii. 27).—The more spiritual knowledge the more prayer in Christ's name.—The true prayer-life is the product of the full knowledge-life.—Access to the Father through Him is to be a characteristic of their higher state under the dispensation of the Spirit.

I do not say, &c. This cannot mean that they might be so certain

He would pray for them that He need not assure them of it : for the next verse excludes such a view.—It means rather : I do not speak of praying for you, for the Spirit will enable *you* to pray in My name.—The idea seems implied that though His prayer will not be necessary, yet that He would pray for them if it should be needed (1 John ii. 1).—He is setting in the strongest light their reconciliation and access to the Father. *Alford.*—Christ's intercession coincides with the immediate prayer of the Holy Spirit within the heart (Rom. viii. 26).—It was not 'necessary for Him to seek to procure them the favour of the Father or the Spirit of sonship.—On the contrary, all these blessings spring from the love of, the Father Himself.

αἰτήσεσθε. Our Lord never uses this word of Himself in respect of that which He seeks on behalf of His disciples from God ; for His is not the petition of the creature to the Creator, but the *request* of the Son to the Father.—The consciousness of His equal dignity, of His potent and prevailing intercession, speaks out in this, that often as He asks, or declares that He will ask, anything of the Father, it is always ἐρωτῶ, ἐρωτήσω, an asking, that is upon equal terms, never αἰτέω or αἰτήσω. *Trench.*—Our Lord's words offer no contradiction to chap. xiv. 16 ; xvii. 19, for the reason that those passages treat of the intercession of Christ previous to the time of the Paraclete. *Meyer.*—But yet John had received the Paraclete when he wrote 1 John ii. 1. *Lange.*

---

27. For the Father himself loveth you, because ye have loved me, and have believed that I came out from God.

The Father, &c. See on chap. xiv. 21, 23.—With the Holy Ghost the love of the Father is also manifested.—In the fulness of the higher spiritual life there is communion between the Father and the heart that receives His love ; yet even this flows from loving the Son, by whom the Father is revealed.—Thus, the highest communion with the Father depends upon our Lord's mediation and the manifestation of Divine love in Him.—The whole mind of the Father toward mankind is LOVE : 1. In Redemption itself (chap. iii. 16) ; 2. In an especial manner by drawing those who come to Christ (chap. vi. 44) ; 3. In this fuller manifestation of His love to those who believe on and love His Son. *Alford.*—Our Lord's words decisively refute the false conception of the Father which attributes to Him *a wrath* which had to be propitiated, and not also that *reconciling love*, which from eternity needed not to be propitiated. *Stier.*—We need to be reminded, " Behold, what manner of love the Father hath bestowed upon us," etc. (1 John iii. 1).

Because, &c. " Because *ye are they* (emphasized) who have loved

Me." *Meyer.*—Love to Christ, in faith in His name, is the medium through which the Father's love is experienced.—Christ is still the efficient cause of the Father's love, and the channel through which it flows.—He loves those who are one with Him in the love of His Beloved.—" The Father loves you, because ye have loved Me; when, therefore, ye fall from My love, ye will straightway fall from the Father's love." *Theophylact.*

And have believed. Note that the order of the words makes faith *follow* love.—Probably to mark emphatically the connection between the Father's love and their love for the Son.—Intimates also the power of love to open the heart and produce conviction of the truth of the Gospel.—Love to Christ cannot be without faith, and where love is it proves faith.

I came out from God. See on verse 28.—Some of the better MSS. read: "*that I came forth from the Father*" (see on chap. viii. 42).—Belief in the Divine personality of Christ was both the foundation and the proof of their love to Christ.—Theirs was a germinant faith, in the form of loving devotion, which unfolded into this faith's knowledge.—" Not merely has the Father Himself already loved them as He loves all the world and every creature, but He loves *them* with that *especial* love which He bears to those in whom He finds Christ's word, and through faith in it Christ Himself, who stand before Him clothed in the garment of His Son's righteousness." *Stier.*

φιλεῖ. The present denotes the proximity of the communication of the Spirit, or, rather, the already beginning ante-celebration of this communication as that of the Spirit of sonship (Rom. viii. 15; Gal. iv. 6). *Lange.*—πεφιλήκατε καὶ πεπιστεύκατε. The Perfect tenses represent their love and faith as completed, and continuing in the present. *Watkins.*—For θεοῦ, πατρός. *Lach., Lange, Treg., Alford, Westcott and Hort.*

---

28. I came forth from the Father, and am come into the world: again, I leave the world, and go to the Father.

I came forth from the Father. He re-affirms His pre-existence and divine origin.—That which the disciples have believed of Him is true (verse 27).—In the background is the ineffable mystery of His Eternal Sonship by eternal generation by the Father. —"Whose goings forth have been from of old, from everlasting" (Micah. v. 2). (See on Matt. ii. 6.)—"Begotten of His Father before all worlds, God of God, Light of Light, Very God of very God, Begotten, not made, Being of one substance with the Father." *Nicene Creed.*

Am come into the world. "Although He be God and Man; yet He is not two, but one Christ; One; not by conversion of the Godhead into flesh; but by taking of the Manhood into God." *Athan. Creed.*—"God manifest in the flesh," a glorious mystery even to the highest intelligences (1 Pet. i. 12).—The *fact* we know; but the *how* is one of "the secret things that belong unto the Lord our God."—Even the mode of the union of mind and body in human personality we cannot understand.—The Incarnation contains in itself the whole mystery of the relation of the Infinite to the finite, the Creator to the creature (see on Matt. i. 23).—Our Lord's words imply that His entrance into the sphere of human life was His own voluntary act.—Of no other human being could this be said.—Contrast "There was a man sent from God" (chap. i. 6) with "I am come into the world."

Again, I leave the world. As His birth was voluntary, so also was His death (see on chap. x. 17, 18).—His ascension also was His own act; His will in all things uniting with the will of the Father. —He left this world at death and entered Paradise, for He said to the penitent malefactor, "This day thou shalt be with Me" (Luke xxiii. 43).—The personality of our Lord was independent of His body; *it* was lying in the sepulchre.—This is the right view of death; it is but *leaving this world*—The "I," the "Me," is not touched by bodily dissolution.—In the *spirit* the essence of our personality lies.—Paul said, "I have a desire to depart."— He knew that *he*, *Paul*, should be with Christ, when his body was mouldering in the grave.—Our Lord left the world finally when, in His resurrection body, He ascended from Olivet (Acts i. 12).

And go to the Father. This follows from what He has said, "I came forth from the Father."—Heaven, not earth, is His proper home.—How keenly He must have felt the absence from His home. —The disciples had accepted the truth of the Incarnation; but that implied the Ascension, and that the gift of the Paraclete, and His own abiding spiritual presence in the Church (see on verse 7 and chap. xiv. 14-18).—The one half of His life, the way from heaven to earth. demands the other half.—His personal coming, as the Son of God, from the Father, is the key to His going, in divine glory, to the Father.—Three births of our Lord worthy our adoring wonder and our praise: 1. His eternal outgoing, or birth from the Father; 2. His coming and being born in the flesh as man; 3. His birth of glorification by means of His death, resurrection and ascension. *Gossner.*—A threefold way Christ trode for our salvation: 1. The way of love (from heaven to earth); 2. The way of obedience (unto the death upon the cross); 3. The way of glory (return to the Father). *Gerhard.*—Of all our Lord's

trials the severest must have been the apparent conflict between
the Fatherhood of God and the course of Providence toward
Him.—This appears in the first recorded temptation (see on Matt.
iv. 3), and comes into view, with dreadful distinctness, in the final
agony (see on Matt. xxvii. 46).—Even *then* His faith triumphed, and
His last words were, "*Father*, into thy hands I commend my
spirit" (Luke xxiii. 46).—How blessed therefore must have been
His return to His Father!—What sublime joy was His as He
entered that glorious presence.—All His conflicts past, and henceforth full, perfect, eternal communion with His Father.—So also
with the Christian as to his trials ; and so also as to his heavenly
blessedness.—In that land of rest there will be no temptation to
doubt the fatherly character of God.—No conflicts between reason
and faith.—No questionings, "Why hast Thou dealt with me
thus?" No bitter cry, "Show me wherefore Thou contendest
with me."—In that place of glorious vision, "before the throne,"
all the Divine attributes resolve themselves into LOVE, and all the
Divine works and ways into the FATHERHOOD of God.—"This
verse furnishes a simple, grand summary of His whole personal
life." *Meyer.*—Mark the symmetry of the four clauses: "I came
forth, I am come, I leave, I go." *Schaff.*

---

29. His disciples said unto him, Lo, now speakest thou plainly, and speakest no
proverb.

Lo. Gr., *behold.*—They perceive with astonishment that He speaks
to them in this new way.

Now. Emphatic.—The words He has just spoken give them, for
the first time, a clear view of His entire life.—They have caught
a glimpse of the truth and hastily infer that the pentecostal time
had already come.—They mistake this momentary view for the
beginning of an uninterrupted enlightenment of the Spirit.—They
fancied they *now* understood what had seemed so dark.

Plainly (see on verse 25). They had, at least, realized that, as He
had come forth from God, He was about to return to Him, in
heaven.

No proverb. Gr., *no parable* (see on verse 25). He had said that
the hour would come when He would speak to them no more in
parables; and, as His last words have shed a beam of light upon
their minds, they fondly imagine the time of the promised illumination has come.—It seemed as if He had already fulfilled His
promise to speak clearly, and without metaphor, to them.—In
obtaining from their Lord their first general view of His entire

life, they experienced a foretaste of the Holy Spirit.—For the
Holy Spirit is given with the Lord's life, and is the Interpreter of
that life, so far as any soul has any right idea of it.—They had a
glimpse of Pentecost, but it was only a glimpse.—Their new-born
enthusiasm must first pass through sore suffering before it could
set into fruit (see on verse 32).

'Ἴδε, &c. They did so little understand Him as not even to understand that they did
not understand, for they were as babes. *Augustine, Tholuck, Lücke.*—They go so far as
to contradict Christ and dispute His plain words, and deny that He was speaking
enigmatically to them. *Lampe.*—Their remark was made in weakness, however true
their persuasion, and heartfelt their confession. *Alford.*—These criticisms are too
severe.—The Lord Himself evidently recognises that some great thing is now going
on within them (verse 31).—They had caught a glimpse of the truth and hastily inferred
that the time had come for fulfilment of the words in verse 25. *Lange. Schaff, Geikie,
Watkins.*—*Exultant ante tempus perinde acsi quis nummo uno aureo divitem se putaret.*
Calvin.

---

30. Now are we sure that thou knowest all things, and needest not that any man
should ask thee : by this we believe that thou camest forth from God.

Now are we sure. Gr., *we know.*—The *now* is emphatic, as in the
previous verse.

Thou knowest all things. See on verse 19, and on chap. ii. 24,
25.—His knowledge of their thoughts convinced them of His
omniscience.—They felt they were standing before the great
Searcher of all hearts.—His " eyes as a flame of fire " had pierced
their inmost soul (Rev. i. 14).—To Him all things are "naked
and opened " (Heb. iv. 13).—They saw He could anticipate by His
disclosures every question they could desire to ask.—Awed and
powerfully impressed, they felt a fresh corroboration of their
belief in Him.—Thus His words to Nathanael, " Before that
Philip called thee, when thou wast under the fig-tree, I saw
thee," drew forth, " Rabbi, thou art the Son of God, thou art the
King of Israel " (see on chap. i. 48, 49).—Thus also His knowledge of what Thomas had said, and the invitation to carry it out,
drew forth " My Lord and my God " (see on chap. xx. 28).—The
disciples rush to the conclusion that the day has come when they
shall not need to inquire of Him any more (see on verse 23) ; for
as He knows all things, He will now surely communicate the truth
to them in all its fulness.

By this, &c. That is, *by reason of this.*—This proves that they
understood His word in its fundamental thought. *Lange.*—They
had believed that He came forth from God before this (verse 27),
but their faith has now received enlargement and strength.—The

new evidence of His Divinity, afforded them, has produced, so to speak, *new* faith.—Thus faith and knowledge should always go together in Christian experience.—From the belief that He had personally and miraculously come forth from God, they draw the deduction, and are reconciled to the fact, that He would leave the world and return to the Father.—Yet their faith had an element of imperfection in it, in that it was begotten rather by the act of His proving His omniscience than by His word.—The solid word of God is the only solid ground for a solid faith.—" When weak beginners get any measure of knowledge or faith, they are in peril to run upon the extremities of rashness and presumptuous conceit; for with this was their profession here hinted, wherein they speak as if they had attained to a full measure, and needed not depend on the promise of the Spirit." *Hutcheson.*

---

31. Jesus answered them Do ye now believe?

Do ye now believe? Better, *Now ye do believe* (compare verse 27 and xvii. 8).—Christ recognises their present faith, but shows how weak it was.—*Now* is emphatic, as if He had said, *Now* ye believe, but how soon will your faith be shaken! *Godet.*—Our Lord did not doubt their faith, but He knew that the hour of their full illumination had not come.—Their present light was but as the flash of a meteor : brilliant, but transient.—The clear and abiding light was in the future of which He had spoken.—Between this and that time lay a night of darkness and bitter sorrow.—" It is true that ye do believe, but how soon will My passion make manifest your real and great weakness." *Stier.*—An hour was at hand that would put their faith to a fiery test.—Our Lord's recognition of their faith shows how precious it is in His sight, even though it be mixed with ignorance and be imperfect.—It is an humbling thought that we are so long before we believe, so slow to accept the Divine word in its entirety and fulness.—The Lord hates presumption and carnal confidence, even in His dearest children, and hence the warning which follows.—Low thoughts of our own faith are becoming, for even at the best it has many defects, and falls far short of the standard in Scripture.

"Ἄρτι πιστεύετε. Not a question, but a concession. *Luther, Lange, Meyer, Alford, Stier, Godet Schaff, Lücke, Bengel, &c.*—A question. *Euth. Zig., Calvin, De Wette, Tisch., Ewald, Hengst.*—These critics overlook the fact that our Lord has actually acknowledged their faith. verse 27, a fact evidenced by the warning that follows. *Lange.*—Here, as in chap. i. 50 the words do not necessarily ask a question, and a sense more in harmony with the context is got by understanding them as an assertion. *Watkins.*

32. Behold, the hour cometh, yea, is now come, that ye shall be scattered, every man to his own, and shall leave me alone: and yet I am not alone, because the Father is with me.

The hour cometh. See on Matt. xxvi. 31.—The hour when their faith should fail to stand the test.—The impulse and inspiration of faith must mature into the setttled mind of faith.

Is now come. The approaching crisis is so close that He regards it as present.—He speaks of he hour as already come to arouse them from their dream.— He would startle them out of their self-confidence and fancied security.—Humility, watchfulness, and prayer could alone prepare them for that inevitable hour.—Thus it often happens in Christian life, that times of rapturous joy or high enthusiasm, are quickly followed by times of painful sifting and severe conflict.—Like David : " And in my prosperity I said, I shall never be moved ; Lord, by Thy favour Thou hast made my mountain to stand strong."—But soon he had to sing another kind of song: "Thou didst hide Thy face ; I was troubled " (Psa. xxx. 6, 7).—An illustration of the words, " Every branch in Me that beareth not fruit He taketh away ; and every branch that beareth fruit He purgeth (pruneth) it, that it may bring forth more fruit" (see on chap. xv. 2).—The baptism of fire is promised, as well as the baptism of the Spirit (see on Matt. iii. 11).

Scattered. See on Matt. xxvi. 31.—" I will smite the Shepherd, and the sheep shall be scattered " (Zech. xiii. 7).—" The wolf cometh and scattereth the sheep " (see on chap. x. 12).—One betrays Him, another denies Him, all abandon Him.—These things being foretold has fortified the faith of God's suffering servants in every age.—The fulfilment of the prophetic words is God's seal upon His claims to be the Messiah.—Though *scattered*, the Lord did not forsake them.—His prayer for Peter that *his* faith might not fail (*wholly fail*) extended, we doubt not, to the rest of the eleven (Luke xxii. 31, 32).

His own. The margin renders it, " to his own home."—The sense of the Greek word depends upon the connection : in chap. xix. 27, it means John's home ; in chap. i. 11, it means the Jewish people.—*Here* we are to understand more generally their own ways and interests which the disciples had left to follow Christ (Luke xviii. 28). *Meyer, Alford, Schaff. &c.*—A man's peculiar possessions were no hindrance to *fellowship*, but fellowship *was* shaken by every man seeking safety in his own way. *Lange.*—Union with Christ can alone hold men together in bonds of brotherly love.— They forsook *each other* as well as their Master (Psa. lxix. 20).— Self-seeking, which is the very opposite to Christ, separates men from one another, and produces alienation and discord amongst brethren—often pitiably seen in Churches!—*Scattering* from the Church of God in times of trouble is both a weakness and a sin. —Many will seek to follow Christ *when His religion goes forth in silver slippers. Bunyan.*—None will endure to the end who "*seek their own,* and not *the things which are Jesus Christ's*" (Phil. ii. 21).

Ye shall leave me alone. To this extent did their faith fail.— "*Going one's own way,* and *leaving Christ alone,* are reciprocal ideas." *Lange.*—His words imply a rebuke, most gently and lovingly expressed, but all the more deeply and humbly to be felt afterward. —As a man, our Lord was keenly alive to the law of sympathy (see on Matt. xxvi. 36-45).—Hence their temporary desertion of Him in the hour of need (when true friendship proves itself) must have wounded Him to the heart.—Pain is alleviated and suffering mitigated by the presence and tenderness of friends— but *Jesus Christ died forsaken.*—There are those who "crucify to themselves the Son of God afresh, and put Him to an open shame" (Heb. vi. 6).—What bitter sorrow it must have cost the disciples afterward, and how great His love that could overlook and forgive all (see on chap. xx. 17).—How cowardly and un- grateful the conduct of those upon whom the Lord has showered His favours, to forsake His cause when it is distressed by enemies! —And what shall be said of those to whom He has given outward prosperity, who forsake Him in the hour of success for the so- called pleasures of the world!—One hope remains: all such deserters of Jesus must ever after be *miserable in soul,* till they return to their Lord.—If they have ever drunk of the water which *He* gives, it is impossible they could really enjoy the world again (see on chap. iv. 13, 14).—How wonderful is that love which forgives and restores, "*and upbraideth not*" (James i. 5).

I am not alone, the Father is with me. Words indescribably touching, and yet one of the profoundest and sublimest sayings. —Our Lord as man came under the ordinary conditions of human life, while in this world.—In proportion as one rises above his fellows in greatness of thought, loftiness of purpose, and purity of life, he is liable to the painful sense of *loneliness.*—It is a penalty of true greatness, and to a mind peculiarly sensitive and affec- tionate the most painful penalty of all.—To be misunderstood and misrepresented, even by one's dearest friends; to struggle on for the attainment of a great object without appreciation or encou- ragement, this is a lot hard indeed to be borne.—Yet such was the lot of Christ; and as His mind was the most perfect, His heart the most loving, His work the most generous and noble, so His lone- liness was the greatest that man could suffer.—Even their leaving

Him could scarcely have added to His sense of loneliness.—He was, even when surrounded by them, *always alone.*—His thoughts were so infinitely beyond them, that the true sympathy which binds souls in companionship was impossible.—And yet He *was never alone,* for His life was one of constant communion with the Father (see on chap. viii. 29).—Thus the absence of human helpfulness was more than made up by the constant presence of God. —In the clear consciousness of that presence He dwelt calm and peaceful; in that He had His abiding *home.*—The apparent desertion implied in the cry upon the cross is perfectly consistent with His words here (see on verse 28, and on Matt. xxvii. 46).—God never forsook His Son, even in the darkest hour.—" And this is the privilege of all believers through their union with Christ: 1. When solitude is their *choice;* 2. When solitude is their *affliction.*" *Henry.*—Alone and not alone: It was so in the human life of Jesus, and it is so in the life of His followers.—There is a sense in which each one is alone! and there is a sphere of being into which no human friend can ever enter.—There is a loneliness which leads to despair, if God is not sought and found.—Perhaps this is the key to that state of mind which leads many to suicide.—Out of the depths of loneliness the Christian stretches his hands to his Saviour, and finds everlasting consolation in His love.—He can die, saying, My Jesus is with me, My God is my portion for ever. —God is with him, as He was with Christ in the suffering hour, in His *essential* presence, in His *gracious* and *supporting* presence. —" Whosoever will ponder this, will hold firm his faith though the world shake, nor will the defection of all others overturn his confidence; we do not render God His full honour, *unless He alone is felt to be sufficient to us.*" *Calvin.*—John Hus, in his lonely dungeon, often comforted himself with this saying of our Lord.

καί—adversative, and *yet,* an emphatic and pathetic use of καί, accompanied by a pause and unexpectedly introducing the opposite, as often in John. *Meyer, Alford, Schaff.*

---

33. These things I have spoken unto you, that in me ye might have peace. In the world ye shall have tribulation: but be of good cheer; I have overcome the world.

These things. To be taken as referring to the whole of the farewell discourses.

In me. See on chap. xv. 7.—This presupposes the return from the scattering in verse 32.—The branches are again gathered into the vine. *Alford.*—While Christian faith has regard to the whole of the revelation of God, it yet fixes itself and is fixed upon the Personal Living Christ.—"The life which I now live in the flesh I live by the faith of the Son of God, who loved me, and gave himself for me" (Gal. ii. 20).

In me; not in Hierarchies, or Councils, or Theological systems, or Ceremonies, or the Church.—Only as the Christ of the Gospels is the centre and life of systems and forms can they be helpful to any soul.

Peace. See on chap. xiv. 27.—*Peace in Christ* as opposed to the *tribulation* prepared for them by *the world.*—Peace embraces all that constitutes rest, contentment, and true happiness of heart on the foundation of the Christian salvation and vital union with Christ.—The happiness of Christians in this life is subject to frequent interruptions from their own remaining infirmities and sins as well as from an ungodly world.—Yet deep down at the bottom peace continues to reign, however much the ocean of life may be agitated by wind and storm. *Schaff.*—This peace on earth, is heaven begun.

Tribulation. Persecution from without and distress from within.—A general statement of their relation to the world and of Christian life while in it.—*Peace in Christ, tribulation in the world*—the two clauses answer to each other.—The one defines the principle of their *inner*, the other of their *outer life.*—The life in the world is what is seen by men, the true "life is hid with Christ in God" (Col. iii. 3).—The life in the world is often a life of failure, of disappointment, of adversity.—Judged by outward circumstances Christians often appear to be " of all men most miserable " (1 Cor. xv. 19).—But the life in Christ is rich in a never failing peace which no tribulation can reach, a birthright and a joy which no one can deprive them of.—The thought is clearly allied to that of the last verse, *alone and not alone; troubled, and yet having peace.* (2 Cor. iv. 8-18).—What a mystery Christian life must ever appear to a world that judgeth everything by carnal sense !—" The trouble is but *in the world;* but the peace is in *Him*, who weighs down thousands of worlds." *Leighton.*—Peace in Christ is that on which all Christian life reposes : this peace shall have no end in time but is itself the end of all holy endeavours. *Augustine.*— It is well to remember that the oppositions of the world could not interrupt peace were it not for weakness of faith and sinful desire. —The Christian is like the woman in travail (verse 21), who has anguish *from within* and *of herself. Stier.*

Be of good cheer; I have, &c. See on verses 11, 20, and on chap. xii. 31.—The " I " is emphatic ; "I Myself have overcome."

—What is yet wanting to the fulness of peace will be supplied by this thought.—Peace is made entire by cheerful confidence, as salvation through patience (Rom. viii. 25) —*Overcome the world*, not only *before* you, but *for* you, that you may also overcome (1 John v. 4, 5).—Christ's victory secures all subsequent victories and makes His people "more than conquerors."—He says, *I have overcome*, for His whole course had been a victory over the world. —The threefold victory over its *lust*, "the lust of the flesh, the lust of the eyes, and the pride of life" (1 John ii. 16), was decided in the great conflict in the wilderness (see on Matt. iv 1-11).— The first of the three great victories over the *tribulation* of the world was decided in the triumph over Judas (see on chap. xiii. 31).—These were the pledges of the full accomplishment of His victory.—Here is the ground for encouragement and good cheer. —The Captain of Salvation has already Himself encountered the foe and even now that foe is a captive at the wheels of the Conqueror's chariot.—The farewell discourses of the Lord : discourses speaking *peace, warning, consolation, victory*.—Yet how could we derive comfort from the thought that the Lord has overcome the world, if we were not assured that He has overcome it in our hearts (see on chap. xiv. 30).—"Who is he that overcometh the world ? " Where is there such a one ? " except he that believeth that Jesus is the Son of God " (1 John v. 5).—"In Him all overcome who rejoice to be the world overcome by Him."— In these last words He condenses the sum of the instruction which He had ministered to the disciples at the last supper. *Nitzsch*.— The Christian should find constant strength, courage, and hope, in the fact, that our Lord closed His farewell discourses with A CHEERING SHOUT OF VICTORY.

For ἕξετε read ἔχετε. *Cod Sin. Meyer, Tisch., Alford, Lange, Schaff.*—θλῖψις. See critical notes, Matt. vii 14; xxiv 9.

John 17

1. These words spake Jesus and lifted up his eyes to heaven, and said, Father, the hour is come; glorify thy Son, that thy Son also may glorify thee.

We have now come to what may be called The Holy of Holies of Divine Revelation. With solemn awe and deep humility we approach it. It seems to carry us within the veil, and to bring us within hearing of The Great High Priest as He maketh intercession in His Father's presence. The cheering shout of victory with which He closes His farewell discourses (see on chap. xvi. 33), was an anticipation of faith, to be real zed by the omnipotent power of God. Hence going forth to the last and decisive conflict He pours out His heart in prayer for Himself, His disciples, and the Church to the end of time. This chapter contains that prayer, properly called the *Sacerdotal* Prayer of our Lord, because He here intercedes for His people and enters upon His office as the High Priest in offering His own life as a perfect sacrifice for the sins of the world. Spoken in the stillness of the night, under the starry heavens, before the wondering disciples, in view of the approaching consummation of His work, this prayer is peculiarly His own. It could be uttered only by Christ, and even by Him only once in the world's history, as the Atonement could occur but once, though its effect vibrates through all the ages. It is not so much the petition of a dependent suppliant, as the communion of an equal, and a solemn declaration of His will concerning those He came to save. He prays as the Mighty Intercessor and Mediator standing between earth and heaven. He looks backward and forward, and comprehends all His present and future disciples in one holy and perfect fellowship with Himself and His Father. It is the simplest, the profoundest, and the sublimest portion of Holy Scripture. The words are as clear and calm as a mirror, but the thoughts as deep and glowing as God's fathomless love to man : Hence all efforts to exhaust them are in vain. *Schaff.* " If in any human speech divinity is manifest, and sublimity is joined to condescending humility, it is in this prayer." *Tholuck.* " A prayer such as the world never heard nor could hear. Sentence rushes upon sentence with wonderful power, yet the repose is never disturbed." *Ewald.* " The noblest and purest pearl of devotion in the New Testament." *Meyer.* " Neither in the Scripture nor in the literature of any nation can there be found a composition which in simplicity and depth, in grandeur and fervour, may be compared to this prayer. It could not be invented, but could proceed only from such a con-

sciousness as the one which speaks here. But it could be preserved
and reproduced by a personality so wholly devoted and conformed to
the personality of Jesus as the Evangelist." *Luthardt.* "A prayer
wherein He discovereth both unto us and to the Father, the abysses
of His heart and poureth forth its treasures. Plain and simple in
sound, it is yet so deep, rich and broad that no one can fathom it."
Luther. Spener would never preach on this chapter: he declared
that a true understanding of it mounted above the ordinary degree
of faith which the Lord is wont to communicate to His people on
their pilgrimage. The evening before his death, however, he caused
it to be read to him three times in succession. *Canstein.* So John
Knox, in his last illness, directed his wife and his secretary that one
of them should every day read to him, in a distinct voice, this
chapter. *McCrie.* The key to the thought of the prayer is in the
presence of the Spirit who shall guide into all truth (see on chap.
xvi. 26).

These words spake Jesus. This expression connects the prayer
of our Lord with His farewell discoures, making it the seal.
—Prayer is the blossom of holy speech ; meditation the root of
prayer.—This is the climax and consummation of all His discourses,
pressing nearest to heaven and most immediately breathing of its
mysteries.—A triumphantly and serenely bright "*It is finished*,"
before the darkness surrounding Him upon the cross.—The most
glowing mystic and the most *careful thinker* finds each his own language
in these words, embracing both opposites in one. *Stier.*—Our
Lord prayed aloud, partly from the strength of emotion which
seeks utterance in speech, partly for the benefit of His disciples
(verse 13).—He would lift them up to the throne of grace and
reveal to them and to His Church the love and sympathy of His
heart.—Such reflection, especially in a prayer of intercession for
others, is in perfect harmony with the deepest spirit of devotion
(see chap. xi. 42).

And lifted up his eyes to heaven. John very seldom depicts
the gestures or looks of our Lord, as here.—But this was an occasion of which the impression was indelible and the upward look
could not be passed over. *Alford.*—With eyes upraised, to show that
He seeks His home above, where His Father is.—Heaven, as the
place where the divine glory is manifested, constitutes the *above*,
in antithesis to Earth.—In prayer the eye of faith is instinctively
lifted to heaven, as heaven is everywhere open, and the angels
are ascending and descending.—Heaven is the abode of the Hearer
of prayer and Giver of every good and perfect gift (James i. 17).
—Every prayer of faith is a spiritual ascension.—He who would

understand this prayer must approach it with eyes and heart up-lifted to the God to whom and by whom it was spoken.

Father. Christ addresses God simply as " *Father,*" six times in this prayer.—Not " *Our* Father," as in the Prayer given in the Sermon on the Mount, which is intended for the disciples.—Nor yet " *My* Father," where He prays for Himself only.—He is the Only Begotten of *His* Father, we the common children of *our* Father (see on chap. xx. 17, and on Matt. ii. 6; iii. 17).—It is the most en-dearing and encouraging Name by which we can know and address God (see on Matt. vi. 9).—It calls out every feeling of filial trust, and gratitude and love.—Our Lord probably used the Aramean word, *Abba,* which passed into the devotional language of Christians.—Through Him all believers receive the Spirit of adoption, and cry. as He cried, " Abba, Father" (Rom. viii. 15; Gal. iv. 6)—In this Great Name, *Father,* the whole mystery of redemption is summed up.—In the prayer-life of Jesus, the perfect truth of His human nature has approved itself.—He who, as the Son of God, is complete revelation, is, as the Son of Man, complete religion.

The hour is come. See on chap. xii. 23, 27; xiii. 1.—The great hour of decision by death and resurrection, which are inseparable. —The hour whose aim and consummation is the glorification of which He had spoken (see on chap. xiii. 31, 32).—The most momentous hour in the history of the world; probably in the history of the universe (1 Pet. i. 12).—The hour of which, Nature, from the first dawnings of life, had unconsciously prophesied, and to which all points.—The hour in which the types and figures of the law and the predictions of the prophets found fulfilment and consummation.—The grand central point of the divine dispensa-tions to which all preceding ages looked forward, and upon which all succeeding ages look back.—The key to human history in the past, and to the course of humanity to the end of time.—Note how Jesus, for everything that is to happen, knows, chooses, and defines *time* and *hour.*—Being sensible of His *eternity,* He is sensible of His *moment.*—Thus He invariably does and suffers that which is proper for each hour.

Glorify thy Son, &c. See on chap. xiii. 31, 32.—" *Thy* Son," to give force to the petition which, being the prayer of the Only Be-gotten, cannot be refused.—He explains in verse 5, the state of glory into which He asks to be conducted.—But He must pass through the dark valley of death before that glory can be attained. —The glorification of the Son was fulfilled in His Resurrection and Ascension.—The glorification of the Father by the completion of the Messianic work, by the mission of the Paraclete, and the

establishment of the Church and of the gospel ministry.—The Son
glorifies the Father, not by adding to His glory, but by making it
known to men through the Holy Spirit, who thus makes known
and glorifies the Son. *Schaff.*—The Son desires His own glorification not *egotistically*, but solely to *the end* that He again may
glorify the Father, and give back to Him the might, honour, and
praise which Himself should receive.—These words are a proof
that the Son is equal to the Father as touching His Godhead.—
" What creature could stand before his Creator, and say, ' Glorify
Thou me, that I may glorify Thee'? " *Stier.*—The glorification of
God and Christ being the redemption of humanity ; it follows
that this redemption is the foundation of our glorification.—Christ
in the heart is the seed of glory, the earnest of the inheritance,
the pledge and foretaste of perfect glory (1 Pet. iv. 14 ; Eph. i.
14 ; Rom. viii. 29, 30.)—In Phil iii. 21, the most definite conception of this glorification appears.—1. Christ prays for His own
glorification (verses 1-5) ; 2. For the preservation of His disciples (verses 6-19) ; 3. For the congregation of believers, which
they are to lead to Him ; (*a*) for their unity and perfection in
the kingdom of glory; (*b*) that the whole world may believe
through them ; (*c*) may attain unto knowledge and (as world)
vanish out of existence (verses 20-24). *Lange.*—The connecting
idea : The work of God, 1, as accomplished by Christ ; 2, as
carried on by the Apostles ; 3, as completed in the Church, to the
glory of God. *Schaff.*

ταῦτα The foregoing discourse. *Alford.*—ἐλάλησεν. λελάληκεν. *Cod. Sin.*—ἐπάρας
without καὶ, instead of the *text. rec.* Lach., Treg., Tisch., Alf., Lange, &c.—εἶπεν. This
prayer probably uttered as they were preparing to leave the chamber after supper.
Watkins.—The time indicated with the going forth over the brook Kedron (chap,
xviii. 1).—The crossing of the brook was the act and sign of final decision.—It is not
necessary to understand the going forth as a going forth from the Supper-room, for
the precincts of the city probably extended, in single residences, down into the valley.
Lange. (See note, chap. xiv. 31.)—Renan disposes of all the parting discourses (chap.
ii.-xvii) in a short foot-note (*Vie de Jésus*), categorically declaring that they cannot
b historical, but must be a free fiction of John in his own language.—So also Strauss,
Weisse, Baur, Schotten, &c.—Such a view, which stands and falls with the whole
fiction theory of the Johannean discourses of Christ, is not only revolting to all religious feeling, but plainly incompatible with the depth and height, the tenderness and
fervour of this prayer.—If John, or whoever was the author of the Gospel, invented
it, he must have been conscious of his own fiction and intention of deceiving the
reader.—That a person in such a frame of mind and heart could produce such a prayer
as this is a psychological and moral impossibility.—That the prayer, as the discourses
of Christ generally, was not only translated from the Hebrew into the Greek, but
freely reproduced in John's mind, and received his peculiar colouring, may be admitted
without impairing the faithfulness as to the thoughts and spirit, especially if we take
into consideration that the Paraclete reminded the apostles of Christ's words and
opened to them their full meaning (chap. xiv. 26 ; xv. 26 ; xvi, 13, 14) *Lange.*—The
internal miracle of a faithful reproduction of the long discourses of Christ is less in-

1204 / Gospel of John

explicable than the artificial composition or fiction of such a masterpiece. *Godet, Schaff.—The very words of our Lord Himself, faithfully rendered by the beloved Apostle in the power of the Holy Spirit.*—If such a promise as xiv. 26 was made, *and fulfilled*, then these must be the words of the Lord Himself ; and the *Greek form* of them only, if even that, can be regarded as bearing evidence of the style and manner of John. *Alford.*

---

2. As thou hast given him power over all flesh, that he should give eternal life to as many as thou hast given him.

As thou hast given him power. Gr., *According as thou gavest Him power.*—This is the ground on which the prayer in verse 1 is based (see on chap. xiii. 3).—The glory He asks is in accordance with the Father's purpose which appointed His Messianic work.— The glorification, the *end*, must correspond to the *beginning*, to the sending, the preparation, the office of the Son. *Lücke.*

Over all flesh. An Old Testament expression, not found elsewhere in John.—A solemn declaration of the universality of His office for the whole human race.—Its especial signification denotes humanity in its weakness and imperfection.—Indicates also the susceptibility of mankind for salvation.—This " power " is expressive of the greatness of His expectations with regard to the spread of His gospel (Phil. ii. 6, &c).—" Authority over *all flesh,* obtained by His becoming a man *in the flesh,* and the Head of our race, the Lord received with joy from the Father." *Stier.*—Of all flesh, *mankind* is the head and crown, and in the *full* blessing of Christ's office, mankind only can share.—But to Him, the Second Adam, belongs the right to rule and judge the *whole creation,* for all things are put under his feet, &c., because " by the grace of God He tasted death for everyone " (Heb. ii. 8, 9).

That he should, &c. Gr., *That all whom Thou gavest Him, He may give to them eternal life* (see on chap. vi. 37, 39).—In the wide gift of power over all flesh, there is a more special gift —The word " all " is in the Greek a neuter singular, and signifies collectively the whole body of humanity given to Christ.—The word translated " to them " is masculine and plural, and signifies the individual reception on the part of those to whom eternal life is given. *Watkins.*—The " all " is necessarily broken up into individual members, for every man must *singly* attain to saving faith. —Yet this individualisation is but conducive to a far higher unity (see on verse 21).—Christ's glorification, though an end in itself, aims at the bliss of believing humanity ; the one design is inseparable from the other.—The bestowal of salvation in Christ, the gift of *eternal life,* glorifies the Father.—That *real* life which is *eternal;* that fellowship with God which begins with living faith, and is con-

summated in the full blessedness of eternal glory (see on verse 3).
—This ineffable gift is imparted to those who believe on Him
and to them alone, for it can only come by union with Him, and
faith is the divinely ordained means of that union.—" Our election
to eternal life is something hidden in God ; yet we may know it
if we lay hold on Christ in true faith, perseveringly continuing
therein." *Canstein.*

---

3. And this is life eternal, that they might know thee the only true God, and Jesus Christ, whom thou hast sent.

Life eternal. No New Testament writer uses these momentous
words so frequently as John (chap. iii. 15, 16, 36 ; v. 24, 39 ;
vi. 27, 40, 47, 54, 68; x. 28; xii. 25, 50 ; 1 John i. 2 ; ii. 15 ;
iii. 15 ; v. 11, 13, 20).—*Life eternal* is not merely *conscious existence,* nor yet merely *endless existence :* it is *the life belonging to
eternity,* the highest *kind* and *state* of being of which the creation
is capable.—Chr'st's life communicated to believers, through the
Spirit, is the great impulse and might of eternal life.—The believer
has life in the eternity of God ; and the eternity of God in the
power of life —The unity of eternity in the manifoldness of life,
and the manifoldness of life in the unity of eternity. *Lange.*—
Perfect inward bliss, and the glorification of the finite life in the
Divine. *Tholuck.*—"God is the life of the soul, as the soul is the
life of the body; hence Eternal Life is not a thing to be begun
hereafter; it is begun now, for the Life of Glory is the Life of
Grace continued." *Marriott.*
Might know. Gr., *might recognize.*—This is no mere head or heart
knowledge, the mere information of the mind or excitation of
the feelings.—It is the living reality of knowledge and personal
realization, oneness in will with God and partaking of His nature.
—The knowledge, love, enjoyment of Him who is infinite, and
therefore themselves infinite.—Eternal Life involves an eternal,
unobstructed reaching toward a goal continually attained and as
continually set afresh.—This is implied in its very nature, for it is
an eternal *knowing* of God.—What a glorious field for the exercise
of the powers of the immortal spirit !—An eternal *knowing* of the
Eternal One ; an infinite knowing of the Infinite One.
Thee the only true God. See on chap. xv. 1.—The only *essential,*
real God.—*True,* in antithesis to the unreal and mythical deities
of the world, and of later Judaism also, in its apostasy from the
God of Scripture.—The *true God* as the God of revelation in
Christ, the God and Father of Christ (Eph. i. 3).—The *true* God

in opposition to all false and obscuring beliefs of God.—The first clause sets forth the distinctive truth of the Old Testament; the next, the distinctive truth of the New.—"To know Thee is perfect righteousness; yea, to know Thy power is the root of immortality" (Wisdom xv. 3).—Knowledge of God in the Scripture sense does not mean *apprehension*, or *thinking* in cold speculation ; nor is it *belief* as mere admission and credence. but a living, conscious possession of fellowship with Him.—This is the highest good possible to man, and it is that for which man was made.

And Jesus Christ. " Not Moses. not a prophet, could have been named in this co-ordination, by the side of God, but He only who could say, *He that hath seen Me hath seen the Father.*" *Tholuck.* —The knowledge of God and the knowledge of Christ are not distinct and separate ; in reality they are one (see on chap. xiv. 9). —Where God is rightly known, He is known as *the only true God;* where Jesus is rightly known, He is known as the Sent of God, *the* Christ.—Our Lord Himself is called "the true God and eternal life" (1 John v. 20).—It is agreeable to the idea of personal knowledge that we know God *and* Christ as well as God *through* Christ.—The Divinity of Christ, and His humanity as the manifestation of that Divinity.—"The very juxtaposition of Jesus Christ here with the Father, and the knowledge of both being defined to be eternal life, is a proof by implication of the Godhead of Christ. The knowledge of *God and a creature* could not be eternal life, and the juxtaposition of the two would be inconceivable." *Alford.*—"The two opposites to the knowledge of the true God here referred to, were in their historical manifestation at that time, 1. *Gentile* idolatry, which knew not nor acknowledged even the one true God ; 2. *Jewish* rejection of His Anointed in the person of Jesus. But in their internal and permanent principle, as the Lord here points to it for all futurity, they are ; *Pantheistic* denial of the Personal Supermundane Creator, and deification of the creature which is the root of all heathenism ; and *Deistical* rationalism, which heeds not and rejects Christ." *Stier.*—"To take the Lord for God is the *natural* part of the covenant ; the *supernatural* part is to take Christ for our Redeemer : The former is first necessary, and implied in the latter." *R. Baxter.*—This is the only time that the Lord Himself unites thus simply and immediately His *Christ*-name with His *Jesus*-name ; but the occasion stands alone. —He here confirms, unfolds, explains, and glorifies the central word of the Old Testament, now fulfilled in Him.—He avows in the most solemn manner before the Father that He, *Jesus*, is the *only true Messiah.*—Speaking of Himself in the third person, He declares *His own proper name,* in order that He may show forth

the spiritual meaning which it involv· s.—He who bears the, name
Jesus (see on Matt. i. 25) presents Himself before the Father *in
the full consciousness* of the power and meaning of that name.—
Thus Matthew's record of the *conception*, and John's of the *departure*,
coincide in *the name of Jesus. Stier.*—'' Verily thou art a God that
hidest thyself '' (Isa. xlv. 15); and had Christ not come into the
world, God had remained a hidden God; but because Christ hath
glorified and revealed Him, we can know God clearly in His
Son. Trusting knowledge is faith; *cognitive personal knowledge is
love;* perfected, seeing knowledge is the felicity of the blessed;
in all stages, however, it is life eternal, in respect of its beginning,
progress, and consummation. *Lange.*

γινώσκωσι. γινώσκουσιν *A. D. G L. &c., Tisch., Tregelles.*—Probably an ancient
error in transcrio ion. *Meyer.*—May be a dogmatical correction.—γινώσκωσι seems to
denote the impulse of a striving a'ter the perfect knowledge of God and Christ charac-
terizing such impulse as the beginning of eternal blessedness. *Schaff*—γινώσκωσι
Lach., Alford, Westcott and Hort, Lange, &c., Cod. Sin., B. C. X. Origen.— Ἰησοῦν Χριστόν.
A difficulty has been found in the use of this name *by the Lord Himself;* a .d inferences
have been hence made that we have *J hn's own language* here; but surely without any
ground.—He who said σου τὸν υἱόν (verse), might well here, before the ἐγώ of verse 4, use
t'at prophetic Name which had been Divinely given Him as the Saviour of men, and
its weighty adjunct Χριστός, in wh ch Names are all the hidden treasures of that
knowledge of which He here speaks—And as to the later use of the two names together having led to their insertion here by the Apostle, what if *the converse were the
case,* and this solemn use of them by our Lord had given occasion to their subsequent
use by the Church? *Alford.*

---

4. I have g'orified thee on the earth : I have finished the work which thou gavest
me to do.

I have glorified thee, &c. Gr., *I glorified thee on the earth: I
finished the work.*—The former sentence is explained by the latter.
—God was glorified in the completion of the Messianic work (see
on chap. v. 36; ix. 4; x. 25).—This is the foundation of the petition
in verse 1.—The Son, by His glorification of the Father, has prepared the moment of His own glorification.—He is justified in
expecting such glorification as a recompense according to the fundamental law of the kingdom of love and righteousness.—In His
doctrine and life He had manifested the Father conformably to
the grace and truth of the Father (chap i. 17).—He could therefore lay this work before the Father as finished and complete.—
He stands by anticipation at the end of His accomplished course,
and looks back on it all as past.—His *work* was His *whole* Life,
with all its manifestations of humility and holiness; with all its
benefits and blessings to the world.—'' How doth He say that He

hath finished the work of man's salvation since He hath not yet
climbed the Cross? Nay, but by the determination of His will,
whereby He hath resolved to endure every article of His mysterious passion, He may truly proclaim that He hath finished
the work." *Polycarp.*—"In this *finished,* before the fulfilment on the Cross, consists the preeminent wonder of this
prayer, which *anticipates* the heavenly mediation and intercession."
Stier.—Learn : 1. It is *work* that glorifies God ; 2. Each one has
his proper work assigned him by God ; 3. This work must be
finished here upon earth ; 4. It is a blessed thing at the hour of
death to be able to say, " I have glorified thee on the earth," &c.
—Every Christian should have his work accomplished, so that
when the hour of death approaches, he, like his Lord, may have
nothing to do but die and go to his Father in heaven.—As Christ's
supreme object was the glorification of His Father, so Christians
should aim at the glory of God in all things (Col. iii. 17).—This is
best accomplished by each one devoting himself to the work to
which he is called, and doing it " as to the Lord, and not to
men " (Eph vi. 7).

ἐτελείωσα. τελειώσας. *Cod. Sin.* and the best modern authorities.—τελειώσας explains
εδόξασα. *Schaff.*

5. And now, O Father, glorify thou me with thine own self with the glory which I
had with thee before the world was.

Glorify me. See on chap. xiii. 31, 32.—His glorification by death,
resurrection and ascension.—Henceforth our Lord conducts
Himself passively ; the Father assumes the *active.*
With thine own self. The Greek preposition denotes closest
proximity and equality with personal distinction ; " With Thyself
as Thy fellow." *Schaff.*—Thus we read, "The Word was *with*
God " (see on chap. i. 1, 2, and on Matt. ii. 6 ; iii. 17).—" *With
Thyself,*" *i. e.,* not simply in heaven, but in His going to the
Father, in His being in God (Col. iii. 3), in antithesis to His life
in the world.—He has glorified the Father in and from this world ;
the Father is to glorify Him in and from the other world. *Lange.*
With the glory, &c. Special importance is to be attached to these
words from the fact that they are the words of our Lord Himself,
and in a prayer to the Father.—It is impossible to explain them
save by allowing that He claimed for Himself divine glory
co-eternal with the Father.—He claims that glory in personality

distinct from the Father; but in essence one with Him.—The same Person who had with the Father glory before the world, also glorified the Father in the world, and prays to be again received into that glory.—*A decisive proof of the unity of the Person of Christ*, in His three estates of eternal pre-existence in glory, humiliation in the flesh, and glorification in the Resurrection Body. *Alford.*

Before the world was. See on verse 24.—" Before all creation."
—The glory which He as the Son of God and the Logos, possessed, before the existence of the world (see on chap. i. 1-14).—Springing out of this, and destined from the beginning, He would receive a *new* glory as the Mediator.—The words reach beyond a re-reception of His original glory, and embrace the glory which issues from the work of redemption.—This future divine glory was assured to the Son along with His eternal Logos-glory.—The "physical" attributes of God are, in the Logos, exhibited in the creation of the world: in the redemption of the world, the "moral" attributes are exhibited in the self-humiliation of Christ.—In the glorification of Christ the moral and physical attributes will shine united, as the manifestation of His majesty. —The *new* glory of Christ will be an eternal blending of the mediatorial glory with the primordial glory (Heb. i. 3). *Lange.*— Learn that: 1. Whoever expects to be glorified with God in heaven must glorify Him first here upon earth; 2. After we have glorified Him, we may expect to be glorified with Him, and by Him. *Burkitt.*

For πρὸ του τὸν κόσμου, &c., γενέσθαι. *Cod. D.*

---

6. I have manifested thy name unto the men which thou gavest me out of the world: thine they were, and thou gavest them me; and they have kept thy word.

I have manifested. Gr., *I manifested.*—Here begins the intercession for the disciples.

Thy name. See on Matt. i. 21; vi. 9.—He had made known the Father as the only true God, and glorified Him on earth.—Our Lord's whole life, ministry, works, a manifestation of the Father. —This absolute manifestation of the Father was the completion of His *prophetic* office.—Though the disciples understood not this revelation, it, nevertheless, was finished, as regarded its objective elements. *Lange.*—Christ first preached and testified concerning the Father (see on chap xvi. 25), and in His own person brought down and unfolded this great word.—It was He who taught man how he may, and why he should, call God, FATHER.—Hitherto the question concerning the *name* of God had been answered by the ineffable name JEHOVAH.—But now *eternal being* is plainly revealed to be *eternal love*.—FATHER, and its appropriate honour, man has nothing further to know, to confess, and to praise.—He announced God *first* to be His own, the Son's, Father, and *then* ours, because He hath given to us the Son.—This is the permanent pre-eminence of the Adamic creature over all other "children of God," that they through Christ have GOD as in the most direct and essential manner their FATHER. *Stier.*

Unto the men, &c. He speaks of the disciples as a company separated from the world (see on chap xv. 19), and given to Him by the Father (see on chap. vi. 37).—"God gave them to Him through His election, through the attraction drawing them to the Son, and through the power of His calling." *Lange.*—He intercedes for them as the chosen bearers of the Father's name.—The great work of manifestation must in them be protected and secured.

Thine they were. Implies more than the general sense in which all things belong to God.—They were prepared by the earlier manifestation of God for the fuller manifestation in Christ.—They were God's by a special training, therefore when Christ was revealed to them they recognised Him as the promised Messiah.—Israelites indeed, in whom was no guile (see on chap i. 47 ; iii. 21 ; v. 46; vi. 37 : viii. 47).—It is a mark of divine grace that men yield to the discipline and drawing of God.

Thou gavest them me. See on chap. x. 27.—Made manifest and realized in their obedience to the heavenly call.—Giving them to the Son was only the completion of the Revelation of the Father to them.—*Thou gavest them Me*, as *sheep* to the shepherd, to be *kept;* as *patients* to the physician, to be *cured;* as *children* to a tutor, to be *educated. Henry.*—The full import of the passage has reference to the covenanted inheritance of Christ, known, determined, and provided for, before the foundation of the world. *Owen.*—1. All believers are given to Christ, as His purchase, and as His charge; as His subjects, as His children; as His wife, as the members of His body ; 2. None are given to Christ, but those that were first the Father's ; 3. All those that are given to Christ keep His word. *Burkitt.*—The election of the disciples: 1. Eternal ; 2. Conditional (they have kept His word) ; 3. Elected for the good of the world. *Lange.*

Kept thy word. See on chap. viii. 51; xiv. 23.—Our Lord says, "Thy word," not "My word," in harmony with the thought that the disciples are the Father's.—Moreover, *His* word was the word of the Father who sent Him (see on chap. vii. 16 ; xii. 48, 49).—Though the disciples must be further tried, to His eyes, they do already issue victorious.—They have stood the chief test, and have not been seduced by the treachery of Judas.—The *word* is the instrument in the conversion of all whom the Father gives to Christ (James i. 18).—This distinguishes true and effectual conversion from all counterfeits.—" Being born again, not of corruptible seed, but of incorruptible, by the word of God, which liveth and abideth for ever " (1 Pet. i. 23).—" Such as have found the word effectual to their conversion will be sure to lay it up in their heart as their daily food, and to observe it in their practice, and to do so because of the authority of God shining in it, for this is an evidence of their conversion, ' they have kept Thy word,' that so, they may be nourished by the same means by which they are begotten." *Hutcheson.*—The elect *keep* the Divine Word in their *understanding*, they *hide* it in their *hearts*, they *feel the force* of it in their *souls*, they *express the power* of it in their *lives. Burkitt.*—The keeping of the word of God stands to election in the relation of effect to cause.—" Wherefore by their fruits ye shall know them," &c. (see on Matt. vii. 29, 30.)

---

7. Now they have known that all things whatsoever thou hast given me are of thee.

Now they have known. " They have come to know, and do know."—The result of their spiritual training, in its fulness, is spoken of as if now present.—Fidelity to truth is rewarded by the beginning of a higher faith-knowledge (see on chap xvi. 30).

That all things, &c. His whole words and works, as contemplated in their separate meanings and testimonies. *Alford.*—No limit can be assigned to the extent of these words. *Ellicott.*—They know that everything which has been given to Christ is of the Father ; *i.e. they know God in Christ.*—They know the words of Christ to be divine by the works, the works by the words.—From their *trust* in the divine words *confided* to them by Him, has arisen a true perception of *His divine origin.*—All that He had been teaching them, and which they should soon fully know, was that His words and works, *His whole life*, was a manifestation of the Father.—Christianity alone is pure, full, entire Theism.—" It is a special evidence of true conversion to know Christ savingly and the mystery of redemption, to know Christ's union with the Father, His commission and authority from Him as Mediator, and to see God in Christ." *Hutcheson.*

ἐγνωκαν is text sustained by *A. B. C. D., &c, Lach., Tisch., Treg., Alf., Westcott and Hort.—ἐγνων. Cod. Sin.—ἐγνωσαν. U. X.*

8. For I have given unto them the words which thou gavest me; and they have
received them, and have known surely that I came out from thee, and they have
believed that thou didst send me.

For I have given. See on chap. xv. 15.—An explanation of the way
in which the disciples had attained to the knowledge He has just
spoken of (see on verse 7).—He carefully emphasises His own work
in teaching them, "I have given."

The words which thou gavest me. See on chap. xii. 49.—He
emphasises the matter taught, as not of Himself, but as that which
the Father had committed to Him.—"On the truth of this saying
stands the whole fabric of creeds and doctrines. It is the ground
of authority to the preacher, of assurance to the believer, of existence to the Church. It is the source from which the perpetual
stream of Christian teaching flows. All our testimonies, instructions, exhortations, derive their first origin and continuous power,
from the fact that the Father has given to the Son, the Son has
given to His servants, the words of truth and life." *Bernard,*
" Progress of Doctrine in the N. T."

Have received them. See on chap. i. 12, 16.—He emphasises the
part of the disciples : *Others* had been taught, but did not
receive the word.—The teaching was the same ; the varying effect
was in the heart of the hearer. *Ellicott.*—Their reception of the
truth came from His manifestation of it to them, and their reception was cordial, leading to obedience.—We *receive* the truth when
we *affectionately* embrace Jesus as our Saviour and our Lord, and
make acknowledgment and confession that He is such to us.
Owen.

Have known surely. Gr., *and knew surely* (see on chap. vi. 69 ;
xvi. 30).—This stamps our Lord's approval on *their* knowledge, and
distinguishes it from such knowledge as the bare "we know " of
Nicodemus and his colleagues (see on chap. iii. 2). *Alford.*—" Well
for us, if we do not merely utter our own *we have believed* and *we
have known,* but are also *acknowledged* before the Father by the
' truly' of His Son." *Stier.*

That I came out from thee. See on chap. xvi. 27, 30.—All His
words and works, His whole life, witnessed to His divine origin,
and *their* belief of it was the evidence of their true conversion.

They have believed, &c. Gr., *they believed that Thou didst send Me.*
—A fuller expression, and in part an advance on the words, " I
came out from Thee."—This implies that they believed Him to be
the sent One, the Messiah (see on verse 3).—" Christ is to be
taken up by lost sinners, not as their fancy or fears would point
Him out, but as He hath revealed Himself in His saving word.
He is savingly known when He is known in His person and

offices, and that the Father is in Him, and He His Ambassador. Believers ought to be well rooted in their knowledge of Christ, His person and offices. For settling of believers in the point of knowing Christ, they must not expect such evidences as are usual in natural things, but must submit, and be content with the evidence of faith, which, how obscure soever it seem, is a sure knowledge in its own kind." *Hutcheson.*

και έγνωσαν. Omitted. *A. D., Cod. Sin.*—Bracketed. *Lach.*—A gloss. *Meyer.*—Supported. *Codd. B. C. L, &c*—Retained. *Treg., Lange, Tisch., Alf., Westcott and Hort.*—Has a decided reference to chap, xvi. 30. *Schaff.*

---

9. I pray for them: I pray not for the world, but for them which thou hast given me; for they are thine.

I pray for them. Gr., *I am praying for them.*—" I," and " for them," are both emphatic.—" *I* who have taught them ; " " *they* who have received the truth " (verse 8).—" *I* who am about to leave the world ; " " *they* who will remain in the world " (verse 11).—Our Lord is referring to the prayer He is at this moment uttering, and not to His general practice.—It is from its very nature applicable only to disciples. *Ellicott.*—He here begins to fulfil His promise (Matt. x. 32).—As the typical high priest prayed only for Israel, bore only the twelve tribes on his breast-plate, so there is a corresponding prayer of the Eternal High Priest only for the true people of God. *Stier.*

I pray not for the world. Gr.. *I am not praying for the world.* —I am not praying for the world *now and in this manner. Bengel, Meyer.*—This whole sacerdotal prayer was offered only for His disciples: 1. For those whom He had already called out of the world (verses 6-19) ; 2. For those who should hereafter come out of the world and believe in Him (verse 20).—In verses 14-16, the world appears in the light of a hostile force, against which He asks protection for His disciples.—Yet by the preservation of His Church in unity and holiness, which is the great object of this prayer, the world itself is at last to be brought to believe in His divine mission (verses 21-23).—The exclusion of the world, therefore, is not absolute but relative.—Our Lord *did* pray for the ungodly world, even for His murderers (Luke xxiii. 34).—He commanded His disciples to pray for them who despitefully used them and persecuted them (see on Matt. v. 44).—For Christians we should pray that God may keep them from the world and the evil one ; for the world that it may cease to be worldly and believe in Christ. *Schaff.*—" To pray for the world,

and not to pray for the world, must both be right in their place."
Luther.

But for them, &c. See on chap. vi. 37, 39.—This is the special
claim on which He intercedes for them with the Father.—They
were the Father's before they were given to the Son.—By that
gift they have become more fully the Father's (verses 6-8).—All
things which are the Son's are the Father's, and all things which
are the Father's are the Son's. *Ellicott.*—" Christ's people have
room in His heart and affection, not only because of His interest
in them, and charge of them, but because of the interest the Father
hath also in them, whose beloved Son He is ; for this is not only
a reason why the Father should respect His prayers for them,
but also why He so heartily undertakes to pray for them : 'for
they are Thine;' which should teach all, in their stations, heartily
to respect and care for those persons or things wherein God hath
an interest." *Hutcheson.*

τοῦ κόσμου. The misconceptions which have been made of this verse as implying
a decree of exclusion for the vessels of wrath, may be at once removed by considering
the use of ὁ κόσμος in this Prayer.—The Lord *does pray* distinctly for ὁ κόσμος, verses
21, 23, that they may believe and know that the Father hath sent Him.—He cannot,
therefore, mean here that He does not pray (absolutely) for the world, but that He is
not *now* praying for the world, does not pray *this thing* for the world. *Alford.*—He
must pray for the world for the sake of those *who are yet to come forth from the world.*
—St. Paul was certainly of the world, when he persecuted and killed Christians; yet
St. Stephen prayed for him and he was converted.—Thus, too, Christ Himself prayed
on the Cross (Luke xxiii. 34).—It is thus true that He prayed for the world, and does
not pray for the world; but this is the distinction: In the same way and in the same
degree in which Christ prays for them that are His, He does not pray for the world.
Luther.—The expression is doubtless of *dogmatic* moment; it is, however, destitute
of a *predestinarian* import.—It is significant of the *purely dynamical* view of the world
and arrangement of the gospel.--By means of this dynamical principle first concentrated in Christ and henceforth to be concentrated in His apostles, *the world, as world,
is to be clean done away with.* But the expression of Christ has also an *affectionate*
emphasis: I pray, above all things for these, who are Thine as the *fruits* of the Old
Testament, and Mine as the firstlings of the New Testament; similarly, the expression
has a *religious* force; the δόξα of Thy name is concerned; that δόξα is henceforth
entrusted to them; it must be secured in them, must, through them, become universal
in the world as the principle of the world's glorification. *Lange.*

---

10. And all mine are thine, and thine are mine; and I am glorified in them.

And all mine, &c. See on chap. xvi. 15.—Gr., *And all My things
are Thine, and Thy things are Mine.*—The Authorised Version
leaves the impression that *persons* only are meant, while *all things,*
the God-head itself included, are meant. *Schaff.*—The words
assert absolute community in *all things* between the Father and
the Son.—He gives prominence to the worth possessed by the dis-

ciples as the objects of His intercession.—As the Son's property, they are the property of the Father : As the Father's property, they are the property of the Son.—" It were not so much if He had only said, ' All mine is Thine ; ' for that we may all say, that all we have is God's. But this is a far greater thing, that He inverts this and says, ' All Thine is Mine.' This can no *creature* say before God." *Luther.*—" There is a communion and reciprocal interest in all things betwixt the Father and His Son, who is heir of all things (Heb i. 2), and betwixt the Father and Christ as Mediator, in the elect. This communion and interest tends much to the advantage of God's people, as having interest both in the Father and the Son ; so that Christ will not neglect those who are not only His own peculiar property, entrusted to Him, but His Father's also, and will have a care to make them forthcoming to the Father ; and the Father will respect those, and His Son in interceding for them, who are not only His beloved Son's charge, but His own also." *Hutcheson.*—Every Christian may in the joyful confidence of faith utter the same word to Christ, " All that is thine is mine " (1. Cor. iv. 21-23).

And I am glorified in them. See on chap. xv. 8.—Not " by *their means,*" but *in them* (verse 23).—The life of the vine is in the branches ; so that the fruit of the branches is the glory of the vine, by the sap of the vine living in the branches. *Alford.*—The fact that Christ is *glorified in them* forms a second reason for His special prayer for them.—The tense of the Greek word implies that He has been already in part glorified (verses 6-8).—But this will be more fully accomplished in the gift of the Spirit, which, all through this prayer, He regards as present.—Since He is glorified in them, the glory of Christ, which is the glory of the Father, must be protected in them.—" The more our endeavour and aim be to glorify God and Christ, we have the clearer ground to expect the acceptation of our prayers " *Hutcheson.*—Those shall have an interest in Christ's intercession, in and by whom He is *glorified. Henry.*

---

11. And now I am no more in the world, but these are in the world, and I come to thee. Holy Father, keep through thine own name those whom thou hast given me, that they may be one, as we are.

Now I am no more. Gr., *And I am henceforth no more in the world.* —This is the motive for his urgent, provident petition.—He is going out of the world ; they remain in the world, and so will be needing special protection.—Our Lord speaks as if that which was close at hand were already present.—The words have a special

1216 / Gospel of John

reference to **vue** int*e*rval between His de**a**th and the day of Pentecost.—That would be for the disciples a time of darkness and danger, when they would have special need of the Father's care. *Ellicott.*

In the world. " Not said of *place* alone, for He is still *here*. The words are descriptive of *state*, the *state of men in the flesh ;* sometimes viewed on its darker side, as overcoming men and bringing in spiritual death; sometimes, as here, used in the most genera) sense." *Alford.*—Although in some degree still remaining *in* His disciples, He yet *leaves* them on going to the Father.—And this thought touches His heart with the feeling of *their* future *need.*— *For Himself*, His words contain the anticipation of His victory over the world.

I come to thee. See on chap. xvi. 28.—Not a mere repetition of the declaration, " I am no more," &c.—Implies H s ascension to heaven and perfect fellowship with His Father.—The position and work of the disciples in the world will be assured by Christ's *coming* to His Father in His intercessory office.—In the first place, His *going away* is expressed as perilous for the disciples who remain here ; and, secondly, His *g ing home* is intimated as the indemnification for the disciples, whose position and task are here. *Lange.*—Those who love God are happy at the thought of *coming* to Him, even though it be through the valley of the shadow of death.—Our Lord's leaving the world would not sever the bond of love that united Him to His disciples.—On the contrary, the Perfected. glorified One in the o*t*her world would care for the unperfected ones in this world.—Why should it not be the same with our friends who have gone to be " for ever with the Lord "?

Holy Father. See on verses 1, 25.—God is to be the Holy Father to Christians in this world when Christ is gone away. *Lange.*—What a blasphemous profanation to call a mortal, sinful man, like the pope, " Holy Father!" *Schaff.*—There is a special fitness in the word " Holy " here, as in opposition to the world.—The disciples though left *in* the world, were not *of* the world (see on chap. xv., 19) ; they were spiritually God's children and He commits them to the Holy Father, that He may keep them.—The preservation of the disciples is a work of God's *holiness.*—"*Holy*, as applied to God, peculiarly expresses that *penetration of all His attributes by* LOVE, which He only who here uttered it sees through in its length, breadth, and height." *Alford.*—This formula, *Holy Father*, condenses the Old and New Testament expressions into *one*, uniting the deepest word of the past revelation with the new name which was now to be revealed, and both being *one* in their meaning. *Stier.*—God, in His holiness, is entirely separat*e*d from the

unholy world, that He may belong entirely to those who are to
be sanctified.—" Confidence of interest in God should be seasoned
with much reverence in prayer, and we should close with such
attributes in God as are suitable to our conditions and petitions,
and may help our confidence; for both these causes doth Christ
add that epithet, 'Holy Father,' to teach us that as He is a Father,
so He is holy and reverend, and that none who draw near to Him
should entertain motions or desires contrary to His holiness; and
to assure us that a petition for preservation from the evil of the
world cannot but be acceptable to a Holy God; and that He who
is the Holy God is able to preserve and continue them holy, and
will not make void His promise to His Son concerning His given
ones. Thus is His holiness engaged in every promise (Psa. lx.
6; lxxxix. 35)." *Hutcheson.*

Keep through, &c. Gr., *keep them in Thy name.*—The most important MSS. read, " *Thy name, which Thou hast given Me* " (see
note).—Viewed in this light the *name* would mean the essential
revelation which the Father made to the Son, and the Son to the
world. *Luthardt.*—" The *Name* of God is that which was to be *in
the Angel of the Covenant* (Ex. xxiii. 21). This Name, not the
essential God-head, but the covenant name, JEHOVAH OUR RIGHT-
EOUSNESS, the Father hath *given to Christ* (Phil. ii. 9). It is the
being kept in this, the truth and confession of this, for which He
here prays." *Alford.* (See on Matt. i. 22; vi. 9.)—" The thought
appears to be that the revelation of the nature of God by Christ
to the world (verse 6) was that which He Himself received from
the Father." *Ellicott.* (See on chap. xii. 49.)—" The motive of the
prayer is: *Whom Thou hast given Me.* As the name of the Father
is given Him for the disciples, so the disciples are given Him for
the name." *Lange.*—" Christ, who bears in Himself and brings to
the world the name of the Father, prays as if He should say,
Keep them *in Me*." *Stier.*—The words import " both that God's
name, or what He hath revealed of Himself, is a strong tower to
which they may flee, there being sufficiency of power, wisdom,
mercy, immutability, &c., in Him to keep them safe on all hands;
as also that He will preserve them because His name is called upon
them, and for His name's sake, and because His glory is engaged,
and will shine in so doing, whatever they may be in themselves;
and because He can reveal His name, and make His name known
unto them, that they may cleave to Him and be preserved."
Hutcheson.—" 1. Keep them *for Thy name's sake. Thy* name and
honour are concerned in their preservation as well as *Mine;* 2. *In
Thy name.* Keep them *in* the knowledge and fear of *Thy name;*
keep them *in* the profession and service of *Thy name;* 3. *By or*

through Thy name. Keep them by *Thine own* **power**, in *Thine own* hand, keep them *Thyself.*" *Henry.*

That they may be one. Not merely harmony of will or of love, but oneness by the indwelling of the Spirit of Christ, and ultimately oneness of nature (1 Cor. vi. 17 ; 2 Pet. i. 4). *Alford.*—Throughout this prayer the *oneness* of the disciples is made the sign of matured discipleship.—It is the evidence that they are one in the name of the Father of Christ, for this clause depends upon the words, " Keep them in Thy name."—The living, known *name* of God has this unifying power.—As it is the bond of union between the Father and the Son, it is, in like manner, to be the bond of union among the disciples.—One among themselves, because one with Me and Thee, with Us.—" Then will our unity be truly happy when it shall bear the image of God the Father and of Christ, as the wax takes the form of the seal which is impressed upon it." *Calvin.*—The strength of their preservation is *His name;* and the purpose, unity, the personal kingdom of love (see on verse 21).— " Whatever be the bonds tying Christians together (Eph. iv. 4-6), and whatever prudential considerations and motives they have to induce them to obey the command of God in keeping together in unity (as Gal. v. 15 and elsewhere), yet it is only the power of God that can keep the bond of unity inviolable; and unless He keep them near Him, and free from the evils of the world, their union will break, and their being overpowered with flesh will break out in the bitter fruits of strife and division. Therefore, saith He, ' Holy Father, keep them, that they may be one, as we are.' " *Hutcheson.*

τήρησον. *To keep an eye upon, to watch,* and hence *to keep, to guard. Robinson*—The reading ᾧ (referring to ὄνομα) instead of οὓς (referring to αὐτούς), rests upon *A. B. C., Cod. Sin.,* &c., and is decisively established.—It is adopted by *Treg., Tisch., Lach,, Scholz, Alford, Westcott and Hort, Schaff, Meyer,* &c.

---

12. While I was with them in the world, I kept them in thy name ; those that thou gavest me I have kept and none of them is lost, but the son of perdition ; that the scripture might be fulfilled.

While I was with them. A further explication of verse 11 (see Comm.).—During His presence with them He watched over them with tenderest care.—There was not this special need for commending them to His Father's protection.—Now He is as a parent blessing and praying for His children before He is taken from them (see on chap. xiii. 33).

I kept them. " I," with solemn emphasis and dignity.—The Lord here compares *His* keeping of His own, to that by *the Father*, in a way only accountable by both persons being of equal power and glory. *Cyril.*—Their natural inclination tended ever out of the bounds constituted by the consciousness of God and by Christ's view of the world ; but His faithfulness held them fast within these limits. *Lange.*—" Concerning all saints, it is implied that 1. They are weak, and cannot keep themselves ; 2. They are in God's sight valuable and worth keeping ; 3. Their salvation is designed, for to that it is that they are kept (1 Pet. i. 5) ; 4. They are the charge of the Lord Jesus." *Henry.*—A celebrated Scotch Evangelist desired that this word " kept " might be placed on his tombstone.—This keeping is in harmony with moral freedom, " Kept by the power of God *through faith* " (1 Pet. i. 5).—" Let no man depend upon the keeping of the Father and the Son, or upon the intercession of the High Priest, as upon an *irresistible grace* which will render *being lost* impossible." *Stier.*—Yet all the glory of salvation, when consummated and perfected, is due to God alone.

In thy name. The most important MSS. read here, as in verse 11, " *I kept them in Thy name which Thou gavest Me* " (see on verse 11 and see note).

Thou gavest me. See on verses 2, 6, and on chap. vi. 37.

I have kept. Gr., *I have guarded ;* not the same word as that rendered " kept," in the first clause.—This is an intensified expression of His vigilant care over them.—*Guarded* or *kept as with a military guard.*—The first " kept " points to their preservation in the truth revealed to them ; the second to the *watchfulness* by means of which this result was obtained.—The former may be compared to the feeding of the flock, the latter to the care which protects from the wild beasts around (see on chap. x. 28-30). *Ellicott.*—He guarded them as the faithful Shepherd of the souls entrusted Him by the Father.

And none of them is lost, but the son of perdition. Gr., *none of them perished, except the son of perdition :* the tense of the Greek verb is the same as that of the word " guarded."—The Good Shepherd watched His flock, and such was His care that none perished but " the son of perdition."—Of him the words carefully state that " he perished."—Yet for him there was the same preservation, and the same guardianship as for those who remained in the fold.—The sheep wandered from the flock and was lost by his own act. *Ellicott.*—Christ does not say, " *I lost none* " (see chap. xviii. 9, where no exception is made).—" Judas lost himself."—Even after the betrayal he might have been saved *if* he had in true penitence fled to the cross. *Schaff.*—The "if" involves the whole question; a man may reach a state of hardness in which true penitence becomes impossible.—God has promised pardon to the penitent, but *penitence* implies *grace* (see on Matt. xii. 31, 32).—There is no "keeping in God's name" independently of "keeping God's word," and this Judas did not do (see on verse 6).—"Although a child of Satan, he is at the same time the author and father of his own sin and his own perdition." *Stier.* (See also on chap. vi 70, 71; xii. 4-6; xiii. 2, 30; xviii. 2; and on Matt. xxvi. 14; xxvii. 3.)—Our Lord, at this solemn moment, is rendering a faithful account of those committed to Him, therefore His reference to Judas is most admonitory.—To how many who bear the Christian name might the words be addressed, "We beseech you that you receive not the grace of God in vain" (2 Cor. vi. 1).—Judas an awful example of the words, "If the salt have lost his savour wherewith shall it be salted?" &c. (see on Matt. v. 13.)

The son of perdition. A well known Hebrew idiom, by which the lack of qualitative adjectives is supplied by the use of the abstract substantives, which express that quality. *Ellicott.*—Thus a disobedient child is "a son of disobedience;" other common instances are "children of light," "children of darkness."—A "son of perdition" implies *the quality* expressed by "perdition." —The *property* of perdition, the *prey* of perdition. *Lange.*—"And none of them perished except him whose nature it was to perish." *Ellicott.*—The "man of sin" is also called "the son of perdition" (2 Thess. ii. 3).—The same term is applied to Satan in the Apocryphal Gospel of Nicodemus.—As the other disciples, by the true *keeping* of the Divine word (verse 6) given to them, rose from being natural men to be the children of God, so Judas, through want of the same, sunk from the state of the natural man to that of the lost, the children of the devil. *Olshausen.*—Many like Judas have called Christ Lord, and seemed to be the children of God, who at length proved "sons of perdition."—Such examples should excite to serious self-examination and prayer; but should not distress the believer, who, though he cannot do the things he would, is conscious of integrity in his professed repentance and faith in Christ, and desire of living to His glory. *Scott.* —"Peter fell from grace, but Judas had no grace to fall from." *Calvin.*—"His election was to the apostleship *only*, and it was from *that* he fell" (Acts i. 25). *Owen.*

That the scripture, &c. (See note).—Here as in other places consolation is found in contemplating the decree of divine judg-

ment (see on chap. xii. 38 ; xiii. 18).—We must not suppose that
Judas was fated to become a "son of perdition ; " but that, as
such, he should be lost from the circle of disciples in accordance
with the righteous judgment of God. *Lange.*—"Jesus caused
it not, still less the Scripture, least of all God." *Braune.*—" He
perished *in order that the Scripture might be fulfilled*. But the
Scripture would not have been written by God, unless God had
foreseen that he would perish. And this divine Prescience, though
it foreknew and foretold that he would perish, did not in any
way *cause* him to perish. Why then was this Scripture written ?
In order that even his perishing might be an evidence of God's
foresight ; and so the traitor himself, even in the hands of Satan,
and betraying Christ, might be a witness of the truth, even by
his perishing : and Judas, "the son of perdition," might still
even in his perdition, be an Apostle of the Son of God." *Wordsworth.*

ἐν τῷ κόσμῳ. Omitted. B. C. D. L., Cod. Sin., &c.—Rejected. Lach., Tisch., Alford.
—οὒς. ὣ. Codd. B. L., Tisch., Treg.. Alf., Westcott and Hort, Ellicott, Schaff, Meyer, &c.—
οὐδεὶς ἐξ αὐτῶν. Judas *then* was included in "them which Thou gavest Me" Ellicott,
Alford —Not implied here, but rather the contrary (chap. xiii. 18).—It is just as in
Luke iv. 26, 27, where we are not to suppose that the woman of *Sarepta* (in Sidon) was
one of the widows of *Israel*, nor Naaman the *Syrian* one of the lepers in Israel. though
the language, the same as here. might seem to express that. *Webster and Wilkinson,
D. Brown.*—ὁ υἱὸς τ. ἀπ. It is difficult to express the meaning in English, because we
have no verb of the same root as the abstract substantive "perdition," and no abstract
substantive of the same root as the verb "perish." *Ellicott.*—ἡ γραφὴ. What portion
of Scripture is here intended ? Psalm xli. 10, on account of the citation of that passage
in chap. xiii. 18. *Lücke. Meyer. Godet.*—Psalm cix. 8, on account of the citation in Acts
i. 20. *Euthy. Zig., Alford.*—The whole mass of prophecies relative to the death of
Jesus. *Kuinoel.*—The passage I-a. lvii. 12 is the one meant; it treats specifically, in
typical prophecy, of the perdition of the destroyer. *Lange.*

13. And now come I to thee; and these things I speak in the world, that they might
have my joy fulfilled in themselves.

And now. In contrast with "while I was with them" of verse 12.
—Implies, " But I shall be here to keep them no more : and therefore I pray this prayer in their hearing, that," &c. *Alford.*—I
can no longer watch over them, as I have done hitherto, in visible individual intercourse. *Lange.*

These things, &c. Being still in the world, and heard by them as
well as by the Father, He confidentially presents His petition.—By
this they will have the comfort and support of knowing that He had
thus solemnly committed them to His Father's care (see on verses
9, 10).

My joy fulfilled. See on chap. xv. 11; xvi. 24.—"Not simply :
through My intercession they shall be assured of Thy protection

and hence be filled with perfect gladness, but rather: My intercession shall awaken the spirit of prayer in them and open their
hearts for the reception of the Holy Spirit of perfect joy, for
whom I am suing on their behalf. And if Thou *keep* them thus,
by the bestowal of the Spirit of joy, He will *watch* over them as
I have done until now." *Lange.*—*His* joy which came from the
unfailing presence of His Father, shall become perfect in them,
and be their guard.—That perfect consciousness of God which
was so emphatically *His* joy, shall be imparted to them by the
Holy Ghost.—There is a double care which Christ takes of His
people; a care of their *graces*, and a care of their *joy and comfort.*
—It is not enough for Christ that His people be perfectly *safe;* He
will have them also perfectly *happy.*—That which the intercession
of Jesus prayed for and assured to His own, is made in the hands
of the Spirit a blessing distributed in ever increasing measure to
all.—Whoever speaks and writes under the benediction of this
discourse of Jesus increases and fulfils the *joy* of those who hear and
read. *Stier.*—"Christ doth not only take care to give His people
cause of joy, but to make them rejoice in it also, and that with an
inexpressible joy, whereof others are ignorant; therefore will He
have it 'fulfilled in themselves '—that is, their hearts filled with it,
and feeding on that hidden manna whereof strangers are not partakers (Prov. xiv. 10)." *Hutcheson.*—"When believers confess their
sins they should confess their *want of joy in the Lord,* as one of the
saddest fruits of unbelief and carnality." *Flavel.*—"If we scan all
the doctrines, all the institutions, all the precepts, all the promises
of Christianity, will not each appear pregnant with matter of *joy?*
Will not each yield great reason, and strong obligation, to this
duty of ' *Rejoicing* evermore ? '" *Barrow.*

---

14. I have given them thy word: and the world hath hated them, because they are
not of the world, even as I am not of the world.

Thy word. Mark how He attributes His teaching as well as His
works to the Father, and that in speaking to the Father.—As
Christ's word is the word of the Father, rejection of that word
is not only rejection of Christ, but of the Father Himself; hence
the guilt of unbelief and its dreadful doom.—On the other hand,
reception of Christ's word is reception of the Father Himself;
hence the blessedness of faith and its glorious reward (see on
chap. xiv. 23).

The world hath hated them. See on chap. xv. 18, 19.—Gr., *hath
conceived a hatred for them.*—Christ's word causing their separa-

tion *from* the world, procures for them the world's hatred.—The divine consciousness of Christ and His people, gravitating in its impulse of faith and love, toward the absolute personality of God, is odious to the world. *Lange.*—Because the doctrine of a living, personal, holy God flames forth from every page of the Bible men hate it, for the ungodly consciousness of the world ever gravitates outwards into the *impersonal.*—Manifestly this is the root of the infidelity of many of those who found their unbelief upon what they call "scientific grounds."—The world's hatred is the true livery of Christians which they wear on earth. *Luther.* —The hatred of the world is the always resulting consequence, in the degree in which the word has been given to us. *Stier.*—Those that receive Christ's *good will* and *good word*, shall have the world's *ill will* and *ill word.*—Where the word of Christ is faithfully preached, the hatred of the world, *within the Church*, will soon show itself.—The popular preacher may be an unfaithful preacher; the faithful preacher may be unpopular.—The "last day" will reverse the judgment of many professing Christians upon this and upon other points.

They are not of the world. See on chap. xv. 18.—After the creation of the new man, which is now their proper *person*, after their union with Christ through the regeneration of the word, they are no longer of the world.

Even as I am not. "It should encourage believers, in this conflict, that in their state and suffering they have a conformity with Christ their Head, conformity with whom is a great dignity; for by this also doth He encourage them, 'They are not of the world, even as I am not of the world.' He or His Kingdom are not of this world more than they are, and their suffering on this account redounds to Him, who is first hated, and for whose sake, and because of conformity with Him, they are hated." *Hutcheson.*— Those that keep the word of Christ's patience, are entitled to special protection in the hour of temptation (Rev. iii. 10).—That cause which makes a martyr may well make a joyful sufferer. *Henry.*

---

15. I pray not that thou shouldest take them out of the world, but that thou shouldest keep them from the evil.

I pray not. Said mostly for their sakes, for whom it was necessary that they should abide yet in the flesh, to do God's work, and to be sanctified by God's truth (verse 17). *Alford.*—The disciples may have thought that the most effectual way to be kept from the world's hatred would be to leave the world with Him.—But *their* work was not finished; *His* work was.—Christ has glorified the Father on the earth (verse 4), and they are to glorify Him by a life of consecration to Christ's service.—" What I want is not that they also should pass out of the world with Me, for I have still more to accomplish by means of them; they must increase My little flock." *Luther.*

That thou shouldest take them. This is our Lord's view of the death of His people; it is God *taking* them.—" Enoch walked with God; and was not; for God *took* him " (Gen. v. 24).—Whatever the secondary cause may be, or however mysterious, the death of the Christian is to be resolved into an act of Divine will.— " Precious in the sight of the Lord is the death of his saints " (Psa cxvi. 15).—" I have the keys of hell (*hades*) and death " (Rev. i. 18).—Christ is "Lord both of the dead and the living " (Rom. xiv. 9).—This thought affords unutterable comfort amid " the changes and chances " of this mortal life.—A father sends for his children to bring them *home*; so is it with death to the children of God.

Out of the world. See on chap. xvi. 28.—That would certainly secure their safety, but it would deprive the world of their services.—Neither by actual death nor by ascetic mortifications does He desire their removal from the world.—Christ has here rejected *Monkery*, as a form of life unsuited to His disciples, they having attained their majority. *Lange.*—They are to be *in* the world but not *of* the world.—He said they were "the salt of the earth," and " the light of the world " (see on Matt. v. 13, 14).— " Because it is the vocation of the disciples to diffuse heavenly life on earth, they may not live retired from the world, or still less, quit it already by death." *Lisco.*—Christ has work for them, and they are of use to Him, *for a time*, in the world ; and till their work be done, Christ's love will not, and the world's malice cannot, remove them hence. *Burkitt.*—The disciples of Christ should be *willing* to die, but not *impatiently long* for it. *Scott.*—Paul had a desire to depart and to be with Christ, but this desire was kept in subservience to the welfare of the Church (Phil. i. 21-25). —" Christ is ' come into the world '; and therefore thou needest not ' go out of the world ' to meet Him. He doth not call thee *from* thy calling, but *in* thy calling. The dove went up and down from the ark, and to the ark, and yet was not disappointed of her olive leaf. Thou mayest come to the house of God at due times, and mayest do the business of the world in other places too ; and still keep thy olive, thy peace of conscience (Gen. xxiv. 27 ; 1 Cor. v. 10)." *Donne.*—Reasons for which it was better that they should remain : 1. Believers are to continue the witness and work of the Lord in the world ; 2. Only in the struggle to accomplish this, are they perfected and *sanctified. Stier.*—Men forget, that separation from society is not separation from the world, for the world is *in their own heart* (1 John ii. 16). *Bates.*

Keep them from the evil. *The evil* is really the same comprehensive term here as in the Lord's Prayer (see on Matt. vi. 13). —Therefore His prayer here may be interpreted in the same sense as the words in which He taught them to pray.—Hence it may be better to read, " that Thou shouldest keep them from *the evil one,*" with reference to " the Prince of this world " (see on chap. xii. 31 ; xiv. 30 ; xvi. 11 ; and compare 1 John ii. 13, 14 ; iii. 12 ; v. 18, 19). *Meyer, Alford.*—If we add to these passages chap. viii. 44, we find that John merges the whole world in personal relations, as regards evil also ; the world, as world, lies in the Wicked One ; it has its pole in Satan. *Lange* (see on Matt. iv. 1-11).—The words may be regarded as embracing *all kinds of evil,* all that is hurtful to the true welfare of His children ; more particularly the sins, temptations, and snares of the world.—As it was chiefly by these Satan assailed our Lord Himself, so it is by these he assails His followers.—All experience shows that these are the Christian's most common, most dangerous, most deadly foes.—The Christian's renunciation of the world is no flight from it, but a stand in it to overcome it (see on chap. xvi. 32).—It is much easier to withdraw from the world than to live in it and be a witness for Christ's truth ; but the ease is purchased at a sad cost.—A spiritual *victory* over evil is more to be preferred than total *exemption* from it.—The great *prize,* the *full fruit* of our discipline is this, to be able to say throughout the conflict and at the end, " More than conquerors " (Rom. viii. 37).—Our Lord's ideal " is not freedom from work, but strength to do it; not freedom from suffering, but joy in an abiding sense of the Father's love ; not absence from the world, but grace to make it better by our presence ; not holy lives driven from the world, and living apart from it, but holy lives spent in the world and leavening it." *Ellicott.* —Men wonder when a believer falls; but it is a far greater cause of wonder that he should hold fast to the end.—What with the world, the flesh, and the devil, no arm but that of Omnipotence could "keep" him from falling.—The preservation of the planets in their courses round the sun is not so wonderful as the preservation of the Christian to the end.—Those huge unconscious bodies are held fast in the iron grasp of law, but the believer is a conscious moral agent, placed amid temptations and trials of keen and powerful influence.—The keeping of such an one, so weak and helpless in himself, "faithful unto death," is only to be accounted for by the fact that "underneath are the everlasting arms" (Deut. xxxiii. 27).—Yet this Divine keeping is in perfect harmony with the voluntariness of the believer's own spirit.—We cannot explain the relation of the Infinite to the finite, or of omniscience and omnipotence, with human freedom, but we know that *both* are true.—"I give unto them eternal life," said Christ, "and they shall never perish;" but He is speaking of those whom He calls " His sheep " and of whom He says " *They hear My voice and follow Me* " (see on chap. x. 27, 28).—It is God "who worketh in us, both to will and to do of His good pleasure," therefore, we are to "work out our salvation with fear and trembling" (Phil ii. 12, 13).—The Christian keeps the divine word (verse 6), and is kept through it; but that very keeping of the word is of the Spirit's influence upon his heart.—Thus the commencement, the carrying on, and the consummation of salvation is of grace, therefore all the glory is due to God alone.

ἐκ τοῦ πονηροῦ.   See critical note to Matt. vi. 13.

16. They are not of the world, even as I am not of the world.

Not of the world.   See on chap. xv. 19.—This is repeated from verse 14, and is the ground of the foregoing petition.—They are already not of the world, above the world, so that they need *not be removed from it* in order to distinction from it.—They are already clean (chap. xiii. 10), and hence He prays that they may be kept from pollution.—Their fitness for *sanctification* (verse 17) is affirmed in this verse.—They no longer have their vital principle in the world, but, like Christ and through Him, in the Father.—" Christians are children of another world, of the heavenly Adam, a new race, children of the Holy Ghost, of light, brothers of Christ ; they are *not of this* world." *Macarius.*—Hence He prays that they may be *sanctified* according to their divine birth and kind.—Separation from the world, as the cause of the world's enmity, the common mark of Christ and His people.—Many are now endeavouring to obliterate this mark of distinction, in the hope of making Christianity acceptable to the world.—To have what is called "a respectable Church " is their ambition.—This is seen in the choice of persons to places of influence in the Church, and in the means which are adopted to carry on Church work.—The spiritual interests of the Church are sacrificed to the claims of worldly "respectability."—This is a far more dangerous enemy to true religion than open and avowed infidelity.—The world's favour has destroyed more Christians than ever its violent persecutions did. *Law.*—" Believers' disconformity with the world and conformity with Christ is a sure pledge that the Father will keep them from the evil of the world, and will not lose those good things which grace has begun in them; for this is an argument why He should 'keep them from the evil' (verse 15), 'They are not of the world,'" &c. *Hutcheson.*

---

17. Sanctify them through thy truth : thy word is truth.

Sanctify them. The idea at the root of the Greek word rendered " sanctify " is not holiness, but separation.—It is opposed not to what is impure, but to what is common, and is constantly used in the Greek of the Sept. for the consecration of persons and things to the service of God.—Hence our Lord uses it of Himself in chap. x. 36, and also in verse 19 of this context. *Ellicott.*—The word as applied to the disciples, this setting apart and consecration, was a long and gradual process, to be accomplished by conflicts, and the deeper sinking in of the Truth by the blows of affliction, and the purifying fire of the Spirit. *Alford.*—There is still something of the *world* in them; they are still *in the evil;* therefore they need to be *sanctified:* 1. For their own sake and in themselves ; 2. For the sake of the world, and for their mission to it (see on verse 18). *Stier.*—"As sanctification is the duty of believers laid upon them by God, so it is also His work in them who principleth them for it, and works it in them, when they, in the sense of their own inability, do put it upon Him ; for Christ, by prayer, seeketh it of the Father." *Hutcheson.*

Through thy truth. Gr., *in Thy truth.*—The truth is the *element* in which the sanctification takes place.—Make them holy *through* the gift of the Holy Ghost, and by true doctrine. *Godet.*—Make them *truly* holy, in distinction from the present *imperfect* holiness. *Luther.*—It implies that He would furnish them, in this their vital sphere of truth, with holy *consecration, i.e.,* inspiration, illumination, through the Holy Ghost. *Meyer.*—The consecration of the Holy Ghost is to the end that the word may for them be rendered living truth, at once the vital sphere and the instrument of their sanctification.—Apostolic sanctification is always both moral and official. *Lange.*—Through Christ they had received the Father's word (verse 14), which is truth, and had become separate from the world ; and He now prays that the Father would preserve them in *that truth*, and also make it more fully instrumental in preparing them for their mission. *Ellicott.*—" As the truth of God is the rule of true sanctification, nothing being holiness in God's account, how specious however it be, unless it be according to that truth, so the truth of God, which is the instrument of regeneration, hath also a special influence in the matter of daily sanctification (1 Pet. ii. 2) ; the word of command being made effectual to press the duty, the word of promise to encourage it (2 Cor. vii. 1 ; 2 Pet. i. 4), and the word and doctrine of the Cross of Christ holding out virtue enabling to duty (1 Cor. i. 18), and exciting faith, which purifieth the heart (Acts xv. 9). In both these respects He prayeth, ' Sanctify them through (or in) Thy truth,' both as the *rule* and *touchstone* of sanctification, and as a mean and instrument of it." *Hutcheson.*—The reality of sanctification must be proved by the truth which was instrumental in it, and whatever efficacy the truth hath, it comes from God. *Baxter.*

Thy word is truth. " *Thy*," emphatically.—The Word of God is pure truth, a living word, the source of light ; and so, what it is in itself, it must become in the disciples (see on chap. iv. 24 ; xviii. 37).—The word must sanctify us ; it divides everything like a two-edged sword, and Satan, in his servants, is always seeking to make it a secondary affair, or to hustle it out of the way altogether. *Gossner.*—" *Thy* word " and " *Thy* truth " embrace even here every Old Testament word also, concerning which the Psalmist gloried : " Thy word is true from the beginning," *i.e.*, The sum, the essential substance of Thy word is Truth (Psa. cxix. 160).—The word is consecrated to be the sanctifying medium of the Holy Spirit.—The Son sanctifies us in Himself; the Father sanctifies us through the Son in the Spirit ; specifically and conclusively therefore it is the Spirit, as the living truth of God, who sanctifies. *Stier.*—*Thy word* in its inner subjective power. *Alford.*—" They who are true disciples of Christ live and move in the word of truth as their element; they *breathe* it." *Schauffler.*—Christ Himself is the true sanctifying Word, by union to whom men become holy, separate from the world, united to God, and partakers of the Divine nature. *Lewis.*—The living word of inspiration, that is, the revelation which the Incarnate Logos made of God, is the divinely appointed means of sanctification. *Jacobus.*—Sanctification is: 1. Through the truth ; 2. By the word ; 3. An act of God.—Ministers should remember that God's revealed truth can alone contribute to sanctification.—A lesson to revivalists as to the true instrumentality for quickening the Church.

σου. Omitted. *Lach. Alford, Lange.*

18. As thou hast sent me into the world, even so have I also sent them into the world.

As thou hast sent me. See on chap. x. 36.—Gr., *As Thou didst send Me.*—Christ is the great Messenger of God, in whom God's whole apostolate to the world is contained.—Christ did not *of Himself* undertake the office of Mediator, He is the Sent of the Father. —It follows, therefore, that we may have the most entire and unreserved confidence in the person and work of Christ.—The very fact that He was sent by the Father guarantees His supreme fitness for His mission, and its complete success.—As He Himself in the flesh overcame through conflict, and by true obedience sowed the seed which was now to produce the full harvest of his glory, so also it is with us.—In this we have the strongest reason why He will not take His own out of the world; why we should not wish to forsake the society of men, and be at rest *before the time;* why we should rather persevere in our mission, as He did. *Stier.*—"Christ is the great apostle of our profession (Heb. iii. 1), sent to us by the Father; so that we need not think shame of a profession which is owned by such an one as He is." *Hutcheson.*

So have I also sent them. See on Matt. x. 5; Luke vi. 13.— Gr., *I also sent them.*—He does not merely *leave* them in the world but *sends* them into it, to witness to this same truth of God. *Alford.*—The complete fulfilment of these words is recorded in chap. xx. 21.—From Him, the Divinely consecrated Messenger of the Father, they are now to go forth consecrated as His messengers to all the world.—Their commission had its beginning simultaneously with their calling (see on Matt. x.), and continued in gradual development until its perfection (see on chap. xx. 21; and on Matt. xxviii. 19; and compare with Acts i. and ii.).—The name "Apostle" shows the nature of their office, but Christ is here speaking of the *wider mission* immediately before them.—*His* mission is placed first, because it is the basis and degree of *theirs.*—Their mission: 1. From Christ; 2. Through Christ from God; 3. Like Christ from God. *Lange.*—"Men appeal in vain to these words of the Lord and to the divine authority of their office, in support of their claim to be respected and heard like Christ, unless they are anointed like Christ, filled with His Spirit and the fulness of God, blessed, called, and sent by Him, as He was sent by the Father, by means of an internal mission and anointing, not simply by outward calling and installation." *Gossner.*—"Whom Christ sends He will stand by, and interest Himself in those that are employed for Him; what He calls us out to, He will fit us out for, and bear us out in." *Henry.*

19. And for their sakes I sanctify myself, that they also might be sanctified through the truth.

And. The sense of "and" here is, "And to make their sanctification possible," &c.

For their sakes. In a special sense for *theirs*, but in a wider sense for all mankind.—"And He is the propitiation for our sins; and not for ours only, but also for the sins of the whole world" (1 John ii. 2).

I sanctify myself. See on verse 17.—The consecration here thought of is, the offering Himself as a sacrifice.—The word was often used in the special sense of an offering set apart for God.— Thus St. Paul in Rom. xv. 16, "That the offering up (Gr., *the sacrificing*) of the Gentiles might be acceptable, being sanctified by the Holy Ghost."—In our Lord's case it means His pure and entire self-consecration by His submission to the Father's holy will; the complete possession of His sinless humanity with the living and speaking truth of God, which should be both the efficient cause and the pattern of their sanctification.—Such an High Priest *became us* (Heb. vii. 26), who are to be ourselves priests unto God (Rev. xx. 6). *Alford.*—As He is already sanctified by the Father in coming into the world (see on chap. x. 36); He now sanctifies Himself unto the Father in leaving the world and, by His death, going unto the Father, on behalf of His disciples, in order to lay the foundation for their sanctification. *Lange.*—As both Priest and Sacrifice, He will enter into the Holy of Holies of the heavenly temple, and from thence will send the Holy Ghost who will consecrate them. *Ellicott.*—"Sanctify" as applied to Christ can only mean to *consecrate;* whereas, applied to the disciples, it signifies to *consecrate* with the *additional idea* of previous sanctification, since nothing but what is holy can be presented as an offering to God. *D. Brown.*—The whole self-sacrificing work of the disciples appears here as a mere *result* of the offering of Christ. *Olshausen.*—Mark the difference between the active, "*I* sanctify Myself" (Gr., *mine ownself*), and the passive, "that they may be sanctified."—Christ sanctifies Himself by His *inherent* holiness, Christians are sanctified by another power. *Schaff.*—Christ sanctifies Himself *for* His people.—*His* was a sacrificial death of self-sacrificing love for their benefit.— That death, being expiatory, made His people capable of sanctification through the Spirit, and as a death of self-sacrificing love, called them to a consecration unto the same life of love in the world.—The foundation of the entire Apostolic mission, of the entire Church, is the self-sacrifice of Christ. *Lange.*

They also, &c. See on verse 17.—Gr., *may be sanctified in truth.*—

What truth, is evident from verse 17, where the article is also wanting in the Greek.—The omission of the article is explained by the fact that *truth* is not to be conceived of here as an independent cause, but as the medium of the effect emanating from Christ.—In that Christ sanctifies Himself, His disciples are sanctified in the blessing of truth that proceeds from Him.—His expiatory power is the element of truth that pours from Him in His Spirit, in order to present them as sanctified persons.—Their consecration by *truth* stands out in antithesis to Old Testament *priestly* consecration. *Lange.*—In proportion as *sin* becomes to us, through the fellowship of His holy and willing Spirit, a *bitterness*, we also are sanctified *in the truth*, essentially *in truth.*—The *truth* of God is the objective element and goal of actual, essential sanctification. *Stier.*—The word of truth as the outward and ordinary means which the Holy Spirit employs : the written word, worship, the preaching of the Gospel. *Macdonald.*—"Christ doth approve of no sanctification but that which is truly such, and abhors all counterfeits of it, and such as rest on outside sanctification, or shadows of true holiness only ; for that is His aim, that they may be sanctified in truth. True sanctification flows only from the application of Christ's sacrifice, and it is that which makes the word of truth effectual for sanctifying of them truly ; for upon His sanctifying Himself it followeth that they are sanctified in truth, and ' through the truth.' " *Hutcheson.*

ἁγιάζω. A customary term for the offering of a sacrifice in the Old Testament (Deut. xv. 19 ff. ; 2 Sam. viii. 11). *Lange* —Cannot refer to spiritual sanctifica i n, but has necessarily the Old Testament sense of holy *self consecration* to His sacrific al death. *Calvin.*—I offer Myself as an oblation, as a holy victim to Thee.—I sacrifice Myself for them that they may be truly consecrate to present themselves a sacrifice (Rom. xii. 1). *Chrys., Meyer.*—That they also may be consecrated to sacrificial brotherly love. *O'shausen, &c.*—The official consecration of Christ is to result in the official consecration of the disciples. *Heumann, Semler, &c.*—Christ has a human nature with human inclinations, of which He was constantly making a holy offering of obedience to God to be completed in death. *Godet, Luthardt.*—Christ's consecration to His holy deed of love is to have for its result the corresponding consecration of the disciples. *De Wette.*—The word ἁγιάζειν is diverse in both sentences : I consecrate Myself to death, that they may be sanctified in the truth, or, truly ; *a.* To righteousness in faith. *Luther ; b.* To *obedientia nova. Calvin, Lampe.*—We must secure'y grasp the two imports of the conception, ἁγιάζειν.—Christ sanctifies Himself, in the negative sense, in that by His sacrificial death He separates Himself utterly from the world, is crucified to the world and goes unto God ; positive'y, in that He thereby gains the power to come again into the world in the power of the Holy Ghost. He sanctifies Himself negatively for His people in that He presents His 'ife for them as an expiation for their guilt ; positively, in that, by this highest love-offering, He exercises a quickening reflex-influence over them and *establishes a principle of suffering out of which their martyr sufferings shall develop. as do their works out of His works* (Col i. 24). *Lange.* It is clear against all Socinian inferences from this verse that all that part of ἁγιάζειν implied in chap. x. 36 is here excluded ; and only that intended which is expressed Heb. ii. 10 by διὰ παθημάτων τελειῶσαι. Of this, His death was the crowning

1232 / Gospel of John

act, and was also the one to which the ὑπὲρ αὐτῶν most directly applies: but the whole is included. *Alford.*—ἐν ἀληθείᾳ. The term (*in truth*) is *adverbial* and means *truly* sanctified. *Chrys., Beza, Calvin, Bengel, Ellicott, Meyer : a.* In antithesis to the Jewish consecration, the *sanctimonia cæremonialis. Ancient Exegetes, Godet : b.* The eminent consecration in antithesis to every other ἁγιότης in human relations. *Meyer.*—The term (*in truth*) is to be construed sub-tantively, as if. *in the truth*, as verse 17. *Some Ancient Exegetes. Erasmus, Bucer, Lücke, Olsh., De Wette, Brückner, Ewald, Alford, D. Brown, Lange, Schaff.*

---

20. Neither pray I for these alone, but for them also which shall believe on me through their word.

For these alone. See on verse 9.—Our Lord now intercedes for future believers.—" The view expands in space and, verse 24, also in time." *Tholuck.*—Time and space go on mutually expanding until the supreme consummation.—The thought of the work to which the Apostles are to be consecrated and sent leads on to the thought of the Church which shall believe through their word, and the prayer is enlarged to include them.—From the prayer for Himself proceeds the prayer for the disciples, and from that the intercession for the whole body of the faithful.

Them also which shall believe. See on chap. i. 7 ; vii. 38.—The best MSS. read, "*but for them also which believe.*"—The future is again spoken of as if actually present, as no doubt it was, in our Lord's thought.—He, to whom a thousand years are as one day, "calleth those things which be not as though they were" (Rom. iv. 17).—To *His* mind every believer was present to the end of time, and therefore comprehended in this prayer, which is the beginning and pledge of His continual intercession in the presence of God for us (Heb. vii. 25).

On me. See on chap. iii. 18.—Saving faith is personal as to its exercise and personal as to its object (see on chap. xvi. 33).—As Christ is the centre of all divine revelations, so also is He the centre of Christian faith (see on chap. i. 29).—Christian faith is distinguished from every kind of belief in that it looks to Jesus and to Him alone.—Hence He is called "the Author and Finisher of faith" (Heb. xii. 2).—A man may be a great theologian and a great Biblical scholar, as well as a great ecclesiastic, and yet lack the faith of a true Christian.—It was only on his deathbed that the author of the celebrated "Analogy," Bishop Butler, realized the nature and blessedness of *Christian* faith.—Everything is gathered up in that one utterance of the heart, "*He loved me, He gave himself for me*" (Gal. ii. 20).

Through their word. Their witness concerning Him through which men should believe (see on chap. xv. 27).—That which they had "heard and seen," the Spirit would enable them to declare to others (1 John i. 1-3).—*Their* word would be *His* word, and His word was the *Father's* word (see on chap. xiv. 26 ; xv. 13, 14 ; and on verses 6, 8).—" All faith in all ages comes *through the word;* this, on the one hand, maintains the doctrine of prevenient grace, the grace of Him who calls, as universal for the world and as special for the individual (without which faith were entirely out of the question) : while, on the other hand, it recognises the freedom of our own decision, for *through the word* means the free way of light and conviction." *Stier.*—" True faith is begotten by and grounds itself upon the word of God delivered by the Apostles, without doting on signs or wonders, or expecting any other revelation of the mind of God ; while such as are taught to discern the divine authority of the word will not stumble at the despicableness or meanness of the instruments carrying the same." *Hutcheson.*—" We may justly write this comfortable text in letters of gold, as it relates to us all. For it is our glory and consolation, our treasure and pearl ; so that for us, Gentiles, the whole Scriptures do not afford a more comfortable saying than this (Isa. liv. 6-14)." *Luther.*

πιστευσόντων. In accordance with *A. B. C. D., Sin*, &c., all critical editors read πιστευόντων.—The present participle expresses the *state* of faith in which all believers are found : the future of the text. rec. would refer more to the act of belief by which that state is begun. But perhaps it is best to take the present as proleptic. It is strikingly set forth here that *all* subsequent belief on Christ would take place through the apostolic word (Rom. x. 16, 17). *Alford.*

---

21. That they all may be one; as thou, Father, art in me, and I in thee, that they also may be one in us : that the world may believe that thou hast sent me.

All may be one. The whole body of believers in all times and places.—In this grand conception of the unity of the whole Church He expresses the fulness of the purpose of His prayer.— He has asked that they may be kept in God's name and sanctified by God's truth ; and if this be so, their unity with the Son and the Father follows (1 John i. 3).—The unity He prays for is a unity in faith and love proceeding from oneness of spiritual life. —Unity in the one Holy Ghost, who is the same in all, is more than moral unity.—The Church is not merely a Society, or an Association, as some seem to think ; the Church is a *Family* (Eph. iii. 15).—But family life rests upon a common participation of nature by *birth.*—No organization, or agreement in opinions, or bonds of friendship can make individuals into a *family.*—So in the Church.—It is not holding the same creed, or the adoption

of the same order, or worshipping in the same place that constitutes membership ; but the *new birth* (see on chap. iii. 3). "To as
many as received Him, to them gave He power to become the sons
of God, even to them that believe on His name: who were born,
not of blood, nor of the will of the flesh, nor of the will of man,
but of God" (see on chap. i. 12, 13).—The one Word on which
faith rests, the one end of the one way in following the one Lord
and Shepherd, the one Spirit by whom all have access to one
Father, make the essential unity of all who believe. *Stier.*—"This
unity has its true and only *ground* in faith in Christ through the
word of God as delivered by the apostles ; and is therefore not
mere outward uniformity, nor can such uniformity produce it.
At the same time its effects are to be real and visible, such that
the world may see them." *Alford.*—This unity may consist with
a variety of *form*, but it cannot consist with diversity of *spirit.*—
The stalk and root of the Vine are one, so that the branches
should be one also, by having all of them a vital relation to the
Vine, and deriving of its one life. *Jacobus.*—Our Lord teaches
that unity among His followers is the goal to be attained ; but it
is *unity in truth.*—"There be two false peaces or unities : the one,
when the peace is grounded but upon an implicit ignorance ; for
all colours will agree in the dark : the other, when it is pieced up
upon a direct admission of contraries in fundamental points. For
truth and falsehood, in such things, are like the iron and clay in
the toes of Nebuchadnezzar's image ; they may cleave, but they
will not incorporate." *Bacon.*

As thou, Father, &c. Gr., *as Thou, Father, in Me, and I in Thee.*
—He prays that the union of His followers may be of the same
essential nature as that between the Father and Himself.—Yea, that
the union of the Church may result from the union of individual
members with the Father through the Son.—The Father in the
Son and the Son in the Father ; both Father and Son taking up
their abode in the believer, and the believer, therefore, in the
Father and the Son.—This is our Lord's ideal of the unity of His
Church ; and if this union with God is realized by each individual,
it necessarily follows that all the individuals will be one with
each other (see on chap. xiv. 23 ; xv. 4-10). *Ellicott.*—"This
oneness is precisely the opposite of a pantheistic obliteration of
personal distinctions. Our Lord gives utterance to this truth in
setting up His oneness with the Father, as the type. They are
just as decidedly distinct one from the other as they are One.
In accordance with this, *Their* oneness, therefore, Christians are
to become one in individuals. Where there is no Christian distinction of character, there is no true union. Uniformity is the

negation of unity. On the other hand, the making of distinctions and the distinctions themselves between believers are bad, if they do not serve to promote unity." *Lange.*—"As the Father and Son have been distinct from eternity, and yet are One through the Eternal Spirit of love, who proceedeth from both, so God hath, by the Son, created a world full of contrasts which His Spirit continually transfigureth into a glorious unity in love. Sin hath banished this harmonizing Spirit from man, hath perverted the contrasts into contradictions and rent men one from the other, as from God. But the work of Christ, the completion of His redemption, is that the Father's unity with the Incarnate Son becometh a unity wherein the whole human race that believeth on the Son, is one with the Father. Jesus prays for future believers also, to the end that these may, with His then existing disciples, form one communion in holy love. With these words the Lord declares the whole essence of His Church on earth. He comes to restore unity to the disrupted human race, by means of their reconciliation to God." *Gerlach.*—"As the Father and Son are one not only by equality of substance, but also in will, so they, between God and whom the Son is Mediator, may be one not only by the union of nature, but by the union of love." *Hilary.*

Be one in us. See on verse 11.—He prays for, 1. The unity of all; 2. A unity such as the unity between Father and Son; 3. Unity in the unity of the Father and Son.—The design is triply intensified: 1. All one; 2. One as We; 3. One in us. *Lange.*— This unity is not merely "with," but *in*, the Son and the Father; because the Spirit proceeds from *the Father and the Son*, and "He that is joined to the Lord is one Spirit." *Alford.*—"The *being one* of believers is not only a being one after the *similitude* of the Father and the Son, but it is *bound up with* their being one; it is at the same time a being one *with* Father and Son, *since* God through Christ and His Spirit essentially dwells in them." *Meyer.* —The unity of the Father and Son is, therefore, not simply a *type*, but a true and effective *cause*, of the oneness of Christians. —"Who can hear this petition from the heart and voice of Jesus without thinking of the word, *Let Us make man in Our image*"? *Mallet.*

That the world, &c. See on verse 9.—"That this their testimony, being borne by them all, and in all ages, may continue to convince the world, so that many in the world may believe." *Alford.* —The Church, as the communion of saints, is an end to herself; but she is also a means to an end as a mission community for the world.—True, immediate prayer for Christians is, therefore, true,

immediate prayer for the world. *Lange.*—"If the Church of
Christ stood forth as a harmonious community of brethren, where
nought but order, love and peace ruled, it would be so unique a
phenomenon in our egotistical world that every one would be
forced to acknowledge that here was a divine work, and to see in
it the government of a higher Spirit, the Spirit of Christ. All
doubts as to, and accusations against, Christianity must perforce
hold their peace." *Heubner.*—"The Lord (1) testifies now at the
end *His own* desire and will that all the world might believe ; (2)
He suggests this aim of universal, all-seeking grace to *His Church*,
and would teach His people to regard this as the goal, however
unattainable in itself, of all the efforts of their united love—*that
the world may believe.* That *unity* which alone gives power to its
missions, and those *missions* which rest solely upon *unity* are in their
union the end of the Church. An intimation from above, that
the greatest obstacle to the world's believing is the want of manifest unity in faith and love on the part of the imperfect Church."
Jacobus.—It was not the unity of *essence* which our Lord prayed
for, that *already* existed, and was *complete* and *invisible ;* but that
of *perfection* (verse 23) which might be broken, was susceptible
of *increase*, and was *apparent* in the world.—The union contemplated was one immediately of *individuals*, and not of *denominations.*—That which Christ prayed for, it is the Church's duty to
strive after.—"The brotherhood of Christians has ever been the
witness to their common Fatherhood in God. The divisions of
Christendom have ever been the weakness of the Church and the
proof to the world that, in that they are divided, they cannot be
of God (chap. xiii. 35)." *Ellicott.*—The world in her disunity, is
Babel ; the Church of unity is the eternal, ideal Zion ; the Holy
Ghost is the Mediator of this union (Eph. iv. 13). *Lange.*—"That
Thou hast sent Me" implies belief in the whole Work and Office
of Christ. Here our Lord certainly *prays for the world. Alford.*

ἐν before ὦσιν is wanting in *Codd. B. C. D., &c.,* in *the Itala, &c.,* in *Hilary.*—Is
supported by *Cod., A., Origen* and, very decidedly, by the subsequent sentence. The
world can see that Christians are one, but it cannot see that they are in God. *Schaff.*—
Is supported also by *Cod. Sin.*, but all the latest critical editions drop it, except *Lach.*—
This verse and verse 23 are the classical passages on Christian union, or the communion of saints.—The following points seem to be implied in the text : 1. Christian
union presupposes the *vital union* of believers with Christ, and is conditioned by it.
2. It is a reflection of the union which subsists between the Father and the Son, consequently not merely a *moral* union of sympathy, but a community of *spiritual life* ;
all partaking of the life of Christ, as the branches of the vine (compare chap. xv.).
3. It *centres* in *Christ* and the *Father* who are one.—Christ is the divine harmony of
all human discord, and Christians are one among each other just in proportion as
they are one with Him.—There is no intimation whatever of a visible centre of unity
on earth, such as Rome claims to be, or of a particular form of government, or form

of worship, as a necessary condition of such union, or means of its promotion.—There was considerable difference in the apostolic age between the Jewish-Christian and the Gentile-Christian type of Christianity, between the doctrinal system of Paul and of James, &c., and yet there was essential unity and harmony.   4. Hence Christian union is *free* and implies the greatest *variety* (but no contradictions) of types and phases of Christian life.—Christian union and Christian liberty are not contradictory, but complimentary and mutually sustaining forces (compare chap. viii. 36; Rom. viii. 2; Gal. v. 1).   5. The unity must *manifest* itself in some outward form. so that the world may perceive it and be impressed by it.—This was the case already in the Apostolic Church (Acts ii. 47: iv. 32), and in the times of persecution, when the heathen used to exclaim: "How these Christians love one another. and how they are ready to die for one another."—Even among the sectarian strifes the spiritual union of Christians has never been lost; and it will deepen and expand, and be fully realized at last, like all the other attributes of the Church (catholicity and holiness, &c.). with the glorification of the body of believers (verses 23, 24).—To promote the union for which our Saviour so frequently prayed. is the duty and privilege of every Christian. *Schaff.*—"Corporeality is the end of God's ways." *Œtinger.*

---

22. And the glory which thou gavest me I have given them; that they may be one, even as we are one.

The glory, &c. Gr., *hast given Me.* See on chap. xiii. 32.—The glory which our Lord here speaks of is that for which He prays in verse 5 (see Comm.).—The fulness of glory which awaits Him at His Father's right hand is thought of as already given to Him.—Here, as all through this Prayer, the future is regarded as present.

I have given them. Tho "I" is emphatic : "I have on My part given to them."—The glory of Christ as *the only-begotten Son*, full of grace and truth (see on chap. i. 14), by virtue of His exaltation and the unity of all believers in Him through the Spirit, has become theirs (Eph. i. 18 ; ii. 16 ; Rom. viii. 30).—Not yet fully, nor *as it is His*, but as each can receive and show it forth, while the perfection of it is described in verse 24. *Alford.*—Believers who have become, and will become, one with Him, are spoken of as even now sharers in His glory.—" Heirs of God, and joint-heirs with Christ, &c., that we may be also glorified together " (Rom. viii. 17).—" Beloved, now are we the sons of God, and it doth not yet appear what we shall be : but we know that, when he shall appear, we shall be like him ; for we shall see him as he is " (1 John iii. 2).—Christ gave His disciples the glory of full fellowship with Him in His glorified state, by giving them the principle of future glory in His word (1 Pet. iv. 14). *Lange.*—This glory is contained in the gift of eternal life, which the believer already possesses (see on verses 2, 3).—Glorification is the complete revelation of a form of life either abstractly or relatively perfect.—A bud is glorified when it bursts its envelope and comes forth a flower.—Grace is heaven in the bud ; glory is begun in the prayer, " God be merciful to me the sinner."—So far as Christ dwells in

any soul He aas given that soul His glory.—There is but *one* glory
for all Christians, high or low, rich or poor, learned or unlearned,
and that is the glory of Christ.—" Even the slightest glimmering
of heavenly light which begins to shine out of the countenance of
a justified publican, is an outbeaming of his future glorification
and so is the still brighter angel-face of the crowned martyr at his
trial (Acts vi. 15)." *Stier.*—Who has not seen on the face of some
Christian, especially when near his end, some rays of this coming
glory ?—What, but the nearness of heaven, could give the countenance the look of unearthly peace and beauty, which it often
wears at the last hour ?—Though the full consummation   this
glory is reserved for the resurrection, yet even here below, it reveals
its divine origin.—What the perfected glory shall be, we may learn
from Rev. i., for we are told that our body shall be like unto His
glorious body (Phil. iii. 21).—" What believers have in and from
Christ doth advance them to a glorious estate, and is their begun
glory and salvation, so that none but they have any true glory,
nor is anything enjoyed by men truly glorious but the grace and
other privileges they enjoy in and from Him." *Hutcheson.*—" Regard each other, at least, O believers, with respect ! Learn, ye
children of God, to stand in awe of your own dignity, that ye defile
not yourselves with sin ! Let your *thanksgivings* for what hath
been already given, invigorate your prayer and effort after holiness
and perfection." *Stier.*—And all this *through faith !*—" A drop of
faith is far more noble than a whole sea of mere science, though it
be the historical science of the Divine word." *Francke.*

That they may be one, &c. See on verse 21.—This is the purpose
for which He has given His people the glory which the Father has
given Him.—The word of the Spirit, with which the Spirit comes,
is the bond of union and peace, and is designed to be this bond.—
The union of believers by the indwelling Spirit with the Father
and Son from whom the Spirit proceeds, entitles them through
grace to participate in the *glory* given to Christ.—" It is not enough
we know what we have in Christ and from Him, unless we also
take up the end for which it is allowed, and improve it accordingly ;
therefore doth He subjoin, ' I have given them that glory, that
they may be one.' " *Hutcheson.*—Divisions and dissensions amongst
Christians deprive them of this glory, and make void the fruit of
all the Lord's communications : whereas those who long for union
and endeavour to promote it are thereby sharers of His glory, even
as He and the Father are one. *Owen.*—We see but little of this
union now, but wherever it exists, it is heaven begun.—All believers should earnestly desire and pray for it, and above all should
seek to give it practical effect, as far as possible ; and even if they

should not be successful, the Lord of the Church will honour the effort, for He says to such, as He did to David, " Thou didst well that it was in thine heart " (1 Kings viii. 18). *Flavel.*

---

23. I in them, and thou in me, that they may be made perfect in one ; and that the world may know that thou hast sent me, and hast loved them, as thou hast loved me.

I in them, &c. A parenthesis more explicitly setting forth the union between the Father and Himself, and His people.—It is the thought which He has uttered again and again, and which, nevertheless, seems incapable of full expression in human language.—All the way through this Prayer we are reminded of the parable of the Vine and the Branches (see on chap. xv. 1-7).—" Albeit there can be no union betwixt God and fallen man immediately, yet through Christ this union is made up ; and Christ being in us, and we united to Him, the Father also, in Him, is in us, and we in Him ; for thus is our union here with God made up." *Hutcheson.* —As the Father is in Christ, so is Christ in believers, and they in Him ; the Father is in Christ in respect of His Divine nature, essence, and attributes ; and Christ is in believers, by the inhabitation of His Holy Spirit. *Burkitt.*—1. Union with Christ ; 2. Union with the Father through Him ; 3. Union with each other, resulting from those. *Henry.*

Made perfect in one. Gr., *perfected unto one.*—The unity is the result of their being made perfect (Heb. x. 14 ; 1 John ii. 5 : iv. 12, 17, 18).—A completeness and perfection of unity, according to the pattern of that which subsisted between the Father and the Son.—The blessedness of believers consisteth in their *oneness ;* in being *one* with the Father through Christ, and *one* amongst themselves.—This *oneness* is holy, spiritual, intimate, indissoluble. —As the children of one Father, united to Him through the Firstborn, believers repose upon a sure foundation of unity.—" There are three most admirable unions, proposed to our faith in the Christian religion. The Unity of Essence, in the Trinity ; the Unity of Person, in Jesus Christ ; and the Union, between Christ and His Church. The first of these is an ensample and prefiguration, as it were, to the second ; and the second, to the third. For we cannot better represent the Union with His Church, than by the Hypostatic Union, or by the Union of the Word with human Nature (1 John iv. 8)." *Norris.*—" There is one remarkable difference between nature and Grace ; for nature of one makes many ; for we are all but one in Adam, but Grace of many makes one ; for the Holy Ghost, who is as fire, melts all the faithful into one mass or lump, and makes of many one Body, in

the unity of God (Acts. ii. 3, 44 ; iv. 32 ; xvii. 26)." *W. Dell.*—
" Whatever excellency the Lord confer upon every particular believer, yet their perfection consists in their union among themselves, and with Christ their Head and Storehouse, and with the
Father in His fulness through Him ; for no one member hath the
perfection of the whole body, but of a part only, nor hath it that
perfection separate from the body, but in it, and being united with
it, to supply its proper function ; and the whole body, thus united,
hath its perfection in and from Christ and the Father ; for so doth
Christ's conjoining of all these teach us." *Hutcheson.*

The world may know. See on verse 21.—Gr., *may recognize.*—The
world seeing in its midst believers living in holy unity would recognize the power as of God.—Parallel to "that the world may
believe " (verse 21), and implies, that saving knowledge by which
from time to time the children of the world are called by God to
become the children of light.—It is the third time this word is
used, and in all three places the recognition is that of *love:* in
chap. xiii. 35, of the disciples one to another ; in chap. xiv. 31, of
Jesus to the Father ; here, of the Father to believers, as perfected
into unity in the Son of His love. *Alford.*

Hast sent me. Gr., *didst send Me* (see on verses 3, 21).—That the
world recognizing this unity as of God, may accept for themselves
the message of love which the "Sent of God" has brought them.

And hast loved, &c. Gr., *didst love,* or, *lovedst them, as Thou didst
love,* or, *lovedst Me.*—The evidence of the Father's love for believers, is here declared to be the great love which they manifest
for one another, and the unity and harmony of purpose and aim
which pervades their life.—" God's life in Christ through the
Holy Spirit founds the ever richer life of Christ in believers ; this
founds their ripening to perfection (Eph. iv. 13) ; this brings with
it their unity ; this, finally, is instrumental towards the *full* conversion of the world, when it not only *knows* the Christ, but also
knows living Christians in their dignity, as beloved of the Father."
Lange.—" The Father's love to believers doth resemble His love
to His Son ; for though His love to His eternal and only Son be
matchless and necessary, not voluntary, as His love to us is ; nor
are we loved for our own sakes as He is ; nor is He capable of
some effects of love we receive ; yet this love doth most resemble
it of any." *Hutcheson.*—As the love of the Father for His Son is
eternal, unchangeable, everlasting, so is His love for those united
to His Son.—Christ would have the world know the greatness of
the Father's love for the children of men (see on chap. iii. 16),
and of this, the surest and most powerful evidence is, *the unity of
His Church in holy love.*—Hence it was that this union so occupied

our Lord's mind as He drew near to death.—According to this Prayer, the unity of the Church means *the conversion of the world*, that is, the manifestation and consummation of the kingdom of love.—Surely every Christian should strive after this by endeavouring to keep, towards all his fellow Christians, "the unity of the Spirit in the bond of peace."

ἵνα. We have the same recurrence of ἵνα as in verse 21, and the same dependence.—The second of them here expresses not merely the similarity of their unity to that of the Son and Father, but the *actuality of its subsistence*, in Christ abiding in them and the Father in Christ.—The καὶ before ἵνα omitted. *Lach.*, *Tisch.*, *Meyer*, *Alford*, *Lange, &c.*

---

24. Father, I will that they also, whom thou hast given me, be with me where I am; that they may behold my glory, which thou hast given me; for thou lovedst me before the foundation of the world.

Father. See on verses 1, 11, and on chap. xvi. 28, 32.—Our Lord takes pleasure in repeating this delightful name of God.—The frequent thought of so tender and blessed a relation would sweeten His heart, and renew His ardour and affection. *Owen.*

I will. An expression of will founded on acknowledged right. *Alford.*—The familiar communication of His wish, as the equal of Him whom He is addressing.—It expresses the consciousness that His will was that of His Father, and is the request of Him who is one with the Father.—He had before said, "I pray" (verses 9, 20), but the thought of the union with the Father, expressed in verse 23, leads to the fuller expression of His confidence.—"The Lord, when He reaches this point, elevates His tone, changes His petition into an *authorized demand*, and sets it before the hearers of His prayer in the form of a strong promise. This '*I will*' is no other than a *testamentary word* of the Son, who in the unity of the Father, is *appointing* what He wills." *Stier.*—"It imports that He was making His latter will and testament, and leaving His legacies, which He was sure would be effectual, being purchased by His all-sufficient merits, and prosecuted by His intercession. And so it teacheth us, that as all these things sought in this prayer are believers' duty to study after them, so are they Christ's legacies, purchased and earnestly prayed for by Him, which will certainly be forthcoming to them." *Hutcheson.*—When He says "I will," He speaks a language peculiar to Himself; He declares: 1. The authority of His intercession in general; He intercedes as a King, for He is a Priest upon His throne (like Melchisedek). 2. His particular authority in this matter; He had power to *give eternal* *life* (verse 3). *Henry.*—Sometimes, when He prayed for Himself, it was "Not as I will, but as Thou wilt ; " but, when He intercedes for His people, it was peremptory, and as one, that would take no denial. *Hurrion.*—This word teaches us that the utmost sanctification human nature can attain to (verse 17), carries in it no presumption to heaven ; but that this is a title, that rises simply from the prevalence of our Lord's mediation. *Young.*

That they also, &c. The best MSS. read : "*Father, I will that that which Thou hast given Me, even they may be with Me where I am.*"— The neuter has a peculiar solemnity uniting the whole Church together as *one gift* of the Father to the Son.—Then the "*even they*" resolves it into the great multitude whom no man can number, and comes home to the heart of every individual believer with inexpressibly sweet assurance of an eternity with Christ. *Alford.* (See on chap. vi. 39.)—The Church is thought of as a collective whole, and the members as individuals composing the whole. *Ellicott.* (See on verse 2.)

Be with me. *Now* He is *with them* in His ordinances, in His word, and at His table; *ere long* they are to be *with Him*, as His friends, as His spouse, as His companions in His kingdom. *Burkitt.*—Our *love* teaches us that to be *with Christ* would be in itself fully sufficient for blessedness : love desires, even in heaven, nothing beside for its unutterable joy.—The same *love* here also speaks in Christ, "I will and must have all My children with Me." *Francke.*—This is the joy and the crown of His *Jesus-heart*, that His saved ones may be eternally *with Him. Stier.*

Where I am. See on chap. xii. 26 ; xiv. 3.—"I am," the *essential* present ; in My true place, *i.e.*, in the glory of the Father. (See on chap. viii. 58.)—Not the subject matter of a petition, but the consequence of a familiar expression of will.—In the presentiment of His heavenly stand-point, He takes possession of His Church as objects bestowed by the Father.—With His ascension, the goal of perfected believers shall be with Him in heaven (see on chap. xiv. 1, 2).—To be with Christ *where He is*, imports union and communion with Him, and in this the chief blessedness of heaven consisteth. *Baxter.*—Christ will never rest satisfied till the spiritual communion begun with Him on earth is perfected in the glory of heaven. *Hutcheson.*

May behold my glory, &c. See on verse 5.—That it is the glory of the divine-human nature of our Lord which is specially referred to, appears from the words "which Thou hast given Me."—Moreover His *essential* Divine glory as the only-begotten of the Father, could not be shared.—It is the Son of Man who is glorified (see on chap. xiii. 31, 22), and therefore it is that human nature is made capable of sharing it.—This is the completion of verse 22, the open beholding of His glory (1 John iii. 2), which shall be coincident with the change into His perfect image.—The word translated "behold" is to *see* and *partake*, the very case supposes it; for no *mere spectator could see* this glory (Rom. viii. 17 ; 2 Cor. iii. 18). *Alford.*—This is a beholding whereby the beholder becometh one with the Beheld, whereby the glory of the Lord doth itself pass into him. *Gerlach.*—"As for me, I will behold thy face in righteousness : I shall be satisfied, when I awake, with thy likeness" (Psa. xvii. 15).—"We should let this utterance of our Lord be our soul's pillow and bed of down, and with joyful heart resort thereunto when the sweet hour of rest is at hand." *Luther.*—"This is the resolution of the contest between *disinterested love* and the *regard to reward;* with the supremest majesty Christ here speaks of *His own glory* and the *beholding* it, as the highest blessedness of His glorified ones (Ex. xxxiii. 18). He does not, however, say 'My glory' otherwise than as He appoints it to be shared by *us.* '*Behold*' is an experiencing and tasting (chap. viii. 51), for, according to verse 22, the Lord had *given* to us already His glory." *Stier.*—"Be it observed that the prayer of Christ from this·point does not issue in a human doxology of God, but in a divine dialogue with the Father." *Lange.*

For thou lovedst me, &c. Gr., *because Thou didst love me.*—Not a question merely of the Trinitarian love of the Father for the Son, but the eternal complacency of God in Christ in anticipation of His obedience unto death, in which complacency God appointed Him this state of exaltation (Eph. i. 19 ; Phil. ii. 6, &c.). *Meyer.*—"The most glorious part of this sight of glory will be to behold the whole mystery of Redemption unfolded in the glory of Christ's person, and to see how, before the being of the creature, that eternal Love was, which gave the glory to Christ of which all creation is but the exponent." *Alford.*—The heavenly kingdom which appeared at the end of time, was grounded, before the beginning of time, in the love of God to the Son.—Thus the mediatorial work of Christ was no *after thought*, but the purpose of God from everlasting (1 Cor. ii. 7 ; Eph. i. 4 ; Col. i. 15-20 ; 1 Pet. i. 20, &c.).—What a sure ground of confidence this reveals to the believer!—"Jesus the Mediator is beloved of the Father with an eternal love, evidenced in His exalting Him to glory, that so sinners may expect to be accepted in Him." *Hutcheson.*

οὕς. *Cod. A., &c.,* sanctioned by *Cyprian* and *Hilary,* adopted by *Lachmann.*—δ. *Codd. B. D., Sin* ; adopted by *Tisch., Treg., Alford, Westcott and Hort, Lange, Schaff, &c.* —δέδωκας. The E. V. is by no means consistent in the rendering of the tenses, and repeatedly confounds the aorist and perfect in this chapter. *Schaff.*

25. O righteous Father, the world hath not known thee: but I have known thee, and these have known that thou hast sent me.

O righteous Father. See on verses 1, 11, 24.—In these closing words of His prayer, our Lord again solemnly appeals to His Father.—But now the special thought presented is that of His Father's righteousness.—" This thought follows upon the prayer that those whom the Father had given Him may be where He is, and behold the Divine glory ; and the connection seems to be in the thought that sinful humanity cannot see God and live." *Ellicott.*—" *Righteous* is connected with the final clause of verse 24. The Righteousness of the Father is witnessed by the beginning of Redemption, and by the glorification of the elect from Christ ; but also by the final distinction made by His Justice between the *world* and *His.*" *Alford.*—" In chap. xvi. 10, He says, ' *Of righteousness because I go to the Father.*' It is agreeable to the righteousness of God and Christ that a separation should be made betwixt the perfected Christ and this present world in its blindness—that Christ should be exalted to heaven." *Lange.*—" The work of divine holiness (verse 11) would otherwise fail of its final consummation and manifestation." *Meyer.*—" He appeals to the righteousness of God against the evil world, and in favour of His people." *Webster and Wilkinson.*—" The righteousness of the Father is the ground upon which He asks for the fulfilment of the promises both to Himself and His people." *Owen.*—He calls God " Holy Father " when He prays for their sanctification ; He calls Him " Righteous Father " when He asks for their glorification. *Henry.*—Our Lord first addresses God as " Father," then as " Holy Father," and lastly as " Righteous Father."—Note that *Holiness* and *Righteousness* flow from the *Fatherhood* of God.—Note also that the manifestation of the divine *Fatherhood* is consummated in the manifestation of the divine *Righteousness.*—" In our prayers we ought to ground ourselves well upon the knowledge of God in His attributes, that as we may be ashamed to seek such things as beseem not such a God to give, so we may be encouraged in what we are allowed to seek ; therefore doth Christ give this title to God, it being a righteous and approven petition, and God, who is righteous, engaged to Christ, and to believers in Him, by His promise to grant it." *Hutcheson.*

The world, &c. See on chap. xv. 21 ; xvi. 3.—The world has not *known* God, either in His general revelation through nature and history, or in the mission of Christ.—It has no *living* knowledge of God as the *Righteous Father,* the *Holy Father.*—This is its own proper *guilt,* on account of which God can manifest Himself to it only in His *justice.*—" Even the nominally Christian world *knoweth* *not* the righteous Father, knoweth not the Lord who revealeth Him ; although naming and calling upon both, like the Jews with their God and their Messiah." *Stier.*

I have known thee. " I have known Thee as working in Me, and revealing Thyself through Me ; known Thee by direct immediate knowledge."—Christ, even as man, has known God in His whole revelation.—His thorough knowledge of the righteous Father is a reason for His exaltation above the world.—He confides the righteousness of God as one that rewards, that shall translate Him to heaven.—" Christ doth perfectly know the Father, that He may cover and rectify all our ignorance, in our uptaking of Him and addresses to Him, and that we may be assured He will give no false character of Him ; for it is recorded, for the disciples' behoof and advantage, ' *I have known Thee.'* " *Hutcheson.*

These have known. They knew Him as sent of the Father (as Christ) and as His Son, and thus through Him and in Him they knew God as *His* Father, holy and righteous.—This they knew *with Christ,* in opposition to the world, from which they are saved. —By this knowledge they had passed through a moral change, and were no longer of the world, but were sons of God (see on chap. i. 12).—Because they have known that He was sent from God, and thereby have begun to know the righteousness of God, they too belong on His side ; and after they have performed His work in the world, they must come to Him into His heaven.— The knowableness of God : 1. Simply unknowable for the world in its ungodliness ; 2. Conditionally knowable and known for the disciples in the beginnings of their life and faith ; 3. Absolutely knowable and known of Christ ; this knowledge the goal of Christians (1 Cor. xiii. 2) —The steps of this knowledge are at once the steps of the kingdom of love and eternal life (see on verse 3). *Lange.*—" Whatever degrees of ignorance saints lie under, yet it doth commend them to God if they know Christ as Mediator and Ambassador of the Father, and so know God in Christ, and in order to salvation ; for in this Christ commends His rude disciples, ' *these have known that Thou hast sent Me.'* " *Hutcheson.*

πατήρ. *A. B.*; πάτερ. *Codd. Sin. C. D. L.. Schaff*—καὶ, δέ. Forms an antithesis to what precedes : Righteous Father, Thou art righteous, Thou givest such good things, *and yet* the world hath not known Thee. *Chrys., Meyer, Luthardt.*—A deduction from the preceding in a predestinarian sense : *Quia justus es ideo te non cognovit mundus. Augustine, Lampe.*—As announcing a subsequent antithesis : on the one side, on the other side. *Heumann, Lücke, Tholuck* —He glances back upon the former antithesis : *Thou didst love Me, &c.*—This contrast of the eternal Christ to the upright world constitutes the first motive for His exaltation.—To it there is now added the second corresponding contrast, that the sinful world has also not known the righteous Father, whilst He has. *Lange.*—The first καί contrasts with the δέ immediately following; the more classical construction would be τε—δέ —The second καί merely couples the preceding to the following as depending upon it. *Alford.*

---

26. And I have declared unto them thy name, and will declare it: that the love wherewith thou hast loved me may be in them, and I in them.

Declared. Gr., *and I made known.*—Belief in the divine source and character of His mission, the first reason for the elevation of believers to participation in His heavenly glory.—This continued in the second, viz., that He has made known unto them the Father's name, and will still make it known until the perfect revelation of it.—To these the third is added; the love of God for the Son must also be in them, *Christ Himself being thereby in them*, through the Holy Ghost. *Lange.*

Thy name. See on verse 6, and on chap. xii. 28; also on Matt. i. 22; vi. 9.—His whole teaching a making known of the name, character, and will of God to them.—They had received this in part, but in part only.—The first steps in this great spiritual lesson had been taken. *Ellicott.*

Will declare it. Gr., *will make it known.*—By His presence in the Paraclete He will guide them into all truth.—He will make known to their hearts, prepared for the revelation, the love of God which passeth knowledge.—And not to the apostles merely, but the whole body of believers.—Note, that it is through the Spirit, the Church was to be fully led to the knowledge of the Father.—This promise has been in fulfilment through all the history of the Church.—"Albeit the knowledge and grace of believers be but small, yet if it be growing it will not want the reward of a larger measure; therefore doth He undertake for the increase of their knowledge, 'I will declare Thy name,' that upon this consideration they may be admitted to partake of this prayed-for mercy." *Hutcheson.*

That the love, &c. See on chap. xv. 9.—The great result of this manifestation of the Father's name is, the wonderful love wherewith the Father loved Christ, dwelling in them.—The perfect, living knowledge of God in Christ, which reveals this love, and in fact is this love. *Alford.*—*Love* (not faith, not eternal life, not glory), only *love* is the last word here! let every one ponder this and feel it.—"With this end of creation, redemption and sanctification, the Redeemer closes His High-priestly Prayer. Love created the world, love took compassion upon the sinful world, love will unite in one the sanctified. Love is the eternal essence of God, and the principle of His dealings." *Fikenscher.*—" The indwelling of His love is not simply 'the *practical* end' of the knowledge of the name and nature of God; but *the love being in them* is itself the living, consummate *knowledge.*" *Stier.*—" The thought in this verse is expanded in St. Paul's prayer in Eph. iii. 17–19. It is more than that God may love the disciples, even as He loved the Son; it is that they may so know the nature of God that this love may be in them, dwelling in them as the prin′ciple of their life." *Ellicott.*—" The consummation of the kingdom, a consummation in love through the consummate proclamation of the name of God." *Lange.*

I in them. He does not say " *Thou* in them," but " *I in them and Thou in Me* " (see on verse 23).—Christ dwelling in their hearts by faith, and renewing and teaching them by His Spirit.—They must be utterly lifted up to Christ in order to be perfected in the communion of the Triune God (2 Pet. i. 4).—Going from them, to be yet with them; not to be with them only as a person without, but as a power *within.*—"I in them," with all the fulness of My love and the Father's love.—As the Son was loved of the Father, His indwelling presence secured for His followers a participation in His Father's love.—The love of the Father dwelleth in us only through the mediation of the Son; we know and we have the Father only as the Father of Christ, nor shall we possess Him throughout eternity otherwise.— Christ in us, the love of the Father in us, is no other in its truth and power than the *communion of the Holy Ghost,* who bringeth through the grace of Christ the love of God to man.— Thus the *last word of all* after the last is, I IN THEM.—This is the last and most appropriate word of this sublime Prayer, a better seal than any doxology or Amen. *Stier.*—The words remain in all their comfort for them in whom " Christ is formed "; in all their encouragement for doubting hearts seeking to know God; in all their warning for hearts that do not seek His presence. *Ellicott.*— The prayer was richly answered in the experience of the apostles; nothing could separate them from the love of Christ (Rom. viii. 39), and Christ ever remained with them and in them by His Spirit, and will remain with believers to the end, their strength and comfort and peace. *Schaff* —" The contrast between the dejected, faint-hearted, materializing Galilæan fishermen and peasants of the Gospels, and the heroic, spiritual confessors of Pentecost and after times, is, itself, a miracle, great beyond all others. The illumination of soul, the grandeur of conception, the loftiness of aim, are a transformation from a lower to an indefinitely higher mental and moral condition, as complete as the change from early twilight to noon, and find their only solution in the admission that they must have received the miraculous spiritual enlightenment from above which Jesus had promised to send them." *Geikie.*—" Chap. xvii. : That all things which He prays for and promises may be Yea and Amen, the Lord of glory went, after these words, to the woe of Gethsemane, to the death of the Cross, and, through the death endured for our sins, to His holy and righteous Father. This death is the centre of all that grace and truth of which the word bears witness to faith ; out of this death cometh life, and love, and sanctification, and unity, and eternal glory." *Stier.*

John 18

1. When Jesus had spoken these words, he went forth with his disciples over the brook Cedron, where was a garden, in'o the which he entered, and his disciples.

When. See on chap. xiv. 31.—We now come upon ground common to John and the earlier Gospels.—Each of the Evangelists has given a narrative of the trial and crucifixion of Jesus.—But each naturally differs by greater or lesser fulness, or as he regarded the events from a point of view peculiar to himself.—These differences (having their ground in varieties of mental constitution or in circumstances) have, under the guidance of the Holy Spirit, secured to us a much more complete picture of that wonderful life than could otherwise have been obtained.—It is in the *fourfold* Biography that the fulness and unity of that life is seen, so far as it was possible to present it in human language.— The reader is referred to our Commentaries upon the other Gospels for the treatment of those facts and incidents, in this part of our Lord's history, common to each : our work here relates to those peculiar to John's narrative.

Went forth. See note to chap. xiv. 31.—Jesus now left the city precincts.—He *went forth* to the awful conflict in Gethsemane, and to the betrayal.—Knowing all that was to happen His sufferings were doubled.—It is an unspeakable mercy that God has concealed the future from *our* view.—Jesus a perfect example of surrender to the will of God, simply as His will, irrespective of consequences.—He took His work before Him : the office of the priest was to teach, and pray, and offer sacrifice ; having taught and prayed He now applies Himself to make atonement.—Having prepared Himself and His disciples by prayer, for the hour of trial, He now courageously goes forth to meet it.—When He had put His armour on, He entered the lists, but not till then.

The brook. Gr., *the winter torrent Kedron* (see note).—These words are found in the Sept. Version of 2 Kings xv. 23, and 3 Kings xv. 13.—*Kedron* is formed from a Hebrew word which means " black."—It was the "Niger" of Judæa, and was so called from its turbid waters, and perhaps from the darkness of the chasm through which they flowed.—The blood of the sacrifices flowing into it, in the time of the temple-worship, added to its dark and gloomy appearance.—Our Lord's passage over this brook, a step of the highest, world-historic import.—An expression of his constrainedness in spirit, His freedom of will, His decision of heart.—Over this brook David once fled from Absalom (2 Sam. xv. 23). **A garden.** At once suggests Gethsemane (see on Matt. xxvi. 36; Luke xxvii. 39).—Though John does not record our Lord's passion there, this notice indicates its place in the history.—John is careful to present most striking instances of the trouble of our Lord's soul by the suffering before Him (see on chap. xii. 23-27; xiii. 21).—The "garden" as John paints it, presupposes the Gethsemane of the Synoptists, and from the latter it is possible to deduce the former.—In the kingdom of God, a mighty assurance of victory admits the inference of a mighty conflict, and a mighty conflict that of a mighty assurance of victory. *Lange.*—Some suppose that the owner of the garden was a friend of Jesus. *Lücke.* —*Paradise* and the *garden :* the first and the second Adam : the serpent and the traitor : the defeat and the victory.—In the garden of Eden man fell, through lust and pride ; in the garden of Gethsemane he was to be raised up again through mourning, anguish and humiliation. *Gossner.*

He entered, &c. See on Matt. xxvi. 36; Mark xiv. 32; and Luke xxii. 39, where the scene is described.

χειμάρρου *flowing in winter, a stormbrook, a wintry torrent,* which flows in the rainy season or winter, but dries up in summer. *Robinson.*—κέδρων. Evidently a Greek corruption of the Hebrew word.—If there were cedars in the ravine the corruption could be easily accounted for.—Instances of the practice of changing foreign names into other words bearing sense in the new language are common in all countries.— This being so, it is perhaps safer to follow the best MSS., even against our own conviction, that John can hardly have written τῶν κέδρων. *Alford.*—The plural seems to have originated in a misapprehension on the part of the transcribers.—Cedar brook instead of Black brook.—It is evidently a Greek corruption of the Hebrew word, under the impression that it means cedars.—There is no evidence that cedars grew on the brook. —John can hardly have sanctioned such a mistake, and therefore I would decide here from internal probability against the authority of MSS.—The error may have been made by the first Greek copyist, who was ignorant of Hebrew. *Schaff.*— κῆπος. John omits the directions of Jesus to His disciples as to their conduct in Gethsemane ; the Passion of His soul ; the reproof of His sleeping disciples ; the kiss of Judas ; the reference of Peter to the twelve legions of angels: the protest of Jesus against His seizers; the healing of Malchus, recorded by Luke; the episode of the fugitive youth related by Mark.—On the other hand, he gives prominence to the fact that Jesus went voluntarily to meet His apprehenders; that the multitude fell to the ground at the sight of His majesty ; that He surrendered Himself prisoner, while securing a free exode to His disciples.—He names Peter as t .e one who drew the sword, mentions the name of the servant, Malchus, who was wounded by him, and, with the words, "who drew the sword," refers the saying of Jesus, "shall I not drink the cup?" &c., to His psychical passion. *Lange.*

2 And Judas a'so, which betrayed him, knew the place: for Jesus ofttimes resorted thither with his disciples.

Judas. See on chap. vi. 70, 71; xii. 4-6; xiii. 2, 26-30.

Betrayed. Gr., *who was betraying Him.*—The original word is a present participle, and marks the Betrayal as actually in progress. *Ellicott.*

Knew. Even this knowledge and recollection of his disciple-life becomes his ruin.—A fearful judgment overtakes the misuse of spiritual experiences.—No one hates Christ and His people more bitterly than a hypocrite who has been unmasked (see on chap. xiii. 26, 27).—The wickedness of Judas was all the greater by his betraying Jesus to death in the very place where he had seen His deeds and heard the words of life from His lips.—Evil men often take advantage of their knowledge of the movements of the godly to injure them; therefore we should take care in whom we confide (Psa. lvii. 6).—The Lord has hallowed even the kind of suffering that His children endure when they must allow unfaithful souls a knowledge of their circumstances (Psa. xli. 6; 9). *Starke.*

Resorted, &c. See on chap. viii. 1; Luke xxi. 37.—These accurate notices of John are especially found in this last portion of his Gospel (compare verses 13, 24, 28; chap. xix. 14, 20, 41, &c.). *Alford.*—All the Evangelists narrate the coming of Judas; but John only remembers that the spot was one frequented by Jesus and His disciples.—Shows how exact the knowledge of John as to all the incidents of the Jerusalem life of our Lord.—Love had imprinted even the minutest incident deep in his mind and heart. —The baseness of Judas is seen in his reckoning that Jesus, in His divine strength of character and fidelity to prayer, would assuredly be found, even on this occasion, in Gethsemane.—How well and yet how poorly he knew his betrayed Lord: 1. His place of prayer and fidelity to prayer, but not the blessing of His prayer; 2. His power, but not His superiority and omnipotence; 3. His innocence, yet not His holiness; 4. His clemency, yet not His love and earnestness; 5. His human dignity, but not His divine majesty.—The betrayer of Christ, a traitor out and out: 1. To the sanctuary; 2. To his fellow-disciples; 3. To his nation; 4. To humanity; 5. To himself. *Lange.*—Christ's holy religion is often *wounded in the house of its friends.*

πολλ ἰκις. According to Luke, it was a habit of Jesus to go thither.—The Synoptists jointly say that He there collected His thoughts in prayer.—According to John, the place also served as a meeting ground for Jesus and His disciples; probably He was wont to be met there by His adherents generally.—Mark, whose mother had a house in Jerusalem, may have owned a country seat at the foot of the Mount of Olives, perhaps even the garden of Gethsemane. *Lange.*—John's remark refers to previous festal visits. *Meyer.*

---

3. Judas then, having received a band of men and officers from the chief priests and Pharisees, cometh thither with lanterns and torches and weapons.

Band, &c. See on Matt. xxvi. 47; Luke xxiii. 47, 52.—Gr., *the band, and officers, &c.*—The other Gospels speak of a " great multitude."—John uses the technical name for the Roman cohort.— It was the garrison band from Fort Antonia, at the north-east corner of the Temple.—This well-known band is mentioned again in the New Testament (verse 12; Matt. xvii. 27; Mark xv. 16; Acts xxi. 31).—The A. V. misleads, by closely connecting in one clause two distinct things, "a band of men and officers."—The band was Roman; the "officers" were the Temple servants, of whom we read in chap. vii. 32 and 45 (see Comm.).—These were sent, here, as there, by the chief priests and Pharisees, with Judas for their guide, and their authority was supported by the civil power. *Ellicott.*—The strength of the cohorts conformed to circumstances.—Some of those under Titus contained 1000 men, others 613 foot-soldiers and 120 horsemen. *Tholuck.*—Not necessary to suppose that the whole garrison of the fortress, whether it consisted of 1000 or only of 300 men, was present; a small detachment with the captain (verse 12) was sufficient.—The objection that Roman soldiers would not have led Jesus to the chief priests is groundless; for He was to be condemned first by the ecclesiastical authorities.—Thus the combined power of the Romans and the Jews was brought to capture the one unarmed gentle Jesus.—That such military preparations should have been thought necessary shows the bad conscience of Judas and the Sanhedrim. *Schaff.*

Lanterns, &c. Gr., *with torches and lamps* (see on Matt. v. 15) *and arms.*—" Torches " would be any blazing substance held in the hand; " lamps," lights, fed with oil; the " arms " or " weapons " were swords and staves (Matt. xxvi. 47).—Torches and lamps were part of the regular military equipment for night service.— They are not mentioned in the other Gospels.—Though it was full moon, the lights were not unnecessary, as, in searching for a prisoner, they might have to enter dark places.—" The array of myrmidons against Jesus : 1. Called out by mendacious and vain fear ; 2. Terrible in its weapons and lamps, over against the Defenceless One; 3. Made a laughing-stock through the light of truth with which Christ goes to meet it ; 4. Shown up in its impotence ; 5. Limited in its operation ; 6. Given free course in its plot, but only in order to the carrying out of the counsel of God." *Lange.*

---

4. Jesus therefore, knowing all things that should come upon him, went forth, and said unto them, Whom seek ye?

Knowing all. See on Matt. xxvi. 45.—Dear to John was the fact of our Lord's omniscience, and dear it is to every Christian (see on chap. ii. 25 ; xvi. 30 ; xxi. 17).

Should come. Gr., *were coming upon Him.*—Hence He suffered both prospectively and actually, making His whole life a martyrdom.—But He saw through those sufferings, what they should be and what they would tend to, and therefore was not afraid.— Consideration of the inevitableness of trouble, in this life, should produce humble resignation, especially when we have had experience of former gracious dealings of God with us, and of the spiritual benefit accruing from our trials. *Sibbes.*

Went forth. Probably from the garden itself (verse 26). *Ellicott, Meyer.*—Out of the depths of the garden : from the shade of the trees into the moonlight. *Tholuck, Alford.*—Out of the circle of disciples, in advance of them, in order to protect them—this is indicated by the question, "Whom seek ye ?" *Lange.*—"When men sought Jesus to make Him a king, He fled : now that they seek Him to put Him to death, He goes forth to meet them." *Stier.*—He baffles the plots of His enemies by freely meeting and anticipating them.—Why so calm, so grand in His surrender? Because He is conscious that He is not abandoning Himself to the malice of His foes, but confiding Himself to the care of His Father (see on chap. xvi. 32).—Note here the sublime freedom of spirit with which our Lord resigns His outward freedom.—The kiss of Judas mentioned in all the earlier Gospels, must be placed here between "went forth" and "said unto them." *Ellicott.* (See on Matt. xxvi. 48, 49 ; and on Luke xxii. 47, 48.)

Whom seek ye? "He put this question, to the end that the temple-officers might learn His name and that it might consequently be rendered impossible to put Him out of the way anonymously." *Hug.*—He boldly faces the danger, and directs it upon Himself, that the disciples may be saved from it (see on verse 8). *Ellicott.*—"They are to be dismayed at the distinct consciousness of their intention to seize Jesus, and, their commission being thus narrowly defined, they shall be in duty bound to let the disciples go." *Lange.*—"To carry reproof to the consciences of those addressed (see on Matt. xxvi. 50), and also to obtain for so solemn an act as the delivering Himself up to them, the formal declaration of their intention to take Him." *Alford.*—Imports that they should have considered whom they were seeking, which if they had they had not done as they did (1 Cor. ii. 8). *Hutcheson.*

Instead of ἐξελθὼν εἶπεν, εξῆλθενκαὶ λέγει. *Lach., Tisch., Alford, Schaff, &c.*

5. They answered him, Jesus of Nazareth. Jesus saith unto them, I am he. And Judas also, which betrayed him, stood with them.

Answered, &c. As He was known to many of them (chap. vii. 32, 46 ; Matt. xxvi. 55) the answer was probably an official declaration.—Or, more likely, because they *feared* to say "Thee." *Lange.*

I am he. Gr., *I am* (see on chap. viii. 58 ; xii. 26 ; xiv. 3. On the name Jehovah see on Matt. i. 22).—A great and significant expression, never without the most powerful effects.—Spoken to His astonished disciples as He walked on the waves ; and as, at the sound, the raging storm instantly subsided, so a flood of peace and joy poured itself into their hearts (chap. vi. 20 ; Mark vi. 50).—Spoken to the Samaritan woman at Jacob's well ; and immediately she left her waterpot and hastened back to Sychar, as the first evangelist to the Samaritans (chap. iv. 26-30).—Spoken at the bar of the Sanhedrim ; and the conviction that He was really the Messiah smote the minds of His judges so powerfully that it was only by means of the stage-trick of rending his clothes that the high-priest was able to save himself from the most painful embarrassment (Mark xiv. 62).—Spoken here ; and the whole band of officers start, give way, stagger backward, and fall to the ground as if struck by an invisible flash of lightning (see on verse 6).—Spoken to His terrified disciples when He appeared to them after His resurrection ; and the most blessed effects followed (Luke xxiv. 39).—A word of unutterable comfort and joy to His friends and of unutterable alarm and misery to His foes.—What will be the effect of the same *I am*, when spoken by the Lord of glory in the day of judgment?—Those who have heard His voice as *Saviour* will then hear Him as *Judge*, to their eternal peace (see on chap. vi. 20).

Judas also. See on verse 2.—Evidently the words of an eye-witness; John detected Judas standing among them, and records it.—How vivid must have been the impression of the whole scene upon the mind of the beloved disciple!—Judas, who had been one of them, who had often been in that place with them, who had sat at the table and received bread from the Master's hand that *very night*, was now standing with the band and officers, who had come to capture Him; yea, had led them to the spot!—It would seem as if he had advanced to give the signal of the kiss, and had again retreated (see on verse 4).—The position of the words suggests also that the traitor was in some way connected with the overthrow of the band, as though the fear that shot through his soul upon hearing the words "I am," had passed from him to those with him. *Ellicott.*

---

6. As soon then as he had said unto them, I am he, they went backward, and fell to the ground.

As soon, &c. Not necessary to suppose any *special* exercise of miraculous power in the effect following our Lord's words.—The majesty of His person, the calmness of His reply, the announcement of the unutterable name, I AM (Jehovah, see on Matt. i. 22), and the consciousness of the wickedness of the errand they had come on, overwhelmed them.—"A miracle *consequent upon* that which Christ said and did, and the state of mind in which His enemies were." *Alford.*—"Not a physical, but a moral miracle." *Schaff.*—"A divine operation, yet with a human instrumentality. At the same time an expression of His freedom in His surrender, which freedom, according to the Synoptists, He also declared by a decided protest. The channel of the miracle was terror of conscience, as was the case in the death of Ananias. On New Testament ground the following belong here: Luke iv. 30; John viii. 59; vii. 44-46; x. 39; Matt. xxviii. 4; Acts v. 5, 10, in reference to a bad conscience. Analogous phenomena occurred even in the circle of Jesus' friends, according to Luke v. 8; Matt. xxviii. 9, 17, &c. Analogous effects of the manifestation of Jehovah, of the Angel of the Lord, or Christ, see in the Old Testament in the history of Balaam, Manoah, Isaiah, Daniel, as also in the New Testament at the commencement of Revelation." *Lange.*—The chief stress is to be laid on the *moral* force, the same which in the temple made His enemies recoil. *Godet.* (See on chap. ii. 15).—"A miracle of Jesus, by which He meant to prove the freedom of His self-surrender." *Meyer, &c.*—"Even before this, they were paralyzed, as it were, with awe of Him; now, when they would fain seize Him, a horror overpowers them and recoiling, they fall, one upon another." *Tholuck, &c.*—"It may be, He revealed a momentary glimpse of His transfiguration splendour, to show that He freely surrendered Himself." *Geikie.*—"Guilt trembled before the calmness of innocence. Man fell to the ground before the presence of God." *Ellicott.*—His hour had come, and therefore He will surrender Himself, but His life no one could take from Him (see on chap. x. 18).—Their prostration in the dust before Him, points out to unbelievers the situation in which they will one day be found.—"If His lamb's voice was so terrible, how dreadful will He be when He roars as a lion? and if that sweet word, which comforted the disciples, be their terror, how terrible will it be when He speaks to them as they deserve?" *Hutcheson.*

---

7. Then asked he them again, Whom seek ye? And they said, Jesus of Nazareth.

Asked, &c. Their fear soon passed away, and this second question in conjunction with His self-surrender, encouraged them to do the errand on which they came.—The influence of terror is transient, and probably the sudden repulse was represented by the leaders as effected by demoniacal agency at the instance of Jesus. *Owen.*— There are hearts so hardened in unbelief that not even the most wonderful manifestations of God's power seem to touch them.— Yet though the instruments of a godless, diabolical plot against the Holy One, they were also, on the other hand, the ministers of an existing order of things, and the instruments of Divine Providence (Acts ii. 23; iv. 27, 28).—His thought is still of saving His disciples. —In the midst of all the peril threatening Himself, care for those with Him has the first place in His mind.

They said. His question calls forth the same formal answer as in verse 5.—They have no warrant for the apprehension of any one else.

---

8. Jesus answered, I have told you that I am he; if therefore ye seek me, let these go their way.

I am he. Gr., *I am* (see on verse 5, and on chap. vi. 20; viii. 48; xiv. 3).

If. He seeks to bind them to their commission according to their own avowal.—Probably some of the Roman cohort, not knowing Jesus, were already laying hands on some of the disciples. *Bengel.*—The inclination for such a step is evinced by the episode of the fleeing youth (Mark xiv. 51) and by the maid who denounced Peter in the history of the denial.

Let, &c. Partly a deduction from their admission and partly a command.—It is, at the same time, the disciples' discharge from the present outward alliance of suffering.—But the great utterance has also a deeper background (Isa. lxiii. 3). *Lange.*—Reasons for His words : 1. Because He wished the disciples preserved for a greater work; 2. Because *His* death, and His *alone*, could secure the redemption of mankind; 3. Because they were not yet strong enough to withstand temptation ; 4. Because He would prove His power and authority over His enemies. *Zeisius.*—He commands His foes, and they do what He commands; they permit them to go away, whom He would preserve.—Our fate does not depend upon the might or number of our enemies, but upon the permission which they receive from God (2 Chron. xxxii. 7).—So tender is the Lord that He will not impose trials upon those not prepared for them.—Herein He gives us great encouragement to follow Him ; for though He has appointed us sufferings, yet He considers our frame (Ps. ciii. 13, 14 ; Heb. iv. 15).—"The power of this authoritative word shows itself down to the present day. The enemy had not left a disciple on earth if this word was not still in force. This is the cause of the continued existence of disciples." *Heubner.*

---

9. That the saying might be fulfilled, which he spake, Of them which thou gavest me have I lost none.

Saying. See on chap. xvii. 12.—John is content with giving the *substance* of our Lord's words.—This is in agreement with the usual practice of New Testament writers when making a quotation. —The quotation shows that in the thought of John, the prayer recorded in chap. xvii. is no *résumé* of the words of our Lord, but an actual record of His prayer: he quotes the "saying" as fulfilled, just as he would have quoted a passage from the Old Testament. *Ellicott.*

Fulfilled. Unquestionably our Lord's words had a deeper meaning than any belonging to this occasion.—To "*fulfil*" a prophecy is not to *exhaust* its capability of being again and again fulfilled.— Divine words have many stages of unfolding.—The temporal deliverance of the disciples now, was but a part in the great spiritual *safe-keeping* which the Lord asserted by anticipation. *Alford.*— John applies to temporal persecution that which had been spoken of spiritual.—An illustration of the kind of way in which words are said to be "fulfilled" in more than one sense.—*Striking* words fix themselves in the mind, and an event occurs which illustrates their meaning, and it is said therefore to fulfil them, though of each fulfilment it can be only part. *Ellicott.* (See on chap. ii. 17; xii. 38.)—John in his charity does not repeat all the declaration which our Lord pronounced that evening, the dreadful part of which was now also fulfilled; as if leaving to the awful reflections of those that hear it, the concluding words of the sentence (Luke iv. 20). *Williams.*—Nothing can occur contrary to the divine plan; not even the mad fury of His foes can overreach His wisdom, or overmatch His providence. *Jacobus.*—Scripture fulfilled: 1. In the most universal sense; 2. In the most special sense (see also on chap. xiii. 18; xvii. 12).

Gavest me. Gr., *hast given* (see on chap. vi. 37, 39, 44; xvii. 2, 6, 12).

Lost none. Gr., *I lost none*, or, *not a single one of them. Schaff.*— "The keeping of the disciples from being lost consisted finally in their preservation from captivity in the present situation, since the overmighty temptation might have been the ruin of the souls of some among them." *Lange.*—"The preservation of the disciples on this occasion is viewed as part of that *deeper preservation* undoubtedly intended in the saying quoted." *D. Brown.*—"Where Christ undertakes the charge of men's souls He will also have a charge of their body and outward condition, in subserviency to their soul's welfare. He will respect their very bodies and outward man, and will not expose them to hazards, save when it is for their soul's good, and when He is to be served thereby. And He will make it evident at last, that He is not prodigal of their bodies, nor casts them away when He exposeth them to suffering." *Hutcheson.*

---

10. Then Simon Peter having a sword drew it, and smote the high priest's servant, and cut off his right ear. The servant's name was Malchus.

Simon Peter. See on chap. i. 40-42; and on Matt. x. 2; and Luke vi. 14.—Gr., *Simon, then, Peter.*—Simon in this rash and hasty act.—John carefully emphasizes the *Simon* by the insertion of "*then*" between the names.—To *Simon* it was natural to act in the way related. *Lange.*

Smote. See on Matt. xxvi. 51, and on Luke xxii. 50.—All the Evangelists record this fact, but John alone gives the name of Peter.—The Synoptists, who wrote earlier, may have had prudential reasons for not mentioning the name.—Doubtless Peter intended, by this blow, to prove his readiness to make good his vow (see on chap. xiii. 37).—Probably it was also his design to give a signal to the friends of Jesus and the Lord Himself to rise in arms against the foe.—His zeal was honest and well-meaning, but impulsive and imprudent, and mistaken in the selection of means.—The drawing up of the world against Christ, and the sword-stroke of Peter for Him : symbols of the impotence of His fleshly opposers, as of His fleshly defenders. *Lange.*—The Church of Rome has imitated Peter in his weakness rather than his strength, and often invoked the arm of the secular power in the bloody persecution of those she has condemned as *heretics;* thus making herself responsible for it in spite of her professed principle: *Ecclesia non sitit sanguinem. Schaff.*

Malchus. Similarly to the mention of Peter, John alone mentions the name of the servant.—One of the circumstantial details so frequent in John's account of the history of the Passion which confirms his authorship.—John knew the high priest (see on verse 15), and so probably also his servant ; for Malchus was the personal servant of the high priest, and not one of the bailiffs or apparitors of the Sanhedrim.—John is careful to note, as Luke does too, that it was the "right ear ; " but Luke, the *physician,* is the only one of the writers who mentions the act of healing.—"When Peter should have watched, he slept : and when he should have been quiet, he made resistance through carnal zeal; thus we always have by nature a sufficient leaning towards evil. But the Lord overrules even the errors of His children, so that no greater harm shall result from them than He has resolved to permit (Gen. xx. 2, 6)." *Zeisius.*

For ὠτίον of the text. rec., ὠτάριον. *Cod. Sin., &c., Tisch., Alford.*

---

11. Then said Jesus unto Peter, Put up thy sword into the sheath : the cup which my Father hath given me, shall I not drink it ?

Unto Peter. It is again significant that John here makes use only of the name Peter (without Simon).—*Simon* took the sword, *Peter* received the reprimand.

Put up, &c. See on Matt. xxvi. 52 ; Luke xxii. 51.—"Christ's deliverance against the action of Peter, as given by John, does not exclude the words related by Matt. from conforming the more closely to the original expressions. As recorded by John, the words of Jesus are expressive of His voluntary surrender to the will of the Father, and they most decidedly look away from the doing of men. Mark passes over the direct disapproval awarded to Peter ; Luke relates how Christ remedied the offence ; Matt.

brings out the theocratical points in our Lord's saying." *Lange.* —John's narrative is more vivid than Matthew's.

The cup. See on Matt. xx. 22; xxvi. 39; Luke xxii. 42.—An echo of the prayer in Gethsemane, which is not recorded by John. —Peter's act was one of opposition to what Jesus knew to be the appointment of His Father.—In His prayer He has solemnly bound Himself to drink the cup.—The image of the "cup" nowhere else occurs in John, and is a striking allusion to the words uttered in the garden.—" Afflictions are measured by God to His people, both for quantity and quality; therefore are they called a 'cup.'" *Hutcheson.*

My Father, &c. It is this living trustfulness which takes the bitterness from the cup.—That which His Father hath appointed Him to suffer must be right and good.—Yet who can conceive of what was contained in that *cup?*—Christ's people are called to know the "fellowship of His sufferings" (Phil. iii. 10).—As the Father gave His only-begotten and well-beloved Son a bitter cup to drink, so also He often gives a bitter cup to those who are one with His Son.—" We must *pledge Christ* in the *cup* that He *drank of:* 1. It is but a *cup*, a small matter comparatively, be it what it will; 2. It is a cup that is *given us;* 3. It is a cup given us by *a Father.*" *Henry.*—It is the Father to whom He has prayed (see on chap. xvii. 1), and solemnly committed His disciples (see on chap. xvii. 11).—It is the Father whose presence never leaves Him (see on chap. xvi. 32).—It is the Father into whose hands, dying upon the cross, He commends His spirit (see on Luke xxiii. 46).—The believer's bitterest potions come not from God as a Judge, but as a Father, a Father in gracious covenant relationship.—Holding fast this precious truth, no believer can suffer shipwreck.—" Herein is the faith and patience of the saints."—Love to God and faith in His love inspire submission to all His holy will ordains, and that upon the ground that nothing but good can come from Him.—Christian resignation, therefore, is the opposite to stoicism; it springs from an intelligent trust in the perfect wisdom and love of God, and its cry is, "Though he slay me, yet will I trust in him" (Job xiii. 15).

σου after μάχαιράν omitted. *Cod. Sin.. &c., Tisch.. Treg., Alford, &c.*—ὁ πατήρ, without μου, is the proper reading. *Schaff, Tisch.. Alford, &c.*

---

12. Then the band and the captain and officers of the Jews took Jesus, and bound him.

Band, &c. See on verse 3.—Gr., *then the band and the captain,* *and the officers of the Jews, &c.*—The "band and the captain" were the Roman cohort and their tribune (Mark vi. 21).—The "officers of the Jews" were the Temple servants, and the apparitors of the Sanhedrim.—Both the Jewish guard and the Roman soldiers take Jesus prisoner in concert.—Thus both Jews and Gentiles, representatives of the whole human race, took part in putting the Lord to death.

Bound him. See on Matt. xxvi. 50 ; xxvii. 2, and Luke xxii. 54. —"He before whose aspect and '*I am*,' the whole band had been terrified and cast to the ground, now suffers Himself to be taken, bound, and led away. To apprehend and bind *one*, all gave their help. Only by the aid of all did they feel themselves secure. And thus it was ordered, that the disciples might escape with the more safety. Jesus suffered Himself to be bound, to show thereby the complete surrender of His will, and also in this form of suffering to be our example (Gen. xxii. 9 ; Psa. cv. 18)." *Luthardt.*— Hands so powerful, so beneficent, are bound.—Our love of an unbound liberty had to be atoned for by the bonds of the Son of God (Psa. ii. 3). *Starke.*—Christ seems betrayed, but the kingdom of darkness has betrayed itself ; He seems surprised, but henceforth He stands sovereign in the midst of the camp of the foe ; He seems a captive, but the adversary *is* the captive. *Lange.*

---

13. 14. And led him away to Annas first; for he was father in law to Caiaphas, which was the high priest that same year.—Now Caiaphas was he, which gave counsel to the Jews, that it was expedient that one man should die for the people.

Annas. See on Luke iii. 2.—Annas, appointed high-priest in his thirty-seventh year, A.D. 7, by Quirinus, governor of Syria, was obliged to give way to Ismael, A.D. 14.—After two more changes, Joseph Caiaphas, the son-in-law of Annas, was appointed to the office, and continued till A.D. 37.—Annas seems to have retained the title and part of the power of that office.—In Luke iii. 2, he is mentioned before Caiaphas, and in Acts iv. 5, he is called high-priest.—Some hold that he was high-priest *de jure*, Caiaphas *de facto. Schaff.*—Both were at the head of the Jewish hierarchy ; Caiaphas as actual high-priest, Annas as president of the Sanhedrim. *Wieseler.*—The preliminary leading of Jesus to Annas is recorded by John alone, and is distinct from the formal trial before Caiaphas, narrated in the earlier Gospels.—Highly probable they occupied different departments of the same (official) palace ; hence the sending from one to the other.—" Whether officially, or personally, or both, he was, from the Jewish point of view, a person whose counsel and influence were of the utmost importance, and

to him they bring Jesus for this doctrinal investigation (**verse 19**);
while it is necessary that He should be sent to the legal high-
priest for official trial in the presence of the Sanhedrim (**verse 24**),
before being handed over to the civil power (**verse 28**). It does
not follow that Caiaphas was not present at this investigation;
but it was altogether of an informal character." *Ellicott.*—"For
John the greatest weight attached to the pre-examination by
Annas; for Matthew and Mark to the official chief examination
by Caiaphas; for Luke to the legalizing final examination in the
morning." *Lange.*—What took place before Annas is unknown:
it would seem to have been a secret inquisitional trial, aiming
probably at the ascertainment of secret transgression on Christ's
part.

Same year. See on chap. xi. 49-52.—" The expression relative to
Caiaphas; 'high-priest of that year,' appearing here for the
second time, it would seem that the Evangelist had adopted it as
an ironical characterization, current in the popular mouth, of the
high-priesthood as desecrated by the Romans." *Lange.* (See also
on Matt. ii. 4.)

Now it was, &c. See on chap. xi. 49-52.—John quotes the prophecy, for its fulfilment is at hand.—An intimation of the fate
impending over Jesus at the hands of these men.—It was an evil
omen that He was to be taken before Caiaphas, who had already
doomed Him to death.—Appropriately John informs his readers
that the malignant old Annas was father-in-law to the murderous
Caiaphas.—The sentence of such judges may easily be anticipated.

"Άννας. The narrative evidently rests upon some arrangement with regard to the
High Priesthood now unknown to us, but accountable enough by foreign influence and
the deterioration of the priestly class through bribes and intrigues, to which Josephus
and the Talmud sufficiently testify. *Friedlieb.*

---

15. And Simon Peter followed Jesus, and so did another disciple: that disciple was
known unto the high priest, and went in with Jesus into the palace of the high priest.

Followed. Gr., *And Simon Peter was following Jesus* (see on Matt.
xxvi. 58).

Another disciple. John's modest designation of himself, as in chap.
xx. 2, 3, 4, 8.—At first the disciples all fled, but afterwards, these,
at least, returned.—A trait in the friendship of these two that
they here go voluntarily together.—Peter, as was his wont, takes
the lead; but at the street-door of the court, their relative posi-
tions change.

Known, &c. How he was known we have no means of conjectur-
ing.—It is to be noted, however, that the name "John" occurs
among the names of the kindred of the high-priest in Acts iv. 6.
Ellicott.—The probability of John's acquaintance with the high-
priest is strengthened if we may suppose, from chap. xix. 27, that
he owned a house in Jerusalem. *Tholuck.*

The palace. Gr., *into the court of the high-priest* (see on Matt.
xxvi. 3, 58, 69 ; Luke xx. 54).—It is the same word as that which
is used in chap. **x.** 1, 16, for the sheepfold.—The palace of the
high-priest was probably the dwelling of both Annas and Caiaphas (see on verse 13).—The apparent difficulty is met by the
explanation that Annas was father-in-law to Caiaphas.—"It is a
stroke of John's greatness, that he does not think it necessary to
justify himself in regard to his singular acquaintanceship in the
house of the high-priest." *Lange.*

ὁ ἄλλος. The article is omitted by *A. D., &c.*, but attested by a majority of authorities.—The insertion is more readily accounted for than the omission, and may have
been conformed to xx. 2, 3, 4, 8, where the article occurs.—There is no doubt that no
other than John is meant.—In using this self-designation for the first time, he may have
omitted the article. *Schaff.*—No reason to doubt the universal persuasion that by this
name John intends *himself*, and refers to the mention in chap. xiii. 23 of a disciple
whom Jesus loved. *Alford.*—τὴν αὐλὴν. The *court-yard*, around which an oriental
house was built, a rectangular area in the open-air, connected with the street by a
vestibule (Mark xiv. 68), and *portal* (Matt. xxvi. 71), in which was a wicket. *Schaff.*

---

16. But Peter stood at the door without. Then went out that other disciple, which
was known unto the high priest, and spake unto her that kept the door, and brought
in Peter.

Without. Peter stood at the door of the court, mingling with the
crowd.—Jesus, as a prisoner, had entered the court, and John,
as an acquaintance of the high priest, had gone in also.

Her, &c. Acts xii. 13. That the Jews had *portresses* instead of
porters is shown by Josephus.

Brought, &c. John brought Peter in, not she who kept the door.
—"Peter was burdened with the consciousness of a civil offence
against Malchus : this rendered his condition insecure ; John,
though meaning well, was at fault in not sufficiently entering
into the dangerous state of Peter." *Lange.*—A brother may act
indiscreetly out of pure good will, and only injure another by his
services.—It is one of Satan's traps to smooth our way sometimes
to such places as he would keep us in for his advantage. *Quesnel.*
—Stay away from that place where thou hast nothing to do ; mere

curiosity can readily get thee into danger and misfortune.—Let a man but step out of the way of God, and every step brings him nearer to his fall. *Starke.*—Peter, doubtless, thought it a piece of good fortune, but it was his misfortune ; so things often happen to us in this life.—His following at all was presumptuous, since Jesus had said : *Let them go their way* (see on verse 8).—It was, therefore, a wrong following, entered upon without reflection and in his own strength.—The repairing to mixed companies in the homes of the great is to the weak generally a cause of their falling ; intercourse with unsanctified men ofttimes seduces Christians from the right path. *Heubner.*—Peter should have noticed the difficulties God had put in his way, when left standing without at the door.—"It is of general verity that impediments laid in our way call us to examine it, though it prove not always ill, because impeded, but the Lord thereby would only exercise our dependence and grace." *Hutcheson.*—Satan uses every artifice to render the entrance into temptation easy, and the retreat difficult and hazardous (Prov. vii. 10-23 ; Matt. vii. 13). *Rambach.*

---

17. Then saith the damsel that kept the door unto Peter, Art not thou also one of this man's disciples? He saith, I am not.

Art not? See on chap. xiii. 38, and on Matt. xxvi. 69-75, and Luke xxii. 54-62.—Gr., *Art thou also (one) of the disciples of this man?*—"Thou as well as thy friend, whom I know?"—According to Mark, the girl does not say this until she has fixed her eyes upon Peter ; according to Luke, not until she has examined him by the light.—The question implies that the other disciple had already been recognised as a follower of Jesus, and had escaped annoyance. *Luthardt.*—It would appear as if she had now grown doubtful as to whether she should have let Peter in, or whether she ought not to denounce him. *Lange.*—She does not seem to have inferred the discipleship of Peter from the mere fact alone of his connection with John.

Of this man. A contemptuous way of speaking.—Had they only known that "this man" was the Lord of glory ! (1 Cor. ii. 8).—Some think that John had gone with Jesus into the chamber of examination. *Meyer.*—But this is improbable, though he occupied a position which enabled him to see what was going on in the chamber as well as what passed in the hall. *Lange.*

I am not. On the subject of Peter's denials, see on Matt. xxvi. 69-75, and on Luke xxii. 56-62.—Conscious that he had attempted to kill, and had actually wounded one of the high-priest's servants, he dreads this recognition and instantly denies.—Thus the desire to hide a fault committed often becomes the occasion of greater sins.—Perhaps, however, this first denial was the result of shame, rather than fear. *Alford.*

Mὴ and μήτε, in interrogative sentences, imply a negative answer, the English *not* like the Greek οὐ and the Latin *nonne*, an affirmative answer.—The παιδίσκη (maid-servant) was apprehensive of an affirmative answer and wished politely to anticipate Peter's denial; or the negative form of the question reveals the feeling that she ought not to have admitted John as a disciple of Jesus except for his being an acquaintance of the high-priest. *Schaff.*

18. And the servants and officers stood there, who had made a fire of coals; for it was cold: and they warmed themselves: and Peter stood with them, and warmed himself.

Servants. These were the household servants (slaves) of the high-priest.

Officers. These were the Temple servants (see on verse 3).

Stood there. In the rectangular area, the *court-yard.*

Fire of coals. Gr., *live coal;* the word means *a glowing fire* (Rom. xii. 20).—John alone mentions the material ("charcoal") of which the fire was made, and the reason for a fire, the coldness of the night.

Cold. It was April, and the night was chilly.—How every particular of that memorable night was engraven on John's memory!

Stood. Gr., *was standing.*—The fact of his now *standing,* now *sitting,* seems to testify to the inward disquiet of Peter's mind.

With them. With the enemies of his Master.—He may have got himself among the servants and officers to bear out his denial. *Lücke.*—Or it may have been that he thought to stand aloof would bring further notice upon himself.—The measure of freedom of entrance into such circles is diverse for Christians: 1. Not the same for everyone; 2. Not the same in all moods; 3. Not the same in all external temptations.

Warmed. He *warmed* himself and yet grew all the while *colder.*—We may not seek to grow warm by the fires of the Lord's foes.—While the fire was warming his body the fire of love was smothering in his heart.—"They that warm themselves with evil-doers soon become cold towards good people and good things; and they that are fond of the devil's fireside, are in danger of the devil's fire." *Henry.*—"The conscience of a child of God may be strangely deadened and laid by for a time, by a sin against light, and not become soon tender again; for though he had denied his Master, and the cock had crowed once (as is elsewhere recorded), to give him warning, yet he 'stood with them,' and went not out to mourn. Thus was it with David in the matter of Bathsheba and Uriah ; and in Peter it is especially to be observed that his care and tossing about his own preservation hindered his conscience to do its duty, which testifieth that that care was a snare unto him." *Hutcheson.*

---

19. The high priest then asked Jesus of his disciples, and of his doctrine.

High-priest. Probably this refers to Caiaphas (see on verse 15), though this preliminary investigation was held before Annas, and in his house, or that part of the palace occupied by him. *Ellicott.*—Seems to have been intended to induce Jesus to criminate Himself, that thus they might have something wherewith to accuse Him of before the Sanhedrim. *Alford.*

Disciples. His followers form the first subject of inquiry.—The high-priest wants to find what is to be thought of, or, perchance, feared from, the Lord's followers, hoping from the answers to obtain some colour of charge against Himself.—We may conjecture that the questions had respect to the number of His followers, who they were, and for what purpose collected.

Doctrine. That is, what principles had He taught His followers. —There is plainly the implied charge, that Jesus had founded a *secret* society by means of *secret* doctrines ; this is evident from His answer (see on verse 20).—"The examination before Annas is a type of the ever-recurring plot of hierarchical governments to tax, first, Christianity generally, then Protestantism, and all decidedly evangelical social life with conspiracy, revolution, secret crimes and criminal complots. But as Christ defended Himself against this insinuation by appealing to His public ministry, so the like has been done and may be done by all His true confessors. Here we also have it demonstrated how decidedly Christianity has renounced all the impure, secret machinations of fanatical spirits and sects." *Lange.*—The present Pope, Leo XIII., has just issued an Encyclical (Jan. 1879) in which he solemnly charges upon the Reformation, the Socialism, Communism, Atheism, and other vices, of the age.

---

20. Jesus answered him, I spake openly to the world ; I ever taught in the synagogue, and in the temple, whither the Jews always resort; and in secret have I said nothing.

Openly. "*I* (emphatic) *have spoken frankly,*" *without reserve, plainly.*

—Our Lord does not directly answer the question about His followers, but His words imply that all may have been His disciples.—"I am one who spake plainly and to all men."—Whatever others may have done, My followers have not been initiated into any secret mysteries, nor made members of any political association.

The world. Means in the first place, the Jewish world, and characterises it in respect of the two central-points of publicity : in the synagogues and in the temple. *Lange.*—Publicity was the character of our Lord's life, and it is the character of His religion (Acts xxvi. 26).—"Christianity knows nothing of secret-mongery, mysteries of an order ; it would be entirely public, because it diffuses *the truth*, which is common property of all." *Heubner.*

Resort. Gr., *where all the Jews assemble.*—Our Lord's constant custom was to teach in the synagogue, and when in Jerusalem, in the temple itself.—Thus His teaching could not fail to come under the notice of the officers of the synagogue and the leaders of the people.—Of course, this does not exclude His teaching in other places ; on the mountain, in the field, by the lake.

In secret, &c. There may be allusion to Isaiah xlv. 19 ; xlviii. 16; in the last of which places the Messiah is speaking. *Stier.*—There is no conflict between these words and Matt. x. 27, or with the fact that our Lord taught His disciples in confidential intercourse. —For there was nothing in His teaching, no matter where or when He taught, such as they understood by "secret teaching." —The warnings against the Pharisees in the Sermon on the Mount He Himself publicly repeated in the temple.—What He repudiates is the insinuation of mischievous sectarian or seditious secrecy.—All true Christian ministers can say with Paul, "We have renounced the hidden things of dishonesty, not walking in craftiness" (2 Cor. iv. 1).—And saith the same apostle, "Prove all things ; hold fast that which is good" (1 Thess. v. 21).— See also how he denounces those who "creep into houses," &c. (2 Tim. iii. 6).

The best authorities omit the article τῇ (text. rec.) before συναγωγῇ, very properly; for there are many synagogues, and but one temple. *Schaff.*—The synagogue is spoken of collectively, as a unitous institution ; hence, neither the synagogues in Jerusalem, nor the provincial synagogues, are exclusively referred to. *Lange.*

21. Why askest thou me? ask them which heard me, what I have said unto them: behold, they know what I said.

Why? The emphasis is on the "*Why?*"—As much as to say, "For what purpose dost thou ask Me?"

Ask. If you want to know of My doctrine why not ask those who have heard Me teach?

hey. Gr., *behold, these know what I said.*—He may have indicated by a gesture some who were present (see on chap. vii. 32, 46). —The high-priest had righteously deserved this sharp and severe dealing.—Moreover, it rendered his intention evident; it unmasked and rebuked his hypocrisy.—Our Lord here appears to approve of the principle of our judicature that the accused person shall not be questioned, but that proof of the accusation shall be established by witnesses.

Know. It is the duty of hearers to be able to give an account of what they hear, as they are called to it; for Christ supposeth this of those who had heard Him, though it is to be feared that but few hearers attain to so much. *Hutcheson.*

---

22. And when he had thus spoken, one of the officers which stood by struck Jesus with the palm of his hand, saying, Answerest thou the high priest so?

Struck. From Acts xxiii. 2 it appears that a blow on the face was a customary punishment for a supposed offence against the dignity of the high-priest.—But in that case it was ordered by the high-priest himself, and the fact that it was here done without authority by one of the "officers" confirms the opinion that this was not a legal trial before judicial authority. *Ellicott.*—"This maltreatment of Jesus must be distinguished from that which He experienced on His examination before Caiaphas, subsequently to His condemnation (Matt. xxvi. 37); as, similarly, this last must in its turn be distinguished from the maltreatment narrated by Luke (chap. xxii. 63, 64); although Matt. has summed up in one the two latter acts. The maltreatment recorded by Luke occurred whilst Jesus, after His condemnation before Caiaphas in the night, was retained under arrest until the final examination on the next morning." *Lange.*—The dastardly conduct of this "officer," before the eyes of these spiritual judges, clearly shows what manner of men *they* were.—Wicked rulers never want wicked servants to carry out their designs against those whom they wish to persecute.—With shuddering horror we read of these indignities inflicted upon our Blessed Lord; yet, above all their cruelties and crimes, rises His prayer, "Father, forgive them; for they know not what they do" (Luke xxiii. 34).—And. after His resurrection, when commissioning His apostles to preach repentance and forgiveness of sins in His name, He commanded them *to begin at Jerusalem* (Luke xxiv. 47).—Surely, if *Jerusalem sinners* could be forgiven in *His name*, no penitent need despair!—O love of Christ! inexhaustible and unchangeable as the eternal heart of God.

Palm. The Greek word originally meant a blow from a rod or stick.—It occurs again in the New Test. only in chap. xix. 3, and Mark xiv. 65.—It is uncertain, therefore, whether the blow was given with the hand or with a rod, but the former is more probable.

Answeredst thou? Gr., *Is it thus that Thou answerest the high-priest?*—"The prohibition, Ex. xxii. 28, had been extended into an ordinance instilling a bigoted veneration for superiors, and for the high-priest especially. In the present instance, the officer makes an application of this prohibition, with indiscretion, hypocritical eye-service, and brutality." *Lange.*—Our Lord's answer was regarded as a violation of the priestly dignity; and hence the blow: just as the primitive Christians were always treated as unmannered boors when they frankly confessed the truth. *Gossner.*—Hypocrites attach great importance to outward formalities; yet behind their so-called "grace and good breeding," so much untruth is concealed, that the truth itself becomes tainted and loses its virtue. *Braune.*

ῥάπισμα. They had staves, and perhaps thus used them. *Alford.*

---

23. Jesus answered him, If I have spoken evil, bear witness of the evil: but if well, why smitest thou me?

If. Our Lord's reply fully corresponds to the nature of the situation.—He is a prisoner on trial, and if He has spoken in an improper manner, let it be dealt with as it deserves.—Let the evidence which the law required be brought forward.—It was neither lawful nor right to punish before conviction and sentence.—This reprimand indirectly applied to the high-priest also, who permitted such conduct upon the part of the "officer."—This answer shows how His words, particularly Matt. v. 39 (see Comm.), are in spirit to be interpreted.—"He did not here fulfil *literally* His own precept; He owed to His innocence this answer full of sweetness and dignity." *Godet.*—"He here gives us the best interpretation of Matt. v. 39, that it does not exclude the remonstrating against unjust oppression, provided it be done calr patiently." *Alford.*—" An *angry* man may turn, in sullenness, the other cheek visibly to the smiter ; better is he who makes a true answer with mildness, and prepares his heart in peace to endure greater sufferings." *Augustine.*—"Christ forbids self-defence with the hand (violence), not with the tongue." *Luther.*

---

24. Now Annas had sent him bound unto Caiaphas the high priest.

Now, &c. Better, *Annas therefore sent Him, bound.*—He was still bound, as He had been from verse 12 ; or else Annas had caused the fetters·to be put upon Him again.—The preliminary investigation was at an end, having resulted in the confounding of Annas and his party.—But this had made no impression upon the wicked old man, and so he despatches Jesus to Caiaphas for formal examination.—Forwarding Him *chained* was a speaking sign how he craved to have Him put to death.—As Annas had found it impossible to stamp Jesus as a secret conspirator, recourse is now had to false witnesses (see on Matt. xxvi. 60).

Caiaphas. See on verses 13, 14, and on chap. xi. 49-53.—The distinction between the examination before Annas and that before Caiaphas is obvious.—At the latter they sought to prove that He was a *public blasphemer* against the sanctuary, &c.—The three spiritual examinations wherein Christ stood : the first was unauthorized and private ; the second, with false witnesses ; the third, a mere mockery.—How the world has warped judgment in all forms over the head of Christ, His Gospel, and His people.

οὖν. The omission of οὖν by some MSS. and editors, appears to be exegetical.—The Johannean οὖν, however, is quite characteristic here.—Other exegetical apprehensions of the passage substituted δέ and καὶ.—The pluperfect rendering of ἀπέστειλεν, *had sent* (A.V.) is ungrammatical, inconsistent with οὖν (which for this reason was omitted by some MSS.), and owes its origin to the desire to harmonize John with the Synoptists.—The apparent discrepancy disappears if we assume that Annas and his son-in-law Caiaphas occupied different departments in one and the same official palace, which is intrinsically all the more probable as they in some way shared the high-priestly dignity (see on verse 13). *Schaff.*—John had no need to relate the hearing before Caiaphas, for he has related chap. xi. 47 ff. : and we have ere this been familiarized with the habit of John not to narrate any further the outward process, where he has already by anticipation substantially given us its result. *Luthardt.*

---

25. And Simon Peter stood and warmed himself. They said therefore unto him, Art not thou also one of his disciples? He denied it, and said, I am not.

Stood. Gr., *And Simon Peter was standing and warming himself* (see on verse 18).—The hall for both examinations must therefore have been the same.—Luke speaks only of a house of the high-priest (Luke xxii. 54). *Lange.*—John's object in repeating this was to draw attention to the fact that Peter was standing in the court at the time when Jesus was sent from Annas unto Caiaphas.—The passage would be from one wing of the quadrangular building across the court to the other. *Ellicott.*—Luke records that "the Lord turned and looked upon Peter" (Luke xxii. 61).—"This fire could not impart fresh warmth to Peter's zeal and fidelity to Jesus. If he had warmed himself by God in prayer, he would not have fallen." *Gossner.*—"Such as cast themselves in unwarrantable company, and continue among them, partaking of their accommodations do not readily escape without a soul trial and slip. Men are so much the nearer a fall as they continue among snares and temptations, when the Lord is eminently calling them to their duty, and to mourn for their former failings." *Hutcheson.*

Art not? See on verse 17.—"It may surprise us that John remains unmolested while Peter's temptations are repeated; but the reason of this should be sought less in the timorous embarrassment of Peter than in the boldness with which he stepped in amongst the servants." *Tholuck.*—But an *assumed* boldness is ever a characteristic symptom of fear.

I am not. This is the *second* denial.—Matthew tells us that this took place at the moment when Peter wished to withdraw from the fire in order to approach the entrance hall; from him also we learn that the men questioned him at the instigation of another maid (see on Matt. xxvi. 71; and on Luke xxii. 58).—"As Satan is ready to tempt and assault sliding disciples, so they, being once entered in a course of defection, are ready to persist and go yet further wrong, especially when they are not sensible of their former failings." *Hutcheson.*

---

26. One of the servants of the high priest, being his kinsman whose ear Peter cut off, saith, Did not I see thee in the garden with him?

One, &c. This was about an hour after the former (see on Luke xx. 59).

Kinsman. This man had probably gone with Malchus to the arrest.—He had noticed Peter in the garden, but does not seem to have known that it was he who had dealt the sword-blow.

Did not? &c. He is not to be silenced by a simple denial; for his question is that of one certain he is not deceived.—"John distinctly brings out the increase of danger in the charges. First it is a single maid who does but doubtingly question him. Then

it is the officers around the coal-fire who more decidedly interrogate him. Finally a kinsman of Malchus, whose ear he cut
off, pretends to recognize him, as one whom he had already seen
in the garden with Jesus. While John plainly depicts the intensifications of the temptations, he, in common with Luke, permits the intensifications of Peter's guilt (most vividly portrayed
by Matthew) to recede from view. Matthew, the apostle of the
Jews, and Mark the disciple of Peter, represent the magnitude
of the denial in the most regardless manner; while John and
Luke manifest the greatest clemency, Luke being especially
tender." *Lange.*—In reference to this kinsman of Malchus it may
be noted how God sometimes brings men into the company of
those they would fain never see more; suddenly and unexpectedly
they run into their hands.—"Therefore do thou cut off no person's ear if thou wouldst never be dismayed at the sight of him."
Gossner.

---

27. Peter then denied again: and immediately the cock crew.

Denied again. On the *thrice* repeated denial, see on Matt. xxvi.
75.—"The denial of Peter does not mean that he intended to
renounce Jesus *inwardly*, but that he designed to escape a mortal
peril by means of a so-called white lie. But in the light of
Christ it was a deep fall. The *repentance of Peter* is set forth by
John with sufficient distinctness in the later signs of his conversion. It is remarkable that John seems to have done nothing to
warn Peter. Whether he was not near enough to him, or whether
he entertained too high an opinion of his practical abilities, cannot be determined; at all events he appears unwilling to exalt
himself at his brother disciple's expense in the account which he
gives of the sad transaction." *Lange.*—"Let him that thinketh
he standeth take heed lest he fall" (1 Cor. x. 12).—"As it is
Satan's element to sin and draw others to multiply sin after sin,
so saints especially may expect that when they slip they will be
most of any incessantly pursued to add sin after sin; it being the
devil's delight to engage them especially in sin against God,
and by the throng of temptations to keep them from recovering their feet; therefore thus doth he pursue Peter the *third*
time." *Hutcheson.*

Crew. Gr., *a cock crew* (see on Matt. xxvi. 74, and on Luke xxii.
60).—Mark alone has recorded the *first* cock-crow after the *first*
denial (Mark xiv. 68).—That warning also involved an aggravation of Peter's guilt passed over by John.—Neither does John

mention Peter's attempt to withdraw, an attempt which presents him in a condition of utter, helpless perplexity.—How true it is that even the meanest creature, if it be God's will to use it as His instrument, may become a means of arousing the conscience of the sinner.—The first crowing of the cock made no impression, but the third, accompanied by the *look of Jesus,* pierced the heart of the fallen disciple.—" In the kingdom of God a defeat may bring more blessings than a victory; and more costly fruits often spring from stumbling than from the most apparently successful strivings after holiness. But woe unto him whom this truth would render reckless." *Krummacher.*—(Upon the law of the Association of Ideas or Suggestion, as illustrated in Peter's case, see on the account in Matthew.)

---

28. Then led they Jesus from Caiaphas unto the hall of judgment : and it was early ; and they themselves went not into the judgment hall, lest they should be defiled; but that they might eat the passover.

Led. Gr., *They, therefore, lead.*—As this refers to verse 24, the *" therefore "* is here very expressive ; it means that with the fact of Annas sending Jesus *bound* to Caiaphas, everything further, even to the leading Him into the heathen Prætorium, was decided. *Lange.*

Hall. Gr., *the Prœtorium* (see on Matt. xxvii. 27).—The translators have given various renderings of this word : here, " hall of judgment," or " Pilate's house," and " judgment hall; " in verse 33, " hall of judgment," without the marginal alternative ; in chap. xix. 9, " judgment hall; " in Matt. xxvii. 27, " common hall," or " governor's house ; " in Mark xv. 6, " prætorium " (the original word Anglicised) ; in Acts xxiv. 10, " judgment hall; " in Phil. i. 13, " palace." *Ellicott.*—The Prætorium was originally the tent of the general in the Roman camp ; here it is the governor's residence.

Early. In the fourth night watch, towards the break of day ; between cock-crowing and sunrise, about from three to six o'clock.—As Pilate had sent the band (verse 4), it is reasonable to believe he was expecting their return with Jesus as a prisoner

Went not, &c. The Jews present would not go into the heathen Prætorium, but sent Jesus in under the Roman guard.

Defiled. For a Jew to enter into the house of a Gentile was to be ceremonially unclean till the close (sunset) of that day.—This was not their only motive, though they hypocritically took cover under it as if it were —" If Pilate tried Jesus' cause *within* the palace, the Sanhedrists would lack the aid of the popular faction which

1274 / Gospel of John

they had driven together, and upon which they could securely
count *outside*, in front of the palace." *Lange.*—These men feared
being "defiled" by the judgment hall of a heathen governor,
but they feared not to murder an innocent brother.—They would
keep the legal Passover holy, but they would kill the Holy One
of God!—Extreme devotion to ritual combined with the most
atrocious wickedness, often repeated since.

Passover. See on chap. ii. 13.—That is, to observe or carry out
the eating of the passover: specific terms for a more general procedure grow into use everywhere in the ritual sphere. *Lange.* (See
note, and see on Matt. xxvi. 17-19.)

φάγωσιν τὸ πάσχα. In reference to the apparent conflict between the statements of
the Synoptists and John as to the time of our Lord's last passover, the following explanations have been propounded: 1. The term "passover" sometimes comprises the *whole
paschal festival*, or the feast of unleavened bread which began with the passover
proper; therefore, the expression "to eat the passover" may mean "to keep the
paschal festival"; and the "preparation of the passover," John xix. 14, denotes simply
the customary "preparation" *for the Sabbath*, which occurred in that paschal week.
*Andrews, Davidson, Fairbairn, Hengst., Lewin, Lange, Milligan, Lightfoot, Robinson,
Stier, Tholuck, Olsh., Wieseler, &c.*—2. The Lord and His disciples *anticipated* the passover by one day, partaking of a substitute upon the thirteenth of Nisan.—There were
probably two distinct days, both legal (one *real*, the other *apparent* time) for keeping
the passover; or the Jews may have fallen behind a day in the computation, and our
Lord corrected their error; or at this time they purposely delayed a day. *Alford.
Bleek. De Wette, Ebrard, Ellicott, Ewald, Lücke, Meyer, Tisch., Winer, &c.*—The former
explanation appears the more satisfactory. *Author.*—The critical and careful *Robinson* states his conclusion on this vexed question as follows ("Harmony," p. 222): "After
repeated and calm consideration, there rests upon my own mind a clear conviction,
that there is nothing in the language of John, or in the attendant circumstances, which
upon fair interpretation requires or permits us to believe, that the beloved disciple
either intended to correct, or has in fact corrected or contradicted, the explicit and
unquestionable testimony of Matthew, Mark, and Luke."

---

29. Pilate then went out unto them, and said, What accusation bring ye against
this man?

Pilate. See on Matt. xxvii. 2, and on Luke xxiii. 1, 52.—He was
the sixth Roman *procurator* of Judæa, and held the office for ten
years during the reign of Tiberias.—By many supplementary
touches John presents us with the clearest view of the *secular
trial* of Jesus before Pilate.—He distinctly brings out the gradation of the Jews' accusation: 1. They charge Jesus with being
an ecclesiastical criminal, already condemned by them, whose
sentence Pilate has but to confirm; 2. In the most ambiguous
sense, with making Himself the King of the Jews; 3. With
being a blasphemer, because He had made Himself the Son of
God; 4. With being a political revolutionist, because He claimed
to be their king.—These form two accusations, a Jewish one and

a Roman one.—John also brings to light the conflict maintained between Pilate and the high-priests throughout the entire procedure.—He has, however, passed over, together with minor features, the trial in the morning (Matt. xxvii. 1); the dream of Pilate's wife (Matt. xxvii. 19); Pilate's washing of his hands, and the self-execration of the Jews (Matt. xxvii. 24, 25); the reed (Matt. xxvii. 29); and the bespitting on the part of the soldiers (Matt. xxvii. 30).—Similarly, the sending of Jesus to Herod, and the resultant friendship of Herod and Pilate (Luke xxiii. 6-12); finally, the notice that Barabbas had perpetrated a sedition in the city (Mark, Luke). *Lange.*

Then. Gr., *Pilate, therefore, went out unto them.*—As he must pay some respect to the Jewish customs, he comes forth to meet them.

Accusation. Whatever knowledge Pilate might have of their charges against Jesus, he must call upon them formally to state them.—It is evident they imagined that he would immediately order the execution of Jesus.—But, as the *Roman governor,* he was bound to know what crime Jesus has committed against *Roman law.*—So shrewd a man also would observe that in coming to him in a pompous procession they intended to overawe him, the better to gain their end, and his demand was aimed at thwarting their design.

---

30. They answered and said unto him, If he were not a malefactor, we would not have delivered him up unto thee.

If, &c. They bring no legal charge against Jesus; they only assert that they had condemned Him to death and assume that this ought to be sufficient warrant for Pilate to order His execution.—True, they call him a "malefactor," yet in the trial before Caiaphas no attempt had been made to shew that He had committed any evil deed.—They hope to obtain by their number and clamour the ratification of their sentence, for they were sensible how difficult it would be to make the false accusation, charging Jesus with a political crime, good before Pilate, and they knew that he would not condemn to death merely on the charge of religious or ecclesiastical offences.—Pilate, therefore, is asked blindly to order Jesus to death upon *their sentence.*

We. Though they were seeking to murder the innocent, yet, forsooth, it must be right because *they* have decided upon it!—*They,* the great officials and rulers of the Jewish Church, have determined to slay the Son of God, *therefore* He ought to be put to death without inquiry or delay!

Delivered, &c. This was a sort of flattery intended as compensation for their illegal demand.—As much as to say : If we come before thy tribunal, that is an honour for thee, in return for which thou surely canst do us the honour to recognise our sentence without further ceremony. *Lange.*—Thus Israel delivers up its Messiah, its King, the sum of all the promises, to the Gentiles to be put to death as a malefactor.

---

31. Then said Pilate unto them, Take ye him, and judge him according to your law. The Jews therefore said unto him, It is not lawful for us to put any man to death.

Take. Pilate proceeds upon their own word : they claim the right to condemn this man ; let them exercise it.

Ye. Gr., *then take Him yourselves:* If He is to be treated as a criminal upon *your* sentence then deal with Him according to *your* law.—As they will have it, that it was within *their* power to condemn, Pilate casts upon *them* the responsibility as to what may follow.—*He*, as the Roman governor, can only execute a sentence pronounced by *himself*, and that only after a formal trial.—He meets their fanatical presumption with frigid sarcasm.

Judge. The word denotes judicial proceedings in general, inclusive of punishment, but to be regulated by their law and right.

The Jews therefore. The "therefore" indicates that Judaism must now come out openly. *Lange.*

Not lawful, &c. They are compelled to confess that they had no power to put Jesus to death, though they claimed the right to sentence Him.—Pilate must be the executioner of their murderous designs, for under the dominion of the Romans the Jews had lost the power of life and death.—The Talmud says this took place forty years before the destruction of Jerusalem. *Lightfoot.*—It was so from the time Archelaus was deposed, and Judæa became a Roman province (A.D. 6 or 7).—Disciplinary punishment pushed to the verge of capital punishment; and proposal for capital punishment, still remained in the power of the Sanhedrim.—If the Roman governor confirmed their sentence they could *stone to death*, according to Jewish custom.—If the Roman governor took cognizance of the case and pronounced the sentence, the criminal was executed according to Roman custom, or, if extreme punishment was resorted to, crucified.—Consequently, the stoning of Stephen was an illegal act ; as also the execution of James, according to Josephus.—Now, from all appearance, there was the prospect of Christ being *stoned:* But this was not so to be, as John explains in the next verse.—"The Lord hath a

supreme hand and providence in the least things which concern
Christ and His followers, and especially in their sufferings; for
that they want power, and He is left in Pilate's hand, there was
a providence in it." *Hutcheson.*

---

32. That the saying of Jesus might be fulfilled, which he spake, signifying what
death he should die.

Saying. See on chap. iii. 14; xii. 32; and Matt. xx. 19, where
Christ foretold His crucifixion.

What death. Gr., *signifying by what manner of death He should die.*
—Had the Jews possessed the power of life and death they
would have stoned Him, according to their law against false
prophets and blasphemers (see on chap. viii. 59; x. 31).—
"Crucifixion was not a Jewish punishment, and it was in the fact
that He was executed, not by Jewish authority and on the charge
of blasphemy, but by Roman authority and on a charge of high
treason, that His own prophecy of the manner of His death was
fulfilled." *Ellicott.*—Jesus, on account of His Messianic claims,
must have appeared to Pilate as a rebel; for crucifixion, the most
cruel and disgraceful kind of death, was not inflicted on Roman
citizens; only on the lowest criminals.—This whole section, from
verse 28 to 32, shows how the purpose of God was accomplished.—
"1. Christ is a faithful keeper of His word, and will not fail to
see that performed which He speaks therein; 2. Christ is the true
Messiah, as being sent into the world, when now the sceptre was
departed from Judah, according to the prophecy (Gen. xlix. 10);
for He foretold this death, and His delivering to the Gentiles to
be crucified, when the Jews wanted power, as here they confess;
3. Christ would be put to a most cursed, ignominious and painful death, that He might testify His love to His own; 4. Christ
also, by His posture in this death, being lifted up with His arms
stretched out upon the Cross, would invite all His people to look
and come to Him who stands with open arms ready to receive
them, and make them partakers of His purchase." *Hutcheson.*

---

33. Then Pilate entered into the judgment hall again, and called Jesus, and said
unto him, Art thou the King of the Jews?

Then. Gr., *Pilate therefore entered into the Prætorium again, and
called Jesus.*—This must have been a private interview, so far as
the Jews were concerned (see on verse 28).

Art thou? Pilate knew of the accusation made against Jesus

when he permitted the Roman band to arrest Him.—The question
need not necessarily be regarded as prompted by mere derision
and scorn.—Pilate may have thought : If His only offence is one
of words, He may repudiate those words ; on the other hand, If
He is a dangerous fanatic, He will be forward to assert His
claims.—Doubtless, however, there was a concealed sarcasm in
the question : *Art thou a King?* thou a poor man, without rank,
or money, or arms, or followers ? *Thou* a King?

Of the Jews. The charge the Sanhedrim preferred against Jesus,
that He claimed to be King of the Jews, was forged out of the
avowal of His Messiahship.—It was a charge based on falsehood,
since He had no intention of becoming a political leader ; and it
was also treason against their national Messianic hope, which
they now abandon (see on verse 36).

---

34. Jesus answered him, Sayest thou this thing of thyself, or did others tell it thee
of me?

Sayest ? We cannot suppose, with Meyer, that our Lord's object
was simply to know the real author of the charge.—" Christ did
not ask for information, which He did not need, but to bring out
the distinction in the mind of Pilate, who seems to have suspected
that Jesus was really what He was charged with being." *Schaff.*
—By the phrase " King of the Jews " Pilate could understand
nothing but a political seditionary urged by fanatical motives.—
The Jewish party knew this; but they also knew that Jesus
claimed the Messiahship in another sense, and they now made use
of the Messianic name to give colour to the false accusation.—
Jesus could not acknowledge the Messianic conception of Pilate,
but neither could He disown the true Messianic conception; hence
this distinction was to be made thoroughly clear.—Our Lord's
object, therefore, was to bring out the sense in which Pilate put
the question : *whether in a Gentile-political,* or a *Jewish-theo-
cratical sense. Lange, Godet, Alford, &c.*—In the political sense,
the only sense in which the claim could be brought against Him
in Roman law, Jesus was not King of the Jews.—In the theocratic
ense, the sense in which a Jew would use that title, He was
deed the King of the Jews.—" It was necessary for Pilate to see
at they were trying to deceive him by means of a perfidiously
terpreted religious idea. And thus in the Middle Ages and in
time of the Reformation (even down to the present day)
Hierarchs have, with evil consciousness, stamped reformation
revolution." *Lange.*

35. Pilate answered, Am I a Jew? Thine own nation and the chief priests have delivered thee unto me: what hast thou done?

Am I a Jew? " You surely do not suppose that *I* am a *Jew?* "— The Roman pride of Pilate takes fire at the bare possibility of such a thought.—He was the governor of the Jews, and neither knew of nor cared for their questions and distinctions.—He held it, therefore, absurd to suppose that *he* would put the question in the Jewish sense.—Proudly and indignantly he repudiates all connection with Jewish expectations and views, which he despises as wild fanaticism.

Own nation. Probably said with a sneer, Jewish nationality not standing for much in Pilate's estimation.

Chief priests. Pilate means that his question (verse 33) was based upon the accusations of the Sanhedrists.

What? Become impatient, Pilate asks the definite question, *What hast Thou done?*—Here the genuine Roman character appears.— Evidently he surmises there is something yet to be explained.

---

36. Jesus answered, My kingdom is not of this world: if my kingdom were of this world, then would my servants fight, that I should not be delivered to the Jews: but now is my kingdom not from hence.

My kingdom. Manifestly this answer was contemplated from the very beginning, in the question of Jesus (verse 34), and introduced by that question.—Jesus acknowledges He *has* a kingdom, and then for Pilate's satisfaction affirms that it " is not of this world."—" Not only hath Christ, as God, a universal kingdom of power and providence, even over the highest of men (Dan. ii. 21; 1 Tim. vi. 15; Prov. viii. 15, 16), but, as Mediator, He hath a donative Kingdom in and over His Church, to the preservation and propagation whereof His Kingdom of power is subservient (Matt. xxviii. 18, 19); for so is here imported, that even in His state of humiliation He hath a Kingdom." *Hutcheson.*—" Christ's Kingdom twines its blessing around all kingdoms, all circumstances; it is the flying bee, clinging with quiet diligence to the fast-fading flowers and their perishable glory, that it may extract honey from them for its kingdom of the future, creating, meanwhile, not the slightest disturbance in the garden of the world. But it is likewise the great power that in all the migrations of nations, in great wars, and the ruins of the kingdoms of the world, proves itself active in advancing the eternal kingdom of peace." *Braune.*—Christ is a King: we are, therefore, not in error who wear His uniform, and have trusted our life and destiny to His hands (see on Matt. ii. 2, 11)

Not of this world. The Greek preposition (ἐκ) relates to *origin and nature.*—"It *is not of this world* as to its principle; it lays, therefore, in respect of its tendency, no claims to this world, and does not, in respect of its character, come into collision with the existent secular empire of the Romans." *Lange.*—In the sense in which Rome claimed to rule the world, He had no kingdom.—He is not a king in the political sense; He is a king in the spiritual sense (see on verse 37).—His answer brings out clearly the distinction between the purely theocratic idea and the purely political.—Yet His kingdom, though not *of* this world, is yet *in* this world and *over* this world.—"He does not say that His kingdom makes no claim eventually to the dominion of the whole world; He only asserts that His government was not of *this* world, and clearly intimates by laying the emphasis on ' *this*,' that another æon than the present would certainly see His delegates seated on the thrones, and His word and Gospel the Magna Charta of all nations. The word ' *now* ' evidently refers to a period in which His kingdom should occupy a position very different from what it did at that time." *Krummacher.*—" His kingdom makes the kingdoms of the world subject unto itself, in order to abolish and absorb the entire old form of the world in the kingdom of heaven." *Olshausen.*—" His words not only deny, they affirm : if not of this world, then *of another world;* He asserts this other world before the representatives of those who boasted of their ' orbis terrarum.' " *Alford.*—1. Its rise is *not from this world:* it is not by succession, election, or conquest, but by the immediate and special designation of the divine will and counsel ; 2. Its nature is not worldly : it is a kingdom within men ; 3. Its guards and supports are not worldly : its weapons are spiritual ; 4. Its tendency and design are not worldly ; 5. Its subjects, though they are *in* the world, yet are not *of* the world. *Henry.*

If, &c. Proof that His kingdom is not *of* this world : "If it *were,* I should have fighters after the manner of such kingdoms, who would prevent the surrender of My person to the Jews."

My servants. Gr., *then would My servants have been fighting.*—His *disciples* (chap. xii. 26 ; 1 Cor. iv. 1 ; 1 Tim. iv. 6), who are themselves not *of* this world (see on chap. xvii. 16), though *in* this world. *Meyer.*—His disciples would be in this relation to Him if He were a temporal king, and the crowds such as those who had sought to make Him king (see on chap. vi. 15) and had filled Jerusalem with the cry, "Hosanna " (see on chap. xii. 13). *Ellicott.*

Delivered. The fact that His servants had made no attempt to deliver Him must have been to Pilate a striking proof of His innocence.—If they would not fight to prevent their King being given up to His enemies, much less would they use force for the establishment of His kingdom.—One of them had drawn the sword (see on verse 10), but Jesus had instantly reprimanded him for so doing, and commanded him to return the sword into the sheath.—Had Jesus chosen to stir up the popular feeling, neither the Roman band nor the Jewish officers could have arrested Him.

Not from hence. This was proved by His standing there *bound, a prisoner*, in the presence of the Roman governor.—Had His kingdom been destined to be a worldly kingdom, it would have taken its rise at that very point in the crisis of the sufferings of the cross. *Lange.*—Christ's words are both a defence and an accusation.—His kingdom in its heavenliness and spiritualness : 1. How it differs from the kingdoms of the Romans ; 2. How it differs from the government of the Priests.—The " MY " which occurs *four* times in this one verse, *thrice* of His *kingdom*, and *once* of His *servants*, is put in the emphatic form.

ὑπηρέται. The servants that I *have ;* angels. *Stier.*—Angels and disciples. *Luthardt, Lampe.*—The servants, followers, that I then *should* have. *Tholuck, Hengst., Alford.*—The disciples. *Meyer, Lange, Schaff, Ellicott, &c.*—νῦν. Has been absurdly pressed by the Romanist interpreters to mean that at some time His kingdom would be ἐντεῦθεν—*i.e.,* ἐκ τοῦ κόσμου τούτου—as if its essential character could ever be changed.—νῦν implies, "as the case now stands"; a demonstratio ad oculos from the fact that no servants of His had contended or were contending in His behalf. *Alford.*

---

37. Pilate therefore said unto him, Art thou a king then? Jesus answered, Thou sayest that I am a king. To this end was I born and for this cause came I into the world, that I should bear witness unto the truth. Every one that is of the truth heareth my voice.

Art thou? " So, then, *Thou* art a king ? " Pilate asks more out of curiosity, and with the attention of an inquisitor, than with any mocking designs. *Tholuck.*—The words are both a question and an inference.—Our Lord had spoken of His "kingdom," and Pilate asks, not without sarcasm, "Does it not follow then that *Thou* art a king ?"—" Not that Pilate had any fear of His kingdom, but to try if He would adhere to such a ridiculous-like profession, which might expose Him to mockery and contempt." *Hutcheson.*

Thou sayest. See on Matt. xxvi. 25.—" *Thou sayest what is true;*

for I am a king." *Meyer.*—"So *Thou* art a king?" questions Pilate with ironical emphasis. "Thou sayest; for *I* am a king," answers Jesus, with the accent of sublime self-assurance.—He acknowledges the correctness of Pilate's deduction.—"From 'My kingdom' thou rightly inferrest My kingly dignity."—The Royal confession of Christ: A king am I.—The *good confession* which our Lord Jesus witnessed before Pontius Pilate (1 Tim. vi. 13).

To this end, &c. Gr., *Unto this end have I been born, and unto this end have I come into the world.*—"To be a king have I been born, and to be a king came I into the world, in order that I may bear witness unto the truth." *Ellicott.*—He affirms that He was *born* a king, and that He was born with a definite purpose.—A pregnant proof of an Incarnation of the Son of God.—This is still further expressed in the words, "I have come into the world."—"I'was *born*, but not therein commenced my being: I *came into* the world." *Alford.* (See on chap. viii. 58; xvi. 28.)

Bear witness. See on chap. i. 8.—Christ is "the faithful and true Witness" (2 Cor. i. 20; Rev. iii. 14; see on Matt. v. 18).—He came to be a witness (a martyr) to the truth, and to send forth others to be witnesses and martyrs to the same truth.—He says to His Church, "Ye are my witnesses" (Isa. xliii. 10).

The truth. See on chap. xvii. 17, 19.—Not "the truth," so that what He said should be *true*, but to THE TRUTH. in its objective reality.—"Our Lord here preached the Truth of His mission, upholding that side of it best calculated for the doubting philosophic mind of the day, of which Pilate was a partaker. He declares the unity and objectivity of Truth; and that Truth must come from above, and must come through a Person sent by God, and that that Person was Himself. The Lord sets forth here in the depth of these words the very idea of all kinghood. The *King* is the representative of the truth: the truth of dealing between man and man; the truth of that power, which in its inmost truth belongs to the great and only Potentate, the King of kings. Again, the Lord, the King of manhood and the world, the second Adam, came to testify to the *truth* of manhood and the world, which sin and Satan had concealed. This testimony to the Truth is to be the weapon whereby His kingdom will be spread." *Alford.* —Christ was *born* such a king; in Him person and office are one. —"His kingdom is founded upon truth, God's promises; it is erected by truth, testimony concerning them; it is enjoyed in truth, obedience towards them; truth is universally disseminated by it." *Braune.*

Of the truth. See on chap. iii. 21; vi. 44; viii. 47.—Having witnessed as to His Kingdom. He now witnesses as to His subjects.

—These include every one who has an ear to hear the voice of truth, and a heart that owns its power.—" *Of the truth* " betokens an inward preparation for the reception of the Gospel which is the work of the Holy Spirit (see on chap. xvi. 8-11).

Heareth, &c. See on chap. x. 5, 27.—" Why does He say this to Pilate? Manifestly He marks the moment in which Pilate is confronted with salvation, and the form under which salvation advances towards him. It is the form in which He is able to preach the Gospel to this man in this position. If thou art of the truth, if the impulse of truth is the vital impulse that influenceth thee, thou wilt know Me, and thou art saved." *Lange.*
—There are minds that ring loud and clear when the truth touches them ; they are *of the truth.*—As it is the conscience, the sense of truth, that is operated upon to draw men into Christ's kingdom, that kingdom must be from God.—The *fitness* of the Gospel to the soul of man clearly reveals the divine origin of the Gospel.—He who gave the soul its faculties, susceptibilities and laws, speaks to it in His word, and the soul responds to that voice.
—The voice of Christ is the voice of " truth unto a knowledge of the Father, truth unto an assurance of the forgiveness of sins, truth unto everlasting comfort through grace, truth unto strength in all holy conversation and godliness." *Rieger.*—How strikingly were these words of our Lord illustrated during His ministry!
—" The royal Kingdom of Truth : 1. The Kingdom of the King : Truth in its profoundest essence, as a revelation of God ; in its highest power, as the Gospel ; in its broadest extent, as the uniting bond of all life ; in its bodily appearance, as the Person of Christ. 2. The King of the Kingdom : Christ, personal Truth itself, as the light-centre of all life, thoroughly at one with itself, and therefore the Light of the world. 3. The title of the King : Perfect agreement of His birth and His office ; His ideal and His historical vocation. 4. His government : The faithful Witness, with His testimony ; the Host-leader of all faithful witnesses. 5. Increase of the Kingdom : The Word received as His voice by all who are of the truth." *Lange.*

σὺ λέγεις. A formula neither classical nor found in the Sept., but frequent in the Rabbinical writings. *Schöttgen.*—It seems best to punctuate at λέγεις, and regard ὅτι as the reason for the affirmation. *Alford, Lange, Schaff.*—ἀκούει. Our Lord designs explaining to Pilate why He finds so few adherents. *Calvin.*—He is appealing to the Roman consciousness, which is more susceptible than that of a Caiaphas. *Chrys.*—Provocat a caecitate Pilati ad captum fidelium. *Bengel.*

38. Pilate saith unto him, What is truth? And when he had said this, he went out again unto the Jews, and saith unto them, I find in him no fault at all.

What? Unhappily Pilate did not belong to the class which Jesus had just spoken of.—He was not *of* the truth, and had no ear for its voice.—His celebrated question reveals indifferentism rather than scepticism.—" It expresses, not without scoff and irony, that truth can never be found: and is an apt representative of the state of the polite Gentile mind at the time of our Lord's coming. It was rather an inability than an unwillingness to find the truth. It was no real question, any more than any other, behind which a negation lies hid." *Alford.*

When, &c. " ' What is truth ? ' said jesting Pilate, and would not wait for an answer." *Bacon.*—John plainly intimates what the question was worth by recording that Pilate turned about, as soon as he had uttered the words, and went out.—No pause, no waiting for a reply is even hinted at.—The instant the word was spoken he wheeled around upon his heel to go out and speak to the Jews.—Pilate's question might have led to his *salvation*, if he had spoken inquiringly and submitted himself to the answer.—But it became the *judgment* of his life because he spoke it triflingly and scornfully, desiring no answer.—His end corresponded to the state of mind he manifested upon this occasion ; in adversity, having no faith to sustain, he committed suicide (see on Matt. xxvii. 24 ; Luke xxiii. 1).—" The light-minded worldliness and dull scepticism of so-called culture lead to a despair of truth." *Braune.*—Pilate's question is often heard in the present day : but in most cases it is the expression of the superficial, hopeless unbelief of men, whose god is the world.—Like many others, the Roman governor thought *tru'h* a poor thing to help a man up in life.—" The world shrugs its shoulders, saying : 'Truth ? Bah ! one can't be so particular.' " *Gossner.*—This question may be considered according to its divine meaning : 1. As the sneering exclamation of the impious scoffer ; 2. As the mere declaration of a frivolous worldling ; 3. As the doubting question of an earnest investigator ; 4. As the vital question of a longing heart. *Lange.*—" Christ and His followers may seem ofttimes great fools in their sufferings, as suffering for things of no moment in the esteem of men, who, as the Lord ofttimes draweth the controversy for which the godly suffer to a very small hair and point of truth, so they account it great folly for men to suffer for any divine truth ; for so much doth Pilate's question import." *Hutcheson.*

No fault. On the perfect sinlessness of Jesus, see on Matt. i. 18,

20, 23.—Gr., *I find no crime in Him.*—" *I*," emphatically : opposed
to "*ye*," who had found fault in Him.—" I find no ground for the
legal charge (verse 33). Whatever He may be, there is no proof
of treason against the majesty of Cæsar." *Ellicott.*—Pilate seems
to have taken Jesus to be a good-natured but guiltless, perhaps
rather tiresome, fanatic.—But notwithstanding this declaration,
he was soon after entangled fatally in the net of a wretched
policy.—Here follows the sending of Jesus to Herod Antipas,
recorded by Luke (see on Luke xxiii. 12).—" Pilate mocks both,
the Witness of the Truth and the haters of the Truth. His
conduct presents a pitiable specimen of the moral weakness of
that spirit of worldly power, which reached its culminating point
in the Roman empire." *Alford.*—Pilate, like Judas, was compelled to acknowledge the innocency of Jesus (see on Matt.
xxvii. 4).

Tί. Probably Pilate thought that Jesus professed only to add one more to the list of
philosophies, or systems of ideas, and turned away from it in sickness of heart. *Grant.*
—He has evidently no suspicion of subjective vital truth, and he understands, by
truth, merely an objective school problem about which a practical man of business
need not puzzle his wits. *Lange.*—αἰτίαν. John uses this word only in this place.—It
is used by Matt. (xxvii. 37) for the technical "accusation written, This is Jesus, the
King of the Jews," and this seems to be the sense here. *Ellicott.*—The word means,
in a forensic sense, *an accusation of crime, a charge. Robinson* —At this place comes in
Matt. xxvi. 12-14; the repeated accusation of Jesus by the chief priests and elders, to
which He answered nothing ; and Luke xxiii. 5-17, the sending to Herod, and second
proclamation of His innocence by Pilate, after which he adopts this method (verse 39)
of procuring His release (Luke xxiii. 17). *Alford.*

39. But ye have a custom, that I should release unto you one at the passover : will
ye therefore that I release unto you the King of the Jews?

A custom. See on Matt. xxvii. 15 ; Luke xxiii. 17.—Supposed to
have arisen from the paschal feast having been regarded as a time
for reconciliation. *Tholuck.*—More probably a kind of dramatic
Easter play, intended, perhaps, to illustrate the sparing of the
Jewish first-born. *Lange.*

Will ye? Pilate thinks to outwit the Jews, but they outwit him.
—He ought simply to have administered justice, and this would
have compelled the release of Jesus.—Instead of this, he proposes to concede to them the power to release Him themselves, in
consideration of their custom.—The consequence of this half-

measure is ruinous to Pilate.—With the first deviation from rectitude, a man enters upon the road to calamity.

The king, &c. The mockery, implied in these words, is not at Jesus, but at the Jews.—" This is your king; such is your national subjection, that your king is bound, my prisoner : Shall I release this king?" *Ellicott.*

---

40. Then cried they all again, saying, Not this man, but Barabbas. Now Barabbas was a robber.

Again. John, though he has not mentioned any clamour before, evidently implies that recorded in Mark xv. 8, and in Luke xxiii. 5-10.—They cried this time, and that *en masse* or with one voice.

Barabbas. See on Matt. xxvii. 16, and on Luke xxiii. 18.—Probably was the son of a Rabbi, as Abba was a Rabbinic title of honour. *Ewald.*—Appears to have been a leader in the insurrection (Mark xv. 7) against Pilate, arising out of his misappropriation of a part of the Temple revenues to the construction of an aqueduct. *Josephus.*—This may explain the eagerness with which the Sanhedrim and the people demanded his release.—According to Matthew, Pilate placed Barabbas beside Jesus and bade the people choose, hoping thus to make the release of Jesus more sure (chap. xxvii. 21, 26).—" Pilate stands as a warning example of the consequence of endeavouring to satisfy God and the world. We meet with Pilate under various forms; many a one has placed himself, like him, in a situation in which he must either set Barabbas free, or give up the Saviour, because he was deficient in courage to brave every danger for Christ's sake. Many reckoning, like Pilate, on the instinctive moral feelings of the multitude, with whom they do not wish to be at variance, have cowardly asked, ' Which will you choose, right or wrong?' and the unexpected reply has been thundered back, ' We choose rebellion and treason.'" *Krummacher.*—" ' *Not this man:* ' Thus was Jesus the goat upon which the Lord's lot fell, to be offered for a sin-offering." *Luthardt.*—(See more fully on Matt. xxvii. 16.)

Robber. See on chap. x. 1.—The word implies unrestrained violence, which often leads to murder.—There is a solemn irony in the words of John—a *Robber !*

> " Thou who condemnest Jewish hate,
> For choosing Barabbas, a murderer,

Before the Lord of glory ;
Look back upon thine own estate,
Call home thine eye (that busy wanderer)—
That choice may be thy story." *Herbert.*

" Sin is *a robber*, every base lust is *a robber*, and yet foolishly chosen rather than Christ, who would truly enrich us." *Henry.*

" Every sinful action is an open rejecting of our Lord and Master, and a preferring of some vile Barabbas to Him (Josh. xxiv. 15; Psa. lxxiii. 24, 25 ; xliv. 20, 21.)" *Hare.*

παντες. Omitted. *Cod. Sin.*, *Tisch.*, *Westcott and Hort.*—Retained. *Lange*, *Alford.*

John 19

1. Then Pilate therefore took Jesus, and scourged him.

Therefore. The connection and force of "therefore," not shown
by John, is explained in Luke xxiii. 21, 23.—John omits the
sending of Jesus to Herod, and the hand-washing of Pilate
which belong here.

Scourged. See on Matt. xxvii. 26.—The Roman mode of scourging
is here meant, which was much more cruel than the Jewish.—
It was never inflicted upon Roman citizens, but only upon
foreigners and slaves, either to extort a confession or as preparatory to crucifixion.—The body was stripped, tied in a stooping
posture to a low block or pillar, and the bare back lacerated by an
unlimited number of lashes with rods or twisted thongs of leather,
so that the poor sufferers frequently fainted and died on the spot.
(See note).—By subjecting Jesus to this disgraceful and horrible
punishment, Pilate hoped to satisfy the vindictiveness of the Jews,
perhaps even to excite their compassion.—And this all the more,
since, according to his ideas, Jesus, by this ignominious treatment,
would be stripped of all dignity in the eyes of the people and His
influence destroyed.—By this, Pilate intended to avert the crucifixion of Jesus ; but, instead of that, it was the beginning of His
crucial sufferings.—Pilate having surrendered *truth* first (see on
chap. xviii. 38), afterwards surrenders *justice.*—Why inflict *scourging*
upon one whom he had already pronounced *innocent ?*—" As his
official administration is without consistency, his justice without
any foundation of truth, his wit without wisdom, so his humanity
is destitute of the fear of God, of strength, and of blessing."
Lange.—This pain and shame Christ submitted to *for our sakes :*
1. That the Scriptures might be fulfilled (Isa. liii. 5, &c.) ; 2. That
by His stripes we might be healed (1 Pet. ii. 24) ; 3. That stripes,
for His sake, might be sanctified, and made easy to His followers.
Henry.

ἐμαστίγωσε. The whips were either rods or thongs, to the ends of which lead or
bones were attached, to increase the tension of the lash, and render the blow the more
fearful.—The backs of the prisoners were completely flayed by this process.—They
frequently fainted and sometimes died.—The soldiers would not inflict the punishment
mildly, for they were the cruel ones who mocked Him afterward —It was, moreover, the policy of Pilate that Jesus shou'd be perfectly disfigured. *Lange.*—It is a

matter of controversy whether bones, iron teeth, or leaden balls, were inserted among
the thongs of the lash ; but that such lashes are mentioned, is not to be doubted.
Heubner.—"Go, bind his hands, and let him be beaten," was the order for this terrible
prelude to crucifixion.—Roman citizens were still exempted, by various laws, from this
agonizing and painful punishment, which was employed sometimes to elicit confessions, sometimes as a substitute for execution, and, at others, as the first step in capital
sentences.—It was in full use in the provinces, and lawless governors did not scruple
to enforce it even on Roman citizens, in spite of their protests that they were so.—The
victim was beaten (till the soldiers chose to stop) with knots of rope, or plaited leather
thongs, armed at the ends with acorn-shaped drops of lead, or small, sharp-pointed
bones.—In many cases not only was the back of the person scourged, cut open in all
directions: even the eyes, the face, and the breast, were torn and cut, and the teeth
not seldom knocked out.—The judge stood by, to stimulate the executioners, by cries
of "Give it him."—Under the fury of the countless stripes, the victims sometimes
sank, amidst screams, convulsive leaps, and distortions, into a senseless heap: sometimes died on the spot : sometimes were taken away an unrecognisable mass of bleeding
flesh, to find deliverance in death from the inflammation and fever, sickness and
shame.—The scourging of Jesus was of the severest, for the soldiers employed as
lictors, in the absence of these special officials, who were not allowed to procurators,
only too gladly vented on any Jew the grudge they bore the nation, and they would,
doubtless, try if *they* could not force out the confession, which His silence had denied
to the governor.—Besides, He was to be crucified, and the harder the scourging the
less life would there be left to keep them on guard at the cross, afterwards.—What He
must have endured is pictured to us by Eusebius in the Epistle of the Church in
Smyrna.—"All around were horrified to see them (the martyrs)," says he, "so torn
with scourges that their very veins were laid bare, and the inner muscles and sinews,
and even the very bowels, exposed" (Euseb., Hist. xv.). *Geikie.*

2, 3. And the soldiers platted a crown of thorns, and put it on his head, and they
put on him a purple robe, and said, Hail, King of the Jews ! and they smote him
with their hands.

Thorns. See on Matt. xxvii. 29.—The word is too vague to
enable us to identify the plant with certainty.—Most scholars
have fixed on the *Zizyphus Spina Christi*, known locally as the
Nebk, or *Nubk*, a shrub growing plentifully in the valley of the
Jordan.—Even yet it grows, on dwarf bushes, outside the walls
of Jerusalem. *Tristram.*—It has branches pliant and flexible,
with leaves of a dark, glossy green, and sharp, prickly thorns.—
Very likely it was found in the garden of the governor's palace.
—The soldiers twisted it into a mock laurel wreath, like that
worn at times by the Cæsars, and forced it down, with its close
sharp thorns, on our Lord's temples.—"A most unquestionable
token this, that His kingdom was not of this world, when He
was crowned only with thorns and briars, which are the curse of
the earth." *Lightfoot.*—Yet as the rose groweth out of the thorn,
so out of this thorny crown hath sprung unto Him a crown of
glory and honour, and crowns unto His followers. *Hutcheson.*

Robe. See on Matt. xxvii. 28, where the robe is called "scarlet."
—The "purple" of the ancients was "crimson," and thus the
same colour might easily be called by either name.—Probably
some cast-off cloak of Pilate's own, or possibly, that in which

Herod had before arrayed Him (Luke xxiii. 11).—It was but too common a practice to subject prisoners before execution to this kind of outrage.—Here the point of the mockery lay in the fact that their Victim had been condemned as claiming the title of a king.

Hail. The oldest MSS. read, *And they kept coming to Him and saying, &c.*—They kept drawing near and bowing before Him, in mock reverence, as to a crowned monarch.

Smote. See on chap xviii. 22.—The derisive blow on the cheek is substituted for the kiss.

πορφύρος. Purple, *i.e.*, reddish purp'e. *Robinson.*—This colour was obtained from the secretion of a species of shell-fish the *Murex trunculus* of Linnæus, which was found in various parts of the Mediterranean Sea.—It is difficult to state with precision the tint described under the Hebrew name,—The Greek equivalent was, we know, applied with great latitude, not only to all colours extracted from the shell-fish, but even to other brilliant colours.—The same may be said of the Latin *purpureus.*—Generally speaking, however, the tint must be considered as having been defined by the distinction between the purple *proper* and the other purple dye (A. V. "blue"), which wa produced from another species of shell-fish.—The latter was undoubtedly a dark violet tint whi e the former had a light red ish tinge. *Smith's* Dict.—For καὶ ἐλεγον, read καὶ ἤρχοντο πρὸς αὐτόν καὶ ἔλεγον. *Codd. Sin.,B. L. U. X., &c., most versions, Augustine, &c. Lach., Tisch., Alford, Lange, Schaff, &c.*—Was probably erased as not being understood by transcribers. *Schaff, Alford.*

---

4. Pilate therefore went forth again, and saith unto them, Behold, I bring him forth to you, that ye may know that I find no fault in him.

Went forth. Pilate had returned to the palace, and had ordered the scourging in the court-yard (Mark xv. 15, 16). *Ellicott.*—According to Matthew (chap. xxvii. 26), the scourging had been consummated before the eyes of the people (not "in the court of the Prætorium") : for after the scourging the soldiers had led Him into the Prætorium, probably in a mocking procession, as though the King were being brought into His castle. *Lange.*

Behold, &c. Pilate now goes forth with Jesus wearing the crown of thorns and the purple robe, hoping by the spectacle to move the sympathy of the people.—If he could satisfy the multitude by showing them the mockery and degradation to which He who claimed to be their king had been subjected, he might then be able to save His life.—But whoso yields once to godless, unscrupulous men, and does their pleasure, must and will do it the second time, must do everything they demand, and so Pilate found it.

Know. The return of the person of Jesus to the Jews was a declaration that He was free from the offence with which they charged Him.

No fault. See on chap. xviii. 38.—An unconditional assertion of His innocence.—He is compelled to proclaim, "*I find no fault in Him.*"—So also Judas, "*I have betrayed the innocent blood*" (see on Matt. xxvii. 4).—Alas! it was discoursing to the wolves concerning the innocence of the Lamb.

---

5. Then came Jesus forth, wearing the crown of thorns, and the purple robe. And Pilate saith unto them, Behold the man!

Then, &c. This is the accurate and graphic delineation of an eye-witness.—The verse pictures the scene as the writer remembered it.—The spectacle of that Lord whom he so devotedly loved, thus led forth before the people, was one which left its mark for ever on John's mind.

Behold the man! The words seem to express compassion; evidently they were designed to excite it.—"There is no doubt as to the sense: there ye have Him again, and what a pitiable object." *Lange.*—"That picture of suffering—is it not enough? Will none in that throng lift up a cry for mercy, and save Him from the death for which the Sanhedrim are calling?" *Ellicott.*— "Pilate turning to the figure at his side, drawn together with mortal agony, and looking at the pale, worn, and bleeding face, through which there yet shone a calm dignity and more than human beauty that had touched his heart, and might touch even the heart of Jews, exclaims, 'Behold the man.' Would they let the scourging and mockery suffice, after all?" *Geikie.*—"See this man who submits to and has suffered these indignities. How can He ever stir up the people, or set Himself up for king? Now cease to persecute Him; your malice surely ought to be satisfied." *Alford.*—The words of Pilate, unconsciously to himself, assume, like his superscription and the sentence of Caiaphas, a significance corresponding to the great situation.—It is an involuntary prophecy of heathenism, as the word of Caiaphas was an involuntary prophecy of hostile Judaism (see on chap. xi. 51, 22). *Schaff.*—Pilate perceives not that Jesus is the Man, the one perfect Man, who, through his wicked pliancy, steps forth so outraged in His outward appearance.—Who could be able to form a correct idea of the spectacle, and yet believe that divine justice rules the world, if we were permitted to behold Jesus only in His own person, and not at the same time as Mediator and High Priest. *Krummacher.*

"Ἴδε. Ἰδοὺ. *Codd. Sin.*, *B. L.*, *Tisch.*, *Alford*, *Lange*, *Schaff.*—*Ecce Homo)* words of many meanings —One of the choicest paintings in the Düsseldorf Gallery was an *Ecce Homo* with the Latin inscription : *All this I did for thee : what doest thou for Me ?* Zinzendorf was greatly affected at the sight of this picture: he is minded that he would not be able himself to make much response to this query, and he prays his Saviour to bring him forcibly into the fellowship of His sufferings if he be inclined to remain without. *Heubner.*

---

6. When the chief priests therefore and officers saw him, they cried out, saying, Crucify him, crucify him. Pilate saith unto them, Take ye him, and crucify him : for I find no fault in him.

Chief priests, &c. See on chap. xviii. 3.—These act as leaders and the multitude follow.

Saw. The spectacle, so far from moving their pity, excites them to wild fury.—No passion so fierce and cruel as that of religious hatred.

Crucify. See on Matt. xxvii. 22, and Luke xxiii. 21.—Every other cry that might arise is drowned in this one dreadful cry.—No revenge will satisfy them so long as still more can be had.—The sight of their victim has redoubled their rage, and priests and people answer Pilate's appeal for pity by deafening shouts of "Crucify! Crucify!"

Take, &c. "Crucify Him, if you dare to do so ; there is no charge on which I can condemn Him ; and I will be no party to your act." *Ellicott.*—As if Pilate wished to say, "I will not be your mere tool."—As in chap. xviii. 31, he delivers the matter entirely into their hands.—Probably this occurred after he had received the message from his wife (see on Matt. xxvii. 19).—The words indicate vacillation between his own sense of the innocence of Jesus and his fear of displeasing the Jews and their rulers. *Alford.*—He had not courage enough to act according to his conscience, and his cowardice betrayed him into a snare.—Yet the heathen governor showed far more humanity than the chief priests of a nation, the most highly favoured of God.

No fault. See on verse 4, and on chap. xviii. 38. So often does Pilate publicly attest His innocence, yet suffers Him to be more and more cruelly maltreated, and even commits the innocent Lamb to the wolves again, and all through want of faith in the Kingdom and King of Truth (see on chap. xviii. 37, 38).—He who fears not God will never have much concern for the rights of his fellow men.—Hence infidelity generally becomes in the end the enemy of all moral and social order.—Many in our own day pronounce eulogies on our Lord's moral character who scorn the thought of relying on Him for salvation.

7. The Jews answered him. We have a law, and by our law he ought to die, because he made himself the Son of God.

Answered. The political accusation had failed and is dropped.— But the priests are determined to have His life and forthwith demand it on a new ground.

A law. See on Matt. xxvi. 65, 66, and Luke xxii. 70, 71.—They feel the bitter sarcasm of Pilate's taunt, and appeal to their own law.—According to that they affirm Him to be guilty of death, as a blasphemer of God (Lev. xxiv. 16), and doubtless also as a false prophet (Deut. xviii. 20).—They put " *We have,*" *&c.*, against Pilate's " *I find no fault in Him.*"—In harmony with the general Roman policy, their own law was left in force in all matters which did not directly affect the imperial government.—So they change the accusation from one of treason to one of a purely religious character, in which they claim to be judges.—Here they feel confident of Pilate's obligation to respect their law.

Son of God. See on chap. v. 18 ; x. 30-36.—They would kill Him for the very reason for which they ought to have worshipped Him. *Chrys.*—God's Son must die because He was God's Son, and *acknowledged and affirmed Himself to be the Son of God.*

ἡμῶν. Omitted. *Cod. B and some others, Lach., Ellicott.*—Retained. *Alford, Lange,*

8. When Pilate therefore heard that saying, he was the more afraid.

Afraid. Their words produced the opposite effect to that they intended.—Hitherto Pilate had been restrained by a *fear of conscience or of law* alone ; now *religious fear* supervened, *fear of Jesus's personality* itself.—The words "Son of God " would confirm the omen already furnished by the dream of his wife (see on Matt. xxvii. 19).—He could not have been ignorant of some of the current impressions as to Christ's life and words, and he had himself heard Him claim a kingdom which is not of this world (see on chap. xviii. 36).—This superstitious fear of Pilate is a characteristic trait of the unbeliever ; and shows the indissoluble connection between unbelief and superstition.—"But after all, the unbelieving Pilate is more believing than the superstitious high-priests in the consummate unbelief with which they reject Christ. Of the threefold terror of Pilate : his terror at the law, his terror of conscience, his religious terror, there appears no trace in these practical atheists, who have donned the mask of the holiest zeal." *Lange.*—The heathen Procurator again puts the descendants of Abraham to shame.—Like Gamaliel, he is seized with a salutary apprehension " lest haply he be found even to fight against God." *Andrews.*

9. And went again into the judgment hall, and saith unto Jesus, Whence art thou? But Jesus gave him no answer.

Went. He had brought Jesus out to the people (verse 4), and he now leads Him back into the Prætorium in order to fresh, private examination.

Whence? The inquiry is indefinitely framed, in accordance with the accusation of the Jews and Pilate's fear.—Not "from what province?" for he knew this (Luke xxiii. 6, 7); nor, "of what parents?" but WHENCE? in reference to His origin and nature. —The question was intended with respect to His claim to be a Son of God, of which he had just heard (see on chap. viii. 14). (See note.)

No answer. Jesus was silent, "as also before Herod and Caiaphas, because He had already testified enough for the susceptible; and for him who had turned his back upon the King of Truth, neither could another testimony avail." *Tholuck.*—Our Lord foresaw that this transaction would lead to nothing.— " Pilate, with his question, abandoned his judicial position, for he was bound to acquit Jesus, not on account of His danger-menancing God-head, but on account of His *protection-demanding human innocence.*" *Lange.*—"This silence was the most emphatic answer to all who had ears to hear it, was a reference to what He had said before (chap. xviii. 37), and so a witness to His divine origin. Would any *mere man*, of true and upright character, have refused an answer to such a question, so put? Let the modern rationalist consider this." *Alford.*—" Pilate's question was one which to him could not be answered in reality, and therefore was not answered in appearance. The answer had, indeed, already been given (chap. xviii. 37), but he had treated it with the impatience which showed he could not receive it now. Not *of the truth*, he could not hear the voice of the Son of God, and therefore that voice did not speak." *Ellicott.*—" 1. Pilate's seeking of light in this particular flowed not from love, and such seeking hath no promise to come speed. 2. He had slighted truth when it had been revealed to him before, and such as do so are justly deprived of further information. 3. By this refusal of an answer Christ would discover some naughtiness in his heart, as appeareth from the following verse. And this is Christ's usual way with those that converse with Him, to try and cause them discover what is in their bosom ; and He doth this very often by suspending the satisfaction of their desires, at least for a time." *Hutcheson.*—Our Lord, in His silence, was acting according to His own precept (Matt. vii. 6). (See Comm.)

πόθεν. Pi'ate pictures to himself the υἰὸς θεοῦ after the analogy of the heathen *heroes*, and fears the vengeance of the Jewish God Jehovah. *Meyer.*—Religious awe, in a moment of superstitious exc'tement, pictures to itself all manner of things, however, and nothing quite distinctly.—Whether He were a Magus or a hero, an angel, after the religion of the land, or a divine apparition, it now seemed very possible to him that there might be something superterrestrial in the appearance of the Man ; and he had so unconcernedly caused Him to be scourged.—In any case celestial vengeance seemed to threaten him. *Lange.*—The fear of Pilate is not mere superstition, nor does it enter into the Jewish meaning of υἱὸς θεοῦ; but arises from an indefinite impression made on him by the Person and bearing of our Lord—We must not therefore imagine any fear of Him as being a "son of the gods," in Pilate's mind : this gives a wrong direction to his conduct and misses the fine psychological truth of the narrative. *Alford.*—ἀπόκ. οὐκ. He would not answer him in order that He might not step in the way of God's will. *Luthardt.*—If the answer had been a moral duty, no religious duty would have stood in the way of it,—God had power, notwithstanding any answer of His, to accomplish His will.—Under such a supposition as Luthardt's, Jesus would in no case have dared to answer anything. *Lange.*

---

10. Then saith Pilate unto him, Speakest thou not unto me ? knowest thou not that I have power to crucify thee, and have power to release thee?

Speakest, &c. ? Gr., To *me* dost Thou not speak?—The position of the "*me*" is strongly emphatic in the original.—Pilate at once recoils from his better thoughts and feelings into the state-pride of office (see on chap. xviii. 35).—His momentary tenderness turned into lowering passion.—"Do you refuse to answer ME ? " he asked, in sudden anger.—Power, when it feels itself in the wrong, is the more ready to drown conscience by violence towards the weakness it outrages.—A moment before Pilate had trembled at the thought of a Being from another world, and now, as Roman governor, he expects that Being to tremble before him.—A striking illustration of the vacillation that marked his character and led to his ruin.

Power, &c. The better MSS. read, *Have power to release Thee, and have power to crucify Thee.*—This is the more natural order of thought, as *releasing* appeals more to the prisoner, and *crucifying* follows as the other alternative.—"Thy life is in my power ; yea, and Thy death also." *Ellicott.*—Full of fear himself, he tries to impress considerations of fear on Jesus.—Boasting of his power instead of remembering his duty, and of his freedom to release Jesus, while the weight of temptation drives him in his impotence resistlessly forward. *Lange.*—"Albeit in his conscience he had absolved Christ as innocent, and therefore would have had Him released as one he might not wrong, yet when his pride is aloft, he thinks he may do what he pleaseth." *Hutcheson.*—After having so plainly declared his own absolute, unfettered authority, how he condemns himself in servilely yielding to a popular clamour !

Codd. A. B., Lach., Tisch., Treg., Alf., Westcott and Hort, Ellicott, Schaff, &c., give the ἀπολῦσαι first.

---

11. Jesus answered, Thou couldest have no power at all against me, except it were given thee from above: therefore he that delivered me unto thee hath the greater sin.

Answered. Jesus is no longer silent; yet had Pilate been able to ponder things aright, he would have seen an answer to his question in that silence.—He, in whose lips no deceit was ever found, would, on the instant, have honourably confessed that He was only a man, had He been no more.—His very silence was a testimony to His divine dignity. *Lücke.*

No power. Twice had Pilate, in pride of office, announced his "power."—Jesus replies that he had of himself *no power against Him*, but that which was given to him.

Given. For the accomplishment of the purpose of God which rendered the death of Jesus necessary.—Even though abusing the power committed him, Pilate was an instrument of divine Providence.—Our Lord here expresses the same thought as that contained in His rebuke to Peter (see on chap. xviii. 11).—Here He takes His stand: even in the midst of Jewish malignity and Gentile injustice, the pure will of God remaineth serene for Him, as the sky letteth its blue be seen through clouds. *Braune.*—But a distinction ever remains between the will of God and the actions of men (Acts ii. 23).—" The providence of God was remarkable in so ordering affairs, that a man, flexible and yielding like Pilate, should be entrusted with power in Judæa. God so works that the *true character* of men shall be *brought out*, and makes use of that character to advance His own great purpose." *Barnes.*

From above. See on chap. iii. 31.—This is a precise answer to the " Whence art Thou? " of Pilate (verse 9).—It is equivalent to "from God," or "from My Father," but this Pilate would not have understood.—The power Pilate boasted of would have been vain had not Jesus submitted to it of His own will (see on chap. x. 17, 18).

He. "Thine own nation and the chief priests have delivered Thee unto me" (see on chap. xviii. 35).—It was the Sanhedrim, and especially Caiaphas, the high-priest, who, professing to represent God on earth, had delivered up the Son of God, and had declared that by the law He ought to die (see on chap. xi. 49 ; xviii. 14-28). *Ellicott.* (See note.)

Delivered. Gr., *delivereth*, the present, because the act is just going on.

Greater sin. An implied reference to a higher Judge, nay, that

Judge Himself speaks. *Alford.*—Pilate sinned, for he acted against his conscience; but not the greater sin, for he did not act against the full light of truth.—Pilate was an ignorant Gentile, the deliverer Jewish; moreover the Jews, with some show of legal title, demanded that he should execute *their* sentence (see on verse 7).—"Pilate had to do, not with a Roman, but with a Jew, and not with a civil law, but with a religious accusation, in regard to which the Jewish tribunal had already decided. This might readily mislead him in his simple judicial duty, and it was his fatality. His guilt would be still less than it really was, had he not been aware that they had delivered Jesus for envy, had not Jesus made so strong an impression on him, and had he not really known it to be his duty to release Him." *Lange.*—Our Lord, as the holy Judge, manifests both righteousness and clemency: It seems as if He felt sympathy with the judicial fate of the weak Pilate.—The Sanhedrim, against the clearest evidence, had rejected the Messiah: Pilate's sin was that of weakly submitting to their clamour.—They were God's chosen people, and had God's word of prophecy before them; Pilate, the blind instrument of their deliberate malice.—"Your sin, though great, in condemning Me against your conscience, and exercising on Me the power granted you by God, is not so great as that of others; for you are only an instrument in His hands to carry out His counsels. The chief guilt lies on those who have delivered Me to you to force you to carry out their will against Me." *Geikie.*—This last testimony of the Lord before Pilate is a *witness to the truth:* opening in a wonderful manner the secret of Pilate's vaunted power, of His own humble submission, and the sinfulness of His enemies. *Alford.*

ἐξουσίαν. Judicial authority: Because thou hast this authority from above, the misuse of it is sin; but the authors of this offence, the Jews, have the greater guilt. *Luther. Calvin, Baur,* &c.—Actual power: It is the providence of God that I, through the obduracy of My people, have fallen into thy hands. *Beza, Gerhard, Tholuck.*—δεδομένον. The neuter is more general, and embraces in itself the whole delegation from above, power included. *Alford.*—ἄνωθεν. From the Roman emperor. *Usteri.*—From the Sanhedrim. *Semler.*—From God. *Grotius, Olsh., Lange, Heubner, Schaff, Meyer, Lampe, Alford, Ellicott, Geikie,* &c.—We must not dream of any allusion to *Rome* or the *Sanhedrim,* in this ἄνωθεν, as the sources of Pilate's power: the word was not so meant, nor so understood, see verse 12. *Alford.*—ὁ παραδιδούς. The highpriest Caiaphas. *Bengel, Meyer, Lampe, Hengst., Ewald.*—Cannot mean Judas, as some have supposed, for he is nowhere mentioned in this connection, and is excluded by the words "unto thee." *Ellicott, Lange, Schaff,* &c.—The hardened Jewish nation. *Tholuck.*—Beyond question, *Caiaphas,* to whom the initiative on the Jewish side belonged.—At the same time the whole Sanhedrim are probably included under the guilt of their chief. *Alford, D. Brown, Ellicott,* &c.—μείζονα. Pilate's guilt rests more upon softness and weakness. *Euthymius.*—Because he could not know, as well as the Jews, who Jesus was. *Grotius.*—Because the Jews had not received this power from God. *Lampe.*—Because thou hast the disposal of Me not from any sovereign power of thine own, but by divine authorization. *Meyer.*—Pilate had no insight into the character which He claimed, as the Jews had. *Alford.*—The Sanhedrim had a better insight into religion, into God's counsel and promise, Jesus's deeds and holiness. *Huebner.*

---

12. And from thenceforth Pilate sought to release him: but the Jews cried out, saying, If thou let this man go, thou art not Cæsar's friend: whosoever maketh himself a king speaketh against Cæsar.

Thenceforth. Better, *for this reason, for the sake of this saying.* "It cast a bright, accidental light upon his obscure, fateful, perilous situation, that for an instant marked the path of duty as a path of deliverance." *Lange.*

Release. The words seem to indicate that Pilate was on the point of ordering His release. *Lange.*—Perhaps he commanded the guard to fall back, or he might have told the Jews that he would take Jesus under his own protection.—At all events, this is the decisive moment in the great tragedy.

Cried out. Pilate's determination, however it was manifested, provoked the most decided outburst on the part of the Jews.—At first the high-priests and officers led the voices; now the entire multitude unite to swell the clamour.—In the uproar thus created the whole storm of hell rises.

If, &c. The demoniacal argument they now urge could hardly have originated with the multitude.—Doubtless it proceeded from the hierarchs, who must have felt it was their last and only chance of success.

Not Cæsar's friend. This was an argument against which no Roman governor was proof.—Once more the political accusation is brought to the front, and this time in a manner which ensures them the victory.—"Jesus is a revolutionist against the emperor, and if thou let Him go, thou bringest thyself under suspicion of treason."—Tiberias was emperor, and his jealous fear had made "treason" a crime, of which the accusation was practically the proof, and the proof was death.—Pilate knew the suspicious character of Tiberias, and feared the more, because his conscience accused him of having abused his office by every form of injustice. —Moreover, he was well aware of the deceitful cunning and fanatical boldness of the Jewish priests.—They would say: Here was a man who had claimed to be a king; and Pilate is seeking to release Him.—His continued refusal might involve the charge of disloyalty against himself, and an appeal to Rome.

A king. They knew perfectly well that our Lord claimed to be a king in a sense wholly different from that by which they attempted to alarm Pilate.—But it was the only weapon that remained to them, and it answered their purpose.

Speaketh against. "He *declareth* against the Emperor." *Meyer.* —This was true; but their application of it to Jesus was a wicked lie.—But *words,* not *facts,* are taken into account by tyrants, and this Pilate knew.—Hence he was ready for any act of weak unrighteousness rather than brave the censure of the emperor, far less the risk of his vengeance.

ἔκραζον. ἐκραύγαζον the stronger form. *Codd. A. B. L. M., Lach., Tisch., Schaff.*— φίλος Καίσαρος. A predicate of honour, since the time of Augustus, conferred by the emperor himself and by others, partly upon prefects and legates, partly upon allies. *Tholuck, Ernesti.*—The term means simply: *loyal* to the emperor. *Meyer, Alford.*— Unfavourable to this view is the technical use of the predicate, *amicus Cæsaris.*—Even if Pilate did not formally possess the title, it is alluded to. *Lange.*—ἀντιλέγει. Is at variance with the emperor, *Lange.*—He *rebelleth* against. *Kuinoel.*—The pages of Tacitus and Suetonius abound with examples of ruin wreaked on families in the name of the "law of treason."—On the extortions and outrages committed by Pilate see Josephus.

---

13. When Pilate therefore heard that saying, he brought Jesus forth and sat down in the judgment seat in a place that is called the Pavement, but in the Hebrew, Gabbatha.

Saying. Better, *these sayings,* the sayings of the previous verse.

Brought, &c. Pilate's time for playing with the situation is gone; now the situation plays with him.—First he said, not asked, "What is *truth?*" Now his frightened heart, to which the emperor's favour is the supreme law of life, says, "What is *justice?*" *Lange.*—He who fears not God above all things is condemned to fear man. *Tholuck.*—Only he is truly free and independent of men, who feels bound in God and dependent on Him.—Pilate no longer hesitates about the course to be taken.—His own position and life may be in danger should he persist in refusing the appeal of the Jews.—Doubtless he tried to make himself believe that he could not, in *any* case, save Christ's life (verse 7).—Perhaps also he comforted himself with the thought that he had acted with exceptional uprightness.—He would think he must after all look to his own interests first.—Should he bring down on himself a recall (perhaps banishment, or even worse) to save a Jew, because justice demanded his doing so?—"Who, in my position, would dream of committing such a folly. Shall I sacrifice myself for any one? No!"—Since the last examination (verse 8) Jesus had been left in the Prætorium.

Judgment seat. The Greek word means an elevated place to which the ascent is by steps.—It is the name used for the seat or throne in the theatre at Cæsarea, on which Herod sat (Acts xii. 21).

Pavement. The judgment seat stood on a floor of Mosaic.—The Greek word means "stone-paved," the name for the tesselated floor of marble and coloured stones with which the Prætorium was adorned —Such a tesselated pavement Julius Cæsar is said to have carried about on his expeditions. *Suetonius.*—Here the word "place" conveys the impression that this was a fixture in front of the Prætorium at Jerusalem on which the Bema (judgment seat) stood.—Josephus says that the whole of the Temple mountain was paved with this kind of Mosaic work.

Gabbatha. The Hebrew or Syro-Chaldaic name, meaning, "an elevated place." The one name was given it from its form, and the other from the material of which it was made.—Both words occur here only, and are instances of John's minute knowledge of the localities in Jerusalem. *Ellicott.*

τοῦτον τόν λόγον. τῶν λόγων τούτων. *Codd. Sin. A. B. L., &c., Lach., Tisch., Alford, Lange, Schaff, &c.*

14. And it was the preparation of the passover, and about the sixth hour : and he saith unto the Jews, Behold your King!

The preparation. See on chap. xviii. 28, particularly the critical note.—Friday in the passover season, or paschal week, as a day of preparation for the Sabbath.—The terms Friday and Sabbath preparation were of necessity synonymous to the Jews.—It was so called from the Jewish habit of preparing the meals on Friday for the Sabbath, since it was forbidden to kindle a fire on the Sabbath (Ex. xvi. 5; *Josephus*).—"This is the uniform meaning of the Greek word in all other passages of the N. T. where it occurs, viz., in this very chapter, verses 31, 32; Matt. xxvii. 62; Luke xxiii. 54 ; Mark xv. 42 (where it is expressly explained for non-Jewish readers as 'the day before the Sabbath'). Why then should the passage in the text be an exception? The addition ' of the passover,' which John always uses in the wider sense for the whole feast (not for the eating of the paschal lamb), makes no difference ; it is simply the *Paschal Friday,* or *Easter Friday,* as we speak of *Easter Sunday, Easter Monday, Easter Tuesday.* We have here a very significant hint that after all John is in perfect accord with the

Synoptists on the day of Christ's death, which was not the 14th, but the 15th of Nisan, or the first day of the paschal festival. John probably chose this very term to expose the awful inconsistency and crime of the Jews in putting the Lord to Death on the day when they should have prepared for the holy Sabbath, doubly sacred now as being at the same time the first day of the great passover." *Schaff.*

Sixth hour. See on Matt. xxvii. 45, and on Luke xxiii. 44.—John's statement of time (twelve o'clock) seems opposed to that of Mark, who states that the crucifixion took place at the "third hour" (nine o'clock).—There are three leading explanations of this difficulty. 1. That the two Evangelists give the extreme limits of time, Mark referring to the beginning of the preparations, and John pointing to the completion of the tragedy. The words of Mark, "it was the third hour," may denote indefinitely that *the third hour was past;* while the words of John, "about the sixth hour," may mean simply that it was *approaching* the sixth hour. *Ewald, Lange, Godet, Schaff.*—2. John writing in Asia Minor, may have used the Roman official mode of computation, reckoning from midnight, so that the "sixth hour" would be 6 a.m. From this time to 9 a.m. (the "third hour," according to the Jewish reckoning) was occupied by the preliminaries, and by the passage of the procession forth to Golgotha. *Ebrard, Gardiner, Hug, Olshausen, Tholuck, Wieseler, Wordsworth, &c.*—3. That it is a copyist's mistake in John. *Bengel, Beza, Eusebius, Robinson, &c.*—Others leave the difficulty unsolved. *Meyer, Ellicott.* (See note.)

Behold your king. Words of bitter irony, by which Pilate not only *masks* his failure but also *avenges* it.—" It may be that these words unfold even this threatening thought : your *King,* then, shall first be crucified, and after Him, *yourselves.*" *Lange.*—It is no longer, *Behold the Man !* to excite their sympathy and effect His release.— Alas for Pilate, every emotion of tenderness, every principle of honour and justice, is now sacrificed to the desire to evince his loyalty to Cæsar.

ὥρα δὲ ὡσεί. ὥρα ἦν ὡς. *Codd. A. B. D.,* Lach., *Tisch., Lange, Schaff, Alford, &c.*— ἕκτη. Without any laboured theory about difference of calculation, how easily might the Greek numeral γ (3) have been changed by accident into ϛ' (6), in the MSS. of John's Gospel, from which ours have been copied (*Lücke*).—But even this is not needed, for as Ewald points out, John likely speaks of the time of the actual nailing to the cross, the other Evangelists of the starting to it.--The preparations, the march, &c., may well have taken up the interval till noon. *Geikie.*—The apostles did not count with the watch in their hands. *Godet.*—" *It was going on towards the sixth hour,*" is the correct reading. — It was past nine o'clock and approaching noon when Pilate spoke the final words upon which the procession to Golgotha immediately followed.—John's employment of the *later* indefinite hour-date is accounted for by the thought—they now hastened to the close, because, with noon, the second, already more Sabbatic, half of the παρασκευή was approaching.—Mark's choice, on the other hand, of the *earlier* indefinite hour-date is accounted for by the significant antithesis which he wishes to institute between the third and the sixth hour. *Lange.*—ἕκτη. Codd. A. B. E. K., &c.—τρίτη. Codd. D L. X., &c. The Alexandrian Chronicle assures us that accurate copies and the authentic MS. preserved at Ephesus give τρίτη.—A conformation to Mark xv. 25, due to the too literal apprehension of the Johannean expression. *Schaff.*

---

15. But they cried out, Away with him, away with him, crucify him. Pilate saith unto them, Shall I crucify your King? The chief priests answered, We have no king but Cæsar.

Away, &c. "At this last moment there is still a mutual effort to shuffle off the legal responsibility upon each other. Pilate's meaning is: If He is to be executed, *ye* may execute Him. The meaning of the Jews is: *thou* shalt have Him, *thou* shalt crucify Him. It was only in this way that they could be assured of Pilate's inability to institute later a review of the proceedings." *Lange.*—The brief, passionate exclamation expresses the exasperation with which they resented the irony of Pilate, "Behold *your* King!"

Shall I? In the order of the Greek words, "your King" comes emphatically first: "*Your* King! shall I crucify *Him?*"—The taunt is uttered in its bitterest form. *Ellicott.*—"Not merely a *reverberation* of the preceding derisive words, but also a distincter expression of the same idea: If He is to be crucified as your King in your sense, He must, according to your law, die as a *religious* criminal. Hence the high-priest's reply." *Lange.*—"It will not satisfy conscience that men have others more concerned and knowing than themselves (upon whom they think they may lay the blame of any evil), so long as they suffer anything to be done contrary to their trust and power; for this is another shift of Pilate, that since the Jews, who were more concerned in their king, and understood these things better than he, will have Christ crucified, he thinks they should bear the blame. But it was his duty to have employed his authority and power to hinder injustice." *Hutcheson.*

No king. "A degrading confession from the *chief priests* of that people of whom it was said, 'The Lord your God is your King' (1 Sam. xii. 12)." *Alford.*—A confession not only degrading; in their mouths it was false.—They will have it that He shall and must die as a political demagogue; but to accomplish this purpose, they are driven to a denial of their dearest and highest hopes.—They who gloried in the Theocracy, and looked for a temporal Messianic reign which should not only free them from the power of Rome, but raise them to the highest place among all nations, proclaim that Cæsar was their only king.—In this consummation of their godless perfidy they disclaim their own Messianic hopes, deny the Messianic claims, traduce the Lord as a seditionary, and feign a zeal of the most loyal fidelity to Rome. —" With one accord they denied the kingdom of God, and God suffered them to fall into their own condemnation ; for they rejected the kingdom of Christ, and called down upon their own head that of Cæsar." *Chrys.*—Some of these very men who here made this hypocritical show of loyalty to carry their point and make a tool of Pilate, perished afterwards most miserably in rebellion against Cæsar.—They said, We have no king, and their saying has come to be such earnest that ever since they have had to remain without a king. *Luther.*—Yet even this judgment of hardening must, according to Rom. ix., redound to the salvation of the world.—The suffering of the Lord in Pilate's tribunal : 1. In view of Pilate tottering to his fall; 2. In view of the priests of His nation in their obduracy and craftiness; 3. In view of the infatuated, raging people.—The temptation of Christ in these sufferings, and His victory. *Lange.*

ἆρον ἆρον No comma between. *Tisch., Alford, Westcott and Hort, Schaff.*

---

16. Then delivered he him therefore unto them to be crucified. And they took Jesus, and led him away.

Then. Gr., *Then therefore he delivered Him.*—The words of the chief-priests (verse 15), like those in verse 12, were evidently intended to compel Pilate to comply with their demands, under dread of an appeal to Rome.—This repeated threat completes the conquest of Pilate.—He fears less to put the Son of God to death, than to risk the emperor's displeasure.—From the moment he constituted himself and his authority constable of the hierarchy, his ruin was inevitable.—Similar was the fate of the Maccabæan house, and, since then, of several European dynasties.—The hierarchy here begets a *revolution* and allies itself to it, in order to shake the political authority.—Hierarchy, popular insurrection, and political authority, in wicked alliance, sentence the King of the Kingdom of God and Protector of all holy order and authority, the High Priest and true Friend of the People, to death upon the cross, as a kindler of rebellion. *Lange.*

Delivered. Pilate ascends the tribunal, and finally pronounces the desired condemnation.—So ends his share in the greatest crime

which has been committed since the world began.—We learn
from Josephus that his anxiety to avoid giving offence to Cæsar
did not save him from political disaster.—"The Samaritans were
unquiet and rebellious. Pilate led his troops against them, and
defeated them easily enough. The Samaritans complained to
Vitellius, then president of Syria, and he sent Pilate to Rome to
answer their accusations before the emperor. When he reached
Rome he found Tiberius dead, and Caius (Caligula) on the throne,
A.D. 36. Eusebius adds that soon afterwards, ' wearied with mis-
fortunes,' he killed himself. As to the scene of his death, there
are various traditions. One is that he was banished to Vienna
Allobrogum (Vienne on the Rhone), where a singular monument,
a pyramid on a quadrangular base, fifty-two feet high, is called
Pontius Pilate's tomb. Another is that he sought to hide his
sorrows on the mountain by the lake of Lucerne, now called
Mount Pilatus ; and there, after spending years in its recesses, in remorse and despair, rather than penitence, plunged
into the dismal lake which occupies its summit. We learn from
Justyn Martyr, Tertullian, Eusebius, and others, that Pilate
made an official report to Tiberius of the Lord's trial and condemnation ; and in a homily ascribed to Chrysostom, though marked
as spurious by his Benedictine editors, certain *Acta*, or *Commen-
tarii Pilati* are spoken of as well-known documents in common
circulation. The *Acta Pilati* now extant in Greek, and two Latin
epistles from him to the emperor, are certainly spurious." *Smith's*
"Dictionary of the Bible."

Unto them. That is, the chief priests.—The soldiers who executed
the decree of crucifixion acted under the direction of the Sanhedrists.—No doubt it was at the time of the delivery of Jesus that
Pilate performed the symbolical act of hand-washing (see on
Matt. xxvii. 24).

Took Jesus. The taking was accompanied with the cry, "His
blood be on us, and on our children " (see on Matt. xxvii. 25).
—The glory of Jerusalem and the glory of Rome sink away in one
ordeal in which they judge the Lord of the world, and with them
the glory of the whole old world. *Lange.*

καὶ ἀπήγαγον. Omitted. *Codd. E. L. X., &c., Lach , Tisch., Alford, Westcott and Hort.*
—Omitted probably on account of the exegetical consideration that the word here refers
to the Jews, while in Matt. xxvii. 31, it has reference to the soldiers. *Schaff*—Verse 16
ought to close with σταυρωθῇ, and παρέλαβον begin the next section. *Tisch., Alford,
Lange, Westcott and Host, Schaff, &c.*

17. And he bearing his cross went forth into a place called the place of a skull, which is called in the Hebrew Golgotha.

And. John's account of the crucifixion, though brief, contains several original details of the deepest import.—Both in that, and in the account of the Lord's burial, he gives special prominence to the fulfilment of Biblical prophecies and types (see on Matt xxvii. 32, and on Luke xxiii. 26).

Bearing. Better, *bearing His own cross, carrying the cross for Himself.*—" As conquerors bear their own trophies, so Christ bears the symbol of His own victory." *Schaff.*—Tradition reports that our Lord sank to the ground beneath the load.—It is evident, however, that He bore His cross the greater part of the way, and this probably is the reason why John omits mention of the circumstance recorded by the Synoptists, as to Simon the Cyrenian. "Though called *His,* the cross He bore was *ours,* which He appropriated to Himself, as though it were His own. He embraced it with such love and patience as it had been His life, and it brought Him death, but *to us life.*" *Gossner.*—" Whatever cross He calls *us* to bear *at any* time, we must remember that *He* bore the cross first." *Henry.*

Went forth. Out of the city, "without the gate," Heb. xiii. 12 (out of the old communion).—A centurion on horseback, called by Tacitus *exactor mortis,* headed the company ; and a herald going in front of the condemned, proclaimed his sentence.—" What a procession! What a spectacle! To the profane a laughing-stock, to the pious a mystery. Profaneness sees a King bearing a cross instead of a sceptre ; piety sees a King bearing a cross, thereon to nail Himself, and afterwards to nail it on the foreheads of Kings." *Augustine.*—" Christians must make many a painful pilgrimage out of the city, out of the land, for the sake of their faith ; but courage! press onward! ye have a noble Predecessor." *Starke.*

Skull. Probably a small, round and barren elevation in the shape of a skull, and derived its name from its globular form.—Jerome, on Matt. xxvii. 33, mentions the tradition that the place derived its name from Adam, the *head* (skull) of the human family, supposed to have been buried there (hence, probably, the skull introduced in early pictures of the crucifixion).—Jerome discredits the tradition, and thinks that it was so called as a place of execution, on account of the skulls of criminals.—But in this case the corresponding Greek name would have been "place of skulls," instead of " place of a skull," still less " a skull," as in Hebrew, and in the Greek of Luke xxiii. 33.—Moreover, skulls were not allowed to lie on the place of execution unburied, but were covered up.—Neither is there any record that the Jews had a *special place* for public execution ; besides, it is extremely unlikely that a rich man like Joseph of Arimathæa, would have kept a garden in such a place, for the sepulchre of Christ was near the place of crucifixion (see on chap. xix. 41). *Schaff.*—The spot may have been chosen by the priests as a deliberate insult to Joseph, because he had refused to share their policy, and was suspected of discipleship. *Ellicott.*

Golgotha. *Skull.*—The Syro-Chaldaic form of the word, that which was common in John's time.—In the three places where *Golgotha* occurs, viz., Matt. xxvii. 33, Mark xv. 22, and here, the E. V. retains the original form.—The Vulgate translates the word in all cases *Calvaria* (fem., *i. e.*, *skull*), from which our *Calvary* is derived.—The E. V., following the Vulgate, uses *Calvary* only once, Luke xxiii. 33.—The popular expression " *Mount Calvary*," is probably of monastic origin, and has no foundation in the Evangelists.—Golgotha is not mentioned by any Jewish writer, and yet the Evangelists speak of it as though it were a well-known locality.—We only know that it was " nigh to the city " (see on verse 20), and therefore outside the walls (Heb. xiii. 12).—A tradition, traceable to the fourth century, has identified the spot with the building known as the "Church of the Holy Sepulchre." —That building is now *within* the walls of the city ; but at the time of the crucifixion the site was outside.—It was afterwards enclosed by the third wall built by Agrippa II.—Fergusson, in Smith's " Bible Dictionary," has propounded the theory that the place of crucifixion was Mount *Moriah*, on the spot where now stands the Mosque of Omar ; and also, that this building is the identical " Church of the Holy Sepulchre " which Constantine erected over the rocky tomb of Jesus.—But to speak of nothing more, this theory is untenable " by the extreme improbability that the temple area was outside of the city, and a place of execution." *Lange.*—After all, it appears a wise arrangement of Providence that the real locality should be unknown.—" It is too holy to be desecrated by idolatrous superstitions and monkish impostures and quarrels such as, from the time of Constantine to this day, have disgraced the Church of the Holy Sepulchre, to the delight of Mohammedan Turks, and to the shame and grief of Christians. The Apostles and Evangelists barely allude to the place of the Lord's birth, death, and resurrection ; they fixed their eyes of faith and love upon the great facts themselves, and upon the ever-living Christ in heaven." *Schaff.* (See on verse 20.)

τὸν σταυρὸν αὐτοῦ. αὐτῷ τὸν σταυρὸν. *Codd. Sin. B. L. X*, *Vu'gate, Ita'a, Origen, Lach., Tisch, Alford, Lange, &c.*—As regards the *Via dolorosa*, or *Via crucis*, or the Lord's road from the Prætorium to Golgotha, mention was first made of it in the fourteenth century. *Krafft.*—The real way trod by our Lord must have lain somewhat more to the south. *Lange.*—If the trial was at the palace of Herod on Mount Zion, He could not have passed along the *Via dolorosa. Andrews.*—"There is a beautiful tradition which assigns the perpetual shiver of the aspen to the fact of the cross having been of this tree. But Lipsius, who has displayed such wealth of erudition on this subject, thinks that it was of oak, which was common in Judæa. There is another tradition that the cross consisted of three kinds of wood: cypress, pine, and cedar. And still another that it consisted of four kinds: cedar, cypress, palm, and olive. That it was wood is certain, but of what wood no evidence remains." *Macdonald.*

18. Where they crucified him, and two other with him, on either side one, and Jesus in the midst.

Crucified Him. See on Matt. xxvii. 35, and Luke xxiii. 33.—See also on chap. iii. 14; xii. 32, 33; xviii. 32.—"The cross pieces were nailed in their places on the upright posts, sometimes before, sometimes after, the posts themselves had been set up. Jesus and His fellow-sufferers, in either case, were now stripped once more, as they had been before they were scourged, a linen cloth at most being left round their loins (see note). The centre cross was set apart for our Lord, and He was laid on it either as it lay on the ground, or lifted and tied to it as it stood upright, His arms stretched along the two cross beams, and His body resting on the projecting pin of rough wood, misnamed a seat. The most dreadful part then followed; for though even the Egyptians only tied the victims to the cross, the Romans and Carthaginians added to the torture by driving a huge nail through the palm of each hand into the wood. The legs were next bent up till the soles of the feet lay flat on the upright beam, and then they, too, were fastened, either separately, by two great iron nails, or over each other, by one. Meanwhile the fierce heat of a Syrian noon beat down upon the cross. The suffering in crucifixion, from which death at last resulted, rose partly from the constrained and fixed position of the body, and of the outstretched arms, which caused acute pain from every twitch or motion of the back, lacerated by the scourge, and of the hands and feet, pierced by the nails. These latter were, moreover, driven through parts where many sensitive nerves and sinews come together, and some of these were mutilated; others violently crushed down. Inflammation of the wounds in both hands and feet speedily set in, and ere long rose also in other places, where the circulation was checked by the tension of the parts. Intolerable thirst, and ever increasing pain, resulted. The blood, which could no longer reach the extremities, rose to the head, swelled the veins and arteries in it unnaturally, and caused the most agonising tortures in the brain. As, besides, it could no longer move freely from the lungs, the heart grew more and more oppressed, and all the veins were distended. Had the wounds bled freely, it would have been a great relief, but there was very little lost. The weight of the body itself, resting on the wooden pin of the upright beam ; the burning heat of the sun scorching the veins, and the hot wind, which dried up the moisture of the body, made each moment more terrible than that before. The numbness and stiffness of the more distant muscles brought on painful convulsions, and this numbness, slowly extending, sometimes through two or three days, at last reached the vital parts, and released the sufferer by death." *Richter in Herzog, Winer, Geikie.*—But all the ordinary sufferings of crucifixion give us but a faint idea of the sufferings of the sinless Redeemer (see on Matt. xxvii. 35).—Constantine the Great, from motives of humanity, and especially from respect to the cross of Christ, abolished crucifixion in the Roman Empire, and since that time it has almost disappeared from Europe.—What a wonderful change ! Through the death of Christ, the cross has been transfigured into a symbol of glory and victory.—" Calvary, so full of horrors, has become transformed into ' the hill from whence cometh our help,' whose mysteries many kings and prophets desired to see. Upon this awful hill our roses blossom, and our springs of peace and salvation burst forth. The pillar of our refuge towers upon this height. The Bethany of our repose and eternal refreshment here displays itself to our view." *Krummacher.*

Two other. See on Matt. xxvii. 38, and Luke xxiii. 33, 39-43.— Meyer thinks that this was an arrangement of the Jews, the Jews being the crucifiers.—But the two robbers were not executed as Jewish heretics, and the carrying out of the crucifixion, as a Roman punishment, must have been left to the Romans.—It was evidently Pilate's arrangement and designed to mock the Jews. *Lange.*—These malefactors, between whom the Lord was crucified, represent the two classes of the human family.—Both are guilty and justly condemned before God, but the one repents and is saved by faith in the atoning Redeemer; the other remains impenitent and unbelieving.

ἐσταύρωσαν. "Hase and Meyer distrust the proofs of any covering, and the Fathers, Athanasius, Ambrose, and Origen, speak of entire nudity. The body cloth seems to have been restricted to inflictions of death by the Jews. The Romans had no such tenderness. Polycarp was martyred entirely naked (Euseb.), The soldiers would hardly lose any part of their perquisites of the clothes for the sake of delicacy. The

Jews. like the Romans, stripped those about to be put to death ; but the Mishna prescribes that a person crucified is to wear a cloth round his loins (Sepp).—Schenkel
thinks that Jesus was stripped entirely naked. Hug, quoted by Winer, was of ʰepp's
opinion. Keim also thinks crucified persons were stripped entirely naked." *Geikie.*
—Each foot was probably nailed to the cross separately, and not both by one nail.—In
earlier p'ctures of the crucifixion, Christ was attached to the cross by three or four
nails indifferently.—Early tradition speaks of four nails.—After the thirteenth century
the practice prevailed of representing the feet as lying one over the other and both
penetrated by only one nail. It is possible that the crown of thorns remained upon
His head as represented by painters, since Matthew and Mark mention the removal of
the purple robe by the soldiers, but not of the crown. *Friedlieb, Andrews. Schaff.*—The
old traditional view of the Church, that the feet of the Lord were nailed as well as His
hands, was contradicted since 1792 by Paulus, who maintained that the feet of Jesus
were only bound. But this assertion has been disproved by Hengstenberg, Hug, Bähr,
Tholuck and others. The first proof that feet and hands were both fastened by nails
is supplied by Luke xxiv. 39, where Jesus, after His resurrection, showed the disciples
His hands and feet (with the marks in them). Again, we have the testimonies of the
oldest Church Fathers, who wrote at a time when this punishment was still practised.
Further, heathen writers testify that the feet as well as the hands were nailed. *Lange.*

---

19. And Pilate wrote a title, and put it on the cross. And the writing was, JESUS
OF NAZARETH THE KING OF THE JEWS.

Wrote. See on Matt. xxvii. 37, and Luke xxiii. 38.—Gr., *Pilate wrote also,* or, *moreover Pilate wrote.*—Pilate first arranged the manner of the crucifixion, between two thieves, and then wrote the superscription. *Lange.* (See on verse 18.)

A title. This was the common Roman term for an inscription of the kind.

On the cross. The "title" was borne before Him, or hung from His neck, and then nailed on the projecting top of the cross, over His head. *Geikie.*—The object of the "title" was to give information of the nature of the crime for which this punishment had been awarded.—Matthew calls it the "accusation" (xxvii. 37) ; Mark, "the superscription of the accusation" (xv. 26) ; Luke, "the superscription" (xxiii. 38).—John gives the exact word, τίτλος, from the Latin *titulus,* an *inscription.*

The writing was, &c. Gr., *Jesus the Nazarene the King of the Jews.* —All four Evangelists give the "title" but with slight variations. —In each the fundamental idea is preserved under all the various forms.—It will be seen that John's statement includes the other three.—Not at all likely that three inscriptions, in three different languages, should correspond word for word.—Very probably thus : The Aramaic (Hebrew), JESUS, THE NAZARENE, KING OF THE JEWS ; The Greek, THIS IS JESUS, THE KING OF THE JEWS ; The Latin, THE KING OF THE JEWS. *Geikie.* (See on verse 20.)— "In the sense of the man Pilate, this 'title' meant : Jesus, the king of the Jewish fanatics, crucified in the midst of Jews, who should all thus be crucified. In the sense of the Jews: Jesus, the seditionary, the king of rebels and false prophets. In the sense of the political judge: Jesus, for whose execution the Jews, with their ambiguous accusation, may answer. In the sense of the divine irony which ruled over the expression: Jesus, the Messiah, by the crucifixion become in very truth THE KING OF THE PEOPLE OF GOD." *Lange.*—His enemies meant it to denote His *offence*, and Pilate the *occasion* of His death, intending it as a mockery of the Jews.—But in the sense of Scripture it denotes His *divine ordination to death*, and in the sense of the Spirit, the *eternal gloriousness* and *fruit of His sacrifice.*—As in his saying, "Behold the Man!" little did Pilate suspect what was involved when he wrote, in the three great languages of the world, this sermon over the cross.—It is God's challenge to all unbelieving Jews and all mankind to acknowledge this Jesus of Nazareth as their King.—All *languages,* all tongues, are to resound with His praise and confess that He is Lord, to the glory of God the Father.—" Thou mayest recognise Him as King by the victories He achieves even on the fatal tree " (see on verse 20).

τίτλος. The Evangelists, in dealing with a written inscription, in which there could have been neither doubt nor difficulty, have not been careful to give us the exact words. The fact is significant, as bearing upon the literary characteristics of the Gospels, and upon the value which the writers set upon exact accuracy in unimportant details. The reason of the variations may be traced to the fact that one or more of the accounts may be a translation from the Hebrew inscription. *Ellicott.*

---

20. This title then read many of the Jews: for the place where Jesus was crucified was nigh to the city: and it was written in Hebrew, and Greek, and Latin.

Read. Thus they had opportunity to reflect upon their treason to their national Messianic hopes.—The word concerning Christ is still read by many who, like these Jews, continue in unbelief.

Nigh. See on verse 17.—" Only this is more or less certain from the Gospels, viz.: That the place of the crucifixion was *out* of the city (John xix. 17; Matt. xxviii. 1); yet *near* the city (John xix. 20); apparently near a thoroughfare and exposed to the gaze of the passing multitude (as may be inferred from Mark xv. 29 and John xix. 20); probably on a little conical elevation ('skull'); and that it was near the Lord's sepulchre (John xix. 41), which was in a garden and hewn in a rock (Matt. xxvii. 60)." *Schaff.*—"On Sunday afternoon the populace are fond of walking out of the city, particularly in the direction of new suburbs. So the Jews, on *their* festivals. Towards Golgotha the beginnings of the now city were forming." *Lange.* (Lange is disposed to identify Golgotha with the hill Goath (Jer. xxxi. 39), which was outside of the city, east of the Sheep Gate.—Prof. Hitchcock says that by personal examination in 1870 he came independently to the same conclusion. *Schaff.*) (See on verses 41, 42).

Written, &c. See on Luke xxiii. 38.—" Hebrew," that is, the current Syro-Chaldaic, was the language of the people generally. (The precise form which occurs here is used in the N. T. only by John, chap. v. 2; xix. 13, 17, 20; xx. 16; Rev. x. 11; xvi. 16.)—" Greek" was the most widely known language of the time.—" Latin " was the official language of the Roman Empire. *Ellicott.*—" Here also the Evangelist has in view the triumph of the Divine Spirit over human sin and malice. The inscription, in this threefold form, must symbolize the preaching concerning the Crucified One in the three principal languages of the world : in the language of religion (Hebrew), of culture (Greek), and of the State (Latin), the language of law and government." *Lange.*— These three were the languages most known then : The Hebrew, on account of being used in the worship of the Jews ; the Greek, in consequence of the spread of Greek philosophy ; the Latin, from the Roman empire being established everywhere. *Augustine.* —Points to the language of the New Testament, as it was written in *Greek* by *Jews* in a Jewish land, under the dominion of the *Romans. Hamann.* — Written in the three great *theological* languages, that all the world may read and understand. *Krummacher.* —Among the early writers of the Church are many allusions to the languages of the Superscription in almost every discourse and treatise upon the Pentecostal gift of tongues.—These languages were also an early recognized symbol of the Trinity in Unity : *Three* to meet the cry of divers nations to bring them to the *One* household of faith.

γεγραμμένον. Ἑβραϊστὶ, Ῥωμαϊστὶ, Ἑλληνιστί. *Cod. Sin., Tisch., Treg., Meyer, Alford, Westcott and Hort.* The order of the text rec. *Codd. A. D., Syriac Vulgate,* Retained. *Lach., Lange.*

---

21. Then said the chief priests of the Jews to Pilate, Write not, The King of the Jews ; but that he said, I am King of the Jews.

Then. Gr., *Therefore said, &c.*—The connection of "therefore" is with the sentence in the preceding verse, "This title then read many of the Jews."

Chief priests. The expression, "chief priests of the Jews," occurs

only here in the N. T.—Perhaps in contrast to the title, "King of the Jews," to indicate that their anxiety came from them as representatives of the national honour. *Ellicott.*

Write not. They feel the sting of the inscription : it exposes the Messianic title to scorn and contempt.—Yet they had hounded Pilate on to take the Lord's life, by the cry, "We have no king but Cæsar."—They had prevailed by urging that He had set Himself up for a king ; and Pilate has taken care to remind them of it : Hence their complaint and his answer.—They want the inscription altered so as to have Jesus more distinctly described as a seditionary, whom Pilate himself had sentenced.

---

22. Pilate answered, What I have written I have written.

What, &c. A formula signifying that the thing was done and could not be undone.—Pilate once more assumes the air of authority and of the firm Roman.—" His declaration contains the continuation of the idea that he lays the dark riddle of this crucifixion upon their consciences, that he does not acknowledge Jesus to be guilty in their sense, and that they need reckon upon no forbearance on his part." *Lange.*—It is an indignant refusal that Jesus should be characterised in the inscription as a deceiver. —" O ineffable working of divine power, even in the hearts of ignorant men ! Did not some hidden voice sound from within, saying to Pilate, 'Alter not the inscription of the title'? " *Augustine.*—" God's decree concerning the kingdom of Christ is immutable, nor will He have the glory of it obscured or borne down by any opposition ; for so much also doth this answer point out, that as Christ was the King of the Jews, however they fretted, so the Lord in His Providence would not have the publication thereof on the cross hindered by any entreaty of theirs." *Hutcheson.*—Most wonderful, that he who before was so vacillating, is now fixed as a pillar of brass. *Flavel.*—The remonstrance of all the world against Christ's royal dignity could avail nothing (Psa. ii.).

γέγραφα, γέγραφα. The first perfect denotes the past action ; the second that it was complete and unalterable. *Alford.*

---

23. Then the soldiers when they had crucified Jesus, took his garments, and made four parts, to every soldier a part; and also his coat: now the coat was without seam, woven from the top throughout.

His garments. See on Matt. xxvii. 35, 36, and Luke xxiii. 34.—

John's account is more complete than any of the others.—By the Greek word may be understood the upper garment, the girdle, the sandals, perhaps the linen shirt; these are divided among the Roman guard, consisting of *four* men (Acts xii. 4).—The only earthly leavings of the Redeemer do not fall to the share of His people, but, in accordance with Roman law, to those who executed the death sentence. *Tholuck.*

The coat. The *tunic*, an inner garment, worn to the skin like a shirt, mostly without sleeves, fastened round the neck with a clasp, and usually reaching to the knees.—Sometimes two were worn for ornament or comfort. *Schaff.*—It was probably a priest's garment, and was woven of linen, or perhaps of wool.—John seems to see in this body-vest a homely work of art, wrought by loving hands.

Without seam. This seems to have been the rule with the priestly tunics.—The Christian Fathers saw in the Lord's seamless coat a symbol of the unity of the Church.—" Neither can the robe of Christ's righteousness be divided; every soul must have it whole." *Gossner.*

---

24. They said therefore among themselves, Let us not rend it, but cast lots for it, whose it shall be: that the scripture might be fulfilled, which saith, They parted my raiment among them, and for my vesture they did cast lots. These things therefore the soldiers did.

Lots. See on Matt. xxvii. 35, and Luke xxiii. 34.—Casting of lots, a universal custom, not condemned by Holy Scripture, was specially characteristic of the Roman soldiery.—All the Evangelists notice both the partition and casting of lots.—John alone explains why both acts were done, when one might seem to exclude the other.—The visible inheritance left by Jesus, and the inheritance left to His spiritual heirs: 1. The visible inheritance; a booty of Gentile soldiers, for which they gamble, and squander their time; 2. The spiritual inheritance: His righteousness, His peace, His word and sacrament. *Lange.*—Christ's poverty our wealth, His nakedness our covering. *Luther.*

Fulfilled See on chap. xvii. 12; xviii. 9; and on Matt. i. 22, &c.—The references to the *fulfilments of Scripture* in Christ's sufferings are heavenly lights shining into the darkness.—" All is spiritualized by the Spirit, in order to be by the Spirit glorified, as God's counsel and judgment upon the blindness of the world, glorified unto salvation." *Braune.*

Parted, &c. The passage is taken from Psa. xxii. 18, closely following the Sept.—The prophecy in the Psalm is of a typical nature.

These things, &c. See on chap. xii. 16.—As the soldiers knew
nothing of the Scripture, its accomplishment is the more manifestly
of God.—Thus all Christ's enemies and persecutors are seen to
work together for the fulfilment of the divine word and purpose.
—" A dying bed presents itself to our view, an individual at the
point of death, a legacy and the heirs : 1. The *Testator ;* Jesus of
Nazareth, (1) the poorest of the poor, (2) the King of the Jews,
the King of kings, the Son of the living God, the Alpha and
Omega, God blessed for ever ; 2. The *Legacy ;* His clothing, (1)
the upper garment which symbolizes the outwardly operating fulness of the Saviour's power and life, and, in a second signification,
the spiritual endowment intended for us—this is divisible ; (2)
the vesture or body-coat of the Man of Sorrows, which He used to
wear under the mantle ; beneath the resplendent robe of His
wonderful and active life, the Saviour wore another, the garment
of a perfect obedience : it is the robe of righteousness of the Son
of God, which is symbolized by the coat without a seam (indivisible), for which the lot is cast at the foot of the cross ; 3. The
heirs, (1) the executioners, (2) *one* of the murderers inherits the
costly robe. This circumstance tells us that no wickedness, however great, excludes unconditionally from the inheritance ; it only
depends upon this, that the symbolical position of these executioners, with respect to the body, should be essentially fulfilled in
us : 1. They know how to value the preciousness of the seamless
vestment ; 2. They perceive that only in its undivided whole it
was of value ; 3. They are satisfied to obtain possession gratui-
tously, without any merit of their own." *Krummacher.* (See on
verse 18.)

---

25. Now there stood by the cross of Jesus his mother, and his mother's sister, Mary
the wife of Cleophas, and Mary Magdalene.

Now. This and the two following verses are peculiar to John.—They
describe " a scene of unique delicacy, tenderness and sublimity.
A type of those pure and spiritual relationships which have their
origin in heaven, and are deeper and stronger than those of blood
and interest. The cross is the place where the holiest ties are
formed, and where they are guarded against the disturbing influences of sin. A few simple touches reveal a world of mingled
emotions of grief and comfort. The mother pierced in her soul
by the sword (Luke ii. 35), the beloved disciple gazing at the cross,
the dying Son and Lord uniting them in the tenderest relation.
The first words furnished the key note to that marvellous *Stabat
Mater dolorosa* of Jacopone (1306), which, though disfigured by

Mariolatry, describes with overpowering effect the intense sympathy with Mary's grief, and is the most pathetic, as the *Dies Iræ* is the most sublime, product of Latin hymnology. It is the text for some of the noblest musical compositions, which will never cease to stir the hearts of men." *Schaff.*

By the cross. According to Matthew (xxvii. 55) and Mark (xv. 40), the women mentioned stood afar off.—This is harmonized with John by distinguishing two stages in the proceedings attendant upon the crucifixion: (1) the tumult of the crucifixion itself amidst which no friends could approach; and (2) the subsequen sufferings on the cross.—The nearer Christ, the nearer the cross, and the heavier the afflictions of His people.—But fervent love regardeth no danger.—Here the weaker sex are seen to be the stronger; standing by the cross when the disciples fly.—" If the man's is the splendid deed, the woman's is enduring patience; if to the former belongs the heroism which cuts the knot, to the latter (which is the greater of the two) belongs the silent self-sacrifice which is faithful unto death. Thus in the midst of rage and fury, love stands near Jesus in His dying moments, and lifts up to Him its tearful and affectionate eye. Behold a lovely little company in the midst of the bands of Belial, a hidden rose-bud under wild and tangled bramble-bushes, a splendid wreath of lilies around the death-bed of the Redeemer. In that mourning group we see only the first divinely-quickened germs of the future kingdom of the Divine Sufferer." *Krummacher.*—These faithful women an example to all Christians, admonishing them never to be ashamed of Jesus and His cross.

His mother. See on verses 26, 27. See also on chap. ii. 1, and on Matt. i. 16, 18.—" Eve stood in Paradise beside the pleasant tree of the knowledge of good and evil. Mary stands beside the ignominious tree of the cross. The former looked upon the forbidden tree, and its fruit conduced to her death; the latter looks upon the promised tree of life, and is refreshed by its fruit in her mortal anguish." *Rambach.*

Mary. Gr., *Mary the* (wife) *of Clopas.*—This Clopas is usually identified with Alphæus (see on Matt. x. 3).—" The question arises, Are there three or four women mentioned here? Is ' Mary the wife of Clopas,' sister of Mary the mother of our Lord? or does John mean by ' His mother's sister ' an unnamed woman, who may not improbably be his own mother, Salome, whom he nowhere mentions? The question cannot be answered with certainty; but upon the whole, the balance of evidence inclines to the view that we have four persons here mentioned in two pairs: ' His mother and His mother's sister; Mary the wife of Clopas, and Mary Magdalene.' " *Ellicott.* (See note.)

Mary Magdalene. See on chap. xx. 1. See also on Matt. xxvii. 56, and Luke viii. 2.—Of her it may truly be said, that having been forgiven much, she loved much (Luke vii. 47).

εἱστήκεισαν. *" His mother* (Mary) *and His mother's sister* (Salome) ; then *Mary—the wife of Clopas—and Mary Magdalene."* Lach., Tisch., Lücke, Ewald, Meyer, Wieseler, Alford, Lange, Schaff, Geikie, Westcott and Hort, &c.—The Syriac, Ethiopian, and Persian translations insert καί between *sister of His mother* and *Mary*, thus making them two distinct persons.—Thus we have not *three* women, but *four*, arranged in two pairs: Mary and her sister (Salome), Mary of Clopas and Mary the Magda'ene. (See the list of the Apost'es, Matt. x 2 ff.; Luke vi. 16 ff.)—Consequently John, the son of Salome, was a cousin of Jesus and a nephew of His earthly mother.—This double relationship explains the more readily the fact that Jesus intrusted her to John rather than to His "brethren," who at the time were yet unbelieving.—The above hypothesis is supported by the following facts: 1. It is not supposable that two sisters had the same name. 2. In a precisely similar manner John elsewhere paraphrases his own name. Nor does he introduce his brother James by name. 3. According to Matt. **xxvii. 56**; Mark **xv, 40**. Salome really was among those women who stood by the cross; and it is not likely that John should have omitted his own mother, the less so as he introduced himself. Lange., Schaff.—Κλωπᾶ may be the same with the Κλεόπας mentioned in Luke xxiv. 18. Schaff.—On the whole, it seems safer to doubt their identity. Smith's "Dict of the Bible."—Commonly identified with Ἀλφαῖος, Matt. x, 3. Meyer, Lange, &c.—Not certain that ἡ τοῦ means the *wife of*; it may also mean the *daughter of*. Ewald.

---

26. When Jesus therefore saw his mother. and the disciple standing by, whom he loved, he saith unto his mother, Woman, behold thy son!

The disciple, &c. See on chap. xiii. 23.—The last sight we have of John, before the crucifixion, is in the courtyard of the high priest (see on chap. xviii. 16).—" He had seen Jesus led away to Pilate, and had, apparently, followed Him to the palace, waiting in the angry crowd till the weak time serving procurator had given Him up to the cross. He may have left as soon as the end was known, to hasten into the city with the sad news to those anxious to hear ; above all, to tell her whose soul the sword was now about to pierce most keenly. Mary, very likely, heard her Son's fate from his lips. She had come to Jerusalem to be near Him, but we do not know when ; for she was not one of the group of pious Galilæan women who habitually followed Him, though she was with them at this moment. How many were together is not told ; but Mary, at least, on hearing John's words, determined, in her love, to go at once to Calvary, and some round her resolved to go with her. John, faithful as a woman, would not stay behind." *Geikie.*—Evidently, none of our Lord's "brothers or sisters" were there, for His resurrection was first to win them to His cause —As His eyes wandered over the crowd, He saw, through the gloom, John standing by His mother's side.—He knew John's heart, and, indeed, his presence there proclaimed it. —Those who enter into the fellowship of Christ's shame and suffering find, like John, that it is the way to honour and reward.

Woman. See on chap. ii. 4.—Here denotes particularly the character of *woman* in her helplessness and need of comfort.—Mary also deserved the name of "*woman*" in the *ideal sense*.—As Christ was the Son of Man, or the Man, so she, though approximately only, not in the perfection of sinlessness, was the ideal woman. *Lange.* —The second Eve, *the Woman*, whose *Seed* had bruised the head of the serpent (Gen. iii. 15).—Thus this name given to her who in spirit shares His agony, is a title of *dignity*.—Moreover, He would not have exposed Mary to the mockery or persecution of the enemy by saluting her with the title of "mother."—It may be hoped that the day is now past, when anything other than thoughts of reverence and honour is to be connected with the title "Woman," least of all from the lips of the Son of Man.—Were proof needed of the tenderness which underlies the word as used by Him, it would be found in the other instances which the Gospels supply (see Matt. xv. 28; Luke xiii. 12; John iv. 21: xx. 13, 15, &c.).— "The sight of his mother in tears; true even in death; in spite of danger, or of her broken heart, or of the reproaches rising on every side; the remembrance of Nazareth; the thought of the sorrows that so often, in these last years, had pierced her soul, and of the supreme grief that had now overwhelmed her; the recognition of the true faith in Him, shining out in these last hours, as the child, borne by miracle to be a Saviour, the holy Son of God; and the thought that His earthly relations to her were closed for ever, filled His heart with tender emotion." *Geikie.*—"The presence of the Godhead in our Lord's person did not efface and outshine the essential feelings of a human heart. It did but quicken and strengthen all those affections and sympathies which are still left as remnants of the heavenly image, and the groundwork of its renewal within us." *Hobhouse.*

Thy son. The silence of the history concerning Joseph presupposes that he was dead.—Mary will therefore be left without her Son as well as without her husband.—And in the tenderness of an undying love, He commits her to the care of him whom He Himself had loved beyond others.—The *friend* of Jesus was fitted to be the *son* of Mary.—As John alone stood by her in this awful moment, as her support; so should he stand by her from this time forth.— Doubtless there were those of nearer earthly relationship, but Jesus regards whosoever doeth the will of His Father in heaven as "brother and sister and mother" (see on Matt. xii. 50).—It was as if He had said, "In him at thy side thou hast thy Son given back to thee."—"Therefore, let those who would envy John the pleasing task of being a support to the mother of Jesus know that the way to the same honour lies open to them." *Krummacher.*

---

27. Then saith he to the disciple, Behold thy mother! And from that hour that disciple took her unto his own home.

Thy mother. "The solemn committal is a double one: the loving heart of the disciple should find, as well as give, sympathy and support in the love of the mother." *Ellicott.*—"Behold thy son!" signifies: in him shall be thy support; "Behold thy mother!" thou shalt become a sharer in her maternal blessings.—As if He had said: "To thee I trust My mother; let her be *thy* mother for My sake."—On both sides love and blessing are one in personal relationship.—Though the burden of the world's redemption lay upon His soul, and boundless anticipations of the glory to be obtained filled His spirit, yet He had room for the exercise of the minutest care.—This thoughtfulness for others rather than Himself, in this His time of greatest need, shows that He was still what He had always been.—Looking up to Him, John saw the light of higher than earthly victory on His pale features.—A double reward to John's love: 1. The new nearness to Jesus by the relationship he was henceforth to sustain to His mother; 2. A confirmation of his faith for ever.—How stupendous a legacy was this for Divine Piety to bequeath, and for human love to inherit!—And what a Son was Jesus! true both to His Father in heaven, and to His mother on earth.—These words to Mary and John, from the cross, contain the record of the institution of a new family relationship, in which Jesus is the Head, and all His people the members.

Took her. The words, "from that hour," may imply that John at once removed Mary from the dreadful scene.—If so, he must soon have returned (verse 35), and the whole account is evidently that of an eye-witness.

His own home. Gr., *his own* (see on chap. xvi. 32).—John may have had a house of his own in Jerusalem (see on chap. xviii. 15). —"If he received Mary into his *dwelling*, into his *family circle*, consisting of Salome and perchance his brother, the words would be perfectly correct." *Meyer.*—The meaning undoubtedly is that whatever was *his* home became hers.—"It was for the Apostle in his later years a sweet reward to recall vividly every such minute detail, and for his readers it is, without his intention, a sign that he alone could have written all this." *Ewald.*—"As GOD, our

Lord might have removed His mother to the best of those 'many mansions' which are prepared for those that love Him. But it was *as* GOD He willed that she should stay awhile on earth : while *as Man*, He both provided a home for her, and called the human feelings of a friend into play on her behalf, while He did so." *Hobhouse.*—" Some say she lived with John at Jerusalem, and there died ; and others say that she died in the twelfth year after the resurrection of Christ, being fifty-nine years of age, and was buried by John in the garden of Gethsemane." *Gill.*—But it has pleased God to envelop all this in doubt and mystery, and with this we are to be satisfied.—Nay, more, being taught by the errors of the Church of Rome in regard to Mary, we may mark the wisdom of God in wrapping up the matter thus.—" With these words on the cross, the Lord Jesus (1) intended to show how He beareth on His heart a care even for our bodily circumstances, and considereth such care a part of His mediatorial office ; He therewith (2) designed to confirm the fifth Commandment, and to set all children a good example, as to how they should care for their poor and forsaken parents ; He hath therewith (3) shown that it is not contrary to the sense of the fifth Commandment if we extend its limit somewhat farther than the letter of it seemeth to require ; He hath (4) designed to hallow the natural love existing between friends and relatives ; He hath (5) sanctioned guardianships ; He hath (6) approved of testaments ; He hath (7) taught thereby how every one ought to strive to make this painful life more endurable to his neighbour by rendering him loving aid ; He hath (8), particularly in the person of John, enjoined it upon the hearts of all the teachers of His Church to have a care for poor and destitute persons; He hath (9) shown how we should seek to accomplish through others the good that we ourselves are unable to perform ; He hath (10) assured all whom He recognizeth as His mother and his brethren that He will not forsake or neglect them either." *Osiander.*

η μήτηρ σου. The solemn and affecting commendation of her to John is doubly made, and thus bound by the strongest injunctions on both.—The Romanist idea, that the Lord *commended all His disciples as represented by the beloved one*, to the patronage of His mother, is simply absurd.—The converse is true: He did solemnly commend the care of her, especially indeed to the beloved disciple, but in him to the whole circle of disciples, among whom we find her, Acts iv. 14.—No certain conclusion can be drawn from this commendation, as to the " brethren of the Lord " believing on Him or not at this time.—The reasons which influenced Him in His selection must ever be far beyond our penetration: and *whatever relations to Him we suppose those brethren to have been*, it will remain equally mysterious why He passed them over, who were so closely connected with His mother.—Still, the presumption that they did not

then believe on Him, is one of which it is not easy to divest one's self ; and at least
may enter as an element into the consideration of the whole subject, beset as it is with
uncertainty. *Alford.*—John's relation to Mary as established beneath the Cross, was
that of a sacred friendship and spiritual communion, and interfered neither with John's
relation and duty to his natural mother Salome, nor with Mary's relation to the
"brethren" of Jesus, whatever view we may take of them. *Schaff.*—Wherever John
dwelt he doubtless regarded the solemn committal of Mary to his care as binding
while she lived.– If we may accept the traditions which place her death in the year
A.D. 48 as approximately true, it may account for the fact that John is not mentioned
with Peter and James as in Jerusalem during Paul's visit after his conversion, about
A.D. 38 (Gal. i. 18, 19) ; but he is so mentioned, and is regarded as one of the " pillars
of the Church," at the visit to the council in A D. 51 (Gal. ii. 9). *Ellicott.*—Observe
how imperturbable our Lord is during His crucifixion, talking to John of His mother,
fulfilling prophecies, giving good hope to the thief ; whereas, before His crucifixion,
He seemed in fear.—The weakness of His nature was shown *there*, the exceeding
greatness of His power *here*.—He teaches us too, herein, not to turn back, because we
may feel disturbed at the difficulties before us ; for when we are once actually under
the trial, all will be light and easy for us. *Chrysostom.*

---

28. After this, Jesus knowing that all things were now accomplished, that the
scripture might be fulfilled, saith, I thirst.

After this. Not necessarily immediate.—Here we must suppose
the words " My God, my God, why hast thou forsaken me ? " to
have been said meantime, and the three hours' darkness to have
taken place.

Knowing. On our Lord's omniscience, see on chap. ii.· 24, 25 ;
xvi. 30 ; xviii. 4 ; xxi. 17.

Accomplished. Gr., *finished* (see on verse 30).—In the original the
words for " accomplished " and " fulfilled," in this verse, are
derived from the same root.

Scripture, &c. The Greek is not the ordinary formula of quotation, such as is found in chap. xiii. 18 ; xvii. 12, &c.—The clause
might be rendered " knowing that all things were now finished
that the Scripture might be completed."—Jesus is conscious that
His passion is finished, *i. e.*, finished unto the accomplishment of
Scripture.—The margin of the A. V. assumes that the fulfilling
of Scripture is connected with the words " I thirst," and refers to
Psa. lxix. 21.—But against this it may be urged : (1) John's custom is to quote the fulfilment of Scripture, as seen in the event
after its occurrence ; (2) he does not here use the ordinary words
which accompany such a reference ; (3) the actual meaning of
" knowing that all things were now accomplished " seems to exclude
the idea of a further accomplishment, and to refer to the whole
life which was an accomplishment of Scripture ; (4) the context
of words as they occur in the Psalm (verse 22, &c.), cannot be
understood of our Lord.—There seems to be good reason, therefore, for understanding the words " that the Scripture might be

completed," of the events of the whole life, and not of the words
which immediately follow. *Ellicott.* (But see note.)—The expression, "that the Scripture might be accomplished," does not mean
that He passed through all these things to fulfil Scripture, but,
that in the fulfilment of Scripture as the expression of the will of
His Father, He found that which was His comfort and support in
view of all these things (Luke xxii. 22; Matt. xxvi. 54).

I thirst. The stupefying draught usually presented to sufferers
by crucifixion, He had refused (see on Matt. xxvii. 34, 48).—The
torment of thirst, caused by raging fever, was one of the most
dreadful elements in the agony of the cross.—Hitherto His mind
had been so absorbed in the great mysterious work of redemption,
that He had forgotten this burning thirst which preyed upon Him.
—But now that all has been accomplished, and with the presentiment of victory in His soul, His bodily condition makes itself felt.
—At the close of the forty days' temptation in the wilderness, He
was an *hungered*, and so here, at the close of the awful conflict on
the cross, He *thirsts*.—Thirst is the child's first appetite, and the
last physical sensation of the dying when leaving earth behind.—
Since the Passover Cup of the evening before, He had tasted no
refreshment.—Six hours have elapsed since He refused the vinegar
mingled with gall.—A touching complaint from the lips of the
Incarnate Word, who had for others changed water into wine, and
who was Himself the Rock whence Israel in the desert was
refreshed (1 Cor. x. 4).—A Christian poet has imagined how, on
this exclamation from the God-man, "all the cool brooks falling
down over the rocks stood still a moment in their course, then
rushed down into the depths below, loudly complaining that they
had not been permitted to assuage the thirst of their Creator in
His human form."—But what is the representation beside the
terrible reality?—Thirst, more dreadful than hunger, is now
endured upon a cross, and by the Son of God!—"The *thirst of
Jesus*, His last suffering. A sign (1) that He has passed through
all His sufferings, and may now receive the draught of refreshment; (2) that He departs from earth, and from those who have
crucified Him, not proudly and coldly, but humbly, warmly, and
lovingly; (3) that He would be no pattern in self-chosen torments and penances ; (4) that He still speaks in the consciousness
of His divine spiritual power, as if it were at once an entreaty and
a command; (5) that He is making preparation for the end."
Lange.—If God's Son hungered and thirsted while on earth, the
servant should not complain if he fare no better than his Lord.—
"And after what does His soul thirst most? A Father of the
Church has said with truth : 'He thirsts after our thirst.' Yea,

He thirsts after the salvation of the world, after the glorifying of the Father, after the *close;* but above all, after the *result* of the struggle. He thirsts after the song of redemption: 'The Lamb that was slain is worthy to receive glory, and honour, and power.' Oh, that this last complaint of the dying Saviour might draw forth from many hearts in reply: 'My soul thirsteth after God, after the living God!' This thirst will most assuredly be quenched with something better than gall and vinegar. Even here the saying passes into fulfilment: 'They shall hunger no more, neither shall they thirst any more;' and hereafter: 'The Lamb, which is in the midst of the throne, shall feed them, and shall lead them *unto living fountains of water.*'" *Oosterzee.*

ἵνα. Is referable to λέγει διψῶ. Since He knew that all things were accomplished, He said, in order to fulfil the Scripture in that particular also, "I thirst." *Chrys., Theoph., &c.*—This manner of fulfilling the Scripture is in accordance neither with the view of the Lord nor the delineation of John (see verse 24).—Then, too, it would have to read thus: As He knew that the Scripture was fulfilled, with the exception of one particular, He said, in order that this one thing also might be fulfilled, &c. *Lange.*— Christ did not drink for the sake of fulfilling the Scripture, but the Evangelist interprets His drinking as a fulfilment of Scripture; ἵνα, &c., is therefore a parenthesis, containing the explanation of the Evangelist. *Pisc., Grotius, Lücke.*—Having it in view to leave no pre-appointed particular of the circumstances of His suffering unfulfilled, Jesus, speaking doubtless also in intense present agony of thirst, but only speaking because He so willed it, and because it was an ordained part of the course He had taken upon Him, said, "I thirst." *Alford.*—The sentence ἵνα, &c., is not parenthetic, nor is it to be applied to what follows, but to that which precedes it. *Michaelis, Semler, Knapp, Tholuck, Meyer, Lange, Schaff, &c.*

---

29. Now there was set a vessel full of vinegar: and they filled a spunge with vinegar, and put it upon hyssop, and put it to his mouth.

Vinegar. The ordinary sour wine, or vinegar and water, the common beverage of the Roman soldiers.—Christ's complaint, His last craving, must not fail of satisfaction; therefore provision had been made beforehand.—The mention of the sponge and hyssop indicates that the vessel of wine had been placed there for this purpose.

Hyssop. Noticed by John only.—No plant mentioned in the Scriptures has given rise to greater differences of opinion than this.—It is named in one other passage of the New Testament (Heb. ix. 29), and is frequent in the Septuagint version of the Old Testament.—But whether the Greek word was adopted as that most nearly resembling the Hebrew in sound, or as the true representative of the plant indicated by the latter, cannot be decided.—Hyssop was used to sprinkle the doorposts of the Israelites in Egypt with the blood of the paschal lamb (Ex. xii. 22). It was employed in the purification of lepers and leprous houses (Lev. xiv. 4, 51), and in the sacrifice of the red heifer (Num. xix. 6).—In consequence of its detergent qualities, or from its being associated with the purificatory services, the Psalmist prays, "purge me with hyssop" (Ps. li. 7).—It is described in 1 Kings iv. 33, as growing on or near walls.—Bochart decides in favour of marjoram, or some plant like it, and to this conclusion all tradition points.—The stalks, from a foot to a foot and a half high, would be sufficient to reach to the cross.

Mouth. Moistening His parched lips: evidently the act of one or the soldiers.—No angel, as at Gethsemane, no friend's hand tenders Him this last service.—Refreshment from such hands, with such a wretched draught, is all the world has to offer the Lord of glory! —The evening draught which the great Labourer takes as He quitteth work!

ὕσσωπος. A low plant or shrub, put in antithesis with the cedar as growing out of the wall or rocks, 1 Kings iv. 33.—Under the names ēzôb and ὕσσωπος, the Hebrews appear to have comprised not only the hyssop, *hyssopus officinalis*, but also other similar aromatic plants, as lavender, and especially origanum or wild marjoram, called by the Arabs *Zattar*, and found in great abundance around Mount Sinai. *Robinson.*—In the present state of the evidence there does not seem sufficient reason for departing from the old interpretation, which identified the Greek ὕσσωπος with the Hebrew ēzôb. *Smith's* ' Dict. of the Bible."

30. When Jesus therefore had received the vinegar, he said, It is finished : and he bowed his head, and gave up the ghost.

It is finished. The Greek is but a single word, and no greater or profounder ever fell upon the human ear.—This is the last but one of the seven sayings upon the cross.—The order is (1) "Father, forgive them; for they know not what they do" (Luke xxiii. 34) ; (2) "Verily I say unto thee, To-day shalt thou be with me in paradise" (Luke xxiii. 43); (3) "Woman, behold thy Son," "Behold thy mother" (John xix. 26, 27); (4) "Eli, Eli, lama sabachthani?" (Matt. xxvii. 46; Mark xv. 34); (5) "I thirst" (John xix. 28); (6) "It is finished" (John xix. 30); (7) "Into thy hands I commend my spirit" (Luke xxiii. 46).

Finished. See on chap. xvii. 1, 4.—He had *finished* the work which the Father had given Him to do.—"Jesus knowing that all things were now *finished*" (see on verse 28).—It is possible that He required the reviving refreshment of the vinegar-wine to aid Him in pronouncing this sublime word.—"All things were done which the law required, all things established which prophecy predicted, all things abolished which were to be abrogated, all things obtained in order to be bestowed which had been the subject of promise. All things were suffered which were to be suffered, all things were done and accomplished, nothing was left wanting. The theology of ages has striven to embrace this ' *all* ' and to develop it; and strives to this day in vain to express it perfectly." *Stier.*—Everything appertaining to the purchase of our salvation is expressed and concluded in this ONE WORD.—" At the very moment when, for the Hero of Judah, all seems lost, He declares that all is won and accomplished. Listen! At these words you hear fetters burst, and prison walls falling down ; barriers as high as heaven are overthrown, and gates which had been closed for thousands of years again move on their hinges. With this heraldic and conquering cry, He turned once more to the world. It was His farewell to earth, a farewell such as beseemed the Conqueror of Death, the Prince of Life, the Lord of all." *Krummacher.*—" But was He already risen for our justification ? He had not yet sent the Comforter. Yet in the holy instant of death, by the light of eternity, His eye beheld the finished work of redemption, in its readiness for prosecution and spiritualization. Thus through suffering and tribulation is attained the triumph of the kingdom of God." *Braune.*—IT IS FINISHED : 1. *It*, not this and that : *all* that lays the foundation of the new, eternal world of God ; 2. It *is*, not it *is being* (Heb. x. 14) ; 3. *Finished.* As a spiritual act, as a vital conflict, as a mortal suffering, as a triumph of Christ and the salvation of God—conducted to the goal ($\tau\epsilon\lambda o\varsigma$). IT IS FINISHED : 1. As the Evangel of Christ ; 2. As the confession of the Church ; 3. As the jubilation of the believing heart; 4. As an excitation to every work of faith; 5. As a prophecy of the Last Day.—It is (1) a prophetic word (all Scripture fulfilled) ; (2) a high-priestly word (the expiatory sacrifice completed) ; (3) a kingly word (the kingdom of heaven founded) ; (4) a unitous word (the work of redemption accomplished as the founding of the new creation, the world of the eternal Spirit.) *Lange.*

Bowed. The mention of this is peculiar to John, as he alone of the Evangelists was an eye-witness of the scene.—The attitude of the Lord in His last moment was powerfully impressed upon the mind of the beloved disciple.

Gave. Gr., *and yielded up His spirit* (see on Matt xxvii. 50, and Luke xxiii. 46).—All the accounts affirm the *voluntary* action of His death.—It was a *free* dying.—In the ethical sense His death was not a *suffering*, but a *deed* (see on chap. x. 17, 18).—Death had no power to lay its icy hand upon His heart : *He gave up His life.* —"The Lord's death : 1 The result of the world's most deadly hate; an unparalleled murder and death. 2. The result of Christ's unconquerable love; the all-comprehensive death, in that'all died in the One. 3. The result of God's grace; it was the world's redemption (its atonement, deliverance, illumination, sanctification). The sublimity of the atoning death of Jesus, as it appears: 1. Towering above the most fearful and terrific guilt; 2. Overcoming the most terrible temptation (the struggle against abandonment by God). 3. Bursting through the most formidable barriers (the feeling of death). 4. Displaying boundless and eternal efficacy (extending as far as the highest height of heaven, the depths of Sheol, the depths of the Gentile world, the depths of the human heart)." *Lange.*—Even the infidel Rousseau exclaimed: "If Socrates lived and died like a sage, Jesus of Nazareth lived and died like a God."—Our death too, when God calleth, must be voluntary.—It is the Christian's art to die willingly. *Heubner.*

παρέδωκεν. Our Lord's death occurred on Friday the 15th of Nisan (April 7th) shortly after 3 o'clock in the afternoon. *Smith's* "Dict. of the Bible."—Chronological calculations show that in the year 30, the 15th Nisan actually fell on a F.iday, which was the case only once more between the year 28-36. *Wieseler.*—In a work by W. Stroud, M.D., on the *Physical Cause of Christ's Death and its Relation to the Principles and Practice of Christianity,* the author endeavours to demonstrate that the immediate cause of the Saviour's death must be traced neither to the ordinary effects of crucifixion, nor the wound inflicted by the soldier's spear nor an unusual degree of weakness, nor the interposition of supernatural influence, but to the vicarious agony of His mind culminating in the exclamation. "My God, My God," &c., and producing *rupture of the heart,* which is intimated by a discharge of blood and water from His side, when it was afterwards pier ed by a spear—The late Sir James Y. Simpson, in an appendix to the second edition, has expressed his approval of Dr. Stroud's work.—The same view is maintained by others.—"In a death from heart rupture 'the hand is suddenly carried to the front of the chest, and a piercing shriek uttered.' The hands of Jesus were nailed to the cr ss, but the appalling shriek is recorded. Jesus literally died of a broken heart." *Dr. Walshe,* quoted by *Sir J. Y. Simpson,* in *Hanna; Ewald, Geikie.* (See also on verse 34.)

---

31. The Jews therefore, because it was the preparation, that the bodies should not remain upon the cross on the sabbath day, (for that sabbath day was an high day,) besought Pilate that their legs might be broken, and that they might be taken away.

Therefore. From verse 31 to 37 is peculiar to John.—The "therefore" characteristically indicates the next concern which troubled the Jews.—The observance of the ceremonial law was their *first* thought after the dreadful crime had been accomplished (see on chap. xviii. 28).

Preparation. See on verse 14.—They must make ready for keeping holy the Sabbath, while their hands are red with the murder of the Son of God.

Not remain. It was the Roman custom to allow the bodies to hang upon the cross till they wasted away, or were consumed by the birds of prey.—" To feed the crows on the cross," was a familiar expression.—Jewish law knew nothing of crucifixion, but it had not been uncommon to hang up the body of a criminal after death. —It was not permitted, however, that it should be exposed after sunset : burial the same day was enacted, " that the land should not be defiled " (Deut. xxi. 23). *Geikie.*

That Sabbath. Gr., *For great was the day of that Sabbath.*—No bodies were allowed to remain hanging on the tree on the Sabbath day.—But this was not simply a Sabbath day ; its sanctity was increased by its falling in the Paschal season.—Three corpses seen on the cross, so near the Temple and the Holy City, on a day so sacred, would make great commotion, as polluting the whole place. —A stroke of that Jewish hypocrisy which strains out gnats and swallows camels, similar to chap. xviii. 28.—These men considered themselves strictly bound to observe every jot and tittle of an outward ordinance ; but never scrupled to violate the most weighty precepts of the moral law.—They made no conscience of murdering an innocent person, and yet could not think of letting His dead body hang upon the cross upon the Sabbath day.

Besought. Doubtless by a deputation of the Temple authorities.— In the case of Jesus they are particularly anxious to have His body removed " out of sight and mind " of the people.—With His corpse they would bury His very name, and their deed also, in the grave for ever.—But here, as in the composition of the superscription, contingencies occur, which cross, modify and enfeeble their plots.—They cannot frustrate the purpose of God that Jesus shall be significantly distinguished from the thieves, and honourably entombed.—Their desire for the removal of the bodies may be viewed : 1. As the expression of a legal, slavish zeal ; 2. As an act of hypocritical sanctimoniousness ; 3. As showing a bad conscience.

Broken. They were anxious to get Pilate's sanction for putting any of the three to death who might yet be alive.—It follows from this general way of preferring their request, that as yet they had no certain knowledge of Christ's death.—In such a case the common mode of procedure was in keeping with Roman cruelty : The legs were shattered by means of clubs.—This punishment, which was known by the name of *crurifragium*, was as harsh and brutal as crucifixion itself.

καταγῶσιν. The *crurifragium* was sometimes appended to the punishment of crucifixion, but does not appear to have been inflicted for the purpose of causing death,

which indeed it would not do. *Alford.*—It is not clear that its effect would be to cause death, but this is the impression derived from the present context (verse 33). *Ellicott.* —The term appears to have involved in it the "*coup de grace*," which was given to all executed criminals; and the piercing with the spear was this death-blow, which was also inflicted on the thieves *Friedlieb.*—In accordance with the presentation in our Gospel, the breaking of the legs must be conceived of as a deadly process. *Lange.* — The shock, by the blows of the clubs, would, generally, produce death. *Geikie.*

---

32. Then came the soldiers, and brake the legs of the first, and of the other which was crucified with him.

Soldiers. Undoubtedly the quaternion by whom the crucifixion was carried out (see on vers 23).—Their dreadful duty having been accomplished, they had naturally fallen back from the crosses.—Now they appear again upon the scene to complete the work of cruelty and death.

The first, &c. They formed two pairs, and simultaneously broke the legs of the thief on the right and the thief on the left.—One of these *thieves* was a penitent, and had received from Jesus an assurance that he should shortly be *with Him in Paradise*, and yet died in the same pain and misery that the *other* did : the extremity of dying agonies is no obstruction to the living comforts that wait for believers on the other side of death. *Henry.*—"All things outward may come alike to all, and however men may be in different conditions before God, yet He may let their outward lot be equal. And albeit where the Lord pardons sin there remains no satisfactory punishment to be paid by the sinner to justice, yet the Lord may see it fit to pursue pardoned men with rods, for their own exercise, and the instruction of others ; for although the one was saved, yet he not only suffered death, but his legs were broken." *Hutcheson.*

---

33. But when they came to Jesus, and saw that he was dead already, they brake not his legs.

Dead. This is the explanation of their not breaking the legs of Jesus.—They had fully intended to break His legs, but God had determined otherwise (see on verse 36).—"Whatever devices are in men's hearts, the counsel of the Lord, that shall stand" (Prov. xix. 21).

Already. By an act of His own will He had committed His spirit into the hands of His Father (see on verse 30) —He *hastened* His death by a voluntary self-surrender, which the Father accepted. *Lange.*—"That He was so soon dead before the other two, doth not only evidence that He, having death at His command, might die when He listed, and when He had done His work ; but also, that He had more upon Him than any of them, and therefore was the sooner dispatched by death." *Hutcheson.*

---

34. But one of the soldiers with a spear pierced his side, and forthwith came there out blood and water.

Pierced. The soldiers " saw that He was dead," but to make assurance doubly sure one of them pierced Him with his lance.—The soldier stood with his right hand opposite the left side of Jesus.— Painters are wont to picture the soldier on horseback, but this is not correct.—The word rendered " pierced," occurs nowhere else in the N. T., but it is certain, from chap. xx. 27, that the act caused a deep wound, and that the point of the lance therefore penetrated to the interior organs of the body. *Ellicott.*—It has been inferred that the wound was the breadth of a man's hand. *Tholuck.*—" His death is thus doubly and trebly warranted : once by the cognition of the soldiers, then by the mortal spear-stroke, finally by His burial on the part of His friends." *Lange.*—Here, again, in the act of this unsuspecting soldier, we see the fulfilment of prophecy (see on verse 37).—" Through this window, opened in *Christ's side*, you may look into His heart, and see love flaming there, *love stronger than death* ; see our own names written there. When *Christ, the second Adam, was fallen into a deep sleep upon the cross*, then was *His side* opened, and out of it was His Church taken which He espoused to Himself." *Henry.*—*Our Lord's pierced side :*—

> " If ye have anything to send or write
> (I have no bag, but here is room),
> Unto My Father's hand and sight
> (Believe Me) it shall safely come.
> That I shall mind, what you impart ;
> Look, you may put it very near My heart.
> Or if hereafter any of My friends
> Will use Me in this kind, the door
> Shall still be open ; what he sends
> I will present, and somewhat more,
> Not to his hurt. Sighs will convey
> Anything to Me. Hark, despair, away."
>
> *—George Herbert.*

Blood and water. It is evident from verse 37, that the Evangelist regarded the fact as one of great moment.—All attempts to explain it as a merely natural event, and upon physiological grounds, are wholly unsatisfactory : we therefore infer that it was *supernatural.*

(See Note.)—"This flowing of the blood and water together from
the wound of the spear, made a deep impression on John ; nothing
in the scene of the crucifixion seems to have made a deeper impression. It was in particular reference to this that he makes his
testimony so strong and emphatic. He makes it thus emphatic,
because the testimony is so important : important not only as part
of the conclusive evidence that the death of Christ was a real
death, but because the beloved disciple saw something eminently
significant, as we learn not only from the manner in which the
record is made, but also from his first epistle, in the two-fold
stream of water and blood which flowed from the wounded side of
Christ. We learn from that epistle (1 John v. 6-8) that the
water and the blood belong to a ternary of witnesses to the efficacy of faith in Jesus Christ. In them is the evidence that He is
an all-sufficient Saviour. The water and the blood flowing
together from the same fountain, are symbolical of the sinlessness
and the sufferings of the Redeemer, which cannot be separated in
His work of atonement. And they are at the same time significant of the two great benefits, sanctification and justification,
which also cannot be separated in believers who partake of the
benefits of His atoning work. This passage in his epistle, written
late in life, shows how deep was the impression on the mind of
John made by the events of which he was a witness on the day
of crucifixion, and how he was qualified thereby to become an
inspired teacher of the Church." *Macdonald,* "The Life and Writings of St. John."—"The blood and water significant : 1. Of the
two great benefits which all believers partake of through Christ—
justification and sanctification ; *blood* for remission, *water* for
regeneration ; *blood* for atonement, *water* for purification ; 2.
Of the two great ordinances of Baptism and the Lord's Supper.
Now was *the Rock smitten* (1 Cor. x. 4), now was *the fountain
opened* (Zech. xiii. 1), now were *the wells of salvation digged*
(Isa. xii. 3). Here is *the river*, the streams whereof make glad
the city of God." *Henry.*—"In the water and the blood are
represented the most essential elements of salvation : the *water*
has a remote reference to baptism, but it chiefly symbolizes the
moral purifying power of the word of Christ ; the *blood* points
out the ransom paid for our guilt, as well as the atoning sacrifice.
The blood flowed separately from the water ; *justification* must
not be mingled with, much less exchanged for, personal amend-
ment." *Krummacher.*

αἷμα καὶ ὕδωρ. 1. The modern explanation of the fact as a NATURAL phenomenon.
[This interpretation is made the more difficult by the circumstance that the blood

does not flow out of dead bodies, neither does it separate into blood and water (or placenta and serum), as it does in a vessel after venesection. *Lange.*) The blood issued from the heart, the water from the pericardium, *i.e.* the membrane which envelops the heart. *Gruner, Kipping. Watson, Webster and Wilkinson, Owen, Barnes.* To this theory it is objected that the quantity of liquid or reddish lymphatic humour in the pericardium is usually so minute as to be scarcely perceptible. " Haller states that a small quantity of water, not exceeding a few drachms, has frequently been found in the pericardium of executed persons; but, except under very peculiar and morbid circumstances, the eminent anatomists John and Charles Bell deny the occurrence altogether. . . . Naturally the pericardium exhibits scarcely anything which deserves the name of liquid ; but after some forms of violent death, more especially when attended with obstructed circulation, it may contain a little serum, either pure or mixed with blood. . . For the statement, that after death accompanied with anxiety the pericardium is full of water, there is no evidence." *Stroud.* Death was produced by the spear-thrust, and the forth-flowing of the blood (or of a reddish lymph) must demonstrate Christ's corporeality, in contradiction of the Docetæ. *Hammond, Kuinoel, Olshausen.* (This view is combated by the presupposition of the disciple and the ancient Church that Jesus was dead, and by the separation of blood and water. *Lange.* It is certain, however, that, had not Christ been already dead, the infliction of such a wound in the heart must have produced death; and this fact in any case sets aside the Gnostic view according to which Christ suffered and died only in appearance, as well as the older rationalistic view that Christ recovered from the effects of the crucifixion, and that His resurrection was merely an awakening from a trance. *Schaff.*) 2. The apprehension of the fact as a MIRACLE. *Origen. Theophylact and the ancient Church generally, Luthardt, Meyer, Bengel, Alford, Macdona'd.* 3. Between the assumption of a miracle unassisted by any physiological instrumentality, and that of a natural phenomenon, there lies the assumption of a PRIMITIVE PHENOMENON, *i.e.* a unique appearance based upon the unique situation. The body of Christ was undergoing a process of *transformation*, and hence the phenomenon : (1) After the death of Jesus, either corruption or transformation must have been preparing. (2) Corruption He did not see, hence it is transformation that was in course of preparation. (3) If this was preparing, the fact must of necessity make itself known by a sign transpiring in His wounded body, a sign such as we are unacquainted with in other corpses. (4) That this sign is a *unicum*, concerning which we can find nothing in the history of extravasations, pericardia, &c., is a circumstance perfectly in order. *Lange.* 4. SYMBOLICAL and ALLEGORICAL interpretations. A symbol of the two sacraments of grace. *Apollinaris, Ambrose, Augustine, Roman Catholic exegetes, Luther, Wordsworth.* The death of Jesus symbolized as the source of spiritual life. *Baur, Luthardt.* Reference of the *blood* to expiation; of the *water* to *regeneration. Calvin. &c.* "The question is properly one for physicians to settle, but they differ as much as theologians. The work of Dr. Stroud (referred to in note to verse 30) is the best upon the subject and contains some curious information. As has been already mentioned he traces the physical cause of the death of Christ to a sudden *rupture of the heart,* produced by intense agony of mind endured in behalf of sinners. He uses this verse as an argument for his theory. Rupture of the heart is followed by an effusion of blood (sometimes as much as a quart or much more) into the pericardium, where it quickly separates into its solid and liquid constituents, technically called *crassamentum* and *serum,* but in ordinary language *blood* and *water.* The soldier, in approaching the body of Christ and inflicting the wound for the purpose either to ascertain or insure His death, would purposely aim at the heart, and, transfixing the lower part of the left side, would open the pericardium obliquely from below ; that capsule being distended with crassamentum and serum, and consequently pressed against the side, its contents would, by force of gravity, be instantly and completely discharged through the wound, in a full stream of clear watery liquid intermixed with clotted blood, exactly corresponding to the sacred narrative : ' and immediately there came forth blood and water.' The difficulties of commentators have arisen mostly from the gratuitous assumption that the blood which flowed from the wound of Christ was liquid and the water pure, and, to account for so marvellous an occurrence, recourse was had either to miraculous agency, or to other equally untenable suppositions. ' Blood and water' simply denote the crassamentum and serum of blood which has separated in its constituents." *Schaff.* (See *Lange* on John, Amer. Edit.) Whatever solution we adopt, it is clear that death had taken place some time previously (verse 30), and that, while we cannot say which physical explanation is the true one, there is within the region of natural occurrences quite sufficient to account for the impression on the mind of John which he records here. *Ellicott.*

---

35 And he that saw it bare record, and his record is true : and he knoweth that he saith true, that ye might believe.

He. John speaks of himself in the third person, a form which gives solemnity to his words.—He makes a distinction between an oral, evangelistic testimony, continued during many years, and his written iteration of the same at a later period, conscious that his testimony contains an extraordinary statement. *Lange.*

Saw. He lays stress upon the specially important fact that it was an eye-witness who testified, and one therefore who knew it to be true.

Record. See on chap. i. 7, 19, 32, 34, &c.—Gr., *witnessed.*—The word " witness," with its cognate forms, is one of the key-notes to the Johannine writings, recurring alike in the Gospel, the Epistles, and the Apocalypse.—Unhappily this is partly concealed from the general reader by the various renderings " record," " testimony," &c., for the one Greek root.

True. See on chap. i. 9; xv. 1.—This is the emphatic word for " ideally true," which is so familiar to readers of this Gospel.—He distinguishes between the *substance* of his testimony as essential truth, and the *form* of his testimony.

Saith true. The witness was *ideally true*, and therefore the things witnessed were *actually true. Ellicott.*

Believe. See on chap. i. 7 ; vii. 38, &c.—This is the end for which the testimony was given.—Not merely faith in the death of Jesus, as an event which really transpired, or in the true corporeality of Christ, but for the consummation and confirmation of faith in the divine nature of Christ, and His sufficiency and efficiency as the Saviour of the world.—" As faith loveth not to walk on slippery and unsure grounds, so the word affordeth sufficient ground of certainty for faith to fasten upon."·—" Such as are made witnesses of anything concerning Christ, it is their duty, and will be their care (if they be affected therewith), to publish the same in their stations, to the edification of others." *Hutcheson.*

---

36 For these things were done, that the scripture should be fulfilled, A bone of him shall not be broken.

These things. The testimony in the preceding verse is not to be confined to the *one* fact of the flowing of the blood and water from the Lord's pierced side.—It includes those other facts in which

Scripture was accomplished, and the Divine seal put upon His claims to be the Messiah.

Fulfilled. See on chap. xvii. 12; xviii. 9.—It was no mere accident that the soldiers brake not the legs of Jesus: It was no mere accident that they parted His raiment and cast lots for His vesture (see on verse 24): It was no mere accident that the soldier pierced His side.—These things were part of the Divine order, which the prophets had foretold.

Above, &c. The first fulfilment mentioned is of a *negative* kind.— The reference is to the Paschal lamb, in which the Baptist had already seen a type of the Lamb of God (see on chap. 1. 29).— Here we find the meaning of the typical ordinance that not a bone of that lamb should be broken (Ex. xii. 46; Num. ix. 12).—As the suffering Christ was the antitype of the Paschal lamb (1 Cor. v. 7), it was necessary that this typical trait should be fulfilled in Him.—It is possible that Psa. xxxiv. 20 (Sept.) may also be referred to as a poetic adaptation of the words in Exodus (see note).

ὀστοῦν. We assume that the provision originally belonged to the expression of the *most hurried* preparation of the paschal lamb, as at the instant of fl'ght or departure. Then at the same time it was expressive of the utterly undivided participation of the house-congregation or domestic church in fellowship and sacrament. This type was fulfilled in Christ. The hurried removal from the cross an expression of the Sufferer's speedy tra sporta'ion to glory) prevented the breaking of the legs, and henceforth the *whole undivided* Christ should be the spiritual and vital food of the Church of His salvation. *Lange.* He would have none of His bones broken or taken off from the communion of His natural Body, to note the indissoluble union, which was to be betwixt Him and His members. *Reynolds.*

---

37 And again another scripture saith, They shall look on him whom they pierced.

Another. The Old Testament is a continuous witness to Christ.— We read that after His resurrection, on the way to Emmaus, "beginning at Moses and all the prophets, He expounded unto them in all the Scriptures the things concerning Himself" (Luke xxiv. 27).—And again : "These are the words which I spake unto you, while I was yet with you, that all things must be fulfilled, which were written in the law of Moses, and in the prophets, and in the psalms, concerning me " (verse 44).

Shall look. The second fulfilment mentioned is of a *positive* kind. —The passage referred to is found in Zech. xii. 10, "*They shall look up to me whom they have pierced.*"—"But the reading which John has followed is that of many MSS., and is adopted by many Rabbinic and many modern authorities. The Greek translation

(Sept.) of the prophet avoided the strong word 'pierced,' as applied to Jehovah, and substituted for it 'insulted.' John translates the original Hebrew freely for himself, and gives the undoubted meaning of the Hebrew word, translating it by the same Greek word which is used by Aquila, Theodotian, and Symmachus. He thinks of the prophecy which spoke of Jehovah as pierced by His people, and sees it fulfilled in the Messiah pierced on the cross." *Ellicott.*—"The passage is one of the exceedingly pregnant Messianic passages of the second half of Zechariah. The Messiah here appears in the light of the self-manifesting Jehovah Himself. The *piercers* are the Jews, standing as representatives of the human race. 'They have pierced Me,' *i. e.*, they have consummated their enmity against My highest manifestation and approach. 'They shall look upon Me whom they have pierced,' *i.e.*, their eyes shall be opened in regard to their conduct, and they shall perceive whom they have outraged. They shall regret it, or it shall become a matter of regret to them. This prophecy has had a general fulfilment in the turning of the *believing world* to the Crucified One. It shall, however, be fulfilled in the most universal sense, in regard to the whole world, at the Last Judgment" (Rev. i. 7). *Lange.* (See Note.)—The revelation of Christ as *pierced* by the sinner, can alone lead to repentance.—Nothing but the sight of *His* breaking heart can melt the stony heart of sin.—" God commendeth His love toward us, in that, while we were yet sinners, Christ died for us" (Rom. v. 8).—He will draw all men unto Him, and that by the power of the very cross upon which He was crucified and pierced (see on chap. xii. 32).—In every penitent who believes "He loved me, He gave Himself for me," these words are fulfilled.—Doubtless there is a prophetic reference also to the future conversion of Israel.

"Οψονται, &c. The Evangelist has given the literal and, as now acknowledged, true sense of the Hebrew word. *Lücke, Alford, &c.*—The beginning of this consternation of the world upon discovering that it has thrust at God, whilst it supposed itself to be piercing a criminal, in dealing the Messiah the heart-thrust, is significantly seen by the Evangelist.—The spear-thrust was the final heart-blow and death-blow which, after many blows and stabs, the whole race of man inflicted upon the Messiah; it was therefore the concentrated symbol of His crucifixion in general.—Hence, there immediately appeared a sign, such as is not met with in other corpses; a sign in which the higher nature of Christ, the incipient manifestation of His glory, announced itself. —That which is related concerning murdered persons, namely, that their wounds bleed afresh when the murderer approach their bodies, did actually happen here in the highest sense.—That the phenomenon made one of the many signs that perplexed and dismayed the people at Golgotha, may be securely assumed from the prominent mention which this occurrence and its effect receive at the hands of John.—This involves the complete overthrow of the *natural* (rationalistic) explanation.—An ordinary appearance could not thus have operated (see chap. viii. 28; xii. 32; Acts ii.). *Lange.*—The stab was given by one soldier only, and here it says : *They* have pierced Him. How is this? The soldier was but the instrument ; *they, sinners,* all of them, from the first to the last, did guide the soldier's hand and the crime is imputed to them. *Gossner.*

---

38. And after this Joseph of Arimathæa, being a disciple of Jesus, but secretly for fear of the Jews, besought Pilate that he might take away the body of Jesus : and Pilate gave him leave. He came therefore, and took the body of Jesus.

Joseph. See on Matt. xxvii. 57-61, and Luke xxiii. 50-56.

Secretly. This is the only additional fact supplied by John with regard to Joseph.—It was Joseph's *honour* that he was a disciple of Christ, his weakness that he was so *secretly.*—Now, however, that the termination of his Master's course seems to have stamped Him as a pitiable fanatic, he comes forward and honours Him as his King before all men.—The germ of faith which, all at once, manifests itself so gloriously, and so fully developed, had long lain in his heart.—Wonderful to tell, from out the dark thunder-cloud that brooded over Calvary, the fruitful shower has descended upon his soul.—A sure sign of the presence of the Holy Spirit, when Christ *crucified* becomes the object of holy affection.—Joseph's love breaks through all fear of man, and now when there is most to fear, his fear has vanished.—Publicly he espouses the cause of *Him* who was hanged on a tree, rejected by the world, and apparently forsaken of God!—Beautiful fruit of the death of Jesus, His *secret* disciples were made *open* ones, the weak strong.—A believing view of that great Sacrifice drives all doubt and timidity from the heart.—" Abraham's faith was great, the thief's was great, the centurion's was great. The first saw Christ in life, the second in dying, the last in death, and amid many miracles. But there is nothing to surpass the faith of Joseph ; *he believes on Him in the grave.*" *Hedinger.* (See on verse 39.)

Besought. We learn from Mark (chap. xv. 44) that Pilate marvelled when he heard that Jesus was already dead.—Evidently he expected that death would not come on before the hour when the soldiers would break the legs of the crucified : hence his sending for the centurion.—According to Jewish law, the body should have been taken away and buried in the place set apart for criminals, and this the Sanhedrists intended to do.—According to Roman law, the body might be given to any one who claimed it.—But it was not allowed to remove a body from the cross without formal permission from the procurator.—Mark how God rescues the body of His Son from the ignominy His enemies would have put upon it, gives it stately burial, and fulfils the word of prophecy.—In Isa. liii. 9, the A. V. reads : " And he made his grave with the wicked, and with the rich in his death ; " the more correct reading is, "They had made or appointed Him a grave with the despised; and among the honoured did He obtain it in His death." *Lange.*— The Sanhedrists designed to have Him buried in the spot where common criminals were interred.—Thus they would have cast the last reproach possible, upon His name and memory.—And had He not numbered among His disciples such men as Joseph and Nicodemus, their intention would have been carried out.—When God has a work to do He can find out such as are proper to do it, and strengthen them for it.—"And in the same way He is able to raise up quickly unto His people, though they be, with Christ, forsaken of all men, persons who interest themselves for them with the greatest care and diligence, such as they would never have thought on. In sorest need, therefore, take heart (Jer. xxxviii. 7, &c.)." *Zeisius.*

Took. "After the Jews had induced Pilate to have the bodies taken down, Joseph presented his request, and arrived at precisely the right moment to take the corpse, which had been accorded him, down from the cross." *Lange.*—A written order, or a verbal command to the centurion, would be sufficient.—Mark says (chap. xv. 45), that Pilate "gave the body to Joseph."—A hint that he gave it up without receiving a bribe; an unusual act for him.— May imply some remains of the feeling which had led him to resist the demands of our Lord's enemies.—Joseph's love leaps over all considerations and scruples about touching a dead body, and that the corpse of a reputed malefactor.—One Joseph is appointed to take charge of Jesus in His infancy, and another is raised up to provide for his burial.

μετὰ ταῦτα. Not "immediately after this," but, "soon after." *Alford.*—τοῦ 'Ιησοῦ. αὐτόν. *Lach., Treg., Alf., Westcott and Hort, Schaff.* αὐτου *Tischendorf.*—The narrative implies, though it does not mention (as Mark and Luke do), that Joseph himself took down the body from the cross. *Alford.*—It was no light matter Joseph had undertaken; for to take part in a burial at any time, would defile him for seven days, and make everything unclean which he touched; and to do so now involved his seclusion through the whole paschal week, with all its holy observances and rejoicings. *Geikie.*

---

39. And there came also Nicodemus, which at the first came to Jesus by night, and brought a mixture of myrrh and aloes, about an hundred pound weight.

Nicodemus. See on chap. iii. 1, 2; vii. 50.—No other Evangelist mentions Nicodemus.—Owing to the prominent part taken by Joseph *he* is mentioned by all the Evangelists, in connection with our Lord's burial.—The remarks concerning Joseph (see on verse 38) equally apply to Nicodemus.—John says, " which *at the first*

came to Jesus by night," designing thus to wipe away that stain
from the character of Nicodemus.—It is as if he had written:
" Though *at the first* he was timid and time-serving, yet *at the last*
he was bold and decisive. Behold, he now comes openly, by day,
and before the world, bearing the costly tribute of his faith
and love." *Ford* —" The association of Joseph of Arimathæa
and Nicodemus : A sign showing how the complete development
of malice and unrighteousness impels all nobler natures into the
camp of Christ; and how the darkest hours of the Kingdom of
God are invariably the natal hour of a new discipleship. That
glory of the Jewish world, to which they cleaved, being turned to
shame in their eyes, they are become free from their earthly goods,
and know not how better to spend them than in the service of the
love of Christ. One offers the abundance of his precious spices,
which constituted an important household treasure among the
Orientals; the other offers his garden and his family-vault to be
the resting place of an excommunicate, outlawed, crucified Man;
both sacrifice their safety, position, authority, their old associa-
tions, and, greatest sacrifice of all, their old Jewish hierarchal
pride, and their old Messianic hope and entire view of the world.
To them all things are involved in midnight gloom; but the innocence and righteousness of Jesus they see, shining as the broad
day in the midst of this darkness." *Lange.*

A mixture. The myrrh and aloes were pulverised and mixed
together.

Myrrh. See on Matt. ii. 11.—The gum of an aromatic plant.—" In
the gifts of the wise men at His birth, the gold is considered to
imply His Kingship, and the frankincense His Divinity, and the
myrrh His Humanity ; now the *myrrh* alone of them is found. It
is our Lord's Humanity, which is embalmed (Mark xvi. 19; Acts
ii. 24, 27)." *Williams.*

Aloes. Not elsewhere mentioned in the N. T., but joined with
myrrh in the Messianic Psalm xlv. 8.—It is the name of various
sorts of aromatic wood in the East.—That referred to is entirely
different from the plant which produces the aloes of the shops.—
It is used by the Orientals as a perfume, and was employed by
the Egyptians for the purposes of embalming.—Chips of the
better kind are now said to be worth their weight in gold. *Ellicott.*

An hundred pound. It is recorded of the burial of Asa, that they
" laid him in the bed which was filled with sweet odours
and divers kinds of spices prepared by the apothecaries' art."
(2 Chron. xvi. 14.)—An hundred pounds is a large quantity; but,
perhaps, the whole body was encased, after the wrapping, in the
mixture, and an outer wrapper fastened over all. *Alford.*—A

proof of the greatness of their love produced by the Lord's death.—Thank offerings which immediately glorify the redemptive and expiatory offering of Christ.—As this love to Jesus was called out by the might of His love, so His death is still the power which constrains men.—Thus this act of love is a testimony for Jesus, and for the future effect of His death.—And thus the Evangelist mentions the weight of the spices ; because it is a witness to the depth and fulness of their love (see on verse 38).

λίτρας ἑκατόν. The proceeding was hurried, on account of the approaching Sabbath : and apparently an understanding entered into with the women, that it shou'd be more completely done after the Sabbath was over.   This p'entiful application of the aromatic substances may therefore have been made with an intention to prevent the body, in its lace·ated state, from incipient decomposition during the interval. *Alford.* — The hundred pounds of myrrh and aloes must have been bought beforehand, and may have been stored up from the time when he knew that the leading members of the Council had resolved upon the death of Jesus. *E'licott.*

---

40. Then took they the body of Jesus, and wound it in linen clothes with the spices, as the manner of the Jews is to bury.

Linen.   See on chap. xi. 44, and Luke xxiii. 53.—Not a shroud, nor a garment, but winding sheets in which the body was wrapped.— Probably an entire piece at first, and afterwards divided for the purpose of rolling.

The spices.   The pieces of linen were wrapped around the limbs in such a way as to enclose the powdered spices.—Doubtless after the last usual rites, the ablution, the last kiss impressed on the lips by mother and dearest friends.—The ends of the bandages were apparently secured on the inner side with gum.—A white cloth was finally laid over the face.—When shrinking from the outward accompaniments of death (the grave-clothes, the grave, the loneliness), we may find comfort in the thought, that all these have been around the Lord Himself, who died, and is now alive for evermore.

Manner.   See note to verse 41.—See also on chap. xi. 44, and Luke vii. 12 ; xi. 47.—The manner of the Egyptians, which was to take out the brains and bowels, or to steep the body seventy days in natron, was designed for the preservation of the bodies as mummies.—The Jewish manner formed a consecrated and beautiful transition from death to decomposition.—The mode of interment, a picture of the religion of a people ; 1. Among the heathen ; 2. The Jews ; 3. The Christians.—In conformity to this example, regard ought to be paid to the dead bodies of Christians.—The resurrection of the saints will be in virtue of Christ's resurrection, and therefore in burying them we should have an eye to Christ's burial. *Henry.*—God watcheth over His own in death as in life.

όθονίοις. *A smaller linen cloth, bandage,* in N. T. only of bandages in which dead bodies were swathed for burial *Robinson.*—It was probably of the nature of muslin rather than linen, and seems to have been specially used by the Egyptians for folding round their mummies. *Ellicott.*

---

41. Now in the place where he was crucified there was a garden; and in the garden a new sepulchre, wherein was never man yet laid.

Place. On the place where the crucifixion occurred, see on verses 17, 20; see also note to verse 42.—John's words "are *so far* in favour of the traditional site of the Holy Sepulchre, that Calvary and the Sepulchre are close together, under the roof of the same church. And those who have found an objection in that circumstance, have forgotten this testimony." *Alford.*

A garden. See on chap. xviii. 1.—We learn from Matt. xxvii. 60, that it was Joseph's garden (see also on Luke xxiii. 53).—Profitable subjects for meditation in garden walks: In a *garden* sin was first committed, first expiated, and finally triumphed over. *Ford.* —In a garden our Lord began His passion, and from a garden He would rise, and begin His exaltation.—"Christ changes the valley of the shadow of death into a garden. Christ's human body was laid in a natural *garden*. His human soul was in a spiritual *garden* (Luke xxiii. 43), and by His death and burial He has prepared a *garden* for the souls and bodies of all who depart hence in the Lord; and He will make them to be like the dew of herbs (Isa. xxvi. 19), and to rise up and blossom in a glorious springtime. He provides Paradise, or a *garden*, for the departed soul (Luke xxiii. 43), and He makes the grave itself to be a garden of Paradise; from which, at the great Day, the bodies of the faithful, which have been sown in hope, will rise in vernal beauty, and be united for ever in unfading glory to their souls." *Wordsworth.*— "In a *garden* there is something emblematic and suitable, where Nature dies and is again renewed; where the seed perishes and is quickened, and brings forth an hundredfold." *Williams.* (See also on chap. xii. 24.)

A new sepulchre. See note.—Matthew (chap. xxvii. 60) alone relates that it was Joseph's *own* tomb.—All the Evangelists, except Mark, notice the *newness* of the tomb.—*New,* and therefore given for the purpose, so that the additional particular not here mentioned, that it *belonged to Joseph*, is almost implied. *Alford.*—"The statement of John, that the tomb was in a garden *near* the place of crucifixion, and was chosen on account of the necessary haste, is not contradictory of the statement that the grave was the property of Joseph. It must have been exactly the location of his newly-formed family-tomb that led him to propose his grave, and yield it up as an offering." *Lange.*—John's account implies that of the earlier Gospels; and the burial, under the circumstances, required both that the sepulchre should be at hand, and that its owner should be willing that the body should be placed in it. *Ellicott.*—Not likely that the body of a crucified person could be laid in a new tomb, without the previous consent of the owner.—" *A new sepulchre:* this was so ordered: 1. For honour ; He that was born from a virgin-womb, must rise from a virgin-tomb ; 2. For the confirming the truth of His resurrection." *Henry.*

Never man, &c. See on Matt. xxvii. 60, and Luke xxiii. 53.—In this there was evidently a special, Divine interposition, that nothing might interfere with the clearest evidence of his resurrection.—This absolutely cuts away every conceivable ground for the evasions of unbelief.—" All suspicion of any other's rising instead of Christ, or of His rising by the virtue of any other, was prevented by His being buried in 'a new sepulchre, wherein was never yet man laid ; ' and so none could rise out of it but He, nor could He be raised by any virtue from any other buried there before Him, as a man was raised at the touch of Elisha's bones (2 Kings xiii. 21)." *Hutcheson.*—Thus as He rode into Jerusalem on an ass, " *whereon never before man had sat,*" so now He shall lie in a tomb *wherein never man before had lain,* that from these specimens it may be seen that in all things He was " separate from sinners (Heb. vii. 26)." *D. Brown.*

μνημεῖον. It was a great disgrace among the Jews if any one had not a burying-place of his own ; and so it came to be considered an act of charity to bury neglected dead bodies.—Josephus mentions as among the abominable deeds of the Zealots and Idumeans, that they left their dead unburied.—It was one of the most loved remembrances of the hero Tobit, in the old times of the first exile, that he had buried any Jew whom he found cast out dead round Nineveh (Tobit i. 17, 19). *Friedlieb, Geikie.*— Among the Jews the hopes of the future were closely connected with the careful preservation of the body after death.—Like the Egyptians, they attached supreme importance to the inviolability of the tomb either by time or violence, and, no less, to the checking of natural decay, by embalming. — To perpetuate their existence on earth, at least in the withered mockery of the grave, and to lie in the Holy Land, in the midst of their fathers, had, at all times, been the most sacred wish of the Jews.—In the days of Jesus, however, an additional motive for burial in Palestine, and a careful preservation of the body, was found in the belief of the Resurrection, which was to take place first in Judæa, commencing in the valley under the east of the Temple.—

Even now an Israelite always seeks to have some of the soil of the Holy Land laid in his grave, that the spot where he rests may be counted part of the sacred ground ; if, indeed, his body has not, before the Judgment, made its way through land and sea, to the home of his fathers.—The same feeling was all-powerful in the days of our Lord, for in the great sieges of Jerusalem, many Jewish fugitives came back to the city, in spite of the horrors they had already striven to escape, that they might count on at least the last of all blessings, a burial in its holy bounds. *Geikie.*—The Jews placed their graves outside their towns.—It was only kings and prophets and priests who might be interred inside the walls.—Commonly, these graves were excavations, or grottoes in gardens, or in spots planted with trees: sometimes natural caves; often, as in this case, expressly hewn out (a costly method), and sometimes built up.—These tombs were sometimes very roomy, and provided with passages.—The sepulchres were either made with steps downward, or placed horizontally; while the particular graves inside were hollowed out, either lengthwise or crosswise, in the walls of the tomb. *Winer, Schultz, Lange.*

---

42. There laid they Jesus therefore because of the Jews' preparation day ; for the sepulchre was nigh at hand.

There. In a garden, amid the fresh shrubbery and the early spring flowers.—Anemones, the star of Bethlehem, tulips, and numerous varieties of the scarlet flowers for which Palestine is celebrated, and which have suggested the touching and significant name of " the Saviour's blood drops," were blooming, and shedding their delicate fragrance on the air.—The figs and olives were covered with fresh leaves, and afforded grateful shade, and the vines hung in graceful festoons from the trellises, or clambered along the terraces of the hills.—John, no doubt, as well as the women of Galilee, saw what was done.—There we leave His body till the promised morning comes.—*There laid they Jesus.*—The great calm after the great storm : 1. The quiet Sufferer ; 2. The quiet grave; 3. The quiet Sabbath ; 4. The quiet mystery of life ; 5. The quiet presentiment; 6. The quiet turning of all things. *Lange.*— The garden of struggle (Gethsemane) is converted into the garden of rest.—His rest on that Sabbath a type of the believer's spiritual rest.—His burial, a work of: 1. Grateful acknowledgment ; 2. Holy love ; 3. Praiseworthy confession. *Brandt.*—It manifests : 1. The believer's courage ; 2. Love's power ; 3. Truth's seal ; 4. The mourner's consolation. *Kuntze.*—It proclaims the amazing depth of His humiliation, *from* what and *to* what His love brought Him, even from the bosom of the Father to the bosom of the grave.—It is our comfort against the fear of death, He has changed the grave from a loathsome dungeon into a perfumed bed.—It inspires our hope of the resurrection, for as the grave could not long keep Him, the Head, neither will it be able to hold His people, His members.—Evening upon Golgotha ; a holy stillness prevails : 1. The quiet rest of the perfected Endurer ; 2. The quiet repentance of the convulsed world ; 3. The quiet labour of the loving friends ; 4. The quiet peace of the honoured grave. *Gerok.*—The repose of Jesus at once a slumber of death and a mystery of transformation unto resurrection. *Schaff.*

Because. Hints that if circumstances had not been urgent, they would have given Him more honourable burial in another place.— *Thus the very haste of the preparation-day was providential.*

Preparation. See on verses 14, 31, and chap. xviii. 28.—The pious observance of the Sabbath on the part of His friends, a testimony against those who, with the charge of Sabbath-breaking, had commenced the persecution which terminated in His death (see on chap. v. 16).

Nigh. "The Lord also did so order that every passage about Christ's burial, and even those which His friends would have done otherwise, did contribute to His great scope of glorifying Christ; for therefore also was it ordered that they, being hastened, laid Him in the sepulchre which was 'nigh at hand,' so that He might *rise* in the view of all His enemies, where they had the stone sealed, and a guard to keep Him in: whereas, had He been carried further off, the matter had been more obscure, and might have seemed more doubtful. And thus also doth He bring about His glory by that wherein His people could little expect it should be so." *Hutcheson.*

ἐκεῖ. Instead of the traditional site of the holy sepulchre on Mount Acra, within the walls of the modern city being the true one, the new tomb in which Jesus was laid was near Calvary, or "in the place where Jesus was crucified."—Calvary was an elevation or hill, having in the distance, as seen from the Mount of Olives, the shape of a human skull, situated just beyond the present Damascus Gate, which is supposed to occupy the identical spot where the northern exit was in the days of Christ.—The hill is so steep in front of the gate that the path winds in order to reach its top. *Macdonald.*—μνημεῖον. From the Gospel narratives concerning the sepulchre of Christ, we may infer: (1) that it was entirely new ; (2) that it was near the spot of the crucifixion ; (3) that it was not a natural cave, but an artificial excavation in the rock ; (4) that it was not cut downward, after the manner of our graves, but horizontally, or nearly so, into the face of the rock. *Alford, Schaff.*

John 20

1. The first day of the week cometh Mary Magdalene early, when it was yet dark, unto the sepulchre, and seeth the stone taken away from the sepulchre.

The first day. See on Matt. xxviii. 1-8. and Luke xxiv. 1-12.— Gr., *And*, or, *But on the first (day) of the week (Sabbath week).*— Henceforth properly called the *Lord's Day*, on account of His Resurrection (Rev. i. 10).—" It has taken the place of the Jewish Sabbath : the substance remained (weekly day of holy rest), the form changed (from the seventh to the first day) with reference to that great event whereby our redemption, or the new creation, was completed. On that day the Lord appeared to His disciples with His peaceful greeting, and on that day He sent His Holy Spirit, and founded the Christian Church. The Christian Sabbath blends the memories of creative and redemptive love, is the connecting link between Paradise lost and Paradise regained, the continuation of Pentecost, and the preparation and pledge of the eternal Sabbath-feast (Heb. iv. 9) in heaven." *Schaff.*—The resurrection morning, the end of the old Sabbath ; the creation becomes spiritual, a spiritual world ; the rest becomes a festival ; the law becomes life.—On the first day of the creative week, light came into being, and on this first day life and immortality were brought to light in the Gospel.—The first in the new creation, the first in which the access to heaven was effected, the first in the dispensation of life.—Easter, the great Sunday, ever returning in the Christian Sabbath, the eternal Easter. (See note.)

Mary. See on chap. xi. 2 ; xix. 25.—Gr., *Mary the Magdalene.*— Matthew has, " Mary Magdalene and the other Mary " (xxviii. 1); Mark, "Mary Magdalene, and Mary the mother of James, and Salome " (xv. 1) ; Luke, " The women which had come with him from Galilee" (xxiii. 55), and enumerates them in xxiv. 10, as "Mary Magdalene, and Joanna, and Mary the mother of James, and the others with them."—John mentions Mary Magdalene only, though verse 2 seems to hint at others.—This prominence may be accounted for by the undoubted fact, that of all the women that ministered to our Lord, her love was the most fervent. *Augustine.* —This is beautifully illustrated in John's narrative, and yet this is the woman " out of whom he had cast seven devils " (Mark xv. 9). —A wonderful testimony to the power of Christ as a Saviour, and

full of comfort and hope for all true penitents.—"Neither nature
nor circumstances, but *love alone*, rules in the kingdom of God."
Owen.—" Good proof gave she of that love ; she was last at His
cross, and first at His grave : stayed longest *there*, was soonest *here ;*
could not rest till she were up to seek Him : sought Him while it
was yet dark, before she had light to seek Him by." *Andrewes.*—
To this loving-hearted woman was vouchsafed the *first* and one
of the most remarkable manifestations of the Risen Lord.

Early. It may be supposed that Mary Magdalene arrived first (so
John) ; soon the other Mary arrives (so Matthew) ; then Salome
comes (so Mark) ; finally, the " other women " make their appearance (so Luke).—This hypothesis removes the difficulty as to the
time of the visit to the tomb.

Yet dark. Mark has, "at the rising of the sun" (xvi. 2).—If
Mary Magdalene came *first* and *alone she* may have come " when
it was yet dark ; " while the others did not arrive till the " rising
of the sun."—Or, of the two parties of women, Mary Magdalene
with her friends may have come at the earlier, the others at the
later time.—Or, in the loose popular sense, the expression, " rising
of the sun," may denote *the early dawn*, when the rays of the
approaching luminary just begin to redden the east.—Thus in
Psa. civ. 22, it is said, respecting young lions : " The sun ariseth,
they gather themselves together, and lay them down in their
dens ; " yet it is well known that wild beasts do not wait for the
actual appearance of the sun, but at the break of day retreat to
their lairs. *Haley.*—Or, in the impatience of her longing, Mary
Magdalene had hastened in advance of the other women.—Upon
any of the above hypotheses, there is no discrepancy, but the latter
appears the most natural and satisfactory.—Not the least doubt
that, if *all* the circumstances were known, those which we *now*
know would be seen to fit perfectly into their appropriate places
in the history.—No one of the Evangelists gives, or intended to
give, *all* the circumstances ; but each has selected those particulars which seemed to him most important, passing by intermediate
incidents.—" The *diversities*, like the *intertwinings*, of the single
features of the *resurrection history* in the accounts of the four
Evangelists, are the *highest proof* of the *truth* and the infinitely
powerful *effect* of the *fact*." *Lange.* (See note.)

Unto the sepulchre. Gr., *To the tomb.*—Love to Christ raises her
above fear of the Roman guard ; above fear of night and the
terrors of the grave ; above fear of spirits, and of the other world
itself.—It is the glory of woman that she seldom forsakes those
she loves, even when things are darkest.—Mary followed Jesus
faithfully, when His disciples cowardly forsook Him ; she stood

near to His cross, and accompanied His bier to the grave, and now before day she hastens to His sepulchre.—Her object, and that of her companions, was to complete the embalming of the body begun by Nicodemus, but left unfinished through the approach of the Sabbath.—Evidently they had resolved to reach the grave by sunrise, which would take place about a quarter before six, and hence must have slept outside the city gates. *Greswell.*—The grey dawn had hardly shown itself when they were afoot on their errand, to perform the last offices of love.—The undying devotion of these holy women to the Lord, clothes their sex with immortal glory.—Doubtless Mary, mother of Jesus, was too sorely stricken and broken to join them.

The stone. The stone had been fitted *into* the mouth of the tomb, which was hewn in a rock (Mark xv. 3, 4).

Away. It now lies sideways by the opening of the tomb, which is conceived of as a perpendicular elevation (see on chap. xix. 41).— Matthew relates that there was a great earthquake; and that an angel from heaven rolled back the stone from the door of the sepulchre (see on Matt. xxviii. 2).—The Crucified One had come forth, unseen by the terrified soldiers, and had presently vanished. —The Christian Fathers held that Jesus rose while the grave was still closed, and that the tomb was opened merely to prove the resurrection.—Some suppose that while the Lord could have rolled back the stone by His own power, He chose to have it done by an angel, to signify that He did not break prison, but had a fair and *legal discharge* from heaven. *Henry, Burkitt.*—" In the case of Lazarus the stone was removed from the grave before he was raised by Christ to a new natural life. But the stone could hardly be a hindrance to Him who raised Himself by His own power to an eternal heavenly life, and who afterward appeared to the disciples through closed doors. The stone may have been rolled away merely for the sake of the women and the disciples, that they might go into the empty tomb and see the evidence of the resurrection. This, at all events, is the more usual orthodox interpretation." *Schaff.* (See on verses 19, 20.)—The fact of the resurrection, an invisible mystery, rendered glorious by visible signs : 1. The invisible working of Omnipotence, and its visible action ; 2. The invisible entrance into existence of the new life of Christ, and the visible earthquake (the birth-pangs of earth); 3. The invisible entrance of the heavenly King into His spiritual kingdom, and the visible angelic messengers ; 4. The invisible overthrow of the kingdom of darkness, and the visible guards (the servants of that kingdom) as dead men ; 5. The invisible, new, victorious kingdom of Jesus, and the beginning of its revelation. *Lange.*—The fact of the removal of the stone is made emphatic in all the accounts (see on Luke xxiv. 2).—And yet *this stone* was the great trouble which occupied their minds by the way (Mark xvi. 3, 4).—Thus our difficulties, as thought of in the distance, often appear insurmountable; but when we come nearer they have vanished—Providence has removed them, or made them easy.—Mary finds the stone taken away, but the body is gone!— " So long as we continue in unbelief, and in our mistakes of Christ, the change of our condition, or removal of apprehended difficulties, will not serve our turn, but will rather beget new sorrows and doubts." *Hutcheson.*—Yet the mistakes of a soul stirred with love must themselves become guiding stars to truth.—" *Who shall roll us away the stone?* " the great symbol of all the sighs of humanity, in its longing for the revelation of immortality.—The FIRST SIGN of the Resurrection, *the stone rolled away.*—The SECOND SIGN of the Resurrection, *the empty sepulchre.*—The THIRD SIGN of the Resurrection, *the fairly disposed and ordered grave-clothes* (see on verses 9, 14).

μιᾷ τῶν σαββάτων. The first day was regarded by the Jews as specially holy.— " That day has ten crowns. It is first in the work of creation, first for the princes of the people (who met on that day to consecrate the Temple), the first for the priesthood, first in the Levitical service, the first on which fire from heaven consumed the sacrifice, the first on which the Shechinah descended (on the Tabernacle), the first in which Israel received the benediction, and the first in the order of months." *Schoettgen* in "Speaker's Comm."—ἡ Κυριακὴ Ἡμέρα (Rev. i. 10).—The general consent both of Christian antiquity and of modern divines has referred this to the week'y festival of our Lord's resurrection, and identified it with ' the first day of the week," or "Sunday," of every age of the Church.—Results of examination of the principal writers of the two centuries after the death of John : 1. The Lord's Day existed during these two centuries as a part and parcel of Apostolical, and so of Scriptural Christianity.—2. It was never defended, for it was rever impugned.—3. It was never confounded with the Sabbath, but carefully distinguished from it.—It was not an institution of severe Sabbatical character, but a day of joy and cheerfulness.—Religiously regarded it was a day of solemn meeting for the Holy Eucharist, for united prayer, for instruction, and for almsgiving.—Four years before the Œcumenical Council of Nicæa, it was recognised by Constantine in his celebrated edict as "The Venerable Day of the Sun."—The Fathers assembled at the Council of Nicæa, A.D. 325, assume the Lord's Day as an existing fact, and only notice it incidentally in order to regulate an indifferent matter, the posture of Christian worshippers upon it. *Smith's* "Dict. of the Bible."—The plural, σαββάτων, is probably used here in reference to the seven weeks that were to be reckoned to Pentecost, and that began to be reckoned from this day in particular; for these were peculiarly denominated *weeks*, and hence Pentecost was called the Feast of Weeks. *Starke.*—σκοτίας. It is impossible to harmonise the differences between John and the Synoptists, and those between the latter, but the grand fact itself and the principal features of the history stand out all the more sure. *Meyer, Alford.*—It is to be regretted that some eminent Christian scholars should have exaggerated the difficulties and apparent "discrepancies" in the history of the Resurrection.—A judicious critic will only oppose a *forced* harmony (see on verse 16).—The differences between the accounts of the first announcement of the Resurrection, found in the four Gospels, are an important testimony, when exactly weighed, to the truth of the history of the resurrection.—It is no doubt remarkable, that literal, or external, protocol-like certainty, should be wanting, exactly in the place where the Christian

faith seeks and does actually find the beginning of the confirmation of all its certainties.
—Faith, even here, is not to be supported upon the letter, but upon the substance,
upon the real essence of the facts.—This essence, this spirit, comes out here most distinctly, and is manifested exactly through the differences themselves because these are
the indications of the extraordinary effect produced by the Resurrection on the band
of disciples. The Evangelical records give no narration of facts, simply for the sake of
the facts, and apart from their effects ; but they present us with a history, which has
individualised itself to the view of the Evangelist.—And hence the Easter occurrences
are retained and rehearsed as reminiscences never to be forgotten ; and differ accordingly, as the standpoints of the disciples vary, and yet preserve a great degree of
harmony.—In this way it is that we are to explain the remarkable individualities and
variations to be found in the accounts of the Resurrection and manifestations of the
Risen Lord ; and in these accounts is contained for all time the joyous fright of the
Church, caused by the great tidings of the Resurrection.—Just as, in a festive *motetto*,
the voices are *apparently* singing in confusion, seemingly separate, and contradict one
another, while, *in reality* they are bringing out one theme in a higher and holier
harmony: so is it here. The *one Easter history*, with its grand unity, meets, when all
the different accounts are combined, the eye in all its clearness and distinctness. *Lange.*
(See also on verse 9.)

---

2. Then she runneth, and cometh to Simon Peter, and to the other disciple, whom
Jesus loved, and saith unto them, They have taken away the Lord out of the sepulchre,
and we know not where they have laid him.

Runneth. So soon as she perceives the stone rolled away, and the
sepulchre open, she instantly concludes that the body is stolen.—
Hence she becomes at first the messenger of alarming news.—Thus
often it happens, that through despondency and unbelief, that
which should bring comfort and joy, is productive but of terror
and dismay (Luke ii. 9).

Simon Peter. Matthew has, "to His disciples;" Luke, "to the
eleven, and to all the rest."—John relates only that of which he
had personal knowledge.—The note of this coming to Peter and
to himself, a characteristic historical trait.—The last time we saw
Peter, was in the court-yard of the high-priest, when he had just
denied his Master the third time (see on chap. xviii. 27).—But
now he is the repentant Peter, soon to be restored by the Risen
Lord (see on chap. xxi. 15-17).—"The hasting of the Magdalene
to Peter and John, and the cleaving together of these two, gives
us an impression of the gentle, placable spirit which the suffering
of Christ had developed in the hearts of the disciples. Peter is
not shunned now by a Magdalene's and a John's enthusiasm for
the Lord, although he *had* denied Him. In a similar manner the
whole band of disciples bear with the doubting Thomas until he
has arrived at the full resurrection faith." *Lange.*—A lesson for
Christians and Churches how to act toward penitent backsliders
(Gal. vi. 1) and honest-hearted sceptics (see on verses 24-29).

The other disciple. See on chap. i. 35-40; xviii. 15.—John deliberately omits all mention of his own family, but his writing is the

record of events in which he had himself taken part, and in this lies its value.—His own personality cannot therefore be suppressed : he is present in all he writes, and yet the presence is felt, not seen.

Jesus loved. See on chap. xiii. 33 ; xix. 26 ; xxi. 7.—A name given to him, it may be, by his brethren, and cherished by him as the most honoured name man could bear.—A veil rests over it ; but beneath the veil lives the person of John, the son of Zebedee and Salome, and the Apostle of the Lord. *Ellicott.*—In these words John indicates what was his pride, his crown, his highest boast.—At the same time they point out the source whence he derived all his consolation, hope, and strength ; this source was *love*, not the love with which he embraced the Lord, but that with which the Lord embraced him.—" He who can sign himself the disciple whom Jesus loves, has a sure guaranty for all that he needs, and for all that his heart can desire. He may call himself the man that is tossed with tempests, yet if he is loved by Jesus, what more can he have ? " *Krummacher.*—It should be noted that the word here used of John is that which is used of Lazarus in chap. xi. 3 (see Comm.), and is not the word which occurs in chaps. xix. 26 ; xxi. 7, 20.

Taken away. " A forejudgment of fear in the love not yet perfect ; an error, starting up and vanishing on the way to truth." *Lange.* —Here we see the mistake of the *disconsolate* Magdalene, and also in verse 15 : in verse 17 we see the mistake of the enraptured Magdalene.—A nature like the Magdalene's is liable to extremes of depression and exaltation ; but in the end Divine love is sure to prove a sufficient guide.—It might have been expected that the first thought would be, *Surely the Lord is risen.*—Mary's state of mind *a picture of our own dulness and forgetfulness in the cloudy and dark day.*

The Lord. Some Greek MSS. have, " my Lord," which is "more expressive of love, and of the feelings of an handmaiden." *Augustine.*—"She puts the part for the whole ; she had come only to seek for the body, and now she laments that her Lord, the whole of Him, is taken away." *Gregory.*—" Even in the greatest fits of saints' unbelief, a right discerner may yet read some faith ; as may be gathered to be in Mary from her calling Him her Lord. So in the Church's complaint, Isa. xlix. 14, ' my Lord,' is not only the language of affection, regretting that such a one had forgotten her, but the language of faith also, cleaving to an interest in Him, though she discern it not. Thus also, Mary's acknowledging Him 'the Lord,' doth refute her present mistake." *Hutcheson.* (On the title ' Lord ' see on verse 28, and on Matt. i. 23.)

1348 / Gospel of John

Know not. The "*we*" may include the other women with herself, and thus John's narrative imply that of the earlier Gospels.— Or it may be nothing more than (in her feeling of despair) a cry generally of the utter hopelessness of human effort, whether her own or that of others.

Laid him. An outburst of passionate moaning from her woman's heart.—"They have not only crucified the Lord, but have robbed the body of the resting-place which love had provided for it, and of the tender care with which love was seeking to surround it. And now we know not to what fresh indignity their hatred, against which even the grave is no protection, has subjected the body of Him whom we have loved." *Ellicott.*—Nothing on earth or in heaven can compensate the soul that "knows the love of Christ," for *His absence.*—Of much modern preaching it may be said, "They have taken away the Lord, and we know not where they have laid Him."—Yet of what worth can any preaching be in which Jesus is not Alpha and Omega?—*A Christianity without Christ* even an honest infidel will scorn and despise.

ἐφίλει, *loved as a friend*; otherwise ὅν ἠγάπα, **xix.** 26 ; **xxi.** 7, 20.

---

3. Peter therefore went forth, and that other disciple, and came to the sepulchre.

Went forth, &c. Peter and John appear to have lodged that night in a place separate from the other Apostles.—At this time the Apostles seem to have been scattered throughout the city among those who were friendly to their cause. *Griesbach.*—Peter and John were the first to go forth, because they loved most. *Gregory.*— Peter's association with John, the disciple whom Jesus loved, an evident proof of the sincerity of his repentance.—And John's reception of Peter to confidence and affection an evident proof how deeply he had drunk in of the Master's spirit.—"When Christ is missing believers should bestir themselves to seek a good account of that dispensation ; while such as have fresh sense of their own frailty and of Christ's love will be most active to inquire after an absent and missed Christ. And it may be that, therefore, Peter only is named in this undertaking (Luke xxiv. 12), because the fallen man's diligence and recovery was specially remarkable." *Hutcheson.*—"How the disciples of Jesus go to His sepulchre: 1. How differently (Magdalene otherwise than the two men; Peter otherwise than John); 2. How unanimously (disciples, both male and female, and the women even in advance. Fallen ones and less guilty ones)." *Lange.*

Came. The tense of the verb in the original expresses the continuance of the journey towards the sepulchre. *Ellicott.* (On the points of connection and difference between Peter and John, see Introduction.)

---

4. So they ran both together: and the other disciple did outrun Peter, and came first to the sepulchre.

They ran. Gr., *And they were running.*—The details of the visit of these two apostles (verses 3-10) are peculiar to John.—The liveliness, circumstantiality, and inner truth of this narrative indicate most unmistakably the record of an eye-witness.

Both together. The going turns to running, and the moderate speed, to running with all their might.

Outrun. John is most graphic in his account.—Its simplicity and naturalness must impress every unprejudiced mind with all the force of reality.—So vivid is the description that the whole scene appears before us.—The greater speed of John was probably the result of more youthful activity.—According to some, Peter's consciousness of his late dreadful fall, retarded his progress. *Lampe, Luthardt.*—There may be some truth in this conjecture, for nothing so paralyzes the powers of body and mind, as a sense of guilt.—Yet this assumption seems contradicted by verse 6, though at *that* moment the sight of the empty sepulchre may have lifted the load from his heart and conscience. *Lange.*

Came first. " He that got *foremost* in the race was *the disciple whom Jesus loved* in a special manner, and who, therefore, in a special manner loved Jesus. Sense of Christ's love to us, kindling love in us to Him again, will make us *excel in virtue.*" *Henry.*—"Albeit affection will put believers to all the diligence they can, yet every one is not to be tried by another's measure of expressing his affection; for one may be as affectionate as another, who yet may be retarded, and come short in expression of what that other attaineth unto. John being young, and of a nimble body, did outrun Peter, who yet loved Christ as well as he, and was running as fast as he could. And thus, also, may many be borne down in their activity in respect of others, by reason of their infirmity of body, troubles of mind, or other frailties, whose affections, notwithstanding, are as fervent towards Christ." *Hutcheson.*

Note the change of the Aorists and the descriptive imperfects in verses 3 and 4; compare chap. iv. 30.

---

5. And he stooping down, and looking in, saw the linen clothes lying; yet went he not in.

Stooping down. Gr., *And stooping down, he seeth.*—The word means *to stoop down* or to *bend forward*, in order to look at anything more closely.—The E. V. has expressed here the intention, and in verse 11, by adding in italics, *and looking in.*—The form of the verb still describes the scene as it actually occurred.—The word is used again in the N. T. only in verse 11, James i., 25, and in 1 Peter i. 12.—Here, in a literal sense, was the longing, eager, searching, inquiring look into the mysteries of our Redemption. *Ford.*—He, that will not stoop at Christ's grave, shall never be partaker of His death and resurrection.—None but humble men and meek men can see these mysteries. *Marlorate.*

Linen clothes. See on chap. xix. 40.—These laid aside, the signs of a change of apparel in the sleeping chamber of the grave.

Not in. Gr., *yet did he not go in.*—John had outrun Peter; but on arriving at the tomb he is restrained from entering by what he sees.—He seems to be fettered first by the apprehension of a sad discovery, then by awe, and his wonder at the orderly disposal of the burial clothes.—We cannot suppose that either fear of defilement (*Ammon*), or natural dread (*Meyer*) prevented him entering; the former view is contradicted by his stooping down, the latter by his close observation of the signs of the sepulchre. *Lange.*—John was constitutionally contemplative and reverent, and these traits of character appear here.—It was perfectly natural to him to stand still, lost in reflection, as he gazes upon the new signs that present themselves.

παρακύψας. It meant originally, to stoop sideways, and was used, *e.g.*, of a harp-player; then, to stoop over, peer into, inquire into. *Ellicott.*

6, 7. Then cometh Simon Peter following him, and went into the sepulchre, and seeth the linen clothes lie, and the napkin, that was about his head, not lying with the linen clothes, but wrapped together in a place by itself.

Went in. Natural reverence, and the awful mystery before him, kept John from entering; but no such diffidence checked the impulsive Peter.—Less reverent and endowed with more practical decision, he hesitates not.—Passing under the low door *he went* in, undismayed.—This incident is in perfect harmony with Peter's character as disclosed in the Gospel history.—Precisely similar is the trait presented in chap. xxi. 7, where John is the first to recognize the Lord, Peter the first to hasten to Him, in the water. —*Hence*, it would seem, Peter alone is mentioned in Luke xxiv. 12. *Lange.*—John could outrun Peter, but Peter could out-dare John.

Seeth. Gr., *beholdeth* —The word is not the same as that which is used in verse 5, in reference to John.—Peter closely observed the linen clothes, John did but see them from without.

Linen clothes. It is to be noted that these coverings of our Lord's body are never called "grave clothes," as in the case of Lazarus.

Napkin. See on chap. xi. 44.—The cloth placed round the forehead and under the chin, but probably not covering the face.

Not lying. This was not seen by John from without, because, perhaps, on the inner side of the sepulchre.—In the minute knowledge of the description we see the undeniable stamp of an eye-witness.—Three signs giving proof of the peacefulness of that which had occurred in the sepulchre in contrast to what would have taken place had the body been violently removed : 1. The grave clothes are not carried off as they naturally would have been if the body had been stolen ; 2. The linen clothes and the napkin are laid away in an orderly manner ; 3. The napkin is lying, wrapped together, in a place by itself.—Signs of the ruling of the highest, clearest presence of mind amid the horrors of the night-darkness of the tomb. *Lange*—The order and heavenly repose reveal the dignity of the Risen One and the glory of His Resurrection.—When Lazarus arose, he came forth with his grave-clothes about him ; but when Christ arose He left His behind Him, because He dies no more, death has no more dominion over Him.— The believer, rising from the death of sin to the life of righteousness, must put off the grave-clothes of his corruptions. *Henry.*

The E. V. obliterates the distinction between βλέπει, the cursory glance of John (verse 5), and the stronger θεωρεῖ, the intense gaze of Peter (verse 6).—The position of ὀθόνια in verse 6 corresponds to τὸ σουδάριον (verse 7). *Schaff.*

---

8. Then went in also that other disciple, which came first to the sepulchre, and he saw, and believed.

Then. Gr., *Then, therefore, went in also the other disciple.*—The act of Peter puts an end to the awe-struck, contemplative attitude of

John.—Doubtless Peter had called to John, informing him of the strange signs within the tomb.

Went in. Following his friend, John now enters the sepulchre, and sees that the signs are precisely as Peter had reported.—How completely the remembrance of Peter's shameful denial, seems to have been erased from John's mind!—What wonderful spiritual changes the death of the Lord has wrought in the disciples, and what wonderful changes the Cross works still!—Only by the power of the Cross do we learn to *forget*, as well as *forgive*, the sins of our brethren.

Saw. The Greek word for "saw" is different from either of those used before in verses 5 and 6.—" It is not that he saw, as from a distance, nor yet that he beheld that which was immediately presented to his gaze; it is not that he saw in any merely physical sense, but that he saw with the eye of the mind, and grasped the truth which lay beneath the phenomena around him." *Ellicott.*

Believed. See on chap. i. 7.—*Believed*, not merely what the Magdalene reported, but *that Jesus was risen from the dead.*—John received into his mind, embraced with his assent, THE FACT OF THE RESURRECTION, *for the first time.*—The spark of faith kindled up at the signs within the tomb.—The Resurrection signs preceding the appearance of the Risen One: 1. As signs of the weakness of the disciples; of their need of this leading from faith to sight; 2. As signs of the wisdom of God; sight is not to bring about faith, but faith sight. *Lange.*—The progress of faith in the disciples: 1. Faith through signs; 2. Faith through knowledge of the Scriptures; 3. Faith through spiritual life.—Nothing is said of Peter: Did he *believe* too?—It appears *not;* and that John modestly suppresses it.—Luke tells us that Peter " departed, *wondering* in himself at that which was come to pass " (chap. xxiv. 12).—Peter sees and *wonders:* John sees and *believes.*—A mind disposed to contemplation may perhaps sooner receive the evidence of divine truth than a mind disposed to action. *Henry.* —This may be so; but John's greater readiness to believe must be resolved into that greater spiritual receptivity which comes of love.

ἐπιστευσεν *What* did John believe ? Was it merely that the body had been taken away as the Magdalene had reported? (*Augustine, Bengel, Stier, Ebrard, &c.*)—Surely not ; John does not so use the word πιστευειν. *Alford.*--He believed in the resurrection signs. *Chrysostom, Euthymius, Lücke, Alford, Lange; Schaff, &c.*—The *two* disciples were satisfied, from the orderly condition in which they found the tomb, that it had not been rifled. They yielded to the evidence before them, in that empty tomb, that their Master had risen from the dead. *Macdonald.*—Some think Peter believed also ; but there is no evidence of his faith, in the Gospel history. *Author.*

9. For as yet they knew not the scripture, that he must rise again from the dead.

As yet. Gr., *For not even yet did they know (understand) the Scripture.*—This explains in what sense John now believed: His faith rested on the ocular testimony before him.—As yet they understood not the Scripture so as to be *antecedently* convinced that He should rise from the dead.—Our Lord's frequent declarations concerning His resurrection (chap. ii. 21 ; viii. 28 ; x. 18 ; xii. 24, 32, &c.) could only have become doubtful to them as to their literal meaning.—It is very likely that a figurative interpretation had suggested itself to their little faith, recollecting, as they did, the figurative phraseology in which He was wont to express Himself. —Yet but these signs, here given, were needed to inspire John with the resurrection faith, and henceforth the meaning of the Scripture might become clear to them.—John, writing many years afterward, meekly acknowledges that they had not taken heed to and pondered those things which were revealed in Scripture, so as to feed upon them by faith. *Hutcheson.* (See on verse 25.)

The scripture. See on chap. ii. 22 ; v. 39.—Refers to types such as Gen. xxii., and Jonah: to Scripture sayings such as Psa. ii.; xvi. ; cx.; Isa. liii. 11 ; Dan. ix. 25 : to sayings in regard to death, such as Isa. xxv. 8 ; Hos. xiii. 14 ; compare Acts ii. 25-34 ; viii. 32, 33 ; xiii. 33, 35.—As the O. T. Scripture prophetically points forward to the life of Jesus, so that life points back to the Scripture concerning His resurrection.—Christ's life is the key to the Old Testament. —The disciples did not sufficiently understand the scope and meaning of the O. T. to induce them, on the strength of its literal predictions, to expect a literal resurrection of Messiah.

Must rise. See on chap. ii. 22 ; xii. 24, and on Luke xxiv. 26, 44.— The necessity was founded upon the immutable word and promise of God (Psa. xvi. 10), upon the principle of life inherent in Jesus as the eternal Son of God, and upon the redemptive economy, by which Christ was to rise from the dead, and become the firstfruits of them that slept (1 Cor. xv. 20).—No event of history is so well attested as the resurrection of Jesus: it proves itself; it is proven by the strongest proofs ; those proofs appeal to our faith, love and hope.—It is the Father's attestation of His claims to be the Son of the living God.—It is the sign to the human race that in His death He made a perfect atonement for sin.—It is the revelation of immortality and eternal life to man.—It pours a clear and steady light over all that is painful in His life, and over the dark mysteries of this sad world.—Through it the cross of the *curse* has become the cross of *reconciliation*, and that which was the sign of the deepest *disgrace*, has been turned into the sign of the highest *glory* (see on verse 29).

ἀναστῆναι. "Nothing stands more historically certain than that Jesus rose from the dead and appeared again to His followers, or than that their seeing Him thus, again, was the beginning of a higher faith, and of all their Christian work in the world. It is equally certain that they thus saw Him, not as a common man, or as a shade or ghost risen from the grave ; but as the one Only Son of God, already more than man at once in nature and power; and that all who thus beheld Him, recognized at once and instinctively His unique divine dignity, and firmly believed in it thenceforth. The Twelve and others had, indeed, learned to look on Him, even in life, as the True Messianic King and the Son of God, but from the moment of His reappearing, they recognized more clearly and fully the divine side of His nature, and saw in Him the Conqueror of death. Yet the two pictures of Him thus fixed in their minds were in their essence identical. That former familiar appearance of the earthly Christ, and this higher vision of Him, with its depth of emotion and ecstatic joy, were so inter-related that, even in the first days or weeks after His death, they could never have seen in Him the Heavenly Messiah, if they had not first known Him so well as the earthly." *Ewald.* (This testimony from so eminent a scholar and critic as Ewald, is all the more valuable on account of his well-known rationalistic tendencies and habits of mind. *Author.*)

10. Then the disciples went away again unto their own home.

Then. Gr., *So the disciples went away again unto their home.*—More exactly, *to their lodgings in Jerusalem.*—The object of their visit to the sepulchre was accomplished.—Tranquilized in mind in respect to the dismal tidings by the Magdalene, and awaiting further disclosures, for which they were now prepared.—One of them at least had realized that the Lord was risen, and he must have told his thoughts to his companion.—Probably the special appearance of Jesus vouchsafed to Peter on that day (Luke xxiv. 34 ; compare verse 12 ; 1 Cor. xv. 5), served not only for his peace in respect to his fall, but also for the confirmation of *his* faith in the Risen Lord.—"Each one was initiated into this wondrous mystery in a peculiar manner : Magdalene, after a scrupulous trial by the angels and then by means of the first personal manifestation of Jesus ; Peter and John, who should have been the first to believe, by the sight of the sepulchre ; the weaker women by the angels ; the disciples on the way to Emmaus, with anxious, comfort-seeking, burning hearts, by the circumstance of Jesus's opening the Scriptures to them ; then all the still unbelieving disciples by Christ's appearance in their assembly. In each of these dispensations there lies a peculiar, tender regard for the persons whom it concerns." *Gerlach.*

11. But Mary stood without at the sepulchre weeping: and as she wept, she stooped down, and looked into the sepulchre.

Mary. See on verse 1.—She had followed Peter and John, but had proceeded more slowly than they (see on verse 4).—We are not told whether she met them at the sepulchre.

Stood. Gr., *was standing.*—She stations herself in front of the sepulchre, as though she would become its guardian.—Where there is *true love* to Christ, there will be a constant adherence to Him, and a resolution with purpose of heart to cleave to Him. *Henry.*—The disciples went to their home (vers 10), but Mary's love kept her waiting at the sepulchre, and so, notwithstanding her mistakes, she is rewarded with the first sight of the Risen One.—What encouragement to all seeking the Saviour, to wait for Him.

Weeping. She weeps because she thinks the body of the Lord has been stolen.—Who can tell how much misery our ignorance and unbelief inflict upon us?—Our misapprehensions of God and of His ways, is the source of our greatest trouble.—" O how many peek and pine without cause ! " *Hall.*—" The case of Mary Magdalene is our case oftentimes : in the error of our conceit, to weep where we have no reason ; to joy where we have as little. Often where we have cause to joy, we weep ; and where to weep, we joy. False joys and false sorrows, false hopes and false fears, this life of ours is full of." *Andrewes.*—Even emotions good in themselves, if too much indulged, become a snare (see on Luke xxiv. 17).—Christ needs not our sympathy : " Weep not for *Me,* but *weep for yourselves, and for your children* " (see on Luke xxiii. 28). —In all the Magdalene's desolation, love for the Lord remained the light of her faith and her hope.—" Blessed are they that mourn : for they shall be comforted," a promise conspicuously fulfilled in her case (see on Matt. v. 4).

Stooped. See on verse 5.—Doubtless, through her blinding tears, she often glanced toward the empty place where He had lain. —But glances are not enough for such love as Mary's.—Holy longings ever gain strength by delay ; did they not, they would not be *longings.*—Weeping must not hinder seeking ; though she *wept,* she *stooped down,* and *looked in.*—Those are likely to *seek and find,* who seek with *affection,* and *in tears. Henry.*—Though she was seeking the living One among the dead, where He was not to be found, her love was rewarded.—A glorious vision rises before her, such as was not vouchsafed even to John and Peter.—How precious is love to Christ in God's sight, even though it be mixed with errors and frailties.

---

12. And seeth two angels in white sitting, the one at the head, and the other at the feet, where the body of Jesus had lain.

Seeth. Gr., *beholdeth,* the same word as that used in verse 6 (see Comm.).

Two angels. See on chap. i. 51, and on Matt. i. 20, 21 ; ii. 13, 19 ; xxviii. 5-7 ; Luke xxiv. 4-8.—It may appear strange that the two Apostles saw no angels here, and that the other women saw but one ; but this only shows that such visions are conditioned by the spiritual state of those beholding them.—The slight impression which these appearances seem to have made upon Mary at the time, goes to establish the reality of the vision.—" If we admit the earlier vision of angels, of which there were several witnesses, there can be no reason for rejecting this ; and if the evidence was at the time sufficient to convince the Evangelist, who himself had seen no such vision, but was guided by the Spirit to accept and record this, as seen by Mary, we have a decisive judgment of higher authority than any which criticism can attain." *Ellicott.*—The angelic world merges into view in all great epochs in the Kingdom of God.—Angelic appearances at the Birth, Passion, Resurrection and Ascension of the Lord, mark these moments as the great epochs in His life.—Their appearance in the resurrection history is a sign of the new and wonderful character of this event. —Doubtless the angelic hosts were thronging around the sepulchre ; hence one angel appeared at one time, and at another two.

In white. All the Evangelists notice the *white* or *shining* appearance of the garment.—Symbolical of the purity and festal joy of the heavenly kingdom.—The redeemed before the throne are arrayed in *white* robes, but those robes have been washed and made white in the blood of the Lamb (Rev. vii. 9, 13, 14).

Sitting. In the vision described by Matthew, the angel " *sat upon the stone,*" which he had rolled away (chap. xxviii. 2).—In that by Mark, "*they saw a young man sitting on the right side,*" within the sepulchre (chap. xvi. 5).—In that by Luke, "*two men stood by them in shining garments,*" within the sepulchre (chap. xxiv. 4).— In that by John, "*two angels were sitting, the one at the head, and the other at the feet, where the body of Jesus had lain.*"—They sit, not as defending, but peacefully watching the Body —" At the *head* and the *feet*, for the Body of the Lord was from head to foot in the charge of His Father and of His servants." *Luthardt.*—It would show Mary there was no ground for fear of any outrage, for God had given His angels charge concerning Him.—" This position of our Lord was set forth by the Ark of the Covenant, *between the two cherubim* (Psa. xci. 1)." *Andrewes.*—What a contrast between the repose of the angels, and the painfully conflicting emotions of Mary and the others.—But the angels belonged to heaven, where all things are seen in divine light ; whereas Mary and the others belonged to earth, where we only " see as through a glass, darkly."

13. And they say unto her, Woman, why weepest thou? She saith unto them, Because they have taken away my Lord, and I know not where they have laid him.

Say. Doubtless in the Aramaic or Syro-Chaldaic tongue, which was then commonly spoken by the Jews.—It would seem to be one of the attributes of angels to be able to speak in any language; and this may be the case with us also when we become "equal unto the angels" (Luke xx. 36).

Woman. On the meaning of this term, in address, see on chap. ii. 4; xix. 26.

Why? The inquiry of the angels concerning a thing which they know, is to be understood similarly with Christ's question to the blind men: "What will ye that I should do unto you?"—Grief, when uttered, makes the heart more susceptible of consolation. *Gerlach.*—To speak comfortably to the afflicted is praiseworthy, and in accordance with the custom of angels, yea, of the great God Himself (Luke viii. 13; 1 Thess. v. 14). *Hall.*

My Lord. The passionate feeling expressed in verse 2 (see Comm.), is again repeated, only it is here more intensified.—She is not now speaking to her friends, and the Lord's disciples, therefore she says, "They have taken away *my* Lord, and I know not where they have laid him."—She is here alone, speaking to strangers, and may, therefore, have used the singular (*I*), whether she went in the early morning with the other women or not. *Ellicott.*—It cannot fail to strike the reader how unmoved Mary appears to be by this angelic appearance.—When the mind is deeply absorbed in some great feeling, it becomes indifferent to surrounding objects.—What were angels to Mary, in the absence of Christ Himself?—The best company in the universe will not satisfy or content those who are seeking the Lord, when they find not Him whom their souls love.—Note the concentration of her heart upon Jesus, in the words, "*my* Lord."—"*Mine,*" as if no other creature had any claim or right to Him.—Thus Thomas, "*My* Lord and *my* God."—Thus Paul, "He loved *me*; He gave Himself for *me.*"—True faith, however imperfect, is personal and appropriative: Its language is, *My* Saviour, *My* Lord, *My* God.—It is a blessed sense of the absence of Christ which causes our love to Him to grow from "the Lord" (verse 2) to "*My* Lord."

---

14. And when she had thus said, she turned herself back, and saw Jesus standing and knew not that it was Jesus.

Turned. Doubtless the angels would have assured her, as they did the women before, but this is prevented by her turning back.—

Whether her turning so quickly, was due to some external cause, it is impossible to say.—More likely, however, it was in a kind of hopeless despair she turned; turned from every creature, even from the angels, to find and see—*Jesus Himself standing!*

Knew not. Various explanations of this have been given: 1. It was still the grey dawn, the light was not clear, and hence objects were not distinctly seen; 2. Her tears have for the moment blinded her, and she cannot see anything more than a dim outline or shadowy form; 3. Jesus has altered: He is the Risen, the Transformed One; 4. As in the case of the disciples journeying to Emmaus, her eyes were holden; 5. He was clothed in the dress of the gardener; 6. Her faculties were concentrated within; she was in a visionary mood, unfavourable to acute observation; 7. She was wholly absorbed in the thought of the dead Lord; 8. Her mind was not in the slightest degree predisposed to expect His appearance, not understanding that He was to rise again.—Not *expecting* a *living* Christ, was, perhaps, the principal cause why she did not discern Him.—"The Lord is nigh to them that are of a broken heart" (Psa. xxxiv. 18), nearer than they are aware. —The greater the sorrow, the nearer Christ is, but often mental gloom hides Him from us.—Many a tender and humbled soul mourns over the loss of its Saviour, and yet He, the while, is close at hand (Cant. iii. 1-4). *Hall.*—Love hides itself, in order that it may, on discovering itself, occasion us the more surprise and joy.— What ist his whole life of trial and misery—exile? A hiding of the heavenly Father's love. *Heubner.*

---

15. Jesus saith unto her, Woman, why weepest thou? whom seekest thou? She, supposing him to be the gardener, saith unto him. Sir, if thou have borne him hence, tell me where thou hast laid him, and I will take him away.

Woman. See on chap. ii. 4; xix. 26.—*Our Lord's first recorded words after His resurrection.*—He addresses her as the angels did (see on verse 13).—But how different are these words as spoken by Jesus, from the same words spoken even by *His* angels.— Friends may ask the same question, in our moments of anguish; but they can give no relief, and no arguments of theirs can heal the inward wound.—But our Lord reveals Himself in words of grace which go to the heart's wound, and divinely heal.

Seekest? He knew perfectly; but He will draw her out to tell *what* she wants and *whom* she seeks.—Though Christ knows His people are seeking Him, yet He will know it *from themselves;* so pleased is He to hear any poor sinner say, *I seek Jesus.*—"Christ may, for a time, seem to carry Himself strangely, even towards those whom He loveth dearly, that so He may bring out more of their affection, and more of their weakness also, both which are useful for them; therefore doth He at first speak like a stranger." *Hutcheson.*—" *Why?* " Is thy weeping for a cause sufficient to call forth such sorrow?—" *Whom?* " Is that thou seekest worthy the affection of thy soul?

The gardener. Evidently supposing that the only person there at that early hour would be the keeper of the garden.—Whoever he was he would have been a servant of Joseph of Arimathæa, and may have become known to Mary at the time of the entombment. —" Jesus wearing the loin-strip, which crucified persons wore, and which was similar to that which field and garden labourers were in the habit of wearing, might have led her to this opinion." *Lange.*—" We must believe the clothing of our Lord's risen Body to have been *that which He pleased to assume;* not earthly clothing, but perhaps some semblance of it. Certainly, in this case, He *was clothed;* or she must at once have recognized Him." *Alford.*— Whatever *kind* of clothing it may have been, it is plain that it appeared to Mary like that worn by the humbler classes.—" Perhaps, however, the woman was right in believing Jesus to be the gardener. Was not He the *spiritual* Gardener, who by the power of His love had sown strong seeds of piety in her heart?" *Gregory.*—He who tendeth the heavenly plants of His Father, *was* in a certain sense *the Gardener. Heubner.*—Troubled spirits, in a cloudy and dark day, are apt to misrepresent Christ to themselves, and to put wrong constructions upon the methods of His providence and grace. *Henry.*

Sir. The Greek word rendered " Sir " denotes respect; but like the corresponding word in most languages it was also used to a stranger, and even to an inferior.—The " gardener," moreover, corresponded more to what we should call a "steward" or " bailiff." *Ellicott.*

Him. A characteristic of ardent affection, Mary does not name Jesus.—To her He is " *Him*," as if there were no other on the face of the earth.—Hence thrice she speaks of " *Him* ": " If thou have borne *Him* hence, tell me where thou hast laid *Him*, and I will take *Him* away."—When one loves a person, one never imagines that any one else can be ignorant of him.—She takes it for granted that every one is thinking of *Him* only.—Of course if the supposed gardener *had* secretly removed the Body (and this is what her words imply), he would understand her allusion: otherwise it were necessarily unintelligible to him. *Meyer.*

I will, &c. In the intensity of her love, she speaks as if *she* has sufficient strength to enable her to carry the corpse and deposit it in a place of safety.—She neither dreads opposition nor fears danger, nor yet sees that the task would be physically impossible. —"Affection towards Christ will not stand to consult with ability, but with itself and its desires, and accordingly will undertake and endeavour to do Him service, though never so far above its strength." *Hutcheson.*

---

16. Jesus saith unto her, Mary. She turned herself, and saith unto him, Rabboni; which is to say, Master.

Jesus saith. To that devoted love, the characteristics of which we have been tracing, the first words of the Risen One were spoken. —Not to His mother, nor to the beloved disciple, but to this Magdalene, who had once been the bond slave of Satan and sin (see on verse 1).—" He who knew her whole past, and knew that her devotion to Him had sprung from the freedom from the thraldom of evil which He had wrought for her, is near to that woman weeping by the grave-side, while Apostles, even the true-hearted Peter and the loving John, have gone to their own homes." *Ellicott.* (See on verse 18.)

Mary. He but utters the familiar name.—To Him she is Mary still, notwithstanding that He has passed through the solemn mystery of death, and to her, His voice has the same unique sound as before.—Whatever changes death and resurrection may have made upon the conditions of His existence, evidently they have not sundered the ties of love, or obliterated the memory of earthly friendship.—Surely this fact may well inspire delightful thoughts in regard to the hope of recognition and re-union beyond the grave.—" With one word, and that one word *her name*, the Lord awakens all the consciousness of His presence : calling her in that tone doubtless in which her soul had been so often summoned to receive divine knowledge and precious comfort." *Alford.*—As the voice of every human being in a healthy condition is the expression of the man within him, we can infer the *impressiveness* of *Jesus's* voice without having a more definite conception of it. *Lange.*—It is well-known that recollections of things that address themselves to the ear are the most enduring.—Thus the fact of Mary's recognizing the Lord by her *ear*, rather than by her *eye*, is entirely in agreement with the laws of manifestation.—But it is also a testimony to the spiritual and divine character of her affection for Him.—She *knows Him* by the tone in which *He calls her name.*—A beautiful illustration of the words : " He calleth his own sheep by name, and they know his voice " (see on chap. x. 3, 4).

—" I have called thee by thy name, and thou art mine," is the gracious word spoken to Israel (Isa. xliii. 1).—Through the human call she becomes aware of the divine call.—It is one thing for God to take notice of a name; another thing to," call by name": the former denotes His omniscience, the latter His special favour. *Hall.*—The *loving heart,* rather than the *understanding head,* always hears the voice of God the most quickly. *Baxter.*—A little thing, yea, even one word, when Christ blesseth it, will bring comfort to mourning souls, and will open their eyes, and wipe away their tears.—Many find Him not because they look for Him to come in some supernatural way, or in some great and wonderful manner or event; whereas He delights to reveal Himself by the ordinary means, and through the common conditions of life.

Turned. This seems to imply that she had not been looking *direct* at Him before.

Rabboni. The oldest MSS. read: *and saith unto Him in Hebrew, Rabboni.*—The only other passage in the N. T. where "Rabboni" occurs is Mark x. 51.—It is "the Master," or, as the Hebrew word means, "*My* Master"; and some render, "My great Master." *Macdonald.*—"The title existed in the Jewish schools under a threefold form: Rab, *master,* the lowest degree of honour; Rabbi, *my master,* of higher dignity; Rabboni, *my great master,* the most honourable of all, publicly given to only seven persons, all of the school of Hillel and of great eminence." *Robinson.*—The pouring out of her gratitude and joy in this *one* word, is in accordance with the deepest psychological truth.—It is an outburst of *complete loyalty* to Christ, as *her* LORD absolutely and supremely, for ever. —And as in the case of the Magdalene, so every true Christian confesses Jesus as *Master* for time and for eternity.—He is *Master* of the reason, the conscience, the affections, the life, and this by the free and loving surrender of all to Him (see on chap. xiii. 13).—*Mary* and *Rabboni,* these two words constitute the entire heart-conversation but they are words full of power.—A dialogue most brief and yet most pregnant.—Thus the *first* manifestation of the Risen Lord was made to the Magdalene (see on verse 1).—Some *harmonists* think His first appearance was to the women as they hastened into the city, but Mark's testimony (chap. xvi. 9) seems decisive, and John's account agrees with it.—" If we compare the Gospel narratives with that of St. Paul, we see *ten* appearances of Christ, which probably took place in the following order: (1) Mary Magdalene sees the Lord first, on coming to the grave the second time (Mark xvi. 9; John xx. 16), after having told Peter and John that the stone is rolled away, and the grave empty. (2) The other women, Mary the mother of James, and Salome, having heard the

angel's joyful message, hurry back in fear and great joy, whereupon the Lord meets them (Matt. xxviii. 9, 10). (3) He also
appears in the course of the same day to Peter (Luke xxiv. 34;
1 Cor. xv. 5); (4) in the evening, to two disciples on their
way to Emmaus (Luke xxiv. 15); (5) and after this to the
ten apostles (without Thomas) assembled in Jerusalem (Luke
xxiv. 36; John xx. 19). (6) On the Sunday following, He appears
to the apostles, with Thomas (John xx. 26). All these appearances took place in *Jerusalem and the neighbourhood,* shortly after the
resurrection. Then come those between Passover and Pentecost,
when the pilgrims to the former feast had returned to *Galilee,*
viz. : (7) at the Lake of Tiberias (John xxi. 1) to seven disciples;
(8) the great manifestation on a mountain in Galilee to all the
disciples (Matt. xxviii. 16 ; Mark xvi. 15 ; Luke xxiv. 49), and
probably at the same time to the five hundred mentioned in 1 Cor.
xv. 6; (9) the special appearance accorded to James ' the brother
of the Lord ' (1 Cor. xv. 7), when, perhaps, the disciples were
exhorted to return earlier than usual to keep the feast of Pentecost at Jerusalem. (10) The final appearance is that to the
apostles on the Mount of Olives, which concluded with the
Ascension (Mark xvi. 19 ; Luke xxiv. 50 ; Acts i. 4). In this
manner the various appearances, although not fully enumerated
in any one record, may be brought together. We may well say
that *the differences in these accounts exclude all idea of an intention to
deceive.* If the Evangelists had been consciously inventing, the
simplest prudence would have made them avoid all traces of differences in their narratives." *Christlieb.* (See note to verse 1 ; also
on verse 29.)

The addition, 'Εβραϊστί, is in accordance with *Codd. Sin.*, *B. D. L. O. X.*, and is
received by *Tisch.*, *Treg.*, *Scholz*, *Alf.*. *Westcott*, *Lange*, *Schaff.*—Most MSS. read
'Ραββουνί (so *Tisch.*, *Alf.*, *Treg.*) ; some 'Ραββουνεί (so *Westcott*) ; some 'Ραββωνεί,
some 'Ραβουνί. *Schaff.*—διδάσκαλε, *Teacher;* the Greek equivalent of Rabbi, and is
used exclusively, as such, by Luke. *Geikie.*—The solemnity of the passage is not contained in the explanatory supplement, but in the " Rabboni." *Lange.*

---

17. Jesus saith unto her, Touch me not; for I am not yet ascended to my Father:
but go to my brethren. and say unto them, I ascend unto my Father, and your Father;
and to my God, and your God.

Touch me not. We infer from this that Mary had fallen at His
feet and embraced them.—The Greek word translated " touch "
occurs thirty-five times in the N. T., and is uniformly thus rendered in the A. V.—But it may also mean to " cling to," to
" fasten on," to " grasp " an object.—Evidently it was not the

mere act of touching, as such, that the Lord reproved; for, in
verse 22, He says to Thomas, "Reach hither thy finger," &c., and
in Luke xxiv. 39, He says, "Handle Me," &c., and Matthew
relates (chap. xxviii. 9) how that the women to whom He appeared
shortly after this "came and held Him by the feet, and worshipped
Him," *unforbidden.*—Was it, therefore, in the motive or in the
act itself that the ground of the prohibition lay?—Was her touch
for the purpose of examining whether it were really Himself, in
the body, or His glorified spirit? *Meyer, Lücke.*—Or, as the tense
of the word is present, is it the *continuance* of the act, the *habit*, that
He prohibits? *Ellicott.*—Or, were her thoughts too earthly, and does
He say: Seek not thy comfort in My *present appearance by terrestrial
contact, but by spiritual communion?* *Augustine.*—This seems the
more satisfactory interpretation of these mysterious words, and
is maintained substantially by *Grotius, Neander, Calvin, Melancthon, De Wette, Tholuck, Luthardt, Hengstenberg, Godet, &c.*—
Mary appears to have thought that she had now gotten Him again
never to be parted from Him.—Her state of mind was similar to
that of Peter on the Mount of Transfiguration, when he exclaimed,
"Let us make three tabernacles," &c.—Our Lord would dissipate
the illusion that every difficulty was past, and that external intercourse with Him is to continue, and is the highest good.—"Her
act supposed a condition which had not yet been accomplished.
He had not returned to earth to abide permanently with His
disciples in the presence of the Paraclete (chap. xiv. 8), for He
had not yet ascended to the Father. There should come a closeness of union in His presence in the soul; but the spirit which
her act was manifesting was one which would prevent this
presence. The coming of the Paraclete depended upon His going
to the Father (chap. xvi. 7), but she would cling to a visible
presence, and had not yet learnt the truth, 'It is expedient for
you that I go away'" (chap. xvi. 7). *Ellicott.*—"Thou shalt
possess Me again, but not as before; it shall be from this time
and for ever *in the spirit.* The time of exalted and divine relationship is come." *Stier.*—"In no moment of blissful ecstasy may we
forget that we are still on earth, and still have a mission here.
Even Mary must attain to a consciousness of the situation. The
fact that she had not yet reached the goal is gently expressed by
His saying that He Himself had not reached it. At the same
time He intimates that *spiritual* communion with Him is the
highest good." *Lange.*—In the background of the reproof another
and a far more blessed *touching* is implied, when He shall have
ascended to the Father. *Alford.*

My brethren. Precious words, seeing they imply the unbroken continuance of His human nature.—The glorious resurrection-life upon which He has entered has not put an end to His brotherly feeling.—"Though Christ be high, yet He is not haughty ; notwithstanding His exaltation, He disdains not to own His poor relations." *Henry.*—"He is not ashamed to call them brethren" (Heb. ii. 11), though He might well have been so, for they had all forsaken Him and fled (see on chap. xvi. 32).—But He is *the same Jesus,* unchanged in love as in personality.—He speaks of them in the heavenly peace of the *new* reconciliation.—He greets them in the dignity of their *new* life, in which He will soon make them glad through the Spirit of adoption.—They are co-brothers and co-heirs in the *new* kingdom that is now founded.—The relation of humanity to God is changed, the *new* Paradise is opened, and, together with the *new* Man, is born, His brethren, of whom, nevertheless, He remains the Lord and King. *Tholuck.*

And say. As if every manifestation of love to Himself must be kept in abeyance till His brethren are comforted by His message. —O love of Christ ! that neither Peter's denial nor desertion by all could shake or change.—Such love belongs not to any creature ; it can be nothing less than the infinite, eternal love of God.—This commission to the Magdalene was a far greater honour than that which He had refused her.—Thus it is, whenever the Lord denies His children anything, it is for their good, and that He may bestow a richer blessing.

I ascend. Gr., *I am ascending ;* I am on My way.—He speaks of His ascension as already present.—He has entered upon the new heavenly state which is the condition of ascension.—He does not speak of His resurrection ; His eye is directed to the supreme goal.—"This teaches us that *resurrection* is nothing, if *ascension* go not with it. Never take care for resurrection ! *That* will come of itself, without any thought-taking of thine. Take thought for ascension ! Set your minds there ! Better lie still in our graves, better never rise, than rise, and, rising, not ascend." *Andrewes.*

My Father. He does not say to *Our Father.*—Jesus is the Son of God in a sense in which no creature could possibly be (see on chap. i. 14, 34, 49, and on Matt. ii. 6 ; iii. 17).—He is the *only begotten* in a sense in which there is no other.—Son from all eternity ; Son by nature ; Son of the same essence with the Father (see on chap. xvi. 28).—His Sonship is of an eternal immediate relation to the Father ; theirs of a relation in time and mediate.—Hence He distinguishes : " *My* Father, *your* Father."

Your Father. *My* Father is also *your* Father now : ye shall be

glorified along with me.—An assurance that the going to the
Father, of which he had so often spoken to them, was about to be
realized.—The victory over death has been accomplished.—This
appearance on earth is the earnest of his return to heaven.—" My
victory over death was the victory of man, whose nature has in
Me conquered death. My ascension into heaven will be the ascension of human nature, which in Me goes to the Father." *Ellicott.*
My God. As the former words imply His *divine* nature, so these
imply His *human* nature, with the same contrast again on both
sides.—His consciousness of God is specific and altogether peculiar, and the source of theirs (Eph. i. 3).—As in His resurrection,
the Father has demonstrated Himself to be *His* almighty God, so
in future, in their course of life and victory, He will prove Himself to be *their* God also.—He designates His glorification as an
ascension *to His Father*, in His character as the Son of God ; *to His
God*, in His character as the glorified Son of Man.—In each case
He connects His relation to God with that of His brethren, and
yet carefully distinguishes between the two. *Lange.*—" Jesus had
called God habitually His *Father*, and on one occasion, in His
darkest moment, His *God* (Matt. xxvii. 46). Both are here united,
expressing that full-orbed relationship which embraces in its vast
sweep at once Himself and His redeemed. Yet, note well, He
says not, *Our* Father and *our* God. All the deepest of the early
Christian writers were wont to call attention to this, as expressly
designed to distinguish between what God is to Him and to us :
*His father essentially, ours not so : our God essentially, His not so :
His God only in connexion with us : our God only in connexion with
Him."* *D. Brown.*—" Christ is the bond of union : like the corner
stone, wherein both sides of the building unite ; or, like the ladder,
whereon Jacob saw angels ascending and descending. All inter-
course betwixt Heaven and earth, God and man, is in and through
Him. If any grace come from God to us, it is by Christ : if any
glory come from us to God, it is by Christ too." *Sanderson.*—
Nothing can afford such consolation as the assurance that *Christ's*
Father is *our* Father, *Christ's* God our God.

Μή μου ἅπτου. Jesus demands a greater reverence for His body now that it has
become divine. *Chrys., Erasmus, &c.*—He was still bodiless, a mere spiritual apparition. *Weisse.*—He as yet appeared only as a mere Man, being not yet re-united to the
Logos, and therefore adoration was unseasonable. *Hilgenfeld.*—Because the new,
glorified corporeality of Jesus was still so tender as to shun every vigorous grasp.
Schleier., Olshausen.—He reproves her gesture as unsuited to the time, and the nature
of His present appearance. *Alford.*—Tarry not with Me, but make haste and discharge
the message; time enough later for handling, greeting. holding. *Beza, Calov., Bengel.*—
Jesus was on the point of ascending, and did not desire to be detained by Mary : one

of the numerous ascensions occurring in the period of the forty days was about to be performed. *Baur, Kinkel.*—Hold Me not as though we were in the perfection of the existence of that world beyond us, for *I* am not yet ascended, &c., to say nothing of *thyself. Hofmann, Luthardt, Tholuck, Lange, &c.*—Cleave not to Me in My bodily appearance ; do not touch Me carnally, but learn to touch Me spiritually.—When the power of the bodily touch ends, then the spiritual touch begins, and that touch most honours Christ and profits us. *Wordsworth* (who applies the words to Christ's presence in the Eucharist which is spiritual, not carnal).—Old familiarities must now give place to new and more awful, yet sweeter, approaches, but for these the time has not come yet. *D. Brown.*—This is not the moment to *attach* yourself to Me as I am before you in My human individuality. *Godet.*—Death has now set a gulf between us.—Touch not, as you once might have done, this body which is now glorified by its conquest over death, for with this body I ascend to the Father. *Euthy., Theoph., Thomson* in *Smith's* " Dictionary of the Bible."—Our Lord's words seem founded in a reference or allusion to some prior conversation ; for the want of knowing which, His meaning is hidden from us.—This very obscurity, however, is a proof of genuineness: no one would have forged such an answer. *Lightfoot, Paley.*—The first μου omitted. *B. D. X., Itala, Tisch., Treg., Alford, Westcott, Lange,*—It was probably supplemented in imitation of the subsequent μου. *Schaff.*

---

18. Mary Magdalene came and told the disciples that she had seen the Lord, and that he had spoken these things unto her.

Came.   Gr., *Mary the Magdalene cometh.*—The coming is described from the point of view of the writer, who was one of the disciples. *Ellicott.*—She was obedient to the command, " Go to My brethren."—When God comforts us, it is with this design, that we may comfort others.—She sought the Body of Jesus to anoint it and received the anointing of the Spirit from the Risen One. —The first appearance of the Angel of the Lord, in the Old Testament, was to Hagar, the bondmaid of Sarah ; and the first appearance of Christ, after His resurrection, was to the Magdalene, once the bondmaid of sin.—Both, at the time, sorely needed consolation, and both were mentally disposed to receive it.—In the hour of utmost distress is evolved the ability to perceive providential help.—Supreme salvation is nigh unto extreme hopelessness, if the latter will but patiently wait for the Lord.—Then, however, salvation comes to hopelessness always from *above*, as a *gift* of deliverance.—Hopelessness may prophesy of salvation, may prepare a place for it, but it cannot be the parent of it.— Thus it was with Mary and the disciples at the time of the Resurrection, and thus it is with all who seek the Saviour.

Told.   Gr., *announceth,* or, *bringeth tidings.*—First she converses with the angels, then with the Lord, now with the disciples.— Her grief was so changed into joy that she became a messenger of life to the whole Church of Christ in all ages.—The first Easter sermon: 1. The *preacher ;* a soul nigh unto despair, a woman who had been a great sinner, penitent and pardoned ; 2. The *manner* of the sermon ; she speaks of her blessedness (" I have seen the Lord "), then faithfully reports His message.—Thus in the true preaching of Christ, the testimony of experience and the commanded Word must accompany each other. *Lange.*—To the glory of sovereign grace it is recorded, that the first preacher of restored, eternal righteousness and life, was Mary *the Magdalene.*

---

19. Then the same day at evening, being the first day of the week, when the doors were shut where the disciples were assembled for fear of the Jews, came Jesus and stood in the midst, and saith unto them, Peace be unto you.

Evening. Gr., *When therefore it was evening on that day.*—The first sight of the Risen One was granted to penitent love, in the person of Mary, *early* in the morning of the Resurrection day.—To less perfect repentance and a more wavering faith, as exhibited in the persons of the Apostles, the same glorious spectacle was not allowed, till the *evening.*—With the early God will be early; and, according to the measure and capacities of every man's faith and love, hope and expectation, shall be his Beatific vision of the Lord Jesus, even in this present world (Psa. xviii. 24-26). *Ford.*

First day. Gr., *The first of the week* (see on verse 1).—In the interval between the last verse and this, the bribing of the Roman guard occurred (Matt xxviii. 11-15), and the conversation on the way to Emmaus (Luke xxiv. 13-35).

Doors were shut. Gr., *The doors had been shut,* or, *the doors being shut.*—John carefully emphasizes this remarkable fact, as also in verse 26.—Evidently with the intention of showing that the appearance of our Lord was supernatural.

Fear. Naturally enough, fear of the Sanhedrists followed the condemnation and crucifixion of their Master.—They would also remember His words, in which He had warned them of the hatred of the world, and of the persecution to which they would be exposed (see on chap. xv. 18-21; xvi. 1-4).—Moreover, it is probable that the Jewish rulers had threatened the disciples and friends of the Crucified One.—Their position, therefore, was such as to excite grave apprehension and alarm.—How lonely, desolate, depressed and helpless they must have felt.—But it was only the gloom which precedes the breaking of the day.—The Sun of Righteousness had arisen, and was coming to them " with healing in His wings."—No doors can prevent Christ's access to His people. —Yea, when the doors are the most completely shut to the world, then are they, in the highest sense, open to the Lord.

Came Jesus. The supposition that the doors were miraculously opened is opposed to the general impression of the context.—

Moreover, John would not have been likely to omit such an incident, had it occurred.—The words, honestly interpreted, imply that Jesus appeared among them while the doors were shut.—The body of the risen Lord was the body of His human life, but it was no longer subject to the conditions of that life.—It was now altogether superior to laws of gravitation and material resistance. —The description leads to the conception " of an unconfinedness to the limits of space." *Tholuck.*—It shows the power of His resurrection life to move unrestrainedly, to appear and disappear at will.—Like every primal generation, the nature of the resurrection body of Him who was "the first-fruits of them that slept," must remain a mystery.—"We cannot form any clear conception of the process by which the corpse of Christ was transmuted into a glorious body, nor can we understand the nature of the latter. We can only recall to our minds that heavy water is changed into light vapour, or dark flint into transparent glass, by heat; or that the caterpillar, which slowly crawls along the ground, at length grows into an airy butterfly. And thus the glorified body of Christ was not altered as regards its fundamental components ; it was *the same body*, with the marks of the nails and the wound in its side; but in a new *spiritual form of existence, and therefore standing under other laws.* It therefore appears—until the Ascension, when its transformation was completed—as an elementary, earthly, material body ; but its elements are no longer bound by space, and it can go here or there, make itself visible or invisible ; in fact, shape itself outwardly according to the internal will. And this is possible because the body is *spiritualized through and through;* it has become an adequate expression of the spirit, and its willing instrument. The body no longer opposes its own laws (of space, gravitation, motion, &c.) to the volitions of the spirit ; it does not hinder nor limit them ; but implicitly obeys. All strife is at an end. If the spirit *will* to transport itself to any place, it can do so together with the body; the body no longer hinders it, for it is saturated with vital force and immortality. This is what the Scriptures (1 Cor. xv. 44-46) call a ' *spiritual body* ' in contradistinction to the '*natural body.*' In this resurrection body the Lord stands during those forty days, as it were, on the boundary line of both worlds ; He bears the impress of this as well as a future state of existence. It is therefore no contradiction (as Strauss would have it) that this body sometimes manifested the force of repulsion (when touched), and at other times not (when penetrating through closed doors) ; for it could do so or not, according to the will of the spirit. Doors could not keep out that which is in a *spiritual* state of existence. Since

all matter, too, is well known to be porous, it can form no absolute barrier for the spirit. We cannot wonder, moreover, that
this body, being formed from the same essential elements as the
former earthly one, should be capable of eating food (Luke
xxiv. 43; Acts x. 41), though not needing it, especially as the
same thing is mentioned in the case of angels (Gen. xviii. 8).
Our Lord does not ' digest ' this food, as Strauss coarsely puts it,
but He assimilates it in some way or other, and transmutes it into
His spiritual form of existence, so that it cannot hinder Him from
disappearing. For we must not forget that it is not earthly
matter *per se* which is incapable of being developed into a
spiritual state of existence, but only the defilement which cleaves
to it in our fallen condition that prevents this. *The terrestrial
body as such is destined to be spiritualized;* but if this is its destiny,
it must also possess the *capability.* This shows us at the same
time the reason why the sinless body of Christ could be immediately transmuted. Its purity was the possibility of its transformation .In this manner we see that the enigma of our Lord's
resurrection body, with its wondrous appearances, no longer contains any inexplicable contradiction." *Christlieb.*

Stood. See on verse 20.—That is, He appeared *standing in their
midst without motion thither.*—How calm and tranquil the life of
the risen Lord, blissfully moving within itself, like God Himself.
—This is the first great fulfilment of His promise, " Where
two or three are gathered together in My name, *there am I in
the midst of them* " (see on Matt. xviii. 20).

Peace. See on chap. xiv. 27; and Luke xxiv. 36.—He concluded
His farewell discourses with this word (see on chap. xvi. 33), and
now, in His resurrection life, it is the first He speaks to them.—
A self-revealing word, as the utterance of her name was to Mary.
—Not a mere greeting but the bestowment of the blessing of
peace.—As He hushed the stormy sea by this word, so now He
hushes their fears and calms their troubled hearts.—It is a message from the spirit world, a voice from the darkness beyond the
grave, and that voice proclaims *peace.*—It is the message of Him
who has conquered death for us, and who, hereby, assures us of
the victory.—It is the preaching of the atonement (at-one-ment),
announcing the peace which flows from pardoned sin and complete reconciliation with God.—The word is filled with the fulness of the resurrection-message and all that proclamation of
salvation therewith connected.—Christ's disciples must receive
His peace into their own hearts before they can become apostles
of peace to mankind.—No claim of " orders " or " ordination "
can possibly constitute a man a minister of Christ's gospel of

peace, whose heart, unrenewed by the Holy Spirit, remains in its natural state of enmity against God (Rom. viii. 7).—What sovereign would send a man as his ambassador who was in rebellion against himself and his government?—Surely, therefore, it may be assumed that the Lord Jesus sends no men to preach His word of reconciliation who are themselves unreconciled to God.—This bestowal of peace upon the disciples was a gracious fulfilment of the promise, chap. xiv. 27.—The day of Christ's heavenly birth from the dead, the birthday of all Christian blessings.—Though Christ may upbraid for unbelief (Mark xvi. 14), yet to speak peace is the object of His coming, and the sign of His presence. *Hutcheson.*

συνηγμένοι. Omitted. *Cod. Sin., &c., Lach., Tisch., Alford, Lange, Tregelles, &c.*

20. And when he had so said, he shewed unto them his hands and his side. Then were the disciples glad, when they saw the Lord.

He showed, &c. Luke's Gospel (chap. xxiv. 39) has " My hands and my feet," thus furnishing an undesigned coincidence with John (verse 25).—The piercing of our Lord's side is recorded by John only (see on chap. xix. 34, 35).—It would appear from the words of John (1 Epistle i. 1) that the disciples had been permitted to handle Him.—Showing them His hands, with the print of the nails, and His side, with the wound caused by the spear, was to convince them that His resurrection was a reality, not a mere appearance.—The conditions of the problem must remain, however, transcendental and mysterious.—It is outside the sphere of our knowledge, beyond the province of our science.—A state of life is brought before us of which we have no experience.— That there is a real corporeity is evident, and yet there is manifest superiority to the ordinary laws of bodily existence.—" One characteristic is common to all the appearances recounted : they never pass outside the purely spiritual bounds we instinctively associate with the mysterious existence on which Jesus had entered. Even when most closely touching the material and earthly, He is always seen speaking and acting only as a spirit, coming suddenly, revealing Himself in an imperceptibly increasing completeness which culminates at last in some unmistakable sign, and presently vanishing, as suddenly as He appeared. He no longer acts or suffers as before His death, and even when condescending most to the seen and material, only does so to prove Himself, beyond question, the same Jesus as formerly, who in common human life, shared all the experiences and wants of His followers." *Ewald, Geikie.*—For the healing of doubting hearts, the marks of the wounds were still preserved. *Augustine.* (See on verse 19.)

Glad. Gr., *The disciples therefore were glad, when they saw the Lord.*— At first they thought they saw a spirit and were terrified and affrighted (see on chap. vi. 19; and Luke xxiv. 37).—But the well-known voice and greeting, and the sight of the wounds in His hands, and the spear mark, assured them that it was indeed the Lord: Hence their *gladness.*—Whatever hopes may be entertained as to a future life, the resurrection of Christ alone can give certainty and confidence to the mind.—Here we see the continuousness of life, through the dread mystery of death and the grave, and with his re-appearing the identity of that life for He is *the same Jesus.*—*Peace* and *joy*, two particular precious fruits of His resurrection and of His spiritual kingdom.—All blessings ensue from the "*Peace be unto you*" of the Risen One.—A church of secret, fugitive disciples, is turned into a church of festive, glad believers.—How different the experience of the disciples from what it was in the morning.—Let all tempted and afflicted ones take courage; a few hours may change the whole character of events.—"At *evening time* it shall be light" (Zech. xiv. 7).

The Lord. See on verse 28; see also on Matt. i. 22.—A believing view of Jesus, as the once crucified, but now risen and exalted Lord, is the true source of all spiritual joy and gladness.—And if such be the case here, when seeing Him only as "through a glass, darkly," when the eye is often dimmed with tears, what will be the rapture of heaven when we shall "see Him as He is"?— "Looking unto Jesus" is *salvation* now; "seeing the King in His beauty" will be *glory* (see on chap. xvii. 24).

---

21. Then said Jesus to them again, Peace be unto you: as my Father hath sent me, even so send I you.

Peace. He repeats the benediction of verse 19, as the introduction to the sending which follows.—He would impress upon them that *His* disciples and ministers are to be pre-eminently messengers of peace.—Christ speaking peace, makes peace; peace with God, peace in the heart, peace with one another.—Paul could only pray for peace: Christ imparts it.—Some understand the words in verse 19 as those of greeting, and these as the words of farewell.— Other words had intervened as we know from Luke's account (chap. xxiv.).

As. See on chap. xvii. 18.—This commission was not now first given them, but now first fully assured to them.—Their sending forth by Him, their glorified Head, was to be, in character and process, like that of Himself by the Father.—He identifies them with Himself in His mediatorial work.—They are ambassadors for Christ, to whom He commits the ministry of reconciliation (2 Cor. iv. 18).—He stands in the same relation to the Father as that in which they stand to Him.—The Father now sends Him out of the kingdom of resurrection and reconciliation to them ; so likewise the Son sends them out of this kingdom to the world. *Lange.*— Their mission from Him is measured in accordance with His mission from the Father.—He declares to them, and they in His name are to declare to the world, the fulness of the Father's love, and the peace between man and God, testified to in His life and death.—In addition to the commission given them at the first, henceforth they are to be witnesses for the Crucified and Risen One.—His words contain the assurance that they shall find in His presence, as He had ever found in the Father's presence, the support which will ever bring peace to their hearts.—Note the union of familiarity and majesty in the first manifestation of the risen Lord in the church.—The great word : Sent from Christ as Christ was sent from the Father.—Can those who claim to be the successors of the apostles thus speak of their appointment and ordination?—He who is *sent* of Christ must needs have received the peace of Christ, and also the Spirit of Christ, for so it is here.— " By their *fruits* ye shall know them," said Christ, and not by their pretensions and claims (see on Matt. vii. 20).—" In the evening and at night Jesus did take in hand many momentous things for our sake : He was born in the night, He instituted the Lord's Supper in the night, He was taken prisoner in the night, and in the evening, when He was risen from the dead, He instituted the ministry of the New Testament." *Starke.*

καθώς. He confirms and grounds their Apostleship on the present glorification of Himself, whose Apostleship (Heb. iii. 1) on earth was now ended, but was to be continued by this sending forth of them. *Alford.*—As at the first bestowal of apostolic dignity, Peter took precedence of the others, so now the general restitution of the whole body precedes a more explicit restitution of Peter. *Lange.*—Christ *sent them* authorised with a divine warrant, armed with a divine power; *sent them* as ambassadors to treat of *peace*, and as heralds to proclaim it; *sent them* as servants to *bid to the marriage :* hence they were called *Apostles, men sent. Henry.*—As God sent Me to preach, to be persecuted, and to suffer; to make known His will, and to offer pardon to men; so I send you. *Barnes.*

22. And when he had said this, he breathed on them, and saith unto them, Receive ye the Holy Ghost.

Breathed. The Greek word translated "breathed" occurs nowhere else in the New Testament.—It is used in the Sept. to express the act of God in the original communication of life to man (Gen. ii. 7).—"He breathed into his nostrils the breath of life," evidently denotes something which is common both to God and man, something which goes forth from God and enters into man.—John describes this act of the risen Lord by the remarkable word used to describe the impartation of life from God to man at the first.—"This breathing is now by God incarnate repeated, sacramentally, representing the infusion of the new life, of which He is become by His glorified humanity the source to His members: see Job xxxiii. 4; Psa. xxxiii. 6; 1 Cor. xv. 45." *Alford.*—"John writes as one who remembered how the influence of that moment on their future lives was a new spiritual creation, by which they were called, as it were, out of death into life. It was the first step in that great moral change which passed over the disciples after the crucifixion, and of which the day of Pentecost witnessed the accomplishment." *Ellicott.*—"He breathes on them"; like a *friend's breath* upon the cheek, shall the Holy Spirit of God come upon man's spirit. *Braune.*—The action of our Lord may have shown emblematically that the Holy Ghost *proceedeth from the* SON. *Augustine.* (See on chap. xv. 26.)—May also intimate that He who now breathed upon the disciples breathed the breath of life into man at the first. *Cyril.*—"That grace which man enjoyed at first, because God breathed into his nostrils, that same grace did Christ now restore." *Eusebius.*—"At the first institution of certain mysteries of the faith, there was not wanting the outward emblem of an inward grace; which grace was afterwards conveyed without any such visible demonstration. Thus at the Baptism of Christ, the Holy Ghost descended *in a bodily shape like a dove* upon Him. And now, at the ordination of His apostles, our Lord is found to have *breathed* into their faces, when He would convey to them the gift of the same Blessed Spirit."—"As if He had said, As ye perceive the breath to proceed from My Body, so understand, that the Holy Spirit proceeds from My Person, even from the secret of My Deity." *Anselm.*—"He had Himself compared the influence and entrance of the Spirit to the breathing of the wind, and, now, prefaces His intended words by the symbolical act of breathing upon them." *Geikie.*

Receive. Not simply a promise of the gift of the Spirit: the words are a definite imperative, referring to the moment when they

were spoken.—He uses the very word which He had used at the
last supper, "Take (*receive ye*), eat; this is My Body" (see on
Matt. xxvi. 26).—This word would come to them with a fulness
of sacred meaning.—The command implies the power to obey.

The Holy Ghost. Gr., *Receive Holy Spirit.*—See on chap. xiv. 26,
and Matt. i. 20; iii. 16.—This is not to be regarded as the promised advent of the Paraclete (see on chap. xiv. 16).—The gift
of the Spirit could not be bestowed till Jesus was glorified (see
on chap. vii. 39; xvi. 7).—Our Lord had given them a sign and
with it the foretaste and pledge of that which was to come.—His
breathing upon them, which was a sacramental act, was accompanied with the inward and spiritual grace.—As His presence with
them *now* was a slight and temporary fulfilment of His promise
to return to them; so the imparting of the Spirit *now*, was the
symbol and first fruits of Pentecost.—This giving of the
Spirit was not the Spirit's *personal* imparting of Himself, but only
a partial instilling of His influence from our Lord in His risen
Body. *Alford.*—"The relation of this saying to the effusion of the
Spirit is the same which chap. iii. bears to Baptism, chap. vi. to
the Lord's Supper, chap. xvii. to the Ascension, &c." *Luthardt.*

λάβετε. Simply the prophetico-symbolical heralding of the Holy Ghost. *Theod.
Mopsueste, Bullinger, Kuinoel, Lampe, &c.*—This view is contradicted by the act, and
by the Aorist Imperative λάβετε. *Lange.*—It is *Holy Spirit* (πνεῦμα ἅγιον, without the
article), but not yet *the* Holy Spirit. *Gess, Hofmann, Luthardt.*—*Grace to prepare* them
for the Apostolic office. *Theoph., Maldon., &c.*—A precursive communication of the Spirit,
in accordance with Christ's not yet perfected state of glorification. *Origen, Calvin,
Neander, Stier, Tholuck.*—A veritable ἀπαρχή (*first fruits*) of the Holy Ghost. *Meyer,
Bengel, Brückner, Hengst., Godet, Ewald, Alford, Lange, &c.*—The apostles have not yet
the gift of communicating the Holy Ghost, but they do possess that of discerning the
Holy Spirit when already communicated. *Lange.*—The absence of the article before
πνεῦμα may indicate the *partial* or *preparatory* inspiration, as distinct from the Pentecostal effusion. *Schaff.*

---

23. Whosoever sins ye remit, they are remitted unto them; and whosoever sins
ye retain, they are retained.

Remit, &c. See on Matt. xvi. 19.—Note that the term, *remit sins*,
is akin to the term, *loose*, used in Matthew; and the term, *retain*,
or *retain together*, is akin to the term, *bind.*—Our Lord here inverts the expression putting redemption (*remission*) in the foreground.—Forgiveness of sins is pre-eminently the fruit of the
resurrection of Christ.—"He was delivered for our offences, and
was raised again for our justification" (Rom. iii. 25).—His triumph
over death was also a triumph over sin, the cause of death.—

Hence the Lord puts forgiveness of sins in the forefront of the apostolic embassy.—This power is here immediately connected with the representative character of the disciples as apostles sent by Christ, as He was Himself sent by the Father (verse 21).— Its validity is dependent upon their reception of the Holy Ghost (verse 22), by whom Christ Himself is present in them (see on chap. xiv. 18 ; xvi. 7-11).—Their remitting of sin and retaining of sin will, as a prophetically ministerial act, rest upon corresponding acts of God, already accomplished in the Spirit.—The apostles will be influenced in these acts by Christ ; they will not influence Him. *Lange.*—*Their acts would be, not creative, but declarative of the preceding acts of Christ and the Holy Spirit. Schaff.*—He intimates that it is not *they*, but the Holy Ghost by them, that puts away sin : *" For who can forgive sin, but God only ? " Augustine.*— As if He said : "The government of the Church is committed to your charge. As a special gift for your work as founders of My Kingdom, divine insight is granted you to ' discern the spirits ' of men (1 Cor. xii. 10), so that you may know their true state before God. Through you, therefore, henceforth, as through Me till now, the Holy Spirit will announce the forgiveness of sins, and it will be granted by God to those to whom you declare it. Through you, moreover, He will make known to others that their sins are not forgiven, and to him to whom you are constrained to speak thus, to him his sins will not be forgiven by God till you announce their being so." *Geikie.*—" God has promised forgiveness wherever there is repentance ; He has *not* promised repentance wherever there is sin. It results from every declaration of forgiveness made in the name of the Father through Jesus Christ, that hearts which in penitence accept it receive remission of their sins, and that the hardness of the hearts which wilfully reject it is by their rejection increased, and the very words by which their sins would be remitted become the words by which they are retained." *Ellicott.*—*What* was conferred in verse 22 is explained here.—Our Lord reassures them of the authority given in Matt. xviii. 18, to discern spirits and pronounce on them, and to discern the mind of the Spirit in such cases as may come before them.—" Both these, however, were only temporary and imperfect. That *no formal gifts of Apostleship were now formally conferred, is plain by the absence of Thomas*, who in that case would be no apostle in the same sense in which the rest were." *Alford.*—" In any *literal* and *authoritative* sense *this power was never exercised by one of the apostles*, and plainly *was never understood by themselves as possessed by them or conveyed to them.* In the *actings* of His ministers, the real nature of the power committed to them is seen in the exercise of *church discipline.*" *D. Brown.*—This power involves : 1. The preaching of the gospel ; 2. Establishment of the preliminary conditions of reception; 3. Reception into the church ; 4. Penitential discipline in the real sense of the term. *Lange.*—Romish priests and others who claim to have the power, *officially* and *literally,* of *binding* and *loosing,* of *remitting* and *retaining sin,* should show : 1. That any apostle ever assumed any such power ; 2. That *they* have been sent by Christ as He was sent by the Father ; 3. That *they* have received the Holy Ghost.— The doctrine of apostolical succession, by episcopal ordination, which Whately, Alford, and other divines of the Church of England have pronounced a *fiction,* was not held by the Reformers.— "It was re-introduced from Rome, thirty years after the Reformation, by Bancroft, afterwards Archbishop of Canterbury, but then Rector of St. Andrew's, Holborn, 1589, to the astonishment of England, He preached it first in a sermon at Paul's Cross. So free from this doctrine was the Church, that Presbyterian ordination was accepted as valid till 1662." *Brodie, Herzog, Geikie.*— This doctrine involves the assumption that the Holy Ghost is inseparably tied to Episcopal ordination, no matter how ignorant the candidate may be of spiritual truth, no matter how wicked in heart or life.—At the same time, it denies the ministerial authority of those not episcopally ordained, no matter how wise, how holy, how useful they may be.—If a bishop puts his hands on the man's head, he is a true minister, no matter how lacking he may be in gifts and fitness for the ministry.—Without this, no enlightenment by the Holy Spirit, no seal of God in the conversion of sinners and the edification of believers, accounts for anything.—The Church of Rome claims to have it and denies it to the Church of England.—The Church of England claims to have it and denies it to the Nonconformists.—"Go ye," said Christ, " and disciple all nations, &c. ; teaching them to observe all things whatsoever I have commanded you : and, lo, I am with you alway, even unto the end of the world."—Here is the divine constitution of the Christian Ministry ; here the true Apostolical succession.—Wherever *the Apostolic faith* and *the Apostolic spirit* are found, there is Christ.—And the ministers whom HE calls and qualifies are known by these marks ; they hold and preach *that faith ;* they are animated and governed by *that spirit* (see on verse 22).—Our Lord's words reach beyond the Apostles and extend to all ages of the Church.—With the gift and real participation of the Holy Spirit, comes the conviction, and therefore the *knowledge,* of *sin,* of *righteousness,* and *judgment.*—This knowledge becomes more perfect, the more men are filled with the Holy Ghost.—Hence

those who are pre-eminently filled with His presence are pre-
eminently gifted with the discernment of sin and repentance in
others, and by the Lord's appointment are authorized to pronounce pardon of sin and the contrary.—The Apostles had
this in an especial manner, and by the full indwelling of the
Spirit were enabled to discern the hearts of men, and to give
sentence on that discernment (see Acts v. 1-11; viii. 21; xiii. 9).
—And this gift belongs to the Church in all ages, and especially
to those who by divine grace are set to minister in the
Churches of Christ.—Not however to them exclusively, though
for decency and order it is expedient that the outward and formal
declaration should be so. —In proportion as *any disciple* shall have
been filled with the Holy Spirit of wisdom, is the inner discernment, the κρίσις (judgment), his. *Alford.*

ἀφίενται, text. rec. *Alford.*— ἀφέωνται. *Codd. A. D. L. O. X., Lach., Tisch., Treg.,
Westcott and Hort, Lange.*—ἀφέωνται is also found in Matt. ix. 2 5; Mark ii 5; Luke
v. 20, 23 ; vii. 47 ; 1 John ii. 12.—On individual words in this text it is important to
note that in the better text the ten e of that rendered "are remitted" is a strict present, while that rendered "are retained" is in the perfect-present. —The difference is
not easy to preserve in English, but the thought seems to be. " Whose soever sins ye
remit, a change in their condition is taking p ace, their sins are being remitted by
God ; whose soever ye retain, their condition remains unchanged, they have been, and
are retained." *Ellicott.*

**24. But Thomas, one of the twelve, called Didymus, was not with them when Jesus
came.**

Thomas. See on chap. xi. 16; xiv. 5; Matt. x. 3; Luke vi. 15.
Not with them. Thomas's absence could hardly have been accidental.—It gives rise to the inference that he was wandering
about solitary and gloomy.—He had spoken of the Lord's return
to Jerusalem as leading to death (chap. xi. 16), and it had turned
out as he feared.—He seems to have abandoned all hope; the
evidence of the death of Jesus was too strong to allow the thought
of restoration to life, and evidently he had no idea of His resurrection.—All this is in harmony with his character as already
presented in this Gospel.—"Thomas's place among the apostles,
though inferior to John and Peter, is yet an important one. He
represents, within the Church, the principle, *knowledge precedes
faith,* which is not necessarily incompatible with the higher principle, *faith precedes knowledge.* His is the type of the honest,
earnest, inquiring, truth-loving scepticism, which anxiously craves
tangible evidence, and embraces it with joy when it is presented.

This is essentially different from the worldly, frivolous scepticism of indifference or hostility to truth, which ignores or opposes the truth in spite of evidence. The former wants knowledge in order to faith, the latter knowledge without or against faith. The inquiring spirit of Thomas, having a moral motive and aim, is a wholesome, propelling principle in the Church, and indispensable in scientific theology. It dispels prejudice, ignorance, and superstition, and promotes knowledge and intelligence. Yet, practically and spiritually, it is defective as compared with the child-like spirit of faith with which alone we can enter the kingdom of heaven. For salvation we must go to Christ, not as reasoning logicians, or learned theologians, or pleading lawyers, or calculating merchants, but as the child goes to the mother's bosom, as heart goes to heart, and love to love—with unbounded confidence and trust. Faith is the true mother of true knowledge in divine things, and even in philosophy, which starts in *love* of wisdom, and consequently implies its existence. It is only in a very qualified sense, in matters of historical inquiry and philosophic and scientific research, that doubt may be called the father of knowledge." *Schaff.* (See on verse 25.)

When. Christians who absent themselves from the assembly of disciples, often lose blessed manifestations of the Lord.—Thomas, by his absence, was deprived, not only of the good news which Mary and others brought them, but of that comfortable sight of the Lord also which they got, and he is left in many snares and doubtings, from which they are delivered. *Hutcheson.*

---

25. The other disciples therefore said unto him, We have seen the Lord. But he said unto them, Except I shall see in his hands the print of the nails, and put my finger into the print of the nails, and thrust my hand into his side, I will not believe.

Have seen. See on verse 20.—"Disciples ought to be communicative in their station of what they have received; and when their hearts are refreshed with a sweet sight of Christ, they cannot but make it known, as they have a calling and opportunity." *Hutcheson.*

The Lord. See on verse 28, and on Matt. i. 23.—"What is the holy expectation of faith, the thing a Christian longs for at the Resurrection? It is the *seeing* of his Saviour, the beholding his God, the enjoying of his Redeemer. It is not, that we shall live ever, but ' be ever *with* the Lord.' It was small joy for Absalom to dwell at Jerusalem, and not to be admitted to see the King's face. The good women at the sepulchre saw a vision of Angels;

but that contented them not till Christ appeared." *Brownrig.* (See on chap. xii. 21.)

Except. See on verse 24.—Thomas was the Rationalist among the apostles. *Olshausen.*—Yet this trait in his mental character was used by God for the strengthening of his own faith, and of that of multitudes who should come after him.—The others have seen the risen Lord and have no doubt of His identity : but he naturally thinks it more probable that they have been deceived than that the Crucified is really alive.—He demands to examine the wound-marks, to trace the prints of the nails, the opening made by the spear-thrust.—In all this he requires no more than had been granted to the rest : but he had *their testimony in addition.*—Nor is it in this particular case only that he is sceptical : it is his habit, as is evidenced in our Lord's reproof, " Be not faithless " (see on verse 27).—Thomas' scepticism, however, was not that of the heart, but that of the understanding.—The former will *not* look at the hands and the side, because it is determined not to be moved morally and spiritually as they would move the honest soul.—The latter insists on seeing the wound-marks, because it wants to know the precise truth, and therefore avails itself of whatever evidence God has given.—The scepticism of the heart hates the light, and will not come to the light, lest its deeds be reproved.—The scepticism of the understanding is that which refuses to believe without sufficient evidence.—Such a mind needs only to have the evidences of Christianity rightly presented, to yield to it cordial and entire faith.—Many of the firmest believers, many of the ablest defenders of the truth as it is in Jesus, belong to this class of minds.—In this sense, Lardner, Paley, Pascal, and Butler, whose contributions to the Christian evidences are invaluable, were pre-eminently sceptical.—They would not believe without examining the hands and the side, trying all the witnesses, testing the objections against Christianity with the opposing arguments, weighing coolly and impartially the evidence, real or pretended, on either side ; and the result was a faith in Christ, which sight could hardly have rendered clearer or stronger. *Peabody.*—Much mischief is often caused by not distinguishing between the scepticism of the heart and that of the understanding.—There is an important difference between the simple *absence* of belief, and *unbelief* or *disbelief. Chalmers.*—Our Lord's treatment of Thomas a lesson to all Christian teachers as to how to deal with the honest, inquiring sceptic.

The print. The demand that he should be permitted to put his finger into the print of the nails, and thrust his hand into His side, sounds more than coarse, even shocking.—But the circumstances should be taken into account as well as the mental character of the speaker.—All common probability was against the supposition of a resurrection, especially with such conditions of life as the disciples described, viz. : the sudden appearance in the room, the doors being closed, and the sudden vanishing.— Thomas had seen Lazarus raised by the miraculous power of Jesus, but the conditions of life were the same *after*, as *before*, death.—What he wants to be convinced of is, the *corporeality* of the Risen One, and the *identity* of that *corporeality* with the Crucified One ; hence his demand for *visual* and *tangible* evidence. —Moreover, belief in the resurrection of Messiah was to all intents and purposes a *new* belief.—" The Messianic expectations of the Jews contained no idea corresponding to it." *Weizsäcker.*— We see the Resurrection in the light of New Testament teaching, and in the light of the faith of the Church for eighteen hundred years; Thomas, and the disciples generally, had no such light.—Because Thomas does not name the Feet, it does not follow that they were not nailed to the cross (see on chap. xix. 18).—The Hands and Side would more naturally offer themselves to his examination than the Feet, to which he would have to stoop. *Alford.*

Not believe. Gr., *I will by no means believe;* the determination is expressed in the strongest form.—For the time he seems to have forgotten the words, " Except ye see signs and wonders ye will not believe " (see on chap. iv. 48).—But God was graciously working through all, and a great and glorious confirmation of the Resurrection was at hand.—This very incredulity was overruled to result in tl e grandest confession of Christ on record, and in the establishment of the faith of the Church to the end of time.— Though Thomas's unbelief, particularly in its obstinacy, is to be condemned, yet in some things he is to be commended : 1. He would not make a profession of belief *merely because others did so ;* many do this in our day, who, notwithstanding their profession, have no true faith, but are often secret unbelievers ; 2. He held fast the *possibility of belief ;* if granted certain evidence he *would believe,* a reproof to a large class of sceptics, who show a very different disposition ; 3. He put himself in *the way of obtaining the evidence* and therefore of *attaining belief* (see on verse 26).

τόπον, text rec., *Alford, Lange, Westcott and Hort. &c.*—τόπον. *Origen, Vulgate, Lach., Tisch.*—τόπον weakens the solemnity of the expression *Schaff.*—Copyists may easily have taken one for the other.—If we read τόπον, it answers to the touch of the finger, as τύπον does to the sight of the eye; but, on the other hand, there is in the repetition an expression of determination, almost, we may say, amounting to obstinacy, which corresponds with the position Thomas is taking. *Ellicott.*

26. And after eight days again his disciples were within, and Thomas with them : then came Jesus, the doors being shut, and stood in the midst, and said, Peace be unto you.

Eight days. See note.—That is, on the octave of the first appearance to them ; as we should say now, on the first Sunday after Easter. *Ellicott.*—The first testimony of the recurring day of the Resurrection being commemorated by the disciples.—The beginning of an observance, which has been continued ever since by the Christian Church (see on verse 29).—It forms an interesting opening of the history of the Lord's Day, that Christ Himself should have thus selected and honoured it. *Alford.*—That day has been pointed out and set apart by His special presence as the day of Christian communion and worship, and as such it will remain till time shall be no longer.—God's Word and the Lord's Day are inseparable companions, and the pillars of God's Church. *Schaff.* (See on verse 1 ; see also on Luke vi. 1, 5.)

Within. Evidently the same place as that in which they were met when the Lord first appeared to them (see on verse 20).—It is probable they had thus assembled daily since that time.—But the fact of all the disciples being now present indicates that already they had begun to attribute special importance to *the first day.*

Thomas. See on verses 24, 25.—Although still an unbeliever in the Resurrection, yet that he is *willing to believe,* his presence with the disciples proves.—His conduct condemns many in our day who profess themselves ready to believe if they could only find evidence sufficient and satisfactory.—But instead of attending the house of God, where the Lord has promised to manifest Himself to humble, longing hearts, these professed sceptics regard Christian worship and the ordinances of the Church with cold indifference, if not with contempt and derision.—This shows that their scepticism is not *honest,* that they have no *love* for the truth, and no *desire* to attain to faith.—They ask, " What is truth ? " but like Pilate, are not " of the truth," and therefore neither *care* for it, nor *seek* it (see on chap. xviii. 37, 38).—Thomas's case was altogether different ; it really seems as if he could not, would not, believe, *for sorrow ;* just as the others at first believed not, *for joy* (Luke xxiv. 41).—And the all-important point is this : *love for the Lord* was the ground of *his sorrow,* as it was also of *their joy.*

The doors were shut. Doubtless for the same reason as that assigned in verse 19.—Fear of spies from the Sanhedrists, would compel the disciples to take every precaution.—But this also was made to conduce to the glory of the Risen One.

In the midst. See on verses 19, 20, 25.—Viewed from the conditions of our earthly life this appearance, under such circumstances, must be described as *supernatural;* but viewed from the conditions of the resurrection life, it was doubtless perfectly *natural.*—This is the *second* great fulfilment of the promise, Matt. xviii. 20 (see Comm.).

Peace. See on verse 19.—This is the salutation of the Risen One now and always.—It is no mere repetition ; but significant of the abundant and assured peace which Christ bestows, and of its abiding continuance with His people.—The soul that hath heard its Lord once speak *Peace,* will crave again and again the comfortable word.—As Thomas was not present when this word was spoken before, doubtless it was specially intended for him.—Who can imagine the feelings of the doubting disciple at this moment, when the characteristic greeting, in the well-known voice, fell upon his ear and upon his heart?—To the others, after a week of reflection and prayer, it must have come full of a new meaning, and with increased power.

ὀκτώ. The second appearance of Christ, on the first Sunday after the resurrection-day, in the midst of the disciples, at Jerusalem, is entirely in accordance with the festal circumstances.—Easter day (Sunday) was the third day of the paschal celebration.—The next Friday, therefore, was the eighth.—The disciples were not permitted to set out on their homeward journey on the Sabbath.—On Sunday they either would not, or could not, set out, because this had now become their feast-day, and Thomas was not convinced.—It was probably the evening before their departure for Galilee, whither, as the place where all His disciples should see Him again, Christ had at first ordered the Apostles. *Lange.*

---

27. Then saith he to Thomas, Reach hither thy finger, and behold my hands; and reach hither thy hand, and thrust it into my side: and be not faithless, but believing.

Then. Gr., *Therefore saith He to Thomas.*—Immediately after the peace salutation the Lord turns to Thomas.—It is with him He has now to do, since he, in his doubting spirit, is not only unhappy in his own mind, but a hindrance to the whole body of disciples. —Of so much importance does the Lord count the solitary individual who still believes not, though all the others are already believing.—He will let none of his children be lost, and hence He waits for the slow, who come eight days behindhand with their faith. *Gossner.*—Observe, Christ did not appear to Thomas till He found him in company with the other disciples.—Thus the Lord not only honoured the first day of the week, but honoured the meeting of His people on that day.

Reach. We see three things in this appeal calculated to produce immediate and complete conviction : 1. The Lord's perfect know-

ledge of Thomas' state of mind, and of the very words he had
uttered (see on verse 25); 2. His amazing grace in condescending
to give the satisfaction Thomas had demanded; 3. The divinely
loving spirit with which He offers Thomas that satisfaction.—
*These things were self-revealing, for they were eminently and gloriously
characteristic of the Lord Jesus.*—With what shame, and yet with
what joy and gratitude, must Thomas have heard these words from
his Lord.

My hands. See on chap. xix. 18.—The words imply that the marks
were no *scars*, but *the veritable wounds themselves.*—The Lord is
silent about the print of the nails; He would not recall the
malice of His *crucifiers.*—He points simply to the wounds themselves, as the abiding monuments of His love unto death.

My side. See on chap. xix. 34.—Seems to imply that the wound
in His side was as large as a man's hand.—"This of itself would
show that the resurrection body was *bloodless.*" *Alford.*—"Handle
me, and see; for a spirit hath not flesh and bones (He does not
say flesh and *blood*), as ye see me have" (Luke xxiv. 39).—Paul
affirms "that flesh and *blood* cannot inherit the kingdom of God"
(1 Cor. xv. 50).—"The blood is the life," or animating principle
of the body, in our present state.—"The blood is the basis, the
element of the nerve-life, and in this sense, the soul." *Lange.*—
But the animating principle of the resurrection body is not psychical, but pneumatical, "a *spiritual* body," and therefore *bloodless.*
Delitzsch.—Our Lord might, if He pleased, have wiped all spot
and trace of wound from His resurrection body; but these wounds,
inflicted by His enemies, are converted by Divine controlling
power and wisdom into proofs of His resurrection, and marks of
His personal identity.—They are indelible evidences of His love,
and glorious trophies of His victory over death and sin and hell.

Be not. Gr., *and become not faithless.*—Not merely as to the fact
of the Resurrection, but the truth of God generally.—He had not
been *faithless* hitherto, but he was in danger of *becoming so.*—Our
Lord distinguishes between *doubt* and *faithlessness.*—Thomas's
habit of *doubting* might, however, grow into *faithlessness.*—This is
the danger attaching to that habit, as all experience shows.—
Doubting, when encouraged and cherished, results in a state of
hardened unbelief.—Let no one suppose that our Lord here censures inquiry, examination, investigation: He only reprehends
an arbitrary and stubborn demand for proof.—Jesus wants neither
credulity nor thoughtless superstition; but neither will He have
self-willed unbelief.—He desires a faith which reposes upon the
Word of Life, and the knowledge of that Truth which makes the
spirit free.—He would have us rest, not on the testimony of sense,

1384 / Gospel of John

but on the intuition of the Spirit —No demand is ever made in the Word of God for *blind* faith.—Here we are warned not to miss opportunities of having our scruples removed, and above all, not to close our eyes to the evidences God gives us of truth.—" Religious belief, which demands the support of sensuous perception, runs the risk of making shipwreck of faith." *Tholuck.*—" Nevertheless, the *sincere heart that needs and craves belief*, receives even in the hour of temptation the right signs which save it from the danger which threatens it. Such was the experience of Thomas. His faith was saved; the great sign of Christ's appearance quickly made the sickly plant burst forth into fairest bloom." *Lange.*

Believing. God's way of educating men is by faith: yet "many labour with all their strength to the end that not faith but knowledge may have the mastery in the case of every truth contained in the Holy Scriptures." *Bengel.*—Our Lord's words manifestly presuppose that the exercise or non-exercise of faith is dependent upon a man's moral and spiritual state.—At the same time it must be admitted that believing is much easier to some persons than to others.—There are those who, through constitutional and other causes, find it exceedingly difficult to believe, except upon the clearest and most irrefragable evidence.—Where the logical understanding predominates, and there is a deficiency in the imaginative power, this difficulty is certain to make itself felt.—And though faith in Christ is the gift of God (Eph. ii. 8), the effect of the Holy Spirit's influence upon the heart, yet it will always be conditioned in its manifestations by these natural and other causes.—Some "mount up with wings as eagles," some "run," some "walk" (Isa. xli. 31).—Some bring "forth an hundredfold, some sixtyfold, some thirtyfold" (see on Matt. xiii. 8). But all are required to believe, therefore all, in their measure and degree, are capable of faith, and the grace of the Holy Spirit is obtainable by prayer in the name of the Lord Jesus.—" The more difficult any one finds it to believe, the more earnest should he be in prayer for divine grace, and the more careful and attentive in the use of all appointed means for the increase of faith." *Chalmers.*—" Minds of every natural complexion are called to the exercise of Christian faith. The principle of faith—the disposition to receive the Word of God as such, to embrace and to walk by it—is not indeed the gift of nature, but of grace; but its operation in each individual mind is modified by that mind's peculiar cast or temperament; and to every class of mind there are sufficient motives presented for the willing admission of the truth whereby we are sanctified and saved." *Mill.*—Unhappily, in the present day, doubt has come to be regarded as the normal state, at least of cultivated minds, respecting the teachings of the Bible.—Scepticism and mental power have become synonyms with popular writers and speakers. —Believers are deemed a " feeble folk," whose faith in God's word has grown up without thought or inquiry.—This has largely been brought about by the timid, half-hearted, apologetic tone of Christian teachers themselves, when speaking or writing of the truths of the Gospel.—Now we have no hesitation in avowing our conviction that unbelief should be regarded as a disease, and not a state of health ; a sign of weakness, and not of strength.—We hold, that faith, in the revelation of God, as in nature, is the normal state of a full grown mind.—It is the only legitimate state of an educated mind.—The most symmetrical and vigorous intellects the world has ever seen have been the most profound and capacious believers.—But if the Gospel is to be successful it must be preached with the living force of *personal conviction* and *experience.*—Men will turn from the preacher of an *apologetic* gospel as from a bewildered guide, whose own distrust creates unbelief.

28. And Thomas answered and said unto him, My Lord and my God.

Answered. Evidently Thomas did *not* apply his finger or his hand to the Lord's person.—He was convinced without using the tests which Jesus had offered him (see on verse 27).—This is shown by the words of the next verse, " Because thou hast *seen Me*," &c.

My Lord and my God. See note.—An address of Thomas to Christ ; compare Christ's address to His Father, Mark xv. 34.— The highest Apostolic confession of faith in the Lordship and Divinity of Christ.—An echo of the beginning of this Gospel, "The Word was God" (chap i. 1), and an anticipation of its closing statement (chap. xx. 30, 31).—The great object of this Evangelist is to place in full light the fundamental truth of the true and proper God-head of the Son of Man; and by this closing confession, he shows how the testimony of Jesus to Himself had gradually deepened and exalted the Apostles' conviction, from the time when they knew Him only as the son of Joseph (chap. i. 46), till now, when He is acknowledged to be their LORD and their GOD. *Alford.*—The excitement of feeling with which Thomas utters this adoring word in glorification of Christ, does not affect the definiteness and fulness of his acknowledgment of His Divinity. —And this homage which unconditionally is due to the Lord, He accepts without reserve.—Yet it is only, indeed, well-pleasing to Him when the emphasis is laid upon the *My* of faith ; and thus the confession is the expression, not of intellectual conviction only, but of inward life experience (see on " Rabboni," verse 16). —We now see the end of the discipline which Thomas passed through, and may well say with some of the Christian Fathers, that the unbelief of this one disciple was over-ruled for greater profit to the faith of the Church than the belief of the others.— The confession of the sceptical Thomas, when convinced, is the grandest on record: no sublimer words could be uttered on earth or in heaven.—From the examples of Mary Magdalene and Thomas, we learn two several duties to the risen Lord.—From Mary's case : to see Him who is invisible; to touch Him by faith; to ascend to Him with heart and mind; to cling to Him as our great High Priest in heaven; to adore Him as God.—Therefore to her he said, "Touch ME not, *for* I am not ascended."—The *touch* of faith is what He requires; that is the touch by which He is to be held, and by which we may have His presence with us.— From Thomas's case : faith in our Lord's resurrection; faith in our own future resurrection; faith in the *identity* of our own bodies to rise hereafter.—Therefore to him He said, "Touch ME." —Thus we are taught the true faith in His Divinity, Humanity, and Personality, by His providential and gracious correction of the *too material* yearnings of a woman's love, of the *too spiritual* doubts of an Apostle's fear. *Wordsworth.* (See also on the case of Nathaniel, chap. i. 46-51.)

Ὁ κύριός μου καὶ ὁ θεός μου. The Socinian view, that these words are *merely an exclamation*, is refuted—(1) By the fact that no such exclamations were in use among the Jews.—(2) By the εἶπεν αὐτῷ.—(3) By the impossibility of referring ὁ κύριός to another than Jesus : see verse 13.—(4) By the New Testament usage of expressing the vocative by the nominative with an article.—(5) By the utter psychological absurdity of such a supposition : that one just convinced of the presence of Him whom he deeply loved, should, instead of addressing Him, break out into an irrelevant cry.—(6) By the further absurdity of supposing that *if such were* the case, the Apostle John, who of all the sacred writers most constantly keeps in mind the object for which he is writing, should have recorded anything so *beside that object.*—(7) By the intimate conjunction of πεπίστευκας (verse 29). *Alford.*—The Socinian view is worse than absurd, it turns an act of adoration into an irrelevant and profane exclamation unrebuked by the Lord ! There is no instance of such profane use of the name of God in exclamations. *Schaff.*— Κύριός. As this is the word into which the Greek of the Sept. renders the name "Jehovah," in all passages in which Messias is called by that peculiar title of Divinity, we have the authority of this version to apply it, in its full and highest signification, to Jesus, who is Himself that Messias.—For this reason, and also because, as men inspired, they were directed to fit and proper terms, the writers of the New Testament apply this appellation to their Master, when they quote these prophetic passages as fulfilled in Him.—They found it used in the Greek version of the Old Testament, in its highest possible import, as a rendering of Jehovah.—Had they thought Jesus less than God, they ought to have avoided, and must have avoided, giving to Him a title which would mislead their readers; or else have intimated, that they did not use it in its highest sense as a title of Divinity, but in its very lowest sense as a term of merely human courtesy, or, at best, of human dominion.—But we have no such intimation ; and, if they wrote under the inspiration of the Holy Spirit, it follows, that they used it as being understood to be fully equivalent to the name "Jehovah" itself.—This will be shown by their quotations.—The Evangelist Matthew (iii. 3) quotes and applies to Christ the celebrated prophecy of Isa. xl. 3: "For this is he that was spoken of by the prophet Esaias, saying, The voice of one crying in the wilderness, Prepare ye the way

of the Lord, make His paths straight."—The other Evangelists make the same application of it, representing John as the herald of Jesus, -the "Jehovah" of the Prophet,
and their Κύριός —It was, therefore, in the highest possible sense that they used the
term, because they used it as fully equivalent to Jehovah.—So again. in Luke i. 16, 17:
"And many of the children of Israel shall he turn unto the Lord their God, and he
shall go before Him in the spirit and power of Elias "—"*Him*" unquestionably refers to
"the Lord their God ; " and we have here a proof that Christ bears that eminent title
of Divinity, so frequent in the Old Testament, "the Lord God," *Jehovah Aleim ;* and
also that Κύριός answered, in the view of an inspired writer, to the name "Jehovah."
On this point St. Paul also adds his testimony; " Whosoever shall call upon the name
of the Lord shall be saved " (Rom. x. 13), which is quoted from Joel ii. 32, "Whosoever
shall call on the name of Jehovah shall be delivered."—Other passages might be added,
but the argument does not rest upon their number; these are so explicit that they are
amply sufficient to establish the important conclusion, that, in whatever senses the
term " Lord " may be used, and though the writers of the N. T., like ourselves, use it
occasionally in a lower sense, yet they use it also in its highest possible sense, and in
its loftiest signification when they intend it to be understood as equivalent to Jehovah ;
and, in that sense, they apply it to Christ.—But, even when the title " Lord " is not employed to render the name " Jehovah," in passages quoted from the O. T., but is used
as the common appellation of Christ, after His resurrection, the disciples so connect it
with other terms, and with circumstances which so clearly imply Divinity, that it
cannot reasonably be made a question but that they themselves considered it as a
divine title, and intended that it should be so understood by their readers.—In that
sense they applied it to the Father; and it is clear, that they did not use it in a lower
sense when they gave it to the Son. *Watson, Waterland, Bull.* (See also on Matt. i.22)—
Bishop Pearson, on the Second Article of the Creed, thus concludes a learned note on
the etymology of κύριός, " Lord ": ' From all which it undeniably appeareth, that the
ancient signification of κυρω is the same with ειμι, or υπαρχω, *sum,* ' I AM.' "—Thomas
saw Christ, as man ; but believed in Him, and confessed Him, as God. *Augustine.*

---

29. Jesus saith unto him, Thomas, because thou hast seen me, thou hast believed :
blessed are they that have not seen, and yet have believed.

Because. Some read these words interrogatively : *Because thou hast
seen Me, hast thou believed? Meyer. Ellicott.*—But this would seem
to infuse a tone of doubt as to the faith of Thomas. *Lücke.*—
Evidently the Lord recognizes and commends the faith just confessed ; while He gently blames the slowness and required ground
of the faith. *Alford.*—And after all, it was not the mere seeing of
Him *outwardly* which had wrought such full and complete conviction in his soul (see on verse 27).

Believed. *Thou hast become believing, a believer.*—The divine mercy
ordained that a doubting disciple should, by seeing in his Master
the wounds of the flesh, heal in us the wounds of unbelief. *Gregory.*
—Thus the Lord causeth not only the wrath of enemies, but the
weakness and faults of His children, to serve Him.—Happy are
all they in whose heart and life unbelief is but a passing cloud,
dispelled by the Sun of Righteousness.

" Let no one take my crown, O Lord !
Or—if too much this be—
Say only, faith has failed in word,
Yet hast Thou loved me."

Blessed. See on Matt. v. 3.—Gr., *Blessed are they that saw not, and
believed,* or, *who never saw, and yet became believers.*—The blessedness
is thought of as existing from the moment of believing, and the
act of faith is therefore spoken of in the past tense. *Ellicott.*—The
words relate not to different *degrees* of faith, but to the *way* in
which the faith is arrived at.—The contrast is between those who
see by the eye of the spirit and those who depend upon sense.—
Between those who perceive the evidence of the truth in the truth
itself, and those resting upon *outward* evidence.—It cannot be
applied in any special manner to the Ten, for they had also seen
and had believed.—It embraces all who become believers without
having seen.—" Wonderful indeed, and rich in blessing for us
who have not seen Him, is this, the closing word of the Gospel."
Alford.—Our Lord looks forward to the founding of His Church
by the testimony of Scripture and the presence of the Spirit.—
" All the appearances of the forty days were mere preparations
for the believing without seeing." *Stier.*—" Whom having not
seen, ye love ; in whom, though now ye see Him not, yet believing, ye rejoice with joy unspeakable and full of glory : receiving
the end of your faith, *even* the salvation of *your* souls" (1 Pet. i. 8).
—He who pinneth faith to bodily sight, to the earthly and visible,
doth indeed expose it to change, since all things visible are temporal, and only the invisible is eternal (2 Cor. iv. 18). *Gerlach.*—
" Those are blessed who, against the things of sense, the temptations of the world and Satan, the perplexities of the natural mind,
the misgivings of a fearful, and the lacerations of a wounded,
heart, have opposed a firm faith in facts remote in Time, but indelible and eternal in effect." *W. H. Mill.*—" One proselyte is
more acceptable to God than all the thousands of Israel that
stood before Mount Sinai ; for they saw and received the law, but
a proselyte sees not, and yet receives it " (A Rabbi quoted by
Lightfoot).—Our Lord's words have a special importance for the
times we are living in.—The tendency of modern thought, both
in science and within the Church, is to dwell much upon outward
appearances.—The visible, the tangible, that which appeals to the
senses, has now more than ordinary prominence.—We are persuaded that the only corrective for this is to be found in putting
greater emphasis on *inward* realities.—*Spirituality of mind* is the cure
for *materialism,* whether it come in the form of Ritualism or philosophy.—A warning also lies in these words, for those who make
feeling the standard of Christian character, as well as for those
who make *visible* success a rule for Christian work.—" We walk
by faith, not by sight," is the great law of Christian life here
below (2 Cor. v. 7).—Such a life is not perfect, but it is essentially

a great and glorious life; for whoever desires it must be born of God and be united with Him (see notes).—GROUNDS FOR FAITH IN THE RESURRECTION OF CHRIST:—1. From the nature of His *Person.*—As the sinless and holy Son of God, He could not see corruption.—Death could not bind Him, since He had life in Himself; and in laying down His life He manifested Himself as eternal LOVE, which must live eternally because itself is LIFE; 2. From *the omnipotence and justice of the Divine Government,* which would have been annihilated had it left the Holy One of God (in whose crucifixion sin and the power of darkness had celebrated their greatest triumph) to corrupt in the grave; had it not crowned Him with glory and honour; 3. From the *work of Christ,* the crown of which would be wanting, unless through His resurrection He confirmed His death as being a sacrifice *for us,* and not for Himself, and thereby overcame the last enemy, death; 4. From the *presence of the Holy Ghost,* whom Christ imparts, and sends in consequence of His resurrection and ascension; and from the personal experience of believers, who, through the same Holy Ghost, constantly experience the sanctifying influence of the Lord's resurrection-life; 5. From the *internal coherence in the history of God's Kingdom,* for with the resurrection of Christ, the second spiritual period of man's history begins, which will be fully realized at the end of this age; 6. From the *idea of the world's consummation;* the resurrection and transformation of Christ being the divine pledge of that general resurrection and transformation in which, as its aim and end, the history of mankind, as well as that of nature, is eventually to be merged, when this earthly sphere shall be transformed into a heavenly.— DIFFICULTIES WHICH UNBELIEF INVOLVES:—1. Difficulties *exegetical:* there is the clear testimony of St. Paul, and the great distinction made by New Testament writers between the description of visions and the narratives of our Lord's appearances; 2. Difficulties *psychological:* all likelihood is wanting for the supposition that so many and such differently constituted persons should, even by hundreds at a time, have been simultaneously predisposed to see visions; there is the sudden and thorough change in the disciples' frame of mind, especially the sudden conversion of St. Paul; and finally, the speedy cessation of our Lord's appearances; 3. Difficulties *dogmatical:* arising from the question, Whence should the idea of an isolated resurrection, hitherto foreign to their belief, arise in the minds of the disciples? 4. Difficulties *chronological:* unanimous historical evidence points to the "third day," and this leaves no space for the gradual development of visions, or for the translocation of the first

1390 / Gospel of John

appearances to Galilee; 5. Difficulties *topographical*: there, in a well known spot, stands the empty tomb, with its loud question, Where is the body? which neither Jew nor Roman attempts to answer, though investigation would have been easy; 6. Difficulties *historical*: there is the firm and immovable belief of the disciples in their Lord's resurrection, their preaching so full of victorious joy and martyr's courage; there is the Christian Sunday, a continual celebration of the first Easter victory; there is the Christian Church, founded and victoriously growing on the rock of her belief in the crucified and risen Saviour; 7. Difficulties *moral*: there is the moral regeneration of the world which proceeded from the preaching of the Apostles. (See *Christlieb*, "Modern Doubt and Christian Belief.")—Now which is the more reasonable, Belief or Unbelief? —Faith still hears Christ say, "Fear not; I am the First and the Last: I am He that liveth and was dead; and, behold, I am alive for evermore" (Rev. i. 17, 18).

Θωμᾶ, after ἑώρακάς με, omitted. *Codd. Sin. A. B. C. D., Tisch., Treg., Alford, Westcott and Hort, Lange, Schaff*—οἱ μὴ ἰδόντες, &c. The aorists, as often in such sentences (see Luke i. 45), indicate the present state of those spoken of, grounded in the past. *Alford.*—This saying of our Lord is so constructed as 1. to intimate a peculiar praise of the other disciples who first believed, as well as to touch them, likewise, in its blame; 2. it, however, does not exclude Thomas from this blessedness, inasmuch as he too commenced to believe before he had seen; it establishes 3 a general rule destined for the beatification of the believing Church of a later period; at bottom, however, it is 4. generally declarative of the innermost essence of faith.—Christ did not reject that *belief* which seeks and finds confirmation in the way of doubt and investigation; neither, therefore, did He reject the correspo d ng *way* of belief: He did, however, point out the danger of that way, in which it is possible for doubt to separate itself from a trust in spiritual experience, and, in consequence of the impulse after sensuous experience, to turn into unbelief and apostasy. *Lange.*—That faith is more blessed, which, supported by the Word and the inner demonstrative power of the Word, believes, as St. Paul has it, παρ' ἐλπίδα ἐπ' ἐλπίδι, Rom. iv. 18; compare John iv. 48. *Tholuck.*—A distinction between belief in something which has occurred, *with* and *without* one's own sensuous perception. *Meyer.*—If any are disposed to regard it as an inferior privilege, to accept this truth (of the resurrection) through *faith* rather than *sight*, this great utterance of Jesus should fully correct such an erroneous view. *Owen.*—By how much our faith stands in less need of the external evidence of sense, the stronger and the more acceptable it is, provided what we believe be revealed in the Word of God. *Burkitt.*

---

30. And many other signs truly did Jesus in the presence of his disciples, which are not written in this book.

Signs. See on chap. ii. 11, 23; iii. 2; iv. 48; vi. 30.—Gr., *Yea, and indeed many other signs did Jesus.*—Some understand these "signs" not of the proofs of the Resurrection only, but of the works wrought during our Lord's whole life.—Miracles in the most general sense, by which Jesus proved His Messiahship.—Hence they regard these

verses (30 and 31) as the conclusion of the original Gospel, and
chap. xxi. as a postscript or appendix.—Others consider that John
here concludes the history of the Passion and Resurrection, inasmuch as that history was designed to perfect the faith of the disciples, and refer the words to the Resurrection signs.—The latter
view appears the more natural and satisfactory, for the following
reasons: 1. Because John has already submitted his *résumé* relative to the earlier signs (chap. xii. 37); 2. Because he is here
speaking of signs done by the Risen One in the presence of the
disciples; 3. Because of the necessity which the other view involves for regarding chap. xxi. as a foreign addition or appendix,
and this in the absence of otherwise sufficient grounds. *Lange.*—
(See note.)

Not written. Shows *the immeasurable fulness* of our Lord's life (see
on chap. xxi. 25).—All that John and the other Evangelists could
do was to present a selection of the more significant facts in that
life.—But that selection, both as to the matter and manner of the
record, was under the superintending influence of the Holy Spirit.
—This is seen, 1, in the character of that which *is recorded*, its
nature, meaning, design; 2, in the *silence* of the writers upon so
many points that must have excited the utmost wonder and curiosity; 3, in the *simple and unimpassioned* style in which they relate
the most astonishing events.—To be willing to be ignorant of what
the Divine Inspirer has thought proper to conceal, is no small
part of Christian learning.—In this verse and that which follows,
John gives the key to the construction of his gospel, and the
Evangelical history generally.—Here is the explanation of the
diversity and unity of the fourfold Biography of the Incarnate
Word.

μὲν οὖν. Intended to guard against taking this Gospel as a *complete account* of the
signs of Jesus. *Schaff.*—ἄλλα σημεῖα. R-surrection signs, signs in at'estation of the
Resurrection. *Chrys., Theophyl., Euthym., &c., Kuinoel, Lücke, Olshausen, Lange, &c.*
—Against this view it is objected by Meyer and others: 1. The term σημεῖα is too
general to support such an interpretation. (But this verse speaks only of such signs as
were wrought by Jesus *in the presence of His disciples,* in the circ.e of the eleven
in particular; Acts i. 3. *Lange.*)—2. πολλὰ καὶ ἄλλα contradicts it; Christ, according to the Gospel, as well as according to 1 Cor. xv., having appeared a few times
only. (But the words are not spoken of the appearances in themselves but of the
σημεῖα which occurred on the occasion of these appearances. To these σημεῖα, then,
there must be reckoned His making of Himself known to Thomas by means of a
miracle of knowledge, to Mary through the word of recognition, her *name.*—But besides
these signs, recorded by John, yet others must be added to the list, *viz.* : His making
of Himself known to the Emmaus disciples through the *breaking of bread* ; to Peter, as
to James, in a mode with which we are unacquainted ; to the five hundred brethren in
Galilee, by a majesty of sudden appearance which threw many of them upon their
knees ; to the disciples on the Mount of Olives by His Ascension; to Paul, by His
manifestation from heaven.—These instances certainly might justify the expression of
the Evangelist. *Lange.*)—3. ἐποίησεν contradicts it ; the word cannot be used concerning

appearances. (It may, however, be applied to manifestations of miracu'ous knowledge, of celestial might, of divine Providence, which manifestations accompanied every appearance. *Lange.*)--4. The words ἐν τῷ βιβλίῳ τούτῳ indicate that John had in view the contents *of his entire Gospel*) Since the Evangelist is speaking of resurrection signs, he has reference to that part of the book which contains statements relative to the resurrection. *Lange.*)—The view of Meyer that the "signs" refer to the whole of our Lord's life, is held also by *Jansen, Wolf, Bengel, Tholuck, Lampe, Godet, Alford.*

---

31. But there are written, that ye might believe that Jesus is the Christ, the Son of God; and that believing ye might have life through his name.

These. These *signs*, these manifestations of the glory of Christ.

Are written. Gr., *have been written.*—John now states the purpose of the Resurrection history and of this Gospel; and indeed of the four Evangelists, and the whole of Scripture.—That purpose is definite and distinct, and pervades the entire Bible from Genesis to Revelation.—All other subjects, however interesting and important in themselves, are secondary, and held subservient to *one* great purpose.—Had this been kept in view, many serious mistakes respecting the Scriptures would have been prevented.— The Bible was never intended to teach men that which they might learn by observation and the application of their own reason.— " It has a *religious purpose*, and is therefore written from a religious impulse, in a religious spirit, under the guidance of the Spirit of God. And all the religious truth of Holy Writ aims at the truth of God in Christ. He is the marrow and star of Holy Scripture." *Lange.*—To teach the way of salvation by our Lord Jesus Christ, is the great and primary object for which the Bible was given, and it must be read in the same spirit in which it was written.

Believe. See on verse 29.—See also on chap. i. 7.—This was John's purpose in writing his narrative, and this is the purpose of revelation generally.—Here, more particularly, to confirm faith in Christ by faith in His resurrection.—True faith conducts the soul not only to peace and joy, but also to light and truth.—Peter says, " We have believed and are sure " : *faith leads on to knowledge*, of which it is itself the first beginning (see on chap. vi. 69).— Rationalists say that everything must first be proved and known before it can be believed; whereas true science shows that faith is really a preliminary and medium of all cognizance, and that all knowing is conditioned by an act of believing.—For is not every act of knowledge based upon an act of faith, namely, the belief that we *are*, and that we *think ?*—It is by the direct testimony of our own minds that we are convinced of the fact that we exist, think, wake, and dream; and this fact neither needs nor is capable of proof; we merely *believe* it.—So also in every act of learning, a believing must be presupposed; some belief in the authority of

the teacher, and in the truth of that which is taught.—Justly
therefore has it been said : *He who believes nothing, knows nothing.*
—"As its ultimate basis, even the most radical unbelief has one
and the same principle of knowledge with Christianity and every
other positive religion, the principle of belief in given matters of
fact, on the ground of the original and direct testimony of the
human mind." *Fabri.*—Faith, as an undoubting and assured conviction of the unseen (Heb. xi. 1), is the organ for the immaterial
world, and for our knowledge of it.—Hence it is not knowledge but
unbelief which is opposed to faith ; the resolve neither to accept
nor to be convinced of the reality of the supersensuous and its influence on the world.—So that in religious things, the antithesis is
not that of faith and knowledge, but that of faith and unbelief, or of
religious knowledge and *religious* ignorance ; and not seldom that of
religious belief and knowledge on the one hand, and *irreligious* belief
and knowledge on the other.—Revelation and reason, therefore, no
more than faith and knowledge can, in principle, contradict one
another.—"True Christianity consists in the submission as well
as in the use of reason. It is Reason's last step to acknowledge
that there is an infinity of things which transcend her powers.
She remains weak till she comes to the acknowledgment of this
her own insufficiency. Doubt and assert we all must at times,
but we must learn at proper times to submit also. He who cannot
do this, knows not yet the true strength of Reason." *Pascal.*—
And Christian faith being the submission of the soul to Divine
revelation, no creature need be ashamed of receiving help from
its Creator.—The law therefore in respect to religious truth is not,
First understand and then accept, but, First submit and accept
the truth, then you will be able to understand.—Finite reason
must submit itself to the infinite ; the weak and imperfect human
understanding must yield to the perfect truth which proceeds
from God.—Instead of scepticism being a sign of *strength,* as
many seem to think, it is just the *contrary* (see on verse 29).—
"Doubt in its innermost nature is a wrong compliance, a weakness,
a cowardly dread of ventures and difficulties ; whereas the innermost source of faith is the courage which bravely seizes and
steadfastly holds to that which is invisible. A sceptic is like a
traveller who should refuse to cross a puddle or to step over a twig,
till all were smoothed down and filled up. Who would think such
a man wise ? Faith takes up all that it can get, and marches courageously onward ; unbelief is the direct opposite of this. In studying the Bible, we must do like the courier who hurries over pools
and hillocks the nearest way to his destination, and does not first
seek to level every clod. That which is difficult at last comes of

its own accord. The most important controversies are those which a man finds in his own heart." *Bengel.*—But these latter point to the place where Thomas had to learn *his* faith—*the wounds of Christ.*—Only there can any soul learn the truth which makes free.—There only does unbelief, even to this day, learn to surrender and humbly confess: "My Lord and my God."—He who will not seek for the truth *there* will never find it.—All that can be done for the sceptics of the present day is to make the way there as easy for them as may be, in order that the sign of Jonah given by our buried and risen Lord, may be to them a rock of salvation and not of offence. *Christlieb.* (See also on Matt. ii.)

The Christ, the Son of God. Belief that Jesus is both these in the fullest meaning of the words (see on chap. i.).—The Incarnation of the Eternal Word, the actual coming in the flesh of the Son of God, born, dead, and risen for our salvation, is the sole foundation of Christianity.—This *great* FACT, and not any particular proposition concerning it, is the real *Article of a standing or falling Church. W. H. Mill.*—The faith here spoken of is not the *miracle-faith*, so often reproved by our Lord, but faith in HIMSELF as the Messiah, the Son of the Living God, of which His Resurrection is the triumphant proof.—Enough has been written by the Evangelist to be a ground, sufficient and sure, for such a faith.—And what is said of this Gospel applies to Scripture generally: "It is able to make wise unto salvation" (2 Tim. iii. 15).—This is its Divine peculiarity and glory that it contains "all things which pertain unto life and godliness" (2 Pet. i. 4).

Believing. That is, *as believers.*—This Gospel was written for the confirming of believers in the faith.—To John, his task as an historian was the same with his task as an Apostle—SALVATION IN CHRIST.—It is the aim of all sound preaching and theological writing, by the faithful exhibition of truth, to produce and to strengthen faith in Christ.—John has traced step by step the development of faith in the Apostles themselves, till it has reached its highest stage in the grand confession of Thomas, "MY LORD AND MY GOD."

Life. See on chap. i. 4; iii. 15, 16; xvii. 2, 3, &c.—Entire, perfect, eternal life in the name perfected through the resurrection.

Name. Gr., *in His name.*—The NAME, the revealed being of Christ, divine essence in human form, is the *object* of faith, and the *ground* of the life. *Schaff.* (See on chap. v. 39.)—Eternal life is obtained in virtue of the claim established by Him in whom we believe.—The *name* of Christ in believers is the full, clear, ideal contemplation of Christ in lively knowledge; with which the full truth, certainty, vigour and blessedness of the new *life* is given. *Lange.*—Thus these words bring us back again to the words of the first chapter (see on chap. i. 4, 12).

αἰώνιον after ζωήν. *Cod. Sin.* Omitted. *Treg., Tisch., Alford, Westcott and Hort, Lange.*—Not satisfactorily established. *Schaff.*—ταῦτα γέγραπται. Clement of Alexandria is quoted by Eusebius, as saying, "John, last of all, perceiving that what had reference to the body in the gospel of our Saviour was sufficiently detailed; and being encouraged by his familiar friends and urged by the Spirit, he wrote a spiritual gospel." And Eusebius himself says, "The three Gospels previously written having been distributed among all, and also handed to John, they say that he admitted them, giving his testimony to their truth; but that there was only wanting in the narrative the account of the things done by Christ among the first of His deeds and at the commencement of the Gospel. . . . For these reasons the Apostle John, it is said, being entreated to undertake it, wrote the account of the time not recorded by the former Evangelists, and the deeds done by our Saviour which they have passed by."—Jerome tells us, that when the Ebionites and Cerinthians endeavoured by various ways to refute or render disputable the Divinity of our Lord, John recounted to the elders of the Churches in Asia some passages of His life and conversation, omitted by the other Evangelists : whereby that Divinity was placed beyond the reach of question or cavil. —On hearing these the Elders solicited him to give the Church a fourth Gospel, wherein might be authenticated and recorded the aforesaid important passages ; not that the other three Evangelists had been silent on the subject; but because the authority of John was qualified to make it a still clearer point.—His answer was, that he was then too old to undertake the work. However. being pressed by their entreaties, and by the urgent necessity of the business. he desired them to fast and pray for the Divine assistance requisite.—They obeyed ; and he wrote the Gospel which bears his name. (See Introduction.)

John 21

1. After these things Jesus shewed himself again to the disciples at the sea of Tiberias; and on this wise shewed he himself.

After. This expression implies no fixed date.—It denotes not immediate succession, but rather an interval during which other events have taken place.—Several days must have elapsed since the last appearance of the Risen Lord, recorded in chap. xx. 26.—The disciples had in the meantime, according to His direction, returned to Galilee (Matt. xxviii. 7, 10, 16; 1 Cor. xv. 6).—Afterwards they again proceeded to Jerusalem, to witness His Ascension from Mount Olivet (Luke xxiv. 50; Acts i. 1-12), and to receive the promised gift of the Paraclete (Acts ii.). —Some suppose that the events described in this chapter occurred just a week or two weeks after the last appearance, and therefore on the first day of the week, the *Christian* Sabbath. *Macdonald.*

These things. Those which had taken place in Jerusalem, narrated in the preceding chapter, by which the faith of the disciples in the Resurrection of Jesus had been established.

Shewed. Gr., *manifested Himself.*—The Greek word is used elsewhere of our Lord's appearance only in Mark xvi. 12, 14 (in the passive form), and in verse 14 of this chapter.—It occurs only once besides in the Synoptic Gospels (Mark iv. 22), while it is distinctly a Johannine word (chaps. i. 31; ii. 11; iii. 21; vii. 4; ix. 3; xvii. 6; 1 John i. 2 (twice); ii. 19, 28; iii. 2 (twice), 5, 8; iv. 9; Rev. iii. 18; xv. 4).—The reflective expression, "*manifested Himself,*" is also in John's style (compare chaps. vii. 4 and xi. 33). *Ellicott.*

Again. Connecting this manifestation with those recorded in chap. xx. 19, 26.—It may also be a glance back at the *first* manifestation of His glory at the same Lake, of which we have an account in chapter vi.

Tiberias. See on chap. vi. 1, 23.—The name, " Sea of Tiberias," is found only in this Gospel.—The appearances of the Risen One still connect themselves with the old life-order of the disciples.— Without further occupation or instruction, they are waiting for the Lord; but in the meantime they must find a livelihood.— Hence we meet these busied again with their old calling.—The old life in the new light of the resurrection : 1. The old persons

(Peter, &c.); 2. The old occupation (fishing); 3. The old surroundings (the Sea of Galilee); 4. The old vicissitudes and the old need (caught nothing); 5. The old connection (Christ); 6. The old miracles (the draught of fishes); 7. The old feasts (the repast).—Transformation of the old form of life into the new in the kingdom of the Risen One: 1. The old calling becomes a new symbol of life; 2. The old home a new vestibule of heaven; 3. The old need a new divine blessing; 4. The old labour a new religious service; 5. The old partnership a new fellowship in Christ; 6. The old discipleship a new apostolate. *Lange.*

On this wise. Gr., *and He manifested Himself in this manner.*— Refers to the miraculous way in which He made Himself known to them, and communed with them (see on chap. xx. 19, 20).— After His resurrection He did not associate freely and constantly with His disciples, as before His death.—As no one saw Him rise from the tomb, and as He did not appear to His enemies and rejecters at all, so to His chosen Apostles He appeared only a few times.—But though few, those appearances were sufficient, for it is recorded that " He showed Himself alive after His passion *by many infallible proofs* " (Acts i. 3).

The Johannean origin of this chapter is denied or doubted by *Grotius, Clericus, Hammond, Semler, Paulus, Lücke, De Wette, Credner, Bleek, Baur, Keim, Scholten.* It is defended by *Wetstein, Lampe, Eichhorn, Kuinoel, Hug, Guericke, Tholuck, Schleiermacher, Olshausen, Luthardt, Ebrard, Hengstenberg, Godet. Alford, Westcott, Wordsworth, Lange, Schaff, Meyer, Ellicott, Thomson, Macdonald, &c*—The only argument worth mentioning against its Johannean origin, is derived from a few rare and unimportant expressions. But these peculiarities are natural and easily explained from the context, and are more than counterbalanced by the number of Johannean words and phrases, as well as by the unanimous testimony of the manuscripts and ancient Versions, which *contain the whole chapter as an integral part of the Gospel. Schaff.*—" In every part of it the hand of John is plain and unmistakable ; in every part of it, his character and spirit is manifested in a way which none but the most biassed can fail to recognize." *Alford.*—It is generally regarded as an Appendix; but this view arises from a " non-apprehension of the connection between the 20th and 21st chapters. Had it been an appendix afterward added, we should have had two distinct editions of the Gospel, whereas now all the MSS. contain it." *Wordsworth.*—It is the Epilogue which corresponds to the Prologue (chap. i. 1-18), and presents, in typical outline, the *post-resurrection history* of Christ, His perpetual, spiritual presence in, and guidance of, the Church ; as the Prologue presents His history *before the Incarnation*, and the body of the Gospel His *earthly history.*—The significant manner in which John, seemingly by way of supplement, relates this single and unique meeting of the Risen One with the seven disciples by the Galilean Sea, culling it out of all the later showings of Jesus after His resurrection, and emphasizing the individual, momentous items of the event, induces the conviction that from the first he designed it to form *the conclusion of his Gospel. Lange.*—It is a picture of Christian life, and the life of the Church, with its contrasts and changes, festive joy and hard work, poverty and abundance, failure and success, humility and loftiness, activity and rest, losing and finding the Lord, longing for Him and rejoicing in His presence. *Schaff.*—'Ἰησοῦς. Omitted. *Alford, Ellicott, &c.* —Retained. *Tisch., Treg., Westcott, Lange, &c.*—There is no good reason for its omission, but there is for its insertion. *Schaff.*

2. There were together Simon Peter, and Thomas called Didymus, and Nathanael of Cana in Galilee, and the sons of Zebedee, and two other of his disciples.

Together. Witnesses of the Resurrection, and recipients of the Holy Ghost (see on chap. xx. 22), they had returned to their humble homes in Galilee.—The future was still unknown to them; but they held themselves ready to receive the command of their Lord.—Evidently they had no idea that this visit to their homes was the last they should ever make to them as such.—Little did they think that within a few weeks they would remove to Jerusalem, to stay there for a time, and then go forth to preach the Gospel to every creature (Mark xvi. 15).— These seven are now *fishing together*, and probably for *the last time!*

Simon Peter. See on chap. i. 40-42.—Doubtless that which follows was intended to prepare Peter for the conference which took place afterward (verses 7-14).

Thomas. See on chap. xi. 16; xiv. 5; xx. 24-29.—Thomas is not named by the other Evangelists except in the list of the Apostles. —Never more will it be said that "Thomas, one of the Twelve, called Didymus, was not with them when Jesus came."—It is well if losses by our neglects make us more careful afterward not to slip opportunities.

Nathanael. See on chap. i. 45-51.—Nathanael is named only by John.—There is good reason for identifying him with the "Bartholomew" of the earlier Gospels (see note, chap. i. 45).

Of Cana. See on chap. ii. 1.—This is added as a descriptive note.

Sons of Zebedee. James and John; but *nowhere named* in this Gospel (see on Matt. x. 2, and Luke vi. 14). It is the only place wherein John introduces himself and his brother in a list with others.—In the lists in the other Gospels, and the Acts, James and John are uniformly placed in the first group.—But *here*, next to Peter are ranged Thomas, the apostolic searcher, and Nathanael, the representative of apostolic sincerity and simplicity. *Lange.*—The position of the sons of Zebedee here agrees with the Johannean origin of the chapter. *Ellicott.*—Perhaps mentioned as in reminiscence of the *draught of fishes which occurred before* (Luke v.). *Alford.*

Two other. It might be inferred from chap. i. 40, 43, that these were Andrew, the brother of Peter, and Philip, the friend of Nathanael.—But as they are not named, some conclude that they were disciples in the wider sense (*Meyer, Ellicott, Luthardt*); though verse 1 seems opposed to this view.—Christ doth not esteem men nor deal with them according as they are of note among others, provided they be honest, and disciples indeed; for He sheweth Himself to these as to the rest, though their names be not expressed, as the others are. *Hutcheson.*—The number *seven* being *a sacred number*, these *seven disciples* may be regarded as representing the Apostolic Church.

δύο. John may have omitted the names of the two disciples for two reasons: 1. Because he would otherwise have been obliged to mention the sons of Zebedee by name. also: 2. Because, it was his desire, by speaking, at the close, of *two* disciples, to induce his readers to make the computation of the *seven.*—Or is their anonymousness to serve the symbolical purpose of the Epilogue? Or was he unwilling, by naming the two, to give prominence to the four remaining ones, who had no part in this feast? *Lange.*

---

3. Simon Peter saith unto them, I go a fishing. They say unto him, We also go with thee. They went forth, and entered into a ship immediately; and that night they caught nothing.

I go. Characteristic of Peter; foremost in outside enterprises, and thoroughly decided in his own mind, without consulting the others.—The vivid picturesque representation of the whole scene shows unmistakably the hand of John (see on chap. xx. 3, &c.).

Fishing. See on Matt. iv. 18.—During the time they were to remain in Galilee, between the feasts of the Passover and Pentecost, they would naturally employ themselves in their old occupation to obtain a livelihood; and perhaps this was the first occasion of doing so.—The Apostles were not forbidden by their apostleship from earning their living by a lawful craft, provided they had no other means. *Augustine.*—The craft which was exercised without sin before conversion, was no sin after it; wherefore after his conversion Peter returned to fishing; but Matthew sat not down again at the receipt of custom. *Gregory.*—It was commendable in them to *go a fishing;* for they did it to *redeem time* and not be idle; and that they might help to *maintain themselves* and not be burthensome to any. *Henry.*—Moreover, their occupation was symbolical of the great work to which Christ had called them (see on Matt. iv. 19).

We, &c. Gr., *We also come with thee.*—Expressive of their cordial, friendly cleaving to Peter.—Neither his proposal nor their ready consent is to be interpreted as if they were desponding of the Master's cause.—On the contrary, Peter's proposal and their cheerful acquiescence indicate a calm assured happy state of mind, while waiting for the promised manifestation.—In addition to the motive to work for their living, they doubtless loved the Sea where in earlier life they had passed so many days.

Went forth. Perfect unanimity is the character of their fellowship. —Prompt, energetic and persevering in their trade, they were all the better fitted for the work to which the Lord had called them.— Their secular occupation was a training for spiritual service, as it ever should be.—Christ has hallowed all things into symbols of the universal activity incumbent upon us in His Kingdom.—In every calling His Spirit may be obtained, just *in* that calling; men need not fly to woods or cloisters.—True religion sanctifies the profession or situation in which God's providence has placed us. —It makes lawful work a ladder upon which the soul may ascend to Heaven.—The odour of sanctity can diffuse itself through every engagement and relation of life.—Nothing that is right is mean, however humble; only that which is sinful is dishonourable.—The Son of God was a carpenter, and His Apostles were fishermen.

Night. The most advantageous time for fishing on the lake (Luke v. 5).—Yet there were unsuccessful nights, and such a one this proved to be.

Caught. The Greek word does not occur in the other Gospels, but is found again in verse 10, and six times in the earlier chapters of this Gospel (vii. 30, 32, 44; viii. 20; x. 39; xi. 57.—It occurs also in Rev. xix. 20).

Nothing. A similar failure is recorded in Luke v. 5.—An instructive fact, the Lord's disciples failing in their lawful occupation!— Even good men may come short of desired success in their honest undertakings: we may be in the way of our duty, and yet not prosper.—It seemeth often unto godly Christians as if their diligence and labour were utterly in vain, and yet such seasons are but meant for the trial of their faith. *Starke.*—God often *disciplines and educates* His children *by failure.*—But though He suffer them to fail, He does not forsake them, but overrules the failure for their spiritual welfare and greater usefulness afterward.—A lesson to those Christian ministers and Churches who judge of every one and every work by the standard of *visible success.*—A minister or other Christian professor, may be *succeeding for time*, and yet, *failing for eternity.*—A man's *success*, as it is called, may be and often is the cause of his *ruin.*—While many a man that the world, and the Church also, have looked upon as a *failure*, will be found to occupy at last a high place in God's Kingdom.— All God's dealings with His children contemplate their *spiritual* and *eternal* welfare, and the only way to that glorious consummation often lies through *earthly failure.*—" It may please the Lord ofttimes to deny His people success in their lawful employments; and that, either when their hearts are too eager and keen upon the world He doth justly cross them, to teach them mortification and sobriety; or because, if success were constant, God would not be so clearly seen in His bounty, and therefore He crosseth that we may acknowledge Him more; or because, He is to appear eminently for His people, therefore He makes way for His appearing, by denying success upon their endeavours." *Hutcheson.*— This failure of the disciples, "a symbol of the times of waiting, of the apparently fruitless struggling and hoping, whereby the labourers of God are tried in their work. These trials are connected with the fact that the disciples must first be freed from their self-consciousness and brought to the point of fully renouncing their work and relinquishing all expectation of shining results. These humiliations are connected with the necessity for distinguishing between an activity based upon human authority (Peter) and one drawing its inspiration from the Word of Christ. A human and legal running produces no abiding fruit." *Lange.*—A picture of the utter failure of the fishers of men without Christ, as verse 6 illustrates their abundant success with Him.—The fishing was made unsuccessful, in order to prepare the way for the miracle. *Gregory.*

εὐθύς. Omitted. *Cod. Sin., &c., Tisch., Treg., Alford, Lange, Schaff, &c.*—The correspondence of this account with that in Luke v. 5, is very remarkable, as is also their entire distinctness in the midst of that correspondence.—The disciples must have been powerfully reminded of that their former and probably last fishing together.—And after the "*fishers of men*" of that other occasion, the whole could not but bear to them a spiritual meaning in reference to their apostolic commission: their powerlessness without Christ, their success when they let down the net at His word.—Their present part was not to go fishing of themselves, but "wait for the promise of the Father" (Act. i. 4). *Alford.*—"In the night-time, before the presence of the Sun, Christ, the Prophets took nothing; for though they endeavoured to correct the people, yet these often fell into idolatry." *Theophylact.*

---

4. But when the morning was now come, Jesus stood on the shore: but the disciples knew not that it was Jesus.

But. Gr., *But when the morning had already dawned.*—It was at the dawn, after a night of unsuccessful toil, that the risen Lord appeared to the help and comfort of His disciples.—And so in Christian life; after a night of spiritual darkness and trial, the Sun of Righteousness arises "with healing in his wings" (Mal. iv. 2).—The *beams* of the Sun are his "wings;" the words set forth the swiftness with which Christ appears to the relief of His people.

Stood. See on chap. xx. 19, 20, 26.—Describes His sudden appear-ance without any indication of motion hither.—Instantly He is seen standing on the shore, as He was seen to be in the room when the doors were shut.—Christ is always near His Apostolic Church on this side of eternity.—From the shore of the other world—the beyond—His eye is fixed upon His people.—A symbol of the Eternal Morning, when Jesus will at last appear : for the Church as yet waiteth, " until the day break and the shadows flee away."—No longer in the ship with them, He is seen standing on the immovable shore ; thither they shall go to Him, but thence He shall not return to them.—Christ's time of making Himself known to His people is when they are most *at a loss;* when they think they have *lost themselves,* He will let them know that they have not *lost Him.*—It is a comfort to us, when our passage is rough and stormy, to know that our Master is on the shore, and that we are hastening to Him. *Henry.*

Knew not. See on chap. xx. 14, 15.—They saw the form standing on the shore, but did not perceive that it was the Lord (see on Luke xxiv. 16).—Christ is always near His people, especially in times of trouble, but owing to natural frailty and unbelief we do not recognize our Divine Saviour and Friend.—It will never be known how near Jesus has been to us, through all life's journey, till we reach the realms of light.—We forget that His promise is, " I will never leave thee (His *presence*) ; I will never forsake thee (His *help*)," (Heb. xiii. 5).—But He comes to us in forms and ways unlooked for and unexpected, and this has much to do with our misapprehension and ignorance.—To *see the Lord* in *all the events* and *changes* of life, is the privilege of His children, though but realised by few.

γενομένης, text. rec., *Cod. Sin., Lach., Alford, &c.* – γινομένης. *Treg., Tisch., Westcott and Hort.*

5. Then Jesus saith unto them, Children, have ye any meat? They answered him, No.

Children. The Greek word is used in addressing others only by John (1 John ii. 14, 18).—It is a different word from that used in chap. xiii. 33, where our Lord speaks to His disciples in terms of affectionate tenderness.—Here, as He has not yet revealed Him-self, *that* word would not be appropriate.—*This* word may indeed express His love for them (chap. iv. 49), but it appears also to

have been used to workmen or inferiors, not unlike our own words
"boys" or "lads."—They seem to take it in this sense, as though
some traveller passing by had asked the question with a view to
purchase some of their fish. *Ellicott.*—"Jesus, wishing in His
character of the Unknown One to address them first as a stranger,
speaks to them in the universal, familiar language of seafaring
men, with the dignity, we may conjecture, of a superior." *Lange.*

Meat. The Greek word occurs here only in the N. T.—It denotes
anything to eat with bread, but especially *fish.*—The idea is that
of some article of food added to what is regarded as the chief
part of the meal.—The term *relish*, in one of its significations,
more nearly expresses it than any other English word. *Schaff.*—
Evidently the question was intended to prepare the way for the
miracle which followed.—Christ knew perfectly well that they
had been unsuccessful, but He will have them acknowledge their
want.—He takes cognizance of the *temporal* necessities of His
people, and has promised them not only *grace* sufficient, but *food*
convenient.—Yet often He sorely tries their faith ; so that they
seem to the judgment of *sense* to be forsaken of God.—But all
experience proves that "man's extremity is God's opportunity."—
"Trust in the Lord, and do good (do *the right*) ; and verily thou
shalt be fed" (Psa. xxxvii. 3).—As a rule, He does not manifest
Himself, either in temporal or spiritual necessity, until a time of
preparation and expectation, and even of painful disappointment,
has been gone through.

No. See on chap. xx. 15.—They all confess their need unanimously, but without complaint or murmur.—"So our Lord first
makes us know, feel, and acknowledge our spiritual poverty ;
and then He feeds us out of the exceeding riches of his grace, to
the surprise and joy of our hearts (see on chap. ii. 3; v. 13; vi.
5; xi. 39, 40)." *Ford.*—Whenever Christ discourses with His
Church concerning her poverty, want of success, unavailing
labour and fatigue, the moment of a new bestowal of blessing is
being prepared. *Lange.*

παιδία. Young men! Boys! 2 Macc. viii. 20. *Nonnus, Tholuck.*—It was nothing
strange that a person should come to them as they were landing, to buy their catch.
—The simple habits of the East, made it common to sell even single fish, which were
prepared and cooked on the spot, in the open air, by the buyer.—They thought nothing,
therefore, of the stranger asking them, with a kindly familiarity not unusual in
antiquity in addressing the humbler classes, "Children, have ye anything to eat?"
as if wishing to buy for his morning meal. "Nothing at all," cried the fishermen.
Geikie. Meyer, Tholuck.—προσφάγιον. Said by the grammarians to be the Hellenic
form equivalent to the Attic ὄψον, signifying anything eaten as an additament to bread,
but especially fish.—So that here the best rendering would be, "Have ye any fish?"
Alford.

6. And he **said** unto them, Cast the net on the right side of the ship, and ye shall find. They cast therefore, and now they were not able to draw it for the multitude of fishes.

Cast. In the miracle recorded in Luke v. 4, He commanded the disciples to *launch out into the deep.*—Here He commands them to cast the net *on the right side of the ship.*—Very probably they had given up all hope of success for the time, and had drawn the net up out of the water with the intention of steering towards the shore.—The season for fishing appointed by Nature had transpired: It was now the season appointed by Grace.—Meantime the necessity of human exertion is not to be *superseded* by the promise of divine help.—Though He will bring the fish to their hand, yet He will not cast them into the ship, but leaves that for them to do. *Hutcheson.*—Paul must plant, and Apollos water, though God must give the increase.

The net. It is always the *old* net that Christ commands His people to cast in a *new* way, in a *new* direction.—A lesson to ministers and others as to the means to be employed to secure the salvation of men.—In times of non-success the temptation to adopt other agencies and means than those Christ has appointed, is great.—But the command, *Preach the gospel to every creature,* continues in force under all circumstances.—The earnest faithful ministry of the Word is the *old net* which Jesus bids His disciples *Cast* into the sea.

Right side. See on Luke i. 11.—Not only *when* He commands, but *as* He commands, if we would be successful.—In things to all appearances indifferent, the Lord's command overcomes all other considerations, and must be implicitly obeyed, to inherit the blessing.—His servants must follow His positive directions as to *when* and *where* and *how,* without first inquiring the *why* and *wherefore.*—Herein is a sure test by which to try whether we have the *principle* of obedience or not. —Not in great things only is the Divine Will to be accepted, but in every thing, however small or insignificant the matter may appear. —" He that is faithful in that which is least is faithful also in much: and he that is unjust in the least is unjust also in much " (see on Luke xvi. 10).—Those are likely to speed well who follow the rule of the Word, the guidance of the Spirit, and the intimations of Providence; for that is *casting the net on the right side. Henry.*

They cast. They think the speaker who stands on the shore sees some indication of fishes, for He is still as a stranger to them, and yet they at once obey Him. *Ellicott.*—May it not be inferred that His Spirit, unconsciously to them, is influencing their hearts?— What brought and kept them together but their common relation to Him who is the centre of all their hopes and wishes?—Is it not the love which united them which has mysteriously inclined them to obey the unknown Man on the shore?

Not able. Not able to drag the net up into the ship, so great was the draught.—Evidently the fish had been brought there by the control of Christ.—"All things were made by Him, and for Him; and by Him all things consist" (Col. i. 16, 17).—His sufferings and death had not lessened His power for the help of His people.—He is not only a God near at hand, but a God afar off also, and can do as much for His children at a distance as when He is close by: for He wrought the like miracle when He was with them (Luke v. 4), but now He works this when He is upon the shore, and they in the ship. *Hutcheson.*—Their *not being able to draw the net*, should teach believers to be contented with the ordinary allowances which their wise and all-sufficient Lord alloweth them. *Donne.*

Multitude. How soon Christ can by His blessing repay His people for the painful labour that they have deemed lost.—An encouragement to His ministers to continue their diligence in their work; one happy draught, at length, may be sufficient to repay many years' toil at the Gospel net. *Henry.*—The Sea of Galilee, formerly the scene of Christ's first miracles, acts, and sufferings, is now the mirror of His glory.

τὰ δεξιά. In Luke v. 4, neither right, nor left, was specified: but here it is, *Cast ye the net on the right side.*—On the former occasion, there was set forth in figure the Church visible, the net spoken of in the parable, as "gathering of every kind," and being "filled with bad and good": and the net therefore is thrown at random, neither to the right nor left.—But here, when the Church invisible of the Elect is represented, such, as is filled only with those, that are finally saved and come to the land of everlasting life, it is said, "Cast ye in on the *right* side."—Here is choice and election, as designed in secret knowledge by Christ Himself (Matt. xxv. 34; Ezek. iv. 4, 6; Psa. xlviii 10; cviii. 6). *Augustine, Gregory, I. Williams.*—The *right side* is that of the elect.—When the net is cast on that side, the fish enter the net of themselves.—The blessing that God puts in the mouth of the preacher along with His Word, is really the source of all the fruit he produces. *Gossner.*

---

7. Therefore that disciple whom Jesus loved saith unto Peter, It is the Lord. Now when Simon Peter heard that it was the Lord, he girt his fisher's coat unto him, (for he was naked,) and did cast himself into the sea.

That disciple. See on chap. xix. 26; xx. 2.—We meet here the same traits of character in John and Peter, which have been already noted (see on chap. xx. 5-8).

The Lord. See on chap. xx. 28.—John first recognizes Him, with the mind's eye, by His manner of acting; then, with the bodily ear, by His speech, as also, with the bodily glance, by His specific appearance. *Lange.*—True to his habit of contemplation, John is the first to trace in the present miracle an analogy with the earlier one, and to discern that the Master who spoke then is present now. *Ellicott.*—" A friend knows his friend by his walk, his step ; so John knew the Lord by the successful draught. Ah, thought he, the Lord hath played us this loving trick; I know Him, that is His way." *Gossner.*—To note and point out the divine in life is a precious and important service.—But this can only be done by those who love God; for love is the organ by which the soul *knows God.*—So enveloped was our Lord's risen body with something that was Divine that divine love alone could discern it.—Hence it was the disciple whom *Jesus loved,* who was the first to discern *the presence of Jesus.*—Our Lord was teaching them to walk by *faith* and not by *sight.*—The *miracle* was the evidence that it was He.

Peter. True to his habit of prompt and immediate action, Peter is the first to rush to the Master.—John is in advance with the swift motion of love, the eagle glance of recognition ; Peter with the spirited, decisive act.—Some are useful as the Church's *eyes,* others as the Church's *hands;* both equally for the good of the Body.—" If all the disciples had done as Peter did, what had become of their fish and their nets? And yet if Peter had done as they did, we had wanted this instance of holy zeal. Christ was well pleased with both, and so must we." *Henry.*

He girt. The Greek words imply that he put on the garment which workmen customarily used.—It seems to have been a kind of linen frock worn over the shirt, without sleeves.—As it reached to the knees, the girding was to enable him to swim more easily.—Some think he walked upon the water as aforetime, but of this there is no evidence.

Naked. The common usage of the Greek and Hebrew words answering to our word " naked," makes it probable that Peter was wearing some under-garment.—Perhaps the usual loin-cloth, or even a fisherman's shirt.—His *reverence* for the Lord is indicated by the careful observation, even in such a moment of excited feeling, of the petty proprieties of clothing.

Into the sea. At the former draught (Luke v. 8) he cried out, " Depart from me; for I am a sinful man, O Lord."—He said this in the weakness of his faith and of his knowledge, and in the confusion of his mind, as though the nearness of the Holy One brought danger to him.—This feeling he had surmounted ; though conscious still of being a sinful man, he was more strongly convinced that the nearness of Jesus is always and everywhere salutary. *Gerlach.*—John, calmer than Peter, while his emotions were deeper, tranquilly remained with the rest in the boat.—But their faces were all set toward the Lord in one love ; and all were filled and made happy with the one thought of His presence.— John and Peter, or Love and Zeal : Love always makes the sweetest discoveries of Christ ; Zeal plunges even into the sea to reach the Master.

οὖν. The οὖν here seems distinctly to allude to the former occasion—the similarity of the incident having led the beloved disciple to scrutinize more closely the person of Him who spoke to them. *Alford.*

8. And the other disciples came in a little ship ; (for they were not far from land, but as it were two hundred cubits,) dragging the net with fishes.

Little ship. Gr., *in the small boat;* the word is used in the Gospels for the small fishing vessels on the Sea of Galilee (Mark iii. 9 ; iv. 36 ; John vi. 22, 23).

Not far. About one hundred English yards from land.—The Greek preposition used with "cubits" ("cubits *off*"), is used of distance only by John (chap. xi. 18 ; Rev. xiv. 20).—*Not far from land:* not far from the eternal shore ; so near are we, even in this troublous world, to the land of Everlasting Rest, and to Him who there abideth.

Dragging. The shortness of the distance explains how they were able to do this.—There are several ways of bringing Christ's *disciples to shore* to Him from off *the sea* of this world ; some are brought to Him by a violent death, as the martyrs, who *threw themselves into the sea*, in their zeal for Christ ; others are brought to Him by a natural death, *dragging the net*, which is less terrible ; but both meet at length on the safe and quiet shore with Christ. *Henry.*

πλοιάριον. The small boat attached to the larger vessel. *Macdonald*—The two words "ship" and "boat" (πλοῖον and πλοιάριον) are interchanged here, as in chap. vi. 17 *et. seq. Ellicott.*—πῆχυς. *The fore arm*, from the wrist to the elbow. In N. T. *a cubit*, the common ancient measure of length, equal to the distance from the elbow to the tip of the middle finger, and usually reckoned at 1½ foot. *Robinson.*

9. As soon then as they were come to land, they saw a fire of coals there, and fish laid thereon, and bread.

Saw. The tenses in the Greek are present : *They see a fire of coals,* *and fish lying thereon, and bread.*—The scene is presented with the vividness peculiar to John, and as it was impressed on his mind even after so many years.

A fire. See on chap. xviii. 18.—Caused to be there by the Lord Himself, or by the ministry of angels at His bidding.—We do not see how the incident can be understood in any other light than that of the *supernatural* —As the Master and Father of the house, He has provided a breakfast for them.—There is the *fire* to *warm* them ; the *fish* and the *bread* to *feed* them.—Must have powerfully affected their minds with a sense of His tender care for them, and strengthened their faith as to the future.—" This twofold miracle of the draught of fishes, and the broiled fish and bread made ready for their repast when their labours were ended, symbolize the fidelity, zeal, and reliance upon Chri-t for success, with which the Apostles and all who succeed them in the ministry of the Word, were to labour in the work of saving souls, and the watchful providence with which He, in whose service they are engaged, will supply all their temporal and spiritual wants." *Stier.*

ἀνθρακιὰν. A miracle. *Chrysostom, Augustine, Theophylact, Grotius, Calovius, Stier, Alford, Macdonald, &c.*—Prepared by the ministry of angels. *Nicephorus, Luthardt. &c.* —Jesus either conveyed the meal thither Himself, or procured others to place it there. *Meyer.*—But had not Jesus friends everywhere along the lake?—Could He not appear to them, and, in a mysterious manner, arrange something similar to the making-ready of the she-ass in Bethphage and of the furnished room in Jerusalem ?— To this day Christ often, through the medium of wonderful providences, cares thus for the maintenance of His people by operating influentially upon foreboding souls. *Lange.*—Rationalistic interpretations are all out of place here : This was as much a miracle as the draught of fishes ; let any child reading the chapter, be the judge. *Stier, Alford* —This miracle was not wrought out of subject matter, already in existence, like His others. . . Those, so wrought before His crucifixion were in character with that dispensation. *Chrysostom.*—ὀψάριον. See on chap. vi. 9, 11.—A word *peculiar to John. Alford.*—In this passage and in verse 13 only it occurs in the singular, but it seems clear that it may be collective, as our word " fish." *Ellicott.*

---

10. Jesus saith unto them, Bring of the fish which ye have now caught.

Bring. They are commanded to add some of the fish which they, by His direction alone, had caught.—In order to assure them of the reality of the miraculous draught. *Euthymius.*—In order to the completion of the meal. *Meyer.*—Also, in order to the revelation of a new order of things.—Christ prepares refreshment for them from a *union* of His *gift of blessing*, and their *blessed labour. Lange.*— " The Lord would hereby teach us to use what we have ; the benefits He bestows upon us are not to be *buried* and *laid up*, but to be *used* and *laid out.* Ministers, who are *fishers of men*, must bring all they catch to their Master." *Henry.*—God's grace, which is the fruit of Christ's Resurrection, does not supersede our endeavours, but rather excites them, and works with them.— Both together prepare us for the Heavenly Feast. *Ford*—*His grace goes before,* and our works follow : Happy day ! when Christ's ministers may bring to Heaven of the multitudes whom they have caught by His grace. *Barnes.*—Christ's faithful servants will have an augmentation of bliss from seeing the happiness of those to whom in life it was their privilege to minister.

---

11. Simon Peter went up, and drew the net to land full of great fishes, an hundred and fifty and three: and for all there were so many, yet was not the net broken.

Went up. At the Lord's command Peter went up into the ship.— His natural disposition is become sanctified by love to Christ ; this is seen in his ready obedience.

Drew. The ship was now lying on the shore with one end of the net attached to it, and Peter drew the remainder of the net to the shore.—Not for himself does he seize the net, but to place it at the disposal of Christ.

Great fishes The greatness would be noted, because in any ordinary draught of fishes a considerable proportion would be small and valueless.—John's intention in speaking of the size and number evidently is to render prominent the remarkable fact that the net was not broken—He mentions the exact number, *an hundred fifty and three;* for it is a peculiarity of John, already noticed, that he carefully states numbers (verse 8; chap. vi. 10, &c.).—This number (153), as a number, is not symbolical, a fact which speaks very decidedly in favour of the historic truthfulness of the narrative.—But although the *number* may not be symbolical, the *numbering* has been regarded in that light.—"The elect, who form the main element of the Church, are great and numbered fishes." *Lange.*—"The church is continually edified by the number of true converts and believers who have received a new name, not by her unnumbered masses." *Schaff.*

Not broken. See on Luke v. 6.—The net was not rent, notwithstanding the size and number of the fishes.—One of the details which show that the writer was an eye-witness.—"Great and numerous as the elect may be, they are not the ones who break the net of the Church. It is the maxim of all the elect: First Christ, then the Church. The true spiritual net of the eternal Church has never yet been broken." *Lange.*—"The net of the Church breaketh not, though never so many great fishes be

in it, when it is drawn at the command of Jesus and by apostolic
hands. But when men arbitrarily pull at the net, and one pulleth
right and another left, it breaketh. And now, alas! what men
usually call the net of the Lord is sorely broken. But the Lord
hath *His* net, the which is not broken." *Gossner.*—The net of
the Gospel is still as mighty as ever to bring souls to God.

ἑκατὸν πεντη. Expressive of the jubilee of the true Israel of beatified saints in
heaven. *Wordsworth*—We have no clue to any mystical in·e pretation of this number,
and it is probably not intended to convey one.—The various meanings which men have
read into it, such as that it represents one of every kind of fish known to the natural
history of the day ; or that one hundred represents the Gentile nations, fifty the Jews,
and three the Trinity ; or that there is a reference to the 153,600 proselytes of 2 Chron.
ii. 17; or that it expresses symbo'ica.ly the name of Simon Peter, t·ke their place
among the eccentricities of exegesis. *Ellicott.*—Betokens the careful counting which
took place after the event, in wh:ch the narrator took a part. *Alford.*

---

12. Jesus saith unto them, Come and dine. And none of the disciples durst ask him,
Who art thou? knowing that it was the Lord.

Dine. See on Luke xi. 37.—It was the early morning meal,
what we call *breakfast* (see on verse 5).—Christ the Master of
the House gives the invitation to the feast.—"A type of that
nearness and fellowship, to which the Lord would in future times
condescend in His invisible relations with His people." *Stier.*—
Points also to the time when the redeemed shall "*sit down* with
Abraham, and Isaac, and Jacob, in the Kingdom of Heaven"
(see on Matt. viii. 2).

Durst ask. See on chap. iv. 27.—The Greek word rendered
"ask" means to "prove," to "inquire."—It occurs nowhere else in
the writings of John, or in the N.T., except in Matt. ii. 8 and
x. 11.—Neither is the word rendered "durst" found again in
John's writings, but its use in the Gospels is almost wholly confined to the expression of the reverence which dared not question
the Lord (compare Matt. xxii. 46; Mark xii. 34; Luke xx. 40).—
In all the instances it is used with a negative, and with a verb of
inquiry, as here. *Ellicott.*—They sat down to the meal in silence,
wondering at, while at the same time they well knew, Him who
was thus their Host. *Alford.*—They know Him to be the Lord, and
yet desire to hear it from Himself, but do not dare to ask.—Not
doubt, but deepest reverence, in connection with a quiet blissful
assurance in regard to His presence. *Lange.*—"The speechless
awe that dares not move, and all the silent heaven of love."
C. Wesley.

The Lord. See on chap. xx. 13, 28, and on Matt. i. 22.—Though He appeared to them as a man, they confessed within themselves that He was THE LORD. " Wherefore is it that thou dost ask after my name ? " said the Divine Man to Jacob (Gen. xxxii. 29). —The believer cannot learn the name of the Lord in any theoretic manner, but only through the experience of faith.—Hence we read, " And He blessed him there ; " that was the Divine answer to Jacob's question.—The Christian must learn to know his Lord by His power upon his heart.—The school of the Cross is the most glorious school : 1. It reveals his God to the Christian ; 2. It reveals also the Christian heart before God and the world.

---

13. Jesus then cometh, and taketh bread, and giveth them, and fish likewise.

Cometh. From the place where they first saw Him standing.— They have been on *this* side of the coal fire (to which He had called them to approach), and He has been on the *other* side.—He now advances to distribute the meal which He had prepared for them.

Taketh. This word brings to mind the account of the institution of the Last Supper.

Bread. Gr., *the bread*, that mentioned in verse 9.

Giveth. The disciples do not *help themselves* to food : It is still Christ that *taketh*, Christ that *giveth*.—All the spiritual refreshment of heaven will still be *His* gift.—The very bliss of the redeemed will be altogether from *Him*.

Fish. Gr., *and the fish likewise*, those mentioned in verses 9 and 10. —Why was the customary thanksgiving omitted ?—" Our Lord no longer does things according to a man, showing that on the former occasions He had done them by condescension." *Chrysostom.*—" The table-communion of Jesus with His people is a silent one in this æon." *Luhardt.*—" The Evangelist is not describing a regular repast, such as is spoken of, Luke xxiv. 30, but a *breakfast*, that was partaken of standing." *Meyer.*—" The meal had been provided by *miraculous* power." *Fritzsche.*—" He did not intend to make Himself known as yet by the expression of the prayer of thanksgiving. Peter, who has denied Him, declaring that he knew Him not, must be made to recognise Him again, as the Anonymous One, by His conduct." *Lange.*—Although it is not expressly stated that our Lord did eat with them, yet it is implied in His invitation. —He appears as the Host, the House-father of His little Church.— There are continually recurring festive moments when Christ holds a feast with His people, as though upon the heights of the new world.—This breakfast a type of the *early meal* of the great resurrection morning, which will be followed by a permanent day of eternal joy. *Stier.*

---

14. Th's is now the third t'me that Jesus shewed himself to his disciples, after that he was risen f:om the dead.

Third. See on chap. xx. 16, 19, 26.—John is giving his own testimony, and therefore reckons only the appearances of the Risen One "to the disciples."—First, to the Ten on Easter-Day ; second, to the Eleven the Sunday following; third, this appearance to the Seven.—This internal trait of consistency adds to the evidence of the genuineness of this chapter.—Christ's present favours should be a mean to bring His former mercies to remembrance, that use may be made of all together. *Hutcheson.*—It is good to keep account of the Lord's gracious visits ; for He keeps account of them, and they will be remembered against us, if we walk unworthily of them. *Henry.*

Shewed. Gr., *manifested Himself* (see on verse i.).—Each appearance was a distinct *revelation* of the Lord Jesus.—The manifestations of the glor.fied Christ are ever more glorious.—The two Easter feasts in Galilee : 1. The Apostles' feast by the sea ; 2. The Church's feast on the mountain (Matt. xxviii. 16).—He manifests Himself to the Apostles by the sea ; for they must plunge into the sea of nations ; He manifests Himself to the Church on the mountain, for it is to be the firm city, stablished upon the mountain of the Lord.—The Risen One in the gradualness of His glorious manifestation : 1. The strange form in the morning twilight on the shore ; 2. The sympathising question ; 3. The confident direction ; 4. The mysterious preparation of a fire ; 5. The condescending community of goods *(bring hither of the fish)*; 6. The glorious invitation ; 7. The complete manifestation in its familiarity and sublimity.—Christ considered in respect to the riches of His life amongst His people : 1. Mysterious and familiar ; 2. Master and Servant; 3. Host and Guest; 4. A heavenly Apparition and a festive Companion. *Lange.* (See note.)

Risen. See on chap. xx. 9, 29.—In spirit, He came forth from the invisib e world, and in body, from the grave.—He was dead, but it was "not possible that He should be holden of death ;" He was buried, but the grave had no power to retain *Him.*—Anticipating the burial of His dead body, and the descent of His spirit into Hades, He had spoken, long before His Incarnation, with infinite assurance, saying by the mouth of David: "Thou

wilt not leave My soul in hell, neither wilt Thou suffer Thine
Holy One to see corruption. Thou wilt show Me *the path of life.*"

ἐφανερώθη. " Without agreeing with all the allegorical interpretations of the Fathers,
I cannot but see much depth and richness of meaning in this whole narrative. The Lord
appears to His disciples busied about their occupation for their daily bread; speaks
and acts in a manner wonderfully similar to His words and actions on a former
memorable occasion, when we know that by their toiling long and taking nothing, but
at His word enclosing a multitude of fishes, was set forth what should befall them as
fishers of men. Can we miss that application at this far more important epoch of their
apostolical mission? Besides, He graciously provides for their present wants, and invites them to be His guests : why, but to show them that in their work hereafter they
should never want but He would provide? And as connected with the parable, Matt.
xiii. 47 ff., has the net *enclosing a great multitude and yet not broken,* no meaning? Has
the ' taking the bread and giving to them, and the fish likewise, no meaning, which
so closely binds together the miraculous feeding, and the institution of the Lord's
Supper, with their future meetings in His Name and round His Table? Anyone who
recognizes the *teaching* character of the acts of the Lord, can hardly cast all such applications from him; and those who do not, have yet the first rudiments of the Gospels
to learn." *Alford.—*ἐγερθείς, not elsewhere in John, but the participial construction is
found in chap. iv. 54. *Alford.*

---

15. So when they had dined, Jesus saith to Simon Peter, Simon, son of Jonas, lovest
thou me more than these? He saith unto him, Yea, Lord; thou knowest that I love
thee. He saith unto him, Feed my lambs.

So. The refreshment by the meal, provided by the Lord, was a
preparation for a solemn conversation and revelation.—Thus when
Elijah had deserted his duty through fear of Jezebel, and had fled
into the wilderness, before God manifested Himself, the errant
prophet was made to eat and drink and sleep (1 Kings xix).—
He who made man recognizes the laws of his constitution, and restores the body before proceeding to restore the soul.—" He
knoweth our frame ; He remembereth that we are dust " (Psa.
ciii. 14).

Saith. That which follows evidently has reference to the fall of
Peter, its object being the re-institution of that disciple.—Note
the threefold address, and the threefold inquiry by the Lord ; also
Peter's three replies, and the Lord's three injunctions in answer.
—The threefold inquiry and the three replies of Peter—the
counterpart of the threefold temptation and denial.

Simon. See on chap. i. 42, and Matt xvi. 17, 18.—Thrice the Lord
addresses him as *Simon, son of Jonas* (or, *son of John,* see note).—
A delicately expressed reminder that he had fallen from the steadfastness of Peter (the Rock), and had been true rather to his
natural than to his apostolic name.—In Matt. xvi. 17, he is called
Simon Barjona, in connection with the mention of his natural
state of flesh and blood, which had not revealed to him the great

truth he had just confessed.—And when Jesus warned him of the approaching temptation, it was, "Simon, Simon," to remind him of his natural weakness (Luke xxii. 31).—A lesson to note well and watch against "the sin which doth so easily beset us" (Heb. xii. 1), and which in most cases derives its power from constitutional causes.—In addition to the general tendency to sin, common to all, each has in himself some peculiarly weak point of character, which the Christian should carefully observe and guard.—It is through this natural infirmity that temptation often assails us, as is seen in the history of the Apostles.—James and John, "the sons of thunder" (Mark iii. 17), would have called down fire from heaven to consume the Samaritans (Luke ix. 54).—Thomas's gloomy, doubting turn of mind led him to make the painful demand recorded in chap. xx. 25 (see Comm.).—And Peter's errors, and sins, and dangers, may be traced to natural descent.— Hence the emphatic, *thrice-repeated* address, *Simon, son of Jonas.* —Our comfort is that our individual frailties are known to the Lord, who "was in all points tempted like as we are, yet without sin"; and who is, therefore, "a *merciful* and *faithful* High priest, to make reconciliation for the sins of the people. For in that He Himself hath suffered being tempted, He is able *to succour* them that are tempted" (Heb. ii. 17, 18).—"Let us therefore come boldly unto the throne of grace, that we may *obtain mercy*, and *find grace to help* in time of need" (Heb. iv. 15, 16).

Lovest? See note.—The Greek word is used of the higher, reverential, constant, unwavering love, such as we ought to have to God as well as to man, and such as Christ had to John (verse 20) and His Church. *Schaff.*—"Dost thou in the full determination of the will, in profound reverence and devotion, love Me?" *Ellicott.*—No question is made of faith, because love *is* faith, in a developed form.—Every element of genuine repentance is comprehended in this one vital question.—There is no formal rebuke of Peter for the denial of his Lord; that was already forgiven; this asking about his love was at farthest a most gentle and affectionate reproof. *Stier.*—Herein Christ has given us a most encouraging instance of His tenderness towards penitents, and has taught us, in like manner, to "restore such as are fallen in a spirit of meekness" (Gal. vi. 1).—The practice of the Lord was entirely different from the subsequently invented Church-penance, ccording to the canons of which, Peter would have been forced to kneel outside of the Church-door for at least fifteen years. *Heuner.*—"Let me fall now into the hand of the LORD; for very great are His mercies: but let me not fall into the hand of man" (1 Chron. xxi. 13).

Me. The main thing is *personal* love, true, real love for the Person of Jesus.—This is the characteristic of His called servant: 1. As the condition of the recognition that the sheep are His; 2. As the condition of true discrimination in attending to the flock; 3. As the condition of true pastoral fidelity. *Lange.*—Love to Christ is the decisive fundamental condition of the pastoral office.—Whatever a man may have, if he have not *that*, he is not fitted for the office.

More. Three interpretations have been given: 1. Lovest thou Me more than thou lovest *these persons, the other disciples?*—2. Lovest thou Me more than thou lovest *these occupations, fishing, &c.?*—3. Lovest thou Me more than *these love Me, more than any of the rest of the disciples love Me?*—The obvious reference is to Peter's *own* comparison of himself with his fellow-Apostles: "Though all shall be offended because of Thee, yet will I never be offended" (Matt. xxvi. 33).—"It may not be fanciful to trace significance, even in the external circumstances under which the question was asked. By the side of the lake after casting his net into the water had Peter first been called to be a fisher of men (see on Matt. iv. 14). The lake, the very spot on the shore, the nets, the boat, would bring to his mind in all their fulness the thoughts of the day which had been the turning-point of his life. By the side of the 'fire of coals' (see on chap. xviii. 18, the only place where the word occurs) he had denied his Lord. As his eye rests upon the 'fire of coals' before him, and he is conscious of the presence of the Lord, who knows all things (verse 17), burning thoughts of penitence and shame may have come to his mind, and these may have been the true preparation for the words which follow." *Ellicott.*

Thou knowest. A threefold expression of humility: 1. No making of comparisons now; no setting up of himself above his fellow-disciples; 2. The appeal to the knowledge of Christ; 3. The choice of the term of personal attachment. *Lange.*

I love. This is a less strong expression than that which our Lord had used.—The word means personal, emotional love and friendship.—A less exalted word, and one implying a consciousness of his own weakness, but also a persuasion and deep feeling of personal attachment. *Alford.*—It seems to say: "Thou knowest me; I dare not now declare this fixed determination of the will, but in the fulness of personal affection I dare answer, and Thou knowest that even in my denials it was true, 'I love Thee.'" *Ellicott.*—It would appear as if Peter felt that the form of the question put him at a comparative distance from his Lord, and therefore in his answer he substitutes this word, which amounts to, "I love Thee dearly."

Feed. As if there were no way of Peter's showing his love to Jesus, but by being a faithful pastor.—As though He said : Be it the office of love to feed the Lord's flock, as it was the effect of fear to deny the Shepherd. *Augustine.*—"Perhaps the *feeding of the lambs* was the furnishing the Apostolic testimony of the resurrection and facts of the Lord's life on earth to the first converts. The *shepherding* or ruling *the sheep* (verse 16), the subsequent government of the Church as shown forth in the early part of the Acts. The *feeding of the sheep* (verse 17), the furnishing the now maturer Church with the rich food of the doctrine contained in the Epistles." *Alford.*—To provide wholesome food for the flock of Christ is the first and last thing in the pastoral office.— This *food* is *the truth of God*, rightly divided, so as to give to each "their portion of meat in due season" (Luke xii. 42 ; 2 Tim. ii. 15).—But he who is to feed others with the truth must himself feed upon the same.—Love to Christ will ensure faithfulness both as to the food and the manner of imparting it.—How evident it is that the Apostolic office consisteth not in *worldly dominion*, but in the *feeding* of the flock of Christ.—Those who have been greatly tempted, and have had humiliating knowledge of their frailty and sinfulness, and who have had much forgiven them, generally prove the most tender and attentive pastors, and the best guides of young converts.—The Lord often leads those whom He loves to pass through painful conflicts, as well as much experience of His compassion, in order to render them more gentle to the weak brethren, and the lambs of His flock. *Scott.*—How deeply this injunction of the Risen Lord impressed Peter's heart is manifest in his Epistles.—When an old man he wrote to the elders of the Church : "Feed the flock of God" (1 Pet. v. 2).

My lambs. Gr., *My little lambs.*—Christ speaks thus as the Chief Shepherd (1 Pet. v. 4).—An expression of His tender affection for His flock.—What is said to Peter, is said to all the Apostles : Not *thy* lambs or *thy* sheep, but " *My* lambs and *My* sheep."—A solemn thought for the pastor of souls, that the "lambs" and the "sheep" are not *his* but *Christ's.*—Not *his ;* therefore, like Jacob with the flock of Laban, he should be prepared to give account for all.—Not *his ;* therefore, must there be One above him, to whom they are a care as well as to himself, who careth alike for *him* and for *them.*—They who feed Christ's sheep as if they were their own, not Christ's, show plainly that they love themselves, not Christ ; that they are moved by lust of glory, power, gain, not by the love of obeying, ministering, pleasing God. *Augustine.*—In

Christ's flock some are *lambs,* young and tender and weak, others are *sheep,* grown to some strength and maturity ; the shepherd here takes care of both, and of the *lambs* first.—It is not merely, therefore, the *privilege,* it is the solemn *duty* of ministers of the Gospel to encourage and support Sunday schools. *Barnes.*—They should carefully distinguish between *lambs* and *sheep, i.e.,* children, youths and old persons, communicating to each his food : to the lambs, milk ; to the adults in faith, strong meat (Heb. v. 12).— Our Lord having *first* recommended the *lambs* to Peter's feeding, it follows that Christian teachers should consider youth and simplicity as specially recommended to their care. *Starke.*—*Feeding* implies personal application to their respective state and case.—It is a notable proof and evidence of love to Christ when ministers show special attention to the religious training of the young. *Baxter.*—In the smallest sphere as well as in the greatest, a man can only be a *good shepherd* over the souls of others in so far as he is himself a *good sheep* of the Great Shepherd.—And the best evidence of a minister's love to Christ, is his conscientious care to *feed* the whole flock of Christ, lambs and sheep, weak and strong. —Parents and others may well be encouraged and comforted by this proof of the Lord's peculiar affection for the young.

'Ιωνᾶ. 'Ιωάννου or Ιωάνου here and in verses 16, 17. *Codd. Sin., B.C.D.L., Vulgate, Jerome, Ambrose. Lach., Tisch., Treg., Alf., Westcott and Hort.* 'Ιωνᾶ is from Matt. xvi. 17. *Schaff.*—'Ιωνᾶ is adopted by *Lange.*—The significant difference between ἀγαπᾶν and φιλεῖν which runs through this section, cannot well be rendered in English, unless we translate φιλῶ σε : *I dearly love Thee.*—The Vulgate renders the former always by *diligere,* the latter by *amare* and *osculari.*—In the Hebrew and Syriac there are not the same shades of difference, but the Lord may have expressed it by an additional word or emphasis; at all events we have to account for the difference in the Greek of John. *Schaff.*—The distinction seems to be that ἀγαπᾶν is more used of that reverential love, grounded on high graces of character, which is borne towards God and man by the child of God ; whereas φιλεῖν expresses more the personal love of human affection. *Alford.*—" Formerly Peter had professed ἀγαπᾶν, but it proved to be only a short-lived φιλεῖν. Now he only professes φιλεῖν, but Christ knows that it will be a long-lived ἀγαπᾶν, an ἀγάπη in old age (verse 18), an ἀγάπη stronger than death." *Wordsworth.*— Βόσκε. A further and higher setting forth of the Apostolic office than that first one, Matt. iv. 13 ; both as belonging to all of the disciples on the present occasion, and as tending to comfort Peter's own mind after his fall, and reassure him of his holding the same place among the apostles as before, owing to the gracious forgiveness of his Lord. *Alford.* (See notes to verses 16, 17.)

---

16. He saith to him again the second time, Simon, son of Jonas, lovest thou me? He saith unto him, Yea, Lord; thou knowest that I love thee. He saith unto him, Feed my sheep.

He saith. The Lord repeats the question in the same form, except that He does not continue the comparison " more than these."

Lovest? Again He uses the same word for the higher, more reverential love.—" Lovest thou Me with all the power of thy soul above all other love? "—" This is the question of life and conscience which He incessantly puts to each one of those who once with Peter have experienced: 'Lord, to whom can we go? Thou hast the words of eternal life.' Anything higher we feel that Jesus cannot ask; nay, the claim would be as little allowable as the fulfilment, if He who thus speaks were anything less than God's own Son, the Saviour of a sinful world, the Sovereign of God's Kingdom, who has an unconditional right to the whole hearts of His subjects. And yet nothing less can He claim from us, if He in truth confess us as His disciples; because not only, or specially, by the professing lips, the busy hand, the ready feet, but by the loving heart, the disciple of the best of Masters may be known. Of such a love there evidently can be no question so long as no personal relation subsists; only the pardoned sinner, like Peter, is in a state and condition to exhibit it, for it is the first and most precious fruit of a humble and grateful faith. Where this faith really lives in us, and shows the blessed consciousness that mercy has been bestowed on us, there this love, however defective, cannot possibly be utterly absent. Even beneath the penetrating eye of the Searcher of hearts it is conscious of itself, in no degree of its perfection, but not the less of its sincerity; it abides the scrutiny of Him who loveth truth in the inward part; and so well-pleasing is it in His holy eyes, that where the first word is heard the second will not be delayed." *Oosterzee.*

Yea, Lord, &c. Peter replies by the same declaration of personal attachment, and the same appeal to Christ's knowledge.—It is the expression of a humbled soul, a soul made sensible of its weakness and need of grace.—Not the most confident profession constitutes the highest proof of love to Christ.—Already the salutary effect of painful discipline is evident in Peter.—For the rest of his life he will speak and act with more diffidence: trust less to self and more to grace.

Feed. See on verse 15.—The Greek word here is not the same as that used in verse 15.—This is a more comprehensive term and includes the former.—In Matt. ii. 6, where it is applied to Christ, it is translated "rule."—It may be rendered "Tend" or "Shepherd," *i.e.,* "Perform all a shepherd's duties" by them; "Feed the flock, *like a shepherd;*" do all that should be done by a "*shepherd of the sheep.*"—Not only "Feed;" "*Guide and guard My sheep.*" (See note.)—" It is not sufficient that ministers be able to feed unless they also govern and rule the people committed to their charge, and do every other duty of a good shepherd unto them." *Hutcheson.*—To *feed*, and *shepherdize*, include every provision for the spiritual wants of the flock, and every kind of supervision and care required.—All that is needed for the soul's health and strength, is here especially referred to.

My sheep. See on verse 15.—" If we call our sheep *ours*, as the sectarists call them *theirs*, Christ hath lost His sheep." *Augustine.* —" Woe be to the shepherds of Israel that do feed themselves! Should not the shepherds feed the flocks?" (Ezek. xxxiv. 2.)

Ποίμαινε. The difference between βόσκω (*to feed, to pasture*) and ποιμαίνω (from ποιμήν, *to pasture, to tend, to provide for, to rule*, a flock or herd), is obliterated in the E.V.—βόσκω occurs nine times in the N.T., and is always translated *to feed* in the E.V., except Matt. viii. 33.—ποιμαίνω occurs eleven times and is rendered *to rule*, or *to feed*. —βόσκειν has reference mainly to the *feeding, nourishing* care, and applies therefore specially to the lambs, while ποιμαίνειν is more general, and covers the providing and governing activity; compare Matt. ii. 6; Acts xx. 23; 1 Pet. v. 2; Rev. ii. 27; vii. 17; xii. 5; xix. 15. *Meyer, Schaff.*—πρόβατα. *Codd. Sin., A.D.X., &c., Lach., Treg., Meyer, Lange.* προβάτια has the authority of *B.C.*, and is adopted by *Tisch., Alford, Westcott.*

---

17. He saith unto him the third time, Simon, son of Jonas, lovest thou me? Peter was grieved because he said unto him the third time, Lovest thou me? And he said unto him, Lord, thou knowest all things; thou knowest that I love thee. Jesus saith unto him, Feed my sheep.

He saith. For the *third* time the Lord repeats the question.—No less than *thrice* must be profess love to the Lord, who is made the representative of those to whom He commits His lambs and sheep. *Austin.*

Lovest? In this case the Lord does *not* use the word found in verses 15, 16; He now uses Peter's *own word*.—Instead of the twice repeated " Lovest thou Me?" His word is, " Dost thou *love Me dearly?* "—He asks with that word which Peter feels will alone express all that is in his heart.—This last a searching entering into the twice-repeated assurance of Peter.—" To the *ethical* love for Christ (verses 15, 16), there must be added a *personal* love for Him, resting upon historically grounded *knowledge*." *Lange.*

Grieved. Not merely on account of the repetition of the question, but because of the *third* time, the number of his own denials of Christ. *Alford.*—Moreover, from the manner of the question it might seem as if his love for his Lord were doubted.—We must not reckon it an affront to have our sincerity questioned, when

we ourselves have done that which makes it questionable. *Henry.*
—Christ was now laying deeply in Peter's heart the foundation
of character on which his future usefulness was to be built.—
There is no better sign of a work of grace in the soul than
extreme sensitiveness to every suspicion of want of love to Christ.
—We must welcome the pain which it will cost us to see ourselves
now, in the light of God.—It is a blessed pain, for the pain which
God's Light gives us, is God's own method of quickening the soul
to seek His cleansing, healing grace.—Hence we must love God
more for what chastises us, than for what pleases us.—No one can
read the Acts of the Apostles, and the Epistles of Peter, without
seeing the blessed spiritual fruit of this loving chastening of the
Lord (Heb. xii. 6).

Thou knowest, &c. See on chap. vi. 64; xvi. 30; xviii. 4.—Peter
now appeals in more solemn words than before to the Lord's
knowledge of his inmost heart.—" *Thou knowest all things; Thou
knowest that I love Thee.*"—It is the appeal of one smarting beneath
a wound: or rather the cry of a sufferer under the deep probing
of the Physician.—But with this the trial terminates, for the end
is accomplished.—Jesus, the Searcher of hearts, a comfort in
every cross, temptation, and persecution.—It ought never to be
terror to the true Christian, for His all-searching eye can trace
His own likeness wherever it is to be found, in the deepest depths
of the soul (see on chap. ii. 25).—But it should prevent indulgence
of sin even in thought, for there is nothing hid before Him, nor
doth ought remain unpunished (Rev. ii. 23).

Feed. The Lord now returns to the word used in verse 15.—The
command to supply wholesome food to the flock is repeated: this
stands first and last in the pastor's office. (See note.)

My sheep. Love must take care of them; Love must govern them;
Love must feed them: for Love redeemed them (chap. x. 17;
Acts xx. 28; Eph. iv. 15, 16).—The Schoolmen apprehended
the thrice repeated feeding as feeding by doctrine, by example,
by hospitality.—The same careful attention to the soul's cravings
and needs, which was enjoined on behalf of the "lambs" of the
fold, is here enjoined on behalf of the "sheep" also.—The love of
the shepherd who tends, and leads, and guards, and lays down
his life for the flock, is the central spring of all, which shows
itself in these outward acts.—" Ministers ought to look upon
Christ's people as very seriously recommended to them, and
therefore should very seriously mind their work about them; for
therefore is this charge *thrice* laid on Peter, that he may mind it
much." *Hutcheson.* (See notes to verses 15, 16.)

πρόβατά, text. rec. *Codd. S'n., D X., Lachmann.*—προβάτια. *Codd. A.B C., Syriac,
Tisch., Treg., Alford, Westcott.*—*Pace agniculos meos, pasce agnos meos, pasce oviculas
meas. Ambrose.*—If προβάτια were better sustained in verse 16, and πρόβατα in verse
17, there would be a beautiful rising climax: *little lambs, sheeplings. sheep. Schaff.*—
The first and most necessary thing is to provide for the *lambs, i.e.,* those of tender age
in the faith, with spiritual sustenance, to lead them to the spiritual pasture (the office
of a catechist).—It is more difficult to guard and guide the full-grown sheep, mature
Christians, to make them seek the right pasture, find the true spiritual food ; most
difficult of all : to offer to these full-aged members appropriate spiritual food. *Lange.*
—The gradation : 1. *Feed my lambs, i.e.,* help the weak ; 2. *Guide and guard My sheep,
i.e.,* counsel the strong ; 3. *Feed My sheep, i.e.,* help the strong, for they too need feeding
with the divine food of the word. *Crosby.*—The *Romish* Peter has made a κατακυριεύειν
of the βόσκειν and ποιμαίνειν ; he has treated the προβάτια as ἀρνία. and has so
thoroughly forgotten the instruction to provide spiritual nourishment for the πρόβατα,
even as βόσκων, as to have, on the contrary, continually *withdrawn* such nourishment
from them more and more, and *forbidden* it under various penalties. *Lange.*—Those
must strangely miss the whole sense, who dream of an exclusive primatial power here
granted or confirmed to Peter.—A sufficient refutation of this silly idea, if it needed
any other than the ἐλυπήθη of this passage, is found in the συμπρεσβύτεροι of 1 Pet. v. 1,
where he refers apparently to this very charge by the Lord. *Alford.*

---

18. Verily, verily, I say unto thee, When thou wast young, thou girdest thyself, and
walkedst whither thou wouldest : but when thou shalt be old, thou shalt stretch
forth thy hands, and another shall gird thee, and carry thee whither thou wouldest
not.

Verily. This form of assurance is peculiar to John (see on chap. i.
52).—The Lord now proceeds to announce to Peter the end of
that pastoral office in which he has been reinstated.—The love
which has been so ardently professed is to be tested by the
martyr's death.—A proof that " all things " are indeed known to
Jesus, as Peter has just confessed.—A contrast also to the denial
of which he has been so gently reminded.—But the words may
be regarded as having a deeper meaning, and as pointing to the
development and future of Peter's *spiritual man*, under the figure
of his natural life. *Lange.*

Young. Gr., *Thou wast younger.*—Peter was at this time a vigorous
man, in the middle years of life, occupying, therefore, a position
betwixt youth and old age.—The prophecy attaches itself to this
fact, just as the contrast of youth and old age is frequently made
a symbol in the O. T. also (Is. xl. 30, 31 ; Ezek. xvi. ; Hos. xi. 1).
—The Lord employs the homeliest figure for the most mysterious
disclosure. *Lange.*

Girdest. As in verse 7, he had girt his fisher's coat unto him.—
That the younger man girds himself is agreeable to nature.—But
if we here find only the martyrdom predicted, the figure of the
young man seems really incongruous. *Tholuck.*—It undoubtedly
denotes the youthful conduct of Peter in his discipleship.—He

girded himself in the acts of self-will of which the Gospel history
testifies; and finally in self-will trod the way of denial. *Lange.*

Wouldest. "The thing which nature, especially while men are
young and in vigour, would still be at, is to be their own masters,
not subject to the law of God, nor to the tossing providences
about the world; for this was Peter's way, and what he delighted
in then." *Hutcheson.*

Old. Gr., *But when thou hast grown gray.*—Indicates both the close
of Peter's life (2 Pet. i. 14), and the last stage of Christian
development (1 John ii. 13).—"That Christ promiseth he shall
not suffer till he be old, He teacheth, partly that the timing of
His people's suffering is in His hand, and He can when He
pleaseth give them a fair time wherein to serve Him, before He
calls them to seal the truth by their sufferings; and partly, that
Christ may call His people to suffer when their visible ability is
least, that so the power carrying them through may be seen to be
of Him." *Hutcheson.*—"In *youth*, in the fulness of intellectual
power, zealous (but also in many respects self-willed) activity for
the Lord is shown; in *old age*, however, manifold hindrances (but
also purifications) are at work, and the highest pitch of self-denial
is death for Christ." *Lisco.*—"Christ reminds Peter of his former
life, because whereas in worldly matters a young man has powers,
an old man none; in spiritual things, on the contrary, virtue is
brighter, manliness stronger, in old age; age is no hindrance to
grace." *Chrysostom.*

Stretch. This also is in accordance with nature; but the traits:
Thou didst walk, as a young man, whither thou wouldest, as an
old man thou shalt be led whither thou wouldest not, in themselves point to the prophetic meaning.—John gives the interpretation in verse 19; but the meaning was not fully disclosed till
Peter's martyrdom took place.—The Church Fathers and some
modern Commentators refer these and the following words to the
crucifixion of Peter.—Tradition states that he was crucified at
Rome (see note), and hence the stretching forth of the hands has
been interpreted to apply to the extension of the arms upon the
cross; and the girding has been considered to mean the binding
upon the cross, or the girding of a cloth about the loins (see on
chap. xix. 18).—But against this interpretation it is objected:
"(1) that the girding (with chains) would precede, not follow,
the crucifixion; (2) that it would be more natural to speak of
another stretching forth his hands if the nailing them to the cross
is intended; (3) that the last clause, 'carry thee whither thou
wouldest not,' could not follow the stretching of the hands on the
transverse beam of the cross. It seems impossible therefore to

adopt the traditional reference to crucifixion, and we must take the
words, 'stretch forth thy hands,' as expressing symbolically the
personal surrender previous to being girded by another. To
what exact form of death the context does not specify." *Ellicott.*—
The words are symbolical of submission to another's power, and
this is significantly reflected in the outstretching of the hands of a
crucified martyr.—Spiritually understood, it is a picture of an
aged Christian resigning himself wholly to the control of the Lord.
Lange. (Acts xx. 22.)

Another. The *other* unqualified; a figure of Divine Providence
working through human instruments.—The comfort to the
Christian lies in the truth that every instrument and event is in
the hand of God.—Faith sees that our life is a plan of God, and
this vision carries order and beauty into the clash and confusion
of the world (Rom. viii. 28).

Gird thee. In contrast to "thou girdest thyself," he shall make thee
ready for thy last journey.—"The girdle, as the symbol of *free*
will, shall be changed into a fetter, as a symbol of the *unfree* will
of a prisoner." *Lange.*

Carry thee. Shall lead thee away to martyrdom.—Some suppose
that leading to the death of the cross is directly intended. *Calvin,*
&c.—At all events a *violent* death is evidently symbolized.—" It
was the word of the Master, whose own violent death had just
consisted in crucifixion, and who had now purposely selected the
figure of the outstretching of the hands, in order to express submission to the extremest fate." *Lange.*

Wouldest not. Refers to the shrinking back of weak humanity
from a violent death; not to the unwillingness of Peter to die for
his Lord.—Grace does not destroy those *natural* instincts which
God has planted in us all.—Even our Lord Himself prayed, "If
it be possible, let this cup pass from Me " (see on Matt. xxvi. 39).
—Spiritually it represents the old, expiring self-will, which often
dies hard.—"How utterly distinct a character a man bears so
long as he is bent upon being his own master; he follows his own
self-will, the corrupt will; how different the man when his will
has been taken away by grace and he belongs to God. Then the
self-will of the flesh is entirely captive to the will of the Spirit."
Heubner.—A picture of the ministry in its youthful, and in its
matured character; *Youthful:* Girding one's self, choosing
one's own ways, making great pretensions; *Matured:* Denying
one's self, suffering one's self to be led, submitting to the guidance
of the Lord.—A life picture also of the leading which the Lord
bestows upon every individual servant in his vocation. *Lange.*

ἀμήν. See on Matt. v. 18 —ἐκτενεῖς. "The evidence of Peter's martyrdom, at Rome, is complete, while there is a total absence of any contrary statement in the writings of the early Fathers. Clement of Rome, writing before the end of the first century, speaks of it, but does not mention the *place*, that being of course well known to his readers. Ignatius, in the undoubtedly genuine Epistle to the Romans (chap. iv.), speaks of Peter in terms which imply a special connection with their Church. In the second century, Dionysius of Corinth, in the Epistle to Soter, bishop of Rome (ap. Euseb. *H. E* ii. 25), states, as a fact universally known, and accounting for the intimate relations between Corinth and Rome, that Peter and Paul both taught in Italy and suffered martyrdom about the same time. In short, the Churches most nearly connected with Rome, and those least affected by its influence, which was as yet but inconsiderable in the East, concur in the statement that Peter was a joint founder of that Church, and suffered death in that city. The time and manner of the Apostle's martyrdom are less certain. The early writers imply, or distinctly state, that he suffered at, or about the same time with Paul, and in the Neronian persecution. *All agree that he was crucified.* Origen says that at his own request he was crucified with his head downward." *Smith's* "Dict. of the Bible."—The Lord Jesus, by connecting the question concerning love toward Him with the announcement of Peter's imminent sufferings, indicates that by the willing assumption of sufferings inflicted for His Name's sake, the sincerity and faithfulness of love, and, consequently, also, the steadfastness of faith, are to be proved. *Lange.*—οὐ θέλεις. Ambrose relates that Peter, not long before his death, being overcome by the solicitations of his fellow Christians to save himself, was flying from Rome when he was met by our Lord, and on asking, "Lord, whither goest Thou?" received the answer, "I go to be crucified afresh."—On this he returned and joyfully went to martyrdom.—The Church called "Domine quo vadis," on the Appian Way, commemorates the legend.

---

19. This spake he, signifying by what death he should glorify God. And when he had spoken this, he saith unto him, Follow me.

This spake. The Evangelist's explanation of this dark saying, and in John's style (compare ii. 21; vi. 6; vii. 29; xii. 33; xviii. 32).

Death. Gr., *By what manner of death.*—Indicates generally the martyrdom of Peter as distinct from a natural death. *Ellicott.*—Brings to view not only the kind of death, martyrdom, but also the distinguished species of *that* death. *Lange.*—When John wrote this Gospel the martyrdom of Peter (67 or 68 A.D.) must have been well known in the Churches (see note to verse 18).

Glorify God. See on chap. xiii. 31; xvii. 1.—This expression was later a customary term for martyrdom. *Suicer.*—The crucifixion of the Lord had invested martyrdom with a peculiar lustre.—Peter knew that he should follow his Master through shame to glory; and to him the cross was a token of honour.—No death so glorious as that which is suffered for Christ's sake, the King of all kings.—Clement of Alexandria says that Peter's wife also suffered martyrdom, her husband encouraging her to be faithful unto death, with the words, "Remember, dear, our Lord."—"To suffer for Christ is to glorify God; but there is a martyrdom of life as well as of death; by the former John, by the latter Peter

and Paul glorified God." *Schaff.*—" The consideration that God
is glorified by *any* lot should put a lovely face upon it." *Hutcheson.*—"That God in *all things* may be glorified through Jesus
Christ, to whom be praise and dominion for ever and ever. Amen"
(1 Pet. iv. 11).

Follow me. See note.—It seems from the next verse, that our
Lord withdrew from the circle of disciples, and by some gesture
signified to Peter that he should follow Him.—But these words
must have had for Peter a much deeper meaning.—It was by the
side of that lake he had first heard the command " Follow Me "
(see on Matt. iv. 19).—It was to his question at the Last Supper
that the answer came, " Whither I go, thou canst not follow Me
now ; but thou shalt follow Me afterwards " (see on chap. xiii. 36).
—And now the command has come again with the prophecy of
martyrdom.—A clear announcement that the way of the *Cross*
still remains and must remain the way to glory.—A call to follow the Lord in suffering and death itself, and through the dark
path which He had trodden, to follow Him to heaven.

Follow me. See on chap. i. 43; xii. 26.—This is the sum and
substance, the beginning and end of Christian life.—The whole
business of a servant of Christ is comprehended in the business
of *following* Him.—Follow, not only on the path of *action*, but
especially of *suffering.*—Follow, not merely in the general sense
in which it is addressed to each disciple, but in that more peculiar sense, in which it makes distinction between Peter and John
(see on verse 22).—Nay, even further, the distinction which
makes a different demand on the Peter of the time then present,
than on the Peter of an earlier period.—Follow the call of Jesus,
each in his own sphere and vocation ; the guidance of Jesus, each
in his own course of life; the footsteps of Jesus, each in his own
special cross.—This is not easy, much less pleasing to flesh and
blood, yet it is honour, duty, happiness.—No one ever yet
repented, who, on this injunction, humbly and cheerfully went
forth after Jesus.—But it is alone possible to *follow* thus unconditionally when we have attained rightly to *serve;* and we cannot
serve without true *love*, and least of all can *love* without belief
and grace. *Oosterzee.*

θανάτῳ. Among the various points of peculiar interest, which belong to the Gospel
of John, must be reckoned the few but expressive references to the future lives and
deaths of the Apostles. *Medley.*—δοξάσει. " The revelation of God unto the world by
the Gospel, is called ' the light of the knowledge of the Glory,' that is, of the manifestation of God, in the face of Jesus Christ; and in 1 Pet. iv. 14, those that suffered for
Christ are said, in allusion to the Shechinah, to have 'the glory and Spirit of God to

rest upon them'; because, I conceive, God appeared as eminently in them in their confessions and sufferings, as if His glory had descended upon them in lambent fires, and rested upon their heads" (Isa. xxiv. 15 ; Matt. v. 11). *Hickes.*—Ακολουθει μου. Follow Me in doctrine and till death. *Cyril, Theophylact.*—In the death of the cross. *Euthymius.*—As œcumenical bishop or teacher. *Chrysostom.*—Refers both to the guidance of the Church and to martyrdom. *Ewald.*—In a martyr's death. *Meyer.*—The words are to be taken literally : the Lord leads Peter aside in order to a confidential communication. *Kuinoel, Tholuck. &c.*—The context, and the immediately subsequent words, "Peter turned himself about and saw," &c, are decisive in favour of the primarily literal sense.—Peter could not understand this saying of Jesus as distinctly referring to martyrdom. if he did not understand the previous saying as referring to the same.—We suppose, however, the significance of this literal sense to have lain in the fact that Jesus retired to the background of the scene, as if for departure to the invisible world, and hence that the summons to Peter was a trial.—The literal expression, therefore, has likewise a symbolical background.—He must prepare himself for the possibility of the immediate decision of his fate ; *i.e.,* stand a test of absolute submission *Lange, Luthardt.*—"One of the most mysterious moments in the whole resurrection-history. In a symbolical act Peter must follow the Lord into the background of the scene, as if he were now to be translated with him from the visible earth across the boundaries of the spirit-realm. Thus is the unconditional following, the readiness for death, of the servant of Christ, presented in a symbolical act ; the type of martyrdom in the Church." *Lange.*—"It appears from verse 20, that Christ rose from the rest of the company, and went away when He gave this command. And this He did, not so much for any present journey. as by calling him to obey this present command. to leave all his enjoyments and company, and follow Him wherever He goeth, He takes proof of his sincerity, and whether he is resolved indeed to follow Christ in suffering, when he shall be called to it, and would have him begin to practice that lesson in time, that he might be the more fit for it when it came to a push ; and so we will find it made use of, verse 20." *Hutcheson.*—Probably He went towards that mountain where He had appointed to meet His assembled followers. *Macdonald.*

---

20. Then Peter, turning about, seeth the disciple whom Jesus loved following ; which also leaned on his breast at supper, and said, Lord, which is he that betrayeth thee ?

Turning. Indicates that Peter had retired with Jesus, and that John seeing this had followed them.

The disciple, &c. See on chaps. xiii. 23 ; xix. 26 ; xx. 2.—This is evidently inserted by John to explain his following, and is a strong token that he wrote this chapter (see on verse 1).—It was this love which enabled him to enter so deeply into communion with his Lord.

Following. John had been the companion and friend of Peter, and this "following" was the involuntary impulse of affection. —It shows that he did not understand the Lord as wishing to make an exclusively confidential communication to Peter.—"The Lord speaks to Peter ; John hears ; at once applies the word to himself and *follows.* The sensitive conscience of an advanced Christian catches at the first intimation of a duty, however indirectly made ; nor does it fail to do so, when, as here, there is a call to suffering. Trials, undertaken in this spirit, the ready ventures of a true faith and love, show our wills to be united to the Will of God (Psa. lxxxv. 8 ; Acts xxi. 11-14)." *Ford.*—"Much

love to Christ, and much of the sense of His love, will make a
man an earnest pursuer after Christ, and to cleave to Him, even
when Christ seems to take no notice of him ; therefore John
followed, when Christ had bidden only Peter follow Him, and
when it seems the rest did not stir." *Hutcheson.*

Leaned, &c. See on chap. xiii. 23-25.—A further explanation
by John of his following.—He intimates that as the confidant of
Jesus at the Last Supper, it was allowable for him now, *as the*
confidant of Jesus, freely to join Him.—*Lange.*

δè. Omitted. *Lach., Tisch., Alford, Westcott and Hort.*—Retained. *Cod. Sin., Lange.*—
ὅς καì, &c. Intended to bring to mind the incident (chap. xiii. 23 ff.) when John inquired of the Lord on Peter's behalf, and to show that Peter has now grown far bolder,
insomuch that he himself questions Christ in behalf of John. *Chrysostom, &c.*—An
intimation that a lot so full of suff-rings as Peter's might not be intended for the
disciple so pre-eminently loved by Jesus. *Meyer.*—As if Jesus in partiality protected
His particular friends from sufferings! *Lange.*—Introduced by John to justify his
following the Lord and Peter. *Alford, Schaff, &c.*—John understood the summons as
the prelude to a love-test to be administered at Christ's withdrawal into concealment.
Lange.—John may well think that for him too there was some glimpse into the
future, some declaration of what his path should be; or in that ming ing of act and
thought, of sign and thing signified, which runs all through these verses. his following
may indicate that he too, though he had never dared to say so, was ready to follow
wherever the Master went. *Ellicott.*

---

21. Peter seeing him saith to Jesus, Lord, and what shall this man do?

Lord. For the meaning of this title as applied to Jesus, see on
chap. xx. 28.

What, &c. *"But how will it be with this?"* *Lange.*—This shows
that Peter had rightly understood the Lord's prophecy (see on
verse 18).—He now desires to know what is to be the future of
his friend and companion.—The motive prompting the question
was probably that of loving interest.—Doubtless the two had often
talked of their Master's predictions and wondered what was in
store for themselves.—Peter had just learned that he was to
follow his Lord through suffering and death, and he longs for
some light upon the future of his friend.—Though the question
was well meant, our Lord's reply shows that it was not wholly
warranted (see on verse 22).

οὗτος. How shall it be with this my fellow combatant? *Euthymius.*—Is he to be
with us now? *Paulus.*—What kind of a fate shall *this* man have in his calling? *Tholuck,
Luthardt.*—If Peter saw in the mysterious walk a test of joyful following, his first
thought would be : John, without being called, exposes himself to a moment of

difficulty. The question, Shall this man go too? had at the same time, then, the back-ground: What shall become of this man? *Lange.*—Peter's motive in asking the question was special love for John. *Chrysostom, Erasmus, Luthardt.*—Prompted by curiosity and a certain jealousy. *Lücke, Meyer.*—Disapprobation of a supposed unauthorised accompanying. *Paulus, &c.*—Curiosity and interest as to John's fate. *Tholuck.*—Not mere *idle* curiosity, but that longing which we all feel for our friends. *Alford, Bengel.*—Prompted by close regard, and the well-known love of Jesus for John. *Macdonald.*—The *self-consciousness* with which Peter receives the disclosure and summons of the Lord, turns to *compassion* for *John,* whose present and future task Jesus apparently fails to appoint.—Between Jesus and John everything is understood of itself, tacitly, as it were, while between Jesus and Peter everything has to be expressed, discussed, in a degree stipulated.—Now, thinks Peter (in all noble mindedness, we may say), the same course must be pursued with John, else will he come short in somewhat: he, therefore, must receive his instructions for now and for the future.—*Lange.*

---

22. Jesus saith unto him, If I will that he tarry till I come, what is that to thee? follow thou me.

If I will. See on chap. xvii. 24.—Christ appeals to His *will,* not to a distinct instruction, though at the same time indicating the substance of His will.—He here claims absolute disposal over human life.—"He is Lord both of the dead and the living" (Rom. xiv. 9).—He has "the keys of hell (Gr., *hades*) and of death" (Rev. i. 18).—"Whether we live, we live unto the Lord; and whether we die, we die unto the Lord: whether we live there-fore, or die, we are the Lord's" (Rom. xiv. 8).—Christians are *His possession,* and it belongs to Him to appoint their earthly life and lot:—"It is a sin to be anxious or too much careful about what Christ will do with His beloved people." *Hutcheson.*—He who has redeemed us at so great a price, and to whom we have com-mitted our eternal interest, may well be trusted with everything else.—"He has sovereign authority to dispose of His own, and to keep them longer or shorter time in the world, and give them ease or trouble, as He pleaseth, without giving an account of His dealing to any."—"My times are in *Thy* hand," a truth full of unutterable comfort (Psa. xxxi. 15).—"Precious in the sight of the Lord is the *death* of His saints" (Psa. cxvi. 15); therefore their death must be by Divine appointment (see on chap. xvii. 15).—Christ the Master of His servants: 1. In the establishment of their vocation; 2. In the foreknowledge of their history. *Lange.*

Tarry. Gr., *remain.*—It is the word rendered "abide" in chap. xii. 34 (see Comm.)—It is opposed to "Follow me," which was to be accomplished through *martyrdom,* and means *to be preserved alive* (compare Phil. i. 25; 1 Cor. xv. 6). *Meyer.*—In these words our Lord enwraps the prophecy concerning John.—As "the disciple whom Jesus loved," it might have been supposed that John would have been the *first* to be taken home, instead of which he was the *last* (see Introduction, page xv.).—With his contemplative, stately, ideal mind, he went angel-like through life.—Christ's presence is continued in the world and Church through the medium of the love of His friends.—It was much easier for a man like Peter to act, dare, sacrifice, than to wait, suffer, passively stand still.—"John was to wait patiently, to linger on year after year in loneliness and weariness of spirit, to abide persecution, oppression and wrong (Rev. i. 9), to endure the enmity of the wicked (1 John iii. 13), and the sight of heresies abounding in the Church (1 John ii. 18, 19-26), as if to exemplify in himself all classes of the faithful, and the various modes of drinking the cup of Christ." *Jacobus.*—The Lord appoints different careers to His people, yet decides for all aright. —Inscrutable and mysterious are the ways by which He leads us, until we are come to the end of them.—Many who seem ripe for heaven, for good and wise reasons are left to linger on.—" John was earlier than the other disciples prepared for the death of martyrdom, as the most perfect sacrifice of obedience to God, and of love to God and man ; but that was the very reason why he was not to taste the martyr's death. John consummated in his life and natural death what the martyrs sealed in their final sacrifice, namely, the victorious manifestation of the love of God and man." *Stier.*

Till I come. See note. See also Introduction, page xv.—The spirit of John shall never perish; it shall ever renew itself ; never shall there be wanting loving and beloved Johannean souls. *Heubner.*—"There shall always be friends of God, friends of Christ, inward subjective intuitive Christians, in accordance with the characteristic of John, representative of the innermost presence of Christ in the Church. In this form the Christian spiritual life shall remain until Christ returns." *Lange.*

What ? These words imply a rebuke.—Our Lord reproves the spirit which would inquire into another's life and work, with the effect of weakening the force of its own.—" Here, as in all the earlier details of Peter's life, his character is emotional, earnest, loving, but wanting in depth, and not without self-confidence. The words ' Follow Me,' the meaning of which he has not missed, may well have led him to thoughts and questions of what that path should be, and the truth may well have sunk into the depths of his heart, there to germinate and burst forth in principle and act. But he is at once taken up with other thoughts. He is told to follow, but is ready to lead. He would know and guide his friend's life rather than his own. To him, and to all, there comes the truth that the Father is the husbandman, and it is He who trains every branch of the vine. There is a spiritual companionship which strengthens and helps all who join in it; there is a spiritual guidance which is not without danger to the true strength of him that is led, nor yet to that of him who leads." *Ellicott.*—Peter is reminded of each man's position and obligation before God.—"*John's* appointed lot is no element in *thy* onward course." *Alford.*—There is a natural desire in men to search into the affairs of others, and to neglect their own; and to be more concerned about things to come, than about present duty.—"Not that Christ condemns solicitude for our brethren which floweth from charity, but that He is ill pleased with this diversion of his mind from the command just given." *Baxter.*—We may concern ourselves about our Christian friend: 1. As to his spiritual welfare, but not as to the external form thereof; 2. As to the will of God concerning his way, not as to a human regulation of that way; 3. In divine sympathy, not in human comparison or in human rivalry. *Lange.*

Follow. See on verse 19.—*Thou* and *Me* are emphatic: It is ME that *thou* must follow.—"They, measuring themselves by themselves, and comparing themselves among themselves, are not wise" (2 Cor. x. 12).—Thy brother's life is no matter for thy care: Thy work is for thyself to follow Me. *Ellicott.*—The mind is thus called away from the problem which perplexes, the prospect which discourages, the thought which distracts and paralyzes, and is fixed upon the one great object, *following Christ.*—An imitation of *His life* in its sinless perfection, its divine-human character, its prophetic, priestly, and kingly office, and in its states of humiliation and exaltation from the cross to the crown, must be the first and last aim of every true Christian.—Not *speculation* is enjoined, but *practice;* not *knowledge,* but *obedience;* not *another's* matters, but *our own.*—Each *must do his own duty,* which is not another's, and whether another shall do his own duty or not.—Such as would avoid curiosity, and much needless and vain exercise, ought closely to follow their own work and calling; therefore doth Christ withdraw Peter from all these inquiries by bidding him again, "Follow *thou* ME." *Hutcheson.*—"Vain man would be wise;" many spend time and strength, "exercising themselves in great matters, in things too high for them" (Psa. cxxxi. 1), who neglect or disregard practical religion.—"The secret things belong unto the Lord our God: but those things which are revealed belong unto us and to our children for ever, that we may *do* all the words of this law" (Deut. xxix. 29).—"Not everyone that saith unto me, Lord, Lord, shall enter into the kingdom of heaven: but he that *doeth* the will of my Father which is in heaven" (see on Matt. vii. 21).—"Whosoever shall *do* the will of my Father which is in heaven, the same is my brother, and sister, and mother " (see on Matt. xii. 50).—Obedience to Christ's command is the true test of love: " If a man love Me, he will *keep My words* " (see on chap. xiv. 23-24).—Those who *follow Christ* are ready for *His coming*, whether at death, or in the glory of His Second Advent.—" What is that to thee ?" which of us has not deserved the *rebuke ?*—" Follow thou Me :" which of us does not require the *counsel?*

ἕως ἔρχομαι. Until Christ returned from His walk with Peter. *Paulus.*—To lead him out of Galilee to apostolic work. *Theoph.*—In the destruction of Jerusalem. *Wetstein, &c.*—Refers to the near Parousia of Christ. *Meyer, Lücke, De Wette.*—After the destruction of Jerusalem began that mighty series of events of which the Apocalypse is the prophetic record, and which is in the complex known as the *coming of the Lord,* ending, as it shall, with His glorious and Personal Advent. *Alford;* so also *Bengel, Luthardt, Stier.*—The sentence hypothetically declares that not even the longest extension of the life-term of Peter's fellow disciple ought to be the occasion of jealousy. *Tholuck;* so also *Trench.*—The coming of Jesus to take John to heaven through the medium of an easy natural death. *Rupert, Grotius, Olshausen, Lampe, Ewald, Wordsworth.*—This interpretation a'one forms a real antithesis; if ἀκολουθεῖν here mean, to follow the home-returning Jesus through the medium of *martyrdom,* and μένειν, on the other hand, signify, *to remain alive,* then to remain alive until I come, means also, until I come to take him.—The destruction of Jerusalem, for instance, forms no contrast to martyrdom; neither does the Parousia itself.—Such a contrast is presented, however, by a natural death.—Natural death is the *individual type,* continuing throughout N. T. times, of the Parousia for the individual Christian (Matt. xxiv. 44; John xiv. 3, &c.); and the Parousia of Christ in the death of believers is a warranty to them of their participation in the general Parousia (1 Cor. xv. 51 ; 1 Thess. iv. 15). *Lange.*—The interpretation which verse 23 suggests is that our Lord made no statement, but expressed a supposition, "If I will," "If it even be that I will;" and this both gives the exact meaning of the Greek, and corresponds to the remainder of our Lord's answer,—He is directing Peter to think of his own future, and not of his friend's; and He puts a supposition which, even if it were true, would not make that friend's life a subject for him then to think of.—Had our Lord told him that John should remain on earth until His coming, in any sense of the word, then He wou'd have given an answer, which He clearly declined to give. *Ellicott.*—It seems more natural to consider our Lord as intending to give *no positive indication* of John's fate at all, but to signify that this was a matter which belonged to the Master of both, who would disclose or conceal it as He thought proper. *D. Brown.*

23. Then went this saying abroad among the brethren, that that disciple should not die: yet Jesus said not unto him, He shall not die; but, If I will that he tarry till I come, what is that to thee?

This saying. Gr., *This report therefore went, &c.*—A striking instance of the vanity and uncertainty of oral tradition.—Even a saying of Jesus to His disciples was interpolated through error, without any fraudulent design.—Shows also how prone sometimes we are to construe the promises of God in a mere temporal or worldly sense.—And we are the more inclined to do this, if by such interpretations we can save ourselves from the necessity of suffering (Psa. cxix. 25; John iv. 15, 33, 34; 2 Cor. v. 16, 17). *Ford.*

Brethren. An expression of later date than any usually occurring in the Gospels; but frequent in the Acts.—The key to it is in our Lord's words to Mary Magdalene (see on chap. xx. 17).—The Church of Christ is a family of which God is the Father (see on chap. xvii. and on Matt. xxiii. 8).

Not die. See Introduction, page xvi.—A tradition which not even this correction has been able utterly to do away with. (See note.)

Said not. This defence of the Lord's exact words is of great importance.—It warrants the conclusion that John was still living when this was written; that consequently it must have been written by him.—Had John been dead, another writer would have expressed himself much more strongly against the mistake of the brethren.—Very probably also he would have given *his* own interpretation of the saying at the same time.—But John would not anticipate the mysterious purport of his Lord's word, which was as yet unfulfilled. *Lange.*—A proof of John's humility, he would not allow so great an honour to be ascribed to him.—A proof of his love, he is anxious to free the brethren from error.—How liable have men been in all ages to put false constructions on the sayings of Scripture.—How necessary to fall back upon the Word *itself*, to study its precise terms, and bring out its teaching in its own exact language.—According to our light and knowledge, this we have endeavoured faithfully to do in this Commentary.—We have long believed that a better understanding of the Scriptures can alone purify the Church from its errors and strengthen and establish wavering faith.—It is of little consequence to know what fallible men have said: It is of immense consequence to know what God Himself has said.—Hence the importance of exposition in Christian instruction.—How many errors have been built upon single texts and sentences which an understanding of the Divine Word in its logical, spiritual connection would have prevented.—"The grossest errors have sometimes shrouded themselves under the umbrage of incontestable truths." *Henry.*—But a better knowledge of the Word of God will strip these errors of their disguises, and expose those perversions of Christianity by which the Church has been hindered growing "up in all things into Him who is the Head."

But. The mistake chiefly arose from not attending to the force of the "**If.**"—They took as a statement what had been said as a supposition, and understood it in the then current belief that the Second Advent would come in their own generation (comp. 1 Cor.

xv. 51, 52; 1 Thess. iv. 17). *Ellicott.*—" The simple recapitulation of the words of the Lord shows that their sense remained dark to the writer, who ventured on no explanation of them ; merely setting his own side of the Apostolic duty over against that of Peter, who probably had already by following his Master through the Cross, glorified God, whereas, the beloved disciple was, whatever that meant, to tarry till He came." *Alford.*—" The Holy Spirit by *commenting* here on a *fulfilled* prophecy, that concerning Peter, teaches us to attend to the fulfilment of prophecy in our own times. And by *only correcting* an *error* with regard to an *unfulfilled* prophecy, that concerning John, He teaches us not to speculate curiously on *unfulfilled prophecies ;* but to wait patiently, till Christ comes to us in the events of history, and interprets His own prophecies by fulfilling them." *Wordsworth.*

οὐκ ἀποθνήσκει. If written by another person after John's death, we should certainly, in the refutation of this error, have read, ἀπέθανεν γὰρ, καὶ ἐτάφη, as in Acts ii. 29. *Alford.*—" The opinion, that John did not die, is found in Sulpitius Severus. I have frequently met with it in Greek legends, monologues, and chronicles, with this addition, *viz.,* that the dust upon his grave is moved by the breath of his mouth. In a work of the Patriarch Ephraim, of Antioch, it is positively affirmed that John is still living : that he has vanished, and that in his grave nought was found but a delicious odour and a precious spring of healing balm." *Johannes Mueller,* quoted in *Lange,* Amer. Edit.

---

24. This is the disciple which testifieth of these things, and wrote these things : and we know that his testimony is true.

The disciple. See on chap. xx. 30, 31.—A self-designation of John.—Five times in this Gospel he calls himself a *disciple* (chaps. xiii. 23 ; xix. 26; xx. 2 ; xxi. 7, 23).—Indicates the remarkable simplicity and humility of his character.—To be a *disciple* of Jesus and to be *loved* by Him was John's highest honour.

Testifieth. See on chap. xix. 35.—The tense of the Greek word is present; the testimony continues.—Little did John think that in this testimony to his Lord and Master, he was immortalizing himself.

These things. The words are too wide to be limited to the Epilogue, and must be taken as referring to all that has preceded.

Wrote. The tense describes the writing as an accomplished act.— The words imply that he who wrote was still living and bearing witness to the truth.—He is *still testifying* to the things of which *he wrote.*—There is a tradition that this Gospel was written many

1434 / Gospel of John

years before the Apostle permitted its general circulation.—*Smith's* " Dict. of the Bible."

We know. Some suppose the plural " we" indicates that these words are not the words of John, but the additional witness of persons knowing him and testifying to his writing.—But it appears more reasonable to accept them as the words of the Evangelist. —The use of the " we " is explained by supposing that he here makes himself one with his readers; compare chap. i. 14; 1 John iv. 14, 16 ; v. 18.

We know. See on chap. xx. 31.—The testimony of Christian consciousness is a witness to the truth of the Gospel (see on chap. **iv.** 42; vi. 69 ; vii. 17).—*We know ;* because we not only believe it, we *experience it.*—Here is the philosophy of Christian success, the secret of all past Christian conquests.—The conversion of the world will not be accomplished by argument, but by the old Gospel process of bringing men to God through Christ, and so creating within them the testimony of their own consciousness. —The guarantee of the perpetuity of Christianity is found in the supernatural life which it produces.—The great Defender of the Faith is the Holy Spirit dwelling in the heart.—As long as God answers prayer offered in the name of Jesus ; as long as, through Christ, He inducts men into conscious communion with Himself, so long will men believe in Christianity.—As long as men show the peace and power of the Christian religion, so long will others yearn to possess it also.—" All history but repeats the scene enacted seven-and-twenty centuries ago upon a mountain in Palestine. As there and then, so through the age-long life of man, false altars and false priests have stood confronting and opposing God's. As there and then, so always and everywhere, observant humanity has watched and waited for the God ' that answereth by fire.' And whensoever on inner or on outer altar, at the prayer of any true prophet, the fire has fallen, even the onlooking world have lifted multitudinous voices with the awed yet glad confession : ' THE LORD HE IS THE GOD, THE LORD HE IS THE GOD.'" *Warren.*

True. *True* in spite of all the objections and contradictions of the world ; *true* in the might of the Spirit that hath overcome the world. *Lange.*

οἴδαμεν. Probably a later addition from the Ephesian Church. *Lange.*—A contemporaneous addition : the words are found in every important MS. and version, and are an undoubted part of the original text. *Ellicott.*—They are the words of John himself. *Meyer, Alford, Wordsworth.*

25. And there are also many other things which Jesus did, the which, if they should be written every one. I suppose that even the world itself could not contain the books that should be written. Amen.

Many other. See on chap. xx. 30.—Refers to the numerous unrecorded miracles performed by Him who "went about doing good" (Acts x. 38).—We may see in Matt. ix. how many He wrought in one single day.—No mention is made in any of the Gospels of the performance of miracles at Chorazin, nor are we even told that Jesus was ever there; and yet "the mighty works," as our Lord calls them, done in that city, would have been sufficient to make the people of Tyre and Sidon repent, had they seen them (see on Matt. xi. 20, 21).—"It is probable that those recorded were more remarkable than the rest, either for the number of the witnesses, who were present at them, or for the character and quality of these witnesses; or for the places, where they were performed; or for the consequences they gave rise to; or for the reports, which went out concerning them, and the fame, which accrued to Jesus from them." *Macknight.*—The miracles recorded by John are remarkable for the momentous truths they demonstrated and ushered in, and for their important practical results.—It may be one of the employments of the Redeemed in heaven to hold converse together on "all that Jesus began to do and to teach," in the days of His humiliation on earth. *Ford.*

I suppose. Some infer that this is the individual testimony of an amanuensis, who, from personal knowledge of the life of Christ, or from knowledge derived from John or from others, feels that full beyond all human thought as this Gospel is, it is but a part of the greater fulness. *Ellicott.*—But we agree with those (*Lange, Alford, Wordsworth*) who regard the words as those of the Evangelist.

The world, &c. See note.—A somewhat similar expression occurs in Eccl. xii. 12: "Of making many books there is no end." —Most expositors look upon these words as simply figurative and hyperbolical; as much as to say, any number of books would not exhaust the subject.—But we think they also imply, that the world would be spiritually incapable of grasping such books.— *Jerome, Augustine, Bengel.*—Such is the infinite glory of the life of the Incarnate Word, that even of heavenly intelligences no more than this is said: "Which things the angels desire to look into" (1 Pet. i. 12).

Should be written. That is, the books that then would be written *continually.*—The wisdom and goodness of God are seen not only in the *matter* of the Gospel history but in its *size.*—How thankful

should we be that the "things which Jesus did," and which have
been written, are recorded in a form which brings the Word of Life
within the study of all.—"Though but little has been written on
the life of Christ by the Evangelists, that little is of more account
than all the literature of the world, and has been more productive
of books, as well as thoughts and deeds, than any number of
biographies of sages and saints of ancient and modern time
The Gospels, and the Bible generally, rise like Mount Arara
high above the flood of literature; they are the sacred librar
for all nations, the literary sanctuary for scholars and the commoi
people; they combine word and work, letter and spirit, eartl
and heaven, time and eternity." *Schaff.*

Amen. A liturgical or devotional addition (see on Matt. v. 18).—
It is not found in the better MSS., and in no part of the writter
text.—"It is the natural prayer of some copyist, as it is the
natural prayer of every devout reader that the writer's purpose
may be fulfilled." *Ellicott.*

All known MSS., except the Sinaitic Codex, contain this verse, though many state ii
a note that it was regarded by some as a later addition. *Schaff.*—ἄλλα πολλά. "Th'
Evangelist thinks it important that he should remind his readers that he has no
written as a chronicler, but has selected and arranged things in conformity to a:
organizing principle, as did also his predecessors, though not in the equal power of ι
concentrated, unitous, ideal view." *Lange.*—"The purpose of this verse seems to be tι
assert and vindicate the fragmentary character of the Gospel, considered merely as aι
historical narrative; for that the doings of the Lord were so many. His life so rich iι
matters of record, that, in a popular hyperbo'ɔ, we can hardly imagine the world con
taining them all, if singly written down: thus setting forth the superfluity and cun
brousness of anything like a perfect detail, in the strongest terms, and in terms whic
certainly look as if fault had been found with this gospel, for want of completeness, by
some objeciors." *Alford*—οἶμαι. Perhaps Andrew, who, with John, was the oldes
disciple of Christ. *Godet, Ellicott.*—χωρῆσαι. No place in literature. *Ebrard.*—Even thι
Christian *Gramma* may err in the way of profuse book-making. Against this th
Christian spirit of a John opposes its final words of warning. *Lange.*—If it be aske
why ιhe gospels are not larger, it may be answered, 1. It was not because *they had ea
hausted their subject*; 2. But (1) it was not *needful* to *write* more; (2) it was nc
possible to *write all*; (3) it was not *advisable* to write *much*. *Henry.*—The chief MSʃ
have a subscription appended to the Gospel. "According to John." *Vatican.* "Gospι
according to John." *Sinaitic, Alexandrine, Paris, Basle.*